PERGAMON GENERAL PSYCHOLOGY SERIES
EDITORS
Arnold P. Goldstein, Syracuse University
Leonard Krasner, Stanford University & SUNY at Stony Brook

HANDBOOK OF
PSYCHOLOGICAL ASSESSMENT

(PGPS-131)

Pergamon Titles of Related Interest

Bellack/Hersen BEHAVIORAL ASSESSMENT: A Practical Handbook, Third Edition

Johnson/Goldman DEVELOPMENTAL ASSESSMENT IN CLINICAL CHILD PSYCHOLOGY: A Handbook

Hersen/Bellack DICTIONARY OF BEHAVIORAL ASSESSMENT TECHNIQUES

Karoly/Jensen MULTIMETHOD ASSESSMENT OF CHRONIC PAIN

Oster/Caro/Eagen/Lillo ASSESSING ADOLESCENTS

Williamson ASSESSMENT OF EATING DISORDERS: Obesity, Anorexia, and Bulima Nervosa

Related Journals
(Free sample copies available upon request)

BEHAVIORAL ASSESSMENT
BEHAVIOUR RESEARCH AND THERAPY
CLINICAL PSYCHOLOGY REVIEW
JOURNAL OF BEHAVIOR THERAPY AND
   EXPERIMENTAL PSYCHIATRY
PERSONALITY AND INDIVIDUAL DIFFERENCES

HANDBOOK OF PSYCHOLOGICAL ASSESSMENT

Second Edition

Edited by

GERALD GOLDSTEIN
Veterans Administration Medical Center, Pittsburgh

MICHEL HERSEN
University of Pittsburgh School of Medicine

PERGAMON PRESS
Member of Maxwell Macmillan Pergamon Publishing Corporation
New York • Oxford • Beijing • Frankfurt
São Paulo • Sydney • Tokyo • Toronto

Pergamon Press Offices:

U.S.A.	Pergamon Press, Inc., Maxwell House, Fairview Park, Elmsford, New York 10523, U.S.A.
U.K.	Pergamon Press plc, Headington Hill Hall, Oxford OX3 0BW, England
PEOPLE'S REPUBLIC OF CHINA	Pergamon Press, 0909 China World Tower No. 1 Jian Guo Men Wei Avenue, Beijing, 100004
FEDERAL REPUBLIC OF GERMANY	Pergamon Press GmbH, Hammerweg 6, D-6242 Kronberg, Federal Republic of Germany
BRAZIL	Pergamon Editora Ltda, Rua Eça de Queiros, 346, CEP 04011, Paraiso, São Paulo, Brazil
AUSTRALIA	Pergamon Press Australia Pty Ltd., P.O. Box 544, Potts Point, NSW 2011, Australia
JAPAN	Pergamon Press, 8th Floor, Matsuoka Central Building, 1-7-1 Nishishinjuku, Shinjuku-ku, Tokyo 160, Japan
CANADA	Pergamon Press Canada Ltd., Suite 271, 253 College Street, Toronto, Ontario M5T 1R5, Canada

Copyright © 1990 Pergamon Press, Inc.

Library of Congress Cataloging in Publication Data
Handbook of psychological assessment / edited by Gerald Goldstein, Michel Hersen. -- 2nd ed.
    p.   cm. -- (Pergamon general psychology series : 131)
    Includes bibliographical references.
    ISBN 0-08-035866-7
    1. Psychometrics. 2. Psychological tests.   I. Goldstein, Gerald, 1931- . II. Hersen, Michel.   III. Series.
BF39.H2645   1990
150$'$.28$''$7--dc20   89-27356
                                                        CIP

Printing: 1 2 3 4 5 6 7 8 9   Year: 0 1 2 3 4 5 6 7 8 9

Printed in the United States of America

CONTENTS

Part X. SPECIAL TOPICS

Preface

The first edition of the *Handbook of Psychological Assessment* appeared in 1984. This second edition was written with several goals in mind. First, there appeared to be the need to update the material presented in the first edition since the field of psychological assessment is a rapidly growing one (e.g., development of the Minnesota Multiphasic Personality Inventory-2). Second, the editors wanted to provide the opportunity for distinguished authorities in various areas of assessment who did not contribute to the first edition to write chapters concerning their areas from their own perspectives. Therefore, some of the chapters in the second edition are on the same topics as they were in the first edition, but are written by different authors. Finally, the editors wanted to present chapters on two important topics not covered in the first edition; testing of minority group members and computer-assisted psychological testing.

We would like to thank our contributors whose work appeared in the first edition for their conscientious and detailed updating of their chapters as well as our new contributors for their provision of new perspectives on topics previously covered by other contributors, or for their introduction of areas of psychological assessment not reviewed in the first edition. The senior editor would again like to acknowledge the support of the Department of Veterans Affairs in the preparation of this work, as well as the assistance of Adelaide Goertler. The junior editor thanks Mary Newell and Mary Anne Frederick for their technical assistance. We both would again like to express our appreciation to Jerome Frank, our editor at Pergamon, for his sustained encouragement, patience, and support.

The editors wish to express their bereavement concerning the passing of Julia R. Vane during the preparation of this book.

Gerald Goldstein
Michel Hersen
Pittsburgh, PA

PART I

INTRODUCTION

CHAPTER 1

HISTORICAL PERSPECTIVES

Gerald Goldstein
Michel Hersen

INTRODUCTION

"A test is a systematic procedure for comparing the behavior of two or more persons." This definition of a test, offered by Lee Cronbach (1949, 1960) many years ago probably still stands as a means of epitomizing the major content of psychological assessment. The invention of psychological tests, then known as mental tests, is generally attributed to Galton (Boring, 1950) and occurred during the middle and late nineteenth century. Galton's work was largely concerned with individual differences, and his approach was essentially the opposite of what was the general case for psychologists of his time. Psychologists then were largely concerned with the exhaustive study of mental phenomena in a few subjects, while Galton was more interested in somewhat less specific analyses of large numbers of people. Perhaps the first psychological test was the "Galton whistle," which evaluated high tone hearing. Galton also appeared to have the statistical concept that errors of measurement in individuals could be canceled out through the mass effect of large samples.

Obviously, psychologists have come a long way from the simple tests of Galton, Binet, and Munsterberg, and the technology of testing has already entered the computer age, with almost science fictionlike extensions, such as testing by satellite. Psychometrics is now an advanced branch of mathematical and statistical science, and the administration, scoring, and even interpretation of tests have become increasingly objectified and automated. While some greet the news with dread and others with enthusiasm, we may

be rapidly approaching the day when most or all testing will be administered, scored, and interpreted by computer. Thus, the nineteenth-century image of the school teacher administering paper-and-pencil tests to the students in her classroom and grading them at home has changed to the extensive use of automated procedures administered to huge portions of the population by representatives of giant corporations. Testing appears to have become a part of Western culture, and there are indeed very few people who enter educational, work, or clinical settings who do not take many tests during their lifetimes.

In recent years, there appears to have been a distinction made between testing and assessment, assessment being the broader concept. Psychologists do not just give tests now; they perform assessments. The title of this volume, the *Handbook of Psychological Assessment*, was chosen advisedly and is meant to convey the view that it is not simply a handbook of psychological testing, although testing will be covered in great detail. The term assessment implies that there are many ways of evaluating individual differences. Testing is one way, but there are also interviewing, observations of behavior in natural or structured settings, and recording of various physiological functions. Certain forms of interviewing and systematic observation of behavior are now known as behavioral assessments, as opposed to the psychometric assessment accomplished through the use of formal tests. Historically, interest in these two forms of assessment has waxed and waned, and in what follows we will briefly try to trace these trends in various areas.

INTELLIGENCE TESTING

The testing of intelligence in school children was probably the first major occupation of clinical psychology. The Binet scales and their descendants continue to be used, along with the IQ concept associated with them. Later, primarily through the work of David Wechsler and associates (Wechsler, 1944), intelligence testing was extended to adults and the IQ concept was changed from the mental age system (Mental Age/Chronological Age × 100) to the notion of a deviation IQ based on established norms. While Wechsler was primarily concerned with the individual assessment of intelligence, many group-administered paper-and-pencil tests also emerged during the early years of the twentieth century. Perhaps the old Army Alpha and Beta tests, developed for intellectual screening of inductees into the armed forces during the First World War, were the first examples of these instruments. The use of these tests progressed in parallel with developments in more theoretical research regarding the nature of intelligence. The English investigators, Burt, Pearson, and Spearman, and the Americans, Thurstone and Guilford, are widely known for their work in this area, particularly with factor analysis. The debate over whether intelligence is a general ability (g) or a series of specific abilities represents one of the classic controversies in psychology. A related controversy that is still very much with us (Jensen, 1983) has to do with whether intelligence is primarily inherited or acquired and with the corollary issue having to do with ethnic-racial differences in intellectual ability.

Another highly significant aspect of intelligence testing has to do with its clinical utilization. The IQ now essentially defines the borders of mental retardation, and intelligence tests are widely used to identify retarded children in educational settings (DSM-III [American Psychiatric Association, 1980]). However, intelligence testing has gone far beyond the attempt to identify mentally retarded individuals and has become widely applied in the fields of psychopathology and neuropsychology. With regard to psychopathology, under the original impetus of David Rapaport and collaborators (1945), the Wechsler scales became clinical instruments used in conjunction with other tests to evaluate patients with such conditions as schizophrenia and various stress-related disorders. In the field of neuropsychology, the use of intelligence testing is perhaps best described by McFie's (1975) remark, "It is perhaps a matter of luck that many of the Wechsler subtests are neurologically relevant" (p. 14). In these applications, the intelligence test was basically used as an instrument with which the clinician could examine various cognitive processes, on the basis of which inferences could be made about the patient's clinical status.

In summary, the intelligence test has become a widely used assessment instrument in educational, industrial, military, and clinical settings. While in some applications the emphasis remains on the simple obtaining of a numerical IQ value, it would probably be fair to say that many, if not most, psychologists now use the intelligence test as a means of examining the individual's cognitive processes, of seeing how he or she goes about solving problems, of identifying those factors that may be interfering with adaptive thinking, of looking at various language and nonverbal abilities in brain-damaged patients, and of identifying patterns of abnormal thought processes seen in schizophrenic patients. Performance profiles and qualitative characteristics of individual responses to items appear to have become the major focuses of interest, rather than the single IQ score.

PERSONALITY ASSESSMENT

Personality assessment has come to rival intelligence testing as a task performed by psychologists. However, while most psychologists would agree that an intelligence test is generally the best way to measure intelligence, no such consensus obtains within the realm of personality evaluation. In long-term perspective, it would appear that two major philosophies have emerged and perhaps three assessment methods. The two philosophies can be traced back to Allport's (1937) distinction between nomothetic versus idiographic methodologies and Meehl's (1954) distinction between clinical and statistical or actuarial prediction. In essence, some psychologists feel that personality assessments are best accomplished when they are highly individualized, while others have a preference for quantitative procedures based on group norms. The phrase "seer versus sign" has been used to epitomize this dispute. The three methods referred to are the interview, the projective, and the objective tests. Obviously, the first way psychologists and their predecessors found out about people was to talk to them, giving the interview historical precedence. But following a period when the use of the interview was eschewed by many psychologists, it has made a return. It would appear that the field is in a historical spiral, with various methods leaving and returning at different levels.

The interview began as a relatively unstructured conversation with the patient and perhaps an informant, with varying goals, including obtaining a history, assessing personality structure and dynamics, establishing a diagnosis, and many other issues. Numerous publications have been written about interviewing (e.g., Menninger, 1952), but in general they provided outlines and general guidelines as to what should be accomplished by the interview. However, model interviews were not provided. With or without this guidance, the interview was viewed by many as a subjective, unreliable procedure that could not be sufficiently validated. For example, the unreliability of psychiatric diagnosis based on studies of multiple interviewers had been well established (Zubin, 1967). More recently, however, a number of structured psychiatric interviews have appeared in which the specific content, if not specific items, has been presented, and for which very adequate reliability has been established. There are by now several such interviews available, including the Schedule for Affective Disorders and Schizophrenia (SADS) (Spitzer & Endicott, 1977), the Renard Diagnostic Interview (Helzer, Robins, Croughan, & Welner, 1981) and the Structured Clinical Interview for DSM-III or DSM-III-R (SCID or SCID-R) (Spitzer & Williams, 1983). These interviews have been established in conjunction with objective diagnostic criteria including DSM-III itself, the Research Diagnostic Criteria (Spitzer, Endicott, & Robins, 1977), and the Feighner Criteria (Feighner, Robins, Guze, Woodruff, Winokur, & Munoz, 1972). These new procedures have apparently ushered in a "comeback" of the interview, and many psychiatrists and psychologists now prefer to use these procedures rather than either the objective- or projective-type psychological test.

Those advocating use of structured interviews note that in psychiatry, at least, tests ultimately must be validated against judgments made by psychiatrists. These judgments are generally based on interviews and observation, because there really are no biological or other objective markers of most forms of psychopathology. If that is indeed the case, there seems little point in administering elaborate and often lengthy tests when one can just as well use the criterion measure itself, the interview, rather than the test. There is no way that a test can be more valid than an interview if an interview is the validating criterion. The structured interviews have made a major impact on the scientific literature in psychopathology, and it is rare to find a recently written research report in which diagnoses were not established by one of them. It would appear that we have come full cycle regarding

this matter, and until objective markers of various forms of psychopathology are discovered, we will be relying primarily on the structured interviews for our diagnostic assessments.

Interviews of the SADS or Diagnostic Interview Schedule type are relatively lengthy and comprehensive, but there are now several briefer and more specific interview or interview-like procedures. Within psychiatry, perhaps the most well-known procedure is the Brief Psychiatric Rating Scale (BPRS) (Overall & Gorham, 1962). The BPRS is a brief, structured, repeatable interview that has essentially become the standard instrument for assessment of change in patients, usually as a function of taking some form of psychotropic medication. In the specific area of depression, the Hamilton Depression Scale (Hamilton, 1960) plays a similar role. There are also several widely used interviews for patients with dementia, which generally combine a brief mental status examination with some form of functional assessment, particularly with reference to Activities of Daily Living. The most popular of these scales are the Mini-Mental Status Examination of Folstein, Folstein, and McHugh (1975) and the Dementia Scale of Blessed, Tomlinson, and Roth (1968). Extensive validation studies have been conducted with these instruments, perhaps the most well-known one having to do with the correlation between scores on the Blessed, Tomlinson, and Roth scale during life and the senile plaque count determined on autopsy in patients with dementia. The obtained correlation of .7 quite impressively suggested that the scale was a valid one for detection of dementia. In addition to these interviews and rating scales, numerous methods have been developed for assessment of psychopathology by nurses and psychiatric aides based on direct observation of ward behavior (Raskin, 1982). The most widely used of these rating scales are the Nurses' Observation Scale for Inpatient Evaluation (NOSIE-30) (Honigfeld & Klett, 1965) and the Ward Behavior Inventory (Burdock, Hardesty, Hakerem, Zubin, & Beck, 1968). These scales assess such behaviors as cooperativeness, appearance, communication, aggressive episodes, and related behaviors, and are to be based on direct observation rather than reference to medical records or the report of others. Scales of this type supplement the interview with information concerning social competence and capacity to carry out functional activities of daily living.

Again taking a long-term historical view, it is our impression that after many years of neglect by the field, the interview has made a successful return to the arena of psychological assessment, but the interviews now used are quite different from the loosely organized, "free-wheeling," conversation-like procedures of the past. First of all, their organization tends to be structured, and the interviewer is required to obtain certain items of information. It is generally felt that formulation of specifically worded questions is counterproductive; rather, the interviewer, who should be an experienced clinician trained in the use of the procedure, should be able to formulate questions that will elicit the required information. Second, the interview procedure must meet psychometric standards of reliability and validity. Finally, while the structured interviews tend to be atheoretical in orientation, they are based on contemporary scientific knowledge of psychopathology. Thus, for example, the information needed to establish a differential diagnosis within the general classification of the affective disorders is derived from the scientific literature on depression and the related affective disorders.

The rise of the interview appears to have occurred in parallel with the decline of projective techniques. Those of us now in a chronological category that may be roughly described as middle-aged may recall that their graduate training in clinical psychology probably included extensive course work and practicum experience involving the various projective techniques. Most clinical psychologists would probably agree that even though projective techniques are still used to some extent, the atmosphere of ferment and excitement concerning these procedures that existed during the 1940s and 1950s no longer seems to exist. Even though the Rorschach technique and Thematic Apperception Test (TAT) were the major procedures used during that era, a variety of other tests emerged quite rapidly: the projective use of human figure drawings (Machover, 1949), the Szondi Test (Szondi, 1952), the Make-A-Picture-Story (MAPS) Test (Shneidman, 1952), the Four Picture Test (VanLennep, 1951), the Sentence Completion Tests (e.g., Rohde, 1957), and the Holtzman Inkblot Test (Holtzman, 1958). The exciting work of Murray and his collaborators reported on in *Explorations in Personality* (Murray, 1938) had a major impact on the field and stimulated extensive utilization of the TAT. It would probably be fair to say that the sole survivor of this active movement is the Rorschach. Many clinicians continue to use the Rorschach, and the work of Exner and his collaborators has lent it increasing scientific respectability (see Erdberg, chapter 17).

There are undoubtedly many reasons for the decline in utilization of the projective techniques, but in our view they can be summarized by the following points.

1. Increasing scientific sophistication created an atmosphere of skepticism concerning these instruments. Their reliability and validity were called into question by numerous studies (e.g., Swensen, 1957, 1968; Zubin, 1967), and it was felt by a substantial segment of the professional community that the claims made for these procedures could not be substantiated.
2. Developments in alternative procedures, notably the MMPI and other objective tests, convinced many clinicians that the information previously adduced from projective tests could be gained more efficiently and less expensively with the objective methods. In particular, the voluminous MMPI research literature has demonstrated its usefulness in an extremely wide variety of clinical and research settings. When the MMPI and related objective techniques were pitted against the projectives during the days of the "seer versus sign" controversy, it was generally demonstrated that the sign was as good as or better than the seer in most of the studies accomplished (Meehl, 1954).
3. In general, the projective techniques are not atheoretical and, in fact, are generally viewed as being associated with one or another branch of psychoanalytic theory.

While psychoanalysis remains a strong and vigorous movement within psychology, there are numerous alternative theoretical systems at large, notably behaviorally and biologically oriented systems. As is implied in the section of this chapter covering behavioral assessment, behaviorally oriented psychologists pose theoretical objections to the projective techniques and make little use of them in their practices. Similarly, the projective techniques tend not to receive high levels of acceptance in biologically oriented psychiatry departments. In effect, then, utilization of the projective techniques declined for scientific, practical, and philosophical reasons. However, the Rorschach, in particular, continues to be productively used, primarily by psychodynamically oriented clinicians.

The early history of the objective personality tests has been traced by Cronbach (1949, 1960). The beginnings apparently go back to Sir Francis Galton, who devised personality questionnaires during the latter part of the nineteenth century. We will not repeat that history here, but rather will focus on those procedures that survived into the contemporary era. In our view, there have been three such major survivors: a series of tests developed by Guilford and collaborators (Guilford & Zimmerman, 1949), a similar series developed by Cattell and collaborators (Cattell, Eber, & Tatsuoka, 1970), and the MMPI. In general, but certainly not in all cases, the Guilford and Cattell procedures are used for individuals functioning within the normal range, while the MMPI is more widely used in clinical populations. Thus, for example, Cattell's 16PF test may be used to screen job applicants while the MMPI may be more typically used in psychiatric health care facilities. Furthermore, the Guilford and Cattell tests are based on factor analysis and are trait oriented, while the MMPI in its standard form does not make use of factor analytically derived scales and is more oriented toward psychiatric classification. Thus, the Guilford and Cattell scales contain measures of such traits as dominance or sociability, while most of the MMPI scales are named after psychiatric classifications such as paranoia or hypochondriasis.

Currently, most psychologists use one or more of these objective tests rather than interviews or projective tests in screening situations. For example, many thousands of patients admitted to Veterans Administration psychiatric facilities take the MMPI shortly after admission, while applicants for prison guard jobs in the state of Pennsylvania take the Cattell 16PF. However, the MMPI in particular is commonly used as more than a screening instrument. It is frequently used as a part of an extensive diagnostic appraisal, as a method of evaluating treatment, and in numerous research applications. There is little question that it is the most widely used and extensively studied procedure in the objective personality test area. Even though the 566 true or false items in the first edition have remained the same since the initial development of the instrument, the test's applications and clinical interpretation have evolved dramatically over the years. We have gone from a perhaps overly naive dependence on single-scale evaluations and overly literal interpretation of the names of the scales (many of which are archaic psychiatric terms) to sophisticated configural interpretation of profiles, much of which is based on empirical research (Gilberstadt & Duker, 1965; Marks, Seeman, & Haller, 1974). Correspondingly, the methods of administering, scoring, and interpreting the MMPI have kept pace with technological and scientific advances in the behavioral sciences. Beginning with sorting cards into piles, hand scoring, and subjective interpretation, the MMPI has gone to computerized administration and scoring, interpretation based at least to some extent on empirical findings, and even computerized interpretation

(Fowler, 1979, and chapter 23, this volume). As is well known, there are several companies that will provide computerized scoring and interpretations of the MMPI.

Since the appearance of the first edition of this handbook, there have been two major developments in the field of objective personality assessment. First, Millon has produced a series of tests referred to as The Millon Clinical Multiaxial Inventory (Versions I and II), The Millon Adolescent Personality Inventory and the Millon Behavioral Health Inventory (Millon, 1982, 1985). Second, the MMPI has been completely revised and restandardized, and now is available as the MMPI-2. Chapter 16 in this volume by Keller, Butcher, and Slutske describes these new developments in detail.

Even though we should anticipate continued spiraling of trends in personality assessment, it would appear that we have passed an era of projective techniques and are now living in a time of objective assessment with an increasing interest in the structured interview. There also appears to be increased concern with the scientific status of our assessment procedures. In recent years there has been particular concern with reliability of diagnosis, especially since distressing findings appeared in the literature suggesting that psychiatric diagnoses were being made quite unreliably (Zubin, 1967). The issue of validity in personality assessment, however, remains a difficult one for a number of reasons. First, if by personality assessment we mean prediction or classification of some psychiatric diagnostic category, we have the problem of there being essentially no known objective markers for the major forms of psychopathology. Therefore, we are left essentially with psychiatrists' judgments. DSM-III and its revision have greatly improved this situation by providing objective criteria for the various mental disorders, but the capacity of such instruments as the MMPI or Rorschach to predict DSM-III and DSM-III-R diagnoses has not yet been evaluated and remains a research question for the future. Some scholars, however, even question the usefulness of taking that research course rather than developing increasingly reliable and valid structured interviews (Zubin, 1984). Similarly, there have been many reports of the failure of objective tests to predict such matters as success in an occupation or trustworthiness with regard to handling a weapon. For example, objective tests are no longer used to screen astronauts, since they were not successful in predicting who would be successful or unsuccessful (Cordes, 1983). There does, in fact, appear to be a movement within the general public and the profession toward discontinuation of use of personality assessment procedures for decision making in employment situations. We would note as another possibly significant trend a movement toward direct observation of behavior in the form of behavioral assessment. The zeitgeist definitely is in opposition to procedures in which the intent is disguised. Burdock and Zubin (1985), for example, argue that "nothing has as yet replaced behavior for evaluation of mental patients."

NEUROPSYCHOLOGICAL ASSESSMENT

Another area that has an interesting historical development is neuropsychological assessment. The term itself is a relatively new one and probably was made popular through the first edition of Lezak's (1976) book with that title. Neuropsychological assessment is of particular historical interest because it represents a confluence of two quite separate antecedents: central and eastern European behavioral neurology, and American and English psychometrics. Neurologists, of course, have always been concerned with the behavioral manifestations of structural brain damage and the relationship between brain function and behavior. Broca's discovery of a speech center in the left frontal zone of the brain is often cited as the first scientific neuropsychological discovery, because it delineated a relatively specific relationship between a behavioral function, speech, and a correspondingly specific region of the brain (the third frontal convolution of the left hemisphere). Clinical psychologists developed an interest in this area when they were called upon to assess patients with known or suspected brain damage. The first approach to this diagnostic area involved utilization of the already existing psychological tests, and the old literature in the area deals primarily with how such tests as the Wechsler scales, the Rorschach, or the Bender-Gestalt test could be used to diagnose brain damage. More recently, special tests were devised specifically for assessment work with patients having known or suspected brain damage.

The merger between clinical psychology and behavioral neurology can be said to have occurred when the sophistication of neurologists relative to the areas of brain function and brain disease was combined with the psychometric sophistication of clinical psychology. The wedding occurred when reliable, valid, and well-standardized measurement instruments began to be used to answer complex questions in neurological diagnosis and differential diagnosis. Thus, clinicians who ultimately identified themselves as clinical neu-

ropsychologists tended to be individuals who knew their psychometrics, but who also had extensive training and experience in neurological settings. Just as many clinical psychologists work with psychiatrists, many clinical neuropsychologists work with neurologists and neurosurgeons. This relationship culminated in the development of standard neuropsychological test batteries, notably the Halstead-Reitan (Reitan & Wolfson, 1985) and Luria-Nebraska batteries (Golden, Hammeke, & Purisch, 1980), as well as in the capacity of many trained psychologists to perform individualized neuropsychological assessments of adults and children. Thus, within the history of psychological assessment, clinical neuropsychological evaluation has recently emerged as an independent discipline to be distinguished from general clinical psychology on the basis of the specific expertise members of that discipline have in the areas of brain-behavior relationships and diseases of the nervous system. In recent years, there have been expansions of both the standard batteries and the individual neuropsychological tests. An alternate form (Golden, Purisch, & Hammeke, 1985) as well as a children's version (Golden, 1981) of the Luria–Nebraska Neuropsychological Battery are now available. Prominent among the newly published or revised individual tests are the series of tests described in detail by Arthur Benton and collaborators in *Contributions to Neuropsychological Assessment* (Benton, Hamsher, Varney, & Spreen, 1983), the California Verbal Learning Test (Delis, Kramer, Kaplan, & Ober, 1987), and the newly revised and thoroughly reworked Wechsler Memory Scale (WMS-R) (Wechsler, 1987).

BEHAVIORAL ASSESSMENT

Over the last three decades behavioral assessment has been one of the most exciting developments to emerge in the field of psychological evaluation (Bellack & Hersen, 1988). Although its seeds were planted long before behavior therapy became a popular therapeutic movement, it is with the advent of behavior therapy that the strategies of behavioral assessment began to flourish (cf. Hersen & Bellack, 1976, 1981). As has been noted elsewhere (Barlow & Hersen, 1984; Herson & Barlow, 1976), behavioral assessment can be conceptualized as a reaction to a number of factors. Among these were the (a) problems with unreliability and invalidity of aspects of the DSM-I and DSM-II diagnostic schemes, (b) concerns over the indirect relationship between what was evaluated in traditional testing (e.g., the projectives) and how it subsequently was used in treatment planning and application, (c) increasing acceptance of behavior therapy by the professional community as a viable series of therapeutic modalities, and (d) parallel developments in the field of diagnosis in general involving greater precision and accountability (e.g., the problem-oriented record).

We will briefly consider each of the four factors in turn and see how they contributed historically to the development of behavioral assessment. To begin with, DSM-I and DSM-II were the targets of considerable criticism from psychiatrists (Hines & Williams, 1975) and psychologists alike (Begelman, 1975). Indeed, Begelman (1975), in a humorous vein, referred to the two systems as "twice-told tales." They were "twice told" in the sense that neither resulted in highly reliable classification schemes when patients were independently evaluated by separate psychiatric interviewers (cf. Ash, 1949; Sandifer, Pettus, & Quade, 1964). Problems were especially evident when attempts to obtain interrater reliability were made for the more minor diagnostic groupings of the DSM schemes. Frequently, clinical psychologists would be consulted to carry out their testing procedures to confirm or disconfirm psychiatrists' diagnostic impressions based on DSM-I and DSM-II. But in so doing, such psychologists, operating very much as x-ray technicians, were using procedures (objective and projective tests) that had only a tangential relationship to the psychiatric descriptors for each of the nosological groups of interest. Thus, the futility of this kind of assessment strategy over time became increasingly apparent. Moreover, not only were there problems with the reliability for DSM-I and DSM-II, but empirical studies documented considerable problems as well with regard to external validity of the systems (Eisler & Polak, 1971: Nathan, Zare, Simpson, & Ardberg, 1969).

Probably more important than any of the above was the fact that the complicated psychological evaluation had a limited relationship to eventual treatment. At least in the psychiatric arena, the usual isomorphic relationship between assessment and treatment found in other branches of therapeutics did not seem to hold. The isolated and extended psychological examination frequently proved to be an empty academic exercise resulting in poetic jargon in the report that eventuated. But its practical utility was woefully limited. Treatment seemed to be unrelated to the findings in the reports.

All of the aforementioned resulted in attempts by clinical psychologists to measure the behaviors of interest in direct fashion. For example, if a patient presented with a particular phobia, the objective of evaluation was not to assess the underlying "neurotic complex" or "alleged psychodynamics." Quite the contrary, the primary objective was to quantify in distance how close our patient could approach the phobic object (i.e., the behavioral approach task) and how his heart rate (physiological assessment) increased as he got closer. In addition, the patient's cognitions (self-report) were quantified by having him assess his level of fear (e.g., on a 1–10 point scale). Thus, the behavioral assessment triad, consisting of motoric, physiological, and self-report systems (Hersen, 1973), was established as the alternative to indirect measurement.

Commenting on the use of direct measurement, Hersen and Barlow (1976) argue that

> whereas in indirect measurement a particular response is interpreted in terms of a presumed underlying disposition, a response obtained through direct measurement is simply viewed as a sample of a large population of similar responses elicited under those particular stimulus conditions. . . . Thus, it is hardly surprising that proponents of direct measurement favor the observation of individuals in their natural surroundigs whenever possible. When such naturalistic observations are not feasible, analogue situations approximating naturalistic conditions may be developed to study the behavior in question (e.g., the use of a behavioral avoidance test to study the degree of fear of snakes). When neither of these two methods is available or possible, subjects' *self-reports are also used as independent criteria*, and, at times, may be operating under the control of totally different sets of contingencies than those governing motoric responses. (p. 116)

We already have referred to the tripartite system of direct measurement favored by the behaviorists. But it is in the realm of motoric behavior that behavior therapists have made the greatest contributions as well as being most innovative (see Foster, Bell-Dolan, & Burge, 1988; Hersen, 1988; Tryon, 1986). With increased acceptance of behavior therapy, practitioners of the strategies found their services required in a large variety of educational, rehabilitation, community medical, and psychiatric settings. Very often they were presented with extremely difficult educational, rehabilitation, and treatment cases, both from assessment and therapeutic perspectives. Many of the clients and patients requiring remediation exhibited behaviors that previously had not been measured in any direct fashion. Thus, there were few guidelines with regard to how the behavior might be observed, quantified, and coded. In many instances, "seat-of-the-pants" measurement systems were devised on the spot but with little regard for psychometric qualities cherished by traditional testers.

Consider the following example of a measurement strategy to quantify "spasmodic torticollis," a tic-like disorder (Bernhardt, Hersen, & Barlow, 1972):

> A Sony video recorder model AV-5000A, an MRI Keleket model VC-1 television camera, and a Conrac 14-inch television monitor were employed in recording torticollis. A Gra Lab sixty-minute Universal Timer was used to obtain percentage of torticollis. . . . A lightolier lamp served as the source of negative feedback. Two to three daily ten-minute sessions were scheduled during the experiment in which the subject was videotaped while seated in a profile arrangement. A piece of clear plastic containing superimposed Chart-Pac taped horizontal lines (spaced one-quarter to one-half inch apart) was placed over the monitor. A shielded observer depressed a switch activating the timer whenever the subject's head was positioned at an angle where the nostril was above a horizontal line intersecting the external auditory meatus. This position was operationally defined as an example of torticollis, with percentage of torticollis per session serving as the experimental measure. Conversely, when the horizontal line intersected both the nostril and auditory meatus or when the subject's nostril was below the horizontal line he was considered to be holding his head in a normal position. (p. 295)

If one peruses the pages of the *Journal of Applied Behavior Analysis, Behaviour Research and Therapy, Journal of Behavior Therapy and Experimental Psychiatry,* and *Behavior Modification,* particularly in the earlier issues, numerous examples of innovative behavioral measures and more comprehensive systems are to be found. Consistent with the idiographic approach, many of these apply only to the case in question, have some internal or face validity, but, of course, have little generality or external validity. (We will further comment on this aspect of behavioral assessment in a subsequent section of this chapter.)

A final development that contributed to and coincided with the emergence of behavioral assessment was the problem-oriented record (POR). This was a system of recordkeeping first instituted on medical wards in general hospitals to sharpen and pinpoint diagnostic practices (cf. Weed, 1964, 1968, 1969). Later this system was transferred to psychiatric units (cf. Hayes-Roth, Longabaugh, & Ryback, 1972; Katz & Woolley, 1975; Klonoff & Cox, 1975; McLean & Miles, 1974; Scales & Johnson, 1975), with its relevance to behavioral assessment increasingly evident (Atkinson, 1973; Katz & Woolley, 1975). When applied to psychiatry, the POR can be divided into four sections: (a) data base, (b) problem list, (c) treatment plan, and (d) follow-up data. There can be no doubt that this kind of recordkeeping promotes and enhances the relationship of assessment and treatment, essentially forcing the evaluator to crystallize his or her thinking about the diagnostic issues. In this regard, we previously have pointed out that

> despite the fact that POR represents, for psychiatry, a vast improvement over the type of record-keeping and diagnostic practice previously followed, the level of precision in describing problem behaviors and treatments to be used remedially *does not* yet approach the kind of precision reached in the carefully conducted behavioral analysis. (Hersen, 1976, p. 15)

However, the POR certainly can be conceptualized as a major step in the right direction. In most psychiatric settings some type of POR is currently being used and, to a large extent, has further legitimized the tenets of behavioral assessment by clearly linking the problem list with specific treatment (cf. Longabaugh, Fowler, Stout, & Kriebel, 1983; Longabaugh, Stout, Kriebel, McCullough, & Bishop, 1986).

ASSESSMENT SCHEMES

Since 1968 a number of comprehensive assessment schemes have been developed to facilitate the process of behavioral assessment (Cautela, 1968; Kanfer & Saslow, 1969; Lazarus, 1973). Because a very detailed analysis of these schemes is much beyond the scope of this brief historical overview, we will only describe the outlines of each in order to illustrate how the behavioral assessor conceptualizes his or her cases. For example, Cautela (1968) depicted in his scheme the role of behavioral assessment during the various stages of treatment. Specifically, he delineated three stages.

In the *first stage* the clinician identifies maladaptive behaviors and those antecedent conditions maintaining them. This step is accomplished through interviews, observation, and self-report questionnaires. The *second stage* involves the selection of the appropriate treatment strategies, evaluation of their efficacy, and the decision when to terminate their application. In the *third stage* a meticulous follow-up of treatment outcome is recommended. This is done by examining motoric, physiologic, and cognitive functioning of the client, in addition to independent confirmation of the client's progress by friends, relatives, and employers.

A somewhat more complicated approach to initial evaluation was proposed by Kanfer and Saslow

(1969), which involves some seven steps. The *first* involves a determination as to whether a given behavior represents an excess, deficit, or an asset. The *second* is a clarification of the problem and is based on the notion that in order to be maintained, maladjusted behavior requires continued support. *Third* is the motivational analysis in which reinforcing and aversive stimuli are identified. *Fourth* is the developmental analysis, focusing on biological, sociological, and behavioral changes. *Fifth* involves assessment of self-control and whether it can be used as a strategy during treatment. *Sixth* is the analysis of the client's interpersonal life, and *seventh* is the evaluation of the patient's socio-cultural-physical environment.

In their initial scheme, Kanfer and Saslow (1969) viewed the system in complementary fashion to the existing diagnostic approach (i.e., DSM-II). They did not construe it as supplanting DSM-II, but they did see their seven-part analysis as serving as a basis for arriving at decisions for precise behavioral interventions, thus yielding a more isomorphic relationship between assessment and treatment. Subsequently, Kanfer and Grimm (1977) have turned their attention to how the interview contributes to the overall behavioral assessment. In so doing, suggestions are made for organizing client complaints under five categories:

> (1) behavioral deficiencies, (2) behavioral excesses, (3) inappropriate environmental stimulus control, (4) inappropriate self-generated stimulus control, and (5) problematic reinforcement contingencies. (p. 7)

Yet another behavioral assessment scheme had been proposed by Lazarus (1973), with the somewhat humorous acronym of BASIC ID: B = behavior A = affect, S = sensation, I = imagery, C = cognition, I = interpersonal relationship, and D = the need for pharmacological intervention (i.e., drugs) for some psychiatric patients. The major issue underscored by this diagnostic scheme is that if any of the elements is overlooked, assessment will be incomplete, thus resulting in only a partially effective treatment. To be fully comprehensive, deficits or surpluses for each of the categories need to be identified so that specific treatments can be targeted for each. This, then, should ensure the linear relationship between assessment and treatment, ostensibly absent in the nonbehavioral assessment schemes.

Despite development of the aforementioned schemes and others not outlined here (e.g., Bornstein, Bornstein, & Dawson, 1984), there is little in the way of their formal evaluation in empirical fashion. Although these schemes certainly appear to have a good

bit of face validity, few studies, if any, have been devoted to evaluating concurrent and predictive validity. This, of course, is in contrast to the considerable effort to validate the third edition of DSM (i.e., DSM-III, APA, 1980; Hersen & Turner, 1984) and its revision (i.e., DSM-III-R; APA, 1987).

In a somewhat different vein, Wolpe (1977) has expressed his concern about the manner in which behavioral assessment typically is being conducted. Indeed, he has referred to it as the "Achilles' Heel of Outcome Research in Behavior Therapy." He is especially concerned that too little attention has been devoted to evaluation of the antecedents of behaviors targeted for treatment, thus leading to a therapeutic approach that may be inappropriate. For example, in treating anxiety, Wolpe (1977) rightly argues that

> A treatment like systematic desensitization, designed for the deconditioning of anxiety, has very little informational content. It can therefore be expected to have little or no effect on phobic cases that call for cognitive solutions. Such cases should properly be weeded out when the efficacy of desensitization is the topic of research. Until now, as far as I know, such weeding out has not been undertaking in any outcome study involving desensitization. (p. 1)

The same analysis, of course, holds true for disorders, such as depression (Wolpe, 1986) and agoraphobia (Michelson, 1984, 1986). Blanket treatment that does not take into account antecedents undoubtedly should fail (Wolpe & Wright, 1988). But here too, the necessary research findings to document this are as yet forthcoming (see White, Turner, & Turkat, 1983).

CHANGES IN BEHAVIORAL ASSESSMENT

Contrasted to the field of psychological assessment in general, behavioral assessment as a specialty has had a history of about three decades. However, in these years we have witnessed some remarkable changes in the thinking of behavioral assessors. Probably as a strong overt reaction to the problems perceived by behavioral assessors in traditional psychological evaluation, many of the sound psychometric features of that tradition were initially abandoned. Indeed, in some instances it appears that "the baby was thrown out with the bath water." As we already have noted, consistent with the idiographic approach to evaluation and treatment, little concern was accorded to traditional issues of reliability and validity. (The exception, of course, was the obsessive concern with high interrater reliability of observations of motoric behavior.) This was particularly the case for the numerous self-report inventories developed early on to be consistent with the motoric targets of treatment (e.g., some of the fear survey schedules).

There were many other aspects of traditional evaluation that also were given short shrift. Intelligence testing was eschewed, norms and developmental considerations were virtually ignored, and traditional psychiatric diagnosis was viewed as anathema to behavior therapy. However, since the late 1970s this "hard line" has been mollified. With publication of the second and third editions of *Behavioral Assessment: A Practical Handbook* and emergence of two assessment journals (*Behavioral Assessment* and *Journal of Psychopathology and Behavioral Assessment*), greater attention to cherished psychometric principles has returned. For example, the external validity of role playing as an assessment strategy in the social skill areas has been evaluated by Bellack and his colleagues (cf. Bellack, Hersen, & Lamparski, 1979; Bellack, Hersen, & Turner, 1979; Bellack, Turner, Hersen, & Luber, 1980) instead of being taken on faith. Also in numerous overviews the relevance of the psychometric tradition to behavioral assessment has been articulated with considerable vigor (e.g., Adams & Turner, 1979; Cone, 1977, 1988; Haynes, 1978; Nelson & Hayes, 1979; Rosen, Sussman, Mueser, Lyons, & Davis, 1981). Looking at behavioral assessment today from a historical perspective, it certainly appears as though the "baby" is being returned from the discarded bath water.

Also, in recent years there have been several calls for a broadened conceptualization of behavioral assessment (e.g., Hersen, 1988; Hersen & Bellack, 1988; Hersen & Last, 1989). Such broadening has been most noticeable with respect to the use of intelligence tests in behavioral assessment (Nelson, 1980), the relevance of neuropsychological evaluation for behavioral assessment (Goldstein, 1979; Horton, 1988), the importance of developmental factors especially in child and adolescent behavioral assessment (Edelbrock, 1984; Harris & Ferrari, 1983; Hersen & Last, 1989), and the contribution that behavioral assessment can make to pinpointing of psychiatric diagnosis (Hersen, in press; Tryon, 1986).

DSM-III, DSM-III-R, AND BEHAVIORAL ASSESSMENT

In the earlier days of behavioral assessment, traditional psychiatric diagnosis was for the most part eschewed. Behavioral assessors saw little relationship between what they were doing and the overall implicit

goals of DSM-II. Moreover, as we have noted, categories subsumed under DSM-II had major problems with reliability and validity. So, consistent with cogent criticisms about the official diagnostic system, behavioral assessors tended to ignore it when possible. They continued to develop their strategies independently of DSM-II and the then-emerging DSM-III. In fact, some (e.g., Adams, Doster, & Calhoun, 1977; Cautela, 1973) advocated totally new diagnostic formats altogether, but these never had a chance of being accepted by the general diagnostic community, given the political realities.

In spite of its problems and limitations, with the emergence of DSM-III (APA, 1980), behavioral therapists and researchers appear to have retrenched and assumed a somewhat different posture (cf. Hersen, 1988; Hersen & Bellack; 1988; Hersen & Turner, 1984; Nelson, 1987). Such positions have been articulated by a number of prominent behavior therapists, such as Nathan (1981) and Kazdin (1983). But the issues concerning DSM-III and behavioral assessment are most clearly summarized by Taylor (1983), a behavioral psychiatrist:

> The new Diagnostic and Statistical Manual of the American Psychiatric Association is a major improvement in psychiatric diagnosis over previous classification systems. Where symptomatic diagnoses are useful, as in relating an individual's problem to the wealth of clinical and research data in abnormal psychology or in identifying conditions which require specific treatments, DSM-III represents the best available system. Many conceptual and practical problems remain with DSM-III; for instance, it retains a bias toward the medical model, it includes many conditions which should not fall into a psychiatric diagnostic system, and it includes descriptive axes which have not been adequately validated. Nevertheless, behavior therapists are well advised to become familiar with and use DSM-III as part of behavioral assessment. (p. 13)

We, of course, would argue that the same holds true for DSM-III-R and its eventual successor, DSM-IV. We are fully in accord with Taylor's comments and believe that if behavior therapists wish to have an impact on the accepted nosological system, they are urged to work from within rather than from without. In this connection, Tryon (1986) has presented the field with a marvelous outline for how motoric measurements in both children and adults will enable the DSM categories to gain greater precision. He clearly shows how many of the diagnostic categories (e.g., depression; attention deficit-hyperactivity disorders) have motoric referents that could be evaluated by behavioral assessors. However, much work of a normative nature (to determine lower and upper limits of normality) will be required before any impact on the DSM system will be felt (Tryon, 1989). We believe that such evaluation represents an enormous challenge to behavioral assessors that could result in a lasting contribution to the diagostic arena.

SUMMARY

We have attempted to provide a brief historical overview of several major areas in psychological evaluation: intellectual, personality, neuropsychological, and behavioral assessment. Some of these areas have lengthy histories, and others are relatively young. However, it seems clear that the tools used by psychologists as recently as 25 years ago are generally different from those used now. Behavioral assessment techniques, structured psychiatric interviews, and standard, comprehensive neuropsychological test batteries are all relatively new. Furthermore, the computer is at least beginning to make significant inroads into the assessment field, with online testing, scoring, and interpretation a reality in some cases. Serious efforts have been made in recent years to link assessment more closely to treatment and other practical concerns. We may also note a trend away from indirect methods to direct acquisition of information and observation. The structured interview is an example of the former approach, and many behavioral assessment techniques would exemplify the latter one. Similarly, while neuropsychological assessment is still heavily dependent on the use of formal tests, there is increasing interest in the use of those tests in rehabilitation planning and in the association between neuropsychological test results and functional activities of daily living. We also note a corresponding decrease in interest in such matters as brain localization, particularly since the CT scan and related brain imaging procedures have solved much of that problem. We would prognosticate that psychological assessment will be increasingly concerned with automation, the direct observation of behavior, and the practical application of assessment results.

REFERENCES

Adams, H. E., Doster, J. A., & Calhoun, K. S. (1977). A psychologically based system of response classification. In A. R. Ciminero, K. S. Calhoun, & H. E. Adams (Eds.), *Handbook of behavioral assessment.* New York: Wiley.

Adams, H. E., & Turner, S. M. (1979). Editorial. *Journal of Behavioral Assessment, 1,* 1–2.

Allport, G. W. (1937). Personality: *A psychological interpretation.* New York: Holt.

American Psychiatric Association. (1980). *Diagnostic and statistical manual of mental disorders* (3rd ed.). Washington, DC: Author.

American Psychiatric Association. (1987). *Diagnostic and statistical manual of mental disorders* (3rd ed. rev.). Washington, DC: Author.

Ash, P. (1949). The reliability of psychiatric diagnosis. *Journal of Abnormal and Social Psychology, 44,* 272–276.

Atkinson, C. (1973). Data collection and program evaluation using the problem-oriented medical record. Miami: Association for Advancement of Behavior Therapy.

Barlow, D. H., & Hersen, M. (1984). *Single-case experimental designs: Strategies for studying behavior change* (2nd ed.). Elmsford, NY: Pergamon Press.

Begelman, D. A. (1975). Ethical and legal issues in behavior modification. In M. Hersen, R. M. Eisler, & P. M. Miller (Eds.), *Progress in behavior modification* (Vol. 1). New York: Academic Press.

Benton, A. L., Hamsher, K. deS., Varney, N. R., & Spreen, O. (1983). *Contributions to neuropsychological assessment: A clinical manual.* New York: Oxford University Press.

Bellack, A. S., & Hersen, M. (1988). Future directions. In A. S. Bellack & M. Hersen (Eds.), *Behavioral assessment: A practical handbook* (3rd ed.). Elmsford, NY: Pergamon Press.

Bellack, A. S., Hersen, M., & Lamparski, D. (1979). Role-playing tests for assessing social skills: Are they valid? Are they useful? *Journal of Consulting and Clinical Psychology, 47,* 335–342.

Bellack, A. S., Hersen, M., & Turner, S. M. (1979). Relationship of role playing and knowledge of appropriate behavior to assertion in the natural environment. *Journal of Consulting and Clinical Psychology, 47,* 679–685.

Bellack, A. S., Turner, S. M., Hersen, M., & Luber, R. (1980). Effects of stress and retesting on role playing tests of social skill. *Journal of Behavioral Assessment, 2,* 99–104.

Bernhardt, A. J., Hersen, M., & Barlow, D. H. (1972). Measurement and modification of spasmodic torticollis: An experiment analysis. *Behavior Therapy, 3,* 294–297.

Blessed, G., Tomlinson, B. E., & Roth, M. (1968). The association between quantitative measures of dementia and of senile change in the cerebral grey matter of elderly subjects. *British Journal of Psychiatry, 114,* 797–811.

Boring, E. G. (1950). *A history of experimental psychology.* New York: Appleton-Century-Crofts.

Bornstein, P. H., Bornstein, M. T., & Dawson, B. (1984). Integrated assessment and treatment. In T. H. Ollendick & M. Hersen (Eds.), *Child behavioral assessment: Principles and procedures.* Elmsford, NY: Pergamon Press.

Burdock, E. I., Hardesty, A. S., Hakerem, G., Zubin, J., & Beck, Y. M. (1968). *Ward behavior inventory.* New York: Springer.

Burdock, E., & Zubin, J. (1985). Objective evaluation in psychiatry. *Psychiatric reference and record book* (2nd ed.). New York: Roerig Laboratories, Inc.

Cattell, R. B., Eber, H. W., & Tatsuoka, M. M. (1970). *Handbook for the sixteen personality factor questionnaire.* Champaign, IL: Institute for Personality and Ability Testing.

Cautela, J. R. (1968). Behavior therapy and the need for behavior assessment. *Psychotherapy: Theory, Research and Practice, 5,* 175–179.

Cautela, J. R. (1973, September). *A behavioral coding system.* Presidential address to the seventh annual meeting of the Association for Advancement of Behavior Therapy, Miami.

Cone, J. D. (1977). The relevance of reliability and validity for behavioral assessment. *Behavioral Therapy. 8,* 411–426.

Cone, J. D. (1988). Psychometric considerations and the multiple models of behavioral assessment. In A. S. Bellack & M. Hersen (Eds.), Behavioral assessment: A practical handbook (3rd ed.). Elmsford, NY: Pergamon Press.

Cordes, C. (1983). Mullane: Tests are grounded. *APA Monitor, 14,* 24.

Cronbach, L. J. (1949). *Essentials of psychological testing.* New York: Harper & Brothers (2nd ed., 1960).

Cronbach, L. J. (1960). *Essentials of psychological testing* (2nd ed.). New York: Harper & Brothers.

Delis, D. C., Kramer, J. H., Kaplan, E., & Ober, B. A., (1987). *CVLT: California verbal learning test: Research Edition,* manual. San Antonio: The Psychological Corporation Harcourt Brace Jovanovich.

Edelbrock, C. (1984). Diagnostic issues. In T. H. Ollendick & M. Hersen (Eds.), *Child behavioral assessment: Principles and procedures* (pp. 30–37). Elmsford, NY: Pergamon Press.

Eisler, R. M., & Polak, P. R. (1971). Social stress and psychiatric disorder. *Journal of Nervous and Mental Disease, 153,* 227–233.

Feighner, J., Robins, E., Guze, S., Woodruff, R., Winokur, G., & Munoz, R. (1972). Diagnostic criteria for use in psychiatric research. *Archives of General Psychiatry, 26,* 57–63.

Folstein, M. F., Folstein, S. E., & McHugh, P. R. (1975). Mini-mental state. A practical method for grading the cognitive state of patients for the clinician. *Journal of Psychiatric Research, 12,* 189–198.

Foster, S. L., Bell-Dolan, D. J., & Burge, D. A. (1988). Behavioral observation. In A. S. Bellack & M. Hersen (Eds.). *Behavioral assessment: A practical handbook.* New York: Pergamon Press.

Fowler, R. D. (1979). The automated MMPI. In C. S. Newmark (Ed.), *MMPI clinical and research trends.* New York: Praeger.

Gilberstadt, H., & Duker, J. (1965). *A handbook for clinical and actuarial MMPI interpretation.* Philadelphia: Saunders.

Golden, C. J., Hammeke, T. A., & Purisch, A. D. (1980). *The Luria–Nebraska Battery manual.* Los Angeles, CA: Western Psychological Services.

Golden, G. (1981). The Luria–Nebraska children's battery: Theory and formulation. In G. W. Hynd & J. E. Obrzut (Eds.), *Neuropsychological assessment and the school-aged child: Issues and procedures.* New York: Grune & Stratton.

Golden, C. J., Purisch, A. D., & Hammeke, T. A. (1985). *Luria–Nebraska neuropsychological battery: Forms I and II,* manual. Los Angeles: Western Psychological Services.

Goldstein, G. (1979). Methodological and theoretical issues in neuropsychological assessment. *Journal of Behavioral Assessment, 1,* 23–41.

Guilford, J. P., & Zimmerman, W. (1949). *Guilford-Zimmerman Temperament survey.* Los Angeles, CA: Western Psychological Services.

Hamilton, M. (1960). A rating scale for depression. *Journal of Neurology, Neurosurgery and Psychiatry, 23,* 56–62.

Harris, S. L., & Ferrari, M. (1983). Developmental factors in child behavior therapy. *Behavior Therapy, 14,* 54–72.

Hayes-Roth, F., Longabaugh, R., & Ryback, R. (1972). The problem-oriented medical record and psychiatry. *British Journal of Psychiatry, 121,* 27–34.

Haynes, S. N. (1978). *Principles of behavioral assessment.* New York: Gardner Press.

Helzer, J., Robins, L., Croughan, J., & Welner, A. (1981). Renard Diagnostic Interview. *Archives of General Psychiatry, 38,* 393–398.

Hersen, M. (1973). Self-assessment and fear. *Behavior Therapy, 4,* 241–257.

Hersen, M. (1976). Historical perspectives in behavioral assessment. In M. Hersen & A. S. Bellack (Eds.), *Behavioral assessment designs: Strategies for studying behavior change*. Elmsford, NY: Pergamon Press.

Hersen, M. (Ed.). (1988). Behavioral assessment and psychiatric diagnosis. *Behavioral Assessment, 10*, 107–121.

Hersen, M., & Barlow, D. H. (1976). *Single-case experimental designs: Strategies for studying behavior change*. Elmsford, NY: Pergamon Press.

Hersen, M., & Bellack, A. S. (Eds.) (1976). *Behavioral assessment: A practical handbook*. Elmsford, NY: Pergamon Press.

Hersen, M., & Bellack, A. S. (1981). *Behavioral assessment: A practical handbook* (2nd ed.). Elmsford, NY: Pergamon Press.

Hersen, M., & Bellack, A. S. (1988). DSM-III and behavioral assessment. In A. S. Bellack & M. Hersen (Eds.), *Behavioral assessment: A practical handbook* (3rd ed.). Elmsford, NY: Pergamon Press.

Hersen, M., & Last, C. G. (1989). Psychiatric diagnosis and behavioral assessment in children. In C. G. Last & M. Hersen (Eds.), *Handbook of child psychiatric diagnosis*. New York: Wiley.

Hersen, M., & Turner, S. M. (1984). DSM-III and behavior therapy. In S. M. Turner & M. Hersen (Eds.), *Adult psychopathology: A behavioral perspective*. New York: Wiley.

Hines, F. R., & Williams, R. B. (1975). Dimensional diagnosis and the medical students' grasp of psychiatry. *Archives of General Psychiatry, 32*, 525–528.

Holtzman, W. H. (1958). *The Holtzman inkblot technique*. New York: Psychological Corporation.

Honigfeld, G., & Klett, C. (1965). The Nurse's Observation Scale for Inpatient Evaluation (NOSIE): A new scale for measuring improvement in schizophrenia. *Journal of Clinical Psychology, 21*, 65–71.

Horton, A. M. (1988). Use of neuropsychological testing in determining effectiveness of ritalin therapy in an DDRT patient. *The Behavior Therapist, 11*, 114–118.

Jensen, A. R. (1983, August). *Nature of the white-black differences on various psychometric tests*. Invited address, American Psychological Association Convention, Anaheim, CA.

Kanfer, F. H., & Grimm, L. G. (1977). Behavior analysis: Selecting target behaviors in the interview. *Behavior Modification, 1*, 7–28.

Kanfer, F. H., & Saslow, G. (1969). Behavioral diagnosis. In C. M. Franks (Ed.), *Behavior therapy: Appraisal and status*. New York: McGraw-Hill.

Katz, R. C., & Woolley, F. R. (1975). Improving patients' records through problem orientation. *Behavior Therapy, 6*, 119–124.

Kazdin, A. E. (1983). Psychiatric diagnosis, dimensions of dysfunction, and child behavior therapy. *Behavior Therapy, 14*, 73–99.

Klonoff, H., & Cox, B. (1975). A problem-oriented system approach to analysis of treatment outcome. *American Journal of Psychiatry, 132*, 841–846.

Lazarus, A. A. (1973). Multimodal behavior therapy: Treating the "basic id." *Journal of Nervous and Mental Disease, 156*, 404–411.

Lezak, M. (1976). *Neuropsychological Assessment*. New York: Oxford University Press.

Longabaugh, R., Fowler, D. R., Stout, R., & Kriebel, G. (1983). Validation of a problem-focused nomenclature. *Archives of General Psychiatry, 40*, 453–461.

Longabaugh, R., Stout, R., Kriebel, G. M., McCullough, L., & Bishop, D. (1986). DSM-III and clinically identified problems as a guide to treatment. *Archives of General Psychiatry, 43*, 1097–1103.

Machover, K. (1949). *Personality projection in the drawing of the human figure: A method of personality investigation*. Springfield, IL: Charles Thomas.

Marks, P. A., Seeman, W., & Haller, D. L. (1974). *The actuarial use of the MMPI with adolescents and adults*. Baltimore: Williams & Wilkins.

McFie, J. (1975). *Assessment of organic intellectual impairment*. London: Academic Press.

McLean, P. D., & Miles, J. E. (1974). Evaluation and the problem-oriented record in psychiatry. *Archives of General Psychiatry, 31*, 622–625.

Meehl, P. E. (1954). *Clinical vs. statistical prediction*. Minneapolis: University of Minnesota Press.

Menninger, K. a. (1952). *A manual for psychiatric case study*. New York: Grune & Stratton.

Michelson, L. (1984). The role of individual differences, response profiles, and treatment consonance in anxiety disorders. *Journal of Behavioral Assessment, 6*, 349–367.

Michelson, L. (1986). Treatment consonance and response profiles in agoraphobia: Behavioral and physiological treatments. *Behaviour Research and Therapy, 24*, 263–275.

Millon, T. (1982). *Millon Clinical Multiaxial Inventory* (3rd ed.). Minneapolis, MN: National Computer Systems.

Millon, T. (1985). The MCMI provides a good assessment of DSM-III disorders: The MCMI-II will prove even better. *Journal of Personality Assessment, 49,* 379–391.

Murray, H. A. (1938). *Explorations in personality.* New York: Oxford University Press.

Nathan, P. E. (1981). Symptomatic diagnosis and behavioral assessment: A synthesis. In D. H. Barlow (Ed.), *Behavioral assessment of adult disorders.* New York: Guilford Press.

Nathan, P. E., Zare, N. C., Simpson, H. F., & Ardberg, M. M. (1969). A systems analytic model of diagnosis: I. The diagnostic validity of abnormal psychomotor behavior. *Journal of Clinical Psychology, 25,* 3–9.

Nelson, R. O. (1980). The use of intelligence tests within behavioral assessment. *Behavioral Assessment, 2,* 417–423.

Nelson, R. O. (1987). DSM-III and behavioral assessment. In C.G. Last & M. Hersen (Eds.), *Issues in diagnostic research.* New York: Plenum Press.

Nelson, R. O., & Hayes, S. C. (1979). Some current dimensions on behavioral assessment. *Behavioral Assessment, 1,* 1–16.

Overall, J. E., & Gorham,, J. R. (1962). The brief psychiatric rating scale. *Psychological Reports, 10,* 799–812.

Rapaport, D. (1945). *Diagnostic psychological testing.* Chicago: Year Book Publications.

Raskin, A. (1982). Assessment of psychopathology by the nurse or psychiatric aide. In E. I. Burdock, A. Sudilovsky, & S. Gershon (Eds.), *The behavior of psychiatric patients: Quantitative techniques for evaluation.* New York: Marcel Dekker.

Reitan, R. M., & Davison, L. A. (1974). Clinical neuropsychology: Current status and applications. Washington, DC: V. H. Winston and Sons.

Reitan, R. M., & Wolfson, D. (1985). *The Halstead-Reitan neuropsychological test battery: Theory and clinical interpretation.* Tucson, AZ: Neuropsychology Press.

Robins, S. L., Helzer, J., Croughan, N. A., & Ratcliff, K. (1981). National Institute of Mental Health Diagnostic Interview Schedule. *Archives of General Psychiatry, 38,* 381–389.

Rohde, A. R. (1957). *The sentence completion method.* New York: Ronald Press.

Rosen, A. J., Sussman, S., Mueser, K. T., Lyons, J. S., & Davis, J. M. (1981). Behavioral assessment of psychiatric inpatients and normal controls across different environmental contexts. *Journal of Behavioral Assessment, 3,* 25–36.

Sandifer, M. G., Jr., Pettus, C., & Quade, D. (1964). A study of psychiatric diagnosis. *Journal of Nervous and Mental Disease, 139,* 350–356.

Scales, E. J., & Johnson, M. S. (1975). A psychiatric POMR for use by a multidisciplinary team. *Hospital and Community Psychiatry, 26,* 371–373.

Shneidman, E. S. (1952). *Make a picture test.* New York: Psychological Corporation.

Spitzer, R. L., & Endicott, J. (1977). *Schedule for affective disorders and schizophrenia.* Technical Report. New York: New York State Psychiatric Institute, Biometrics Research Department.

Spitzer, R. L., Endicott, J., & Robins, E. (1977). *Research diagnostic criteria (RDC) for a selected group of functional disorders.* Bethesda, MD: National Institute of Mental Health.

Spitzer, R. L., & Williams, J. B. W. (1983). *Instruction manual for the structured clinical interview for DSM-III (SCID).* New York: New York State Psychiatric Institute, Biometrics Research Department.

Swensen, C. H. (1957). Empirical evaluations of human figure drawings, 1957–1966. *Psychological Bulletin, 54,* 431–466.

Swensen, C. H. (1968). Empirical evaluations of human figure drawings. *Psychological Bulletin, 20,* 20–44.

Szondi, L. (1952). *Experimental diagnostics of drives.* New York: Grune & Stratton.

Taylor, C. B. (1983). DSM-III and behavioral assessment. *Behavioral Assessment, 5,* 5–14.

Tryon, W. W. (1986). Motor activity measurements and DSM-III. In M. Hersen, R. M. Eisler, P. M. Miller (Eds.), *Progress in behavior modification: Vol. 20.* New York: Academic Press.

Tryon, W. W. (1989). Behavioral assessment and psychiatric diagnosis. In M. Hersen (Ed.), *Innovations in child behavior therapy.* New York: Springer.

VanLennep, D. J. (1951). The four-picture test. In H. H. Anderson & G. L. Anderson (Eds.), *An introduction to projective techniques.* New York: Prentice-Hall.

Wechsler, D. (1944). *The measurement of adult intelligence.* Baltimore, MD: Williams & Wilkins.

Wechsler, D. (1987). *Wechsler Memory Scale-Revised.* New York: Psychological Corporation.

Weed, L. L. (1964). Medical records, patient care, and medical education. *Irish Journal of Medical Sciences, 6,* 271–282.

Weed, L. L. (1968). Medical records that guide and teach. *New England Journal of Medicine, 278,* 593–600.

Weed, L. L. (1969). *Medical records, medical education, and patient care.* Cleveland, OH: Case Western Reserve University Press.

White, D. K., Turner, L. B., & Turkat, I. D. (1983). The etiology of behavior: Survey data on behavior therapists' contributions. *Behavior Therapist, 6,* 59–60.

Wolpe, J. (1977). Inadequate behavior analysis: The Achilles' heel of outcome research in behavior therapy. *Journal of Behavior Therapy and Experimental Psychiatry, 8,* 1–3.

Wolpe, J. (1986). The positive diagnosis of neurotic depression as an etiological category. *Comprehensive Psychiatry, 27,* 449–460.

Wolpe, J., & Wright, R. (1988). The neglect of data gathering instruments in behavior therapy practice. *Journal of Behavior Therapy and Experimental Psychiatry, 19,* 5–9.

Zubin, J. (1967). Classification of the behavior disorders. *Annual Review of Psychology, 18,* 373–406. Palo Alto, CA: Annual Review, Inc.

Zubin, J. (1984). Inkblots do not a test make. *Contemporary Psychology, 29,* 153–154.

PART II

PSYCHOMETRIC FOUNDATIONS

CHAPTER 2

TEST CONSTRUCTION

Charles J. Golden
Robert F. Sawicki
Michael D. Franzen

INTRODUCTION

Recent years have witnessed a proliferation of psychological assessment instruments. Many of these instruments assess single constructs such as androgyny (Bem, 1974, 1977), assertion (Galassi, Delo, Galassi, & Bastien, 1974), and depression (Carroll, Fielding, & Blashki, 1973). Other tests focus on multiple traits, including the Personality Inventory for Children (Lachar & Gdowski, 1979), the Millon Personality Inventory (Millon, 1982), and the Luria-Nebraska Neuropsychological Battery (Golden, Hammeke, & Purisch, 1980).

Due to space limitations, it is not possible to review all of the work done on test development by persons like Anastasi (1982) or Fiske (1978) within this chapter. Rather, the intent is to present an overview of the major steps in test construction, with special attention to the practical considerations inherent in scale development and validation in order to provide an appreciation of the issues underlying this process, and encourage test-oriented research in the future.

There are at least three approaches to scale construction (Wiggins, 1973). The analytic approach relies most heavily on theory to determine the selection of items, procedures, and criteria for assessing individuals. Under this approach, items are chosen on the basis of whether they appear to tap an aspect of the construct under consideration. For example, if the theory specifies that an important aspect is the age at which a person was toilet trained, then a question regarding that information would be included in the scale.

Under the empirical approach, the first step in scale construction is to select an operational index of the construct to be measured. For example, in devising the first edition of the Minnesota Multiphasic Personality Inventory (MMPI), the authors of the test used psychiatric diagnosis as the operational index. The second step was to select items that were assumed to be associated with the index. With the MMPI, the authors asked clinicians to generate items that corresponded to the psychiatric diagnoses. Next, the method of contrasted groups was used to see which items discriminated among the diagnostic groups. It is clear that under this approach, items are chosen on the basis of empirically demonstrated relationships with the criterion, and theory plays less of a role than under the analytic approach.

A third strategy is the rational approach or, as Jackson (1975) has labeled it, the sequential system approach. The sequential system model tries to combine the features of the analytic and the empirical approaches in a logical sequence as well as evaluating the psychometric properties of the resultant scales. It operates under the guidance of four principles, which are (a) the importance of psychological theory, (b) the necessity for suppressing variance due to response style, (c) the balance of scale homogeneity with generalizability, and (d) the evaluation of convergent and discriminant validity. Items are originally generated on the basis of a coherent theory but are retained on the basis of their psychometric properties and empirical relationships. Because of its flexibility and applicability, the sequential system model is the method most often used today in scale construction and is the approach that provides a broad outline for the discussion in this chapter. Because the authors are most familiar with neuropsychology, many of the examples are drawn from that field. However, the discussion is broad enough to be applicable to other areas in psychology for which scale construction is an issue.

INITIAL ITEM SELECTION

The first step in the development of any test is to determine what domain the test responses will represent. A thorough understanding of what the test is expected to measure will guide both initial validation research and later clinical interpretation of individual results. Such theoretical understanding of what a given test is expected to produce also guides the development of an initial item pool.

Since the initial item pool is selected to maximize data gathering along some trait or skill dimension, it is useful for persons who are designing their first test to construct a Table of Specifications (Hopkins & Antes, 1978) in order to increase their chances of identifying an item pool that will represent their domain of interest. Initially many more items are selected than actually necessary. This set of items is then pared down by the validation process.

The Table of Specifications can be described as a two-dimensional matrix where one dimension represents the skills or traits of interest and the other the behaviors representative of these characteristics. This blueprint can be used to determine both the number of items that will be selected to represent each aspect (behavior) of the domain of interest and the type of items that will be used. Thus a comprehensive test battery may include diverse and seemingly unrelated items. A limited purpose test may include only very specific and highly similar items. Table 2.1 provides

Table 2.1. Specifications

| | TASK | |
FUNCTION	SIMPLE	COMPLEX
Motor Organization	Items 1–4 28–31	Items 21–27 32–33
Tactile-Motor Integration	Items 5–6	Items 7–8
Visual-Spatial-Motor Integration	Items 9–18	Items 36–47
Verbal-Motor Integration	Items 19–20	Items 48–51

specifications for the Luria-Nebraska Motor Scale. This table has been greatly simplified for descriptive purposes. In actual practice the functions could be further subdivided into much smaller skill areas (e.g., Motor Integration, Oral) and topic areas could be weighted by the theoretical importance of a given subarea (e.g., 30% of the items would be selected to represent motor organization).

Items are most often chosen by face validity. In the best of cases, items are derived from a comprehensive theory that dictates the types of items that may be necessary for a given test. In other instances, item selection may be based on "professional nomination," the result of suggestions by experts, or simply by sampling many items used in other tests or clinical practice. In general, since some items will probably be dropped subsequent to validation, it is better at this stage to be overinclusive in the selection of items. It is recommended that the original item pool include from two to four times the number that one wishes to include in the final version of the test. Overall limitations on the number of items in the initial pool will occur as a factor of practical issues: tests that will require individual administration (i.e., IQ tests) will probably start out with a smaller pool than those that permit group administration (i.e., personality inventories).

ITEM FORMATS

Items may either be open-ended or restricted in terms of response options. Restricted items are defined here as forced choice (e.g., true/false) or multiple choice items. Such items are more popular with group administered tests. Open-ended items allow more projective responses from patients; however, by necessity, they must be individually administered and scored because of the infinite variety of answers that must be evaluated by an examiner. Open-ended item construction requires careful selection due to the amount of interpretation that will be required of an examiner to accurately score such items. These items are less likely to meet the requirements for standardization as they are discussed below.

Item content or presentation is not limited by the type of response format chosen. For example, inkblots may be used in tests that are open ended. However, we could design an inkblot test that was multiple choice: Is the above inkblot [a] a. bat; b. person; c. two persons; d. dying swan. Whether such a test would measure the same thing as the more open-ended format is, of course, a question of construct validity that must be empirically explored. The item format influences the amount of information gathered from a given item. Open-ended/projective items are more useful when the clinician wishes to observe and analyze the process a patient uses to arrive at a response, while forced choice and multiple choice items are more concerned with the resulting pattern of responses than the process. The interpretive meaning of such a pattern is determined by empirically derived correlates.

Items may also be classified as objective or projective. Objective items include not only the forced choice and multiple choice items but also items that allow more flexible responses, for which there are consensually determined correct answers. An example of the latter is the question, "What does the word 'summer' mean?" Projective items, on the other hand, are deliberately vague and ambiguous. There is a wide range of correct responses to which an interpretive system must be applied in order to derive meaningful scoring. Although some writers would exclude such ambiguous material from the arena of standardized tests, the present authors see no reason to do this as long as the set of items meets the general criteria for a standardized test.

Limitations to Item Formats

In deciding the item format to use within a test, one must be cognizant of the limitations of each format type. Such limits must be weighed against the amount of useful information that a particular format will generate. Though multiple choice items can be scored quickly, provide greater interrater reliability, and sample a larger content area, they are open to interpretive error due to guessing and random response sets. Such tests also take longer to construct, because both test items and distractors must be designed. In the initial stages of test construction, such items may also be misplaced on a scale, because the researcher must intuitively determine the level of difficulty of each item before it is seen by a patient (Hopkins & Antes, 1978). Similar criticisms may be applied to the true/false format. In addition, the forced choice format is greatly affected by the wording used within items. Poorly stated items undermine a test's clinical usefulness.

Although the open-ended/projective items may be constructed more quickly, do not permit guessing, and allow the clinician to observe the problem-solving process, they require that examiners have extensive training in a scoring system so that responses may be validly interpreted. In addition, scoring takes much longer and "styles" of scoring may limit the overall reliability of the open-ended test.

Standardization: Administration

At this point in the test construction process, there are two major requirements for standardization: (a) standard administration and (b) standard scoring. An item must lend itself to both of these processes in order to be acceptable at this stage of development. Forced choice and multiple choice items meet such criteria without difficulty. The patient is read or reads the item and chooses a response alternative or states his or her answer. If additional material is used (e.g., pictures), these are identical for all patients. Such structure facilitates group applications for such items.

Open-ended items can (but do not need to) present more difficulties for standard administration. Standardization is achieved by having the examiner state the test instructions in a standard form and as much as possible say "root" demands in a standard manner. Again, whenever possible, each patient handles the same set of ancillary test materials. Problems arise with open-ended items on two occasions: (a) when an examiner attempts to elicit further information within an item procedure rather than first getting a scoreable response, then goes back to test the limits of a response; and (b) when the patient produces an entirely novel response that does not fit into any established scoring criteria. Open-ended questions are also more open to questioning by a patient, thus offering the possibility of disrupting the administration procedure.

The first difficulty usually arises when an examiner does not completely understand the intent of an item. Such a problem raises the possibility that the item itself may contain unintended ambiguity. Thus an individual examiner's interpretation of the item's intent may break standard administration and invalidate the item.

This problem can be handled in one of several ways. The most common approach has been to demand strict adherence to rigid administration rules regardless of outside concerns. Examiners are instructed to adopt testing the limits procedures after eliciting a scoreable response in order to gain sufficient additional information that is needed to avoid interpretive difficulties.

A second more complex approach is to allow more flexible examination procedures within a standard administration format. For example, the administration of an item requiring a motor response (e.g., finger tapping) may begin with the standard verbal demand. If the patient does not comprehend the task requirements, the examiner may follow up with an alternative verbal explanation, followed by an actual demonstration until the patient understands what is necessary to make a scoreable response to the item. Again, the issue is one of being very clear on what the intent of an item is and offering assistance only to the degree that it does not invalidate the item. By writing such procedures into the standardized administration instructions, one can offer both flexibility and standardization. For this to be functional, more detailed training of examiners is necessary to insure that not only the item procedure, but also the item intent is comprehended by the clinician.

In writing such procedures, the item author must be personally aware of the intent of an item in order to maintain scoring and interpretive integrity. For example, a demonstration could not be allowed when testing a patient's ability to follow spoken instructions, but is quite appropriate in the previous finger tapping example. Similarly, written instructions could be used as an additional procedure for an item measuring verbal comprehension, but not for an item requiring auditory analysis.

In all cases, item materials must be identical. Small differences in legibility, color, shape, size, or other dimensions can create wide, artifactual variations in response to items. In cases where identical materials cannot be easily or reliably employed (for whatever reason), research must identify the effect of such differences on subject responses. Such study is intended to identify the salient aspects of stimuli in order to make subsequent interpretation of patient data more meaningful. For example, it may not matter which type of tape recorder is used to present auditory stimuli for an item, but the quality of reproduction across tape recorders may create unintended differences in the overall results of a set of items measuring subtle tonal discrimination. Thus quality control becomes an important issue not only for individual items but also for any ancillary test materials employed.

Standardization Scaling

A number of scaling methods may be used with items, depending on the domain of interest that the test is intended to measure. Scaling methods can roughly be characterized into three types: nominal, ordinal, or interval scales. Ratio scales have not been applied to psychological data.

Nominal scaling reflects regrouping responses into arbitrarily defined categories, which are only meaningful in the context of the measure within which they were created. Such categories are not assumed to have characteristics of counting numbers. It is usually the frequency of responses within a given category that provides the focus of interest for the clinician. This method of scaling is most often used when scoring represents an analysis of the process used to achieve an answer rather than the tabulation of the answer alone. The scoring system of the Rorschach Inkblot Test (Exner, 1974) is an example of such a scaling system. Responses may be regrouped under such category headings as "Form," "Location," "Shading," and so forth. Some neuropsychological tests may count the number of responses that may be classified as "perseveration," "neglect," or "impulsiveness."

Ordinal scaling reflects a ranking of responses along some underlying dimension (e.g., adequacy of performance). Thus an item may be scored as "0" (normal), "1" (borderline), "2" (mild impairment), "3" (moderate impairment), and "4" (severe impairment). Ordinal scaling does not assume that the distance between numbers is equal, only that the ranking is meaningful. Thus, the change in severity from 0 (normal) to 1 (borderline) is not assumed to have similar magnitude as the change in severity from 3 (moderate impairment) to 4 (severe impairment). Because there is generally a lack of empirical support for quantifiable parallel increases between psychometric data and behavioral changes, most psychological data could be classified as ordinal in nature.

Interval scaling is also ordered, but the distances between data points are assumed to be equal. The distances between points are meaningful; that is, the difference between "1" and "3" is twice as large as the difference between "1" and "2." The zero point is determined arbitrarily and does not necessarily indicate the absence of the quality measured. Psychophysiological measures serve as the best example of such scaling. Though one would be hard pressed to identify assessment instruments that meet such a scaling criteria, most psychological data is treated as though it were on an interval scale.

Gaito (1970) defends the assumptions that indicate that a set of scores may take on the characteristics of more than one type of scaling. He suggests that scaling descriptions are guidelines and that rigid adherence only promotes the wasting of data. In an example he states,

the same data may be considered to have the properties of two or more scales, depending on the context in which it is considered. For example, if we look at the response of one subject (*S*) to a single item, the properties of the data are those of a nominal scale, i.e., right or wrong. However, if we concentrate on the total score for one *S* or the total scores for a group of *S*'s, we have at least an ordinal scale. (p. 65)

Gaito emphasizes that it is not the property of a given scale which has overriding importance but the degree to which items produce data that are normally distributed in a large sample of subjects. This matter is an important point for the use of parametric tests to describe the reliability and validity of a set of items that have undergone a scaling transformation. It may be that few of the assumptions underlying parametric tests need be met with any great accuracy, although this point is debated by some (e.g., Hays, 1973).

Item Analysis: Administration Difficulties

After the initial items have been designed and written, it is best to administer them to several normal individuals to see how they "work." This can be a valuable step, saving much time later, as one will find that some of the items simply do not perform as expected. In some cases, administration as envisioned will be demonstrated to be impossible on a practical level. This may be because subjects cannot comprehend the instructions, the administration is too difficult for an examiner without three arms, or other related possibilities.

Different examiners may be unable to agree on scoring. For example, in the development of the Luria-Nebraska, we initially had an item, "Show me how to frown." While it appeared simple on the surface, we were unable to come up with scoring criteria from which to get reliable data. Items may require more time than expected. Subjects may balk at an item's content or fail to comprehend an item's demand, no matter how it is presented.

In all of these instances, items may be revised or eliminated prior to starting a full validation project. Many of these difficulties are much less frequent with group-administered tests, such as personality inventories.

ITEM ANALYSIS: ITEM EFFICIENCY

After these initial steps have been completed, the test may be administered to a sample of interest. This step should include a minimum of two to three times the number of subjects as test items. If the test is aimed at several different groups, testing with a sample from each group will be necessary. In administering the items, it is important to ensure that the conditions of testing, as well as the items, are standardized. Lighting conditions, ambient noise, distractions, and other environmental conditions should be closely controlled. Even a factor such as room temperature can severely interfere with the interpretability of initial test results if it is not closely observed.

Items should be administered in the same order to all subjects. Examiners must be thoroughly trained to ensure that the test is administered identically to all subjects. Subjects selected for initial pilot studies of the new item set should be cooperative and strongly encouraged to provide their most valid, honest, and accurate performance. An attempt must also be made to select an initial subject pool that is representative of the population to whom the test will later be applied.

After this step has been completed, several analyses may be used to evaluate items further. The *Item Difficulty Index* results from a simple analysis, which demonstrates the relative efficiency of items in groups that do and do not possess the characteristic of interest. In its simplest form, the Item Difficulty Index represents the percentage of a given group that fails an item. If one were testing a given ability that was assumed to be randomly distributed within a population and using a sample randomly drawn from that population, the expected item difficulty for any given item would be .50. As the item difficulty level moves toward 1.0, a given item is too difficult, since at 1.0 no one is passing the item. As the item difficulty approaches 0.0, a given item is too easy, since hardly anyone is missing the item. Items that are too easy or difficult are useless in a test, since they offer no discriminations among subjects. Understanding what is communicated by item difficulty in a psychological test is a little more complex.

When analyzing items from a psychological instrument, it is useful to compute difficulty indices for both the sample of interest and the comparative or control sample. Before performing the computations, one must understand that passing or failing an item must be redefined as responding in the scoreable direction or responding otherwise. Thus, if one has designed a set of true/false items that are expected to identify depression, the scoreable direction is the way in which a depressed person would endorse an item. Therefore, if one has designed a perfect set of items, one expects that difficulties for the depressed group approach 1.00, while difficulties for the comparison (nondepressed) group would tend toward 0.0, suggesting that the items discriminate between the two groups. The total hypothetical sample (both depressed and not depressed) of difficulty indices would approach .50 given the within-group disparities.

On neuropsychological tests where items also involve some ability dimensions, one expects that item difficulty in a heterogeneous sample of brain impaired will be at .50 or greater, while unimpaired controls ought to have difficulty indices of .30 or less. The latter may be expected in a heterogeneous group of unimpaired normals due to the biological variance for performance measures that is assumed in the general population. Thus, one may see that item difficulty is computed by dividing the number of persons who responded in the scoreable direction by the total number of persons who responded to the item. The formula (Hopkins & Antes, 1978, p. 187) below would be applicable to an item that can be scored correct/incorrect. By the nature of the test it is the incorrect response that serves to discriminate among subjects.

$$\text{Item Difficulty} = \frac{\text{Number of subjects who failed the item}}{\text{Number of subjects who responded to item}}$$

Since the Item Difficulty Index is severely affected by the characteristics of the sample, the initial subject pool must be carefully screened for underlying characteristics that may bias the findings. Thus, deriving such an index from an impaired sample that has a great proportion of Alzheimer's patients will produce a set of results that are an artifact of the sample rather than descriptive of item efficiency in a generalizable sense. Similarly, using a sample of normals with below-average cognitive abilities will also create incorrect impressions about item difficulty.

In an appropriate sample those items with difficulties below .2 and above .8 must be closely examined before inclusion in the final test. Again, in an appropriate, heterogeneous sample, item difficulty ought to approach .5 for maximum discrimination on the variable of interest. In order to include a broad base of items, item difficulties should be gathered from samples who contain greater and lesser amounts of the variable of interest. Thus, one would intentionally test very bright and less bright people as separate groups if one were creating a test of cognitive efficiency in order to select items that would discriminate accurately along the full spectrum of cognitive abilities.

In examining the item difficulties for neuropsychological tests, one expects that in a heterogeneous sample of brain impaired item difficulties will approx-

imate .5. One may use such knowledge to observe item difficulties in more homogeneous samples of brain-impaired persons in order to get a sense of the functions that are impaired within such a homogeneous group. Items that showed difficulty indices above the .7 to .8 range would indicate a localized impairment, which one hopes would be consistent with the known impairment of the homogeneous group. Such findings could then be used to support the content validity (which will be discussed later in the chapter) of sets of items.

The *Discrimination Index* is a method of differentiating persons high on a given variable from those low on such a characteristic. Thus, if one assumes that a high overall score on the motor scale of the Luria-Nebraska indicates greater impairment in the higher cortical functions associated with motor movements, one would select two sets of subjects from the sample: those having the highest one third of the scores on the Motor Scale and those having the lowest one third on the Motor Scale and compare item efficiency in these two groups. The formula for the discrimination index (Hopkins & Antes, 1978, p. 189) is

$$\text{Discrimination Index} = \frac{\text{Number in the Upper Group} - \text{Number in the Lower Group}}{\text{Number of Subjects in Either Group}}$$

When a greater number of subjects in the upper group respond in the scoreable direction than the number of subjects in the lower group, the discrimination index is positive. On the other hand, when a greater number of subjects in the lower group respond in the scoreable direction the discrimination index is negative, and one may assume that there is either something wrong with the item or the sample on whom it is being tested. According to Hopkins and Antes (1978) the discrimination index may take on values from -1.0 to $+1.0$; values above .40 suggest effective items, while values between $+.20$ and $+.39$ are considered satisfactory. It must be remembered that items with negative discrimination indices are discriminating in the wrong direction and ought to be reconsidered.

An alternative way to compare high and low scoring groups is to compare a Phi-coefficient. This coefficient is based on a correlation between group membership (high score and low score) and item score (pass, fail). Like all correlation coefficients it may vary between -1.0 and $+1.0$, with higher scores indicating greater discrimination. High negative scores indicate substantial discrimination but in the wrong direction. This may suggest a scoring or criterion problem.

Tables for calculating this coefficient may be found in Jurgensen (1947).

The *Validity Index* is a correlation between a score on a given item and some criterion variable. For example, one may dummy code a criterion variable as 1 = unimpaired and 2 = impaired and correlate each item response with such a variable. In this case items correlating positively would be related to impairment, while items correlated negatively would be related to performance by the unimpaired group. If the test is intended to describe impairment, negatively correlated items will need to be reconsidered. It is up to the researcher to determine the level at which a validity coefficient is acceptable. Because it is a correlation coefficient, it can be squared in order to determine the approximate shared variance between the criterion variable and any given item.

A final method used by test developers to observe item efficiency is to calculate a point biserial correlation between an item and the overall test score in order to discern the degree to which an item represents what the test measures as a whole. Because the item contributes to the general test score, the test score must be recalculated without the given item before the computation is performed. This avoids artificially inflating the item-test relationship.

Items should be positively correlated with the overall test performance. The exact size of the ideal correlation again varies with the intent of the test. In a test measuring a broad skill or personality category, correlations may be in the .4 to .6 range; in a test that purports to measure a single, highly specific skill, correlations should be substantially higher. In the actual selection of items for the final form, intercorrelations among items must also be considered in the manner discussed later in this chapter.

Within multiple-choice tests, analyses may also be performed on the distractors from which the subject must select the correct alternative. One may compute a discrimination index for each distractor. In general, alternatives that are not endorsed are useless, and alternatives that are endorsed to high degrees by subjects who do not contain the characteristic of interest also need to be reevaluated. Obviously such indices will again vary with the characteristics of the subject pool and the overall item difficulty.

A much more complex model of item analysis has been suggested by various theorists based on latent trait models (Anastasi, 1982; Baker, 1977; Weiss & Davison, 1981; Wright & Stone, 1979). These models assume nothing more than a mathematical existence for the characteristic being measured. Based on theoretical models that differ in underlying assumptions,

these models can be used to establish item characteristic curves that represent a comparison of item difficulty against the expected scores of the hypothesized trait (usually estimated by the total test score). From these curves, several parameters of item difficulty may be established. In particular, the one parameter logistic model (Rasch model) holds promise for future developments (Rasch, 1966). A more detailed discussion of such methods is not within the scope of this chapter.

Further item analyses may be performed by observing scale characteristics. This discussion will be included within the context of the broader discussion of scale development.

SCALE DEVELOPMENT

A major difference among tests relates to the number of subscales present within a given test. Item scores may be assembled in a variety of ways, each of which has examples in the literature and in clinical and research applications. More recent tests (e.g., Millon Personality Inventory, Luria-Nebraska Neuropsychological Battery) as well as modifications over the years of tests such as the MMPI illustrate a growing recognition that a test can recombine items that were initially validated and created by different methods.

The most intuitive method of scale construction is simple face validty. The most basic case of this method is the single scale that is assumed to describe a single dimension. Items are chosen because they are assumed to measure this dimension, and such items usually vary only in difficulty levels. In some cases, there is the assumption that items may be ranked according to difficulty within the scale, so that missing a simpler item implies that more difficult items will also be failed. An example of such a test is the Bender-Gestalt Test (Bender, 1938). Each item is assumed to be a measure of a basic visuo-integrative skill that is also related to visual-motor integration. While items vary in complexity (difficulty), they are assumed to all measure the same ability. Thus, items appear to be arranged in order of difficulty.

A face-valid depression scale could be put together by picking items that represent the apparent symptoms of depression (e.g., "I feel sad"; "My appetite has decreased"). In this method, the scale may be based simply on the impressions of the test developer, other experts, or it may reflect an underlying theory of what "depression" is assumed to be. In general, scales that have a strong theoretical background are preferred, because this allows the application of more sophisticated validation techniques.

In summing items to represent scales, all items must be represented on the same scaling system. This may necessitate transforming some items within a test so that they are all similarly scaled, since an item that is only scored "right/wrong" cannot be meaningfully added to another item that represents the number of correct responses within a given time limit. In addition to the type of scaling already discussed, linear transformations of data may also be performed in order to make individual item results more comparable. One may use z scores or, if one wishes to avoid negative values, t scores.

Further, frequencies within nominal categories may be summed to form scales drawn from responses to all items. Thus, on the Rorschach the *Pure Form* scale represents the total number of occurrences of unmodified form responses across all responses. Similarly, in neuropsychology, one could identify a *Perseveration* scale. Although the initial data are nominal, the summing process creates at least ordinal data (Gaito, 1970). In order to make further comparisons among subjects, these raw sums can then be transformed into some form of standard score (e.g., t score).

In addition to the face validity approach to scale formation, scales may also be identified on the basis of empirical properties of the items. These scales are usually based on three basic methodologies: (a) a set of items that discriminate maximally between two groups, (b) a set of items that show high correlations with an external representation of the variable of interest, and (c) a set of items that group together empirically as the result of a factor analytic procedure.

The first methodology may be illustrated by the construction of the original *Depression* scale of the MMPI. This scale was formed by comparing the responses of a group of psychiatrically diagnosed depressed patients with the responses derived from a control group. Items selected for the scale were those that maximally discriminated the two groups. Another example would be a screening test for brain damage, which could be put together from a set of items that are observed to maximally separate the brain impaired from unimpaired persons.

In the second case, items are selected on the basis of their correlation with an outside criterion. Thus, a depression scale may be formed by correlating item performance with psychiatric ratings of depressed persons on a scale from 1 to 7. If one were more biologically inclined, correlations could be calculated between the results of the dexamethasone suppression test and a set of items assumed to measure depression. This would link the diagnosis of depression to a specific biological marker rather than clinical impression alone. A test of brain damage could be developed by correlating items with ventricular size as derived from a cranial computed tomograph.

The validity of the scales developed by these first two methods is dependent on the adequacy of the group or the external criteria selected. This, however, is not always the case. The original MMPI is a perfect example of a test that has been criticized for its method of norm group definition but has been found to have enormous clinical value as the result of later empirical study. However, in such cases the empirically based method of interpretation may not resemble the original procedures intended by the test makers.

In the third method, scales are factor analytically derived based on the intercorrelations among items within an item pool. Items that load on the same factor are assumed to relate to an underlying trait that can be represented by a factor score. By orthogonally rotating the initial solution and employing some criterion factor loading, sets of items that load on given factors can be identified as a group of independent scales.

An additional factor analytic method that may be used to create a scale includes the use of marker variables: that is, variables that are known to be representative of a given trait. With this method, a depression scale may be constructed from a general pool of items by factor analyzing these items along with a set of variables known to be associated with depression. Items that share factors with the marker variables can then be included in the depression scale.

There are several limitations to the factor analytic procedures that must be considered in using such a methodology. First, one must thoroughly understand the theory that guided the initial item selections or constructions, since the resulting factors can be interpreted accurately only within the context of a theoretical base. Second, each factor solution and rotational method carries with it a set of theoretical assumptions that guides its meaningful application. It is up to the test designer to determine which analysis will create the least distortion in the original data while producing interpretable results. Thus, in choosing a rotational method one must understand, for instance, that the computational method in a Varimax rotation conserves variance down columns and thus creates a large first factor, partially as a consequence of the computational procedure.

Third, an exploratory (initial) factor analytic solution may be unstable across groups. Therefore, it is important to replicate factor analytically derived dimensions across groups in order to feel some assurance that one is observing a stable (reliable) structure; that is, that items are not simply going together as an artifact of the study at hand.

A fourth limitation to the factor analytic method results from the sample employed. Because dimensions are formed based on how items (variables) covary, the presence of subgroups in the sample that show both great within-group similarity on a set of items and great between-group differences on the same set of items offer the possibility of identifying dimensions that reflect the a priori group differences. This is a problem if it is unintended by the investigator. It can be a benefit if within-group characteristics are being used as marker variables.

Underlying characteristics that may bias responses may also create artificial factor dimensions. Thus, factors may actually reflect such variables as scoring approach, age, education, socioeconomic status, cultural, or gender differences.

Finally, the results of a factor analysis are influenced by the items available for the analysis. Thus, underrepresentation of certain skills or traits in the item pool will prevent such variables from emerging as meaningful factors, even if such skills are important to the domain of the test. The best way to avoid such difficulties is to start with the Table of Specifications, which was described earlier in this chapter, as a blueprint for item construction.

Scales may, of course, be created by a combination of any of these methods. For example, original items may be chosen by screening based on face validity, then confirmed by correlational analysis. The resultant items may then be factor analyzed in an attempt to validate assumptions about the structure of the test. This would be an example of Jackson's (1975) sequential model, which was referred to earlier.

The latter process may also be used to create new scales from the existing pool of items within a test. For example, the original items on the Luria-Nebraska were selected based on face validity and validated by item-scale correlations. Localization scales were derived from comparisons among groups with known characteristics (localized brain injury), and factor scales were identified from the test-item pool.

After initial creation of scales, further item analysis can be performed. For example, items within a scale that are redundant (highly intercorrelated) may be eliminated. Other items may be eliminated due to their overall lack of relationship with the total score of the scale. For scales validated against outside criteria, items showing the least relationship with these criteria may be removed from the scale. Scale factors analyt-

ically derived may be shortened by determining the least number of items that maximize prediction of the characteristic of interest.

The final decisions regarding scale length must result from several considerations: (a) theoretical concerns, which are an attempt to insure that the domain of interest is being adequately sampled; (b) practical concerns (e.g., time for administration); (c) procedural concerns, that is, the elimination of items that create excessive administrative difficulty while yielding limited clinical information; (d) psychometric concerns or the need to maintain adequate levels of reliability and validity. Though we are speaking of making some final decisions about an instrument at this point, it is optimally useful to enter the next phase of study with several versions of a scale (differing usually only in length) to see which is the most useful for the intended purpose of the test.

Reliability

Once a scale has been established, attention can be directed toward the analysis of the psychometric properties of the scale itself. As has been previously suggested, additional item analyses may be performed during this phase, but this topic will not be further addressed in the following sections. Within the following sections, the topic areas will focus on reliability, validity, and methods of norming the test battery.

Kerlinger (1973) suggests several synonyms for reliability. They are dependability, stability, consistency, predictability, or accuracy. He describes reliability as the rating of the precision of a given instrument. Theoretically, the number, which we observe as the reliability estimate of a given test, represents the degree to which our constructed test overlaps a perfect measure of the characteristic of interest. Psychometrically, reliability is the squared correlation between the observed scores and the true scores for the trait of interest (Allen & Yen, 1979). The true score is a theoretical concept that can only be inferred and not directly measured. Each of the computational methods to estimate reliability are in fact an estimate of this relationship between the perfect measure of a given characteristic and our test.

There are several computational forms of reliability that are used depending on the characteristic that a test purports to measure, the type of items, and the needs of the test user. All of these forms are actually methods to estimate the precision (reliability) of the instrument by systematically controlling for potential sources of error. For example, test-retest reliability methods attempt to partial out the amount of error associated with the passage of time.

Test-Retest Reliability

The most obvious type of reliability deals with the *stability* of test scores over time. In this method, scores from an initial administration are correlated with scores on the same instrument after some interval. To use this method of describing the reliability of a test, one must start with the assumption that the characteristic measured by the test has some temporal stability. Thus, the test-retest method would be a poor estimate for an instrument used to assess state anxiety or one designed to assess degree of acute impairment after a head injury. No test, even of a stable trait, should be expected to demonstrate perfect test-retest reliability, as there are many factors that influence test scores other than what the test purports to measure. These include (a) fatigue, which may create differential concentration and motivation levels between two administrations; (b) differential environmental conditions, such as temperature, outside noise, ambient distractions, scheduling demands, unexpected personal events between sessions; (c) administration errors on the part of the examiner. Test-retest reliability will also be affected by the sample. If homogeneous samples showing either very high or very low scores on the initial administration are used for the second administration, the extremity of their initial scores will capitalize on chance fluctuation and will in all likelihood underestimate the stability of the test.

Another important aspect of evaluating test-retest reliability is estimating the extent to which test scores change in level over time. The calculation of a correlation coefficient will only estimate the extent to which individual scores remain in their relative positions in the distribution of scores. Therefore, it is recommended that a repeated-measures analysis of variance also be conducted in order to evaluate the extent to which level of score has changed (Franzen, 1989).

In interpreting a test-retest coefficient the following limitations must be taken into account. The experience of the first administration may affect the subject's performance during the second administration. Such carry-over effects can work either to underestimate or overestimate an instrument's stability (Allen & Yen, 1979). The length of time between tests creates differential effects depending on the characteristic being measured. Allen and Yen (1979) indicate that short intervals create effects due to memory, practice, or mood; longer intervals create effects due

to the possibility of acquiring new information and changes in mood. In summary, test-retest estimates of reliability are most appropriate for tests involving abilities rather than achievement or personality traits that are assumed to be stable.

Alternate-Form Reliability

This method is similar to test-retest stability except another form of the test is administered at the second session. Thus, this coefficient represents both temporal stability as well as the degree of redundancy across forms. One must remember that the maximum alternate-form reliability will be limited by the test-retest reliability.

Adequate alternate-form reliability suggests that the items on the two forms are both samples from the same population of items that represents a hypothesized trait or skill. Low alternate-form reliabilities suggest that the two test forms are not measuring the same thing. If the tests sample from the same item population but different components of that population, the correlation may also be small. As an example, let us hypothesize alternate-form scales that sample from the universe of motor skills. If one scale is weighted heavily with finger dexterity tasks and the other is weighted with hand strength tasks, the two scales may exhibit small correlations.

Alternate-form reliability has many of the same limitations as test-retest reliability. Thus, one may expect this computational type to show effects from both carry-over and length of interval between sessions. These latter factors may be most evident in a test that requires a specific cognitive style for problem solving or demands a cognitive set that is applicable to both forms.

Split-Half Reliability

In split-half reliability, a type of alternate-form reliability is produced by dividing a single scale into two halves. This computational method estimates the degree of consistency across items. Though it does not measure temporal stability, it offers the advantage of a single administration. This method assumes that all of the items contribute equally to the measurement of a central construct.

The major problem with this method rests on the issue of how to split the items. In general, the most convenient method is to correlate odd-numbered items with even-numbered items (odd-even split). Alternatively, one may correlate the first half of the test items with the latter half; however, this method is inadequate with speeded tests, where the subject may not reach the second half, or with tests that arrange their items by degree of difficulty, where the latter part of the test is much more difficult than the first part. Halves may also be created by random selection, without replacement, but this is a cumbersome and usually unnecessary procedure.

Because this method uses only one half of the items that are seen in the other reliability measures, split-half reliabilities may be lower than other reliability estimates. The Spearman-Brown formula may be used to estimate the correlation if the number of items has not been reduced. The estimated correlation is equal to

$$\frac{2r}{(1 + r)}$$

where r represents the correlation of the two halves.

The more general form of the Spearman-Brown formula can be used to estimate the effects on reliability by increasing or decreasing the number of items for a scale. The general formula is

$$\frac{n\,r}{1 + (n - 1)\,r}$$

where n is the ratio of the number of items in each form. Thus, if the number of items started at 60 and $r = .5$ and one is interested in the effect on reliability of increasing the number of items to 150, n would equal 150/60 or 2.5, and the estimated increased reliability would be .71. Such calculations allow one to estimate quickly the effects on scale reliability from either adding or removing items before going to the work of actually constructing the items.

Internal Consistency Reliability

Although split-half reliability is a measure of internal consistency, it looks at only one possible division of items instead of all possible splits. Other formulas have been developed to make more conservative estimates of internal consistency reliability. These are the Kuder-Richardson 20 formula (KR20) and coefficient alpha (Cronbach, 1951; Ebel, 1965; Kaiser & Michael, 1975; Kuder & Richardson, 1937).

The KR20 formula is generally intended for tests with items that have only two possible alternatives (e.g., true/false, right/wrong), while coefficient alpha is usually applied to test items that have multiple possible answers. The results of these techniques represent an average of all possible split-half reliabilities formed by all possible combinations of items. Formulas for these coefficients may be found in the above references.

Coefficient alpha has a number of additional properties that are useful to note for the purposes of test construction. Alpha is a low estimate of the reliability of a test, which is a less than perfect estimate of the true score for the characteristic of interest; it is the upper estimate of the variance accounted for by the first factor, when the test is factor analyzed (Allen & Yen, 1979). It is this latter characteristic of alpha that allows the degree of homogeneity among test items to be inferred. Obviously, since the first factor accounts for a greater amount of variance (larger alpha reliability), the test may be described more unidimensionally. This is also one of the limits of the alpha reliability estimate. It will tend to underestimate the reliability of a heterogeneous test.

It should be emphasized, however, that there is no particular virtue in raising or lowering the results of these calculations. In a case where the domain of interest is multidimensional, a heterogeneous scale may be more useful. Perfectly homogeneous sets of items do not exist, since multiple skills go into the performance of any item. Often, an extremely homogeneous scale will fail to correlate well with external criterion variables. Usually, there is a need to compromise between a desire to make the scale as internally consistent as possible and demands that the test be useful in the real world.

The more common methods of assessing internal consistency reliability assume that the items are parallel, that is, that the items measure a single construct equally. The above example of relatively heterogeneous scales is easily seen to be an example of this notion. However, it is also true that rarely do the items of a scale measure the construct to the same extent. In those cases, factor analysis may be useful to help estimate reliability. The factor loading can give an indication of the extent to which an item is correlated with the factor and comparison of loadings for different factors in the same item can give an idea of the extent to which an item is uniquely related to the factor. Carmines and Zeller (1979) recommend the use of coefficient theta as the reliability coefficient in principal-components factor analysis and the use of coefficient omega in common factor analysis. In those cases where the items are parallel, coefficients alpha, theta, and omega will all be equal. In other cases, coefficient alpha will have the lowest value and coefficient omega will have the highest value.

Interscorer Reliability

Another estimate of a test's reliability may be derived by the use of multiple examiners to score the same protocol of responses. In most tests, except for the simplest, it is useful to analyze the effect on the test created by a variety of scorers. This is especially important for standardized tests as discussed here, because we are assuming that administration and scoring will provide a consistent base across clinicians for interpretive purposes. This becomes a crucial issue for projective tests of personality and open-ended tests, both of which require the examiner to perform subjective analyses of behavior.

Interscorer reliability can be determined from either (a) obtaining protocols and having them scored by two different investigators, (b) having two examiners observe and score the performance of the same patient at the same time, or (c) having two scorers independently evaluate data from the same patient. In the latter case, a better evaluation of the effects of different administration techniques is achieved, but a poorer measure of scoring errors occurs because of complications by test-retest effects. The first two methods do not estimate the effects of different administrators at all, since the test is given only a single time.

In summary, all of the above methods of evaluating reliability assume a univariate structure underlying the test; however, many scales are multidimensional. For example, the assertion scale of Galessi et al. (1974) can be broken down into expression of positive affect, expression of negative affect, and asking one's needs to be met. If one wishes to observe the internal consistency reliability of such a test, Bentler's (1975) procedure, which is applicable to these multidimensional situations, may be applied.

Analyzing Variance

Anastasi (1982) has observed that these different estimates of reliability can be used to parcel out test variance among subjects, which is true variance (due to the characteristic of interest) from that attributable to error variance (effects unrelated to the characteristic of interest). She identifies the following techniques as measuring specific types of error variance: (a) test-retest—variance due to time interval; (b) alternate form, immediate administration—variance due to content; (c) alternate form, delayed administration—variance due to both time and content; (d) split-half—variance due to content sampling; (e) KR20 and alpha—variance due to content sampling and heterogeneity; (f) interscorer—variance due to examiner and administration style.

Because the difference between the square of a reliability coefficient and 1.0 represents the percentage of variance we can attribute to a specific factor, we can calculate the total amount of explained and error variance from this information if we assume that the test under consideration is perfectly reliable. For example, if the test-retest reliability is .9, we can calculate that $1.0 - (.9)^2$ or $1.0 - .81$ or an estimated

19% of the variance is due to time. If in the same test, the KR20 is .8, we can calculate that item content and heterogeneity account for $1.0 - (.8)^2$ or 36% of the total variance. Finally, if the interscorer reliability is .95, we can estimate that the examiner effect is responsible for 9.75% of the variance. If these percentages are summed, the total amount of variance attributable to error factors is 64.75%, which leaves, theoretically, 35.25% as true variance.

Further, since true variance can be translated into a theoretical reliability for this scale, the correlation would be the square root of .3525 or just less than .6. Because most test designers find a test with a reliability in the .7 to .8 range to be adequate, it may be inferred that the amount of error variance in most tests is between 30% and 50%. However, one must note that the previously described method of estimating error contributions to a test may inflate the error estimate, since components of that error effect may overlap between estimation methods (i.e., both alternate form and test-retest are affected by time interval).

Limits of Correlational Estimates

Because all measures of reliability are correlational in nature, all are affected by the way variance is distributed across both items and subjects. First, as the sample being tested becomes more homogeneous, the correlation between measures will decrease to the restricted range of variance available in one or both measures. Second, tests for which speed is a factor (only subsets of items are completed due to the time limitations of the test and the subject's abilities) make calculation of inter-item and internal consistency measures impossible, without altering procedures such as correlating item performance during one time period (the first 10 minutes) with performance in another time period (the last 10 minutes) as a way to get around such difficulties.

Correlational estimates will also differ within ability levels. For example, the Luria-Nebraska correlates .84 with the WAIS IQ in a sample whose average IQ was under 115 but correlates less than .2 in a sample with IQs greater than 120. Such factors suggest the need to observe the scales' performance in relation to traits which it is not intended to measure. The multi-trait multimethod approach to validity is one way to respond to such issues and will be discussed in the next section.

Validity

The issue of validity answers the questions "Does the test measure what it was intended to measure?"

and "Does the test produce information that will be useful to clinicians?" The majority of research with a test usually focuses on validity issues. Consequently, this is also the area of investigation that breeds the most controversy. The major types of validity of concern to the researcher are content validity, criterion-related validity, and construct validity. Each of these will be discussed separately later.

It is important to interject here a short discussion of the concept of validity. Validity concerns do not actually refer to the test itself, but instead to the inferences derived from the use of a test (APA, AERA, & NCME, 1985). Although this may at first seem to be an unnecessary bit of semantics, the change in language can help us avoid potential problems. When we say that a test is valid, we are actually overstating the interpretation of research results. By instead saying that it is valid to infer clinical levels of anxiety in a Caucasian, middle-class individual who is an outpatient in a psychological clinic, we are reminded of the limits of the use of the test used to generate those inferences.

Construct validity relies on a consideration of more than one study. Until recently, the evaluation of different studies was conducted in a qualitative fashion. Recently, a group of statistical procedures called meta-analysis has become popular in evaluating disparate studies (Hedges, 1985). Although the complete mechanics of meta-analysis cannot be presented here, some of the basic notions can be described. The general idea is to combine the results of independent studies in such a way as to allow single conclusions to be drawn regarding the variables under consideration. There are advantages in applying meta-analysis to evaluations of test validity (Hedges, 1988). Some of the limitations of meta-analysis are related to its assumptions that all evaluations of the test have been identified and are available for combination and that the tests are of equal methodological rigor. Because of the sampling that occurs in the publication process and because of the variability in research skill of different investigators, these assumptions may not be completely met. However, meta-analysis is a potentially viable avenue for evaluating validity.

Yet another recent development in validity research is the concept of validity generalization. Like meta-analytic approaches, validity generalization attempts to combine results across different studies in order to obtain a best estimate of the extent to which a test generates valid inferences. Validity generalization also attempts to provide an estimate of the variability of validity coefficients across situations (Jones & Applebaum 1989).

Content Validity

Content validation starts as the initial items are selected for a test. It is easiest to demonstrate when the test has been built from a well-defined theoretical orientation, and the designer has started from a Table of Specifications in order to sample adequately a representative group of items.

Subsequent analysis of content validity may differ markedly from the original validation. Subsequent investigators may assume a different underlying theory or support a different set of representative items. When items or scales are shown to have limited content validity, it is usually a result of either incomplete understanding of the underlying theory, lack of a theory, or a tendency to overgeneralize in item construction. Thus, for example, one may assume that a person capable of doing short-term memory tasks is also capable of doing tasks requiring long-term storage, an assumption that is not accurate. Selection of items that only demonstrate long-term storage will not be effective in determining short-term memory impairment.

Content validity becomes more of an issue for tests of achievement or ability and less a concern for tests of personality, where high content validity may limit the overall usefulness of the test. It is also useful for tests of cognitive skills that require an assessment of a broad range of skills in a given area.

Content validity is commonly confused with a form of validity called "face validity." Face validity does not deal with what a test actually measures but rather with what a scale appears to measure based on the reading of various items. The researcher will often find that what an item appears to measure on the surface will differ considerably from what the scale measures in actual practice. What an item actually measures in a test will depend not only on the structure of the item, but the conditions under which it is administered and scored. Changes in timing, instruction, and scoring procedures can cause relationships with external correlates to vary considerably. Thus, face validity is essentially a limited concept that may not reflect intended content.

Despite this fact, face validity does play a role in test construction. While it is not important to the professional, face validity is the characteristic through which the subject receives an impression of what the test is measuring. If a test appears too easy, too hard, inappropriate to what the patient wants, or unnecessarily intrusive, it may affect the patient's test-taking attitude (e.g., level of cooperation, honesty, etc.). These factors should also be taken into account in order to insure the widest usefulness for the test.

Criterion-Based Validity

Criterion validity is extremely important and used widely throughout the construction of psychological tests. This form of validity deals with the ability of test scores to predict behavior, either as represented by other test scores, observable behaviors, or other accomplishments such as grade point averages.

Criterion validity can be subdivided into two types: concurrent and predictive. The difference between these forms of criterion validity lies primarily in the temporal relationship between the test and the external criterion. Concurrent validity involves prediction to an alternative method of measuring the same characteristic of interest, while predictive validity attempts to show a relationship with future behavior. For example, concurrent validity would assume a relationship between a new test and an existing test if both are assumed to be sensitive to a dementing process. On the other hand, a design involving predictive validity would attempt to classify future dements based on their performance on the new instrument. The accuracy of such a classification over time would serve as the measure of predictive validity. Because designs involving concurrent validity are generally easier to operationalize due to the absence of the temporal constraint, concurrent procedures are occasionally substituted, though the intent is clearly predictive. Thus, we may assess anxious students already referred to a college counseling center to validate a test with a group of high-anxiety students. Patterns identified during such a study could then be used to predict which freshman students are likely to develop anxiety disorders during their college experience. Care must be taken in such cases, because the assumed predictive relationship is not confirmed by the current data and awaits the passage of time.

The existence of concurrent relationships between criterion variables and the results of psychological tests is one of the main advantages of employing psychological tests, because they usually are less expensive and take considerably less time to perform. Using a neuropsychological example, one may note that the presence of brain damage can be determined reasonably well by collecting an incisive history, a CT scan, EEG, PET scan, NMR, and regional cerebral blood flow measures, along with other appropriate biochemical tests; however, such a workup costs thousands of dollars. Thus, the existence of concurrent relationships between the results of a neuropsychological battery and the results of such broad-based physiological measures allow the possibility of saving both time and money. Further predictive relationships between neuropsychological findings and changes in function after brain injury provide information in addition to the information delivered by the physiologically based tests. This is not to suggest that a neuropsychological battery should be rotely substituted for the extensive physical workup. Rather, it is suggestive of the complementary nature of the two forms of evaluation and an indication of the ideal relationship between any new form of assessment and existent instruments and procedures.

Tests should be validated against as many criteria as there are behaviors that may reasonably be predicted from the data. Generally such research will identify the limits of a test; that is, test scores will be better predictors for some events and worse for others. Such a pattern of findings helps to identify the appropriate test for a given need. Both clinical users and research users must recognize that no test is appropriate in all circumstances or for all purposes, and it is the purpose of assessment research to clarify those limits for each test.

Both predictive and concurrent validities are accepted by deciding the appropriate level of validity coefficient or correlation between a test score and some criterion variable. The appropriate acceptance level depends on the intended use of the test. For example, if one wishes to predict group membership, a classification analysis, or a similar technique that determines placement, accuracy based on test scores would be appropriate. This is a noncorrelational method of validation. Whatever technique is used, the research must take into account the limitations and strengths of the statistic that will be employed.

Construct Validity

Construct validity is the most newly recognized type of validity (see Cronbach & Meehl, 1955). This approach is much more complex than the other forms of validity that we have discussed, requiring an accumulation of data over a long period of time. Construct validity involves studying test scores in their relationship not only to variables that the test is intended to assess, but also to variables that should have no relationship to the domain underlying the instrument. Thus, one builds a nomothetic net or inferential definition of the characteristics that a test is measuring. Hypotheses may be generated in a wide variety of ways depending on the characteristic of interest.

For example, when cognitive skills are studied, theories can be used to predict developmental changes that are expected in a trait over time. Such changes are then sought in test scores given at different age levels. This research can obviously be extended over the total life span and is not limited to children only.

A second approach includes predictions to other tests that are assumed to measure the same underlying trait as well as those measures that describe unrelated traits. Thus, we may predict that a specific intellectual skill should have a moderate correlation with a measure of hypochondriasis, and a strong correlation to another test measuring the same intellectual skill. It should be clear that in examining such interrelationships the efficacy of the research depends on the accuracy of the original hypothesis, which in turn is related to the investigator's comprehension of the trait under study. Researchers and consumers must be careful not to confuse a researcher's misunderstanding of either the intention of an instrument or the underlying theory with the inefficiency of the instrument itself.

In a major paper, Campbell and Fiske (1959) expanded these notions into an analytic model that includes the concepts of discriminant and convergent validity. Discriminant validity includes those tests that should show little or no relationship to the test at hand, while convergent validity represents concurrent relationships with the test at hand. Based on this model, they proposed the use of a multitrait/miltimethod design. In such a design, the trait under study is measured in a number of alternative ways, which include the test that is being evaluated. At the same time measures of assumed unrelated traits are also included. The pattern of intercorrelation among the various measures creates a multitrait/multimethod matrix. The validity of a test is supported if it shows moderate to high relationships with instruments assumed to measure a similar characteristic, while demonstrating low to zero correlations with instruments measuring unrelated characteristics.

Although the Campbell and Fiske (1959) article represents an important consideration in the evaluation of a psychological test, their suggested methodology can be improved. Jackson (1969) has raised criticisms of the methodology and has suggested an alternative evaluation model. Most of Jackson's (1969) criticisms center around the fact that Campbell and Fiske's (1959) methodology compares individual criterion correlations and does not examine the overall structure. Pattern correlations between traits may be influenced by the method of variance engendered in measuring the traits under consideration.

Jackson (1969) instead recommends a factor analysis of the monomethod matrix. In such an analysis, the matrix is first orthogonalized and submitted to a principle components analysis, followed by a varimax rotation. The expected number of factors is set equal to the number of traits under consideration. Although Jackson's analysis helps meet certain shortcomings of the earlier methodology, it is also open to criticism. Because Jackson's procedure capitalizes on the discrepancy between the characteristics of interest, it is not useful for conceptually related traits. Because it uses a monomethod matrix, it cannot be used to examine the influence of different methods. Therefore, these two methods of validational analysis (i.e., Campbell & Fiske's and Jackson's) may be seen as being complementary to each other, and it is advisable to use both in the complete analysis of an assessment instrument.

A further development in the evaluation of multitrait/multimethod matrices involves the use of the structural equations approach. Kallenberg and Kluegel (1975) describe three advantages of this method. The structural equations approach provides a mechanism for describing the correlation between trait and method factors. It provides a mechanism for describing the relationships of both trait and method factors under consideration. Finally, in order to use the structural equations method, one must first specify one's assumptions regarding the construct under consideration.

Another way to study construct validity is through factor analysis. One may postulate a factorial structure for a specific instrument given one's assumptions about both the trait that is being measured and the theory from which it was derived. A confirmatory factor analysis is then performed to test the hypothesis. For cxample, in our own work with the Luria-Nebraska, predictions were made from Luria's theory of brain functioning. Such predictions were operationalized in terms of item interrelationships, and the factoring process is used to test such hypotheses (see Golden et al., 1982, for an example).

In the case of tests in which a limited number of scores or a single score is generated, marker variables with meanings that are more completely understood may be included in the analysis. Factorial relationships with such marker variables can then be used to determine the meaning of the new test scores. In such analyses and all factor analytic procedures, it is useful to perform a series of factor analyses in order to determine whether the factor structure and the factorial relationships are stable across time and across groups.

Test Bias

There has been much recent interest in the concept of test bias. Because the use of psychological tests is involved in everything from access to educational resources to the placement of individuals in job positions, the context for the evelution of these tests has expanded from the pages of research journals to the pages of the popular press, to the legislative bodies of our political units, and to the courts. Most of the activity is secondary to attempts to insure that test scores do not impinge on our political values of equality. Unfortunately, there is no small degree of misunderstanding of the concept of bias in the more recent contexts. Bias does not refer to a difference of average scores across different groups, for then every test would be "biased." Bias refers to a difference of relations among variables across groups. The issue is not that different racial groups score differently on a test of IQ, but that scores on an IQ test predict academic achievement with differential degrees of validity for the two grups (Kaplan, 1985).

Reynolds (1982) has reviewed some of the different methods available to investigate the possibility of bias. In order to investigate the possibility of bias in construct validity, one can conduct factor analyses separately for the groups and then compare the correlation matrices, use a goodness of fit statistic, determine the degree of similarity between factors in the group solutions, or assess for the possibility of significant differences between factors loadings. Alternately, the researcher can compare internal consistency estimates across groups or evaluate for the presence of differences in rank order of item difficulties. In order to evaluate for bias in predictive or criterion-related validity, one must compare the regression equations relating the variables of interest, derived separately for the two groups. A complete discussion of the concepts and methods of evaluating for test bias is beyond the scope of this chapter and the reader is referred to Berk (1982).

Normative Data

Once the items of a test have been established, normative data can be obtained. However, before this topic is explored, several comments are in order. First, although the above test construction process has been laid out in a linear manner by necessity, the actual process is much more dynamic and integrated. Because no test is a perfect measure of what it is trying to assess (behavior), the process of test refinement may be an endless one. Validity data may lead one back to earlier stages of the design process, necessitating revision of the instrument. Because perfection is not likely attainable, the constructor must work with the test until validity and reliability are suitable for the

intended purpose of the instrument. Suitable endpoints will differ in relation to the intended use of the measure.

Moreover, even after a test is completed, additional work may be done in terms of providing alternate or improved versions of the test. One of the unfortunate drawbacks of this area has been the tendency for tests to stagnate even after research has shown defects that could be corrected. This inertia is usually explained as the need for users to have an unchanging instrument, the unwillingness of users to change administration methods, or the difficulty involved in renorming or revalidating a new version of a test. Even though the practical problems of such work are appreciated by the authors, this general attitude undermines the effectiveness of the field by permitting errors to be endlessly repeated. Moreover, it leads many consumers to the erroneous conclusion that a given technique is perfect because it has been around a long time without change. The science of test construction is better served by an attitude that the design of any instrument is an ongoing process that demands continuous reevaluation in the context of both validational research and feedback from consumers.

After the test has reached an acceptable initial form, normative data may be established. In some cases, this may be done as an integral part of the previously mentioned validation investigations or in a separate phase. Such a decision usually depends on the constraints that the test designer faces as well as the initial results of validation efforts. Several approaches may be taken to form normative data.

Norms will differ depending on the scaling scheme used for a scale or for individual items, a topic that has been discussed earlier. As indicated, a given scaling approach is dependent on the type of information desired and the inferences that will be drawn from the data. Similarly, the eventual scoring system employed, whether percentiles, t scores, z scores, or the like, will depend on many of the same factors. Of greater importance to this chapter is the issue of relativity of norms.

Norms for a given test may differ considerably depending on the characteristics of the standardization sample that was used. In addition, the future sample to which the instrument is applied may differ considerably from the group on whom it was normed, even though both may be from the same general population. This presents serious problems for the test designer as well as the test user.

Although attempts are made to gather representative samples whose characteristics will be appropriate to a wide variety of subjects, this is essentially a futile task, since any limited sample cannot hope to represent adequately a broad population like "the American student," for example, or even more restricted groups like "all 10-year-olds." Individuals within such groups are simply too diverse. A large number of factors will affect individual scores: motivation, environment, culture, age, developmental level, language, training, educational quality, personal experience, gender, and attitude to name a few. Although such factors may average out across a large group, they grossly affect the interpretation of an individual protocol. Thus, even if a sample of 3,000 subjects were to include the same percentage of American Indians as exists in the population as a whole, to argue that the mean scores of such a sample are as representative of an individual Native-American's performance as the modal subject's performance is of questionable validity. The degree to which such an assumption is accurate may be determined only by norming the test within subgroups that exist within the majority population. The investigator should keep well in mind that no single set of norms can be used in all circumstances, and that norms must take into account both individual and group factors in order to be meaningful.

Such an understanding results in a greater emphasis on the use of local or specific norms aimed at individual groups. The degree to which these groups must be precisely described is determined to a great extent by the trait or skill that is being measured. For example, if we wish to look at the population of college-educated individuals, fewer persons are necessary in the sample and less discrimination in subject selection is needed if the task to be measured is reading the word "cat," a skill for which there will be limited within-group variation in such a population. On the other hand, a complex skill requiring the comprehension of nuclear engineering will be strongly affected by individual coursework and in turn will affect the norms that are derived. Care must be taken in situations where different cultures or language backgrounds will limit exposure to the domain that a test is intended to assess. Thus, in selecting samples in order to create norms, the factors that will vitiate the characteristic being measured must be considered.

Local or specific group norms may be established in two ways. First, norms may be defined in reference to a given subgroup. Thus, on an IQ test, one may establish that Group A has a mean score of 92 and a standard deviation of 18, rather than the more general mean of 100 and a standard deviation of 15. For a member of such a group, we would consequently define a score of 65 as within two standard deviations

of normal (92 ± 36), while we would not have done so using the more general norm (i.e., 100). Alternately, we could equate an IQ of 92 in our group with an IQ of 100, using appropriate tables to redefine every other score within our group in a similar manner. This latter method has the advantage of allowing the same interpretive statements to be applied to members of the subgroup; however, it loses the relative information conveyed by the difference between the scores of our group and the more general norm group.

An example of this may be seen in tests of memory. If we were to put together special norms for individuals with IQs below 70, we could redefine what would be a "normal" score for such a group. But this would obscure the fact that a person with such an IQ may have poor memory functions. The latter issue becomes important if we are attempting to make recommendations for treatment or rehabilitation of an individual. Use of the same norms but different interpretations, which take into account vitiating factors, allows greater flexibility to deal with such issues.

For example, although standard scores are used across all scales on the Luria-Nebraska, interpretations regarding the absence or presence of brain impairment are modified based on the presence or absence of certain demographic factors. Thus, a score of 70 on the Reading scale generally suggests poor reading in English but does not indicate impaired performance in an individual who has never been formally educated. The same score for a college graduate with a degree in English literature would indicate impaired performance. Such a system based on a common scoring scheme has the advantage of allowing one simultaneously to correct for multiple extraneous factors without the need to create a multitude of tables in order to anticipate every novel subject characteristic.

In such a system, the reference group serves only to anchor the norms and need not be representative of any specific population. Interpretation is not based on any assumptions regarding such a norm group or its representativeness. Rather, interpretations are derived from a sample of interest: that is, a group that is high on the characteristic being described by the instrument. Such an interpretive reference group should not have any unusual characteristics that would mitigate against accurate comprehension of resulting protocols. For example, if the interpretive reference group were individuals with an average IQ of 12, too many groups will score several standard deviations from the reference norms, creating interpretive difficulties due to the exaggerated differences between individuals.

Another advantage of such a system is the ease with which other investigators may develop local or specific group norms, which may be communicated to other researchers in simple and understandable terms. This also permits one to develop alternate test forms with scores that can be related to the original reference group, which further insures comparability of scoring across forms.

The use of such locally derived subgroup norms in relation to a fixed reference group produces a situation in which one is never done collecting normative data. Future investigators may develop norms for their own samples of interest, which may be quite divergent from the original reference sample. They may also investigate the effects of variables such as age, education, anxiety, and so on in order to further refine the limits of interpretation.

A related issue is the use of a national anchor group to insure comparability of scores across tests (rather than within a single test form only). Such an anchor group insures comparability by defining scores on an alternative measure in terms of the scores of the original test. Scores on the new test are assumed to be equal to the scores achieved on the earlier test.

FUTURE DIRECTIONS IN TEST CONSTRUCTION

There are likely to be multiple changes in test construction in the near future. We are currently in an era where the hegemony of classical test theory is being increasingly challenged and where both new statistical models and new psychometric theories are being proposed. Additionally, we are witnessing synthetic activities where two areas are being combined to provide new tests, such as the application of self-report inventories to behavioral assessment in which the scale scores are being treated as indices of probabilistic relations among classes of behaviors rather than as indices reflective of underlying constructs. Crystal ball predictions have notoriously low reliability and poor validity; however, certain predictions may be likely to become realized.

The use of meta-analysis will become more widespread as more researchers become familiar with the methodology. There is likely to be increased test construction and evaluation using item-response theory (IRT). Most of the publications related to IRT can presently be found in methodological journals such as *Psychometrika*. Initial applications of IRT have been in the area of achievement tests, but there have been signs of the use of IRT in evaluating instruments for contemporary clinical practice such as the Knox Cube

Test (Stone & Wright, 1980). Another important new direction is related to the use of computers to administer psychological tests. In some instances, IRT is used to construct adaptive tests where the sequence of items presented is related to the skill of the individual in answering the previous items (Weiss, 1985). The legal arena is likely to mandate changes in test construction and use based on studies of test bias, and the evaluation of potential bias will become an essential component of test construction. In a related vein, there will be more widespread dissemination and use of local norms.

All of the above predictions are based on assumptions that there will be professionals who will be looking for ways to improve tests and testing. If the current trend of public and political interest in tests continues, the interest may be related to a desire to survive as well as a desire to improve.

SUMMARY

As the reader can see, test construction is ideally a set of interrelated steps ranging from theoretical description of a measure, to item development and selection, to psychometric investigation, to normative studies. This is an on-going process that must continue beyond the initial development of the test as items, scores, and normative data are further refined in order to increase the overall usefulness of an instrument across a wide variety of needs and people. Such work is characterized by the recognition that the ideal test does not exist and can only be approximated. And each setting, need, and group may have its own variation on such an approximation. Ideal development of tests must include research that insures the appropriateness of a given test to given samples and clinical issues, as well as empirical feedback that points the direction in which each test must evolve in order to provide maximum clinical utility.

REFERENCES

Allen, M. J., & Yen, W. M. (1979). *Introduction to measurement theory*. Monterey, CA: Brooks/Cole.

American Psychological Association, American Educational Research Association, & National Council on Measurement in Education. (1985). *Standards for educational and psychological testing*. Washington, DC: Author.

Anastasi, A. (1982). *Psychological testing*. New York: Macmillan.

Baker, F. B. (1977). Advances in item analysis. *Review of Educational Research, 47,* 151–178.

Bem, S. L. (1974). The measurement of psychological androgyny. *Journal of Consulting and Clinical Psychology, 42,* 155–162.

Bem, S. L. (1977). On the utility of alternative procedures for assessing psychological androgyny. *Journal of Consulting and Clinical Psychology, 45,* 196–205.

Bender, L. (1938). A visual motor gestalt test and its clinical use. *American Orthopsychiatric Association, Research Monographs,* No. 3.

Bentler, P. M. (1975). A lower bound method for the dimension free measurement of internal consistency. *Social Science Research, 60,* 1–9.

Berk, R. A. (1982). *Handbook of methods for detecting test bias.* Baltimore: Johns Hopkins University Press.

Campbell, D. T., & Fiske, D. W. (1959). Convergent and discriminant validation by the multitrait-multimethod matrix. *Psychological Bulletin, 56,* 81–105.

Carmines, E. G., & Zeller, R. A. (1979). *Reliability and validity assessment.* Beverly Hills, CA: Sage Publications.

Carroll, B. J., Fielding, J. M., & Blashki, T. G. (1973). Depression rating scales: A critical review. *Archives of General Psychiatry, 28,* 361–366.

Cronbach, L. J. (1951). Coefficient alpha and the internal structure of tests. *Psychometrika, 16,* 297–334.

Cronbach, L. J., & Meehl, P. E. (1955). Construct validity in psychological tests. *Psychological Bulletin, 52,* 281–302.

Ebel, R. L. (1965). *Measuring educational achievement.* Englewood Cliffs, NJ: Prentice-Hall.

Exner, J. E. (1974). Rorschach: A comprehensive system (Vol. 1). New York: Wiley.

Fiske, D. W. (1978). *Strategies for personality research.* San Francisco: Jossey-Bass.

Franzen, M. D. (1989). *Reliability and validity in neuropsychological assessment.* New York: Plenum Press.

Gaito, J. (1970). Scale classification and statistics. In E. F. Heermann & L. A. Braskamp (Eds.), *Readings in statistics for the behavioral sciences.* Englewood Cliffs, NJ: Prentice-Hall.

Galassi, J. P., Delo, J. S., Galassi, M. D., & Bastien, S. (1974). The college self-expression scale: A measure of assertiveness. *Behavior Therapy, 5,* 165–171.

Golden, C. J., Hammeke, T. A., & Purisch, A. D. (1980). *The Luria-Nebraska Neuropsychological Battery manual.* Los Angeles, CA: Western Psychological Services.

Golden, C. J., Hammeke, T. A., Purisch, A. D., Berg, R. A., Moses, Jr., J. A., Newlin, D. B., Wilkening, G. N., & Puente, A. E. (1982). *Item interpretation of the Luria-Nebraska Neuropsychological Battery.* Lincoln: University of Nebraska Press.

Hays, W. L. (1973). *Statistics for the social sciences.* New York: Holt, Rinehart, & Winston.

Hedges, L. V. (1985). *Statistical methods for meta-analysis.* New York: Academic Press.

Hopkins, C. D., & Antes, R. L. (1978). *Classroom measurement and evaluation.* Itasca, IL: F. E. Peacock.

Jackson, D. N. (1969). Multimethod factor analysis in the evaluation of convergent and discriminant validity. *Psychological Bulletin, 72,* 30–49.

Jackson, D. N. (1970). A sequential system for personality scale development. In C. D. Spielberger (Ed.), *Current topics in clinical and community psychology.* New York: Academic Press.

Jones, L. V., & Appelbaum, M. I. (1989). Psychometric methods. In M. R. Rosenzweig & L. W. Porter (Eds.), *Annual review of psychology.* (Vol. 40). Palo Alto, CA: Annual Reviews.

Jurgenson, C. E. (1947). Table for determining phi coefficients. *Psychometrika, 12,* 17–29.

Kaiser, H. F., & Michael, W. B. (1975). Domain validity and generalizability. *Educational and Psychological Measurement, 35,* 31–35.

Kallenberg, A. L., & Kluegel, J. R. (1975). Analysis of the multitrait multimethod matrix: Some limitations and an alternative. *Journal of Applied Psychology, 60,* 1–9.

Kaplan, R. M. (1985). The controversy related to the use of psychological tests. In B. B. Wolman (Ed.), *Handbook of intelligence: Theories, measurement, and application.* New York: Wiley.

Kerlinger, F. N. (1973). *Foundations of behavioral research.* New York: Holt, Rinehart, and Winston.

Kuder, G. F., & Richardson, M. W. (1937). The theory of estimation of test reliability. *Psychometrika, 2,* 151–160.

Lachar, D. L., & Gdowski, C. L. (1979). *Actuarial assessment of child and adolescent personality: An interpretive guide for the Personality Inventory for Children profile.* Los Angeles, CA: Western Psychological Services.

Millon, T. (1982). *Millon Clinical Multiaxial Inventory manual*. Minneapolis, MN: National Computer Systems.

Rasch, G. (1966). An individualistic approach to item analysis. In P. F. Lazarsfeld & N. W. Henry (Eds.), *Readings in mathematical social sciences*. Cambridge, MA: MIT Press.

Reynolds, C. R. (1982). Methods for detecting construct and predictive bias. In R. A. Berk (Ed.), *Handbook of methods for detecting test bias*. Baltimore: Johns Hopkins University Press.

Stone, M. H., & Wright, B. D. (1980). *Knox's Cube Test (manual)*. Chicago: Stoelting.

Weiss, D. J. (1985). Adaptive testing by computer. *Journal of Consulting and Clinical Psychology, 53,* 774–789.

Weiss, D. J., & Davison, M. L. (1981). Test theory and methods. *Annual Review of Psychology, 32,* 629–658.

Wiggins, J. S. (1973). *Personality and prediction: Principles of personality assessment*. Reading, MA: Addison-Wesley.

Wright, B. D., & Stone, M. H. (1979). *Best test design: Rasch measurement*. Chicago: Mesa Press.

CHAPTER 3

SCALING TECHNIQUES

Mark D. Reckase

INTRODUCTION

When assessment instruments are administered, the goal is to gather information about the characteristics of the individual being assessed. The characteristics may be directly observable, such as height, weight, or hair color, and the assessment instrument may be merely a form that is used to record the results of the observations. A more complex situation exists when the characteristics are not directly observable or when the required observations are much too extensive to be practical. In those cases, the information obtained from the assessment instrument is used to infer the characteristics of the person. Examples of these kinds of characteristics include intelligence, aptitude for foreign language, artistic interests, repression, and anxiety. The vast majority of psychological assessment instruments describe characteristics that fall into the latter category.

In addition to merely gathering information about an individual's characteristics, there is usually interest in determining the relative amount of each characteristic that a person has. This interest implies that the recording scheme used must quantify observations in some way. The resulting numerical scores not only give an indication of the relative amount of each characteristic, but also allow comparisons to be made between persons and give a convenient procedure for summarizing observations. The numerical scores also lend themselves to further analyses that may help disclose relationships that exist among different characteristics. That is, the numerical values are used to infer relationships among the underlying causative variables (hypothetical constructs) that explain or describe a person's behavior.

The discovery of relationships between quantitative measures of hypothetical constructs is a necessary first step in the development of an area of science. It is hard to imagine any area of science that has not required quantitative information for its development. For example, proportions of phenotypes were needed to develop the area of genetics, and atomic weights were needed to develop the molecular theory in chemistry. So it is also with psychology. The advances in the quantification of psychological variables have facilitated both the theory and practice of psychology (for example, see Cattell, Eber, & Tatsuoka, 1970; Guilford, & Hoepfner, 1971; Holland, 1966).

The process that is used to assign numbers to observations is the topic of this chapter. This process is called *scaling*. If scaling is successful, the numerical score that is obtained from an assessment instrument can be used to infer accurately the characteristics of a person and the relationships among the characteristics. In a very basic psychological sense, scaling can be defined as the assignment of meaning to a set of numbers derived from an assessment instrument.

The purpose of this chapter is to present some basic information about the characteristics and use of numerical scales developed to describe psychological constructs. The chapter is organized around two major topics: (a) the theory behind scale formation, and (b) the relationship of that theory to the scales produced by several psychological scaling procedures. This chapter will not merely present a catalog of scaling procedures, although some procedures will be described. Rather, it offers a basic philosophy of scale development that can be used to develop new scales for the assessment of psychological traits. Although practical methodologies will be presented, the results of these methodologies will always be related to the basic philosophy of scale formation.

SCALING THEORY

The basic concept in the theory of scale formation is that of a property (see Rozeboom, 1966, for a more abstract development of the concepts presented here). A property can be thought of in at least two different ways. It is commonly used to denote a characteristic, trait, or quality of an entity. Human beings are mammals; being a mammal is a property of human beings. This usage of the term *property* is sufficient for conversational use, but it is not precise enough for use in scaling theory.

For the purposes of this chapter, a *property* will be defined by a set of entities, the entities of interest usually being people. Any set of entities defines a property, but some sets are more interesting in a psychological sense than others. For example, the set of all persons who are alcoholics defines the property "alcoholic." If a person belongs to that set, he or she is an alcoholic. Theoretically, we can determine whether a person is an alcoholic by checking whether he or she is a member of the set (see Figure 3.1). A less interesting property, X, might be made up of some random selection of entities. Then, each entity in that set has the property that it is a number of X. Although the sets "alcoholic" and "member of X" are equally good definitions of properties, the random set does not have psychological meaning. The process of defining a scale will require that properties be defined in a meaningful way.

The definition of a property used here is very similar to that of a concept in the psychological study of concept formation. Just as persons are presented with exemplars and nonexemplars of a concept until they develop a personal, empirically useful definition of the concept, members of a property set can be thought of as exemplars and those not in the set as nonexemplars. These two groups define the property. The "concept" that a person forms in studying the characteristics of the two groups is an abstract generalization that summarizes the property for the person, but the abstraction is not itself the property. Only the two sets, the exemplar group and the nonexemplar group, contain all the nuances of the property.

When used in a psychological context, the sets of people that define properties are often more restricted in their definition than the "alcoholics" example given above. Most psychological characteristics exist at a number of levels. Therefore, psychological properties are usually defined by sets of people having the same level of the characteristic of interest rather than membership in a global, single class. For example, a set of people who all have the same amount of test anxiety defines the property of that level of test anxiety. Another set of people defines another, different level of test anxiety. A different set of people is hypothesized to exist for each different level of test anxiety, and each of those defines a property. Thus, when a person is said to have a high anxiety level, in theory that means the person belongs to the set of people who

Figure 3.1. Alcoholics/Not alcoholics

are as highly anxious as the person in question. All the people in that set have the property of having a high level of anxiety.

Defining a Property

The actual process required to define a property is that of determining equivalence. All persons who have a property are equivalent on the characteristic of interest and are different in at least the level of the characteristic from those persons who do not have the property. If a procedure can be developed to determine whether two individuals are equivalent on the characteristic of interest to some practical level of precision, then the first step toward scale formation has been taken.

An example of the formation of the sets of people that form properties can easily be given if height is used as the characteristic of interest. Imagine a room full of people of varying heights. It would not be a difficult task to sort the people into groups of individuals who have approximately the same height. Each of the groups would define a property of being an individual of a particular height.

Definition of a Natural Variable

A further step toward the formation of a scale can be demonstrated using the height example given above. If the room full of people contained the total population of people of interest as far as the characteristic "height" is concerned, the sets of people of equal

height contain all the possible properties related to the concept *height*. This situation is depicted in Figure 3.2. Further, each person belongs to only one set, and every person belongs to a set, even if that person is standing alone because no one else is of the same height. Sets containing one person are perfectly legitimate. Thus, each person has a height-property and no person has more than one.

The collection of sets that define the properties for different levels of height together define a concept called a *natural variable*. A natural variable is a collection of properties in which every entity is included in a property and no entity is in more than one property. The variable is called "natural" because it is defined using the actual objects of interest and it does not depend on abstract symbols such as numbers.

All the variables that are commonly dealt with in psychology are assumed to be natural variables. When the variable "intelligence" is used, it is assumed that at any moment in time numerous groups could be formed, each of which contain persons who are equivalent in their level of intelligence. All persons are assumed to have some level of intelligence, and no person is assumed to have more than one level of intelligence at a given time. This set of conditions holds for any psychological trait for which a scale can be formed.

Of course, the procedure described above for forming a natural variable is impractical in reality. The example was given only to illustrate the concept of a variable that is commonly used in psychology. A variable is merely a collection of sets of individuals

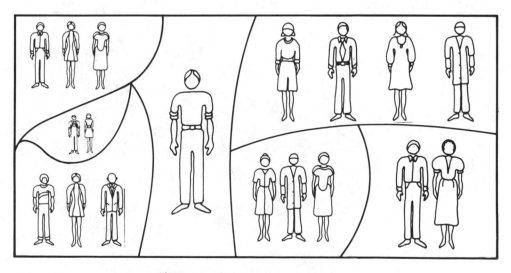

Figure 3.2. The Natural Variable *Height*

such that individuals in a given set are equal on the trait of interest. In order for the concept of *variable* to be of use, some means must be determined to identify the particular set to which a person belongs without going through the physical sorting process. The general procedure that will be proposed is to assign a number to each property set and then to develop a set of rules for determining the number that goes with each person so that their property set can be uniquely determined.

Definition of a Scaled Variable

Up to this point, rather cumbersome language has been used to describe a property and a natural variable. These concepts can be simplified considerably if abstract symbols are used to represent actual individuals. Suppose, in the height example given above, that each person in the room had been randomly assigned a number between 1 and 10. The individuals could then be grouped according to the number that had been assigned to them to form a collection of sets. If each person is given one number, and no person receives more than one number, this collection of sets forms a variable that can be called "the number assigned to each person." However, this variable is not a natural variable because it was not defined using naturally occurring features. This variable may or may not have a connection to an underlying trait. It is strictly an abstract variable. This type of variable will be labeled a *scaled variable* (see Figure 3.3).

An infinite number of scaled variables are possible. Any numbers can be assigned to a set of individuals, and if the conditions of a property and a variable are met by the assignment (i.e., each person gets one number and no person gets more than one), then the result is a scaled variable. If, however, the properties in the scaled variable are related to the properties in a natural variable, a very powerful result is obtained.

Definition of a Scaling

If each person having the same height property is assigned the same number, then the grouping of sets that defines the natural variable "height" is exactly the same as the grouping of sets that defines the scaled variable. If this relationship between the variables occurs, the result is called a *scaling* or a *nominal scaling* of the variable height. The relationship between a natural variable and a scaled variable for a nominal scaling is shown in Figure 3.4.

The scaling of a natural variable yields a very powerful result. The individuals no longer have to be physically present for one to know whether they are equal in height. The numbers assigned to them need only be compared. If two persons have been assigned the same number, they are equal in height. If they have been assigned different numbers, they are different in height.

It should be clear that the critical part of scaling a variable is the procedure for assigning the numbers. If the numbers are assigned in such a way that persons

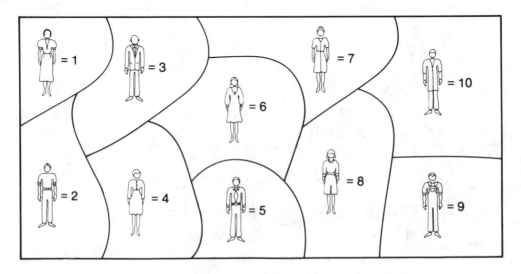

Figure 3.3. A Scaled Variable

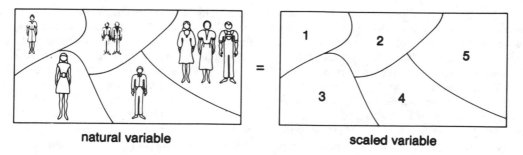

natural variable = **scaled variable**

Figure 3.4. An Example of a Nominal Scaling

with the same number have the same property on the trait of interest, a perfect scaling results, and the information present in the natural variable is present in the scaled variable. For most natural variables of interest to psychologists, it is not possible to assign numbers so that every member of a property set gets the same number because of errors in the assignment process. In most cases, the scaling would be considered successful if most persons in a property were assigned the same number. To the extent that the correct assignment is made, the numerical assignment is said to be valid. The greater the frequency of persons assigned the wrong numbers, the more invalid is the numerical assignment. The numerical values assigned to the properties are called *measurements* when the assignment is reasonably valid.

Scale Types

When the results of the scaling of a psychological variable are used, more information is usually desired than a mere indication of whether a person does or does not have a property (i.e., belong to a property set). Information about the magnitude of the level of the trait of interest is also desired. For this information to be obtained, it must first be possible to order the properties of the natural variable. For the height example given above, the procedure for doing the ordering is quite obvious. Persons with the various height properties can be compared and ranked according to height. If the numbers assigned to the property sets have the same order as the properties in the natural variable, the scaling that results will contain information about the ordering and is called an *ordinal scale*.

Still more information can be included in the scaling of a natural variable if an assumption can be made about the properties in the natural variable. If it can be assumed that when the ordered properties of a natural variable differ by an equal amount, the numerical

values in the corresponding scaled variable also differ by an equal amount, the resulting scaling is called an *interval scale*. That is, if numbers are assigned in such a way that when the distances between sets of numerical values are equal, the psychological differences in the elements of the corresponding properties of the natural variable are also equal, an interval scaling is the result.

The measurement of temperature using the Celsius scale is a common example of measurement at the interval-scale level. When Anders Celsius developed this scale he assigned 0 to the freezing point of water and 100 to the boiling point of water and divided the temperature range between into 100 units. This numerical rule defined the scaled variable now labeled Celsius temperature. The equal units on the Celsius scale correspond to the increase in the temperature of one cubic centimeter of water brought about by the application of one calorie of heat. The physical sets of objects of equal temperature define the properties in the natural variable. Thus, for this temperature scale, equal differences in the natural variable correspond to equal numerical differences on the Celsius scale. Therefore, the Celsius temperature scale is an interval scale.

The classification of scales as ordinal or interval takes on importance because psychometric theorists (e.g., Stevens, 1959) have pointed out that many common statistical procedures (e.g., the mean, standard deviation, etc.) require interval scale measurements for proper application. These procedures use the difference between scores to compute the descriptive statistics. Because the distance between scores does not provide information about the difference in properties on the natural variable for ordinal scales, the interpretation of the statistics computed on these scales is questionable.

The opposing point of view is that most psychological scales give a reasonably close approximation to interval scales and therefore that interval based statistics can be applied. Labovitz (1970) performed a study that supported this point of view. He demonstrated that only if the size of the scale intervals varied by great amounts were the statistics adversely affected. Adams, Fagat, and Robinson (1965) also argued that it is the interpretations of the natural variable that are important. If the scaled variable and the statistics applied to it yield useful information about the natural variable (e.g., the scaled variable is found to correlate with other variables of interest), the level of measurement is not a concern. Few psychologists are very dogmatic about the relationship between scale type and the use of particular statistical procedures. However, scale types should still be considered when interpreting the results of an analysis.

One other type of scale has been included in the typology of scales developed by Stevens (1959). In this type of scale, one of the property sets is defined by the group of individuals who quantitatively have none of the variable of interest. This property defines the true zero point of the scale. In addition to the existence of the property defining the true zero point, the natural variable must also meet all of the requirements for an interval scale. That is, equal differences in the numbers assigned to the properties must correspond to equal psychological differences in the properties. Of course, the entities in the true zero property must be assigned the number zero.

If all of these conditions are met, the resulting scaling is called a *ratio scale*. Ratio scales are relatively rare when psychological traits are scaled because of the difficulty in defining the zero point. While objects approaching zero height are relatively easy to find (e.g., very thin paper), persons approaching zero intelligence are hard to imagine. Even if an object such as a rock is defined as having zero intelligence, the equal steps of intelligence required to get the interval properties of the scale are difficult to determine. For example, is the difference in intelligence between a dog and a rock the same as the difference between a person and a dog? At some point in the future we may be able to develop psychological scales with ratio scale properties, but currently the best that can be expected are interval scales.

Definition of Validity

Up to this point, various scale types have been defined, and the relationship between scaled variables and natural variables has been considered. However, as was mentioned earlier, the match between the scaled variable and the natural variable is seldom exact. In some cases, a scaled variable can be formed that has properties that do not conform at all to the properties of the natural variable in question. In these cases, there is more of a problem than occasionally misclassifying a person—the sets clearly do not match. Such a case is illustrated in Figure 3.5.

When the sets do not match, the scaling does not result in a *valid* measure of the natural variable. The scaled variable does not give useful information about an entity's membership in the properties of the natural variable. Obviously, the most important task in forming a scale is insuring that a valid scale is the result. The next section deals with the techniques that are available for forming scales and checking their validity.

There can be scaled variables that are reproducible in that assignment of numbers at different times or with different techniques yields the same set of scaled variable properties, but that are not valid because the properties do not match those in the natural variable. These scalings are *reliable* because the assignment is consistent, but they are not valid. Fairly consistent assignments of numbers are a minimal condition for validity but they do not guarantee validity. The sets from the scaled and natural variables must match for the scaling to be valid.

TECHNIQUES FOR SCALE FORMATION

Guttman's Scalogram Approach

According to Guttman's scalogram approach to the formation of a scale, the properties in a natural variable can be ordered in such a way that individuals in a higher-level property include all the characteristics of those in lower-level properties plus at least one more. That is, if the properties in a natural variable are labeled in increasing order starting with a_1 to a_{n-1}, then those individuals in property a_n have all the characteristics of the persons in properties a_1 to a_{n-1} plus at least one more. The task involved in scale formation is to find a series of behaviors such that all those persons who exhibit a particular set of behaviors belong to the same property, and those in the next higher property exhibit at least one additional behavior.

The classic example of a Guttman scale is the measure of fear developed for use with soldiers in World War II (Stouffer, 1950). For that scale, those who did not experience "violent pounding of the heart" formed the lowest property set, while those who did formed the next higher property in the natural

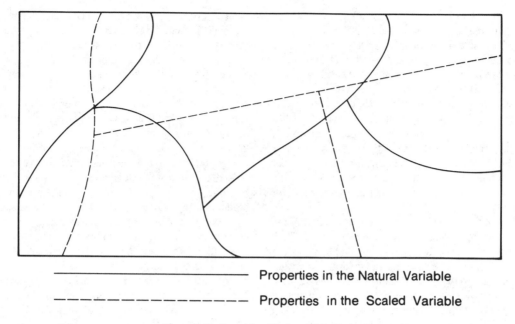

———————————————————— Properties in the Natural Variable

— — — — — — — — — — — — — — — Properties in the Scaled Variable

Figure 3.5. Example of an Invalid Scaling

variable. If a sinking feeling in the stomach as well as a violent pounding of the heart were reported, the person belonged in the next higher property. If, in addition to the other two characteristics, trembling all over was reported, the person belonged in the next higher property level on the natural variable "fear" (see Figure 3.6). In all, 10 fear properties were defined in this way.

The scaled variable corresponding to the natural variable was formed by simply counting up the number of characteristics that were present. If no characteristics were present, the person was assigned a numerical score of 0. If only violent pounding of the heart were present, a score of 1 was assigned. If both violent pounding of the heart and a sinking feeling in the stomach were reported, a score of 2 was assigned. Because of the cumulative nature of this type of natural variable, the case where a person has a sinking

feeling in his or her stomach but does not have a pounding heart occurs infrequently. Therefore, the meaning of a score of one is unambiguous.

The scaled variable is formed by grouping together into a property all the individuals who have been assigned the same numerical score. If all the individuals with the same numerical score have the same level of the trait (belong to the same property of the natural variable), a scaling results. Usually this scaling is of at least the ordinal level because of the cumulative nature of the Guttman procedure. If the added characteristics that distinguish the different levels of the properties indicate an equal amount of change in the trait level from a psychological point of view, an interval scale is formed.

The relationship between the properties in the natural variable and the presence of characteristics is usually shown by a two-way table. Across the top of

Property Characteristics

None	Violent pounding of heart	Violent pounding Sinking feeling	Violent pounding Sinking feeling Trembling all over

Figure 3.6. Characteristics of Individuals in Four Property Sets of the Natural Variable, *Fear*

the table are listed the characteristics of the individuals that are used to classify them into the properties. Down the side of the table are listed the properties in the natural variable. In the body of the table, a 1 is placed at the intersection of a property and a characteristic if all persons in the property have the characteristic. An example of such a table is presented in Figure 3.7. If all persons in a property do not have the characteristic, a 0 is placed in the table. If a Guttman scale is present, the 1's in the table form a triangular pattern when the properties are arranged by order of magnitude of the trait being measured and the characteristics are arranged according to their level of severity.

In reality, we do not know the composition of the properties of the natural variable and must substitute the properties of the scaled variable for the rows of the table. In this case, the perfect triangular form may not be present. To the extent that the relationship between the scaled variable and the characteristics cannot be put into the triangular form, a scaling has not taken place. There are two possible reasons why a proper scaling might not be accomplished. First, the trait for which the measure is being developed may not easily be put into the hierarchical form required by the Guttman procedure. For example, holding liberal political beliefs does not mean that a person also holds all the beliefs of a person of conservative bent, even though the properties in the natural variable defined by political beliefs can generally be ordered along a continuum. The second reason a scaling may not be possible is that the properties of the scaled variable do not match the properties of the natural variable because of errors in the assignment of the numerical

values. A person may not report a characteristic when it is really present, an observer may miss an important activity, or a record may be inaccurately kept.

In order to judge whether the scaled variable matches the natural variable sufficiently closely to form a scaling, Guttman (1950) suggested that a statistic called the coefficient of reproducibility be computed. This coefficient is simply the proportion of ones and zeros in the person-by-characteristic table that are in the appropriate places to produce the triangle form when the rows and columns have been ordered according to the total number of ones in them. If a one or zero is not in the appropriate place to produce the triangular form, the perfect Guttman scale will not be possible. The number of inappropriately placed zeros and ones is given by the number of ones below the diagonal and the number of zeros above the diagonal. In Figure 3.8, the number of inappropriately placed zeros and ones is 3 out of a total of 30 entries. The number of appropriate values is then $30 - 3 = 27$. The coefficient of reproducibility is $27/30 = .90$. Guttman felt that the coefficient of reproducibility should be at least .90 for the scaling to be considered reasonable.

Since Guttman's early work, procedures for determining the quality of a Guttman scale have become much more elaborate (see McIver & Carmines, 1981, and White & Saltz, 1957, for examples). However, these procedures are all conceptually related to the coefficient of reproducibility. They all check to determine whether the properties of the scaled variable have the necessary cumulative relationship with the observed characteristics.

An analysis of the assumptions of the Guttman

Characteristics

	Pounding	Sinking	Trembling	Sick	Weak
a_5	1	1	1	1	1
a_4	0	1	1	1	1
a_3	0	0	1	1	1
a_2	0	0	0	1	1
a_1	0	0	0	0	1
a_0	0	0	0	0	0

Properties in Natural Variable

Figure 3.7. Representation of a Perfect Guttman Scale

Characteristics

1	0	1	1	1
0	1	1	1	1
0	0	1	1	1
0	0	1	0	1
0	0	0	1	0
0	0	0	0	1

Persons

Figure 3.8. An Imperfect Guttman Scale

Scalogram procedure can be used to determine whether this approach should be used to form a scale. The first step in this process is to evaluate the properties of the natural variable in question to determine whether they have the required cumulative relationship. If they do not, the Guttman procedure should not be used. One of the other methods given later in this chapter may be an appropriate alternative. If the necessary cumulative relationship does exist among the properties, the next step is to determine the characteristics that distinguish the properties of the natural variable. For example, a particular type of self-destructive behavior may distinguish one type of psychological disorder from another. This behavior can then be used as one of the items to assign the score to form the scaled variable. Usually a number of different behaviors are tentatively selected and only those that can be used to form the triangular pattern of responses shown above are used to form the scale. It is usually difficult to find more than five or six behaviors that have the required cumulative relationship.

Once the behaviors have been selected and data have been collected on the presence or absence of the behavior for a new group of individuals, a variant of the reproducibility coefficient is computed to determine whether a reasonable Guttman scale has been obtained. If the value of this coefficient is sufficiently high, the scaling is accepted.

Thurstone's Method of Equal-Appearing Intervals

Guttman's method of scale formation is fairly limited in its application because of the requirement of cumulative properties in the natural variable. Many natural variables do not have the cumulative property.

Yet, the properties in the natural variable are distinguishable. In order to identify the persons belonging to each property, Thurstone (1927) developed a model of the interaction between a person and statements describing possible attitudes toward an object. Thurstone's model indicates that a person who is a member of a particular property set will endorse some attitude statements and not others. Persons in a different property set will endorse a different, although possibly overlapping, set of alternatives. Those persons who endorse similar sets of statements are hypothesized to belong to the same property set.

By merely sorting persons into categories on the basis of the responses to a set of attitude statements, a variable can be defined, but this variable does not contain any information about the level of an attitude toward an object. All that is obtained is groups of individuals, each of which is composed of persons with similar attitudes. In order to add the information about the relative level of attitude into the scaling, Thurstone suggested that the attitude statements themselves first be scaled.

The scaling of the attitude statements is performed in a very straightforward manner. A set of 11 properties is hypothesized for the natural variable of interest. These properties range from sets of statements that are very unfavorable to the object of interest to those that are very favorable. The sixth property is assumed to contain those statements that are neutral. The 11 properties can be arranged in order from very unfavorable through neutral to very favorable. This set of properties is the scaled variable for the attitude statements.

To determine which statements belong in each of the property sets, a number of judges (Thurstone used 300) are asked to sort the statements (usually over

100) into the appropriate sets (see Figure 3.9). The judges were instructed to perform this sorting on the basis of the favorableness or unfavorableness of the statements, not on the statements' level of agreement with the judges' position. If the statements differed solely on their degree of favorableness, and if the judges were totally consistent in their judgments, it would be expected that a statement would be put into the same property set by each judge. In reality, variations in the classifications are found which Thurstone called discriminal dispersion. In other words, the placement of the statements into the property sets is not perfectly reliable.

Because there usually is variation in the placement of the statements, a procedure is needed for forming a scaled variable using the statements. The procedure suggested by Thurstone first assigns the numbers 1 to 11 to the properties. When a statement is sorted into one of the properties by a judge, the corresponding number is assigned to the statement. After all the judges classify all the statements, the median and quartile deviations are computed using the numbers assigned to each statement.

If the quartile deviation for a statement is large, the statement is ambiguous in some sense, as indicated by the fact that the judges could not agree on the property set into which the statement should be placed. For a statement with a low quartile deviation, the median value is used as the scale value for the statement. The numbers that are assigned in this way are used to form the scaled variable for the statements. Two statements that have been assigned the same number are assumed to fall into the same property set. The statements and their associated scale values are used to produce the instrument that is used to assign numerical values to individuals and thereby form the scaled variable for people.

Recall that individuals who endorse roughly the same sets of statements are assumed to come from the same property on the natural variable. If the mean scale value for these statements were computed, each person in the same property set would obtain the same mean scale value. Thus, Thurstone decided to form the scaled variable on people by assigning each person the mean scale value of the statements that they endorsed. In order to have a sufficient range of statements for all the persons who are being measured, Thurstone suggested producing the measuring instrument by selecting two statements from each of the 11 property sets. This results in an attitude-measuring device consisting of 22 statements. To use it, a person is asked simply to check the statements with which they agree. Their score is the average scale value for the statements endorsed.

Of course, there is some error in the procedure because persons can obtain approximately the same score although agreeing with different sets of statements. To the extent that this occurs, the scaled variable does not match the natural variable and the results of the scaling are invalid.

The level of scaling of the scores obtained from the Thurstone equal-appearing interval procedure depends on the quality of the judgments made concerning the attitude statements. Clearly a person who endorses favorable statements has a more positive attitude toward the topic in question than one who endorses less favorable statements. Therefore, the procedure results in at least an ordinal scale. Whether an interval scale is achieved depends on whether the 11 properties of the natural variable used to classify the attitude statements are equally spaced. Thurstone and Chave (1929) contended that the judges would subjectively make adjacent properties equally distant when they classified the items. To the extent that this conjecture is true, the scaling procedure results in an interval scale.

At this point, an example of the application of the Thurstone equal-appearing interval technique may prove useful in clarifying the steps in this procedure. Suppose it were desirable to develop a measuring instrument for determining attitudes toward nuclear power. The first step in the process would be to write

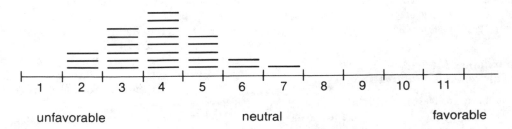

Figure 3.9. Judgments for a Statement With a Scale Value of About 4

more than 100 statements that vary in their degree of favorableness toward nuclear power. These should be statements of opinion, not fact. For example, the statement "Nuclear power will vastly improve the quality of life" is a favorable statement. "The use of nuclear power will destroy this country" is a negative statement. After these statements have been produced, several hundred individuals should be asked to rate the statements, based on their attitudes toward nuclear power, using the 11-point scale. Next, the median and quartile deviations of each statement are computed. Those statements with large quartile deviations are dropped and, from the statements remaining, two statements are selected from each of the 11 categories. For this purpose, the median for the statement is used as a scale value. The resulting 22 statements form the measuring device for attitudes toward nuclear power.

To use the measuring instrument that has been developed, individuals are asked to check the statements with which they agree. Each person's attitude score is the average of the scale values for the statements they have checked.

Item Response Theory

Within the last 10 years, a new approach to the formation of scales of measurement has become popular. This approach, called item response theory or IRT (Lord, 1980), has been applied mostly to aptitude and achievement measurement, but it can also be used for other types of psychological assessment problems (see Kunce, 1979, for example). As with the Guttman and the Thurstone procedures, this scaling procedure assumes that the properties in the natural variable can be arranged along a continuum based on the magnitude of the trait possessed by the persons in each property set. If a test item is administered to the persons in one of these properties, this model assumes that all the persons will have the same probability of responding correctly or endorsing the item, but that they may not all give the same response to the item because of errors in measurement.

For example, suppose the item "Define democracy" is given to all the persons in a particular property set. Because of errors in the persons' responses, ambiguities in the question, problems in deciding whether the answer is correct or incorrect, and so on, some of the persons miss the item and others answer it correctly. However, the IRT model assumes that all persons in that property set have the same probability of answering the item correctly. Persons in a different property

set will have a different probability of a correct response. If the probability of a person's correct response to an item is known, then the person can be classified into the appropriate property of the natural variable.

One of the basic assumptions usually made for IRT models is that if the properties are ordered according to the probability of correct response to an item, they are also ordered according to increasing trait level on the natural variable. That is, the probability of a correct response is assumed to have a monotonically increasing relationship to the trait of interest. Thus, if persons can be placed into the properties on the basis of the probability of correct response, at least an ordinal scale results.

If the natural variable has properties that are evenly spaced, the relationship between the ability properties and the probability of a correct response for persons in a property is assumed to have a particular form. The mathematical forms commonly used for this purpose are the one-parameter logistic model (Rasch, 1960), the two-parameter logistic model (Birnbaum, 1968), the three-parameter logistic model (Lord, 1980), and the normal ogive model (Lord, 1952). However, other forms, including ones that are nonmonotonic, are also being considered. The usual practice is to assume one of these forms for all the items in the measuring instrument to be produced. Figure 3.10 presents an example of the relationship typically found between the properties of a natural variable and the probability of a correct response.

The relationship shown here assumes that the probability of a correct response increases with increased magnitude of the trait. This type of model is most appropriate for items that have a single positive or correct response that is more likely for persons belonging to property sets defining high magnitudes of the trait. Other models are more appropriate for rating scale type items (Masters, 1988; Samejima, 1969). These models assume that the probability of a particular response to the rating-scale item first increases and then decreases as the level of the trait increases. This relationship is shown in Figure 3.11.

As with the other two procedures described earlier, the purpose of the IRT analysis procedures is to determine the property in the natural variable to which a person belongs. If the probability of a person's responses to a single item could be observed, the determination of the appropriate property could be accomplished with one item. Of course, when a person is administered an item, a discrete score is obtained (usually a 0 or a 1), and no probability is observed. Therefore, a person cannot be classified

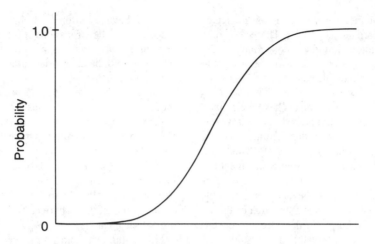

Figure 3.10. Properties of the Natural Variable

into a property using one item if IRT methods are used. Instead, an instrument composed of many items is administered, and a person is classified into the property that has the highest probability of giving the observed responses to the set of items.

For example, suppose two items are administered to the persons in two different property sets. Suppose further that the probability of a correct response for the two items for persons in the two properties is given in Figure 3.12.

If a person answered the first item incorrectly and the second correctly, that set of responses would have a probability of $(1 - .1) \times .6 = .54$ for those in property A but a probability of $(1 - .7) \times .9 = .27$ for those in property B. Because the probability of the responses was higher for property A, the examinee would be estimated to belong in property A. This principle of classification is called maximum likelihood trait estimation.

In practice, the properties of the scaled variables are indexed by numerical values, and the probability of a correct response to each item is determined by a mathematical formula. For example, the formula for the two-parameter logistic latent trait model is given by

$$P(x_{ij} = 1) = \frac{e^{a_i(\theta_j - b_i)}}{1 + e^{a_i(\theta_j - b_i)}},$$

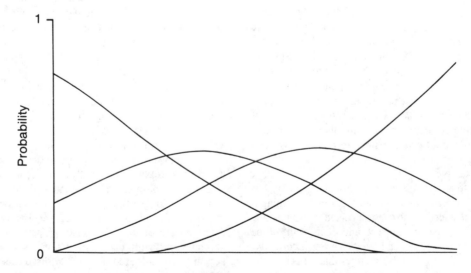

Figure 3.11. Properties in the Natural Variable

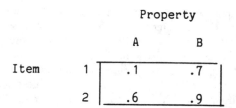

		Property	
		A	B
Item	1	.1	.7
	2	.6	.9

Figure 3.12. The Probability of a Correct Response to Two Items for Persons in Different Properties

where $P(x_{ij} = 1)$ is the probability of a correct response for person j on item i, e is the constant, 2.718 . . . , θ_j is the ability of person j, and a_i and b_i are the item parameters that control the shape of the mathematical function. The estimate of θ_j indicates the property on the scaled variable to which the person belongs.

The values of a_i and b_i for an item are determined in much the same way as the scale values in Thurstone's equal-appearing interval procedure. A set of test items is administered to a large number of individuals and values of a_i and b_i are computed from the responses. The values of b_i are related to the proportion responding correctly to the item, and the values of a_i are related to the correlation between the item score and the values of the scaled variable (see Lord & Novick, 1968, for a discussion of this relationship). These values are determined from a scaling of each item along two dimensions, while the ability estimates are a scaling of the people responding to the items. The process of determining the values of a_i and b_i for a set of items is called *item calibration*.

The use of item response theory for the process of scaling is conceptually more complicated than use of the Guttman or Thurstone procedures because of the complex mathematics involved. In practice, however, the procedures are simpler because computer programs are available to perform the necessary analyses. Suppose we want to measure a personality characteristic by administering a series of items with instructions to the examinee to check those that apply to him or her. If this scale is to be developed using item response theory, the items would first be administered to a large number of individuals who vary on the trait of interest. The resulting data are analyzed using one of the available calibration programs to determine the item parameters. The calibration program is selected depending on which of the item response theory models is assumed. If the items are assumed to vary only in their rate of endorsement, the one-parameter logistic model may be appropriate, and a program

such as BICAL (Wright, Mead, & Bell, 1979) can be used to obtain the item parameters. If the items are assumed to vary also in their discriminating power, the two-parameter logistic model is appropriate, and the BILOG program (Mislevy & Bock, 1983) can be used for calibration. If there is a non-zero base rate for positive responses to the items, the three-parameter logistic model is appropriate, and the LOGIST (Wingersky, Barton, & Lord, 1982), BILOG or ASCAL (Vale & Gialluca, 1985) programs can be used for item calibration. Finally, if a rating-scale item form is used, a program like MULTILOG (Thissen, 1986) may be appropriate. New programs are constantly being produced for these methods, and the literature should be checked for the most current versions for a particular model before the item calibration is performed.

After the items are calibrated, the items for the measuring instrument are selected. A procedure similar to Thurstone's can be used if the population to be measured ranges widely on the trait of interest. The items may also be selected on the discriminating power if high precision is required. Many of the computer programs also give measure of fit between the models and the data. These fit measures may also be used to select items to insure that the model being used is appropriate.

Once the items for the instrument are selected, an estimation program or a conversion table can be used to obtain an estimate of the level of the trait for each person. In general, as with the Guttman and Thurstone procedures, those persons with similar patterns of responses will receive a similar trait estimate. These trait estimates form the scaled variable for the trait in question. As with any of the other procedures, this scaled variable must be checked to determine whether it matches the natural variable and therefore yields a reliable and valid measure.

Likert Scaling Technique

Another commonly used procedure for forming attitude measuring instruments was developed by Likert (1932). This procedure also begins by assuming a natural variable with properties that can be ordered according to the magnitude of the trait possessed by the persons in each property set. The form of the item used by the Likert procedure is a statement concerning the concept in question, followed by five answer choices ranging from *strongly agree* to *strongly disagree*. It is assumed that the five answer choices divide the natural variable into five classes that are ordered with respect to the attitude toward the concept.

If only one item is used in the measuring instrument, the five categories are numbered from 1 (strongly disagree) to 5 (strongly agree) and each person is assigned the score corresponding to the response selected. If the statement being rated has a negative connotation, the scoring is reversed. The score assignment forms the scaled variable for this procedure.

In reality, more than one item is usually used with the Likert procedure. Each of these items is assumed to divide the natural variable in a similar, but not exactly the same, way. Thus, for two items the natural variable may be divided up as shown in Figure 3.13. In this figure, the boundaries between the sets of properties are not exactly aligned. Therefore, it is possible for one person to respond with *strongly agree* responses to two items, while another person may respond with *strongly agree* and *agree*. The latter person has a slightly lower trait level than the former. To indicate this fact on the scaled variable, the scores on the two items are simply summed. The first person receives a score of 10 on the scaled variable while the second receives a 9.

As more items are added to the instrument, the score for each person is obtained by simply summing the numbers assigned to each response category. Because the division of the natural variables into five categories is seldom exactly the same, each additional item brings about a greater subdivision of the natural variable. If 20 items were used in an instrument, the natural variable could be divided into as much as $(5 - 1)20 + 1 = 81$ categories. Each of these would be assigned a score which is the sum of the item scores. The persons with the same score would constitute properties in the scaled variable. To the extent that the properties in the scaled variable match those of the natural variable, a valid scaling is the result.

Although for the 20-item example given above each score is assumed to result from only one pattern of responses (one region on the natural variable), in reality there are many ways to obtain the same score. A total of $5^{20} = 9.5 \times 10^{13}$ patterns of responses are possible. To the extent that categories other than the 81 mentioned above are present, the underlying model does not hold. These response patterns are usually attributed to errors of measurement and result in a mismatch between the scaled score and natural variable reducing the reliability of the results of the scaling. The Likert procedure tends to be robust to the violations, however, and items that result in many inappropriate responses are usually removed at a pretesting phase in instrument construction. This is done by correlating the score for each item with the total score on the instrument and dropping those that have a low correlation.

The level of scaling obtained from the Likert procedure is rather difficult to determine. The scale is clearly at least ordinal. Those persons from the higher level properties in the natural variable are expected to get higher scores than those persons from lower properties. Whether an interval scale is obtained depends on a strong assumption. In order to achieve an interval scale, the properties on the scaled variable have to correspond to differences in the trait on the natural variable. Because it seems unlikely that the categories formed by the misalignment of the five response categories will all be equal, the interval scale assumption seems unlikely. However, as the number of items on the instrument is increased, each property of the scaled variable contains a smaller proportion of the population, and the differences in category size may become unimportant. Practical applications of the Likert procedure seem to show that the level of scaling for this method is not an important issue. That is, treating the scores as if they were on an interval scale does not seem to cause serious harm.

An example of the construction of an attitude scale using the Likert procedure should clarify all the issues discussed. As with the Thurstone procedure, the first step in producing a Likert-scaled attitude instrument

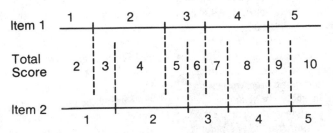

Figure 3.13. Score Categories for a Two-Item Likert Scale

is to write more statements about the concept of interest than are expected to be used. In this case, about twice as many statements as are to be used should be enough. These should be statements of opinion, not fact, and both positive and negative statements should be included in approximately equal numbers. The five response categories (strongly agree, agree, neither agree nor disagree, disagree, strongly disagree) are then appended to each statement. For positive statements the categories are scored 5, 4, 3, 2, and 1, and for negative statements they are scored 1, 2, 3, 4, and 5.

If a measure of body image were desired, one item might be the following:

I have a well-proportioned body.
(a) strongly disagree
(b) disagree
(c) neither agree nor disagree
(d) agree
(e) strongly agree.

A negatively phrased item might be

I am noticeably overweight.
(a) strongly disagree
(b) disagree
(c) neither agree nor disagree
(d) agree
(e) strongly agree.

For the first item, (a) would be scored as 1, (b) as 2, (c) as 3, (d) as 4, and (3) as 5. For the second item, the scoring would be reversed: (a) 5, (b) 4, (c) 3, (d) 2, (e) 1.

The attitude items are next tried on a sample of approximately 100 individuals who represent the population of interest. For each statement, the correlation is computed between the score on the statement and the sum of the scores on all the statements. If the correlation is negative, the phrasing for the statement has probably been misclassified as to whether it is positive or negative. If it has not been misclassified, the statement should be deleted from the instrument as being ambiguous. Statements with low correlations (less than .3) are also dropped from consideration because the correlation indicates that these statements do not form a scaled variable that is consistent with the other items. From the items that meet the above criteria, 10 to 20 are selected with about equal numbers that are positively and negatively phrased. Both positively and negatively phrased items are needed to reduce response bias. The items selected constitute the measuring device.

THE REQUIREMENTS FOR SCALE FORMATION

In the formation of measurement devices presented, there is a common starting point for all the techniques. In all cases, a natural variable is hypothesized to exist. Without this initial step, the concept of instrument validity is meaningless because the focus of the instrument is unknown. Once the natural variable has been defined, the scale construction task becomes one of devising a method for determining which persons belong in each of the property sets of the natural variable. Conceptually this could be done by developing a detailed description of the persons in each property set and then observing each individual until he or she could be accurately classified into a property. This is essentially the procedure that is used for some infant intelligence scales.

The more common procedure is to develop a series of items and use these items to obtain a highly structured sample of behavior (i.e., item responses). Those persons who exhibit similar behavior are assigned the same numerical score and are assumed to belong to the same property of the natural variable. For the Guttman procedure, behaviors that are cumulative in nature are used, and the numerical assignment rule is based on a count of the number of behaviors present. For the Thurstone procedure, the behavior is the endorsement of an attitude statement, and the numerical assignment rule is based on the average scale value of the items endorsed. The IRT approach is very similar to Thurstone's procedure in that the items are first scaled, and the results are then used to determine the estimate of the trait level for a person. For Likert's procedure, the behavior used in the scaling is the rating of attitude statements, and the numerical assignment is based on the sum of the ratings.

Note that for all the procedures some sort of pre-screening of items is required. The Thurstone and IRT procedures require a scaling of items and some measure of fit to the underlying model. The Guttman and Likert procedures also use a measure of fit: the reproducibility coefficient in the former case and the item total score correlation in the latter. The presence of these procedures for evaluating the quality of the items in the measuring instruments reflects the fact that merely assigning numbers to persons does not result in the meaningful measurement of a trait.

The numbers must be assigned in a way that is consistent with the natural variable. The procedures described for each of the methods provide a check on the consistency. Even when the scales produced by these methods are shown to be internally consistent, this fact does not insure that measurements obtained from the instruments are valid. The measures must still be shown to interact with other variables in ways suggested by an understanding of the natural variable. If this is not the case, a good measure has been developed of some unknown quality.

REFERENCES

Adams, E. W., Fagat, R., & Robinson, R. E. (1965). A theory of appropriate statistics. *Psychometrika*, *30*, 99–127.

Birnbaum, A. (1968). Some latent trait models and their use of inferring an examinee's ability. In F. M. Lord & M. R. Novick, (Eds.), *Statistical theories of mental test scores*. Reading, MA: Addison-Wesley.

Cattell, R. B., Eber, H. W., & Tatsuoka, M. M. (1970). *Handbook for the sixteen personality factor questionnaire*. Champaign, IL: Institute for Personality and Ability Testing.

Galton, F. (1870). *Hereditary genius: An inquiry into its laws and consequences*. London: D. Appleton.

Guilford, J. P., & Hoepfner, R. (1971). *The analysis of intelligence*. New York: McGraw-Hill.

Guttman, L. L. (1950). The basis for scalogram analysis. In S. A. Stouffer, L. Guttman, E. A. Suchman, P. W. Lazarsfeld, S. A. Star, & J. A. Clausen, *Studies in social psychology—World War II* (Vol. 4). Princeton, NJ: Princeton University Press.

Holland, J. L. (1966). *The psychology of vocational choices*. Waltham, MA: Blaisdell.

Kunce, C. S. (1979). *The Rasch one-parameter logistic model applied to a computerized, tailored administration of Mini-Mult scales*. Unpublished doctoral dissertation, University of Missouri-Columbia.

Labovitz, S. (1970). The assignment of numbers to rank order categories. *American Sociological Review*, *35*, 515–524.

Likert, R. (1932). A technique for the measurement of attitudes. *Archives of Psychology*, *140*, 44–53.

Lord, F. M. (1952). A theory of test scores. *Psychometric Monograph*, 1.

Lord, F. M. (1980). Applications of item-response theory to practical testing problems. Hillsdale, NJ: Lawrence Erlbaum Associates.

Lord, F. M., & Novick, M. R. (1968). *Statistical theories of mental test scores*. Reading, MA: Addison-Wesley.

Masters, G. N. (1988). Measurement models for ordered-response categories. In Langeheine, R., & Rost, J. (Eds.), *Latent trait and latent class models*. New York: Plenum Press.

McIver, J. P., & Carmines, E. G. (1981). *Unidimensional scaling*. Beverly Hills, CA: Sage Publications.

Mislevy, R. J., & Bock, R. D. (1983). *BILOG: Marginal estimation of item parameters and subject ability under binary logistic models*. Chicago: International Educational Services.

Rasch, G. (1960). *Probabilistic models for some intelligence and attainment tests*. Copenhagen: Danish Institute for Educational Research.

Rozeboom, W. W. (1966). Scaling theory and its nature of measurement. *Synthese*, *16*, 170–233.

Samejima, F. (1969). Estimation of latent ability using a response pattern of graded scores. *Psychometrika* (Monograph Supplement No. 17).

Stevens, S. S. (1959). Measurement. In C. W. Churchman (Ed.), *Measurement: Definitions and theories*. New York: Wiley.

Stouffer, S. A. (1950). An overview of the contributions to scaling and scale theory. In S. A. Stouffer, L. Guttman, E. A. Suchman, P. W. Lazarsfeld, S. A. Star, & J. A. Clausen, *Studies in social psychology—World War II* (Vol. 4). Princeton, NJ: Princeton University Press.

Thissen, D. (1986). *MULTILOG version 5 user's guide*. Mooresville, IN: Scientific Software.

Thurstone, L. L. (1927). Psychophysical analysis. *American Journal of Psychology*, *38*, 368–389.

Thurstone, L. L., & Chave, E. J. (1929). *The measurement of attitude*. Chicago: University of Chicago Press.

Vale, C. D., & Gialluca, K. A. (1985, November). *ASCAL: A microcomputer program for estimating logistic IRT item parameters* (Research Report ONR-85-4). St. Paul, MN: Assessment Systems Corporation.

White, B. W., & Saltz, E. (1957). Measurement of reproducibility. *Psychological Bulletin*, *54*(2), 81–99.

Wingersky, M. S., Barton, M. A., & Lord, F. M. (1982, February). *LOGIST user's guide*. Princeton, NJ: Educational Testing Service.

Wright, B. D., Mead, R. J., & Bell, S. R. (1979). *BICAL: Calibrating items with the Rasch model*. Research Memorandum No. 23B. Chicago: University of Chicago, Department of Education, Statistical Laboratory.

PART III

ASSESSMENT OF INTELLIGENCE

CHAPTER 4

ASSESSMENT OF CHILD INTELLIGENCE

Mitchel D. Perlman
Alan S. Kaufman

INTRODUCTION

Over the centuries, many definitions of intelligence have been postulated attempting to explain this elusive construct. This chapter provides a context in which to understand children's intelligence by including a chronology of historical landmarks, by expounding on popular intelligence measures, and by looking at future trends in intelligence testing. In the first part, a brief history of mental measurement is sequenced to provide an overview of its development. The second part is partitioned into two subsections and describes tests currently available to measure children's intelligence (infancy through adolescence). The first subsection provides detail on the three major intelligence tests for children: Wechsler Intelligence Scale for Children-Revised (WISC-R), Kaufman Assessment Battery for Children (K-ABC), Stanford-Binet (Fourth Edition). The second subsection describes other popular tests of mental measurement. The third part focuses on the directions intelligence testing appears to be moving. It discusses cultural trends and their impact upon the purposes for which intelligence tests might be utilized, as well as on possible format changes.

A CHRONOLOGY

Classifying and categorizing individuals is by no means a novel concept. From the beginning, so we are told, Adam was classified as being "man" and Eve was classified as being "woman." This fascinating but evasive concept of "intelligence," while called many things, is a concept that has been with us throughout time and has been used both positively and negatively to set mankind apart from beasts and to differentiate within the broad category of mankind itself. Measuring intelligence is not only complex, but historically is a sensitive issue that has not been done without abuse.

Measuring intelligence emerged out of both theoretical interest and societal need. Theoretical interest relates to the desire to understand individual differences. Societal need involves the utilization of this understanding to solve practical problems. The evolution of the measurement of intelligence, therefore, did not emerge in a vacuum, but rather, by the interplay in the development of several paradigms: psychology, sociology, psychometrics, and law. The brief historical review that follows highlights landmark events in those areas and relates them to the birth and development of intelligence.

It is difficult to pinpoint when intelligence testing was born, but certainly it was conceived prior to the 1800's. Aristotle, for example, attempted to understand how people behaved by dividing mental functions into a cognitive (cybernetic) and a dynamic (orectic) category. Cybernetic functions are thought processes, orectic functions are emotional and moral processes (Das, Kirby, & Jarman, 1979). Since the time of Aristotle, whenever personality is conceptualized, attempts are still made to keep separate these two functions, but the difficulty in doing so has been well recognized (Das et al., 1979; Perlman, 1986; Shapiro, 1965). Others, such as Firtzherbert in 1510, Huarte in

1575, Swinbourne in 1610, and Thomasius in 1692 gave credence to testing one's cognition. They proposed various definitions of cognition and gathered information on human mentality (Sattler, 1988).

The 1800s ushered in several important advances in intelligence testing. In fact, interest in cognition and in the measurement of cognition in the nineteenth century was part of the scientific movement that brought psychology into being as a separate and respected discipline. Esquirol (1828) focused on distinguishing between mental retardation and emotional disturbance. It was he who coined terms such as *imbecile* and *idiot* to describe diverse levels of mental deficiency. He pointed out that idiots never developed their intellectual capacities, whereas mentally deranged persons lost abilities they once possessed. After studying different methods of measuring intelligence, he concluded that language usage was the most dependable criterion: a philosophy prevailing in most intelligence measures today.

Seguin's (1907) philosophy was quite different. He stressed sensory discrimination and motor control as aspects of intelligence. The Seguin Form Board, which requires rapid placement of variously shaped blocks into their correct holes, is an application of his theory. Many of the procedures he developed were adopted or modified by later developers of performance and nonverbal tasks. It was during this time that intelligence testing and education had their first formal courtship, for Seguin convinced the authorities of the desirability of educating the "idiots" and "imbeciles." He is credited for beginning the first school for the feebleminded and for being the author of the first standard book dealing with educating and treating them (Pintner, 1949). Also, his methods provided the inspiration for Maria Montessori's approach to education.

Galton's (1869) approach was similar to Seguin's in that he also stressed discrimination and motor control. In accordance with his commitment to the notion that intelligence is displayed through the uses of the senses—sensory discrimination and sensory motor coordination—he believed that those with the highest IQ should also have the best discriminatory abilities. Therefore, he developed tasks such as weight discrimination, reaction time, strength of squeeze, and visual discrimination. Galton is credited both with establishing the first comprehensive individual intelligence test and with introducing two basic notions of intelligence: the idea that intelligence is a unitary construct (which eventually led others to postulate the notion of general intelligence, or the "g" factor), and that individual differences in intelligence are largely genetically de-

termined (possibly influenced by the theory of his cousin, Charles Darwin) (Cronbach, 1970; Das et al., 1979; Pintner, 1949). Perhaps Galton's greatest contributions to the field of intelligence testing, though, were two crucial psychometric concepts that he originated: regression to the mean and correlation. His concepts allowed for studying intelligence over time, as well as for studying relationships between intelligence scores of parents, children, etc. (a concept for which, on the basis of Galton's work, Pearson developed the product-moment correlation and other related formulas).

James McKeen Cattell (1888), an assistant in Galton's laboratory, brought Galton's concepts to the United States. He shared his mentor's philosophy that intelligence is best measured by sensory tasks, but expanded his use of "mental tests" (a term coined first by Cattell in the literature) to include standardized administration procedures. He pleaded for standardized procedures, and urged the necessity for the establishment of norms. Cattell's valuable contribution to psychology was that he took the assessment of mental ability out of the field of abstract philosophy and showed that mental ability could be studied experimentally and practically. Under Cattell's direction, the Pearson correlation technique seems to have been used for the first time for comparison of test with test, and tests with college grades.

By the late 1800s diverse notions of intelligence were conjectured, standardized procedures and norms were urged, and interest in classification had been implemented. Societal need provided the final impetus which led to the development of the individually administered Binet-Simon Scale in 1905. With the specific appointment by the French minister of public instruction to study the education of retarded children, the notion to separate mentally retarded and normal children in the Paris public schools arose. Binet, assisted by Theophile Simon and Victor Henri, rejected Galton's notions of what made up intelligence and proposed that tasks utilizing higher mental processes—memory, comprehension, imagination, etc.—would be more effective measures. Binet did, however, retain Galton's idea of general intelligence ("g"), which is reflected in his battery. This 1905 scale might be considered the first *practical* intelligence test.

The Binet has gone through a number of modifications and revisions throughout the years including the eventual introduction of the term "intelligence quotient" in Terman's 1916 version, the Stanford-Binet (this ratio IQ was computed by dividing mental age by chronological age, and multiplying by 100). While these single IQ scores have become a popular means of classifying individuals, it is a clear departure from Binet's notion of intelligence as "a shifting complex of inter-related functions" (Tuddenham, 1962, p. 490). In fact, some doubt whether Binet would have accepted the concept of a single IQ score even with Terman's elaborate standardization (Wolf, 1969). In 1986, Thorndike, Hagen, and Sattler developed a completely modified version of the Stanford-Binet. The test incorporates Wechsler's "point-scale" format, and departs so much from the previous test that one wonders whether it merits the same name.

An important note is that this first major intelligence test battery arose to classify individuals. Classification has been fundamental to the history of mental assessment. It is no wonder that this philosophy continues today with such fervor, despite earnest attempts to move beyond single IQ scores in a desire to individualize profile analysis.

Like Binet, David Wechsler included the concept of global intelligence in his Wechsler-Bellevue Scale (published in 1939). Instead of having one global score, however, his battery included three separate IQ scores: namely, a Verbal IQ, a Performance IQ, and a Full Scale IQ. The Full Scale IQ, for Wechsler, is an index of general mental ability ("g").

While the formats from the Stanford-Binet and the Wechsler Scales differ considerably, the subtests themselves do not. Wechsler's tasks weren't novel concepts at all, but rather, borrowed from other tests of cognitive abilities. In many ways, Wechsler combined the philosophies of Esquirol and Seguin, and the psychometrics of Cattell and Terman. As equal components of intelligence, the Verbal Scale roughly capitalizes upon a person's language abilities (Esquirol), while the Performance Scale roughly capitalizes upon a person's nonverbal and motoric abilities (Seguin). Wechsler's main ideas for the verbal tasks were the Stanford-Binet and the Army Group Examination Alpha. Ideas (and often specific items) for the performance tasks came primarily from the Army Group Examination Beta and the Army Individual Performance Scale Examination. The Army Alpha and Army Beta tests, published by Yerkes in 1917, were group administered intelligence tests developed to assess United States military recruits. The Wechsler Scales have gone through a number of revisions, but the basic test has remained structurally intact.

Although the Stanford-Binet and Wechsler scales were powerful tools to measure cognitive ability, theories of intelligence continued to be introduced and refined. In 1936, Piaget published *Origins of Intelligence*. He conceived of intelligence as a form of biological adaptation of the individual to the environment. Just as living organisms adapt to their environments biologically, individuals adapt to their environments through cognitive growth. Cognitive stages, therefore, emerge as a function of psychological structures reorganizing and/or developing out of organismic-environmental interactions (Piaget, 1950). Piaget's model of intelligence is developmental and hierarchical in that he believes individuals pass through four predetermined, invariant stages of cognition, each more complex than the preceding one: *sensorimotor* (birth–2 years), *preoperational thought* (2 years–7 years), *concrete operations* (7 years–11 years), *formal operations* (11 years–adult).

With the advancement of psychometrics, factor analytic theories of intelligence emerged espousing either a general-factor theory ("g") or a multiple-factor theory. Each method can be reduced to the other by either accepting the unrotated first factor, or by rotating the factors by various methods. Within this domain, J. P. Guilford (1959) developed a complex multifactor theory. His three-dimensional *Structure of Intellect* model (Guilford, 1967; Guilford & Hoepfner, 1971) posited five different *operations*, four types of *content*, and six *products* resulting in 120 possible factors ($5 \times 4 \times 6$). Also following the factor analytic model were Raymond B. Cattell and John Horn (Cattell, 1963) who postulated a structural model that separates fluid from crystallized intelligence. Fluid intelligence traditionally involves relatively culture-fair novel tasks and taps problem solving skills and the ability to learn. Crystallized Intelligence refers to acquired skill: knowledge and judgments which have been systematically taught. The latter type of intelligence is highly influenced by formal and informal education and often reflects cultural assimilation. Tasks measuring fluid ability may involve more concentration and problem solving than crystallized tasks which tap retrieval and application of general knowledge.

Another theoretical approach conceptualizing intelligence is an information-processing model focusing on the strategies individuals use to complete tasks successfully. Within this approach is the neuropsychological processing model which originated with the neurophysiological observations of Alexsandr Luria (1966a, 1966b, 1973) and Roger Sperry (1968), the psychoeducational research of J. P. Das (1973; Das et al., 1975, 1979), and the psychometric research of A. S. and N. L. Kaufman (1983). This model possesses several strengths relative to previous models in that it (a) provides a unified framework for interpreting a wide range of important individual-difference variables; (b) rests on a well-researched theoretical base in clinical neuropsychology; (c) presents a processing, rather than a product-oriented, explanation for behavior; and (d) lends itself readily to clear remedial strategies based on relatively uncomplicated assessment procedures (Das et al., 1979; Kaufman & Kaufman, 1983; McCallum & Merritt, 1983; Perlman, 1986).

This neuropsychological processing model describes two very distinct types of processes which individuals use to organize and process information received in order to solve problems successfully: successive or sequential, analytic-linear processing versus holistic/simultaneous processing (Levy & Trevarthen, 1976; Luria 1966a). These processes have been identified by numerous researchers in diverse areas of neuropsychology and cognitive psychology (Perlman, 1986). Successive processing refers to the processing of information in a sequential, serial order. The essential nature of this mode of processing is that the system is not totally surveyable at any point in time. Simultaneous processing refers to the synthesis of separate elements into groups. The essential nature of this mode of processing is that any portion of the result is at once surveyable without dependence on its position in the whole. The model assumes that the two modes of processing information are available to the individual. The selection of either or both modes of processing depends on two conditions: (a) the individual's habitual mode of processing information as determined by social-cultural and genetic factors, and (b) the demands of the task (Das et al., 1975).

Many laws and judicial decisions have addressed the need for the development of nonbiased IQ tests for those having various learning deficiencies and those in minority groups. These laws and opinions underscore some of the controversy surrounding the appropriate use of intelligence tests and place ethical, if not legal, responsibility on clinicians for determining the adequacy and appropriateness of intelligence tests for children. The American Psychological Association clearly addresses this issue in their Ethical Principles of Psychologists and, under Principle 2–Competence, requires clinicians to recognize differences among people (age, sex, socioeconomic, and ethnic backgrounds) and to understand test research regarding the validity and the limitations of their assessment tools (American Psychological Association, 1974).

Attending to these legal, ethical, and practical concerns, Alan and Nadeen Kaufman (1983) published the Kaufman Assessment Battery for Children (K-ABC). The K-ABC was developed in response to

contemporary assessment needs not being met by other intelligence test batteries. It was developed to be sensitive to the needs of psychoeducational assessment of children (including nonbiased assessment of minority groups, learning impaired, and hearing impaired), as well as to complement a neuropsychological evaluation. Underpinning the K-ABC is its commitment to a theoretical rationale for the battery based on a thorough research foundation in cognitive psychology, developmental psychology, clinical psychology, neuropsychology, and neurology.

Intelligence, as measured by the K-ABC, is the ability to process information sequentially and/or simultaneously. It is a definition based upon an individual's style of solving problems and processing information and combines information-processing, factor-analytic, and developmental models of intelligence. By separating the intelligence scale from the achievement scale, the battery makes a clear distinction between fluid intelligence (Mental Processing Scales) from crystallized knowledge (Achievement Scales). Not all tasks on the K-ABC are administered at every age level, for unlike the Wechsler scales, a premium was placed on the developmental appropriateness of the tasks. Taking into account that abstract, hypothetico-deductive reasoning (Piaget's Formal Operations stage) begins between the ages of 12 to 14, the test battery appropriately taps children's intelligence between the ages of 2½ to 12½. According to Anastasi (1988), "the K-ABC is an innovative, cognitive assessment battery whose development meets high standards of technical quality" (pp. 269–270).

CURRENT MEASURES

Intelligence tests are administered for a variety of reasons including *identification* (of mental retardation, learning disabilities, other cognitive disorders, giftedness), *placement* (gifted and other specialized programs), and as a cognitive adjunct to a *clinical evaluation*. The Wechsler Scales, K-ABC, and Stanford-Binet are the most commonly used and most widely accepted individual intelligence measures. Administration of one of these more traditional measures is recommended for the assessment of intelligence when a child has the necessary physical capacities to respond to test questions, when the child meets age requirements of the test, and when there are no time restraints. When verbal responses cannot be elicited from a child, when sensory and/or motor impairments place limits on a child's performance, or when time is at a premium, other measures become necessary. A review of these three tests follows with a summary of other general cognitive measures and tests designed for special populations (infants and preschoolers, mentally retarded, hearing and language impaired, visually impaired, orthopedically impaired, cultural minorities). The list of measures reviewed is by no means exhaustive, but represents the ones that are commonly used in the field today.

Three Major Intelligence Scales[1]

Wechsler Intelligence Scale for Children–Revised (WISC-R)

Theory. Wechsler (1974) puts forth the definition that "intelligence is the overall capacity of an individual to understand and cope with the world around him" (p. 5). His tests, however, were not predicated on this definition. Tasks developed were not designed from well-researched concepts exemplifying his definition. In fact, as previously noted, virtually all of his tasks were adapted from other existing tests.

Like the Binet, Wechsler's definition of intelligence also ascribes to the conception of intelligence as an overall global entity. He believed that intelligence cannot be tested directly, but can only be inferred from how an individual thinks, talks, moves, and reacts to different stimuli. Therefore, Wechsler did not give credence to one task above another, but believed that this global entity called intelligence could be ferreted out by probing a person with as many different kinds of mental tasks as one can conjure up. Wechsler did not believe in a cognitive hierarchy for his tasks, and he did not believe that each task was equally effective. He felt that each task was necessary for the fuller appraisal of intelligence.

Standardization and Properties of the Scale. Standardization procedures followed the 1970 U.S. Census data. The manual provides information by geographic region, urban versus rural residence, race, and parental occupation. Stratification figures reported follow closely the census data.

The WISC-R yields three IQ scores: a Verbal Scale IQ, a Performance Scale IQ, and a Full Scale IQ. All three IQs are point-scale standard scores (mean of 100 and standard deviation of 15) obtained by comparing an individual's score with those earned by the representative sample of age peers. Both scales consist of

six tasks, five regular and one supplementary (12 tasks total). The dichotomy of the test into verbal and performance tasks is, according to Wechsler (1974), a way of identifying two principal modes by which human abilities are expressed.

Construct validity was obtained by factor analytic procedures, criterion validity by correlations with other intelligence measures. Factor analysis reveals that three, instead of two, factors efficiently describe the WISC-R: Verbal Comprehension, Perceptual Organization, and Factor III (Kaufman, 1979).

Verbal Comprehension involves verbal knowledge and the expression of this knowledge. Perceptual Organization, a nonverbal dimension, involves the ability to interpret and organize visually presented material. Factor III has been described as freedom from distractibility since common among tasks is the ability to focus, to concentrate, and to remain attentive. Other interpretations have included facility with numbers, short-term memory, and sequencing because the three tasks which comprise the factor all involve a linear process whereby numbers are manipulated. Success is either facilitated by or wholly dependent on memory (Kaufman, 1979). While the WISC-R manual provides standard scores only on the three IQ scales as mentioned above, procedures and tables for obtaining standard scores on the three factors are readily available in other texts (Sattler, 1988). Taken together, the Verbal Comprehension and Perceptual Organization factors offer strong support for the construct validity of the verbal and performance IQs; substantial loadings on the large, unrotated first factor ("g") supports the construct underlying Wechsler's Full Scale IQ.

The manual reports correlations between the Full Scale IQs of the WISC-R with the WPPSI at age 6 and the WAIS at age 16 (.82 and .95, respectively). Since publication of the manual, literally hundreds of studies have given solid support for the WISC-R's concurrent, predictive, and construct validity (Kaufman, 1979; Quereshi & McIntire, 1984; Sattler, 1988). The WISC-R is truly "king" among children's intelligence tests, and remains the criterion against which other tests are compared.

Kaufman Assessment Battery for Children (K-ABC)

Theory. The K-ABC is a battery of tests measuring intelligence and achievement of normal and exceptional children ages 2½ through 12½ years. It yields four scales: two mental processing scales, a composite

---

[1]Adapted from Perlman and Kaufman (in press).

processing scale, and an achievement composite. When developing the K-ABC, its authors (Kaufman & Kaufman, 1983) relied on their experience in clinical evaluation, graduate student training, empirical research, and test construction to understand the limitations of existing clinical instruments and areas where improvement in assessment procedures was essential. Primary goals, therefore, were (a) to measure intelligence from a strong theoretical and research basis; (b) to separate acquired factual knowledge from the ability to solve unfamiliar problems; (c) to yield scores that translate to educational intervention; (d) to include novel tasks; (e) to be easy to administer and objective to score; and (f) to be sensitive to the diverse needs of preschool, minority group, and exceptional children (Kaufman & Kaufman, 1983).

Intelligence, as measured by the K-ABC, is the ability to process information sequentially and/or simultaneously. The Sequential Processing and Simultaneous Processing Scales represent two types of mental functioning that have been identified independently by cerebral specialization researchers (Bogen, 1975; Gazzaniga, 1975; Kinsbourne, 1978), by Luria (1966a) and his followers (Das et al., 1979), and by cognitive psychologists (Neisser, 1967). Sequential processing involves analysis of stimuli in terms of details and features. It is a linear process whereby the result is dependent upon its position in the whole. Each task on the Sequential Processing Scale presents a problem which requires linear abilities in order to be most successful: tasks are linearly and temporally related. Simultaneous processing deals with more global properties and patterns. It is a holistic process whereby the result is *not* dependent upon its position in the whole. Each task on the Simultaneous Processing Scale presents a problem which requires input to be integrated and synthesized simultaneously in order to be most successful: tasks tend to be spatial and analogic.

Because theoretical relevance was the primary consideration when developing each processing scale and the subtests it comprises, the authors' first goal was fulfilled. Furthermore, because research evidence is in strong support of the two information-processing styles which form the theoretical foundation of the K-ABC, the paths toward fulfilling the remaining goals were clearly paved. For example, because the theory focuses on process rather than on content, it was logical and natural to separate problem solving (mental processing scales) from the acquisition of knowledge and facts (achievement scales). Separating process from content in this manner is also congruent

with the previously discussed theory expounded upon by Cattell and Horn (Horn, 1979).

Additionally, separating abilities in this manner helps identify a child's capacity to problem solve, and to pinpoint his or her relative strengths and weaknesses in the two processing styles. The way to translate test scores into strategies for academic intervention, then, becomes readily apparent. One works primarily with the child's processing strength to make academic achievement gains (Biggs, 1978; Gunnison, 1982; Gunnison, Kaufman, & Kaufman, 1982).

To measure processing abilities it was necessary to develop new tasks and to adapt previously well-researched tasks. The resulting test is easy to administer and avoids unnecessary complexities by reducing the emphasis on speeded performance and by using consistent administrative procedures for each task. The final goal of measuring the needs of preschool, minority groups, and exceptional children was an extensive undertaking and is thoroughly discussed in the interpretive manual (Kaufman & Kaufman, 1983). Careful consideration has been given to addressing the needs of these populations (a) by developing tasks that are fun and that would hold the interest and attention of young and/or hyperactive children; (b) by including a representative sample of this population in the standardization; (c) by combining the standardization sample with additional African-American children above the proportional number to develop sociocultural norms; (d) by minimizing the role of language; (e) by providing a nonverbal scale; (f) by providing teaching items for all processing tasks to ensure that children understand what is expected of them; and (g) by standardizing the test using flexible directions (e.g., a foreign language can be used to teach the tasks).

Whether the K-ABC's authors succeeded in measuring sequential and simultaneous processing and in separating cognitive ability from achievement has been the frequent subject of research, speculation, and often heated controversy (Kamphaus & Reynolds, 1987; Miller & Reynolds, 1984).

Standardization and Properties of the Scale. Stratification of the K-ABC standardization sample was excellent and very closely matched the 1980 U.S. Census data in age, gender, geographic region, community size, socioeconomic status, race and ethnic group, and parental occupation and education. Additionally, unlike other intelligence measures for children, stratification variables also included educational placement of the child (see Table 4.1).

Reliability and validity data are impressive. Test-

Table 4.1. Representation of the Standardization Sample by Educational Placement (N = 2,000)

EDUCATIONAL PLACEMENT	K-ABC STANDARDIZATION SAMPLE		U.S. SCHOOL-AGE POPULATION[a]
	N	%	%
Regular Classroom	1,862	93.1	91.1
Speech Impaired	28	1.4	2.0
Learning Disabled	23	1.2	2.3
Mentally Retarded	37	1.8	1.7
Emotionally Disturbed	5	0.2	0.3
Other[b]	15	0.8	0.7
Gifted and Talented	30	1.5	1.9[c]
Total K-ABC Sample	2,000	100.0	100.0

[a] Data from U.S. Department of Education, National Center for Education Statistics, 1980. Table 2.7, *The Condition of Education,* Washington, DC, U.S. Government Printing Office.
[b] Includes other health impaired, orthopedically impaired, multihandicapped, and hard of hearing.
[c] Data from U.S. Office for Civil Rights, 1980, *State, Regional, and National Summaries of Data from the 1978 Civil Rights Survey of Elementary and Secondary Schools,* p. 5, Alexandria, VA, Killalea Associates.

retest reliability coefficients for the Mental Processing Composite are .83 for age 2 years, 6 months–4 years, 11 months; .88 for ages 5 years, 0 months–8 years, 11 months; and .93 for ages 9 years, 0 months–12 years, 5 months. Construct validity was established by looking at five separate topics: developmental changes, internal consistency, factor analysis (principal factor, principal components, and confirmatory), convergent and discriminant analysis, and correlations with other tests. Factor analysis of the Mental Processing Scales offered clear empirical support for the existence of two, and only two, factors at each age level; and the placement of each preschool and school-age subtest on its respective scale. Analyses of the combined processing and achievement subtests also offered good construct validation of the K-ABC's three-scale structure (Kaufman & Kamphaus, 1984).

Correlations between the K-ABC and the WISC-R for normal and specialized populations also strongly supports the scale's validity. In fact, even more impressive is the minimization of differences between whites and cultural minorities. A comparison of the K-ABC and the WISC-R when testing cultural minorities is presented in Table 4.2. Hispanic-white differences on the K-ABC are virtually nonexistent. Differences between African-Americans and whites on the K-ABC are approximately half as large as on the WISC-R and other conventional intelligence tests. Cultural variables affecting performance on the Mental Processing Scales may have been successfully minimized by the rigorous item development and standardization procedures, by deemphasizing the role of language, and by putting achievement-oriented tasks on a separate scale. The *K-ABC Interpretive Manual* (Kaufman & Kaufman, 1983) provides a wealth of psychometric data on the battery; Kamphaus and Reynold's (1987) text on the K-ABC presents a research update on the battery, as well as sophisticated clinical and psychometric approaches to profile interpretation.

The Stanford-Binet: Fourth Edition

Theory. Like its predecessor, the Fourth Edition is based on the principal of a general ability factor, "g," rather than on a collection of separate functions. It argues for a wide range of cognitive tasks which, when increased in range and in number, will render an individual's standing on the composite performance more completely dependent on "g" as factors specific to single tasks decrease (Thorndike et al., 1986). The Fourth Edition has maintained, albeit to a much lesser degree, its adaptive testing format. No examinee takes all the items on the scale, nor do all examinees of the same chronological age respond to the same tasks. Like its predecessor, the scale provides a continuous appraisal of cognitive development from ages 2 through adult.

One of the criticisms in the previous version is that it tended to underestimate the intelligence of examinees whose strongest abilities did not lie in verbal skills (or overestimate intelligence of those whose verbal skills excelled). Therefore, consideration when developing this Fourth Edition was to give equal credence to several areas of cognitive functioning. The authors set out to appraise verbal reasoning, quantitative

Table 4.2a. Hispanic-White Differences on the K-ABC and WISC-R

INTELLIGENCE SCALE	MEAN SCORE WHITES	MEAN SCORE HISPANICS	DIFFERENCE
K-ABC			
Sequential Processing	101.2	98.7	+ 2.5
Simultaneous Processing	102.3	99.5	+ 2.8
Mental Processing			
Composite	102.0	98.9	+ 3.1
WISC-R			
Verbal IQ	102.0	87.7	+14.3
Performance IQ	103.8	97.9	+ 5.9
Full Scale IQ	103.1	91.9	+11.2

Note: Data for the K-ABC are based on the following number of 2½ to 12½-year-old children in each ethnic group: whites (1,569), Hispanics (160). Data for the WISC-R are based on the following number of 5 to 11-year-old children in each ethnic group: whites (604), Hispanics (520). Source of WISC-R data: Mercer, J. R. (1979). *SOMPA Technical Manual,* Table 43. New York: Psychological Corporation.

Table 4.2b. Black-White Differences on the K-ABC and WISC-R

INTELLIGENCE SCALE	MEAN SCORE WHITES	MEAN SCORE BLACKS	DIFFERENCE
K-ABC			
Sequential Processing	101.2	98.2	+ 3.0
Simultaneous Processing	102.3	93.9	+ 8.4
Mental Processing			
Composite	102.0	95.0	+ 7.0
WISC-R			
Verbal IQ	102.0	87.8	+14.2
Performance IQ	102.2	87.2	+15.0
Full Scale IQ	102.3	86.4	+15.9

Note: Data for the K-ABC are based on the following number of 2½ to 12½-year-old children in each ethnic group: whites (1,569), blacks (807). Data for the WISC-R are based on the following number of 6 to 16-year-old children in each ethnic group: whites (1,870), blacks (305). WISC-R data are obtained from the standardization sample for that IQ test. Source: Kaufman, A.S., & Doppelt, J. E. (1976) Analysis of WISC-R standardization data in terms of the stratification variables. *Child Development, 47,* 165–171.

reasoning, abstract/visual reasoning, and short-term memory (in addition to a composite score representing "g").

This model is based on a three-level hierarchical model of the structure of cognitive abilities. A general reasoning factor is at the top level ("g"). The next level consists of three broad factors: crystallized abilities, fluid analytic abilities, and short-term memory. The third level consists of more specific factors: verbal reasoning, quantitative reasoning, and abstract/visual reasoning.

The selection of these four areas of cognitive abilities came from the authors' research and clinical experience of the kinds of cognitive abilities that correlate with school progress. This foundational emphasis on academic cognition continues the philosophy of the original Binet which did not extend to measuring adult intelligence as did later versions including this Fourth Edition. One wonders whether the same emphasis should be used when measuring adult intelligence. While subtests change (with considerable overlap) for various age groups, and while selection reportedly has been subjected to rigorous research, there is considerable dispute whether children and adults utilize the same intellectual processes. After all, any task can be developed and normed for a variety of ages, but does that mean that each age group is calling upon the same processes to accomplish this task?

This Fourth Edition contains previous tasks combining old with new items and some completely new tasks. In general, test items were accepted if (a) they proved to be acceptable measurements of the construct; (b) they could be reliably administered and scored; (c) they were relatively free of ethnic and/or gender bias and; (d) they functioned adequately over a wide range of age groups (again, not making philosophical distinctions between intelligence of children and adults).

Standardization and Properties of the Scale. Standardization procedures followed 1980 U.S. Census data. There appears to be an accurate sample representation from geographic region, size of community, race/ethnic group, and gender. The standardization falls short, however, in terms of age, parental occupation, and parental education. The age representation extends from 2 years, 0 months to 23 years, 11 months. The concentration of the sample is on children 4 to 9 years old (41%). Not only were adults 24 years and older not represented, but representation beyond age 17 years, 11 months is negligible (4%).

In order to assess characteristics of socioeconomic status (SES), information regarding parental occupation and parental education was obtained. A review of Table 4.3 demonstrates that children whose parents came from managerial/professional occupations and/ or who were college graduates and beyond were grossly overrepresented in the sample. In other words, the norms are based on a tremendous excess of children whose parents were from upper-socioeconomic classes. In order to adjust for this discrepancy,

an after-the-fact weighting procedure was applied, which makes the norming sample suspect. Unquestionably, SES has been shown time and again to be the single most important stratification variable regarding its relationship to IQ (Kaufman & Doppelt, 1976).

Construct validity for "g" and for the four factors was studied using a variant of confirmatory factor analysis. The sublists had impressive high to substantial loadings on g (.51–.79). Unfortunately, the four factors were given weak support by the confirmatory procedure. Additionally, exploratory factor analysis gave even less justification for the four Binet Scales; only *one* or *two* factors were identified by Reynolds, Kamphaus, and Rosenthal (1988) for 16 of the 17 age groups studied. Clearly, the factor analytic structure does not conform to the theoretical framework used to construct the test. Therefore, once again one is left with the composite score as the only possible valid representation of a child's cognitive abilities.

Correlational studies, using non-exceptional children, between the Fourth Edition and the Stanford-Binet (Form L-M), WISC-R, .WAIS-R, WPPSI, K-ABC have ranged from .80 to .91 (comparing full-scale composites). Correlational studies using exceptional children (gifted, learning impaired, mentally retarded) produced generally lower correlations, probably because of restricted variability in the test scores. For example, for gifted students, the mean composite score on the Fourth Edition correlated .69 with the WISC-R full scale IQ. These data and data from similar validity investigations are presented more extensively in the *Technical Manual* for the new Binet (Thorndike, et al., 1986). Despite the presentation of ample evidence of concurrent validity, the severe problems with construct validity, the irresponsibly gathered normative data, and other difficulties with the Fourth Edition have led at least one reviewer to recommend that the battery be laid to rest (Reynolds, 1987): "To the S-B IV, *Requiescat in pace*" (p. 141).

Other General Cognitive Measures

Many other cognitive measures have been developed throughout the years, often to test populations for which standard intelligence measures were inappropriate. These include assessing (a) infants and preschoolers, (b) mentally retarded, (c) hearing, language, and/or speech impaired, (d) visually impaired, (e) orthopedically impaired, and (f) minority cultural groups.

When looking at cognitive development of infants and preschoolers (birth to approximately six years),

Table 4.3. Representation of the Stanford-Binet, Fourth Edition

	SAMPLE PERCENT	U.S. POPULATION PERCENT
By Parental Occupation		
Managerial/Professional	45.9	21.8
Technical Sales	26.2	29.7
Service Occupations	9.7	13.1
Farming/Forestry	3.2	2.9
Precision Production	6.7	13.0
Operators, Fabricators, Other	8.3	19.5
Total	100.0	100.0
By Parental Education		
College Graduate or Beyond	43.7	19.0
1 to 3 Years of College	18.2	15.3
High School Graduate	27.5	36.5
Less Than High School Graduate	10.6	29.2
Total	100.0	100.0

many of the assessment procedures are, in fact, norms and inventories of developmental and behavioral tasks which have been grouped by respective average age levels. Many of these scales are not tests, per se, but are observations of children's behaviors in a variety of situations and assess a combination of motor, social, and cognitive skills. Tests for this population are normally used for two purposes: (a) to determine a child's developmental status at the time of the examination; and (b) to predict future developmental and intellectual functioning. A considerable body of research has demonstrated that there is virtually no predictive value of cognitive assessments when the child is under 18 to 24 months of age (McCall, 1979). There may be some validity in predicting preschool test scores (.23–.47), but essentially no validity for predicting IQ scores obtained beyond the preschool level. Reasons for the low predictive value of these scales is thought to include behavioral characteristics of infants and preschoolers (short attention span, susceptibility to fatigue) and the fact that the nature and composition of intelligence changes rapidly during these ages. Despite their poor preditive value, experienced clinicians can reap benefits from going beyond the numerical scores and analyzing performance on the various parts to arrive at an understanding of a child's current mental, motor, and social-emotional development.

The American Association on Mental Deficiency (AAMD) defines mental retardation as significantly subaverage general intellectual functioning which exists concurrently with deficits in adaptive behavior, and that is manifested during the developmental period (Grossman, 1973). In other words, to be classified as mentally retarded a child must display deficiencies both in intellectual functioning and in adaptive behavior. In response to this requirement, a number of comprehensive measures have been developed to assess adaptive functioning to complement cognitive measures.

There is a fundamental difference between tests for hearing-impaired children and those for language-impaired children. While both minimize the role of language, tests for hearing impaired minimize receptive language; tests for language impaired minimize expressive language. Note that many of the tests developed for language-impaired children also minimize the role of receptive language. Some like the Peabody Picture Vocabulary Test-Revised (PPVT-R), do not. The PPVT-R minimizes only the role of expressive language and requires children to understand verbal directives.

As noted in recent court decisions, of growing concern is the possible inadequacy of standard intelligence tests for assessing the intellectual functioning of minority groups. A number of test developers, therefore, have been sensitive to these concerns and have attempted to develop culture-fair tests. Typically, in their attempts to eliminate cultural biases, three areas have been closely examined: language, speed, content (Anastasi, 1982).

While there have been batteries developed for the visually and orthopedically impaired populations, it is common for examiners to administer one of the major intelligence measures and to discard (or discount) those tasks which are obviously inappropriate. It is, in fact, useful sometimes to determine the extent of the impairment by measuring the limited ability on a well-standardized scale. So, for example, a visually impaired child may be administered both the Verbal and Performance Scales of the WISC-R. The astute examiner, then, may gain an *estimate* of the child's intellectual functioning from the Verbal Scale, and an estimate of the child's visual impairment from the Performance Scale. When measuring an individual with orthopedic limitations, an estimate of the potential and the limitation can be obtained by comparing those tasks which require motor coordination with those tasks which do not.

The K-ABC, as detailed in the previous section, certainly addresses some of these specialized needs: preschool, hearing and language impaired, minority cultural groups. Other tests that are in popular use are briefly detailed below.

Bayley Scales of Infant Development

Based on results of the Berkeley Growth Study (an extensive longitudinal research investigation), this scale was carefully developed to assess infants and toddlers ages 2 to 30 months (Bayley, 1969). Three separate scales are offered; (a) the Mental Scale addresses perception, memory, language, problem solving, verbal communication, and abstract thinking (resulting in a Mental Developmental Index Standard Score); (b) the Motor Scale addresses the child's gross motor abilities and some finer motor control (resulting in a Psychomotor Developmental Index Standard Score); and (c) the Infant Behavioral Record addresses the child's emotional, social, and personality development.

Both the mental and motor scales have been subjected to extensive longitudinal research. The standardization for these two scales is, according to Damarin (1978), excellent, especially for this population. Data on the Infant Behavior Record are less complete. This measure does, however, require considerable practice and experience to administer and to interpret. Shortages of interpretive material in the manual (only 1½ pages out of 185) are incongruent with Bayley's assertion that assessing developmental status is a fundamental clinical task with children at these ages. Therefore, the examiner must be trained not only in the mechanics of the instrument, but also in the principles underlying normal infant development and its deviations. Nevertheless, the Bayley Scales are, at present, regarded as the best measure of infant development, providing valuable information regarding patterns of early mental development (Sattler, 1988).

Columbia Mental Maturity Scale (CMMS)

This third edition (Burgemeister, Blum, & Lorge, 1972) is a pictorial classification test designed to tap general reasoning ability of children 3 years, 6 months to 9 years, 11 months. This task is unique in that it requires neither fine motor skills nor verbal responses. Thus, while the first edition was originally developed for children with cerebral palsy, it also has tremendous utility for children who have speech, language, and/or hearing impairments. Additionally, the successful attempt by the authors to include reasonably fair items suggests the test has utility for children of minority group cultures as well.

Unlike many tests of general cognitive ability, flexibility is built into the directions for administration (e.g., the examiner may use many different phrases in order to communicate the nature of the task). Also, each task contains three sample items which should enable most children to understand what is expected of them. This feature is especially helpful in trying to assess children with specialized needs in communication (e.g., receptive language deficits, bilingual). On a less positive note, the necessity of administering more than 50 items to a child, regardless of his or her success on the items, may be a very frustrating experience for many young children.

The CMMS was standardized carefully matching the 1960 U.S. Census data with regard to sex, racial group, geographic region, and parental occupation. The normative tables presented in the manual are derived from a highly representative and meticulously selected sample, and will, therefore, tend to yield meaningful scores. Kaufman (1978) suggests only one potentially serious flaw with the CMMS. Its multiple choice format means that chance guessing may exert a considerable influence on the score earned by any child. With a little bit of luck, a "guesser" can earn a score in the average range.

Split-half reliability coefficients computed from standardization data yielded values from .85 to .90; test-retest coefficients were about .85 regardless of subject age (Kaufman, 1978; Ratusnik & Koenigsknecht, 1976; Ritter, Duffey, & Fischman, 1974). In light of the scale's multiple-choice format and its relatively brief administration time, these internal consistency and stability estimates are more than adequate. Validity studies correlating other cognitive measures and tests of achievement are lower than values typically obtained by hour-long ability tests with a varied item content. These values underscore limitations of this brief test with homogeneous content.

Despite the authors' descriptions of the composite score as "general reasoning," "general mental maturity," and "mental ability," the CMMS samples a rather narrow spectrum of behavior. The authors recommend that this test be used as a quick screening device prior to administration of a thorough diagnostic battery. Additional abilities need to be measured to supplement the abilities assessed. According to Kaufman (1978), the CMMS "is undoubtedly the best brief instrument (verbal or nonverbal) available, and it ranks as one of the finest tests for assessing preschool children" (p. 301). At this time, these same claims can be made for the PPVT-R, which was published three years after Kaufman's (1978) review of the CMMS.

McCarthy Scales of Children's Abilities (MSCA)

The MSCA was designed for children 2½ to 8½ years old. It consists of 18 subtests that are grouped into six overlapping scales (Verbal, Quantitative, Perceptual-Performance, General Cognitive, Memory, and Motor). The General Cognitive Scale, based on 15 of the subtests, is similar to other measures of general intellectual development. Because the MSCA includes a number of very easy items, it is useful for assessing the strengths and weaknesses of mentally retarded school-age children.

The MSCA was well standardized with the sample closely matching the 1970 U.S. Census data with regard to race, geographic region, and father's occupational status. While McCarthy deliberately avoided the term *IQ*, the functional definition of the GCI is so similar to the descriptive classifications associated with the WISC-R that their functions are virtually identical (Sattler, 1988).

The internal consistency of the MSCA is very good. Reliability estimates averaged .93 across 10 age groups between 2 ½ to 8 ½ for the GCI and between .79 and .88 for the other five scale indices. A key issue for preschool tests, however, is stability because of the appreciable fluctuation in the test behaviors of young children. Stability estimates for the MSCA were also good. Test-retest reliability over a one-month period on a stratified sample averaged .90 for the GCI and from .69 to .89 for the other scales. While these estimates are quite adequate, it is noteworthy that few children under age 5 were included and stability for exceptional children was not examined (even though such children constitute the majority of children in need of testing).

Concurrent validity, as assessed by correlations with the Stanford-Binet (Form L-M), WISC-R, WPPSI, and K-ABC, is quite acceptable; coefficients ranged from .45 to .91 (Mdn r = .75) (Sattler, 1988). Construct validity for the factors is variable, depending on the specific population sampled (Kaufman, 1975; Keith & Bolen, 1960; Naglieri, Kaufman, & Harrison, 1981; Purvis & Bolen, 1984; Trueman, Lynch, & Branthwarte, 1984; Wiebe & Watkins, 1980).

The MSCA has major strengths that place it among the best of available general cognitive instruments for preschool children. (a) It has an outstanding manual that elaborates information about the test's psychometric soundness, the standardization process, and guidelines for administration and interpretation with a clarity that facilitates assurance among test users. (b) Unlike the WPPSI, the MSCA's subtests are game-like. While administration time is often 60–90 minutes, this quality can stretch the attention span of preschool children, for they often enjoy the activities. These features may especially enhance rapport with shy, nonverbal, and minority children (Kaufman & Kaufman, 1977).

Unfortunately, exceptional children were excluded from the standardization. This limitation has affected test users' confidence in understanding the meaning of scores for exceptional children relative to normal children. Other limitations identified by Kaufman and Kaufman (1977) include (a) lack of social comprehension and judgment tasks; (b) problems in testing older school-age children because the scale lacks a measure of verbal reasoning; (c) difficulties pertaining to scale interpretations due to overlap in content between some of the scales and a limited floor and ceiling. Because of this latter limitation, the MSCA should not be used for assessing younger retarded children or older gifted students. Paget (1985), when reviewing the MSCA,

concluded that "for preschool children aged 3 to 6½, the technical contributions and advantages of the battery far outweigh the disadvantages" (p. 923).

Peabody Picture Vocabulary Test-Revised (PPVT-R)

This scale provides a rough estimate of intelligence by measuring receptive vocabulary and replaces the original Peabody Picture Vocabulary Test (PPVT) published in 1959 (Dunn & Dunn, 1981). This revised version retains many of its predecessor's best features: it consists of two equivalent forms, allows for a verbal or nonverbal response, and is untimed. The examinee is shown plates with four pictures on each and is to point to the picture that best illustrates the meaning of the stimulus word spoken by the examiner. The PPVT-R is appropriate for individuals aged 2½ through adult who can hear the stimulus word, see the drawings, and respond in some manner.

While the original PPVT was normed on a large but restricted sample, the PPVT-R norms were based on a nationwide data gathering effort which, for children, was representative of the 1970 U.S. Census data with regard to sex, age, geographic region, occupational background, race and ethnic background, and urban-rural distributions. Because only 828 adults (ages 19 through 40) in contrast to 4,200 children were included in the standardization, the manual suggests careful interpretation of scores for individuals above 18 years, 11 months. Minority groups were included in the normative sample and are also included on the test plates. Sex and ethnic stereotyping, a problem with the old PPVT, has been virtually eliminated. The pictorial stimuli associated with items were redrawn to reflect a more appropriate racial, ethnic, and gender representation. Following the trend of other new or revised tests, the PPVT-R has adopted conversion of raw scores to either percentile ranks, age equivalents, or standard score equivalents (mean = 100; standard deviation = 15).

The test manual reports moderate internal consistency (.61 to .88) and alternate form reliability estimates (.71 to .91) for the standardization sample. The degree of equivalence of the two forms was established for a subsample of 642 children. Coefficients of equivalence ranged from .73 to .91 (median = .82). Correlations of the PPVT-R with other intelligence composites typically range from .40 to .60 (Dunn & Dunn, 1986; Kaufman & Kaufman, 1983; McCallum, 1985). These modest concurrent validity estimates suggest limited shared variance. Therefore, the PPVT-R should not be interpreted as equivalent to intelligence test scores.

In sum, the PPVT-R is an easy to use test of receptive language, providing content that is current and that contains appropriate racial, ethnic, and gender representation. The national representative standardization for the educationally critical age range (2½ to 19 years) responds to requirements set by P.L. 94-241 (Wiig, 1985) and psychometric characteristics of this latest revision appear adequate to excellent (McCallum, 1985). Facilitation of interpretation has also been improved by providing the ability to convert raw scores to percentile ranks, age equivalents, and standard score equivalents.

Slosson Intelligence Test (SIT)

The SIT evaluates 2 to 18-year-olds' mental ability in a brief period of time (10 to 15 minutes), and is best used as an estimate of their intelligence. No specific theoretical rationale is offered for the SIT and test items came mainly from the Stanford-Binet (Form L-M) and from the Gesell. It was first published in 1963 and renormed in 1981, with expanded norms published in 1985 (Jensen & Armstrong, 1985). In 1981, the SIT provided the ability to compute a deviation IQ in addition to the ratio IQ and mental age.

This test places a premium on language production. For people over four years of age, all questions are presented verbally and require verbal responses. For children under four, language skills are still given extreme emphasis which may render it invalid for young children whose language is merely delayed, or for others who are limited in their use of the English language. It has equal limitations for those with visual acuity disabilities.

Standardization and psychometric properties of the scale are, at best, highly questionable. No sample demographic characteristics were reported to determine the extent to which the sample represented the U.S. population. The sample was not randomly selected and included only individuals residing in the New England states. Additionally, true validity studies and internal consistency reliability coefficients are not presented in the 1981 manual. A review of this scale by Oakland (1985) found that many of the author's statements in the manual equating the SIT with the Stanford-Binet (L-M) and the WISC were incorrect and misleading. Furthermore, he concluded that placement decisions should never be based on SIT data.

Vineland Adaptive Behavior Scales (Vineland)

The Vineland Adaptive Behavior Scale was termed by its authors a revision of the Vineland Social Maturity Scale. Because this new revision dramatically exceeds the original Vineland in many important areas one reviewer (Campbell, 1985) was led to state, "This is somewhat like calling the space shuttle a revision of the DC-3" (p. 1661). Important revisions include improvements in (a) the applicable age ranges and/or populations, (b) item-selection procedures, (c) standardization, and (d) norming and psychometric properties.

Clinical use of the Vineland suggests greatest value for children, adolescents, and mentally retarded individuals. Items are arranged linearly on the basis of normal-life behavioral progressions in eight categories of behavior related to *social competence*: general self-help, self-help in eating, self-help in dressing, self-direction, occupation, communication, locomotion, and socialization.

Three forms are available: the Survey Form, the Expanded Form, and the Classroom Edition (Sparrow, Balla, & Cicchetti, 1984). With the Survey Form, a clinician or a paraprofessional interviews the parent or caregiver. The semistructured interview typically lasts from 20 to 60 minutes. The Expanded Form offers a more comprehensive assessment of adaptive behavior and, perhaps more importantly, a systematic basis for preparing individual educational, habilitative, or treatment programs. It too is administered in a semistructured interview with a parent or caregiver and takes from 60 to 90 minutes. The Classroom Edition is administered in the form of a questionnaire that is independently completed by a child's teacher. Completion of the questionnaire takes about 20 minutes.

Both the Survey and Expanded Forms provide information on individuals from birth to 18 years, 11 months old or on low-functioning adults. The Classroom Edition provides information on individuals from 3 years to 12 years, 11 months. The obtained scores on all three versions yield standard scores (mean = 100; standard deviation = 15), percentile ranks, stanines, adaptive levels, and age equivalents. In addition, for the Survey and Expanded Forms, supplementary norm-group percentile ranks and adaptive levels are provided. These supplementary scores are based on the performance of supplementary standardization samples of mentally retarded, emotionally disturbed, visually handicapped, and hearing-impaired individuals. Thus, examiners can obtain a percentile rank on a handicapped individual that shows his or her relative standing compared with others with the same handicap. Finally, the optional Maladaptive Behavior domain of the Survey and Expanded Forms determines whether an individual exhibits a significant number of maladaptive behaviors compared with others in the same age group of the national standardization sample or with others of the supplementary norm groups (mentally retarded, etc.).

The norming sample of the Vineland was based on the 1980 U.S. Census data and for each of the three forms, 3,000 individuals were included. Because there is substantial overlap in the norming samples of the Vineland and the K-ABC, when used in concert with each other, the Vineland and K-ABC represent powerful tools for diagnosing mental retardation and for making decisions regarding placement or institutionalization.

The Survey and Expanded Forms have both received positive reviews for assessing adaptive behavior (Campbell, 1985). A word of caution, however, was noted concerning the authors' suggestion for generating rehabilitation planning programs based on the Expanded Form analyses. While this latest revision greatly improved upon the previous edition, it also inherited one of the former's weaknesses. The developmental ordering of the items results in too few items at some age levels. For example, for the Expressive subdomain (within the Communication domain), only 16 items are included to measure the entire age range from 6 to 18+. The Personal subdomain (within the Daily Living Skills) has a similar limitation. Not surprisingly, reliability coefficients decrease sharply for both these subdomains beginning at age 8. Therefore, designing educational/rehabilitative programs by breaking down the subdomains and the clusters may be ill-advised unless examiners familiarize themselves with the numbers of items and the reliability figures for the various ages.

Wechsler Primary and Preschool Intelligence Scale (WPPSI)

The WPPSI was developed as a downward extension of the WISC-R. Like the other Wechsler Scales, the WPPSI is also not based on any particular research theory of cognitive development, but rather, all but two tasks were adapted directly from the children and the adult scales. It was designed to measure the intelligence of children aged 4 to 6½ years.

This scale was well standardized with reliability estimates ranging from .93 to .96 for the three IQ scales. Concurrent validity studies demonstrated a correlation of .81 with the Stanford-Binet (Form L-M). While yielding IQs somewhat higher than those produced by the WISC-R at the upper age levels, the two tests correlated highly both in normal and deviant populations. Predictive validity was found to be adequate for both white and African-American children

on a number of achievement measures, but inadequate for Mexican-American children. In general, correlations between the WPPSI and achievement measures was more variable with ethnic minority and lower socioeconomic status children than for white middle-class children (Paget, 1985). The factor structure of the WPPSI is similar to that of the WISC-R in that it supports both a Verbal Comprehension and a Perceptual organization factor (Sattler, 1988). Factor III, commonly referred to as Freedom from Distractibility, does not emerge as a separate factor on the WPPSI—perhaps because the WPPSI does not include two of the three subtests (Digit Span and Coding) which make up this factor on the WISC-R.

Several limitations of the WPPSI have been noted. These include (a) long administration time which may fatigue young children for whom the test was developed; (b) a limited floor and ceiling. A child can obtain a scaled-score with a raw score of zero which presents serious problems when assessing children with significant developmental difficulties. Therefore, information is not tapped that may have been quite useful for diagnostic and remedial puposes. (c) Six of the subtests have inadequate difficulty level for many gifted children (Hawthorne, Speer, & Buccellato, 1983).

The WPPSI is currently being revised and restandardized.

FUTURE TRENDS

If history is a predictor of future trends, intelligence testing is likely to see a combination of the old with the new. Inertia seems to be ever present with us. While researchers seem committed to advancing theory, clinicians (who are the consumers of the products) accept change with great reticence. Clinicians are trained, rather well, to be better than the tests they use. Many clinicians feel comfortable accepting instruments' limitations (so long as they are not debilitating) and combine history, behavioral observations, and clinical judgment to arrive at diagnoses and treatment considerations.

Nevertheless, social influences and legal decisions behoove refinement of our instruments. Certainly the APA's ethical code imposes on test publishers and clinicians alike the responsibility of demonstrating reliability and validity for the instruments they develop and utilize. As theories of intelligence change or become more refined, it necessitates the refinement of our instrumentation; otherwise, validity becomes questionable at best.

It seems, therefore, when looking at intelligence testing of the future, one can expect changes in both the purpose for testing and in the shape these tests will take. Intelligence tests gained public support when classification between individuals became important (in Binet's time). Future purposes are likely to be quite different as the trend appears to be away from classification *between* individuals toward identification *within* each individual of his or her own mental processes and abilities. Additional purposes will include prediction and prescription. The shape intelligence testing will take is likely to be influenced by theory, research, cultural changes, and technological advances.

Intelligence tests of the future are likely to derive from the need to assess the complex learning capacities which characterize adult thinking (Horn, 1979; Sattler, 1988). Their original development addressed a pragmatic need by predicting academic success or failure. Not surprisingly, they accomplish this function exceptionally well (they predict about 25% of the variance in grades and about 50% of the variance in number of years of education) because items on intelligence tests are often representative of the types of issues which dominate school curricula (Detterman, 1979). In developing intelligence tests which reflect adult thinking, tasks are likely to be based on theories of cognition which include constructs that go beyond academic intelligence: critical life experiences and adaptation outside school. This move is reinforced to some degree by the wide acceptance of industrial psychology as a viable discipline. Corporations have often been disillusioned by the "grade point average" and want to know if an individual has what it takes to succeed, with training, beyond the confines of the four walls of academia.

Assessment of intelligence within a given culture or subculture is likely to receive continued attention in the future. This cultural component may take the form of a separate scale which reflects dominant values of the culture in which the measurement occurs. Providing a separate "cultural" scale might afford an understanding of a child's or an adult's intellectual capacity (a) without cultural influences, (b) when dominant cultural influences are present, and (c) when current (nondominant) cultural influences are present. This type of assessment certainly has invaluable utility for diagnostic consideration and for treatment recommendations. Therefore, whether the cultural component is labeled intelligence or applied intelligence (i.e., achievement), assessment batteries need to include tasks that are culturally saturated and relevant. To strip cultural aspects from psychological measures is to neglect assessing qualities of intellectual functioning that reflect values of a culture, and to neglect a part of intelligent behavior that many, particularly in applied settings, regard as most important.

What is suggested above may be a heavy burden for future test developers. For this feat to be accomplished, there is likely to be a continued deemphasis on measuring a single general factor of intelligence and an increased emphasis on measuring separate capacities that fall under the rubric of intelligence. We are likely to see intelligence tests which provide separate scores on a variety of abilities such as mental processing (e.g., sequential, simultaneous, planning) and achievement (academic, daily living). Certainly the move in this direction has already begun. The K-ABC, for example, provides separate standard scores on sequential processing, simultaneous processing, and academic achievement. Even the Stanford-Binet (Fourth Edition) attempted, albeit unsuccessfully, to move away from a single IQ score. The abilities measured in the future are also likely to be standard scores which will constitute an integrated theory of intelligence. This integration may not, however, include a statistical composite score labeled "IQ" which proposes to explain *intelligence*.

Certainly, the wave of the future is shifting attention away from performance on tests themselves (which essentially defines intelligence as the ability to do well on IQ tests), to the learning processes that underlie both skillful test performance and skillful school performance (Resnick, 1979). Current tests make assumptions. For example, a low score on the WISC-R information subtest reflects, to some extent, a poor fund of factual knowledge that is normally acquired incidentally or through formal education in the cultural environment of the United States. It *may* point, *indirectly*, to an inability to pick up essential elements in one's environment. Future measures may be able to measure directly, and more precisely, what we now measure indirectly.

Current intelligence measures predict academic success and failure rather well. Unfortunately, reliable prediction does not always extend downward to include preschool populations. Most of the current instruments are not sensitive enough to distinguish between developmental delay, mental retardation, and learning handicaps at young ages. Because the legal criteria for a formal diagnosis of a learning disability is interpreted to mean a disparity between intelligence and achievement, a diagnosis of learning disability is nigh to impossible until approximately second or third grade where achievement levels have had an opportunity to be sufficiently raised—too late

Figure 4.1.

to intervene before cognitive deficits create an emotional disruption which further clouds the diagnostic picture.

Besides being predictive, intelligence tests need to be prescriptive. The inability to provide adequate translation of intelligence test scores to academic remediation may be a function of most intelligence tests not being founded on any theory to suggest remedial strategies given certain profiles. Previous intelligence tests, therefore, are little different from predictions of a fatal disease for which there is no cure. The K-ABC attempted to remedy this gloomy outcome by founding subtests on state-of-the-art theory which logically permits generation of remedial techniques. Most intelligence measures, at best, have exhibited only the most casual theoretical foundation, if any at all. Future measures will likely involve tests that attempt to link sound theory and experimental research with assessment tasks.

As stressed above, there is a component to intelligence that is integrally linked with the values and demands of a culture. Intelligence of the future, therefore, must reflect aspects of that culture including the manner information is transmitted and received. In the Western society, information transmitted through moving images—television, video, computer terminal—is becoming the norm. With the acculturation of the microcomputer in this climate, assessment measures of the future are likely to capitalize on their utility—not just in scoring and administrative ease, but in the types of tasks and in methods of delivery that heretofore were prohibited.

Historically, technology has always advanced to ease our burden and to maximize our efficiency. No doubt this trend will find its way into assessment practices. Computerized scoring will continue to make the clinician's task more efficient, and computerized administration will minimize clinician-client contact. The latter certainly can easily lead to an abuse of computerized assessment. For example, it may be tempting to many clinicians to accept the modification of current tasks for computerized administration, resulting only in a loss of clinician contact. Data gained from individual administration by a skilled clinician are an invaluable part of the assessment procedure. If the clinician's role is minimized, invaluable data may be lost.

We see the elegance of computerized testing to be (a) to develop tasks that could not otherwise be administered, (b) to standardize oral tasks by audio-visual presentations, (c) to permit an economy of testing time by administering a tailor-made set of tasks to each individual based on his or her success (or failure) on each item administered, and (d) to administer tests of complex learning ability along with a permanent record (computer printout) of every correct and incorrect decision made during the learning process. If computerized assessment procedures also succeed in reducing the clinician's time spent with the client, then it is incumbent on the clinician to interact with the client in other meaningful ways. These notions have limitless capabilities. We might be able to refine the way we tap visual-spatial abilities, for example. Additionally, response-contingent tasks can be developed in which one's response determines which of several possible items will appear next. If a subject fails to obtain a correct answer, an easier item appears. Also, programs can be generated to test the ability to learn by providing hints and/or immediate feedback to responses.

It will be imperative for future test developers to blend the known benefits of computer technology with the time-honored clinical benefits of direct observation of a person's test-taking behavior.

REFERENCES

American Association on Mental Deficiency. (1974). *Adaptive Behavior Scale: Manual*. Washington, DC: Author.

American Psychological Association. (1974). *Standards for educational and psychological tests and manuals*. Washington, DC: Author.

Anastasi, A. (1982). *Differential psychology*. New York: Macmillan.

Anastasi, A. (1988). *Psychological testing* (6th ed.). New York: Macmillan.

Arlin, P.K. (1979). Cognitive development in adulthood: A fifth stage? *Developmental Psychology, 11*, 602–606.

Bayley, N. (1933). *The California First-Year Mental Scale*. University of California Syllabus Series, No. 243. Berkeley: University of California Press.

Bayley, N. (1969). *Bayley Scales of Infant Development: Birth to two years*. San Antonio: Psychological Corporation.

Biggs, J.B. (1978). Genetics and education: An alternative to Jensenism. *Educational Researcher, 7*, 11–17.

Bogen, J. E. (1975). Some educational aspects of hemispheric specialization. *UCLA Educator, 17*, 24–32.

Brazelton, T. B. (1973). *Neonatal Behavioral Assessment Scale*. Philadelphia: J. B. Lippincott.

Brown, A. L., & French, L. A. (1979). The zone of potential development implications for intelligence testing in the year 2000. In R. J. Sternberg & D. K. Detterman (Eds.), *Human intelligence* (pp. 217–235). Norwood, NJ: Ablex.

Burgemeister, B. B., Blum, L. H., & Lorge, I. (1972). *Columbia Mental Maturity Scale* (3rd ed.). San Antonio: Psychological Corporation.

Butcher, H. J. (1973). *Human intelligence: Its nature and assessment*. New York: Harper & Row.

Buros, O. K. (Ed.). (1978). *Eighth Mental Measurements yearbook*. Highland Park, NJ: Gryphon.

Buros, O. K. (Ed.). (1985). *Ninth Mental Measurements yearbook*. Highland Park, NJ: Gryphon.

Campbell, I. A. (1985). Review of Vineland Adaptive Behavior Scales. In O. K. Buros (Ed.), *Ninth Mental Measurements yearbook* (pp. 1660–1662). Highland Park, NJ: Gryphon.

Cattell, J. McK. (1988). As cited in Pintner, R. (1949). *Intelligence testing: Methods and results*. New York: Henry Holt.

Cattell, P. (1940). *The measurement of intelligence of infants and young children*. New York: Psychological Corporation.

Cattell, R. B. (1963). Theory of fluid and crystallized intelligence: A critical experiment. *Journal of Educational Psychology, 54*, 1–22.

Cronbach, L. J. (1970). *Essentials of psychological testing*. New York: Harper & Row.

Damarin, F. (1978). Bayley Scales of Infant Development. In O. K. Buros (Ed.), *Eighth Mental Measurements yearbook* (pp. 206–207). Highland Park, NJ: Gryphon.

Das, J. P. (1973). Structure of cognitive abilities: Evidence for simultaneous and successive processing. *Journal of Educational Psychology, 65*, 103–108.

Das, J. P., Kirby, J. R., & Jarman, R. F. (1975). Simultaneous and successive synthesis: An alternative model for cognitive abilities. *Psychological Bulletin, 82*, 87–103.

Das, J. P., Kirby, J. R., & Jarman, R. F. (1979). *Simultaneous and successive processes*. New York: Academic Press.

Detterman, D. K. (1979). A job half done: The road to intelligence testing in the year 2000. In R. J. Sternberg & D. K. Detterman (Eds.), *Human intelligence* (pp. 245–256). Norwood, NJ: Ablex.

Dunn, L. M., & Dunn, L. M. (1981). *Peabody Picture Vocabulary Test-Revised*. Circle Pines, MN: American Guidance Service.

Esquirol, J. E. D. (1828). Observations pour servir a l'histoire de l'idiotie. [Observations to ser the history of idiocy]. *Les Malidies Mentales.*

Eysenck, H. J. (1979). *The structure and measurement of intelligence*. New York: Springer-Verlag.

Eysenck, H. J., & Kamen, L. (1981). *The intelligence controversy,* New York: Wiley-Interscience.

Figurelli, J. C., & Keller, H. R. (1972). The effects of training and socioeconomic class upon the acquisition of conservation concepts. *Child Development, 43*, 293–298.

Freeman, F. S. (1953). *Theory and practice of psychological testing*. New York: Henry Holt.

Galton. (1869). As cited in Sattler, J. M. *Assessment of children*. San Diego: Jerome M. Sattler.

Gazzaniga, M. S. (1975). Recent research on hemispheric lateralization of the human brain: Review of the split-brain. *UCLA Educator, 17*, 9–12.

Gesell, A. (1925). *The mental growth of the preschool child*. New York: Macmillan.

Gesell, A., & Amatruda, C. S. (1947). *Developmental diagnosis* (rev. ed.). New York: P. B. Hoeber.

Gesell, A., & Thompson, H. (1938). *The psychology of early growth*. New York: Macmillan.

Goldschmid, M. L. (1973). A cross-cultural investigation of conservation. *Journal of Cross-Cultural Psychology, 4*, 75–88.

Grossman, H. (Ed.). (1973). *Manual on Terminology and Classification in Mental Retardation*. Washington, DC: AAMD.

Guilford, J. P. (1959). Three faces of intellect. *American Psychologist, 14*, 459–479.

Guilford, J. P. (1967). *The nature of human intelligence*. New York: McGraw-Hill.

Guilford, J. P. & Hoepfner, R. (1971). *The analysis of intelligence*. New York: McGraw-Hill.

Gunnison, J. A. (1982). Remediation strategies based on the roles of simultaneous and successive processing in reading. *Journal of Educational Neuropsychology, 2*, 36–69.

Gunnison, J. A., Kaufman, J. L., & Kaufman, A. S. (1982). Sequential and simultaneous processing applied to remediation. *Academic Therapy, 17*, 297–307.

Hawthorne, L. W., Speer, S. K., & Buccellato, L. (1983). Appropriateness of the Wechsler Preschool and Primary Scale of Intelligence for gifted children. *Journal of Consulting and Clinical Psychology, 51*, 463–464.

Hersen, M. (Ed.). (in press). *Innovations in child behavior therapy*. New York: Springer Publishing.

Horn, J. L. (1979). Trends in the measurement of intelligence. In R. J. Sternberg & D. K. Detterman (Eds.), *Human intelligence* (pp. 191–201). Norwood, NJ: Ablex.

Jensen, J. A., & Armstrong, R. J. (1985). *Slosson Intelligence Test (SIT) for children and adults: Expanded norms tables application and development*. East Aurora, NY: Slosson Educational Publications.

Kamphaus, R. W., & Reynolds, C. R. (1987). *Clinical and research applications of the K-ABC*. Circle Pines, MN: American Guidance Service.

Kaufman, A. S. (1975). Factor structure of the McCarthy Scales at five age levels between 2½ and 8½. *Educational and psychological measurement, 35*, 641–656.

Kaufman, A. S. (1978). Review of the Columbia Mental Maturity Scale. In O. K. Buros (Ed.), *Eighth Mental Measurements yearbook* (pp. 299–301). Highland Park, NJ: Gryphon.

Kaufman, A. S. (1979). *Intelligence testing with the WISC-R*. New York: Wiley-Interscience.

Kaufman, A. S., & Doppelt, J. E. (1976). Analysis of WISC-R standardization data in terms of the stratification variables. *Child Development, 47*, 165–171.

Kaufman, A. S., & Kaufman, N. L. (1977). *Clinical evaluation of young children with the McCarthy Scales*. New York: Grune & Stratton.

Kaufman, A. S., & Kaufman, N. L. (1983). *Interpretive manual for the Kaufman Assessment Battery for Children*. Circle Pines, MN: American Guidance Service.

Kaufman, A. S., & Kamphaus, R. W. (1984). Factor analysis of the Kaufman Assessment Battery for Children (K-ABC) for ages 2½ through 12½ years. *Journal of Educational Psychology, 76*, 623–637.

Keith, T. Z., & Bolen, L. M. (1980). Factor structure of the McCarthy Scales for children experiencing problems in school. *Psychology in the Schools, 17*, 320–326.

Kinsbourne, M. (Ed.). (1978). *Asymmetrical function of the brain*. Cambridge, MA: Cambridge University Press.

Levy, J. & Trevarthen, C. (1976). Metacontrol of hemispheric function in human split-brain patients. *Journal of Experimental Psychology: Human Perception and Performance, 2*, 299–312.

Luria, A. R. (1966a). *Higher cortical functions in man*. New York: Basic Books.

Luria, A. R. (1966b). *Human brain and psychological processes*. New York: Harper & Row.

Luria, A. R. (1973). *The working brain: An introduction to neuro-psychology*. London: Penguin Books.

McCall, R. B. (1979). The development of intellectual functioning in infancy and the prediction of later IQ. In J. D. Osofsky (Ed.), *Handbook of infant development* (pp. 707–741) New York: Wiley.

McCallum, S. (1985). Review of Peabody Picture Vocabulary Test-Revised. In O. K. Buros (Ed.), *Ninth Mental Measurements yearbook* (pp. 1126–1128). Highland Park, NJ: Gryphon.

McCallum, R. S., & Merritt, F. M. (1983). Simultaneous-successive processing among college students. *Journal of Psychoeducational Assessment, 1*, 85–93.

McCarthy, D. A. (1972). *Manual for the McCarthy Scales of Children's Abilities*. San Antonio: Psychological Corporation.

Mercer, J. R. (1973). *System of Multicultural Pluralistic Assessment (SOMPA)*. New York: Psychological Corporation.

Miller, T. L., & Reynolds, C. R. (1984). Special issue . . . The K-ABC. *Journal of Special Education, 18*(3).

Naglieri, J. A., Kaufman, A. S., & Harrison, P. L. (1981). Factor structure of the McCarthy Scales for school-age children with low GCIs. *Journal of School Psychology, 19*, 226–232.

Neisser, U. (1967). *Cognitive psychology*. New York: Appleton-Century-Crofts.

Oakland, T. (1985). Review of Slosson Intelligence Test. In O. K. Buros (Ed.), *The Ninth Mental Measurements Yearbook* (pp. 1401–1403). Highland Park, NJ: Gryphon.

Paget, K. D. (1985). Review of McCarthy Scales of Children's Abilities. In Buros, O. K. (Ed.), *Ninth Mental Measurements yearbook* (pp. 922–926). Highland Park, NJ: Gryphon.

Perlman, M. D. (1986). *Toward an integration of a cognitive-dynamic view of personality: The relationship between defense mechanisms, cognitive style, attentional focus, and neuropsychological processing*. Unpublished doctoral dissertation, California School of Professional Psychology-San Diego.

Perlman, M. D., & Kaufman, A. S. (In press). Intelligence testing. In M. Hersen (Ed.), *Innovations in child behavior therapy*. New York: Springer Publishing.

Piaget, J. (1950). *The psychology of intelligence*. New York: Harcourt Brace.

Pintner, R. (1949). *Intelligence testing: Methods and results*. New York: Henry Holt.

Pintner, R., & Patterson, D. G. (1925). *A scale of performance*. New York: Appleton.

Porteus, S. D. (1959). *The Maze Test and clinical psychology*. Palo Alto, CA: Pacific Books.

Purvis, M. A., & Bolen, L. M. (1984). Factor structure of the McCarthy Scales for males and females. *Journal of Clinical Psychology, 40*, 108–114.

Quay, L. C. (1971). Language, dialect, reinforcement, and the intelligence test performance of Negro children. *Child Development, 42*, 5–15.

Quay, L. C. (1972). Negro dialect and Binet performance in severely disadvantaged black four-year-olds. *Child Development, 43*, 245–250.

Quereshi, M. Y., & McIntire, D. H. (1984). The comparability of the WISC, WISC-R and WPPSI. *Journal of Clinical Psychology, 40*, 1036–1043.

Ratusnik, D. L., & Koenigsknecht, R. A. (1976). Cross-cultural item analysis of the Columbia Mental Maturity Scale: Potential application by the language clinician. *Language, Speech, and Hearing Services in Schools, 7*, 186–190.

Resnick, L. B. (1976). *The nature of intelligence*. Hillsdale, N. J.: Lawrence Erlbaum Associates.

Resnick, L. B. (1979). The future of IQ testing in education. In R. J. Sternberg & D. K. Detterman (Eds.), *Human intelligence* (pp. 203–215). Norwood, NJ: Ablex.

Reynolds, C. R. (1987). Playing IQ roulette with the Stanford-Binet, 4th edition. *Measurement and Evaluation in Counseling and Development, 20*, 139–141.

Reynolds, C. R., Kamphaus, R. W., & Rosenthal, B. L. (1988). Factor analysis of the Stanford-Binet Fourth Edition for ages 2 years through 23 years. *Measurement and Evaluation in Counseling and Development, 21*, 52–63.

Ritter, D., Duffey, J., & Fischman, R. (1974). Comparability of Columbia Mental Maturity Scale and Stanford-Binet, Form L-M, estimates of intelligence. *Psychological Reports, 34*, 174.

Sattler, J. M. (1988). *Assessment of children*. San Diego: Jerome M. Sattler.

Seguin E. (1907). *Idiocy: Its treatment by the physiological method.* (reprinted from original addition of 1866). New York: Bureau of Publications, Teachers College, Columbia University.

Shapiro, D. (1965). *Neurotic styles*. New York: Basic Books.

Slosson, R. L. (1983). *Slosson Intelligence Test (SIT) and Oral Reading Test (SORT) for children and adults*. East Aurora, NY: Slosson Educational Publications.

Sparrow, S. S., Balla, D. A., & Cicchetti, D. V. (1984). *Vineland Adaptive Behavior Scales*. Circle Pines, MN: American Guidance Service.

Sperry, R. W. (1968). Hemisphere deconnection and unity in conscious awareness. *American Psychologist, 1968, 23*, 723–733.

Sternberg, R. J., & Detterman, D. K. (Eds.). (1979). *Human intelligence: Perspectives on its theory and measurement*. Norwood, NJ: Ablex.

Terman, L. M. (1921). Intelligence and its measurement. *Journal of Educational Psychology, 12*, 127–133.

Thorndike, R. L., Hagen, E. P., & Sattler, J. M. (1986). *Technical manual, Stanford-Binet Intelligence Scale: Fourth Edition*. Chicago: Riverside Publishing.

Torgesen, J. K. (1979). What shall we do with psychological processes? *Journal of Learning Disabilities, 12*, 514–521.

Trueman, M., Lynch, A., & Branthwaite, A. (1984). A factor analytic study of the McCarthy Scales of Children's Abilities. *British Journal of Educational Psychology, 54*, 331–335.

Tuddenham, R. D. (1962). The nature and measurement of intelligence. In L. J. Postman (Ed.), *Psychology in the making* (pp. 469–525). New York: Knopf.

Wechsler, D. (1967). *Manual for the Wechsler Preschool and Primary Scale of Intelligence*. San Antonio: Psychological Corporation.

Wechsler D. (1974). *Manual for the Wechsler Intelligence Scale for Children-Revised*. San Antonio: Psychological Corporation.

Wiebe, J. J., & Watkins, E. O. (1980). Factor analysis of the McCarthy Scales of Children's Abilities on preschool children. *Journal of School Psychology, 18*, 154–162.

Wiig, E. H. (1985). Review of Peabody Picture Vocabulary Test-Revised. In O. K. Buros (Ed.), *Ninth Mental Measurements yearbook* (pp. 1126–1128). Highland Park, NJ: Gryphon.

Wolf, R. H. (1960). The emergence of Binet's conceptions and measurement of intelligence: A case history of the creative process. Part II. *Journal of the History of the Behavioral Science, 5*, 207–237.

Yerkes, R. M. (1917). The Binet versus the point scale method of measuring intelligence. *Journal of Applied Psychology, 1*, 111–122.

CHAPTER 5

ASSESSMENT OF ADULT INTELLIGENCE

James E. Lindemann
Joseph D. Matarazzo

The application of measures of intelligence to adults is a complex function with a multitude of goals. It demonstrates the breadth and depth of useful information that can be obtained from interacting with a subject during the administration of a standardized set of cognitive tasks. It transcends the generation of "an IQ." The traditional task of grade placement is usually irrelevant. *Because they are available*, intelligence tests have been put to use for a broad range of purposes. This chapter will describe commonly used adult intelligence tests, with emphasis on the Wechsler Adult Intelligence Scale-Revised (WAIS-R). This test and its predecessor, the Wechsler Adult Intelligence Scale (WAIS) are today's most frequently used adult tests. The chapter will describe a diversity of applications, including individual evaluation and career counseling, psychodiagnosis and assessment of functional impairment of cognitive ability, neuropsychological evaluation, assessment of mental retardation, and measurement of intelligence as a genetic marker. Case materials from each of these areas will be included to illustrate the richness of utility that can be obtained from standardized administration, careful observation, and detailed analysis of results.

HISTORICAL FOUNDATIONS

Since the dawn of civilization, men and women have subjectively assessed or tested their abilities (intelligence) against others. Survival itself is a test, as are most "games." Raw measures of physical superi-ority soon became measures of individual difference; "Omar is the best tentmaker; Anna the best keeper of goats."

As tests moved from unstandardized *in situ* observation of performance to more objective samples of traits, (e.g., "quickness of mind") or specific achievements as in ancient Greece (Doyle, 1974), China (DuBois, 1970), or the Ottoman Empire (Inalcik, 1973), they were closely associated with selection for ability to learn. Therefore, it should be no surprise that the first modern attempt to construct an intelligence scale was related to school placement, and that age (and closely associated grade placement) became the criterion against which Binet and Simon validated their 1905 test.

The scholarly roots of the study of intelligence lie in the discussion of early philosophers who did little to operationalize its definition, let alone to consider its measurement. Galton (1869) wrote about ability, general and specific, but limited his attempts at measurement to psychophysical methods. William James (1890) was interested in the nature and attributes of "intellect" without reference to measurement. In the years that followed, psychologists have generated many definitions of intelligence without consensual agreement, reflecting the inferential nature of the concept. We measure what people have learned or how they perform, and from that we infer intelligence.

It was Alfred Binet who first began systematically to identify items of achievement and performance that would reflect intellectual development. Like any good pragmatist, after a decade of effort he eventually discerned a criterion that, although crude, was readily available and objective: the cognitively differentiable attributes necessary for the progressive grade placement of school children. From the rudimentary scale developed by Binet and Theodore Simon in 1905 came the Binet-Simon scales of 1908 and 1911, each of which incorporated the concept of *mental age*. In 1912 William Stern suggested that mental age could be divided by chronological age, thus bringing into existence the concept of IQ—*intelligence quotient*. The simplicity of that numerical statement has made IQ a common household word and has done more to bring about the use and misuse of intelligence tests than any other single factor.

The development of age-scale tests of intelligence suitable for assessment of the *individual* was carried forward in 1916 by Terman and in 1937 and 1960 by Terman and Merrill (1973). Wechsler (1939, 1944, 1955, 1974, 1981) dropped the mental age and introduced the deviation quotient for determining the IQ. He deliberately set out to incorporate different ways of measuring individual intelligence within one scale. The measurement of different cognitive skills in vertical tests within a scale has been adopted in the fourth edition of the Stanford-Binet Intelligence Scale (Thorndike, Hagen, & Sattler, 1986). This recent revision of the Stanford-Binet also substitutes Standard Age Scores for the traditional IQ.

Concurrent with the creation of individually administered tests of intelligence has been the development of group measures, many of them batteries measuring multiple factors. The measurement of intelligence with application to large groups was given impetus during World War I, when Robert Yerkes and others (1921) developed two group tests, the Army Alpha (for literates) and the Army Beta (for the non-English speaking). From this second development has flowed a whole movement of group ability testing applied to diagnostic evaluation for the educational placement of school children, industrial and military selection, and vocational and educational planning for individuals bound for college, technical, graduate, and professional schools.

THEORETICAL UNDERPINNINGS

While Binet in Paris was pragmatically constructing a test of "intelligence," Spearman (1904) was striving to understand its nature and to define it (in London). His correlational studies led him to the conclusion that intelligence is a unitary factor, which became known as *g* for *general intelligence*, with secondary *specific* or *s* components. In New York, Thorndike and his colleagues (Thorndike, Lay, & Dean, 1909) interpreted their data quite differently, finding only minimal correlations among various measures of ability. This position was advanced by Thurstone and Thurstone (1941) who developed measures of *primary mental abilities*. Theirs was essentially a multiple (specific) factor theory of intelligence, although their measures could be statistically analyzed in ways that suggested the influence of a general factor. The conflict between proponents of general- and multiple-factor theories of intelligence—with analysis and reanalysis, interpretation and reinterpretation, often of the same data—continues after 75 years. Happily, a great deal of *pragmatically* useful information has been accumulated that psychologists can apply in their professional activity while simultaneously collecting further data for the scientific quest.

Significant positions on the contemporary stage of intelligence theorizing are occupied by Guilford, Cattell, and their respective colleagues. Guilford has advanced a tridimensional model of the structure of intelligence (Guilford & Hoepfner, 1971) derived from factor analysis. Intelligence is conceptualized by means of a three-dimensional cube, which includes *contents* (four variables), *operations* (five variables), and *products* (six variables). The result is a theoretical model of 120 different kinds of "abilities," for some of which measures have yet to be devised. In contrast to this multiple-variable theory, Cattell (1971) postulates only two major dimensions of intelligence: *fluid intelligence* (*Gf*), which is an ability to perceive relationships based on the individual's unique physiological structures and processes, and *crystallized intelligence* (*Gc*), which is a product of original fluid ability plus the effects of cultural and educational experiences. Cattell's theory has been elaborated and advanced by Horn (1986), especially in the study of adult development, with a major focus on the postulated decline of fluid intelligence during the "vital years of adulthood" from ages 20 to 60.

Some researchers recently (e.g., Sattler, 1982, 1988) have made the interpretive assumption that the Performance Scale tests of the WAIS-R may be viewed as measures of fluid intelligence and the Verbal Scale tests as measures of crystallized intelligence. Kaufman and Kaufman (1983) have used the Cattell-Horn theory in the development of the Kaufman Assessment Battery for Children. This battery contains an Achievement Scale which is intended to measure crystallized abilities and two Mental Processing Scales which are intended to measure fluid abilities. The recently constructed Fourth Edition of the Stanford-Binet Intelligence Scale (Thorndike et al., 1986) also uses the constructs of crystallized abilities and fluid-analytic abilities as part of a three-level hierarchical model which includes the concept of *g*, or general reasoning ability. Thus these concepts seem to be achieving pragmatic recognition in applied measurement.

On the forefront of some exciting new approaches to the conceptualization of intelligence is a group of modern theorist-psychologists whose backgrounds are in research in cognition, computers, artificial intelligence, and information processing. Their approach to theory building in intelligence involves study of the strategies employed in learning new material rather than in psychological assessment or psychometrics. On the surface these developments bear no linear relationship to those of Binet or the succession of theorists from Spearman through Guilford and Cattell. The interested reader will find the writings of leaders in this newest development, such as Detterman, Glaser, and Hunt, in the pages of *Intelligence: A Multidisciplinary Journal* and in books by these and other authors (e.g., Sternberg & Detterman, 1986). Although it is early to speculate, the findings of these modern researchers in the field of intelligence (more correctly, *cognition*) may prove to be related and compatible with the views of Spearman and earlier theorists.

We shall now turn to a discussion of tests available for the assessment of adult intelligence.

ADULT INTELLIGENCE TESTS DESCRIBED

Wechsler's Scales

The composition of Wechsler's scales directly reflects David Wechsler's (1944) definition of intelligence as "the aggregate or global capacity of the individual to act purposefully; to think rationally, and to deal effectively with his environment" (p. 3). Impelled by his conviction that intelligence should include the ability to handle practical situations as well as to reason in abstract terms, Wechsler proceeded to select a group of tests that up to now, at least, have effectively withstood the test of time as well as the analysis of theoreticians, psychometricians, and factor analysts. The 11 tests that made up the original Wechsler-Bellevue Scale (Wechsler, 1939, 1944) were retained with revision in the Wechsler Adult Intelligence Scale (1955) and, with further revision, in the Wechsler Adult Intelligence Scale-Revised

(1981). Six tests comprise the Verbal Scale: Information, Digit Span, Vocabulary, Arithmetic, Comprehension, and Similarities. The remaining five make up the Performance Scale: Picture Completion, Picture Arrangement, Block Design, Object Assembly, and Digit Symbol. In the WAIS, all six verbal tests were administered consecutively, followed by the five performance tests. In the WAIS-R they are systematically alternated on the assumption that varying the task will help to maintain the subject's interest.

The WAIS tests have been described by Wechsler (1939, 1955). Additionally, Matarazzo (1972) and Zimmerman and Woo-Sam (1973) provide extensive coverage of the interpretation and relevant research findings on the WAIS and its subtests. House and Lewis (1985) and Sattler (1988) have described the WAIS-R subtests and reviewed much of the research regarding the psychometric properties and factorial structure of the scale. Leckliter, Matarazzo, and Silverstein (1986) have published a review of the findings from all the factor analytic studies published on the WAIS-R to date. The following sections will include an abbreviated description of each WAIS-R subtest, the factors it is presumed to measure, the revisions that were made from WAIS to WAIS-R, and the correlation of the WAIS-R test with Full Scale, Verbal Scale, and Performance Scale scores for the combined nine age groups included in the WAIS-R standardization. The reader should note that such correlations differ from one age level to another, and reference should be made to the WAIS-R manual (Wechsler, 1981) for precise application at a specific age level. This is especially recommended when the WAIS-R is used as an aid in decision making involving assessment under any of the currently extant federal guidelines that require an assessment of individual intelligence. The reader wishing a concise up-to-date review of research with the WAIS-R will find it in Sattler (1988).

WAIS-R Verbal Tests

Information

The WAIS-R Information test includes 29 questions that sample the subject's range of general information and are related to intellectual alertness, motivation, and retention of information. Eight WAIS items were replaced because they were technically unsuitable or unfair to some subgroups. Some new questions reflect a concern for cultural balance in item selection, for example, "Who was Louis Armstrong?" and "What was Marie Curie famous for?"

Correlation with the WAIS-R Full Scale Score is .76, Verbal Score .79, and Performance Score .62, each corrected for "contamination" (i.e., the effect of being part of the total score with which it was correlated).

Digit Span

The Digit Span test measures memory for series of digits, forward and backward, increasing in difficulty up to seven digits, and is related to auditory recall, attention, and freedom from distractibility. The content of WAIS is identical with that of WAIS-R. WAIS-R administration (and scoring) is changed to include administration of two series of digits at each level of difficulty. Correlation (corrected for contamination) with the WAIS-R Full Scale Score is .58, Verbal Score .57, and Performance Score .50.

Vocabulary

The Vocabulary test includes 35 words to be defined and tests understanding of words. This test is considered to be an excellent measure of general intelligence and is commonly believed to be influenced by education and cultural opportunities. Seven words have been eliminated from the WAIS and two added. Correlation (corrected for contamination) with the WAIS-R Full Scale Score is .81, Verbal Score .85, and Performance Score .65.

Arithmetic

The Arithmetic test includes 14 orally presented, timed, arithmetic "story" problems and is believed to measure arithmetic reasoning, ability to comprehend verbal instructions, concentration, and freedom from distractibility. Performance on this test is believed to be influenced by education. One WAIS item was eliminated, one added, and bonus point scoring was modified. Correlation (corrected for contamination) with the WAIS-R Full Scale Score is .72, Verbal Score is .70, and Performance Score is .62.

Comprehension

This test consists of 16 questions about aspects of everyday living and social situations and is sometimes called a test of common sense. It requires evaluation of past experience, application of judgment to practical situations, and ability to verbalize. Two items were eliminated from the earlier WAIS and four were added. Some new items are "What are some reasons why many foods need to be cooked?" and "Why is a free press important in a democracy?" Correlation (corrected for contamination) with the WAIS-R Full Scale is .74, Verbal Score .76, and Performance Score .61.

Similarities

In this test the subject is asked to abstract and report what is alike about 14 paired items. This task requires perception of essential features, associative thinking, and conceptual judgment. One WAIS item has been modified, two eliminated, and three new items added (e.g., "In what way are a button and a zipper alike?"). Correlation (corrected for contamination) with the WAIS-R Full Scale is .75, Verbal Score .74, and Performance Score .64.

WAIS-R Performance Tests

Picture Completion

This test includes 20 pictures in which some important feature is missing. It requires ability to recognize familiar objects and to differentiate essential from nonessential details. Six items from the WAIS were dropped, and five new ones added. Correlation (corrected for contamination) with the WAIS-R Full Scale is .67, Verbal Score .61, and Performance Score .65.

Picture Arrangement

The Picture Arrangement test consists of 10 sets or series of pictures that the subject is required to put in the proper sequence to tell a story, as in cartoon strips. This task involves the ability to assess and comprehend a total, primarily social, situation, which may be influenced by social-cultural background. Two WAIS items were eliminated and four new ones added. Time bonuses have been eliminated on the WAIS-R, and administration is discontinued after four consecutive failures. Correlation (corrected for contamination) with the WAIS-R Full Scale is .61, Verbal Score .57, and Performance Score .56.

Block Design

This test includes nine designs to be constructed from red and white blocks following patterns presented on cards. It measures form perception, problem solving, visual-motor integration, and speed of performance. One item was eliminated from the WAIS, and rules of scoring were revised to allow greater additional credit for quick, accurate completion. Correlation (corrected for contamination) with the WAIS-R Full Scale is .68, Verbal Score .61, and Performance Score .70.

Object Assembly

The Object Assembly test consists of four simple jigsaw puzzles with large pieces to be assembled into a *Manikin*, a *Profile*, a *Hand* and an *Elephant*. It measures visual analysis, ability to synthesize parts into wholes, and assembly skill. The *Manikin* figure from the WAIS was modified. Correlation (corrected for contamination) with the WAIS-R Full Scale is .57, Verbal Score .49, and Performance Score .62.

Digit Symbol

This test requires the subject to mark, in a series of squares, symbols presented in association with the numbers 1 through 9. It measures speed and accuracy, ability to learn an unfamiliar task, and visual-motor dexterity. The number of sample items was slightly reduced and the number of performance items slightly increased in the WAIS-R. Correlation (corrected for contamination) with the WAIS-R Full Scale is .57, Verbal Score .54, and Performance Score .52.

Stanford-Binet

The Fourth Edition of the Stanford-Binet Intelligence Scale (Thorndike et al., 1986) has been standardized on populations ranging from 2 to 24 years of age, and thus is primarily intended for use with children. It is given brief mention here because there are occasions when it may be the instrument of choice (or necessity) for adults. These occasions are the measurement of intelligence of a moderate or severely retarded adult, where an IQ lower than 45 (lowest possible on the WAIS-R) is anticipated, or where it is anticipated that the test subject would achieve a raw score of zero on a substantial number of subtests of the WAIS-R. Using the Stanford-Binet for such subjects, one may derive Standard Age Scores, following the recommendation of the *Examiner's Handbook* (Delaney & Hopkins, 1987, p. 71), and reporting that the subject's performance was referenced to the 17–11–16 to 23–11–15 age sample. The user should also bear in mind that, similar to the slightly less-than-perfect relationship between the WAIS and the 1960 Binet, the WAIS-R mean IQ of 73 exceeds the Fourth Edition mean composite Standard Age Score of 63.8 for a group of mentally retarded subjects, administered both tests, as reported in the Stanford-Binet *Technical Manual* (Thorndike et al., 1986).

While the 1986 Fourth Edition of the Stanford-Binet (S-B) is a descendant of the scale devised by Binet and Simon (1905, 1908, 1911; see Kite, 1916 translation) and the revisions by Terman and Merrill (1973), it differs from its predecessors as it does not follow the age-scale format but, somewhat akin to the Wechsler Scales, consists of a variety of vertical tests of different cognitive skills. It also substitutes Stan-

dard Age Scores for the concept of IQ. It is based on a three-tier hierarchical model, and its 15 tests are grouped into four areas: Verbal Reasoning, Abstract/Visual Reasoning, Quantitative Reasoning, and Short-Term memory. For a more extended discussion of the Stanford-Binet as a child intelligence test, the reader is referred to Kaufmann and Perlman's chapter in the present volume.

Other Adult Intelligence Tests

In addition to the Wechsler Scales and the Stanford-Binet, the *Ninth Mental Measurements Yearbook* (Mitchell, 1985) lists four individual intelligence tests which are intended for use with adults. The Slosson Intelligence Test (Slosson, 1981) is an abbreviated test based in part on the Stanford-Binet, Third Edition. The Detroit Tests of Learning Aptitude (Baker & Leland, 1967) are an extensive battery of tests with a very limited standardization population. The Peabody Picture Vocabulary Test (Dunn, 1965) is a pictorial test which measures primarily verbal comprehension. The Test of Nonverbal Intelligence (TONI) (Brown, Sherbernou, & Dollar, 1982) is described as a language-free measure of cognitive ability. It is a brief (15–30 minute administration) test based on a relatively small normative population.

SELECTED RESEARCH FINDINGS

Research on the structure and application of the Wechsler-Bellevue Intelligence Scale, Wechsler Adult Intelligence Scale, and Stanford-Binet has been voluminous and has been summarized many times (e.g., see Matarazzo, 1972, and Sattler, 1988). The present review of research findings is restricted to studies of the Wechsler Adult Intelligence Scale-Revised, which has rapidly replaced its predecessor, the WAIS.

The norms of the WAIS-R (Wechsler, 1981) are based on a group of 1,880 adults, ranging in age from 16 years to 74 years, 11 months. This sample was stratified on the basis of age (nine groups), sex, race (white, nonwhite), geographic region (Northeast, North Central, South, West), occupation (six groups), education (five levels), and urban-rural residence, following 1970 census reports. The scaled scores for each of the 11 tests in the scale were derived for each age group from the scores of the 500 standardization subjects in the 20- to 34-year age groups. As in the WAIS these *scaled scores* were converted to a mean of 10 and a standard deviation of 3, allowing for comparison of the score of any subject with the 20–34 reference group. This is in contrast to IQ scores, which are directly comparable from one age group to another, although derived in relation to each subject's own age group. Thus, as in the WAIS, IQs were derived so that the mean IQ for each of the nine age groups is 100, with a standard deviation of 15.

The reliability of the WAIS-R has been computed by split half and test-retest methods as well as computations of the standard error of measurement. Split-half reliability was computed for nine of the subtests across all nine age groups. Test-retest reliability of two subtests (Digit Span and Digit Symbol) was calculated from repeated testing of four age groups. Across all nine age groups the average reliability coefficients of the six Verbal tests range from .83 (Digit Span) to .96 (Vocabulary). The average reliability coefficients of the five performance tests range from .68 (Object Assembly) to .87 (Block Design). The average reliability coefficients, as derived from all nine age groups of the standardization population, are .97 for Verbal IQ, .93 for Performance IQ, and .97 for Full Scale IQ.

Test-retest reliability (stability) was examined by administration of the WAIS-R twice (with 2 to 7 weeks intervening) to 71 subjects aged 25 to 34, and 48 subjects aged 45 to 54. The test-retest reliability coefficients for Verbal IQ, Performance IQ, and Full Scale IQ ranged from .89 to .97. Despite these seemingly high test-retest reliability coefficients for the *group* of 119 individuals, an analysis of change from test to retest for each of the 119 *individuals* revealed surprisingly wide magnitudes of losses and gains; a finding of considerable importance for the practitioner who is evaluating and planning for a single individual (Matarazzo & Herman, 1984).

The standard errors of measurement (SEMs) for the 11 WAIS-R tests ranged from .61 scaled score points on Vocabulary to 1.54 scaled score points on Object Assembly, Average SEMs of the Verbal, Performance, and Full Scale IQs were 2.74, 4.14, and 2.53 IQ points, respectively.

The WAIS-R manual (Wechsler, 1981) offers little in the way of original validity data, pointing instead to the continuity of its structure with its predecessors, the WAIS and Wechsler-Bellevue. Each of the earlier scales included the same 11 tests with similar and often identical content. These scales were originally validated on the basis of correlations with other tests of intelligence, ratings by experienced clinicians, and studies of groups of known intellectual level, among many other criteria (Matarazzo, 1972). The 1981 WAIS-R manual does provide a comparison of the

WAIS and WAIS-R as administered to 72 adults, aged 35–44. Correlations across the WAIS and WAIS-R pairs of scores of the 11 tests ranged from .50 (Picture Arrangement) to .91 (Vocabulary). Correlation of the WAIS and WAIS-R Scales were Verbal IQ .91, Performance IQ .79, and Full Scale IQ .88. Thorndike et al. (1986) report a correlation of .91 between the WAIS-R Full Scale IQ and the Composite Standard Age Scale score of the Fourth Edition of the Stanford-Binet. Mean Full Scale IQ of 102.2 on the WAIS-R was 3.5 points higher than the Mean Standard Age Scale Score of 98.7 on the Stanford-Binet for this group of 47 adults.

For the WAIS-R population mentioned in the preceding paragraph (ages 35–44), the counterpart WAIS Verbal, Performance, and Full Scale IQ scores for the 72 adults were approximately 7, 8, and 8 points higher, respectively, than their WAIS-R counterparts (Wechsler, 1981, p. 47). Unfortunately, this tendency for WAIS scores to be higher may not be the full extent of the problem in comparing WAIS and WAIS-R scores. On the WAIS-R, unlike its predecessors, the standard deviations of the sums of scaled scores varied among the nine age groups of the standardization population, and some of the differences between standard deviations reached significance. Because these differences were adjusted in constructing IQ tables, the practical implication for any single WAIS-R IQ is insignificant. It may *be* significant, however, in comparing WAIS and WAIS-R scores at various age and intelligence levels, especially when the same individual is examined and then reexamined on the same scale years later, when he or she is older and will be compared with the norms of another group. Until such differences are further explored, the clinician should consider making such comparisions by use of the scaled-score equivalents of raw scores at the appropriate age levels, as found in the WAIS and WAIS-R manuals. At the very least, the clinician should be aware of this statistical problem whenever dealing with a client at or near an IQ value mandated by law in quasi-judicial examinations.

The structure of the WAIS-R has been explored by numerous factor analytic studies which have been summarized by Leckliter, Matarazzo, and Silverstein (1986). They conclude that these studies provide corroboration for "a global general factor (g), a robust Verbal Comprehension factor, a Perceptual Organization factor, and a weaker, but still seemingly robust Memory/Freedom from Distractibility factor" (p. 340). They observe that Vocabulary, Information, and Comprehension load highly and uniquely on the Verbal Comprehension factor. Similarities also loads highly on this factor, but additionally has a moderate loading on the Perceptual organization factor. Block Design and Object Assembly load highly and uniquely on Perceptual Organization, as well. Digit Span and Arithmetic consistently load highest on the Memory/ Freedom from Distractibility factor, and Picture Arrangement contributes to this factor in some studies. Leckliter et al. (1986) conclude that whether a study yields a two-factor or three-factor solution depends upon the statistical approach employed. Noting that the third factor (Memory/Freedom from Distractibility) may be more of a nonintellectual "personality" or "brain-behavior" variable, they suggest that the three-factor solution may provide the clinical neuropsychologist practitioner or the applied investigator with a potentially richer source of hypotheses.

Much of the research utilizing the WAIS-R standardization sample data is addressed to the problem of making valid comparisons among the subtests and scales. Thus, Naglieri (1982), using the standard errors of measurement given in the WAIS-R manual, has computed the intervals needed for the 85%, 90%, 95%, and 99% levels of confidence in statistically based, psychometric comparisons of the Verbal, Performance, and Full Scale IQ scores. Naglieri recommends that confidence intervals be routinely stated in order to address the psychometric properties of the test.

Silverstein (1982) discusses the statistical problems in making multiple comparisons of subtest scores and presents a solution based on the standard error for comparing a subject's scores on each of the Verbal or Performance subtests with the average Verbal or Performance subtest score or the overall average. The differences required for significance at the .05 and .01 levels in comparing WAIS-R subtest scores are presented in Table 5.1. Silverstein presents similar data for the WAIS, WISC, WISC-R, and WPPSI, and the reader is referred to the original article for that information.

Matarazzo and Herman (1985) have made an extensive analysis of Verbal IQ-Performance IQ (VIQ-PIQ) differences as found in the WAIS-R standardization sample. They note a marked discrepancy between the magnitude of a VIQ-PIQ difference required for statistical reliability versus the magnitude of VIQ-PIQ differences actually observed empirically in the WAIS-R standardization sample. For example, while the magnitude of difference of 13 points is required to demonstrate that a VIQ-PIQ difference is *statistically* reliably different from zero at the .01 level, they note that nevertheless such a 13-point VIQ-PIQ difference (or greater) was found in 24.3% of the 1,880 individuals in the WAIS-R standardization sample of community-living normals. In fact, in two of these 1,880 normals, a VIQ-PIQ difference of 30 points was found. Matarazzo and Herman conclude that the rule of thumb that a 15-point discrepancy in Verbal versus Performance IQ should be further examined and clarified by reference to the history and other laboratory and test data is merely a rule of thumb: a finding which should be pursued in some cases and put aside in

Table 5.1. Differences Required for Significance When Comparing Each WAIS-R Subtest Score with an Average Subtest Score

SUBTEST	VERBAL AVERAGE		PERFORMANCE AVERAGE		OVERALL AVERAGE	
	0.5	.01	.05	.01	.05	.01
Information	2.4	2.8	—	—	2.6	3.1
Digit Span	2.9	3.5	—	—	3.4	3.9
Vocabulary	1.8	2.1	—	—	1.9	2.2
Arithmetic	2.8	3.3	—	—	3.1	3.7
Comprehension	2.9	3.4	—	—	3.3	3.8
Similarities	3.0	3.5	—	—	3.4	4.0
Picture Completion	—	—	3.0	3.5	3.4	4.0
Picture Arrangement	—	—	3.2	3.9	3.8	4.4
Block Design	—	—	2.5	3.0	2.8	3.2
Object Assembly	—	—	3.5	4.2	4.1	4.8
Digit Symbol	—	—	3.0	3.6	3.5	4.0

Note: Adapted with permission from "Pattern Analysis as Simultaneous Statistical Inference" by A. B. Silverstein, 1982, *Journal of Consulting and Clinical Psychology, 50,* 237.

others. Statistical significance should not be substituted for clinical experience and professional judgment.

As to the effect of age on intellectual performance, Matarazzo (1972) and many others have pointed out a likely methodological flaw in early studies of aging and intelligence: the conclusion that intelligence declines gradually with age, beginning at about age 28. These early studies, based on cross-sectional samples at various ages, failed to take into account the differences in educational level in the various generations represented. Flynn (1984) has examined the Stanford-Binet and the Wechsler scales from 1932 to 1978, finding that each standardization sample has established norms of a higher standard than its predecessor and that the accumulation of these differences suggests an IQ "gain" of 13.8 points in that time period. He points out the confounding effect of this on research studies (e.g., of parents and children), whether the differences are assumed to be a statistical artifact, or to be real.

Horn (1986) and others have refocused the study of aging and intelligence by reference to the concept of fluid and crystallized intelligence, postulating that crystallized intelligence may actually *increase* with age, while fluid intelligence may be expected to decline. Additionally, working on the assumption mentioned earlier in this chapter, that the WAIS-R Verbal tests may be equated with crystallized intelligence and the Performance tests with fluid intelligence, Sattler (1982) has examined the scaled-score

points assigned to identical raw scores at various age levels. Table 5.2 presents the additional scaled-score points given at each age level for a score which in the reference group (age 25–34) would be assigned a scaled score of 10. As can be seen, a raw score on a Performance test that would be assigned a scaled score of 10 for a subject aged 25–34 would receive a scaled score of 14 to 16 for a subject in his or her 70s. A similar comparison with Verbal tests would yield much smaller differences with the 70-year-old receiving scaled scores from 11 to 13. Sattler concludes that fluid intelligence shows a much more severe decrement with age than does crystallized intelligence.

Matarazzo and Herman (1984) have discussed the problem of estimating premorbid IQ of neurologically impaired patients for whom information on measured intelligence, per se, is unavailable. Using the WAIS-R standardization sample, they calculated correlations between years of education and Full Scale IQ of .63 for the 25–44 year age group and .62 for the 45–74 year age group. The mean IQs for the 25–44 and 45–74-year-old group who had completed different numbers of years of education are shown in Table 5.3. Matarazzo and Herman suggest that these data be used only when no other estimate is available, and caution against the use as a regular practice, inasmuch as an individual's earlier school transcripts often contain more useful measures of premorbid intellectual ability (e.g., scores on the Otis, California Mental Maturity Scale, the Scholastic Aptitude Test, etc.).

Barona, Reynolds, and Chastain (1984) developed

Table 5.2. Additional Scaled-Score Points by Age Awarded to WAIS-R Subtests when the (25–34 Year Old) Reference Group Receives a Scaled Score of 10

	AGE GROUP				
TEST	35–44	45–54	55–64	65–69	70–74
Verbal Scale					
Information	0	0	0	0	1
Digit Span	0	0	1	1	1
Vocabulary	−1	0	0	0	1
Arithmetic	0	0	1	1	1
Comprehension	0	0	0	1	1
Similarities	1	1	1	2	3
Performance Scale					
Picture Completion	1	1	2	2	4
Picture Arrangement	1	1	2	4	5
Block Design	1	1	2	3	4
Object Assembly	0	1	2	4	4
Digit Symbol	1	2	3	5	6

Note: "Age effects on Wechsler Adult Intelligence Scale-Revised Tests," by J. M. Sattler, 1982, *Journal of Consulting and Clinical Psychology, 50,* 786. Reprinted with permission.

Table 5.3. Mean Verbal, Performance, and Full Scale IQs on the WAIS-R, by Age Group and Years of Education for the Standardization Sample

| YEARS OF EDUCATION COMPLETED | AGE GROUP | | | | | |
| | 25–44 (n = 550) | | | 45–74 (n = 730) | | |
	VIQ	PIQ	FSIQ	VIQ	PIQ	FSIQ
0–8	77.3	82.5	78.4	88.8	91.0	89.0
9–11	88.4	91.5	88.8	96.8	99.5	97.6
12	97.4	98.6	97.6	103.6	103.0	103.5
13–15	105.2	105.4	105.6	109.5	105.2	108.2
16+	114.0	110.7	113.8	119.2	111.9	117.8

Note: WAIS-R = Wechsler Adult Intelligence Scale-Revised; VIQ = Verbal IQ; PIQ = Performance IQ; FSIQ = Full Scale IQ. Adapted with permission from "Relationship of Education and IQ in the WAIS-R Standardization Sample" by J. D. Matarazzo and D. O. Herman, 1984, *Journal of Consulting and Clinical Psychology, 52,* 633.

a more complex, demographically based index of premorbid intelligence for the WAIS-R, using age, sex, race, education, occupational status, urban-rural residence, and geographic region as variables on a regression equation. They found education, race, and occupation to be the most powerful of these demographic predictors, with age and occupation also contributing. Eppinger, Craig, Adams, and Parson (1987) have cross-validated the index of Barona et al. (1984) on neurologically normal and brain-impaired patients. The reader is referred to their study for use of this index. Eppinger et al. (1987) point out that the Barona Index is not applicable at the upper and lower extremes of intelligence and, similar to Matarazzo and Herman, caution that such an estimate be used only as a screening device.

CLINICAL APPLICATIONS OF INDIVIDUAL ADULT INTELLIGENCE TESTS

This section describes the following uses of adult intelligence tests: as part of an assessment battery in individual evaluation and career counseling; in psychodiagnosis, such as evaluation for possible mental retardation; in examination for indices of emotional or psychotic processes as seen in thought disorders accompanying serious psychiatric illness; in neuropsychological evaluation; and in determining the overall intellectual level and more discrete dimensions of cognitive processes in individuals identified as being at risk for genetic disorders.

The generation of an IQ score and its subtest profile is an important and useful product yielded by the standardized individual intelligence evaluation. The clinical usefulness of the IQ score and profile is rivaled, however, by the rich observational material that becomes available to the skilled clinician while interacting with the client/patient during this structured cognitive task. Goals of this section are to present guidelines within which these qualitative observations can be systematized, as well as to comment on some uses that appear to have received minimal attention in the literature of individual intelligence testing: namely, their applications in career counseling as well as in the investigation of genetic disorders. Illustrative case histories are included.

Individual Evaluation and Career Counseling

The literature in the field of vocational evaluation and career counseling makes regular reference to the individual intelligence test, usually endorsing its use as an instrument to predict the client's potential for reaching a certain educational or occupational level. The capacity of intelligence tests to predict one's educational attainment has been long established. Indeed, at lower age levels intelligence test scores and school grade placements have a chicken-egg relationship, because many of the items included in the first tests of intelligence were chosen because they successfully differentiated students at increasingly higher grade (and age) levels. Furthermore, the relationship between intelligence test scores and occupational level has been documented in many studies (e.g., the one reported by Harrell & Harrell, 1945, which related the Army General Classification Test to 64 civilian occupations). A review of that literature may be found in Matarazzo (1972). Herman (1982) points out that the standardization data of the WAIS-R show a moderately strong relationship between mean IQ and occupational level, with a spread of 22 points between the average IQs of subjects in occupational groups 1 and 5 (the highest and lowest categories of employed persons that were included).

The literature of vocational psychology usually makes a gesture toward individual intelligence tests as they relate to educational and occupational levels and then refers the reader to multiple aptitude or special aptitude tests. Thus, Cronbach (1960) recommended tests of specialized aptitude for vocational guidance, and Super and Crites (1962) suggested that the use of intelligence test scores be limited to total or verbal scores as a rough index of the educational or occupational level that the person may *actuarially* be expected to attain. Although the authors of textbooks on vocational psychology typically are sophisticated psychologists, there is rarely mention in such textbooks of the potential contribution of qualitative observations, obtained from client-examiner interaction, to the process of vocational evaluation and career counseling. Tyler seems to adopt a slightly different stance. Commenting on the search in the 1930s for prototypical evidence that different occupations were characterized by their own occupational ability profiles, Tyler (1978) wrote: "What proved discouraging, however, was that success in the occupation did not seem related to whether or not one possessed the proper profile and that a wide variety of profiles existed within any occupation" (p. 95). Although seeing possible utility in some general aptitude battery profiles, Tyler mentions a number of other interesting possibilities in measuring human ability. For instance, she suggests that psychologists might consider assessing *direction* of development (e.g., what *kinds* of competency) in addition to *levels* of intelligence. Tyler also observes that "it requires a certain level of the ability intelligence tests measure to *enter* one of the more prestigious occupations, but once one gets in, how successful one is depends on factors other than intelligence" (p. 80). For example, published frequency distributions of the IQ levels of a sample of young physicians in the United States as well as a sample of faculty members at the University of Cambridge reveal a range in IQ from 111 to 150 in each sample (Matarazzo, 1972). Tyler (1978) has also emphasized cognitive and conceptual styles (e.g., analytic-descriptive, reflective-impulsive) as important dimensions of individual difference that need assessment.

Despite these problems, it is our opinion that the individual adult intelligence test contributes more to effective career counseling than appears to be recognized in the literature, and that its contribution could be potentially greater, given recognition of this fact and increased systematic investigation of vocational applications. The authors are aware, from their own practices and their service as consultants to agencies which utilize vocational psychological evaluations, that the use of individual intelligence tests as part of such evaluations is almost universal. This should not be surprising, in view of the findings of Brown and McGuire (1976) and Lubin, Wallis, and Paine (1971), which reported the WAIS to be the third and second most frequently used psychological test, respectively, at the time of their studies. More recently Lubin et al. (1985) found that the WAIS and WAIS-R are the tests second most frequently used by psychologists, and Reynolds (1979) reported that psychologists ranked the WAIS second in psychometric quality (after the WISC) among the 10 most used tests. It is clear that psychologists both respect and rely heavily upon the individual adult intelligence test as one of the main tools in their assessment batteries, and it is the authors' observation, supported by the findings of Lubin et al. (1985), that this extends to vocational psychological assessment.

The psychological assessment used to evaluate potential for employment typically includes observations about the client's approach, demeanor, cognitive style, response to challenge and failure, and other relevant characteristics manifested during the test session. Such an assessment also includes arrival at an estimate of the client's potential for success at various levels of educational or occupational attainment, as these are predicted by the total IQ score, as well as inferences about more specific abilities such as verbal, spatial, and (with appropriate qualification) numerical ability. In some instances, such vocational evaluations may include tests of special aptitudes (e.g., verbal reasoning, numerical reasoning, clerical aptitude, manual dexterity).

The use of the standardized test as a controlled instrument by which to observe variability of behavioral response is hardly a new idea. Psychologists have done it regularly. Garner (1966) cites Terman's 1924 comparison of the standardized test administration to the controlled experiment. What remains to be done even today is to systematize and study the relevant variables of such observations, so that they may be subjected to verification and refinement. As an example, Table 5.4 includes some descriptions of cognitive style that are used by one of the authors (JEL) to help systematize the observation (and later reporting) of client behavior in the testing situation, as

Table 5.4. Descriptors of Cognitive Style

1. *Persistence.* Keeps trying? Gives up easily? Declines to attempt difficult items? Puzzles and works at difficult or failed items—even becomes obsessed and keeps going back to them?

2. *Anxiety.* General anxiety about being tested? Reacts to failure with anxiety, flustering, blocking? Becomes anxious or blocks about a specific set of items, e.g., arithmetic?

3. *Reaction to failure.* Won't attempt when unsure of an item? Gets flustered and upset at failure? Gives arbitrary answers just to "satisfy" the situation?

4. *Approach.* Methodical or systematic? Block design—trial and error, analytic-insightful, a combination of both? Reasoned or impulsive responses? Comprehensive or fragmented associations? Whole to part, or part to whole?

5. *Concentration.* On simple material, e.g., digit span? On complex material, e.g., difficult arithmetic questions, block designs, comprehension or picture arrangement?

6. *Pace.* Fast or slow? Erratic?

7. *Verbal expression.* Articulate, well spoken? Awkward, imprecise?

8. *Attitude.* Casual or serious about the whole thing? Competitive?

9. *Reaction to authority.* Ability to conform to the demands of the task as presented by the examiner?

well as for teaching such observation procedures to psychology interns.

From this brief treatment of the subject, it no doubt is clear to the reader that there is a need for a greater rapprochement between those psychologists who regularly use individual intelligence tests and those who study and advise regarding entry into occupations. Such a marriage would facilitate the development of a pool of empirical findings on the utility of intelligence test subscales for measuring abilities relevant to occupational success, *insofar as success can be predicted from such cognitive measures.*

The following brief case histories were chosen to highlight some of the ways an intelligence test provides useful information in career planning. All names used are pseudonyms and information that might identify the subjects has been withheld or modified.

Case History—A Determined Achiever

Henry J. was 17 years old when he was seen for evaluation and career counseling at the request of his mother. He was near the end of his junior year in a small-town high school in rural Oregon. He has cerebral palsy (mild spastic quadraparesis). He can walk unassisted and has relatively good use of arms, hands, and fingers, although with some awkwardness and diminished coordination both in ambulation and dexterity.

Henry was of medium height and dark haired, with a prominent case of teen-age acne. He was sociable, friendly, and cooperative throughout the evaluation. There was obvious mutual fondness with Mom, and she volunteered the information that he applied himself well academically.

Henry had attended a city school for handicapped children from age 3 through 10, and had been in regular classrooms in a small school district since then. His classmates were primarily from blue-collar families (as he was), and among them he felt most comfortable with "the academic ones." He spent long hours studying, had a 3.0 grade-point average on a four-point scale, and made the National Honor Society. His favorite subject was "Yearbook Class," in which he did design layout and title writing. His least favorite subjects were chemistry, physics, and "any science." He was a member of the Student Council. He worked as a volunteer at the public library, where he did filing.·

On interview, Henry expressed interest in working at data processing, bookkeeping or other clerical work. He said he was able to maintain close-to-average speed in a typing class. He said that he has some difficulty making his handwriting legible when he has to fit things into small spaces.

The results of the psychological evaluation are seen in Table 5.5. The lowered Performance IQ reflects the difficulty in space perception and motor coordination that is frequently (but not always) found in persons with cerebral palsy. This was explained to Henry and his mother, and accompanied by further discussion of common problems of cerebral palsy (e.g., emotional overflow and difficulty in carrying out more than one cognitive/motor task simultaneously). It is the authors' experience that when information is couched in an explanation of the general effects of cerebral palsy, affected persons are relieved to understand the cause for problems which may have bothered them all their lives, and are also willing to accept cognitive limitations which may have significance for their vocational choice. The findings here suggested that in helping Henry to consider a career decision we should avoid vocations which require unimpaired space perception and motor coordination. Observation during the Digit Symbol Test and in other parts of the evaluation suggested that the lower Digit Symbol score reflected motoric slowness rather than impaired speed of asso-

Table 5.5. Psychological Assessment Findings in the Case of a Determined Achiever

WAIS-R		CAREER ASSESSMENT INVENTORY
VIQ 104		*Highest Theme Score*—Conventional
PIQ 76		*Lowest Theme Score*—Realistic, Investigative
FSIQ 91		
		Highest Basic Interest Scales—Office Practices, Clerical
Information	10	*Lowest Basic Interest Scales*—Agriculture, Nature/Outdoors, Arts/Crafts
Digit Span	9	*Highest Occupational Scales*—Bank Teller, Bookkeeper, Data Entry,
Vocabulary	10	Operator, Accountant, Secretary, Card/Gift Shop Manager, Hotel/Motel
Arithmetic	7	Manager, Travel Agent
Comprehension	9	
Similarities	9	*Lowest Occupational Scales*—Those in Realistic, Investigative, Arithmetic
		and Social Occupations.
Picture Completion	8	
Picture Arrangement	9	Fine Arts—Mechanical Score: 56
Block Design	5	Occupational Extroversion:
Object Assembly	6	Introversion: 68
Digit Symbol	4	Education Orientation: 2
		Variability of Interests: 34

Peabody Individual Achievement Test

	GRADE EQUIVALENTS
Mathematics	12.9
Reading Recognition	9.4
Reading Comprehension	12.9

ciative learning. His career decision should also avoid tasks requiring manual speed as well as significant physical activities. With these limitations in mind, a career choice could be aimed at the higher level of ability reflected by the Verbal IQ. The Full Scale IQ reflecting, as it does, a combination of disparate abilities, is of little significance in this particular case.

The Verbal tests reflect Henry's strengths. He has good verbal reasoning and judgment about practical everyday matters. Scattered successes on the Information test show that he has not read broadly and comes from a limited educational/cultural milieu. He has a good vocabulary, although he tends to be wordy. Inspection of his Arithmetic test reveals a significant finding that is not apparent from the scaled score. On items reflecting only basic arithmetic operations (addition, subtraction, multiplication, and division) Henry was fast and accurate. All the first nine items were done correctly and in seven seconds or less (most of them in only one or two seconds). Henry failed all the complex items which required that variables be manipulated mentally. Thus we see that he has the kind of arithmetic ability that is utilized for bookkeeping or elementary data processing and we understand his difficulty with and aversion for subjects like chemistry and physics, which often require complex mathematical operations. This finding was confirmed

by observation of his performance on the mathematics subtest of the Peabody Individual Achievement Test.

Henry's scores on the Career Assessment Inventory suggest a strong interest in clerical work—that is, work that is well structured and routine, performed in an office setting, and includes working with numbers, such as in data processing. There is also the suggestion of interest in clerical/managerial work such as might be involved in a small retail store or motel. He is not at all interested in things that are mechanical, involve large physical activity, or are technical-scientific. He does not like classroom learning and apparently would not like occupations in which he had continued close dealings with people.

The ability and interest test results are compatible with Henry's expressed interest in going to a business college to learn data processing and other clerical skills. It was pointed out that he might have difficulty in a clerical job which called for speed of productivity. Given that he is a reasonably social and very responsible young man, it was suggested that he consider combining clerical-bookkeeping-data processing work with minor managerial or business administrative work (thus using his verbal reasoning and practical judgment skills as well). He might have some responsibility in a motel, small retail store, or service station for some service to customers while also doing clerical work such as recordkeeping or inventory, which could be done more at his own pace, interspersed with his other activities.

The time of this writing is three years after Henry's initial evaluation and counseling. He has completed high school and, with assistance from the Vocational Rehabilitation Division (VRD), two years of business college. He accepted temporary employment doing bookkeeping for a small chain of book stores. He found it difficult maintaining the pace of productivity expected there. He is currently seeking (again with the assistance of VRD) employment in a retail setting such as described in the preceding paragraph. Despite his initial disappointment he remains determined and fundamentally optimistic.

Next to be examined is the case of a mid-career vocational choice in a person without significant handicap.

Case History—Middle-Age Malaise

Mr. Hurst is 42 and self-referred for career planning assistance. He has held a secure, well-paying job as an accountant for a small firm for four years and is "bored." He is tall, heavy set, and talkative with a resonant voice; he appeared for each appointment in casual dress. His opening social conversation was relaxed and friendly. However, as the interview progressed to more personal levels, he became increasingly guarded and almost obsessive in seeking the "right words" to describe his thoughts.

He related that his parents had been strict and that he found his father "difficult," so had avoided him when he could. He did well in grade and high school without trying very hard. He worked for awhile in the family carpeting business and enjoyed himself when he reflected on a job well done. For several years he went to community college and "fooled around." He worked for a time as a policeman. Upon returning to college he discovered accounting and remained on the dean's list thereafter. After college graduation he held a government job for seven years, leaving it when his marriage failed. He took a trip around the world, returned and tried selling real estate, then settled into his present accountant's job. He does his job effectively and enjoys his standard of living. He has a stable relationship with a woman to whom he is engaged. He says his job is not challenging and that he would like to work with his hands in a field like architecture or engineering.

The results of Mr. Hurst's psychological evaluation are summarized in Table 5.6. During the WAIS-R administration his need to be precise, observed previously during the interview, was even more exaggerated, and it became evident that Mr. Hurst's preciseness stemmed from the fear of making a mistake. His final verbal productions were good, but he frequently showed obsessive indecision in formulating verbal descriptions. In dealing with numbers, he was rapid and accurate. When confronting the complexities of the more difficult Block Design and Object Assembly

Table 5.6. Psychological Assessment Findings in a Case of Middle-Age Malaise

WAIS-R		STRONG-CAMPBELL INTEREST INVENTORY
VIQ	126	*Highest Theme Score*—Realistic Investigative, Artistic
PIQ	117	
FSIQ	126	*Highest Basic Interest Scales*—Agriculture, Nature, Mechanical Activities, Science, Medical Science, Medical Services, Music/Dramatics, Art,
Information	14	Domestic Arts
Digit Span	16	*Highest Occupational Scale Scores*—Optometrist, Engineer, Radiological
Vocabulary	12	Technician, Computer Programmer, Math-Science Teacher, Architect,
Arithmetic	14	Musician, Photographer, Physical Sciences, Health Fields Physical
Comprehension	14	Sciences, Health Fields
Similarities	13	*Academic Comfort Scale*—53
Picture Completion	10	
Picture Arrangement	15	*Introversion-Extroversion Scale*—57
Block Design	14	
Object Assembly	9	
Digit Symbol	10	

Edwards Personal Preference Schedule

High Needs: Endurance, Heterosexuality, Succorance
Low Needs: Deference, Autonomy, Abasement, Affiliation, Dominance

items, he became highly anxious and aware of being timed but nevertheless was able to maintain sufficient organization to be reasonably effective. Throughout it was evident that he was most comfortable working with highly structured tasks where the "rules" were clear, as in numerical operations. He could not make precise formulations of ambiguous problems and became anxious when he met complexity. The latter qualities were most evident on the WAIS-R when he was dealing with spatial relations and assembly materials. The Strong-Campbell Interest Inventory results shown in Table 5.6 suggested interests that are technical-creative, indicating a wish to work with tangibles in a creative way. Interest in the visual arts was strong. He displayed a desire not to work closely with people or to have supervisory responsibility. The Edwards Personal Preference Schedule suggested avoidance of highly independent or dominant roles and an orientation toward achievement through persistence.

It appeared to the psychologist that Mr. Hurst's aspiration to creativity (as expressed on the interest test) was at odds with his insecurity in the face of ambiguity and consequent difficulty in making judgments and decisions. Interestingly, this need for structure and certainty seemed to prevail only in his employment setting or when he perceived a decision as "serious." He was able to be casual in ordinary social interaction and to enjoy changes in his life situation.

Based on his history and the test findings in Table 5.6, Mr. Hurst was counseled and helped to identify his need for change through a move to a new job setting (but not occupation), and to seek creative expression through avocational pursuits. Face-to-face observation of his cognitive style aided significantly in arriving at this recommendation, and Mr. Hurst was able to recognize the validity of this observation in the course of counseling.

At this writing, just a few months after Mr. Hurst was seen, he is seeking a change to an accounting position in a company whose products and procedures are markedly different from those of the employer with whom he is presently affiliated.

Psychodiagnosis

Mental Retardation

The individual intelligence test, compassionately and intelligently used, can be extremely useful in the overall assessment of mental retardation and in determination of the areas of strength around which the person with retardation may be helped to build a more fulfilling life. Such a test possesses a degree of structure and objectivity that ordinarily exceeds opinions based on nonsystematic observation. Along with an index of measured intelligence, the requirement of a complementing measure of adaptive behavior for the diagnosis of mental retardation adds a valuable dimension and helps in detecting those instances where the true strengths of the individual may not be adequately measured by the intelligence test alone. Certainly the results obtained with the test need to be evaluated in terms of the cultural background of the individual and the conditions of its administration. Litigation during the past decade provides evidence that there have been misapplications of intelligence tests and misinterpretations of their results. In the experience of the authors, errors of this type have rarely been attributed to psychologists who are fully trained and qualified in the utilization of standardized individual tests.

The most common use of intelligence tests to assess possible mental retardation is for school placement, and this typically involves the administration of a test designed for use with children. Subsequently, adult intelligence tests are used to monitor the functioning of the retarded adult over time, to document the existence of retardation where the person may be eligible for benefits either in his or her own right or as a "dependent child", to assist in determining competence (or incompetence) to handle funds, to assist in determining employability, and to identify assets for use in vocational planning.

Where a formal determination of mental retardation is mandated by law or semijudicial requirements, standards for classification have been established by the American Association on Mental Retardation (Grossman, 1973). These specify *mild* mental retardation as falling between two and three standard deviations below the mean of the test being utilized, *moderate* between three and four standard deviations below the mean, *severe* between four and five standard deviations below the mean, and *profound* below six standard deviations below the mean. The IQ ranges for these classifications using the WAIS-R and Stanford-Binet are found in Table 5.7. A case history follows.

Case History—Retarded Identical Twins

Linda and Rhonda Robertson are the 35-year-old daughters of a disabled laborer and his wife. They were referred for psychological evaluations to determine whether they could be considered "dependent children" for purposes of compensation.

Table 5.7. AAMR Classification of Mental Retardation

CLASSIFICATION	RANGE IN STANDARD DEVIATION UNITS	I.Q. RANGE	
		STANFORD-BINET S.D. 16	WAIS-R S.D. 15
Mild	−2.01 to −3.00	52–67	55–69
Moderate	−3.01 to −4.00	38–51	40–54
Severe	−4.01 to −5.00	20–35	25–39
Profound	Below −5.00	0–19	0–24

Linda promptly and proudly announced that the sisters are "mirror," in that she is left handed and Rhonda is right handed. They are extremely similar in appearance, each short, overweight, with a round, red face. Each talked rapidly and was easily excited. They differed slightly in that Linda would become argumentatively defensive when threatened by difficult material, and Rhonda would sigh anxiously and act put upon.

The sisters grew up in a rural area, and their mother stated that there was no special education in their little school. They had difficulty with their lessons from the earliest grades, were frequently teased, and left school at the seventh grade. Later they spent a few years in the state institution for the retarded, but the girls did not like being away from their family and were allowed to return home. In recent years they have been enrolled in sheltered workshops, but (they rationalized) "Mom needed us worser at home." At home they help with housework and the dishes. During the psychological assessment each independently named the other as her best friend. They differed in their attitudes toward boys. Linda was indifferent, and Rhonda showed disdain. They both like to watch television.

The results of the psychological assessment of Linda and Rhonda are summarized in Table 5.8. They displayed their individualized characteristics in the test situation—Linda responding defensively to difficulty and Rhonda with ineffective, random trial-and-error methods. Each had a low frustration tolerance and thus occasionally had to be "nursed" through one or another part of the evaluation. Each could, however, be directed to task, and the measures obtained appeared to be representative.

Despite some differences, there was much more similarity than difference in the twins' overall WAIS-R response pattern. As is seen in Table 5.8, Linda scored somewhat higher, with better verbal reasoning skills and was generally more assertive. Linda showed some

Table 5.8. Psychological Assessment Findings of Linda and Rhonda—Identical Twins

WAIS-R			VINELAND SOCIAL MATURITY SCALE		
	Linda	Rhonda		Linda	Rhonda
VIQ	67	61	Total Score	78	75.5
PIQ	72	71	Age Equivalent	10.3	9.5
FSIQ	68	63	Social Quotient	41	38
Information	5	4			
Digit Span	2	1			
Vocabulary	4	3			
Arithmetic	2	2			
Comprehension	5	3			
Similarities	5	3			
Picture Completion	5	5			
Picture Arrangement	4	4			
Block Design	5	4			
Object Assembly	4	3			
Digit Symbol	3	4			

ability to approach performance tasks systematically, while Rhonda proceeded strictly on random trial and error for much of the test. The most striking similarity in their responses came on the Comprehension question "Why are child labor laws needed?" Linda—"some kidnapping and stuff"; Rhonda—"kidnapping, picking up people's kids." They were examined in succession, without contact in the interim, and thus had no opportunity to compare notes. When the second one had been evaluated, the first was waiting outside the office door. Without a signal, each moved beside the other, the left arm of one, and the right arm of the other shot around the partner's waist, and they made off in stride down the corridor, chattering like very close but much younger best friends.

In addition to the WAIS-R, the Vineland Social Maturity Scale was administered with the mother serving as informant. Again, as summarized in Table 5.8, the sisters' capacities were parallel. Thus, although they take care of their own dressing and hygiene needs, and are relatively good at self-help and household chores, their communication, socialization, recreation and self-responsibility skills are very limited. The result is that each achieved a Social Quotient (41 and 38, respectively) some 25–27 points below her own Intelligence Quotient.

The diagnosis of mild mental retardation was thus made on the basis of combined intelligence and behavior measures (i.e., 68 and 41 for Linda, and 63 and 38 for Rhonda—scores in the lower 1% of the adult population). In view of the twins' demonstrated inability to function independently out of the family setting and the results of this more standardized appraisal, they were eligible to be viewed under existing legislation as dependent "children." Even though they were seen as not having the potential for competitive employment, some contact out of the home, such as in an activity center, was recommended in order for them to develop better social skills and flexibility, which will be helpful to them in making the transition to another sheltered living setting at the time when it is no longer possible for them to live with their parents.

Functional Cognitive Impairment

The interrelationship and inseparability of personality characteristics, cognitive styles, and personal preferences in individual functioning is a commonly accepted idea, notwithstanding the prevalence of standardized psychological tests whose scores are interpreted as representing measures of independent "traits." The experienced clinical psychologist relates findings about various aspects of the person in ways that reflect this functional unity, and rightly so. Our earlier discussion of cognitive style, the listing of "descriptors" in Table 5.4, and interpretation of elements relevant to career directions in individuals each reflected this. Just as "normal" characteristics will, to some degree, influence all aspects of behavior, it is recognized that characteristics considered to be deviant or pathological will also manifest themselves in one or another dimension of a person's behavior. In general, the more influence those characteristics—such as neuroticism, sociopathy, depression, or psychosis—exert on a person's intellectual functioning, the greater will be the degree of pathology seen. Hunt and his associates studied various aspects of disorganization in thinking, and Hunt and Arnhoff (1955) published what have become widely used scales of disorganization in thinking based on vocabulary items from the Binet and Wechsler-Bellevue Scales and comprehension items from the Wechsler-Bellevue. They used ratings by skilled clinicians to develop their final, pedagogically useful list of scaled gradations of schizophrenic thought disorganization. Excerpts from these scales are included in Table 5.9. As one moves down from a scaled-test item reply of 1 (normal) to items scored as 7, note how each successive item mirrors more and more psychopathology.

Psychopathology may be reflected in many aspects of cognitive functioning, including those tapped by performance tests. The patient may approach the block design task in a compulsive or ritualistic fashion. Examiner-solicited associations to picture arrangement cards may be bizarre. However, pathology appears to be more frequently observed in respect to verbal tasks, although research on this topic is lacking. In addition to the work of Hunt and Arnhoff (1955), Zimmerman and Woo-Sam (1973) provide examples of clinical interpretations of responses to comprehension items on the WAIS. These include responses that may indicate phobia ("germs kill you"), self-reference ("I never see a train"), literalness ("but I don't pay taxes"), passive dependence ("wait until found") or negativism ("not true!"). Matarazzo (1972) lists some unusual modes of response to vocabulary items in those who have thinking disturbances. These include (a) overelaboration—giving irrelevant details; (b) overinclusion—mentioning attributes that are shared by many objects, e.g., "has cells"; (c) ellipsis—omitting words necessary to the meaning of a phrase; (d) self-reference—incorporating personalized elements; and (e) bizarreness—idiosyncratic associations or juxtaposition of disconnected ideas. An illustrative case history follows.

Table 5.9. Excerpts from Hunt-Arnhoff Standardized Scales for Disorganization in Schizophrenic Thinking

SCALE POINT*	RESPONSE	MEAN	SD
Vocabulary Scale			
1	Gamble—To take a chance, a risk	1.00	0.00
	Seclude—To go away and be alone, to seclude oneself	1.50	0.63
2	Gown—Garment you wear for lounging	1.75	0.93
	Shrewd—Careful in a sneaky, clever way	2.19	0.75
3	Join—Has to do with organization	2.62	0.96
	Peculiarity—Action one doesn't usually engage in	3.00	1.15
4	Espionage—Crooked, not truthful	4.12	1.09
	Seclude—To put somewhere in the dark	3.81	1.11
5	Juggler—Acts in front of a person, respects himself as a juggler	5.00	0.82
	Espionage—A type of sinful devilment	5.44	0.89
6	Nail—Metal I guess let's say a metal which is made scientifically for purpose of good and bad use	5.75	0.93
	Diamond—A piece of glass made from roses	6.44	0.63
7	Cushion—To sleep on a pillow of God's sheep	6.75	9.45
	Fable—Trade good sheep to hide in the beginning	6.81	0.40
Comprehension Scale			
1	Envelope—Deposit it in the mail box	1.06	0.25
2	Land in the city—Because they got more accommodations in the city than in the country	2.00	0.96
3	Envelope—Pass it by or mail it	2.87	0.81
	Theatre—Turn in an alarm so that everyone wouldn't get burned up	3.00	0.82
4	Marriage—Proof and identification so you wouldn't get someone else's wife	3.00	0.82
5	Laws—It is reasonable to a group of people to come in some agreement and acceptance of a common good and to aid what has proven to be the best for the many; that is, they are made to prevent illegal activities	4.87	0.96
6	Marriage—For ownership you might say and to take care of each other according to health	5.87	0.96
7	Forest—I'm not good at telling directions. Just walk uphill and when you get to the top it is easier going down.	6.31	0.71
	Marriage—For scientific purposes and for the identification of siblings, siblings of the association of the parents		

*Disorganization rated from none (1) to maximum (7).

Note: Adapted from "Some Standardized Scales for Disorganization in Schizophrenic Thinking" by W. A. Hunt and F. N. Arnhoff, 1955, *Journal of Consulting Psychology, 19,* pp. 171–74.

Case History—An Avoidant Personality with Depression and Dependency

Bill Smithers, 22 years old, was referred for an evaluation of the level of his emotional stability and to determine his intellectual potential. He was a "late" child, the youngest of elderly but successful parents. His father was a businessman and his mother an artist-homemaker. In his youth he was diagnosed as maladroit and suffering from being a member of "a high-expectation family." He completed high school with difficulty and subsequently took a few community college courses. He held two jobs briefly: one was temporary and obtained for him by his aunt; one he left in order to go on vacation. He has no car as he has been unable to pass the driver's test. He stays home and occasionally plays tennis or volleyball.

During the opening interview Bill was soft spoken and mild. He was inconsistent and frequently did not understand the intent of questions until they were made very explicit. He was reluctant to make judgments or generalizations about any aspects of his life.

The results of the psychological evaluation are summarized in Table 5.10. On the WAIS-R, Bill was inconsistent and erratic. He failed simple items and passed more difficult ones, thus displaying intratest "scatter." His reasoning was generally good as long as

Table 5.10. Psychological Assessment Findings in an Avoidant Personality with Depression and Dependency

WAIS-R		16PF TEST	
VIQ	91	*High Score Descriptions*—Astute (not forthright). Outgoing, Tender-minded,	
PIQ	89	Apprehensive, Self-sufficient	
FSIQ	89		
Information	8	*Low Score Descriptions*—Sober, Expedient, Shy, Undisciplined self-conflict,	
Digit Span	8	Less intelligent	
Vocabulary	10	Trailmaking	
Arithmetic	9	Part A	10 credits
Comprehension	4	Part B	6 credits
Similarities	12	Part C	16 credits
Picture Completion	10		
Picture Arrangement	8		
Block Design	9		
Object Assembly	11		
Digit Symbol	7		

Peabody Individual Achievement Test

	GRADE EQUIVALENTS
Mathematics	12.9
Reading Recognition	9.4
Reading Comprehension	12.8
Spelling	12.9

Bender
Primitive, but not suggestive of perceptual impairment

Rotter Incomplete Sentences Blank
Perplexed, Directionless. Self-blame—feels immobilized. People
puzzling. Independence seen as threatening. Suppressed anger
toward parent.

he had only a limited number of concepts to deal with. He did well on similarities and basic arithmetic functions but poorly on complex arithmetic problems. He clutched the pencil like an ice-pick and consequently was slow and made primitive productions. He was anxious, with poor tolerance for stress of any kind, and desperate to please. When he could not answer immediately, his pace became frantic, he paid little attention to detail, and in verbal response he would confabulate answers to "please" the examiner. Some unusual verbal responses were: *Sanctuary*—"a place safe [sic];" *Evasive*—"afraid of somebody, trying to get away from;" *Fortitude*—"a strong attitude;" *Deaf People*—"they can't sound it out," (Q. tell me more) "they can if they look at paper and see how it is divided into syllables."

Bill's medical history, his older mother, the 8-point (almost 3 standard deviation) intertest "scatter" between his scores on the Comprehension and the Similarities subtest, and his difficulty in word finding and organizing verbal concepts collectively warranted

further study regarding the possible presence of a neurological impairment that was interfering with his verbal expression and verbal organization. It is possible that the academic and social difficulties stemming from this postulated dysfunction may well have been the stimulus early in his life for family overprotection as well as rejection and sometimes ridicule from peers. At the present time Bill's passivity, dependence, ineptness, depression, and withdrawal represent greater impediments than this possible underlying organic impairment. Bill is being provided supportive therapy to help him make the transition from the family home into a sheltered residential setting and to help him find work where options are clear, changes from routine are minimized, and time is available to absorb new instructions.

Neuropsychological Evaluation

Large-scale systematic attempts to use intelligence tests to measure cognitive impairment due to organic brain dysfunction followed the publication of the Wechsler-Bellevue Scales. Wechsler identified the subtests on which he believed functioning would be impaired by organic brain damage and suggested a deterioration index that was the ratio of such "don't hold" to "hold" subtests. That this index was not satisfactorily validated may have been related as much to the unreliability of neurological and neurosurgical diagnoses as it was to the neuropsychological instrument.

Neuropsychological assessment was carried forward by Ralph Reitan, who built on the earlier work of Ward Halstead as well as Wechsler. Reitan validated neuropsychological measures against groups of patients who were carefully (neurologically) diagnosed as having left-hemisphere, right-hemisphere, or diffuse brain lesions. He helped develop what later was called the Halstead-Reitan Battery of Neuropsychological Tests (Reitan & Davison, 1974), of which the Wechsler scales are a part.

A history of some of the research pertinent to the use of the Wechsler scales in neuropsychological assessment has been published by Matarazzo (1972). In their review of factor analytic studies of the WAIS-R, Leckliter, et al. (1986) note that studies which include scores from the Halstead-Reitan Neuropsychological Battery (HRNB) reveal that their first factor has loadings from Wechsler's Verbal subtests and from the Aphasia HRNB Screening test, the second factor has loadings from Wechsler's Performance subtests and the HRNB Tactual Performance Test, and a third factor, although more variable, generally includes loadings from Wechsler's Digit Span and Arithmetic subtests. Clinical neuropsychologists agree that the WAIS-R is sensitive to some aspects of organic impairment, and that a large difference between the Verbal IQ and Performance IQ, and large differences in subtest to subtest scores, typically should alert the clinician to search for medical, personal history, and other extra-test evidence (if any) of organic brain dysfunction. Studying sex differences in the WAIS-R, Matarazzo, Bornstein, McDermott and Noonan (1986) reported base rates for the magnitude, frequency, and direction of VIQ-PIQ discrepancies found for the 940 males and 940 females who make up the WAIS-R standardization sample. They noted no differences of consequence in male versus female VIQ-PIQ discrepancies nor in VIQ, PIQ, and FSIQ for these 1880 normal subjects. Noting the absence of research based on large samples of well-matched brain-injured subjects, they concluded that, based on the limited WAIS-R evidence available, a patient's sex need not be a variable to which practitioners assign

unusually strong weight in the interpretation of VIQ-PIQ discrepancies.

The research in neuropsychological assessment with intelligence tests and other instruments is burgeoning and is too voluminous for inclusion in this overview chapter on measures of adult intelligence. However, the interested reader will find more detailed discussion of this important topic in the section of the book devoted to neuropsychological assessment.

Measurement of Intelligence as a Genetic Marker

Even though the relative role of inheritance in individual intelligence has been a matter of bitter debate, the relationship between intellectual impairment and certain inherited genetic disorders (e.g., Down's syndrome) has been generally accepted. Early studies of the relationship between intelligence and specific genetic disorders frequently utilized measures of intelligence that varied from the standardized individual test to casual observation based on interview. As genetic research became more sophisticated, the need for reliable and more finely discriminating measures became apparent.

Jackson (1981) has summarized the psychological findings in four major genetic disorders: phenylketonuria (PKU), Turner's syndrome, Klinefelter's syndrome, and Huntington's disease. Because of the development of a simple and cost-effective screening method, it has become possible to identify individuals with phenylketonuria within a few days of birth and, with proper dietary measures, to avoid the brain damage that results in mental retardation in untreated PKU. Intellectual evaluation involves examination of siblings as well as the identified patient, and continued monitoring of these individuals as dietary controls are changed over time.

Turner's syndrome is found in females who lack one of the two X sex chromosomes (XO instead of XX). A consistent pattern of intellectual deficit has been found, in that patients with Turner's Syndrome typically score lower on performance (spatial) abilities while not differing from siblings or controls in verbal abilities. Such patients may also have difficulty carrying out arithmetic functions. The case history following this section provides a representative example of cognitive functioning in Turner's syndrome. Recently, Rovet and Netley (1982) have begun to examine more closely the earlier recognized impairment of spatial abilities in Turner's syndrome, with results suggesting that speed of response on rotational tasks (where transformation of spatially presented information is required) is primarily responsible for the deficit in Performance IQ.

Klinefelter's syndrome involves males with an extra X chromosome (XXY instead of XY). Here the intelligence test findings are the obverse of those in Turner's syndrome, with those affected typically having an impaired Verbal IQ, while their Performance IQ is unaffected relative to controls and siblings. Robinson, Lubs, Nielsen, and Sorensen (1979) also describe delayed speech development, delayed emotional development, and school maladjustment in patients with Klinefelter's syndrome.

Huntington's disease usually has its onset between ages 35 and 45 and eventually results in gross intellectual deficit. The normal-appearing individual whose parent is affected is "at risk," with a 50:50 chance of having inherited the disease. Retrospective studies show that those members of the "at risk" group who *later* develop the disease show IQ values that are lower than those of controls, but psychological measures in general have not been satisfactory for such predictive purposes. Josiassen, Burry, Roemer, De-Bease, and Mancall (1982) report a consistent pattern in *recently diagnosed* Huntington's patients (in comparison with those "at risk"), with impairment in Arithmetic, Digit Span, Digit Symbol, and Picture Arrangement subtests.

The relationship between intelligence theory and measurement and genetic research is not necessarily a unidirectional one. Even though intelligence test results have demonstrated value in helping to identify genetic syndromes, continuing genetic research may well produce significant contributions to our understanding of intelligences, especially the thorny problem of the relationship between heredity and intelligence. A case history follows.

Case History—A Young Lady with Turner's Syndrome

Tanya Metsgy was referred for consultation at age 17, when she was a senior in high school. She was a tiny girl, alert and spontaneous during the interview. Although she was bright and had a good sense of humor, she had experienced a great deal of teasing from fellow students because of her diminutive size. She had a comfortable but mildly dependent relationship with her parents.

Tanya listed her physical problems as poor finger dexterity, trouble standing for prolonged periods, and the problems attendant on being short. Her grades were average, although she had to struggle to pass a general math course. The formal results of her psychological evaluation are summarized in Table 5.11.

Table 5.11. Psychological Assessment Findings in a Young Woman with Turner's Syndrome

WAIS		STRONG-CAMPBELL INTEREST INVENTORY
VIQ	118	*Higher Theme Score*—Social
PIQ	99	*Highest Basic Interest Scales*—Medical Service, Social Service
FSIQ	110	
		Highest Occupational Scale Scores—Elementary Teacher, Director of Christian Education
Information	14	
Comprehension	15	*Academic Orientation Scale*—99
Arithmetic	7	
Similarities	13	*Introversion-Extroversion Scale*—46
Digit Span	9	
Vocabulary	15	
Digit Symbol	8	
Picture Completion	9	
Block Design	9	
Picture Arrangement	10	
Object Assembly	8	

Peabody Individual Achievement Test

	GRADE EQUIVALENTS
Mathematics	5.7
Reading Recognition	12.9+
Reading Comprehension	12.9+
Spelling	12.9+

Tanya's pattern of intellectual functioning as seen on the WAIS appears to be classic for Turner's syndrome. Vocabulary and verbal reasoning are superior. She had moderate difficulty with visual-spatial relationships (see her low scores on the five Performance subtests), relying on trial-and-error methods to solve space relations problems. In addition, limitations in arithmetic ability were observed on the WAIS as well as on the Peabody Individual Achievement Test (PIAT).

The test results (which included a Verbal IQ of 118) were interpreted as suggesting that Tanya should be able to function with average expenditure of effort in a four-year college of average academic standards, although she might have difficulty with math requirements. She had expressed interest in nursing or teaching. She was encouraged toward teaching because of the relatively difficult physical demands and math requirements in nursing and because her interest-test profile was more compatible with teaching.

Six years after the evaluation shown in Table 5.11 it was learned that Tanya was in her last quarter of work toward a B.A. in history. College had been difficult, and she had dropped out for several brief periods. She had changed her major from education because she could not successfully complete the required math. She is living independently and expresses satisfaction with her social adjustment. Her plans are to seek a position in the occupational world commensurate with her B.A. degree, and her chances for success appear to be relatively good.

FUTURE DIRECTIONS

Future directions for exploration of the nature of intelligence, its measurement, and its application may be conceptualized in terms of two major forces: those that may bring us closer to understanding the neuromolecular, biochemical, and physiological correlates of intelligence and those directed toward its most effective application.

Research in molecular biology, neurochemistry, neurobiology, genetics, neuropsychology, and developmental psychology may be expected to enlighten us further on the physiological correlates of memory, information processing, and related components of human cognition; how "intelligent" characteristics are inherited and the patterns in which they are inherited; how these characteristics help receive sensory input, store it in short- or long-term memory, process it for the immediate task at hand, or retrieve it at a later date; and how intelligent behaviors unfold in the biological and social developmental process. It is hoped that such research will allow us to develop strategies and

tests for assessing intelligent behavior and intellectual abilities beyond those that have been intuitively included in intelligence tests to date. Such future research also may well provide us with the capacity to measure intellectual potential more directly, for example, at a physiological, neurochemical, or even anatomical level. Assuming the future existence of such measures, however, one might note that as long as the goal of measurement is the use of intelligence in environments where motivation and personal style impinge on its application, measures of *intelligent behavior* as well as *intellectual capacity* will be required.

Research using computer models and concepts of "artificial intelligence" are showing considerable potential to contribute to our knowledge of the most effective way to apply one's intelligence. The direction of these efforts includes study of strategies of learning and the procedures involved in information processing. In addition to developing an understanding of the strategies and procedures, they may also help to expand the mechanical limits of intellectual processing, thus reducing some of the "reality" limitations to learning and creative analysis.

SUMMARY

This chapter traces the development of the intelligence test from the rudimentary age scale of Binet and Simon to the publication of the Wechsler Adult Intelligence Scale-Revised. The historical conflict between proponents of general and multiple specific-factor theories of intelligence is reviewed, noting the development of pragmatically useful knowledge and instruments, despite the continuing debate. The more recent concepts of *fluid* and *crystallized* intelligence are described, as is their relationship to studies of the factor analytic structure of intelligence tests.

A number of intelligence tests intended for adult populations are listed and briefly annotated, including the recently published Fourth Edition of the Stanford-Binet. Major attention is then focused on the WAIS-R. Recently published findings regarding the reliability, validity, and factor analytic structure of the WAIS-R are reviewed, and some differences in statistical properties between the WAIS and WAIS-R are noted.

Applications of adult intelligence test are described, including their use in individual evaluation for career counseling; evaluation of mental retardation or thought disorders; neuropsychological assessment; and evaluation of individuals at risk for genetic disorders. Illustrative case histories are included.

The chapter concludes by noting two major directions for the future: exploration of neuromolecular, biochemical and physiological correlates of intelligence, and development of more effective methods for the application of human intelligence. These are related to ongoing research in genetics, neuropsychology, developmental psychology, and concepts of "artificial intelligence."

REFERENCES

Baker, H., & Leland, B. (1967). *Detroit Tests of Learning Aptitude*. Indianapolis: Bobbs-Merrill.

Barona, A., Reynolds, C. R., & Chastain, R. (1984). A demographically based index of pre-morbid intelligence for the WAIS-R. *Journal of Consulting and Clinical Psychology, 52*(5), 885–87.

Binet, A., & Simon, T. (1905). Application des méthodes nouvelles au diagnostic du niveau intellectuel chez des enfants normaux et anormaux d'hospice et d'école primare. [Application of new methods to diagnose intellectual levels of normal and abnormal children in hospitals and primary schools.] *L'Annee Psychologique, 11*, 245–336.

Binet A., & Simon, T. (1908). Le développement de l'intelligence chez les enfants. [The development of intelligence in children.] *L'Annee Psychologique, 14*, 1–94.

Binet, A., & Simon, T. (1916). *The Development of Intelligence in Children (The Binet-Simon Scale)* E. S. Kite, Trans.). Baltimore: Williams & Wilkins.

Brown, L., Sherbernou, R. J., & Dollar, S. J. (1982). *Test of nonverbal intelligence*. Austin, TX: PRO-ED.

Brown, W. R., & McGuire, J. M. (1976). Current psychological assessment practices. *Professional Psychology, 7*, 475–484.

Cattell, R. B. (1971). *Abilities: Their structure, growth and action*. Boston: Houghton-Mifflin.

Cronbach, L. J. (1960). *Essentials of psychological testing* (2nd ed.). New York: Harper & Row.

Delaney, E. A., & Hopkins, T. F. (1987). *The Stanford-Binet Intelligence Scale: Fourth Edition, Examiner's handbook*. Chicago: Riverside Publishing.

Doyle, Jr., K. O. (1974). Theory and practice of ability testing in ancient Greece. *Journal of the History of the Behavioral Sciences, 10*, 202–212.

DuBois, P. H. (1970). *A history of psychological testing*. Boston: Allyn & Bacon.

Dunn, L. (1965). *Peabody Picture Vocabulary Test*. Circle Pines, MN: American Guidance Service.

Eppinger, M. G., Craig, P. L., Adams, R. L., & Parsons, O. A. (1987). The WAIS-R index for estimating premorbid intelligence: Cross-validation and clinical utility. *Journal of Consulting and Clinical Psychology, 55*(1), 86–90.

Flynn, J. R. (1984). The mean IQ of Americans: Massive gains 1932 to 1978. *Psychological Bulletin, 95*(1), 29–51.

Galton, F. (1869). *Hereditary genes: An inquiry into its laws and consequences*. London: Macmillan.

Garner, A. M. (1966). Intelligence testing and clinical practice. In I. A. Berg & L. A. Pennington (Eds.), *An introduction to clinical psychology*. New York: Ronald Press.

Grossman, H. J. (1973). *Manual on terminology and classification in mental deficiency*. Washington, DC: American Association on Mental Retardation.

Guilford, J. P., & Hoepfner, R. (1971). *The analysis of intelligence*. New York: McGraw-Hill.

Harrell, T. W., & Harrell, M. S. (1945). Army General Classification Test scores for civilian occupations. *Educational and Psychological Measurement, 5*, 229–239.

Herman, D. O. (1982). Demographic factors in performance on WAIS-R. In D. Herman (Chair), *WAIS-R factor structures and patterns of performance in various groups*. Symposium presented at the ninetieth annual convention of the American Psychological Association, Washington, DC.

Horn, J. L. (1986). Intellectual ability concepts. In R. L. Sternberg (Ed.), *Advances in the psychology of human intelligence* (Vol. 3, pp. 35–77). Hillsdale, NJ: Lawrence Erlbaum.

House, A. E., & Lewis, M. L. (1985). Wechsler Adult Intelligence Scale-Revised. In C. S. Newmark (Ed.), *Major psychological assessment instruments* (pp. 323–379). Boston: Allyn & Bacon.

Hunt, W. A., & Arnhoff, F. N. (1955). Some standardized scales for disorganization in schizophrenic thinking. *Journal of Consulting Psychology, 19*, 171–174.

Inalcik, H. (1973). *The Ottoman Empire*. New York: Praeger.

Jackson, R. H. (1981). Other genetic disorders. In J. E. Lindemann, *Psychological and behavioral aspects of physical disability*. New York: Plenum Press.

James, W. (1890). *The Principles of psychology*. New York: Dover.

Josiassen, R. C., Curry, L., Roemer, R. A., De Bease, C., & Mancall, E. G. (1982). Patterns of intellectual deficit in Huntington's Disease. *Journal of Clinical Neuropsychology, 4*(2), 173–83.

Kaufman, A. S., & Kaufman, N. L. (1983). *Kaufman Assessment Battery for Children: Interpretive manual*. Circle Pines, MN: American Guidance System.

Leckliter, I. N., Matarazzo, J. O., & Silverstein, A. B. (1986). A literature review of factor analytic studies of the WAIS-R. *Journal of Clinical Psychology*, 42(2), pp. 332–342.

Lubin, B., Larsen, R. M., Matarazzo, J. D., & Seever, M. (1985). Psychological test usage patterns in five professional settings. *American Psychologist*, 40, 857–861.

Lubin, B., Wallis, R. R., & Paine, C. (1971). Patterns of psychological test usage in the United States: 1935–1969. *Professional Psychology*, 2, 70–74.

Matarazzo, J. D. (1972). *Wechsler's measurement and appraisal of adult intelligence* (5th ed.). Baltimore: Williams & Wilkins.

Matarazzo, J. D., Bornstein, R. A., McDermott, P. A., & Noonan, J. V. (1986). Verbal IQ versus performance IQ difference scores in males and females from the WAIS-R standardization sample. *Journal of Clinical Psychology*, 42(6), 965–974.

Matarazzo, J. D., & Herman, D. O. (1984). Relationships of education and IQ in the WAIS-R standardization sample. *Journal of Consulting and Clinical Psychology*, 52(4), 631–34.

Matarazzo, J. D., & Herman, D. O. (1985). Clinical uses of the WAIS-R: Base rates of differences between VIQ and PIQ in the WAIS-R standardization sample. In B. B. Wolman (Ed.), *Handbook of intelligence: Theories, measurements, and applications*. New York: Wiley.

Mitchell, Jr., J. V. (Ed.). (1985). *Ninth Mental Measurements yearbook*. Lincoln, NB: University of Nebraska Press.

Naglieri, J. A. (1982). Two types of tables for use with the WAIS-R. *Journal of Consulting and Clinical Psychology*, 50, 319–21.

Reitan, R. M., & Davison, L. A. (Eds.). (1974). *Clinical neuropsychology: Current status and applications*. Washington: Winston.

Reynolds, W. M. (1979). Psychological tests: Clinical usage versus psychometric quality. *Professional Psychology*, 3, 324–329.

Robinson, A., Lubs, H. A., Nielson, J., & Sorensen, K. (1979). Summary of clinical findings: Profiles of children with 47,XXY,47,XXX and 47,XYY Karyotypes. *Birth Defects: Original Article Series*, 15(1), 261–266.

Rovet, J., & Netley, C. (1982). Processing deficits in Turner's Syndrome. *Developmental Psychology*, 18(1), 77–94.

Sattler, J. M. (1982). Age effects on Wechsler Adult Intelligence Scale-Revised Tests. *Journal of Consulting Clinical Psychology*, 50(5), 785–786.

Sattler, J. M. (1988). *Assessment of children* (3rd ed.). San Diego: Jerome M. Sattler.

Silverstein, A. B. (1982). Pattern analysis as simultaneous statistical inference. *Journal of Consulting and Clinical Psychology*, 50(2), 234–240.

Slosson, R. L. (1981). *Slosson Intelligence Test*. East Aurora, NY: Slosson Educational Publications.

Spearman, C. (1904). "General intelligence," objectively determined and measured. *American Journal of Psychology*, 15, 201–293.

Stern, W. L. (1912). Über die psychologischen methoden der intelligenzprufüng. [About the psychological methods of intelligence testing.] *Ber V. Kongress Exp. Psychol.*, 16, 1–160. (American translations by G. W. Whipple, The psychological methods of testing intelligence. *Education Psychology Monographs*, 13, Baltimore: Warwick & York.)

Sternberg, R. J., & Detterman, D. K. (1986). *What is intelligence: Contemporary viewpoint on its nature and definition*, Norwood, NJ: Ablex.

Super, E. E., & Crites, J. O. (1962). *Appraising vocational fitness by means of psychological tests* (rev. ed.). New York: Harper.

Terman, L., & Merrill, M. (1973). *Stanford-Binet Intelligence Scale*. Boston: Houghton-Mifflin.

Thorndike, E. L., Lay, W., & Dean, P. R. (1909). The relation of accuracy in sensory discrimination to general intelligence. *American Journal of Psychology*, 20, 364–369.

Thorndike, R. L., Hagen, E. P., & Sattler, J. M. (1986). *The Stanford-Binet Intelligence Scale: Fourth Edition*. Chicago: Riverside Publishing.

Thurstone, L. L., & Thurstone, T. G. (1941). Factorial studies of intelligence. *Psychometric Monographs*, 2. Chicago: University of Chicago Press.

Tyler, L. E. (1978). *Individuality*. San Francisco: Jossey-Bass.

Wechsler, D. (1939, 1944). *The measurement of adult intelligence*. Baltimore: Williams & Wilkins.

Wechsler, D. (1955). *Manual for the Wechsler Adult Intelligence Scale*. New York: Psychological Corporation.

Wechsler, D. (1974). *Wechsler Intelligence Scale for Children-Revised*. New York: Psychological Corporation.

Wechsler, D. (1981). *Wechsler Adult Intelligence Scale-Revised*. New York: Psychological Corporation.

Yerkes, R. M. (Ed.). (1921). Psychological examining in the U.S. Army. *Memoirs of the National Academy of Sciences*, 15.

Zimmerman, I. L., & Woo-Sam, J. M. (1973). *Clinical interpretation of the Wechsler Adult Intelligence Scale*. New York: Grune & Stratton.

CHAPTER 6

GROUP INTELLIGENCE TESTS

Julia R. Vane
Robert W. Motta

Group intelligence tests have a long history and have been administered under different names in one form or another for many centuries. Lin Chuan-tin (1980) has found that the Chinese were using some form of mental testing for appointment to the Imperial Court as early as the third century. At that time the belief was that the speed of speaking and writing could be used as an index of intelligence. By the seventh and eighth centuries sentence completion items were widely used in the imperial examination, and various methods of paired antithetical phrases were used, similar to the opposite analogies found in present-day individual and group intelligence tests. A seven-piece puzzle also was developed as a nonverbal intelligence test, comparable in nature to the differentiation of shapes and forms that appears today on many group tests of nonverbal intelligence. Even then concern was expressed about the predictive value of the test results and how the results were being used.

Group intelligence tests are used throughout the world, although some countries make greater use of them than others. For example, for the past 30 years countries such as Belgium, France, the Netherlands and Norway have regularly tested all young men entering military service, and countries such as Australia, Canada, East Germany, Great Britain, and New Zealand have regularly conducted large-scale group intelligence testing of school children as a matter of course (Flynn, 1987). Group intelligence tests are used at all educational levels from kindergarten through professional schools and in many employment settings. Because group intelligence testing is so pervasive, it affects the lives of many individuals. For

this reason, testing and the use of test results are subjects of interest to the public and professionals.

HISTORICAL PERSPECTIVE

The impetus for the widespread use of group intelligence tests in the United States began with the entrance of this country into World War I in 1917. At this time, the American Psychological Association, whose president was Robert Yerkes, offered its services to the United States Army. The Army was interested in a rapid means of sorting and classifying recruits for different levels of training. Psychologists, such as Terman, Yerkes, Otis, and others, developed what came to be known as the Army Alpha Intelligence Test, which was designed for literate recruits, and the Army Beta Intelligence Test designed for illiterate recruits. Testing was carried out in 35 camps, and 1,726,966 men were tested. The experience with these tests was considered to be so successful that at the end of the war the psychologists urged expansion into civilian testing. Within a short time various versions of the Army Alpha and similar group tests had been given in many hundreds of schools. At this stage, group intelligence testing was acclaimed as an educational aid that helped to identify the abilities of students more accurately than the traditional methods of teacher evaluation and marks. It was seen also as a means of discovering talented individuals and as a way of opening doors for the talented poor. There was concern as well for identifying bright children who were forced to maintain an average pace in the classroom and dull children who were urged to work at a level beyond their ability. This orientation won general acceptance in educational circles, and group intelligence testing became part of the general school routine with classes of children being tested on a regular basis, often once a year. In addition, the use of such tests was extended to the selection of candidates for college and professional school admission and to screen applicants for employment.

The growth was so rapid that by 1923 Pintner published a book, *Intelligence Testing,* in which he was able to list 37 group intelligence tests, among which were five non-language and six nonverbal tests. The non-language tests were entirely pictorial in nature, and the directions were given in pantomime and by samples demonstrated by the examiner. The nonverbal tests were pictorial in content and did not require a knowledge of reading or writing on the part of the test takers. At this time it was assumed that intelligence was a recognizable, inherent ability that could be assessed through the use of intelligence tests, although it was not measurable in the same sense as physical attributes such as height or weight. Also, the level of tested intelligence was thought to be stable over the individual's life span.

Despite the general acceptance of group intelligence tests, controversy was touched off by the incautious conclusions drawn by professionals and even more by articles in the popular press. The conclusions were often less than scientific and to some minds highly inflammatory. There were suggestions that the level of mental maturity among the men in the Army was about 12 to 13 years, and that certain ethnic groups who did well on the tests, particularly those with English and Scottish backgrounds, were superior to those who did poorly, namely individuals from southern and eastern European countries. Little account was taken of the language, cultural, and environmental differences experienced by these groups.

Cronbach (1975) and Haney (1981) provide extensive descriptions of the controversy that erupted in the early 1920s with Walter Lippman (1922a, 1922b, 1923) leading a press attack on the concept of IQ testing with articles such as "The Mental Age of Americans," "Tests of Hereditary Intelligence," and "Rich and Poor, Girls and Boys." Rebuttals were undertaken by Freeman (1923), Terman (1922a, 1922b), Brigham (1923), and Yerkes (1923).

It would be a mistake to believe that the controversy was limited to professionals on one side and the public and press on the other. Many professionals did not agree with the position that intelligence tests measured innate potential, and a series of studies followed that indicated that environmental influences play a part in affecting tested intelligence. In 1923 the work of Gordon (Vernon, 1979) in England with canal-boat and Gypsy children showed that the IQ levels of these children were depressed, and the level of depression appeared related to the amount of schooling they had received, which was usually very little. Five years later studies by Freeman, Holzinger, and Mitchell (1928), as well as those of Burks (1928), showed that when orphans were placed in good foster homes there was an improvement in their tested intelligence.

Following this show of interest by the public in the 1920s, professionals continued to debate the relative influence of nature and nurture on tested intelligence, but public curiosity waned. Despite the fact that more than twice as many men were tested for military assignments in World War II than had been tested in World War I, little attention was paid to the results in the popular press.

In 1958, following the launching of Sputnik by the Russians, group intelligence and aptitude tests were encouraged by the passage of the National Defense Education Act, which provided funds to the states to "establish and maintain a program for testing aptitudes and abilities of students, and . . . to identify students with outstanding aptitudes and abilities" (Goslin 1963, p. 71). In this same year the National Merit Scholarship Corporation was established to identify high school students of exceptional ability. As testing expanded, a number of critical articles appeared challenging the "tyranny of testing," as Hoffman (1962) phrased it. After another short, quiet period, a significant upturn of public interest occurred in the late 1970s and has continued to the present.

Similar concerns can be found in articles published in other countries. As an example, half a century ago Lommatzsch (1929) discussed a study done at a school in Dresden in which group intelligence tests were found to predict school performance no better than previous school grades. Lommatzsch questioned the value of the tests and noted, "The Saxon Philological Society is now undertaking a number of investigations for the further elaboration of the problem" (p. 346).

Cronbach (1975), in his article which chronicled the cycles of public acceptance and rejection of intelligence testing in the United States, indicated that there is always potential for heightened public interest in professional findings that impinge upon the lives of the public, but the form this interest will take usually is dependent upon the mood of times. A good example of a challenging idea regarding testing that appeared at the wrong time was the work of Eels, Davis, Havighurst, Herricks, and Tyler (1951), who developed a "culture-fair" test to identify bright children from the lower class that other tests and the educational system failed to locate. This effort would have been highly interesting in the 1970s and 1980s, but it elicited little attention from the press, public, or educators at that time. In contrast, when Rosenthal and Jacobsen (1968) presented their view that teacher expectations strongly influence how well school children perform on tests, the idea was readily exploited by the press and reached a receptive audience. Although Rosenthal's data were weak and most of the conclusions have not been substantiated, this point of view is still widely accepted in educational and popular circles because it is a notion that many individuals find attractive.

In viewing the present controversy regarding testing, Cronbach (1975) suggests that it is just another example of a cycle. Linn (1982), however, sees the present attacks as different. In the earlier cycles, the attacks were limited to professional journals and the popular press, in which the debates took place. The most recent attacks, which began in 1970, have gone beyond the earlier ones and today are being debated on the national level and in state legislatures. The outcomes have been more serious than before in curtailing the use of both individual and group intelligence testing.

MAJOR OBJECTIONS TO INTELLIGENCE TESTING

That standardized testing in general and intelligence testing in particular have engaged the interest of the public and the press for so many years is perhaps a reflection of the power that test results are perceived to exert over society, from early school entry to later opportunities for employment and promotion. The tone of the information on the issues purveyed to the public can be seen in the titles of some of the articles and books published in the last 20 years: *They Shall Not Pass* (Black, 1962), *The Brain Watchers* (Gross, 1962), "Born Dumb?" (Newsweek, 1969), "How Racists Use 'Science' to Degrade Black People" (Rowan, 1970), *The Stranglehold of the IQ* (Fine, 1975), "The War on Testing: David, Goliath and Gallup" (Lerner, 1980), *The Reign of ETS: The Corporation That Makes Up Minds* (Nairn, 1980), and "Soul Searching in the Testing Establishment" (Fiske, 1981).

Attacks on intelligence testing, both group and individual, by the pubic and professionals usually fall into three categories: criticisms of the way in which tests are used, criticisms of the conclusions drawn from the results of testing and the theories underlying these conclusions, and criticisms of the tests themselves.

CRITICISMS OF HOW TESTS ARE USED

Criticism of some of the ways in which tests are used or misused has been well founded. Misuses often cited have included classification of bilingual and foreign-born students as retarded on the basis of tests given in English, group tests administered and interpreted by poorly trained personnel, and employment tests that have little relation to the jobs for which the applicants are applying. Those who criticize often suggest that misuses of testing are so widespread that there should be a ban on all testing, particularly intelligence tests. The major complaint is that such tests discriminate against minorities, especially African-Americans, Hispanics, Native-Americans, and individuals from low socioeconomic backgrounds. These groups cite examples such as the observation that in California in 1970 the enrollment in special classes for the mildly retarded was about 25% African-American, whereas the total African-American population of students was only about 10%. In 1981, an analysis of the New Jersey schools revealed that African-American and Hispanic students, respectively, made up only 18% and 7% of the total student body but constituted 43% and 14% of the enrollment in classes for the mildly retarded (Reschly, 1981).

Not only in the United States are the public and professionals concerned that group intelligence tests may discriminate against minorities. Zeidner (1988), in discussing fairness in testing among school children in Israel, notes that representatives of Israeli minority groups, whose children consistently score below their Western counterparts on standardized ability tests, have launched a vehement antitest campaign. On the other hand, Madge (1979) defends group intelligence tests in a reply to an article criticizing South African testing measures as being biased against migrant and other subgroups in the culture. She claims that these criticisms do not apply in South Africa because different tests are constructed and standardized for the various groups.

As a result of the activity and court suits brought by various groups in the United States, there is now a moratorium on IQ testing in the schools in California, Minneapolis, New York City, and Philadelphia. However, when methods rather than IQ testing were used to evaluate California children for special class placement, the same percentage of minority children was found to be in need of special class placement as had been determined when IQ testing was used. The proportion of these children dropped only after a rigid quota system was imposed by the court on placement of minorities in these classes.

As may be noted from the last example, to ban testing is a nonsolution because the alternatives suggested, namely teacher evaluation, past grades, achievement tests, assessment of motivation, and cultural background, have a greater potential for producing biased decisions than do the tests they are meant to replace. Although past performance and grades have been shown to be fairly good predictors of future performance, intelligence tests benefit those individuals who may have good ability as demonstrated on the tests but are handicapped by poor past performance and/or a dismal academic record. Even Gordon and Terrell (1981), who strongly criticize the misuse of standardized tests, state: "To argue that standardized testing should be done away with or radically changed simply because ethnic minorities and disadvantaged groups do not earn as high scores as do middle-class whites is an untenable position" (p. 1170). The authors do suggest, however, that the use of standardized tests be greatly reduced because they do not believe these tests serve a useful purpose. They propose the development of alternate devices and procedures that would be "process sensitive instruments designed to elicit data descriptive of the functional and conditional aspects of learner behavior" (p. 1170).

It would be naive to suppose, however, that if tests were developed that would do all the things Gordon and Terrel and other critics suggest, these tests would be above criticism.

As a subject that invites debate and controversy, tests and their uses must rank with religion, politics and sex. Tests, at least in part, are designed to do a dirty job: they help us make discriminating judgments about ourselves, about others, about levels of accomplishment and achievement, about degrees of effectiveness. They are no less controversial when they perform their tasks well than when they perform them poorly. Indeed, it can be argued that the better the test, the more controversial its use becomes. (Hargadon, 1981, p. 1113)

CRITICISMS OF CONCLUSIONS BASED UPON RESULTS OF INTELLIGENCE TESTING

The conclusions drawn from the results of large scale intelligence testing usually arouse the greatest passion because these conlcusions often suggest that one group of citizens is inferior to another based on the inheritance of intelligence. In the past decade professionals and the public have become sensitive to these theoretical positions through the controversy generated by articles by Jensen (1969), Herrnstein (1971), and others, which suggested that aspects of general intelligence may be inherited and may be present to a greater or lesser degree in some ethnic groups. As was noted earlier, this theoretical position was strongly held in the 1920s, and although it created a furor at that time, it eventually died down without having such far-reaching effects as it has today.

It is possible to make use of group intelligence testing without embracing such positions with respect to them. As Carroll and Horn (1981) state, "While questions about the heritability of human abilities are probably worthwhile scientific issues they are irrelevant to consideration about the use of tests in placement and selection" (p. 1013). In other words, one can use tests to select and differentiate without necessarily subscribing to any particular position with respect to the heritability of intelligence or to the extent to which intelligence is a single characteristic, a multiple characteristic, or a trait modifiable by the environment.

Present theories about human abilities do not provide a sound basis for the assertion that a particular IQ score represents a hereditary defect, but the theories do provide a reasonable basis for the probabilistic statement that individuals obtaining a particular IQ score are not likely to do a good job in an occupation where the abilities represented in the IQ test have been shown to be related to good performance in that occupation. (Carroll & Horn, 1981, p. 1017)

CRITICISMS OF THE TESTS THEMSELVES

Tests are criticized with the claims that they do not predict adquately what they are designed to predict, that they tend to favor groups who are sophisticated test takers, that the test scores are subject to improvement with coaching or repetition, that they emphasize unimportant aspects at the expense of aspects crucial for success in school or employment, and that they have not been standardized adequately on certain populations.

Any evaluation of the criticism of group intelligence tests requires some understanding of test constriction and the theory underlying it. Most of the widely used standardized group intelligence tests are developed and distributed by professional testing agencies that use accepted procedures prescribed for designing an effective test. It is true that testing is big business as the critics maintain, but to meet the standards set by the court, legislators, and professional agencies, it is necessary for test developers to have a large staff of highly trained experts. The American Psychological Association (1985) has published a revised set of standards for educational and psychological testing as a guide for those who construct tests, as well as for test users and test administrators. These standards require that large-scale research be carried out to establish test reliability and validity, and that the test be normed on large samples representative of the population with whom the tests are to be used. In addition, a test manual, as well as technical supplements, must be provided to permit the qualified user to make sound judgments regarding the use and interpretation of test scores. Anyone ordering sample tests will be supplied with this information, although technical manuals must be requested as they do not usually come with the specimen sets.

Criticisms that intelligence tests do not predict adequately what they have been designed to predict or that they have not been standardized adequately on certain populations are attacks upon the validity of the tests. As has been established in earlier articles, a test's validity is the extent to which scientifically valuable or practically useful inferences can be drawn from the scores. There are, as we know, four types of validity: content, criterion, concurrent, and construct.

Content validity, also known as face validity, is most relevant to achievement tests, job knowledge tests, and work sample tests. A test has content validity when the items in the test appear, on the face of it, to be relevant to the performance the test is designed to measure. For example, on a test of mechanical knowledge, not mechanical aptitude, the items would have to represent a broad range of mechanical information. Many items on group intelligence tests do not seem to be related to the public's idea of how intelligence should be measured. It is often difficult for some to understand how certain items, such as analogies involving figures, really measure intelligence.

Criterion validity, also known as correlational or predictive validity, is measured by the ability of the test scores to predict performance in some criterion external to the test itself. For example, an elementary school intelligence test would be said to have good criterion validity if the test scores correlated highly with achievement scores or grades in school, because students who score high on an intelligence test are expected to achieve well in school and those who score on the low end are not expected to achieve well. Critics attack the criterion validity of group intelli-

gence tests by giving examples of individuals who did poorly on tests, but turned out to be successful in college, professional school, or in later life. No one who supports testing disagrees that the tests do not predict perfectly, but they make the point that, on the whole, tests predict better than other measures. If the correlation between the intelligence test score and the criterion measure were perfect, namely 1.00, human beings would be perfectly predictable in the area tested. Correlations between intelligence and achievement tests tend to range between .50 and .80. These correlations take into account not only errors due to misclassification as the result of poor test construction, but also errors that occur because of poor motivation, poor testing conditions, and a number of other factors that enter into the test taking. Test publishers, as well as those who do research in this area, have offered extensive evidence of test validity based on large-scale studies of representative samples of the population. Critics of test validity, however, usually base their claims of poor validity on isolated examples of individuals who have been misclassified. Snyderman and Rothman (1987), who did a survey of experts in the field, state, "These claims may well be true, but they are rarely made with sufficient supporting evidence" (p. 137).

An example of a study used to determine criterion validity is one in which 5,000 elementary school pupils in Milwaukee were given an intelligence test in the fourth grade. These results were compared with the results of an achievement test given in the sixth grade. The correlation between the two was .75 (Crano, Kenny, & Campbell, 1972). Another study by the same authors showed that the correlation between the results of the Lorge Thorndike Intelligence Scale given in the fourth grade and the Iowa Tests of Basic Skills, an achievement test, given in the sixth grade, was .73 for a sample of 3,900 suburban children and .61 for a sample of 1500 inner-city children. It is difficult, however, to find studies of elementary school or high school students that attempt to predict success in other than academic areas, because whether children are achieving in terms of their academic potential is a major interest to the schools.

Concurrent validity is the correlation of a previously unvalidated test with an already validated test. This is rarely the only method used to validate a published test, but if this should be so, the user should exercise caution in its use until further data are supplied.

Construct validity is most important from the standpoint of science, just as criterion validity is most important in terms of the practical use of the tests. Construct validity is used to determine whether the test predicts behavior in specific situations that would be deduced from a theory. For example, if a theory of intelligence involved the idea that ability to deal effectively with abstractions was the measure of intelligence, then an intelligence test should involve items measuring abstract reasoning. As has been indicated, one need not subscribe to any particular theory to use an intelligence test, but if general conclusions are to be drawn from the results, the user should be aware of the theory espoused by the test designer.

THEORIES OF INTELLIGENCE

It is not possible in this chapter to do more than mention some of the well-known theories of intelligence. Most have been derived by factor analyzing large numbers of different kinds of tests given to large samples of the population. One of the earliest attempts to explain intelligence was the *two-factor* theory of Spearman (1927), who posited a general factor or "g" and a number of specific factors. Somewhat later, Thurstone (1938) proposed that intelligence was composed of seven "primary mental abilities," each independent of one another. He was not able to demonstrate this independence, however, since the abilities tended to intercorrelate, indicating the presence of "g" or a general factor. Guilford (1959) developed a *structure of intellect* model of intelligence which hypothesized 120 abilities under three categories: content, operations, and products. Guilford believed that the most commonly used group intelligence tests were limited. This limitation resulted because the tests measured only convergent thinking, since the questions required a single correct answer. Under his model Guilford included tests of divergent thinking to measure aspects such as creativity. These items had no correct answers and therefore were difficult to score. Like Thurstone, Guilford attempted to measure abilities that were independent of one another, but many of his tests were shown to correlate with other group tests of intelligence that indicated the presence of a substantial amount of "g." Cattell's (1963) work suggested that intelligence was composed of "fluid" and "crystallized" intelligence. The former was measured by tests that have little informational content, but require the ability to see relationships; the latter was measured by tests of acquired knowledge such as vocabulary and information. Sternberg (1981, 1984, 1985) has begun to look at intelligence in terms of the cognitive processes involved in solving some of the problems presented on intelligence tests. This work is an exten-

sion of that done earlier by French (1965) and MacLeod, Hunt, and Mathews (1978), who showed that different subjects use different cognitive strategies to solve the same kinds of problems. For example, subjects who are good at perceptual ideation may use a perceptual approach to a spatial ability problem, whereas other subjects may use reasoning to solve the problem. Frederiksen (1986), in reviewing this type of research, highlights the limitations of many of our present-day group intelligence tests and the theories underlying them. He concludes that

> the structure of intellect in the future will include a much broader spectrum of intelligent behaviors. Furthermore, it will not be a static model but will be one that recognizes the interactions involving test formats, subject characteristics and the settings in which the problems are encountered. (p. 451)

The many intelligence tests in use today bear certain similarities in content and format, although they use a number of different types of test items. These test items, when combined into a single score, are considered to be a measure of intelligence or general ability known as "g." Most group intelligence tests correlate highly with one another suggesting that although there are differences among them, the "g" factor is being tapped in a number of different ways. Even tests with quite different titles, such as the Scholastic Aptitude Test, the Medical College Admission Test, the Law School Aptitude Test, and the Graduate Record Examination, are almost as highly correlated with one another as are equivalent forms of the same test. For example, Fricke (1975) reported a correlation of .80 between the Scholastic Aptitude Test score taken by 1400 students for college admission and the scores obtained on the Graduate Record Examination four years later.

TEST CONTENT

When test content is considered, the large range of items that can be employed in constructing group intelligence tests becomes apparent. One form of test item is based on knowledge of vocabulary and is usually presented as follows:

> *generous* means charitable openhanded lovingcareful

Vocabulary items are frequently criticized because they are said to measure an individual's education and background. This is true to some extent, but these items show the highest correlation with different types of items that have been found to be good measures of general intelligence. Acquisition of vocabulary is not just a matter of learning and memory, but also requires discrimination, generalization, and education. During childhood and life nearly everyone hears more different words than ever become part of his or her vocabulary. Some people, however, acquire much larger vocabularies than others, and this is true even among siblings of the same family. Vocabulary items can be presented in pictorial form to be used with children and nonreaders; they sometimes appear on group intelligence tests in the lower grades.

Items to tap an individual's range of general information may also be used on group intelligence tests and are open to the same criticism applied to vocabulary items. They correlate highly with other noninformational measures of intelligence because an individual's range of knowledge is a good indication of ability. These items provide the most problems with respect to cultural differences because of the difficulty in determining the range of information an individual from a different culture might be expected to know. For this reason vocabulary items and general information items do not appear as frequently on many group intelligence tests today as they once did.

The most common items on group intelligence tests are those classified as requiring reasoning ability. These may be problems presented in verbal form, numerical form, or pictorial form. For example, an analogies item in verbal form would be as follows:

WOOD is to TREE as PAPER is to: LAKE
IRON   PEN   MILL   PULP

Analogies in a figural format would be similar to those below:

Other types of verbal reasoning items include similarities, an example of which is shown below:

SMART means the same as: LIVELY   HAPPY
AGREEABLE   CLEVER

Another type of item called oddities, or Odd Man Out in British terminology, is as follows:

Underline the word that does not belong with the others: BOOK PENCIL PEN PAD WRITING

Logical reasoning is another type of item that is popular, as in the example below:

Mary is shorter than Ellen.
Joan is taller than Mary.
Who is shortest?

Items that depend upon reasonable inferences and judgment based on the information given are called inferential conclusions. These items are similar in form to items of reading comprehension, except that when used in intelligence tests, the level of vocabulary and reading difficulty are kept simple so that items are not dependent upon vocabulary or reading per se. An example of this kind of item, reported by Jensen (1980, p. 151) and taken from Womer (1970) is as follows:

In a particular meadow there are a great many rabbits that eat the grass. There are also many hawks that eat the rabbits. Last year a disease broke out among the rabbits and most of them died. Which one of the following things most probably occurred?

a) The grass died and the hawk population decreased.
b) The grass died and the hawk population increased.
c) The grass grew taller and the hawk population decreased.
d) The grass grew taller and the hawk population increased.
e) Neither the grass nor the hawks were affected by the death of the rabbits.

In a random sample of the adult population in the United States, 52% chose the correct answer, which was "c." Other test items involve numbers such as those shown below:

Numerical reasoning:
Tom is twice as old as Jim, who is four years old. How old will Tom be when Jim is 15 years old?
Number series:
Write the number that will complete the following series:
3   8   13   18   23   _____

Most of these items fall into the category of multiple-choice items. Critics decry their use on the grounds that such items tap only surface knowledge. Multiple-choice items can be good or bad depending upon the amount of thought put into developing them. The amount of knowledge or reasoning required depends upon the level of the item itself. As may be seen from the item quoted from Womer, a high level of reasoning is involved. Another sample is given by Glaser and Bond (1981). They contrast two multiple-choice questions; both require similar knowledge, but the first item requires only knowledge, the second requires knowledge and reasoning.

1. The mean of a set of values is
   a. the lowest value
   b. the average value
   c. the middle value
   d. the most frequent value
2. The correlation of SAT-verbal or SAT-math among all test takers is about .5. For a group of applicants admitted to Harvard, the correlation is probably
   a. greater than .5 b. about .5 c. less than .5
   d. Anything—no basis for guess

For the second question the student would have to reason that since Harvard is highly selective, the group admitted would have relatively homogeneous test scores, so the correlation will be lower than that of the national group.

There are many other types of verbal and nonverbal test items, all of which have been shown to make a contribution to "g." Jensen (1980) has an exhaustive list of these. When tests must be administered to large groups, as most group intelligence tests are, issues such as ease of administration and ease of scoring become important factors, and these influence the selection of items.

Commonly Used Group Intelligence Tests

One of the more popular group intelligence tests which is intended to provide a measure of "g," or the general intellectual factor, is the Otis-Lennon Mental Ability Test (Otis & Lennon, 1969). The OLMAT is an outgrowth of the original Army Alpha Examination, which was used in classifying World War I recruits. The current test reflects many characteristics of the earlier version but is more refined with regard to psychometric properties. The kindergarten-level form of this test taps areas such as following directions, quantitative reasoning, and comprehension of verbal concepts. Here we can see something of an intuitive arrangement of areas of reasoning that are contributors to and reflect the operation of "g." Scales applicable up to the third-grade level would include more difficult items in these categories but would also involve reasoning-by-analogy items. At higher grade levels, various types of verbal and nonverbal items sample a wide range of mental processes, all believed to reflect and contribute to the general intellectual ability factor. Items are hand or machine scored, and the final score is a normalized standard score (called a deviation IQ), which has a mean of 100 and a standard deviation of 16. Although an IQ is derived, the authors of the test

appear to take a tentative stand on whether the test is, in fact, a measure of intelligence. At one point the test is called a measure of general mental ability, yet at a later point, the reader is informed that the tests do not measure native endowment. Despite the issue of whether group intelligence tests do measure intelligence, virtually all these measures report statistically significant reliability and validity figures. The OLMAT, for example, yields reliability coefficients from about .84 to .90, with the variation a function of the particular age and grade level being assessed. The OLMAT, like most of the group intelligence tests in wide use, is based on a large standardization sample. The OLMAT includes a standardization sample of 200,000 children in kindergarten through high school in 117 school districts throughout the country, and has validity coefficients of .73 and .78 with the individual Wechsler Scales.

A further outgrowth of the Otis series of tests is the Otis-Lennon School Ability Test (Otis & Lennon, 1977). Like its predecessor, the OLMAT, the OLSAT is a paper-and-pencil, multiple-choice test that is group administered and objectively scored. The test is a multilevel battery that is suitable for school settings (grades 1 through 12) and is designed to measure abstract thinking and reasoning ability. The purposes of the OLSAT are to assess examinees' ability to cope successfully with school learning tasks, to classify them for school learning functions. The tight focus on school learning dispenses with the potential interpretational problems that arise when terms such as *mental ability, intelligence,* or *mental maturity* are used. In fact, there is a change from Deviation IQ (DIQ) as used in the OLMAT to the School Ability Index (SAI) on the OLSAT. Nevertheless, the OLSAT, like the OLMAT, is designed to assess a verbal educational factor, and the SAI has the same psychometric and statistical properties as the DIQ. The OLSAT, like its predecessor, the OLMAT, is based on a respectable standardization procedure. In this case it involved 130,000 students in 70 school districts. Reliability estimates range from .84 to .95, depending on the level within the test that is assessed and the method of computing reliability. Validity coefficients range from .40 to .60, and these values are typical of well-constructed psychological tests. The Primary I level of the test consists of objects familiar to the child—ice cream cones, animals, stars, etc., and is thereby helpful in holding the child's attention. Some sample items of the Primary levels are displayed by Anastasi (1982, p. 308).

The Lorge Thorndike Intelligence Test is another popular group-administered scale that is applicable to grades 3 through 13. This test is clearly stated to be a measure of "abstract intelligence," and like the OLMAT, contains both verbal and nonverbal items. The verbal battery is made up of five subtests that include vocabulary, verbal classification, sentence completion, arithmetic reasoning, and verbal analogies. The nonverbal battery contains subtests of pictorial classifications, pictorial analogies, and numerical relationships.

The current edition, called the Multi-Level Edition, has more representative norms than the earlier Separate Level Edition. Validity estimates are readily established as the Lorge-Thorndike was normed on the same samples used for the Iowa Test of Basic Skills, a group-administered test for grades 3 through 8, and the Tests of Academic Progress for grades 9 through 12. Correlations with school performance are typical of the various group tests, and in one case are reported to be .87 with reading and .76 with math. Moderate but significant correlations are found between the Lorge-Thorndike and WISC and Stanford-Binet, and range from .54 to .77. The conglomerate of different types of verbal and nonverbal items again appears to represent an attempt to assess "g" by utilizing some arrangement of tests that correlate with each other and which therefore are assumed to share a common global or general intellectual process.

The Short Form Test of Academic Aptitude (SFTAA), which was published in 1970 and which evolved from the Short Form of the California Test of Mental Maturity (1963), is designed specifically for use in grades 1.5 through 12. The developers of the SFTAA claimed that a number of items on the California Test were ambiguous, unreliable, and not sound predictors of academic performance. Thus, items were dropped and replaced by more robust and reliable items resulting in an 85-item test, compared with the 100 items of the SF-CMMT. These items sampled areas of vocabulary, analogies, sequences, and memory. The test includes items called inferences and are of the following type:

A is shorter than B
B is shorter than C
Who is the shortest, A, B, or C?

Also included are number series, like those of the OLMAT, and numerical quantities, which are items requiring the student to solve arithmetic problems. Finally, in the verbal concepts the student is required to select from four choices the word that is synonymous with the key word. IQs can be obtained from verbal, nonverbal, and total scores.

The recently developed Test of Cognitive Skills (1981) is the latest step in the series and retains many of the features of the earlier tests. The Test of Cognitive Skills (TCS) is applicable to grades 2 through 12. The test's developers claim that this test is a major revision of the SFTAA, yet two of the four major areas of the TCS—Sequences and Analogies—remain the same as those of the SFTAA in structure and rationale. The SFTAA vocabulary test has been replaced by a verbal reasoning test on the TCS. Some of the verbal reasoning items involve inferring relationships among ostensibly unrelated words, identifying essential aspects of objects or concepts, drawing logical conclusions from information given in a short passage, etc. This modification appears to have been effected in order to make comparisons between the TCS and achievement batteries commonly given in schools. Although the SFTAA and TCS both contain a memory test, the two subtests do differ. On the former test, a story is read at the beginning of the test period. Recall items require not only the ability to recall facts and ideas, stated or implied, but also the ability to make inferences and to recall the logical flow of the story. On the TCS, the memory test is designed to provide a measure of memory that is not dependent on reasoning or reading comprehension skills. At upper levels of the TCS, 20 obscure words and their definitions are presented to the students. At some later point, students are required to associate the definition with the appropriate word after having been presented with a set of obscure words.

In testing for college entrance, one test dominates the field: the College Entrance Examination Board's Scholastic Aptitude Test (SAT). This test is given by the College Board to all high school students throughout the nation who wish to take it. The results are then sent to the colleges the student wishes to enter. Most selective colleges require SAT scores, but in many colleges the scores are only one of the factors used in admitting students. Most colleges, however, do have minimum cutoff scores.

The SAT is a paper-and-pencil test containing 150 multiple-choice items with five choices each. There is a verbal section involving reading comprehension, antonyms, verbal analogies, and sentence completion. The mathematics section consists of numerical and quantitative reasoning items, but does not tap formal mathematical knowledge per se. The SAT would undoubtedly load very heavily on the "g" factor in any factor analytic study that included other mental ability tests. The verbal section has been found to correlate higher than the mathematics score with grade point average in college.

The validity of the SAT scores in predicting scores of minority group students has frequently been challenged. In a study by Stanley and Porter (1967), students in three African-American, coeducational, four-year state colleges were compared with students in 15 predominantly white state colleges in Georgia. Correlations of the combined scores with freshman grade point averages was .72 for white females, .63 for African-American females, and .60 for both white and African-American males, suggesting that the prediction for white females is better than for the other three groups. A number of studies have shown that high school grade point averages predict college grade point averages better than the SAT for whites, but not for African-Americans (Cleary, 1968; McKelpin, 1965; Munday, 1965; Peterson, 1968).

In the area of employment, tests have been used in making employment decisions in the United States for over 70 years. Although there are many content-validated job knowledge tests and job sample tests, such as typing tests, the most commonly used have been measures of cognitive skills, called either aptitude or ability tests. According to Schmidt and Hunter (1981), who performed a meta-analysis of a large number of studies in the field of employment testing, the results show that

> professionally developed cognitive ability tests are valid predictors of performance on the job and in training for all jobs in all settings . . . [and that] cognitive ability tests are equally valid for minority and majority applicants and are fair to minority applicants in that they do not underestimate the expected job performance of minority groups. (p. 1128)

The authors offer considerable evidence of the money saved by the use of group tests of general ability. They report that about 10 years ago one large company responded to pressure from the government and dropped all tests of job aptitude. Like many other large companies, this one had a policy of promoting from within. After about seven years the company found that a large percentage of the people they had hired were not promotable, so that the problem was transferred from the hiring level to the promotional level. Schmidt, Hunter, and Pearlman (1981) report the results of a study of 370,000 clerical workers, which showed that the validity of seven cognitive abilities was essentially constant across five different clerical job families. All seven abilities were highly valid in all five job families. The article by Schmidt and Hunter contains a great deal of information about the value

and validity of employment testing and should be read by all interested in this area.

One of the group intelligence tests designed for use in employment selection is the Wonderlic Personnel Test. The author intentionally uses the term *personnel* rather than *intelligence* to reduce the anxiety of those who must take the test. Despite this, the test manual clearly indicates that the intended use of the instrument is to assess mental ability so that a suitable match can be made between the applicant's ability and the ability demanded for a particular job area. One of the advantages, from a personnel screening standpoint, is that the test is administered in only 12 minutes. There are 50 questions, which examinees usually do not finish; they require the examinee to reason in terms of words, numbers, and symbols, and to think using ideas. The test has 14 different forms and has been standardized in business situations, using large numbers of people and test sites. Minimum scores are reported for professions ranging from custodian to administrator and executive. The score reported is the number correct instead of an IQ, thus reducing some of the controversy evoked by the latter term. Norms are available based on sex, age, race, and educational level.

A sampling of items includes the following:

> Assume the first two statements are true. Is the final statement (1) true, (2) false, (3) not certain _____
> _____ Harry is the same age as John. John is younger than Tom. Harry is older than Tom.

It is of interest to note that this item is quite similar to one which might be found in the Inference section of the Short Form of the California Mental Maturity Scale, although the two tests were designed for different purposes.

Other types of items that are similar to those found on the Wonderlic are the following:

> How many square inches are there on a panel that measures 1 foot by 2 feet?
> Are the meanings of the following sentences (1) similar, (2) contradictory or (3) neither _____
> _____? Still water runs deep. You can't tell a book by its cover.

One may ask how valid an instrument can be if it claims to do in 12 minutes what other, more established, measures do in an hour or more. In a study by Dodrill (1981), the Wonderlic was given to a varied group of 120 adults along with the WAIS and other measures. Correlations between the two tests ran from

.91 to .93. Dodrill concluded that when groups of normal individuals are considered, the average error is about 1 IQ point. When persons are considered individually, the Wonderlic yields IQ scores within 10 points of the WAIS 90% of the time. In a later study Dodrill (1983) found that the Wonderlic showed a test-retest reliability of .94. This high degree of stability and similarity with Wechsler scores was attained even with scorers who were not professionally trained.

Edinger, Shipley, Watkins, and Hammett (1985) conducted a study in which the Wonderlic and the WAIS-R were administered to psychiatric patients and found only moderate correlations between the two tests. These authors conlcuded that the Wonderlic was "not an acceptable alternative to the WAIS-R" (p. 937). Dodrill and Warner (1988) criticized this study on methodological grounds and stated that they had used psychiatric, neurological, and normal subjects and had found a high degree of correspondence between the WAIS and Wonderlic. They conlcude that the results "point to the Wonderlic as a measure of general intelligence" (p. 146).

Drawbacks of the Wonderlic are that reading skill is required to take the test and speed is a factor. As a result, it would penalize those with psychomotor deficits. Because the test provides only a single score, it may not be as diagnostically useful as longer tests. These disadvantages are offset by the obvious benefits of a reliable and valid group measure of intelligence that is easily administered and scored. If used in the right context, it is a valuable test.

Not only are group intelligence tests used for educational purposes and for employment, but as indicated earlier, the Armed Forces employ a test of general ability for use in selecting and classifying men in the services. This is the Armed Forces Qualification Test, a 100-item multiple-choice group test. The results classify men into five categories. Category I includes men with scores of 80–10; II, 74–88; III, 53–73; IV, 25–52; and V, 1–24. Those falling in category V are rejected.

A study by Grunzke, Guinn, and Stauffer (1970) compared men in Category IV who were inducted into the Air Force with men in the top three categories. The results showed that the category IV men were less likely to complete basic training, had more undesirable discharges, and were less likely to attain the required levels of skill needed on the job. Correlation between test scores and job training grades was about .50, but this dropped to about .30 for ratings of performance on the job. It was found also that men scoring low on the test had a greater tendency to become disciplinary cases.

Another type of group intelligence test is represented by the Cattell (1973) Culture Fair Intelligence Tests. There are other tests that aim to be culture-fair, culture free, or culture reduced. Davis and Eels developed a test in this area in 1951, but it never gained popularity. Cattell (1940) listed a group of highly universal concepts that would span most cultures and provide a common basis for developing reasoning questions. Among them were common objects: the human body and its parts, footprints, trees (a concept unsuitable for Eskimos), four-legged animals, earth, sky, clouds, sun, moon, stars, lightning, fire, smoke, water, parents, children. In addition, he proposed using common processes, such as breathing, choking, coughing, sneezing, eating, drinking, sleeping, and so on. Despite this original interest in common objects and processes, the items in the Cattell tests are entirely content free and are composed of abstract figural items forming sets of problems in series progression, classification, matrices, and discovering common properties. An example of an item similar to those that appear on the Cattell Culture Fair Test is shown below.

The tests are in paper-and-pencil format and have time limits for each subtest. Scale 1 is intended for children 4 to 8 years old and retarded adults. It has eight subtests, each with a time limit varying from 2 to 4 minutes. There are lengthy instructions for each subtest and although the test time is only 22 minutes, the total time is 60 minutes. Scale 2 is for ages 8 to 13 and average adults, and Scale 3 is for high school, college, and superior adults. The subject's total working time is only 12½ minutes, but the total time is about 30 minutes. Criticisms of this test are strong with respect to the lengthy instructions which cause children to lose attention and become bored. Another problem is that bright adults with learning disability deficits, particularly left-right and reversal difficulties, obtain low scores on this test.

A number of studies done with Cattell's tests have produced mixed results. It has been shown that there are moderate correlations from .20 to .50 with scholastic achievement, and predictive validities have been fairly impressive for certain groups and criteria. Correlations with other intelligence tests are mostly in the .50 to .70 range, suggesting that the test is measuring the "g" factor. The tests have been administered to many culturally different groups outside the United States, producing comparable scores even across quite dissimilar groups—for example, children in the United States, France, England, Hong Kong, and Taiwan. Although the tests show somewhat lower correlations with socioeconomic status than culture loaded or verbal tests, and some bilingual immigrant groups score higher on these tests than on conventional IQ tests, the Cattell does not necessarily reduce the magnitude of the racial differences found with other tests or yield higher scores, on the average, with native-born culturally disadvantaged groups, particularly African-Americans.

Another test that might be considered to be culture fair or culturally reduced is the Raven's Progressive Matrices (Raven, 1941, 1981, 1985). All the test items are composed of geometric figures that require the test taker to select among a series of designs the one that accurately represents the one shown in the stimulus material. The test items are presented in graded levels of difficulty; there are chromatic and achromatic versions and there are test booklets for different age levels. The test was introduced in 1938 and has gone through many revisions. Because it is nonverbal and in most situations requires little more than having the examinee point to the correct item, it is often used in situations where examiners want a measure of ability that is not biased by educational background or by cultural or linguistic deficiencies. Test-retest reliabilities usually range from .80 to .90 depending upon the retest interval and sample. Validity measures involving the correlation of the Raven with the Binet and Wechsler Scales range from .54 to .86 (Raven, Court, & Raven, 1983, pp. 8–9). The authors indicate that "the scales can be described as 'tests of observation and clear thinking.' . . . By themselves they are not tests of 'general intelligence'. . . . They should be used in conjunction with a vocabulary test" (p. 3). Despite this caution, the Progressive Matrices have been viewed as measures of intelligence and have been widely used in many countries to test military groups because they are considered to be independent of prior learning.

An unusually extensive investigation involving Raven's Matrices and other ability tests was carried out by Flynn (1987). In this study, Flynn attempted to track IQ trends from one generation to the next in various cultures. Data were obtained from 14 nations involving samples of tens of thousands of subjects in order to determine whether IQ gains had occurred as had been suggested by previous studies in different

countries. After reviewing the results, Flynn noted that there were large gains in measured IQ over a 30-year period and that the gains on the culturally reduced tests such as Raven's Matrices were twice the size of gains with tests involving verbal ability. Based on this data he concluded: "The [Raven's] test does not measure intelligence but rather a correlate with a weak causal link to intelligence" (p. 187).

At the other end of the continuum are those tests that are designed to reflect a unique knowledge of a given culture. An example of this type of scale is the BITCH Culture Specific Test by Williams (1972). The acronym stands for Black Intelligence Test of Cultural Homogeneity. The author of this test set out to demonstrate that one's performance on a test can be affected by prior cultural experience. The test contains a vocabulary that reflects African-American slang and, as might be expected, African-Americans score significantly better on it than do whites. The test's value probably is that it sensitizes us to the extent to which one's performance can vary due to prior knowledge; its major drawback is that it does not correlate with known measures of intelligence (Matarazzo & Weins, 1977). The latter finding can, of course, be countered by the notion that one would not expect to find a correlation between popular standardized intelligence tests that are considered by some to be culturally biased in terms of the dominant culture and one that is biased in favor of a minority group.

In general, the standardized group intelligence tests predict reasonably well the ability of most individuals to succeed in the dominant culture; the use of other instruments at this point has not been able to do as well in predicting this success. Whether these same group intelligence tests are useful in predicting the ability of individuals from minority cultures to succeed in early education, college, professional schools, and later life is too large an area to treat in this chapter. Many aspects of this problem are addressed by the 1980 book by Jensen, *Bias in Mental Testing,* as well as "Critical Factors in Testing Hispanic Americans" by Padilla (1979), "Diverse Human Populations and Problems in Education Program Evaluation via Achievement Testing" by Gordon (1977), and "The Futility of a Comparative IQ Research" by Garcia (1975). All these writings contain extensive references and supporting data. There can be no doubt that it is in the best interest of all concerned citizens that tests affecting the lives of so many be designed and used so that they provide a fair evaluation. Professionals, educators, and the public have an obligation to look at research findings and outcomes on both sides of the question, not only the side to which they have an emotional attachment.

LEGISLATED CHANGES

A review of some of the changes made in response to criticisms of group intelligence testing offers some perspective on a field in flux. Some of the changes have resulted in improvements; others have not had such a favorable outcome. As mentioned previously, there are court-ordered moratoriums on group intelligence testing in California and other large cities of the nation. In addition, in California there is a court mandate that no more than a certain percentage of minority children may be placed in special classes for the retarded. In Chicago (Cordes, 1983), the school system, as part of its court-approved desegregation plan and in an attempt to meet the objections of the critics, adopted a ban on standardized intelligence tests and made a commitment to reassess all children classified as mildly mentally retarded, using other methods. To do so, school psychologists developed a battery including psychometric tests, assessment of adaptation, clinical techniques, behavioral observations, consultations, and team discussions. No cutoff scores on any measures were used. Although the critics originally had objected to the use of standardized intelligence tests, at this juncture they are bringing suit because the present battery has not been standardized and validated and because there are no cutoff scores. It is apparent that it is easy to legislate changes, but the changes do not always improve the situation, even in the eyes of the critics.

Another legislated change took place in New York State in 1980. This was passage of the "truth-in-testing" law, aimed at giving the consumer more knowledge regarding the product being utilized. Under this law, the questions and answers that determine an examinee's score on college and professional school admission tests must be disclosed within 30 days of release of test scores. Many of these are group intelligence tests, although they are not always labeled as such. As soon as this law went into effect, the Association of American Medical Colleges brought suit against the state of New York on the grounds that there is a limited number of high-quality questions that can be designated for a test such as the Medical College Admissions Test. Within a month a federal judge ordered a preliminary injunction exempting this test from the New York State law until the legal merits of the case could be considered in court. Also as a reaction to this law, the Psychological Corporation,

publishers of the Miller Analogies Test, stopped administering it in New York; the Educational Testing Service reduced the schedule for administration of the Graduate Record Examinations and eliminated entirely certain sections of this examination for New York. Students who wish to take some of these examinations must do so in neighboring states. The actions of these companies were based on their claim that they cannot continue to construct new, reliable questions, which they would have to do if test questions and answers were made public on a regular basis.

The difficulty of developing highly discriminating, effective test items was highlighted in a number of well-publicized incidents resulting from the "truth-in-testing" law. The newspapers and those opposed to testing reveled in the report that a school boy in Florida was able to demonstrate that his answer on one question on the Scholastic Aptitude Test was the correct one; although it was not the answer designated as correct by the publishers of the test, the Educational Testing Service. "Youth outwits merit exam, raising 240,000 scores," stated *The New York Times* of March 17, 1980. As Haney (1981) reports, there were several other incidents of this type involving an SAT mathematics question, two faulty items on the Graduate Record examination, and another on a Law School Admissions Test. Clearly, incidents of this kind are bound to make those who develop and review the test questions very careful, but the relevance of errors of this sort is questionable with respect to the larger issues involved.

CHANGES MADE BY TEST DEVELOPERS AND PUBLISHERS

One of the criticisms directed at the tests themselves is that some groups have more experience and are better prepared to take tests than others, and that the test scores improve with better preparation and with practice. Research supporting these criticisms has shown that short orientation and practice sessions can be effective in equalizing test sophistication (Millman, Bishop, & Ebel, 1965) and that significant mean gains have been shown when alternate forms of the same test have been administered over time within a range of one day to several years (Angoff, 1971; Droege, 1966). To answer this criticism the large test companies—such as the Psychological Corporation, the Educational Testing Service, and the College Board—as well as the United States Employment Service, have prepared booklets on how to take tests. In addition, the United States Employment Service has introduced a more extensive orientation for educationally disadvantaged applicants (U.S. Department of Labor, 1968, 1970, 1971).

To assess the impact of a new booklet, *Taking the SAT,* that it had prepared (Alderman & Powers, 1980), the College Board sent a prepublication copy to a sample of 1,000 high school juniors who had registered for the SAT. This group also received a copy of an earlier booklet, *About the SAT.* A control group of 1,000 comparable registrants received only the earlier booklet. The new booklet contained detailed analyses of different item types included on the SAT along with suggestions for answering the items. In addition, there was a complete form of the SAT—accompanied by a scoring key—that the student could take under standard testing conditions. After the actual administration of the SAT both groups were asked to complete questionnaires. The results showed that nearly all respondents in the experimental sample reported some use of the booklet, but only 38% had read the entire booklet. Only 36% reported having tried to answer all the questions, and 23% had answered none. Significantly more experimental than control subjects believed that their test performance had been helped by the material they had received, but their actual scores showed no difference between the groups. It would appear that the original material was as effective as the more extensive material in terms of outcome. However, studies have shown that test-retest with alternate forms improves scores; therefore, the results might have been different if 100% of the experimental group had taken the sample test.

The criticism that test scores improve as the result of coaching is not new and has been the subject of considerable research. Anastasi (1981) covered many of these studies, some of which were done in the United States, and some in England over a long period. The British studies were concerned with the examinations given there to all 11-year-old school children as a means of assigning them to different types of advanced education. In general, these studies showed that the extent of improvement depended on the ability and earlier educational experiences of the examinees, the nature of the tests, and the type of coaching. Children with poor educational background benefited most from special coaching; the closer the similarity between test content and coaching material, the greater was the improvement in test scores.

At the present time there are many coaching courses offered in the United States for those preparing to take college entrance examinations as well as professional examinations in areas such as law and psychology. Studies conducted by the College Board on the effects of coaching courses on subsequent scores showed that the usual short high school coaching programs yielded average gains of approximately 10 points in SAT Verbal scores and approximately 15 points in SAT Mathematics scores. More intensive and longer commercial programs showed gains as high as 20 points on the Verbal scores and 30 on the Mathematics scores.

Most of the gains achieved through coaching are shortlived because knowledge obtained through intensive drill does not translate into increased ability to do well on the criterion measure, which is usually college or professional school performance. It takes a long time to accumulate the relevant knowledge that is part of what many psychologists consider intelligence and that contributes to a person's readiness to learn more advanced material. When coaching improves test performance without adding to the individual's permanent store of knowledge, it reduces test validity and the test becomes a poorer measure of the broad abilities it was designed to assess. Well-constructed tests employ items least susceptible to drill and short-term coaching, so that the tests may continue to be an accurate means of ascertaining whether the individual has acquired the skills and knowledge necessary for success in the criterion.

One of the problems in meeting the criticisms made of group intelligence tests is the difficulty of finding satisfactory substitutes for them. As was seen in the Chicago schools, the new evaluation techniques found no more favor with the critics than did the original tests. Another example of this was reported in *The New York Times* on March 20, 1983. The story by Treaster is headlined "New Police Test is Called Unfair"; it reports: "Scores of New York City police sergeants are charging that a new Police Department examination that was designed to overcome racial and sexual biases was unfair to them. Four lawsuits have been filed." According to the article, the new test was designed to overcome the objections of the courts that previous police examinations were discriminatory because they consisted entirely of multiple-choice questions and the test was similar to a group intelligence test. The new test was a departure from the usual pencil-and-paper tests. In the first part the candidates were given a basket of papers that the department said was typical of what a lieutenant would find when he reported for work at a precinct station; they were asked to respond to the problems raised in the papers by indicating answers to 47 multiple-choice questions. The second part consisted of 75 multiple-choice questions about police procedures and regulations. In the third part the candidates were asked to assume the role of a lieutenant and conduct a 30-minute meeting with a person playing the role of a police sergeant who, the candidate was told, had been experiencing some job performance problems. This part was videotaped and graded at the headquarters of the company that had designed the test. On the new test, the pass rate for white males was 30%, for women was 29%, for Hispanics was 23%, and for African-Americans was 20%. Almost no women, Hispanics, or African-Americans had passed the previous tests. As may be seen, innovative methods of testing can be developed to meet the criticisms leveled at group intelligence tests; however, they are expensive to construct and give, they need to be validated by on-the-job performance, and they are clearly not beyond challenges.

SUMMARY

A review of the history of testing suggests that it is unlikely that testing will disappear despite attacks and actions by legislatures and courts. In highly developed countries, such as our own, as well as in emerging cultures there is a continuing demand for some means of evaluation and selection to aid in personal decisions in the area of education and employment. Articles written in other cultures indicate these countries are struggling with the same problems concerning group intelligence tests that we are in the United States. For example, Watkins and Astilla (1980) reported on a followup of 1149 freshmen at a major Filipino university. Their findings showed that the college entrance examination, the Otis-Lennon Mental Abilities Test, and the high school grade point average were only moderately successful predictors of college performance. When they looked at nonintellectual factors, however, such as socioeconomic status, scholastic expectations, family constellation, and results of the California Personality Inventory, they found these had no value as predictors.

Another attempt to find predictors for success in completing the West African School Certificate Examination was reported by Obemesta (1980) in the *West African Journal of Education and Vocational Measurement*. One group of secondary school students was given a preliminary test in Yoruba and a control group was given the test in English. Five years later their progress was checked, and it was found that both tests showed moderate correlations with success on the Certificate examination, but that the tests given in Yoruba predicted no better than the tests given in English.

It is clear that tests will continue to be a part of modern life. Therefore, one can hope that users of group intelligence tests will be sensitive to the social context within which the tests are to be used, the professional manner in which they should be used, and the adequacy of their construction. The public and professional controversies that have been reviewed have been valuable in highlighting some of the problems associated with testing. Perhaps these controversies will serve as an impetus for psychologists to look at testing in new and creative ways and work to develop tests that will serve the public good.

REFERENCES

Adlerman, D. L., & Powers, D. E. (1980). The effects of special preparation on SAT-verbal scores. *American Educational Research Journal, 17*, 239–253.

American Psychological Association. (1985). *Standards for educational and psychological tests.* Washington, DC: Author

Anastasi, A. (1981). Coaching, test sophistication, and developing abilities. *American Psychologist, 36*, 1086–1093.

Anastasi, A. (1982). *Psychological testing* (5th Ed.). New York: Macmillan.

Angoff, W. H. (Ed.). (1971). *The College Board admissions testing program: A technical report on research and development activities relating to the Scholastic Aptitude test and achievement tests.* New York: College Entrance Examination Board

Black, H. (1962). *They shall not pass.* New York: Random House.

Born dumb? (1969). *Newsweek, 73*(13), 84.

Brigham, C. C. (1923). *A study of American intelligence.* Princeton, NJ: Princeton University Press.

Burks, B. S. (1928). The relative influences of nature and nurture upon mental development. *27th yearbook of the National Society for the Study of Education* (Vol. 1), 219–316.

California Short-Form Test of Mental Maturity. (1963). Monterey, CA: CTB McGraw-Hill.

Carroll, J. B. & Horn, J. L. (1981). On the scientific basis of ability testing. *American Psychologist, 36*, 1012–1020.

Cattell, R. B. (1940). A culture free intelligence test, Part I. *Journal of Educational Psychology, 31*, 161–179.

Cattell, R. B. (1963). Theory of fluid and crystallized intelligence: A critical experiment. *Journal of Educational Psychology, 54*, 1–22.

Cattell, R. B. (1973). Cattell Culture Fair Intelligence Tests. Champaign, IL: Institute for Personality and Ability Testing.

Cleary, T. A. (1968). Test bias: Prediction of grades of negro and white students in integrated colleges. *Journal of Educational Measurement, 5,* 115–124.

Cordes, C. (1983). Chicago school reassessment renews debate on role of tests. *APA Monitor, 14,* 14–15.

Crano, W. D., Kenny, D. A. & Campbell, D. T. (1972). Does intelligence cause achievement? A cross-lagged panel analysis. *Journal of Educational Psychology, 63,* 258–275.

Cronbach, L. (1975). Five decades of public controversy over mental testing. *American Psychologist, 3,* 1–14.

Dodrill, C. B. (1981). An economical method for the evaluation of general intelligence in adults. *Journal of Consulting and Clinical Psychology, 49,* 668–673.

Dodrill, C. B. (1983). Long-term reliability of the Wonderlic Personnel Test. *Journal of Consulting and Clinical Psychology, 51,* 316–317.

Dodrill, C. B., & Warner, M. H. (1988). Further studies of the Wonderlic Personnel Test as a brief measure of intelligence. *Journal of Consulting and Clinical Psychology, 56,* 145–147.

Droege, R. C. (1966). Effects of practice on aptitude scores. *Journal of Applied Psychology, 50,* 306–310.

Edinger, J. D., Shipley, R. H., Watkins, E. C., Jr., & Hammett, E. B. (1985). Validity of the Wonderlic Personnel Tests: A brief IQ measure in psychiatric patients. *Journal of Consulting and Clinical Psychology, 53,* 937–939.

Eels, K., Davis, A., Havighurst, R. J., Herricks, V. E., & Tyler, R. (1951). *Intelligence and cultural differences.* Chicago: University of Chicago Press.

Fine, B. (1975). *The stranglehold of the IQ* New York: Doubleday.

Fiske, E. (1981, April 28). Soul searching in the testing establishment. *New York Times.*

Flynn, J. R. (1987). Massive IQ gains in 14 nations: What IQ tests really measure. *Psychological Bulletin, 101,* 171–191.

Frederiksen, N. (1986). Toward a broader conception of human intelligence. *American Psychologist, 41,* 445–452.

Freeman, F. N. (1923). A referendum of psychologists. *Century Illustrated Magazine, 107,* 237–245.

Freeman, F. N., Holzinger, K. J., & Mitchell, B. C. (1928). The influence of environment on the intelligence of school achievement and conduct of foster children. *27th yearbook of the National Society for the Study of Education* (Vol. 1), 103–217.

French, J. W. (1965). The relationship of problem solving styles to the factor composition of tests. *Educational and Psychological Measurement, 25,* 9–28.

Fricke, B. G. (1975). *Report to the faculty: Grading, testing, standards and all that.* Ann Arbor: Evaluation and Examinations Office, University of Michigan.

Garcia, J. (1975). The futility of a comparative IQ research. In N. A. Buchwald & M. A. Brazier (Eds.), *Brain mechanisms in mental retardation.* New York: Academic Press.

Glaser, R., & Bond, L. (1981). Testing: Concepts, policy, practice and research. *American Psychologist, 36,* 997–1000.

Gordon, E. W. (1977). Diverse human populations and problems in educational program evaluation via achievement testing. In J. J. Wargo & D. R. Green (Eds.), *Achievement testing of disadvantaged and minority students for educational program evaluation.* New York: CTB/McGraw-Hill.

Gordon, E. W., & Terrell, M. D. (1981). The changed social context of testing. *American Psychologist, 36,* 1167–1171.

Goslin, D. (1963). *The search for ability.* New York: Russell Sage.

Gross, M. (1962). *The brain watchers.* New York: Random House.

Grunzke, N., Guinn, N., & Stauffer, G. (1970). *Comparative performances of low-ability airmen.* Technical Report 74. Lackland AFB, TX: Air Force Human Resources Laboratory.

Guilford, J. P. (1959). Three faces of intellect. *American Psychologist, 14,* 469–479.

Haney, W. (1981). Validity, vaudeville and values. *American Psychologist, 36,* 1021–1034.

Hargadon, F. (1981). Tests and college admissions. *American Psychologist, 36,* 1112–1119.

Herrnstein, R. (1971, September). I.Q. *Atlantic-Monthly,* 43–64.

Hoffman, B. (1962). *The tyranny of testing.* New York: Collier.

Jensen, A. R. (1969). How much can we boost IQ and scholastic achievement? *Harvard Educational Review, 39,* 1–123.

Jensen, A. R. (1980). *Bias in mental testing.* New York: Free Press.

Lerner, B. (1980). The war on testing: David, Goliath and Gallup. *Public Interest, 60,* 119–147.

Chuan-ting, Lin. (1980). A sketch on the methods of

mental testing in ancient China. *Acta Psychologica Sinica, 12,* 75–80.

Linn, R. L. (1982). Admissions testing on trial. *American Psychologist, 37,* 279–291.

Lippman, W. (1922a). The mental age of Americans. *New Republic, 32,* 213–215.

Lippman, W. (1922b). Tests of hereditary intelligence. *New Republic, 32,* 328–330.

Lippman, W. (1923). Rich and poor, girls and boys. *New Republic, 34,* 295–296.

Lommatzsch, H. (1929). Sur frage der intelligenzprüfungen. [On the question of intelligence testing.] *Hohere Schule i Sachsen, 7,* 345–347.

Lorge, I., Thorndike, R. L., & Hagen, E. (1966). The Lorge-Thorndike Intelligence Tests. New York: Riverside Publishing.

MacLeod, C. M., Hunt, E. B., & Mathews, N. N. (1978). Individual differences in the verification of sentence-picture relationships. *Journal of Verbal Learning and Verbal Behavior, 17,* 493–507.

Madge, E. M. (1979). *The intelligent use of intelligence tests.* Pretoria, South Africa: Human Science Research Council Institute for Psychometric Research.

Matarazzo, J. D., & Wiens, A. N. (1977). Black Intelligence Test of Cultural Homogeneity and Wechsler Adult Intelligence Scale scores of black and white police applicants. *Journal of Applied Psychology, 62,* 57–63.

McKelpin, J. C. (1965). Some implications of the intellectual characteristics of freshmen entering a liberal arts college. *Journal of Educational Measurement, 2,* 161–166.

Millman, J., Bishop, C. H., & Ebel, R. (1965). An analysis of test-wiseness. *Educational and Psychological Measurement, 25,* 707–726.

Munday, L. (1965). Predicting college grades in predominantly Negro colleges. *Journal of Educational Measurement, 2,* 157–160.

Nairn, A. (1980). *The reign of ETS: The corporation that makes up minds.* Washington: Nader.

Obemesta, J. O. (1980). A verbal intelligence test in the mother tongue as a predictor of success in the School Certificate Examination. *West African Journal of Educational and Vocational Measurement, 5,* 7–12.

Otis, A. S., & Lennon, R. T. (1968). *Otis-Lennon Mental Ability Test: Manual for administration.* New York: Harcourt Brace Jovanovich.

Otis, A. S., & Lennon, R. T. (1969). Otis-Lennon Mental Ability Test. New York: Harcourt, Brace, & World.

Otis, A. S., & Lennon, R. T. (1977). *Otis-Lennon*

School Ability Test. New York: Harcourt Brace Jovanovich.

Padilla, A. M. (1979). Critical factors in the testing of Hispanic Americans. In R. W. Tyler & S. H. White (Eds.), *Testing, teaching and learning: Report of a conference on testing.* Washington, DC: National Institute of Education.

Peterson, R. E. (1968). Predictive validity of a brief test of academic aptitude. *Educational and Psychological Measurement, 28,* 441–444.

Pintner, R. (1923). *Intelligence Testing.* New York: Henry Holt.

Raven, J. C. (1941). Standardization of Progressive Matrices. *British Journal of Medical Psychology, 19,* 137–150.

Raven, J. C. (1981). *Manual for Raven's Progressive Matrices and Mill Hill Vocabulary Scales* (Research Supplement No. 1). London: H. K. Lewis.

Raven, J. C., Court, J. H., & Raven, J. (1983). *Manual for Raven's Progressive Matrices and Vocabulary Scales. Standard Progressive Matrices (Sect 1.).* London: H. K. Lewis.

Raven, J. C., Court, J. H., & Raven, J. (1985). *Manual for Raven's Progressive Matrices and Vocabulary Scales. Standard Progressive Matrices (Sect 3.).* London: H. K. Lewis.

Reschly, D. J. (1981). Psychological testing in educational classification and placement. *American Psychologist, 36,* 1094–1102.

Rosenthal, R., & Jacobsen, L. (1968). *Pygmalion in the classroom.* New York: Holt, Rinehart, and Winston.

Rowan, C. T. (1970). How racists use "science" to degrade black people. *Ebony, 25,* 31–40.

Schmidt, F. L., & Hunter, J. E. (1981). Employment testing: Old theories and new research findings. *American Psychologist, 36,* 1128–1137.

Schmidt, F. L., Hunter, J. E., & Pearlman, K. (1981). Task differences and validity of aptitude tests in selection: A red herring. *Journal of Applied Psychology, 66,* 166, 185.

Short Form Test of Academic Aptitude, (1970). Monterey, CA: CTB/McGraw-Hill.

Snyderman, M., & Rothman, S. (1987). Survey of expert opinion on intelligence and aptitude testing. *Amerian Psychologist, 42,* 137–144.

Spearman, C. (1927). *The abilities of man.* New York: MacMillan.

Stanley, J. C., & Porter, A. C. (1967). Correlation of Scholastic Aptitude Test scores with college grades for Negroes versus whites. *Journal of Educational Measurement, 4,* 199–218.

Sternberg, R. J. (1981). Nothing fails like success:

The search for an intelligent paradigm for studying intelligence. *Journal of Educational Psychology, 73,* 142–155.

Sternberg, R. J. (Ed.). (1984). *Human abilities: An information processing approach.* New York: Freeman.

Sternberg, R. J. (1985). *Beyond IQ: A triarchic theory of human intelligence.* New York: Cambridge University Press.

Test of Cognitive Skills. (1981). Monterey, CA: CTB/McGraw-Hill.

Terman, L. M. (1922a). The great conspiracy. *New Republic, 33,* 116–120.

Terman, L. M. (1922b). The psychological determinist: Or democracy and the IQ. *Journal of Educational Research, 6,* 57–62.

Thurstone, L. L. (1938). *Primary mental abilities* (Psychometric Monographs, No. 1). Chicago: University of Chicago Press.

Treaster, J. B. (1983, March 20). New police test called unfair. *New York Times,* p. 24.

U.S. Department of Labor, Employment and Training Administration. (1968). *Pretesting orientation exercises* (Manual; Test Booklet). Washington, DC: U.S. Government Printing Office.

U.S. Department of Labor, Employment and Training Administration. (1970). *Pretesting orientation on the purposes of testing* (Manual: Illustrations). Washington, DC: U.S. Government Printing Office.

U.S. Department of Labor, Employment and Training Administration. (1971). *Doing your best on aptitude tests.* Washington, DC: U.S. Government Printing Office.

Vernon, P. E. (1979). Intelligence testing: 1928–1978. *British Journal of Educational Psychology, 49,* 1–14.

Watkins, D., & Astilla, E. (1980). Intellective and non-intellective predictors of academic achievement at a Filipino University. *Educational and Psychological Measurement, 40,* 245–249.

Williams, R. L. (1972). *The BITCH Test (Black Intelligence Test of Cultural Homogeneity).* St. Louis, MO: Black Studies Program, Washington University.

Womer, F. B. (1970). National assessment says. *Measurement in Education, 2,* 1–8.

Wonderlic, E. F. (1945). Personnel test. New York: The Psychological Corporation.

Wonderlic, E. F. (1978). *Wonderlic Personnel Test manual.* Northfield, IL: E. F. Wonderlic & Associates.

Yerkes, R. M. (1923). Testing the human mind. *Atlantic Monthly, 131,* 358–370.

Youth outwits merit exam, raising 240,000 scores. (1980, March 17). *New York Times,* p. 17.

Zeidner, M. (1988). Culture fairness in aptitude testing revisited: A cross-cultural parallel. *Professional Psychology: Research and Practice, 19,* 257–262.

ACHIEVEMENT, APTITUDE, AND INTEREST

CHAPTER 7

ACHIEVEMENT TESTING

Lynda J. Katz
Gregory T. Slomka

INTRODUCTION

During the mid-1970s the use of standardized tests among a variety of elementary, secondary, and post-secondary educational programs came under severe criticism. It had been reported that the use of standardized achievement tests in particular involved over 80% of American school children, with some of these children taking 26 achievement tests during a school career (National School Boards Association, 1977). It has been postulated that this national concern with standardized tests has resulted from competition among the "baby boom" generation children of the late 1940s and early 1950s for "scarce slots in the choicest schools and businesses," so that their stakes of doing well or poorly on tests went up. Second, those same baby boomers were looking back on their experiences with years of taking standardized tests and were very sensitive to the perceived abuses of such testing (Strenio, 1981, p. XVIII). The main criticisms of these tests have centered around the quality of the tests themselves, the use to which they are put, the behavior of the test industry (some 40 to 50 test publishers responsible for 90% of the tests used in the country today), and the consequences for society of the misuse of these tests. In addition, major court cases and federal legislation for exceptional children have addressed specifically the use of tests and testing as part of the overall assessment process (*Larry P. v. Riles* and P.L. 94-142), again in response to these same criticisms.

In November, 1975, at a conference on testing sponsored by the National Association of Elementary School Principals and the North Dakota Study Group on Evaluation, 25 national organizations including the U.S. Office of Education drafted the following statement:

> We believe that the public, and especially educators, parents, and children, need fair and effective assessment processes that can be used for diagnosing and prescribing for the needs of individual children.
>
> We also believe that the use of fair, effective assessment practices is one way of being held accountable for providing quality education for all students.
>
> We have grave reservations, however, about any continued use of so-called IQ tests.
>
> In regard to standardized achievement tests, we have agreed on the following recommendations:
>
> 1. The profession needs to place a high priority on developing and putting into wide use new processes of assessment that are more fair and effective than those currently in use and that more adequately consider the diverse talents, abilities, and cultural backgrounds of children.
> 2. Parents and educators need to be much more actively involved in the planning and processes of assessment.
> 3. Any assessment results reported to the public must include explanatory material that details the limitations inherent in the assessment instruments used.
> 4. Educational achievement must be reported in terms broader than single-score national norms, which can be misleading.
> 5. Information about assessment processes should be shared among the relevant professions, policy makers, and the public so that appropriate improvements and reforms can be discussed by all parties.
> 6. Every standardized test administered to a child should be returned to the school for analysis by the teachers, parents, and child.

7. Further, the standardized tests used in any given community should be made publicly available to that community to give citizens an opportunity to understand and review the tests in use.

8. The professions, the public, and the media need to give far greater consideration to the impact of standardized testing on children and young people, particularly on those below the age of ten.

9. A comprehensive study should be conducted on the actual administration and use of standardized tests and the use of test scores in the schools today. (National School Boards Association, 1977, p. 18)

Thus, it is relevant and timely more than a decade later to

- review the historical development, classification, and psychometric properties of traditional achievement tests;
- update their status and use in terms of contemporary educational and clinical research and practice;
- consider the relationship of achievement testing to ecological and sociocultural variables and their use with special population groups; and
- take a futuristic look at the impact of modern computer technology on test construction and utilization.

Such a discussion may determine whether these recommendations regarding the use of achievement tests long since made, have been or will need to continue to be addressed.

Historical Development of Achievement Tests

The standardized objective achievement test based upon a normative sample was first developed by Rice in 1895. His spelling test of 50 words (with alternate forms) was administered to 16,000 students in grades 4 through 8 across the country. Rice went on to develop tests in arithmetic and language, but his major contribution was his objective and scientific approach to the assessment of student knowledge (DuBois, 1970). Numerous other single-subject-matter achievement tests were developed in the first decade of the twentieth century, but it was not until the early 1920s that the publication of test batteries emerged: in 1923, the Stanford Achievement Test at the elementary level, and in 1925, the Iowa High School Content Examination (Mehrens & Lehmann, 1975). Since the 1940s, there has been a movement toward testing in broad areas as well, such as the humanities and natural sciences rather than in specialized, single-subject-

matter tests. Moreover, attention has been directed toward the evaluation of work-study skills, comprehension, and understanding, rather than factual recall per se. In the 1970s, standardized tests were developed that were keyed to particular test books, the use of "criterion-referenced" tests (CRTs) emerged (their dissimilarity from norm-referenced tests will be addressed in the next section), and the development of "tailored-to-user specifications" tests (Mehrens & Lehmann, 1975, p. 165) was initiated.

Now in the 1990s, the literature on achievement testing is concerned with latent-trait theory, item-response curves, and an assessment of learning achievement that is brief into the instructional process. The intrinsic nature of achievement tests themselves is changing. Computer-adaptive testing is not the computerization of standardized norm-referenced paper-and-pencil tests but a radically different approach. The approach is based on a concept of a continuum of learning and where a particular child fits on that continuum so that his or her experience with testing is one of success rather than failure. To appreciate fully this dramatic shift in the conceptualization of the assessment of achievement it is first necessary to understand (a) the nature of tests which fall under the domain of achievement; (b) the psychometric underpinnings of achievement tests; (c) the basis for criterion-referenced as opposed to norm-referenced measurement; and (d) particular issues which arise when achievement tests are used for particular purposes.

Classification of Achievement Tests

Achievement tests have generally been categorized as single-subject tests, survey batteries, or diagnostic tests and further dichotomized as group or individually administered tests. Reference to the *Ninth Mental Measurement Yearbook* (1985) reveals the prevalence of multitudinous published objective tests, and elsewhere it has been reported that some 2,585 standardized tests are in use (Buros, 1974). Table 7.1 is a listing of the most commonly used achievement tests. They have been categorized as (a) group administered, (b) individually administered, and (c) modality specific tests of achievements, which can be either group or individually administered.

Typically one administers achievement tests in order to obtain an indication of general academic skill competencies or a greater understanding of an individual's performance in a particular area of academic performance. In this regard achievement tests are specifically designed to measure "degree of learning"

Table 7.1. Commonly Used Achievement Tests

Group Administered Achievement Tests

California Achievement Tests	CTB/McGraw Hill. (1984). California Achievement Tests. Monterey, CA: Author.
Iowa Test of Basic Skills	Hieronymus, E. F., Lindquist, H. D., Hoover, D., et al. (1978). Iowa Test of Basic Skills. Chicago, IL: Riverside Publishing.
Metropolitan Achievement Tests	Balow, I. H., Farr, R., Hogan, T. P., Prescott, G. A. (1978). Metropolitan Achievement Tests (5th ed.). Cleveland, OH: Psychological Corporation.
Stanford Achievement Test	Gardner, E. G., Rudman, H. C., Karlson, B., & Merwin, J. C. (1982). Stanford Achievement Test. Cleveland, OH: Psychological Corporation.
SRA Achievement Services (SRA)	Naslond, R. A., Thorpe, L. P., & Lefever, D. W. (1978). SRA Achievement Series, Chicago, IL: Science Research Associates.

Individually Administered Achievement Tests

Basic Achievement Skills Individual Screener (BASIS)	Psychological Corporation. (1983). Basic Achievement Skills Individual Screener. San Antonio: Author.
Kaufman Test of Educational Achievement	Kaufman, A. S., & Kaufman, N. G. (1985). Kaufman Test of Individual Achievement. Circle Pines, MN: American Guidance Service.
Peabody Individual Achievement Test—Revised	Markwarat, F. C. (1989). Peabody Individual Achievement Test. Circle Pines, MN: American Guidance Service.
Wide Range Achievement Test	Jastak, S., & Wilkinson, G. S. (1984). Wide Range Achievement Test—Revised. Wilmington, DE: Jastak Associates.
Woodcock Johnson Psychoeducational Battery	Woodcock, R. W. (1977). Woodcock Johnson Psychoeducational Battery: Technical Report. Allen, TX: DLM Teaching Resources.

Modality Specific Achievement Tests

Reading

Classroom Reading Inventory	Silvaroli, N. J. (1986). Classroom Reading Inventory (5th ed.). Dubuque, IA: Wm. C. Brown.
Diagnostic Reading Scales	Spache, G. D. (1981). Diagnostic Reading Scales. Monterey, CA: CTB/McGraw-Hill.
Durrell Analysis of Reading Difficulty	Durrell, D. D., & Catterson, J. H. (1980). Durrell Analysis of Reading Difficulty (3rd ed.). Cleveland, OH: Psychological Corporation.
New Sucher-Allred Reading Placement Survey	Sucher, F., & Allred, R. A. (1981). New Sucher-Allred Reading Placement Inventory. Oklahoma City: Economy Company.
Gates-MacGinitie Reading Tests	MacGinitie, W. H., et al. (1978). Gates-MacGinitie Reading Tests. Chicago, IL: Riverside Publishing.
Nelson-Denny Reading Test	Brown, J. I., Bennett, M., & Hanna, G. (1981). Nelson-Denny Reading Test. Chicago, IL: Riverside Publishing Co.
Stanford Diagnostic Reading Test	Karlson B., Madden, R., & Gardner, E. F. (1976). Stanford Diagnostic Reading Test (1976 ed.). Cleveland, OH: Psychological Corporation.

Mathematics

Enright Diagnostic Inventory of Basic Arithmetic Skills	Enright, F. E. (1983). Enright Diagnostic Inventory of Basic Arithmetic Skills. North Billerica, MA: Curriculum Associates.

Table 7.1. Commonly Used Achievement Tests (*Continued*)

Modality Specific Achievement Tests (*Continued*)

Keymath Diagnostic Arithmetic Test	Connolly, A. J., Nachtmam, W., & Pritchett, E. M. (1971). The Keymath Diagnostic Arithmetic Test. Circle Pines, MN: American Guidance Service.
Sequential Assessment of Mathematics Inventories	Reisman, F. K. (1985). Sequential Assessment of Mathematics Inventories. San Antonio, TX: Psychological Corporation.
Stanford Diagnostic Mathematics Test	Beatty, L. S., Madden, R., Gardner, E. G., Karlsen, B. (1976). Stanford Diagnostic Mathematics Test. Cleveland, OH: Psychological Corporation.

in specific content areas. There are several distinct applications of achievement tests which vary as a function of the setting in which they are applied. Tests such as the Metropolitan Achievement Tests, Stanford Achievement Tests, California Achievement Tests, and Iowa Tests of Basic Skills represent instruments which typically consist of test category content in six or more skill areas. The benefit of the battery approach is that it permits comparison of individual performances across diverse subjects. Because all the content areas are standardized on the same population, differences in level of performance among skill areas can reflect areas of particular strength or deficit. Many of these instruments provide a profile as well as a composite score that allows ready comparison of levels of performance between tests. The representative content of these batteries typically includes core assessment of language, reading, and mathematics abilities. The extensiveness of the coverage of allied curricula, that is, science, humanities, and social studies, varies significantly. Sax (1974) provides a description of the major differentiating characteristics of 10 of the most commonly used achievement test batteries.

In contrast to the "survey" type tests or screening batteries described above are the more content focused diagnostic achievement tests. Although any of the survey instruments is available to identify areas of academic strength or weakness (Radencich, 1985), they are not in themselves sufficient for diagnostic or remediation planning purposes. Their use in screening large groups helps to identify those individuals in need of more specific individualized diagnostic evaluation. Through the use of a diagnostic battery an area of identified deficit is examined in a more extensive fashion to determine what factors contribute to the academic dysfunction. Typically, these tests include a broad enough sampling of material so that areas of need are specified in order to develop remedial instructional objectives. For example, the Woodcock

Reading Mastery Test (Woodcock, 1973) provides five subtests which examine component processes associated with overall reading ability. These include Letter Recognition, Word Attack, Word Recognition, Word Comprehension, and Passage Comprehension. More in-depth examination at this level permits hypothesis generation regarding the nature of the specific academic deficit to be further tested. Similar tests are available to assess other aspects of academic performance: mathematics, spelling, writing, language skills, etc. Refined assessment at this level is necessary for differential diagnosis and remedial intervention. Screening batteries simply do not permit sufficient evaluation of an area for this kind of decision making to take place.

Although most achievement tests have the potential to be used as screening instruments to identify individuals in need of remedial instruction, fewer instruments are actually used for diagnostic purposes. In a national survey, Goh, Teslow, and Fuller (1981) reported that the Wide Range Achievement Test and the Peabody Individual Achievement served as the general achievement batteries most commonly utilized by school psychologists. In the area of specific achievement tests, the Key Math Diagnostic Achievement Test, Illinois Test of Psycholinguistic Abilities, and Woodcock Reading Mastery Tests ranked as the instruments used most frequently for the assessment of specific academic content areas.

Criterion-Referenced versus Norm-Referenced Achievement Tests

One other highly significant dichotomy must be addressed when discussing the classification of achievement tests and certain of their psychometric properties, namely, the distinction between criterion-referenced tests (CRTs) and norm-referenced tests (NRTs). While it is not possible to differentiate one from the other in terms of visual inspection (a criterion-referenced test can also be used as a norm-referenced test: for example, Basic Achievement Skills Individual Screener), there are intrinsic differences between the two approaches to achievement testing. Traub and Rowley (1980) described the decade of the 1970s as a time when "the notion of criterion-referenced measurement captured and held the attention of the measurement profession unlike any other idea" (p. 517). Mehrens and Lehmann (1975) asserted that the issues of accountability, performance contracting, formative evaluation, computer-assisted instruction, individually prescribed instruction, and mastery learning created a need for a new kind of test, the criterion-referenced test.

The concept of criterion-referenced achievement measurement was first detailed in the 1963 paper by Robert Glaser entitled "Instructional Technology and the Measurement of Learning Outcomes: Some Questions." In that landmark publication Glaser wrote:

> Underlying the concept of achievement is the notion of a continuum of knowledge acquisition ranging from no proficiency at all to perfect performance. An individual's achievement level falls at some point on this continuum as indicated by behaviors he displays during testing. The degree to which his achievement resembles desired performance at any specified level is assessed by criterion-referenced measures of achievement or proficiency. . . . Criterion levels can be established at any point in instruction. . . .
>
> Criterion-referenced measures indicate the content of the behavioral repertory. . . . Measures which assess student achievement in terms of a criterion standard . . . provide information as to the degree of competence attained by a particular student which is independent of reference to the performance of others. (p. 519).

Glaser further stated that achievement measures are appropriately used to provide information regarding a student's capability in relation to the capabilities of his or her fellow students as well. Where an individual's relative standing along the continuum of attainment is the primary concern, the appropriate achievement measure is one that is norm referenced. Whereas both CRTs and NRTs are used to make decisions about individuals, NRTs are usually employed where a degree of selectivity is required by a situation, as opposed to situations in which concern is only with whether an individual possesses a particular competence and there are no constraints regarding how many individuals possess that skill. Thus, at the core of the difference between the two kinds of tests is the issue of variability. "Since the meaningfulness of a norm-referenced score is basically dependent on the relative position of the score in comparison with other scores, the more variability in the scores the better" (Popham, 1971). This obviously is not a requirement of the criterion-referenced measure.

Because of basic differences in the theories underlying test construction, there have been several hundred publications on CRTs dealing with such issues as test reliability, determination of test length (Millman, 1973), score variability (Hambleton & Cignor, 1978; Hambleton, 1980), and test validity (Linn, 1982). The psychometric properties of CRTs have undergone close scrutiny and one of the most critical dimensions reviewed has been the issue of validity. In the words of Linn (1980):

> Possibly the greatest short-coming of criterion-referenced measurement is the relative lack of attention that is given to questions of validity of the measures. The clear definitions of content domains and well-specified procedures for item generation of some of the better criterion-referenced measures places the content validity of the tests on much firmer ground than has been typical of other types of achievement tests. Content validity provides an excellent foundations for a criterion-referenced test; but . . . more is needed to support the validity of inferences and uses of criterion-referenced tests. Unfortunately, the accumulation and reporting of evidence to support the uses and interpretations of criterion-referenced tests is the exception rather than the rule.
>
> In their review of 12 commercially prepared criterion-referenced tests, Hambleton and Eignor (1978) did not find a single one that had a test manual that included satisfactory evidence of validity (Hambleton, 1980). Validity has too often been assumed by both developers and users of criterion-referenced tests. This is no more acceptable for a criterion-referenced test than it is for any other test. It is time that questions of validity of the uses and interpretations of criterion-referenced tests be given the attention they deserve. (p. 559)

Despite these criticisms from the point of view of traditional test construction theory, criterion-referenced measurement has been found to have major utility with respect to the development of computer-assisted, computer-managed, and self-paced instructional systems. In all of these instructional systems, testing is closely allied with the instructional process, being introduced before, during, and after the completion of particular learning units as a monitoring, diagnostic, and prescriptive mechanism (Anastasi, 1982). Moreover, it has had practical application with respect to concerns with minimum competency testing (Hunter & Burke, 1987; Lazarus, 1981) and mastery testing (Harnisch, 1985; Kingsbury & Weiss, 1979).

Curriculum-Based Measurement

In addition to criterion-referenced and norm-referenced tests of achievement, one additional "hybrid"— which appears to be surfacing, particularly in the area of special education—*curriculum-based measurement* (CBM), merits a brief note in this review. From the Institute for Research on Learning Disabilities at the University of Minnesota, Deno (1985) and his colleagues have proposed a method of measurement which lies somewhere between the use of commercialized tests and informal teacher observations. Their initial research with the procedure in the areas of reading, spelling, and written expression, and concerns with reliability, validity, and limitations are reviewed by Deno. Among the limitations are its utility only with the domain of reading at present, its lack of stability estimates as indicative of reliability, and its lack of generality that enables aggregation across curricula.

However, one aspect of CBM that appears to mark a distinct embarkation from traditional achievement testing is the concept of frequent measurement. In addition to the work of Mirkin, Deno, Tindal, and Kuehnle (1982) on the measurement of spelling achievement with learning disabled students, Le Mahieu (1984) has reported on the extensive use of a program of frequent assessment known as the Monitoring Achievement in Pittsburgh (MAP) which began in 1980 and involves 81 schools with a total enrollment of 40,000 students. Students are tested every six weeks with curriculum-based measures developed by committees of teachers. Serious risks in this kind of achievement testing involve the potential for teachers to narrow the curriculum and to teach to the assessment instrument as well as for students themselves to develop and refine test-wise behaviors as opposed to attaining specific academic skills.

USE OF ACHIEVEMENT TESTS

Achievement Tests in Education

Within the context of educational programs there is a continual process of evaluation which also includes teacher-made tests and letter-grade performance standards. The continuous monitoring of student performance within a particular academic content area provides means not only to assess student progress but also to link instructional strategies and learning objectives with identified student learning needs and/or skill deficits. The periodic administration of achievement tests has traditionally been viewed as an educationally sound procedure by professionals in the field despite criticisms with respect to the misuse or inappropriate use of these tests.

From a positive perspective, Anastasi (1988) provides a summary of their usefulness in educational settings. First, their inherent objectivity and uniformity provide an important tool in assessing the significance of grades. While individual classroom performance measures can be susceptible to fluctuation due to a number of variables, their correlation with achievement test scores provides a useful comparative validity criterion for grades. They are especially useful in the identification of students whose limited progress in a content area will require remedial intervention. Within this context, individualization of specific needs can be identified so that individual and group curricula can be modified. In this regard, the use of achievement tests prior to the initiation of training can become particularly efficacious. When these measures are utilized at the end of an instructional period they have the potential to serve as a means for assessing the quality of instructional programming and aiding in programmatic evaluation.

In general, then, achievement tests are used to make decisions, decisions which may involve instructional, guidance, or administrative issues. For example, what is the efficacy of a particular method of instruction? What are the specific outcomes of learning? Is there a need for remediation? Are grading practices accurate? Is the curriculum responsive to the acquisition of basic and/or specific academic skills? Is counseling appropriate for any given student? Is appropriate placement a concern? Thus, the breadth of the assessment will be predicated upon the rationale for the use of particular achievement measures. Table 7.2 illustrates the types of questions or problems which may be addressed and the expected benefit(s) to be derived from the testing process.

Achievement versus Aptitude

One further point which any review of achievement tests must certainly address with respect to their classification and use is the notion of aptitude versus achievement. This contrast dates back to the preoccupation of educational psychologists in the 1920s and 1930s with the role of heredity versus environment in the learning arena. This early simplistic notion that innate capacity or potential could be measured by aptitude tests independent of an individual's learning history or "reactional biography" (Anastasi, 1984, p. 363) has been disavowed. Replacing the traditional concepts of aptitude and achievement in psychometrics is the concept of "developed abilities," the level of development attained by an individual in one or more

Table 7.2. Achievement Tests: Purpose and Outcome

PURPOSE OF TESTING	OUTCOME CRITERION
Screening:	Identification of students potentially eligible for remedial programming
Classification/Placement:	Specific academic deficiencies have been ascertained. Question now arises regarding whether student meets eligibility criteria.
Prescriptive Intervention:	A specific developmental arithemtic disorder is manifested in a child identified with visuo-perceptual processing problems. What curriculum adjustments appear warranted?
Program Evaluation:	Administrators seek to evaluate benefits of an accelerated reading program for gifted students

abilities (Anastasi, 1982, p. 395). In line with this conceptualization of the measurement of abilities, Anastasi provides a continuum of testing in terms of the "specificity of experiential background" that particular tests presuppose. The continuum ranges from course-oriented achievement tests to broadly oriented achievement tests to verbal-type intelligence to "culture-fair" tests. This continuum more accurately reflects the overlapping of aptitude and achievement tests. This analysis has been demonstrated empirically over and over in terms of the high correlations between achievement and intelligence tests. "In some instances, in fact, the correlation between achievement and intelligence tests is as high as the reliability coefficients of each test" (Anastasi, 1982, p. 395).

Finally, Anastasi notes that the continued labeling of some tests as aptitude or achievement measures has led to misuses of test results—in particular, the identification of certain children as underachievers when their respective achievement test scores are lower than their scholastic aptitude or intelligence test scores. In the words of Anastasi:

> Actually, such intraindividual differences in test scores reflect the universal fact that no two tests . . . correlate perfectly with each other. . . . Among the reasons for the prediction errors in individual cases are the unreliability of the measuring instruments, differences in content coverage, the varied effects of attitudinal and motivational factors on the two measures, and the impact of such intervening experiences as remedial instruction or a long illness. (p. 396)

Scoring Systems Associated with Tests of Academic Achievement

Before further discussion of the application of achievement test data, it is necessary to consider how the results of these tests are conveyed. Raw scores derived from achievement tests are typically converted to age or grade equivalent scores, standard scores, or percentile scores. Hoover (1984) makes a useful distinction between two scoring dichotomies. *Developmental scores* compare individual performance to that of a series of reference groups that differ systematically and developmentally in average achievement, with developmental scores being expressed as age or grade equivalent scores. *Status scores* compare test performance with a single normative reference group and are expressed as standard scores and percentiles. It is important to distinguish between the two types of measurement as each has unique strengths and limitations.

Developmental Scores

Age Equivalent Scores. Educational Age (EA) represents a scoring criterion which has come under significant criticism and is used very infrequently in reporting educational test data. The scaling of items on some achievement tests is presented in a developmental sequence such that a particular score represents mean level of performance for a specific age reference group. An individual who attains a specific score on the test is reported to function at a particular age level. This system of score reporting is useful for descriptive purposes, especially for "measuring growth." As in grade equivalent scores which will be discussed next, serious flaws are encountered when one attempts to utilize such scores for comparative purposes, however.

Grade Equivalent Scores. A grade equivalent score (GE) reflects the presumed level of performance of an average student at a particular grade level. For example, if the mean score of a group of sixth graders on an achievement test is reported as $\overline{m} = 6.2$, children who attain the same score are imputed to function at a level of performance commensurate with sixth graders in general. Although it is quite important to have available a continuous scale describing developmental level as a means to demonstrate progress in attainment and growth, the GE represents one of the most frequently misinterpreted sources of educational data. First, it should be noted that GE scores are reported in a format that reflects both grade level and month. The typical school year is approximately 10 months. Hence, scores of 6.2 and 6.9 contrast levels of performance commensurate with the beginning and end of the school year. There are, however, limitations on direct interpretation of GE scores. The scaling of achievement test data is rarely a continuous process. Scores for many grade equivalents are frequently extrapolated or interpolated and consequently do not reflect actual derived scores. They are in fact estimations based on a hypothetical grade equivalent curve. The use of such a scale also presumes that the teaching of such skills is a continuous process reflected across grades. This is not, however, reflected in the reality of the educational experience. Gains made by students are more realistically seen as a combination of spurts and plateaus, and not as a continuous process as is mathematically interpolated in scale construction.

The most significant limitation in the use of GE scores appears to arise because they are ordinal measures. The difference between a one-year gain in proficiency at a lower grade level in comparison to that same gain at a higher grade level may be significant. Further, because most of the basic core academic competencies are taught within the first through eighth grades, one cannot presume that grade equivalent scores associated with the terminal stages of the educational career are equivalent. Finally, it must be noted that relatively small differences in performance can result in exaggerated differences in grade-level equivalency owing to the nature of scale construction.

The most frequently cited problem with using GE scores is the potential for misinterpretation of significant differences in level of performance. For example, a fourth grader obtains a score of 6.7 in reading. One cannot directly compare this youngster to other sixth graders. It is an erroneous assumption to state that this child's reading ability is commensurate with that of a sixth grader. His reference group remains fourth graders. He clearly demonstrates well-above-average performance in comparison to this reference group. One cannot, however, compare him to sixth graders who by the nature of their development and experience with reading, are different from our fourth

grader. Because of the inherent potential for parents to set inappropriate standards of performance for their children based on such scores, the use of scores has been abandoned in many quarters.

Status Scores

A wide variety of standard score methodologies are available for reporting test results. These represent scores scaled along a continuum which permits one to ascertain where a particular score may fall in comparison to other scores in a distribution. There are two distinct advantages to the utilization of this scoring system. Standard scores permit the opportunity to compare individual performance to a normative standard, and they make possible the comparison of individual performance across two or more different tests. The latter represents an important criterion for the application of achievement tests within the context of a larger test battery.

Percentiles. Percentile rank represents a point in a distribution at or below which the scores of a given percentage of subjects fall. If a student scored at the 95th percentile, this would mean his or her score was better than 95% of the other students who took the same test. When clearly conveyed in the context of a psychological report, this scoring methodology represents one of the most readily understandable forms of test description. The potential for inappropriate comparisons of level of performance as reflected in the GE score example is significantly reduced.

Standard Scores. Standard scores represent raw scores which have been scaled relevant to a constant mean and standard deviation. As a function of the magnitude of the standard deviation, one can through linear transformation readily ascertain how far from the mean performance lies. Most tests standardize scores within defined age groups. Therefore, regardless of the age of the subjects under evaluation, a specific standard score will have the same meaning. For example, if two students, ages 8 and 10, obtain the same standard score on a reading test, relative to the normal curve, one can readily distinguish that in comparison to their age mates, they are functioning at equal distance from the mean. Standard score conversions also include z scores, t scores, and occasionally stanine scores which can be interpreted in like manner. In general, standard scores are considered the more accurate and precise means of reporting test results. Finally, it is not uncommon for test developers to provide multiple methods for performance description. For example, the Wide Range Achievement

Test-Revised provides grade equivalent scores, age-based standard scores, and percentiles.

Achievement Test Scores and the Diagnosis of Learning Disabilities

The relevance of understanding the scoring systems utilized in the interpretation of achievement test results can be dramatically illustrated when one considers the educational diagnosis of a specific learning disability. Learning disabilities have become the dominant handicap of school-age children in the country with some 42% of all students ages 3 to 21 in special education programs diagnosed as learning disabled (Databank, 1985).

A basic assumption underlying learning disabilities is the failure of the student to acquire primary academic skills at levels expected for age, grade placement, and level of intellectual functioning. The identification of individuals with learning disabilities has traditionally been based on the notion of a "significant discrepancy" between ability level and demonstrated academic skill attainment. Regardless of which of the many formulas is used to diagnose a learning disability, all require data from standardized achievement tests. Thus, the use of achievement testing has become an integral component in the differential diagnosis of learning disabilities. In this regard, the concept of "significant discrepancy" has been an important one for it forms the basis for distinguishing specific learning disability diagnoses from conditions such as underachievement or mental retardation.

Under Public Law 94-142, the Education for All Handicapped Children Act of 1975, it was specified that a team could render a determination of specific learning disability if a child does not achieve at his or her ability level when provided with appropriate educational instruction and if a severe discrepancy exists between intellectual ability and achievement in one or more of seven areas of achievement including oral expression, listening comprehension, written expression, basic reading skills, reading comprehension, mathematics calculation, or reasoning. Specifically excluded along with mental retardation were other factors which could impinge on limited academic proficiency, such as peripheral sensory or motor handicaps, emotional disturbance, or socioeconomic or cultural disadvantage. The actual specification of the means of ascertaining discrepant performance is left vague in this definition. Algozzine, Ysseldyke, and Shinn (1982) emphasize that the field of learning disabilities has always suffered a definitional dilemma. Federal guidelines have not appreciably corrected this situation. No clear consensus across school districts exists nationally for arriving at workable definitions of learning disability diagnoses.

In spite of the lack of consensus regarding definition, the notion of severe discrepancy has been defined most frequently by the use of an ability-achievement discrepancy. Inherent in this conceptualization of learning disability is the potential for at least average intellectual functioning with academic performance well below expectations. A number of strategies have been applied in an attempt to operationalize criteria representative of a severe discrepancy.

Deviation from grade level. A commonly encountered criterion to define a potential learning disability might be "grade level performance in academic achievement two grade levels below expectation for age." This criterion has been criticized as inadequate for a number of reasons. First, as previously discussed, grade-level equivalents represent the weakest psychometric criterion upon which to base comparisons of academic performance. Second, utilization of such a constant criterion fails to take into consideration the significance of discrepant performance at various points in the continuum of educational programming. For example, performance two grade levels below expectation in a third grader can be far more significant than the same magnitude of score deficit in an eighth grader. Further, in the assessment of adult populations, the efficacy of grade equivalent scores lose predictive validity. It is extremely difficult to ascertain whether eighth-grade academic skills in a 40-year-old are indicative of any significant disparity in level of performance.

Finally, problems have been identified with potential identification of learning disabled students. Use of grade-level discrepancy criteria tends to overidentify children whose intellectual functioning is low average and to underidentify those students who may be above average. A student with an IQ of 82 might in fact be functioning at a grade level which is not discrepant for his or her overall level of intellectual functioning. On the other hand, a fourth grader who is reading just below grade level, but who has an IQ in the superior range, who should clearly be reading at well above grade level expectations, would be excluded.

Standard Score Discrepancy Models. The process of comparing standard scores derived from academic and intelligence tests holds apparent benefits over grade discrepancy scores on purely psychometric grounds. Typically, a criterion level is arbitrarily selected, a 1 or 2 standard deviation point discrepancy between general ability and achievement test score. This methodology can, however, also impose bias into the discrimination process. Many such models do not take into consideration the regression of IQ on achievement. One cannot assume direct correspondence between IQ and standard score equivalents. It can be demonstrated that academic achievement test scores fall somewhat short of IQ for individuals manifesting above-average performance, and in lower-functioning individuals, academic achievement scores are actually higher. The use of a simple discrepancy score formula implicitly assumes a perfect correlation between general ability and achievement tests which in fact does not exist. It would also require that each test be based on the same standard score distribution.

Regression Equations. The most sophisticated methodologies available for determining significant score discrepancies are based upon complex computations or tables designed from formulas based upon regression equations. A number of strategies have been developed, each with unique distinguishing properties. A number of reviews are available (Forness, Sinclair, & Guthrie, 1983; Reynolds, 1984; Wilson & Reynolds, 1984) which describe the characteristics of these methodologies. There remains, however, no one mathematial model which is commonly accepted or in fact utilized.

Reynolds (1984) reports on the findings of the Work Group on Measurement Issues in the Assessment of Learning Disabilities, a study section formed in 1983. This group was delegated the responsibility of addressing questions directed toward identification of "best practice" solutions to the learning disabilities definitional dilemma. In their findings, models of discrepancy analysis based upon grade-equivalent scores were rejected outright. Factors related to their imprecision and their ready misinterpretation were noted. Most critical, however, was the inherent lack of the mathematical properties necessary for conducting comparative analyses that are associated with this scoring system. The group concluded that age-based standard score discrepancy models represent potentially the best methodology available. However, while developmental standard scores are to be preferred over grade level of status standard scores, their value has been challenged also because they require greater growth for below-average children than for average or above-average children (Clarizio & Phillips, 1986).

One cannot, however, focus exclusively on the concept of discrepancy as the sole basis for the diagnosis of a learning disability. To quote Reynolds (1984), "The establishment of a severe discrepancy is a necessary but insufficient condition for the diagnosis of a learning disability" (p. 468). A host of factors other than specific learning disability can contribute to significant academic underachievement. Among these are limited sociocultural opportunity, dysmotivation, sensory-perceptual dysfunction, or functional psychiatric impairment. It is Reynolds' bias, however, that only when a severe discrepancy can be demonstrated is a child considered eligible for a diagnosis of LD.

Some Thoughts on the Validity Issue

There are, among educators and researchers, those who question the focus on the *reliability* of the discrepancy between IQ and achievement rather than on its *validity* (Shepard, 1983). In a study by Shepard and Smith (1983), which evaluated the identification practices of psychologists and teachers within the state of Colorado involving 1,000 student files and 2,000 specialists, 50% of those professionals surveyed were unaware that an IQ of 90 falls at the 25th percentile. For children with IQs of 90, the expectation was that achievement would be at grade level (the 50th percentile) because the IQ was "in the normal range" (Shepard, 1983). The authors continued that these specialists were also unaware that after the first or second grade it is not uncommon for large numbers of children to have grade-equivalent scores below their grade placement. Other technical problems identified in this study also complicate the identification of LD: (a) Most of the tests used in the diagnosis of LD are technically inadequate with the exception of the WISC-R and one or two achievement batteries; (b) Many clinicians were unaware of the differences between technically adequate and inadequate tests; (c) Specialists often selected technically inadequate measures even when more valid instruments were available, their choices tending to follow traditional preferences associated with each professional group; (d) Many clinicians continued to apply inaccurate conventional wisdom regarding the symptoms of the disorder (relying on interpretations of subtest scatter, underestimating normal patterns of difference, etc.).

Reynolds (1984) and the Task Force advanced a number of recommendations which attempted to bridge this validity-reliability gap with respect to the diagnosis of LD:

1. Instruments applied should meet criteria defined in PL 94-142.
2. Well-standardized national norms should form the

basis for statistical comparison of individual level of performance.

3. Normative comparisons should be based upon co-normed samples. The ideal scenario is one in which the two tests compared are normed on the same sample. Where this is not possible, the two normative groups should be clearly comparable.

4. Only individually administered tests of achievement and intellectual ability should be utilized.

5. Age-based standard scores based upon a common scale represent the most statistically robust means for score comparison.

6. Measures employed should conform to acceptable criteria for validity and reliability.

7. Special technical considerations should be addressed when using performance based measures of achievement (e.g., writing skill).

8. Bias studies should have been conducted and reported.

In summary, while the psychometrics involved in scoring and interpreting the results of achievement tests can be fraught with complexity and controversy, as illustrated in the case of the diagnosis of learning disabilities, the consequences of the resolution of the issues involved are even further reaching. Consider the effects of labeling, the contraction of teacher competence to deal with a variety of learning styles in the classroom, the allocation of resources available to those students with the most severe disability, and the costs of providing for special education resources themselves (Shepard, 1983). All of these can be viewed as negatives. It is not difficult nor unrealistic to extrapolate these same issues to include diverse groups of students in educational programs today. Thus, we are left with ethical responsibilities to insure the appropriate utilization of achievement tests based on the most current thinking and research available which is macrocosmic rather than microcosmic in nature.

Messick (1980) has argued this point in his "Test Validity and the Ethics of Assessment." He had written earlier, with specific reference to the measurement of personality, that tests should be evaluated not only in terms of their measurement properties but also in terms of their potential social consequences (Messick, 1965). Messick emphasized the importance of construct validity, arguing "that even for purposes of applied decision making reliance upon criterion validity or content coverage is not enough" (Messick, 1975, p. 956), and that "the meaning of the measure must also be comprehended in order to appraise potential social consequences sensibly" (Messick,

1980, p. 1013). He defined test validity as an overall evaluative judgment of the adequacy and appropriateness of inferences drawn from test scores, opining that values questions arise with any approach to psychological testing whether it be norm referenced or criterion referenced, a construct-based ability test or a content-sample achievement test. This evaluative judgment of test validity is based on (a) convergent and discriminate research evidence as to the test scores interpretability in terms of the particular construct under review, (b) an appraisal of the value implications of that interpretation, (c) justification of the relevance of the construct and its utility of the particular application proposed, and (d) dealing with the potential social consequences of the proposed use as well as the actual consequences upon implementation of the testing procedure.

> Intervening in the model between test use and the evaluation of consequences is a decision matrix to emphasize the point that tests are rarely used in isolation but rather in combination with other information in broader decision systems. The decision process is profoundly influenced by social values and deserves, in its own right, massive research attention beyond the good beginning provided by utility models. (Messick, 1980, p. 1025)

Messick concluded his remarks by paraphrasing Guion: "The formulation of hypotheses is or should be applied science, the validation of hypotheses is applied methodology, but the act of making . . . [a] decision is . . . still an art" (p. 1025).

The Use of Achievement Tests in Clinical Practice

Achievement testing conducted with clinical populations is generally regarded as an extension of intelligence and aptitude testing. It provides one further means to ascertain "general ability level." Results are typically utilized for drawing inferences regarding the capacity of the individual under evaluation to apply knowledge or native intelligence in practical problem-solving situations. One equates intelligence and exposure to educational opportunity with the ability to conform with the demands of achievement testing at commensurate levels of success. Typically, one is not engaging in achievement testing with this population in anticipation of identification of potential performance discrepancies, but to gauge overall adaptive competency. The identification of any significant discrepancies would of course result in further clinical investigation. Cognitive as well as noncognitive variables would then be explored.

Achievement Test Results Applied in Neuropsychological Evaluation. Achievement tests play a definitive role in the administration of standard neuropsychological test batteries. For example, a number of extended versions of the Halstead-Reitan Neuropsychological Test Battery include an administration of the Wide Range Achievement Test or other age-appropriate screening battery within the test protocol. Data derived from such tests offer clinical utility beyond discrepancy analysis. They can be used as a method to infer an estimated level of premorbid intellectual functioning (Lezak, 1983). As basic academic skill competencies are generally not susceptible to significant deterioration in mild to moderate generalized cerebral dysfunction, standard scores derived from general achievement test measures offer one means to interpolate a coarse estimation of premorbid functioning when other means of documentation are not available.

Achievement test results can be incorporated in the pattern analysis of other neuropsychological test variables to aid in the specification of the effects of focal lesion processes. For example, problems exclusively with the spatial components of arithmetic processes in an individual manifesting no evidence of linguistic defects would help suggest a post-Rolandic lesion of the right cerebral hemisphere, when other markers of right hemisphere dysfunction are present. It is not uncommon to consider achievement test performance within the context of a formal aphasia examination as a means to extend the assessment to the integrity of lexical skill functions and writing ability.

Beyond their application in the documentation of the effects associated with focal lesion processes, such test results hold even greater potential utility in aiding in the development of hypotheses regarding functional limitations associated with cerebral dysfunction. As primary academic skill competencies are intimately related to aspects of autonomous functioning in a number of instrumental activities associated with daily living, the degree of preservation of such primary skills as reading and arithmetic abilities can be important prognostic indicators associated with long term recovery and adaptation.

Achievement Test Results Applied to Rehabilitation Assessment Methodologies. In the areas of both psychiatric and vocational rehabilitation, the specification of the degree to which core academic competencies are developed holds a number of prognostic

implications. With low-level functioning individuals, the specification of primary literacy skills is an important determinant of the level of complexity of programming in which they might participate. The degree to which a learning curriculum might emphasize effective reading comprehension might be potentially exclusionary, for example.

An important component of the rehabilitation assessment is determination of the degree to which any remedial intervention might be required prior to implementing programming. Inadequate educational opportunity or underachievement related to psychosocial factors must be distinguished from developmental academic disorders and conditions which cause a loss of previously attained ability. Intervention strategies to remediate or supplant deficient academic skills are determined by the thorough analysis of their cause. Prognostically, it is important to identify those individuals functioning at their plateau versus those who have the potential to develop these skills further.

In summary, with the use of achievement testing in clinical settings the focus is typically divested towards two lines of inquiry: (a) obtaining knowledge of the degree to which basic academic skill competencies are developed in a particular individual, and (b) examining individual performance within a particular area of academic performance. The basic referral question in large measure determines what armamentarium of techniques will be brought to bear in the assessment. It will also influence how test scores will be compared and interpreted.

COGNITION, METACOGNITION, AND ACHIEVEMENT TESTING

The application of cognitive theory research to educational psychology can be traced back as early as 1960 with the publication of David Ausubel's paper "The Use of Advance Organizers in the Learning and Retention of Meaningful Verbal Material," the later work of Rothkopf (1965) on mathemagenic behaviors, Ausubel's (1968) test, *Educational Psychology: A Cognitive View,* Anderson's (1972) work on how to construct achievement tests to assess comprehension, and the work of Martin and Säljö (1976a, 1976b) who argued that a description of what is learned is more important than a summary of how much is learned (Clarke, 1982). Glaser (1981) reviewed current research in cognitive and developmental psychology addressing its potential influence on the development of new psychometric methodology. He cited Bartholomae's (1980) work on error analysis with college students in remedial writing programs and Siegler's (1976) work on rule assessment in the acquisition of scientific concepts as illustrative of the "necessary interrelationships between the analytical assessment of performance and effective instruction" (Glaser, 1981, p. 929). Interest in the assessment of mastery or competence can be traced also to developments in cognitive psychology, artificial intelligence, and language understanding. Herein the works of Chase and Simon (1973) on the chess master and the work of Larkin, McDermott, Simon, and Simon (1980) on problem solving in the area of elementary physics were cited by Glaser.

Finally, research in the realm of metacognition— the knowledge, regulation, and management of one's own cognitive processes and products (Flavell, 1976)—has led to a concern with the measurement of these self-regulatory skills in terms of predicting successful problem solving which then leads to learning. Metacognitive abilities develop with maturity, and current research in learning instruction has demonstrated that these skills may be less well developed in those individuals who have learning disabilities.

Thus, it becomes quite clear that an understanding of the learning process and its assessment can yield more fruitful data than those traditionally obtained by achievement tests. This is particularly important in light of the social-educational demands outlined by Glaser (1981) which will shape and mold the future of educational assessment:

- the shift from a selective educational system to one designed to help individuals succeed in educational programs (zero-reject system)
- the requirement for improved levels of literacy and problem-solving ability in a variety of knowledge and skill domains (minimum competency and mastery certification)
- the need to understand individual differences in the process of measurement so that abilities can be improved to facilitate further learning (cognitive, sociocultural, gender specific)

The application of cognitive and metacognitive principles with respect to the measurement of learning have been detailed in the areas of reading (Curtis, 1980; Curtis & Glaser, 1983), spelling (Henderson & Beers, 1980; Nolen & McCartin, 1984), and foreign language (Fischer, 1981; Stevenson, 1983; Terry, 1986). Curtis and Glaser (1983) describe the current level of understanding and the theoretical framework utilized to study the process of learning to read, a process which involves a complex of interrelated skills (word decoding, accessing semantic word information, sentence processing, and discourse analysis), proficiency in one affecting success in the others. The results of traditional reading achievement tests have made it impractical to diagnose reading problems in terms of remediation or instructional strategies thus far. However, current theory on efficiency in word identification, the qualitative features of semantic knowledge, and research on schemata can be utilized as a form of construct validity and thus allow measurement of achievement that reflects both the development of competence and the process of instruction. "With developing knowledge of reading it should be possible to establish standards of performance . . . [and] . . . combined enterprise representing test design based on knowledge of human learning and performance, psychometric requirements, and studies of test use should improve our ability to link testing and instruction" (Curtis & Glaser, 1983, p. 144).

Diagnostic Applications of Achievement Test Results

As an illustration of the application of cognitive and metacognitive strategies in the process of achievement testing, the remainder of this discussion focuses on an expanded level of analysis that can be undertaken in the clinical setting for purposes of both diagnosis and remediation interventions.

Reading. Assessment of the skills brought to bear by a reader in decoding words generally represents the first level of analysis in diagnostic assessment. One is interested in determining how sophisticated word attack skills may be relative to age and intellectual ability. Two types of decoding activities are typically utilized in reading: (a) a "phonetic" approach in which words are systematically analyzed based on the blend of their phonological properties, and (b) a visually based process in which whole words or word parts are immediately recognized, that is, "sight recognition" vocabulary. Typically in normal readers whole word recognition skills increasingly supplant the need to decode individual words phonologically. As the lexicon of sight recognition vocabulary increases with reading experience, semantic and contextual cues become incorporated in the reading process. It is usually only on confrontation with unfamiliar words that a reader has to resort to phonological decoding (Curtis, 1980).

A major portion of diagnostic reading assessment focuses on the sophistication and accuracy of decoding skills. This assessment is accomplished through the presentation of reading material presented as isolated phonemes, nonsense words, familiar and unfamiliar words, as well as words presented "in context," that is, in the form of sentences or complex paragraphs. At a first level of analysis the rule-out of basic visuo-perceptual dysfunction is necessary. The reader must be able to appreciate fully the visuo-symbolic configuration of letters and words. Here one is concerned with the rule-out of visual-sequential and modality specific attentional deficits which could prevent the accurate assimilation of the written material. Perceptual errors such as reversals (reading "b" for "d" or "p" for "q") would also be excluded.

With the rule-out of primary perceptual dysfunction, analysis of grapheme-phoneme correspondence is undertaken. Basic decoding ability is ascertained for vowels, consonants, and consonant blends of letter combinations. Increasing the level of complexity of syllabic blends permits analysis of any sequential information-processing deficits that may be present. One is interested in the capacity not only to analyze and decode written material sequentially, but aural material as well.

There are tasks which tap auditorization or syllabication, that is, the ability to decode the component phonetic properties of a word. On the Auditory Analysis Test, for example, one is asked to say "Germany" without the "ma" sound, thus transforming the remaining syllables to "journey." Some individuals, who on a task like the Word Attack subtest of the Woodcock Reading Mastery Tests are reasonably successful in reading isolated phonemes, have great difficulty blending these same sounds into their appropriate phonological expression when confronting them in complex words. For example, when asked to read "phonological," the student struggles to isolate-"pho" . . . "no" . . . "loge" . . . "ee" . . . "cal" only to pronounce the word then as "phonograph," a word more embedded in auditory memory. Frequently the effort required to analyze words laboriously in this fashion is exacted at great expense in terms of comprehension and memory for material read.

Assessment techniques which require rapid identification of words serve as a means to assess sight recognition vocabulary. Speed of recognition is not a factor controlled for in many types of reading tests. "Automatic recognition" represents the most sophisticated and efficient means of reading. Reading performed at this level taxes working memory minimally and frees the reader to focus on the semantic organization of the material for greater understanding and for committing textual information to memory. There

are, however, individuals who have not attained adequate levels of sight recognition skills. They maintain a more labored phonologically based reading style. These individuals may present a variety of deficits which impede their ability to process complex visuo-symbolic material. This might involve visual inattention, visuo-perceptual processing problems, spatial or gestalt recognition deficits, or weak visual memory. An analysis of the approach taken during "word attack" can be helpful in isolating the contributing deficit or deficits.

Within this context, the overall complexity of the word presented can be important. Errors encountered with relatively simple reading material can suggest problems in processing the basic visual morphology of written material. In terms of the simultaneous processing of visual input, there may be a finite limit on how complex a word can be for it to be realized. In attempts to compensate, some children "guess" at the whole word by processing only the prefix or first few syllables. Poor visual gestalt functions or whole word recognition skills are usually typified by gross lexical "word substitution" errors. Here words which share a similar visual gestalt to the word at hand are substituted, often resulting in flagrant misreading. In this regard it is necessary to rule out impulsivity as a contributing factor. The absence of other evidence of attention deficit disorder symptoms in ancillary testing or observation is particularly helpful.

Finally, comparisons of the relative efficiency of oral and silent reading under timed conditions can be potentially useful. A sample of oral reading of both word recognition material and passage material can be extremely beneficial. Dramatic improvement in passage versus isolated word reading immediately suggests the potential for the reader to compensate via the use of semantic cues. There are students whose oral reading efficiency can be significantly compromised by anxiety or inhibition. Far greater efficiency can be expressed by them in silent reading.

Spelling. Standardized spelling tests permit an opportunity to ascertain whether skills are developed at levels commensurate with age and grade level expectations. Individualized assessment of spelling ability requires obtaining a broad sample of actual oral or written spelling skills. Multiple-choice format tasks characteristic of some achievement tests are inadequate for they permit the use of opportunistic compensatory strategies that could potentially mask true spelling deficits. In assessing spelling abilities it is useful to combine both the use of graded word lists as well as a sample of spelling in context, for example a brief paragraph written to oral dictation. Diagnostic spelling assessment attempts to ascertain whether there are any consistencies in error patterns within misspellings. Most commonly, a mixed pattern of errors is confronted in the student who is a weak speller. The identification of a distinct spelling dysfunction, however, flags the need for potential specialized remedial intervention.

The development of spelling skills closely parallels the development of primary linguistic skills as well as reading skills. Deficits in either or both of these areas can signal potential problems in spelling. Frequently the elucidation of the nature of reading impairment suggests the modal pattern of deficits that can be anticipated in spelling. Using the model proposed by Boder (1973) of dysphonetic, dyseidetic, and mixed types of reading disability one can expect corollary difficulties in spelling. The dysphonetic reader encounters problems in basic grapheme-phoneme correspondence. Prominent phonetic errors in spelling can be anticipated. Dysphonetic spelling errors can be viewed along a continuum of severity. At the gross impairment level, it is expected that primary errors are associated with an inability to form basic sound-symbol relationships. Lesser degrees of impairment would be reflected in the ability to form close phonetic approximation to the real spelling so that words could be recognized by the examiner. These errors are primarily orthographic. There are also dysphonetic spellers whose deficiencies are not in phoneme-to-grapheme correspondence. They are in fact very accurate phonetic spellers, but they lack appropriate development of the higher order rules which govern spelling.

Another subclass of spelling errors is those that predominantly relate to sequential information-processing errors. Here syllables or letters are transposed in ordinal position or actually left out. Observation of the spelling process reflects a laborious, piecemeal attack. The most unusual spelling pattern exhibited is that of the dyseidetic speller. In the dyseidetic reader, phonological processing abilities necessary for word recognition are critically underdeveloped, hence, a strong reliance on visual association cues is utilized. In spelling, this takes the form of gross spelling errors secondary to word substitution errors arising from "wild guesses" at visual gestalts of words ensconced in the speller's visual lexicon of word memory. These misspellings are unique for their lack of phonological relation to the target word.

It is also useful to assess spelling in the context of dictation to lexical material. This permits assessment of the "automaticity" of spelling. The speller is also forced in this paradigm to attend to issues which relate to grammar and syntax. Under these conditions subtle spelling errors might be elucidated which were not seen on word list dictation strategies. Here especially, errors which may be secondary to attentional dysfunction and limited self-monitoring ability are seen.

Reading Comprehension. Examination of reading comprehension is generally undertaken via the reading of a paragraph and the answering of questions about the content. A quantitative score is applied based on the number of correct responses and an estimation of reading comprehension level is ascertained. This procedure does not in itself reflect the myriad factors which can contribute to comprehension difficulties. Reading comprehension is not an auditory ability. Rather, a number of discrete abilities contribute to performance. Level of investment can be a significant factor. Motivation can be influenced by interest in the factual material presented as well as general investment in reading as a preferred learning modality. Basic reading proficiency in terms of adequate word recognition skills will also influence comprehension. Without strategies for the decoding of unfamiliar or complex reading material, adequacy of understanding will suffer. There is also a number of higher cognitive skills that influence performance including linguistic proficiency, memory, cognitive flexibility, and semantic organization skills. In order to ascertain where on a continuum of contributing factors comprehension problems lie, a number of informal strategies have been recommended to augment the reading comprehension examination (Aaron & Poostay, 1982; Levine, 1987).

These strategies focus on the reading of restricted passages of known grade level difficulty with the examiner focusing on a number of direct questions that permit an informal task analysis of potential contributions to comprehension failure. For example, Levine (1981) recommends beginning with the oral reading of simple sentences as the starting point. Limiting the amount of information to be assimilated restricts the degree to which active memory and semantic organizational skills are required, thus permitting direct access to potential problems based on decoding lexical information. At this level, basic questions regarding word recognition errors, limited functional vocabulary, and problems with understanding morphology and syntax can be ascertained. Increasingly more complex lexical material is then presented. With each passage a number of profiles are presented in which the reader is asked to recall details, sequence events, and identify main ideas. More sophisticated demands can be made such as summarizing the overall content of the passage. Responses can be evaluated on a continuum of literal to inferential depending on their level of complexity. It is also of value to compare general level of performance on oral comprehension and memory tests to determine whether reading comprehension is related to more generalized cognitive impairment.

Mathematical Abilities. The major objective of conducting diagnostic standardized testing in mathematics abilities is to ascertain areas of strength and deficits relative to developmental level. In order to accomplish this objective, more than a general screening of mathematical calculation abilities is necessary. Assessment in areas related to multiple aspects of applied mathematics is required. For example, in obtaining a score on the Peabody Individual Achievement Test or Wide Range Achievement Test-Revised, two grade levels below expectation or obvious difficulties with arithmetic ability are ascertained, but their nature is not immediately evident. While one could attempt to determine whether there were any commonalities of errors or clustering of errors in a particular domain of arithmetic functions, the sample of abilities assessed on such screening batteries is limited. Reliance on one of the diagnostic arithmetic tests offers far more information on which to base inferences. Table 7.3 describes the domains of function assessed by the

Stanford Diagnostic Arithmetic Test and the Keymath Diagnostic Arithmetic Test.

The expanded domains of functioning included in diagnostic arithmetic batteries permit analysis of "profiles" of mathematics abilities, thus allowing for the more immediate and direct identification of patterns of strength and deficit.

It is important, also, to conceive of mathematical skills as sequentially developed abilities which are intrinsically related to the overall level of cognitive maturation of the individual. Hence, a developmental perspective must be maintained in approaching the analysis of mathematical skills—not only so that an understanding of how failure to develop cumulative skills might interfere with performance, but also to consider how cognitive deficits differentially expressed over the course of development can affect performance. Unfortunately, not all standardized achievement tests reveal an immediately discernible logical progression through the formal operations associated with mathematics skill development. Further, the standardized curriculum utilized in instruction may not conform to the developmental sequence of abilities measured on the achievement test. Thus, considerable flexibility is required in application of the results to remedial instructional strategies.

There are a number of secondary factors that can indirectly affect performance in mathematics. Functional impairment secondary to anxiety or primary

Table 7.3. Domains of Mathematical Abilities Assessed on Diagnostic Arithmetic Batteries

STANFORD DIAGNOSTIC ARITHMETIC TEST (LEVEL II)	KEYMATH DIAGNOSTIC ARITHMETIC TEST
Measures:	Measures:
Concepts—Number systems and operations	Content 　Numeration 　Fractions 　Geometry
Computation—Addition, subtraction, multiplication, and division	
Common Fractions—Understanding and computation	Operations 　Addition 　Subtraction
Decimal Fractions and Percent	Multiplication 　Division
Number Facts—Addition, subtraction, multiplication, division, and carrying	Mental Computations 　Numerical Reasoning
	Applications 　Word problems 　Missing elements 　Money 　Measurement 　Time

Table 7.4. Deficits in Higher Cortical Functioning Associated with Mathematics Difficulties

Visuo-perceptual dysfunction	"Static" or "kinetic" reversals in number recognition or writing (example: reading 6 for 9) leading to calculation errors.
Spatial processing problems	Deficits in the ability to appreciate spatial properties could lead to difficulty in learning concepts such as borrowing or carrying. Failure might be seen in the linear ordering of the operations associated with long division or multiplication. Concepts associated with geometry and higher-level mathematics may be conceptually too demanding.
Sequential information processing deficits	Tasks involving complex multistep operations are failed.
Attention deficit disorder	Failure to appreciate the full ramification of a problem with impulsive errors noteworthy, i.e., missed steps or procedures in routine problem solving well within the respective area of ability.
Memory dysfunction	Failure to acquire skills reliant upon rote memorization such as "times-tables" or deficiencies in efficient discursive reasoning problems because of weak immediate memory. Persistent requests for repetition of material.
Language dysfunction	Failure to appreciate the nuances of complex "statement problems" because of the complexity of their logico-grammatical structure or failure to develop working vocabulary of mathematical terminology.

psychopathology can significantly influence general efficiency. Individuals who manifest attention deficit disorder diagnoses may be especially error prone. Their impulsivity results in inadequate assimilation of all aspects of the problem or faulty planning in that all sufficient steps for task completion are not carried out. In this regard, developmental models of pragmatic and conceptual skills associated with mathematical skills acquisition as proposed by Reisman (1982) are helpful.

At different age levels, differing cognitive styles may be brought to bear in problem resolution. More than one means to go about solving a particular problem can be chosen. The level of sophistication of the processes brought to bear in task resolution can in itself be diagnostic. Even though a correct answer is ultimately obtained, the strategies utilized in reasoning may be developmentally deficient, hence affecting overall efficiency in performance. Greater "automation" and use of "formal operations" with maturity are anticipated. Lack of expression of efficient problem-solving strategies can be diagnostically important.

Standardized achievement tests are helpful, therefore, in identifying both the failure to develop appropriate numerical reasoning or problem-solving strategies as well as in identifying their type. Multiple pathways can lead to the expression of developmental arithmetic problems, however. It is important for the assessment of mathematical ability to be tied to the larger domain of higher cognitive functioning. This would involve more rigorous assessment than a comparison with IQ scores. The identification of any associated cognitive dysfunction could affect very significantly the design of remedial or adaptive instruction. A number of discrete developmentally based higher cognitive processing problems have been identified in Table 7.4 and their functional implications discussed.

As can be seen from this brief sampling of deficits associated with higher cognitive functioning, a number of discrete deficits can follow from developmentally based or acquired cerebral dysfunction. Functional psychopathology and anxiety effects can selectively compromise performance and should be ruled out as well.

ACHIEVEMENT TESTING WITH SPECIAL POPULATIONS

Exceptional Children

Under the educational opportunity safeguards included within Section 504 of the Rehabilitation Act and P.L. 94-142 are specific components dealing with the process of evaluation. What is mandated by law is that all students who potentially have an educational disability receive a comprehensive evaluation that fairly assesses their abilities and does not discriminate against them because of cultural or racial factors or a disabling condition. Moreover, in all areas of exceptionality, federal and state legislation require the development of individualized education plans (IEPs) for handicapped students. Educational assessment data from standardized tests provides one necessary source of information used in the development of strategies for diagnostic prescriptive teaching. Here diagnostic achievement testing plays a particularly important role not only in identifying areas in need of remediation but also in placement and classification decisions. With the importance attached to assessment in the identification, diagnosis, placement, and instruction of children with disabling conditions, it is no surprise that the use of achievement tests, particularly the use of norm-referenced measures, has come under increasing criticism (Fuchs, Fuchs, Benowitz, & Barringer, 1987; Fuchs, Fuchs, Power, & Darley, 1985; LaGrow & Prochnow-LaGrow, 1982; Ysseldyke et al., 1980; Ysseldyke & Shinn, 1981).

Fuchs et al. (1987) conducted an extensive study of the 27 most well-known and commonly used tests in special education in order to determine the degree of participation of children with handicaps in the creation of test norms, and item selection, and in the establishment of their reliability and validity. Fourteen of these tests were measures of achievement classified as either screening (battery) or diagnostic (content specific). The user manual and/or technical supplement of each test was then analyzed in terms of (a) norms, (b) item development, (c) internal and test-retest reliability, and (d) concurrent and predictive validity. In only two of the achievement measures were children with handicaps included in the norming process and on only one measure were they included in item development. Otherwise, no other information was available. Such findings led the authors to state: "[I]f, in fact, test constructors have not validated their instruments for use with handicapped people, they 'should issue cautionary statements in manuals and elsewhere regarding confidence in interpretation' based on these tests" (p. 269. Note: The quotation in Fuchs is taken from Standard 14.2, p. 79, the Standards for Educational and Psychological Testing, 1985).

Numerous studies have analyzed the performance on standardized tests of academic achievement of students with learning disabilities (Caskey, 1986; Estes, Hallock, & Bray, 1985; McGue, Shinn, & Ysseldyke, 1982; Shinn, Algozzine, Marston, & Ysseldyke, 1982; Webster, 1985), behavioral disturbances (Altrows, Maunula, & LaLonde, 1986; Eaves

& Simpson, 1984), and hearing impairments (Allen, White, & Karchmer, 1983; Karchmer, Milone, & Wolk, 1979; Trybus & Karchmer, 1977), as well as students who are gifted (Karnes, Edwards, & McCallum, 1986). The findings from these studies and others demonstrate empirically (a) the variability in test results across achievement measures; (b) particular item biases where low SES is a factor; (c) the influence of the examiner on the testing process; (d) the differential effect of diagnosis; and (e) the roles of time pressure, anxiety, and sex (Doolittle, 1986; Plass & Hill, 1986). It is critical that the professionals who utilize these tests be aware of the significant validity issues involved when assessing persons with disabilities or other areas of exceptionality.

Minority Children

Cautionary comments have been made also by those persons concerned with the standardized testing of minority students. Critics of the testing movement assert that tests which purport to measure achievement, among other things, are biased against certain ethnic/racial groups. Those in favor of testing regard test misuse as the real problem. Underlying the debate is the belief by the critics that the model used to assess performance and competence in society is monocultural. "A main criticism is that the model ignores the relevance of culturally different experiences that foster other equally important competencies essential to the survival of the group or individual" (Williams, 1983, p. 192). Similarly, Green and Griffore (1980) report that in one study 46% of the errors made on Gray's Oral Reading Test by minority children were due to dialect differences. Others have suggested that lack of "test-wiseness" (Millman, Bishop, & Ebel, 1965) may serve to lower the scores of minority students on tests of aptitude and achievement. Johnson (1979), commenting about the variables that may invalidate test scores for African-Americans and other minorities, wrote:

Many factors operate to attenuate or lower test scores, and these factors tend to have their greatest effects on Blacks and other minority applicants. These include factors which affect the actual performance of individuals on the test, such as socioeconomic status, differences in educational opportunity, motivation, narrowness of content of the tests, atmosphere of the testing situation, and the perceived relevance of the test to success. They also include factors that affect the test score more directly such as the composition of the group used for item tryouts and item selection and analysis which precede the actual standardization, composition of the standardization or normative group, and the techniques and procedures employed in item construction. Also, the validity or appropriateness of tests often differ for Black and white applicants, in relation to the same future performance of criterion. (p. 3)

In addition, it has been substantiated that minority and white children are exposed to different curricula through the practice of ability tracking (Coleman, 1966; Findley, 1974; Green & Griffore, 1980; Mc-Partland, 1969). Reviewers of the hundreds of ability grouping studies conducted since the 1920s have concluded that while superior students may benefit from this method of curricular offering, students with lower class ranking may not. The primary areas of concern are exposure to undemanding curricula and the social stigma attached to students in low-ability groups.

In a study by Abadzi (1985), the effects on both academic achievement and self-esteem of students placed in ability grouping classrooms were investigated with a population of 767 students from grades 4 to 8 in a large Texas school district. Contrary to earlier studies, her findings were that high-ability students did not maintain in the long run the performance gains made in the first year of grouping. Only the lower-level high-ability students in grouped classes were to benefit from the educational and social opportunity provided the highest-ability students. Students near the cutoff score in all groups were the ones most influenced by grouping in terms of both achievement and self-concept. Support for these findings was provided in spite of a general downward trend in performance at the end of elementary school that was characteristic of the school district's test scores and those of other districts as well. The author hypothesized that the steady drop in scores with the high-ability students may have been the result of reduced achievement motivation brought on by a "sense of invincibility, which the high status of the program combined with nonexistent exit criteria helped reinforce" (Abadzi, 1985, p. 39).

The concept of achievement motivation raised in Abadzi's conclusions has been systematically studied since the publication of David McClelland's *The Achievement Motive* (1953). This concept has been defined as a learned motive, unconscious in nature, resulting from reward or punishment for specific behavior. While studies utilizing this definition of achievement motivation have been conducted across racial groups, they have been criticized because of their ethnocentric design, methodology, and instrumentation. Castenell (1984) suggests that future research incorporate the definition espoused by Katz

(1969) and Maehr (1974) which posits that (a) achievement motivation is conscious, (b) the need to achieve is universal to all groups, but (c) "because different groups have different life experiences it is likely that situations or a set of tasks will evoke different group responses" (p. 442).

This section on special populations concludes with guidelines set forth by Williams (1983) that are highly reminiscent of the recommendations put forth in 1975 and cited at the beginning of this chapter. They would appear to encompass concerns regarding the use of achievement tests regardless of students' race, color, national origin, or handicap.

- Test constructors should foster an awareness of the limitations of the tests and the meaning attributed to test scores.
- Test constructors should educate their consumers in selecting tests in terms of particular goals and objectives of educational evaluation.
- Test constructors should bear responsibility for including minorities in all aspects of test development and not limit this to the standardization sample.
- Test consumers must assume some responsibility for developing skills in administering tests and interpreting results in light of the culturally diverse experiences that pupils bring into the testing situation.
- The educational community should minimize or eliminate intelligence testing or substitute appropriately modified assessment techniques and interpretive procedures that consider cultural differences.
- The educational community should focus on achievement rather than intelligence or aptitude testing to eliminate pernicious connotations and unfair placement practices that limit future educational attainment and opportunity. (p. 205)

THE FUTURE OF ACHIEVEMENT TESTS

Computer Adaptive Testing

The final section of this chapter is a discussion of the growth and impact of computerized adaptive testing on the measurement of achievement and what this product of modern technology means to the field of measurement. This is a fitting topic to conclude the previous narrative because computer adaptive testing is the direct result of advances in the fields of psychometrics, mathematics, cognitive learning theory, educational measurement, human engineering, and science technology. It relies as heavily on Glaser's criterion-referenced measurement as it does on Ausubel's cognitive approach to learning, Deno's curriculum-based measurement, Messick's concern with test validity, and Anastasi's continuum of testing.

Overall, educational research and development is most currently preoccupied with enhancing the instructional value of tests, or as Haney (1985) describes it, "making testing more educational" (p. 4). He states that one need not be a dyed-in-the-wool social Darwinist to recognize that the use of standardized testing is increasing because it serves some important social functions. However, certain deficits that currently exist tend to negate the value of these tests: (a) Most testing programs violate the one nearly universal desideratum in all learning theories—in order to learn, an individual needs to receive rapid and specific feedback; (b) Most standardized tests have a very uncertain relationship to the specific teaching and learning that occurs in particular schools and classrooms; (c) The frequent concern to keep standardized testing programs secure limits their educational utility. It is these deficits, both narrowly and broadly defined, that the process of adaptive testing can be seen to rectify.

Adaptive testing is based on the premise that a measurement continuum should parallel a learning/teaching continuum, and if this learning continuum could be adequately measured by an underlying scale extending through its entire range, a student could enter and exit the measurement continuum at points appropriate to his or her current development regardless of age or grade levels (Forbes, 1986). This test development system is based on a measurement model popularly named the Rasch Model after its originator. This model is also referred to as a one-parameter model in contrast to three-parameter models of latent traits which are based not only on item difficulty (single parameter) but also on item discrimination (slope of the difficulty) and on the level of chance performance (guessing).

All item-response theory models must have an item data bank from which test items are drawn in the process of test construction. These items are computer stored and are then retrieved following a logical format. Utilizing a computer, the test can be presented to the student on a video screen with the computer keyboard serving as the response mechanism. Under such a procedure, the computer presents one preconstructed test selected from a group of such tests. The test is tailored so that the computer "jumps" the person to the appropriate item-difficulty range and then gives a preselected sequence of items based on the correctness or incorrectness of the previous response. Generally, fewer items are required to measure performance at a predetermined level of measurement error than is the case with traditional testing procedures. Computerized adaptive tests have been shown also to take less than half the testing time required by traditional achievement tests and to provide more precise ability estimates across the entire ability range. Because the ability estimates and the item parameters are calibrated on a common scale, these estimates are theoretically independent of the particular sample of persons taking the test and the particular sample of items selected by each examiner.

Seminal work done by Weiss (1980) focused on applying computerized adaptive testing to the measurement of achievement, using a methodology to extend beyond the aptitude measurement to which this type of testing had been limited previously. In addition to extending the use of item-characteristic curve theory (ICC) methods from ability testing to the problems of achievement testing, the project was also concerned with developing solutions to unique problems raised in achievement testing, that is, assessment in multiple content areas, mastery testing, the issue of stability of measurement over time, and the effects of immediate feedback as to the correctness or incorrectness of test responses. The findings of this three-year research project supported the use of ICC theory and methods and computerized adaptive testing for the measurement of achievement. However, many new questions were raised in addition to those originally addressed by the research that were in need of further study.

Finally, one of the first studies to compare and equate achievement scores from three alternative methods of testing—paper-administration, computer-administration and computerized adaptive testing—was conducted by Olson (1986) with all students in grades 3 to 6 within three California school districts. A total of 575 students were involved in ,the study. Results of the study indicated that (a) analysis of variance showed no significant differences among the three measures in terms of the comparability of measurement precision; (b) computerized adaptive testing (CAT) required only one fourth of the testing time required by the paper-administered test; (c) the computerized adaptive test provided a more precise ability estimate with smaller variance than either of the other two measures; and (d) the ability estimates calculated from a 20-item CAT tended to show more precision than tests of 55 to 62 items used with the other two measures.

This section on adaptive testing concludes with the

futuristic predictions raised by Hsu and Sadock (1985) in their review, *Computer-assisted Test Construction: The State of the Art*. The authors foresaw the following as commonplace in testing of the future:

1. The development of item construction theories that take advantage of artificial intelligence and the phrase recognizability of the computer.
2. The development of item banks in the area of criterion-referenced achievement tests and in conjunction with textbook publication.
3. Item calibration and test design available on microcomputer.
4. The regular use of computers in test administration.
5. The application of IRT in test design by non-measurement specialists.
6. The use of computerized adaptive and diagnostic testing in the classroom.

Writing about achievement tests in the 1984 edition of the *Handbook of Psychological Assessment,* Fox and Zerkin concluded: "[While] standardized tests are not perfect and can be misused and misunderstood . . . they are currently the best instruments educators have available for assessing the quality of curriculum and for individualizing and improving instructional programs for each child" (p. 130). These conclusions no longer hold.

It is no longer possible to call these standardized measures of achievement the "best" instruments available. It is hoped that the present discourse has led the reader to question practices of the present because of knowledge of the present and to look to the future with eager anticipation. Tests can be a flexible passport into that future or a rigid barrier bound to the past. It is our job as professional educators, in the broadest sense, to insure the former. When describing the failure of the testing profession to inform the public about the meaning of "objective" standardized tests, Strenio (1981) states: "At a minimum, testers have an obligation to avoid placing their particular jargon in any context that makes it even harder for the layman to interpret than it already is" (p. 65). The authors of this chapter hope that they have not been guilty of this same failing.

"Then you should say what you mean," the March Hare went on.

"I do," Alice hastily replied; "at least—at least I mean what I say—that's the same thing, you know."

"Not the same thing a bit!" said the Hatter; "why, you might just as well say that 'I see what I eat' is the same thing as 'I eat what I see!' "

—Lewis Carroll
Alice's Adventures in Wonderland

REFERENCES

Aaron, I., & Poostay, E. (1982). Strategies for reading disorders. In C. Reynolds & T. Gutkin (Eds.), *Handbook of school psychology.* New York: Wiley.

Abadzi, H. (1985). Ability grouping effects on academic achievement and self-esteem: Who performs in the long run as expected. *Journal of Educational Research, 79*(1), 36–40.

Algozzine, B., Ysseldyke, J., & Shinn, M. (1982). Identifying children with learning disabilities: When is a discrepancy severe? *Journal of School Psychology, 20*(4), 299–305.

Allen, T. E., White, C. E., & Karchmer, M. A. (1983). Issues in the development of a special edition for hearing-impaired students of the Seventh Edition of the Stanford Achievement Test. *American Annals of the Deaf, 128,* 34–39.

Altrows, I. F., Maunula, S., & LaLonde, B. D. (1986). Employing teachers' ratings in selection of achievement tests in reading and mathematics with a behaviorally disturbed population. *Psychology in the Schools, 23,* 316–319.

Anastasi, A. (1982). *Psychological testing* (5th ed.). New York: MacMillan.

Anastasi, A. (1984). The K-ABC in historical and contemporary perspective. *Journal of Special Education, 18*(3), 357–366.

Anastasi, A. (1988). *Psychological testing* (6th ed.). New York: MacMillan.

Anderson, R. C. (1972). How to construct achievement tests to assess retention of meaningful verbal material. *Review of Educational Research, 42*(2), 145–170.

Ausubel, D. P. (1960). The use of advance organizers in the learning and retention of meaningful verbal material. *Journal of Educational Psychology, 51,* 145–170.

Ausubel, D. P. (1968). *Educational psychology: A cognitive view.* New York: Holt, Rinehart, and Winston.

Bartholomae, D. (1980). The study of error. *College Composition and Communication, 31,* 253–269.

Boder, E. (1973). Developmental dyslexia: A diagnostic approach based on three atypical reading-spelling patterns. *Developmental Medicine and Child Neurology, 15,* 663–687.

Buros, O. (1974). *Tests in Print II.* Highland Park, NJ: Gryphon Press.

Caskey, W. E. (1986). The use of the Peabody Individual Achievement Test and the Woodcock Reading Mastery Tests in the diagnosis of learning disability in reading: A caveat. *Journal of Learning Disabilities, 19*(6), 336–337.

Castenell, L. (1984). A cross-cultural look at achievement motivation research. *Journal of Negro Education, 53*(4), 435–443.

Chase, W. G., & Simon, H. A. (1973). A perception in class. *Cognitive Psychology* (Vol. 1), 55–81.

Clarizio, H. F., & Phillips, S. E. (1986). The use of standard scores in diagnosing learning disabilities: A critique. *Psychology in the Schools, 23,* 380–387.

Clarke, A. M. (1982). Psychology and education. *British Journal of Educational Studies, 30*(1), 3–56.

Coleman, J. S. (1966). *Equality of educational opportunity.* Washington, DC: U.S. Government Printing Office.

Curtis, M. E. (1980). Development of components of reading skill. *Journal of Educational Psychology, 72*(5), 656–669.

Curtis, M. E., & Glaser, R. (1983). Reading theory and the assessment of reading achievement. *Journal of Educational Measurement, 20*(2), 133–147.

Databank. (1985). *Education Week, 5,* 16.

Deno, S. L. (1985). Curriculum-based measurement: The emerging alternative. *Exceptional Children, 52*(3), 219–232.

Doolittle, A. E. (1986, April). *Gender-based differential item performance in mathematics achievement items.* Paper presented at the annual meeting of the American Educational Research Association, San Francisco, CA.

DuBois, P. H. (1970). *A history of psychological testing.* Boston: Allyn & Bacon.

Eaves, R. C., & Simpson, R. G. (1984). The concurrent validity of the Peabody Individual Achievement Test relative to the Key Math Diagnostic Arithmetic Test among adolescents. *Psychology in the Schools, 21,* 165–167.

Estes, R. E., Hallock, J. E., & Bray, N. M. (1985). Comparison of arithmetic measures with learning disabled students. *Perceptual and Motor Skills, 61,* 711–716.

Findley, W. (1974). Grouping for instruction. In L. P. Miller (Ed.), *The testing of black students: A symposium.* Englewood Cliffs, NJ: Prentice-Hall.

Fischer, R. S. (1981). Measuring linguistic competence in a foreign language. *International Review of Applied Linguistics, 19*(3), 207–217.

Flavell, J. H. (1976). Metacognitive aspects of problem solving. In L. B. Resnick (Ed.), *The nature of intelligence.* Hillsdale, NJ: Erlbaum.

Forbes, D. W. (1986, April). The Rasch Model as a practical and effective procedure for educational measurement. In *Taming the Rasch tiger: Using item response theory in practical educational measurement.* Symposium conducted at the meeting of the National Council on Measurement in Education, San Francisco, CA.

Forness, S., Sinclair, E., & Guthrie, D. (1983). Learning disability discrepancy formulas: Their use in actual practice. *Learning Disability Quarterly, 6,* 107–114.

Fox, L. H., & Zerkin, B. (1984). Achievement tests. In G. Goldstein & M. Hersen (Eds.), *Handbook of psychological assessment* (pp. 119–131). New York: Pergamon Press.

Fuchs, D., Fuchs, L. S., Benowitz, S., & Barringer, K. (1987). Norm-referenced tests: Are they valid for use with handicapped students? *Exceptional Children, 54*(3), 263–271.

Fuchs, D., Fuchs, L. S., Power, M. H., & Darley, A. M. (1985). Bias in the assessment of handicapped children. *American Educational Research Journal, 22,* 185–197.

Glaser, R. (1963). Instructional technology and the measurement of learning outcomes: Some questions. *American Psychologist, 18,* 519–521.

Glaser, R. (1981). The future of testing. A research agenda for cognitive psychology and psychometrics. *American Psychologist, 36*(9), 923–936.

Goh, D. S., Teslow, C. J., & Fuller, G. B. (1981). The practice of psychological assessment among school psychologists. *Professional Psychology, 12,* 696–706.

Green, R. L., & Griffore, R. J. (1980). The impact of standardized testing on minority students. *Journal of Negro Education, 49,* 238–252.

Guion, R. M. (1976). The practice of industrial and organizational psychology. In M. D. Dunnette (Ed.), *Handbook of Industrial and Organizational Psychology.* Chicago: Rand McNally.

Hambleton, R. K. (1980). Test score validity and standard selling methods. In R. A. Berk (Ed.), *Criterion-referenced measurement: The state of the art.* Baltimore: Johns Hopkins University Press.

Hambleton, R. K., & Cignor, D. R. (1978). Guidelines for evaluating criterion-referenced tests and test manuals. *Journal of Educational Measurement, 15,* 321–327.

Haney, W. (1985). Making testing more educational. *Educational Leadership, 43*(2), 4–13.

Harnisch, D. L. (1985). *Computer application issues*

in certification and licensure testing. (ERIC Document Reproduction Service No. ED 261 079)

Henderson, E. H., & Beers, J. W. (Eds.) (1980). *Developmental and cognitive aspects of learning to spell.* ERIC Document RIE Jan. 1986.

Hoover, H. (1984). The most appropriate scores for measuring educational development in the elementary schools: GE's. *Educational Measurement: Issues and Practices, 3,* 8–14.

Hsu, T., & Sadock, S. F. (1985). *Computer-assisted test construction: The state of the art.* ERIC Clearinghouse on Tests, Measurement, and Evaluation, Princeton, NJ.

Hunter, D. R., & Burke, E. F. (1987). Computer-based selection testing in the Royal Air Force. *Behavior Research Methods, Instruments, and Computers, 19*(2), 243–245.

Johnson, S. T. (1979). *The measurement mystique.* Washington, DC: Institute for the Study of Educational Policy.

Karchmer, M., Milone, M., & Wolk, S. (1979). Educational significance of hearing loss at three levels of severity. *American Annals of the Deaf, 124,* 97–109.

Karnes, F. A., Edwards, R. P., & McCallum, R. D. (1986). Normative achievement assessment of gifted children: Comparing the K-ABC, WRAT, and CAT. *Psychology in the Schools, 23,* 346–352.

Katz, I. (1969). A critique of personality approaches to Negro performance, with research suggestions. *Journal of Social Issues, 25,* 13–27.

Kingsbury, G. G., & Weiss, D. J. (1979). *An adaptive strategy for mastery decisions—Research Report 79-5. Computerized adaptive performance evaluations: Final report, February 1976 through January 1980.* Minnesota University, Department of Psychology (Contact # N00014-76-C-0627). Arlington, VA: Office of Naval Research, Personnel and Training Research Programs Office.

LaGrow, S. J., & Prochnow-LaGrow, J. E. (1982). Technical adequacy of the most popular tests selected by responding school psychologists in Illinois. *Psychology in the Schools, 19*(2), 186–189.

Larkin, J., McDermott, J., Simon, D. P., & Simon, H. A. (1980). Expert and novice performance in solving physics problems. *Science, 208,* 1335–1342.

Larry P. vs. Riles, 343 F. Supp. 1306 (N.D. Cal. 1972).

Lazarus, M. (1981). *Goodbye to excellence: A critical look at minimum competency testing.* Boulder, CO: Westview Press.

LeMahieu, P. G. (1984). The effects on achievement and instructional content of a program of student monitoring through frequent testing. *Educational evaluation and policy analysis, 6*(2), 175–187.

Levine, M. (1987). *Developmental variation and learning disorders.* Cambridge: Educators Publishing Service.

Lezak, M. (1983). *Neuropsychological assessment* (2nd ed.). New York: Oxford University Press.

Linn, R. L. (1980). Issues of validity for criterion-referenced measures. *Applied Psychological Measurement, 4*(4), 547–561.

Linn, R. L. (1982). Two weak spots in the practice of criterion-referenced measurement. *Educational Measurement,* Spring, *12–13,* 25.

Maehr, M. (1974). *Sociocultural origins of achievement.* Monterey, CA: Brooks-Cole.

Marton, F., & Säljö, R. (1976a). On qualitative differences in learning—I: Outcome and process. *British Journal of Educational Psychology, 46*(1), 4–11.

Marton, F., & Säljö, R. (1976b). On qualitative differences in learning—II: Outcome as a function of the learner's conception of the task. *British Journal of Educational Psychology, 46*(2), 115–127.

McClelland, D. C., Atkinson, J. W., Clark, R. A., Lowell, E. L. (1953). *The Achievement Motive.* New York: Appleton-Century-Crofts.

McGue, M., Shinn, M., & Ysseldyke, J. (1982). Use of cluster scores on the Woodcock-Johnson Psycho-educational Battery with learning disabled students. *Learning Disability Quarterly, 5,* 274–287.

McPartland, J. M. (1969). The relative influence of school desegregation and of classroom desegregation on the academic achievement of ninth-grade Negro students. *Journal of Social Issues, 25,* 93–102.

Mehrens, W. A., & Lehmann, I. J. (1975). *Standardized tests in education.* New York: Holt, Rinehart, and Winston.

Messick, S. (1965). Personality measurement and the ethics of assessment. *American Psychologist, 20,* 136–142.

Messick, S. (1975). The standard problem: Meaning and values in measurement and evaluation. *American Psychologist, 30,* 955–966.

Messick, S. (1980). Test validity and the ethics of

assessment. *American Psychologist, 35*(11), 1012–1027.

Millman, J. (1973). Passing scores and test lengths for domain-referenced measures. *Review of Educational Research, 43,* 205–216.

Millman, J., Bishop, C., & Ebel, R. (1965). An analysis of test-wiseness. *Educational and Psychological Measurement, 25,* 707–726.

Mirkin, P., Deno, S., Tindal, G., & Kuehnle, K. (1982). Frequency of measurement and data utilization as factors in standardized behavioral assessment of academic skill. *Journal of Behavioral Assessment, 4*(4), 361–370.

Mitchell, J. V. (Ed.). (1985). *The ninth mental measurement yearbook.* Lincoln, NE: University of Nebraska Press.

National School Boards Association (1977). *Standardized achievement testing* (Report No. 1977-1). Washington, DC: Author.

Nolen, P., & McCartin, R. (1984, November). Spelling strategies on the Wide Range Achievement Test. *The Reading Teacher,* 148–158.

Olson, J. B. (1986, April). *Comparison and equating of paper-administered, computer-administered and computerized adaptive tests of achievement.* Paper presented at the annual meeting of the American Educational Research Association, San Francisco, CA.

P.L. 94-142, The Education for All Handicapped Children Act of 1975, 20 U.S.C. SS1401 et seq., 45 C.F.R. 121(a).

Plass, J. A., & Hill, K. T. (1986). Children's achievement strategies and test performance: The role of time pressure, evaluation, anxiety, and sex. *Developmental Psychology, 22*(1), 31–36.

Popham, W. J. (1971). *Criterion-referenced measurement.* Englewood Cliffs, NJ: Educational Technology Publications.

Radencich, M. C. (1985). BASIS: Basic Achievement Skills Individual Screener. *Academic Therapy, 20*(3), 377–382.

Reisman, F. (1982). Strategies for mathematics disorders. In C. Reynolds & T. Gukin (Eds.), *Handbook of school psychology.* New York: Wiley.

Reynolds, C. R. (1984). Critical measurement issues in learning disabilities. *Journal of Special Education, 18*(4), 451–476.

Rothkopf, E. Z. (1965). Some theoretical and experimental approaches to problems in written instruction. In J. D. Krumbaltz (Ed.), *Learning and the educational process* (pp. 193–221). Chicago: Rand McNally.

Sax, G. (1974). *Principles of educational measurement and evaluation.* Belmont, CA: Wadsworth.

Section 504 of the Rehabilitation Act of 1973, 29 U.S.C. 794. 45 C.F.R. 81, 84.

Shepard, L. (1983). The role of measurement in educational policy: Lessons from the identification of learning disabilities. *Educational Measurement: Issues and Practice, 2*(3), 4–8.

Shepard, L. A., & Smith, M. L. (1983). An evaluation of the identification of learning disabled students in Colorado. *Learning Disability Quarterly, 6*(2), 115–127.

Shinn, M., Algozzine, B., Marston, M. A., & Ysseldyke, J. (1982). A theoretical analysis of the performance of learning disabled students on the Woodcock-Johnson Psycho-educational Battery. *Journal of Learning Disabilities, 15*(4), 221–226.

Siegler, R. S. (1976). Three aspects of cognitive development. *Cognitive Psychology, 5,* 481–520.

Stevenson, D. K. (1983). Foreign language testing: All of the above. In C. J. James, *Practical applications of research in foreign language teaching.* Lincolnwood, IL: National Textbook.

Strenio, A. J. (1981). *The testing trap.* New York: Rawson, Wade.

Terry, R. M. (1986). Testing the productive skills: A creative focus for hybrid achievement tests. *Foreign Language Annals, 19*(6), 521–528.

Traub, R. E., & Rowley, G. L. (1980). Reliability of test scores and decisions. *Applied Psychological Measurement, 4,* 517–545.

Trybus, R. J., & Karchmer, M. A. (1977). School achievement scores of hearing-impaired children: National data on achievement status and growth patterns. *American Annals of the Deaf, 122,* 62–69.

Webster, R. E. (1985). The criterion-related validity of psychoeducational tests for actual reading ability of learning disabled students. *Psychology in the Schools, 22,* 152–159.

Weiss, D. J. (1980). *Computerized adaptive performance evaluation: Final report, February 1976 through January 1980.* Minnesota University, Department of Psychology. Arlington, VA: Office of Naval Research, Personnel and Training Research Programs Office.

Williams, T. S. (1983). Some issues in the standardized testing of minority students. *Boston University Journal of Education, 165*(2), 192–208.

Wilson, V., & Reynolds, C. (1984). Another look at evaluating aptitude-achievement discrepancies in the diagnosis of learning disabilities. *Journal of Special Education, 18*(4), 477–494.

Woodcock, R. (1973). *Woodcock Reading Mastery Tests*. Circle Pines, MN: American Guidance Service.

Ysseldyke, J. E., Algozzine, B., Regan, R., & Potter, M. (1980). Technical adequacy of tests used by professionals in simulated decision making. *Psychology in the Schools, 17*(2), 202–209.

Ysseldyke, J. E., & Shinn, M. R. (1981). Psychoeducational evaluation. In J. M. Kauffman & D. P. Hallahan (Eds.), *Handbook of special education* (pp. 418–440). Englewood Cliffs, NJ: Prentice-Hall.

CHAPTER 8

APTITUDE TESTS IN EDUCATIONAL CLASSIFICATION AND PLACEMENT

Daniel J. Reschly

Psychological and educational tests are used extensively in educational settings for a variety of purposes. This chapter emphasizes the use of aptitude tests to make decisions about student classification and placement.

The use of aptitude tests for these purposes has become increasingly controversial in recent years. The controversies involve fundamental questions about the *utility* of such tests for all student populations: that is, do the tests combined with other information improve decisions? They also concern the *fairness* of these tests to minority students; that is, do such tests unfairly penalize minority students and thereby reduce their opportunities?

The analysis of these issues will require discussion of certain basic features of tests, test uses (and misuses), and empirical research with tests. This part of the chapter, although not simple, is reasonably straightforward. There is fairly broad consensus on how certain groups perform on various tests, and the effects of using tests as part of the decision-making process with these groups. What is unclear, however, is whether we *should* use tests as part of important decisions and whether we ought to provide various compensations for lower-scoring groups. The "should" and "ought" questions, involving deep philosophical issues, reflect concerns about test use as an instrument of social policy. Efforts to resolve these questions, especially by legislation and the courts, will also be discussed in this chapter. First, the nature of classification/placement decisions needs to be explored.

TRADITIONAL CLASSIFICATION/ PLACEMENT DECISIONS

In public school settings, traditional classification/ placement involves two related decisions: (a) Is the individual eligible to be classified as handicapped? In some states, students may also be classified as gifted. If characteristics of more than one handicap are present, a primary handicapping condition must also be specified in most instances. (b) If classified, then the kind of program, usually within special education, must be selected so the individual is provided with an "appropriate education."

Traditional placements in special education may vary from only two or three hours per week to fulltime. The amount of time spent within special education usually is directly related to the severity of the handicap which, in turn, is often related to amount of interaction with normal peers. Fulltime programs often are self-contained classrooms where one teacher is responsible for nearly all the instruction for as few as four or five students to as many as 15 or more. It is important to see special education placements as a continuum from "less restrictive environments," such as individual or small group tutoring for as little as two or three hours per week, to the more restrictive, self-contained classrooms. In addition to less contact with normal peers and regular education activities generally, the more restrictive programs usually reflect less emphasis on intellectual/academic skills and more emphasis on functional (very practical) academic skills and broadly conceived social competencies.

Classification/placement is potentially a very significant event in the lives of children. The decision to classify/place may be critical to the development of compensatory mechanisms which enhance the handicapped person's opportunities to lead a normal life. Many examples could be cited. Tutoring, which enables an otherwise bright, high school student with a learning disability to develop basic reading skills, is likely to increase the student's social and vocational opportunities markedly. Speech therapy that is effective in overcoming stuttering, physical therapy for persons with cerebral palsy, mobility training for the blind, social skills development for withdrawn or aggressive students, and many, many other very beneficial special education services become available only *if* the individual is classified and placed. To be denied these services because the student was not or could not be classified as handicapped might very well significantly limit opportunities for an "appropriate education." Court decisions and legislation at the state and federal levels guarantee the rights of handicapped students to an appropriate education at public expense.

There is another side to classification/placement decisions. Placement of a student can involve, for example, a public school curriculum that is so different from the regular curriculum that pursuit of a college education would be very difficult, if not impossible. Furthermore, classification/placement can expose the individual to the stigma associated with the being "named" something like mildly (educable) mentally retarded or emotionally disturbed. These, too, are significant consequences. Improper classification and misplacement through human error, inaccurate assessment information, or misapplication of eligibility criteria might cause very serious harm to the individual. To call a potential Einstein retarded, or to attach that name to someone of more modest intellect (like D. J. Reschly) would indeed be most unfortunate.

In view of the potentially enormous consequences of classification/placement decisions it is not surprising that carefully constructed safeguards have been developed. These safeguards are designed to ensure that classification/placement decisions in educational settings are proper, that those truly handicapped persons *do* receive the special education services they need, and that classification/placement does not occur with students who are *not* truly handicapped. The

safeguards, now firmly entrenched through court opinions and legislation, have vast implications for psychoeducational assessment of students (Reschly, 1987a). A summary of these principles and the implications for assessment are provided in Table 8.1.

Aptitude testing is almost always a significant part of the process whereby classification/placement decisions are made about students. The nature of aptitudes and the devices used to assess aptitudes are an integral part of classification/placement decisions. Results of aptitude assessment, especially if done poorly, may put a person into an improper classification/placement or deny a needed classification/placement. In view of the consequences of these decisions, it is not surprising that aptitude testing has been scrutinized carefully in recent years.

THE APTITUDE-INTELLIGENCE-ACHIEVEMENT DISTINCTION

Aptitude, achievement, and intelligence as kinds of tests are not easily distinguished. The traditional distinction was that achievement tests reflect the effects of learning whereas aptitude and intelligence tests reflected the individual's potential for success. In this traditional view, both aptitude and intelligence were seen as relatively enduring traits of the individual, not easily modified by experience or special training. In some instances both aptitude and intelligence test results were regarded as indications of innate capacity.

These traditional meanings of aptitude, achievement, and intelligence tests are rejected in all the leading measurement texts from the last decade (e.g., Anastasi, 1988; Brown 1983; Cronbach, 1984). Anastasi also pointed out that these tests were recognized as being essentially the same as early as 1927. Still, the idea that these tests are very different persists, especially in some introductory psychology or educational psychology texts.

Current measurement texts stress certain commonalities among aptitude, achievement, and intelligence tests. All are tests of what now is characterized as "developed abilities," indicating that all these tests reflect the effects of experience or, simply, learning. They also are characterized as being "maximum performance" tests, meaning that the examinees are encouraged to exhibit their very best efforts or to do as well as possible. This is in contrast to "typical performance" measures, for example, interest inventories

Table 8.1. Legal Principles and Education of the Handicapped: Implications for Assessment

PRINCIPLE	EFFECTS	IMPLICATIONS FOR ASSESSMENT
RIGHT TO EDUCATION	—More students classified as handicapped. —New populations of handicapped students entered the public schools.	—Greatly increased need for individual psychoeducational assessment. —Need for specialized skills in assessment of low incident and more severely handicapped.
LEAST RESTRICTIVE ENVIRONMENT	—Handicapped students served in as normal an environment as possible including regular classrooms with support services or parttime special education.	—More emphasis on assessment in the natural environment through observations, etc., and the development and evaluation of interventions in the natural environment.
INDIVIDUALIZED EDUCATIONAL PROGRAM	—Development of detailed plans to guide interventions with learning or behavior problems. —Annual reviews of effects of interventions.	—More emphasis on descriptions of specific educational needs and problem behaviors. —More emphasis on use of assessment information to design interventions and to monitor progress.
DUE PROCESS *PARC v. Pa (1972)*	—Formal procedures to ensure fairness through informed consent, access to records, appeal, and hearing.	—Greater scrutiny of the entire decision making process including psychoeducational assessment. —More emphasis on open communication with parents concerning instruments, results, and recommendations based on assessment data.
PROTECTION IN EVALUATION PROCEDURES	—Numerous guidelines concerning the preplacement and reevaluation of handicapped students: multifactored assessment, multidisciplinary team, valid procedures, appropriate in terms of handicap, primary language, nondiscrimination, etc.	—More emphasis on adaptive behavior, sociocultural status, and primary language, and less emphasis on global measures such as IQ. —More emphasis on determination of specific educational need, and less emphasis on underlying dynamics. —Assessment tailored to nature of child. —Assessment conducted by a team of professionals.

and personality tests, on which examinees are encouraged to respond according to their *usual* thoughts, feelings, or actions.

Perhaps the single most persuasive bit of evidence on the commonalities among these types of tests is that the same type of test item or even the same test battery may be used as a measure of achievement or aptitude at different times with different examinees. This apparently was the case with the Iowa Tests of Educational Development (ITED) which, according to Mercer (1979a), was widely used as an achievement test battery with high school students *and* as an aptitude test in the National Merit Scholarship competition. When the same test is used as an achievement measure in one instance and as an aptitude test in another, it clearly is impossible to argue that the differences among achievement and aptitude reside in characteristics of the test, content, format, or process. A final example to illustrate this point is the often mentioned but, as far as I know, never reported or researched activity of placing the items from group-administered aptitude and achievement tests on cards, mixing up the cards, and then attempting to sort the items according to whether they reflect aptitude or achievement content, format, or process. Presumably, it would be difficult if not impossible to exceed chance in the assignment of items.

If not test type, then what is/are the difference(s) among aptitude, achievement, and intelligence? Snow (1980) argued that each was an important and useful psychological construct and facilitated the development of theory, research, and practice. The most important differences among them have to do with *how* they are used and with assumptions about *antecedent experiences* (Anastasi, 1980; Brown, 1983).

The achievement construct and associated tests are attempts to measure learning that occurred in a specific circumscribed situation. Achievement has a past and present reference (Brown, 1983). In contrast, aptitude has a future reference. The aptitude construct involves general and incidental learning experiences that are related to how persons perform in future learning or training situations (Anastasi, 1988; Brown, 1983). As a construct, aptitude is used quite broadly, especially in the theory and research on aptitude by treatment interactions (ATI) (Cronbach & Snow, 1977; Snow, 1980). Here, aptitude is virtually any psychological characteristic of the person that *predicts* differences among people in later learning or training situations. Included in this very broad conception of aptitude are general ability, specific cognitive skills, and prior achievement, all cognitive or thinking/knowledge characteristics, personality/affective characteristics such as anxiety, achievement motivation, etc.

Obviously, the situation can be very confusing. Conspicuous by its absence in the above discussion is the construct of intelligence, perhaps the most controversial of the aptitude-achievement-intelligence trilogy. Intelligence, sometimes used synonymously with ability, is usually seen as lying somewhere between achievement and aptitude on the continuum of test use and antecedent experiences. Intelligence is often described as having a present reference, reflecting very broad, general learning experiences. Moreover, intelligence as a form of test is often used in diagnostic work with individuals which, as Anastasi (1980, 1988) demonstrates, is essentially the same as prediction.

It now appears we have gone nearly full circle! However, there are trends today in test development which will, if followed consistently in the future, reduce much of the confusion. First, intelligence is rarely used in the names of newly developed tests that are, for all intents and purposes, similar in content and intended use to traditional intelligence tests. The term *IQ* as a kind of score also is used less frequently in the newer tests. The trend away from intelligence and IQ is particularly strong with group-administered tests designed for school-age children (Lennon, 1980). These tests increasingly use names such as *school ability, cognitive ability, scholastic aptitude,* etc. Newly developed individual intelligence tests reflect a similar trend (e.g., Kaufman & Kaufman, 1983). Interestingly, at least part of the acceptance of these newer tests depends on whether they are highly similar to traditional intelligence tests. This was quite apparent in Kaufman and Kaufman's (1977) contention that the General Cognitive Index on the McCarthy Scale of Children's Ability was essentially equivalent in meaning to an IQ score from well-accepted, older intelligence tests such as the Stanford-Binet Intelligence Test or the Wechsler Intelligence Scale for Children.

General Aptitude or Intelligence

In at least one major segment of the testing profession today the terms general aptitude and intelligence are nearly synonymous. The tests used in public education with school age groups to *diagnose* learning problems and to *predict* likely level of academic performance are increasingly called *general aptitude, scholastic aptitude,* or *school ability.* These tests are *not* different in any significant respect from traditional general intelligence tests. The change in name does imply a change in the interpretation of results from these tests, a topic discussed later. Moreover, certain older individual tests such as the Wechsler Intelligence Scale for Children-Revised (WISC-R) and the Stanford-Binet (SB) still use scores called IQs and retain *intelligence* in their names. However, in at least one instance to date, the publisher of the WISC-R, the Psychological Corporation, permitted a seemingly radical change in the name and interpretation of the conventional WISC-R IQ scores. In the System of

Multicultural Pluralistic Assessment (SOMPA) (Mercer, 1979a), the WISC-R IQ score is renamed School Functioning Level (SFL). Thus, the trend away from intelligence and IQ is even apparent with the traditional tests.

Tests of general aptitude or intelligence used in public education settings have the following general characteristics: (a) Heterogeneous item-types and formats are used (usually within the same test). (b) Complex cognitive operations are required (as opposed to simple recognition or memory). (c) Power rather than speed is emphasized. (d) A general factor is apparent, sometimes augmented by less robust, but stable group factors. The WISC-R is a prime example of this kind of test. The WISC-R typically is used to diagnose or to predict, activities which are, as noted earlier, very similar. Clearly, the WISC-R is a test of developed abilities as are all aptitude, achievement, and intelligence tests. The antecedent experiences reflected in the WISC-R are not defined at all precisely and might be characterized generally as "growing up in America in the twentieth century" (Anastasi, 1980, p. 7). As an aside, that characterization might be broadened even further to something like, "growing up in any twentieth-century literate, technological society" since translated versions of the WISC-R are used widely and successfully in Europe and Japan. After a brief section on specific aptitude tests, the discussion of uses of general aptitude tests will continue.

Specific Aptitudes or Tests of Psychological Processes

Tests of specific aptitudes, or what are sometimes called the psychological processes related to learning, are also used in the public schools as part of classification/placement and/or program planning/ intervention decisions. These specific aptitude tests, in contrast to general scholastic aptitude or intelligence tests, usually have fairly homogeneous items that are intended to assess rather specific discrete (presumably independent) abilities. Numerous underlying learning processes have been postulated and even more tests attempting to measure these functions have been developed. Some examples of these special aptitudes are visual-motor memory, auditory discrimination, visual closure, and auditory sequential memory.

The specific aptitude tests have been used for three kinds of decisions in the public schools. First, criteria for classifying students as handicapped sometimes require demonstration of deficits in one or more of these specific aptitudes or processes. This is most likely to be the case with the area of learning disabilities, although the definite trend in that field is toward less emphasis on process variables or specific aptitudes. A second use is to establish objectives for remedial interventions. In this instance the process deficit in, say, auditory closure becomes the educational objective. A wide variety of materials and activities have been designed to develop these processing skills. Finally, the most frequent current use is to choose teaching method or strategy based on apparent strengths in particular processes or "modalities." The most frequent strategy choice is between sight/ whole word versus phonic approaches to teaching reading. Presumably students with strengths in the visual-motor modality and a weakness in the auditory-vocal modality would do best if a sight/whole word method were used. Conversely, phonic methods would be expected to be most beneficial for students with auditory-vocal strengths and visual-motor weaknesses. These predictions are almost identical to our earlier description of an aptitude by treatment interaction (ATI), that is, a psychological characteristic of the learner that predicts different reactions to treatment conditions.

Recent trends toward greater emphasis on neuropsychological explanations and "treatments" of mild learning problems also rely heavily on assumptions of treatment by aptitude interactions (Hartlage, 1986; Hartlage & Reynolds, 1981; Hynd, Obrzut, Hayes, & Becker, 1986; Reynolds, 1986). Here the assumption is that utilization of intact areas of the brain or neurological processing strengths will lead to better educational outcomes. This approach is virtually identical to the third use of specific aptitudes described in the preceding paragraph. Again, the principal application occurs with selection of methods to teach reading.

Specific aptitude, psychological process assessment and teaching, and neuropsychological "treatment" of mild learning problems have not fared at all well in the research conducted over the past 10 years or so. Although various methodological difficulties certainly do exist in this research, collectively it has produced certain nearly inescapable conclusions: (a) Most of the specific aptitude or process measures, including those used in neuropsychological evaluations of children have poor psychometric characteristics, for example, low reliability and doubtful validity (Reschly & Gresham, 1989; Salvia & Ysseldyke, 1988); (b) There is little evidence that the processes can be successfully taught, and even less evidence that improvements in these processes lead to better performance in relevant academic subjects (see Hammill & Larsen, 1974, 1978; Newcomer, Larsen, & Hammill, 1975). (c) There is virtually no evidence for aptitude by treatment interactions using these process measures and currently available teaching strategies (Ysseldyke & Mirkin, 1982). For these reasons, along with the development of other criteria for classifying children as learning disabled, there has been a steady decline in the use of process measures in public school settings. However, the recent expansion of neuropsychological concepts to explain and "treat" learning disorders among school-age children, a revival of process concepts using different terminology and another set of theoretical constructs, will ensure that specific aptitude tests will continue to be used. Overall, specific aptitude tests are not used as widely nor have they been as central to educational classification/placement and program planning/intervention decisions as general aptitude or intelligence tests.

USES OF GENERAL APTITUDE TESTS

General aptitude tests, or what earlier were called tests of intelligence, are used for a variety of purposes in educational settings. A number of group and individually administered tests are available from the major test publishers.

Group Tests

Group tests are probably used less frequently than before. The results of group tests are hardly ever used as a significant part of classification/placement decisions with handicapped students, but they may be a key part of identification of gifted students.

Group tests of academic aptitude may be given to students two to three times during their public school careers. In contrast, group-administered achievement tests are given far more often, usually annually or every other year. It is my impression that the use of group aptitude tests has declined significantly in recent years due to the criticisms of their utility, concerns about labeling effects, and disproportionate impact on minority students. In some areas *group* scholastic aptitude or intelligence tests are banned. Group tests generally have the following characteristics: (a) use of a pencil-and-paper format where the examinee reads the items and selects responses, usually on a machine-scorable answer sheet; (b) use of time limits, although the time limits are generally established so that nearly all examinees can complete

the test; and (c) multiple-choice format where a best or correct answer is selected from a limited number of options. Group scholastic aptitude tests are typically used to establish general expectations for level of academic achievement and as part of the initial stages of identifying students as intellectually gifted. These general screening functions of group aptitude tests are emphasized as opposed to diagnostic or classification/placement decisions.

A definite trend in recent years is the shift from titles or terminology involving mental ability or intelligence to newer terminology that has fewer connotations of innate ability. Two examples are the change of the Lorge-Thorndike Intelligence Test to the Cognitive Ability Test and the change of the Otis-Lennon Mental Ability Test to the Otis-Lennon School Ability Test. The changes in terminology appear to be efforts to delimit interpretations of scores and to restrict inferences to the school setting (Lennon, 1980).

Group aptitude tests are very efficient means of collecting information that, at least for groups, has very high reliability and validity. The results of group intelligence tests would undoubtedly be useful to persons doing individual psychoeducational assessments of students suspected of being handicapped. For example, it is highly unlikely that a student who scores in the average range or above on a group-administered test would obtain a significantly lower score on an individually administered test. An average or above score for a youngster who is referred would then obviate the need for administering the individual intelligence test, an activity that is very time consuming and expensive. However, it should be emphasized that students who obtain low scores on group ability tests should be administered an individually administered test before inferences are made about scholastic aptitude. It is necessary to use the individual test before such inferences are made because the student may have been penalized on the group test due to reading difficulties, inability to work efficiently, or a variety of other reasons. It should be noted that these interpretations have the effect of giving the individual the benefit of doubt or, to put it another way, we accept at face value evidence indicating the individual has average or above average scholastic aptitude but we regard low scores on group tests with considerable skepticism requiring confirmation from individually administered tests and a variety of other information as well.

Group-administered scholastic aptitude tests are used widely with young adults. These tests are typically administered prior to college entrance where they frequently are called scholastic aptitude tests.

More advanced and sophisticated versions of these kinds of tests are administered as part of the process whereby individuals are selected for entrance to professional schools, law, dentistry, and medicine or to graduate programs in a variety of areas. These scholastic aptitude tests are often regarded as being fair to minority students when precise statistical criteria are used to assess fairness (Anastasi, 1988).

Individual Tests

Individual tests are administered only under special conditions. The vast majority of students are never administered an individual test of intelligence and, as noted above, some places do not use group tests of intelligence. Individually administered tests of intelligence typically involve the following: (a) Subtests are presented orally by the examiner to a single examinee. (b) Questions typically are administered one at a time without a great deal of emphasis on speed of response. (c) The individual usually has the opportunity to construct his or her response rather than being required to select a response from a limited number of options. Most individually administered tests must be given by someone who has, at a minimum, a master's degree in a relevant area, most often psychology or school psychology.

Individual scholastic aptitude tests, such as the WISC-R, the Stanford-Binet, McCarthy's Scale of Children's Ability, and the Kaufman Assessment Battery for Children (K-ABC), are typically given in public school settings by school psychologists. There are approximately 21,000 school psychologists working in the public schools in the United States. The major traditional role of these professionals, requiring about two-thirds of their time, is to conduct individual comprehensive evaluations with students who are referred, most often by teachers, because of learning and/or adjustment problems in the classroom (Reschly, Genshaft, & Binder, 1987). School psychologists provide a variety of services in the public schools and the future trends discussed later may lead to substantial changes in assessment procedures and purposes. Nevertheless, administration of individual tests continues to be the dominant role.

A complex, not very well understood process, is involved in classification/placement decisions (Bickel, 1982). Psychoeducational assessment is an important component. However, other steps—failure in the regular classroom, insufficiency of regular education remedial services, referral, screening, etc.—are also very important steps in the process whereby students may be classified as handicapped.

Individual tests are most often important steps in classification decisions with the *mildly* handicapped. Mildly handicapped students most often involve the classifications of learning disability (LD), educable or mild mental retardation (EMR), and emotional/behavioral disorders. These handicaps account for a large percentage of the school-age (5–18) population of handicapped students. These handicaps typically are mild in degree meaning that (a) the learning or adjustment problem is not so severe to render the individual incapable of being involved with regular classroom instruction, (b) the handicapping condition usually is not visible, that is, individuals do not display physical, sensory, or motor disabilities that are easily recognized, and (c) these handicapping conditions usually are identified first in a school setting and the individual so identified may be regarded as normal in other settings and at preschool or adult ages (Reschly, 1987b).

The criteria for classification in the mildly handicapping categories usually require underlying intellectual/aptitude dimensions that often can be examined only through the use of standardized tests. This is particularly true with mild or educable mental retardation where intelligence or scholastic aptitude is fundamental to the classification criteria. Intelligence or scholastic aptitude tests are also used in almost all classification decisions involving children with LD. The emphasis on intelligence with LD classification has increased in recent years as a result of the dissatisfaction discussed earlier with the process criteria and the corresponding greater emphasis on "severe discrepancy" (*Federal Register*, 1977a; Mercer, Hughes, & Mercer, 1985). In LD classification the severe discrepancy almost always means examining the difference between the results from an individual intelligence test and a measure of educational achievement in certain areas (e.g., reading or mathematics). If this discrepancy is large enough to be regarded as "severe," which is a difficult judgment fraught with possible measurement artifacts and logical inconsistencies (Coles, 1978; Salvia & Ysseldyke, 1988), the student may be classified as LD. Recall the earlier discussion of the overlap in the constructs and the tests of achievement and aptitude (intelligence). Depending on the nature of the test and the assumptions about preceding experiences, the search for the severe discrepancy may involve comparing measures of the same attribute. In this instance, by no means entirely unrealistic, it is hard to know what any difference among the measures might mean. Despite these and many other problems in LD classification/placement, the number and percent of students classified as LD continues to expand (*Ninth Annual Report*, 1987), and the more stringent criteria for LD classification, implemented recently in many states, usually establish precise limits for the size of the discrepancy between aptitude and achievement (Mercer et al., 1985).

Individual scholastic aptitude tests are less important in classification of emotional disturbance/behavior disorders, but surveys of school assessment practices indicate that such tests are almost always used with these students. Individual scholastic aptitude tests also are given quite frequently to students who have more visible handicaps (e.g., sensory or physical deficits such as hearing impairment or cerebral palsy). In these areas, though, intelligence tests are not used as part of the basic classification process which, more often than not, is accomplished by medical specialists. Here, the individual test results are used to estimate likely level of academic performance as well as to rule out the possibility of the associated handicap of mental retardation. Intelligence test use with these populations of handicapped persons, that is, the more severely handicapped, is not particularly controversial because there is no significant overrepresentation in these handicapping areas by race, social status, or gender. Use of individual tests with the mildly handicapped has become increasingly controversial in recent years because of concern about fairness to specific sociocultural groups.

APTITUDE TESTING AND MINORITY STUDENTS

The use of intelligence (i.e., general aptitude), tests as part of the process of educational classification/placement was severely criticized in the 1970s by a number of minority educators and psychologists. These allegations have led to litigation in the 1970s and 1980s as well as other challenges with far-reaching implications. Jones and Wilderson (1976) suggested that poor assessment practices and use of biased tests were part of an overall pattern of institutional racism, a theme expanded in Jones and Jones (1987).

Williams (1970) commented, "Ability testing is being utilized to dehumanize, damage, and destroy black children and youth through improperly labeling and classifying them" (p. 5). Samuda (1975) stated that "the implications and consequences of testing for minority group individuals are real, drastic, and pervasive in their effects at all stages in the lives of minority individuals" (p. 69). Finally, Hilliard's remarks (quoted below) mention the major topics in this

section: overrepresentation, litigation, test bias, and concepts of fairness.

> At any point when a certain cultural group is overrepresented in a particular category of special education, the special educator should spare no effort to review the system of assessment for cultural bias. . . . It is a shame and a disgrace that the courts and the legislature are left to overrule the bad practices which are so widespread among us. (Hilliard, 1980, p. 587)

Overrepresentation

Disproportionate representation occurs whenever an identifiable group has significantly greater or fewer members in a particular classsification than would be expected from their actual numbers or percentages in the general population. Some kinds of over- or underrepresentation are well known and widely accepted, for example, more males have problems in learning to read or more economically disadvantaged students, including minority students, are in the Head Start and Chapter 1 programs. Other forms of disproportionate classification are viewed by some as discriminatory.

Disproportionate classification/placement of minority students is likely to be viewed as discriminatory, at least by some people, when the following conditions exist: (a) The classification/placement is associated with a label that is negative (e.g., mentally retarded or behavior disordered). (b) The student is separated from normal peers (e.g., placement in a self-contained special education class or suspension from school). (c) Ineffective or marginally effective programs are provided as a result of the classification/placement. This analysis of disproportionality is similar to the conclusions of the National Academy of Sciences report on minority overrepresentation in special education (Heller, Holtzman, & Messick, 1982). This prestigious panel changed the question from "Why does minority overrepresentation occur?" to "Why is minority overrepresentation viewed as a problem?" They then concluded that overrepresentation is a problem under four conditions: (a) poor regular education instruction, (b) improper or invalid referral decisions, (c) inappropriate or biased assessment procedures, and (d) ineffective special education programs.

A recent report by the National Council of Advocates for Students (1988) concluded that African-American students are considerably more likely than other ethnic groups to be subjected to corporal punishment, suspended from school, and classified as mildly mentally retarded or behavior disordered and placed in special education. These trends were apparent in nearly all states, including certain northern states such as Iowa with low numbers of minority students. A critical and unanswered question is whether educational overrepresentation of African-American students is attributable to the effects of poverty, to discrimination by teachers and others, or to other courses not yet identified and understood. The poverty explanation is particularly cogent and plausible in the area of mild or educable mental retardation (EMR), a phenomenon known for decades to occur more frequently in poverty circumstances regardless of race or ethnicity (Reschly, 1986a; Richardson, 1981).

Overrepresentation of African-American students in special education programs for the EMR has been the most controversial issue to date and the subject of considerable litigation that has vast implications for aptitude assessment. Before examining that litigation and associated issues, we need to examine closely the nature of overrepresentation statistics. Overrepresentation statistics are frequently misunderstood. Consider these undisputed facts from the now famous *Larry P. v. Riles* (1979) trial. African-American students constituted 10% of the total California student population, but 25% of the enrollment in EMR special education classes. The question for the reader to ponder is this: What percent of African-American students were in EMR programs? The answer, to the shock of many, was 1.1%, that is, only 1% of African-American students were in EMR programs. Surprising? The difference in perspective arises from the widely varying impressions created by three statistics: (a) percent of the general population by group (10% African-American), (b) percent of EMR program by group (25% African-American), and (c) percent of group in EMR program (1.1% African-American). Similar findings have been reported for other states and districts (Reschly, 1986a). The point is that the degree of overrepresentation is frequently distorted by use of statistics that are easily misinterpreted to suggest that large percentages of minority students are disproportionately placed in special education or subjected to various punishments such as suspension.

LITIGATION AND LEGISLATION

Over the last 20 years there has been a recognizable cycle of litigation-legislation-litigation (Bersoff, 1982a; Reschly, 1988). The overall effects of a number of court cases and legislative actions have been to establish a set of principles which attempt to guarantee certain rights, establish procedural safeguards, and ensure appropriate assessment procedures. These principles and their implications for assessment practices were presented earlier in Table 8.1. In this section the specific legal influences on aptitude testing are discussed.

Overrepresentation of minorities in EMR programs has provoked suspicion of continued segregation by race in several cases filed in federal district courts. Segregation by race in public educational settings was, of course, ruled unconstitutional in the famous *Brown* decision in 1954. The *Brown* decision usually is cited as the seminal event in judicial scrutiny of the assessment procedures used in educational classification/placement (Bersoff, 1979, 1981, 1982a). The *Brown* decision has been refined and extended by numerous succeeding cases and legislation. The courts now often view practices which have a disproportionate impact on minorities with special scrutiny. At times, this special scrutiny has meant that the burden of proof is shifted to defendants rather than residing with the plaintiffs because the courts are concerned about removing all vestiges of segregation in education. This very complicated legal issue, which continues to evolve as cases are decided through the district courts, the appellate courts, and the U. S. Supreme Court, is parallel in many ways to the competing concepts of fairness to be discussed in a later section. However, the crucial issue is whether discriminatory intent is required or whether the far less stringent criterion of disproportionate impact on minorities is sufficient to establish constitutionally impermissible discrimination. The courts to date have vacillated on this question, mirroring the rather ambivalent views of the entire society on the most appropriate and equitable methods to remove all vestiges of discrimination. But, as we shall see, burden of proof is extremely important in aptitude testing cases because it is virtually impossible to prove unequivocally with the available research either that tests are biased or that tests are fair.

The major classification/placement court cases have been class action suits pressed by minority plaintiffs alleging discrimination in EMR classification/placement. Overrepresentation data, discussed earlier, were used in plaintiffs' arguments that the defendant school districts and state departments of education were using practices that reestablished or preserved segregation by race. In all the placement-bias court cases to date the classification of primary concern was EMR and the objectionable placement was the self-contained special class.

Pre-1975 Litigation

Class action court cases on behalf of African-American, Hispanic, and Native-American students (e.g., *Diana*, 1970; *Guadalupe*, 1971) in the early

1970s either were decided in favor of minority plaintiffs or were settled by consent decrees agreeable to plaintiffs (Reschly, 1987a). Fairness of intelligence tests and use of adaptive behavior were the central issues, and little or no attention was devoted to other aspects of the referral-placement process. The cases settled prior to 1975 generally involved a variety of poor and sometimes unethical practices in addition to the test fairness issue (MacMillan, 1982). For example, some bilingual students were classified as mentally retarded and placed in special education programs on the basis of *verbal* IQ scales that unfairly penalized them for lack of familiarity with English. In other instances, defendant school districts did not even contest plaintiffs' allegations that short-form intelligence scales and even group-administered verbal scales were used by poorly trained personnel as the basis for classification of bilingual students. In addition, parents were at least occasionally not even informed, let alone accorded rights of consent, when their children were referred, evaluated, and placed in a special education program.

The plaintiffs described deplorable conditions in the special education programs. These included little academic emphasis, poor facilities, and inadequately trained teachers (MacMillan, 1982). For obvious reasons, defendants in the early cases (school districts and state departments of education) had little choice but to acknowledge plaintiff complaints and agree to various reforms establishing due process, informed consent, and other protections for parents and children (MacMillan, 1982; Reschly, 1987a).

These early cases also established several requirements concerning assessment practices. Classification decisions were to be based on a broad spectrum of information, including adaptive behavior outside school, not just IQ test scores. The child's primary language was to be determined and assessment devices were to be administered in this language. For bilingual students, more emphasis was to be placed on nonverbal or performance measures. This was particularly relevant for Hispanic and Native-American students. These reforms were entirely consistent with best practice standards and had the effect of eliminating some very poor practices that were probably *not* typical of assessment practices at that time.

Legislation

State and federal legislation in the mid-1970s incorporated many of the key reforms from the early placement-bias cases (Prasse, 1978). The Federal Education for All Handicapped Children Act of 1975 (Public Law 94-142), with the accompanying rules

and regulations (*Federal Register*, 1977b), was the most important and most widely applicable legislative act. The Protection in Evaluation Procedures Provision section of the P.L. 94-142 Rules and Regulations has enormous implications for assessment (see Table 8.2). Many of these requirements have unequivocal language, for example, "must," but no definitions of key concepts; also, criteria for evaluating assessment practices are not provided. No criteria are provided for determining discrimination, nor are there suggestions for the level and kind of validity evidence that might be needed. Is overrepresentation evidence of discrimination? Are nonbiased tests required, or is an equal placement rate sufficient? How valid? Is a correlation of .5 with a relevant criterion sufficient? How specific must the validity evidence be? This latter concern may be a particularly difficult problem due to the very sparse research based on test use with handicapped persons (Sherman & Robinson, 1982). In view of these rather sweeping generalizations, further litigation to define the meaning of these legislative require-

Table 8.2. Protection in Evaluation Procedures of P.L. 94-142

---

a) Nondiscrimination: "Testing and evaluation materials and procedures used for the purposes of evaluation and placement of handicapped children must be selected and administered so as not to be racially or culturally discriminatory."

b) "Full and individual evaluation of the child's educational needs."

c) Use of "child's native language or other mode of communication, unless it is clearly not feasible to do so."

d) Tests and other evaluation devices "have been validated for the specific purpose for which they are used."

e) Administered by trained personnel.

f) "assess specific areas of educational needs and not merely . . . a single general intelligence quotient."

g) *No* single procedure used as sole criterion for classification or placement.

h) Multidisciplinary team.

i) Multifactored assessment required in preplacement evaluation.

j) Reevaluation of classification and placement at least every three years.

Note. Quoted statements are from *Federal Register*, 1977b, pp. 42496-97.

ments was a near-certain outcome. That indeed has been the case over the past decade.

Litigation 1975–1988

Four trials have been heard in the federal district courts in three federal judicial circuits over the issue of overrepresentation of African-American students in special education classes for the educable mentally retarded (EMR). Although each case was slightly different, the same essential issues were argued in each: (a) Did African-American student overrepresentation in EMR programs constitute discrimination, particularly, violation of the P.L. 94-142 prohibition against discrimination (see Table 8.2)? (b) Did the overrepresentation occur due to improper referral practices, inappropriate and biased tests of general intellectual functioning, and inadequate use of adaptive behavior information? Furthermore, all were class action suits filed by minority advocacy groups who clearly harbored additional implicit assumptions about EMR special classes, uses of tests, and the meaning of mild mental retardation (Elliott, 1987; Reschly, 1987a). First, the trials are considered, followed by discussion of implicit issues and implications for psychoeducational assessment.

Larry P. v. Riles (1979, 1984, 1986)

Extensive discussion of The *Larry P*. case has appeared in the literature over the past 10 years (Condas, 1980; Elliott, 1987; Hilliard, 1983; Lambert, 1981; MacMillan & Meyers, 1980; Madden, 1980; Mercer, 1979b; Prasse & Reschly, 1986; Reschly, 1980a; Reschly, Kicklighter, & McKee, 1988b, 1988c; Sattler, 1981, 1982). *Larry P*. will not be discussed as extensively here as the *Marshall v. Georgia* (1984, 1985) case, a lesser known but equally important case dealing with nearly identical issues.

Larry P. was first before the courts in December, 1981. The *Larry P*. case resulted in a lengthy court opinion, federal circuit court of appeals action and at least three injunctions, the most recent in 1986.

Larry P. dealt with the fundamental issues of African-American student overrepresentation in EMR programs. *Larry P*., and a similar case, *PASE v. Hannon*, 1980, were focused almost exclusively on the issue of alleged biases in individually administered tests of intelligence, particularly the Wechsler Intelligence Scale-Revised, and the Stanford-Binet. The *Larry P*. trial involved expert witness testimony from a number of leading American psychologists. The critical issues, as stated by Judge Peckham in his trial

opinion (*Larry P*., 1979), were the degree to which there were cultural biases in IQ tests, whether individual items were biased against African-American students, whether IQ testing was part of a longstanding, historical pattern of racism that continued to the present, whether there was a higher incidence of EMR among African-American students, and whether explanations other than bias in tests could account for the overrepresentation in EMR programs. On all these questions Judge Peckham's ruling adopted the position of the *Larry P*. plaintiffs; specifically, IQ tests were regarded as biased, part of a historical pattern of racism, and that biases in the IQ tests, rather than other explanations such as the effects of poverty, accounted for the overrepresentation of African-American students in EMR programs. Judge Peckham then issued a strongly worded ban on overrepresentation of African-American students in programs for the mildly retarded as well as a prohibition against the use of IQ tests with African-American students considered for the classification of EMR.

The defendant, the California State Department of Education, appealed the *Larry P*. decision to the Ninth Circuit Court of Appeals. In a split, 2–1 decision, the Circuit Court of Appeals upheld the trial opinion in 1984. The prohibition against overrepresentation and the ban on IQ tests was further expanded through an injunction issued by Judge Peckham in 1986. This expanded injunction provided a strongly worded prohibition against virtually any use of IQ tests with African-American students as well as the proviso that the parents of African-American students must not be contacted by schools seeking permission to administer individual intelligence tests.

From *Larry P*. we have a comprehensive ban on the use of individually administered intelligence tests with African-American students. This ban is predicated on an opinion that found IQ tests to be biased and part of a longstanding pattern of discriminatory treatment of African-American students. The trial opinion was upheld by the federal circuit court of appeals, thus strengthening the case law precedent value of the trial opinion.

PASE v. Hannon (1980)

PASE v. Hannon was a federal court case in Illinois dealing with the now familiar issue of African-American student overrepresentation in EMR programs. Like *Larry P*., the *PASE* trial focused almost exclusively on the use of individually administered IQ tests with African-American students. In sharp contrast to *Larry P*., however, Judge Grady's opinion in *PASE* found that IQ tests were, by and large, unbiased.

Moreover, any biases in IQ tests were overcome by the extensive protections established in P.L. 94-142 (see Table 8.2).

PASE does not have the same precedent value as Larry P. or Marshall because it was not heard by a court of appeals and the issues in PASE were rendered moot by actions of the Chicago Board of Education in 1981. Briefly, the Chicago Board of Education, despite having won the PASE decision at the federal district court level, agreed to a comprehensive ban on the use of individually administered IQ tests, thus rendering the basic issue in the case moot. At that point, the PASE plaintiffs withdrew their appeal to the circuit court and the PASE decision then stood at the district court level, with issues having been rendered moot with no possibility of further court action.

Marshall v. Georgia (1984, 1985)

Although lesser known, Marshall v. Georgia has the same case law precedent value as Larry P. Both cases dealt with the fundamental issue of overrepresentation of African-American students in EMR special education programs. Marshall v. Georgia was heard in a lengthy trial in 1983 in Savannah, Georgia. The trial opinion was published in 1984, appealed by plaintiffs later in 1984, then upheld in 1985 in a unanimous decision by the Eleventh Circuit Court of Appeals.

The Marshall plaintiffs, representing a class defined as African-American students placed in Georgia EMR special education programs, alleged violation of federal regulations concerning nondiscrimination. The Marshall defendants were 10, mostly rural, school districts in Georgia and the State Department of Education. The plaintiffs alleged that (a) the assessment of general intellectual functioning and adaptive behavior was improper and inadequate; (b) the districts did not apply state EMR classification guidelines properly; (c) the state failed to monitor properly compliance by local districts; and (d) the state and local districts violated numerous procedural regulations and rules, such as timely reevaluation of students placed in special education programs, adequate parental notice and consent, and appropriate involvement of parents in placement decisions. The plaintiffs provided extensive statistical data establishing patterns of overrepresentation and evidence from a selective review of records of African-American students. Plaintiffs sought a ban on overrepresentation in special education programs, extensive changes in the state rules concerning the assessment and decision making

with individual intellectual functioning and adaptive behavior, strengthened monitoring and compliance mechanisms including a court-ordered monitor who would have extensive authority to govern actions of professional staff in the State Department of Education.

The Marshall court rejected all plaintiffs' claims concerning discrimination. The court was apparently convinced by defendants' claims that they were following conceptions of best professional practices, were in substantial conformance with guidelines established by an authoriatative national and international organization, the American Association on Mental Deficiency (now the American Association on Mental Retardation), that the effects of poverty explained overrepresentation of African-American students in EMR special education programs, and that violations of procedural rules and regulations (e.g., timely reevaluation of students placed in special education programs) occurred with equal frequency with African-American and white students. The court ordered the state to improve monitoring of compliance with procedural rules and regulations, but specifically noted that this order did not establish or confirm plaintiffs' claims of discrimination against African-American students.

Although Marshall has the same precedent value as Larry P., the only analysis of Marshall to appear in the literature to date was provided by Reschly et al. (1988a, 1988b). Marshall deserves considerably more attention because it is a more recent case, involved issues framed somewhat differently for those in Larry P. (see later section), and addressed regular education grouping as well as special education overrepresentation (Reschly, Kicklighter, & McKee, 1988a).

In the regular education grouping side of the case, the state of Georgia and the defendant school districts were again absolved of allegations of discrimination because of their successful defense of grouping practices as educationally beneficial and appropriate for low-achieving white and African-American students. It is important to note that in both sides of the Marshall case disproportionate impact on African-American students was permitted by the court because the defendants were able to defend successfully the outcomes of test use, that is, instruction designed to meet more fully the needs of students with learning and achievement problems. Furthermore, rather than sole reliance on aptitude tests, defendants emphasized the role of daily classroom performance, teacher-made and administered tests, and other measures of achievement.

S-1 v. Turlington (1986)

The fourth trial over the past 10 years, *S-1 v. Turlington*, was conducted in Miami, Florida, in 1986. The *S-1* plaintiffs were a class of African-American students placed in EMR special education programs, represented by attorneys for the Center for Education and Law of Cambridge, Massachusetts. The *S-1* defendant was the Florida Department of Education. *S-1* was highly similar to *Marshall* in terms of basic issues, allegations by plaintiffs, and the defense developed by the Florida Department of Education. In September, 1986, all plantiffs' claims were dismissed by Judge Atkins "with prejudice," meaning that the defendant's case was regarded as insufficient to justify a trial opinion analyzing the merits of the evidence and applying legal principles. The effect of the *S-1* trial and dismissal of plaintiffs' claims was to allow the *Marshall* precedent to stand in the Eleventh Circuit without further comment or revision by another court.

Larry P. and Marshall Differences

A number of significant differences between *Larry P.* and *Marshall*, particularly in how basic issues were framed by the defendants, were identified and discussed in Reschly et al. (1988a, 1988b). The fundamental differences were as follows: (a) The role of IQ tests was seen as primary in *Larry P.* but secondary to severe, chronic achievement problems in *Marshall*. (b) Use of prior educational alternatives before referral for possible consideration of special education placement was stressed in *Marshall*, including placement in other remedial or compensatory education programs, other tutorial services, and grade repetition. (c) There was greater emphasis on adaptive behavior in *Marshall*, particularly a conception of adaptive behavior that included practical cognitive skills. (d) Careful presentation of overrepresentation statistics in *Marshall* ensured that the court understood clearly the differences between percent of group in program versus percent of program by group (see prior section). (e) Compilation of data in *Marshall* showed that African-American students were much more likely to be placed in other remedial or compensatory education programs rather than EMR special education programs (e.g., Head Start, Chapter 1, and LD resource, all of which were used much more frequently than EMR special education placement. (f) Defendants in *Marshall* demonstrated conformance to the American Association on Mental Deficiency (Grossman, 1983) classification scheme. (g) *Marshall* defendants provided an explanation for overrepresen-

tation, specifically the effects of poverty, as opposed to the "agnostic" position on this issue taken by the California defendants. (h) *Marshall* defendants emphasized the results of the National Academy of Science Panel's analysis (Heller et al., 1982) that acknowledged overrepresentation is acceptable if appropriate instruction, among other things, was provided. Although space does not permit in this chapter, Reschly et al. (1988b, 1988c) provided extensive discussion of the critical differences between the *Marshall* and *Larry P.* cases.

Implicit Issues and Assumptions

A careful analysis of the four cases shows that more than IQ tests and overrepresentation were involved in plaintiffs' motives. For example, consider the *Larry P.* opinion that reflected plaintiffs' assertions that (a) IQ tests were biased, (b) IQ and achievement tests "autocorrelated," (i.e., they were the same), and (c) "the customary uses of achievement tests are not questioned by plaintiff, even though black children also tend not to do well on these tests" (p. 120 of *Larry P.* opinion). That reasoning makes little sense unless factors other than IQ tests were of concern. Furthermore, as noted previously, economically disadvantaged, minority students are overrepresented in a variety of educational programs including Head Start, Chapter 1, and Follow Through. This overrepresentation is well known, but apparently, acceptable. An additional incongruity is the substantially larger per pupil expenditure in EMR than in regular education programs and the other apparent advantages of EMR placement such as low student-teacher ratio and greater individualization. The implicit issues and assumptions, discussed briefly here, provide an explanation for these seemingly inconsistent trends in plaintiff's positions.

Nature-Nurture

The debate over the relative effects of heredity and environment in determining intelligence predates the development of measures of intelligence. This very old debate has not been resolved and is not likey to be resolved in the foreseeable future. The controversy was increased dramatically in the 1970s and 1980s with the extension of the hereditarian view to explain differences between racial groups (Jensen, 1969). Because the debate over the source or cause of observed group differences in measured intelligence cannot be resolved with presently available data (Loehlin, Lindzey, & Spuhler, 1975), minority critics have attempted to force a kind of resolution through the courts. Indirectly, the real defendants in the court cases were the advocates of hereditarian explanations of race differences in measured intelligence, for example, Arthur Jensen and William Shockley. Their views were a major component in the motivation of plaintiffs to press these cases, an interpretation substantiated in Elliott's (1987) thorough examination of *Larry P.*

Meaning of IQ Test Results

A number of myths regarding the meaning of intelligence test results have been around for several decades. Of particular concern are the beliefs that IQ test results are predetermined by genetic factors, that intelligence is unitary and is measured directly by IQ tests, and that IQ test results are fixed. The evidence available for nearly three decades has clearly refuted these myths (e.g., Hunt, 1961) and the vast majority of professional psychologists do *not* harbor such misconceptions. Kaufman (1979) provided an excellent discussion of the underlying assumptions and the meaning of intellectual assessment. His views are probably typical of those of most professional psychologists. However, many consumers of IQ test results such as teachers, parents, and the lay public generally hold these misconceptions. A significant portion of the testimony in the litigation was devoted to disproving these myths, which hardly any psychologists believe anyway. However, some judges apparently have been surprised that IQ tests do not measure innate potential, which, in turn, has contributed to judicial skepticism about the fairness and usefulness of such tests (Bersoff, 1982a).

Role of Tests

In several court cases and much of the placement bias literature, it was implicitly assumed that IQ tests were the primary if not the sole basis for the classification of students as mildly retarded (*Larry P.*, 1973, 1979a, 1979b; Mercer, 1979). The role of standardized tests in the classification process has been exaggerated. From reading this literature one might reach the totally erroneous conclusion that classified and placed students were performing well until a psychologist came along and ensnared the unsuspecting children in a pernicious psychometric net. The single most important determinant of classification is the academic failure in the regular classroom leading to referral, a fact stressed by defendants in *Marshall* and *S-1*. It is only in this context that individual IQ tests are given and classification even considered.

Labeling Effects

Implicit in the litigation was the assumption that classification as EMR was potentially stigmatizing and humiliating with probable permanent harmful effects. The controversy over labeling is far from resolved. The available empirical evidence does not support the self-fulfilling prophecy notion, and direct effects of labels on the behavior of children or adults have been difficult to document (MacMillan, 1982; MacMillan, Jones & Aloia, 1974).

Meaning of Mild Mental Retardation

The reasoning in the *Larry P.* decision was that the plaintiffs were not "truly retarded" despite low IQs, low academic achievement, and teacher referral. The effort to identify "true" mental retardation appears to be related to confusion of mild with more severe levels of mental retardation. The criteria for "true" mental retardation are apparently believed to require comprehensive incompetence, permanence, and evidence of biological anomaly (Mercer, 1973; 1979a). In contrast, the American Association on Mental Deficiency (AAMD) classification system does not specify etiology or prognosis (Grossman, 1983). In addition, different domains of adaptive behavior are emphasized depending on the age of the individual. There was little doubt that the plaintiffs in the placement litigation had serious academic problems. The question was whether they were "truly" retarded, or whether they merely performed within the retarded range due to biases in the IQ tests. Confusion over the meaning of mild mental retardation and questions concerning the criteria for adaptive behavior were key issues in all the cases.

Effectiveness of EMR Special Classes

Although the research problem is extremely complex, precious little empirical support exists for the efficacy of EMR classes at the elementary and junior high school grade levels. Any benefits that exist appear to be in the areas of social and personal adjustment, not academic achievement. The doubts about special classes were accepted as fact by the *Larry P.* court. Proper classification followed by poor treatment is quite justifiably viewed negatively. Recent trends toward more emphasis on regular education alternatives before referral and greater use of parttime special education placements as well as evidence that secondary level EMR programs are effective may alleviate some of these concerns.

Meaning of Bias

Many definitions of bias in tests have been proposed in the psychological and educational measurement literature (e.g., Reschly, 1982; Reynolds, 1982). Rather narrow and simplistic criteria have been used by plaintiffs. The difinitions of bias used by the courts have been overrepresentation percentages, the rather simplistic notion of mean differences, and judgments of item bias. On the basis of these criteria, all current measures of achievement and ability would be regarded as biased. However, other criteria such as statistical analyses of item bias, predictive validity, and construct validity have been studied with minority samples using conventional tests. Current tests typically are not biased according to these latter criteria (Jensen, 1980; Reschly, 1982; Reynolds, 1982; Sandoval, 1979).

A number of implicit issues were apparent in plaintiffs' motivation to press palcement bias litigation in the federal courts. These implicit issues need to be recognized and addressed to the extent possible in efforts to improve the use of tests with minority clients.

Concepts of Fairness

Many of the professional and scholarly analyses of aptitude testing with minority students have emphasized fairly narrow criteria, particularly predictive validity. The Cleary, Humphrey, Kendrick, and Wesman (1975) report is typical of the professional-scholarly responses to minority critics of standardized testing. Conventional standardized tests function in about the same way with minority students. Reliability is about the same. Validity coefficients and regression systems are nearly identical. Factor structure is nearly constant across various groups. According to these criteria, conventional standardized tests are fair, and any bias or discrimination from testing is due either to misuse or the general, pervasive bias or discrimination in the entire society. But the tests per se are not blamed in these accounts.

Minority critics of tests usually concede most, if not all, these points. However, their concern is with the sociopolitical effects of test results and the impact of testing on the lives of individual children. Their concerns are, stated more bluntly, "Do tests contribute more to the problem or to the solution of racism?" "Do tests enhance or limit opportunities for individual students who have minority status?" The reactions of Jackson (1975) and Bernal (1975) to the Cleary et al. (1975) report are typical of the views of many psychologists who have minority status. They are concerned with the broad social consequences of test use, not merely whether tests predicted equally well for different groups. Jackson and Bernal were particularly critical of the use of test results to perpetuate negative racial and ethnic stereotypes. Media accounts in recent years of mean differences among groups are especially destructive according to minority psychologists who claim, perhaps with good reason, that such accounts have been used to justify lower governmental expenditures on compensatory education programs. Although Herrnstein (1982) strongly disputed claims of meida bias on minority IQ test results, the fact remains that test results from different groups are often confused and distorted in the media.

The overall impact of standardized tests on the rate and level of minority group progress is very difficult to assess. Certainly, high test performance has been a key to expanded opportunities for many individuals with minority status. These high test scores prove, at a minimum, that there are exceptions to negative stereotypes about racial or ethnic group abilities. This is important, but insufficient. Test results also have been used to establish the case for greater expenditure of monies on educational programs for minority students. Here test use would be, it seems to me, regarded as positive if the educational programs are worthwhile. As was noted with the EMR special classes, the expenditure of more money does not guarantee that educational programs will be perceived as worthwhile or more effective. However, most compensatory education programs *are* very popular with minority critics of testing, and test results are a major part of the case that is made for the need for these programs.

In a real sense, the issue continues to be a matter of test use. Test use is perceived as positive if more monies and, presumably, better opportunities are the outcomes. However, if test use leads to decisions that greater percentages of minority individuals failed to meet certian criteria, as in minimum competency testing for high school diplomas (*Debra P. v. Turlington*, 1979) or lower admission rates to professional schools (law, medicine, and dentistry), then test use often is criticized by minority spokespersons as an instrument that perpetuates discrimination. These rather ambivalent attitudes toward testing are related to different notions of fairness and to different ethical positions.

In recent years, two rather different notions of fairness have emerged from a variety of institutions and disciplines. These notions, called here, equal treatment versus equal outcomes, have different underlying philosophical and ethical assumptions

(Hunter & Schmidt, 1976). These differences lead to sharp contrasts in how tests are used and how various decisions are made (Lerner, 1981).

Equal Treatment

Equal treatment means to use the same selection procedures and criteria regardless of the race, social class, sex, or ethnicity of the individual. Other contemporary names for equal treatment are *color blind* or *nonsexist*. The ethical and philosophical position of qualified individualism (Hunter & Schmidt, 1976) is consistent with the equal treatment notion of fairness. To discriminate is to treat persons differently on the basis of race, sex, or some other demographic variable.

The use of tests for selection, classification, and placement is usually endorsed by equal treatment advocates. Tests are seen as objective, color-blind devices that can eliminate the discrimination, conscious or unconscious, that is likely in more subjective methods such as supervisor rating, recommendations, and personal interviews (Cleary et al., 1975). A useful and fair test has the characteristics of equal validity and equal prediction regardless of group membership (Cleary, 1968). The same test score is related to the same level of performance on some criterion, regardless of group membership. Group differences in means on the test used as a predictor (e.g., an individual intelligence test), are permissible if approximately the same group differences are found on the criterion (e.g., grades or teacher ratings).

This is generally the case with current aptitude tests with a variety of criteria, groups, and tests (Reschly & Sabers, 1979). There are group mean differences on *both* the predictor and the criterion. Validity is virtually the same and prediction is, likewise, nearly identical regardless of group membership.

Applying the equal treatment approach to educational classification/placement with minority students would involve careful examination of referral, screening, preplacement evaluation, and placement decisions. If minority students are treated in essentially the same way at all steps in this classification/placement process, and the tests and other evaluation procedures are equally valid, the entire process would be regarded as unbiased and fair from the equal treatment notion of fairness. Although few studies have examined these variables, the equal treatment criterion appeared to be met in comparisons of African-American and white EMR students in California (Meyers, MacMillan, & Yoshida, 1978) and Georgia (Reschly & Kicklighter, 1985). Such results are essential to the equal treatment notion of fairness.

The problem with the equal treatment approach is that there are group differences at all stages in the classification/placement process leading to unequal outcomes. The equal treatment notion of fairness, for which there is broad support in the general public (Lener, 1981), leads inevitably to minority overrepresentation in EMR classification, and disproportionate selection, classification, and placement at all educational levels, from kindergarten through post-BA graduate and professional schools.

Equal treatment is a rather slow mehtod of eliminating group differences in career patterns, income, and educational levels. Existing group differences (e.g., African-American versus white income levels) are changed so slowly that several decades, perhaps several generations, would be needed before the disparities are eliminated. Impatience with the effects of equal treatment have led to the development of another notion of fairness: equal outcomes.

Equal Outcomes

The equal outcomes notion of fairness is very straightforward: selection, classification, and placement percentages should match the group percentages in the general population. If 10% of the population is African-American, then 10% of any group—EMR, gifted, law school admissions, etc.—should also be African-American. Substantial variations from these percentages are regarded as discriminatory. The equal outcomes notion of fairness is consistent with the ethical position of quotas (Hunter & Schmidt, 1976). Fairness means that all groups should have an equal, that is, proportional, share of whatever rewards are available.

Advocates of equal outcomes have quite different positions on the use of tests. Williams (1974) claimed that aptitude tests and the usual criteria share the same biases, producing a spurious relationship among a biased predictor and a biased criterion. In this view, most standardized tests were regarded as largely useless. The development of pluralistic norms for conventional tests (Mercer, 1979a) is another method of producing equal outcomes. Here, the assumed biases in a conventional test (the WISC-R) are corrected through a complex procedure that results in adding substantial numbers of points to the conventional WISC-R IQ scores of most minority students. This procedure eliminates mean differences and, if followed precisely, reduces disproportionate classification/placement somewhat (Reschly, 1981). Another method of test use with the equal outcomes criterion of fairness is the differential weighting of the aptitude test scores of minority students. Complex methods of establishing the weights have been described (Novick & Petersen, 1976), but the essential idea is the same; test results are treated differently depending on whether the examinee is minority or majority.

The vast philosophical differences and the very important practical implications of equal treatment and equal outcomes need to be emphasized. In one, to treat differently, is to discriminate. In the other, *not* to treat differently, at least to the point of establishing proportional outcomes, is to discriminate. Advocates of equal outcomes argue that racism has existed for so long, is so pervasive, and so deeply rooted that extraordinary measures must be invoked. Therefore, a period, perhaps several decades, of reverse discrimination (or "positive" discrimination) is necessary and just.

Lerner (1981) was very critical of the equal outcomes criterion. She viewed the reverse discrimination that must be followed to produce equal outcomes as particularly unwise from legal, social, and economic perspectives. According to Lerner, classification and placement on some basis other than merit creates mismatches that require further compromise of standards, accommodations, and remedial programming, all of which are potentially disastrous. Finally, equal outcomes and reverse discrimination may very well retard the progress of equal opportunity because the general public is opposed to these measures which have the further dubious effect of "cast[ing] a shadow over the accomplishment of the very large number of black scholars and workers who scorned special preferences and earned their rewards in exactly the same way that their white counterparts did" (Lerner, 1981, p. 9).

As noted in the early portion of this chapter, test use is often a central issue in controversies over how to best achieve equity and fairness. There is little remaining doubt about how various minorities perform on tests. The effects of different methods of using tests also are well known. The critical questions having to do with how tests "ought" or "should" be used cannot be resolved by academic or professional psychologists. Psychologists can present options and estimate the probable effects of different policies on classification/placement decisions. But the policies as such must be determined as part of the broad sociopolitical process involving all citizens and political representatives.

FUTURE DIRECTIONS

Aptitude testing continues to be an important part of educational classification/placement decisions despite

severe criticism from some minority scholars and intense legal scrutiny. Standardized testing generally and aptitude testing specifically have been carefully and critically examined over the past 10 years. The usual result continues to be (a) endorsement of the purposes of aptitude testing, (b) recognition of the value of information from current tests, (c) prohibitions against the use of aptitude test results as the sole or primary basis for important decisions, and (d) attribution of problems in testing to misuse of tests, not the tests per se. These conclusions were prominent in three of the most important recent reviews of standardized testing (Cleary et al., 1975; Heller et al., 1982; Wigdor & Garner, 1982). Three conclusions from the National Academy of Sciences (NAS) Committee on Ability Testing Report are especially pertinent to the future uses of aptitude tests in educational classification and placement.

> Test scores play a central, often a determinative, role in special education placement. Used appropriately, they can help to identify pupils who should be studied individually to determine in what educational setting they will prosper. . . . An unbiased count of the children who are expected to have severe difficulty with instruction at the regular pace would surely find a greater proportion of poor children, including minority children, in that category. Radical social change would have to take place to alter that prediction significantly. (Wigdor & Garner, 1982, p. 176)

> Skepticism about the value of tests in identifying children in need of special eduacation has probably been carried too far; people making those decisions should, whenever practicable, have before them a report on a number of professionally administered tests, in part to counteract the stereotypes and misperceptions that contaminate judgmental information. (p. 179)

Clearly, as indicated in the NAS Panel Report, one of the most important current trends is renewed acceptance of standardized testing. Whatever movement there was to restrict sharply or even ban tests appears to be far less prominent today than 10 to 20 years ago. Part of this change is a matter of pendulum phenomena—the cycle of action and reaction that so often occurs. Beyond that, I believe the greater acceptance of standardized testing today is, at least in part, a result of research indicating that tests do function in about the same way regardless of sociocultural group. These essential findings were not available in the early years of what became a movement to restrict or ban tests. In that era there was serious question about the technical characteristics of conventional tests when used with minority students (Deutsch, Fishman, Kogan, North, & Whiteman, 1964). Minority students were sometimes not included in standardization samples. There was little or no research examining technical characteristics such as reliability, validity, and factor structure with different groups. As noted in an earlier section, findings of recent research indicate that the technical characteristics of conventional tests are nearly constant for the major sociocultural groups in the United States.

There are several current trends which hold promise for improving the technology and the use of aptitude assessment. The trends in test *use* generally involve conceptual clarification, more conservative interpretations of results, lower levels of inference, and greater emphasis on treatment utility (Reschly, 1980b, 1986b). These trends hold promise for improving the outcomes of test use for the student or client.

Conceptual Clarification

There is a subtle, but significant misconception related to our ideas and explanations of how individually administered IQ tests are used in educational classification and placement. In our literature we routinely advance the notion of predictive validity to justify the use of such tests. In fact, individually administered IQ tests are rarely, if ever, used in the sense of *predictive validity*: that is, meaning that the test is given and a prediction made about *future* performance. Indeed, we have very little evidence regarding the actual *predictive* validity of such tests because individually administered tests are rarely given to students who have not been referred due to achievement or behavioral difficulties.

The predictive validity myth became especially apparent during the testimony of one of the plaintiffs' expert witnesses in the *S-1* trial. This witness argued that the differential predictive validity of IQ tests in selecting and assigning students to differential educational treatments had never been established. Of course, to establish such evidence would require a nearly impossible kind of study, random assignment of students eligible for classification as EMR to different educational placements such as regular classroom, parttime resource placement, and special education/special class. Regardless of the merits of attempting to conduct such a study, the point became apparent that we typically use the concept of predictive validity incorrectly in justifying the use of individually administered IQ tests. In fact, such tests are nearly always administered *after*, and only *after*, the student has experienced chronic, servere educational difficulties. Rather than predictive validity, individu-

ally administerd IQ tests are used as part of an effort to diagnose the reasons for the severe, chronic low achievement. If the intellectual functioning is sufficiently low, accompanied by extremely low achievement, assuming other criteria are also met, the problem may be attributed to mild mental retardation or, perhaps, some other educational handicap such as learning disability. The critical issue is *when* the IQ test is given and *how* it is used. It is clearly not used in a predictive validity sense and our continued association of the concept of predictive validity with the justification for using individually administered IQ tests can only further confuse the advantages and disadvantages of individual educational evaluations with referred students (Reschly et al., 1988c). Furthermore, failure to correct the predictive validity myth may cause more difficulties in legal situations where we may be called upon to justify the use of individually administered IQ tests.

A number of other conceptual clarifications are essential to greater progress in the use of tests for the benefit of students. For example, further specification of the meaning of *adaptive behavior* will do much to improve assessment practices and the actual use of such information in educational programs designed to benefit handicapped students. Failure to clarify the meaning of adaptive behavior leads to the continued confusion rampant now in the professional literature and professional practice (Reschly & Gresham, 1987).

Additional conceptual clarification concerning the purposes of assessment is needed in order to guide practitioner selection of assessment approaches and instruments. We still observe, to a far greater extent than appropriate, the application of standard batteries (e.g., one of the Wechsler Scales, the Bender, the Wide Range Achievement Test, and a favorite projective device such as the House/Tree/Person or the Rorschach), regardless of the nature of the presenting problem of the student or client. This use of standard battery, although convenient for the professional psychologist, practically guarantees that much information potentially relevant to the client's problem will not be collected and carefully considered. One of the most important conceptual advances in assessment will be greater attention to very careful matching of assessment purposes, often defined through specification of precise questions, with methods and instruments for collecting information. Thus, for persons referred due to social skills difficulties, it should be rare indeed to see administration of IQ tests; far greater attention would be devoted to appropriate ways to collect information on social skills (Gresham, 1985). The use of standard batteries, an unfortunate tradition in nearly all areas of professional psychology, can be expected to decline as we implement known ways to match assessment procedures and instruments more carefully to the presenting problems of clients or students.

Interpretation of Assessment Information

The major advances in interpretation of assessment information will be apparent in the adoption of a lower level of inference and greater reliance on well-established empirical relationships. These two changes promise to improve current assessment practices dramatically.

Lower Level of Inference

Level of inference refers to the relationship between what is observed and the interpretation of that behavior. For example, reproduction of the Bender designs can be interpreted at various levels of inference ranging from low levels, such as poor copying or impaired visual motor skills, a medium level, such as developmental lag, to very high levels, such as neurological dysfunction, emotional conflict, or psychosexual stage of development. Applied areas of psychology have an unfortunate tradition of using high levels of inference with relatively simple behavioral events. Numerous examples could be cited of these high levels of inference. For example, a very common interpretation of dark, heavy lines on Bender drawings is the assertion of "repressed hostility." Other examples of highly inferential interpretations are interpreting a higher score on digits backward than digits forward scores as examples of "oppositional behavior" or the placement of various bodily parts related to psychosexual stages of development. Many of these interpretations appeared in a highly influential, early text that first appeared in the mid-1940s (Rapaport, Gill, & Schafer, 1945–46, 1968).

The major difficulties with the deeply dynamic and often global assertions about motives and emotions generated from traditional clinical interpretations are the following: (a) Little if any empirical support exists for most of the interpretations. (b) The underlying conditions cannot be treated directly. (c) These "insights" are rarely related to improved validity of treatment selection or implementation. (d) Focus on the deep underlying dynamics often deflects attention from more useful behavior or self-report information from the client that can be used more directly in interventions. The deeply dynamic and highly inferential interpretations are expected to become increasingly less common in the foreseeable future due to a variety of influences, not the least of which is the increased legal scrutiny of the work of professional psychologists (Reschly, 1987a; Ziskin, 1970, 1975, 1981).

Empirical Relationships

A development related to lower level of inference is the increasing availability and use of empirical studies as the basis for interpretation and use of the aptitude test results. There is far more relevant research today, and professional psychologists are increasingly likely to apply this information in work with students or clients.

One of the most important empirical findings related to aptitude testing has been information on base rates for subtest and scale differences on the Wechsler Scales (Kaufman, 1976, 1979). Base rates refer to the naturally occurring rate of some phenomenon in the general population. The central conclusions regarding base rates on the Wechsler Scale are that (a) subtest scatter is normal, *not* abnormal; (b) IQ scale differences such as verbal considerably higher or lower than performance IQ are common; and (c) flat profiles are very unusual. These conclusions are the opposite of traditional beliefs in the clinical literature where scatter, that is, differences in subtests or scale scores, was seen as indicative of cognitive or emotional difficulties. If most persons have a high degree of scatter, then it is impossible for scatter to be a unique, diagnostically significant feature of any syndrome that occurs rarely. Base rates, usually determined from studies of standardization samples, must be known before assertions are made about the clinical significance of aptitude test profiles. Because of base rate research, the general trend now is toward far less use of personality, emotional, or motivational interpretations of aptitude test profiles.

Neuropsychological Interpretations

Neuropsychology appears to be a growing area in professional psychology. Although firm relationships have been established between various behavioral indices in neurological dysfunctions for adults, such relationships are far less well established for children and youth, particularly those exhibiting relatively mild learning problems without developmental histories suggesting neurological insult. Here, various behavioral indices, often drawn from general or specific aptitude tests, are used to suggest the neurological causes of learning problems. Most of these interpretations involve high levels of inference without solid empirical foundations, and reflect complicated base rate phenomena. For example, certain kinds of subtest scatter may be used to suggest particular kinds of neurological dysfunctions (Hartlage, 1981, 1982; Obrzut, 1981). Although these inferences appear to be highly sophisticated, in fact, they lack empirical foundation, most likely involve interpretation of normal scatter, and are often based on instruments with highly questionable technical characteristics (Reschly & Gresham, 1989). Furthermore, there is the underlying assumption of treatment by aptitude interaction. Specifically, neuropsychological interpretations assume that intact areas of the brain can be identified and that those intact areas can be utilized to select teaching methods that will be more effective. Recent reviews as well as empirical studies (Arter & Jenkins, 1979; Ayres & Cooley, 1986; Goodman, 1983; O'Boyle, 1986; Reschly & Gresham, 1989; Ysseldyke & Mirkin, 1982) suggest a high level of skepticism about either identification of specific areas of the brain responsible for mild learning problems or the ability to avoid "dead tissue" in the selection of methodologies to improve instruction. Without such empirical evidence, the neuropsychological interpretation of mild learning problems, with those children without any physical evidence of neurological disorder, must be viewed with great skepticism.

Assessment for Interventions

Perhaps the single most important trend is greater emphasis on selection and use of assessment procedures that are useful as direct measures of behaviorally defined target behaviors in natural settings. These measures are then used continuously in the various phases of an intervention: baseline, treatment design, treatment implementation, monitoring and revising treatment plans, and evaluating outcomes. Recent advances in behavioral assessment and curriculum-based assessment have markedly improved the treatment utility of psychological assessment.

Treatment utility (Heller et al., 1982) or an outcomes criterion (Reschly, 1979, 1986b) are efforts to emphasize the broad effects of psychological assessment for individuals and groups. Essential questions are these: How did test use influence opportunities for the individual? Are the test results useful in developing interventions or treatments? Here, it is very important to recognize the limitations of general aptitude tests. General aptitude tests are useful in identifying persons who are far below or far above average on the kinds of cognitive operations required in academic and other settings. Persons who are far below or far above average often need and benefit from alternative educational programs. Aptitude tests have treatment utility for this very general, but important, kind of decision. General aptitude tests are not very useful in identifying specific educational objectives or strategies.

The trend toward greater emphasis on treatment utility, especially as a means to address the problem of bias against minority students, implies continued, but limited, use of aptitude tests. Use of aptitude tests, along with other information, for general classification/placement decisions was endorsed by the National Academy of Science reports (Heller et al., 1982; Wigdor & Garner, 1982). This endorsement was, however, conditional on the delivery of more effective interventions as a result of classification/placement decisions. In recent discussions of test use, the absence of bias according to statistical criteria was seen as a prerequisite to fair use and treatment utility. Absence of statistical bias is important, but not sufficient. Treatment utility must be regarded as the predominant criterion (Reschly, 1979, 1986b).

Recent advances in behavioral assessment including direct measures of a wide variety of social and academic behaviors provide the technological basis for greater emphasis on treatment utility, (e.g. Deno, 1985; Shapiro & Kratochwill, 1988). These approaches have advantages such as direct reflections of the problem behavior, use in the natural setting, and application to all phases of interventions. Furthermore, these measures, if developed according to known and well-established procedures, have excellent reliability and validity. The disadvantages are that the specific measures have to be invented or, at least, adjusted for each client. Furthermore, use of these measures in classification/placement decisions (e.g., EMR), although promising, requires considerable further study.

SUMMARY

Aptitude testing for the purposes of educational classification/placement is alive and well today, even flourishing. The naive reader may sense a bit of surprise (and cynicism) in that conclusion which is a reaction to the projected imminent demise of aptitude or intelligence assessment that was so popular in the late 1960s and 1970s. Aptitude testing has changed in subtle but important ways. The criticism from minority professionals and the legal scrutiny in the courts, though often misdirected in my view, has prompted subtle changes in interpretation, gradual reform of procedures, and vigorous pursuit of better tests and , sound testing practices. These very positive changes virtually guarantee continued use of general aptitude or intelligence tests in educational classification/placement decisions.

Much remains to be accomplished. The presently available research on validity of aptitude tests needs to be expanded to include more groups of participants and a wider variety of criteria. The issue of treatment utility needs to be addressed in many more studies. The greatest need is for data on program effects with students varying in general aptitude. A variety of program alternatives need to be examined with students now classified as EMR.

These program alternatives should be developed around the results of longitudinal studies, especially of the early adjustment of EMR and borderline ability groups. These studies should significantly augment our knowledge base and technological resources concerning general scholastic aptitude or intelligence. In anticipating those developments, we are building on a solid research base and a rich tradition of using tests to enhance opportunities for individuals.

REFERENCES

Anastasi, A. (1980). Abilities and the measurement of achievement. In W. B. Schrader (Ed.), *Measuring achievement: Progress over a decade. New directions for testing and measurement*. San Francisco: Jossey-Bass.

Anastasi, A. (1988). *Psychological testing* (6th ed.). New York: MacMillan.

Arter, J. A., & Jenkins, J. R. (1979). Differential diagnosis-prescriptive teaching: A critical appraisal. *Review of Education Research, 49*, 517–55.

Ayres, R. R., & Cooley, E. J. (1986). Sequential versus simultaneous processing on the K-ABC: Validity. *Psychoeducational Assessment, 4*, 211–220.

Bernal, E. (1975). A response to "Educational uses of tests with disadvantaged subjects." *American Psychologist, 30*, 93–95.

Bersoff, D. (1979). Regarding psychologists testily: Legal regulation of psychological assessment in the public schools. *Maryland Law Review, 39*, 27–120.

Bersoff, D. N. (1981). Testing and the law. *American Psychologist, 36*, 1047–1056.

Bersoff, D. N. (1982a). The legal regulation of school psychology. In C. R. Reynolds & T. B. Gutkin (Eds.), *The handbook of school psychology*. New York: Wiley.

Bersoff, D. (1982b). *Larry P.* and *PASE*: Judicial report cards of the validity of individual intelligence tests. In T. Kratochwill (Ed.), *Advances in school psychology* (Vol. 2). Hillsdale, NJ: Lawrence Erlbaum.

Bickel, W. E. (1982). Classifying mentally retarded students: A review of placement practices in special education. In K. A. Heller, W. H. Holtzman, & S. Messick (Eds.), *Placing children in special education: A strategy for equity*. Washington, DC: National Academy Press.

Brown, F. G. (1983). *Principles of educational and psychological testing* (3rd ed.). New York: Holt, Rinehart, and Winston.

Cleary, T. A. (1968). Test bias: Prediction of grades of Negro and white students in integrated colleges. *Journal of Educational Measurement, 5*, 115–124.

Cleary, T., Humphreys, L. G., Kendrick, S. A., & Wesman, A. (1975). Educational uses of tests with disadvantaged students. *American Psychologist, 30*, 15–41.

Coles, G. S. (1978). The learning disabilities test battery: Empirical and social issues. *Howard Educational Review, 48*, 313–340.

Condas, J. (1980). Personal reflections on the *Larry P.* trial and its aftermath. *School Psychology Review, 9*, 154–158.

Cronbach, L. J. (1984). *Essentials of psychological testing* (4th ed.), New York: Harper & Row.

Cronbach, L. J., & Snow, R. E. (1977). *Aptitudes and instructional methods*. New York: Wiley (Halstead Press).

Debra P. v. Turlington, Case No. 78-892-Civ-T-C (M. D.Fla. 1979).

Deno, S. L. (1985). Curriculum-based measurement: The emerging alternative. *Exceptional Children, 52*, 219–232.

Deutsch, M., Fishman, J., Kogan, I., North, R., & Whitman, M. (1964). Guidelines for testing minority group children. *Journal of Social Issues, 20*, 129–145.

Diana v. State Board of Education, C-70 37RFP (N. D. Cal. 1970).

Elliott, R. (1987). *Litigating Intelligence*. Dover, MA: Auburn House.

Federal Register. (1977a, December 29). Procedures for evaluating specific learning disabilities (pp. 65082–65085). Washington, DC: Author.

Federal Register. (1977b, August, 23). Regulations implementing Education for All Handicapped Children Act of 1975 (Public Law 94-142) (pp. 42474–42518(b)). Washington, DC: Author.

Goodman, J. F. (1983). Organicity as a construct in psychological diagnosis. In T. R. Kratochwill (Ed.), *Advances in school psychology* (Vol. 3, pp. 101–139). Hillsdale, NJ: Lawrence Erlbaum.

Gresham, F. M. (1985). Social skills. In A. Thomas & J. Grimes (Eds.), *Best practices in school psychology*. Kent, OH: National Association of School Psychologists.

Grossman, H. J. (Ed.). (1983). *Classification in mental retardation*. Washington, DC: American Association on Mental Deficiency.

Guadalupe v. Tempe Elementary School District. (1982). 71-435, District Court for Arizona, January.

Hammill, D., & Larsen, S. (1974). The effectiveness of psycholinguistic training. *Exceptional Children, 41*, 5–14.

Hammill, D., & Larsen, S. (1978). The effectiveness of psycholinguistic training: A reaffirmation of position. *Exceptional Children, 44*, 402–14.

Hartlage, L. C. (1981). Clinical application of neuropsychological test data: A case study. *School Psychology Review, 10*, 362–366.

Hartlage, L. C. (1982). Neuropsychological assessment techniques. In C. R. Reynolds & T. B. Gutkin (Eds.), *Handbook of school psychology* (pp. 296–313). New York: Wiley.

Hartlage, L. C. (1986). Pediatric neuropsychology. In D. Wedding, A. M. Horton, & J. Webster (Eds.), *The neuropsychology handbook: Behavioral and clinical perspectives* (pp. 441–455). New York: Springer.

Hartlage, L. C., & Reynolds, C. R. (1981). Neuropsychological assessment and the individualization of instruction. In G. W. Hynd & J. E. Obrzut (Eds.), *Neuropsychological assessment and the school age child: Issues and procedures* (pp. 355–378). New York: Grune & Stratton.

Heller, K., Holtzman, W., & Messick, S. (1982). *Placing children in special education: A strategy for equity*. Washington, DC: National Academy Press.

Herrnstein, R. J. (1982, August). IQ testing and the media. *Atlantic Monthly*, 68–74.

Hilliard, A. (1980). Cultural diversity and special education. *Exceptional Children, 46*, 584–588.

Hilliard, A. G. (1983). IQ and the courts: *Larry P. v. Wilson Riles* and *PASE v. Hannon*. *Journal of Black Psychology, 10*, 1–18.

Hunt, J. (1961). *Intelligence and experience*. New York: Ronald Press.

Hunter, J., Schmidt, F. (1976). Critical analysis of the statistical and ethical implications of various definitions of test bias. *Psychological Bulletin, 83*, 1053–1071.

Hynd, G. W., Obrzut, J. E., Hayes, F., & Becker, M. G. (1986). Neuropsychology of childhood learning disabilities. In D. Wedding, A. M. Horton, & J. Webster (Eds.), *The neuropsychology handbook: Behavioral and clinical perspectives* (pp. 456–485). New York: Springer.

Jackson, G. (1975). On the report of the ad hoc committee on educational uses of tests with disadvantaged students. *American Psychologist, 30*, 88–92.

Jensen, A. R. (1969). How much can we boost IQ and scholastic achievement? *Harvard Educational Review, 39*, 1–123.

Jensen, A. R. (1980). *Bias in mental testing*. New York: Free Press.

Jones, R. L. (1988). Psychoeducational assessment of minority group children: Issues and perspectives. In R. L. Jones (Ed.), *Psychoeducational assessment of minority group children: A casebook* (pp. 13–35). Berkeley, CA: Cobb and Henry.

Jones, R. L., & Jones, J. M. (1987). Racism as psychological maltreatment. In M. R. Brassard, R. Germain, & S. N. Hart (Eds.), *Psychological maltreatment of children and youth* (pp. 146–158). New York: Pergamon.

Jones, R., Wilderson, F. (1976). Mainstreaming and the minority child: An overview of issues and a perspective. In R. Jones (Ed.), *Mainstreaming and the minority child*. Reston, VA: Council for Exceptional Children.

Kaufman, A. (1976). A new approach to interpretation of test scatter on the WISC-R. *Journal of Learning Disabilities, 9*, 160–168.

Kaufman, A. (1979). *Intelligent testing with the WISC-R*. New York: Wiley.

Kaufman, A., & Kaufman, N. (1977). *Clinical evaluation of young children with the McCarthy Scales*. New York: Grune & Stratton.

Kaufman, A., & Kaufman, N. (1983). *Kaufman Assessment Battery for Children (K-ABC)*. Circle Pines, MN: American Guidance Service.

Lambert, N. M. (1981). Psychological evidence in *Larry P. v. Wilson Riles*: An evaluation by a witness for the defense. *American Psychologist, 36*, 937–952.

Larry P. v. Riles, 343 F. Supp. 1306 (N. D. Cal. 1972) (preliminary injunction). Aff'd 502 F. 2nd 963 (9th cir. 1974); 495 F. Supp. 926 (N. D. Cal. 1979) (decision on merits). Aff'd 80-427 (9th cir. Jan. 23, 1984). Order modifying judgment, C-71-2270 RFP, (September 25, 1986).

Lennon, R. (1980). The anatomy of a scholastic aptitude test. *NCME Measurement in Education, 11*, 1–8.

Lerner, B. (1981). Equal opportunity versus equal results: Monsters, rightful causes, and perverse effects. In W. G. Schrader (Ed.), *Admissions testing and the public interest: New directions for testing and measurement* (Number 9). San Francisco: Jossey-Bass.

Loehlin, J., Lindzey, G., & Spuhler, J. (1975). *Race differences in intelligence*. San Francisco: Freeman.

MacMillan, D. (1982). *Mental retardation in school and society* (2nd ed.). Boston: Little, Brown, & Co.

MacMillan, D., Jones, R., & Aloia, G. (1974). The mentally retarded label: A theoretical analysis and review of research. *American Journal of Mental Deficiency, 79*, 241–261.

MacMillan, D., & Meyers, C. E. (1980). *Larry P.*: An educational interpretation. *School Psychology Review, 9*, 136–148.

Madden, P. B. (1980). Intelligence tests on trial. *School Psychology Review, 9*, 149–153.

Marshall et al. v. Georgia, CV482-233 (S. D. Ga. June 28, 1984). Affirmed 84-8771 (11th cir. Oct. 29, 1985). (Appealed as NAACP v. Georgia.)

Mercer, J. (1973). *Labeling the mentally retarded*. Berkeley, CA: University of California Press.

Mercer, J. (1979a). *System of Multicultural Pluralistic Assessment Technical manual*. New York: Psychological Corporation.

Mercer, J. (1979b). In defense of racially and culturally nondiscriminatory assessment. *School Psychology Digest, 8*, 89–115.

Mercer, C. D., Hughes, C., & Mercer, A. R. (1985). Learning disabilities definitions used by state education departments. *Learning Disability Quarterly, 8*, 45–55.

Meyers, C., MacMillan, D., & Yoshida, R. (1978). Validity of psychologists' identification of EMR students in the perspective of the California decertification experience. *Journal of School Psychology, 16*, 3–15.

National Council of Advocates for Students (1988). *Special analysis of the 1986 elementary and secondary school civil rights survey data*. Boston: National Council of Advocates for Students.

Newcomer, R., Larsen, S., & Hammill, D. (1975). A response to Minskoff. *Exceptional Children, 42*, 144–148.

Ninth Annual Report to Congress on the Implementation of the Education of the Handicapped Act.
(1987). Washington, DC: United States Department of Education.

Novick, M., & Peterson, N. (1976). Toward equalizing educational and employment opportunity. *Journal of Educational Measurement, 13*, 77–88.

O'Boyle, M. W. (1986). Hemispheric laterality as a basis for learning: What we know and don't know. In G. D. Phye & T. Andre (Eds.), *Cognitive instructional psychology: Components of classroom learning*. New York: Academic Press.

Obrzut, A. (1981). A neuropsychological case report of a child with auditory-linguistic dyslexia. *School Psychology Review, 10*, 356–361.

PASE (Parents in Action on Special Education) v. Joseph P. Hannon, 74 (3586) (N. D. Ill. July, 1980).

Prasse, D. (1978). Federal legislation and school psychology: Impact and implication. *Professional Psychology, 9*, 592–601.

Prasse, D. P., & Reschly, D. J. (1986). *Larry P.*: A case of segregation, testing, or program efficacy? *Exceptional Children, 52*, 333–346.

Rapaport, D., Gill, M., & Schafer, R. (1945–46, 1968). *Diagnostic psychological testing* (Rev. ed. by R. Holt). New York: International Universities Press.

Reschly, D. (1979). Nonbiased assessment. In G. Phye & D. Reschly (Eds.), *School psychology: Perspective and issues*. New York: Academic Press.

Reschly, D. (1980a). Psychological evidence in the *Larry P.* opinion: A case of right problem—wrong solution. *School Psychology Review, 9*, 123–135.

Reschly, D. (1980b). School psychologists and assessment in the future. *Professional Psychology, 11*, 841–848.

Reschly, D. (1981). Evaluation of the effects of SOMPA measures on classification of students as mildly mentally retarded. *American Journal on Mental Deficiency, 86*, 16–20.

Reschly, D. (1982). Assessing mild mental retardation: The influence of adaptive behavior, sociocultural status and prospects for nonbiased assessment. In C. Reynolds & T. Gutkin (Eds.), *The handbook of school psychology*. New York: Wiley-Interscience.

Reschly, D. J. (1986a). Economic and cultural factors of childhood exceptionality. In R. T. Brown & C. R. Reynolds (Eds.), *Psychological perspctives on childhoold exceptionality: A handbook* (pp. 423–466). New York: Wiley-Interscience.

Reschly, D. J. (1986b). Functional psychoeducational assessment: Trends and issues. *Special Ser-*

vices in the Schools (Special issue on emerging perspectives on assessment of exceptional children), *2*, 57–69.

Reschly, D. J. (1987a). Assessing educational handicaps. In A. Hess & I. Wiener (Eds.), *Handbook of forensic psychology* (pp. 155–187). New York: Wiley.

Reschly, D. J. (1987b). Learning characteristics of mildly handicapped students: Implications for classification, placement, and programming. In M. C. Wang, M. C. Reynolds, & H. J. Walberg (Eds.), *The handbook of special education: Research and practice.* (Vol. 1, pp. 35–58). Oxford, England: Pergamon Press.

Reschly, D. J. (1988). Alternative delivery stystems: Legal and ethical issues. In J. L. Graden, J. E. Zins, & M. J. Curtis (Eds.), *Alternative educational delivery systems: Enhancing instructional options for all students* (pp. 525–552). Washington, DC: National Association of School Psychologists.

Reschly, D. J., Genshaft, J., & Binder, M. S. (1987). *The 1986 NASP survey: Comparison of practitioners, NASP leadership, and university faculty on key issues.* Washington, DC: National Association of School Psychologists.

Reschly, D. J., & Gresham, F. M. (1987). Adaptive behavior and the mildly handicapped. In T. R. Kratochwill (Ed.), *Advances in school psychology* (pp. 265–298). Hillsdale, NJ: Erlbaum.

Reschly, D. J., & Gresham, F. M. (1989). Current neuropsychological diagnosis of learning problems: A leap of faith. In C. R. Reynolds & E. Fletcher-Janzen (Eds.), *Handbook of clinical child neuropsychology* (pp. 503–519). New York: Plenum Press.

Reschly, D. J., & Kicklighter, R. J. (1985). *Comparison of black and white EMR students from Marshall v. Georgia.* Paper presented at the annual convention of the American Psychological Association, Los Angeles, CA: (Eric Document Reproduction Service No. ED 271 911).

Reschly, D. J., Kicklighter, R. H., & McKee, P. (1988a). Recent placement litigation, Part I: Regular education grouping: Comparison of *Marshall* (1984, 1985) and *Hobson* (1967, 1969). *School Psychology Review, 17*, 7–19.

Reschly, D. J., Kicklighter, R. H., McKee, P. (1988b). Recent placement litigation, Part II, Minority EMR overrepresentation: Comparison of *Larry P.* (1979, 1984, 1986) with *Marshall* (1984, 1985) and *S-1* (1986). *School Psychology Review, 17*, 20–36.

Reschly, D. J., Kicklighter, R. H., McKee, P. (1988c). Recent placement litigation, Part III: Analysis of differences in *Larry P.*, *Marshall*, and *S-1* and implications for future practices. *School Psychology Review, 17*, 37–48.

Reschly, D. J., & Sabers, D. L. (1979). Analysis of test bias in four groups with the regression definition. *Journal of Educational Measurement, 16*, 1–9.

Reynolds, C. R. (1982). The problem of bias in psychological assessment. In C. R. Reynolds & T. B. Gutkin (Eds.), *The handbook of school psychology.* New York: Wiley.

Reynolds, C. R. (1986). Transactional models of intellectual development, Yes. Deficit models of process remediation, No. *School Psychology Review, 15*, 256–260.

Richardson, S. (1981). Family characteristics associated with mild mental retardation. In M. Begab, H. C. Haywood, & H. Barber (Eds.), *Psychosocial influences in retarded performance:* (Vol. 2, pp. 29–43). Baltimore: University Park Press.

S-1 v. Turlington. Trial on Merits, May 19–June 4, 1986, Order on Motion to Dismiss, No. 79-8020-Civ-Atkins (S. D. Fla.) October 9, 1986.

Salvia, J., & Ysseldyke, J. (1988). *Assessment in special and remedial education* (4th ed.). Boston: Houghton-Mifflin.

Samuda, R. J. (1975). *Psychological testing of American minorities: Issues and consequences.* New York: Dodd, Mead, & Co.

Sandoval, J. (1979). The WISC-R and internal evidence of test bias with minority groups. *Journal of Consulting and Clinical Psychology, 47*, 919–927.

Sattler, J. M. (1981). Intelligence tests on trial: An "interview" with Judges Robert F. Peckham and John F. Grady. *Journal of School Psychology, 19*, 359–369.

Sattler, J. (1982). The psychologist in court: Personal reflections of one expert witness in the case of *Larry P. School Psychology Review, 11*, 306–319.

Shapiro, E. S., & Kratochwill, T. R. (Eds.). (1988). *Behavioral assessment in schools: Conceptual foundations and practical applications.* New York: Guilford Press.

Sherman, S. W., Robinson, N. M. (1982). *Ability testing of handicapped people: Dilemma for government, science, and the public.* Washington, DC: National Academy Press.

Snow, R. E. (1980). Aptitude and achievement. In W. B. Schrader (Ed.), *Measuring achievement:*

Progress over a decade. New directions for testing and measurement. San Francisco: Jossey-Bass.

Wigdor, A. K., & Garner, W. R. (1982). *Ability testing: Uses, consequences, and controversies*. Washington, DC: National Academy Press.

Williams, R. (1970). Danger: Testing and dehumanizing the black child. *Clinical Child Psychology Newsletter, 9,* 5–6.

Williams, R. (1974). The problem of match and mismatch in testing black children. In L. Miller (Ed.), *The testing of black students: A symposium*. Englewood Cliffs, NJ: Prentice-Hall.

Ysseldyke, J. E., & Mirkin, P. K. (1982). The use of assessment information to plan instructional interventions: A review of the research. In C. R. Reynolds & T. B. Gutkin (Eds.), *The handbook of school psychology*. New York: Wiley.

Ziskin, J. (1970, 1st ed.; 1975, 2nd ed.; 1981, 3rd ed.). *Coping with psychiatric and psychological testimony* (3rd ed.). Venice, CA: Law and Psychology Press. (Also, *1983 Supplement* to third edition.)

CHAPTER 9

INTEREST INVENTORIES

Jo-Ida C. Hansen

INTRODUCTION

The importance of an individual's interests in job selection was first recognized by educators in the 1900s and shortly thereafter by industry. Early theorists in the field, such as Parsons (1909), hypothesized that occupational adjustment was enhanced if an individual's characteristics and interests matched the requirements of the occupation. As E. K. Strong, Jr., (1943) pointed out in *Vocational Interests of Men and Women*, interests provide additional information, not available from analyses of abilities or aptitudes, for making career decisions. Consideration of interests, along with abilities, values, and personality characteristics, provides a thorough evaluation of an individual that is superior to consideration of any trait in isolation.

HISTORY OF INTEREST INVENTORIES

The earliest method for assessing interests was *estimation*, accomplished by asking individuals to indicate how they felt about various activities. To improve the accuracy of their estimation, people were encouraged to *try out* activities before making their estimates. However, try-out techniques for evaluating interests were time consuming and costly; the search for a more economical assessment method led to the development of interest *checklists* and *rating scales* (Kitson, 1925; Miner, 1922) and eventually to *interest inventories* that used statistical procedures for summarizing an individual's responses to a series of items representing various activities and occupations.

The Earliest Item Pool

Construction of interest inventories is based on several assumptions:

1. A person can give informed responses of degree of interest (e.g., like, indifferent, dislike) to familiar activities and occupations.
2. Unfamiliar activities have the same factor structure as do familiar activities.
3. Therefore, familiar activities and occupations can be used as items in interest inventories to identify unfamiliar occupational interests.

The first item pool of interest activities was accumulated by a seminar taught by Clarence S. Yoakum at Carnegie Institute of Technology in 1919. The 1,000-item pool was developed using a *rational sampling approach* designed to represent the entire domain of interests. Over the years, statistical analyses were performed to determine the worth of each item, and numerous inventories used that original item pool as the foundation for their development (e.g., Occupational Interest Inventory [Freyd, 1923]; Interest Report Blank [Cowdery, 1926]; General Interest Survey [Kornhauser, 1927]; Vocational Interest Blank [Strong, 1927]; Purdue Interest Report [Remmers, 1929]; Interest Analysis Blank [Hubbard, 1930]; Minnesota Interest Inventory [Paterson, Elliott, Anderson, Toops, & Heidbreder, 1930]).

Characteristics of Good Items

Interest inventory items should be evaluated periodically because societal changes can make items obsolete as well as create the need for new items.

Number of Samples

10 –

Percent "Like" Response

| 0 | 10 | 20 | 30 | 40 | 50 | 60 | 70 | 80 | 90 | 100 |

Highest Samples

Recreation Leaders 81%
Home Economics Teachers 79%
Public Relations Directors .. 78%
Restaurant Managers 78%
Life Insurance Agents 77%
Realtors 76%
Dietitians 76%
Funeral Directors 75%

Lowest Samples

Physicists 15%
Farmers 15%
Foresters 16%
Biologists 17%
Geologists 17%
Chemists 17%
Computer Programmers 18%

Figure 9.1. Percent "like" responses to the SCII–SVIC item *Planning a large party* for 137 occupational samples.

Several qualities that contribute to the excellence of items, and ultimately to the excellence of an interest inventory, can be used to assess the value of each item.

First, items should differentiate among groups because the purpose of interest inventories is to distinguish people with similar interests from those with dissimilar interests. The item in Figure 9.1, for example, has the power to spread 137 occupations over a wide range of response percentages. The lowest "Like" response rate for this item, *Planning a large party*, is 15% (meaning that few people in the sample answered "Like" to the item), and response rates ranged up to a high of 81% (meaning that the majority of the sample responded "Like").

Samples with similar interests should have similar item-response rates, and clusters of groups with high or low response rates should make sense. In Figure 9.1, for example, the samples of restaurant managers, public relations directors, home economics teachers, and recreation leaders had high "Like" response rates of 78–81%. Physicists, farmers, and foresters, however, had low "Like" response rates to the same item. Those clusters of high and low response rate samples are intuitively satisfying and illustrate the item's content validity; one expects restaurant managers, for example, to enjoy planning parties. Even the high response rate for the funeral directors makes sense; they do spend the majority of their time making arrangements (e.g., ordering flowers, reserving a hall, arranging transportation, coordinating activities) that are similar in job task to making arrangements for a party.

Items also should be sex fair; no item should suggest that any occupation or activity is more appropriate for one sex than the other. In addition to sex-fair items, all interpretive and instructional materials for interest inventories should be sex fair.

Inventories can be adapted more easily to other cultures for use with ethnic minorities or for international use if the items are culture-fair and unambiguous. Straightforward items also are more likely to have the same meaning for everyone taking the inventory regardless of cultural or occupational orientation, and they will be easier to translate.

The items should be revised periodically to ensure that they are current and familiar to the respondents. The face validity, as well as content validity, of an interest inventory is affected if the item pool contains obsolete items that are unfamiliar to the general population. On the other hand, as new technologies develop, new items should be generated to ensure that the entire domain of interests is represented in the item pool.

Finally, items should be easy to read. All materials that accompany interest inventories (e.g., instructions, profile, interpretive information) and the item pool itself should be easy to read to make the inventory useful for a wide educational and age range in the population.

Theories of Vocational Interest

The earliest interest inventories were developed using the atheoretical, empirical method of contrast groups that is based on an assumption that people with similar interests can be clustered together and, at the same time, be differentiated from groups with dissimilar interests. The inventory that best illustrates this technique is the Strong Vocational Interest Blank (SVIB), now called the Strong Interest Inventory (Hansen & Campbell, 1985), first published by E. K. Strong, Jr., in 1927.

Later, results from empirical investigations of interests were used to develop hypotheses about the structure of interests. Theorists Anne Roe (1956) and John Holland (1959), for example, used the factor analysis of Guilford and his colleagues (Guilford, Christensen, Bond, & Sutton, 1954), who found seven interest factors: (a) mechanical, (b) scientific, (c) social welfare, (d) aesthetic expression, (e) clerical, (f) business, and (g) outdoor work.

CONSTRUCTION OF INTEREST INVENTORY SCALES

Most interest inventories feature either *homogeneous* or *heterogeneous* scales; the Minnesota Vocational Interest Inventory (MVII) (Clark, 1961) and the Strong Interest Inventory are two instruments that combine heterogeneous occupational scales and homogeneous basic interest scales. Heterogeneous scales are more valid for predictive uses of interest inventories (e.g., predicting future job entry or college major), but homogeneous scales are more useful for providing parsimonious descriptions of the structure of a sample's interests.

Homogeneous Scale Development

Items may be selected during scale construction based on internal consistency or homogeneous scaling. Items chosen in this manner have high intercorrelations. Empirical methods such as cluster or factor analyses can be used to identify the related items. The scales of the Vocational Interest Inventory (VII) (Lunneborg, 1976), for example, were constructed using factor analysis. The scales may also be based on rational selection of items; this method uses a theory to determine items appropriate for measuring the construct represented by each scale. For example, the General Occupational Themes of the Strong Interest Inventory were rationally constructed using Holland's theoretical definition of the six vocational types to guide item selection.

Heterogeneous Scale Development

The Occupational Scales of the Strong Interest Inventory and the Kuder Occupational Interest Survey (KOIS) (Form DD) (Kuder, 1966) are composed of items with low intercorrelations and, therefore, are called heterogeneous scales. Heterogeneous scales are atheoretical: the choice of items is based on empirical results rather than an underlying theory. The Strong Interest Inventory uses the empirical method of contrast groups to select items; this technique compares the item-response rates of occupational criterion groups and contrast groups, representing the interests of people in general, to identify items that significantly differentiate the two samples. The KOIS uses a different empirical method that compares an individual's item-response pattern directly to the item-response patterns of criterion samples that represent the interests of various occupations and college majors.

CURRENT INTEREST INVENTORIES

The most frequently used of all interest inventories is the Strong Interest Inventory, the most recent revision of the Strong Vocational Interest Blank. Other widely used inventories include various forms of the Kuder, the Vocational Preference Inventory, and the Self-Directed Search (Engen, Lamb, & Prediger, 1982; Zytowski & Warman, 1982). Less often used instruments, which have somewhat more restricted applications than the Strong, Kuder, VPI, and SDS in terms of appropriate age and appropriate exploration goals, include the Ohio Vocational Interest Survey (OVIS) (D'Costa, Winefordner, Odgers, & Koons, 1969; Winefordner, 1981), the Vocational Interest Inventory (VII) (Lunneborg, 1976), the Career Assessment Inventory (CAI) (Johansson, 1975, 1986), and the Jackson Vocational Interest Survey (JVIS) (Jackson, 1977).

Strong Interest Inventory

The Strong Interest Inventory (Hansen & Campbell, 1985) is the latest version of the Strong Vocational Interest Blank (SVIB). The SVIB has the longest history of all inventories; it has been under continuous research, revision, and use for over 50 years. The first version of the Strong (1927) used the empirical method of contrast groups to construct occupational scales representing the interests of men in 10 occupations. The first form for women was published in 1933, and until 1974 the instrument was published with separate forms for women and men. In 1974, the two forms were combined by selecting the 325 best items from the previous women's (TW398) and men's (T399) forms; in 1981 another revision was completed in an effort to provide matched-sex occupational scales (e.g., male- and female-normed Forester Scales, male- and female-normed Flight Attendant Scales, male- and female-normed Personnel Director Scales).

The completion of the current version of the Strong Interest Inventory in 1985 marked the end of the sex-equalization process which began in 1971. One additional major change in the 1985 revision was the expansion of the breadth of the profile to include more nonprofessional and vocational/technical occupational scales; 32% of the occupational scales now represent occupations with educational requirements less than a college degree and include additions of female (f) and male (m) normed scales such as f and m Bus Driver, f and m Carpenter, f and m Electrician, f and m Emergency Medical Technician, f and m Respiratory Therapist, f and m Chef, f and m Florist, f and m Funeral Director, f and m Optician, f and m Travel Agent, and f and m Food Service Manager.

During each of the recent revisions of the Strong Interest Inventory, there have been efforts to increase the utility of the inventory for users and their clients in an expanding market. A broadened *Interpretive Report* (Hansen, 1989); several guides and aids for improving interpretation (e.g., the *User's Guide for the SVIB-SCII* [Hansen, 1984] and the *Strong-Hansen Occupational Guide* [Hansen, 1987]); series of Strong Interest Inventory Topical Reports (Hansen, 1988b; McAllister, 1988; Meyer, 1988); and microcomputer software for interactive test administration typify the materials and interpretive aids developed to accompany the expanded profile.

Item Pool and Profile

The item booklet for the Strong Inventory includes 325 items, divided into seven sections: Part 1, Occupational Titles; Part 2, School Subjects; Part 3, Work-related Activities; Part 4, Spare-time Activities; Part 5, Types of People; Part 6, Forced-choice Preference Between Two Activities; Part 7, Self-Description Characteristics. The item format requires respondents to indicate the degree of their interest in each item by responding "Like," "Indifferent," or "Dislike"; for example

Actor/Actress   (L)   I   D

Watching an open-heart   L   (I)   D
   operation

Sports pages in the newspaper   (L)   I   D

Outspoken people with new   L   I   (D)
   ideas

The profile includes three sets of scales: 6 General Occupational Themes, 23 Basic Interest Scales, and 207 Occupational Scales that represent professional and nonprofessional occupations (e.g., farmers, geographers, photographers, social workers, buyers, credit managers).

Occupational Scales

The Occupational Scales are a classic example of test construction using the empirical method of contrast groups. The first step in the procedure is to determine the base rate of popularity of each item with contrast samples called Women-in-General (WIG) for female-normed Occupational Scales and Men-in-General (MIG) for male-normed scales. This step is necessary because items vary in popularity. For example, only 30% of WIG say "Like" to the item *Expressing judgments publicly, regardless of what others says*, but 58% of WIG say "Like" to the item *Skiing*. If this variance were ignored, the result would be extremely popular items appearing on most of the scales and unpopular items appearing on very few scales. The WIG and MIG are each composed of 300 subjects selected from a wide variety of occupations. The female and male subjects in the 1985 WIG and MIG are matched on occupational titles; if the MIG sample, for example, included three electricians, so did the WIG sample.

The next step is to collect a national sample of 200 to 300 females and 200 to 300 males from a specific occupation to serve as criterion samples. Subjects included in the criterion sample are at least 25 years old, have been in the occupation at least three years, and are satisfied with their jobs.

The response-rate percentage of the criterion sample to each item is compared to the response-rate percentage of the appropriate-sex contrast sample (i.e., WIG or MIG) to identify items that differentiate the two samples. Usually 50 to 70 items are identified as the interests ("Likes") or the aversions ("Dislikes") of each occupational criterion sample.

The raw scores for an individual on the Occupational Scales are converted to standard scores based on the Occupational criterion sample, with the mean set equal to 50 and a standard deviation of 10. As shown in Figure 9.2, the scores indicate how similar the respondents' interests are to those of the criterion group for each scale.

Every effort has been made to provide matched-sex Occupational Scales on the Strong Interest Inventory profile; only five of the 106 occupations (207 Scales) are represented by just one scale (e.g., f Dental Assistant, f Dental Hygienist, f Home Economics Teacher, f Secretary, and m Agribusiness Manager). The Occupational Scales are ordered on the profile according to their Holland Code, beginning with occupations classified with a primary code of Realistic and continuing with Investigative occupations, then Artistic, Social, Enterprising, and Conventional occupations.

Separate-sex Occupational Scales continue to be developed because interests of women and men are too dissimilar to provide valid combined-sex scales. E. K. Strong, Jr., (1943) attempted combined-sex construction without success, and more recent attempts have been equally disappointing (Campbell & Hansen, 1981; Hansen, 1976; Kuder, 1977; Webber & Harmon, 1978). Until the interests of women and men converge, separate-sex Occupational Scales provide the most valid results and the greatest breadth of interest exploration for both sexes.

General Occupational Themes

The General Occupational Themes (GOT) are a merger of Strong's empiricism with Holland's theory of vocational types. The six homogeneous themes each contain 20 items selected to represent Holland's definition of each type—Realistic, Investigative, Artistic, Social, Enterprising, and Conventional. The GOT correlate highly (.72 to .79) with same-named Vocational Preference Inventory scales (Hansen, 1983); correlations between the GOT indicate that the hexagonal order that Holland proposes to describe the relationship between his types (adjacent types have more in common than do diametrically opposed types) also describes the relationship between the Strong Inventory Themes (Hansen & Campbell, 1985).

Figure 9.2. A portion of the SVIB–SCII profile showing scores on the Occupational Scales.

STRONG CAMPBELL INTEREST INVENTORY OF THE
STRONG VOCATIONAL INTEREST BLANK

PAGE 2   PROFILE REPORT FOR: DATE TESTED:

ID: DATE SCORED:
AGE: SEX: F

OCCUPATIONAL SCALES	STANDARD SCORES F	M	VERY DISSIMILAR	DISSIMILAR	MODERATELY DISSIMILAR	MID-RANGE	MODERATELY SIMILAR	SIMILAR	VERY SIMILAR

SOCIAL

GENERAL OCCUPATIONAL THEME - S   30 40 50 60 70   F / M
36   LOW

BASIC INTEREST SCALES (STANDARD SCORE)

TEACHING   49   AVERAGE
SOCIAL SERVICE   30   VERY LOW
ATHLETICS   58   HIGH
DOMESTIC ARTS   42   LOW
RELIGIOUS ACTIVITIES 33 VERY LOW

Scale	F	M
sa (as) Foreign language teacher	5	(AS)
sa sa Minister	12	26
sa sa Social worker	16	21
s s Guidance counselor	16	23
s s Social science teacher	18	22
s s Elementary teacher	17	18
s s Special education teacher	14	22
sm saa Occupational therapist	36	37
sia sai Speech pathologist	23	34
si (nsr) Nurse, RN	34	(ISR)
sm s/a Dental hygienist	31	N/A
sa sc Nurse, LPN	13	20
(ris) Athletic trainer	(RIS)	31
sm sm Physical education teacher	33	20
sas sm Recreation leader	42	34
sa sa YWCA/YMCA director	21	18
sas sas School administrator	22	22
sas s/a Home economics teacher	5	N/A

ENTERPRISING

GENERAL OCCUPATIONAL THEME - E   30 40 50 60 70   F / M
31   VERY LOW

BASIC INTEREST SCALES (STANDARD SCORE)

PUBLIC SPEAKING   39   MOD LOW
LAW/POLITICS   36   LOW
MERCHANDISING   28   VERY LOW
SALES   36   VERY LOW
BUSINESS MANAGEMENT 29   VERY LOW

Scale	F	M
e e Personnel director	11	17
ea e Elected public official	12	18
ea ea Life insurance agent	12	8
ec e Chamber of Commerce executive	5	16
ec ec Store manager	14	11
e/a eca Agribusiness manager	N/A	5
ec ec Purchasing agent	10	20
ec e Restaurant manager	9	22
(ar) ea Chef	(AR)	29
ec e Travel agent	11	24
eas e Funeral director	16	14
(ece) ea Nursing home administrator	(CSE)	14
ec em Optician	19	22
e e Realtor	2	12
e (ae) Beautician	23	(AE)
e e Florist	25	21
e e Buyer	-4	10
e e Marketing executive	56	52
ea eci Investments manager	56	45

CONVENTIONAL

GENERAL OCCUPATIONAL THEME - C   30 40 50 60 70   F / M
40   MOD LOW

BASIC INTEREST SCALES (STANDARD SCORE)

OFFICE PRACTICES   38   LOW

Scale	F	M
c c Accountant	35	32
c c Banker	18	28
ci ca IRS agent	22	16
cas cas Credit manager	14	17
cas cas Business education teacher	0	3
(cs) cas Food service manager	(CS)	22
(isr) Dietitian	(ISR)	27
cas (sse) Nursing home administrator	14	(ESC)
cas cas Executive housekeeper	20	25
cs (ces) Food service manager	18	(CES)
ca s/a Dental assistant	20	N/A
c s/a Secretary	10	N/A
c (r) Air Force enlisted personnel	21	(R)
cas (rci) Marine Corps enlisted personnel	24	(RC)
cas ca Army enlisted personnel	28	12
ca ca Mathematics teacher	29	32

Strong-Campbell Interest Inventory of the Strong Vocational Interest Blank Form T325
Copyright · 1933 1938 1945 1946 1966 1968 1981 1983 1985 by the Board of Trustees of the Leland Stanford Junior University All rights reserved Printed and scored under license from Stanford University Press Stanford California 94305

CONSULTING PSYCHOLOGISTS PRESS
577 COLLEGE AVENUE
PALO ALTO, CA 94306

ADMINISTRATIVE INDEXES (RESPONSE %)

OCCUPATIONS	26 %	7 %	67%
SCHOOL SUBJECTS	39 %	31 %	31%
ACTIVITIES	47 %	6 %	47%
LEISURE ACTIVITIES	54 %	28 %	18%
TYPES OF PEOPLE	38 %	38 %	25%
PREFERENCES	50 %	30 %	20%
CHARACTERISTICS	79 %	14 %	7%
ALL PARTS	39 %	17 %	44%

Figure 9.2. (Continued).

Figure 9.2 illustrates the score information provided for the General Occupational Themes on the profile; the same information is presented for the Basic Interest Scales. The standard scores are based on a General Reference Sample composed of 300 women and 300 men with mean set equal to 50 and standard deviation of 10. In addition to standard scores, interpretive comments based on distributions for the respondent's own sex are presented, and interpretive bars provide a visual representation of the distribution of Women-in-General (upper bar) and Men-in-General (lower bar), respectively.

The integration of Holland's theory with Strong's empiricism provides the organizational framework for the current Strong profile. The Occupational Scales are coded with one to three Holland types based on the criterion sample's highest scores on the General Occupational Themes. The codes, in turn, are used to order the Occupational Scales on the profile. The Basic Interest Scales (BIS) also are clustered according to Holland types by identifying the Theme with which each Basic Interest Scale has its highest correlation.

Basic Interest Scales

The 23 Basic Interest Scales (BIS) were constructed using the statistical technique of cluster analysis to identify highly correlated items (Campbell, Borgen, Eastes, Johansson, & Peterson, 1968). The BIS were developed to focus on the measurement of only one interest factor per scale and, consequently, are easier to interpret than the heterogeneous Occupational Scales that incorporate items representing several interest factors as well as likes and aversions in each scale.

The BIS scale names, as indicated in Figure 9.2, describe the homogeneous item content and the interest trait measured by each scale. Like the GOT, standard scores based on a combined-sex General Reference Sample and interpretive comments and bars based on Women- and Men-in-General are presented on the profile.

Reliability and Validity. The test-retest reliability of the scales on the Strong profile is substantial over short and long intervals. Median reliabilities over 2-week, 30-day, and 3-year periods for the General Occupational Themes were .91, .86, and .81; for the Basic Interest Scales, they were .91, .88, and .82; and for the Occupational Scales, they were .91, .89, and .87 (Campbell & Hansen, 1985).

Concurrent validity data for the GOT and BIS, which by their homogeneous scaling nature are more useful for description of interests rather than for prediction, include mean scores for hundreds of occupational samples on each scale. Generally, the scales distribute occupations over 2 to 2½ standard deviations, and the patterns of high and low scoring occupations indicate that scores on these scales are related to pursued occupations (Hansen & Campbell, 1985).

Concurrent validity for the Occupational Scales is determined by identifying the power of each scale to discriminate between the criterion samples and the appropriate sex-in-general sample. The median overlap between scores of the criterion and contrast samples is 36%, representing about two standard deviations of separation between the samples.

Because interest inventories are used to make long-term decisions, predictive validity is important. The Strong Interest Inventory has a long history of predictive validity studies, and the finding is that high scores on the Occupational Scales are related to occupations eventually entered; generally, between one-half and three-fourths of the subjects in predictive validity studies enter occupations predictable from their earlier scores (Campbell, 1966; Dolliver, Irvin, & Bigley, 1972; Hansen, 1986; Harmon, 1969; Spokane, 1979). A recent study assessed the usefulness of the Strong Inventory for predicting college majors and found accuracy rates similar to those reported for occupational entry (Hansen & Swanson, 1983).

Kuder's Interest Inventories

The Personal Preference Record-Form A was published in 1939 by Frederic Kuder and included seven almost independent homogeneous scales. Kuder added two more homogeneous scales in 1943 (Form B) and another homogeneous scale in 1948 (Form C). The Kuder General Interest Survey (Form E) (Kuder, 1988), measures the 10 interest areas of Form C but expresses the items in language that is easier to understand. The first edition of the Kuder Occupational Interest Survey (Form DD) was published in 1966; the latest additions and revisions are reported in the *Kuder DD Manual Supplement* (Zytowski, 1985).

General Interest Survey (Form E)

The General Interest Survey (Form E) is composed of homogeneous scales that measure interest in 10 broad areas: Outdoor, Mechanical, Computational, Scientific, Persuasive, Artistic, Literary, Musical, Social Service, and Clerical. Kuder originally developed the scales by grouping related items on the basis of content validity; later he used item analyses to determine groups of items (scales) with high internal consistency.

The item booklet contains 168 forced-choice triads reported to be at the sixth grade reading level. The respondent compares each of the three activities with the other two and ranks them as most preferred (M) and least preferred (L). For example:

a. Take special notice of people when you are traveling	(M)	(L)
b. Watch for beautiful scenes when you are traveling	(M)	(L)
c. Take special notice of the farm crops when you are traveling	(M)	(L)

d. Read lessons to a blind student	(M)	(L)
e. Keep a record of cars passing past a certain place	(M)	(L)
f. Talk with people to find out their opinions for a newspaper	(M)	(L)

The General Interest Survey (KGIS) may be hand scored or machine scored; both techniques produce raw scores that are entered on the profile sheet shown in Figure 9.3. The respondent's raw scores, in turn, are compared with percentile distributions of norm groups of either girls or boys in grades 6 through 8 or grades 9 through 12. The machine-scored KGIS narrative report, shown in Figure 9.3, compares a male client to the grade 9–12 norm group of boys.

The Kuder Preference Record-Vocational (Form C) is an earlier form that was designed for use with students in grades 9 to 12 and with adults. It uses more difficult vocabulary than does Form E but measures the same 10 areas of interest.

Kuder Occupational Interest Survey (Form DD)

The Kuder Occupational Interest Survey (Form DD) is composed of 100 triads of activities similar to those of the Kuder-Form E already described. The profile includes 104 Occupational Scales and 39 College Major Scales that, like the Strong Interest Inventory, compare the respondent's interests to those of people in criterion samples. Unlike the Strong, the KOIS does not use the empirical method of contrast groups for scale construction. Instead, the individual's responses are compared directly to those of the criterion samples, and scores are reported as lambda coefficients, which do not allow comparison of scores across different persons' profiles as can be done with standard scores. Thus, a respondent's KOIS scores derive meaning only from the rank each scale occupies among all the scales.

This form of the Kuder must be machine scored; the respondent receives the profile illustrated in Figure 9.4. The 104 Occupational Scales represent 28 occupations (56 scales) that were developed using both male and female criterion samples, 37 that are based on male criterion samples only, and 11 based on female criterion samples only. The 39 College Major Scales represent 12 majors (24 scales) that are based on female and male criterion samples, 10 based on male samples only, and 5 on female samples.

In 1985, a new profile for the KOIS was designed and 10 Vocational Interest Estimates (VIE scales) were added to the existing Occupational Scales. The VIE section of the profile is described as a short form (i.e., fewer items are included on each scale) of the earlier Kuder instruments that measure homogeneous or global areas of interest. The reliabilities of the new scales are acknowledged by Zytowski (1985) to be lower than those for Form E or Form C, precipitating the decision to call the scales "estimates" of interests.

The VIEs are reported on the profile in rank order with divisions into high (75th percentile), average, and low (25th percentile) portions, as are the Occupational Scales and College Majors, based on percentile ranks (see Figure 9.4). The separate-sex norm samples for the VIEs are composed of high school and college students and individuals from private agencies (N = 1631 women and 1583 men).

The profile also offers instructions for converting the VIE percentiles to Holland codes by combining the various scales. For example, the Outdoor and Mechanical Scales are combined to estimate Holland's Realistic type, and Computational and Clerical are combined to represent the Conventional type.

Reliability and Validity. An inventory, such as the KOIS, which provides rank-ordered results intended to discriminate interests within the respondent rather than to discriminate among people, has special requirements for analyses of reliability. Test-retest reliability can be assessed only in terms of consistency of the order of scores for each subject from one testing to the next. Kuder and Diamond (1979) reported individual two-week test-retest Occupational Scale reliabilities computed for high school and college-age students; the median reliability for all cases was .90. Zytowski (1985), using college students (N = 192),

SRA®

KUDER GENERAL İNTEREST SURVEY
Form E Narrative Report

Name	THOMPSON ALEX	Numeric Grid	343434343434343
Sex	M	Process Number	0001 00011
Level	GRADES 9 - 12	Norm Group	GRADES 9 - 12

Recently you took the KUDER GENERAL INTEREST SURVEY, FORM E. You were (A) asked to indicate which of three activities you most preferred and which you least preferred. Your V score of 006 indicates that you marked your answers carefully and sincerely. This means that you can have confidence in the accuracy of your results.

Your results show how your interest in ten vocational areas compares to that of other students. The numbers in the charts below indicate the proportion of students whose interest in these ten areas is less than (B) yours. Your scores are ranked from highest to lowest and grouped into HIGH, AVERAGE, and LOW interests. The charts below show which of the vocational areas fall within each of these groups. The vocational areas in which your interests are highest extend into the HIGH areas of the chart; those in which your interests are about the same as other students extend only into the AVERAGE area; and those that are lowest extend only into the LOW area. (D)

Compared to other males: Compared to females:

(F)
          Low....Avg..High....   Low....Avg..High....
(G)   (E)
Persuasive 96-------:----:-----   Persuasive 98-------:----:-------
Literary   96-------:----:-----   Scientific 93-------:----:----
Scientific 78-------:----:-   Literary   88-------:----:----
Soc Serv   78-------:----:-   Computat'l 68-------:----:
Musical   66-------:----   Musical   54--------:---
Computat'l 60-------:----   Mechanical 36--------:-
Artistic   21-------   Soc Serv   33--------:-
Outdoor   18------   Outdoor   24-------
Clerical   14------   Artistic   18------
Mechanical 02-   Clerical   07----

Because there are differences in the interests of males and females, (G) results are provided separately by sex. Generally you will be interested in the results for your own sex; however, if your interests are nontraditional, you may learn something from seeing how you compare with the other sex.

A number of reference books in which you may find occupational (H) information are keyed to the following personality type codes: Realistic, Investigative, Artistic, Social, Enterprising, and Conventional. Your scores rank you highest on the following:

Compared to other males: Compared to females:

          Enterprising   Enterprising
          Investigative   Investigative
          Social   Social

For more information on the vocational areas and scores discussed here, read your Interpretive Leaflet. If you have any questions regarding these results, please see your counselor or teacher.

(A) V score (a measure of reliability that flags unusual or doubtful results) is reported and interpreted

(B) Explanation of test and its interpretation

(C) Score ranking by percentile (compared to norm group) on each scale

(D) Every student compared to both male and female norms

(E) Both graphic and numerical results shown

(F) High, average, and low interest graphically differentiated

(G) Every student is encouraged to look at results on both male and female norms

(H) Conversion to RAISEC codes

All information on this report is simulated.

Figure 9.3. Machine scored KGIS Narrative Report.

Note. From Kuder general interest survey by G. F. Kuder. Chicago: Science Research Associates. Copyright 1987, 1963 by Science Research Associates, Inc. Reprinted by permission.

Kuder Occupational Interest Survey Report Form

Name _____

Sex FEMALE   Date _____

Numeric Grid No. _____   SRA No. 00039

1 Dependability

Dependability: How much confidence can you place in your results? In scoring your responses several checks were made on your answer patterns to be sure that you understood the directions and that your results were complete and dependable. According to these:

YOUR RESULTS APPEAR TO BE DEPENDABLE.

2 Vocational Interest Estimates

Vocational Interest Estimates: Vocational interests can be divided into different types and the level of your attraction to each type can be measured. You may feel that you know what interests you have already — what you may not know is how strong they are compared with other people's interests. This section shows the relative rank of your preferences for ten different kinds of vocational activities. Each is explained on the back of this report form. Your preferences in these activities, as compared with other people's interests, are as follows:

Compared with men		Compared with women	
HIGH		**HIGH**	
COMPUTATIONAL	89	COMPUTATIONAL	91
MUSICAL	85	MUSICAL	89
SCIENTIFIC	83	SCIENTIFIC	87
OUTDOOR	81	OUTDOOR	87
AVERAGE		**AVERAGE**	
LITERARY	74	LITERARY	70
CLERICAL	67	MECHANICAL	70
MECHANICAL	27	CLERICAL	55
LOW		**LOW**	
SOCIAL SERVICE	13	SOCIAL SERVICE	03
PERSUASIVE	01	PERSUASIVE	01
ARTISTIC	01	ARTISTIC	01

3 Occupations

Occupations: The KOIS has been given to groups of persons who are experienced and satisfied in many different occupations. Their patterns of interests have been compared with yours and placed in order of their similarity with you. The following occupational groups have interest patterns most similar to yours.

Compared with men		Compared with women	
CHEMIST	.59	COMPUTR PRGRMR	.55
MATHEMATICIAN	.57	ENGINEER	.54
MATH TCHR, HS	.55	THESE ARE NEXT MOST SIMILAR:	
METEOROLOGIST	.54	ACCT, CERT PUB	.48
SCIENCE TCHR, HS	.54	SCIENCE TCHR, HS	.48
THESE ARE NEXT MOST SIMILAR:		VETERINARIAN	.47
STATISTICIAN	.52	MATH TEACHER, HS	.45
FORESTER	.51	DENTIST	.43

Compared with men — MOST SIMILAR, CONT.

ENGINEER	.51
OPTOMETRIST	.47

THE REST ARE LISTED IN ORDER OF SIMILARITY:

X-RAY TECHNICIAN	.46	TRAVEL AGENT	.36
TV REPAIRER	.46	LAWYER	.36
BANKER	.45	ELECTRICIAN	.35
ACCT, CERT PUB	.45	JOURNALIST	.35
PHYS THERAPIST	.44	PODIATRIST	.35
SCHOOL SUPT	.44	MACHINIST	.34
COUNSELOR, HS	.44	RADIO STATOM MGR	.34
BUYER	.44	WELDER	.34
LIBRARIAN	.43	AUTO MECHANIC	.34
POSTAL CLERK	.43	INSURANCE AGENT	.33
EXTENSION AGENT	.43	FILM/TV PROD/DIR	.33
FLORIST	.42	PLUMBER	.32
PHOTOGRAPHER	.41	PERSONNEL MGR	.32
ARCHITECT	.41	CLOTHIER, RETAIL	.32
ELEM SCH TEACHER	.40	SOCIAL WORKER	.31
BLDG CONTRACTOR	.40	PAINTER, HOUSE	.29
FARMER	.39	CARPENTER	.29
PRINTER	.39		
NURSE	.39		
AUDIOL/SP PATHOL	.38		
POLICE OFFICER	.37		
SUPERVSR, INDUST	.37		
REAL ESTATE AGT	.37		
BRICKLAYER	.37		
PLUMBING CMTRAC	.37		

REST, CONT. — Compared with men

PHARMACEUT SALES	.42
AUTO SALESPERSON	.40
TRUCK DRIVER	.40
INTERIOR DECOR	.40
MINISTER	.39

Compared with women — THE REST ARE LISTED IN ORDER OF SIMILARITY:

DENTIST	.66	PHYS THERAPIST	.39
VETERINARIAN	.46	BEAUTICIAN	.38
BOOKSTORE MGR	.45	INTERIOR DECOR	.38
PLANT NURSRY MKR	.45	RELIGIOUS ED DIR	.38
PSYCHOLOGIST	.45	DEPT STORE-SALES	.38
PHYSICIAN	.44	X-RAY TECHNICIAN	.38
BOOKKEEPER	.44	ARCHITECT	.37
PHARMACIST	.44	BOOKKEEPER	.37
X-RAY TECHNICIAN	.44	BANK CLERK	.36
LAWYER	.43	NUTRITIONIST	.36
COUNSELOR, HS	.43	SECRETARY	.36
AUDIOL/SP PATHOL	.43	BOOKSTORE MGR	.34
NURSE	.43	LIBRARIAN	.34
EXTENSION AGENT	.42		
OCCUPA THERAPIST	.41		
OFFICE CLERK	.41		
DENTAL ASSISTANT	.40		
COL STU PERS MKR	.40		
FLORIST	.40		
ELEM SCH TEACHER	.40		
INSURANCE AGENT	.39		
FILM/TV PROD/DIR	.39		
JOURNALIST	.39		
SOCIAL WORKER	.39		

Compared with women (REST, CONT.)

PHARMACEUT SALES	.27
AUTO SALESPERSON	.26
PHYSICIAN	.26
PSYCHOLOGIST	.25
INTERIOR DECOR	.25

4 College Majors

College Majors: Just as for occupations, the KOIS has been given to many persons in different college majors. The following college major groups have interest patterns most similar to yours.

Compared with men

PHYSICAL SCIENCE	.56
MATHEMATICS	.54
ENGINEERING	.51
FORESTRY	.51
THESE ARE NEXT MOST SIMILAR:	
BIOLOGICAL SCI	.48
AGRICULTURE	.45
THE REST ARE LISTED IN ORDER OF SIMILARITY:	
MUSIC & MUSIC ED	.43
PHYSICAL EDUC	.43
BUSINESS EDUC	.42
PREMED/P MAR/DENT	.42
ANIMAL SCIENCE	.39
PSYCHOLOGY	.39
SERV ACAD CADET	.39
ELEMENTARY EDUC	.38
ECONOMICS	.38
BUSINESS ADMIN	.37
FOREIGN LANGUAGE	.36
ARCHITECTURE	.32
SOCIOLOGY	.31
ENGLISH	.30
HISTORY	.28
ART & ART EDUC	.26
POLITICAL SCI	.26

Compared with women

MATHEMATICS	.47
BIOLOGICAL SCI	.42
THESE ARE NEXT MOST SIMILAR:	
HEALTH PROFESS	.37
THE REST ARE LISTED IN ORDER OF SIMILARITY:	
MUSIC & MUSIC ED	.33
PHYSICAL EDUC	.33
BUSINESS EDUC	.32
PSYCHOLOGY	.32
NURSING	.30
FOREIGN LANGUAGE	.28
HOME ECON EDUC	.26
ELEMENTARY EDUC	.26
ENGLISH	.26
HISTORY	.22
POLITICAL SCI	.22
DRAMA	.20
ART & ART EDUC	.19
SOCIOLOGY	.17

Experimental Scales.

V-SCORE 54

M	.45	MBI	.02	F	.40	M	.56	MBI	.04
S	.61	D	.20	RU	.28	M	.39	RU	.28

7-3881

Figure 9.4. KOIS Report Form.

reported profile stability of .80 for the VIEs over a
two-week interval.

A large predictive validity study for the KOIS
(Zytowski, 1976) involved over 800 women and men
who were located 12 to 19 years after taking the
Kuder. Fifty-one percent were employed in an occupation predicted by their scores on the KOIS.

Holland's Interest Inventories

The emergence of John Holland's theory of careers
(Holland, 1959, 1966) began with development of the
Vocational Preference Inventory (VPI) (Holland,
1958). Based on interest data collected with the VPI as
well as data from other interest, personality, and
values inventories and from analyses of the structure
of interests, Holland formulated his theory of vocational life and personality. According to Holland,
people can be divided into six types or some combination of six types: Realistic, Artistic, Investigative,
Social, Enterprising, and Conventional. Holland indicates that the types can be organized in the shape of a
hexagon in the R–I–A–S–E–C order; the types adjacent to one another on the hexagon (e.g., Realistic-
Investigative or Enterprising-Conventional) are more
related than types that are diametrically opposed to
one another (e.g., Realistic-Social or Artistic-Con-
ventional). Attempts to verify Holland's hexagonal
representation of the world of work show in general
that the structure of interests approximates the theoretical organization proposed by Holland (Campbell &
Hansen, 1981; Cole & Hanson, 1971; Edwards &
Whitney, 1972; Prediger, 1982).

Holland's theory has led to development of inventories and sets of scales to measure his six types, for
example, his own Self-Directed Search (SDS) (Holland, 1971), the ACT Interest Inventory (ACT II)
(Lamb & Prediger, 1981), the System for Career
Decision-making (CDM) (Harrington & O'Shea,
1976), and the General Occupational Themes of the
Strong Interest Inventory (Campbell & Holland,
1972; Hansen & Johansson, 1972).

Vocational Preference Inventory

Development of the Vocational Preference Inventory (VPI) was based on a series of theoretical and
empirical reports. Holland surveyed personality, vocational choice, and vocational interest literature;
identified interest-personality factors; and hypothesized how they related to one another. Then, he used
160 occupational titles to develop an item pool that
represented the interest factors or types, for example:

Criminologist	(Yes)	No
Restaurant Worker	Yes	(No)
Photoengraver	Yes	(No)
Wild Animal Trainer	(Yes)	No

The current version of the VPI (Holland, 1985c) has
seven homogeneous scales, constructed in a series of
rational-empirical steps that measure Self-Control
(Sc), plus the six types hypothesized in Holland's
theory: Realistic (R), Investigative (I), Artistic (A),
Social (S), Enterprising (E), and Conventional (C).
Other VPI scales developed using empirical methods
of scale construction include Acquiescence (Ac),
measuring willingness to say "yes" to items; Status
(St), indicating interest in occupational status; Mascu-
linity-Feminity (Mf), measuring interest in occupations traditionally preferred by men or women; and
Infrequency (Inf), assessing the tendency to answer
items in an atypical direction.

The VPI may be hand scored; raw scores are plotted
either on the female profile shown in Figure 9.5 or a
male profile. Even though Holland is a strong propo-
nent of the use of raw scores for predicting occupational membership, the profile is calibrated to provide
standard scores based on either 378 female or 354
male college students and employed adults to provide
comparisons across scales.

Self-Directed Search

The Self-Directed Search (Holland, 1985b, 1987a),
similar to the VPI, was developed to measure Holland's six types. It may be self-administered, self-
scored, and to a limited degree, self-interpreted. The
228-item assessment booklet includes four sections:
Activities the respondent would like to do; Competencies; Occupations; and Self-Estimates. A sample item
from each section is provided below:

		L	D
(Act)	Fix electrical things	■	☐
(Comp)	I can program a computer to study a scientific problem	Y ☐	N ■
(Occ)	Poet	Y ☐	N ■

| | | High | | | | | | Low |
| (S-E) | Teaching Ability | 7 | 6 | 5 | (4) | 3 | 2 | 1 |

The reading level of the SDS is estimated at the
seventh- or eighth-grade level; Form Easy (E), which
has only 203 items, is rated at the fourth grade level.

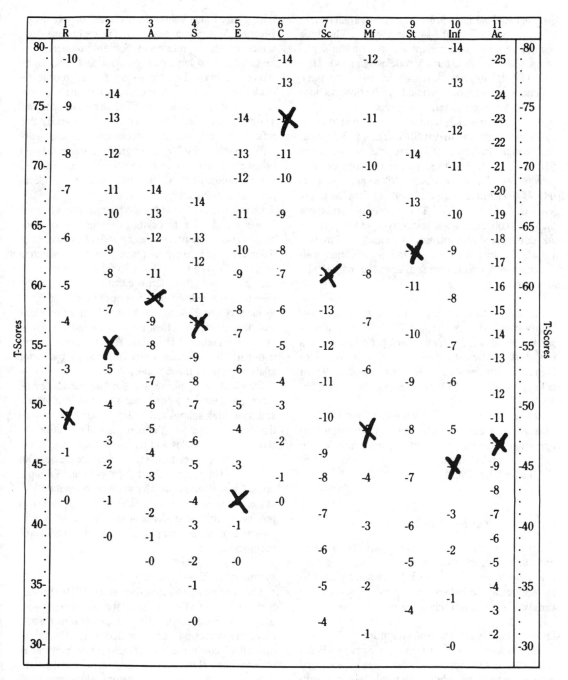

Figure 9.5. Profile for the Vocational Preference Inventory. Standard scores are based on 378 female college students and employed adults.

As illustrated in Figure 9.6, the most important feature of the SDS profile is the summary codes. The three highest raw scores represent the respondent's primary, secondary, and tertiary code assignments. Holland (1979) suggests flexibility in using the three summary codes for occupational exploration, because the codes are approximate, not precise.

A series of materials have been developed to assist in the interpretation of the SDS. The *1987 Manual Supplement* (Holland, 1987a) explains the use of the SDS in individual and group career assistance. *The Occupations Finder* (Holland, 1985a) and *The College Majors Finder* (Holland, 1987b) provide three-letter Holland codes for 1,156 occupations and more than 900 college majors, respectively. Occupational and educational alternatives can be identified by surveying the two booklets to find possibilities with summary codes which are similar to the individual's summary code.

Reliability and Validity. The median test-retest reliability coefficient for the 11 VPI scales over a two-week interval is .72; over the same period the median reliability coefficient for the six SDS scales is .82 for high school students and over 7 to 10 months, .92 for college students (Holland, 1978, 1979, 1985b, 1985c).

Studies of the predictive validity of the VPI and SDS, for choice of occupation and college major over one-, two- and three-year intervals, range from 35% to 66% accuracy (Holland, 1962, 1979, 1985c, 1987a; Holland & Lutz, 1968).

Other Interest Inventories

Several other interest inventories have been developed more recently than the Strong, Kuder, or Holland inventories. They are not as frequently used as the previously described inventories and represent a variety of scale construction techniques.

Jackson Vocational Interest Inventory

The Jackson Vocational Interest Survey (JVIS) (Jackson, 1977), appropriate for high school and college students and adults who need assistance with educational and career planning, is composed of 289 forced-choice items describing occupational activities. The 34 homogeneous scales that measure *work roles* and *work styles* each contain 17 items estimated to be at the seventh-grade reading level. The work-role scales include five that characterize specific occupations (e.g., Engineering, Elementary Educa-

tion) and 21 that represent a cluster of jobs (e.g., Creative Arts, Social Science). The eight work-style scales measure preferences for environments that require certain behaviors (e.g., Dominant Leadership, Accountability). The hand-scored JVIS profile includes only the 34 Basic Interest Scales; the machine-scored profile also includes 10 General Occupational Themes measuring broad patterns of interests that reflect the respondent's *orientation toward work* rather than interests (e.g., Logical, Enterprising); 17 broad clusters of university major fields (Educational Classifications) and 32 occupational clusters (Occupational Classifications).

Development of the 34 homogeneous Basic Interest Scales relied on a theory-based technique of scale construction. The process began with identification of the interests to be measured from previous research in vocational psychology. Then 3,000 items were written to represent the interest constructs. Finally, the item pool was submitted to a series of factor analyses to identify the 289 items that had high correlations with factor scores on their own scales and low correlations with other JVIS scales. The 10 General Occupational Themes later were constructed by factor analyzing the 34 Basic scales.

Standard score norms for the Basic and Theme scales are based on a combined-sex sample of female and male high school and college students. Interpretive bars representing the percentile distributions of scores of the females and males on each scale allow individuals to infer how their scores compare with those of other people. The Educational and Occupational Classifications involve analyses of an individual's entire profile of Basic scales compared to model profiles of college students in various academic majors and of people employed in a wide variety of occupations.

Vocational Interest Inventory

The Vocational Interest Inventory (VII) (Lunneborg, 1976, 1981), designed for use with young people, is similar to the JVIS on several dimensions. First, the interests to be measured were selected on theoretical considerations. The eight homogeneous scales of the VII were developed to represent the eight groups described in Roe's theory of occupational classifications: Service, Business Contact, Organization, Technical, Outdoor, Science, General Culture, and Arts and Entertainment. Second, the scales were constructed using a series of factor analyses that reduced the initial item pool to the final 112 forced-choice items. The eight scales each contain 28 response choices that have high correlations with factor

How To Organize Your Answers

Start on page 4. Count how many times you said L for "Like." Record the number of L's or Y's for each group of Activities, Competencies, or Occupations on the lines below.

Activities (pp. 4-5)

$$\underset{R}{4} \quad \underset{I}{6} \quad \underset{A}{5} \quad \underset{S}{6} \quad \underset{E}{7} \quad \underset{C}{0}$$

Competencies (pp. 6-7)

$$\underset{R}{7} \quad \underset{I}{8} \quad \underset{A}{1} \quad \underset{S}{10} \quad \underset{E}{5} \quad \underset{C}{6}$$

Occupations (p. 8)

$$\underset{R}{2} \quad \underset{I}{6} \quad \underset{A}{10} \quad \underset{S}{1} \quad \underset{E}{2} \quad \underset{C}{0}$$

Self-Estimates (p. 9)
(What number did)
you circle?)

$$\underset{R}{6} \quad \underset{I}{7} \quad \underset{A}{1} \quad \underset{S}{6} \quad \underset{E}{1} \quad \underset{C}{4}$$

$$\underset{R}{6} \quad \underset{I}{6} \quad \underset{A}{4} \quad \underset{S}{4} \quad \underset{E}{4} \quad \underset{C}{4}$$

Total Scores
(Add the five R scores,
the five I scores, the
five A scores, etc.)

$$\underset{R}{25} \quad \underset{I}{33} \quad \underset{A}{21} \quad \underset{S}{27} \quad \underset{E}{19} \quad \underset{C}{14}$$

The letters with the three highest numbers indicate your summary code. Write your summary code below. (If two scores are the same or tied, put both letters in the same box.)

Summary Code

I	S	R
Highest	2nd	3rd

Figure 9.6. Profile for the Self-Directed Search.

scores on their own scales and low correlations with other VII scales. Third, the scales were normed on a combined-sex sample of students. According to the author (Lunneborg, 1981), scores on only two scales were unaffected by sex and thus, the VII may have the problem of bias in interpretation for one sex or the other.

Ohio Vocational Interest Survey

The first edition of the Ohio Vocational Interest Survey (OVIS I) (D'Costa, Winefordner, Odgers, & Koons, 1969, 1970) also was developed for use with young people, especially those in grades 7 through 12. The homogeneous OVIS I interest scales were developed based on the data-people-things model of the *Dictionary of Occupational Titles* (1965). The first scales (e.g., Machine Worker, Crafts, Customer Service, Nursing) were rationally derived; in other words, persons familiar with definitions of the scales to be developed were asked to assign items to, in their estimation, the appropriate scale or scales. After initial rational clustering of related items, a series of factor analyses were employed to refine the item pool, resulting in 280 items that correlated more highly with their own scales than with any other scale.

The OVIS II (Winefordner, 1983) is composed of 253 items, about one-fourth of which came from the OVIS I. The 23 clusters are based on a reexamination of the data-people-things levels of all occupations in the 348 subgroups of the *Guide for Occupational Exploration* (1979). Because the OVIS I and OVIS II clusters are based on different classification schemes, the equivalence between the two sets is not exact; for example, two OVIS I clusters, *Personal Services* and *Caring for People and Animals*, were merged into one OVIS II cluster, *Basic Services*. The OVIS II profile provides percentile ranks for both females and males in three grade groups: grades 7 through 9; grades 10 through 12; and grades 13 through 14. The instrument can be hand scored or machine scored.

Career Assessment Inventory

The first edition of the Career Assessment Inventory (CAI) (Johansson, 1975; Johansson & Johansson, 1978) was developed for use with individuals considering immediate career entry, community college education, or vocational-technical training, and was modeled after the Strong Interest Inventory. In 1982, the decision was made to move from separate-sex to combined-sex Occupational Scales. The enhanced version of the CAI published in 1986 (Johansson, 1986) has been expanded to include several Occupational Scales representing professional occupations.

The enhanced CAI test booklet includes 370 items and the profile, like the Strong profile, reports three sets of scales: 6 homogeneous General Themes, 25 homogeneous Basic Interest Areas and 111 heterogeneous Occupational Scales. The CAI also uses Holland's theory to organize the Basic Interest Areas and Occupational Scales on the profile, clustering together those that represent each of Holland's six types.

The General Themes and Basic Interest Areas are normed on a combined-sex reference sample composed of employed adults and students drawn from the six Holland interest areas; 75 females and 75 males from each of the six groups, for a total of 900 subjects, compose the sample. In addition to the standard scores based on a combined-sex sample, however, the CAI profile presents bars for each scale representing the range of scores for females and males in the reference sample. These additional data help to circumvent the problem of sex differences on some of the homogeneous scales.

The Occupational Scales of the enhanced version of the CAI were developed using the empirical method of contrast samples employed with the Strong Interest Inventory. Unlike the Strong Occupational Scales, however, the CAI Occupational Scales were developed with combined-sex criterion and general reference samples. Many of these "combined-sex" samples fall far short of the goal of equally representing females and males within the sample (e.g., 0 female aircraft mechanics, 0 male medical assistants, 0 female purchasing agents, and 0 male secretaries). The author attempted to improve the psychometrics of the scales by doing separate-sex item analyses if the separate-sex samples were large enough. In most instances, however, the sample representing one sex or the other was too small to produce reliable item analyses (e.g., 22 male bank tellers, 16 female dental laboratory technicians, 12 male bookkeepers, and 20 female enlisted personnel). In fact, 64 of the 111 Occupational Scales were developed using criterion samples that included less than 50 subjects representing one sex or the other (45 scales with < 50 female subjects and 19 scales with < 50 male subjects). Consequently, the exploration validity, for the scales developed with unbalanced female-male ratio criterion samples, is questionable for the underrepresented gender.

STABILITY OF INTERESTS

The degree to which interests are stable is important to the predictive power of inventories. If interests are fickle and unstable, interest inventory scores will not explain any of the prediction variance.

Stability of interests was one of the earliest concerns of researchers in interest measurement (Strong, 1943). Cross-sectional and longitudinal methods have been used in a number of studies to document that interests are stable even at relatively young ages of 15 or 16 years. By age 20, the stability of interests is obvious even over test-retest intervals of 5 to 10 years, and by age 25, interests are very stable (Johansson & Campbell, 1971).

During the long history of the Strong Interest Inventory, over 30 occupations have been tested at least three times: in the 1930s, 1960s, and 1970s/80s. Analyses of these data have shown that interests of randomly sampled occupational groups are stable. Figure 9.7, a profile of interests for chemists collected in the 1930s, 1960s, and 1970s, illustrates the typical finding for all the occupations:

1. The configuration of the interests of an occupation stays the same over long periods of time, and
2. even when interests change to some small extent, the relative importance of various interests stays the same. (Hansen, 1988a)

USE OF INTEREST INVENTORIES

Interest inventories are used to assess interests efficiently by a variety of institutions including high school and college advising offices, social service agencies, employment agencies, consulting firms, corporations, and community organizations such as the YWCA.

Career Exploration

The major use of assessed interests, usually reported as interest inventory scores, is in career counseling that leads to decisions such as choosing a major, selecting an occupation, making a mid-career change, or preparing for retirement. First, counselors use the interest inventory profiles to develop hypotheses about clients that may be discussed, confirmed, or discarded during career exploration. Then, the interest scores and profile provide a framework for interest exploration and a mechanism for helping the client to integrate her or his past history with current interests.

The inventory results serve as a starting point for evaluating interests, as an efficient method for objectively identifying interests, and as a structure for the counseling process. Inventory results help some counselees to increase the number of options they are considering; some use the results to begin to narrow the range of possible choices. Others want only to confirm educational or vocational decisions that they already have made.

Selection and Placement

Interest inventories are also used to assess interests during employment selection and placement evaluations. Among qualified candidates, interest inventories help to identify those most likely to complete the training program and stay in the profession (Berdie & Campbell, 1968; Reeves & Booth, 1979). Even after initial selection, interest inventories may be used to help an employee find the right job within the company (Dunnette & Kirchner, 1965).

Research

Researchers use measures of interests (e.g., checklists, self-estimates, rating scales, interest inventories) to operationalize interest traits, investigate the origin and development of interests, explore changes or stability in society, and understand the relationship between interests and other psychological variables such as abilities, satisfaction, success, and personality. Studies assessing the structure of interests and also the interests of various occupational groups provide information for understanding the organization of the world of work and the relationships among occupations.

Most interest inventories are constructed to measure vocational interests. Recent research, however, indicates that instruments such as the Strong Interest Inventory measure not only vocational interests but also leisure interests (Cairo, 1979; Varca & Shaffer, 1982). Holland (1973) has proposed that instruments measuring his six personality types also can identify a respondent's preferences for environments and types of people as well as job activities.

FUTURE DIRECTIONS

The frequency of test use in counseling has not changed appreciably in the last 25 years; however, the use of interest inventories has increased while the use of other tests (e.g., ability, aptitude, achievement) has decreased (Zytowski & Warman, 1982). A wide variety of new interpretive materials, career guidance packages, and interactive computerized systems for inventory interpretation and career exploration are available. Thus far, evaluations of the use of interest inventories indicate that various modes and mediums of presentation are equally effective (Johnson, Korn, & Dunn, 1975; Maola & Kane, 1976; Miller &

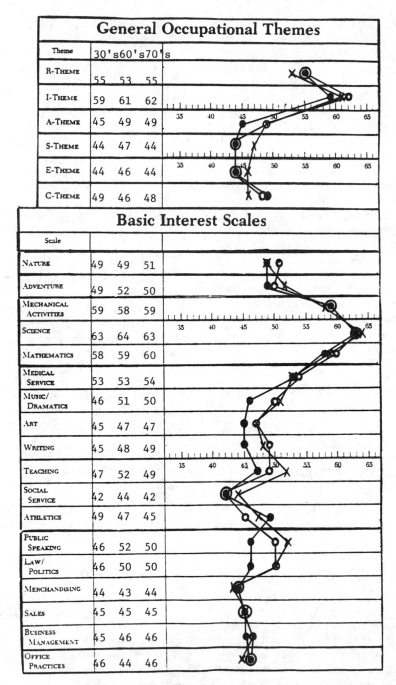

Figure 9.7. Mean interest profile for male Chemists tested in the 1930s (●—●), the 1960s (x—x), and the 1970s (○—○).

Cochran, 1979; Rubinstein, 1978; Smith & Evans, 1973). The trend in the future, with decreasing budgets and personnel in educational institutions, will be toward even greater use of computers for interest inventory administration and interpretation and for integration into computerized career counseling modules.

Techniques for developing reliable and valid interest inventories are available now, and the construction methods have reached a plateau of excellence in reliability and validity. Therefore, publishers can direct their efforts toward an increased emphasis on interpretation and counselor competency. Test manuals traditionally were written to provide data required by the American Psychological Association's (1986) *Standards for Educational and Psychological Testing*; now, interpretive manuals are prepared in addition to technical manuals to help the professional maximize the usefulness of inventory results (Hansen, 1984; Holland, 1971, 1987; Zytowski, 1981).

As the use of interest inventories expands to new populations, research must also move in that direction to aid in understanding the characteristics of the populations as well as the best methods for implementing interest inventories with them. The cross-cultural use of interest inventories also is increasing the demand for valid translations of inventories and for data on the predictive accuracy of inventories normed on U.S. populations for non-English-speaking respondents.

SUMMARY

Interest inventories will be used in the future as in the past to operationalize the construct of interests in research. Attempts to answer old questions, such as the interaction of interests and personality, success, values, satisfaction, and ability, will persevere.

Holland's theory undoubtedly will continue to evoke research in the field. Studies designed to understand educational and vocational dropouts and changers, to analyze job satisfaction, to understand the development of interests, and to predict job or academic success will draw on Holland's theoretical constructs for independent variables and on interest inventories to identify interests.

The exploration of vocational interests always has been a popular topic in counseling psychology; the increased use of inventories and career guidance programs indicates that interest inventories will continue to be an important component in psychological research.

REFERENCES

American Psychological Association. (1986). *Standards for educational and psychological testing*. Washington, DC: American Psychological Association.

Berdie, R. F., & Campbell, D. P. (1968). Measurement of interest. In D. K. Whitla (Ed.), *Handbook of measurement and assessment in behavioral sciences*. Reading, MA: Addison-Wesley.

Cairo, P. C. (1979). The validity of the Holland and Basic Interest Scales of the Strong Vocational Interest Blank: Leisure activities versus occupational membership as criteria. *Journal of Vocational Behavior*, *15*, 68–77.

Campbell, D. P. (1966). Occupations ten years later of high school seniors with high scores on the SVIB life insurance salesman scale. *Journal of Applied Psychology*, *50*, 369–372.

Campbell, D. P., Borgen, F. H., Eastes, S. H., Johansson, C. B., & Peterson, R. A. (1968). A set of basic interest scales for the Strong Vocational Interest Blank for Men. *Journal of Applied Psychology Monograph*, *52*, 1–54.

Campbell, D. P., & Hansen, J. C. (1981). *Manual for the SVIB-SCII* (3rd ed.). Stanford, CA: Stanford University Press.

Campbell, D. P., & Holland, J. L. (1972). Applying Holland's theory to Strong's data. *Journal of Vocational Behavior*, *2*, 353–376.

Clark, K. E. (1956). *Manual for use of the Navy Vocational Interest Inventory*. Minneapolis: University of Minnesota Press.

Clark, K. E. (1961). *Vocational interests of nonprofessional men*. Minneapolis, MN: University of Minnesota Press.

Cole, N. S., & Hansen, G. (1971). *An analysis of the structure of vocational interests*. ACT Research Report No. 40. Iowa City: American College Testing Program.

Cowdery, K. M. (1926). Measurement of professional attitudes: Differences between lawyers, physicians, and engineers. *Journal of Personnel Research*, *5*, 131–141.

D'Costa, A. G., Winefordner, D. W., Odgers, J. G., & Koons, P. B., Jr. (1969). *Ohio Vocational Interest Survey*. New York: Harcourt, Brace, and World.

D'Costa, A. G., Winefordner, D. W., Odgers, J. G. & Koons, P. B., Jr., (1970). *Ohio Vocational Interest Survey Manual for Interpreting*. New York: Harcourt, Brace, Jovanovich.

Dolliver, R. H., Irvin, J. A., & Bigley, S. E. (1972). Twelve-year follow-up of the Strong Vocational Interest Blank. *Journal of Counseling Psychology*, *19*, 212–217.

Dunnette, M. D., & Kirchner, W. K. (1965). *Psychology applied to industry*. New York: Appleton-Century-Crofts.

Edwards, K. J., & Whitney, D. R. (1972). A structural analysis of Holland's personality types using factor and configural analysis. *Journal of Counseling Psychology*, *19*, 136–145.

Engen, H. B., Lamb, R. R., & Prediger, D. J. (1982). Are secondary schools still using standardized tests? *Personnel and Guidance Journal*, *60*, 287–290.

Freyd, M. (1922–1923). The measurement of interests in vocational selection. *Journal of Personnel Research*, *1*, 319–328.

Guilford, J. P., Christensen, P. R., Bond, N. A., Jr., & Sutton, M. A. (1954). A factor analysis study of human interests. *Psychological Monographs*, Whole No. 375, *68*, 1–38.

Hansen, J. C. (1976). Exploring new directions for Strong-Campbell Interest Inventory occupational scale construction. *Journal of Vocational Behavior*, *9*, 147–160.

Hansen, J. C. (1983). *Correlation between VPI and SCII scores*. Unpublished manuscript. Minneapolis: Center for Interest Measurement Research, University of Minnesota.

Hansen, J. C. (1984). *User's guide to the SVIB-SCII*. Stanford, CA: Stanford University Press.

Hansen, J. C. (1986 August). *12-Year longitudinal study of the predictive validity of the SVIB-SCII*. Paper presented at the meetings of the American Psychological Association, Washington, DC.

Hansen, J. C. (1987). *Strong-Hansen occupational guide*. Palo Alto, CA: Consulting Psychologists Press.

Hansen, J. C. (1988a). Changing interests: Myth or reality? *Applied Psychology: An International Review*, *37*, 133–150.

Hansen, J. C. (1988b). *Leisure report for the Strong Interest Inventory*. Palo Alto, CA: Consulting Psychologists Press.

Hansen, J. C. (1989). *Strong Interest Inventory expanded interpretive report*. Palo Alto, CA: Consulting Psychologists Press.

Hansen, J. C., & Campbell, D. P. (1985). *Manual for the SVIB-SCII* (4th ed.). Stanford, CA: Stanford University Press.

Hansen, J. C., & Johansson, C. B. (1972). The application of Holland's vocational model to the Strong Vocational Interest Blank for Women. *Journal of Vocational Behavior*, *2*, 479–493.

Hansen, J. C., & Swanson, J. L. (1983). Stability of interests and the predictive and concurrent validity of the 1981 Strong-Campbell Interest Inventory. *Journal of Counseling Psychology*, *30*, 194–201.

Harmon, L. W. (1969). The predictive power over 10 years of measured social service and scientific interests among college women. *Journal of Applied Psychology*, *53*, 193–198.

Harrington, T. F., Jr., & O'Shea, A. J. (1976). *Manual for the Harrington/O'Shea Systems for Career Decision-Making*. Needham, MA: Career Planning Associates.

Holland, J. L. (1958). A personality inventory employing occupational titles. *Journal of Applied Psychology*, *42*, 336–342.

Holland, J. L. (1959). A theory of vocational choice. *Journal of Counseling Psychology*, *6*, 35–45.

Holland, J. L. (1962). Some explorations of a theory of vocational choice: I. One- and two-year longitudinal studies. *Psychological Monographs*, *76*, 26.

Holland, J. L. (1966). *The psychology of vocational choice*. Waltham, MA: Blaisdell.

Holland, J. L. (1971). *The counselor's guide to the Self-Directed Search*. Palo Alto, Ca: Consulting Psychologists Press.

Holland, J. L. (1973). *Making vocational choices: A theory of careers*. Englewood Cliffs, NJ: Prentice-Hall.

Holland, J. L. (1978). *Manual for the Vocational Preference Inventory* (3rd ed.). Palo Alto, CA: Consulting Psychologists Press.

Holland, J. L. (1979). *The Self-Directed Search professional manual*. Palo Alto, CA: Consulting Psychologists Press.

Holland, J. L. (1985a). *The occupations finder*. Odessa, FL: Psychological Assessment Resources.

Holland, J. L. (1985b). *The Self-Directed Search professional manual—1985 edition*. Odessa, FL: Psychological Assessment Resources.

Holland, J. L. (1985c). *Vocational Preference Inventory (VPI) manual—1985 edition*. Odessa, FL: Psychological Assessment Resources.

Holland, J. L. (1987a). *1987 manual supplement for the Self-Directed Search*. Odessa, FL: Psychological Assessment Resources.

Holland, J. L. (1987b). *The college majors finder*. Odessa, FL: Psychological Assessment Resources.

Holland, J. L., & Lutz, S. W. (1968). Predicting a student's vocational choice. *Personnel and Guidance Journal, 46,* 428–436.

Hubbard, R. M. (1930). Interest Analysis Blank. In D. G. Paterson, R. M. Elliot, L. D. Anderson, H. A. Toops, & E. Heidbrider (Eds.), *Minnesota Mechanical Ability Test.* Minneapolis: University of Minnesota Press.

Jackson, D. N. (1977). *Jackson Vocational Interest Survey manual.* London, Ontario: Research Psychologists Press.

Johansson, C. B. (1975). *Manual for the Career Assessment Inventory.* Minneapolis, MN: National Computer Systems.

Johansson, C. B. (1986). *Career Assessment Inventory: Enhanced version.* Minneapolis, MN: National Computer Systems.

Johansson, C. B., & Campbell, D. P. (1971). Stability of the Strong Vocational Interest Blank for Men. *Journal of Applied Psychology, 55,* 24–26.

Johansson, C. B., & Johansson, J. C. (1978). *Manual supplement for the Career Assessment Inventory.* Minneapolis: National Computer Systems.

Johnson, W. F., Korn, T. A., & Dunn, D. J. (1975). Comparing three methods of presenting occupational information. *Vocational Guidance Quarterly, 24,* 62–65.

Kitson, H. D. (1925). *The psychology of vocational adjustment.* Philadelphia: Lippincott.

Kornhauser, A. W. (1927). Results from a quantitative questionnaire of likes and dislikes used with a group of college freshmen. *Journal of Applied Psychology, 11,* 85–94.

Kuder, G. F. (1939). *Kuder Preference Record-Form A.* Chicago: University of Chicago Bookstore.

Kuder, G. F. (1943). *Vocational Preference Record-Form B.* Chicago: Science Research Associates.

Kuder, G. F. (1948). *Kuder Preference Record-Form C (Vocational).* Chicago: Science Research Associates.

Kuder, G. F. (1966). *General manual: Occupational Interest Survey Form-DD.* Chicago: Science Research Associates.

Kuder, G. F. (1977). *Activity interests and occupational choice.* Chicago: Science Research Associates.

Kuder, G. F. (1988). *Kuder General Interest Survey, Form E.* Chicago: Science Research Associates.

Kuder, G. F., & Diamond, E. E. (1979). *Kuder Occupational Interest Survey: General manual (2nd ed.).* Chicago: Science Research Associates.

Lamb, R. R., & Prediger, D. J. (1981). *Technical report for the unisex edition of the ACT Interest Inventory.* Iowa City: American College Testing Program.

Lunneborg, P. W. (1976). *Manual for the Vocational Interest Survey.* Seattle: University of Washington, Educational Assessment Center.

Lunneborg, P. W. (1981). *Vocational Interest Inventory manual.* Los Angeles: Western Psychological Services.

Maola, J., & Kane, G. (1976). Comparison of computer-based versus counselor-based occupational information systems with disadvantaged vocational students. *Journal of Counseling Psychology, 23,* 163–165.

McAllister, L. (1988). *Leadership Management style report for the Strong Interest Inventory.* Palo Alto, CA: Consulting Psychologists Press.

Meyer, P. (1988). *Organizational specialty report for the Strong Interest Inventory.* Palo Alto, CA: Consulting Psychologists Press.

Miller, M. J., & Cochran, J. R. (1979). Evaluating the use of technology in reporting SCII results to students. *Measurement and Evaluation in Guidance, 12,* 166–173.

Miner, J. B. (1922). An aid to the analysis of vocational interests. *Journal of Educational Research, 5,* 311–323.

Parsons, F. (1909). *Choosing a vocation.* Boston: Houghton-Mifflin.

Paterson, D. G., Elliott, R. M., Anderson, L. D., Toops, H. A., & Heidbreder, E. (Eds.). (1930). *Minnesota Mechanical Abilities Test.* Minneapolis: University of Minnesota Press.

Prediger, D. J. (1982). Dimensions underlying Holland's hexagon: Missing link between interests and occupations? *Journal of Vocational Behavior, 15,* 155–163.

Reeves, D. J., & Booth, R. F. (1979). Expressed versus inventoried interests as predictors of paramedical effectiveness. *Journal of Vocational Behavior, 15,* 155–163.

Remmers, H. H. (1929). The measurement of interest differences between students of engineering and agriculture. *Journal of Applied Psychology, 13,* 105–119.

Roe, A. (1956). *The psychology of occupations.* New York: Wiley.

Rubenstein, M. R. (1978). Integrative interpretation of vocational inventory results. *Journal of Counseling Psychology, 25,* 306–309.

Smith, R. D., & Evans, J. (1973). Comparison of experimental group and individual counseling facilitators of vocational development. *Journal of Counseling Psychology, 20,* 202–208.

Spokane, A. R. (1979). Occupational preferences and the validity of the Strong-Campbell Interest Inventory for college women and men. *Journal of Counseling Psychology*, 26, 312–318.

Strong, E. K., Jr. (1927). *Vocational Interest Blank*. Stanford, CA: Stanford University Press.

Strong, E. K., Jr. (1943). *Vocational interests of men and women*. Stanford, CA: Stanford University Press.

U.S. Department of Labor. (1965). *Dictionary of occupational titles* (3rd ed.). Washington, DC: U.S. Government Printing Office.

U.S. Department of Labor. (1979). *Guide for occupational exploration*. Washington, DC: U.S. Government Printing Office.

Varca, P. E., & Shaffer, G. S. (1982). Holland's theory: Stability of avocational interests. *Journal of Vocational Behavior*, 21, 288–298.

Webber, P. L., & Harmon, L. W. (1978). The reliability and concurrent validity of three types of occupational scales for two occupational groups. In C. K. Tittle & D. G. Zytowski (Eds.), *Sex-fair interest measurement: Research and implications*. Washington, DC: National Institute of Education.

Winefordner, D. W. (1981). *Ohio Vocational Interest Survey: Manual for interpreting* (2nd ed.). New York: Harcourt Brace Jovanovich.

Zytowski, D. G. (1976). Predictive validity of the Kuder Occupational Interest Survey: A 12- to 19-year follow-up. *Journal of Counseling Psychology*, 3, 221–233.

Zytowski, D. G. (1981). *Counseling with the Kuder Occupational Interest Survey*. Chicago: Science Research Associates.

Zytowski, D. G. (1985). *Kuder DD manual supplement*. Chicago: Science Research Associates.

Zytowski, D. G., & Warman, R. E. (1982). The changing use of tests in counseling. *Measurement and Evaluation in Guidance*, 15, 147–152.

PART V

NEUROPSYCHOLOGICAL ASSESSMENT

CHAPTER 10

COMPREHENSIVE NEUROPSYCHOLOGICAL ASSESSMENT BATTERIES

Gerald Goldstein

This chapter is the first of three covering the area of neuropsychological assessment. It will provide a general introduction to neuropsychological assessment and deal specifically with the extensive standard test batteries used with adults. Neuropsychological assessment is a relatively new term that has essentially replaced the older terms *testing for brain damage* or *testing for organicity*. Lezak (1983) indicates that these procedures are used for three purposes: diagnosis, provision of information important for patient care, and research. A significant component of the patient care function is rehabilitation planning and monitoring (Golden, 1978; Goldstein & Ruthven, 1983; Meier, Benton, & Diller, 1987). The focus of neuropsychological assessment has traditionally been on the brain-damaged patient, but there have been major extensions of the field to psychiatric disorders (Goldstein, 1986; Gruzelier & Flor-Henry, 1979; Yozawitz, 1986), functioning of normal individuals (Kimura & Durnford, 1974), and normal aging (Goldstein & Shelly, 1975; Reed & Reitan, 1963).

Perhaps the best definition of a neuropsychological test has been offered by Ralph Reitan, who describes it as a test that is sensitive to the condition of the brain. If performance on a test changes with a change in brain function, then the test is a neuropsychological test. However, it should be noted that comprehensive neuropsychological test batteries should contain not only neuropsychological tests. They should also contain some tests that are generally insensitive to brain dysfunction, primarily because such tests are often useful for providing a baseline against which extent of

impairment associated with acquired brain damage can be measured. Most neuropsychological assessment methods are formal tests, but some work has been done with rating scales and self-report measures. Neuropsychological assessment is rarely conducted through a structured interview outside a test situation.

A comprehensive neuropsychological test battery is a procedure that assesses all the major functional areas generally affected by structural brain damage. We use the term ideally because none of the standard, commonly available procedures entirely achieves full comprehensiveness. Some observers have described the comprehensive procedures as screening batteries because feasibility and time constraints generally require a sacrifice of detailed investigations of specific areas in order to achieve comprehensiveness. In Hamsher's chapter (12), we will learn more about what a clinical neuropsychologist does when asked to explore a particular area in detail rather than do a comprehensive evaluation. While the term *screening* may be justifiable in certain respects, the extensive standard batteries in common use should not be grouped with the brief, paper-and-pencil screening tests used in many clinical and industrial settings. That is, they do not simply screen for presence or absence of brain damage, but also evaluate a number of functional areas that may be affected by brain damage. Because brain damage radically affects cognitive processes, most neuropsychological tests assess various areas of cognition, but perception and motor skills are also frequently evaluated. Thus, neuropsychological tests are generally thought of as assessment instruments for a variety of cognitive, perceptual, and motor skills. That is not to say that brain damage does not affect other aspects of the personality, but traditionally the standard neuropsychological tests do not typically assess these other areas. Perhaps the most important reason for this preference is that cognitive tests have proven to be the most diagnostic ones. While personality changes may occur with a wide variety of psychiatric, general medical, and neurological conditions, cognitive changes appear to occur most dramatically in individuals with structural brain damage.

Numerous attempts have been made to classify the functional areas typically affected by brain damage, but the scheme proposed in what follows is a reasonably representative one. Perhaps the most ubiquitous change is general intellectual impairment. Following brain damage, the patient is not as bright as he or she was before. Problems are solved less effectively, goal-directed behavior becomes less well organized, and there is impairment of a number of specific skills such as solving arithmetic problems or interpreting proverbs. Numerous attempts have been made to epitomize this generalized loss, perhaps the most successful one being Goldstein and Scheerer's (1941) concept of impairment of the abstract attitude. The abstract attitude is essentially a phenomenological concept having to do with the way in which the individual perceives the world. Some consequences of its impairment involve failure to form concepts or to generalize from individual events, failure to plan ahead ideationally, and inability to transcend the immediate stimulus situation. While the loss is a general one involving many aspects of the individual's life, it is best observed in a testing setting where the patient is presented with a novel situation in which some problem must be solved. Typically these tests involve abstraction or concept formation, and the patient is asked to sort or categorize in some way. The Goldstein-Scheerer (1941) tests, perhaps the first neuropsychological battery, consist largely of sorting tests, but also provide the patient with other types of novel problem-solving tasks.

Probably the next most common manifestation of structural brain damage is impairment of memory. Sometimes memory impairment is associated with general intellectual impairment, sometimes it exists independently, and sometimes it is seen as an early sign of a progressive illness that eventually impairs a number of abilities other than memory. In most but not all cases, recent memory is more impaired than remote memory. That is, the patient may recall his or her early life in great detail, but may be unable to recall what happened during the previous day. Often, so-called

primary memory is also relatively well preserved. That is, the patient may be able to repeat immediately what was just presented to him, such as a few words or a series of digits, but will not retain new information over a more extended period of time, particularly after intervening events have occured. In recent years, our capacity to examine memory has benefited from a great deal of research involving the various amnesic syndromes (e.g., Butters & Cermak, 1980; Squire, Slater, & Chace, 1975; Warrington & Weiskrantz, 1982), and we have become quite aware that not all brain-damaged patients experience the same kind of memory disorder (Butters, 1983). A detailed assessment is generally required to identify specifically the various types of memory disorder, and the comprehensive batteries we will be discussing here generally can detect only the presence of a memory disorder and provide an index of its severity.

Loss of speed in performing skilled activities is an extremely common symptom of brain damage. Generally, this loss is described in terms of impaired psychomotor speed or perceptual-motor coordination. While its basis is sometimes reduction of pure motor speed, in many instances pure speed is preserved in the presence of substantial impairment on tasks involving speed of some mental operation or coordination of skilled movement with perceptual input. Thus, the patient may do well on a simple motor task, such as finger tapping, but poorly on a task in which movement must be coordinated with visual input, such as a cancellation or substitution task. Tasks of this latter type are commonly performed slowly and laboriously by many kinds of brain-damaged patients. Aside from slowness, there may be other disturbances of purposive movement that go under the general heading of apraxia. Apraxia may be manifested as simple clumsiness or awkwardness, an inability to carry out goal directed movement sequences as would be involved in such functional activities as dressing, or as an inability to use movement ideationally as in producing gestures or performing pretended movements. While apraxia in one of its pure forms is a relatively rare condition, impairment of psychomotor speed is quite common and seen in a variety of conditions.

A set of abilities that bridge movement and perception may be evaluated by tasks in which the patient must produce some form of construction or copy a figure from a model. Among the first tests used to test brain-damaged patients was the Bender-Gestalt (Bender, 1938), a procedure in which the patient must copy a series of figures devised by Wertheimer (1923) to study perception of visual gestalten. It was found that many patients had difficulty copying these figures, although they apparently preceived them normally. These difficulties manifested themselves in reasonably characteristic ways, including various forms of distortion, rotation of the figure, simplification, or primitivation and perseveration. The copying task has continued to be used by neuropsychologists, either in the form of the Bender-Gestalt or a variety of other procedures. Variations of the copying task procedure have involved having the patient draw the figure from memory (Benton, 1963; Rey, 1941), from a verbal command, for example, "Draw a Circle" (Luria, 1973), or copy a figure that is embedded in an interfering background pattern (Canter, 1970). Related to the copying task is the constructional task, in which the patient must produce a three-dimensional construction from a model. The most popular test for this purpose is the Kohs Blocks or Block Design subtest of the Wechsler Scales (Wechsler, 1955). While in the timed versions of these procedures the patient may simply fail the task by virtue of running out of time, at least some brain-damaged patients make errors on these procedures comparable to what is seen on the copying tasks. With regard to block design type tasks, the errors might involve breaking the contour of the model or incorrectly reproducing the internal structure of the pattern (Kaplan, 1979). Thus, a constructional deficit may not be primarily associated with reduction in psychomotor speed, but rather with the inability to build configurations in three-dimensional space. Often, this ability is referred to as visual-spatial skill.

Visual-spatial skills also form a bridge with visual perception. When one attempts to analyze the basis for a patient's difficulty with a constructional task, the task demands may be broken down into movement, visual, and integrative components. Often, the patient has no remarkable impairment of purposive, skilled movement and can recognize the figure. If it is nameable (the patient can tell you what it is) or if it is not, it can be correctly identified on a recognition task. However, the figure cannot be accurately copied.

While the difficulty may be with the integration between the visual percept and the movement, it has also been found that patients with constructional difficulties, and indeed patients with brain damage in general, frequently have difficulties with complex visual perception. For example, they do poorly at embedded figures tasks (Teuber, Battersby, & Bender, 1951) or at tasks in which a figure is made difficult to recognize through displaying it in some unusual manner, such as overlapping it with other figures (Golden, 1981b) or presenting it in some incomplete or ambiguous form (Mooney, 1957).

Some brain-damaged patients also have difficulty when the visual task is made increasingly complex through adding elements in the visual field. Thus, the patient may identify a single element, but not two. When two stimuli are presented simultaneously, the characteristic error is that the patient reports seeing only one. The phenomenon is known as extinction (Bender, 1952) or neglect (Heilman, 1979).

Many brain-damaged patients also have deficits in the areas of auditory and tactile perception. Sometimes, the auditory impairment is such that the patient can hear, but sounds cannot be recognized or interpreted. The general condition is known as agnosia and can actually occur in the visual, auditory, or tactile modalities. Agnosia has been defined as "perception without meaning," implying the intactness of the primary sense modality but loss of the ability to comprehend the incoming information. Auditory agnosia is a relatively rare condition, but there are many disturbances of auditory perception that are commonly seen among brain-damaged patients. Auditory neglect can exist and is comparable to visual neglect; sounds to either ear may be perceived normally, but when a sound is presented to each ear simultaneously, only one of them may be perceived. There are a number of auditory verbal problems that we will examine in the discussion of language. Auditory attentional deficits are common and may be identified by presenting complex auditory stimuli, such as rhythmic patterns, which the patient must recognize or reproduce immediately after presentation. A variety of normal and abnormal phenomena may be demonstrated using a procedure called dichotic listening (Kimura, 1961). It involves presenting two different auditory stimuli simultaneously to each ear. The subject wears earphones, and the stimuli are presented using stereophonic tape. Higher-level tactile deficits generally involve a disability with regard to identifying symbols or objects by touch. Tactile neglect may be demonstrated by touching the patient over a series of trials with single and double stimuli, and tactile recognition deficits may be assessed by asking the patient to name objects placed in his or her hand or to identify numbers or letters written on the surface of the skin. It is particularly difficult to separate primary sensory functions from higher cognitive processes in the tactile modality, and many neuropsychologists perform rather detailed sensory examinations of the hands, involving such matters as light touch thresholds, two-point discrimination, point localization, and the ability to distinguish between sharp and dull tactile stimuli (Semmes, Weinstein, Ghent, & Teuber, 1960).

The neuropsychological assessment of speech and language has in some respects become a separate discipline involving neuropsychologists, neurologists, and speech and language pathologists. There is an extensive interdisciplinary literature in the area (Albert, Goodglass, Helm, Rubens, & Alexander, 1981), and several journals that deal almost exclusively with the relationships between impaired or normal brain function and language (e.g., *Brain and Language*). Aphasia is the general term used to denote impairment of language abilities as a result of structural brain damage, but not all brain-damaged patients with communicative difficulties have aphasia. While aphasia is a general term covering numerous subcategories, it is now rather specifically defined as an impairment of communicative ability associated with focal damage to the hemisphere of the brain that is dominant for language—the left hemisphere in most people. Aphasia is generally produced as a result of disorders that have a sudden onset, notably stroke and head trauma, but it may sometimes be seen in cases of other localized diseases such as brain tumors and focal infections. Stroke is probably the most common cause of aphasia.

Historically, there have been numerous attempts to categorize the subtypes of aphasia (Goodglass, 1983), but in functional terms, the aphasias involve a rather dramatic impairment of the capacity to speak, to understand the speech of others, to find the names for common objects, to read (alexia), write (agraphia), calculate (acalculia), or to use or comprehend gestures. However, a clinically useful assessment of these functional disorders must go into their specific characteristics. For example, when we say the patient has lost the ability to speak, we may mean that he or she has become mute or can produce only a few utterances in a halting, labored way. On the other hand, we may mean that the patient can produce words fluently, but the words and sentences being uttered make no sense. When it is said that the patient does not understand language, that may mean that spoken but not written language is understood, or it may mean that all modalities of comprehension are impaired. Thus, there are several aphasic syndromes, and it is the specific syndrome that generally must be identified in order to provide some correlation with the underlying localization of the brain damage and to make rational treatment plans. We may note that the standard comprehensive neuropsychological test batteries do not include extensive aphasia examinations. There are several such examinations available, such as the Boston Diagnostic Aphasia Examination (Good-

glass & Kaplan, 1983) and the Western Aphasia Battery (Kertesz, 1979). Even though they may be used in conjuction with a neuropsychological assessment battery, they are rather lengthy procedures in themselves and require special expertise to administer and interpret.

For various reasons, it is often useful to assess attention as part of the neuropsychological examination. Sometimes, an attention deficit is a cardinal symptom of the disorder, but even if it is not, the patient's level of attention may influence performance on tests of essentially all the functional areas we have been discussing. A discussion of attention may be aided by invoking a distinction between *wide aperture* and *narrow aperture* attention (Kinsbourne, 1980). Wide aperture attention has to do with the individual's capacity to attend to an array of stimuli at the same time. Attention may be so narrowly focused that the total picture is not appreciated. Tests for neglect may in fact be assessing wide aperture attention. Narrow aperture attention has to do with the capacity to sustain attention to small details. Thus, it can be assessed by vigilance tasks or tests like the Picture Completion subtest of the Wechsler scales. Brain-damaged patients may manifest attentional deficits of either type. They may fail to attend to a portion of their perceptual environment, or they may be unable to maintain sufficient concentration to complete successfully tasks requiring sustained occupation with details. Individuals with attentional deficits are often described as distractible or impulsive, and in fact, many brain-damaged patients may be accurately characterized by those terms. Thus, the assessment of presence and degree of attention deficit is often a highly clinically relevant activity. Recently, Mirsky (in press) has proposed a useful division, based upon a factor analytic study of attentional tasks, dividing them into tests that evaluate encoding, sustaining concentration, focusing, and shifting attention from one aspect of a task to another.

In summary, neuropsychological assessment typically involves the functional areas of general intellectual capacity, memory, speed and accuracy of psychomotor activity, visual-spatial skills, visual, auditory, and tactile perception, language, and attention. Thus, a comprehensive neuropsychological assessment may be defined as a procedure that surveys at least all of these areas. In practical terms, a survey is all that is feasible if the intent of the assessment is to evaluate all areas. It is obviously generally not feasible to do an indepth assessment of each of these areas in every patient, nor is it usually necessary to do so.

PROBLEMS IN CONSTRUCTION AND STANDARDIZATION OF TEST BATTERIES

It will be assumed here that neuropsychological tests share the same standardization requirements as all other psychological tests. That is, there is the need for appropriate quantification, norms, and related test construction considerations, as well as the need to deal with issues related to validity and reliability. However, there are some special considerations regarding neuropsychological tests, and we will turn our attention to them here.

Practical Concerns in Test Construction

Neuropsychological test batteries must of necessity be administered to brain-damaged patients, many of whom may have severe physical disability, cognitive impairment, or a combination of the two. Therefore, the stimulus and response characteristics of the tests themselves, as well as the stimulus characteristics of the test instructions, become exceedingly important considerations. Neuropsychological test materials should, in general, be constructed with salient stimuli that the patient can readily see or hear and understand. The material to be read should not require high levels of literacy, nor should the grammatical structures be unduly complex. With regard to test instructions, the potential for multimodal instruction giving should ideally be available. If the patient cannot see or read, it should be possible to give the instructions verbally, without jeopardizing the clinician's opportunity to use established test norms. The opportunity should be available to repeat and paraphrase instructions until it is clear that the patient understands them. It is of crucial importance in neuropsychological assessment that the examiner achieve maximum assurance that a test was failed because the patient could not perform the task being assessed, not because the test instructions were not understood. This consideration is of particular importance for the aphasic patient, who may have a profound impairment of language comprehension. With regard to response parameters, efforts should be made to assure that the test response modality is within the patient's repertoire.

In neuropsychological assessment, it is often not the failure to perform some specific task that is diagnostic, but the failure to perform some component of a series of tasks in the presence of intact function in other areas. As an example, failure to read a passage is not specifically diagnostic, because the inability to read may be associated with a variety of cognitive, perceptual, and learning difficulties. However, failure to be able to transfer a grapheme or a written symbol to a phoneme or sound in the presence of other manifestations of literacy could be quite diagnostic. Individuals with this type of deficit may be able to "sight-read" or recognize words as perceptual patterns, but when asked to read multisyllabic, unfamiliar words, they are unable to break the word down into phonemes and sound it out. In perhaps its most elegant form, neuropsychological assessment can produce what is called a double dissociation (Teuber, 1959): a task consistently failed by patients with a particular type of brain disorder accompanied by an equally difficult corresponding task that is consistently passed, and the reverse in the case of patients with some other form of brain disorder. Ideally, then, neuropsychological assessment aims at detailed as possible specification of what functional deficits exist in a manner that allows for mapping of these deficits onto known systems in the brain. There are several methods of achieving this goal, and not all neuropsychologists agree with regard to the most productive route. In general, some prefer to examine patients in what may be described as a linear manner, with a series of interlocking component abilities, while others prefer using more complex tasks in the form of standard, extensive batteries and interpretation through examination of performance configurations. The linear approach is best exemplified in the work of A. R. Luria (1973) and various collaborators, while the configural approach is seen in the work of Ward Halstead (1947), Ralph Reitan (Reitan & Davison, 1974), and their many collaborators. In either case, however, the aim of the assessment is largely that of determining the pattern of the patient's preserved and impaired functions and inferring from this pattern what the nature might be of the disturbed brain function. The difficulty with using complex tasks to achieve that end is that such tasks are really only of neuropsychological interest if they can be analyzed by one of the two methods described here.

Issues Related to Validity and Reliability

Neuropsychological assessment has the advantage of being in an area where the potential for development of highly sophisticated validation criteria has been very much realized in recent years and will surely achieve even fuller realization in the near future. We begin our discussion with this consideration, and are first occupied with the matters of concurrent and predictive validity. A major review of validation studies was accomplished by Klove (1974) and updated by Boll (1981). Reitan and Wolfson (1985) have written an entire volume on the Halstead-Reitan battery, which contains a brief review of pertinent research findings in addition to extensive descriptions of the tests themselves and case materials. These reviews essentially covered only the Wechsler scales and Halstead-Reitan Battery, but there are several reviews of the work with the Luria-Nebraska Neuropsychological Battery as well (e.g., Golden, 1981b). We will not deal with the content of those reviews at this point, but rather focus on the methodological problems involved in establishing concurrent or predictive validity of neuropsychological tests. With regard to concurrent validity, the criterion used in most cases is the objective identification of some central nervous system lesion arrived at independently of the neuropsychological test results. Therefore, validation is generally provided by neurologists or neurosurgeons. Identification of lesions of the brain is particularly problematic because, unlike many organs of the body, the brain cannot usually be visualized directly in the living individual. The major exceptions occur when the patient undergoes brain surgery or receives the rarely used procedure of brain biopsy. In the absence of these procedures, validation is dependent upon autopsy data or the various brain imaging techniques. Autopsy data are not always entirely usable for validation purposes, in that numerous changes may have taken place in the patient's brain between time of testing and time of examination of the brain. Of the various imaging techniques, the CT scan is currently the most fruitful one. Cooperation among neuroradiologists, neurologists, and neuropsychologists has already led to the accomplishment of several important studies correlating quantitative CT scan data with neuropsychological test results (e.g., Hill & Mikhael, 1979). Beyond the CT scan, however, we can see the beginnings of even more sensitive indicators, including measures of cerebral metabolism such as the PET scan (Positron Emission Tomography), the Xenon enhanced CT scan, and the advanced imaging techniques that may develop from the new method of nuclear magnetic resonance (NMR). Recently, more generally available and even more sensitive measures of cerebral metabolism have appeared, including generations of the PET scan allowing for greatly improved resolution SPECT (Single Photon Emission Computerized Tomography) which allows for studying brain metabolism in settings in which a cyclotron is not available, and the evolving method of magnetic resonance imaging spectroscopy. These exciting new developments in brain imaging and observation of brain function will surely provide increasingly definitive criteria for neuropsychological hypotheses and assessment methods.

Within neuropsychological assessment, there appears to have been a progression regarding the relationship between level of inference and criterion. Early studies in the field as well as the development of new assessment batteries generally addressed themselves to the matter of simple presence or absence of structural brain damage. Thus, the first question raised had to do with the accuracy with which an assessment procedure could discriminate between brain-damaged and non-brain-damaged patients, as independently classified by the criterion procedure. In the early studies, the criterion utilized was generally clinical diagnosis, perhaps supported in some cases by neurosurgical data or some laboratory procedure such as a skull X-ray or an EEG. It soon became apparent, however, that many neuropsychological tests were performed at abnormal levels, not only by brain-damaged patients, but by patients with several of the functional psychiatric disorders. Because many neuropsychologists worked in neuropsychiatric rather than general medical settings, this matter became particularly problematic. Great efforts were then made to find tests that could discriminate between brain-damaged and psychiatric patients or, as sometimes put, between "functional" and "organic" conditions. There have been several reviews of this research (Goldstein, 1978; Heaton, Baade, & Johnson, 1978; Heaton & Crowley, 1981; Malec, 1978), all of which were critical of the early work in this field in light of current knowledge about several of the functional psychiatric disorders. The chronic schizophrenic patient was particularly problematic, because such patients often performed on neuropsychological tests in a manner indistinguishable from the performance of patients with generalized structural brain damage. By now, this whole issue has been largley reformulated in terms of looking at the neuropsychological aspects of many of the functional psychiatric disorders (e.g., Gruzelier & Flor-Henry, 1979; Henn & Nasrallah, 1982), largely under the influence of the newer biological approaches to psychopathology.

Neuropsychologists working in neurological and neurosurgical settings were becoming increasingly interested in validating their procedures against more refined criteria, notably in the direction of localization of brain function. The question was no longer only whether a lesion was present or absent, but if present, whether the tests could predict its location. Major basic research regarding this matter was conducted by H.-L. Teuber and various collaborators over a span of many years (Teuber, 1959). This group had access to a large number of veterans who had sustained open head injuries during World War II and the Korean conflict. Because the extent and site of their injuries were exceptionally well documented by neurosurgical and radiological data, and the lesions were reasonably well localized, these individuals were used productively in a long series of studies in which attempts were made to relate both site of lesion and concomitant neurological defects to performance on an extensive series of neuropsychological procedures ranging from measures of basic sensory functions (Semmes, Weinstein, Ghent, & Teuber, 1960) to complex cognitive skills (Teuber & Weinstein, 1954). Similar work with brain-wounded individuals was accomplished by Freda Newcombe and collaborators at Oxford (Newcombe, 1969). These groups tended to concentrate on the major lobes of the brain (frontal, temporal, parietal, and occipital), and would, for example, do contrasts between the performances of patients with frontal and occipital lesions on some particular test or test series (e.g., Teuber, 1964). In another setting, but at about the same time the Teuber group was beginning its work, Ward Halstead (1947) and collaborators conducted a large-scale neuropsychologically oriented study of frontal lobe function. Ralph M. Reitan, who was Halstead's student, adopted several of his procedures, supplemented them, and developed a battery of tests that were extensively utilized in localization studies. Reitan's (1955) early work in the localization area was concerned with differences between the two cerebral hemispheres more than with regional localization. The now well-known Wechsler-Bellevue studies of brain lesion lateralization (see review in Reitan, 1966) represented some of the beginnings of this work. The extensive work of Roger Sperry and various collaborators (Sperry, Gazzaniga, & Bogen, 1969) with patients who had undergone cerebral commisurotomy also contributed greatly to validation of neuropsychological tests with regard to the matter of differences between the two hemispheres, particularly the functional asymmetries or cognitive differences. Since the discoveries regarding the major roles of subcortical structures in the mediation of various behaviors (Albert, 1978), neuropsychologists have also been studying the relationships betweeen test performance and lesions in such structures and structure complexes as the limbic system (Scoville & Milner, 1957) and the basal ganglia (Butters, 1983).

The search for validity criteria has become increasingly precise with recent advances in the neurosciences as well as increasing opportunities to collect test data from various patient groups. One major conceptualization largely attributable to Reitan and his co-workers is that localization does not always operate independently with regard to determination of behavioral change, but interacts with type of lesion or the specific process that produced the brain damage. The first report regarding this matter related to differences in performance between patients with recently acquired lateralized brain damage and those who had sustained lateralized brain damage at some time in the remote past (Fitzhugh, Fitzhugh, & Reitan, 1961, 1962). Patients with acute lesions were found to perform differently on tests from patients with chronic lesions. It soon became apparent, through an extremely large number of studies (cf. Filskov & Boll, 1981) that there are many forms of type-locus interactions, and that level and pattern of performance on neuropsychological tests may vary greatly with the particular nature of the brain disorder. This development paralleled such advances in the neurosciences as the discovery of neurotransmitters and the relationship between neurochemical abnormalities and a number of the neurological disorders that historically had been of unknown etiology. We therefore have the beginnings of the development of certain neurochemical validating criteria (Davis, 1983). There has also been increasing evidence for a genetic basis for several mental and neurological disorders. The gene for Huntington's disease is close to being discovered, and there is growing evidence of a significant genetic factor contributing to the acquisition of certain forms of alcoholism (Steinhauer, Hill, & Zubin, 1987). In general, the concurrent validity studies have been quite satisfactory, and many neuropsychological test procedures have been shown to be accurate indicators of many parameters of brain dysfunction.

A persistent problem in the past has been the possible tendency of neuropsychological tests to be more sensitive than the criterion measures. In fact, a study by Filskov and Goldstein (1974) demonstrated that neuropsychological tests may predict diagnosis more accurately than many of the individual neurodiagnostic procedures commonly used in assessment of neurological and neurosurgical patients (e.g., skull X-ray). It would appear that with the advent of the CT scan and the even more advanced brain imaging procedures, this problem will be diminishing. A related problem involves the establishment of the most accurate and reliable external criterion. We have always taken the position (Goldstein & Shelly, 1982; Russell, Neuringer, & Goldstein, 1970) that no one method can be superior in all cases, and that the best criterion is generally the final medical opinion based on a comprehensive but pertinent evaluation, excluding, of course, behavioral data. In some cases, for example, the CT scan may be relatively noncontributory, but there may be definitive laboratory findings based on examination of blood or cerebral spinal fluid. In some cases (e.g., Huntington's disease) the family history may be the most crucial part of the evaluation. It is not being maintained here that the best criterion is a doctor's opinion, but rather that no single method can stand out as superior in all cases when one is dealing with a variety of disorders. The diagnosis is often best established through the integration by an informed individual of data coming from a number of sources. A final problem to be mentioned here is that objective criteria do not yet exist for a number of neurological disorders, but even this problem appears to be undergoing a rapid stage of solution. Most notable in this regard is the in vivo differential diagnosis of the degenerative diseases of old age, such as Alzheimer's disease. There is also no objective laboratory marker for multiple sclerosis, and diagnosis of that disorder continues to be made on a clinical basis. Only advances in the neurosciences will lead to ultimate solutions to problems of this type.

In clinical neuropsychology, predictive validity has mainly to do with course of illness. Will the patient get better, stay the same, or deteriorate? Generally, the best way to answer questions of this type is through longitudinal studies, but very few such studies have actually been done. Even in the area of normal aging, in which many longitudinal studies have been accomplished, there really have been no extensive neuropsychologically oriented longitudinal studies. There is, however, some literature on recovery from stroke, much of which is attributable to the work of Meier and collaborators (Meier, 1974). Levin, Benton, and Grossman (1982) provide a discussion of recovery from closed head injury. Of course, it is generally not possible to do a full neuropsychological assessment immediately following closed head injury, and so prognostic instruments used at that time must be relatively simple ones. In this regard, a procedure known as the Glasgow Coma Scale (Teasdale & Jennett, 1974) has well-established predictive validity. Perhaps one of the most extensive efforts directed toward establishment of the predictive validity of neuropsychological tests was accomplished by Paul Satz and various collaborators, involving the prediction of reading achievement in grade school based on neuropsychological assessments accomplished during kindergarten (Fletcher & Satz, 1980; Satz, Taylor, Friel, & Fletcher, 1978). At the other end of the age spectrum, there are currently several ongoing longitudinal studies contrasting normal elderly individuals with dementia patients (Danziger, 1983; Wilson & Kaszniak, 1983). However, we do not yet know from these studies and other ongoing longitudinal investigations what the best prognostic instruments are for predicting the course of dementia or for determining whether or not an elderly individual suspected of having dementia will deteriorate or not.

An important aspect of predictive validity has to do with prediction of treatment and rehabilitation outcome. Ben-Yishay, Gerstman, Diller, and Haas (1970) were able to show that a battery of neuropsychological tests could successfully predict length of time in rehabilitation and functional outcome in patients with hemiplegia. There have been several studies (reviewed by Parsons & Farr, 1981) concerned with predicting outcome of alcoholism treatment on the basis of neuropsychological test performance. The results of these studies are mixed, but in general it would appear that test performance during the early stages of treatment may bear some relationship to outcome as evaluated by followup. Before leaving this area, I should mention that there are several not fully documented but apparently reasonable clinical principles related to prediction of treatment outcome. In general, patients with relatively well-circumscribed deficits and perhaps underlying structural lesions, tend to do better in treatment than do patients with more global deficits. Some data suggest that early intervention for aphasic adults, perhaps within two months post-onset, is more effective than treatment initiated later (Wertz, 1983). Ben-Yishay, Diller, Gerstman, and Gordon (1970) have suggested that an individual's level of competence on a task to be trained is related to his or her ability to profit from cues utilized in the training procedure.

In general, studies of predictive validity in neuropsychological assessment have not been as extensive as studies involving concurrent validity. However, the data available suggest that neuropsychological tests can predict degree of recovery or deterioration to some extent and have some capacity to predict treatment outcome. Because many neurological disorders change over time, getting better or worse, and the treatment of neurological disorders is becomimg an increasingly active field (Reisberg, Ferris, & Gershon, 1980), it is often important to have some foreknowledge of what will happen to the patient in the future in a specific rather than general way and to determine whether the patient is a good candidate for some form of treatment. Efforts have also been made to predict functional abilities involved in personal self-care and independent living on the basis of neuropsychological test performance, particularly in the case of elderly individuals (McCue, Rogers, Goldstein, & Shelly, 1987). The extent to which neuropsychological assessment can provide this prognostic information will surely be associated with the degree of its acceptance in clinical settings.

Studies of the construct validity of neuropsychological tests represent a great amount of the corpus of basic clinical neuropsychological research. Neuropsychology abounds with constructs: short-term memory, attention, visual-spatial skills, psychomotor speed, motor engrams, and cell-assemblies. Tests are commonly characterized by the construct they purport to measure; Test A is one of long-term memory; Test B is one of attention; Test C is one of abstraction ability; Test D is a measure of biological intelligence, etc. Sometimes we fail to recognize constructs as such because they are so well established, but concepts like memory, intelligence, and attention are in fact theoretical entities used to describe certain classes of observable behaviors. Within neuropsychology, the process of construct validation generally begins with an attempt to find a measure that evaluates some concept. Let us begin with a simple example, say the desire to develop a test for memory. Memory, as a neuropsychological construct, would involve a brain-behavior relationship. That is, neuropsychologists are concerned with how the brain mediates memory and with how impaired brain function affects memory. There are memory tests available, notably the newly revised Wechsler Memory Scale (WMS-R) (Wechsler, 1987), but without experimental studies, that scale would have only face validity. That is, it appears to be a test of memory on the basis of the nature of the test items. However, if we ask the related question, "Does the patient who does well on the scale have a normal memory?" we would have to know more about the test in regard to how well it assesses memory as a construct. Reasonable alternative hypotheses might be that the scale measures intelligence, educational level, or attention, or that these influences confound the test such that impairment of memory per se cannot be unequivocally identified.

The problem may be approached in numerous ways. A factor analytic strategy may be used in which subtests of the Wechsler Memory Scale are placed into a factor analysis along with educational level and tests of intelligence and attention. It may be found that the memory scale subtests load on their own factor or on factors that receive high loadings from the intelligence and attention tests or from educational level. Another approach may involve giving the test to patients with amnesia and to nonamnesic brain-damaged patients. A more sophisticated study may involve administering the Wechsler Memory Scale to these subjects along with other tests. Studies such as these may reveal some of the following hypothetical findings. The Wechsler Memory Scale is highly correlated with IQ, and so it is not possible to tell whether the scale measures the construct memory specifically or intellectual ability. Some patients cannot repeat stories read to them because they are aphasic and cannot produce words, not because of poor memories. Therefore, interpretation of the measure as an indicator of memory ability cannot be made unequivocally in certain populations. Certain amnesic patients do exceedingly poorly on certain components of the Wechsler Memory Scale, but well on other components. Such a finding would suggest that memory, as a neuropsychological construct, requires further refinement, because there appears to be a dissociation in patients known to have profound loss of memory between certain memory skills that are intact and others that are severely impaired. Still another approach, suggested by Cronbach (1960), is correlation with practical criteria. Individuals given the Wechsler Memory Scale could be asked to perform a number of tasks, all of which involve practical memory in some way, and the obtained data could be analyzed in terms of what parts of the scale predict success or failure at the various tasks.

Another important way of establishing the construct validity of neuropsychological test batteries involves determining capacity to classify cases into meaningful subtypes. In recent years, several groups of investigators have utilized classification statistics, notably R-type factor analysis and cluster analysis, in order to determine whether combinations of test scores from particular batteries classify cases in accordance with established diagnostic categories or into types that are meaningful from the standpoint of neuropsychological considerations. A great deal of effort has gone into establishing meaningful, empirically derived subtypes of learning disability (Rourke, 1985), and there has also been work done in the neuropsychologically based empirical classification of neuropsychiatric patients (Goldstein & Shelly, 1987; Goldstein, Shelly, McCue, & Kane, 1987; Schear, 1987).

It is particularly important to note that, at least in recent years, the construct validation of neuropsychological tests has involved a multidisciplinary effort with colleagues in cognitive psychology, the experimental psychology of memory and learning (utilizing both human studies and animal models), linguistics, and sensory and perceptual processes. For example, aphasia testing has been profoundly influenced by basic research in psycholinguistics (Blumstein, 1981), while memory testing has been correspondingly influenced by recent developments in information theory and the experimental psychology of memory and learning (Butters & Cermak, 1980; Squire & Butters, 1984). These experimental foundations have aided significantly in the interpretation of clinical tests, and indeed, many new clinical tests are actually derived from laboratory procedures.

While neuropsychological tests should ideally have reliability levels commensurate with other areas of psychometrics, there are some relatively unique problems. These problems are particularly acute when the test-retest method is used to determine the reliability coefficients. The basic problem is that this method really assumes the stability of the subject over testing occasions. When reliability coefficients are established through the retesting of adults over a relatively brief time period, that assumption is a reasonable one, but it is not as reasonable in samples of brain-damaged patients who may be rapidly deteriorating or recovering. Indeed, it is generally thought to be an asset when a test reflects the appropriate changes. Another difficulty with the test-retest method is that many neuropsychological tests are not really repeatable because of substantial practice effects. The split-half method is seldom applicable because most neuropsychological tests do not consist of lengthy lists of items, readily allowing for odd-even or other split-half comparisons. In the light of these difficulties, the admittedly small number of reliability studies done with the standard neuropsychological tests batteries have yielded perhaps surprisingly good results. Boll (1981) has reviewed reliability studies done with the Halstead-Reitan Battery; the test manual for the Luria-Nebraska Battery (Golden, Hammeke, & Purisch, 1980) reports reliability data for that instrument. The details of these matters are discussed later in our reviews of these two procedures. In any event, it seems safe to say that most neuropsychological test developers have not been greatly preoccupied with the reliabilities of their procedures, but those who have studied the matter appear to have provided sufficient data to permit the conclusion that the standard, commonly used procedures are

at least not so unreliable as to impair the validities of those procedures.

AN INTRODUCTION TO THE COMPREHENSIVE BATTERIES

The number of generally available comprehensive standard neuropsychological test bateries for adults is not entirely clear. *The Handbook of Clinical Neuropsychology* (Filskov & Boll, 1981) contains chapters on only two batteries: the Halstead-Reitan and Luria-Nebraska. Lezak (1983) lists the Halstead-Reitan, the Smith Neuropsychological Battery, and two versions of batteries derived from Luria's work—one by Christensen (1975a, 1975b, 1975c), and Golden, Hammeke, and Purisch's Luria-Nebraska (originally South Dakota) Battery (1980). Jones and Butters (1983) reviewed the Halstead-Reitan, Luria-Nebraska, and Michigan batteries. Benton, Hamsher, Varney, and Spreen (1983) have produced a manual containing descriptions and instructions for tests these neuropsychologists have been associated with over the years, but there was clearly no intention to present this collection of tests as a standard battery. In this chapter, we will consider only the Halstead-Reitan and Luria-Nebraska procedures. The Michigan Battery (Smith, 1975) will not be reviewed, primarily because it consists largely of a series of standardized tests, all of which have their own validity and reliability literature. This literature is thoroughly reviewed by Lezak (1983).

The Halstead-Reitan Battery

History

The history of this procedure and its founders has been reviewed by Reed (1983). He traces the beginnings of the battery to the special laboratory established by Halstead in 1935 for the study of neurosurgical patients. The first major report on the findings of this laboratory appeared in a book called *Brain and Intelligence: A Quantitative Study of the Frontal Lobes* (Halstead, 1947), the title of which suggests that the original intent of Halstead's tests was to describe frontal lobe function. In this book, Halstead proposed his theory of "biological intelligence" and presented what was probably the first factor analysis done with neuropsychological test data. It is perhaps more significant that the book provides descriptions of many of the tests now contained in the Halstead-Reitan battery. As Reed (1983) suggests, the theory of biological intelligence was never widely accepted among neuropsychologists, and the factor analysis had its mathematical problems. But several of the tests that went into that analysis survived, and many of them are commonly used at present. In historical perspective, Halstead's major contributions to neuropsychological assessment, in addition to his very useful tests, include the concept of the neuropsychological laboratory in which objective tests are administered in standard fashions and quantitatively scored, and the concept of the impairment index, a global rating of severity of impairment and probability of the presence of structural brain damage.

Ralph M. Reitan was a student of Halstead at Chicago and was strongly influenced by his theories and methods. Reitan adopted the methods in the form of the various test procedures and with them established a laboratory at the University of Indiana. He supplemented these tests with a number of additional procedures in order to obtain greater comprehensiveness, and he initiated a clinical research program that is ongoing. The program began with a cross-validation of the battery and went on into numerous areas, including validation of new tests added to the battery (e.g., the Trail Making test), lateralization and localization of function, aging, and neuropsychological aspects of a wide variety of disorders such as alcoholism, hypertension, disorders of children, and mental retardation. Theoretical mattters were also considered. Some of the major contributions included the concept of type-locus interaction (Reitan, 1966), the analysis of quantitative as opposed to qualitative deficits associated with brain dysfunction (Reitan, 1958, 1959), the concept of the brain-age quotient (Reitan, 1973), and the scheme for levels and types of inference in interpretation of neuropsychological test data (Reitan & Davison, 1974). In addition to the published research, Reitan and his collaborators developed a highly sophisticated method of blind clinical interpretation of the Halstead-Reitan Battery that continues to be taught at workshops conducted by Dr. Reitan and associates. The Halstead-Reitan Battery, as the procedure came to be known over the years, also has a history. It has been described as a "fixed battery," but that is not actually the case. Lezak (1976) says in reference to this development, "This set of tests has grown by accretion and revision and continues to be revised" (p. 440). Halstead's original battery, on which the factor analyses were based, included the Carl Hollow Square test, the Dynamic Visual Field Test, the Henmon-Nelson tests of mental ability, a flicker fusion procedure, and the Time Sense test. None of these procedures is now widely used,

although the Time Sense and Flicker Fusion tests were originally included in the battery used by Reitan. The tests that survived include the Category test, the Tactual Performance test, the Speech Perception test, and Finger Tapping. Halstead also used the Seashore Rhythm test, which is included in the current version of the battery, but was not included in the sub-battery used by Halstead in his factor analyses. There have been numerous additions, including the various Wechsler Intelligence Scales, the Trail Making test, a sub-battery of perceptual tests, the Reitan Aphasia Screening test, the Klove Grooved Pegboard, and other tests that are used in some laboratories but not in others. Alternative methods have also been developed for computing the impairment index (Russell, Neuringer, & Goldstein, 1970).

Bringing this brief history into the present, the Halstead-Reitan Battery continues to be widely used as a clinical and research procedure. Numerous investigators utilize it in their research, and there have been several successful cross-validations done in settings other than Reitan's laboratory (Goldstein & Shelly, 1972; Vega & Parsons, 1967). In addition to the continuation of factor analytic work with the battery, several investigators have applied other forms of multivariate analysis to it in various research applications. Several investigations have been conducted relative to objectifying and even computerizing interpretation of the battery, the most well-known efforts probably being the Selz-Reitan rules for classification of brain function in older children (Selz & Reitan, 1979) and the Russell, Neuringer, and Goldstein "Neuropsychological Keys" (Russell et al., 1970). The issue of reliability of the battery has recently been addressed, with reasonably successful results. Clinical interpretation of the battery continues to be taught at workshops and in numerous programs engaged in training of professional psychologists. The most detailed description of the battery available will be found in Reitan and Wolfson (1985).

Structure and Content

Although there are several versions of the Halstead-Reitan Battery, the differences tend to be minor, and there appears to be a core set of procedures that essentially all versions of the battery contain. The battery must be administered in a laboratory containing a number of items of equipment and generally cannot be completely administered at bedside. Various estimates of length of administration are given, but it is probably best to plan on about 6 to 8 hours of patient time. Each test of the battery is independent and may be administered separately from the other tests. However, it is generally assumed that a certain number of the tests must be administered in order to compute an impairment index.

Scoring for the Halstead-Reitan varies with the particular test, such that individual scores may be expressed in time to completion, errors, number correct, or some form of derived score. For research purposes, these scores are generally converted to standard scores so that they may be profiled. Matthews (1981) routinely uses a T-score profile in clinical practice, while Russell et al. (1970) rate all the tests contributing to the impairment index on a six-point scale, the data being displayed as a profile of the ratings. In their system the impairment index may be computed by calculating the proportion of tests performed in the brain-damaged range according to published cutoff scores (Reitan, 1955) or by calculating the average of the ratings. This latter procedure provides a value called the Average Impairment Rating. Russell et al. (1970) have also provided quantitative scoring systems for the Reitan Aphasia Screening test and for the drawing of a Greek cross that is part of that test. However, some clinicians do not quantify those procedures, except in the form of counting the number of aphasic symptoms elicited. We will return to other aspects of the battery's structure after the following description of the component tests.

A. Halstead's Biological Intelligence Tests

1. *The Halstead Category Test*: This test is a concept identification procedure in which the subject must discover the concept or principle that governs various series of geometric forms, verbal, and numerical material. The apparatus for the test includes a display screen with four horizontally arranged numbered switches placed beneath it. The stimuli are on slides, and the examiner uses a control console to administer the procedure. The subject is asked to press the switch that the picture reminds him or her of, and is provided with additional instructions to the effect that the point of the test is to see how well he or she can learn the concept, idea, or principle that connect the pictures. If the correct switch is pressed, the subject will hear a pleasant chime, while wrong answers are associated with a rasping buzzer. The conventionally used score is the total number of errors for the seven groups of stimuli that form the test. Booklet (Adams & Trenton, 1981; DeFillippis, McCampbell, & Rogers, 1979) and abbreviated forms (Calsyn et al., 1980; Russell & Levy, 1987; Sherrill, 1987) of this test have been developed.

2. *The Halstead Tactual Performance Test*: This procedure utilizes a version of the Seguin-Goddard Formboard, but it is done blindfolded. The subject's task is to place all of the 10 blocks into the board, using only the sense of touch. The task is repeated three times, once with the preferred hand, once with the nonpreferred hand and once with both hands, following which the board is removed. After removing the blindfold, the subject is asked to draw a picture of the board, filling in all of the blocks he or she remembers in their proper locations on the board. Scores from this test include time to complete the task for each of the three trials, total time, number of blocks correctly drawn, and number of blocks correctly drawn in their proper locations on the board.

3. *The Speech Perception Test*: The subject is asked to listen to a series of 60 sounds, each of which consist of a double e digraph with varying prefixes and suffixes (e.g., geend). The test is given in a four-alternative multiple-choice format, the task being to underline on an answer sheet the sound heard. The score is number of errors.

4. *The Seashore Rhythm Test*: This test consists of 30 pairs of rhythmic patterns. The task is to judge whether the two members of each pair are the same as or different from each other and to record the response by writing an S or a D on an answer sheet. The score is either number correct or number of errors.

5. *Finger Tapping*: The subject is asked to tap his or her extended index finger on a typewriter key attached to a mechanical counter. Several series of 10-second trials are run with both the right and the left hand. The scores are average number of taps, generally over five trials, for the right and left hand.

B. Tests Added to the Battery by Reitan

1. *The Wechsler Intelligence Scales*: Some clinicians continue to use the Wechsler-Bellevue, some the WAIS, and some the WAIS-R. In any event, the test is given according to manual instructions and is not modified in any way.

2. *The Trail Making Test*: In Part A of this procedure the subject must connect in order a series of circled numbers randomly scattered over a sheet of 8½ × 11 paper. In part B, there are circled numbers and letters, and the subject's task involves alternating between numbers and letters in serial order (e.g., 1 to A to 2 to B, etc.). The score is time to completion expressed in seconds for each part.

3. *The Reitan Aphasia Screening Test*: This test serves two purposes in that it contains both copying and language-related tasks. As an aphasia screening procedure, it provides a brief survey of the major language functions: naming, repetition, spelling, reading, writing, calculation, narrative speech, and right-left orientation. The copying tasks involve having the subject copy a square, Greek cross, triangle, and key. The first three items must each be drawn in one continuous line. The language section may be scored by listing the number of aphasic symptoms or by using the Russell et al. quantitative system. The drawings are not formally scored or are rated through a matching to model system also provided by Russell et al. (1970).

4. *Perceptual Disorders*: These procedures actually constitute a sub-battery and include tests of the subject's ability to recognize shapes and identify numbers written on the fingertips, as well as tests of finger discrimination and visual, auditory, and tactile neglect. Number of errors is the score for all of these procedures.

C. Tests Added to the Battery by Others

1. *The Klove Grooved Pegboard Test*: The subject must place pegs shaped like keys into a board containing recesses that are oriented in randomly varying directions. The test is administered twice, once with the right and once with the left hand. Scores are time to completion in seconds for each hand and errors for each hand, defined as number of pegs dropped during performance of the task.

2. *The Klove Roughness Discrimination Test*: The subject must order four blocks, covered with varying grades of sandpaper and presented behind a blind, with regard to degree of roughness. Time and error scores are recorded for each hand.

3. *Visual Field Examination*: Russell et al. (1970) include a formal visual field examination utilizing a perimeter as part of their assessment procedure. It should be noted that many clinicians, including Reitan and his collaborators, frequently administer a number of additional tests mainly for purposes of assessing personality and level of academic achievement. The MMPI is the major personality assessment method used, and achievement may be assessed with such procedures as the Wide Range Achievement Test-R (Jastak & Wilkinson, 1984) or the Peabody Individual Achievement Test (Dunn & Markwardt, 1970). Some clinicians have also adopted the procedure of adding the Wechsler

Memory Scale (WMS or WMS-R) to the battery, either in its original form (Wechsler, 1945, 1987) or the Russell modification (Russell, 1975a). Some form of lateral dominance examination is also generally administered, including tests for handedness, footedness, and eyedness.

Quantitative Structural Considerations

Factor analysis is probably the clearest way of providing a quantitative description of the structure of a test battery. Many such analyses have been accomplished with the Halstead and Halstead-Reitan Battery, going back to Halstead's (1947) original work. Unfortunately, it is exceedingly difficult to compare one factor analytic study with another, largely because the battery has not remained stable over the years. For example, Halstead's original factor analysis involved the Flicker Fusion and Dynamic Visual Field tests, procedures that are rarely if ever used in current versions of the battery. Similarly, more recent factor analytic studies (Newby, Hallenbeck, & Embretson, 1983; Swiercinsky, 1979) utilized the Wechsler Memory Scale and other procedures that Halstead did not use, nor do many users of the battery. We will therefore take the solution of using some of our own factor analytic work (Goldstein & Shelly, 1971, 1972) as illustrative of the results one might achieve using a reasonably stripped down, core battery involving only Halstead's original tests that remain in common use, the WAIS, and the other procedures added to the battery by Reitan. The first of the two analyses utilized a sample of 50 alcoholic inpatients, while the second utilized a sample of 619 neuropsychiatric inpatients with miscellaneous diagnoses. The rotated factor matrices, presented in Table 10.1, are similar in some respects and dissimilar in others.

In both cases, the WAIS verbal subtests in combination with the aphasia screening test form a grouping (Factor 1) that clearly taps language abilities. There is a second factor largely contributed to by the WAIS performance tests, the Category test, and the speed component of the Tactual Performance test. The Finger Tapping test shows a different pattern in the two studies. In the analysis involving only the alcoholic patients, it loads on a factor along with several other tests, including WAIS Digit Symbol and the Seashore Rhythm test. In the case of the larger, more miscellaneous sample, Finger Tapping essentially achieves simple structure, forming its own factor. Thus, what the two factor analyses have in common are a verbal and a complex problem-solving factor. In the case of the alcoholic sample, there are three other factors: one that we have described as involving

Table 10.1. Two Factor Analyses of the Halstead-Reitan Battery

TEST	ROTATED FACTOR LOADINGS FOR ALCOHOLIC GROUP					ROTATED FACTOR LOADINGS FOR GENERAL PSYCHIATRIC GROUP			
	1	2	3	4	5	1	2	3	4
WAIS Information	.87	.14	−.05	−.04	.06	.81	.20	−.04	.00
WAIS Comprehension	.70	.08	.14	.09	.05	.72	.22	.03	.04
WAIS Similarities	.69	.11	.11	.19	.08	.73	.25	.07	.06
WAIS Vocabulary	.84	−.05	.19	−.02	.20	.88	.12	−.02	.04
WAIS Picture Completion	.68	.37	.30	.22	.02	.52	.56	.18	.14
Aphasia Screening	.51	−.12	.15	.25	.17	.68	.21	.27	.08
WAIS Block Design	.03	.50	.39	.30	.20	.40	.62	.30	.15
WAIS Object Assembly	.13	.82	.41	.05	.16	.29	.63	.27	.11
Perceptual Disorders	.19	.61	.33	.16	.27				
Finger Agnosia—R						.20	.15	.64	.14
Finger Agnosia—L						.14	.24	.66	.09
Finger Writing—R						.07	.32	.60	.17
Finger Writing—L						−.01	.31	.60	.10
Halstead Category	.09	.68	−.03	.10	.25	.38	.55	.34	.07
Trail Making	.04	.64	.44	.17	.18	.42	.51	.32	.11
Tactual Performance Test—Time	−.02	.55	.36	.40	.08	.10	.69	.27	.20
WAIS Digit Symbol	.19	.18	.67	.22	.15	.41	.53	.32	.29
WAIS Picture Arrangement	.33	.25	.52	.11	−.03	.44	.60	.21	.12
Speech Perception	.38	.21	.51	−.11	−.03	.59	.24	.34	.19
Finger Tapping—DH	.06	.14	.71	.15	−.10	.08	.16	.20	.92
Finger Tapping—NDH						.10	.22	.17	.62
Seashore Rhythm	.10	.17	.69	.12	.20	.41	.24	.27	.13
Tactual Performance Test—Memory	.33	.38	.12	.79	−.15	.24	.65	.20	.14
Tactual Performance Test—Location	.09	.14	.20	.61	.04	.21	.60	.16	.07
WAIS Arithmetic	.20	.33	−.02	.07	.63	.64	.30	.23	.02
WAIS Digit Span	.38	.13	.24	−.18	.50	.57	.20	.20	.14
% of Original Variance Explained	18.26	14.86	14.23	7.72	5.03	22.29	17.41	10.75	6.50

Note. Some of the scores have been reflected so that higher scores always indicate above average performance.

perceptual and motor skills, one that receives salient loadings only from the memory and location components of the Tactual Performance Test, and one that receives loadings from the two WAIS numerical tests, Arithmetic and Digit Span. There was a total of only four factors extracted for the large miscellaneous sample: the language and problem-solving factors noted above, a factor that received substantial loadings only from the tactual functions perceptual tests, and a factor that received high loadings only from the Finger Tapping test. While the factor analyses probably differ from each other because of differences in the samples and the specifics of the variables included

(which were not precisely the same), the two analyses taken together provide a reasonably good impression of the abilities tapped by the Halstead-Reitan. They can readily be described as verbal skills, complex problem-solving abilities, and various perceptual and motor skills. In some cases, a purely numerical ability factor may emerge as well as a factor representing the nonverbal memory abilities involved in the memory and location components of the Tactual Performance test. In general, when standard factor extraction termination procedures are used, in our case Kaiser's (1960) rule, the battery seems to be satisfactorily structured into four or five factors. It is interesting to note that the original Halstead (1947) analysis, even with its different tests and different factoring methods, also generated four factors.

Theoretical Foundations

There are really two theoretical bases for the Halstead-Reitan Battery, one contained in *Brain and Intelligence* and related writings of Halstead, the other in numerous papers and chapters written by Reitan and various collaborators (e.g., Reitan, 1966; Reitan & Wolfson, 1985). They are quite different from each other in many ways, and the difference may be partly accounted for by the fact that Halstead was not primarily a practicing clinician and was not particularly interested in developing his tests as psychometric instruments to be used in clinical assessment of patients. Indeed, he never published the tests. He was more interested in utilizing the tests to answer basic scientific questions in the area of brain-behavior relationships in general and frontal lobe function in particular. Reitan's program, on the other hand, can be conceptualized as an effort to demonstrate the usefulness and accuracy of Halstead's tests and related procedures in clinical assessment of brain-damaged patients. It is probably fair to say that Halstead's theory of biological intelligence and its factor analytically based four components (the central integrative field, abstraction, power, and the directional factor), as well as his empirical findings concerning human frontal lobe function, have not become major forces in modern clinical neuropsychology. However, they have had, in my view, a more subtle influence on the field.

Halstead was really the first to establish a human neuropsychology laboratory in which patients were administered objective tests, some of which were semiautomated, utilizing standard procedures and sets of instructions. His Chicago laboratory may have been the initial stimulus for the now common practice of trained technician administration of neuropsychological tests. Halstead was also the first to utilize sophisticated, multivariate statistics in the analysis of neuropsychological test data. Even though Reitan did not pursue that course to any great extent, other researchers with the Halstead-Reitan Battery have done so (e.g., Goldstein & Shelly, 1971, 1972). Thus, though the specifics of Halstead's theoretical work have not become well known and widely applied, the concept of a standard neuropsychological battery administered under laboratory conditions and consisting of objective, quantifiable procedures has made a major impact on the field of clinical neuropsychology. The other, perhaps more philosophical, contribution of Halstead

was what might be described as his Darwinian approach to neuropsychology. He viewed his discriminating tests as measures of adaptive abilities, as skills that assured man's survival on the planet. Many neuropsychologists are now greatly concerned with the relevance of their test procedures to adaptation— the capacity to carry on functional activities of daily living and to live independently (Heaton & Pendleton, 1981). This general philosophy is somewhat different from the more traditional models emanating from behavioral neurology, in which there is a much greater emphasis on the more medical-pathological implications of behavioral test findings.

Reitan, while always sympathetic with Halstead's thinking, never developed a theoretical system in the form of a brain model or a general theory of the biological intelligence type. One could say that Reitan's great concern has always been with the empirical validity of test procedures. Such validity can be established only through the collection of large amounts of data obtained from patients with reasonably complete documentation of their medical/neurological conditions. Both presence and absence of brain damage had to be well documented, and if present, findings related to site and type of lesion had to be established. He has described his work informally as one large experiment, necessitating maximal consistency in the procedures used, and to some extent, the methods of analyzing the data. Reitan and his various collaborators represent the group that was primarily responsible for introduction of the standard battery approach to clinical neuropsychology. It is clear from reviewing the Reitan group's work that there is substantial emphasis on performing controlled studies with samples sufficiently large to allow for application of conventional statistical procedures. One also gets the impression of an ongoing program in which initial findings are qualified and refined through subsequent studies.

It would probably be fair to say that the major thrust of Reitan's research and writings has not been espousal of some particular theory of brain function, but rather an extended examination of the inferences that can be made from behavioral indices relative to the condition of the brain. There is a great emphasis on methods of drawing such inferences in the case of the individual patient. Thus, this group's work has always involved empirical research and clinical interpretation, with one feeding into the other. In this regard, there has been a formulation of inferential methods used in neuropsychology (Reitan & Wolfson, 1985) that provides a framework for clinical interpretation. Four methods are outlined: level of performance, pattern of performance, specific behavioral deficits (pathognomonic signs), and right-left comparisons. In other words, one examines for whether the patient's general level of adaptive function compares with that of normal individuals, whether there is some characteristic performance profile that suggests impairment even though the average score may be within normal limits, whether there are unequivocal individual signs of deficits, and whether there is a marked discrepancy in functioning between the two sides of the body.

In general, then, Reitan's theoretical framework is basically empirical, objective, and data oriented. An extensive research program, by now of about 35 years' duration, has provided the information needed to make increasingly sophisticated inferences from neuropsychological tests. It thereby constitutes to a significant extent the basis for clinical interpretation. The part of the system that remains subjective is the interpretation itself, but in that regard, Reitan (1964) has made the following remark: "Additional statistical methods may be appropriate for this problem but, in any case, progress is urgently needed to replace the subjective decision-making processes in individual interpretation that presently are necessary" (p. 46).

Standardization Research

The Halstead-Reitan Battery, as a whole, meets rigorous validity requirements. Following Halstead's (1947) initial validation the battery was cross-validated by Reitan (1955) and in several other laboratories (Russell et al., 1970; Vega & Parsons, 1967). As indicated above, reviews of validity studies with the Halstead-Reitan Battery have been written by Klove (1974) and Boll (1981). Validity, in this sense, means that all component tests of the battery that contribute to the impairment index discriminate at levels satisfactory for producing usable cutoff scores for distinguishing between brain-damaged and non-brain-damaged patients. The major exceptions, the Time Sense and Flicker Fusion tests, have been dropped from the battery by most of its users. In general, the validation criteria for these studies consisted of neurosurgical and other definitive neurological data. It may be mentioned, however, that most of these studies were accomplished before the advent of the CT scan, and it would probably now be possible to do more sophisticated validity studies, perhaps through correlating extent of impairment with quantitative measures of brain damage (e.g., CT scan density measures). In addition to what was done with Halstead's tests, validity studies were accomplished with tests added to the battery, such as the Wechsler scales, the Trail

Making test and the Reitan Aphasia Screening tests, with generally satisfactory results (Reitan, 1966).

By virtue of the level of inferences made by clinicians from Halstead-Reitan Battery data, validity studies must obviously go beyond the question of presence or absence of brain damage. The first issue raised related to discriminative validity between patients with left-hemisphere and right-hemisphere brain damage. Such measures as Finger Tapping, the Tactual Performance test, the perceptual disorders sub-battery, and the Reitan Aphasia Screening test all were reported as having adequate discriminative validity in this regard. There have been very few studies, however, that go further and provide validity data related to more specific criteria such as localization and type of lesion. It would appear from one impressive study (Reitan, 1964) that valid inferences concerning prediction at this level must be made clinically, and one cannot call upon the standard univariate statistical procedures to make the necessary discriminations. This study provided the major impetus for Russell et al.'s (1970) neuropsychological key approach, which was in essence an attempt to objectify higher-order inferences.

There is one general area in which the discriminative validity of the Halstead-Reitan Battery is not particularly robust. The battery does not have great capacity to discriminate between brain-damaged patients and patients with functional psychiatric disorders, notably chronic schizophrenia. There is an extensive literature concerning this matter, but it should be said that some of the research contained in this literature has significant methodological flaws, leaving the findings ambiguous. It may also be pointed out that the constructors of the Halstead-Reitan did not have the intention of developing a procedure to discriminate between brain-damaged and schizophrenic patients, and the assumption that it should be able to do so is somewhat gratuitous. Furthermore, Heaton and Crowley (1981) find that with the exception of the diagnosis of chronic schizophrenia, the Halstead-Reitan Battery does a reasonably good job of differential diagnosis. They provided the following conclusion:

> The bulk of the evidence . . . suggests that for most psychiatric patient groups there is little or no relationship between the degree of emotional disturbance and level of performance on neuropsychological tests. However, significant correlations of this type are sometimes found with schizophrenic groups. (p. 492)

This matter remains controversial and has become exceedingly complex, particularly since the discovery of cerebral atrophy in a substantial portion of the schizophrenic population and the development of hypotheses concerning left-hemisphere dysfunction in schizophrenics (Flor-Henry & Yeudall, 1979). The point to be made here is that the user of the Halstead-Reitan Battery should exercise caution in interpretation when asked to employ the battery in resolving questions related to differential diagnosis between brain damage and schizophrenia. Some writers have advised the addition of some measure of psychiatric disability, such as the MMPI, when doing such assessments (Russell, 1975b, 1977).

Even though there have been several studies of the predictive validity of neuropsychological tests with children (Fletcher & Satz, 1980; Rourke, 1983) and other studies with adults that did not utilize the full Halstead-Reitan Battery (Meier, 1974), I know of no major formal assessment of the predictive validity of the Halstead-Reitan Battery accomplished with adults. Within neuropsychology, predictive validity has two aspects: predicting everyday academic, vocational, and social functioning and predicting course of illness. With regard to the former matter, Heaton and Pendleton (1981) document the lack of predictive validity studies using extensive batteries of the Halstead-Reitan type. However, they do report one study (Newman, Heaton, & Lehman, 1978) in which the Halstead-Reitan successfully predicted employment status on six-month followup. With regard to prediction of course of illness, there appears to be a good deal of clinical expertise in this regard, but no major formal studies in which the battery's capacity to predict whether the patient will get better, worse, or stay the same are evaluated. This matter is of particular significance in such conditions as head injury and stroke, because outcome tends to be quite variable in these conditions. The changes that occur during those stages are often the most significant ones related to prognosis (e.g., length of time unconscious).

In general, there has not been a great deal of emphasis on studies involving the reliability of the Halstead-Reitan Battery, probably because of the nature of the tests themselves, particularly with regard to the practice-effect problem, and because of the changing nature of those patients for whom the battery was developed. Those reliability studies that were done produced satisfactory results, particularly with regard to the reliability of the impairment index (Boll, 1981). The Category test can have its reliability assessed through the split-half method. In a study accomplished by Shaw (1966), a .98 reliability coefficient was obtained.

Norms for the Halstead-Reitan are available in numerous places (Russell et al., 1970; Vega & Parsons, 1967), but because the battery was never published as a single procedure, there is no published manual to which one can refer for definitive information. Schear (1984) has published a table of age norms for neuropsychiatric patients, but there are no published age- or education-corrected norms for the general population. However, several laboratories have collected local norms. A great deal is known about the influence of age and education on the various tests in the Halstead-Reitan Battery, but this information was never consolidated into tables of norms or through the formulation of equations for calculating appropriate corrections. Similarly, sex differences generally reported appear only on Finger Tapping, with women tapping slightly more slowly than men. It is somewhat unusual for a procedure in as widespread use as the Halstead-Reitan not to have a commercially published manual. However, detailed descriptions of the procedures as well as instructions for administration and scoring are available in several sources including Reitan and Wolfson (1985), Jarvis and Barth (1984), and Swiercinsky (1978).

In summary, the validity of the Halstead-Reitan seems well established by literally hundreds of studies, including several major cross-validations. These studies have implications for the concurrent, predictive, and construct validity of the battery. Reliability has not received nearly as much attention, but it seems apparent that the battery is sufficiently reliable not to compromise its validity. There are few age- or education-related norms, but the relevance of such norms to neuropsychological assessment, particularly with regard to age, is a controversial and unsettled matter. There is no commercially available manual for the battery, and so the usual kinds of information generally contained in a manual are not available in a single place to the test user. However, the relevant information is available in a number of separate sources.

Evaluation

The Halstead-Reitan Battery is without doubt the most widely used standard neuropsychological battery, at least in North America and perhaps throughout the world. Aside from its widespread clinical application, it is used in many multidisciplinary research programs as the procedure of choice for neuropsychological assessment. It therefore has taken on something of a definitive status and is viewed by many experts in the field as the state-of-the-art instrument for comprehensive neuropsychological assessment. Nevertheless, several criticisms of it have emerged over the years, and some of them are reviewed here. Each major criticism is itemized and discussed.

1. *The Halstead-Reitan Battery is too long and redundant.* The implication of this criticism is that pertinent, clinically relevant neuropsychological assessment can be accomplished in substantially less time than the 6 to 8 hours generally required to administer the full Halstead-Reitan battery. Other batteries are, in fact, substantially briefer than the Halstead-Reitan. Aside from simply giving fewer or briefer tests, another means suggested of shortening neuropsychological assessment is through a targeted, individualized approach rather than through routine administration of a complete battery. The difficulty with this latter alternative is that such an approach can generally be conducted only by an experienced clinician, and one sacrifices the clinician time and expense that can be saved through administration by trained technicians. The response to the criticism concerning length is generally that shortening of the battery correspondingly reduces its comprehensiveness, and one sacrifices examination of areas that may be of crucial significance in individual cases. Indeed, the battery approach was, in part, a reaction to the naiveté inherent in the use of single tests for "brain damage." The extent to which the clinician reverts to a single-test approach may reflect the extent to which there is a return to the simplistic thinking of the past. In general, the argument is that to cover adequately what must be covered in a standard, comprehensive assessment, the length of the procedure is a necessity. From the point of view of patient comfort and fatigue, the battery can be administered in several sessions over a period of days if necessary.

2. *The tests in the Halstead-Reitan Battery are insufficiently specific, both in regard to the functions they assess and the underlying cerebral correlates of those functions.* Most of the tests in the battery are quite complex, and it is often difficult to isolate the source of impairment within the context of a single test. Even as apparently simple a procedure as the Speech Perception test requires not only the ability to discriminate sounds, but to read, make the appropriate written response, and attend to the task. Therefore, failure on the test cannot unequivocally point to a specific difficulty with auditory discrimination. Difficulties of this type are even more pronounced in such highly complex procedures as the Category and Tactual Performance tests. This criticism eventuates in the conclusion that it is difficult to say anything meaningful about the patient's brain or about treatment because one cannot isolate the specific deficit. In Luria's (1973) terminology one cannot isolate the

functional system that is involved, no less the link in that system that is impaired. Failure to do so makes it difficult if not impossible to identify the structures in the brain that are involved in the patient's impairment as well as to formulate a rehabilitation program, because one does not really know in sufficiently specific terms what the patient can and cannot do.

This criticism ideally requires a very detailed response, because it implies an approach to neuropsychological assessment substantially different from the one adopted by developers of the Halstead-Reitan. Perhaps the response can be summarized in a few points. The Halstead-Reitan Battery is founded on empirical rather than on content validity. Inferences are drawn on the basis of pertinent research findings and clinical observations rather than on the basis of what the tests appear to be measuring. The fact that one cannot partial out the various factors involved in successful or impaired performance on the Category test, for example, does not detract from the significant empirical findings related to this test based on studies of various clinical populations. In any event, Reitan, Hom, and Wolfson (1988) have shown that complex abilities, notably abstraction, are dependent upon the functioning of both cerebral hemispheres, and not on a localized unilateral system. The use of highly specific items in order to identify a specific system or system link is a procedure that is closely tied to the syndrome approach of behavioral neurology. Developers of the Halstead-Reitan typically do not employ a syndrome approach for several reasons. First, it depends almost exclusively on the pathognomonic signs method of inference to the neglect of other inferential methods, and second, the grouping together of specific deficits into a syndrome is felt to be more often in the brain of the examiner than of the patient. The lack of empirical validity of the so-called Gerstmann Syndrome is an example of this deficiency in this particular approach (Benton, 1961). Another major point is that the Halstead-Reitan Battery is a series of tests in which interpretation is based not on isolated consideration of each test taken one at a time, but on relationships among performances on all of the tests. Therefore, specific deficits can be isolated, in some cases at least, through intertest comparisons rather than through isolated examination of a single test. Returning to our example, the hypothesis that there is impairment on the Speech Perception test because of the patient's failure to read the items accurately can be evaluated through looking at the results of the aphasia screening or reading-achievement test given. Finally, complex tests are likely to have more ecological validity than simple tests of isolated abilities. Thus, the Category test or Tactual Performance test results can tell the clinician more about real-world functioning than can the simpler tests. Simple tests were developed in the context of neurological diagnosis, while the tests in the Halstead-Reitan Battery seem more oriented to assessing adaptive functioning in the environment.

3. *The Halstead-Reitan Battery is not sufficiently comprehensive, particularly in that it completely neglects the area of memory.* The absence of formal memory testing in this battery has been noted by many observers and appears to be a valid criticism. On the face of it, it would appear that the battery would be incapable of identifying and providing meaningful assessments of patients with pure amnesic syndromes (e.g., patients with Korsakoff's syndrome). The absence of formal memory testing as part of the Halstead-Reitan is something of a puzzlement; although memory is involved in many of the tests, it is difficult to isolate the memory component as a source of impairment. Such isolation is readily achieved through such standard, commonly available procedures as list or paired associate learning.

We know of no formal response to this criticism, but the point of view could be taken that pure amnesic syndromes are relatively rare, and the Halstead-Reitan Battery would probably not be the assessment method of choice for many of the rarely occurring specific syndromes. I would view this response as weak in view of the reported significance of memory defect in a number of disorders (Butters, 1983). Apparently, Halstead did not work with patients of those types, particularly patients with Alzheimer's and Huntington's disease, and so may have failed to note the significance of memory function in those disorders. However, this criticism is probably the one most easily resolved, because all that is required is addition of some formal memory testing to the battery. Many clinicians have already added all or parts of the Wechsler Memory Scale or similar procedures.

4. *The Halstead-Reitan Battery cannot discriminate between brain-damaged and schizophrenic patients.* This matter has already been discussed, and most of the evidence (Heaton & Crowley, 1981) indicates that the performance of chronic schizophrenics on the Halstead-Reitan may be indistinguishable from that of the patient with generalized, structural brain damage. There are essentially two classes of response to this criticism. First, there is a disclaimer that the Halstead-Reitan was ever designed for this kind of differential diagnosis, and so it is not surprising that it fails when it is inappropriately used for that purpose. Second, and perhaps much more significant, is the finding that many schizophrenics have brain

atrophy, as assessed by CT scan, and tests of the Halstead-Reitan type can now be viewed as accurately identifying the behavioral correlates of that condition (Weinberger & Wyatt, 1982). Furthermore, there are now several studies indicating that schizophrenia is a neuropsychologically heterogeneous condition, and that there is a lack of relationship betwen neuropsychological test results and psychiatric diagnosis in the case of several psychiatric disorders (Goldstein & Shelly, 1987; Townes et al., 1985.)

5. *Findings reported from Reitan's laboratory cannot be replicated in other settings.* Here we have particular reference to the criticisms raised by Smith of Reitan's early Wechsler-Bellevue laterality studies. In a series of papers, Smith (1965, 1966a, 1966b) presented empirical and theoretical arguments against the reported finding that patients with left-hemisphere lesions had lower verbal than performance IQs on the Wechsler-Bellevue, while the reverse was true for patients with right-hemisphere brain damage. Smith was unable to replicate these findings in patients with lateralized brain damage for whom he had Wechsler-Bellevue data; he also presented theoretical arguments against the diagnostic and conceptual significance of this finding. Klove (1974) analyzed the Smith versus Reitan findings in terms of possible age and neurological differences between the studies. Reviewing the research done to the time of writing, he also concluded that most of the research, with Smith as the only pronounced exception, essentially confirmed Reitan's original findings.

In summary, many criticisms have been raised of the Halstead-Reitan as a comprehensive, standard neuropsychological assessment system. While pertinent and reasonable responses have been made to most or all of these critiques, members of the profession have nevertheless sensed in recent years the desire to develop alternative procedures. Despite the pertinent replies to criticisms, there appear to be many clinicians who still feel that the Halstead-Reitan Battery *is* too long, *does* neglect memory, and in many cases *is* insufficiently specific. Some holders of these views adopted an individualized approach, or modified the Halstead-Reitan, while others sought alternative standard batteries.

The Luria-Nebraska Neuropsychological Battery

History

This procedure, previously known as the Luria-South Dakota Neuropsychological Battery or as A Standard Version of Luria's Neuropsychological

Tests, was first reported on in 1978 (Golden, Hammeke, & Purisch, 1978; Purisch, Golden, & Hammeke, 1978) in the form of two initial validity studies. One could provide a lengthy history of this procedure, going back to Luria's original writings, or a brief one recording only events that occurred since the time of preparation of the two publications cited above. We will take the latter alternative, for reasons that will become apparent. Prior to the past quarter of a century, Luria was a shadowy figure to most English-speaking neuropsychologists. It was known that he was an excellent clinician who had developed his own methods for evaluating patients as well as his own theory, but the specific contents were unknown until translations of some of his major works appeared in the 1960s (e.g., Luria, 1966). However, when these works were read by English-speaking professionals, it became apparent that Luria did not have a standard battery of the Halstead-Reitan type and did not even appear to use standardized tests. Thus, while his formulations and case presentations were stimulating and innovative, nobody knew quite what to do with these materials in terms of practical clinical application. One alternative, of course, was to go to the Soviet Union and study with Luria. In fact, Anne-Lise Christensen did just that and reported what she had learned in a book called *Luria's Neuropsychological Investigation* (Christensen, 1975a). The book was accompanied by a manual and a kit containing test materials used by Luria and his co-workers (Christensen, 1975b, 1975c). Even though some of Luria's procedures previously appeared in English in the *Higher Cortical Functions* (1966) and *Traumatic Aphasia* (1970), they were never presented in a manner that encouraged direct administration of the test items to patients. With Christensen's publications, the English-speaking public had in hand a manual and related materials that could be used to administer some of Luria's tests. These materials did not contain information relevant to standardization of these items. There was no scoring system, norms, data regarding reliability and validity, or review of research accomplished with the procedure as a standard battery. This work was taken on by a group of investigators under the leadership of Charles J. Golden and was initially reported on in the two 1978 papers cited above. Thus, in historical sequence, Luria adopted or developed these items over the course of many years, Christensen published them in English but without standardization data, and finally Golden and collaborators provided quantification and standardization. Since that time, Golden's group as well as other investigators have produced a massive amount of studies with

what is now known as the Luria-Nebraska Neuropsychological Battery. The battery was published in 1980 by Western Psychological Services (Golden, Hammeke, & Purisch, 1980) and is now extensively used in clinical and research publications. An alternate form of the battery is now available (Golden, Purisch, & Hammeke, 1985), as is a children's version (Golden, 1981a).

Structure and Content

The Luria-Nebraska is an evolving procedure, and the details presented here will no doubt change over the years. However, the basic structure of the battery will probably remain essentially the same. The current version contains 269 items, each of which may be scored on a 2- or 3-point scale. A score of 0 indicates normal performance. Some items may receive a score of 1, indicating borderline performance. A score of 2 indicates clearly abnormal performance. The items are organized into the categories provided in the Christensen kit (Christensen, 1975c), but while Christensen organized the items primarily to suggest how they were used by Luria, in the Luria-Nebraska version the organization is presented as a set of quantitative scales. The raw score for each scale is the sum of the 0, 1, and 2 item scores. Thus, the higher the score, the poorer the performance. Because the scales contain varying numbers of items, raw scale scores are converted to T scores with a mean of 50 and a standard deviation of 10. These T scores are displayed as a profile on a form prepared for that purpose. The scores for the individual items may be based on speed, accuracy, or quality of response. In some cases, two scores may be assigned to the same task, one for speed and the other for accuracy. These two scores are counted as individual items. For example, one of the items is a block counting task, with separate scores assigned for number of errors and time to completion of the task. In the case of time scores, blocks of seconds are associated with the 0, 1, and 2 scores. When quality of response is scored, the manual provides both rules for scoring, and, in the case of copying tasks, illustrations of figures representing 0, 1, and 2 scores.

The 269 items are divided into 11 content scales, each of which is individually administrable. In Table 10.2 we present the name of each content scale, a brief description of each scale, and a sample item. In the alternate form of the battery, the names of the content scales have been replaced by abbreviations. Thus, the scales listed in Table 10.2 are referred to as the C1 through C11 scales.

Table 10.2. The Luria-Nebraska Major Scales

SCALE	DESCRIPTION AND SAMPLE ITEM
Motor	Contains items assessing a wide variety of motor skills ranging from simple movements to more complex tasks including pretended movements and movements associated with complex verbal instructions.
	Sample Item: If I knock hard, you knock gently; if I knock gently, then knock hard.
Rhythm	Contains measures of primarily nonverbal auditory perception such as pitch discrimination and appreciation of rhythmic patterns.
	Sample Item: Now you are going to hear two tones on a tape from this tape recorder. I want you to tell me whether the tones you hear are the same or different.
Tactile	This scale is basically a sensory examination and contains measures of light touch localization, two point discrimination, and tactile recognition.
	Sample Item: I am going to touch you with the eraser end of the pencil. Tell me where I am touching you (touching fingers, palm and forearm of each upper extremity).
Vision	Contains items assessing basic visual perceptual skills as well as more complex visual-spatial tasks.
	Sample Item: I am now going to show you several pictures. Tell me what they are. (Subject is presented with cards containing photographs of common objects.)
Receptive Speech	Contains items ranging from perception of single sounds to comprehension of complex grammatical structures.
	Sample Item: Someone has just told you that "Arnie hit Tom." Who was the victim?
Expressive Speech	Contains items assessing ability to repeat sounds, words, and word groups, to name objects, and to produce narrative speech.
	Sample Item: Please make up a speech for me about the conflict between generations.
Writing	Contains items assessing ability to analyze words into letters and to write under varying conditions.
	Sample Item: Please write: physiology; probabilistic
Reading	Contains items assessing ability to make letter to sound transformations and to read simple material.
	Sample Item: I am going to show you several cards. Read the word on each card.
Arithmetic	Contains items assessing knowledge of numbers, number concept, and ability to perform simple calculations.
	Sample Item: Please solve these problems. You may also write them down if you like: (1) $3 + 4$; (2) $6 + 7$
Memory	A brief, formal memory examination including list learning, immediate memory, short-term memory with interference, and paired-associate learning.
	Sample Item: Now I am going to read you a short story. I want you to listen carefully because when I am finished I want you to repeat to me all that you can remember about the story.
Intellectual Processes	A brief intellectual assessment containing sequencing, problem solving, and abstraction items.
	Sample Item: What is meant by these expressions: (1) "iron hand"? (2) "green thumb"?

In addition to these 11 content scales, there are three derived scales that appear on the standard profile form: the Pathognomonic, Left Hemisphere, and Right Hemisphere scales. The Pathognomonic scale contains items from throughout the battery found to be particularly sensitive to presence or absence of brain damage. The Left and Right Hemisphere scales are derived from the Motor and Tactile scale items that involve comparisons between the left and right side of the body. They therefore reflect sensory-motor asymmetries between the two sides of the body.

Several other scales have been developed by Golden and various collaborators, all of which are based on different ways of scoring the same 269 items. These special scales include new (empirically derived) right- and left-hemisphere scales (McKay & Golden, 1979a), a series of localization scales (McKay & Golden, 1979b), a series of factor scales (McKay & Golden, 1981), and double discrimination scales (Golden, 1979). The new right-and left-hemisphere scales contain items from throughout the battery and are based upon actual comparisons among patients with right, left hemisphere, and diffuse brain damage. The localization scales are also empirically derived (McKay & Golden, 1979b), being based on studies of patients with localized brain lesions. There are frontal, sensory-motor, temporal, and parieto-occipital scales for each hemisphere. The factor scales are based on extensive factor analytic studies of the battery involving factor analyses of each of the major content scales (e.g., Golden & Berg, 1983). The factor scales and associated codes are listed below (see Table 10.3). The code consists of an abbreviation for the major content scale followed by the number of the scale (e.g., M3 is the third factor scale derived from the Motor scale).

The new right- and left-hemisphere, localization, and factor scales may all be expressed in T scores with a mean of 50. The double discrimination scales are still in an experimental phase, but have been shown to be effective in diagnosis of multiple sclerosis (Golden, 1979). This method involves development of two scales: one contains items on which patients with a particular diagnosis do worse than the general neurological population; the other contains items on which patients do better. Classification to the specific group is made when scores are in the appropriate range on both scales. There are also two scales that provide global indices of dysfunction and are meant as equivalents to the Halstead Impairment Index. They are called the Profile Elevation and Impairment scales.

The Luria-Nebraska procedure involves an age and education correction. It is accomplished through computation of a cutoff score for abnormal performance based on an equation that takes into consideration both age and education. The computed score is called the critical level and is equal to .214 (Age) + 1.47 (Education) + 68.8 (Constant). Typically, a horizontal line is drawn across the profile at the computed critical level point. The test user has the option of considering scores above the critical level, which may be higher or lower than 60, as abnormal.

As indicated above, extensive factor analytic studies have been accomplished, and the factor structure of each of the major scales has been identified. These analyses were based on item intercorrelations, rather than on correlations among the scales. It is important to note that most items on any particular scale correlate more highly with other items on that scale than they do with items on other scales (Golden, 1981b). This finding lends credence to the view that the scales

Table 10.3. The Luria-Nebraska Factor Scales

CODE	FACTOR SCALES
M1	Kinesthetic-Based Movement
M2	Drawing Speed
M3	Fine Motor Speed
M4	Spatial-Based Movement
M5	Oral Motor Skills
Rh1	Rhythm and Pitch Perception
T1	Simple Tactile Sensation
T2	Stereognosis
V1	Visual Acuity and Naming
V2	Visual-Spatial Organization
Rc1	Phonemic Discrimination
Rc2	Relational Concepts
Rc3	Concept Recognition
Rc4	Verbal-Spatial Relationships
Rc5	Word Comprehension
Rc6	Logical Grammatical Relationships
E1	Simple Phonetic Reading
E2	Word Repetition
E3	Reading Polysyllabic Words
Rg1	Reading Complex Material
Rg2	Reading Simple Material
W1	Spelling
W2	Motor Writing Skill
A1	Arithmetic Calculations
A2	Number Reading
Me1	Verbal Memory
Me2	Visual and Complex Memory
I1	General Verbal Intelligence
I2	Complex Verbal Arithmetic
I3	Simple Verbal Arithmetic

are at least somewhat homogeneous, and thus that the organization of the 269 items into those scales can be justified.

Theoretical Foundations

As in the case of the Halstead-Reitan Battery, one could present two theoretical bases for the Luria-Nebraska, one revolving around the name of Luria and the other around the Nebraska group—Golden and his collaborators. This view is elaborated on in Goldstein (1986). It is to be noted in this regard that Luria himself had nothing to do with the development of the Luria-Nebraska Battery, nor did any of his co-workers. The use of his name in the title of the battery is, in fact, somewhat controversial, and seems to have been essentially honorific in intent, recognizing his development of the items and the underlying theory for their appliction. Indeed, Luria died some time before publication of the battery but was involved in the preparation of the Christensen materials, which he endorsed. Furthermore, the method of testing employed by the Luria-Nebraska was not Luria's method, and the research done to establish the validity, reliability, and clinical relevance of the Luria-Nebraska was not the kind of research done by Luria and his collaborators. Therefore, our discussion of the theory underlying the Luria-Nebraska Battery will be based on the assumption that the only connecting link between Luria and that procedure is the set of Christensen items. Thus, it becomes clear that the basic theory underlying the development of the Luria-Nebraska is based on a philosophy of science that stresses empirical validity, quantification, and application of established psychometric procedures. Indeed, as pointed out elsewhere (Goldstein, 1982, 1986), it is essentially the same epistemology that characterizes the work of the Reitan group.

The general course charted for establishment of quantitative, standard neuropsychological assessment batteries involves several steps: (a) determining whether the battery discriminates between brain-damaged patients in general and normal controls; (b) determining whether it discriminates between patients with structural brain damage and conditions that may be confused with structural brain damage, notably various functional psychiatric disorders; (c) determination of whether the procedure has the capacity to lateralize and regionally localize brain damage; (d) determination of whether there are performance patterns specific to particular neurological disorders, such as alcoholic dementia or multiple sclerosis. In proceeding along this course, it is highly desirable to accomplish appropriate cross-validations and to deter-

mine reliability. This course was taken by Golden and his collaborators, in some cases with remarkable success. Because the relevant research was accomplished during recent years, it had the advantages of being able to benefit from the new brain imaging technology, notably the CT scan, and the application of high-speed computer technologies, allowing for extensive use of powerful multivariate statistical methods. With regard to methods of clinical inference, the same methods suggested by Rietan—level of performance, pattern of performance, pathognomonic signs, and right-left comparisons—are the methods generally used with the Luria-Nebraska.

Adhering to our assumption that the Luria-Nebraska bears little resemblance to Luria's methods and theories, there seems little point in examining the theoretical basis for the substance of the Luria-Nebraska Battery. For example, it seems that there would be little point in examining the theory of language that underlies the Receptive Speech and Expressive Speech scales or the theory of memory that provides the basis for the Memory scale. An attempt to produce such an analysis was made by Spiers (1981), who examined the content of the Luria-Nebraska scales and evaluated it with reference not so much to Luria's theories but to current concepts in clinical neuropsychology in general. However, despite the thoroughness of the Spiers review, it seems to miss the essential point that the Luria-Nebraska is a procedure based primarily on studies of empirical validity. One can fault it on the quality of its empirical validity studies, but not on the basis that it utilizes such an approach. It therefore appears that the Luria-Nebraska Battery does not constitute a means of using Luria's theory and methods in English-speaking countries, but rather is a standardized psychometric instrument with established validity for certain purposes and reliability. The choice of using items selected by Christensen (1975b) to illustrate Luria's testing methods was, in retrospect, probably less crucial than the research methods chosen to investigate the capabilites of this item set. Indeed, it is somewhat misleading to characterize these items as "Luria's tests," because many of them are standard items used by neuropsychologists and neurologists throughout the world. Surely, one cannot describe asking a patient to interpret proverbs or determine two-point thresholds as being exclusively "Luria's tests." They are, in fact, venerable, widely used procedures.

Standardization Research

Fortunately, there are published manuals for the Luria-Nebraska (Golden, Hammeke, & Purisch,

1980; Golden, Purisch, & Hammeke, 1985) that describe the battery in detail and provide pertinent information relative to validity, reliability, and norms. There are also several review articles (e.g., Golden, 1981b; Purisch & Sbordone, 1986) that comprehensively describe the research done with the battery. A brief review of this material shows that satisfactory discriminative validity has been reported in studies directed toward differentiating miscellaneous brain-damaged patients from normal controls and from chronic schizophrenics. Cross-validations were generally successful, but Shelly and Goldstein (1983) could not fully replicate the studies involved with discrimination between brain-damaged and schizophrenic patients. Discriminative validity studies involving lateralization and localization achieved satisfactory results, but the localization studies were based on small samples. Quantitative indices from the Luria-Nebraska were found to correlate significantly with CT scan quantitative indices in alcoholic (Golden, Graber, Blose, Berg, Coffman, & Block, 1981) and schizophrenic (Golden, Moses et al., 1980) samples. There have been several studies of specific neurological disorders, including multiple sclerosis (Golden, 1979), alcoholism (Chmielewski & Golden, 1980), Huntington's disease (Moses, Golden, Berger, & Wisniewski, 1981), and learning-disabled adults (McCue, Shelly, Goldstein, & Katz-Garris, 1984), all with satisfactory results in terms of discrimination.

The test manual reports reliability data. Test-retest reliabilites for the 13 major scales range from .78 to .96. The problem of inter-judge reliability is generally not a major one for neuropsychological assessment because most of the tests used are quite objective and have quantitative scoring systems. However, there could be a problem with the Luria-Nebraska, because the assignment of 0, 1, and 2 scores sometimes requires a judgment by the examiner. During the preliminary screening stage in the development of the battery, items in the original pool that did not attain satisfactory inter-judge reliability were dropped. A 95% interrater agreement level was reported by the test constructors for the 282 items used in an early version of the battery developed after the dropping of those items. The manual contains means and standard deviations for each item based on samples of control, neurologically impaired, and schizophrenic subjects. An alternate form of the battery is available. To the best of our knowledge, there have been no predictive validity studies. It is unclear whether there have been studies addressed to the issue of construct validity. Stambrook (1983) suggested that studies involved with item-scale consistency, factor analysis, and cor-

relation with other instruments are construct validity studies, but it does not appear to us that they are directed toward validation of Luria's constructs. The attempt to apply Luria's constructs has not in fact involved the empirical testing of specific hypotheses derived from Luria's theory. Thus, we appear to have diagnostic or discriminative validity established by a large number of studies. There also seems to be content validity, because the items correlate most highly with the scale to which they are assigned, but the degree of construct validity remains unclear. For example, there have been no studies of Luria's important construct of the functional system or of his hypotheses concerning the role of frontal lobe function in the programming, regulation, and verification of activity (Luria, 1973).

Evaluation

It is well known that the Luria-Nebraska Battery, at this writing, remains a controversial procedure, and several highly critical reviews of it have appeared in the literature. Adams (1980) criticized it primarily on methodological grounds, Spiers (1981) on the basis that it was greatly lacking in its capacity to provide a comprehensive neurophychological assessment, Crosson and Warren (1982) because of its deficiencies with regard to assessment of aphasia and aphasic patients, and Stambrook (1983) on the basis of a number of methodological and theoretical considerations. Replies were written to several of these reviews (e.g., Golden, 1980), and a rather heated literature controversy eventuated. This literature was supplemented by several case studies (e.g., Delis & Kaplan, 1982), in which it was shown that the inferences that would be drawn from the Luria-Nebraska were incorrect with reference to documentation obtained for those cases.

These criticisms can be divided into general and specific ones. Basically, there are two general criticisms: (a) the Luria-Nebraska Battery does not reflect Luria's thinking in any sense, and his name should not be used in describing it; and (b) there are several relatively flagrant methodological difficulties involved in the standardization of the procedure. The major specific criticisms primarily involve the language-related and memory scales. With regard to aphasia, there are essentially two points. First, there is no system provided, nor do the items provide sufficient data to classify the aphasias in terms of some contemporary system (e.g., Goodglass & Kaplan, 1983). Second, the battery is so language-oriented that patients with aphasia may fail many of the non-language tasks because of failure to comprehend the test instructions or to make the appropriate verbal responses indicative of a correct answer. For example, on the Tactile scale, the patient must name objects placed in the hands. Patients with anomia or anomic aphasia will be unable to do that even though their tactile recognition skills may be perfectly normal. With regard to memory, the Memory scale is criticized because of its failure to provide a state-of-the-art comprehensive memory assessment (Russell, 1981). Golden has responded to this criticism through adding additional items involving delayed recall to the alternate form of the battery.

In providing an evaluation of the Luria-Nebraska, one can only voice an opinion, as others have, since its existence has stimulated a polarization into "those for it" and "those against it." I would concur with Stambrook's (1983) view, which essentially is that it is premature to make an evaluation, and that major research programs must be accomplished before an informed opinion can be reached. This research involves more definitive validation with a greatly expanded data base, an evaluation of the actual constructs on which the procedure is based, and assessment of its clinical usefulness relative to other established procedures such as the Halstead-Reitan or individual approaches. The following remark by Stambrook (1983) appears to reflect a highly reasoned approach to this issue: "The clinical utility of the LNNB does not depend upon either the publisher's and test developer's claims, or on conceptual and methodological critiques, but upon carefully planned and well-executed research" (p. 266). In this regard, one might note the discrepancy between the nearly half-century of work with Halstead's test and the barely ten years at this writing of work with Luria-Nebraska. Various opinions have also been raised with regard to whether it is proper to utilize the Luria-Nebraska in clinical situations. My view of the matter would be that it may be so used as long as inferences made from it do not go beyond what can be based on the available research literature. In particular, the test consumer should not be led to believe that administration and interpretation of the Luria-Nebraska Battery provide an assessment of the type that would have been conducted by Luria and his co-workers, or that one is providing an application of Luria's method. The procedure is specifically not Luria's method at all, and the view that it provides valid measures of Luria's constructs and theories has not been verified. Even going beyond that point, attempts to verify some of Luria's hypotheses (e.g., Drewe, 1975; Goldberg & Tucker, 1979) have not always been completely successful. Therefore, clinical interpretations, even when they are based on

Luria's actual method of investigation, may be inaccurate because of inaccuracies in the underlying theory.

SUMMARY AND CONCLUSIONS

In the first part of this chapter, general problems in the area of standardization of comprehensive neuropsychological test batteries were discussed, while the second part contained brief reviews of the two most widely used procedures, the Halstead-Reitan and the Luria-Nebraska. It was generally concluded that these batteries have their advantages and disadvantages. The Halstead-Reitan is well established and detailed but also lengthy and cumbersome, and neglects certain areas, notably memory. The Luria-Nebraska is also fairly comprehensive and briefer than the Halstead-Reitan but is currently quite controversial and is thought to have major deficiencies in standardization and rationale, at least by some observers. I have taken the view that all of these standard batteries are screening instruments, but not in the sense of screening for presence or absence of brain damage. Rather, they may be productively used to screen a number of functional areas, such as a memory, language, or visual-spatial skills, that may be affected by brain damage. With the development of the new imaging techniques in particular, it is important that the neuropsychologist not simply tell the referring agent what he or she already knows. The unique contribution of standard neuropsychological assessment is the ability to describe functioning in many crucial areas on a quantitative basis. The extent to which one procedure can perform this type of task more accurately and efficiently than other procedures will no doubt greatly influence the relative acceptability of these batteries by the professional community.

REFERENCES

Adams, K. M. (1980). In search of Luria's battery: A false start. *Journal of Consulting and Clinical Psychology, 48,* 511–516.

Adams, R. L. & Trenton, S. L. (1981). Development of a paper-and-pen form of the Halstead Category test. *Journal of Consulting and Clinical Psychology, 49,* 298–299.

Albert, M. L. (1978). Subcortical dementia. In R. D. Terry and K. L. Bick (Eds.), *Alzheimer's disease: Senile dementia and related disorders.* New York: Raven Press.

Albert, M. L., Goodglass, H., Helm, N. A., Rubens, A. B., & Alexander, M. P. (1981). *Clinical aspects of dysphasia*. New York: Springer-Verlag/Wein.

Ben-Yishay, Y., Diller, L., Gertsman, L., & Gordon, W. (1970). Relationship between initial competence and ability to profit from cues in brain-damaged individuals. *Journal of Abnormal Psychology, 78*, 248–259.

Ben-Yishay, Y., Gertsman, L., Diller, D., & Haas, A. (1970). Prediction of rehabilitation outcomes from psychometric parameters in left hemiplegics. *Journal of Consulting and Clinical Psychology, 34*, 436–441.

Bender, L. (1938). A visual motor gestalt test and its clinical use. *American Orthopsychiatric Association, Research Monographs*, No. 3.

Bender, M. B. (1952). *Disorders in perception*. Springfield, IL: Charles C. Thomas.

Benton, A. L. (1961). The fiction of the Gerstmann Syndrome. *Journal of Neurology, Neurosurgery and Psychiatry, 24*, 176–181.

Benton, A. L. (1963). *The Revised Visual Retention Test*. New York: Psychological Corporation.

Benton, A. L., Hamsher, K. deS., Varney, N. R., & Spreen, O. (1983). *Contributions to neuropsychological assessment*. New York: Oxford University Press.

Blumstein, S. E. (1981). Neurolinguistic disorders: Language-brain relationships. In S. B. Filskov and T. J. Boll (Eds.), *Handbook of clinical neuropsychology*. New York: Wiley-Interscience.

Boll, T. J. (1981). The Halstead-Reitan neuropsychology battery. In S. B. Filskov & T. J. Boll (Eds.), *Handbook of clinical neuropsychology*. New York: Wiley-Interscience.

Butters, N. (1983, August). *Clinical aspects of memory disorders: Contributions from experimental studies of amnesia and dementia*. Presented at the American Psychological Association, Division 40 Presidential Address, Anaheim, CA.

Butters, N. M., & Cermak, L. S. (1980). *Alcoholic Korsakoff's syndrome*. New York: Academic Press.

Calsyn, D. A., O'Leary, M. R., & Chaney, E. F. (1980). Shortening the Category Test. *Journal of Consulting and Clinical Psychology, 48*, 788–789.

Canter, A. (1970). *The Canter Background Interference Procedure for the Bender-Gestalt Test: Manual for administration, scoring and interpretation*. Iowa City, IA: Iowa Psychopathic Hospital.

Chmielewski, C., & Golden, C. J. (1980). Alcoholism and brain damage: An investigation using the Luria-Nebraska Neuropsychological Battery. *International Journal of Neuroscience, 10*, 99–105.

Christensen, A. L. (1975a). *Luria's neuropsychological investigation*. New York: Spectrum.

Christensen, A. L. (1975b). *Luria's neuropsychological investigation: Manual*. New York: Spectrum.

Christensen, A. L. (1975c). *Luria's neuropsychological investigation: Test cards*. New York: Spectrum.

Cronbach, L. J. (1960). *Essentials of psychological testing* (2nd ed.). New York: Harper & Brothers.

Crosson, B., & Warren, R. L. (1982). Use of the Luria-Nebraska Neuropsychological Battery in aphasia: A conceptual critique. *Journal of Consulting and Clinical Psychology, 50*, 22–31.

Danzinger, W. (1983, October). *Longitudinal study of cognitive performance in healthy and mildly demented (SDAT) older adults*. Paper presented at conference on Clinical Memory Assessment of Older Adults, Wakefield, MA.

Davis, K. (1983, October). *Potential neurochemical and neuroendocrine validators of assessment instruments*. Paper presented at conference on Clinical Memory Assessment of Older Adults, Wakefield, MA.

DeFillippis, N. A., McCampbell, E., & Rogers, P. (1979). Development of a booklet form of the Category Test: Normative and validity data. *Journal of Clinical Neuropsychology, 1*, 339–342.

Delis, D. C., & Kaplan, E. (1982). The assessment of aphasia with the Luria-Nebraska neuropsychological battery: A case critique. *Journal of Consulting and Clinical Psychology, 50*, 32–39.

Drewe, E. A. (1975). An experimental investigation of Luria's theory on the effects of frontal lobe lesions in man. *Neuropsychologia, 13*, 421–429.

Dunn, L. M., & Markwardt, F. C. (1970), *Peabody individual Achievement Test Manual*. Circle Pine, MN: American Guidance Service.

Filskov, S. B., & Boll, T. J. (1981). *Handbook of clinical neuropsychology*. New York: Wiley-Interscience.

Filskov, S. B., & Goldstein, S. G. (1974). Diagnostic validity of the Halstead-Reitan neuropsychological battery. *Journal of Consulting and Clinical Psychology, 42*, 382–388.

Fitzhugh, K. B., Fitzhugh, L. C., & Reitan, R. M. (1961). Psychological deficits in relation to acuteness of brain dysfunction. *Journal of Consulting Psychology, 25*, 61–66.

Fitzhugh, K. B., Fitzhugh, L. C., & Reitan, R. M. (1962). Wechsler-Bellevue comparisons in groups of "chronic" and "current" lateralized and diffuse brain lesions. *Journal of Consulting Psychology, 26*, 306–310.

Fletcher, J. M., & Satz, P. (1980). Developmental changes in the neuropsychological correlates of reading achievement: A six-year longitudinal follow-up. *Journal of Clinical Neuropsychology, 2*, 23–37.

Flor-Henry, P. & Yeudall, L. T. (1979). Neuropsychological investigation of schizophrenia and manic-depressive psychoses. In J. Gruzelier & P. Flor-Henry (Eds.), *Hemisphere asymmetries of function in psychopathology.* Amsterdam: Elsevier/ North Holland.

Goldberg, E., & Tucker, D. (1979). Motor perseveration and long-term memory for visual forms. *Journal of Clinical Neuropsychology, 1*, 273–288.

Golden, C. J. (1978). *Diagnosis and rehabilitation in clinical neuropsychology.* Springfield, IL: C. C. Thomas.

Golden, C. J. (1979). Identification of specific neurological disorders using double discrimination scales derived from the standardized Luria neuropsychological battery. *International Journal of Neuroscience, 10*, 51–56.

Golden, C. J. (1980). In reply to Adams' "In search of Luria's battery: A false start." *Journal of Consulting and Clinical Psychology, 48*, 517–521.

Golden, C. J. (1981a). The Luria-Nebraska children's battery: Theory and formulation. In G. W. Hynd & J. E. Obrzut (Eds.), *Neuropsychological assessment and the school-aged child: Issues and procedures.* New York: Grune & Stratton.

Golden, C. J. (1981b). A standardized version of Luria's neuropsychological tests: A quantitative and qualitative appproach to neuropsychological evaluation. In S. B. Filskov & T. J. Boll (Eds.), *Handbook of clinical neuropsychology.* New York: Wiley-Interscience.

Golden, C. J., & Berg, R. A. (1983). Interpretation of the Luria-Nebraska Neuropsychological Battery by item intercorrelation: The memory scale. *Clinical Neuropsychology, 5*, 55–59.

Golden, C. J., Graber, B., Blose, I., Berg, R., Coffman, J., & Block, S. (1981). Difference in brain densities between chronic alcoholic and normal control patients. *Science, 211*, 508–510.

Golden, C. J., Hammeke, T. & Purisch, A. (1978). Diagnostic validity of the Luria neuropsychological battery. *Journal of Consulting and Clinical Psychology, 46*, 1258–1265.

Golden, C. J., Hammeke, T. & Purisch, A. (1980). *The Luria-Nebraska Battery manual.* Los Angeles: Western Psychological Services.

Golden, C. J., Moses, J. A., Zelazowski, R., Graber, B., Zatz, L. M., Horvath, T. B., & Berger, P. A. (1980). Cerebral ventricular size and neuropsychological impairment in young chronic schizophrenics. *Archives of General Psychiatry, 37*, 619–623.

Golden, C. J., Purisch, A. & Hammeke, T. (1985). Luria-Nebraska Neuropsychological Battery Manual-Forms I and II. Los Angeles: Western Psychological Services.

Goldstein, G. (1978). Cognitive and perceptual differences between schizophrenics and organics. *Schizophrenia Bullentin, 4*, 160–185.

Goldstein, G. (1982, March). Overview: *Clinical application of the Halstead-Reitan and Luria-Nebraska batteries.* Invited lecture, NE-REMC Conference, Northport, NY.

Goldstein, G. (1986). The neuropsychology of schizophrenia. In I. Grant & K. M. Adams (Eds.), *Neuropsychological assessment of neuropsychiatric disorders.* New York; Oxford University Press.

Goldstein, G., & Ruthven, L. (1983). *Rehabilitation of the brain damaged adult.* New York: Plenum Press.

Goldstein, G., & Shelly, C. (1971). Field dependence and cognitive, perceptual and motor skills in alcoholics: A factor analytic study. *Quarterly Journal of Studies on Alcohol, 32*, 29–40.

Goldstein, G., & Shelly, C. (1972). Statistical and normative studies of the Halstead Neuropsychological Test Battery relevent to a neuropsychiatric hospital setting. *Perceptual and Motor Skills, 34*, 603–620.

Goldstein, G., & Shelly, C. H. (1975). Similarities and differences between psychological deficit in aging and brain damage. *Journal of Gerontology, 30*, 448–455.

Goldstein, G., & Shelly, C.(1982). A further attempt to cross-validate the Russell, Neuringer and Goldstein neuropsychological keys. *Journal of Consulting and Clinical Psychology, 50*, 721–726.

Goldstein, G., & Shelly, C. (1987). The classification of neuropsychological deficit. *Journal of Psychopathology and Behavioral Assessment, 9*, 183–202.

Goldstein, G., Shelly, C., McCue, M., & Kane, R. L. (1987). Classification with the Luria-Nebraska Neuropsychological Battery: An application of cluster and ipsative profile analysis. *Archives of Clinical Neuropsychology, 2*, 215–235.

Goldstein, K., & Scheerer, M. (1941). Abstract and concrete behavior: An experimental study with special tests. *Psychological Monographs, 63* (Entire No. 239).

Goodglass, H. (1983, August). Aphasiology in the United States. In G. Goldstein (Chair), *Symposium: History of human neuropsychology in the United States*. Ninety-first annual convention of the American Psychological Association, Anaheim, CA.

Goodglass, H., & Kaplan, E. (1983). *The assessment of aphasia and related disorders* (2nd ed.). Philadelphia, PA: Lea & Febiger.

Gruzelier, J., & Flor-Henry, P. (1979). *Hemisphere asymmetries of function in psychopathology*. Amsterdam: Elsevier/North-Holland.

Halstead, W. C. (1947). *Brain and intelligence: A quantitative study of the frontal lobes*. Chicago: University of Chicago Press.

Heaton, R. K., Baade, L. E., & Johnson, K. L. (1978). Neuropsychological test results associated with psychiatric disorders in adults. *Psychological Bulletin, 85*, 141–162.

Heaton, R. K., & Crowley, T. (1981). Effects of psychiatric disorders and their somatic treatment on neuropsychological test results. In S. B. Filskov & T. J. Boll (Eds.), *Handbook of clinical neuropsychology*. New York: Wiley-Interscience.

Heaton, R. K., & Pendleton, M. G. (1981). Use of neuropsychological tests to predict adult patients' everyday functioning. *Journal of Consulting and Clinical Psychology, 49*, 807–821.

Heilman, K. M. (1979). Neglect and related disorders. In K. M. Heilman & E. Valenstein (Eds.), *Clinical neuropsychology*. New York: Oxford University Press.

Henn, F. A., & Nasrallah, H. A. (1982). *Schizophrenia as a brain disease*. New York: Oxford University Press.

Hill, S. Y., & Mikhael, M. (1979) Computerized transaxial and tomography (CTT) and neuropsychological evaluation in chronic alcoholics and heroin addicts. *American Journal of Psychiatry, 136*, 598–602.

Jastak, J. F., & Jastak, S. P. (1965). *The Wide Range Achievement Test: Manual of instructions*. Wilmington, DE: Guidance Associates.

Jastak, S., & Wilkinson, G. S. (1984). The Wide Range Achievement Test-Revised. Wilmington DE: Jastak Associates.

Jarvis, P. E., & Barth, J. T. (1984). Halstead-Reitan Test Battery: An interpretive guide. Odessa, FL: Psychological Assessment Resources.

Jones, B. P., & Butters, N. (1983). Neuropsychological assessment. In M. Hersen, A. S. Bellack, & A. E. Kazdin (Eds.), *The clinical psychology handbook*. New York: Pergamon Press.

Kaiser, H. F. (1960). The application of electronic computers to factor analysis. *Educational and Psychological Measurement, 20*, 141–151.

Kaplan, E. (1979). Presidential address. Presented at the International Neuropsychological Society, Noordwijkerhout, Holland.

Kertesz, A. (1979). *Aphasia and associated disorders: Taxonomy, localization and recovery*. New York: Grune & Stratton.

Kimura, D. (1961). Some effects of temporal lobe damage on auditory perception. *Canadian Journal of Psychology, 15*, 156–165.

Kimura, D., & Durnford, M. (1974). Normal studies on the function of the right hemisphere in vision. In S. J. Dimond & J. G. Beaumont (Eds.), *Hemisphere function in the human brain*. London: Elek Science.

Kinsbourne, M. (1980). Attentional dysfunctions and the elderly: Theoretical models and research perspectives. In L. W. Poon, J. L. Fozard, L. S. Cermak, D. Arenberg & L. W. Thompson (Eds.), *New directions in memory and aging*. Hillsdale, NJ: Erlbaum.

Klove, H. (1974). Validation studies in adult clinical neuropsychology. In R. M. Reitan & L. H. Davison (Eds.), *Clinical neuropsychology: Current status and applications*. Washington, DC: V. H. Winston.

Levin, H. S., Benton, A. L., & Grossman, R. G. (1982). *Neurobehavioral consequences of closed head injury*. New York: Oxford University Press.

Lezak, M. (1976). *Neuropsychological assessment* (1st ed.). New York: Oxford University Press.

Lezak, M. (1983). *Neuropsychological assessment* (2nd ed.). New York: Oxford University Press.

Luria, A. R. (1966). *Higher cortical functions in man*. New York: Basic Books.

Luria, A. R. (1970). *Traumatic aphasia*. The Hague: Mouton and Co.

Luria, A. R. (1973). *The working brain*. New York: Basic Books.

Malec, J. (1978). Neuropsychological assessment of schizophrenia vs. brain damage: A review. *Journal of Nervous and Mental Disease, 166*, 507–516.

Matthews, C. G. (1981). Neuropsychology practice in a hospital setting. In S. B. Filskov & T. J. Boll (Eds.), *Handbook of clinical neuropsychology*. New York: Wiley-Interscience.

McCue, M., Rogers, J. C., Goldstein, G., & Shelly, C. (1987, August). *The relationship of neuropsychological skills and functional outcome in the elderly*. Paper presented at the annual meeting of the American Psychological Association, New York, NY.

McCue, M., Shelly, C., Golstein, G., & Katz-Garris, L. (1984). Neuropsychological aspects of learning disability in young adults. *Clinical Neuropsychology, 6*, 229–233.

McKay, S., & Golden, C. J. (1979a). Empirical derivation of experimental scales for the lateralization of brain damage using the Luria-Nebraska Neuropsychological Battery. *Clinical Neuropsychology, 1*, 1–5.

McKay, S., & Golden, C. J. (1979b). Empirical derivation of experimental scales for localizing brain lesions using the Luria-Nebraska Neuropsychological Battery. *Clinical Neuropsychology, 1*, 19–23.

McKay, S. E., & Golden, C. J. (1981). The assessment of specific neuropsychological skills using scales derived from factor analysis of the Luria-Nebraska Neuropsychological Battery. *International Journal of Neuroscience, 14*, 189–204.

Meier, M. J. (1974). Some challenges for clinical neuropsychology. In R. M. Reitan & L. A. Davison (Eds.), *Clinical neuropsychology: Current status and applications*. Washington, DC: V. H. Winston and Sons.

Meier, M. J., Benton, A. L., & Diller, L. (1987). *Neuropsychological rehabilitation*. Edinburgh: Churchill Livingstone.

Mirsky, A. (in press). The neuropsychology of attention: Elements of a complex behavior. In E. Perecman (Ed.), *Integrating theory and practice in clinical neuropsychology*. New York: Institute for Research in Behavioral Neuroscience.

Mooney, C. M. (1957). Age in the development of closure ability in children. *Canadian Journal of Psychology, 2*, 219–226.

Moses, J. A., Golden, C. J., Berger, P. A., & Wisniewski, A. M. (1981). Neuropsychological deficits in early, middle, and late stage Huntington's disease as measured by the Luria-Nebraska Neuropsychological Battery. *International Journal of Neuroscience, 14*, 95–100.

Newby, R. F., Hallenbeck, C. E., & Embretson (Whitely), S. (1983). Confirmatory factor analysis of four general neuropsychological models with a modified Halstead-Reitan Battery. *Journal of Clinical Neuropsychology, 5*, 115–133.

Newcombe, F. (1969). *Missile wounds of the brain: A study of psychological deficits*. Oxford: Clarendon Press.

Newman, O. S., Heaton, R. K., & Lehman, R. A. W. (1978). Neuropsychological and MMPI correlates of patients' future employment characteristics. *Perceptual and Motor Skills, 46*, 635–642.

Parsons, O. A., & Farr, S. P. (1981). The neuropsychology of alcohol and drug abuse. In S. B. Filskov & T. J. Boll (Eds.), *Handbook of clinical neuropsychology*. New York: Wiley-Interscience.

Purisch, A. D. Golden, C. J., & Hammeke, T. A. (1978). Discrimination of schizophrenic and brain-injured patients by a standardized version of Luria's neuropsychological tests. *Journal of Consulting and Clinical Psychology, 46*, 1266–1273.

Purisch, A. D., & Sbordone, R. J. (1986). The Luria-Nebraska Neuropsychological Battery. In G. Goldstein & R. E. Tarter (Eds.), *Advances in clinical neuropsychology*, (Vol. 3). New York: Plenum Press.

Reed, H. B. C., & Reitan, R. M. (1963). A comparison of the effects of the normal aging process with the effects of organic brain-damage on adaptive abilities. *Journal of Gerontology, 18*, 177–179.

Reed, J. (1983, August). The Chicago-Indianapolis Group. In G. Goldstein (Chair), *Symposium: History of human neuropsychology in the United States*. Ninety-first annual convention of the American Psychological Association, Anaheim, CA.

Reisberg, B., Ferris, S. H., & Gershon, S. (1980). Pharmacotherapy of senile dementia. In J. O. Cole & J. E. Barrett (Eds.), *Psychopathology in the aged*. New York: Raven Press.

Reitan, R. M. (1955). An investigation of the validity of Halstead's measures of biological intelligence. *Archives of Neurology and Psychiatry, 73*, 28–35.

Reitan, R. M. (1958). Qualitative versus quantitative mental changes following brain damage. *Journal of Psychology, 46*, 339–346.

Reitan, R. M. (1959). Correlations between the Trail Making test and the Wechsler-Bellevue scale. *Perceptual and Motor Skills, 9*, 127–130.

Reitan, R. M. (1964). Psychological deficits resulting from cerebral lesions in man. In J. M. Warren & K. Akert (Eds.), *The frontal granular cortex and behavior*. New York: McGraw-Hill.

Reitan, R. M. (1966). A research program on the psychological effects of brain lesions in human beings. In N. R. Ellis (Ed.), *International review of research in mental retardation.* New York; Academic Press

Reitan, R. M. (1973, August). Behavioral manifestations of impaired brain functions in aging. In J. L. Fozard (Chair), *Similarities and differences of brain-behavior relationships in aging and cerebral pathology.* Symposium presented at the American Psychological Association, Montreal, Canada.

Reitan, R. M., Davison, L. A. (1974). *Clinical neuropsychology: Current status and applications.* Washington, DC: V. H. Winston and Sons.

Reitan, R. M., Hom, J., & Wolfson, D. (1988). Verbal processing by the brain. *Journal of Clinical and Experimental Neuropsychology, 10,* 400–408.

Reitan, R. M., & Wolfson, D. (1985). *The Halstead-Reitan Neuropsychological Test Battery: Theory and clinical interpretation.* Tucson: Neuropsychology Press.

Rey, A. (1941). L'examinen psychologique dans les cas d'encephalopathie traumatique. *Archives de Psychologie, 28,* 286–340.

Rourke, B. P. (1983). Reading and spelling disabilities: A developmental neuropsychological perspective. In U. Kirk (Ed.), *Neuropsychology of language, reading and spelling.* New York: Academic Press.

Rourke, B. P. (Ed.). (1985). *Neuropsychology of learning disabilities: Essentials of subtype analysis.* New York: Guilford Press.

Russell, E. W. (1975a). A multiple scoring method for the assessment of complex memory functions. *Journal of Consulting and Clinical Psychology, 43,* 800–809.

Russell, E. W. (1975b). Validation of a brain damage versus schizophrenia MMPI. *Journal of Clinical Psychology, 33,* 190–193.

Russell, E. W. (1977). MMPI profiles of brain damaged and schizophrenic subjects. *Journal of Clinical Psychology, 33,* 190–193.

Russell, E. W. (1981). The pathology and clinical examination of memory. In S. B. Filskov & T. J. Boll (Eds.), *Handbook of clinical neuropsychology.* New York: Wiley-Interscience.

Russell, E. W., & Levy, M. (1987). Revision of the Halstead Category Test. *Journal of Consulting and Clinical Psychology, 55,* 898–901.

Russell, E. W., Neuringer, C., & Goldstein, G. (1970). *Assessment of brain damage: A neuropsy-*

chological key approach. New York: Wiley-Interscience.

Satz, P., Taylor, H. G., Friel, J., & Fletcher, J. M. (1978). Some developments and predictive precursors of reading disability. In A. L. Benton & D. Pearl (Eds.), *Dyslexia: An appraisal of current knowledge.* New York: Oxford University Press.

Schear, J. M. (1984). Neuropsychological assessment of the elderly in clinical practice. In P. E. Logue & J. M. Schear (Eds.), *Clinical neuropsychology: A multidisciplinary approach.* Springfield, IL: C. C. Thomas.

Schear, J. M. (1987). Utility of cluster analysis in classification of mixed neuropsychiatric patients. *Archives of Clinical Neuropsychology, 2,* 329–341.

Scoville, W. B., & Milner, B. (1957). Loss of recent memory after bilateral hippocampal lesions. *Journal of Neurology, Neurosurgery, and Psychiatry, 20,* 11–21.

Selz, M., & Reitan, R. M. (1979). Rules for neuropsychological diagnosis: Classification of brain function in older children. *Journal of Consulting and Clinical Psychology, 47,* 258–264.

Semmes, J., Weinstein, S., Ghent, L., & Teuber, H.-L. (1960). *Somatosensory changes after penetrating brain wounds in man.* Cambridge, MA: Harvard University.

Shaw, D. (1966). The reliability and validity of the Halstead Category Test. *Journal of Clinical Psychology, 22,* 176–180.

Shelly, C., & Goldstein, G. (1983). Discrimination of chronic schizophrenia and brain damage with the Luria-Nebraska Battery: A partially successful replication. *Clinical Neuropsychology, 5,* 82–85.

Sherrill, R. E. Jr. (1987). Options for shortening Halstead's Category Test for adults. *Archives of Clinical Neuropsychology, 2,* 343–352.

Smith, A. (1965). Certain hypothesized hemispheric differences in language and visual functions in human adults. *Cortex, 2,* 109–126.

Smith, A. (1966a). Intellectual functions in patients with lateralized frontal tumors. *Journal of Neurology, Neurosurgery, and Psychiatry, 29,* 52–59.

Smith, A. (1966b). Verbal and nonverbal test performances of patients with "acute" lateralized brain lesions (tumors). *Journal of Nervous and Mental Disease, 141,* 517–523.

Smith, A. (1975). Neuropsychological testing in neurological disorders. In W. J. Friedlander (Ed.), *Advances in neurology* (Vol. 7). New York: Raven Press.

Sperry, R. W., Gazzaniga, M. S., & Bogen, J. E.

(1969). Interhemispheric relationships: The neocortical commisures; syndromes of hemisphere disconnection. In P. J. Vinkin & G. W. Bruyen (Eds.), *Handbook of clinical neurology*. Amsterdam: North Holland.

Spiers, P. A. (1981). Have they come to praise Luria or to bury him; The Luria-Nebraska Battery controversy. *Journal of Consulting and Clinical Psychology, 49*, 331–341.

Squire, L. R., Butters, N. (Eds). (1984). *Neuropsychology of memory*. New York: Guilford Press.

Squire, L. R., Slater, P. C., & Chace, P. M. (1975). Retrograde amnesia: Temporal gradient in very long term memory following electroconvulsive therapy. *Science, 187*, 77–79.

Stambrook, M. (1983). The Luria-Nebraska Neuropsychological Battery: A promise that may be partly fulfilled. *Journal of Clinical Neuropsychology, 5*, 247–269.

Steinhauer, S. R., Hill, S. Y., Zubin, J. (1987). Event-related potentials in alcoholics and their first-degree relatives. *Alcohol, 4*, 307–314.

Swiercinsky, D. (1978). *Manual for the adult neuropsychological evaluation*. Springfield, IL: C. C. Thomas.

Swiercinsky, D. P. (1979). Factorial pattern description and comparison of functional abilities in neuropsychological assessment. *Perceptual and Motor Skills, 48*, 231–241.

Teasdale, G., & Jennett, B. (1974). Assessment of coma and impaired consciousness: A practical scale. *Lancet, 2*, 81–84.

Teuber, H.-L. (1959). Some alterations in behavior after cerebral lesions in man. In A. D. Bass (Ed.), *Evolution of nervous control from primitive organisms to man*. Washington, DC: American Association for Advancement of Science.

Teuber, H.-L. (1964). The riddle of frontal lobe function in man. In J. M. Warren & K. Albert (Eds.), *The frontal granular cotex and behavior*. New York: McGraw-Hill.

Teuber, H.-L., Battersby, W. S., & Bender, M. B. (1951). Performance of complex visual tasks after cerebral lesions. *Journal of Nervous and Mental Disease, 114*, 413–429.

Teuber, H.-L., & Weinstein, S. (1954). Performance on a form-board task after penetrating brain injury. *Journal of Psychology, 38*, 177–190.

Townes, B. D., Martin, D. C., Nelson, D., Prosser, R., Pepping, M., Maxwell, J., Peel, J., & Preston, M. (1985). Neurobehavioral approach to classification of psychiatric patients using a competency model. *Journal of Consulting and Clinical Psychology, 53*, 33–42.

Vega, A., & Parsons, O. (1967). Cross-validation of the Halstead-Reitan tests for brain damage. *Journal of Consulting Psychology, 31*, 619–625.

Warrington, E. K., & Weiskrantz, L. (1982). Amnesia: A disconnection syndrome? *Neuropsychologia, 20*, 233–248.

Wechsler, D. (1945). *Wechsler Memory Scale Manual*. New York: Psychological Corporation.

Wechsler, D. (1955). *Wechsler Adult Intelligence Scale*. New York: Psychological Corporation.

Wechsler, D. (1987). Wechsler Memory Scale-Revised. New York: Psychological Corporation.

Weinberger, D. R., & Wyatt, R. J. (1982). Brain morphology in schizophrenia: In vivo studies. In F. A. Henn & H. A. Nasrallah (Eds.), *Schizophrenia as a brain disease*. New York: Oxford University Press.

Wertheimer, M. (1923). Studies in the theory of gestalt psychology. *Psychologische Forschung, 4*, 301–350.

Wertz, R. T. (1983). Language intervention context and setting for the aphasic adult: When? In J. Miller, D. E. Yoder, & R. Schiefelbusch (Eds.), *Comtemporary issues in language intervention*. Rockville, MD: American Speech-Language-Hearing Association.

Wilson, R., & Kaszniak, A. (1983, October). *Progressive memory decline in progressive idiopathic dementia*. Paper presented at Conference on Clinical Memory Assessment of Older Adults, Wakefield, MS.

Yozawitz, A. (1986). Applied neuropsychology in a psychiatric center. In I. Grant & K. M. Adams (Eds.), *Neuropsychological assessment of neuropsychiatric disorders*. New York: Oxford University Press.

CHAPTER 11

NEUROPSYCHOLOGICAL ASSESSMENT OF CHILDREN

H. Gerry Taylor
Jack M. Fletcher

INTRODUCTION

Over the last several years neuropsychological testing of children has become increasingly popular. Numerous authoritative summaries on this topic are now available (Obrzut & Hynd, 1986; Rourke, Fisk, & Strang, 1986; Spreen, Tupper, Risser, Tuokko, & Edgell, 1984). Together with the substantial number of research publications in this area, this body of work provides a wealth of information on neuropsychological principles and test procedures. A perusal of the more general assessment literature reveals that neuropsychological methods have a broad appeal and are widely applied—not only to children with neurological disease, but also to those whose disabilities are not accompanied by known brain injury. The latter category consists of children with learning disabilities, hyperactivity, and chronic disease (e.g., diabetes, heart disease, congenital disorders). Neuropsychological testing may even be considered appropriate in evaluating children with more traditional psychosocial or psychiatric disturbances. The nature of the overt disorder is immaterial. So long as there is reason to believe that inherent cognitive problems contribute to or are associated with the child's problems, neuropsychological assessment is usually deemed to be desirable.

Unfortunately, neuropsychological methods are not easily distinguished from other modes of clinical assessment. The standardized measures of intelligence, achievement, and behavioral adjustment employed by the neuropsychologist are not intrinsically neuropsychological. Sensitivity to brain injury in adults is also insufficient grounds for considering test procedures to have utility in child neuropsychological assessment (Fletcher & Taylor, 1984). The neuropsychological relevance of a given test is most fundamentally dependent on the willingness of the examiner to make two assumptions. The first assumption is that the child tested has a disorder with biological-genetic, as opposed to purely environmental, underpinnings. The second supposition is that the child's performance on the test provides a measure of these inherent influences (Taylor, 1988b). Understanding the rationale for making these assumptions is helpful in conceptualizing the purposes and offerings of child neuropsychological assessment.

We begin the present chapter with a critical examination of the historical roots and current status of child neuropsychological assessment. Rational interpretation of test results demands that the premises for making central nervous system (CNS) inferences be clearly understood and that the clinician avoid logical fallacies that would lead to overinterpretation of data. We then describe a "biobehavioral systems" approach to neuropsychological evaluation. This approach acknowledges the lack of well-established brain-behavior relationships in children and it stresses the importance of studying relationships between behavioral variables. Temptation to make direct inferences from behavior to brain are resisted in favor of a multifactorial framework that considers environmental, psychosocial, and developmental influences. Following discussion of the primary features of this approach, we will detail the corresponding assessment process. One contention is that the specialized nature of child neuropsychology accrues primarily from an interest in (CNS) contributions to behavior, but that assessment methods may be drawn from the general community of techniques and procedures of developmental psychology.

ORIGINS OF NEUROPSYCHOLOGICAL APPROACHES TO CHILDREN

Concept of Cerebral Dysfunction

To a great extent, our current conceptualization of the child neuropsychological assessment is an outgrowth of the concept of childhood cerebral dysfunctions. According to the latter concept, certain behavioral deficits in children are viewed as evidence of abnormal cerebral dysfunction, even in children without documentable neurological disorder. The justification for making CNS inferences in such cases was based on two observations dating back to the first part of this century. The first observation was that children with established brain disease frequently suffer from relatively specific cognitive and behavioral sequelae (Benton, 1962); the second was that these sequelae, or cognitive-behavioral patterns analogous to them, may also be found in children without recognizable neurological disorders. In the latter instance, the assessment of cerebral dysfunction was based on the conviction that similar behavioral patterns represented similar etiologies, rather than on any direct proof of abnormal brain status (Taylor, 1984b).

The conviction that some subset of child behaviors reflects brain abnormalities has a long history in psychology and medicine. As early as 1902, Still attributed instances of impulsive, acting-out behavior to subtle brain disorders. He acknowledged that such behavior was frequently associated with general impairment of intellect or recognizable physical disease (e.g., head trauma, epilepsy, or CNS infections). But he also pointed out that these etiologies did not account for all cases. Noting that cases of the latter variety occurred more frequently in males than in females and were associated with a raised incidence of physical stigmata and stressful births, Still (1902) proposed a biological explanation. He referred to these latter instances as "morbid failure of the development of moral control" (p. 1080).

A similar theme is echoed in a classic paper by Kahn and Cohen (1934). In reaction to the pronounced tendency at that time to provide psychoanalytic explanations for all childhood disorders, these authors interpreted certain instances of impulsive, overactive, and unmanageable behavior as a reflection of "organic drivenness." Such behavior was frequently observed in children who no longer displayed pathognomic signs of brain damage, but who had histories of birth trauma, head injury, or encephalitis. Kahn and Cohen argued that the distinct behavioral patterns of these children, combined with abnormal medical histories, implicated a brain-stem syndrome. In contrast to the then prevailing psychogenic accounts of many childhood disabilities, Kahn and Cohen were unwilling to attribute these patterns to faulty interaction with the environment.

The most direct point of origin for the concept of cerebral dysfunction is the work of Strauss and his associates (Strauss & Lehtinen, 1947). Based on work with mentally retarded children, Strauss applied the term *minimal brain injury* to children who displayed combinations of impulsivity, hyperactivity, perseverative response tendencies, perceptual disturbances, and poor abstract reasoning. The concept of minimal brain injury was later extended to all children with similar symptoms, regardless of general intelligence or neurological status, and especially to children with deficiencies in academic achievement (Laufer & Denhoff, 1957). Although the existence of a group of nonretarded children displaying these specific characteristics has never been demonstrated (Baumeister & MacLean, 1979), Strauss's concept of the brain-injured child was highly influential.

A federal task force formed to define the learning and behavior problems subsumed within the category discussed by Strauss relied heavily on his conceptualization of minimal brain injury. Pointing out that actual injury to the brain could not be demonstrated in cases of so-called minimal brain injury, the task force changed Strauss's term to *minimal brain dysfunction* and expanded on the categories included under this rubric (Clements, 1966). For the most part, however, the task force preserved the notion that certain behavior problems represented abnormal brain status (Taylor, 1984b).

The popularity of the concept of minimal brain dysfunction stemmed in part from the support it offered for the then popular notion of a "biological gradient" (Ingalls & Gordon, 1947). According to this notion and to the related concept of a "continuum of reproductive casualty" (Pasamanick & Knobloch, 1960), if serious brain damage can result in death, physical disability, or clear mental retardation, then less serious degrees of damage are held responsible for less extreme forms of mental and behavioral impairment. Learning and attentional problems would be included in this latter category. The basic premise of the biological gradient hypothesis—that is, there is an isomorphism between disorders of behavior and disorders of brain—has been widely criticized (Benton, 1973; Fletcher & Taylor, 1984; Rutter, 1982; Satz & Fletcher, 1980). Nevertheless, the idea that functional (i.e., behavioral) signs can provide a basis for making CNS inferences about children, even when the relationship of those signs to the CNS is not documented, has had an insidious influence on neuropsychological approaches to children. Psychologists evaluating children continue to make unwarranted inferences about the CNS solely on the basis of psychometric test results and behavioral observations, despite the lack of any direct confirmation for these inferences.

Influence of Adult Neuropsychology

Early conceptualizations of brain function proposed by such figures as Lashley (1929) and Goldstein (1939) have also helped to lay the groundwork for contemporary approaches to child neuropsychological assessment. These and other researchers observed qualitatively distinct effects of brain injuries on adult behavior. They interpreted these effects as evidence that certain behaviors or cognitive skills are highly vulnerable to neurological insult. Halstead's tests for biological intelligence and the Halstead Neuropsychological Test Battery for Adults that followed represent early outgrowths of these observations (Reitan & Davison, 1974). More recent developments are summarized in contemporary volumes by Filskov and Boll (1986), Hecaen and Albert (1978), Heilman and Valenstein (1985), and Lezak (1983).

The assumption that certain skills represent more direct reflections of cerebral status than other skills has had a similar influence on child neuropsychological assessment. This influence is represented by (a) the continued search for measures differentially sensitive to CNS dysfunction in children; (b) the frequent use of competence-achievement discrepancies in diagnosing learning problems; and (c) the emphasis on models of adult brain function for interpreting psychometric test results.

Despite the problems associated with wholesale application of adult models to children (Dennis, 1983; Fletcher & Taylor, 1984), these models have been useful in several respects. The application to children of modes of neuropsychological interpretation developed initially for adults is one example. Interpretive modes based on levels of performance, pathognomic signs, lateralization of deficits, and differential patterns of performance across multiple testing procedures have proved helpful in recognizing potential brain-related disorders in children (Rourke, 1975). As a further example, adult neuropsychology's focus on various dissociations in memory, language, and motor skills that occur in brain-damaged adults has brought about an expanded awareness of the organization and complexity of higher cognitive functions. The development of the Halstead-Reitan approach and other adult-based approaches to neuropsychology (Benton, Hamsher, Varney, & Spreen, 1983; Goodglass & Kaplan, 1972; Reitan, 1984) has led to growing recognition of the diversity of effects of brain injury on behavior. Application of these approaches to children has yielded many important empirical discoveries. The value of neuropsychological tests for distinguishing subvarieties of learning disabilities is representative of these findings (Rourke, 1985). In addition, concepts like cerebral dysfunction and organicity have drawn attention to the role of biological factors in common childhood behavior disorders. Learning disabilities and attention deficit-hyperactivity disorder are two important instances. Although direct evidence for physiological abnormality is generally lacking for these conditions, the conviction that such "specific" developmental disabilities are brain related remains warranted (Taylor, 1988b; Taylor & Fletcher, 1983).

Implications for Child Neuropsychological Assessment

The above-noted historical factors have culminated in several distinct approaches to neuropsychological assessment of children. One of these approaches is to apply modified versions of adult-originated tests, or to create tests that attempt to measure abilities analogous to those tapped by adult neuropsychological batteries. The Luria-Nebraska Children's Battery is an example of this approach (Golden, 1981). The second general approach is to make use of more traditional procedures for children, including IQ tests and psychoeducational or psycholinguistic batteries (Wilson, 1987). The practitioners of this second approach vary considerably in terms of tests used and caution applied in making CNS inferences. Many practitioners use test results largely for their diagnostic-prescriptive utility, with statements regarding brain status serving as explanations for the ability deficits observed. A third approach combines the use of standard test batteries with experimental cognitive and linguistic measures—the latter having been borrowed from other areas of psychology or developed anew to understand better specific problems on populations (Fletcher, 1988; Fletcher, Levin, & Satz, in press; Taylor, et al., 1984; Taylor, 1988a). Because a primary focus of this third approach is on ability structures and how these structures change with age, this approach represents the greatest departure from adult-derived methods and from the influence of the concept of minimal brain dysfunction. Dennis (1980, 1983) illustrates this approach in her research on the effects of stroke and hemispherectomy on the organization of cognitive skills in children.

A major limitation of any approach that emphasizes the relationship of test results and behavioral observations to children's brain status is the scant knowledge base in this area (Fletcher & Taylor, 1984; Rutter, 1981). For a wide spectrum of clinical problems, brain status is a virtual unknown, and the study of brain-behavior associations thus unfeasible. By default, an exclusive emphasis on brain-behavior relationships leads either to vague and misleading concepts such as cerebral dysfunction or to an overreliance on methods and models of brain function derived from adult studies.

The way out of this dilemma is to recognize that neuropsychologists are just as interested in relationships between behavioral variables as they are in the relationships of brain to behavior (Benton, 1962). The concordance of verbal comprehension deficits and paraphasic speech in patients with left-hemisphere disease provides a vivid example of the importance of behavioral interrelationships in neuropsychological investigation. As the history of aphasiology shows, behavioral associations and dissociations of this sort typically precede hypotheses concerning underlying brain mechanisms (Benton, 1964). In a similar fashion, analyses of child behavior may well lead the way to discovery of brain-behavior relationships in children (Dennis, 1983; Fletcher & Taylor, 1984; Fletcher & Levin, 1988).

An emphasis on relationships between behavioral variables and on the limitations of knowledge regarding brain-behavior relationships in children suggests the necessity to reformulate child neuropsychological assessment. First, the child neuropsychologist's task is not restricted to that of making CNS inferences. An understanding of behavioral relationships is vitally important to the practice of child neuropsychology. As an example, investigation of language correlates of reading disability can be valuable in determining the type of reading disability and in recommending treat-

ment, even when nothing is known about the CNS basis for either the language disorder or the reading disability. Second, the child neuropsychologist is not always well served by a reliance on adult models. While adult models are heuristic, a focus on the organization of children's abilities is essential. Awareness of how language skills and reading abilities interrelate in normal children, for example, is likely to suggest novel approaches to the study of childhood reading disabilities. Third, the child neuropsychologist must explicitly acknowledge the influence of social and environmental factors on the child's behavior and test performance. Because there is little empirical justification for assuming that most neuropsychological measures are "culture fair," it would seem unwise to interpret test performances without references to social-cultural factors. Fourth, the child neuropsychologist must attempt to incorporate developmental considerations into the assessment process. Developmental analyses require that the neuropsychologist look carefully at the manner in which the disability is manifested at different ages, the nature of parent and teacher expectations of the child, and age-related changes in the pattern of the behavioral correlates of the disability (Taylor, 1988a). With improved knowledge of these correlates and of the social-environmental influences on the disabilities of interest, the neuropsychologist should be better able to evaluate the influence of biological factors per se.

In the next section, we will detail a biobehavioral systems framework for neuropsychological assessment of children. As with attempts to develop "brain-sensitive" measures, this approach makes use of our limited knowledge regarding the influence of CNS abnormalities on child behavior. In addition, however, this assessment model encourages the selection of test instruments according to their value as measures of children's abilities and their sensitivity to problems known to be present in developmentally disabled groups. Although this approach emphasizes behavioral relationships, it assumes that the neuropsychologist has special training and interest in the contributions of CNS factors to behavior. The biobehavioral systems framework is presented not as an alternative to other neuropsychological approaches or to standard intellectual or psychoeducational assessment, but as an integration of existing assessment methodologies. The focus is on thorough study of children's abilities as a means for clarifying etiology, correlates, course, and preferred treatment. This approach has evolved since its initial presentation in Taylor et al., (1984) (see Fletcher, 1988; Fletcher et al., in press; Taylor, 1988a; 1989).

A BIOBEHAVIORAL APPROACH TO CHILD NEUROPSYCHOLOGICAL ASSESSMENT

Neuropsychological assessment is commonly conceptualized as an evaluation of abilities thought to reflect CNS integrity. Attempts at differential diagnosis of emotional versus organic disorders frequently form the basis for these assessments. The emphasis of a biobehavioral systems approach is somewhat different. Within this framework, the primary assessment goal is to evaluate developing cognitive and behavioral skills associated with the disability in question. It is taken for granted that no single set of measures will be either necessary or sufficient in every case. While it may be important to evaluate the same general areas of skill in most cases (e.g., language, attention, memory), different clinical problems require alternative methods. Developmental and psychosocial considerations vary from child to child and necessitate a flexible approach to assessment.

Basic Premises

The working assumptions of the biobehavioral systems approach are presented below in an effort to clarify the model and to distinguish it from other modes of child assessment:

Tenet #1

Neuropsychological evaluation of a developmental disability involves assessment of four types of variables:

1. A descriptive analysis of *presenting problems,* or ways in which the child is failing to meet age appropriate expectations for learning or behavior (i.e., the manifest form of the disability);
2. Assessment of a range of *cognitive and psychosocial traits* characteristic of the child;
3. Consideration of relevance of *environmental, sociocultural, and historical variables;* and
4. Evaluation of *biological and genetic variables.*

Tenet #2

Although the manifest disability is in part a product of weaknesses in basic cognitive competencies, the impact of these weaknesses on the child's ability to learn and behave as expected is also dependent on other child characteristics and on environmental factors. The degree to which cognitive limitations result in manifest disabilities is dependent on these addi-

tional influences, which may serve either to exacerbate or to mute the manifest disability.

Tenet #3

Although covariation in cognitive capacities is usually high, dissociations between skills are characteristic of many disabled children. Skill dissociations are related either to congenital neurological variation or to outright neurological disorder. The study of the child who exhibits variations in basic skills is therefore of value in refining our understanding of the nature of competences and how they are deployed in the more complex learning and behavioral functions that define the manifest form of the disability.

Tenet #4

Child traits differ in the extent to which they reflect neurological versus environmental variability. Those traits which are relatively sensitive to variations in neurological status offer the best means for understanding the neurological basis of the child's manifest disability. However, because child characteristics are influenced by environmental variables and learning history, as well as by biological limitations, the relevance of the CNS can be ascertained only by taking both sets of factors into account.

Notwithstanding some revisions in these postulates over previous versions, the schema depicted in Figure 11.1 is much like that described in these previous publications (Fletcher, 1988; Fletcher et al., in press; Fletcher & Taylor, 1984; Taylor, Fletcher, & Satz, 1984; Taylor, 1988a). As shown in Figure 11.1, neuropsychological evaluation of the presenting problem requires assessment of four sets of variables, each of which is assumed to exercise its influence in a particular way. The first variable set represents the child's manifest disability. Examples include inability to acquire academic skills in an age-appropriate fashion, difficulties in focusing on school tasks or completing assignments, deficiencies in verbal communication skills, or failure to retain or follow through on instructions. What best defines the presenting problem, or manifest form of the disability, is the inability of the child to fulfill age-related expectations that have been set by the family, culture, or school.

The second variable set shown in Figure 11.1 represents what might be regarded as fundamental child traits, classified into cognitive and psychosocial subdomains. Cognitive skills are illustrated by the hyperactive child's performance on attentional tasks and by the perceptual, linguistic, and memory deficits of the disabled learner or child aphasic. Psychosocial variables encompass those behavioral traits that are

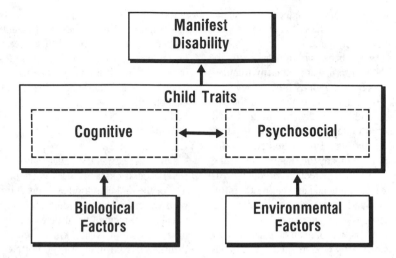

Figure 11.1 Schematic Representation of the Biobehavioral Systems Approach to Child Neuropsychological Assessment

not considered to be primarily cognitive in nature. Included in this subdomain are behavioral adjustment, motivation, self-esteem, socialization, and personality or temperament. As with cognitive abilities, some of the latter traits may be more a function of environmental events or learning history, whereas other traits may have a more constitutional origin. According to the biobehavioral systems model, cognitive and psychosocial subdomains are separable though not totally independent. Together, they comprise the behavioral underpinnings of the child's manifest disability.

Environmental and biological factors, in contrast, exercise their influence on the manifest disability more indirectly, via their effects on child traits. Environmental factors encompass the child's learning history, child management practices, and opportunities for learning and socialization. Biological factors include the presence or absence of chronic medical illness, past or present neurological disorders, placement on medications, and indirect biological indices such as family histories of learning problems, pre- and perinatal risk events, and electrophysiological abnormalities. Environmental factors may occasionally exert a direct influence on the manifest disability, as when a child who is otherwise competent and well motivated has simply not been given the opportunity to learn, or when expectations of the child are unreasonable. These latter possibilities, however, are not represented in Figure 11.1. This is in part because of the relative infrequency of such circumstances and in part because these circumstances generally could not continue long without having an adverse effect on the child's basic competencies and motivation.

Important Features

CNS As One of Several Influences on Learning and Behavior.

One essential feature of the schema presented in Figure 11.1 is that both environmental and biological factors are presumed to influence child characteristics. The model thus discourages brain-behavior isomorphisms, in which behavioral dysfunctions are viewed as direct expressions of neurological endowment. Neurological status is more appropriately described as one of several contributors to the manifest disability. Influences of biological factors are best appreciated by first analyzing the psychological characteristics that underlie the disability. Once these traits have been isolated, biological factors are presumed to operate to the extent that they can account for variation in traits not explained by environmental influences.

More precisely, the model assumes that, although all behaviors are products of both "nature" and "nurture," the proportion of between-child variability accounted for by biological factors is greater for some traits than for others. As an example, the facility with which a child repeats a multisyllabic nonword may be regarded as more subject to native endowment than is the child's ability to repeat a familiar word. In the latter instance, overpractice or established associations between sound patterns and meaning may contribute substantially to the child's success in repeating the familiar word. Although the ability to repeat nonwords is not completely free from the effects of familiarity with sound patterns or from strategies the child may have learned to use in sequencing sounds, nonword repetition is at least less likely to be subject to these factors than repetition of familiar words.

The contrast between behaviors that are primarily CNS-related and behaviors that are more environmentally determined has been drawn by others. Developmental psychologists have long emphasized the importance of both physiological maturation and environmental conditioning accounting for developmental change (McCall, 1981; Spiker, 1966). Hebb (1942) also drew this distinction in contrasting intellectual power with intellectual products. Attempts to separate environmental and biological influences on behavior and on child development are central to child neuropsychological inquiry.

One of the several tactics that can be used to show that a behavior is primarily CNS-related is to demonstrate that variations in skill are independent of environmental conditions. This can be done by demonstrating that skills are invariant across different environments, or, conversely, that environmental differences are not adequate to explain between-child variation in skill levels (e.g., Morrison & Hinshaw, 1988). A second strategy is to link given skills to biological "markers," such as medical risk events, neural imaging studies, family history of learning or behavioral problems, electrophysiological abnormalities, or measures of physical growth (Fletcher & Levin, 1988; Gray & Kavanagh, 1985; Taylor, 1987b; Wolff, 1981). A third tactic for isolating biologically-related behaviors is to study children who have sustained definitive brain disorders. While no skills are categorically immune from the effects of brain damage, studies of brain-injured children suggest that some abilities are more susceptible to early CNS insults than other abilities (Dennis, 1985b; Levin, Ewing-Cobbs, & Benton, 1984; Taylor, 1984a).

Description of the Manifest Form of the Disability.

Another virtue of the schema presented in Figure 11.1 is that it encourages us to take a close look at the manifest form of the disability. A necessary first step in determining the factors that contribute to a child's learning or behavioral problems is to examine the exact manner in which the child is failing to acquire academic skills, attend to schoolwork, or behave in accordance with social expectations. To pick but one example, there are many ways in which children fail to learn how to read. Some disabled readers are able to understand what they read but have difficulty in decoding single words (Johnson, 1980; Perfetti, 1980). Other poor readers show difficulties in both

comprehension and single-word decoding, or may fail to comprehend what they read despite an ability to read constituent words (Isakson & Miller, 1976). Differences in the manifest form of the disability have important implications for treatment and may also provide valuable clues as to the nature of the associated cognitive dysfunction.

Organization of Traits Underlying the Disability.

Direct assessment of underlying child cognitive and psychosocial characteristics is another essential feature of the biobehavioral systems approach. Children with specific learning disorders as well as those having documented brain disease may show any one of a number of basic skill deficits (Benton, 1975; Rourke, 1980; Rutter, 1981). Differentiation of subtypes based on patterns of cognitive impairment may hold promise in identifying etiology, course, and preferred treatment for the individual child (Rourke, 1985). Psychosocial factors also contribute to developmental disabilities, either by affecting the child's adjustment or motivation to perform or through the effects of psychosocial factors on cognitive development (Musser, Conger, & Kagan, 1979; Walsh & Greenough, 1976). Examples of relevant psychosocial traits include premorbid adjustment in children who have sustained brain injuries (Rutter, 1982), and social adaptation and temperament in children experiencing early learning difficulties (Birch, Thomas, & Chess, 1964; Keogh, 1983). The way in which the children respond to, or attempt to cope with, their difficulties is another important psychosocial variable (e.g., Cunningham & Barkley, 1978; Douglas, 1980).

Behavioral Interrelationships.

A further advantage of the model is the encouragement it provides for study of relationships between variables. Among these are (a) the effect of neurological/medical status on the child's cognitive and psychosocial functioning, (b) environmental influences on these same traits, (c) interrelationships between cognitive and psychosocial characteristics, and (d) associations of these latter characteristics to manifest behavior and learning problems.

Studies of the impact of documented brain injuries or chronic diseases on cognitive performances exemplify the first type of investigation (Rourke, Fisk, & Strang, 1986; Rutter, 1981; Taylor, 1987a). The second type of relationship is illustrated by research on the influences of parent and teacher management styles, early childhood experiences, and cultural factors on children's motivation and cognitive abilities

(Kistner & Torgesen, 1987). Relationships between cognitive and psychosocial traits have been the subject of investigations by Rourke and Fisk (1981) and Richman and Lindgren (1981). The latter two investigations have demonstrated that certain patterns of cognitive performance help to predict which children are most likely to have social-adaptational problems, and even the nature of the behavioral disturbance. Associations between cognitive-neuropsychological traits and manifest disabilities have also received recent attention. To illustrate, Rourke and Finlayson (1978) and Sweeney and Rourke (1978) have examined the relationship between types of academic disabilities and patterns of neuropsychological performance in learning-disabled children. The importance of determining which child characteristics are most central to children's learning and behavior problems has been underscored in several analyses of research needs (Benton, 1978; Brown & Campione, 1986; Taylor, Fletcher, & Satz, 1982; Torgesen, 1979). According to Benton (1978),

> It is within this framework of a more adequate description of the disability itself, both in terms of the characteristics of reading performance and of syndromes defined by correlated cognitive performances, that the question of its genetic, neurological, cognitive, and social determinants can be most fruitfully attacked. (p. 476)

Other Areas of Psychology.

One final virtue of the biobehavioral systems model is that it does not wed the examiner to any particular battery of tests. By eschewing a narrow focus on the types of behaviors which we presume discriminate normal from abnormal brain status, and by encouraging study of a broad range of behavioral characteristics, the model encourages application of knowledge from other areas of psychology. To analyze better the psychological substrates of a given disability, the concepts, findings, and methods of cognitive and developmental psychology deserve special consideration.

Common to both cognitive psychology and neuropsychology is the premise that cognitive functions may be decomposed into a relatively limited set of dissociable component processes (Hunt, 1983; Kail & Bisanz, 1982). Dimensions not routinely evaluated in neuropsychological assessment but deserving of closer scrutiny include such concepts as metacognition, executive processing, working memory, deployment of attentional resources, knowledge base, and information acquisition (Brown, Bransford, Ferrara, & Campione, 1983; Kail & Bisanz, 1982; Siegel,

Bisanz, & Bisanz, 1983; Sternberg, 1984). For some time, both neuropsychologists and cognitive psychologists have emphasized the importance of distinguishing tests that demand application of previously acquired information from tasks that require either new learning or active problem solving (Brown, 1975; Rourke, 1980). Torgesen (1980) has shown that learning-disabled children often fail to use problem-solving strategies that, when experimentally induced, can facilitate task performance. Thus, some of these children with learning problems may have sufficient skills to improve their learning; they simply do not put these skills to proper use.

Another information-processing construct that merits further consideration is the concept of attentional resources. Although poorly defined, attentional disorders may be an important correlate of learning failure (Cooley & Morris, in press; Douglas, 1980; Dykman, Ackerman, Clements, & Peters, 1971). Attentional disorders may involve either an absolute inability to sustain attention or control impulses, or inefficient focusing or deployment of available attentional capacity. According to information-processing research, automatization of lower-level skills is required if sufficient attentional resources are to be available for more complex tasks (Kail & Bisanz, 1982; Sternberg, 1984). In the case of the reading-disabled child, reading fluency and comprehension may be hampered by general inattention to the material being read or by more specific failure to automatize lower-level word decoding skills. Consideration of this construct may well lead to new insight with regard to the cognitive basis of some forms of learning disorder.

Child neuropsychological assessment also has much to gain from developmental psychology. Evaluation of how ability structures change with age is necessary both in establishing performance expectations for the child and in identifying cognitive and psychosocial factors influencing the child's ability to acquire academic skills (Kistner & Torgesen, 1987). Early in the reading-acquisition process, knowledge of phonological relationships is fundamental to learning to read. At later stages, semantic and syntactic knowledge may be more critical determinants of reading competence (Gibson & Levin, 1975). The cognitive skills most closely associated with reading ability also change as the child develops (Doehring, 1976; Fletcher, 1981; Taylor, 1988). From the perspective of the child's overall development, a disability in learning or behavior can be viewed as a disruption in the acquisition of skills or behavioral adaptations (Sroufe & Rutter, 1984). Deficits at one age may thus predict later problems, sometimes of a different sort. By virtue of its focus on behavior, the biobehavioral systems model highlights the need to consider developmental change (Siegel et al., 1983), and to make use of existing age-referenced methods for evaluating developmental problems, cognitive and psychosocial competencies, and environmental influences.

THE ASSESSMENT PROCESS

Due to its many positive features, the biobehavioral systems model provides a useful framework for the conduct of child neuropsychological assessments. Reliance on this model makes it possible for the examiner to avoid undue reliance on adult models. The emphasis instead is on all of the factors that contribute to the child's disability. CNS factors are of obvious interest to the neuropsychologist, but can only be weighed against the influence of a number of other variables. The goal of neuropsychological assessment is not limited to determination of biological contributions to the disability. Equally important are relevant behavioral correlates, environmental circumstances, and learning history. The attention the model pays to description of behaviors, cognitive and psychosocial constructs, and relationships among these variables assures that assessment results will be of immediate value in diagnosing the child's problems and in recommending treatment.

The first order of business in following this model is to obtain information on the manifest disability. In our experience, referral for neuropsychological assessment most often stems from concern over the child's failure to meet expectations at school or at home. This failure may be due to inability to make progress in reading, spelling, or arithmetic, or, alternatively, it may involve poor work habits or behavioral transgressions. The neuropsychologist next examines cognitive and psychosocial correlates, as well as potential biological and environmental contributors. Comprehensive assessments demand that the neuropsychologist be conversant in many of the techniques used in child clinical psychology, pediatric psychology, and school psychology. The neuropsychologist need not be an expert in conducting psychoeducational or personality workups, but must at least be able to identify problems within these complementary domains and have a familiarity with their evaluation methodologies. In a sense, the child neuropsychologist operates in a boundary zone among several disciplines. When problems extend into areas not within the neuropsychologist's expertise, appropriate referrals must be made to other child specialists. Child neuropsychologists often work in medical settings where children are likely to be in need of medical care or monitoring. For this reason, an appreciation of medical—especially neurological—disorders and their treatment must be developed. Here again, the effectiveness of the neuropsychologist in understanding the factors that contribute to the child's disability and in recommending appropriate treatment rests heavily on an ability to work in concert with other professionals.

The biobehavioral systems model provides a structure by which to assure that all potential contributors to the child's manifest problems are considered in the assessment process. Following this approach, assessment is broken down into the following components: (a) analysis of the manifest disability, (b) cognitive testing, (c) evaluation of psychosocial functioning, (d) exploration of potential environmental influences, (e) review of evidence for biological relatedness, and (f) interpretation and management of the problems. Each of these components of the assessment process are considered in turn below.

Analysis of the Manifest Disability

Evaluation begins with a review of the reason for referral and a thorough analysis of the child's difficulties. Information on presenting problems can be obtained in at least three ways. Parent and teacher questionnaires, school and medical records, and the results of previous evaluations constitute one source of data. In most cases, these data can be collected before the evaluation session begins. Our standard practice is to request that the parents describe their primary concerns, give information regarding medical history and current medical status, and complete checklists regarding the child's behavior (Taylor, 1988a). Formal checklists such as the Conners Parent Rating Scale (Barkley, 1981) or the Child Behavior Checklist (Achenbach & Edelbrock, 1986) are useful in identifying problem behaviors or areas of maladjustment. Teachers can be asked to provide similar information, and to comment on the programs in which the child is currently involved at school, special management or remedial strategies in use, and other options that may exist for the child within the school system.

Parent interviews provide a second means for obtaining information about the child's problems. The purpose of these interviews is to solicit more detailed descriptions of the nature and history of the child's problems, the context in which these problems arise, parent and teacher expectations of the child, and parental views concerning the origins of the difficulties. To ensure that all potential problem areas are brought to light, parents are routinely questioned about child characteristics and parent-child interactions (e.g., personality, attentional abilities, peer and social interactions, behavior management issues). If the examiner wishes to obtain a more formal rating of the child's developmental standing and adaptive abilities, it may be useful to administer the Vineland Adaptive Behavior Scales (Sparrow, Balla, & Ciccetti, 1984). Based on information provided in a semistructured parent interview, the Vineland Adaptive Behavior Scales yield age-standardized scores in several important areas of functioning (communication, daily living skills, socialization, and motor skills). Ways in which the child and parents are coping with existing problems can also be explored during the interview, along with parent impressions of the child's strengths. By surveying the parents' understanding of the problems, their fears for the child, and the relationships they have had with the child's teachers, the neuropsychologist is in a better position to build rapport. Because parents are the best advocates for their children, the clinician's ability to communicate impressions and recommendations forms the foundation for effective intervention.

The third way in which the clinician can learn more about the child's disability is to probe problem areas. For children with learning problems, the Wide Range Achievement Test-Revised (Jastak & Wilkinson, 1984) surveys word recognition, spelling to dictation, and arithmetic calculation abilities. Other useful tests of academic achievement include the Woodcock Reading Mastery Tests-Revised (Woodcock, 1987), the Gilmore Oral Reading Test (Gilmore & Gilmore, 1968), the Peabody Individual Achievement Test (Dunn & Markwardt, 1970), and the Kaufman Test of Educational Achievement (Kaufman & Kaufman, 1985). Potential difficulties are not limited to lack of skill in reading, spelling, writing, or mathematics, but may also involve incomplete work, ineffective study habits, limited knowledge of content areas (e.g., history, social studies, science), inability to follow directions, failure to organize one's approach to assigned work, noncompliance and misconduct, and lack of initiative or independence. Although formal evaluation of possible problem areas is recommended where possible, informal procedures may also be useful. Examples include observations of how the child approaches a task, what it takes for the child to succeed (testing of limits), and trial teaching. By means of informal observations, the examiner may develop impressions of traits for which formal measures are unavailable (e.g., independence, task orientation, perseverance, initiative, resourcefullness, and use of strategies for remembering, studying, and prolem solving).

It is frequently necessary to evaluate a number of component skills, especially in conducting an academic assessment. Research indicates that, although a given academic deficiency usually portends weaknesses across the board, relatively specific subskill deficits can also occur (Stanovich, 1986; Taylor et al., 1982). Children who are weak in arithmetic, for example, may be able to decode words and spell quite well. Reading problems may entail incomplete knowledge of letter-sound correspondences, limited memory of orthographic patterns, lack of automaticity in word recognition, reading dysfluency, or poor comprehension. Spelling difficulties may also involve limited knowledge of grapheme-phoneme correspondences, or failure to memorize more complex orthographic patterns. Poor written expression may reflect limited vocabulary, poor penmanship or punctuation, slowness in writing, or weaknesses in the child's ability to express or organize ideas on the page. Analysis of the child's academic limitations provides hints about the underlying deficit (e.g., general versus specific language dysfunction), as well as information on skills most in need of remediation.

Cognitive Testing

The basic goals of cognitive-neuropsychological testing are to assist the clinician in formulating hypotheses to explain why the child is having problems in learning or behavior, and what to do about these problems. Specifically, do cognitive weaknesses contribute to the child's difficulties? If so, what are these weaknesses and what other implications do they have for the child's day-to-day functioning? Finally, what are the child's strengths and how can these be put to use in coping with the problem areas?

Test procedures will depend to some extent on the referral issues. For those children who are suffering from learning disabilities, a detailed language evaluation may be the most revealing. In contrast, tests of memory and attention may be more essential for a child with attention deficits—especially if the child's history is consistent with normal linguistic development. Nevertheless, testing must be comprehensive if the examiner is to appreciate strengths as well as pinpoint cognitive deficiencies. Because neuropsychological assessment is constantly evolving, experimental procedures are necessary supplements to more routine and well-standardized measures. Experimental procedures are useful in decomposing a deficit skill area (e.g., breaking the naming deficit down into vocabulary knowledge versus memory retrieval), or in further exploring abilities not tapped by the standard techniques. Observations of the child's approach to test taking and testing of limits are just as appropriate here as they are in assessing the manifest disability.

There is an extensive repertoire of both experimental and more traditional test procedures from which to choose in evaluating cognitive skills. Most tests fall into one of the seven general categories described below. Test rationale limitations and exemplary measures are noted for each category. Specific measures listed by no means exhaust the possibilities; they are mentioned only to give the reader a sampling of the kinds of tasks contained in the child neuropsychologist's test repertoire.

Intelligence.

Standard intelligence tests—most notably the Wechsler Intelligence Scale for Children-Revised (WISC-R) (Wechsler, 1974)—contribute to neuropsychological assessment in several ways. First and foremost, tests like the WISC-R tap a wide range of verbal and nonverbal skills. The child's performance on different subtests of the WISC-R are suggestive of cognitive strengths and weaknesses. Comparisons between performances on the WISC-R subtests requiring primarily verbal, visual-spatial, or attentional skills are often helpful in delineating processing deficits (Kaufman, 1979b; Sattler, 1982). Other IQ test batteries of similar utility include the Kaufman Assessment Battery for Children (Kaufman & Kaufman, 1983), the Stanford-Binet: Fourth Edition (Thorndike, Hagen, & Sattler, 1985), the British Ability Scales (Elliot, Murray, & Pearson, 1983), and, for younger children, the McCarthy Scales of Children's Abilities (McCarthy, 1970). Because these test batteries measure different types of abilities and are well standardized, scores provide estimates of a child's general range of mental functions, points of reference in describing samples of children for research purposes, and documentation for placement recommendations.

The utility of IQ tests is nonetheless overrated. The limitations of IQ tests must be recognized if the results are to be correctly interpreted. To begin with, IQ testing cannot be viewed as a pure measure of learning "potential." Performance on an IQ test reflects past learning history as well as genetic endowment (Bortner & Birch, 1970; Estes, 1981; Liverant, 1960). Related to this issue is the problem of defining some disabilities (e.g., learning disabilities) in terms of

discrepancies between IQ and academic achievement. The fact that those same cognitive deficiencies that make learning difficult may also depress IQ scores challenges the frequent practice of defining learning disabilities in terms of an IQ-achievement discrepancy (Doehring, 1978; Yule, 1978). Similarly, the statistical limitations of computing discrepancies between moderately correlated IQ and achievement tests have received too little attention (Yule, 1978).

Another shortcoming is that IQ tests do not survey all possible areas of competency. These tests fail to measure important aspects of social adaptation, nonverbal problem solving, and information-processing skills (Guilford, 1967; Kaufman, 1979a; Sternberg, 1984). Illustrative of this fact is (a) the finding that correlations between many neuropsychological performances and academic achievement remain robust, even with differences in IQ partialled from the correlation (Taylor et al., 1982); and (b) that IQ scores are not highly predictive of adaptive behaviors in mildly retarded individuals (Brown & French, 1979).

IQ tests are designed for largely pragmatic reasons—that is, to predict learning or achievement outside of the test situation—rather than as measures of distinct processing skills (Hunt, 1980; Kaufman, 1979a). Most IQ subtests demand combinations of skills; consequently, performance offers few clues as to the nature of an individual's component mental abilities. IQ test batteries are also unlikely to be of much use in guiding treatment. There is little reason to believe, for instance, that different educational strategies are appropriate for children with substandard IQs compared to children with average or above-average IQs (Resnick, 1979). In sum, although IQ tests have an important role to play in assessment, they are by no means sufficient in evaluating cognitive abilities.

Language Abilities.

The high frequency of linguistic deficiencies among children with learning problems and brain injuries justifies a more detailed assessment in this area than can be obtained from IQ testing alone (Fletcher & Levin, 1988; Torgesen, 1975). Disabilities in language or learning have been associated with weaknesses in language comprehension, naming and expressive speech, and phonology and sound sequencing (Fletcher, 1981). Tests that can be used to tap these skills include the following: Auditory Analysis Test (Rosner & Simon, 1971), Peabody Picture Vocabulary Test (Dunn & Dunn, 1981), Token Test for Children (DiSimoni, 1978), Expressive One-Word Picture Vocabulary Test (Gardner, 1979),

Word Fluency Test (Gaddes & Crockett, 1975), Pseudoword Repetition Test (Taylor, Lean, & Schwartz, 1989), and Sentence Repetition Test (Golick, 1977). Standardized tests may also be drawn from existing language batteries for children, such as the Sequenced Inventory of Communication Development (Hedrick, Prather, & Tobin, 1975), the Illinois Test of Psycholinguistic Abilities (ITPA) (Kirk, McCarthy, & Kirk, 1968), and the Comprehensive Evaluation of Language Functions Diagnostic Battery (CELF) (Semel & Wiig, 1980). Aphasia batteries such as the Neurosensory Center Comprehensive Examination of Aphasia (Gaddes & Crockett, 1975) merit special consideration in evaluating the brain-injured aphasic child.

As with measures of intelligence, one shortcoming of many language tests is their sensitivity to more than one component skill deficit. Tests of syntactic comprehension of spoken sentences, for instance, often require the child to make distinctions based on word meaning. If the child's semantic knowledge is limited, performance deficits should not be interpreted as evidence of a problem in the area of syntax per se (Fletcher, 1981). Other cognitive deficiencies may also interfere with a child's performance in language testing, such as when an attention deficit results in poor memory for digit sequences or sentences. Overall, however, available language measures are comprehensive and fairly well standardized. Many of them tap isolated language competencies. In view of the fact that language skills are fundamental aspects of academic and social development, testing in this area has special priority in this assessment process.

Visual-spatial and Constructional Performance.

Tests of visual-spatial and constructional skills make up a second grouping of neuropsychological functions. Deficits in this area are measured by procedures that require active manipulation and graphic skills or by procedures that are relatively "motor free." The Recognition-Discrimination Test (Satz & Fletcher, 1982) and the Line Orientation Test (Lindgren & Benton, 1980) illustrate the latter type of task. Tests involving an active motor component inlcude the Bender-Gestalt (Koppitz, 1964), Benton's Three-Dimensional Block Construction Test (Benton et al., 1983), and the Beery Test of Visual-Motor Integration (Beery, 1982).

Longitudinal research by Satz and Fletcher (1982) documents the importance of visual-spatial and constructional abilities in predicting reading failure. Assessment of visual-motor skills has been found to be of additional value in isolating subtypes of learning disabilities (Mattis, French, & Rapin, 1975; Rourke, 1978), and in identifying children with actual brain disorders (Rutter, 1981; Soare & Raimondi, 1977). The fact that WISC-R Performance IQ tends to be more affected than Verbal IQ by early brain injury raises the possibility that brain-damaged children may have special vulnerabilities in this area of function (Taylor, 1984a).

As in the case of other tests of basic skills, a major shortcoming of visual-perceptual tasks is that they are likely to engage multiple competencies (Torgesen, 1975). Factor analytic research shows that measures of visual-spatial and constructional skill load on a common factor and that this factor is distinct from other (e.g., verbal) factors (Fletcher & Satz, 1980). Nevertheless, it is not yet clear whether the value of these tasks stems from their spatial-constructional components or from the fact that they place heavy demands on attention, organization, or other aspects of information processing.

Somatosensory and Motor Functions.

Somatosensory and motor tests are among the more traditional of the neuropsychologist's tools, at least in the sense that these tasks represent extensions of the standard neurological examination. Somatosensory functions include finger localization, stereognosis, graphesthesia, sensory extinction, and right-left orientation. Procedures for measuring these functions are described by Benton et al. (1983) and by Reitan and Davison (1974). Useful test batteries for motor skills assessment include the Klove-Matthews Motor Steadiness Battery (Reitan & Davison, 1974) and the Bruininks-Oseretsky Test of Motor Proficiency (Bruininks, 1978). Tests of fine motor coordination, ocular-motor control, motor overflow, steadiness, and alternating movements that make up assessments of "soft" neurological status may also be employed in evaluating motor functions (Taylor, 1987b). The special value of sensorimotor procedures is their sensitivity to neurological disorders and utility in predicting eventual learning failure in young children (Fletcher & Satz, 1980; Rourke & Orr, 1977). Sensorimotor performance may also be useful in distinguishing subtypes of disabled learners (Fisk & Rourke, 1979; Petrauskas & Rourke, 1979), and as a marker of problems that are brain related (Taylor, 1987b).

A major limitation of testing in this area is the relatively low ceiling of performance on somatosensory and motor tests. Many children with developmental handicaps reach ceiling levels by early to mid-childhood (Fletcher, Taylor, Satz, & Morris,

1982). One is also led to wonder, based on clinical experience with these tests, if problems in attention or motivation may be behind many instances of impaired performance. Moreover, one might question the relevance of test results to treatment decisions.

Attentional Resources.

Clinical impressions suggest that the ability to pay attention and work efficiently is important to everyday functioning and at least partially independent of other higher-order cognitive skills. Because attention deficits come in many different forms and may have multiple etiologies, careful review of this area of functioning is essential. Questions to parents and teachers regarding impulsivity, task persistence, concentration, and compliance with rules and directions provide the basis for making the diagnosis of attention deficit-hyperactivity disorder (Barkley, 1981). Direct observation is also useful. In some cases, attentional difficulties are key constituents of the learning or behavioral disorders. By observing how well children are able to sustain interest in tasks, plan responses, self-correct, and avoid careless mistakes, impressions can be formed as to the adequacy of the child's attentional resources relative to normative expectations. The speed, accuracy, and automaticity with which the child carries out familiar or cognitively unchallenging tasks is also relevant to assessment of attentional skills. More formal assessment involves administration of tests of vigilance, selective attention/psychomotor efficiency, attention shifting, and concentration/freedom from distractibility. The following test procedures are among those that tap the various aspects of the attention construct: Continuous Performance Test (Lindgren & Lyons, 1984); The Children's Checking Test (Keogh & Margolis, 1976); Underlining Test (Rourke & Gates, 1980); Contingency Naming Test (Taylor, Albo, Phebus, Sachs, & Bierl, 1987); arithmetic, digit span, and coding subtests of the WISC-R (Kaufman, 1979b). A wide variety of other procedures is described in Cooley and Morris (in press).

The primary drawback of assessment is the lack of clarity surrounding this construct (Cooley & Morris, in press). Paying attention is variably defined in terms of the capacity to resist distraction, selectively attend to certain aspects of the stimulus array, maintain vigilance, or engage in goal-directed behavior (Hale & Lewis, 1979). It is difficult to know which of these several mental processes is most deserving of assessment. A further issue is how to distinguish attentional deficits from lack of interest or ability. Despite the intricacies of assessment in this area, attentional weaknesses are common in children with learning and behavior disorders. Evaluation of the child's ability to pay attention is fundamental to the diagnosis of attention deficit-hyperactivity disorder (Barkley, 1981). There is also evidence that learning-disabled children pay attention less well than normal learners and that this difference cannot be accounted for by either IQ or outright hyperactivity (Schatz, 1988).

Memory and Learning Skills.

Memory is another area of function that has a pervasive influence on test performances and that defies unitary definition. The information processing concepts of sensory registration, working memory, long-term memory, and information transfer are useful in considering ways in which to decompose memory skills in child neuropsychological assessment. Adult neuropsychological studies support similar decompositions and argue for a distinction between verbal and nonverbal memory systems (Shallice, 1979). Tests available for memory assessment in children include the Benton Visual Retention Test (Benton, 1974) and the Verbal and Nonverbal Selective Reminding Tests (Fletcher, 1985). Fletcher (1985b) found the latter two techniques helpful in differentiating types of learning problems. The advantages of the selective reminding procedures include their provision of separate measures of storage and retrieval abilities and sensitivity to neurological impairment (Levin et al., 1982). Other measures of the ability to acquire new information have been found helpful in the assessment of children with mild mental deficiency (e.g., Budoff, 1964). Measures of serial memory ability (Torgesen, 1978; Torgesen, Rashotte, Greenstein, Houck, & Portes, 1987) and of efficiency of memory retrieval (Denckla & Rudel, 1976) also deserve consideration.

As in the case of so many other areas of assessment, weaknesses on a memory task may be difficult to ascribe to a memory dysfunction per se. Tests of immediate memory and the ability to retrieve information rapidly from long-term storage may be confounded with the child's attentional abilities. The fact that the digit span subtest of the WISC-R loads on the Freedom from Distractibility factor (Kaufman, 1979b) is consistent with this possibility. Performance on memory tasks is additionally determined by the child's ability to employ cognitive strategies such as rehearsal (Torgesen, 1980). Despite these confounds, the efficiency with which a child is able to remember and acquire new information is an important predictor of school performance (Gettinger & White, 1979). Memory tests are likely therefore to figure more prominently in the assessment process than they have in the past (Resnick, 1979).

Problem Solving and Abstract Reasoning.

A final cognitive grouping pertains to the child's ability to make use of component skills in solving more complex problems. This area of ability, while not easily described in terms of a single mental operation, has been referred to by Brown (1975) as *metacognition.* The construct of *executive functions* (Kistner & Torgesen, 1987; Shallice, 1981) refers to a similar set of mental operations. The WISC-R Block Design subtest, the Halstead Category Test, and the Tactual Performance Test exemplify procedures that tap this aspect of cognition (Rourke, 1980). Richman and Lindgren (1981) isolated a similar ability dimension, referred to as *abstract reasoning,* and found that it differentiated subgroups of children with verbal deficiencies. According to the latter investigators, tests loading on abstract reasoning include the similarities and block design subtests of the WISC-R, and the picture identification, picture association, and block patterns subtests of the Hiskey-Nebraska Test of Learning Aptitude (Hiskey, 1966). Rourke, Fisk, and Strang (1986), Kaufman (1979a), and Sternberg (1984) also favor assessment of the child's ability to reason abstractly and to solve novel problems. Subtests of the K-ABC (Kaufman & Kaufman, 1983) and Woodcock-Johnson Psychoeducational Battery (Woodcock & Johnson, 1977) were designed in part to fill this void. The Wisconsin Card Sorting Test (Chelune & Thompson, 1987) may be a useful device for assessing these types of skills. Other procedures can be found in Passler, Isaac, and Hynd (1985) and Welse and Pennington (1988).

A major disadvantage of testing in this area is that a variety of component skills contribute to a child's ability to solve a novel problem. Inefficiency in problem solving may thus reflect component skill deficits rather than poor strategizing or mental disorganization. The potential influence of motivational factors on the child's willingness to acquire or apply higher-order mental processes represents a further confounding influence (Douglas, 1980; Kistner & Torgesen, 1987). Application to children of highly circumscribed problem-solving tasks (e.g., Sternberg, 1977), along with attempts to decipher the impact of moderator variables on task performance, hold promise for improving assessment of problem-solving capacities. Although presently available tests of problem-solving skills may be less than satisfactory, clinical experience suggests that both formal and informal evaluation of these capacities greatly enhances the assessment process.

Evaluation of Psychosocial Functioning

In addition to their cognitive deficits, children referred for neuropsychological assessment tend to have a number of behavioral, social, and motivational liabilities. Many of these children, particularly those with learning problems, are poorly oriented to academic tasks. They lack initiative and perseverance. Their schoolwork is disorganized and frequently incomplete. They tend to be more disruptive and noncompliant than their peers; and they are prone to other behavioral disturbances such as depression, acting-out behaviors, and somatization. They are often poorly motivated, low in self-esteem, and socially imperceptive, and unadaptive (Rourke, Fisk, & Strang, 1986; Taylor, 1988a). In some instances, these psychosocial characteristics have a negative impact on scores obtained in formal testing. Awareness of psychosocial issues is thus mandatory, not only if one is to appreciate all of the variables that contribute to the child's presenting problems, but also in interpreting the results of other portions of the assessment.

Interviews with parents and teachers is one way to survey these aspects of behavior. The Vineland Adaptive Behavior Scales mentioned earlier offer one formal means for assessing social skills. Other methods include parent-teacher rating scales, classroom observations, interview of the child, and self-ratings of attitudes, attributions, or personality style. The following are illustrative: Conners Parent and Teacher Rating Scales (Barkley, 1981), Child Behavior Checklist (Achenbach & Edelbrock, 1986), Perceived Competence Scale (Harter, 1982), Personality Inventory for Children (Wirt, Lachar, Klinedinst, & Seat, 1977).

Difficulties in behavioral, personality, or adaptive functioning tend to exacerbate learning problems, while strengths in these areas help children compensate for cognitive limitations. Still, the relationship between psychosocial and learning problems is far from straightforward. The behavioral or motivational difficulties of some children seem to stem from the frustration associated with consistent failure to meet parent or teacher expectations. In other cases, such failure may have been shortlived had it not been for the child's psychosocial vulnerabilities. For still other children, psychosocial and cognitive difficulties may reflect a common underlying mechanism (Porter &

Rourke, 1985). Whatever the relationship, effective treatment requires that all of the child's problems be attended to.

Exploration of Potential Environmental Influences

To complicate the picture even more, there are many environmental influences on a child's academic and behavioral development. Relevant factors include cultural values, language background, social and educational opportunities, parent attitudes, and the extent to which parent and teacher expectations of the child match the child's capabilities (Keogh, Major, Omori, Gandara, & Reid, 1980; Rutter, 1978). It is also important to identify stress within the family. Family stress may originate from financial or health crises, from marriage difficulties or other interpersonal problems between family members, or from the sheer burden that the child's problem imposes on the family. Spouses may have different opinions as to why problems exist or what to do about them. One parent may blame the child for being unmotivated, while the other parent is overprotective or defensive. Ineffective behavior management—sometimes related to family dynamics—is another common source of stress. If enduring, poor management of the child poses risks for prolonged social maladjustment and academic underachievement (Patterson, 1986).

In cases of traumatic injury, family disruptions may result from resentment concerning the accident, from fear of loss of the child, or from the process of adjustment to the child's needs or changed mental capacities. This type of stress can have a destabilizing effect on family systems, with changed roles and expectations of family members and difficulties in maintaining preexisting family activities. Failure of family members to maintain expectations of the child and to enforce limits may also have negative repercussions (see Ylvisaker, 1985).

Although the best single source of information on environmental variables is the parent interview, more formal measures also deserve consideration. The latter include standardized assessments of life events (Herzog, Linder, & Samaha, 1981); family environment (Sines, 1983); and parents' attitudes, values, and child-rearing practices (Moos & Moos, 1981; Roberts, Block, & Block, 1984).

Review of Evidence for Biological Relatedness

Information regarding neurological and medical evaluations, family history of learning or behavioral problems, and other direct and indirect indications of the biological relatedness of the child's problems should always be gathered as part of the assessment process. Neuropsychological and medical examinations are frequently negative and noncontributory for children with learning and behavior problems, mental retardation, and attention deficit disorders. For example, EEGs and CT scans are rarely abnormal in disabled learners and should be performed only if neuropsychological evaluations or behavioral reports suggest some pathognomic sign of neurological dysfunction. In the more typical cases, biological markers such as minor physical anomalies, developmental delays, pre- and perinatal complications, and family histories of similar problems provide the primary basis for establishing the biological relatedness of the child's problems. Other relevant biological variables include the presence of chronic illnesses such as diabetes and asthma, hearing and visual impairments, and medication side effects. Each of these conditions increases the likelihood of learning or behavioral problems, either by virtue of the neurological consequences of these conditions, or via an increase in the stress or fatigue experienced by the child.

At the same time, it is essential that the neuropsychologist be aware of the signs of actual brain disease and to refer to a pediatric neurologist or other appropriate medical specialist when appropriate. Signs that would indicate referral include any seizure-like behavior or rapid change in mentation that would suggest a behavioral regression. Physical symptoms such as headaches, dizziness, and vomiting also signal referral or consultation. In cases of definitive brain disease or insult, the child's performance should be reviewed in light of findings from neurological and radiological evaluations. Initial medical findings and the post-traumatic course following a head injury, for example, may help to explain the severity of the child's residual deficits (Fletcher & Levin, 1988). Considerable intracranial swelling induced by delays in treatment increases the probability of diffuse insult (Levin, Benton, & Grossman, 1982). Similarly, the presence of any focal injuries on CT scan (e.g., subdural hematoma) may be related to the child's test performances. While most tumors in children are deep in the base of the brain, influences on cortical functions can occur through growth of the tumor or pressure on other brain areas. For child neuropsychologists who work with neurologically disordered patient groups, an awareness of the pathophysiology of these disorders and their course is essential. Knowledge of the child's specific disorder is of assistance in monitoring the patient and in planning rehabilitation.

Neuropsychological evaluation of children in most

respects parallels adult neuropsychological assessment. In both instances, the clinician begins with a thorough description and history of the presenting problems, a review of all available information on neurological status, and a survey of any other concerns and of environmental expectations (Lezak, 1983). The results of cognitive testing are interpreted in light of background information, and this information is useful in forming impressions regarding the bases of the presenting complaints, in monitoring progress, and in making treatment recommendations.

The major difference between adult and child assessment is that many children referred for neuropsychological examination do not have definitive brain disease (Benton, 1973). Investigation of brain-behavior relationships is therefore more problematic. Furthermore, even in cases where brain disease has been established, the damage is usually more diffuse and less easily localized in children than it is in adults. Distinctive clinical syndromes so typical of brain-damaged adults (e.g., a particular type of aphasia or a selective visual-constructional deficit) are rarely seen in children. Another problem specific to neuropsychological evaluation of children is the unavailability of estimates of premorbid abilities. Children's cognitive and learning skills are constantly changing, and learning problems will themselves compromise future acquisition of these skills (Dennis, 1983). These several factors make it more difficult to isolate biological influences on children's skills.

Interpretation and Management of the Problems

Following completion of testing and collection of information pertaining to each of the variable sets depicted in Figure 11.1, the clinician can begin to analyze factors that contribute to the child's problems and form impressions regarding the child's needs. The interpretative, or post-assessment, interview with parents is the first occasion on which these impressions are shared with others. We have found it helpful to begin these sessions with a general summary of our impressions of the child and his or her problems. This presentation allows the clinician to confirm or reformulate the parents' own impression of their child, and to note strengths and weaknesses (psychosocial as well as cognitive) that have been brought to light by the testing. Environmental and biological factors that may be contributing to the child's problems are also reviewed at this time. The purpose of this initial portion of the interpretative interview is to convey hypotheses regarding the origin of the child's problems. Mention of cognitive or psychosocial weaknesses is accompanied by credible explanations of their biological and environmental antecedents. Care is taken to answer parents' presenting questions as directly and honestly as possible. While stressing that skill deficits make children vulnerable to certain problems, we encourage attention to the multiple determinants of skill development and to the fact that children can usually be helped to cope with their deficits.

Because questions pertaining to intervention universally arise following discussion of contributing factors, treatment recommendations are discussed next. Problems that might be anticipated in the future are also shared in order to foster early identification and to help parents realize the need for continued monitoring. Parents are informed that future development is difficult to predict and the best way of helping the child is providing appropriate assistance with current problems. In cases where issues are complex and multifaceted, it is occasionally necessary to assign a priority to some issues and to leave others for later visits. Throughout the family interview, feedback from the child's caregivers helps to establish how much and what type of information the family is ready to absorb. At the end of the interview, followup arrangements are made in cases where monitoring of the child's progress is necessary or where actual treatment by the neuropsychologist has been initiated.

Following the interview, the neuropsychologist may need to make referrals to other specialists or to communicate directly with referral sources. A written report is then prepared to summarize the neuropsychologist's findings and impressions. Recommendations are an important part of the written report. To be profitable for those working with the child, recommendations should include realistic suggestions as to the kinds of educational programs that are likely to benefit the child, appropriate rehabilitational procedures, and behavioral management strategies. Recommendations must reflect an awareness of available school programs and community resources and must address all aspects of the child's problem (Taylor, 1989). Through contacts with teachers, counselors, and other professionals, as well as treatment-oriented followup visits with the neuropsychologist, assessment becomes a basis for action on the child's behalf.

Case Illustrations

The following case summaries demonstrate the types of problems for which children are referred, the basic elements of the assessment, and the issues which the examiner might be expected to address. Due to limitations in space, summaries are restricted to an outline of the referral questions, assessment techniques, and case formulation.

Case #1: Severe Head Injury

Referral Information. The first case is that of a 14-year-old white male who received a severe head injury as the result of a high-speed motor vehicle accident. The child was initially referred during his hospital stay and was subsequently followed at periodic intervals on an annual basis until five years post injury. The initial referral question concerned the extent to which various cognitive skills were impaired by the head injury and the child's capacity for returning to independent functioning. Subsequent referrals were made in an effort to try to clarify the basis for school-related difficulties.

Assessment Techniques. A battery of tests derived from research on various aspects of head injury was employed (Fletcher, 1988). This battery included the following procedures: Grooved Pegboard, Beery Test of Visual-Motor Integration, Recognition-Discrimination, Stereognosis, Word Fluency, Visual Naming, Peabody Picture Vocabulary Test-Revised, Token Test, Verbal Selective Reminding, Non-Verbal Selective Reminding, Continuous Performance, Wide Range Achievement Test-Revised, Peabody Individual Achievement Test, Child History For Child Behavior Checklist, Conners Parent Questionnaire, and Vineland Adaptive Behavior Scales.

Longitudinal Summary of Results. The evaluation stems from the model outlined in Figure 11.1. In terms of cognitive functions (basic competencies), this child demonstrated generally impaired cognitive abilities at the base-line assessment. In addition to a mild aphasia and hemiparesis on the right side, the child had severely impaired memory and attentional skills. Impairments in language and motor functions were consistent with right hemiparesis and aphasia. Other cognitive functions were reduced as a consequence of attentional problems.

By six months, these deficiencies had begun to resolve. Outright aphasia and hemiparesis were no longer present. Sensory functions were intact. However, there was mild residual motor incoordination in the dominant right hand, and mild naming and word retrieval deficiencies. Severe memory and attentional problems persisted, but these had improved since the previous evaluation. Tests of academic achievement showed average development of word recognition and spelling skills but extremely poor computational arith-

metic. This contrasted with performance on previously administered achievement tests. For example, the Stanford Achievement Tests had been administered several weeks prior to the injury; the composite battery was at the 75th percentile. The patient scored poorly relative to premorbid estimates in all subdomains of the Vineland Adaptive Behavior Scales (Communication, Daily Living, and Socialization). The child also attained higher scores on the Externalizing scales of the Child Behavior Checklist relative to initial assessment.

Considerable recovery was apparent at one year post insult. Overall performance continued to be marked by impulsive, inattentive behavior with poor planning and organizational skills. Memory for spatial material was at age-appropriate levels, but there were persistent deficiencies in encoding and retrieving verbal information. Language functions were generally intact except for mild difficulties in word retrieval. Motor and perceptual-motor skills were now intact. Word recognition and spelling abilities had continued to improve, but arithmetic computations remained well below age expectations. Parent reports on the Child Behavior Checklist, in interview, and on the Vineland Adaptive Behavior Scales revealed continued difficulties in concentration, fatigue, feelings of inferiority, poor social judgment, and inadequate school achievement.

Difficulties with verbal memory and computational arithmetic persisted at three and five years post-injury assessments. Attentional skills remained poor. Problems with social judgment, planning, and organization became predominant features of this child's adaptational style. The Vineland Adaptive Behavior Scales composite score showed a constant decline over time.

Psychosocial factors included an accelerated school placement prior to the accident. When the child was able to return to school, both he and his family insisted on returning to this previous and now inappropriate program. The child's adaptation to the head injury was characterized by significant attempts to deny the consequences of the injury, with resulting feelings of failure and poor self-esteem. At the one- and two-year followup intervals, he was clearly depressed about his overall functioning. Although the family had the resources to provide a variety of services, the child was not moved from the accelerated placement until more than one year after the injury. He was then placed in a lower track of a tiered academic system.

Although the child was initially in an inpatient rehabilitation program, few services were provided on discharge despite recommendations to the contrary.

The child did receive some speech therapy on an inconsistent basis. He also continued to receive tutoring after the one year followup, but again inconsistently. Legal action on the child's behalf resulted in a large settlement. By age 18, however, he had dropped out of school and the funds were rapidly depleted. The patient is currently receiving counseling. Plans are to continue in counseling and to attempt college in a program adapted to the needs of persons with learning handicaps.

An assessment of biological factors centers around the head injury. On initial neurological examination, there was an absence of eye opening. This and other oculovestibular signs were consistent with a significant insult to the brain stem. The child did not verbalize and application of painful stimulation produced withdrawal of the extremities. This led to scores of less than 8 on both initial and 24-hour administrations of the Glasgow Coma Scale. Spontaneous eye opening and vocalization were initially observed about eight days post injury. The child was unable to follow commands until about 15 days after the injury. Neural imaging studies on the day of admission were basically within normal limits. A followup scan 12 days post injury was consistent with moderate ventricular atrophy, with most prominent enlargement of the right lateral ventricle. Cerebral atrophy and enlargement of the right lateral ventricle were also apparent on a magnetic resonance scan three years post insult.

Environmental factors included the child's high level of premorbid functioning, child and family denial of the significance of the injury, and their intolerance of attempts to adjust the child's academic program to his ability to function. The family had considerable difficulty accepting the changes in the child's ability to function and was not able to place limits on his behavior when this was necessary. Several attempts at counseling met with denial by the family and with abrogation of any responsibility to advocate for the child's treatment.

Formulation. Problems associated with the effects of the severe head injury included persistent memory and attentional deficits and diminution of the child's capacity for judgment, planning, and insight. Extensive attempts were made to remediate the deficiencies. These entailed various inpatient and outpatient forms of rehabilitation during the first year, and additional supplemental services (counseling) throughout the protracted course of recovery. However, the inability of the child and family to accept the changes brought about by the injury made them relatively unresponsive to recommendations for rehabilitation. This attitude

resulted in a failure to establish appropriate guardianship, and the patient eventually squandered a settlement that could have been used to facilitate his adjustment to adult life.

Case #2: A Learning Disabled Child

Referral Information and Assessment Techniques. This 7½-year-old white female was referred for neuropsychological evaluation of school problems. Assessment procedures paralleled those outlined in Fletcher (1988) and Taylor (1988a). Test instruments included the Grooved Pegboard, Beery Test of Visual-Motor Integration, Judgment of Line Orientation, Word Fluency, Auditory Analysis, Token, Verbal Selective Reminding, Non-Verbal Selective Reminding, Underlining, Woodcock-Johnson Psycho-Educational Test Battery, Child History Form, Child Behavior Checklist, Conners Parent Questionnaire, Children's Apperception Test, and a clinical interview with the parents and child.

Test Results and Interpretations. Assessment of academic achievement revealed that the child had primary impairments in reading and spelling. Her most significant difficulty was in phonics, as reflected in her inability to pronounce nonsense words. Reading vocabulary and written spelling skills were poorly developed despite late second-grade placement. An examination of reading and spelling errors also revealed extremely limited grasp of phonics. Spelling errors were not phonetically constrained. Reading comprehension was also underdeveloped, most probably as a consequence of her deficit in phonics. In contrast, she performed at age-appropriate levels on tests of computational arithmetic.

An assessment of cognitive skills revealed intact motor and perceptual abilities. The child performed well on tests of fine motor coordination, visual-motor and perceptual discrimination skills, and somatosensory abilities. Her difficulties were confined to the language area. Problems were most apparent when she was asked to break down aurally presented words into constituent sounds (phonological segmentation). She was also deficient in generating words within phonologically-based categories. Semantic fluency and language comprehension were within normal limits. Memory for verbal material was less adequate than spatial memory, and attentional skills were also mildly impaired.

Evaluation of psychosocial functioning revealed a child who was somewhat frustrated with her school performance and who had low self-esteem. According to her parents, she was also impulsive and inattentive. Her family was concerned about her, was motivated to provide for her needs, and had good financial resources. An additional environmental advantage was that the child attended a school district with excellent special educational programs.

Biological factors were largely noncontributory. The child had been recently examined by her pediatrician and was in good health. Family history was positive for a maternal grandfather who had school-related problems and a maternal uncle with a reading disorder. There were no neurological abnormalities.

Recommendations were made for special educational placement in the public schools. A remedial reading program was advised which capitalized on the child's well-developed visual memory and perceptual skills. This approach emphasizes visual recognition of morphophonemic units (Rourke et al., 1986). Recognition of these units is drilled and repeated until identification is automatic. The units are then used as building blocks for assembling and disassembling words. Additional emphasis was placed on visual recognition of sight words and various strategies for improving reading comprehension. The family's motivation and resources also permitted referral for individual tutoring in reading to complement the school's special educational program. Discovery of attentional deficiencies prompted behavioral suggestions for improving the structure and consistency of school and home environments. Suggestions included a new classroom placement with a lower student-to-teacher ratio. The possibility of a future referral for medication evaluation (stimulants) was discussed, in case attentional problems became more problematic; counseling was also brought up as a potential treatment strategy if the child's self-esteem did not improve. A followup appointment was scheduled for six months, at which time the plan was to evaluate the child's progress in reading, her attentional abilities, and her overall adjustment.

Formulation. This second case illustrates a common form of reading disability. The disorder was characterized by impairments in reading and spelling and a corresponding deficit in phonological processing skills. Arithmetic computation and spatial abilities were intact. Psychosocial problems were most likely secondary to the child's underachievement. Environmental factors were generally positive, with good school and family resources. Biological factors were limited to a positive family history of learning difficulties. Treatment emphasized the child's strengths, attentional weaknesses, and low self-esteem.

SUMMARY

One of the primary aims of this chapter is to debunk the idea that brain-behavior relationships are the sine qua non of child neuropsychological assessment. Discovery of brain correlates for learning and behavioral disabilities in children is a laudable goal. The problem facing the examiner is that many children referred for neuropsychological assessments either have no demonstrable brain disease (as yet discovered), or they have neurological disorders for which the pathophysiology is ill-defined. Studies of the behavioral implications of discrete or well-delineated brain lesions in children are few and far between. Consequently, there is no established body of brain-behavior correlations from which to draw in making inferences regarding brain status from neuropsychological test findings.

A second and related problem is that the overemphasis on brain-behavior relationships encourages direct extrapolation of adult findings to children. Because children's abilities are structured differently from those of adults, there is every reason to believe that brain-behavior relationships will vary from those observed in adults. Moreover, we would expect these relationships to change with age.

The third major limitation of simplistic brain-behavior models is their promotion of the idea that some behaviors, notably those assessed by neuropsychological tests, are free from social and enviromental influences. While we would agree that some skills and behaviors may be more sensitive to variation in neurologic status than others, it seems reasonable to suppose that all human behavior is to some extent dependent on learning history and social-environmental conditions. In order to evaluate better the influences of CNS variables, it is therefore imperative to consider these influences within the assessment process (Fletcher & Taylor, 1984; Taylor, 1988a).

Our contention is that child neuropsychological assessment must place increasing emphasis on the study of the child's behavior and cognitive development. In support of this contention, we have described a biobehavioral systems framework for child neuropsychological assessment. The latter approach recognizes the need to evaluate behavior as a first step toward linking behavioral and developmental disorders to biological factors. Finer-grained analysis of the child's problems and their developmental and cognitive underpinnings will lead to more appropriate management of the child, and to a better understanding of the significance of indirect biological "markers," such as family history, minor physical anomalies, and pre- and perinatal complications. Improved techniques for behavioral and cognitive analyses of developmental disorders will also allow us to take advantage of advances in brain imaging and neurochemical techniques. By focusing on disorders that are likely to have some biological basis, and on their cognitive and psychosocial correlates, one may hope that the biobehavioral systems will serve as a catalyst for these discoveries.

Another objective of the biobehavioral systems model is to promote an openness to other types of clinical assessment. The methods and concepts of clinical psychology, educational psychology, and speech pathology are frequently employed in comprehensive neuropsychological evaluations. Existing tests of academic achievement, for example, are well standardized and can help to delineate the nature of the child's learning problems. Published tests of language and other basic skills may also be incorporated into the assessment process, along with standardized ratings of adaptive behavior and emotional adjustment. The importance of employing tests that satisfy standard psychometric criteria for reliability and validity cannot be underestimated. This is especially the case in neuropsychology, where these considerations have often been overlooked (Reynolds, 1982).

At the same time the child neuropsychologist cannot afford to ignore more experimental procedures from the fields of cognitive psychology, developmental psychology, or adult neuropsychology. The Buschke (1974) *selective reminding* method for assessing memory functions provides an example of such a procedure. Although originally developed for use with adults and normal children, Levin et al. (1982) and Fletcher (1985b) have found this method useful in assessing children with histories of head injury, leukemia, and learning disabilities. Experimental techniques for examining phonological processing, short-term memory, attention, and problem solving hold similar promise for child neuropsychological assessment (Sternberg, 1984; Taylor, Lean, & Schwartz, 1987; Torgesen, Rashotte, Greenstein, Houck, & Portes, 1987).

Because test findings must always be interpreted with references to the child's level of development, models of normal cognitive growth are also relevant to test selection (Dennis, 1980; Lovett, 1984). These models encourage comprehensiveness and at the same time provide hints as to how to study, or in Shallice's (1979) term *fractionalize,* component cognitive functions. Regardless of the exact procedures employed in child neuropsychological testing, the focus of assessment should be on the analysis of ability structures rather than on the test per se. The tests employed are less important than (a) the constructs being assessed; (b) the utility of these constructs in establishing etiology, correlates, course, and preferred treatment; and (c) the significance of performance deficits in relation to the child's learning and behavioral problems—that is, whether the deficiency leads directly or indirectly to the disability, merely moderates the extent of the disability, or is perhaps better conceived of as a consequence of that disability (Taylor, 1988b).

Paralleling this emphasis on abilities and on the multitude of factors influencing behavior, the biobehavioral systems model has implications for the role of neuropsychologists in assessing childhood problems. In our view, the neuropsychologist's role entails careful examination of the nature of the developmental disability and of the factors contributing to that disability. The emphasis of the biobehavioral systems approach is on a broad assessment of factors potentially contributing to the manifest disability in order to provide a complete formulation of the child's problems. This formulation includes judgments as to the likelihood of biological antecedents, but it also involves consideration of other relevant factors and suggestions as to how the problem should be managed. Fulfillment of this more comprehensive role requires a broad range of assessment skills, an understanding of social and cultural influences on behavior, and an ability to generate effective treatment plans. The need for general clinical skills does not detract from the uniqueness of the child neuropsychologist among other clinicians. Above and beyond this core clinical knowledge, the child neuropsychologist must have a working knowledge of the neurosciences and of behavioral neurology, an understanding of psychological methods from nonclinical areas such as developmental and cognitive psychology, and a thorough acquaintance with the learning and behavior disabilities for which children are referred. With this multidisciplinary perspective, the neuropsychologist is better prepared to appreciate the complexities of child development.

REFERENCES

Achenbach, T. M. (1979). The Child Behavior Profile: An empirically based system for assessing children's behavioral problems and competencies. *International Journal of Mental Health, 7,* 24–42.

Achenbach, T., & Edelbrock, C. (1986). *Manual for the Child Behavior Checklist and Revised Child Behavior Profile.* Burlington, VT: University of Vermont, Department of Psychiatry.

Ackerman, P. T., Dykman, R. A., & Peters, J. E. (1977). Learning-disabled boys as adolescents: Cognitive factors and achievement. *Journal of the American Academy of Child Psychiatry, 16,* 296–313.

Bale, P. (1981). Pre-natal factors and backwardness in reading. *Educational Research, 23,* 134–143.

Barkley, R. A. (1981). *Hyperactive children: A handbook for diagnosis and treatment.* New York: Guilford Press.

Baumeister, A., & MacLean, W. (1979). Brain damage and mental retardation. In N. R. Ellis (Ed.), *Handbook of mental deficiency, psychological theory and research* (2nd ed.). Hillsdale, NJ: Erlbaum.

Beery, K. E. (1982). *Revised administration, scoring and teaching manual for the Developmental Test of Visual-Motor Integration.* Cleveland: Modern Curriculum Press.

Benton, A. L. (1962). Behavioral indices of brain injury in school children. *Child Development, 33,* 199–208.

Benton, A. L. (1964). Contributions to aphasia before Broca. *Cortex, 1,* 314–327.

Benton, A. L. (1973). Minimal brain dysfunction from the neuropsychological point of view. In F. F. de la Cruz, B. H. Fox, & R. H. Roberts (Eds.), *Minimal brain dysfunction.* New York: New York Academy of Sciences.

Benton, A. L. (1974). *Revised Visual Retention Test: Clinical and experimental application* (4th ed.). New York: Psychological Corporation.

Benton, A. L. (1975). Developmental dyslexia: Neurological aspects. In W. J. Friedlander (Ed.), *Advances in neurology.* New York: Raven Press.

Benton, A. L. (1978). Some conclusions about dyslexia. In A. L. Benton & D. Pearl (Eds.), *Dyslexia: An appraisal of current knowledge* (pp. 451–476). New York: Oxford University Press.

Benton, A. L., Hamsher, K. de S., Varney, N. R., & Spreen, O. (1983). *Contributions of neuropsychological assessment: A clinical manual.* New York: Oxford University Press.

Benton, A. L., & Pearl, D. (Eds.). (1978). *Dyslexia: An appraisal of current knowledge.* New York: Oxford University Press.

Birch, H. G. (1964). The problem of "brain damage" in children. In H. G. Birch (Ed.), *Brain damage in children: The biological and social aspects.* Baltimore: Williams & Wilkins.

Birch, H. G., Thomas, A., & Chess, S. (1964). Behavioral development in brain-damaged children: Three case studies. *Archives of General Psychiatry, 11,* 596–603.

Bortner, M., & Birch, H. G. (1970). Cognitive capacity and cognitive competence. *American Journal of Mental Deficiency. 74,* 735–744.

Brown, A. L. (1975). The development of memory, knowing, knowing about knowing, and knowing how to know. In H. W. Reese (Ed.), *Advances in child development and behavior* (Vol. 10). New York: Academic Press.

Brown, A. L., Bradford, J. O., Ferrara, R. A., & Campione, J. C. (1983). Learning, remembering, and understanding. In J. H. Flovell & E. E. Markman (Eds.), *Handbook of child psychology: Cognitive development* (4th ed., pp. 77–166). New York: John Wiley & Sons.

Brown, A. L., & Campione, J. C. (1986). Psychological theory and the study of learning disabilities. *American Psychologist, 14,* 1059–1068.

Brown, A. L., & French, L. A. (1979). The zone of potential development: Implications for intelligence testing in the year 2000. In R. J. Sternberg & D. K. Detterman (Eds.), *Human intelligence: Perspective on its theory and measurement.* Norwood, NJ: Ablex.

Bruininks, R. H. (1978). *Bruininks-Osteretsky Test of Motor Proficiency, examiner's manual.* Circle Pines, MN: American Guidance Service.

Budoff, M. (1964). "Learning potential" as an assessment approach to the adolescent mentally retarded. *Journal of Consulting Psychology, 28,* 433–439.

Buschke, H. (1974). Components of verbal learning in children: Analysis by selective reminding. *Journal of Experimental Child Psychology, 18,* 488–496.

Calfee, R. (1982). Cognitive models of reading: Implications for assessment and treatment of reading disability. In R. N. Malatesha & P. G. Aaron (Eds.), *Reading disorders: Varieties and treatments.* New York: Academic Press.

Chelune, G. J., & Thompson, L. L. (1987). Evaluation of the general sensitivity of the Wisconsin Card Sorting Test among younger and older children. *Developmental Neuropsychology, 3,* 81–89.

Clements, S. F. (1966). *Minimal brain dysfunction in children—terminology and identification* (NINDB Monograph No. 3). Washington, DC: U.S. Public Health Service.

Cooley, E., & Morris, R. (in press). Attention in children: A neuropsychologically-based model of assessment. *Developmental Neuropsychology.*

Cunningham, C. E., & Barkley, R. A. (1978). The

role of academic failure in hyperactive behavior. *Journal of Learning Disabilities, 11,* 15–21.

Dean, R. S. (1986). Neuropsychological aspects of psychiatric disorders. In J. E. Obrzut & G. W. Hynd (Eds.), *Child neuropsychology: Clinical practice* (Vol. 2, pp. 83–112). Orlando: Academic Press.

Denckla, M. B., & Rudel, R. (1976). Rapid "automotized" naming (R.A.N.): Dyslexia differentiated from other learning disabilities. *Neuropsychologia, 14,* 471–479.

Dennis, M. (1980). Language acquisition in a single hemisphere: Semantic organization. In D. Caplan (Ed.), *Biological studies of mental processes.* Cambridge: MIT Press.

Dennis, M. (1983). The developmentally dyslexic brain and the written language skills of children with one hemisphere. In U. Kirk (Ed.), *Neuropsychology of language, reading and spelling.* New York: Academic Press.

Dennis, M. (1985a). Intelligence after early brain injury: I. Predicting IQ scores from medical variables. *Journal of Clinical and Experimental Neuropsychology, 8,* 526–554.

Dennis, M. (1985b). Intelligence after early brain injury: II. IQ scores of children classified on the basis of medical history variables. *Journal of Clinical and Experimental Neuropsychology, 8,* 555–576.

Dennis, M., Fitz, C. R., Netley, C. T., Sugar, J., Harwood-Nash, D. C. G., Hendrick, E. B., Hoffman, H. J., & Humphreys, R. P. (1981). The intelligence of hydrocephalic children. *Archives of Neurology, 38,* 607–615.

DiSimoni, F. G. (1978). *The Token Test for Children.* Boston: Teaching Resources.

Doehring, D. G. (1976). Acquisition of rapid reading responses. *Monographs of the Society for Research in Child Development, 41,* 1–54.

Doehring, D. G. (1978). The tangled web of behavioral research on developmental dyslexia. In A. L. Benton & D. Pearl (Eds.), *Dyslexia: An appraisal of current knowledge.* New York: Oxford University Press.

Doehring, D. G., Trites, R. L., Patel, P. G., & Fiedorowicz, A. M. (1981). *Reading disabilities: The interaction of reading, language, and neuropsychological deficits.* New York: Academic Press.

Douglas, V. I. (1980). Higher mental processes in hyperactive children: Implications for training. In R. N. Knights & D. J. Bakker (Eds.), *Treatment of hyperactive and learning disordered children: Current research.* Baltimore: University Park Press.

Dunn, L. M., & Dunn, L. M. (1981). *Peabody Picture Vocabulary Test-Revised, Manual for forms L and M.* Circle Pines, MN: American Guidance Service.

Dunn, L. M., & Markwardt, F. C. (1970). *Peabody Individual Achievement Test manual.* Circle Pines, MN: American Guidance Service.

Dykman, R. A., Ackerman, P. T., Clements, S. D., & Peters, J. E. (1971). Specific learning disabilities: An attentional deficit syndrome. In H. R. Myklebust (Ed.), *Progress in learning disabilities* (Vol. 2). New York: Grune & Stratton.

Elliott, C., Murray, D. J., & Pearson, L. S. (1983). *The British Ability Scales.* Windsor, England: The NFER-Nelson Publishing Company.

Estes, W. K. (1981). Intelligence and learning. In M. P. Friedman, J. P. Das, & N. O'Connor (Eds.), *Intelligence and learning.* New York: Plenum Press.

Filskov, S. B., & Boll, T. J. (Eds.). (1986). *Handbook of clinical neuropsychology* (Vol. 2). New York: Wiley.

Fisk, J. L., & Rourke, B. P. (1979). Identification of subtypes of learning disabled children at three age levels: A neuropsychological, multivariate approach. *Journal of Clinical Neuropsychology, 1,* 29–310.

Fletcher, J. M. (1981). Linguistic factors in reading acquisition: Evidence for developmental changes. In F. Pirozollo & M. C. Wittrock (Eds.), *Neuropsychological and cognitive processes in reading.* New York: Academic Press.

Fletcher, J. M. (1985a). External validation of learning disability typologies. In B. P. Rourke (Ed.), *Neuropsychology of learning disabilities: Essentials of subtype analysis* (pp. 187–210). New York: Guilford Press.

Fletcher, J. M. (1985b). Memory for verbal and nonverbal stimuli in learning disability subgroups: Analysis by selective reminding. *Journal of Experimental Child Psychology, 40,* 224–259.

Fletcher, J. M. (1988). Brain-injured children. In E. J. Mash & L. G. Terdal (Eds.), *Behavioral assessment of childhood disorders* (Vol. 2, pp. 451–489). New York: Guilford Press.

Fletcher, J. M., & Levin, H. S. (1988). Neurobehavioral effects of brain injury in children. In D. Routh (Ed.), *Handbook of pediatric psychology* (pp. 258–295). New York: Guilford Press.

Fletcher, J. M., Levin, H. S., & Satz, P. (in press). Neuropsychological and intellectual assessment of children. In H. Kaplan & B. J. Sadock (Eds.), *Comprehensive textbook of psychiatry*. Baltimore: Basic Books.

Fletcher, J. M., & Satz, P. (1980). Developmental changes in the neuropsychological correlates of reading achievement: A six-year longitudinal follow-up. *Journal of Clinical Neuropsychology, 2*, 23–37.

Fletcher, J. M., & Taylor, H. G. (1984). Neuropsychological approaches to children: Towards a developmental neuropsychology. *Journal of Clinical Neuropsychology, 6*, 24–37.

Fletcher, J. M., Taylor, H. G., Satz, P., & Morris, R. (1982). Finger recognition skills and reading achievement: A developmental neuropsychological analysis. *Developmental Psychology, 18*, 124–132.

Gaddes, W. H., & Crockett, D. J. (1975). The Spreen-Benton aphasia tests—normative data as a measure of normal language development. *Brain and Language, 2*, 257–280.

Gardner, M. F. (1979). *Expressive One-Word Picture Vocabulary Test*. Novato, CA: Academic Therapy Publications.

Gettinger, M., & White, M. (1979). Which is the stronger correlate of school learning? Time to learn or measured intelligence? *Journal of Educational Psychology, 71*(4), 405–412.

Gibson, E. J., & Levin, H. (1975). *The psychology of reading*. Cambridge, MA: MIT Press.

Gilmore, J. V., & Gilmore, E. C. (1968). *Gilmore Oral Reading Test: Manual of directions*. New York: Harcourt Brace Jovanovich.

Golden, C. J. (1981). The Luria-Nebraska Children's Battery: Theory and formulation. In G. W. Hynd & J. E. Obrzut (Eds.), *Neuropsychological assessment and the school-age child: Issues and procedures*. New York: Grune & Stratton.

Goldstein, K. (1939). *The organism*. New York: American Book Co.

Golick, M. (1977). *Language disorders in children: A linguistic investigation*. Unpublished doctoral dissertation, McGill University, Montreal.

Goodglass, H., & Kaplan, E. (1972). *The assessment of aphasia and related disorders*. Philadelphia: Lea & Febiger.

Gray, D. B., & Kavanagh, J. F. (1985). *Biobehavioral measures of dyslexia*. Parkton, MD: York Press.

Guilford, J. P. (1967). *The nature of human intelligence*. New York: McGraw-Hill.

Guthrie, J. T. (1973). Models of reading and reading disability. *Journal of Educational Psychology, 65*, 9–18.

Hale, G. A., & Lewis, M. (Eds.). (1979). *Attention and cognitive development*. New York: Plenum Press.

Harter, S. (1982). The Perceived Competence Scale for Children. *Child Development, 53*, 87–97.

Hartlage, L. C., & Telzrow, C. F. (1983). The neuropsychological basis of educational intervention. *Journal of Learning Disabilities, 16*, 521–528.

Hebb, D. O. (1942). The effect of early and late brain injury upon test scores, and the nature of normal adult intelligence. *Proceedings of the American Philosophical Society, 85*, 265–292.

Hecaen, H., & Albert, M. L. (1978). *Human neuropsychology*. New York: Wiley.

Hedrick, D. L., Prather, E. M., & Tobin, A. R. (1975). *Sequenced Inventory of Communication Development*. Seattle: University of Washington Press.

Heilman, K. M., & Valenstein, E. (1985). *Clinical neuropsychology* (2nd ed). New York: Oxford University Press.

Herzog, J., Linder, H., & Samaha, J. (1981). *The measurement of stress: Life events and the interviewer's ratings*. Project Competence Report #1. Minneapolis: University of Minnesota.

Hiskey, M. S. (1966). *Hiskey-Nebraska Test of Learning Aptitude*. Lincoln, NE: Union College Press.

Hunt, E. (1980). Intelligence as an information-processing concept. *British Journal of Psychology, 71*, 449–474.

Hunt, E. (1983). On the nature of intelligence. *Science, 219*, 141–146.

Ingalls, T. H., & Gordon, J. E. (1947). Epidemiologic implications of developmental arrests. *American Journal of Medical Science, 241*, 322–328.

Isakson, R. L., & Miller, J. W. (1976). Sensitivity to syntactic and semantic cues in good and poor comprehenders. *Journal of Educational Psychology, 68*, 787–792.

Jastak, S., & Wilkinson, G. S. (1984). *Wide Range Achievement Test-Revised*. Wilmington, DE: Jastak Associates.

Johnson, D. J. (1980). Persistent auditory disorders in young dyslexic adults. *Bulletin of the Orton Society, 30*, 268–276.

Kahn, E., & Cohen, L. H. (1934). Organic driveness: A brain stem syndrome and experience. *New England Journal of Medicine, 210*, 748–756.

Kail, R., & Bisanz, J. (1982). Information processing and cognitive development. In H. W. Reese (Ed.), *Advances in child development and behavior* (Vol. 17). New York: Academic Press.

Kalverboer, A. F. (1976). Neurobehavioral relationships in young children: Some concluding remarks on concepts and methods. In R. M. Knights & D. J. Bakker (Eds.), *The neuropsychology of learning disorders: Theoretical approaches*. Baltimore: University Park Press.

Kaufman, A. S. (1979a). Cerebral specialization and intelligence testing. *Journal of Research and Development in Education, 12,* 96–107.

Kaufman, A. S. (1979b). *Intelligent testing with the WISC-R*. Somerset, NJ: Wiley.

Kaufman, A. S., & Kaufman, N. (1983). *The Kaufman Assessment Battery for Children*. Circle Pines, MN: American Guidance Associates.

Kaufman, A. S., & Kaufman, N. (1985). *Kaufman Test of Educational Achievement*. Circle Pines, MN: American Guidance Service.

Keogh, B. K. (1983). Individual differences in temperament: A contribution to the personal, social, and educational competence of learning disabled children. In J. D. McKinney & L. Feagans (Eds.), *Current topics in learning disabilities*. Norwood, NJ: Ablex.

Keogh, B. R., Major, S. M., Omori, H., Gandara, P., & Reid, H. P. (1980). Proposed markers in learning disabilities research. *Journal of Abnormal Psychology, 8*(1), 21–31.

Keogh, B. K., & Margolis, J. S. (1976). A component analysis of attentional problems of educationally handicapped boys. *Journal of Abnormal Child Psychology, 4,* 349–359.

Kirk, S. A., McCarthy, J. J., & Kirk, W. D. (1968). *The Illinois Test of Psycholinguistic Abilities*. Urbana: University of Illinois Press.

Kistner, J. A., & Torgesen, J. K. (1987). Motivational and cognitive aspects of learning disabilities. In B. B. Lohey & A. E. Kazdin (Eds.), *Advances in clinical child psychology* (Vol. 10, pp. 289–333). New York: Plenum Press.

Koppitz, E. M. (1964). *The Bender Gestalt Test for Young Children*. New York: Grune & Stratton.

Lashley, K. S. (1929). *Brain mechanisms and intelligence*. Chicago: University of Chicago Press.

Laufer, M. W., & Denhoff, E. (1957). Hyperkinetic behavior syndrome in children. *Journal of Pediatrics, 50,* 463–474.

Levin, H. S., Benton, A. L., & Grossman, R. G. (1982). *Neurobehavioral consequences of closed head injury*. New York: Oxford University Press.

Levin, H. S., Eisenberg, H. M., Wigg, N. R., & Kobayashi, K. (1982). Memory and intellectual ability after head injury in children and adolescents. *Neurosurgery, 11,* 668–672.

Levin, H. S., Ewing-Cobbs, L., & Benton, A. L. (1984). Age and recovery from brain damage: A review of clinical studies. In S. Scheff (Ed.), *Aging and recovery of function in the central nervous system* (pp. 169–205). New York: Plenum Press.

Lezak, M. D. (1983). *Neuropsychological assessment* (2nd ed). New York: Oxford University Press.

Lindgren, S. D., & Benton, A. L. (1980). Developmental patterns of visuospatial judgment. *Journal of Pediatric Psychology, 5,* 217–225.

Lindgren, S. D., & Lyons, D. A. (1984). *Pediatric Assessment of Cognitive Efficiency* (PACE). Iowa City: University of Iowa, Department of Pediatrics.

Liverant, S. (1960). Intelligence: A concept in need of re-examination. *Journal of Consulting Psychology, 24,* 101–110.

Lovett, M. W. (1984). The search for subtypes of specific reading disability: Reflections from a cognitive perspective. *Annals of Dyslexia, 34,* 155–178.

McCall, R. B. (1981). Nature-nurture and the two realms of development: A proposed integration with respect to mental development. *Child Development, 52,* 1–12.

McCarthy, D. (1970). *Manual for the McCarthy Scales of Children's Abilities*. New York: Psychological Corporation.

McMahon, R. C. (1981). Biological factors in childhood hyperkinesis: A review of genetic and biochemical hypotheses. *Journal of Clinical Psychology, 37,* 12–21.

Mattis, S. (1981). Dyslexia syndromes in children: Toward the development of syndrome-specific treatment programs. In F. J. Pirozzolo & M. C. Wittrock (Eds.), *Neuropsychology and cognitive processes in reading*. New York: Academic Press.

Mattis, S., French, J. H., & Rapin, I. (1975). Dyslexia in children and young adults: Three independent neuropsychological syndromes. *Developmental Medicine and Child Neurology, 17,* 150–163.

Meichenbaum, D. (1976). Cognitive-functional approach to cognitive factors as determinants of learning disabilities. In R. M. Knights & D. J. Bakker (Eds.), *The neuropsychology of learning disorders: Theoretical approaches.* Baltimore: University Park Press.

Moos, R. H., & Moos, B. S. (1981). *Family Environment Scale manual.* Palo Alto, CA: Consulting Psychologists Press.

Morrison, D. C., & Hinshaw, S. P. (1988). The relationship between neuropsychological/perceptual performance and socioeconomic status in children with learning disabilities. *Journal of Learning Disabilities, 21*(2), 124–128.

Musser, P. H., Conger, J. J., & Kagan, J. (1979). *Child development and personality.* New York: Harper & Row.

Obrzut, J. E., & Hynd, G. W. (1986). *Child neuropsychology: Clinical practice* (Vol. 2). Orlando: Academic Press.

Pasamanick, B., & Knobloch, H. (1960). Brain damage and reproductive casualty. *American Journal of Orthopsychiatry, 30,* 298–305.

Passler, M. A., Isaac, W., & Hynd, G. W. (1985). Neuropsychological development of behavior attributed to frontal lobe functioning in children. *Developmental Neuropsychology, 1,* 349–370.

Patterson, G. R. (1986). Performance models for antisocial boys. *American Psychologist, 41,* 432–444.

Pellegrino, J. W., & Glaser, R. (1979). Cognitive correlates and components in the analysis of individual differences. In R. J. Sternberg & D. K. Detterman (Eds.), *Human intelligence: Perspectives on its theory and measurement.* Norwood, NJ: Ablex.

Perfetti, C. A. (1980). Verbal coding efficiency, conceptually guided reading, and reading failure. *Bulletin of the Orton Society, 30,* 197–208.

Petrauskas, R. J., & Rourke, B. P. (1979). Identification of subtypes of retarded readers: A neuropsychological, multivariate approach. *Journal of Clinical Neuropsychology, 1,* 17–37.

Porter, J. E., & Rourke, B. P. (1985). Socio-emotional functioning in learning disabled children: A subtypal analysis of personality patterns. In B. P. Rourke (Ed.), *Neuropsychology of learning disabilities: Essentials of subtype analysis* (pp. 277–280). New York: Guilford Press.

Reitan, R. M. (1984). *Aphasia and sensory-perceptual deficits in adults.* Tucson, AZ: Neuropsychology Press.

Reitan, R. M., & Davison, L. A. (Eds.). (1974). *Clinical neuropsychology: Current status and applications.* New York: Wiley.

Resnick, L. B. (1979). The future of IQ testing in education. In R. J. Sternberg & D. K. Detterman (Eds.), *Human intelligence: Perspectives on its theory and measurement.* Norwood, NJ: Ablex.

Reynolds, C. R. (1982). The importance of norms and other traditional psychometric concepts to assessment in clinical neuropsychology. In R. N. Malatesha & L. C. Hartlage (Eds.), *Neuropsychology and cognition* (Vol. 2). The Hague: Martinus Nijhoff.

Richman, L. C., & Lindgren, S. D. (1981). Verbal medication deficits: Relation to behavior and achievement in children. *Journal of Abnormal Psychology, 90,* 99–104.

Roberts, G. C., Block, J. H., & Block, J. (1984). Continuity and change in parents' child-rearing. *Child Development, 55,* 586–597.

Rosner, J., & Simon, D. P. (1971). The auditory analysis test: An initial report. *Journal of Learning Disabilities, 4,* 40–48.

Rourke, B. P. (1975). Brain-behavior relationships in children with learning disabilities. *American Psychologist, 30,* 911–920.

Rourke, B. P. (1978). Reading, spelling, arithmetic disabilities: A neuropsychological perspective. In H. R. Myklebust (Ed.), *Progress in learning disabilities.* New York: Grune & Stratton.

Rourke, B. P. (1980). Neuropsychological assessment of children with learning disabilities. In S. B. Filskov & T. J. Boll (Eds.), *Handbook of clinical neuropsychology.* New York: Wiley-Interscience.

Rourke, B. P. (Ed.). (1985). *Neuropsychology of learning disabilities: Essentials of subtype analysis.* New York: Guilford Press.

Rourke, B. P., & Finlayson, M. A. (1978). Neuropsychological significance of variations in patterns of academic performance: Verbal and visual-spatial abilities. *Journal of Abnormal Psychology, 84,* 412–421.

Rourke, B. P., & Fisk, J. L. (1981). Socio-emotional disturbances of learning disabled children: The role of central processing deficits. *Bulletin of the Orton Society, 31,* 77–88.

Rourke, B. P., Fisk, J. L., & Strang, J. D. (1986). *Neuropsychological assessment of children: A treatment-oriented approach.* New York: Guilford Press.

Rourke, B. P., & Gates, R. D. (1980). *The Underlining Test: Preliminary norms.* Windsor: University of Windsor.

Rourke, B. P., & Orr, R. (1977). Prediction of the reading and spelling performances of normal and retarded readers: A four-year follow-up. *Journal of Abnormal Child Psychology, 5,* 9–20.

Rourke, B. P. (1982). Central processing deficiencies

in children. Toward a developmental neuropsychological model. *Journal of Clinical Neuropsychology, 4*, 1–18.

Rutter, M. (1978). Prevalence and types of dyslexia. In A. L. Benton & D. Pearl (Eds.), *Dyslexia: An appraisal of current knowledge* (pp. 3–28). New York: Oxford University Press.

Rutter, M. (1981). Psychological sequelae of brain damage in children. *The American Journal of Psychiatry, 138*, 1533–1544.

Rutter, M. (1982). Syndromes attributed to "minimal brain dysfunction" in childhood. *American Journal of Psychiatry, 139*, 21–33.

Sameroff, A. J., & Chandler, M. J. (1975). Reproductive risk and the continuum of caretaking casualty. In F. Horowitz (Ed.), *Review of child development research* (Vol. 4). Chicago: University of Chicago Press.

Sattler, J. M. (1982). *Assessment of children's intelligence and special abilities* (2nd ed.). Boston: Allyn & Bacon.

Satz, P., & Fletcher, J. M. (1980). Minimal brain dysfunctions: An appraisal of research concepts and methods. In H. E. Rie & E. D. Rie (Eds.), *Handbook of minimal brain dysfunctions: A critical review*. New York: Wiley.

Satz, P., & Fletcher, J. M. (1981). Emergent trends in neuropsychology: An overview. *Journal of Consulting and Clinical Psychology, 49*, 851–865.

Satz, P., & Fletcher, J. M. (1982). *Manual for the Florida Kindergarten Screening Battery*. Odessa, FL: Psychological Assessment Resources.

Satz, P., & Morris, R. (1981). Learning disability subtypes: A review. In F. J. Pirozzolo & M. C. Wittrock (Eds.), *Neuropsychological and cognitive processes in reading*. New York: Academic Press.

Schatz, J. (1988). *Attention deficits in the learning disabled child*. Unpublished honor's thesis, Montreal: McGill University, Department of Psychology.

Schonhaut, S., & Satz, P. (1983). Prognosis of the learning disabled child: A review of the follow-up studies. In M. Rutter (Ed.), *Developmental Neuropsychiatry*. New York: Guilford Press.

Selz, M. (1981). Halstead-Reitan neuropsychological test batteries for children. In G. W. Hynd & J. E. Orbzut (Eds.), *Neuropsychological assessment in the school-age child*. New York: Grune & Stratton.

Semel, E. M., & Wiig, E. H. (1980). *CELF: Clinical Evaluation of Language Functions: Diagnostic battery, examiner's manual*. Columbus, OH: Merrill.

Shallice, T. (1979). Case study approach in neuropsychological research. *Journal of Clinical Neuropsychology, 1*, 183–211.

Shallice, T. (1981). Neuropsychological impairment of cognitive processes. *British Medical Bulletin, 37*, 187–192.

Siegel, A. W., Bisanz, J., & Bisanz, G. L. (1983). Developmental analysis: A strategy for the study of psychological change. In J. Meachum & D. Kuhn (Eds.), *Contributions to human development* (Vol. 8). Basel: Karger.

Siegel, L. S. (1981). Infant tests as predictors of cognitive and language development at two years. *Child Development, 52*, 545–557.

Sines, J. O. (1983). *Home Environment Questionnaire manual*. Iowa City, IA: Psychological Assessment Services.

Soare, P. L., & Raimondi, A. J. (1977). Intellectual and perceptual-motor characteristics of treated myelomeningocele children. *American Journal of Diseases of Children, 131*, 199–204.

Sparrow, S. S., Balla, D. A., & Ciccetti, D. V. (1984). *Vineland Adaptive Behavior Scales: A revision of the Vineland Social Maturity Scale*. Circle Pines, MN: American Guidance Service.

Spiker, C. C. (1966). IV. The concept of development: Relevant and irrelevant issues. *Monographs for the Society for Research in Child Development* (Serial 107), *31*, 40–54.

Spreen, O., Tupper, D., Risser, A., Tuokko, H., & Edgell, D. (1984). *Human developmental neuropsychology*. New York: Oxford University Press.

Sroufe, L. A., & Rutter, M. (1984). The domain of developmental psychopathology. *Child Development, 55*, 17–30.

Stanovich, K. (1986). Cognitive processes and the reading problems of learning disabled children: Evaluating the assumption of specificity. In J. Torgesen & B. Wong (Eds.), *Psychological and educational perspectives in reading disabilities* (pp. 87–131). New York: Academic Press.

Sternberg, R. (1977). *Intelligence, information processing, and analogical reasoning*. Hillsdale, NJ: Erlbaum.

Sternberg, R. J. (1984). What should intelligence tests test? Implications of a triarchic theory of intelligence for intelligence testing. *Educational Researcher, 13*, 5–15.

Still, G. F. (1902). Some abnormal psychological conditions in children. *Lancet, 1*, 1077–1082.

Strauss, A. A., & Lehtinen, L. E. (1947). *Psychopathology and education of the brain-injured child.* New York: Grune & Stratton.

Sweeney, J. E., & Rourke, B. P. (1978). Neuropsychological significance of phonetically accurate and phonetically inaccurate spelling errors in younger and older retarded spellers. *Brain and Language, 6,* 212–225.

Taylor, H. G. (1984a). Early brain injury and cognitive development. In C. R. Almli & S. Finger (Eds.), *Early brain damage: Research orientations and clinical observations* (Vol. 1, pp. 325–345). Orlando: Academic Press.

Taylor, H. G. (1984b). Minimal brain dysfunction in perspective. In R. Tarter & G. Goldstein (Eds.), *Advances in clinical neuropsychology,* (Vol. 2, pp. 207–229). New York: Plenum Press.

Taylor, H. G. (1987a). Childhood sequelae of early neurological disorders: A contemporary perspective. *Developmental Neuropsychology, 3*(2), 153–164.

Taylor, H. G. (1987b). The meaning and value of soft signs in the behavioral sciences. In D. E. Tupper (Ed.), *Soft neurological signs: Manifestations, measurement, research, and meaning* (pp. 297–335). New York: Grune & Stratton.

Taylor, H. G. (1988a). Learning disabilities. In E. J. Mash & L. G. Terdal, (Eds.), *Behavioral assessment of childhood disorders* (2nd ed., pp. 402–450). New York: Guilford Press.

Taylor, H. G. (1988b). Neuropsychological testing: Relevance for assessing children's learning disabilities. *Journal of Consulting and Clinical Psychology, 56*(6), 795–800.

Taylor, H. G. (1989). Learning disabilities. In E. J. Mash & R. A. Barkley (Eds.), *Behavioral treatment of childhood disorders* (pp. 347–380). New York: Guilford.

Taylor, H. G., Albo, V. C., Phebus, C. K., Sachs, B. R., & Bierl, P. G. (1987). Postirradiation treatment outcomes for children with acute lymphocytic leukemia: Classification of risks. *Journal of Pediatric Psychology, 12*(3), 395–411.

Taylor, H. G., & Fletcher, J. M. (1983). Biological foundations of "specific developmental disorders": Methods, findings, and future directions. *Journal of Child Clinical Psychology, 12,* 46–65.

Taylor, H. G., Fletcher, J. M., & Satz, P. (1982). Component processes in reading disabilities: Neuropsychological investigation of distinct reading subskill deficits. In R. N. Malatesha & P. G. Aaron (Eds.), *Reading disorders: Varieties and treatments.* New York: Academic Press.

Taylor, H. G., Fletcher, J. M., & Satz, P. (1984). Neuropsychological assessment of children. In G. Goldstein & M. Hersen (Eds.), *Handbook of psychological assessment* (pp. 211–234). New York: Pergamon Press.

Taylor, H. G., Lean, D., & Schwartz, S. (1989). Pseudoword repetition ability in learning-disabled children. *Applied Psycholinguistics, 10,* 203–219.

Thorndike, R. L., Hogen, E. P., & Sattler, J. M. (1986). *Stanford-Binet Intelligence Scale* (4th ed.). Chicago: Riverside.

Torgesen, J. K. (1975). Problems and prospects in the study of learning disabilities. In E. M. Hetherington (Ed.), *Review of Child Development Research* (Vol. 5, pp. 385–440). Chicago: University of Chicago Press.

Torgesen, J. K. (1978). Performance of reading disabled children on serial memory tasks: A review. *Reading Research Quarterly, 19,* 57–87.

Torgesen, J. K. (1979). What shall we do with psychological processes? *Journal of Learning Disabilities, 12,* 16–23.

Torgesen, J. K. (1980). Conceptual and educational implications of the use of efficient task strategies by learning disabled children. *Journal of Learning Disabilities, 13,* 19–26.

Torgesen, J. K., Rashotte, C. A., Greenstein, J., Houck, G., & Portes, P. (1987). Academic difficulties of learning disabled children who perform poorly on memory span tasks. *Memory and Learning Disabilities: Advances in Learning and Behavioral Disabilities,* Suppl. 2, 305–333.

Walsh, R. N., & Greenough, W. T. (Eds.). (1976). *Environments as therapy for brain dysfunction.* New York: Plenum Press.

Wechsler, D. (1974). *Manual for the Wechsler Intelligence Scale for Children-Revised.* New York: Psychological Corporation.

Weisfeld, G. E. (1982). The nature-nurture issue and the integrating concept of function. In B. B. Wolman (Ed.), *Handbook of developmental psychology.* Englewood Cliffs, NJ: Prentice-Hall.

Welsh, M. C., & Pennington, B. G. (1988). Assessing frontal lobe functioning in children: Views from developmental psychology. *Developmental Psychology, 4,* 199–230.

Werner, E. E. (1980). Environmental interaction in minimal brain dysfunctions. In H. C. Rie & H. D. Rie (Eds.), *Handbook of minimal brain dysfunctions: A critical review.* New York: Wiley.

Wilson, B. (1987). An approach to the neuropsychological assessment of preschool children with developmental deficits. In S. Filskov & T. Boll

(Eds.). *Handbook of clinical neuropsychology* (Vol. 2). New York: Wiley.

Wirt, R. D., Lachar, D., Klinedinst, J. K., & Seat, P. D. (1984). *Multidimensional description of child personality: A manual for the Personality Inventory for Children* (rev. ed.). Los Angeles: Western Psychological Services.

Wohlwill, J. F. (1973). *Study of behavioral development*. New York: Academic Press.

Wolff, P. H. (1981). Normal variations in human maturation. In K. J. Connolly & H. F. R. Prechtl (Eds.), *Clinics in Developmental Medicine No. 77/78: Maturation and development: Biological and psychological perspectives*. London: William Heinemann Medical Books.

Woodcock, R. W. (1987). *Woodcock Reading Mastery Test-Revised*. Circle Pines, MN: American Guidance Service.

Woodcock, R. W., & Johnson, M. B. (1989). *Woodcock-Johnson Psycho-Educational Battery-Revised*. Allen, TX: DLM Teaching Resources.

Yule, W. (1978). Diagnosis: Developmental psychological assessment. In A. F. Kalverboer, H. M. van Praag, & J. Mendlewicz (Eds.), *Advances in biological psychiatry: Vol. 1. Minimal brain dysfunction: Fact or fiction?* Basel: S. Karger.

Ylvisaker, M. (1985) (Ed.) *Head injury rehabilitation: Children and adolescents*. San Diego: College Hill Press.

CHAPTER 12

SPECIALIZED NEUROPSYCHOLOGICAL ASSESSMENT METHODS

Kerry deS. Hamsher, Ph.D.

There are a variety of approaches to neuropsychological assessment. Different styles or systems could be characterized in various ways. They may differ, for example, depending on whether the individual tests are standardized (where the methods of administration and scoring are clear and objective), and how well they are normed (e.g., not at all; according to one reference or standardization group; or simultaneously taking into account variables such as education, age, and other variables that might influence the expected performance levels) (Roberts & Hamsher, 1984). Some authorities emphasize the making of subjective judgments about the patient's approach to the presented problems in conjunction with theories as to what these impressions should mean. In this view, the use of statistical norms which seem to emphasize some global score may be denigrated. The length of the assessment is another dimension on which systems of assessment may differ (referring to both the number of tests given and the time taken for the subject to complete the battery). Advocates for some test batteries may claim their battery is comprehensive but in so doing may actually confuse the concept of "comprehensive" with the quality of being "extensive." There is no limit to the number of tests one could conceivably include in a battery set. Yet it is not necessarily true that each test adds useful information. Nor does merely including a large number of tests guarantee that all relevant domains of behavior for a given case are appropriately assessed by that set battery of tests.

In this chapter we will concern ourselves with formal or objective approaches to neuropsychological assessment. These approaches do not reject or necessarily overlook qualitative aspects of performance. However, objectivity is sought with regard to both qualitative and quantitative aspects of behavior because only through objectivity can one scientifically study the meaning of one's examination results and hopefully advance this science. Similarly, primary emphasis is given to standardized procedures with objective normative criteria.

A once raging but now fading controversy in neuropsychological assessment in the United States was the contrast between neuropsychological approaches dichotomized as the "fixed battery" versus "flexible battery" approach. On the one hand, there is the specialized approach in which the choice of tests is individualized and will depend on the referral question, the clinical history and interview, and the patient's presentation during the examination itself. Arthur Benton (1977b) has called this the "flexible approach," the idea being that it is better to fit the assessment to the patient rather than vice versa as the latter has all the faults of the Procrustean bed. On the other hand, there has been the battery approach wherein there is a defined or fixed set of measures to be administered to all patients for all occasions. The fixed battery approach to clinical assessment is often said to be advantageous because it facilitates the collection of data for research. Nevertheless, while *some* fixed battery (as opposed to *a* fixed battery) is typically used in clinical research projects, the re-

256

searcher more commonly adopts the strategy of the flexible approach in that the research battery is specifically designed for the target clinical group and particular hypotheses to be tested. Since the fixed test battery approach to clinical assessment by definition precludes its modification, such a strategy will fail to make use of new information and advancements in knowledge and techniques. Consequently, the fixed (or so-called comprehensive) battery approach has fallen behind the times and is now passé. For a more comprehensive comparison between these two approaches, the reader may refer to the work of Jones and Butters (1983). This chapter is written within the framework of the flexible, individualized, or specialized approach.

Variations in the goals of assessment may influence the assessment strategy and, therefore, result in differences in approaches. Traditionally, a major concern for neuropsychological assessment was the identification and localization of focal brain lesions. Indeed, in the history of clinical neuropsychology there has been a strong emphasis on studying the behavioral consequences of focal brain lesions as these results bear directly on the issues of hemispheric cerebral dominance and intrahemispheric specialization of function (Benton, 1977a, 1985). However, other neurodiagnostic technologies, such as computerized tomography (CT scan), positron emission tomography (PET scan), and magnetic resonance imaging (MRI scan), are gaining the upper hand (Kent & Larson, 1988). Their accuracy and efficiency for localizing focal lesions in many conditions already surpass the offerings of neuropsychological assessment.

If this were the only assessment issue, then one might wonder what the future holds for clinical neuropsychology vis-á-vis this rapidly evolving and spreading technology in neurological medicine that is ever improving the capability for the identification and localization of structural and physiological abnormalities (Costa, 1983). But one could conceive of these advances as representing another phase in a "bootstrap" operation. Historically, as Benton (1985) has illustrated, it is precisely through the interplay between clinical and experimental studies that a field such as neuropsychology often makes its greatest leaps in knowledge. That is, by adding new and more precise information to the brain side of the brain–behavior equation, we are able to learn more about the behavioral side. Rather than replacing neuropsychology, these exciting technological developments are likely to enhance the neuropsychologist's diagnostic and consultative roles. By more sharply defining disease states through improved sensitivity and accu-

racy, we are better able to overcome sources of confusion or ambiguity and, in a complementary fashion, to more sharply define our behavioral formulations of the effects of disease on nervous system functioning. To remain a sound and fit science, neuropsychology must evolve with and capitalize on the changing technological environment. Besides neuropsychology, fields such as clinical psychology and psychiatry have viewed the present and anticipated future contributions of the neurosciences with favor and optimism.

It is difficult to imagine there would ever be a loss of interest in the contributions of clinical neuropsychologists as our quantified data address questions about the highest levels of human behavior. From an evolutionary standpoint, it is precisely the brain's capacity for the production of rational thought, communication, memory, learning, emotional responsiveness, and social integration that defines the essence of being human. Thus, it is not surprising that the medical definition of death has been restructured to use irreversible loss of brain function (absence of cerebral and brain stem functions) as the major criterion despite the persistence of other vegetative activity. And short of death, consideration of residual cerebral functioning figures prominently in medical decision making. As long as society and the health care system remain concerned with the issues of mental status, there will be a role for neuropsychologists (Hamsher, 1983).

Nor could infrabehavioral data from neurobiology and current imaging technologies replace the neuropsychologists' clinical contributions. There is no more reason to expect neuropsychology's contribution to be diminished than there is to expect neurology to abandon its clinical examination procedures and consultative role in light of these developments. One current challenge for the infrabehavioral data and for the study of brain–behavior relations in general is the fact of behavioral recovery following acute cerebral lesions (Benton, 1985; Kertesz, 1983). Given a structural lesion, we can find in one month that the patient is aphasic (or has some other neurobehavioral disorder) while in another month the same person is speaking normally despite the unaltered appearance of the original structural lesion. Consequently the identification of a structural lesion cannot necessarily imply a particular behavioral state.

Besides identifying focal lesions or elucidating their behavioral effects, a distinctive contribution of clinical neuropsychological assessment can also be appreciated in the study of progressive neurodegenerative disorders. We know, for example, that depletion of acetylcholine (or more precisely its marker substance, choline acetyltransferase) is linked with Alzheimer's disease and a depletion of cells in the basal nuclei of Meynert (Whitehouse, Price, Clark, Coyle, & Delong, 1981; Davies, 1983; Katzman, 1986; Arendash, Millard, Dunn, & Meyer, 1987; Hansen, DeTeresa, Davies, & Terry, 1988)—also known as the nucleus basalis, the ganglion of Meynert, and the "substantia innominata" of Reichert (Lockard, 1977). Were technology to reveal a reduction in cerebral acetylcholine metabolism in some patient, would this mean the patient had dementia? Of course not! Dementia is a neurobehavioral diagnosis that can only be determined from a behavioral assay while Alzheimer's disease is a histological diagnosis which can only be determined from a tissue assay (Henderson & Finch, 1989). The extent to which a diagnosis from one nosological system implies some particular diagnosis in a different nosological system is an empirical question, not something that can be taken for granted.

This does not gainsay the contributions that even limited objective cognitive assessment may provide in certain restrictive clinical contexts to predict disease entities. If one selects an elderly sample with an apparent history of progressive mental decline and if neuroimaging and medical tests are used to exclude cases with contradictory etiologies, then positive (abnormal) results from such brief tests of mental status can be shown to have a high predictive value for identifying the presence of neurodegenerative disorders (Storandt, Botwinick, Danziger, Berg, & Hughes, 1984; Eslinger, Damasio, Benton, & Van Allen, 1985; Morris, McKeel, Fulling, Torack, & Berg, 1988). Such minimal mental status surveys have the advantage that they can be administered by persons with little or no understanding of the intricacies of mental assessment and the neurobiological foundations of mentation. However, without the inclusion and exclusion criteria embedded in a particular clinical context, the sensitivity and appropriateness of these brief measures may be greatly altered. If the goals of the assessment were to differentially diagnose mental states (as opposed to predicting disease categories) or to provide a data base to advance our knowledge of neurobehavioral disorders, then such brief screening devices are not likely to achieve these ends even in delimited clinical contexts.

There are many etiologies resulting in the behavioral state that we classify under the rubric of dementia. Alzheimer's disease, multiple cerebral infarcts and severe head trauma are three examples that may, though not necessarily, produce this neurobehavioral state. Though often mistaken as synonymous with Dementia, it now appears that presumed Alzheimer's disease is more likely to present in the early stages withthe clinical picture of a slowly progressive amnesia. Besides dementia and amnesia, Alzheimer's disease may present as other neurobehavioral disorders as well (Shuttleworth, 1984; Martin et al., 1986; Capitani, Della Sala, & Spinnler, 1986, Friedland, 1988).

The interplay between neurobehavioral assessment and more basic research has recently come to fore with the identification of subgroups of patients with slowly progressive cognitive deterioration of several distinct types. These patients would easily be diagnosed as having "dementia" by many clinicians' clinical criteria and brief global measures of "dementia" would likely support this inaccurate impression. Quantitative neuropsychological examinations have identified one of these as a "Slowly Progressive Aphasia" (Mesulam, 1982). One form has a distinct hereditary component while another has been shown to have neurotransmitter changes that distinguish it from Alzheimer's disease though not from Pick's disease.

In general, neurologic and neuropsychological deficits are determined by the locus of lesion rather than its etiology (e.g., stroke, tumor, infection, trauma). However, if an etiology happened to imply a particular locus, then it may also imply a particular neurobehavioral disorder (e.g., thiamine deficiency and Wernicke's encephalopathy). Evidence is now mounting that points to a particular proclivity for Alzheimer's disease to attack the hippocampal memory system's anatomic relay structures for input from and output to association cortex (Hyman, Van Hoesen, & Damasio, 1984; Hyman, Van Hoesen, Kromer, & Damasio, 1986). Yet when patients with presumed Alzheimer's disease show the picture of Dementia, then it is the parietotemporal association cortex of the two cerebral hemispheres that are implicated as the site of cerebral dysfunction (Duara et al., 1986; Foster et al., 1983).

On the behavioral side of the brain–behavior equation, neuropsychology can be viewed as the study of the behavioral output of the central nervous system. Although it is akin to an assessment of functional capacity, the neuropsychological evaluation differs from the functional assessments provided by other professionals such as vocational and rehabilitation psychologists or occupational and speech therapists. In the latter examples, the functional assessment centers around criteria for task competencies, such as the ability to perform vocational activities, activities of daily living, or the capacity to communicate by oral or other substitutive means. Valuable as these other functional assessments may be, because behavior has multiple determinants, such assessments do not, nor are they intended to, define the precise cognitive and brain mechanisms responsible for observed impairments of function.

It is the province of clinical neuropsychology to relate neurological disease and other neurodiagnostic information to behavioral aberrations that can be understood in terms of involvement of specific brain structures and mechanisms. Indeed, there will be some cases where the lack of correspondence between the identified behavioral deficits and known brain damage will be the key to the diagnosis of a hitherto undetected and/or independent disorder (be it neurologic or psychiatric in origin). In turn, it is also the province of clinical neuropsychology to relate these neurologically specific cognitive and other behavioral disorders to the problems observed in real life or on these other types of functional assessments. Thus, neuropsychological assessment for the diagnosis of neurobehavioral disorders provides the conceptual bridge between brain disease and its associated ecological implications.

More could be said about the role and contributions of neuropsychological assessment and some of these other features will be addressed later in this chapter. So far we have seen that the origins of clinical neuropsychological assessment began in the last century with clinical studies that sought to localize cognitive and conative behaviors to specific anatomic loci within the brain. Up through the early 1970s, when there were few alternative technologies for localization, this remained a dominant theme of neuropsychological assessment. In the past 10 to 15 years, there have been revolutionary technological advances in the *in vivo* imaging of structural brain lesions. Further progress, including the imaging of physiological abnormalities in the nervous system, is expected to become clinically available in the near future. This progress has helped to advance rather than replace the contributions of neuropsychological assessment which has since moved beyond localization issues (Goldstein & Tarter, 1986; Hamsher, 1988; Whitaker, 1988). Thus, aside from the neurological and behavioral diagnostic issues, the product of clinical neuropsychological assessment is directed to a variety of issues that are relevant to patients, their family members, their employers, and others involved in the patient's medical management, nursing care, and functional rehabilitation.

DESCRIPTION OF A SPECIALIZED APPROACH

The specialized or flexible approach to neuropsychological assessment is commonly used in the major neurological training centers in the United States, and it appears to be the dominant approach in western Europe, Great Britain, and the Commonwealth countries. Beaumont (1983) calls it the "individual-centered normative approach" (p. 281). It can be thought of as falling between two extremes for the assessment of mental status. Anchored at one end of this continuum is the informal and individualistic bedside assessment that emphasizes efficiency and practicality (Strub & Black, 1988b). At the other end of the spectrum is the day-long fixed assessment battery where the patient is subjected to a far-reaching assortment of tests that may be either irrelevant to the patient's presenting complaint or redundant with information already established in the patient's medical record—if not internally redundant as well. Nevertheless, as we shall see, there are common themes in the flexible approach that are often repeated in case after case. The collection of tests that reflect these common themes are often referred to as a "core battery." Furthermore, as research continues to identify critical and meaningful behavioral distinctions associated with particular etiologies or neurobehavioral disorders, a specified set of behavioral issues becomes routinely relevant for specified cases. Consequently, the flexible approach takes on the characteristics of containing a core battery plus a specialized battery selected to be appropriate for the referral question or a particular disease entity. A neuropsychologist employing the flexible approach may have any number of specialized batteries for the evaluation of such things as learning disabilities, mental competency, patients with Parkinson's disease, persons with closed head injuries, and the like. But if it should become apparent that one is on the wrong track, the assessment could switch to a more appropriate attack. For example, some assessment of core linguistic functions (i.e., naming, word fluency, comprehension, repetition) is typically included in a dementia assessment battery. If aphasic signs were elicited, then the examiner would switch to an aphasia assessment battery.

SCOPE AND LIMITS

In this chapter, we shall primarily review an approach for the assessment and differential diagnosis of the major nonaphasic neurobehavioral disorders. The core battery is directed to this differential diagnosis. There are many highly interesting disorders that have distinctive clinical presentations, which are pertinent to the development of neuropsychological theory, and which have specific neurological correlates, but which are beyond the purview of this chapter. Unfortunately for many of these we have as yet no standardized assessment methods beyond those employed in the clinical description of the disorders (Kertesz, 1983). While practicing neuropsychologists must be alert to their possible presence, no attempt will be made to address these rare neurobehavioral disorders and their associated assessment issues. For a flavor of what is missing, the interested reader might refer to the following: the sensory agnosias (Bauer & Rubens, 1985); Klüver-Bucy syndrome (Lilly, Cummings, Benson, & Frankel, 1983); frontal lobe emotional disorders (Damasio, 1985; Damasio & Van Hoesen, 1983); alexia without agraphia (Friedman & Albert, 1985; Varney & Damasio, 1982); Balint's syndrome (DeRenzi, 1982); Charcot-Wilbrand syndrome (Critchley, 1953; Murri, Arena, Siciliano, Mazzotta, & Muratorio, 1984); callosal syndrome (Bogen, 1985; Graff-Radford, Welsh, & Godersky, 1987); ideational and ideomotor apraxias (Heilman & Rothi, 1985); reduplicative paramnesia (Benson, Gardner, & Meadows, 1976); misreaching or "optic ataxia" (Damasio & Benton, 1979; Rondot, de Recondo, & Dumas, 1977). Several general reference works may also be of interest (Cummings, 1985a; Frederiks, 1985a; Frederiks, 1985b; Kirshner, 1986; Lishman, 1987; Mesulam, 1985).

Also excluded from detailed consideration in this chapter are the aphasic disorders. In contrast to the rare disorders described above, the aphasic disorders are rather common and are highly localizing, most particularly in the context of a cerebrovascular accident (CVA) or stroke. The aphasic disorders, too, have practical and theoretical significance for clinical neuropsychology. Nevertheless, experience teaches that in order to perform the appropriate differential diagnosis in a reliable fashion, one must acquire a "tutored ear" under supervised clinical training. Also some special and still unresolved problems arise in the cognitive assessment of aphasic patients (Hamsher, 1981; Mohr, 1982). Therefore, the task of covering this very highly specialized area of neuropsychological assessment falls beyond the scope of this chapter. However, a number of resources are available for the reader interested in the assessment and diagnosis of aphasic disorders (see for example, Albert, Goodglass, Helm, Rubens, & Alexander, 1981; Benson, 1979; Brown, 1972; Davis, 1983; Goodglass & Kap-

lan, 1983; Kertesz, 1979; Kirshner & Freemon, 1982; Rose, Whurr, & Wyke, 1988; Sarno, 1981; Tonkonogy, 1986).

GENERAL ASSESSMENT GOALS

The major purposes of neuropsychological assessment are to evaluate the differential diagnoses of the presenting complaints, to objectively establish the current status of the patient's general mentation, to investigate special relevant or associated features, and to relay this information back to the referring source along with the corollary clinical significance of the findings. The clinical significance may relate to neurological issues such as lesion localization, etiological concerns, prognosis, or indications for or against a particular treatment. Clinical significance also encompasses behavioral issues such as mental competency and the need for a legal guardian, suggestions for patient management or rehabilitation, and implications for discharge planning, return to work, or vocational retraining. The neurological implications of the neuropsychological findings are gleaned from clinical research, the preponderance of which is found in the neurological, neurosurgical, psychiatric, and neuropsychological literature. At the present time, there is little in the way of systematic research regarding the behavioral forms of clinical significance. Consequently, one must rely on one's clinical training and experience to address these issues. Ideas along these lines are largely a function of common sense and foresightedness; one could say they depend on the integrity of the neuropsychologist's executive functions. For example, if a patient neglects stimuli on his left, one might recommend that the bed in the hospital be positioned so that visitors and medical personnel address the patient from the patient's right side. It would also seem reasonable that such a patient should not drive or return to a job as a mechanical inspector so long as these symptoms persists (Burns, Halper, & Mogil, 1985).

REQUISITE TRAINING FOR NEUROPSYCHOLOGICAL ASSESSMENT

Preparation for becoming a clinical neuropsychologist (or ethically providing services identified as being neuropsychological in nature) is obviously not a simple matter. The extent of the literature is such that it cannot be adequately conveyed through a series of workshops. Nor can one acquire the prerequisite minimal skills to appropriately process and apply this information in a clinical context without extensive (two or more years) supervised training in an appropriate (viz., a neurological or neurosurgical) setting. These realities are captured in the published guidelines for doctoral, internship, and postdoctoral education and training in clinical neuropsychology (Reports of the INS-Division 40 Task Force on Education, Accreditation, and Credentialing, 1987) and in the current definition of a clinical neuropsychologist (Division of Clinical Neuropsychology, 1989). Moreover, it is difficult to foresee how one could stay current with the necessary literature if one's practice were not largely or entirely devoted to clinical neuropsychology or else narrowly focused within a specialized area.

DEFINING MENTAL STATES

Much attention has been given to the specification of the psychological status of patients and clinical research subjects, that is, to denote whether the subjects manifested psychoses or severe neuroses. Obviously, such conditions could invalidate neuropsychological test results. When such conditions exist, the subjects may not heed the test instructions or they may bias their responses in an unpredictable way. Patients in psychotic states may not be guided by the usual motivations and social demands of the examination situation (and the conditions under which the tests were probably standardized). However, in the absence of severe psychopathology or indications of malingering, examiners generally assume a patient's test responses are veridical and representative of current abilities.

It is unfortunate that less attention has been paid to the specification of patient's neurobehavioral status in clinical neuropsychology. A very important role for clinical neuropsychology is to apply its scientific methodology for the study of behavior to the problem of diagnosing disorders of mental status, that is, defining and identifying neurobehavioral syndromes. This endeavor has implications for both clinical assessment and research. The process is begun by operationalizing the concepts of clinical neurology as they apply to disorders of cognition in accordance with the psychometric and methodological principles of psychological testing (Anastasi, 1988). These data then must be combined to classify the patient's general mental status according to a scheme of well-recognized and validated neurobehavioral (organic brain) syndromes.

DSM-III-R

Most of the major neurobehavioral disorders have been well described in the neuropsychiatric literature. The recent revision (3rd edition, revised) of the Diagnostic and Statistical Manual of Mental Disorders (DSM-III-R) by the American Psychiatric Association (1987) has developed criteria in a manner more nearly acceptable to scientifically oriented clinicians than those given in previous first and second editions. This is likely to further the recognition of the syndromes described in DSM-III-R. Presently, however, the section on the Organic Brain Syndromes (Organic Mental Disorders) leaves much room for improvement if the manual is to be generally applied so as to include the organic mental disorders seen in patients from neurological and neurosurgical services. The listed criteria are stated in terms that lack specificity. Furthermore, this catalog of mental disorders is too limited. Because of these and other problems, if literally applied, most aphasic patients would be classified by DSM-III-R criteria as having dementia. Such a diagnostic strategy would deprive the behavioral diagnosis of dementia from having any specific neurological import. If a diagnostic entity refers to all sorts of things, then it really means nothing.

In DSM-III-R, one could take particular issue with the treatment of amnesia (Amnestic Syndrome) and dementia. Both are described in similar ways as involving a defect of both short-term memory (more at new learning) and long-term memory. The only distinction in DSM-III-R is that in Dementia there is at least one other cognitive defect or personality change. This ignores the empirical literature demonstrating a variety of cognitive defects and personality changes in association with amnesia, even in the classic Korsakoff's syndrome (Butters & Cermak, 1980). Furthermore, DSM-III-R is internally inconsistent in its concept of dementia. In the section on Mental Retardation, this condition is defined as an impairment in general intellectual functioning (as assessed by individually administered general intelligence tests) associated with impairments in adaptive functioning and with an onset before age 18. Yet, "when a similar clinical picture develops for the first time after the age of 18, the syndrome is a Dementia" (American Psychiatric Association, 1987, p. 29). So in one section dementia is cast as essentially an amnestic syndrome and in another it is equated with general intellectual impairment (with no requirement that recent memory be defective). The latter is more consistent with the traditional neuropsychological concept of dementia (Benton, 1985). It would seem that the former concept is an attempt to reclassify the amnestic syndrome that is often seen in the early stages of Alzheimer's disease as a dementia. As a result, DSM-III-R not only blurs these two diagnostic concepts, it essentially defines out of existence the amnestic syndrome because of its overly restrictive criteria. While specific developmental cognitive disorders are recognized among the disorders of childhood and adolescence, specific acquired cognitive disorders presenting in adulthood are not recognized.

HISTORY AND DEVELOPMENT

The Benton Laboratory

Matarazzo has described the early history of the development of neuropsychological assessment in the United States, beginning in the post–World War II era from the vantage point of clinical psychology (Matarazzo, 1972). Notably there were two pioneers, Arthur L. Benton at the University of Iowa and Ralph Reitan at University of Indiana. Each went in his own direction. Reitan pursued the fixed battery approach, now called the Halstead–Reitan Battery, while Benton pursued the problem of blending traditional clinical neurology with psychology's scientific approach to the study and assessment of human behavior, especially cognitively mediated behaviors.

Benton came to the University of Iowa in 1948 as Professor of Psychology and Director of the Clinical Psychology Graduate Training Program. By 1950 he had established a small neuropsychological testing unit in the Department of Neurology, which then grew into one of the major internationally recognized centers for research and clinical training in neuropsychology. Even as a graduate student, Benton had a major interest in the relationships between intellectual functioning and neurological disease. So, he began a study of the neurological concepts of mental activity and the history behind the development of these concepts. He has had a major influence on the development and epistemology of neuropsychology from both research and clinical standpoints. A number of important and representative works of Arthur Benton have been assembled by Costa and Spreen (1985) which no serious student of neuropsychology should overlook.

Although there was no scarcity of tests of neuropsychologic function when Benton began his career, clearly missing from this literature was the notion of standardization and the multiplicity of determinants of cognitive performance. Thus, he began his career by applying the methodology of experimental psychol-

ogy to some of the neurological issues of the time. After some 10 years of controlled, systematic research on arithmetic ability, right–left discrimination, and finger localization, he applied this methodology to the popular notion of the Gerstmann syndrome. He found that there was no scientific basis for calling this symptom tetrad (finger agnosia, right–left disorientation, acalculia, and agraphia) a syndrome (Benton, 1961, 1977c). In explaining the results, he pointed out how biased observations could lead to spurious concepts. This helped to establish new standards of acceptability for behavioral concepts and research in neurology.

Benton urged clinical neurology to do away with some of the traditional bedside tests which were poorly constructed and unreliable and to substitute scientifically validated behavioral assessment instruments in their place. But in this process he would not lose sight of clinical utility. For example, in looking for ways to improve the reliability of the digit span test, a trade off between choosing elaborate psychophysical procedures versus a less time-consuming method suitable for routine clinical use was emphasized (Blackburn & Benton, 1957). Another of the students in his laboratory demonstrated that, for the purposes of identifying patients with brain disease, one need not give the full Wechsler intelligence battery (Fogel, 1964). That is, no further information was to be gained from the full battery than what could be obtained from a single subtest or the combination of a few. With the limited availability of patient time, the decision to give the full battery would have to be at the expense of administering other tasks that could add new information. In the same study, Fogel demonstrated that by comparing a patient's obtained IQ with his expected IQ as estimated from the patient's educational background, predictive accuracy was significantly augmented as compared with using a single cutting score for all subjects. This finding continues to be replicated (Overall & Levin, 1978; Wilson, Rosenbaum, & Brown, 1979).

It was also argued that in evaluating a test for neuropsychological assessment, the common practice of examining cutting scores and hit rates was, for the most part, off target. While appropriate for evaluating screening devices, such tests were not going to advance neuropsychology. Instead, progress was foreseen in:

the prediction of a specific locus of lesion by the use of special methods according to neuropsychological hypotheses. As a rule, such techniques have little value as screening devices for the presence or absence of brain damage in general, although their contribution to the diagnostic evaluation of the individual patient may be of considerable importance. (Spreen & Benton, 1965, p. 332)

Test Development

The tests that were studied or developed in the Benton Laboratory of Neuropsychology were generally introduced to test a hypothesis. As these research topics often came from the clinical literature of neurology and neuropsychology, the transition from research tools to diagnostic instruments was a natural one. Empirical findings determined which tests would be developed for clinical use. In one case, Benton, Levin, and Van Allen (1974) investigated the map localization test which had been used by others to evaluate "disorders of spatial thought" (Critchley, 1953) that were commonly attributed to a right hemisphere lesion. Before this there had been no study that standardized the task or took into account the educational backgrounds of the subjects. The empirical results failed to show an association between defective performance and either right or left hemisphere lesions; however, there was an overwhelming effect due to educational background. Obviously this task was not developed for clinical use.

The development of the Facial Recognition Test (Benton & Van Allen, 1968) went in a different direction. It was introduced as an experimental device to study the syndrome of prosopagnosia. In this syndrome, patients are unable to recognize family members by their faces, and they appear unable to learn to recognize new faces such as those of their attending physician and ward staff (Damasio, Damasio & Van Hoesen, 1982). Although it was subsequently demonstrated that patients with severe prosopagnosia could nevertheless perform normally on this and related tasks (Benton, 1980; Benton & Van Allen, 1972), the test proved to be a valid behavioral sign of acquired neurologic disability with localizing significance in its own right (Benton, Hamsher, Varney, & Spreen, 1983; Hamsher, Levin, & Benton, 1979). In another vein, the test of tactile form perception (Benton et al., 1983) was originally introduced as a control task for subjects who failed tactile naming on the Neurosensory Center Comprehensive Examination for Aphasia (Spreen & Benton, 1969) so as to evaluate the sensory component of the defective performance. Later, defective performances were found to be associated with signs of spatial disturbances as well as contralateral sensorimotor deficits. Consequently, the test was developed for clinical use.

Benton's program encompassed a wide variety of research topics. Thus, interest in the functional properties of the right hemisphere led to investigations such as motor impersistence and proprioception (Levin, 1973), facial recognition, tactile form perception, and constructional praxis (Benton et al., 1983). Inquiries into the relationship between aphasic disorder and cognitive function led to development of two aphasia batteries (Benton & Hamsher, 1983; Spreen & Benton, 1969) and tests of pantomine recognition (Varney, 1978; Varney & Benton, 1982), phoneme dicrimination (Varney & Benton, 1979), and sound recognition (Varney, 1980). A more complete review of the contributions of the Benton Laboratory of Neuropsychology can be found in Hamsher (1985).

THEORY AND RESEARCH: BASIC PRINCIPLES

Nosological Problems

The concept of dementia dates back many centuries. It refers to a state of global deterioration in behavioral performances to such an extent that a person is rendered unable to discharge the responsibilities associated with the intellectual demands of everyday life (Benton, 1985). Unfortunately, this concept is very broad and vague. It sometimes takes on surplus meaning to include an image of drooling and the odors of incontinence. At the other extreme, it may be applied in the face of nearly any acquired cognitive defect, especially in the elderly. Over the past 100 years, a number of distinct disorders have been distinguished from dementia, including the aphasias, amnesia, agnosia, and confusional states (delirium). The latter condition has also been variously called "acute organic brain syndrome" or "reversible dementia" (Cummings & Benson, 1983).

Despite this movement toward a more differentiated view of the neurobehavioral disorders there are others who have extended the concept of dementia to a condition characterized by preserved intellectual functioning but with impaired attention–concentration, psychomotor retardation, and a slowness in information retrieval, called the "subcortical dementias" (Albert, Feldman, & Willis, 1974; Benson, 1983; Joynt & Shoulson, 1985). The concept of "subcortical dementia" has proved to be rather controversial, if not ill-conceived. Albert's description of the disorder (Albert et al., 1974) in patients with progressive supranuclear palsy was behaviorally similar to the presentation of patients described as having pseudodementia (Wells, 1979), that is, the late-life presentation of psychopathology. Indeed, more recently, "subcortical dementia" has been applied to the cognitive manifestation of depression (Cummings & Benson, 1984), schizophrenia-like psychosis, mania and obsessive-compulsive disorder (Cummings, 1985b). Some investigators have failed to replicate Albert's findings in patients with progressive supranuclear palsy (Kimura, Barnette, & Burkhart, 1979) but others have found at least partial support (Pillon, Dubois, Legault, Agid, & Lhermitte, 1986). "Subcortical dementia" is said to also apply to Parkinson's disease, yet some have found no clear behavioral differences between this and the (cortical) dementia associated with Alzheimer's disease (Mayeux & Stern, 1983) while others have (Huber, Shuttleworth, Paulson, Bellchambers & Clapp, 1986). At the same time, there are disorders that principally involve subcortical ganglia, such as Wilson's disease and Huntington's disease, which result in mental changes similar to that seen in Alzheimer's disease rather than what has been described as the clinical presentation of "subcortical dementia" (Benson, 1983). Thus, diagnostic confusion seems to follow when one mixes diagnostic metaphors by intermingling behavioral diagnostic terms with anatomic and disease entities.

From the scientific method, one can infer two general purposes for diagnosis: classification and prediction. With regard to classification, one must keep in mind that this process is dependent on technology. When we classify objects or diseases, the goal is to sort like with like. But, while two objects may look alike with the naked eye, significant differences may be observed with a microscope, and this would cause us to refine our classification scheme. Thus, a limiting factor for any nosology is the assessment technology. A clinical nosology is intended to aid professional communication and to facilitate systematic inquiry. With regard to prediction and in the case of disease states, there are several objectives. We may wish to predict response to treatment, course or prognosis, etiology, and pathophysiological processes (Spitzer, Sheehy, & Endicott, 1977).

No one classification schema may be able to accomplish all these goals at the same time. At any particular time, emphasis will be placed on one or another goal, depending on current knowledge. As new information becomes available, conceptualizations may shift, and diagnostic categories may be split, refined, redefined, or deleted. When clinical lore held that declining mentation in the elderly was the result of "hardening of the arteries of the brain," we had the concept of arteriosclerotic dementia. This concept no longer

exists in the neurological nomenclature, as many of the cases that received this diagnosis in the past would now be considered examples of Alzheimer's disease; however, arteriosclerotic disease may contribute to the presentation of what is now commonly called multi-infarct dementia (Adams & Victor, 1981).

Given all this, it would seem prudent to avoid forcing our behavioral diagnoses into alignment with particular etiologies or presumptive lesion localizations. Linking neurobehavioral diagnoses to etiologies would seem to deny the fact that the behavioral presentation of a disease entity can change over time, as in Alzheimer's disease or closed head injury (Levin, Benton, & Grossman, 1982). And linking behavioral diagnoses to lesion localization may prove difficult to sustain as seen in "subcortical dementia." Thus, for conceptual clarity, it would seem more appropriate to base our classification of mental states on our neuropsychological technology.

Nosological Refinements

Once objectively defined, validity correlates can be developed for the diagnostic groups. Diagnoses can be subdivided when it is shown that the subdivision provides further information. For example, the clinical distinction between dementia of the primary degenerative type versus the multi-infarct type is based on elements of the clinical history that can be tabulated as an "Ischemic Score" (Rosen, Terry, Fuld, Katzman, & Peck, 1980). At this stage of subclassification, other types of data may be incorporated to make subtype distinctions that add to the validity correlates of the basic diagnoses. These other elements could include laboratory, radiological, or physical findings as well as specialized behavioral observations.

Major Disorders

The major neurobehavioral disorders are those in which disturbances of memory and attention are the prominent clinical features. These are dementia, confusional states, dementia with confusion, amnesia, material–specific memory learning defects, and attentional dysfunction (or aprosexia). Included in the differential diagnosis are the aphasic disorders. Other disorders, which have yet to be defined as well-recognized syndromes by objective methodologies, include focal neuropsychological deficits implicating disease of either the right or left hemisphere (not accounted for by any of the above syndromes).

Assessment

The differential diagnosis relies on four types of measurements, assuming an aphasic disorder can be ruled out. In the clinical literature these are called remote memory, recent memory, short-term memory (new learning), and immediate memory. These terms, and the concepts they represent, were derived from clinical observations. More in line with the terminology of the types of tests we shall use to measure these dimensions of mental function, we shall refer to these same constructs as (general) intelligence (psychometric g), recent memory and orientation, verbal and nonverbal learning, and attention–concentration, respectively. In cognitive psychology, general intelligence is represented by the concept of semantic long-term memory, whereas recent memory is akin to episodic long-term memory.

INTELLIGENCE, ATTENTION, AND PSYCHOMOTOR SPEED

The Wechsler Scale

For assessing intelligence, the Wechsler Adult Intelligence Scale–Revised (WAIS–R) is recognized as the standard. As described above, one need not administer the entire battery for neurobehavioral diagnostic purposes. In choosing which subtests to select, we turn to the factor analysis studies. As reviewed by Matarazzo (1972), for the WAIS, the general findings indicate two major factors and one or two additional factors. The first factor is defined by the Information, Comprehension, Similarities, and Vocabulary tests. We shall call it the verbal–conceptual factor, as its more common designation as "verbal comprehension" in the context of a neuropsychological assessment is likely to be confused with language comprehension, a dimension important to the diagnosis of aphasia but quite different from what is being assessed with the WAIS. The second major factor is defined by performances on Block Design, Object Assembly, Picture Arrangement, and Picture Completion. We shall arbitrarily call this the perceptual–constructional factor. The third factor is defined by performances on Digit Span and Arithmetic (occasionally Digit Symbol may load on this factor as well), which we shall designate attention–concentration (excluding Digit Symbol). A similar factor structure has been found with the WAIS-R (Atkinson & Cyr, 1984; Leckliter, Matarazzo, & Silverstein, 1986; Parker, 1983).

Within the first two factors, the combination of any two or three subtests will define the performance level

with clinically adequate stability and reliability. That is, the subtests in the first two factors are highly intercorrelated, and all have substantial loadings on psychometric g. For report writing purposes, these scores can be described in terms of deviation quotients (DQs) by using the age-corrected scaled score equivalents, given in the back of the WAIS–R manual, and applying the formula of Tellegen and Briggs (1967). The advantage of this approach is to purify our measure of verbal and nonverbal intellectual functioning so as not to confound them with attention–concentration and psychomotor speed measures that may be selectively impaired in the brain damaged population. Relative impairments in attention–concentration and psychomotor speed performances also relate to the severity of psychopathology, when present (Overall, Hoffmann, & Levin, 1978). That is, it would be a mistake to identify a patient as manifesting general intellectual impairment when in fact the only performances to fall below expectations were on the attention–concentration and psychomotor speed tests. If averaged in with the other tests in the computation of the traditional Verbal and Performance IQs, this could produce artifactual defective scores on these composite measures.

Because of the very high correlations between Information and Vocabulary, as well as between Block Design and Object Assembly, it would be redundant to include both in an abbreviated battery. Based on McFie's work (1975), looking at patterns of WAIS subtest performance in patients with focal brain lesions, the following selection would seem to provide the most information: Information and Similarities for the computation of the verbal–conceptual DQ; Arithmetic and Digit Span for the computation of the attention–concentration DQ; Block Design and Picture Arrangement for the computation of the perceptual–constructional DQ; and Digit Symbol as a measure of psychomotor (or more precisely, graphomotor) speed. However, an atypical educational history or a history of a learning disability may be reflected in a significantly depressed score on Information (Zimmerman & Woo-Sam, 1973); in such instances it would be wise to include a third verbal–conceptual subtest for balance and stability of measurement.

Interpretation

Interpretation of these results involves a comparison of the obtained IQ (or DQ) values with the expected premorbid values (Benton, 1980b). Wilson et al. (1979) and Overall and Levin (1978) provide formulae for this purpose. The Wilson formula has been cross-validated with adequate results (Goldstein, Gary, & Levin, 1986; Karzmark, Heaton, Grant & Matthews, 1985). An accommodation is needed to translate from the WAIS to the WAIS–R (Barona, Reynolds, & Chastain, 1984), since the two batteries do not give equivalent results (Wechsler, 1981). In my laboratory I found that if Wilson et al.'s recommendation for altering the educational coefficient were followed, then one could use the results from the WAIS–R. Obviously, local norms will always be more desirable for this prediction situation.

Caveat

A general principle to be followed in interpreting intellectual or neuropsychological test results in the context of a neurobehavioral evaluation is to keep one's eye keenly fixed on the referral question. Suppose one were assessing a 35-year-old patient and performance on the verbal and nonverbal scales of the WAIS–R fell significantly below expectations (defined as being at or below the second percentile for the subject's demographic group). The question is, have we demonstrated that the patient has dementia? The answer would, in great measure, depend on the clinical history and the reason for the referral. If we were trying to explain a decline in mental status sufficient to produce significant psychosocial disability that interfered with social and occupational functioning, then the diagnosis of dementia would have to be entertained. Since a primary degenerative dementia would be unlikely at this age, one should look for an etiological event to support the diagnosis, such as a history of severe head trauma with prolonged coma, or severe hypotensive (anoxic–ischemic) cerebral damage (drowning, hanging, carbon monoxide poisoning), or infectious disease of the brain. However, without such a clinical history, the incidental finding of intellectual performances being significantly below expectations, based on the actuarial formulae, would not suggest dementia. Instead, it would raise the question of an error of prediction or call into question the information used to calculate the expected intellectual scores. Alternatively, such results could be an example of the obvious, namely, that by definition, 2% of the general population without a history or evidence of dementia will score at or below the second percentile using these prediction formulae.

COMPARISON WITH CLINICAL ASSESSMENT

In the clinical (bedside) assessment of remote memory, examiners would inquire about the patient's early personal history; however, much of this information is difficult to verify. In substitution, clinical examiners would inquire about various overlearned facts that are acquired in a grade school education, such as questions about major points in history, geography, or measurement (Strub & Black, 1977). Obviously, this is assessing one's general fund of information which, along with vocabulary, is an excellent predictor of general intelligence. Hence, the clinical concept of remote memory can be replaced with measures of general intelligence. The only neurobehavioral disorder in which there is a true defect of remote memory is dementia.

In the clinical mental status examination, attention–concentration is typically measured with a similar digit span task, by asking the patient to perform serial additions, subtractions, or other mental calculations, and by spelling common words backwards. Sustained attention may be measured with the Continuous Performance Test (Gordon & Mettleman, 1988). For other alternate psychometric measures of attention–concentration, as well as the other dimensions of mental functioning to be discussed in this chapter, the reader is referred to Lezak's book (1983).

On the Wechsler Memory Scale (WMS) and the Wechsler Memory Scale–Revised (WMS–R) (Wechsler, 1987), the Mental Control and Digit Span subtests tap the attention–concentration domain (Erickson & Scott, 1977). The Trail Making Test and the Symbol Digit Modalities Test (Lezak, 1983) are commonly used tests that could be substituted for the Digit Symbol Test as measures of psychomotor speed.

RECENT MEMORY AND ORIENTATION

Tests of orientation are intended to assess the contents of recent memory, whereas tests of verbal and nonverbal learning are intended to assess the processes by which such memories are presumed to be acquired. Clinically, the examiner may ask the patient to explain the events leading up to his hospitalization or outpatient referral, to describe recent major news events, or to recount the recent presidents of the United States (Adams & Victor, 1981). Orientation to place and time are also typically included. A sharp division between what is recent memory and what is remote does not exist. Basically, the intent of recent memory testing is to assess the retention of material that is typically forgotten over the course of time through the process of normal forgetting. In this fashion one may be able to determine if there is an abnormal rate of forgetting. Many things influence recent memory capacity, including intellectual level, age, and the significance of the material to be assessed. A foreign war or the death of a foreign government leader may hold intellectual significance for the well educated and therefore be well remembered, but such may be of no consequence to the individual of less than average intelligence. A variety of questions assessing recent memory and orientation are included in the highly abbreviated mental status questionnaires (Pfeiffer, 1975).

Objective and well-standardized tests of recent memory are few in number. The test of temporal orientation by Benton, Van Allen, and Fogel (1964) is quick, easy to administer and score, and it has been extensively normed (Benton et al., 1983). A similar measure intended specifically for head injury victims is also available (Levin, O'Donnell, & Grossman, 1979). Memory for recent presidents (Presidents Test) has been extensively standardarized (Hamsher & Roberts, 1985). Other tests that may be taken from the experimental literature involve assessing memory for famous persons, news events, and television shows (Albert & Kaplan, 1980; Warrington, 1976). On the Wechsler Memory Scale, the Orientation and Information subtests tap this domain (Erickson & Scott, 1977). Defects in temporal orientation are common in patients with bilateral or diffuse cerebral disease (Benton et al., 1983) and in bilateral frontal lobe disease (Benton, 1968).

NEW LEARNING

Tests of verbal and nonverbal learning are legion in the psychology and neuropsychology literature (see Lezak, 1983). On the Wechsler Memory Scale, the Logical Memory, Associate Learning and Visual Reproduction subtests would fall into these categories. With regard to clinical application, nearly all learning tests suffer from the same deficiency: They have not been well standardized. Since the speed of learning and the quantity of material that can be memorized are closely related to intelligence and age in neurologically intact individuals, the normative standards for learning tests must be adjusted according to such

individual differences. Of all our demographic predictor variables, years of educational attainment show the closest relationship with IQ measures (Matarazzo, 1972). Therefore, tests of this sort should be minimally corrected (or separately normed) for educational background along with age. For a verbal learning test, the serial digit learning (or digit supraspan) test fulfills these requirements up through age 74 (Benton et al., 1983; Hamsher, Benton, & Digre, 1980). However, in some age–education categories, the test suffers from "floor effect," such that it can be used to identify normal performances but cannot adequately grade the severity of defective scores (i.e., just below normal limits vs. grossly impaired). The Benton Visual Retention Test, Administration A (Benton, 1974) fulfills the essential normative criteria and can serve as a nonverbal learning test as, apparently, successful performance requires the subject to mentally rehearse the geometric designs. However, the test is also sensitive to disturbances of immediate memory. Performance on both the serial digit learning and visual retention tests drop precipitously with age (Benton, Eslinger, & Damasio, 1981). Both tests are frequently failed by patients with bilateral or diffuse cerebral disease, whereas a minority of patients with unilateral disease perform defectively. There is only a slight bias for a higher failure rate on the verbal learning task by patients with left-sided unilateral lesions. On the nonverbal task, the bias is in the other direction, but again slight.

DIFFERENTIAL DIAGNOSIS

Dementia

From a neurobehavioral and psychometric standpoint, dementia is defined as a generalized decline in intellectual functioning that is associated with a significant impairment in psychosocial or occupational functioning (not due simply to physical limitations). On a reasonably comprehensive assessment battery, one should see widespread cognitive defects, although some aspects of cognitive performance may appear more severely affected than others (Benton, 1980b; Eslinger & Benton, 1983). However, aphasic patients are not intended to be classified in this category, even though they, too, may show multiple cognitive defects secondary to their linguistic disability. While patients with dementia eventually develop severe disorders of recent memory, orientation, and learning, only about 40% have such defects on their initial assessment when diagnosed in this fashion (Benton, Van Allen, & Fogel, 1964). Although attention–concentration may not be normal, it should be no worse than expected for the patient's current intellectual level. As a clinical rule of thumb, the attention–concentration DQ should not fall 15 or more points below the verbal–conceptual DQ.

Confusional State

The hallmarks of a confusional state are disturbances in arousal and attention (Mesulam, 1985; Seltzer & Mesulam, 1988; Strub, 1982). The disturbances in arousal may cause the patient to be overly active (delirium or hyperkinetic confusional state) or underactive (mild lethargy or hypokinetic confusional state). Patients are inattentive and disoriented. Psychotic features are often present in the hyperkinetic phase, and speech may be mumbled or incoherent at times. Often, an inability to maintain a mental set requires that the examiner frequently prompt the patient so as to comply with the test instructions. Presumably, as a consequence of the impairment in attention–concentration, much information does not get registered, producing disturbances in recent memory and learning. Perceptual disturbances are also common. However, there is no loss of general information. While such patients are difficult to assess, when appropriately stimulated so as to maximize their attention, one finds that verbal–conceptual performances are not defective.

Dementia with Confusion

This is a rather common combination. These patients are easily identified because their mental impairments are global. Intelligence, orientation and recent memory, learning, and attention–concentration all suffer. This condition has also been called "beclouded dementia" (Adams & Victor, 1981, pp. 282–283). A patient with a preexisting but unidentified dementia very often comes to clinical attention when the features of an acute confusional state are superimposed. These are the patients who are best captured by the DSM-III-R criteria for dementia and dementia with delirium.

Amnesia

These patients have no significant impairment of intellectual functioning, as in dementia, or of attention–concentration, as in a confusional state, but have a generalized (verbal and nonverbal) learning impairment with evidence of a recent memory defect, disorientation, or both.

Material–Specific Memory Disorder

This is a tenuous diagnostic category. It is intended to capture patients with unilateral temporal lobe lesions who show a disruption of either verbal or nonverbal learning, but not both, and who otherwise appear cognitively preserved. Primarily, such disorders have been reported as a consequence of unilateral temporal lobectomy for the control of intractable seizures (Loring, Lee, Martin & Meador, 1988; Milner, 1974). However, it has not been clearly established whether or not such patients simultaneously manifest associated temporal lobe symptoms, such as naming and other aphasic symptoms with left-sided lesions, or visuoperceptive and spatial disturbances in the case of right-sided lesions. If this were the case, then it may be difficult to parcel out a specific memory disorder that cannot be accounted for in terms of the associated symptomatology.

Attentional Dysfunction (Aprosexia)

Psychometrically, this disorder is characterized by impaired attention–concentration, with preserved intelligence. When severe, learning may also be mildly impaired, but there is no impairment of recent memory or orientation such as seen in confusional states and amnesia. Some psychomotor slowing and slowness in information retrieval are frequently associated symptomatology. This category of abnormal mental status has been overlooked in most modern nomenclatures. In the 1880s it was a recognized disorder, and it was given the name aprosexia (literally meaning a failure to heed). This disorder needs to be differentiated from the disorder of childhood and adolescence called Attention Deficit Disorder with or without hyperactivity. Therefore, it would seem appropriate to resurrect this now archaic term, aprosexia, and apply it to this diagnostic category. Aprosexia is defined in psychiatric dictionaries so as to mean precisely what we would wish it to mean: "Inability to maintain attention. The condition is common in organic states that affect the brain and psychiatric conditions" (Hinsie & Campbell, 1975, p. 60). Among neurology outpatients presenting with complaints of memory problems, this is the most frequent neuropsychologic finding. It is frequently associated with psychopathology.

FOCAL DEFICITS

Small or focal cerebral lesions are not likely to produce a general disturbance in one's cognitive status. In terms of the major neurobehavioral disorders, if the lesion were recent, then one may see an attentional dysfunction (aproxesia) that recedes over time. With focal lesions it would not be unusual to find no evidence of a significant disturbance of memory or attention. However, if the lesion were associated with diffuse pressure or brain edema, as is often the case with mass lesions, then the behavioral picture of diffuse dysfunction, characteristically expressed as a confusional state or pronounced aproxesia, may be present in addition to the focal features.

Exceptions to this rule have been reported when the focal lesions involve certain regions of the thalamus (Castaigne, Lhermitte, Buge, Escourolle, Hauw, & Lyon-Caen, 1981; McFarling, Rothi, & Heilman, 1982) or polymodal association cortex in the right hemisphere (Mesulam, 1981; Mesulam, Waxman, Geschwind, & Sabin, 1976). In these situations, small lesions that were not associated with pressure or edema effects presented as confusional states with focal neuropsychological signs or emotional changes.

Before launching into an unwieldy investigation of neuropsychological signs of an unknown focal cerebral disease, one should formulate a hypothesis about the likelihood of the existence of a focal lesion and its location based on the history, neurological findings, radiographic data, clinical presentation, and the complaints of the patient. With ever-advancing technology in neurological medicine, it is becoming more common for the neuropsychologist to know where the lesion is before starting the examination. In such cases, the question may be, what is the significance of the lesion and in what behavioral context does it occur; that is, what is the patient's mental (or cognitive) status? In contrast, in nonneurological settings, one is often referred patients with a nonspecific history of some behavioral change that the patient either denies knowledge of or is only vaguely able to describe, with a lack of sufficient detail to suggest a particular problem for evaluation. In these cases, one may wish to rule out the major neurobehavioral disorders, screen the major domains of neuropsychological functions, and specifically address the issue of some disturbance of personality functioning (i.e., psychopathology).

Neuropsychological tests are not direct measures of brain functioning. That is, we do not have tests that measure how well the left temporal or right temporal lobe is working. Likewise, a defective test score is not synonymous with an organic brain lesion. The tests can be thought of as challenges to the brain that are made to identify weaknesses and to elicit recognizable signs and symptoms of brain disease in addition to providing objective and quantified behavioral observations. Some of the signs come from incidental observations. For example, neuropsychological studies implicate a role for the superior parietal lobule in visually guided arm–hand movements (Hyvarinen, 1982), and clinical studies in man have shown that superior parietal lobule lesions may produce a characteristic sign called, among other names, misreaching (Damasio & Benton, 1979). Special tests would not be needed to evaluate this sign, as reaching is required in the performance of several neuropsychological tests, for example, in building three-dimensional block models.

The major realms of mental activity for which cognitive tests have been developed for clinical application include: speech and language, somatoperceptual functioning, visuoperceptive ability, spatial orientation, psychosensory and psychomotor functioning (Benton, 1977b). Detailed reviews of the various psychometric signs and symptoms of focal cerebral lesions are provided by Freda Newcombe (1969) and Kevin Walsh (1978). Syndromes of neuropsychological impairment are reviewed in detail in the works of Hécaen and Albert (1978), Heilman and Valenstein (1979), and DeRenzi (1982). A comprehensive review of neuropsychological tests and their validity correlates is provided by Lezak (1983). Some of the tests developed in the Benton Laboratory are described in a recent book that also summarizes their validity data (Benton et al., 1983).

Speech and Language

Speech is assessed by listening to the patient during an examination. Rather than testing speech, the test is rated in terms of various qualities such as fluency, articulation, and prosody, and by listening for errors, such as phonemic or semantic paraphasias. For this purpose, the rating scales for speech characteristics and aphasia severity from the Boston Diagnostic Aphasia Battery are most commonly used (Goodglass & Kaplan, 1983). Intrusions, perseverations, echolalia, and palilalia are other forms of speech disorders of central origin that may be seen in the absence of aphasia (Benson, 1979). Language functions that may be compromised in conditions other than aphasia, such as in dementia, confusional states, or with focal lesions of the left temporal or frontal lobe, include naming, word fluency, and comprehension (Barker &

Lawson, 1968; Chedru & Geschwind, 1972; Mayeux, Brandt, Rosen, & Benson, 1980; Rosen, 1980; Seltzer & Sherwin, 1983). The visual naming, controlled oral word association, and Token Test subtests of the Multilingual Aphasia Examination (Benton & Hamsher, 1976) are useful for these purposes.

Somatoperceptual Functioning

Chief among these are tests of right–left orientation and finger localization (Benton et al., 1983). Both types of performance show a close relationship with aphasia and dementia. The right–left orientation task assesses this discrimination both in relation to the patient's body and that of a confronting person. A generalized defect on both parts of the test is associated with dementia and aphasia, whereas an isolated defect in pointing to a confronting person is found in right-hemisphere disease in addition to the other two major disorders (Ratcliff, 1982). The finger localization task assesses performance in both hands: Bilateral impairment is common in the presence of bilateral disease and aphasia. A unilateral defect on the side opposite the side of the lesion is the most common abnormal performance of nonaphasic patients with unilateral lesions, the majority of whom perform normally on this test.

Visuoperceptive Ability

A variety of visuoperceptive functions may be assessed in a neurobehavioral evaluation. Their localizing significance and historical background are reviewed by Benton (1979), and Ratcliff (1982), and the available tests are reviewed by Lezak (1983) and in Benton et al. (1983). Cancellation tests are used to identify visual inattention and lateralized neglect that may follow lesions of the right parietal lobe (Albert, 1973) or the frontal lobes and basal ganglia on either side (Damasio, Damasio, & Chui, 1980). Disorders of color perception are associated with bilateral occipitotemporal lesions (Damasio, Yamada, Damasio, Corbett, & McKee, 1980; Meadows, 1974), while disorders in associating colors with visual referents (e.g., what color is an apple?) are closely associated with aphasia (Damasio, McKee, & Damasio, 1979; Varney, 1982). Disturbances in facial recognition (i.e., the discrimination of unfamiliar faces) have two correlates when dementia has been excluded: Such impairment is seen in the context of aphasic language comprehension impairment and, thus, is associated

with left hemisphere lesions; in the absence of a significant language comprehension deficit, the disorder is associated with focal right hemisphere lesions, with more frequent posterior than anterior involvement (Hamsher, Levin, & Benton, 1979). Disorders of visual synthesis, pattern identification, and "closure," including the perception of subjective contours and the recognition of incomplete figures, have been associated with right hemisphere lesions (Hamsher, 1978a), with particular involvement of the temporal lobe (Newcombe & Russell, 1969). Disturbances in form discrimination appear sensitive to brain lesions in general (Benton et al., 1983), although there is a bias for patients with posterior parietal and temporal lobe lesions on the right to show more frequent and severe defect (Meier & French, 1965; Ratcliff, 1982). In the context of aphasia, the form discrimination test appears useful in the discrimination of two subtypes of alexia, by identifying a chiefly perceptual defect (Varney, 1981) that may be distinguished from a cognitive or semantic subtype (see below). Disorders of stereoscopic perception (global stereopsis) in the absence of defects in stereoacuity (local stereopsis) are associated with right hemisphere lesions, in fact, almost exclusively so (Hamsher, 1978b).

Spatial Orientation

Spatial ability is often assessed by asking patients to draw figures or copy geometric designs, and by having them assemble models, such as Block Design from the WAIS or three-dimensional block model constructions (Benton et al., 1983). The correlates of defective performance are similar to those noted above for facial recognition (Benton, 1973). Constructional apraxia as measured by the three-dimensional task is also a correlate of bilateral and unilateral right frontal lobe disease (Benton, 1968). More localizing is defective performance on the visual task of judging the spatial orientation of lines (Benton, Varney, & Hamsher, 1978), which, when performance is in the severely defective range, suggests right parietal lobe involvement. In the tactile modality, the identification of abstract tactile forms, for example, tactile-visual pattern matching, appears quite sensitive to the presence of cerebral disease, both bilateral and unilateral (Benton et al., 1983). In addition to identifying a higher-level somesthetic defect in the hand contralateral to the lesion, bimanually defective performances appear to result from a generalized (or supramodal) spatial disability.

Complex Sensory Functions

For neurobehavioral examination purposes, tests of sensory function are chiefly concerned with higher-level disorders of perception and extinction phenomena (i.e., when single stimuli on the right and left are adequately perceived, but double simultaneous stimulation results in a consistent suppression of responses on one side). Tests such as the finger localization and tactile form perception tests provide information about tactile perception in addition to their cognitive components. In the auditory modality, tests of dichotic listening may provide highly localizing information, in the absence of an auditory acuity defect (A. R. Damasio & H. Damasio, 1977; H. Damasio & A. R. Damasio, 1979); extinction on dichotic tests may be related to lesions in the geniculotemporal auditory pathway or in the transcallosal pathway that connects the superior temporal gyri from each hemisphere. Tests of the recognition of meaningful environmental sounds (Varney, 1980) and the discrimination of meaningless sound (such as crackling or buzzing) (Vignolo, 1969) have demonstrated lateralizing value (left versus right hemisphere lesions, respectively). Also, the test of meaningful sound recognition has been useful in the differentiation of subtypes of language comprehension impairment. A perceptual subtype can be identified with a test of phoneme discrimination (Benton et al., 1983), whereas defective sound recognition in the context of preserved phoneme discrimination appears related to a cognitive or semantic subtype (Varney, 1980). Similarly, a test of the recognition of the import of pantomimes (Benton et al., 1983) has been helpful in identifying a subtype of alexia that appears related to a cognitive or semantic disturbance in the visual modality, as opposed to the perceptual subtype mentioned above (Varney & Benton, 1982).

Psychomotor Functioning

In the Benton Laboratory, emphasis was placed on the cognitive components of motor functioning. As a practical matter, it was felt that the neuropsychologist's distinctive contribution was in the assessment of cognitive functions, whereas tests of elementary sensory and motor function were somewhat redundant with the neurologic examination. Three aspects of psychomotor functioning that received considerable research attention were reaction time (Dee & Van Allen, 1971), motor impersistence (Levin, 1973), and gestural apraxia (Dee, Benton, & Van Allen, 1970). Although reaction time has been shown to be sensitive to brain disease in general (Dee & Van Allen, 1972), at the present time it does not appear to contribute to differential diagnosis. However, several studies have found defective reaction times to be predictive of prognosis (e.g., Hamsher, Halmi, & Benton, 1981; Van Zomeren & Deelman, 1978). There are a number of unresolved issues concerning motor impersistence, that is, the inability to sustain voluntary motor acts (Benton et al., 1983). It shows a close relationship with dementia. In the context of unilateral cerebral lesions, it is related to proprioceptive disorders with lesions on the right, but not on the left. Likewise, studies of gestural apraxia have failed to resolve a number of conceptual and procedural issues relating to this putative disorder, which is primarily seen in the context of aphasia (Dee, Benton, & Van Allen, 1970). However, a special form of this disorder that only affects the performance of the left side of the body ("left-limb dyspraxia") has been well established, and it implicates involvement of the transcallosal motor pathways (Bogen, 1979).

DIAGNOSIS

Meier (1981) has stressed the need to establish standards of competency in neuropsychology based on educational and training requirements and a demonstration of current knowledge by objective testing and professional review. Equally important will be the development of a professional consensus of opinion on the standards of practice for neuropsychology (Matthews, 1981). What do we measure, how do we measure it, and what should we say in our interpretive reports? If we are all cognizant of the same body of scientific data, then why would there not be a consensus? As a field develops, it is probably healthy for there to be a divergence of opinion on these issues, but at some point there should be enough data and experience to resolve these issues. I am not suggesting a rigid model that discourages further development and experimentation; nor am I suggesting that every examiner should be using identical testing instruments. Differences in patient populations, base rates, and the purposes for which the neuropsychological services are being requested, along with other considerations, call for some rational diversity of approach in different settings. Hopefully, neuropsychology will continue to receive new and improved tests for clinical use that will sharpen our diagnostic and predictive capabilities, and such evolutionary changes should be encouraged.

OBJECTIVE CRITERIA FOR NEUROBEHAVIORAL SYNDROMES

Recommendations for the future of neuropsychology include the development of a basic framework for neuropsychological assessment geared to the identification of neurologically significant syndromes. Along with this we shall need to develop an objective nosology of neurobehavioral disorders. The chief goal of the nosology is to provide a brief summary statement about states of nature, namely, the cognitive status of patients with brain disease or trauma. With these objective diagnostic categories in mind, we know what it is we are trying to predict from our assessment. This helps to establish a framework for diagnostic reasoning. Criteria for the diagnostic categories are not meant to be etched in stone. In fact, an objective nosology facilitates refinements and modifications of the criteria as new data are published. If an alteration in the criteria is shown to improve or add to the validity correlates for the diagnostic category, it should be adopted.

Once established, the diagnostic categories could be subtyped using objective behavioral or other findings that may be predictive of etiology, prognosis, response to a particular treatment, and so forth. The nosology would enhance both inter- and intraprofessional communications. It would also stimulate the professional development of the practice of neuropsychology by fostering uniform standards of practice based on sound propositions and scientific merit. Likewise, this would provide a focus for the further development of existing or new neuropsychological test instruments.

For research, the benefits would include an individualized control of mental status and demographic factors for both group and idiographic research designs. This would come with the use of standardized tests that took into account a patient's demographic background. In this fashion, demographic variables may be combined to predict an adjusted normal range of variability. Although such adjustments may not apply to all tests, such factors should be investigated in the development of all tests. An objective nosology, so devised, would provide a means by which investigators at different institutions could meaningfully contribute to the body of knowledge associated with each diagnostic category. Finally, this objective nosology would further the study of brain–behavior relationships because those relationships vary with the mental status of the subject. For example, if two patients each suffer a right parietal lobe stroke, but one happens to be demented and the other not, the outcomes are going to be quite different. Test measures that may correlate with each other in the context of dementia may show marked dissociation in the presence of certain focal cerebral lesions.

The major neurobehavioral disorders, defined above, would be a starting point, as they are already well recognized and validated syndromes despite there being some confusion in their differential diagnosis. To this list one would have to add the classical aphasia syndromes and the nonaphasic focal deficit syndromes of the left and right hemisphere. In recent years there has been a growing literature on atypical "aphasia" syndromes attributed to lesions in the internal capsule, basal ganglia, and the putamen (Damasio, Damasio, Rizzo, Varney, & Gersh, 1982; Naeser et al., 1982), which now seem to have the potential for objective behavioral definition. Likewise, cognitive symptoms associated with thalamic lesions may eventually lead to their syndrome definition so as to differentiate them from other causes of similar symptomatology (Henderson, Alexander, & Naeser, 1982; Wallesch, Kornhuber, Kunz, & Brunner, 1983). Emotional changes, devoid of associated cognitive symptoms with localizing value, might one day be developed in an objective fashion so as to deserve the status of neurobehavioral syndrome designations and be added to our nosology. Although some of these emotional changes have been related to focal cerebral lesions, the behavioral concepts are in an early stage of development and still lack objective specificity (Bear, 1983; Damasio & Van Hoesen, 1983). Nevertheless, the future of clinical neuropsychology at this point in time looks quite promising and clearly has the potential for making a major impact on diagnostic conventions and the further study of brain–behavior relationships.

SUMMARY

While the specialized approach to neuropsychological assessment is interested in the localization of brain lesions in the appropriate case material for such study, it is also concerned with a broader perspective, which includes the specification of the patient's general mental status. In neuropsychological assessment one must not only document the signs and symptoms that may reasonably be attributed to focal lesions but also define the behavioral context in which they occur. This is done by determining the patient's neurobehavioral status. The dimensions of assessment that should be incorporated into our nosology of neurobehavioral disorders should be derived from known brain–behavior relationships. To study behaviors without reference to the brain (Geschwind, 1980) would not be neuropsychology.

Efficiency in assessment is also stressed in the flexible approach. Lengthy examinations very often cannot be justified. Examples of tests that may be used to identify focal cerebral lesions were briefly reviewed, particularly those tests used or developed in the Benton Laboratory of Neuropsychology. A psychometric approach for adapting the WAIS for neurobehavioral examination purposes was also described and its rationale explained.

Admittedly, the psychometrically defined neurobehavioral disorders described in this chapter are limited in scope. Some of these conditions can occur in combinations. Clearly more work lies ahead in the enumeration of these disorders. Decisions must take into account which tests to use (which are best suited to the patient population under examination), base rates, and the import of the diagnostic decisions, all of which may vary from one setting to another.

Preoccupations with symptoms of cerebral disease are giving way to broader conceptualization bringing in the role of the diencephalon and basal ganglia in determining cognitive deficits and emotional changes. Limited concepts of brain disease in the form of structural changes are being replaced with more physiological concepts, such as disorders of neurotransmitter metabolism. Such occult disorders have long been implicated in the origin of psychiatric disease and in some neurological disorders such as Parkinson's disease; now a neurotransmitter disorder is being held responsible for neuropsychology's most fundamental syndrome, dementia. All these observations support a strong diagnostic role in neuropsychology's future.

REFERENCES

Adams, R. D., & Victor, M. (1981) Principles of Neurology (2nd ed.) New York: McGraw-Hill.

Adams, R. D., & Victor, M. (1985). *Principles of neurology* (3rd ed.). New York: McGraw-Hill.

Albert, M. L. (1973). A simple test of visual neglect. *Neurology, 23,* 658–664.

Albert, M. L., Feldman, R. G., & Willis, A. L. (1974). The subcortical dementia of progressive supranuclear palsy. *Journal of Neurology, Neurosurgery, and Psychiatry, 37,* 121–130.

Albert, M. L., Goodglass, H., Helm, N. A., Rubens, A. B., & Alexander, M. P. (1981). *Clinical aspects of dysphasia.* New York: Springer-Verlag.

Albert, M. S., & Kaplan, E. (1980). Organic implications of neuropsychological deficits in the elderly. In L. W. Poon, J. L. Fozard, L. S. Cermak, D. Arenberg, & L. W. Thompson (Eds.), *New directions in memory and aging.* Hillsdale, NJ: Erlbaum.

American Psychiatric Association. (1987). *Diagnostic and statistical manual of mental disorders* (3rd ed., Revised). Washington, DC: Author.

Anastasi, A. (1988). *Psychological testing* (6th ed.). New York: Macmillan.

Arendash, G. W., Millard, W. J., Dunn, A. J., & Meyer, E. M. (1987). Long-term neuropathological and neurochemical effects of nucleus basalis lesions in the rat. *Science, 238,* 952–956.

Atkinson, L., & Cyr, J. J. (1984). Factor analysis of the WAIS–R: Psychiatric and standardization samples. *Journal of Consulting and Clinical Psychology, 52,* 714–716.

Barker, M. G., & Lawson, J. S. (1968). Nominal aphasia in dementia. *British Journal of Psychiatry, 114,* 1351–1356.

Barona, A., Reynolds, C. R., & Chastain, R. (1984). A demographically based index of premorbid intelligence for the WAIS–R. *Journal of Consulting and Clinical Psychology, 52,* 885–887.

Bauer, R. M., & Rubens, A. B. (1985). Agnosia. In K. M. Heilman & E. Valenstein (Eds.), *Clinical neuropsychology* (2nd ed.) (pp. 187–241). New York: Oxford University Press.

Bear, D. M. (1983). Hemispheric specialization and the neurology of emotion. *Archives of Neurology, 40,* 195–202.

Beaumont, J. S. (1983). *Introduction to neuropsychology.* New York: Macmillan.

Benson, D. F. (1979). *Aphasia, alexia, and agraphia.* New York: Churchill Livingstone.

Benson, D. F. (1983). Subcortical dementia: A clinical approach. In R. Mayeux & W. G. Rosen (Eds.), *The dementias.* New York: Raven Press.

Benson, D. F., Gardner, H., & Meadows, J. C. (1976). Reduplicative amnesia. *Neurology, 26,* 147–151.

Benton, A. L. (1961). The fiction of the "Gerstmann Syndrome." *Journal of Neurology, Neurosurgery, and Psychiatry, 24,* 176–181.

Benton, A. L. (1968). Differential behavioral effects in frontal lobe disease. *Neuropsychologia, 6,* 53–60.

Benton, A. L. (1973). Visuoconstructive disability in patients with cerebral disease: Its relationship to side of lesion and aphasic disorder. *Documenta Ophthalmologica, 34,* 67–76.

Benton, A. L. (1974). *Revised visual retention test: Clinical and experimental applications* (4th ed.). New York: Psychological Corporation.

Benton, A. L. (1977a). Historical notes on hemispheric dominance. *Archives of Neurology, 34,* 127–129.

Benton, A. L. (1977b). Psychological testing. In A. B. Baker & L. H. Baker (Eds.), *Clinical neurology.* New York: Harper & Row.

Benton, A. L. (1977c). Reflections on the Gerstmann syndrome. *Brain and Language, 4,* 45–62.

Benton, A. L. (1978). The interplay of experimental and clinical approaches in brain lesion research. In S. Finger (Ed.), *Recovery from brain damage.* New York: Plenum Press.

Benton, A. L. (1979). Visuoperceptive, visuospatial and visuoconstructive disorders. In K. M. Heilman & E. Valenstein (Eds.), *Clinical neuropsychology.* New York: Oxford University Press.

Benton, A. L. (1980a). The neuropsychology of facial recognition. *American Psychologist, 35,* 176–186.

Benton, A. L. (1980b). Psychological testing for brain damage. In H. I. Kaplan, A. M. Freedman, & B. J. Badock (Eds.) *Comprehensive textbook of Psychiatry III Vol. 1.* Baltimore: William & Wilkins.

Benton, A. L. (1985). Psychological testing for brain damage. In H. I. Kaplan & B. J. Sadock (Eds.), *Comprehensive textbook of psychiatry/IV* (pp. 535–543). Baltimore: Williams & Wilkins.

Benton, A. (1988). Neuropsychology: Past, present and future. In F. Boller & J. Grafman (Eds.), *Handbook of Neuropsychology,* Vol. 1 (pp. 3–27). Amsterdam: Elsevier.

Benton, A. L., Eslinger, P. J., & Damasio, A. R. (1981). Normative observations on neuropsychological test performance in old age. *Journal of Clinical Neuropsychology, 3,* 33–42.

Benton, A. L., & Hamsher, K. deS. (1976). *Multilingual aphasia examination.* Iowa City: University of Iowa.

Benton, A. L., & Hamsher, K. deS. (1983). *Multilingual aphasia examination.* Odessa, FL: Psychological Assessment Resources.

Benton, A. L., Hamsher, K. deS., Varney, N. R., & Spreen, O. (1983). *Contributions to neuropsychological assessment: A clinical manual.* New York: Oxford University Press.

Benton, A. L., Levin, H. S., & Van Allen, M. W. (1974). Geographic orientation in patients with unilateral cerebral disease. *Neuropsychologia, 12,* 183–191.

Benton, A. L., & Van Allen, M. W. (1960). Impairment in facial recognition in patients with cerebral disease. *Cortex, 4,* 344–358.

Benton, A. L. & Van Allen, M. W. (1968). Impairment in facial recognition in patients with cerebral disease. *Cortex, 4,* 344–358.

Benton, A. L., & Van Allen, M. W. (1972). Prosopagnosia and facial discrimination. *Journal of the Neurological Sciences, 15,* 167–172.

Benton, A. L., Van Allen, M. W., & Fogel, M. L. (1964). Temporal orientation in cerebral disease. *Journal of Nervous and Mental Disease, 139,* 110–119.

Benton, A. L., Varney, N. R., & Hamsher, K. deS. (1978). Visuospatial judgment: A clinical test. *Archives of Neurology, 35,* 364–367.

Blackburn, H. L., & Benton, A. L. (1957). Revised administration and scoring of the digit span test. *Journal of Consulting Psychology, 21,* 139–143.

Bogen, J. E. (1979). The callosal syndrome. In K. M. Heilman & E. Valenstein (Eds.), *Clinical neuropsychology.* New York: Oxford University Press.

Bogen, J. E. (1985). The callosal syndromes. In K. M. Heilman & E. Valenstein (Eds.), *Clinical neuropsychology* (2nd ed.) (pp. 295–338). New York: Oxford University Press.

Brown, J. W. (1972). *Aphasia, apraxia and agnosia: Clinical and theoretical aspects.* Springfield: Charles C Thomas.

Burns, M. S., Halper, A. S., & Mogil, S. I. (Eds.). (1985). *Clinical management of right hemisphere dysfunction.* Rockville, MD: Aspen Systems Corporation.

Butters, N., & Cermak, L. S. (1980). *Alcoholic Korsakoff's syndrome.* New York: Academic Press.

Capitani, E., Della Sala, S., & Spinnler, H. (1986). Neuropsychological approach to dementia. In K. Poeck, H. J. Freund, & H. Ganshirt (Eds.), *Neurology* (Proceedings of the XIIIth World Congress of Neurology) (pp. 61–69). Berlin: Springer-Verlag.

Castaigne, P., Lhermitte, F., Buge, A., Escourolle, R., Hauw, J. J., & Lyon-Caen, O. (1981). Paramedian thalamic and midbrain infarcts: Clinical and neuropsychological study. *Annals of Neurology, 10,* 127–148.

Cermak, L. S. (1982). The long and short of it in amnesia. In L. S. Cermak (Ed.), *Human memory and amnesia.* Hillsdale, NJ: Erlbaum.

Chedru, F., & Geschwind, N. (1972). Disorders of

higher cortical functions in acute confusional states. *Cortex, 8,* 395–411.

Costa, L. (1983). Clinical neuropsychology: A discipline in evolution. *Journal of Clinical Neuropsychology, 5,* 1–11.

Costa, L. D., & Spreen, O. (Eds.). (1985). *Studies in neuropsychology: Selected papers of Arthur Benton.* New York: Oxford University Press.

Critchley, M. (1953). *The parietal lobes.* London: Arnold.

Cummings, J. L. (1985a). *Clinical neuropsychiatry.* Orlando, FL: Grune & Stratton.

Cummings, J. L. (1985b). Psychosomatic aspects of movement disorders. In M. R. Trimble (Ed.), *Interface between neurology and psychiatry.* Basel: Karger.

Cummings, J. L., & Benson, D. F. (1983). *Dementia: A clinical approach.* Boston: Butterworth.

Cummings, J. L., & Benson, D. F. (1984). Subcortical dementia: Review of an emerging concept. *Archives of Neurology, 41,* 874–879.

Damasio, A. R. (1985). The frontal lobes. In K. M. Heilman & E. Valenstein (Eds.), *Clinical neuropsychology* (2nd ed.) (pp. 339–375). New York: Oxford University Press.

Damasio, A. R., & Benton, A. L. (1979). Impairment of hand movements under visual guidance. *Neurology, 29,* 170–178.

Damasio, A., & Damasio, H. (1977). Studies in dichotic listening: Contributions to neuropsychology. In F. C. Rose (Ed.), *Physiological aspects of clinical neurology.* Boston: Blackwell Scientific Publications.

Damasio, A. R., Damasio, H., & Chui, H. C. (1980). Neglect following damage to frontal lobe or basal ganglia. *Neuropsychologia, 18,* 123–131.

Damasio, A. R., Damasio, H., Rizzo, M., Varney, N., & Gersh, F. (1982). Aphasia with nonhemorrhagic lesions in the basal ganglia and internal capsule. *Archives of Neurology, 39,* 15–20.

Damasio, A. R., Damasio, H., & Van Hoesen, G. W. (1982). Prosopagnosia: Anatomic basis and behavioral mechanisms. *Neurology, 32,* 331–341.

Damasio, A. R., McKee, J., & Damasio, H. (1979). Determinants of performance color anomia. *Brain and Language, 7,* 74–85.

Damasio, A. R., & Van Hoesen, B. W. (1983). Emotional disturbances associated with focal lesions of the limbic frontal lobe. In K. M. Heilman & P. Satz (Eds.), *Neuropsychology of human emotion.* New York: Guilford Press.

Damasio, A., Yamada, T., Damasio, H., Corbett, J., & McKee, J. (1980). Central chromatopsia: Be-

havioral, anatomic, and physiologic aspects. *Neurology, 30,* 1064–1071.

Damasio, H., & Damasio, A. R. (1979). "Paradoxic" ear extinction in dichotic listening: Possible anatomic significance. *Neurology, 29,* 644–653.

Davies, P. (1983). An update on the neurochemistry of Alzheimer disease. In R. Mayeux & W. G. Rosen (Eds.), *The dementias.* New York: Raven Press.

Davis, G. A. (1983). *A survey of adult aphasia.* Englewood Cliffs, NJ: Prentice-Hall.

Dee, H. L., Benton, A. L., & Van Allen, M. W. (1970). Apraxia in relation to hemispheric locus of lesion and aphasia. *Transactions of the American Neurological Association, 95,* 147–150.

Dee, H. L., & Van Allen, M. W. (1971). Simple and choice reaction time and motor strength in unilateral cerebral disease. *Acta Psychiatrica Scandinavica, 47,* 315–323.

Dee, H. L., & Van Allen, M. W. (1972). Psychomotor testing as an aid in the recognition of cerebral lesions. *Neurology, 22,* 845–848.

Dee, H. L., & Van Allen, M. W. (1973). Speed of decision-making processes in patients with unilateral cerebral disease. *Archives of Neurology, 28,* 163–166.

DeRenzi, E. (1982). *Disorders of space exploration and cognition.* Chichester, England: Wiley.

Division of Clinical Neuropsychology. (1989). Definition of a clinical neuropsychologist. *The Clinical Neuropsychologist, 3,* 22.

Duara, R., Grady, C., Haxby, J., Sundaram, M., Cutler, N. R., Heston, L., Moore, A., Schlageter, N., Larson, S., & Rapoport, S. I. (1986). Positron emission tomography in Alzheimer's disease. *Neurology, 36,* 879–887.

Erickson, R. C., & Scott, M. L. (1977). Clinical memory testing: A review. *Psychological Bulletin, 84,* 1130–1149.

Eslinger, P. J., & Benton, A. L. (1983). Visuoperceptual performances in aging and dementia: Clinical and theoretical implications. *Journal of Clinical Neuropsychology, 5,* 213–220.

Eslinger, P. J., Damasio, A. R., Benton, A. L., & Van Allen, M. (1985). Neuropsychologic detection of abnormal mental decline in older persons. *Journal of the American Medical Association, 253,* 670–674.

Fogel, M. L. (1964). The intelligence quotient as an index of brain damage. *American Journal of Orthopsychiatry, 34,* 555–562.

Foster, N. L., Chase, T. N., Fedio, P., Patronas, N. J., Brooks, R. A., & Di Chiro, G. (1983).

Alzheimer's disease: Focal cortical changes shown by positron emission tomography. *Neurology, 33,* 961–965.

Frederiks, J. A. M. (Ed.). (1985a). *Clinical neuropsychology.* [In P. J. Vinken, G. W. Bruyn & H. L. Klawans (Eds.), *Handbook of clinical neurology,* Vol. 45.] Amsterdam: Elsevier.

Frederiks, J. A. M. (Ed.). (1985b). *Neurobehavioral disorders.* [In P. J. Vinken, G. W. Bruyn & H. L. Klawans (Eds.), *Handbook of clinical neurology,* Vol. 46.] Amsterdam: Elsevier.

Friedland, R. P. (1988). Alzheimer disease: Clinical and biological heterogeneity. *Annals of Internal Medicine, 109,* 298–311.

Friedman, R. B., & Albert, M. L. (1985). Alexia. In K. M. Heilman & E. Valenstein (Eds.), *Clinical neuropsychology* (2nd ed.) (pp. 49–73). New York: Oxford University Press.

Geschwind, N. (1980). Neurological knowledge and complex behaviors. *Cognitive Science, 4,* 185–193.

Goldstein, F. C., Gary, H. E., & Levin, H. S. (1986). Assessment of the accuracy of regression equations proposed for estimating premorbid intellectual functioning on the Wechsler Adult Intelligence Scale. *Journal of Clinical and Experimental Neuropsychology, 8,* 405–412.

Goldstein, G., & Tarter, R. E. (Eds.). (1986). *Advances in clinical neuropsychology* (Vol. 3). New York: Plenum Press.

Goodglass, N., & Kaplan, E. (1983). *The assessment of aphasia and related disorders* (2nd ed.). Philadelphia: Lea & Febiger.

Gordon, M., & Mettelman, B. B. (1988). The assessment of attention: I. Standardization and reliability of a behavior-based measure. *Journal of Clinical Psychology, 44,* 682–690.

Graff-Radford, N. R., Welsh, K., & Godersky, J. (1987). Callosal apraxia. *Neurology, 37,* 100–105.

Hamsher, K. deS. (1978a). Stereopsis and the perception of anomalous contours. *Neuropsychologia, 16,* 453–459.

Hamsher, K. deS. (1978b). Stereopsis and unilateral brain disease. *Investigative Ophthalmology & Visual Science, 17,* 336–343.

Hamsher, K. (1981). Intelligence and aphasia. In M. T. Sarno (Ed.), *Acquired aphasia.* New York: Academic Press.

Hamsher, K. (1983). Mental status examination in Alzheimer's disease: The neuropsychologist's role. *Postgraduate Medicine, 73,* 225–228.

Hamsher, K. deS. (1985). The Iowa group. *International Journal of Neuroscience, 25,* 295–305.

Hamsher, K. deS. (1988). Beyond localization. *Contemporary Psychology, 33,* 614–615.

Hamsher, K. deS., Benton, A. L., & Digre, K. (1980). Serial digit learning: Normative and clinical aspects. *Journal of Clinical Neuropsychology, 2,* 39–50.

Hamsher, K. deS., Halmi, K. A., & Benton, A. L. (1981). Prediction of outcome in anorexia nervosa from neuropsychological status. *Psychiatry Research, 4,* 79–88.

Hamsher, K. deS., Levin, H. S., & Benton, A. L. (1979). Facial recognition in patients with focal brain lesions. *Archives of Neurology, 36,* 837–839.

Hamsher, K. deS., & Roberts, R. J. (1985). Memory for recent U.S. presidents in patients with cerebral disease. *Jounral of Clinical and Experimental Neuropsychology, 7,* 1–13.

Hansen, L. A., DeTeresa, R., Davies, P., & Terry, R. D. (1988). Neocortical morphometry, lesion counts, and choline acetyltransferase levels in the age spectrum of Alzheimer's disease. *Neurology, 38,* 48–54.

Hécaen, H., & Albert, M. L. (1978). *Human neuropsychology.* New York: Wiley.

Heilman, K. M., & Rothi, L. J. G. (1985). Apraxia. In K. M. Heilman & E. Valenstein (Eds.), *Clinical neuropsychology* (2nd ed.) (pp. 131–150). New York: Oxford University Press.

Heilman, K. M. & Valenstein, E. (Eds.) (1979). *Clinical neuropsychology.* New York: Oxford University Press.

Henderson, V. W., Alexander, M. P., & Naeser, M. A. (1983). Right thalamic injury, impaired visuospatial perception, and alexia. *Neurology, 32,* 235–240.

Henderson, V. W., & Finch, C. E. (1989). The neurobiology of Alzheimer's disease. *Journal of Neurosurgery, 70,* 335–353.

Hinsie, L. E., & Campbell, R. J. (1975). *Psychiatric dictionary* (4th ed.). New York: Oxford University Press.

Huber, S. J., Shuttleworth, E. C., Paulson, G. W., Bellchambers, M. J. G., & Clapp, L. E. (1986). Cortical vs. subcortical dementia: Neuropsychological differences. *Archives of Neurology, 43,* 392–394.

Hyman, B., Van Hoesen, G. W., & Damasio, A. (1984). Cell specific pathology isolates the hippocampal formation in Alzheimer's disease. *Science, 225,* 1168–1170.

Hyman, B. T., Van Hoesen, G. W., Kromer, L. J., & Damasio, A. H. (1984). Perforant pathway changes and the memory impairment of Alzheimer's disease. *Annals of Neurology, 20,* 472–481.

Hyvarinen, J. (1982). *The parietal cortex of monkey and man.* Berlin: Springer-Verlag.

Jones, B. P., & Butters, N. (1983). Neuropsychological assessment. In M. Hersen, A. E. Kazdin, & A. S. Bellack (Eds.), *The clinical psychology handbook.* Elmsford, NY: Pergamon Press.

Joynt, R. J., & Shoulson, I. (1985). Dementia. In K. M. Heilman & E. Valenstein (Eds.), *Clinical neuropsychology* (2nd ed.) (pp. 453–479). New York: Oxford University Press.

Karzmark, P., Heaton, R. K., Grant, I., & Matthews, C. G. (1985). Use of demographic variables to predict Full Scale IQ: A replication and extension. *Journal of Clinical and Experimental Neuropsychology, 7,* 412–420.

Katzman, R. (1986). Alzheimer's disease. *New England Journal of Medicine, 314,* 964–973.

Kent, D. L., & Larson, E. B. (1988). Magnetic resonance imaging of the brain and spine. *Annals of Internal Medicine, 108,* 402–424.

Kertesz, A. (1979). *Aphasia and associated disorders: Taxonomy, localization, and recovery.* New York: Grune & Stratton.

Kertesz, A. (1983). Issues in localization. In A. Kertesz (Ed.), *Localization in neuropsychology* (pp. 1–20). New York: Academic Press.

Kimura, D., Barnett, H. J. M., & Burkhart, G. (1979). *The psychological test pattern in progressive supranuclear palsy* (Research Bulletin #477, Department of Psychology). London, Canada: University of Western Ontario.

Kirshner, H. S. (1986). *Behavioral neurology: A practical approach.* New York: Churchill Livingstone.

Kirshner, H. S., & Freeman, F. R. (Eds.). (1982). *The neurology of aphasia.* Lisse, The Netherlands: Swets & Zeitlinger.

Leckliter, I. N., Matarazzo, J. D., & Silverstein, A. B. (1986). A literature review of factor analytic studies of the WAIS–R. *Journal of Clinical Psychology, 42,* 332–342.

Levin, H. S. (1973). Motor impersistence and proprioceptive feedback in patients with unilateral cerebral disease. *Neurology, 23,* 833–841.

Levin, H. S., Benton, A. L., & Grossman, R. G.

(1982). *Neurobehavioral consequences of closed head injury.* New York: Oxford University Press.

Levin, H. S., O'Donnell, V. M., & Grossman, R. G. (1979). The Galveston orientation and amnesia test: A practical scale to assess cognition after head injury. *Journal of Nervous and Mental Disease, 167,* 675–684.

Lezak, M. D. (1983). *Neuropsychological assessment.* New York: Oxford University Press.

Lilly, R., Cummings, J. L., Benson, D. F., & Frankel, M. (1983). The human Klüver-Bucy syndrome. *Neurology, 33,* 1141–1145.

Lishman, W. A. (1987). *Organic psychiatry* (2nd ed.). Oxford: Blackwell Scientific.

Lockard, I. (1977). *Desk reference for neuroanatomy: A guide to essential terms.* New York: Springer-Verlag.

Loring, D. W., Lee, G. P., Martin, R. C., & Meador, K. J. (1988). Material-specific learning in patients with partial complex seizures of temporal lobe origin: Convergent validation of memory constructs. *Journal of Epilepsy, 1,* 53–59.

Martin, A., Brouwers, P., Lalonde, F., Cox, C., Teleska, P., & Fedio, P. (1986). Towards a behavioral typology of Alzheimer's disease. *Journal of Clinical and Experimental Neuropsychology, 8,* 594–610.

Matarazzo, J. D. (1972). *Wechsler's measurement and appraisal of adult intelligence* (5th ed.). Baltimore: Williams & Wilkins.

Matthews, C. G. (1981). Neuropsychology practice in a hospital setting. In S. B. Filskov & T. J. Boll (Eds.). *Handbook of clinical neuropsychology.* New York: Wiley.

Mayeux, R., Brandt, J., Rosen, J., & Benson, D. F. (1980). Interictal memory and language impairment in temporal lobe epilepsy. *Neurology, 30,* 120–125.

Mayeux, R., & Stern, Y. (1983). Intellectual dysfunction and dementia in Parkinson's disease. In R. Mayeux & W. G. Rosen (Eds.), *The dementias.* New York: Raven Press.

McFarling, D., Rothi, L. J., & Heilman, K. M. (1982). Transcortical aphasia from ischemic infarcts of the thalamus: A report of two cases. *Journal of Neurology, Neurosurgery, and Psychiatry, 45,* 107–112.

McFie, J. (1975). *Assessment of organic intellectual impairment.* London: Academic Press.

Meadows, J. C. (1974). Disturbed perception of colours associated with localized cerebral lesions. *Brain, 97,* 615–632.

Meier, M. J. (1981). Education for competency assurance in human neuropsychology: Antecedents, models, and directions. In S. B. Filskov & T. J. Boll (Eds.), *Handbook of clinical neuropsychology*. New York: Wiley.

Meier, M. J., & French, L. A. (1965). Lateralized deficits in complex visual discrimination and bilateral transfer of reminiscence following unilateral temporal lobectomy. *Neuropsychologia, 3*, 261–272.

Mesulam, M.-M. (1981). A cortical network for directed attention and unilateral neglect. *Annals of Neurology, 10*, 309–325.

Mesulam, M.-M. (1982). Slowly progressive aphasia without generalized dementia. *Annals of Neurology, 11*, 592.

Mesulam, M.-M. (1985). *Principles of behavioral neurology*. Philadelphia: F. A. Davis.

Mesulam, M.-M., Waxman, S. G., Geschwind, N., & Sabin, T. D. (1976). Acute confusional states with right middle cerebral artery infarctions. *Journal of Neurology, Neurosurgery, and Psychiatry, 39*, 84–89.

Milner, B. (1974). Hemispheric specialization: Scope and limits. In F. O. Schmitt & F. G. Worden (Eds.), *The neurosciences third study program*. Cambridge, MA: MIT Press.

Mohr, J. P. (1982). The evaluation of aphasia. *Stroke, 13*, 399–401.

Morris, J. C., McKeel, D. W., Fulling, K., Torack, R. M., & Berg, L. (1988). Validation of clinical diagnostic criteria for Alzheimer's disease. *Annals of Neurology, 24*, 17–22.

Murri, L., Arena, R., Siciliano, G., Mazzotta, R., & Muratorio, A. (1984). Dream recall in patients with focal cerebral lesions. *Archives of Neurology, 41*, 183–185.

Naeser, M. A., Alexander, M. P., Helm-Estabrooks, N., Levine, H. L., Laughlin, S. A., & Geschwind, N. (1982). Aphasia with predominantly subcortical lesion sites: Description of three capsular/putaminal aphasia syndromes. *Archives of Neurology, 39*, 2–14.

Newcombe, F. (1969). *Missile wounds of the brain: A study of psychological deficits*. London: Oxford University Press.

Newcombe, F., & Russell, W. R. (1969). Dissociated visual perceptual and spatial deficits in focal lesions of the right hemisphere. *Journal of Neurology, Neurosurgery, and Psychiatry, 32*, 73–81.

Overall, J. E., Hoffmann, N. G., & Levin, H. (1978). Effects of aging, organicity, alcoholism, and functional psychopathology on WAIS subtest profiles. *Journal of Consulting and Clinical Psychology, 46*, 1315–1322.

Overall, J. E., & Levin, H. S. (1978). Correcting for cultural factors in evaluating intellectual deficit on the WAIS. *Journal of Clinical Psychology, 34*, 910–915.

Parker, K. (1983). Factor analysis of the WAIS–R at nine age levels between 16 and 74 years. *Journal of Consulting and Clinical Psychology, 51*, 302–308.

Pfeiffer, E. (1975). SPMSQ: Short portable mental status questionnaire. *Journal of the American Geriatric Society, 23*, 433–441.

Pillon, B., Dubois, B., Lhermitte, F., & Agid, Y. (1986). Heterogeneity of cognitive impairment in progressive supranuclear palsy, Parkinson's disease, and Alzheimer's disease. *Neurology, 36*, 1179–1185.

Ratcliff, G. (1982). Disturbances of spatial orientation associated with cerebral lesions. In M. Potegal (Ed.), *Spatial abilities: Development and physiological foundations*. New York: Academic Press.

Reports of the INS–Division 40 Task Force on Education, Accreditation, and Credentialing. (1987). *The Clinical Neuropsychologist, 1*, 29–34.

Roberts, R. J., & Hamsher, K. deS. (1984). Effects of minority status on facial recognition and naming performance. *Journal of Clinical Psychology, 40*, 539–545.

Rondot, P. de Recondo, J., & Dumas, J. L. R. (1977). Visuomotor ataxia. *Brain, 100*, 355–376.

Rose, F. C., Whurr, R., & Wyke, M. A. (Eds.). (1988). *Aphasia*. London: Whurr Publishers.

Rosen, W. G. (1980). Verbal fluency in aging and dementia. *Journal of Clinical Neuropsychology, 2*, 135–146.

Rosen, W. G., Terry, R. D., Fuld, P. A., Katzman, R., & Peck, A. (1980). Pathologic verification of the ischemic score in differentiation of dementias. *Annals of Neurology, 7*, 486–488.

Sarno, M. T. (Ed.). (1981). *Acquired aphasia*. New York: Academic Press.

Seltzer, B., & Mesulam, M.-M. (1988). Confusional states and delirium as disorders of attention. In F. Boller & J. Grafman (Eds.), *Handbook of neuropsychology*, Vol. 1 (pp. 165–174). Amsterdam: Elsevier.

Seltzer, B., & Sherwin, I. (1983). A comparison of clinical features in early- and late-onset primary degenerative dementia. *Archives of Neurology, 40*, 143–146.

Shuttleworth, E. C. (1984). Atypical presentations of dementia of the Alzheimer type. *Journal of the American Geriatrics Society, 32,* 485–490.

Spitzer, R. L., Sheehy, M., & Endicott, J. (1977). DSM-III: Guiding principles. In V. M. Rakoff, H. C. Stancer, & H. B. Kedward (Eds.), *Psychiatric diagnosis.* New York: Brunner/Mazel.

Spreen, O., & Benton, A. L. (1965). Comparative studies of some psychological tests for cerebral damage. *Journal of Nervous and Mental Disease, 140,* 323–333.

Spreen, O., & Benton, A. L. (1969). *Neurosensory Center for Comprehensive Examination for Aphasia.* Victoria, B.C.: Neuropsychology Laboratory, Department of Psychology, University of Victoria.

Storandt, M., Botwinick, J., Danziger, W. L., Berg, L., & Hughes, C. P. (1984). Psychometric differentiation of mild senile dementia of the Alzheimer type. *Archives of Neurology, 41,* 497–499.

Strub, R. L. (1982). Acute confusional state. In D. F. Benson & D. Blumer (Eds.), *Psychiatric aspects of neurologic disease.* Volume II. New York: Grune & Stratton.

Strub, R. L., & Black, F. W. (1977). *The mental status examination in neurology.* Philadelphia: F. A. Davis.

Strub, R. L., & Black, F. W. (1988a). *Neurobehavioral disorders: A clinical approach.* Philadelphia: F. A. Davis.

Strub, R. L., & Black, F. W. (1988b). The bedside mental status examination. In F. Boller and J. Grafman (Eds), *Handbook of neuropsychology,* Vol 1 (pp. 29–46). Amsterdam: Elsevier.

Tellegen, A., & Briggs, P. F. (1967). Old wine in new skins: Grouping Wechsler subtests into new scales. *Journal of Consulting Psychology, 31,* 499–506.

Tonkonogy, J. M. (1986). *Vascular aphasia.* Cambridge, MA: The MIT Press.

Van Zomeren, A. H., & Deelman, B. G. (1978). Long-term recovery of visual reaction time after closed head injury. *Journal of Neurology, Neurosurgery, and Psychiatry, 41,* 452–457.

Varney, N. R. (1978). Linguistic correlates of pantomime recognition in aphasic patients. *Journal of Neurology, Neurosurgery, and Psychiatry, 41,* 564–568.

Varney, N. R. (1980). Sound recognition in relation to aural language comprehension in aphasic patients. *Journal of Neurology, Neurosurgery, and Psychiatry, 43,* 71–75.

Varney, N. R. (1981). Letter recognition and visual form discrimination in aphasic alexia. *Neuropsychologia, 19,* 795–800.

Varney, N. R. (1982). Colour association and "colour amnesia" in aphasia. *Journal of Neurology, Neurosurgery, and Psychiatry, 45,* 248–252.

Varney, N. R., & Benton, A. L. (1979). Phonemic discrimination and aural comprehension among aphasic patients. *Journal of Clinical Neuropsychology, 1,* 65–73.

Varney, N. R., & Benton, A. L. (1982). Qualitative aspects of pantomime recognition defect in aphasia. *Brain and Cognition, 1,* 132–139.

Varney, N. R., & Damasio, A. R. (1982). Acquired alexia. In R. N. Malatesha, & P. G. Aaron (Eds.), *Reading disorders: Varieties and treatments.* New York: Academic Press.

Vignolo, L. A. (1969). Auditory agnosia. In A. L. Benton (Ed.). *Contributions to clinical neuropsychology.* Chicago: Aldine.

Wallesch, C. W., Kornhuber, H. H., Kunz, T., & Brunner, R. J. (1983). Neuropsychological deficits associated with small unilateral thalamic lesions. *Brain, 106,* 141–152.

Walsh, K. W. (1978). *Neuropsychology: A clinical approach.* New York: Churchill Livingstone.

Warrington, E. (1976). Recognition and recall in amnesia. In J. Brown (Ed.), *Recall and recognition.* London: Wiley.

Wechsler, D. (1981). *WAIS–R manual.* New York: Harcourt Brace Jovanovich.

Wechsler, D. (1987). *Wechsler Memory Scale—Revised.* San Antonio, TX: Harcourt Brace Jovanovich.

Wells, C. E. (1979). Pseudodementia. *American Journal of Psychiatry, 136,* 895–900.

Whitaker, H. A. (Ed.), (1988). *Neuropsychological studies of nonfocal brain damage: Dementia and trauma.* New York: Springer-Verlag.

Whitehouse, P. J., Price, D. L., Clark, A. W., Coyle, J. T., & Delong, M. R. (1981). Alzheimer disease: Evidence for the selective loss of cholinergic neurons in the nucleus basalis. *Annals of Neurology, 10,* 122–126.

Wilson, R. S. Rosenbaum, G., & Brown, G. (1979). The problem of premorbid intelligence in neuropsychological assessment. *Journal of Clinical Neuropsychology, 1,* 49–53.

Zimmerman, I. L., & Woo-Sam, J. M. (1973). *Clinical interpretation of the Wechsler Adult Intelligence Scale.* New York: Grune & Stratton.

PART VI
INTERVIEWING

CHAPTER 13

CONTEMPORARY PSYCHIATRIC INTERVIEWING: INTEGRATION OF DSM-III-R, PSYCHODYNAMIC CONCERNS, AND MENTAL STATUS

Shawn C. Shea

INTRODUCTION

Interviewing is the backbone of all mental health professions. It is a dynamic and creative process, which represents a somewhat elusive set of skills. The importance of this set of skills has been highlighted by Langsley and Hollender (1982). Their survey of 482 psychiatric teachers and practitioners revealed that 99.4% ranked conducting a comprehensive interview as an important requirement for a psychiatrist. This represented the highest ranking of 32 skills listed in the survey. Seven of the top 10 skills were directly related to interviewing technique, including skills such as the assessment of suicide and homicide potential, the ability to make accurate diagnoses, and the ability to recognize countertransference problems and other personal idiosyncracies as they influence interactions with patients.

It can be seen from this list that the contemporary clinician is being asked to combine an impressive list of complex skills, ranging from structuring techniques and diagnostic explorations using the DSM-III-R to more classic psychodynamic approaches and engagement skills. Such an integrative task can represent a major hurdle for the developing clinician. This educational expectation was somewhat wryly stated by

Sullivan (1970) a few decades ago when he wrote: "The psychiatric expert is presumed, from the cultural definition of an expert, and from the general rumors and beliefs about psychiatry, to be quite able to handle a psychiatric interview." But the ability to handle the psychiatric interview has become a considerably more complicated task ever since the time of Sullivan's quote, for there has been an evolution in psychiatry of immense proportions in the past 20 years.

This chapter is about this evolution and its impact on psychiatric interviewing. Perhaps the single most striking legacy of the evolution is the disappearance of *the* psychiatric interview. Instead, the contemporary clinician must learn to perform an impressive array of interviews suited to the specific clinical task at hand, including assessments as diverse as those required in an emergency room; an inpatient unit; a psychotherapy practice, consultation and liaison setting; and a diagnostic clinic.

This chapter is designed for both academicians interested in the theoretical and research underpinnings of the interview process and clinical students concerned with practical interviewing techniques. It makes no attempt to be an exhaustive overview; instead, the reader is provided with a conceptual guide that provides a wealth of references for more indepth study.

The following areas are discussed: (a) an historical overview and description of the influences that have shaped the evolution mentioned earlier; (b) a practical introduction to two of the major influences on current psychiatric interviewing: the mental status examination and DSM-III-R; and (c) a review of some of the major research efforts with regard to interviewing, including clinician phrasing of responses, nonverbal concerns, alliance issues and empathy, structured interviews, and educational research.

Before proceeding it will be of use to define a few terms that clarify many of the complicated issues regarding interviewing style. The style of any specific clinical or research interview is greatly determined by the following structural factors: (a) the specific content areas required to make a clinical decision or to satisfy a research data base, (b) the quantity of data required, (c) the importance placed on acquiring valid historical and symptomatic data as opposed to patient opinion and psychodynamic understanding, and (d) the time constraints placed upon the interviewer.

With regard to these structural concerns of the interview, two concepts outlined by Richardson, Dohrenwend, and Klein (1965) are useful: *standardization* and *scheduling*. Standardization refers to the extent to which informational areas or items to be explored are specified in the interview procedure. Scheduling refers to the prespecification of the wording and sequence of the interview process.

By utilizing these two concepts, several interview types can be defined. In the free-format interview, the interviewer has little standardization or data base and is highly interested in the spontaneous content produced by the patient. Such free-format interviews place little emphasis on scheduling and tend to follow the natural wanderings of the patient. These interviews are valuable for uncovering patient psychodynamics and revealing patient feelings, opinions, and defenses.

At the opposite end of the spectrum is the fully structured interview that is highly standardized and strictly scheduled. In fully structured interviews the required informational areas are specified in detail and the ways of exploring them are also prescribed. An example of this type of interview is the Diagnostic Interview Schedule (Robins, Helzer, Croughan, & Ratcliff, 1981), developed for community surveys by lay interviewers.

Semistructured interviews represent procedures in which the informational areas to be explored are specified, but the sequence and wording to be used in data gathering are only moderately predetermined. In these interviews, general guidelines about the interview sequence, such as beginning with the chief complaint and following with episodes of the present illness, may be provided, but the clinician is given some latitude to move within this framework. Semistructured interviews are of value in both research and clinical settings. They frequently can provide standardized data bases as pioneered by Mezzich in the Initial Evaluation Form (Mezzich, Dow, Rich, Costello, & Himmelhoch, 1981; Mezzich, Dow, Ganguli, Munetz, & Zettler-Segal, 1986).

The last major type of interview is the flexibly structured interview. The flexibly structured interview represents the most popular clinical interview and, when performed by an experienced clinician, holds promise as a research tool. With the flexibly structured interview, the clinician has a standardized data base (pre-determined by the clinical or research task at hand) but is given total freedom in scheduling. The interview begins with a free-format style in which the clinician moves with whatever topics appear to be most pressing for the patient. Once the engagement is secured the clinician begins to structure the interview sensitively.

With flexibly structured interviews the actual scheduling will be relatively unique to each clinician-patient dyad, for the interviewer fluidly alters the style of scheduling to gather the standardized data base most effectively while working with the specific needs and defenses of the patient. These interviews require a high degree of sophistication from the clinician and allow him or her to insert areas of free format and dynamic questioning whenever expedient. Most experienced clinicians, whether consciously or by habit, utilize a flexibly structured format. The complexities and nuances of the flexibly structured clinical interview have been most recently explored in detail by Shea (1988).

Historically, clinical interview styles have varied in popularity; they have ranged from semistructured interviews that were partially based on the medical model to more free-form analytic interviews and flexibly structured styles. It is to this evolution that attention is now turned.

HISTORICAL FOUNDATIONS

When studying the historical evolution of the interview, it is helpful to look for underlying principles of development. Perhaps the most useful principle is that interview styles tend to evolve out of whatever theoretical knowledge base is most popular in a given age. In particular, the more numerous and syndrome-specific the available treatment modalities are, the more likely it is that a standardized data base will be sought. If the standardized data base requirements become large, there is a gradual shifting toward methods of structuring, whether done by rigid schedule or by flexible maneuvering. This relationship between the availability of treatment modality and interview style is seldom noted but represents a powerful and unifying historical principle.

Early in the century the approach to clinical assessment was rooted in the medical model. Kraepelin had attempted to classify mental illnesses and indeed had been able to differentiate manic depression from dementia praecox (Kaplan, Freedman, & Sadock, 1980). Although there was not an abundance of treatment modalities present, the gestalt of the moment was toward a careful detailing of behaviors and symptoms in an effort to determine specific syndromes and diseases.

At this time the gifted psychiatrist and educator Adolf Meyer proved to be a catalyst in the development of the psychiatric interview. Paradoxically, his interests would move forward both the free-format style and a more semistructured approach. Meyer professed a psychobiological approach to the patient, in which it was deemed important to determine a "biography" of the patient that included biological, historical, psychological, and social influences on the patient's current behavior (Kaplan, Freedman, & Sadock, 1980). His interest in psychological and social influences further advanced a style of interviewing in which there was an appreciation for the value of the free-format style (Siassi, 1984).

On the other hand, Meyer's interest in determining a sharp conceptualization of biological influences as well as a clear presentation of the patient's immediate symptomatology moved him toward an appreciation of semistructured or flexibly structured formats. For instance, Meyer believed that the clinician should begin the interview with a careful exploration of the patient's chief complaint (Kaplan, Freedman, & Sadock, 1980). In his work "Outlines of Examinations" (Meyer, 1951), which was printed privately in 1918, Meyer was the first to define the term *mental status* (Donnelly, Rosenberg, & Fleeson, 1970).

By the end of the first quarter of the century many of the major components of the psychiatric interview had been established. These key content regions included the chief complaint, the history of the present illness, the social history, the family history, the medical history, and the mental status. All of these were related to an underlying attempt to arrive at a diagnostic overview. But a diagnostic system based on mutually agreed upon criteria was not well established and, consequently, most of the interview was not directed primarily toward establishing a specific diagnosis.

Such lack of diagnostic specificity, coupled with a relative paucity of treatment interventions, resulted in a data base that did not require a high degree of scheduling. In the first place, because there were few diagnostic-related interventions, there was not a pressing need to complete the initial assessment quickly. The clinician could spend many hours over many days eliciting the data for the initial interview. In the second place, the diagnostic schema were so limited that there was not a significant need to cover large areas of symptomatology quickly. The resulting relative lack of scheduling and structure was to have a major thrust toward even more emphasis on free format.

Psychoanalysis arrived on the shores of America like a native-born son. By the 1940s it had become well established. Freud's pioneering work had an enormous impact on interviewing technique. His basic theories seemed to move away from emphasis on diagnosis in a medical sense toward a more probing investigation of actual psychological processes. With the development of ego psychology and a further investigation of defense mechanisms by theorists such as Heinz Hartman and Anna Freud, the emphasis further shifted toward an understanding of how the patient's defenses were manifested in the context of the interview itself. Interviewing and therapy seemed to become less distinct.

A free-format style of interviewing became more common. Clinicians became increasingly aware of the value of spontaneous speech as a fertile ground for uncovering patient defenses and conflicts. The elicitation and description of these defenses and a basic description of the patient's ego structure became goals of the interview. Important advances in interviewing technique evolved during this time. Emphasis was placed not only on what the patient said but what the patient either consciously or unconsciously did not say. Resistance came to be seen as a golden door for entering the dynamics and conflicts of the patient. A free-format style of interview provided a rich psychological milieu in which to observe directly the maneuverings of the patient's unconscious defenses.

Several books helped clinicians to adapt to this new emphasis in interviewing style. One was *Listening With the Third Ear* by Theodore Reik (1952). In the section entitled "The Workshop," Reik provides a variety of insights concerning issues such as free-floating attention, conscious and unconscious observation, and the therapist-patient alliance.

Another important analytic contribution was *The Clinical Interview* (Volumes 1 and 2) written by Felix Deutsch and William Murphy (1955a and 1955b). Working out of Boston, Deutsch and Murphy described the technique of *associative anamnesis*. This technique emphasizes a free-format style in which free association and gentle probing by the clinician open a window into the symbolic world that lies "between the lines" of the patient's report.

But perhaps the most influential book dedicated to interviewing from an analytic point is the classic text, *The Psychiatric Interview in Clinical Practice,* by MacKinnon and Michels (1971). This book provided an easily read yet highly rewarding introduction to understanding dynamic principles as they revealed themselves in the initial interview and subsequent therapy. Few if any books describe more lucidly and insightfully the subtle relationships between patient defense mechanisms and clinician style.

In the early 1950s another major force was to have an impact on the psychiatric interview. That force would be a single man; Harry Stack Sullivan. During his life, Sullivan proved to be one of the most gifted interviewers of all time. His book *The Psychiatric Interview* was published posthumously in 1954. (Sullivan, 1970). The book would establish forever the importance of the interpersonal matrix as one of the major areas through which to understand the interview process. Sullivan stressed the importance of viewing the interview as a sociological phenomenon in which the patient and the clinician form a unique and dynamic dyad, with the behavior of each affecting the other.

One of Sullivan's key terms was *participant observation*. This concept emphasized the need of the interviewer to "step aside" during the interview itself in the sense of viewing his or her own behavior and the impact of that behavior upon the patient. Sullivan saw that the measuring instrument itself, in this case the interviewer, could actually change the data base, that is, the patient's behaviors and degree of distortion in relating symptomatology.

Sullivan was also one of the first interviewers to emphasize the importance of structuring, and he discussed specific methods of making transitions during the interview from one topic to another. In this sense Sullivan recognized the importance of free-format style as well as scheduling issues, and essentially developed a flexibly structured style of interviewing

in which these various techniques could be intermixed at the will of the clinician.

Near the time of Sullivan's book, another work appeared entitled *The Initial Interview in Psychiatric Practice* by Gill, Newman, and Redlich (1954). This work was strongly influenced by Sullivan's interpersonal perspective. Innovatively, the book includes three fully annotated transcripts of interviews which were accompanied by phonographic records of the actual patient/physician dialogue. It also contains an excellent history of interviewing technique.

With regard to the interpersonal perspective, Sullivan's classic text had been predated by J. C. Whitehorn. In 1944 Whitehorn published an influential article in the *Archives of Neurology and Psychiatry* entitled, "Guide to Interviewing and Clinical Personality Study." One of Whitehorn's contributions lay in his emphasis on eliciting patient opinion as both a powerful engagement technique and a method of looking at unconscious dynamics. In particular, the patient's opinions concerning interpersonal relations and reasons for caring for others represented major avenues for exploration.

Closely related to the analytic and interpersonal schools was the European-based school of phenomenological psychiatry and psychology. Giants in the field during the first half of this century, such as Karl Jaspers and Medard Boss, emphasized an approach to the patient in which the focus was on developing an understanding of the exact ways in which the patient experienced "being in the world" (Hall & Lindzey, 1978). In this approach, while utilizing a phenomenological style of interview, the clinician delicately probes the patient for careful descriptions of the patient's symptoms, feelings, perceptions, and opinions. Through a shared process of precise questioning and at times, self-transparency, the clinician arrives at a vivid picture of the patient's universe, a picture which sometimes even surprises the patient as defenses and distortions are worked through by the clinician's style of questioning.

In more recent years, authors such as Alfred Margulies and Leston Havens have reemphasized the importance of a phenomenological approach (Havens, 1978, 1979; Margulies, 1984; Margulies & Havens, 1981). A particularly fascinating technique, known as counterprojection, has been described by Havens. The counterprojective technique deflects paranoid projections before they manifest onto the interviewer. Such techniques are valuable in consolidating an alliance with frightened, hostile, angry, or actively paranoid patients (Havens, 1980).

In summary, it can be seen that during the middle

years of this century and later, psychiatrists from the analytic, interpersonal, and phenomenological schools exerted a strong influence on interviewing technique. The next impact would come from a nonmedical tradition.

In the 1950s, 1960s, and 1970s, the fields of psychology and counseling had an enormous impact on clinical interviewing. More than psychiatry, these fields emphasized the need for empirical research, which will be discussed in more detail later. These research approaches opened up an increased awareness of the specific factors, both verbal and nonverbal, which allow the clinician to relate favorably to the interviewee.

Carl Rogers represents one of the most powerful influences in this regard. His *client-centered approach* emphasized empathic techniques. He described empathy as the clinician's ability "to perceive the internal frame of reference of another with accuracy, and with the emotional components and meanings which pertain thereto, as if one were the other person, but without ever losing the 'as if' condition" (Rogers, 1951, 1959).

Rogers is also well known for his concept of *unconditional positive regard*. A clinician conveys this value when he or she listens without passing judgment on the patient's behaviors, thoughts, or feelings. These ideas were pivotal in conveying the idea that the clinician should not appear remote or distant during the interviewing process, for such artificial remoteness could seriously disengage patients. Interviewers were allowed to utilize in a naturalistic sense their social skills and personality.

Other counselors, such as Alfred Benjamin (1969) in *The Helping Interview* and Gerard Egan (1975) in *The Skilled Helper,* carried on this tradition of emphasizing genuineness and common sense in the therapeutic relationship. Benjamin emphasized the need to develop a trusting relationship with the patient, avoiding the tendency to hide behind rules, position, or sense of authority. Egan attempted to help clinicians develop these abilities by describing a concrete language with which to help convey these ideas in an educational sense, highlighted by a self-programmed manual to accompany his text. Most of the interviewing techniques developed by these authors and other counselors are distinctly nondiagnostically focused. Consequently, as one would expect, they tend to be neither highly standardized nor scheduled.

But the fields of counseling and psychology did not ignore the importance of the data base. To the contrary, an emphasis on developing an increasingly sophisticated understanding of the impact of interviewing technique on the validity of data grew out of the empirical studies and behavioral approaches pioneered by nonmedical researchers.

For example, Richardson, Dohrenwend, and Klein (1965) whose schema of standardization and scheduling was mentioned earlier, produced a particularly incisive work entitled *Interviewing: Its Forms and Functions.* The power of the text lies in the authors' attempts systematically to define and study various characteristics of the interview process ranging from the style of questioning (such as open-ended versus closed-ended) to the impact of patient and clinician characteristics on the interviewing process. Their work transformed a process that was heretofore somewhat nebulous in nature into a process that could be studied behaviorally.

Another psychologist, Gerald Pascal (1983), described a technique known as the *behavioral incident.* Although simple in nature, this technique represents one of the most significant and easily taught of all interviewing techniques in the last several decades. The technique is based on the premise that questions can range on a continuum from those that request patient opinion to those that ask for historical or behavioral description. The latter style of questioning is more apt to yield valid information, whereas questions which request patient opinion are dangerously prone to patient distortion.

The behavioral incident provides a more reliable tool for exploring areas of particular sensitivity where patient distortion may be high, as in the assessment of suicide potential, child abuse, substance abuse, and antisocial behavior. For example, a clinician may phrase a lethality probe in this fashion, "Have you ever had any serious suicide attempts?" It is then up to the patient to interpret the notion of what constitutes a "serious" attempt. To the patient, an overdose of 20 pills may not seem serious and consequently may not be reported. Using the behavioral incident technique the clinician asks a series of questions focused directly on patient behaviors: "Tell me exactly what methods of killing yourself you have ever tried, even if only in a small way," and "When you took the pills how many did you take?" With these types of questions the patient is asked to provide concrete information. It is up to the clinician to arrive at an opinion as to what is "serious."

Another significant book concerning the specific phrasing of questions with regard to their impact on data gathering was *The Structure of Magic I* by Grinder and Bandler (1975). Although some of their latter work has been controversial in nature, this early volume was sound, penetrating, and to the point. They described a variety of techniques for phrasing questions in such a manner that the patient's hidden thoughts would be gradually pulled to the surface. The work is based on an understanding of transformational grammar and is enhanced by the self-programmed layout of the book, which literally forces the reader to make actual changes in style of questioning.

Ironically, the most powerful forces to operate on interviewing style in the last several decades were not directly related to attempts to advance interviewing per se by any specific discipline but were related to the theoretical and clinical advances occurring within psychiatry proper. The evolution of the psychiatric interview was the direct result of a revolution in the development of treatment modalities.

In the past 30 years an impressive array of new therapeutic interventions has emerged. These revolutionary advances include modalities such as tricyclic antidepressants, antipsychotic medications, behavior modification, family therapy, group therapy, and more sophisticated forms of dynamic and hypnotic therapies, to name only a few. In the same fashion that the rapid acceptance of analytic thinking resulted in the further development of the free-format style of interviewing, these new interventions, which frequently are chosen in relation to a DSM-III-R diagnosis, have led interviewers to reexamine the importance of developing both a thorough and valid data base.

In order to determine an effective treatment plan and disposition, the contemporary interviewer must gather an amount of concrete information in 50 minutes which might have seemed unmanageable to an interviewer of 40 years ago. Consequently, interviewers have reexamined their approaches to scheduling, moving toward partially scheduled interviews as seen in the semistructured format or toward a method of tracking the data base while maximizing the interviewer spontaneity seen in the flexibly structured format.

The development of new treatment interventions directly spawned the second major force molding the contemporary interview. Researchers and clinicians quickly realized that better diagnostic systems, which would decrease variability and unreliability, needed to be developed, for treatment modalities were being increasingly determined by diagnosis.

One of the most influential of the modern diagnostic systems which resulted was the Feighner criteria (Feighner et al., 1972). These criteria were developed in the Department of Psychiatry at Washington University in St. Louis. This system delineated 15 diagnostic categories by using both exclusion and inclu-

sion criteria. Building on this base, Spitzer, Endicott, and Robins (1978) developed the Research Diagnostic Criteria (RDC). With the RDC system the psychopathological range was increased to include 23 disorders.

Of particular note to the history of interviewing was the subsequent development of a semistructured interview designed to delineate the diagnoses described by the Research Diagnostic Criteria. This interview, the Schedule for Affective Disorders and Schizophrenia (SADS), was developed by Endicott and Spitzer (1978). It was a powerful tool with good reliability and it became popular as a research instrument. A second interview which was both highly standardized and rigidly scheduled was the Diagnostic Interview Schedule (DIS) developed by Robins (Robins, Helzer, Croughan, & Ratcliff, 1981). This interview was designed to be used by lay interviewers and hence was highly scheduled to ensure interrater reliability.

The semistructured and structured formats displayed by the SADS and the DIS, respectively, were not overly popular with clinicians. Such lack of enthusiasm demonstrated that even though clinicians were progressively required to obtain a highly standardized data base, the method to achieve this goal while flexibly engaging the patient and handling resistance was not clear.

The movement toward the need for a highly standardized data base with regard to diagnostic information was given further momentum in the United States by the publication of the third edition of the *Diagnostic and Statistical Manual of the Mental Disorders* (DSM-III) by the American Psychiatric Association (1980). This manual emphasized a multi-axial approach which will be described in more detail later in this chapter. Seven years later the revised edition, the DSM-III-R, appeared (APA, 1987). With the advent of these widely accepted diagnostic systems, interviewers were faced with the necessity of gathering sensitively the data that would be required for a sophisticated differential diagnosis. This would prove to be no easy task.

The lead toward resolving some of the complex integrative tasks facing the contemporary psychiatric clinician came from the Western Psychiatric Institute and Clinic at the University of Pittsburgh. In 1985, Hersen and Turner edited an innovative book entitled *Diagnostic Interviewing*. This book represented one of the first attempts to acknowledge fully that interviewers should become familiar with specific techniques for exploring sensitively the diagnostic criteria from the various diagnoses in the DSM-III. To accomplish this educational task, various experts contributed chapters on a wide range of DSM-III categories from schizophrenia to sexual disorders.

At the same time, also at the Western Psychiatric Institute and Clinic, Shea was developing a novel training program in interviewing that would open new roads into the development of a truly flexible style of clinical interview. The first innovation in the training program was the idea that, in addition to the traditional model of longitudinal supervision, a unified block of highly supervised time should be set aside for trainees in which interviewing skills were intensively studied in an immediately relevant setting, such as an assessment clinic or emergency room. The second innovation was the development of an integrated approach in which phenomenological inquiry, engagement skills, and an awareness of psychodynamic concerns were taught in direct conjunction with approaches to complex clinical tasks, such as sensitively delineating a specific DSM-III-R diagnosis or determining the risk of suicide, homicide, or child abuse. The third innovation consisted of integrating both theory and supervision techniques (such as videotaping, direct supervision, role playing, microtraining, and behavioral self-monitoring) from a variety of disciplines including counseling, psychology, psychiatry, and analysis.

These innovations were expanded on in *Psychiatric Interviewing: The Art of Understanding* (Shea, 1988). This book represented the first attempt to synthesize smoothly the divergent streams of interviewing knowledge developed in the various mental health fields over the last 50 years. In particular, it acknowledged the confusing task facing contemporary clinicians who must synthesize a wide range of important information (including regions such as the chief complaint, history of the present illness, the social history, the family history, the medical history, the mental status, and the DSM-III-R diagnositc regions) into an interview that is naturally flowing and to which appropriate energy can be given to dynamic issues and resistance concerns.

To accomplish this task, Shea developed a supervision language that would provide a readily understandable system with which to study the flow of the interview. This study of the structure and flow of the interview process was named *facilics* derived from the Latin root *facilis* (ease of movement). The study of facilics also includes an examination of the overall structuring of the interview as it relates to time constraints and clinical tasks. To enhance learning further, a graphic supervision system was designed, made up of symbols which depict the various transi-

tions and types of topical expansions. This shorthand system clarifies educational concepts and highlights structural elements while presenting an immediately understandable record of what took place in the interview.

Facilics was not designed as a specific style of structuring. Instead, it is a method of understanding the structuring process so that at any given moment the clinician can consciously affect the information gathering process. The system allows the clinician to structure flexibly, to prevent errors of omission, and to explore specific content regions, such as diagnostic symptom clusters, while carefully attending to patient engagement.

From a historical perspective, psychiatric interviewing has continually evolved and undoubtedly will continue to change as clarifying theories and treatment modalities grow in number and depth. Clinicians have been forced to cope with the realization that the contemporary clinical interview frequently requires a high degree of standardization, as exemplified by the demand for large amounts of data, of both diagnostic and psychosocial importance, to be gathered in relatively short periods of time. At first it appeared that these requirements would necessitate clinical interviews to be tightly scheduled or semistructured in nature. But with the advent of sensitive structuring approaches, such as facilics, clinicians remain free to utilize flexibly structured styles of interviewing. Such styles provide clinicians with methods of gathering thorough data bases in relatively short periods of time, scheduling the interview as they go along, each interview representing a unique creative venture.

With the historical review completed it is valuable to provide a practical introduction to two of the most powerful influences mentioned earlier. The first influence, which dates back to the pioneering work of Adolf Meyer, is the mental status. The second, and much more recent influence, is the development of the DSM-III and its revision, the DSM-III-R.

THE MENTAL STATUS EXAMINATION

The mental status represents an attempt to describe objectively the behaviors, thoughts, feelings, and perceptions of the patient during the course of the interview itself. These observations are usually written as a separate section of the patient's evaluation. The general topics covered by the mental status are categorized as follows: appearance and behavior, speech characteristics and thought process, thought content, perception, mood and affect, sensorium, cognitive ability, and insight. Clinicians may vary on the exact categories that are used, and some clinicians collect all of these observations into a single narrative paragraph. In any case the clinician attempts to convey the state of the patient during the interview itself, as if a cross-section were being taken of the patient's behavior for 60 minutes.

In a sense, the mental status consists of a variety of different clinician activities, ranging from observation to the written record. Part of the mental status occurs informally as the clinician observes various characteristics of the patient while the patient spontaneously describes symptoms or history. The clinician may note whether the patient appears to be shabbily dressed or able to concentrate. Other aspects of the mental status are more formal in nature as the clinician asks direct questions concerning areas of psychopathology, such as inquiries regarding hallucinations or delusions. Finally, certain aspects of the mental status may be quite formalized as is seen during the formal cognitive examination. During this part the patient is asked to perform tasks, such as calculations or digit spans.

All of these clinician activities are synthesized into the written mental status. Indeed, it is by examining the thought processes required to produce a sound written mental status that one can best discuss the more intangible processes at work during the "gathering of the mental status information." Consequently, in this chapter each segment of the mental status is examined as it might appear in a standard written evaluation. An effort is made to summarize commonly utilized descriptive terms, to clarify confusing terms, to point out common mistakes, and to provide an example of a well-written mental status.

Appearance and Behavior

In this section the clinician attempts to describe accurately the patient's outward behavior and presentation. One place to start is with a description of the patient's clothes and self-care. Striking characteristics such as scars and deformities should be noted, as well as any tendencies for the patient to look older or younger than his or her chronological age. Eye contact is usually mentioned. Any peculiar mannerisms are noted, such as twitches or the patient's apparent responses to hallucinations, which may be evident through tracking movements of the eyes or a shaking of the head as if shutting out an unwanted voice. The clinician should note the patient's motor behavior; common descriptive terms include *restless, agitated,*

subdued, shaking, tremulous, rigid, pacing, and *withdrawn.* Displacement activities such as picking at a cup or chain smoking are frequently mentioned. An important, and often forgotten characteristic, is the patient's apparent attitude toward the interviewer. With these ideas as a guide, the following excerpt represents a relatively poor description.

> *Clinician A:* The patient appeared disheveled. Her behavior was somewhat odd and her eye contact did not seem right. She appeared restless and her clothing seemed inappropriate.

Although this selection gives some idea of the patient's appearance, one does not come away with a sense of what it would be like to meet this patient. Generalities are used instead of specifics. The following description of the same patient captures her presence more aptly.

> *Clinician B:* The patient presents in tattered clothes, all of which appear filthy. Her nails are laden with dirt, and she literally has her soiled wig on backwards. She is wearing two wrist watches on her left wrist and tightly grasps a third watch in her right hand, which she will not open to shake hands. Her arms and knees moved restlessly throughout the interview, and she stood up to pace on a few occasions. She did not give any evidence of active response to hallucinations. She smelled bad, but did not smell of alcohol. At times she seemed mildly uncooperative.

This passage presents a more vivid picture of her behavior, a pattern that may be consistent with a manic or psychotic process. Her "odd" behaviors have been concretely described. The clinician has included pertinent negatives, indicating that she shows no immediate evidence of hallucinating, as might be seen in a delirium.

Speech Characteristics and Thought Process

The clinician can address various aspects of the patient's speech, including the speech rate, volume, and tone of voice. At the same time, the clinician attempts to describe the thought process of the patient, as it is reflected in the manner with which the patient's words are organized. The term *formal thought disorder* is utilized to suggest the presence of abnormalities in the form and organization of the patient's thought. The less commonly used term, *content thought disorder,* refers specifically to the presence of delusions, and it is addressed in a subsequent section of the mental status. The more generic term *thought disorder* includes both the concept of a formal thought disorder and of a content thought disorder. In this section of the mental status the emphasis is on the process of the thought (presence of a formal thought disorder), not the content of the speech. Terms frequently used by clinicians include the following:

Pressured speech: This term refers to an increased rate of speech, which may possibly best be described as a "speech sans punctuation." Sometimes it is only mildly pressured, whereas at other times, the patient's speech may virtually gush forth in an endless stream. It is commonly seen in mania, agitated psychotic states, or during extreme anxiety or anger.

Tangential thought: The patient's thoughts tend to wander off the subject as he or she proceeds to take tangents off his or her own statements. There tends to be some connection between the preceding thought and the subsequent statement. An example of fairly striking tangential thought would be as follows: "I really have not felt very good recently. My mood is shot, sort of like it was back in Kansas. Oh boy, those were bad days back in Kansas. I'd just come up from the Army and I was really homesick. Nothing can really beat home if you know what I mean. I vividly remember my mother's hot cherry tarts. Boy, they were good. Home cooking just can't be beat." *Circumstantial thought* is identical in nature to tangential thought but differs in that the patient returns to the original topic.

Loosening of associations: The patient's thoughts at times appear unconnected. Of course, to the patient, there may be obvious connections, but a normal listener would have trouble making them. In mild forms, loosening of associations may represent severe anxiety or evidence of a schizotypal character structure. In moderate or severe degrees, it is generally an indicator of psychosis. An example of a moderate degree of loosening would look like this: "I haven't felt good recently. My mood is shot, fluid like a waterfall that's black, back home I felt much better, cherry tarts and Mom's hot breath keeps you going and rolling along life's highways." If loosening becomes extremely severe it is sometimes referred to as a *word salad.*

Flight of ideas: In my opinion this is a relatively weak term, for it essentially represents combinations of the above terms. This is why most trainees find it confusing. For flight of ideas to occur, the patient must demonstrate tangential thought or a loosening of associations in conjunction with a significantly pressured speech. Usually there are connections between the thoughts, but, at times, a true loosening of associations is seen. A frequently but not always seen characteristic of flight of ideas is the tendency for the patient's speech to be triggered by distracting stimuli or to demonstrate plays on words. When present, these features represent more distinguishing hallmarks of a flight of ideas. Flight of ideas is commonly

seen in mania, but can appear in any severely agitated or psychotic state.

Thought blocking: The patients stop in mid-sentence and never return to the original idea. These patients appear as if something has abruptly interrupted their train of thought and, indeed, something usually has, such as an hallucination or an influx of confusing ideation. Thought blocking is very frequently a sign of psychosis. It is not the same as exhibiting long periods of silence before answering questions. Some dynamic theorists believe it can also be seen in neurotic conditions, when a repressed impulse is threatening to break into consciousness.

Illogical thought: The patient displays illogical conclusions. This is different from a delusion, which represents a false belief but generally has logical reasoning behind it. An example of a mildly illogical thought follows: "My brother has spent a lot of time with his income taxes so he must be extremely wealthy. And everyone knows this as a fact because I see a lot of people deferring to him." These conclusions may be true, but they do not necessarily logically follow. Of course, in a more severe form, the illogical pattern may be quite striking: "I went to Mass every Sunday, so my boss should have given me a raise. That bum didn't even recognize my religious commitment."

In the following excerpt, the speech and thought process of the woman with two watches on her wrist is depicted. Once again the description demonstrates some areas in need of improvement.

Clinician A: Patient positive for loosening of associations and tangential thought. Otherwise grossly within normal limits.

This clinician has made no reference to the degree of severity of the formal thought disorder. Specifically, does this patient have a mild loosening of associations or does she verge upon a word salad? Moreover, the clinician makes no reference to her speech rate and volume, characteristics that are frequently abnormal in manic patients. The following brief description supplies a significantly richer data base:

Clinician B: The patient demonstrates a moderate pressure to her speech accompanied at times by loud outbursts. Even her baseline speech is slightly louder than normal. Her speech is moderately tangential, with rare instances of a mild loosening of associations. Without thought blocking or illogical thought.

Slowly one is beginning to develop a clearer picture of the degree of this patient's psychopathology. More evidence is mounting that there may be both a manic-like appearance and a psychotic process. In any case, the patient's speech coupled with her strikingly disheveled appearance, may lead the clinician to suspect that the patient is having trouble managing herself.

Thought Content

This section refers primarily to four broad issues: ruminations, obsessions, delusions, and the presence of suicidal or homicidal ideation. Ruminations are frequently seen in a variety of anxiety states and are particularly common in depressed patients. Significantly depressed patients will tend to be preoccupied with worries and feelings of guilt, constantly turning the thoughts over in their minds. The thinking process itself does not appear strange to these patients, and they do not generally try to stop it. Instead, they are too caught up in the process to do much other than talk about their problems. In contrast, obsessions have a different flavor to them, although they may overlap with ruminations at times.

The obsession is a specific thought that is repeated over and over by the patient as if he or she is seeking an answer to some question. Indeed, the patient frequently demonstrates obsession over a question and its answer. As soon as the question is answered, the patient feels an intense need to ask it again, as if some process had been left undone. The patient may repeat this process hundreds of times in a row until it "feels right." If one interrupts the patient while this process is occurring, the patient will frequently feel a need to start the whole process again. Unlike the case with ruminations, patients find these obsessive thought processes to be both odd and painful. They frequently have tried various techniques to interrupt the process. Common themes for obsessions include thoughts of committing violence, homosexual fears, issues of right and wrong, and worries concerning dirt or filth. Obsessions may consist of recurrent ideas, thoughts, fantasies, images, or impulses. If the clinician takes the time to listen carefully to the patient, bearing the above phenomenological issues in mind, he or she can usually differentiate between ruminations and obsessions.

Delusions represent strongly held beliefs that are not correct or held to be true by the vast majority of the patient's culture. They may range from bizarre thoughts, such as invasion of the world by aliens, to delusions of an intense feeling of worthlessness and hopelessness.

The fourth issue consists of statements concerning lethality. Because all patients should be asked about current lethality issues, these issues should always be addressed in the written mental status. In general, the clinician should make some statement regarding the presence of suicidal wishes, plans, and degree of intent to follow the plans in an immediate sense. If a plan is mentioned, the clinician should state the degree to which any action has been taken on it. He or she should also note whether any homicidal ideation is present and to what degree, as with suicidal ideation.

Clinician A: The patient is psychotic and can't take care of herself. She seems delirious.

This excerpt is just simply sloppy. The first statement has no place in a mental status, for it is the beginning of the clinician's clinical assessment. The description of the delusion is threadbare and unrevealing. The clinician has also omitted the questioning concerning lethality. Assuming the clinician asked but forgot to record this information, he or she may sorely regret this omission if this patient were to kill herself and the clinician was taken to court to face a malpractice suit for possible negligence. A more useful description is given below.

Clinician B: The patient appears convinced that if the watch is removed from her right hand, the world will come to an end. She relates that, consequently, she has not bathed for three weeks. She also feels that an army of rats is following her and is intending to enter her intestines to destroy "my vital essence." She denies current suicidal ideation or plans. She denies homicidal ideation. Without ruminations or obsessions.

With this description it has become clear that the patient is psychotic, as evidenced by her delusions. The next question is whether hallucinations play a role in her psychotic process.

Perception

This section refers to the presence or absence of hallucinations or illusions. It is of value to note that there is sometimes a close relationship between delusions and hallucinations. It is not uncommon for the presence of hallucinations eventually to trigger the development of delusional thinking, but the two should not be confused. Let us assume that a patient is being hounded by a voice screaming, "You are possessed. You are a worthless demon." If the patient refuses to believe in the reality of the voice, then one would say that the patient is hearing voices but is not delusional. If, on the other hand, the patient eventually begins to believe in the existence of the voice and feels that the devil is planning her death, then the patient is said to have developed a delusion as well. The following description of perceptual phenomena is obviously threadbare.

Clinician A: Without abnormal perceptions.

There is a question concerning the appropriateness in the mental status of using phrases such as, "grossly within normal limits" or "without abnormality." Generally, the mental status is improved by the use of more precise and specific descriptions, but sometimes clinical situations require flexibility. For example, if the clinician is working under extreme time constraints, such global statements may be appropriate; in most situations, however, it is preferable to state specifically the main entities that were ruled out, for this tells the reader that the clinician actually looked for these specific processes. Stated differently, with these global phrases, the reader does not know whether they are accurate or the end result of a sloppy examination. If one has performed a careful examination, it seems best to let the reader know this.

There is another problem with the phrasing used by Clinician A: he or she has stated that the patient does not, in actuality, have hallucinations. It is possible, however, that this patient is simply withholding information out of fear that the voices represent a sickness. Numerous reasons exist for a patient to avoid sharing the presence of hallucinations with a clinician, including instructions to the patient from the voices not to speak about them to the clinician. It may be more accurate to state that the patient denied having hallucinations rather than to report categorically that the patient is without them. A more sophisticated report would be as follows:

Clinician B: The patient denied both visual and auditory hallucinations and any other perceptual abnormality.

Mood and Affect

Mood is a symptom, reported by the patient, concerning how he or she has generally been feeling recently, and it tends to be relatively persistent. Affect is a physical indicator noted by the clinician as to the immediate feelings of the patient. Affect is demonstrated by the patient's facial expressions and other nonverbal clues during the interview itself; it is frequently of a transient nature. Mood is a self-reported symptom; affect is a physical sign. If a patient refuses to talk, the clinician can say essentially nothing about mood in the mental status itself, except that the patient refused to comment on mood. Later in the narrative assessment, the clinician will have ample space to describe his or her impressions of what the patient's actual mood has been. In contrast to mood, in which the clinician is dependent upon the patient's self-report, the clinician can always say something about the patient's affect.

Clinician A: The patient's mood is fine and her affect is appropriate but angry at times.

This statement is somewhat confusing. In which sense is her affect appropriate? Is it appropriately fearful for a person who believes that rats are invading her intestines, or does the clinician mean that her affect is appropriate for a person without a delusional system? The clinician should always first state what the patient's affect is and then comment upon its appropriateness. Typical terms used to describe affect include *normal* (broad) *affect with full range of expression, restricted affect* (some decrease in facial animation), *blunted affect* (a fairly striking decrease in facial expression), *a flat affect* (essentially no sign of spontaneous facial activity), *buoyant affect, angry affect, suspicious affect, frightened affect, flirtatious affect, silly affect, threatening affect, labile affect,* and *edgy affect.* The following description gives a much clearer feeling for this patient's presentation:

Clinician B: When asked about her mood, the patient angrily retorted, "My mood is just fine, thank you!" Throughout much of the interview she presented a guarded and mildly hostile affect, frequently clipping off her answers tersely. When talking about the nurse in the waiting area she became particularly suspicious and seemed genuinely frightened. Without tearfulness or a lability of affect.

Sensorium, Cognitive Functioning, and Insight

In this section the clinician attempts to convey a sense of the patient's basic level of functioning with regard to the level of consciousness, intellectual functioning, insight, and motivation. It is always important to note whether a patient presents with a normal level of consciousness, using phrases such as "The patient appeared alert with a stable level of consciousness," or "The patient's consciousness fluctuated rapidly from somnolence to agitation."

It should be noted that this section of the mental status examination may have evolved from two processes: the informal cognitive examination and the formal cognitive examination. The informal cognitive examination is artfully performed throughout the interview in a noninvasive fashion. The clinician essentially "eyeballs" the patient's concentration and memory by noting the method by which he or she responds to questions. If the clinician chooses to perform a more formal cognitive examination, it can range from a brief survey of orientation, digit spans, and short-term memory, to a much more comprehensive examination, perhaps lasting 20 minutes or so. Clinical considerations will determine which approach is most appropriate. For a fast reading and penetrating discussion of the use of the formal cognitive exam, the reader is referred to *The Mental Status Examination in Neurology* (Strub & Black, 1979). The reader may also be interested in becoming familiar with the 30-point Folstein Mini-Mental State Exam. This exam can be given in about 10 minutes, provides a standardized set of scores for comparison, and is extremely popular (Folstein, Folstein, & McHugh, 1975). With regard to the patient in question, the following description is a weak one and could use some polishing:

Clinician A: The patient seemed alert. She was oriented. Memory seemed fine and cognitive functioning was grossly within normal limits.

Once again this clinician's report is vague. Most important, the reader has no idea how much cognitive testing was performed. No mention has been made regarding the patient's insight or motivation. The following excerpt provides a more clarifying picture:

Clinician B: The patient appeared alert with a stable level of consciousness throughout the interview. Indeed, at times, she seemed hyperalert and overly aware of her environment. She was oriented to person, place, and time. She could repeat six digits forward and four backward. She accurately recalled three objects after five minutes. Other formal testing was not performed. Her insight was very poor as was her judgment. She does not want help at this time and flatly refuses the use of any medication.

When done well, as described above, the mental status can provide a fellow clinician with a reliable image of the patient's actual presentation over the course of the interview. It should be openly acknowledged that, in actual practice, the written mental status may need to be significantly briefer, but the principles outlined above remain important and can help prevent the briefer mental status from being transformed into an inept mental status.

THE DSM-III AND THE DSM-III-R

The importance, with respect to interviewing, of the DSM-III system does not pertain to any specific interviewing technique or mode of questioning. The DSM-III is not a style of interview; it is a diagnostic system. Its impact on interviewing derives from its having established an important set of symptoms that must be covered in order for a thorough assessment of the stated criteria to take place. In this sense the DSM-III has become an important factor in determining the type and amount of data that contemporary clinicians must address. With the advent of the DSM-III, the degree of standardization required in a typical "intake interview" has increased significantly, for the required data base has grown significantly.

In this section a brief outline of the DSM-III system and its revision is provided as an introduction to utilizing the system in practice. An attempt is made to highlight some of the more important conceptual advances of the DSM-III system.

When the DSM-III appeared in 1980, it represented several major advances. First, as compared to the Feighner criteria or the SADS, it was a system designed primarily for clinical practice rather than for application to a research setting. This clinical orientation mandated that all areas of psychopathology be delineated. The actual diagnoses were intended to be distinct from one another. Consequently, a second major advance, in comparison to the DSM-I and the DSM-II systems, was an emphasis on well-defined criteria for almost all the diagnostic categories.

The third major advance, and perhaps the most important, was the utilization of a multi-axial system, in which the patient's presentation was not limited to a single diagnosis. The clinician was pushed to look at the patient's primary psychiatric diagnosis within the context of a variety of interacting systems, such as the patient's physical health, level of stress, and level of functioning. As Mezzich (1985) has pointed out, the DSM-III system evolved from pioneering work with multi-axial systems across the world including England (Rutter, Shaffer, & Shepherd, 1975; Wing, 1970), Germany (Helmchen, 1975; von Cranach, 1977), Japan (Kato, 1977), and Sweden (Ottosson & Perris, 1973).

In the DSM-III-R the clinical formulation is summarized on the following five axes:

Axis I: All clinical syndromes and V codes except for personality disorders and developmental disorders

Axis II: Personality disorders and developmental disorders
Axis III: Physical disorders and conditions
Axis IV: Severity of psychosocial stressors
Axis V: Global assessment of functioning

Each of these axes is examined in more detail below.

Axis I

At first glance Axis I may appear somewhat intimidating because of the large number of diagnostic entities it contains. But the clinician can approach the system in a two-step manner which greatly simplifies the task. In the first step or *primary delineation,* the clinician determines whether the patient's symptoms suggest one or more of the major diagnostic regions of Axis I which are confined to the following 10 easily remembered categories:

1. Mood Disorders
2. Schizophrenia and related disorders
3. Anxiety disorders
4. Organic disorders (including dementia and delirium)
5. Alcohol and drug abuse disorders
6. Somatoform disorders (such as hypochondriasis)
7. Adjustment disorders
8. Other miscellaneous disorders (such as sexual disorders, factitious disorders, sleep disorders, and impulse control disorders)
9. V codes
10. No disorder

Clues to which general categories of disorders are most relevant to the patient in question will arise as the clinician explores the patient's history of the present illness, both spontaneously and with the use of probe questions.

The second step or *secondary delineation* consists of delineating the specific diagnoses under each broad category. In the secondary delineation the clinician clarifies the data base so that an exact DSM-III-R diagnosis can be determined. Thus, if the clinician suspects a mood disorder, he or she will eventually search for criteria substantiating specific mood diagnoses, such as major depression, bipolar disorder, dysthymia, cyclothymia, bipolar disorder not otherwise specified, and depressive disorder not otherwise specified. This secondary delineation is performed in each broad diagnostic area deemed pertinent.

With regard to the interview process itself, the trained clinician performs these delineations in a highly flexible manner, always patterning the questioning in the fashion most compatible with the needs of the patient. Utilizing a flexibly structured format, the clinician can weave in and out of these diagnostic regions, as well as any other areas such as the social history or family history, in whatever fashion is most engaging for the patient. With the flexibly structured format the only limiting factor is that the standard data base must be thoroughly explored by the end of the available time. It is up to the clinician to schedule the interview creatively. When done well, the interview feels unstructured to the patient, yet delineates an accurate diagnosis.

One diagnostic area that warrants further explanation is the concept of the *V code.* V codes represent conditions not attributable to a mental disorder that have nevertheless become a focus of therapeutic intervention. Examples include academic problems, occupational problems, uncomplicated bereavement, marital problems, and others. Sometimes these codes are used because no mental disorder is present and the patient is coping with one of the stressors just listed. They can also be used if the clinician feels that insufficient information is available to rule out a psychiatric syndrome, but in the meantime, an area for specified intervention is being highlighted.

Axis II

Axis II emphasizes the realization that all the Axis I disorders exist in the unique psychological milieu known as *personality.* Many mental health problems are primarily related to the vicissitudes of personality development. Moreover, the underlying personality of the patient can greatly affect the manner in which the clinician chooses to relate to the patient both in the interview and in subsequent therapy.

On Axis II the following diagnostic categories are utilized:

1. Paranoid personality disorder
2. Schizoid personality disorder
3. Schizotypal personality disorder
4. Histrionic personality disorder
5. Narcissistic personality disorder
6. Antisocial personality disorder
7. Borderline personality disorder
8. Avoidant personality disorder
9. Dependent personality disorder
10. Compulsive personality disorder
11. Passive-aggressive personality disorder
12. Personality disorder, not otherwise specified (NOS)

Developmental disorders are also included on this axis. These disorders may reflect limited cognitive delays or more massive disruptions involving both cognitive, affective, and personality disturbances. Examples include developmental arithmetic disorder, mental retardation, and autistic disorder.

This axis also functions in many respects as an important integration center in which diagnostic concerns can be related to psychodynamic principles. For instance, the clinician is asked to look carefully for evidence not only of personality disorders but also of personality traits, many of which are adaptive in nature. These traits can also be listed on Axis II. Along similar lines, the clinician may list specific defense mechanisms that may have been displayed during free-format areas of the interview or as methods of avoiding certain topics raised by the clinician. These defense mechanisms may range from those commonly seen in neurotic disorders, such as rationalization and intellectualization, to those seen in more severe disorders, such as denial, projection, and splitting.

Axis III

On this axis the clinician considers the role of physical disorders and conditions. The clinician is asked to view the patient's psychiatric problems within the holistic context of the impact of these problems on physical health, and vice versa. This axis reinforces the idea that a sound medical review of systems and past medical history should be a component of any complete psychiatric assessment.

In addition, other physical conditions that are not diseases may provide important information concerning the holistic state of the patient. For instance, it is relevant to know whether the patient is pregnant or is a trained athlete, for these conditions may point toward germane psychological issues.

Axis IV

This axis concerns itself with an examination of the current stresses affecting the interviewee. It examines the crucial interaction between the patient and the environment in which he or she lives. Sometimes interviewers are swept away by diagnostic intrigues and fail to uncover the reality based problems confronting the patient. This axis helps to keep this important area in focus.

By way of illustration, on this axis the interviewer may discover that, secondary to a job lay-off, the home of the patient is about to be foreclosed. Such information may suggest the need to help the patient make contact with a specific social agency or the utility of a referral to a social worker. When the clinical task focuses upon crisis intervention, axis IV becomes of primary importance, illustrating the practical value of a multi-axial system of diagnosis.

Axis V

A variety of changes were made in Axis V when the DSM-III was revised into the DSM-III-R. In DSM-III this axis delineated only the highest functioning of the patient over a two-month period in the preceding year. This relatively narrow perspective did not provide an abundance of practical information. Consequently, in the DSM-III-R this axis was broadened. It now includes not only a rating of the highest functioning in the past year, but also a rating of the current functioning, which provides immediate data pertinent to treatment planning and the decision as to whether hospitalization is warranted. These ratings are to be made by combining both symptoms and occupational and interpersonal functioning on a 90-point scale, the Global Assessment Functioning Scale (GAF Scale).

The first rating, the highest level of functioning in the past year which is sustained for at least a two-month period, may help to predict ultimate outcome, for some clinicians feel that higher levels of recent functioning may suggest better hopes prognostically. Probably of more practical importance to the clinician is the window that this axis opens into the patient's adaptive skills and coping mechanisms as reflected in the rating of current functioning.

This brief review of the DSM-III-R system shows that the impact of this new diagnostic system on the interviewing process is manyfold. The multi-axial approach and the thoroughness of the diagnostic schema require the clinician to cover a lot of ground, especially during a one-session intake. But the resulting standardized data base is an illuminating one that highlights a holistic and rigorous approach to understanding the patient's problems and needs. Moreover, the skilled use of a flexibly structured interview allows this informational base to be gathered in an empathic and flowing manner.

RESEARCH ON INTERVIEWING

It is not an exaggeration to state that it would require an entire book to review comprehensively the vast literature related to interviewing. On a more modest level an attempt is made in this chapter to introduce the reader to the main currents of this research area, providing a simplifying schema for categorizing the available literature while referencing specific articles that can be used as stepping stones into the categories described.

One of the confusions facing the reader, as he or she attempts to approach the research on interviewing, is the significant overlap between interviewing research and research done with regard to psychotherapy. This overlap is a healthy one, for it demonstrates that alliance issues are in some respects inseparable from data-gathering issues. There is an intimate relationship between the strength of the initial alliance and the resulting ability to gather valid information and structure the flow of the conversation effectively.

On the other hand, there are differences in emphasis between intake interviews and psychotherapy sessions. As the degree of standardization has increased with the advent of new therapies and new diagnostic systems, these differences have become more apparent. Eventually, such differentiation between interviewing and psychotherapy will probably be reflected more distinctly in the research literature as increased research occurs on structuring techniques and validity concerns. With these qualifications observed, the following major research areas will be discussed: (a) clinician response modes, (b) nonverbal behavior and paralanguage, (c) clinician characteristics as related to alliance issues and empathic communication, (d) reliability and validity concerns as related to structured interviews, and (e) educational techniques.

With regard to the first category, response mode research attempts to examine the type of verbal exchange occurring between clinician and patient, focusing on styles of response such as open-ended questions, reflections, and interpretations. Stiles (1978) notes that it is important to separate response mode research from content research, which focuses on the actual meaning of the words spoken, and research on extralinguistic areas, such as speech characteristics, pauses, and laughter.

It has been estimated that 20- to 30-response mode systems have been developed (Elliott et al., 1987). Much of the pioneering research on response modes was done during the 1950s, 1960s, and 1970s (Aronson, 1953; Danish & D'Augelli, 1976; Goodman & Dooley, 1976; Hackney & Nye, 1973; Hill, 1975; Ivey, 1971; Robinson, 1950; Snyder, 1945, 1963; Spooner & Stone, 1977; Strupp, 1960; Whalen & Flowers, 1977).

In 1978 Clara Hill developed a system which integrated many of the best features of the earlier systems. Her system consisted of 14 categories, including response types such as minimal encourager, direct guidance, closed question, open question, self-disclosure, confrontation, approval-reassurance, and restatement. Hill's system was further developed to include three supercategories that focused on the degree of structuring as seen with low structure (encouragement/approval/reassurance, reflection/restatement, and self-disclosure), moderate structure (confrontation, interpretation, and provision of information) and high structure (direct guidance/advice and information seeking) (Friedlander, 1982).

In 1987, six of the major rating systems were compared when applied to therapy sessions by well-known clinicians such as Albert Ellis and Carl Rogers (Elliott et al., 1987). Interrater reliability was found to be high; when categories in different rating systems were collapsed to the same level of specificity, moderate to strong convergence was found. Studies such as the above point to a bright future for response-mode research when systems with high interrater reliability are applied to various interviewing situations. Different systems appear to shed slightly different light on the data base, and the complementary use of various systems will probably become the preferred approach in the future.

Research with respect to nonverbal communication, the second major research category, spans a variety of perspectives which can best be separated into three areas known as proxemics, kinesics, and paralanguage. Edward T. Hall (1966) first coined the term *proxemics* in his classic book *The Hidden Dimension*. Proxemics represents the study of how humans conceptualize and utilize interpersonal space. Hall was particularly interested in the impact of culture on an individual's sense of interpersonal space. Kinesics is the study of the body in movement including movements of the torso, head, limbs, face, and eyes as well as the impact of posture. The field was pioneered by Ray T. Birdwhistell (1952) in the book, *Introduction to Kinesics: An Annotation System for Analysis of Body Motion and Gesture*. The final realm of nonverbal study is paralanguage, which focuses on how messages are delivered, including elements such as tone of voice, loudness of voice, pitch of voice, and fluency of speech (Cormier & Cormier, 1979).

The impact of these three areas of nonverbal behavior on the issue of social control has received much attention. Ekman has devoted considerable time to the nonverbal constituents of the act of lying (Ekman, 1985; Ekman & Friesen, 1974). In a concise review of the literature concerning nonverbal behavior and social control, including areas such as status, persuasion, feedback, deception, and impression formation, it appears that gaze and facial expression are the most telling factors (Edinger & Patterson, 1983). Scheflen (1972) has described *kinesic reciprocals* which represent display behaviors between two organisms that convey intent, such as mating rituals, parenting behavior, and fighting behavior, all of which also reflect the role of nonverbal behavior in social control.

Another area of active research concerns those nonverbal behaviors that can facilitate the therapeutic alliance. Tepper and Haase (1978) emphasized the importance of considering a multichannel approach to understanding this subtle set of relationships. In one study they reviewed the impact of various factors including verbal message, trunk lean, eye contact, vocal intonation, and facial expression on facilitative concerns such as empathy, respect, and genuineness. Nonverbal components appeared to play a major role in these facilitative processes. Attempts have been made to determine methods of measuring clinician ability to decode the nonverbal behavior of patients. Rosenthal, Hall, DiMatteo, Rogers, and Archer (1979) developed the Profile of Nonverbal Sensitivity (PONS) in this regard. The original PONS consisted of 220 two-second film segments for which subjects were asked to read accurately nonverbal clues, such as facial expression and tone of voice.

The issue of decoding nonverbal cues immediately raises the concept of cross-cultural differences with regard to interpretation of nonverbal behavior. As mentioned earlier, Hall was fascinated by this process and, in recent times, Sue has studied these ramifications in great detail (Sue, 1981; Sue & Sue, 1977).

Issues such as paralanguage and temporal speech characteristics have been carefully studied. Matarazzo and Wiens (1972) have developed a concrete system of exploring such interactions. They have delineated three major temporal speech characteristics: duration of utterance (DOU), response time latency (RTL), and percentage of interruptions (Wiens, 1983). In conjunction with Harper, these same authors provide an insightful review of nonverbal behavior in *Nonverbal Communication: The State of the Art* (Harper, Wiens, & Matarazzo, 1978). As Tepper and Haase have emphasized, the future of nonverbal research probably lies in an integrative approach combining paralanguage concerns, such as those delineated by Matarazzo and Wiens, with other proxemic and kinesic elements as they have impact on the interviewing relationship.

The interviewing relationship is further defined by the third major area of research which focuses on characteristics of the interviewer that affect the thera-

peutic alliance, such as communication style, race, physical attractiveness, and the ability to convey empathy. Because of its broad area of investigation, this type of research overlaps with some of the areas already described. For instance, response modes have been used to correlate client perceptions of clinician empathy with clinician phrasing, responses focused on exploration being strongly associated with perceived empathy (Barkham & Shapiro, 1986). In a similar vein, the child psychiatrist Rutter has developed a system of training clinicians to display four distinct styles ranging from a "sounding board" style to a "structured" style. The impact of these styles on the interview process was then examined (Rutter, Cox, Egert, Holbrook, & Everitt, 1981).

The concept of empathy has received as much, if not more, emphasis than any other single clinician characteristic. As mentioned earlier, Rogers was pivotal in the development of thought related to the empathic process. Historically, another major contribution was made by Truax and Carkhuff (1967) who emphasized qualities such as accurate empathy, nonpossessive warmth, and interpersonal genuineness as critical to the development of a sound therapeutic alliance (Truax & Carkhuff, 1967). The Truax scale itself was a popular measure of empathy but has been attacked on numerous grounds ranging from a lack of specificity concerning the clinician behaviors in question, to the claim that the scale may be measuring more than one thing (Cochrane, 1974; Lambert, DeJulio, & Stein, 1978; Wenegrat, 1974; Zimmer & Anderson, 1968).

One of the more powerful unifying theories is the *empathy cycle* proposed by G. T. Barrett-Lennard (1981). The empathy cycle delineates the empathic process in five specific phases, including such processes as the clinician's ability to perceive the patient's feelings and the patient's ability to provide feedback that the empathic message has been received. The empathy cycle provides a framework from which differing components of the empathic process can be studied (Harmon, 1986). Over the years numerous articles and reviews concerning empathy have spun off from the works previously described as well as the viewpoints espoused by the psychoanalytic community (Berger, 1987; Elliott et al., 1977; Gladstein, 1983; Smith-Hanen, 1977).

When considering the broad region of the impact of clinician characteristics on alliance, one area of progress has been in the development of rating forms with regard to patient satisfaction with the interviewer. In 1975 Barak and LaCrosse developed the Counselor Rating Form which is also available in a shortened form (Barak & LaCrosse, 1975; Corrigan & Schmidt, 1983). Other scales have followed that emphasize the alliance as it develops in the psychotherapeutic relationship (Alexander & Luborsky, 1986; Marmar, Horowitz, Weiss, & Marziali, 1986).

A major thrust in the research dealing with clinician characteristics evolves from the work of Strong. His work with the interpersonal influence theory of counseling has focused attention on the idea that counselors who were perceived as expert, attractive, and trustworthy would possess a more effective means of influencing the behaviors of their clients (Paradise, Conway, & Zweig, 1986; Strong, 1968; Strong, Taylor, Bratton, & Loper, 1971). For example, the physical attractiveness of the clinician appears to have a positive impact in certain situations (Cash, Begley, McCown, & Weise, 1975; McKee & Smouse, 1983; Vargas & Borkowski, 1982).

Other characteristics that have been studied include race (Paurohit, Dowd, & Cottingham, 1982), body movement (LaCrosse, 1975), spontaneity and fluency of speech (Strong & Schmidt, 1970), and the role of displays of accreditation, such as diplomas, on the walls of the clinician's office (Siegel & Sell, 1978).

In concluding a review of the literature describing the impact of clinician characteristics on alliance, it is natural to mention some of the work based on the ultimate measure of clinician impact and compliance with followup. A number of issues have been studied, such as the impact of the degree of directiveness, counselor gender, and counselor experience, as well as the clinician's willingness to negotiate a therapeutic contract. It appears that the ability to convey accurately a sensitive understanding of the patient's problem and the ability to negotiate future treatment plans flexibly are powerful predictors of compliance (Eisenthal, Koopman, & Lazare, 1983; Eisenthal & Lazare, 1977a, b; Epperson, Bushway, & Warman, 1983; Heilbrun, 1974).

The fourth major area of interviewing research leaves the arena of interpersonal dynamics and focuses more on the issue of structured and semistructured interviews and their impact on the thoroughness, reliability, and validity of the data base. Whereas much of the process research previously described has evolved from the fields of counseling and psychology, a large part of the work on structured interviews has been undertaken in the field of psychiatry.

In many respects structured and semistructured interviews grew out of the tradition of psychiatric epidemiology (Helzer, 1983). Examples include the Home Interview Survey (HIS) used in the Midtown Manhattan Study (Srole, Langer, Michael, Opler, &

Rennie, 1962) and the Psychiatric Epidemiological Research Interview (PERI) developed by Dohrenwend (Dohrenwend, Shrout, Egri, & Mendelsohn, 1980). One of the most influential interviews that dealt directly with psychiatric symptomatology and diagnosis was the Present State Examination (PSE) developed by Wing in England (Wing, Cooper, & Sartorius, 1974).

The PSE combines elements of both the recent psychiatric history and the mental status. It represents a semistructured interview which emphasizes the need for the interviewer to cross examine in a flexible manner, when attempting to delineate the presence and severity of a symptom. The PSE has undergone numerous editions, and the ninth edition can be used in conjunction with a computer program CATEGO, which will delineate a diagnosis from the data gathered during the interview. The ninth version contains 140 principal items and its phenomenological approach creates a Western European feel in the interview format (Hedlund & Vieweg, 1981). Numerous studies have been undertaken with regard to the reliability of the PSE (Cooper, Copeland, Brown, Harris, & Gourlay, 1977; Wing, Nixon, Mann, & Leff, 1977).

Several important interviews have already been mentioned during the historical survey earlier in the chapter including the Diagnostic Interview Schedule (DIS) and the Schedule for Affective Disorders and Schizophrenia (SADS). All of these interview formats were developed with the idea of increasing the thoroughness, reliability, and validity of the data base. In some respects, these goals have been at least partially realized. But Sanson-Fisher and Martin (1981) have emphasized an important point. Because these interviews have been shown to be reliable, researchers tend to assume that the interviews will automatically be reliable in the hands of the clinicians working in their protocols. This assumption is not necessarily the case. It is important that reliability studies be used at each research site and in an ongoing fashion if, indeed, the interview format is to function with a high degree of reliability.

Before leaving the area of structured interviews and their impact on reliability and validity concerns, it is important to mention the major role that child psychiatrists have had in the development of interview formats. A variety of interviews have been developed including the Diagnostic Interview for Children and Adolescents (DICA) (Herjanic & Campbell, 1977; Herjanic & Reich, 1982), the Interview Schedule for Children (ISC) (Kovacs, 1983), the Kiddie-SADS (Puig-Antich & Chambers, 1978), the Diagnostic

Interview Schedule for Children (DISC) (Costello, Edelbrock, Kalas, & Dulcan, 1984), and the semi-structured interview developed by Rutter and Graham (1968). The development of such interviewing tools have allowed researchers to address the intriguing questions concerning the correlation between developmental age and the validity of information provided by children (Edelbrock, Costello, Dulcan, Kalas, & Conover, 1985).

The fifth, and final major area in interviewing research concerns developments in educational techniques. This field is both exciting and broad, with contributions from all disciplines of mental health. For the sake of simplicity, it is best to group this research into two large areas: the development of improved supervision techniques and the development of tools for measuring student learning with regard to interviewing skills.

In the same fashion that there has been a striking evolution in the number of treatment modalities now available, there has been an equally remarkable advancement in training techniques over the past several decades. For many years, interviewing training seemed to be stuck on the model of indirect supervision that had evolved from the psychoanalytic tradition. With indirect supervision the trainee sees the patient alone and then reports on "what happened" to the supervisor. Indirect supervision, when done well, can be very effective, providing an intimate and carefully individualized supervision, but it has obvious limitations.

The idea that the supervisor could actually "sit in" with the patient and the interviewer probably developed from a variety of disciplines. For instance, the idea of direct supervision is a popular style of supervision in family therapy. With regard to interviewing an individual patient, numerous advantages appear when comparing direct to indirect supervision (Digiacomo, 1982; Stein, Toksoz, Karasu, Charles, & Buckley, 1975).

Direct supervision removes many of the distorting mechanisms at work with the secondhand information provided by indirect supervision. In direct supervision the supervisor can more accurately evaluate nonverbal interaction, the structuring of the interview, and the handling of resistance. It also provides the trainee with the all-too-rare opportunity to model a more experienced clinician, if the supervisor chooses to demonstrate a technique. Rarely does direct supervision appear to hamper engagement with the patient significantly. In one study more than twice as many patients with direct supervision, compared with indirect supervision, remained in active treatment or successively

completed therapy (Jaynes, Charles, Kass, & Holzman, 1979).

On the heels of direct supervision, the closely related concept of videotape supervision was developed. Such supervision complements both indirect and direct supervision. Like direct supervision it provides an excellent opportunity for feedback on nonverbal and structuring techniques. It also offers the advantage of helping the clinician to develop a more effective observing ego by literally experiencing the process of observing and analyzing his or her own behavior (Dowrick & Biggs, 1983; Jackson & Pinkerton, 1983; Maguire et al., 1973; Waldron, 1973).

The advent of recording technologies, such as audiotape and videotape, provided the foundation for an innovative style of supervision known as Interpersonal Process Recall (IPR). Bloom (1954) was one of the first to experiment with the technique in his attempt to explore the thought processes of college students during discussion sections. Kagan (1975) was the first to apply the technique to the clinical interview in the mental health professions and coined the term *Interpersonal Process Recall*. In IPR the students are asked to reflect upon their internal feelings, thoughts, and reactions that are associated with specific clinical situations observed on videotapes of their own clinical interviews. It is an excellent tool for uncovering countertransference issues and other psychodynamic concerns. IPR is also a powerful method of helping trainees to recapture fleeting impressions that would normally be lost or distorted (Elliott, 1986).

Role playing provides yet another complementary and widely accepted avenue for enhancing specific interviewing skills (Canada, 1973; Errek & Randolf, 1982; Hannay, 1980; Hutter et al., 1977). It may represent the single most effective manner by which to familiarize trainees with various methods of handling hostile or awkward patient questions.

Ward and Stein (1975) pioneered the concept of group supervision by colleagues. In this format the patient is interviewed by the trainee while fellow trainees observe in the same room. It provides a format in which the group identifies emotionally with both the patient and the interviewer, providing a unique window into the processes of engagement and empathy.

Combining many of the advances just described, Ivey (1971) developed the innovative process of microtraining. Microtraining probably represents one of the most extensively studied and empirically proven of all the training techniques currently utilized. In this format, specific skills, such as the use of empathic statements or open-ended questions, are taught in an individualized fashion with a heavy emphasis on behavioral reinforcement. The trainee is videotaped. Immediate feedback is given and problem areas delineated. Concise, goal-directed reading material, related to a well-circumscribed skill, is provided. The trainee then immediately performs further role plays during which the newly acquired skill is practiced until it is perfected, the trainee constantly being given concrete feedback from the supervisor.

The second major area with regard to research on interviewing in education focuses on methods of evaluating interviewing skills. It is interesting to note that much of the empirical work in this area has been done with medical student education as opposed to psychiatric resident education.

One test technique consists of providing trainees with videotape vignettes followed by three possible physician responses. The trainee is asked to select the most appropriate response (Adler, Ware, & Enelow, 1968; Cline & Garrard, 1973). A written test that attempts to examine interviewer decision making with regard to the interview process has been described by Smith (Smith, Hadac, & Leversee, 1980). This instrument, called the Helping Relationship Inventory, consists of 10 brief patient statements. Each statement is followed by five alternative responses categorized as understanding, probing, interpretive, supportive, or evaluative. Liston has developed a tool for assessing the acquisition of psychotherapy skills known as the Psychotherapy Competence Assessment Schedule (PCAS) (Liston & Yager, 1982; Liston, Yager, & Strauss, 1981).

With regard to assessing the skills demonstrated in the initial medical or psychiatric interview, the vast majority of work has moved away from pencil-and-paper tests, focusing instead on direct or videotaped evaluation of actual clinical interviews. This body of literature is relatively large and is well reviewed by Ovadia, Yager, and Heinrich (1982). A representative example of one such format is the Queen's University Interview Rating Scale (QUIRS). This rating process was developed to test the psychiatric interviewing skills of medical students as they rotated on third- and fourth-year clerkships (Jarrett, Waldron, Burra, & Handforth, 1972). The QUIRS consists of 23 items collapsed from a list of 75 skills drawn from the literature. The test items are organized into three supercategories: interview structure, interviewer role, and communication skills. With regard to medical interviewing, Brockway (1978) developed an extensive system for evaluating interviewing skills. This system includes over 50 items ranging from process

items, such as the use of silence, to content items, such as eliciting the patient's rationale for making an appointment.

A paper written by Sanson-Fisher, Fairbairn, and Maguire (1981) provides a good ending point for this section, albeit a somewhat sobering one. In a review of 46 papers dealing with the teaching of communication and interviewing skills to medical students, the majority of the papers revealed methodological flaws. According to Sanson-Fisher, the future of research in this area should include a consolidated effort toward the use of standard research techniques including control groups, reliability studies, student characteristics, patient characteristics, and more sophisticated statistical analyses.

SUMMARY

In this chapter an attempt has been made to provide a sound introduction to the art and craft of psychiatric interviewing. It can be seen that the historical currents of psychiatric interviewing are varied and rich. These currents include medical traditions such as the mental status, diagnostic systems, and psychoanalytic techniques. But they also include a remarkable array of contributions from nonmedical fields such as counseling and psychology.

At the present moment there is a cross-pollination among fields that is unusually promising. Research teams from different disciplines can be assembled to study the interviewing process from a variety of perspectives. These interdisciplinary teams can analyze engagement techniques, nonverbal processes, and structuring principles in the context of specific styles of interaction and characterological functioning, as determined by psychological testing and diagnosis by DSM-III-R criteria. For the first time the role of response modes, empathic statements, and nonverbal techniques can be studied in relation to specific psychopathological states such as paranoia or to specific communication resistances as seen with overly loquacious patients.

This chapter began with an historical note and it seems appropriate to end with an historical perspective as well. In 1806 the psychiatrist Philippe Pinel became renowned for his humanistic treatment of patients in the French institution known as the Asylum de Bicetre. In his book *A Treatise on Insanity* he wrote, "Few subjects in medicine are so intimately connected with the history and philosophy of the human mind as insanity. There are still fewer, where there are so many errors to rectify, and so many prejudices to remove." (p. 3). His point is as penetrating today as it was at the beginning of the nineteenth century. In the past, part of the prejudice blocking our understanding of human nature has been created by a stubborn battle over turf among the various mental health traditions. Contemporary interviewing represents an area in which the disciplines can at last join forces to further our understanding of human nature, both as a function of psychopathology and as a function of health.

REFERENCES

Adler, L., Ware, J. E., & Enelow, A. J. (1968). *Evaluation of programmed instruction in medical interviewing*. Los Angeles: University of Southern California Postgraduate Division.

Alexander, L. B., & Luborsky, L. (1986). The Penn Helping Alliance Scales. In L. S. Greenberg & W. M. Pinsof (Eds.), *The psychotherapeutic process—A research handbook*. New York: Guilford Press.

American Psychiatric Association. (1980). *Diagnostic and statistical manual of mental disorders. (DSM-III)* (3rd ed.). Washington, DC: Author.

American Psychiatric Association. (1987). *Diagnostic and statistical manual of mental disorders (DSM-III-R)* (3rd ed., rev.). Washington, DC: Author.

Aronson, M. (1953). A study of the relationships between certain counselor and client characteristics in client-centered therapy. In W. U. Snyder (Ed.), *Pennsylvania State College Psychotherapy Research Groups: Group report of a program of research in psychotherapy*.

Barak, A., & LaCrosse, M. B. (1975). Multidimensional perception of counselor behavior. *Journal of Counseling Psychology, 22,* 417–476.

Barkham, M., & Shapiro, D. A. (1986). Counselor verbal response modes and experienced empathy. *Journal of Counseling Psychology, 33,* 3–10.

Barrett-Lennard, G. T. (1981). The empathy cycle: Refinement of a nuclear concept. *Journal of Counseling Psychology, 28,* 91–100.

Benjamin, A. (1969). *The helping inteview*. Boston: Houghton-Mifflin.

Berger, D. M. (1987). *Clinical empathy*. Northvale, NJ: Jason Aronson.

Birdwhistell, R. L. (1952). *Introduction to Kinesics: An annotation system for analysis of body motion and gesture*. Louisville: University of Kentucky.

Bloom, B. S. (1954). The thought process of students in discussion. In S. J. French (Ed.), *Accent on teaching: Experiments in general education*. New York: Harper.

Brockway, B. S. (1978). Evaluating physician competency: What difference does it make? *Evaluation and Program Planning, 1,* 211.

Canada, R. M. (1973). Immediate reinforcement versus delayed reinforcement in teaching a basic interview technique. *Journal of Counseling Psychology, 20,* 395–398.

Cash, T. F., Begley, P. J., McCown, D. Q., & Weise, B. C. (1975). When counselors are heard but not seen: Initial impact of physical attractiveness. *Journal of Counseling Psychology, 22,* 273–279.

Cline, D. W., & Garrard, J. N. (1973). A medical interviewing course: Objectives, techniques, and assessment. *American Journal of Psychiatry, 130,* 574–578.

Cochrane, C. T. (1974). Development of a measure of empathic communication. *Psychotherapy: Theory, Research and Practice, 11,* 41–47.

Cooper, J. E., Copeland, J. R. M., Brown, G. W., Harris, T., & Gourlay, A. J. (1977). Further studies on interviewer training and inter-rater reliability of the Present State Examination (PSE). *Psychological Medicine, 7,* 517–523.

Cormier, W. H., & Cormier, L. S. (1979). *Interviewing strategies for helpers—A guide to assessment, treatment, and evaluation*. Monterey, CA: Brooks/Cole.

Corrigan, J. D., & Schmidt, L. D. (1983). Development and validation of revisions in the counselor rating form. *Journal of Counseling Psychology, 30,* 64–75.

Costello, A. J., Edlebrock, C., Kalas, R., & Dulcan, M. K. (1984). The NIMH Diagnostic Interview Schedule for Children (DISC): Development, reliability, and comparisons between clinical and lay interviews. Manuscript in preparation.

Danish, S. J., & D'Augelli, A. R. (1976). Rationale and implementation of a training program for paraprofessionals. *Professional Psychology, 7,* 38–46.

Deutsch, F., & Murphy, W. F. (1955a). *The clinical interview, Vol. 1: Diagnosis*. New York: International Universities Press.

Deutsch, F., & Murphy, W. F. (1955b). *The Clinical Interview. Vol. 2: Therapy*. New York: International Universities Press.

Digiacomo, J. N. (1982). Three-way interviews and psychiatric training. *Hospital and Community Psychiatry, 33,* 287–291.

Dohrenwend, B. P., Shrout, P. E., Egri, G., &

Mendelsohn, F. S. (1980). Nonspecific psychological distress and other dimensions of psychopathology. *Archives of General Psychiatry, 37,* 1229–1236.

Donnelly, J., Rosenberg, M., & Fleeson, W. P. (1970). The evolution of the mental status—Past and future. *American Journal of Psychiatry, 126,* 997–1002.

Dowrick, P. W., & Biggs, S. J. (Eds.) (1983). *Using video: Psychological and social applications.* New York: Wiley.

Edelbrock, C., Costello, A. J., Dulcan, M. K., Kalas, R., & Conover, N. C. (1985). Age differences in the reliability of the psychiatric interview of the child. *Child Development, 56,* 265–275.

Edinger, J. A., & Patterson, M. L. (1983). Nonverbal involvement and social control. *Psychological Bulletin, 93,* 30–56.

Egan, G. (1975). *The skilled helper: A model for systematic helping and interpersonal relating,* Belmont, CA: Brooks/Cole.

Eisenthal, S., Koopman, C., & Lazare, A. (1983). Process analysis of two dimensions of the negotiated approach in relation to satisfaction in the initial interview. *Journal of Nervous and Mental Disease, 171,* 49–54.

Eisenthal, S., & Lazare, A. (1977a). Evaluation of the initial interview in a walk-in clinic. *Journal of Nervous and Mental Disease, 164,* 30–35.

Eisenthal, S., & Lazare, A. (1977b). Expression of patient's requests in the initial interview. *Psychological Reports, 40,* 131–138.

Ekman, P. (1985). *Telling lies—Clues to deceit in the marketplace, politics, and marriage.* New York: W. W. Norton & Company.

Ekman, P., & Friesen, W. V. (1974). Detecting deception from the body or face. *Journal of Personality and Social Psychology, 29,* 288–298.

Elliott, R. (1986). Interpersonal Process Recall (IPR) as a psychotherapy process research method. In L. S. Greenberg (Ed.), *The psychotherapeutic process: A research handbook.* New York: Guilford Press.

Elliott, R., Filipovich, H., Harrigan, L., Gaynor, J., Reimschuessel, C., & Zapadka, J. K. (1982). Measuring response empathy: The development of a multicomponent rating scale. *Journal of Counseling Psychology, 29,* 379–387.

Elliott, R., Stiles, W. B., Mahrer, A. R., Hill, C. E., Friedlander, M. L., & Margison, F. R. (1987). Primary therapist response modes: Comparison of six rating systems. *Journal of Consulting and Clinical Psychology, 55,* 218–223.

Endicott, J., & Spitzer, R. L. (1978). A diagnostic interview: The Schedule for Affective Disorders and Schizophrenia. *Archives of General Psychiatry, 35,* 837–844.

Epperson, D. L., Bushway, D. J., & Warman, R. E. (1983). Client self-terminations after one counseling session: Effects of problem recognition, counselor gender, and counselor experience. *Journal of Counseling Psychology, 30,* 307–315.

Errek, H. K., & Randolph, D. L. (1982). Effects of discussion and role-play activities in the acquisition of consultant interview skills. *Journal of Counseling Psychology, 29,* 304–308.

Feighner, J. P., Robins, E., Guze, S. B., Woodruff, R. A., Winokur, G., & Munoz, R. (1972). Diagnostic criteria for use in psychiatric research. *Archives of General Psychiatry, 26,* 57–63.

Folstein, M. F., Folstein, S. E., & McHugh, P. R. (1975). "Mini mental state": A practical method for grading the cognitive state of patients for the clinician. *Journal of Psychiatric Research, 12,* 189–198.

Friedlander, M. L. (1982). Counseling discourse as a speech event: Revision and extension of the Hill Counselor Verbal Response Category System. *Journal of Counseling Psychology, 29,* 425–429.

Gill, M., Newman, R., & Redlich, F. C. (1954). *The initial interview in psychiatric practice.* New York: International Universities Press.

Gladstein, G. A. (1983). Understanding empathy: Integrating counseling, developmental, and social psychology perspectives. *Journal of Counseling Psychology, 30,* 467–482.

Goodman, G., & Dooley, D. A. (1976). A framework for help-intended communication. *Psychotherapy, Theory, Research, and Practice, 13,* 106–117.

Grinder, J., & Bandler, R. (1975). *The structure of magic I.* Palo Alto, CA: Science & Behavior Books.

Hackney, H., & Nye, S. (1973). *Counseling strategies and outcomes.* Englewood Cliffs, NJ: Prentice-Hall.

Hall, C. S., & Lindzey, G. (1978). *Theories of personality.* New York: Wiley.

Hall, E. T. (1966). *The hidden dimension.* New York: Doubleday.

Hannay, D. R. (1980). Teaching interviewing with simulated patients. *Medical Education, 12,* 246–248.

Harman, J. I. (1986). Relations among components of the empathic process. *Journal of Counseling Psychology, 33,* 371–376.

Harper, R. G., Wiens, A. N., & Matarazzo, J. D.

(1978). *Nonverbal communication: The state of the art*. New York: Wiley.

Havens, L. (1978). Explorations in the uses of language in psychotherapy: Simple empathic statements. *Psychiatry, 41*, 336–345.

Havens, L. (1979). Explorations in the uses of language in psychotherapy: Complex empathic statements. *Psychiatry, 42*, 40–48.

Havens, L. (1980). Experience in the uses of language in psychotherapy: Counterprojective statements. *Contemporary Psychoanalysis, 16*, 53–67.

Hedlund, J. L., & Vieweg, B. W. (1981). Structured psychiatric interviews: A comparative review. *Journal of Operational Psychiatry, 12*, 39–67.

Heilbrun, A. B. (1974). Interviewer style, client satisfaction, and premature termination following the initial counseling contact. *Journal of Counseling Psychology, 21*, 346–350.

Helmchen, H. (1975). Schizophrenia: Diagnostic concepts in the ICD-8. In M. H. Lader (Ed.), Studies in schizophrenia. *British Journal of Psychiatry, Special Publication, 10*, 10–18.

Helzer, J. E. (1983). Standardized interviews in psychiatry. *Psychiatric Developments, 2*, 161–178.

Herjanic, B., & Campbell, W. (1977). Differentiating psychiatrically disturbed children on the basis of a structured interview. *Journal of Abnormal Child Psychology, 5*, 127–134.

Herjanic, B., & Reich, W. (1982). Development of a structured psychiatric interview for children: Agreement between child and parent on individual symptoms. *Journal of Abnormal Child Psychology, 10*, 307–324.

Hersen, M., & Turner, S. M. (1985). *Diagnostic interviewing*. New York: Plenum Press.

Hill, C. E. (1975). Sex of client and sex experience level of counselor. *Journal of Counseling Psychology, 22*, 6–11.

Hill, C. E. (1978). Development of a counselor verbal response category system. *Journal of Counseling Psychology, 25*, 461–468.

Hutter, M. J., Dungy, C. I., Zakus, G. E., Moore, V. J., Ott, J. E., & Favret, A. (1977). Interviewing skills: A comprehensive approach to teaching and evaluation. *Journal of Medical Education, 52*, 328–333.

Ivey, A. E. (1971). *Microcounseling: Innovations in interviewing training*. Springfield, IL: Charles C Thomas.

Jackson, M. G., & Pinkerton, R. R. (1983). Videotape teaching in family practice residencies. *Journal of Medical Education, 58*, 434–435.

Jarrett, F. J., Waldron, J. J., Burra, P., & Handforth,

J. R. (1972). Measuring interviewing skill—The Queen's University Interviewer Rating Scale (QUIRS). *Canadian Psychiatric Association Journal, 17*, 183–188.

Jaynes, S., Charles, E., Kass, F., & Holzman, S. (1979). Clinical supervision of the initial interview: Effects of patient care. *American Journal of Psychiatry, 136*, 1454–1457.

Kagan, N. (1975). *Interpersonal process recall: A method of influencing human interaction*. (Available from N. Kagan, 434 Erickson Hall, College of Education, MSU, East Lansing, Michigan 48824.)

Kaplan, H., Freedman, A., & Sadock, B. (Eds.). (1980). *Comprehensive textbook of psychiatry* (3rd ed.). Baltimore: Williams & Wilkins.

Kato, M. (1977). *Multiaxial diagnosis in adult psychiatry*. Paper presented at the Sixth World Congress of Psychiatry, Honolulu.

Kovacs, M. (1983). *The Interview Schedule for Children (ISC): Interrater and parent-child agreement*. Manuscript submitted for publication.

LaCrosse, M. B. (1975). Nonverbal behavior and perceived counselor attractiveness and persuasiveness. *Journal of Counseling Psychology, 6*, 563–566.

Lambert, M. J., DeJulio, S. J., & Stein, D. M. (1978). Therapist interpersonal skills: Process, outcome, methodological considerations, and recommendations for future research. *Psychological Bulletin, 85*, 467–489.

Langsley, D. G., & Hollender, M. H. (1982). The definition of a psychiatrist. *American Journal of Psychiatry, 139*, 81–85.

Liston, E. H., & Yager, J. (1982). Assessment of clinical skills in psychiatry. In J. Yager (Ed.), *Teaching psychiatry and behavioral science*, New York: Grune & Stratton.

Liston, E. H., Yager, J., & Strauss, G. D. (1981). Assessment of psychotherapy skills: The problem of interrater agreement. *American Journal of Psychiatry, 138*, 1069–1074.

MacKinnon, R. A., & Michels, R. (1971). *The psychiatric interview in clinical practice*. Philadelphia, PA: W.B. Saunders.

Maguire, P., Roe, P., Goldberg, D., Jones, S., Hyde, C., & O'Dowd, T. (1978). The value of feedback in teaching interviewing skills to medical students. *Psychological Medicine, 8*, 695–704.

Margulies, A. (1984). Toward empathy: The uses of wonder. *American Journal of Psychiatry, 141*, 1025–1033.

Margulies, A., & Havens, L. (1981). The initial

encounter: What to do first? *American Journal of Psychiatry, 138,* 421–428.

Marmar, C. R., Horowitz, M. J., Weiss, D. S., & Marziali, E. (1986). The development of the Therapeutic Alliance Rating System. In L. S. Greenberg & W. M. Pinsof (Eds.), *The psychotherapeutic process—A research handbook.* New York: Guilford Press.

Matarazzo, J. D., & Wiens, A. N. (1972). *The interview: Research on its anatomy and structure.* Chicago: Aldine-Atherton.

McKee, K., & Smouse, A. D. (1983). Clients' perceptions of counselor expertness, attractiveness, and trustworthiness: Initial impact of counselor status and weight. *Journal of Counseling Psychology, 30,* 332–338.

Meyer, A. (1951). *The collected papers of Adolf Meyer* (Vol. 3). E. E. Winters (Ed.). Baltimore: John Hopkins Press.

Mezzich, J. E. (1985). Multiaxial diagnostic systems in psychiatry. In H. I. Kaplan & B. J. Sadock (Eds.), *The comprehensive textbook of psychiatry* (4th ed.). Baltimore: Williams & Wilkins.

Mezzich, J. E., Dow, J. T., Ganguli, R., Munetz, J. R. & Zettler-Segal, M. (1986). Computerized initial and discharge evaluations. In J. E. Mezzich (Ed.), *Clinical care and information systems in psychiatry.* Washington, DC: American Psychiatric Press.

Mezzich, J. E., Dow, J. T., Rich, C. L., Costello, A. J. & Himmelhoch, J. M. (1981). Developing an efficient clinical information system for a comprehensive psychiatric institute. II. Initial evaluation form. *Behavior Research Methods & Instrumentation, 13,* 464–478.

Ottosson, J. O., & Perris, C. (1973). Multidimensional classification of mental disorders. *Psychological Medicine, 3,* 238–243.

Ovadia, A. B., Yager, J., & Heinrich, R. L. (1982). Assessment of medical interview skills. In J. Yager (Ed.), *Teaching psychiatry and behavioral science.* New York: Grune & Stratton.

Paradise, L. V., Conway, B. S., & Zweig, J. (1986). Effects of expert and referent influence, physical attractiveness, and gender on perceptions of counselor attributes. *Journal of Counseling Psychology, 33,* 16–22.

Pascal, G. R. (1983). *The practical art of diagnostic interviewing.* Homewood, IL: Dow Jones-Irwin.

Paurohit, N., Dowd, E. T., & Cottingham, H. F. (1982). The role of verbal and nonverbal cues in the formation of first impressions of black and white counselors. *Journal of Counseling Psychology, 4,* 371–378.

Pinel, P. (1988). *A treatise on insanity.* Birmingham, AL: Gryphon Editions. (Original work published 1806)

Puig-Antich, J., & Chambers, W. (1978). *The Schedule for Affective Disorders and Schizophrenia for School-aged Children.* Unpublished manuscript, New York State Psychiatric Institute.

Reik, T. (1952). *Listening with the third ear.* New York: Farrar, Strauss.

Richardson, S. A., Dohrenwend, B. S., & Klein, D. (1965). *Interviewing—Its forms and functions,* New York: Basic Books.

Robins, L. N., Helzer, J. E., Croughan, J., & Ratcliff, K. S. (1981). National Institute of Mental Health Diagnostic Interview Schedule. Its history, characteristics, and validity. *Archives of General Psychiatry, 10,* 41–61.

Robinson, F. R. (1950). *Principles and procedures in student counseling.* New York: Harper.

Rogers, C. R. (1951). *Client-centered therapy.* Boston: Houghton-Mifflin.

Rogers, C. R. (1959). A theory of therapy, personality and interpersonal relationships as developed in the client-centered framework. In S. Koch (Ed.), *Psychology: A study of a science: Formulations of the person and the social context* (Vol. 3). New York: McGraw-Hill.

Rosenthal, R., Hall, J. A., DiMatteo, M. R., Rogers, P. L., & Archer, D. (1979). *Sensitivity to nonverbal communication: The PONS test.* Baltimore: Johns Hopkins University Press.

Rutter, M., Cox, A., Egert, S., Holbrook, D., & Everitt, B. (1981). Psychiatric interviewing techniques IV. Experimental study: Four contrasting styles. *British Journal of Psychiatry, 138,* 456–465.

Rutter, M., & Graham, P. (1968). The reliability and validity of the psychiatric assessment of the child: Interview with the child. *British Journal of Psychiatry, 11,* 563–579.

Rutter, M., Shaffer, D., & Shepherd, M. (1975). *A multiaxial classification of child psychiatric disorders.* Geneva: World Health Organization.

Sanson-Fisher, R., Fairbairn, S., & Maguire, P. (1981). Teaching skills in communication to medical students—A critical review of the methodology. *Medical Education, 15,* 33–37.

Sanson-Fisher, R. W., & Martin, C. J. (1981). Standardized interviews in psychiatry: Issues of reliability. *British Journal of Psychiatry, 139,* 138–143.

Scheflen, A. E. (1972). *Body language and social order*. Englewood Cliffs, NJ: Prentice-Hall.

Shea, S. (1988). *Interviewing: The art of understanding*. Philadelphia: W. B. Saunders.

Siassi, I. (1984). Psychiatric interview and mental status examination. In G. Goldstein & M. Hersen (Eds.), *Handbook of psychological assessment*, New York: Pergamon Press.

Siegel, J. C., & Sell, J. M. (1978). Effects of objective evidence of expertness and nonverbal behavior on client-perceived expertness. *Journal of Counseling Psychology, 25*, 188–192.

Smith, C. K., Hadac, R. R., & Leversee, J. H. (1980). Evaluating the effects of a medical interviewing course taught at multiple locations. *Journal of Medical Education, 55*, 792–794.

Smith-Hanen, S. S. (1977). Effects of nonverbal behaviors on judged levels of counselor warmth and empathy. *Journal of Counseling Psychology, 24*, 87–91.

Snyder, W. U. (1945). An investigation of the nature of nondirective psychotherapy. *Journal of General Psychology, 33*, 193–223.

Snyder, W. U. (1963). *Dependency in psychotherapy: A casebook*. New York: Macmillan.

Spitzer, R. L., Endicott, J., & Robins, E. (1978). Research diagnostic criteria. *Archives of General Psychiatry, 35*, 773–782.

Spooner, S. E., & Stone, S. C. (1977). Maintenance of specific counseling skills over time. *Journal of Counseling Psychology, 24*, 66–71.

Srole, L., Langer, T. S., Michael, S. T., Opler, M. K., & Rennie, T. A. C. (1962). *Mental health in the metropolis: The Midtown Manhattan Study* (Vol. 1). New York: McGraw-Hill.

Stein, S. P., Karasu, T. B., Charles, E. S., & Buckley, P. J. (1975). Supervision of the initial interview. *Archives of General Psychiatry, 32*, 265–268.

Stiles, W. B. (1978). Verbal response modes and dimensions of interpersonal roles: A method of discourse analysis. *Journal of Personality and Social Psychology, 7*, 693–703.

Strong, S. R. (1968). Counseling: An interpersonal influence process. *Journal of Counseling Psychology, 15*, 215–224.

Strong, S. R., & Schmidt, L. D. (1970). Expertness and influence in counseling. *Journal of Counseling Psychology, 17*, 81–87.

Strong, S. R., Taylor, R. G., Bratton, J. C., & Loper, R. (1971). Nonverbal behavior and perceived counselor characteristics. *Journal of Counseling Psychology, 18*, 554–561.

Strub, R. L., & Black, W. W. (1979). *The mental status examination in neurology*. Philadelphia: F. A. Davis.

Strupp, H. H. (1960). *Psychotherapists in action: Explorations of the therapist's contribution to the treatment process*. New York: Grune & Stratton.

Sue, D. W. (1981). *Counseling the culturally different*. New York: Wiley.

Sue, D. W., & Sue, D. (1977). Barriers to effective cross-cultural counseling. *Journal of Counseling Psychology, 24*, 420–429.

Sullivan, H. S. (1970). *The psychiatric interview*. New York: W. W. Norton Company.

Tepper, D. T., Jr., & Haase, R. F. (1978). Verbal and nonverbal communication of facilitative conditions. *Journal of Counseling Psychology, 25*, 35–44.

Truax, C. B., & Carkhuff, R. R. (1967). *Toward effective counseling and psychotherapy: Training and practice*. Chicago: Aldine.

Vargas, A. M., & Borkowski, J. G. (1982). Physical attractiveness and counseling skills. *Journal of Counseling Psychology, 29*, 246–255.

von Cranach, M. (1977). *Categorical vs. multiaxial classification*. Paper presented at the Seventh World Congress of Psychiatry, Honolulu, Hawaii.

Waldron, J. (1973). Teaching communication skills in medical school. *American Journal of Psychiatry, 130*, 579–581.

Ward, N. G., & Stein, L. (1975). Reducing emotional distance: A new method of teach interviewing skills. *Journal of Medical Education, 50*, 605–614.

Wenegrat, A. (1974). A factor analytic study of the Truax Accurate Empathy Scale. *Psychotherapy: Theory, Research and Practice, 11*, 48–51.

Whalen, C. K., & Flowers, J. V. (1977). Effects of role and gender mix on verbal communication modes. *Journal of Counseling Psychology, 24*, 281–287.

Whitehorn, J. C. (1944). Guide to interviewing and clinical personality. *Archives of Neurology and Psychiatry, 52*, 197–216.

Wiens, A. N. (1983). The assessment interview. In I. B. Weiner (Ed.), *Clinical methods in psychology*. New York: Wiley.

Wing, J. K., Cooper, J. E., & Sartorius, N. (1974). *Measurement and classification of psychiatric symptoms*. Cambridge: Cambridge University Press.

Wing, J. K., Nixon, J. M., Mann, S. A., & Leff, J. P.

(1977). Reliability of the PSE (ninth edition) used in a population study. *Psychological Medicine, 7,* 505–516.

Wing, L. (1970). Observations on the psychiatric section of the *International Classification of Dis-* *eases* and the *British Glossary of Mental Disorders. Psychological Medicine, 1,* 79–85.

Zimmer, J. M., & Anderson, S. (1968). Dimensions of positive regard and empathy. *Journal of Counseling Psychology, 15,* 417–426.

CHAPTER 14

STRUCTURED INTERVIEWS FOR CHILDREN AND ADOLESCENTS

Craig Edelbrock
Anthony J. Costello

INTRODUCTION

Interviewing has long been the standard method of assessing children's emotional, behavioral, and social functioning. Direct questioning of parent and child is a universal, and arguably indispensable, component of clinical assessment of children and youth. Yet, it is one of the least trustworthy assessment procedures, subject to broad variations in content, style, detail, and coverage. Interviewers differ in *what they ask* and *how they ask it*. They undoubtedly influence responses directly through the choice of a particular line and style of questioning and indirectly through their verbal and nonverbal reactions. Furthermore, interviewers differ in how they combine, reduce, and interpret interviewees' responses. Interviewing is therefore prone to high "information variance"—variability in what information is *sought* and *elicited* from respondents—which is a major cause of low reliability in the assessment and diagnostic process (see Matarazzo, 1983).

Suppose there were a pool of subjects who were identical in every way. Clinical interviews would not elicit identical information from such clones. Different interviewers would ask different questions in different ways, and would rate and record the responses idiosyncratically. Moreover, interviews conducted by the *same interviewer* might yield quite different information due to variations in interviewing style and content from one clone to the next. If this hypothetical example were a study of diagnostic reliability, the *subject variance* would be eliminated,

because all subjects are identical. The *criterion variance*—variability due to use of different diagnostic criteria—could also be eliminated by the use of one diagnostic system. But information variance would remain as a major threat to reliability. Given the freedom of unstructured interviews, differences in the information obtained would undoubtedly arise and the reliability of diagnoses would be less than perfect.

If interviewing is universal and ultimately indispensable, how can it be made reliable and valid enough for clinical and research purposes? The answer, at least in part, involves structuring the interview. Structuring involves limiting variability in the question-answer transactions between interviewer and respondent. This is accomplished by *defining* the phenomena to be assessed, *limiting* the order and wording of questions, and *standardizing* how responses are rated, recorded, combined, and interpreted.

Historical Foundations

Structured interviews for children and adolescents developed along two distinct historical lines: one *diagnostic* and the other *descriptive*. The diagnostic line of development paralleled the emergence of more differentiated taxonomies of childhood disorders. Prior to 1980 and the publication of the third edition of the *Diagnostic and Statistical Manual of the American Psychiatric Association* (DSM-III) (American Psychiatric Association, 1980), there was little need for diagnostic interview schedules that provided precise, detailed, and reliable assessments of child psychopathology. During the era of the first edition of the DSM (American Psychiatric Association, 1956) there were only two diagnostic categories for children: Adjustment Reaction and Childhood Schizophrenia. Adult diagnoses could be applied to children, but the vast majority of children seen in psychiatric clinics were either undiagnosed or were labeled adjustment reactions (Rosen, Bahn, & Kramer, 1964). More differentiated taxonomies of childhood disorders were provided by the Group for the Advancement of Psychiatry (GAP) (1966) and the second edition of the DSM (American Psychiatric Association, 1968), but both systems lacked explicit diagnostic criteria and operational assessment procedures. Not surprisingly, the reliability of both systems was mediocre (Freeman, 1971; Sandifer, Pettus, & Quade, 1964; Tarter, Templer, & Hardy, 1975).

In 1980, however, the DSM-III provided a differentiated taxonomy, "Disorders Usually First Evident in Infancy, Childhood, or Adolescence," that had more explicit diagnostic criteria. The need for more valid and reliable ways of assessing diagnostic criteria was a primary stimulus for the development of structured interview schedules for children and adolescents. More impetus was gained from the successes in the adult area. Although adult psychiatric disorders had explicit diagnostic criteria, refined through decades of trial-and-error tinkering, the reliability of adult diagnoses was too low for research purposes such as epidemiologic surveys and clinical trials. This prompted the development of structured interview schedules such as the Diagnostic Interview Schedule (Robins, Helzer, Croughan, & Ratcliff, 1981) and the Schedule for Affective Disorders and Schizophrenia (Endicott & Spitzer, 1978), which substantially reduced information variance and boosted diagnostic reliability (see Matarazzo, 1983). Researchers interested in child and adolescent psychopathology were quick to follow suit and, in fact, many interview schedules for children are downward extrapolations of adult interviews.

Apart from diagnostic purposes, there had long been a need for obtaining descriptive data on children's emotional, behavioral, and social problems, but standardized assessment procedures were lacking. In the spring of 1955 Lapouse and Monk (1958) undertook a survey to determine the prevalence and patterning of problem behaviors in a community sample. A standard format was used for interviewing mothers about their children's behavior. This had the obvious advantages of yielding more objective data

than an unstructured clinical interview, and it insured that direct comparisons could be made between subjects assessed by different interviewers. Moreover, the goal was to *describe* children's behavioral problems, rather than to detect prespecified syndromes and disorders. The unresolved questions about the existence and definition of specific childhood disorders were circumvented.

Interviews were conducted with 482 mothers and 193 children aged 6 to 12. The interview comprised 200 questions and took about 90 minutes to complete. Most items had a yes/no response format, but some involved rating the frequency or intensity of the target behavior.

Several findings from this landmark study have been replicated by more recent research. Reinterviews with mothers, for example, indicated high test-retest reliability for items such as thumb sucking, bed wetting, and stuttering. But reliability was low for items such as fears and worries and for items requiring precise estimates of frequency (e.g., number of temper tantrums). Mother-child agreement was low for most behaviors, but was higher for behaviors such as bedwetting, temper tantrums, and biting fingernails. Mothers tended to report more behavior problems that are irksome to adults (e.g., bedwetting, restlessness, overactivity), whereas children tended to report more problems that are distressing to themselves (e.g., fears, worries, nightmares). These findings have been replicated in several recent studies that employed structured interviews for parents and children.

In another pioneering effort, Rutter and Graham (1968) developed structured procedures for directly interviewing the *child*. This was a major departure from the prevailing thought and clinical practice of the time. In clinical settings, direct interview of the child was used primarily as a *therapeutic* rather than as an assessment technique. Moreover, the assessment uses of the interview were largely restricted to uncovering unconscious wishes, fears, conflicts, and fantasies (see Group for the Advancement of Psychiatry, 1957). In contrast, the interview procedures developed by Rutter and Graham were aimed at descriptive assessment of the child's emotional, behavioral, and social functioning and were based on direct questioning of the child (and parent).

The parent and child versions of this interview schedule differ somewhat, but parallel one another in content and rating procedure. Both are semistructured interviews designed for clinically trained interviewers. The exact order and wording of questions is not prescribed. Instead, areas of functioning, such as school performance, activities, and friendships are listed, along with symptom areas such as antisocial behavior, anxiety, and depression. The parent version has more detail regarding the duration, severity, action taken, presumed cause, and expected course of problems reported. The rating of many items requires clinical judgment. Parent and child are interviewed separately. After each interview, the interviewer rates the child's mental status and determines whether the child has *no psychiatric impairment*, *some impairment*, or *definite or marked impairment*.

Two findings from this early work have been replicated in more recent studies. First, higher reliabilities were obtained for ratings of global psychiatric status than for ratings of specific symptoms, syndromes, and disorders. Rutter and Graham (1968), for example, found high interrater reliability ($r = .84$) for the overall ratings of psychiatric impairment based on separate interviews of the child by different interviewers. But reliabilities were mediocre for items pertaining to attention and hyperactivity ($r = .61$), social relations ($r = .64$), and anxiety and depression ($r = .30$). Second, as illustrated by these results, reliabilities were generally higher for problems such as hyperactivity and antisocial behavior, than for problems such as fears, anxiety, and depression.

Structured interview schedules for children and adolescents proliferated in the 1980s as the need for descriptive and diagnostic assessment tools increased. There are now many well-developed interview schedules that are widely used in research and to a lesser extent in clinical practice. A major trend has been toward increasing specialization of interview schedules. Specialization of *purpose*, for example, has resulted in different interview schedules for screening nonreferred populations versus differential diagnosis of identified cases. Specialization in *age range* has resulted in different interview schedules for preschool-aged children, grade schoolers, and adolescents. Interview schedules have also become more specialized in *coverage* and *focus*. Most cover a broad range of symptoms and behaviors, but some are focused on specific syndromes and disorders, such as childhood depression. Last, there has been increasing specialization in *interviewer training* and *qualifications*. Some are designed for clinically sophisticated interviewers, whereas others are designed for lay interviewers having only interview-specific training.

A second major trend has been an increasing emphasis on the *child as informant* regarding his or her own functioning. The assessment of child psychopathology has traditionally depended on reports and ratings by adults, particularly parents. Parents are the most common instigators of child mental health referrals, and they are almost always involved in the assessment of children's functioning. Furthermore, parents' perceptions of their children are often crucial in the implementation of treatments and the evaluation of treatment outcomes. Until recently, directly interviewing children was not considered valuable. It was assumed that children lack insight into their own problems and that they are not cognitively mature enough to understand anamestic or symptom-oriented interviews. These assumptions have been increasingly questioned and numerous schedules have been developed for directly interviewing the child.

Comment

The development of structured clinical interviews for children and adolescents can be traced along two historical lines. First, the emergence of differentiated taxonomies of childhood disorders with more explicit diagnostic criteria necessitated more accurate, precise, comprehensive, and reliable diagnostic interviewing procedures. Diagnostic interview schedules were therefore developed for purposes of differential diagnosis of children already identified as cases. Second, standard interview procedures for assessing children's emotional, behavioral, and social functioning were needed for descriptive, developmental, and epidemiologic studies. Interview schedules aimed at obtaining descriptive information about children's functioning were developed primarily for use with nonreferred populations.

The pioneering studies by Lapouse and Monk (1958) and Rutter and Graham (1968) broke new ground and introduced several innovations in interviewing, including (a) structuring the content of the interview around specific target phenomena, (b) providing prespecified formats for rating and recording responses, (c) focusing on the child's functioning rather than psychodynamic states, (d) directly interviewing the child, and (e) using parallel interview schedules for parent and child.

Research in the past 15 years has amplified and improved upon these methodological innovations. A broad range of interview schedules for children and adolescents are now available and they are widely used in research. These interview schedules have become more specialized in purpose, age range, coverage, and training requirements. Additionally, the child is now viewed as a potentially important source of information, so interview schedules have been developed specifically for interviewing children about their own functioning.

THEORETICAL UNDERPINNINGS

Descriptive interviews have few theoretical underpinnings. Because there is no overarching theory of child psychopathology that dictates what phenomena to assess, items are selected primarily on the basis of face validity. In other words, interview items seem like meaningful descriptors. In the long run, descriptive data from interviews will contribute to more useful theories of child psychopathology, which will in turn influence the focus and content of the interviews themselves.

The diagnostic interviews, of course, are built on the prevailing taxonomic system, which in the United States has been the DSM. Any taxonomic system involves decisions regarding the nature of child psychopathology and how disorders are defined and delineated—which are essentially theoretical preferences. Key theoretical assumptions are (a) that mental disorders exist, (b) that there are distinct diagnostic entities that may be hierarchically arranged in a system of classes, and (c) that the diagnostic criteria are appropriate for detecting and differentiating among disorders.

The DSM has evolved rapidly in the child area. The current revision (DSM-III-R) (American Psychiatric Association, 1987) barely resembles the edition of only a decade ago. At one time, low diagnostic reliability could have been attributed to inadequate assessment procedures, but now the inadequacy appears to be more in the taxonomy itself. Structured interview schedules cannot be expected to yield more valid diagnoses than the taxonomy will allow. There has been considerable taxonomic progress in the child area, but the validity of many diagnostic categories has been questioned, and it is not yet clear if the criteria and diagnostic thresholds proposed in the most recent revision of the DSM-III-R are correct. In a broader view, each revision of the DSM must be seen as provisional, subject to revision and refinement. Research using structured diagnostic interviews will undoubtedly contribute to future taxonomic advancements.

Another key assumption is that informants can report and rate children's emotional, behavioral, and social functioning. That parents can report on their own children's overt behavioral and social functioning is rarely questioned. It is less clear, however, that parents can provide reliable and valid information about covert behaviors that may be intentionally hidden from adults, such as truancy, alcohol and drug abuse, stealing, and vandalism; or about private phenomena such as fears, worries, and anxiety. Conversely, children and adolescents are unimpeachable sources of information regarding their own feelings and covert behaviors—even though a minimum level of cognitive maturity and degree of insight may be required. Whether children can see certain behaviors, such as disobedience, inattentiveness, and stubbornness, as *symptoms* and report them during an interview remains unclear.

DESCRIPTION

A structured interview is a list of target behaviors, symptoms, and events to be covered, guidelines for conducting the interview, and procedures for recording the data. Interview schedules differ widely in degree of structure. A crude, but useful, distinction can be made between *highly structured* and *semistructured* interviews. Highly structured interviews specify the exact order and wording of questions and provide explicit rules for rating and recording the subject's responses. The interviewer is given very little leeway in conducting the interview and the role of clinical judgment in eliciting and recording responses is minimized. In fact, the interviewer is seen as an interchangeable part of the assessment machinery. Different interviewers should ask exactly the same questions, in exactly the same order, and rate and record responses in exactly the same way. Semistructured interviews, on the other hand, are less restrictive and permit the interviewer some flexibility in conducting the interview. The interviewer plays more of a role in determining what is asked, how questions are phrased, and how responses are recorded. Different interviewers should cover the same target phenomena when using a semistructured interview, but they may do so in different ways.

It is not yet known if a high degree of structure yields consistently better data. Each type of interview has its advantages. Highly structured interviews minimize the role of clinical judgment and typically yield more objective and reliable data. But they are rigid and mechanical, and result in a stilted interview style that cannot be adapted to the individual respondent. Alternatively, semistructured interviews try to capitalize on expert clinical judgment and permit a more spontaneous interview style that can be adapted to the respondent. Of course, this flexibility allows more information variance to creep into the assessment process, which compromises reliability to some degree. The key unresolved issues are how highly structured clinical interviews should be and how much they should depend upon clinical judgments by interviewers. These are complex issues, of course, and they may have no simple answer. The more appropriate questions may be, When would it be best to minimize clinical judgment by highly structuring the interview and when would it be best to capitalize on the expertise of clinically trained interviews by providing less structure?

Structured clinical interviews for children and adolescents differ in other ways besides degree of structure. Most interview schedules have been developed for interviewing parents about their children, but parallel versions for directly questioning the child are becoming more common. Interview schedules also differ in length, organization, time requirements, age appropriateness, amount and type of interviewer training, and diagnostic coverage. Last, interview schedules differ in their intended purpose. Some were designed specifically for screening nonreferred populations for emotional and behavioral disorder, whereas others were designed for descriptive and diagnostic purposes within clinically referred populations.

RESEARCH FINDINGS

The following sections briefly describe some of the more widely used interview schedules for children and adolescents. First covered are screening tools and then descriptive and diagnostic interview schedules. The review distinguishes between semistructured interviews and highly structured interviews.

Screening Tools

Two efforts developed interview procedures for screening general populations of children for psychopathology: the Behavioral Screening Questionnaire and the Child Screening Inventory.

The Behavioral Screening Questionnaire.

The Behavioral Screening Questionnaire (BSQ) was developed to identify disturbed preschool children (Richman & Graham, 1971). The BSQ is a parent interview comprising 60 questions about child health, behavior, and development. Questions are designed to be asked verbatim but "may be supplemented until the interviewer feels comfortable about the rating" (Richman & Graham, 1971, p. 7). The BSQ therefore has features of both a highly structured and a semistructured interview. Parents' responses are rated on a 0–1–2 scale, where 0 indicates the behavior is *absent*, 1 indicates it occurs *sometimes or to a moderate degree*, and 2 indicates it occurs *frequently or to a marked degree*. The questions are clearly worded and

are easily understood by most parents. The BSQ takes 20 to 30 minutes to complete, and although it is usually administered by trained clinicians, it can be given by lay interviewers—a necessity in large-scale screening efforts.

The behavior scale of the BSQ was constructed from the 12 items that discriminated best between clinically referred and nonreferred samples. Summing the 0–1–2 responses to all 12 items yields a summary score with a range of 0–24. Interrater reliability for summary scores was $r = .77$ based on two separate interviews with parents, and $r = .94$ for independent ratings of videotaped interviews. Reliabilities for individual items are mediocre (Range = $.15 - .77$; average $r = .44$).

Validity of the behavior scale has been supported by significant discrimination between clinically referred and nonreferred samples. Using referral for services as a criterion, screening performance has been calculated in terms of *sensitivity*, which is the percentage of true cases identified, and *specificity*, which is the percentage of true negative cases identified. Using a cutoff score of 11, sensitivity was 70% and specificity was 91.2%. This is considered very good screening performance, especially because referral for services is a crude and fallible criterion for child psychopathology. The validity of the BSQ behavior scale has been supported in numerous other studies (Earls, 1980a, 1980b; Earls et al., 1982; Earls & Richman, 1980a, b; Richman, 1977; Richman, Stevenson, & Graham, 1975).

Richman (1977) has also developed a paper-and-pencil version of the behavior scale, which has the same items and rating format as the interview version. This checklist version has proven to be slightly more reliable than the interview and to have about the same screening efficiency (Richman, 1977). Because it is self-administered, inexpensive, and can be mailed out, the paper-and-pencil has many advantages over direct interviewing in large-scale screening efforts.

The Child Screening Inventory.

A screening inventory for detecting psychiatric impairment has been developed from a two- to three-hour parent interview covering child behavior and development, family background, the marital relationship, and child rearing practices (Langner et al., 1976). The Child Screening Inventory (CSI) was constructed by first culling 287 interview items from an initial pool of 654 items. Factor analysis of the reduced item pool yielded seven factors labeled self-destructive tendencies, mentation problems, conflict with parents, regressive anxiety, fighting, delinquency, and isolation. The 35-item CSI comprises the five highest loading items from each of the seven factors. It takes only 15 to 20 minutes to administer and yields scores on the seven factor-based scales as well as a total screening score.

The seven scales have low internal consistency (average alpha = .49). The internal consistency of the total screening score is somewhat higher (alpha = .76), but is still mediocre. Validity is also weak. Total screening score correlated .69 with total impairment rating derived from the entire interview, but correlated only .33 with psychiatrists' ratings of impairment based on direct interview of the child. Total screening score was also only moderately related to treatment referral status ($r = .49$). Screening efficiency has been evaluated on a general population sample of 1,034 children aged 6 to 18 in Manhattan, and a sample of 1,000 children of the same age range who were receiving welfare. Psychiatrists' rating of *marked or severe impairment* based on the entire interview was taken as the criterion for psychopathology. In the general population sample, total screening score has a specificity of 91.8%, and a sensitivity of 67.2%. In the welfare sample, specificity was 95.9%, but sensitivity was only 38.5%.

Comment

Although interviews can be used for general population screening, they are costly and time consuming. The paper-and-pencil version of the BSQ performed as well as the interview version and is less expensive, can be self-administered, and can be mailed out. The interview version of the BSQ is recommended only for smaller-scale studies, where more precise and detailed information is required, and where trained interviewers are readily available. The authors of the CSI have also recommended that it not be used as a screening tool (Langner et al., 1976). It seems a poor choice as a descriptive instrument as well because of its low internal consistency and weak validation.

Semistructured Interviews

The following section is a brief review of four semistructured interviews: the Kiddie-SADS, the Interview Schedule for Children, the Mental Health Assessment Form, and the Child Assessment Schedule.

The Kiddie-SADS.

The Kiddie-SADS or K-SADS (Puig-Antich & Chambers, 1978) is a semistructured diagnostic interview schedule for children aged 6 to 17, modeled after the Schedule for Affective Disorders and Schizophrenia (SADS), an interview schedule for adults developed by Endicott and Spitzer (1978). The K-SADS is designed to assess current psychopathology. It is focused on affective disorders but also covers conduct disorder, separation anxiety, phobias, attention deficits, and obsessions-compulsions. The K-SADS is administered by clinically sophisticated interviewers who have had intensive training using the interview schedule and who have expert knowledge about the DSM diagnostic criteria.

The parent is usually interviewed first about the child. Then the child is interviewed and any discrepancies between parent and child reports are addressed. The interviewer may confront the child about discrepancies and attempt to resolve them before making final ratings. The interviews begin with an unstructured section aimed at establishing rapport, obtaining a history of the present problems, and surveying current symptoms. The onset and duration of the current disorder and type of treatment received are then recorded. The interviewer then moves on to more structured sections covering specific symptoms. Each section includes an item (e.g., depressed mood) to be rated by the interviewer on a seven-point scale ranging from *not at all* to *very extreme*. Each section has a series of model questions (e.g., Have you felt sad? Have you cried?) that serve as guidelines for the interviewer. Interviewers are free, however, to ask as many questions as necessary to substantiate their symptoms ratings.

The K-SADS also embodies a *skip structure* whereby sections can be omitted if initial screening questions or "probes" are negative. If depressed mood is not evident, for example, subsequent questions in that section can be skipped. This reduces interviewing time substantially, but results in little lost information.

Following the section on psychiatric symptoms, the interviewer rates 11 observational items (e.g., appearance, affect, attention motor behavior) and rates the reliability and completeness of the entire interview. Finally, the interviewer completes a global assessment scale reflecting overall degree of psychiatric impairment.

The K-SADS yields information on the presence and severity of about 50 symptom areas (depending on the version of the interview). Most of the core areas concern depressive disorder, but somatization, anxiety, conduct disorder, and psychosis are also tapped. Additionally, there are 12 summary scales: four hierarchically related depression scales, five depression-related scales (e.g., suicidal ideation), and scales reflecting somatization, emotional disorder, and conduct disorder. The K-SADS data can also be translated into RDC and DSM diagnostic criteria for major depressive disorder, conduct disorder, and neurotic disorder. Diagnoses are based on the clinician's overview of the interview responses, rather than computer algorithms applied directly to the K-SADS data.

An epidemiological version of the K-SADS (K-SADS-E) is also available for assessing lifetime psychopathology (Orvaschel, Puig-Antich, Chambers, Tabrizi, & Johnson, 1982). It parallels the K-SADS, but most questions are phrased as "Have you *ever* done or had X?" As a preliminary test of validity, 17 subjects having previous depressive episodes were reinterviewed six months to two years later. For all but one subject, the K-SADS-E detected the same diagnosis that was made previously, suggesting accurate retrospective recall of previous psychiatric disturbances.

The K-SADS is widely used in clinical research, and there is a growing body of findings supporting its reliability and validity. Short-term test-retest reliability has been evaluated on 52 disturbed children and their parents (Chambers et al., 1985). Reliabilities averaged .55 (intraclass correlation, range: .09 to .89) for individual items, and averaged .68 (range: .41 to .81) for the 12 summary scales. Internal consistency for the 12 summary scales has averaged .66 (alpha statistic, range: .25 to .86). For diagnoses, agreement over time ranged from .24 to .70 (kappa statistic). Parent-child agreement has averaged .53 (intraclass correlation, range: .08 to .96) for individual items.

The K-SADS was developed primarily to identify children with major affective disorders. Because it is designed to assess diagnostic criteria, the validity of the K-SADS depends upon the validity of the diagnostic system (currently the DSM-III-R). In a sense, the K-SADS has strong content validity because it directly operationalizes DSM criteria. On the other hand, the DSM is evolving rapidly in the child area and the validity of many child psychiatric diagnoses is questionable—so the validity of the K-SADS is necessarily limited. Nevertheless, the K-SADS serves its intended purpose well. It has proven to be very useful in selecting homogeneous subgroups of depressed children from heterogeneous clinic populations (e.g., Puig-Antich, Blau, Marx, Greenhill, & Chambers, 1978). Preliminary investigations also suggest that the K-SADS is useful in research aimed at elucidating the biologic correlates of childhood depression (Puig-Antich, Chambers, Halpern, Hanlon, & Sachar, 1979) and some core depression items are sensitive to treatment effects (Puig-Antich, Perel et al., 1979).

The Interview Schedule for Children.

The Interview Schedule for Children (ISC) (Kovacs, 1982) is a semistructured interview for children aged 8 to 17 and their parents, focused on current symptoms of depression. It is designed for clinically-trained interviewers who are familiar with the DSM diagnostic criteria and who have had extensive training with the interview schedule. Two forms of the ISC are available: one for initial clinical evaluations, the other for follow-up assessments. Parent and child are interviewed separately; then the interviewer makes a final rating based on both interviews.

The ISC begins with an unstructured portion designed to establish rapport and determine the nature of the current disorder. This is followed by a more structured section covering 43 core symptoms such as depressed mood, irritability, and suicidal ideation. Each core symptom is rated on a 0–8 scale ranging from *none* to *severe*. Each step on the scale is anchored by a description of severity. For example, for dysphoric mood, a rating of *minimal* severity (1 or 2) corresponds to "infrequent, occasional sadness, but transient and not marked; not a problem." A rating of *severe* (7 or 8), on the other hand, corresponds to "pronounced dysphoria almost constantly; or acute dysphoric episodes that entail little or no response to affection/distraction; wretchedness is prominent; pronounced impairment in social functioning."

The order of questions may vary if the respondent spontaneously mentions symptoms covered in other areas. The ISC is also designed to confirm children's initial responses before a final rating is made. For many target symptoms, questions are asked more than once in different ways to double check children's answers. This seems particularly important with younger children because their initial responses are occasionally misleading. The ISC also employs standard prompts for the interviewer which are abbreviated on the form. This makes the ISC harder to learn, but results in a smoothly flowing interview once the prompts are mastered.

After the symptom section, the interviewer rates eight mental status items, twelve observational items (e.g., impaired concentration, psychomotor agitation), two developmental milestones (dating and sexual behavior), and five clinical impressions (e.g., grooming, social maturity).

Like the K-SADS, the validity of the ISC rests primarily on strong content validity and usefulness in identifying children with major depression (Kovacs, Feinberg, Crouse-Novak, Paulauskas, & Finkelstein, 1984). Interrater reliability has been evaluated by having one interviewer conduct the ISC interview while another interviewer observed and made ratings independently (Kovacs, 1983). For 39 symptoms having sufficient variability, interrater reliability averaged .89 (intraclass correlation, range: .64–1.00). Reliability averaged .86 for the mental status items, .78 for the observational items, and .77 for the clinical impressions. Parent-child agreement has also been determined for 75 outpatients. For 38 symptoms having sufficient variability, agreement averaged r = .61 (range: .02 to .95). Agreement was higher for fairly overt, easily observable behaviors such as temper tantrums, encopresis, enuresis, and school refusal than for affective and cognitive items such as feelings of pessimism, guilt, and hopelessness.

The ISC is similar to the K-SADS in many ways. It is designed for clinically referred children, is focused primarily on affective disorders, and requires extensive clinical and instrument-specific training. It can be recommended for selecting subjects for research on childhood affective disorders and as an aid in differential diagnosis. Interrater reliability appears adequate. Test-retest reliability has not been established and validity rests primarily on content rather than performance in empirical research.

The Mental Health Assessment Form.

The Mental Health Assessment Form (Kestenbaum & Bird, 1978) was developed to record the results of a semistructured interview with children aged 7 to 12. It covers 168 items organized into two parts: (a) a mental status exam, and (b) a symptom section dealing with affective disturbances, social relationships, dreams and fantasies, self-concept, conscience, and level of adaptation. Most items are rated on a 1 to 5 scale: *no deviation* to *marked deviation*. Guidelines for making item ratings are provided, but the interview depends on a high degree of clinical training and inference. Reliability has been explored using 35 videotaped interviews that were rated by three child psychiatrists. Interrater reliability for symptoms averaged r = .72, which is relatively low for taped interviews. The MHAF represents an early effort to structure child interviews, but it has not been widely adopted, per-

haps due to its mediocre reliability, limited information yield, and weak validation.

The Child Assessment Schedule.

The Child Assessment Schedule (CAS) is a semistructured interview for children and adolescents aged 7 to 12 (Hodges, McKnew, Cytryn, Stern, & Kline, 1982; Hodges, Kline, Stern, Cytryn, & McKnew, 1982). It was originally designed for directly interviewing the child only, but a parallel version for interviewing parents has been developed recently. The CAS is designed for clinically trained interviewers and requires 45 to 60 minutes to administer to each informant (parent and child). It comprises 75 questions about school, friends, family, self-image, behavior, mood, and thought disorder. Most item responses are coded Yes/No. The interview is organized thematically beginning with questions about family and friends, followed by feelings and behaviors, and ending with items about delusions, hallucinations, and other psychotic symptoms. After interviewing the child, the interviewer rates 53 items (e.g., insight, grooming, motor behavior, activity level, speech).

The CAS was intended to facilitate evaluation of child functioning in various areas and to aid in the formulation of diagnostic impressions. It is less structured than other interview schedules, providing a simple outline of target phenomena to be assessed, suggested questions, and a simple format for recording the presence/absence of symptoms. The CAS yields scores in 11 content areas (e.g., school, friends, activities, family) and 9 symptom areas (e.g., attention deficits, conduct disorder, overanxious, oppositional). A total score reflecting total number of symptoms is also obtained.

Clinical interpretation of the CAS is also flexible and requires considerable expertise. The interview was not originally designed to yield DSM diagnoses, although many items correspond to DSM criteria. A diagnostic index has been developed indicating the correspondence between CAS items and DSM criteria. To address DSM criteria more fully, a separate addendum to the interview has been developed for assessing symptom onset and duration. This complicates the interview somewhat, but provides more adequate coverage of DSM criteria for diagnosis of attention deficit disorder, conduct disorder, anxiety disorders, oppositional disorder, enuresis, encopresis, and affective disorders. Diagnoses are based on clinical overview of CAS responses, rather than explicit algorithms.

Interrater reliability based on independent ratings of

53 videotaped child interviews was r = .90 for total symptom score, and averaged r = .73 for content areas, and r = .69 for symptom areas. Reliabilities were somewhat higher for hyperactivity and aggression (average r = .80) than for fears, worries, and anxiety (average r = .60). Interrater reliabilities averaged kappa = .57 for individual items.

The validity of the CAS has been supported by several findings. Total symptom score discriminated significantly between inpatient, outpatient, and normal children and correlated significantly (r = .53, p < .001) with total behavior-problem score derived from the Child Behavior Checklist (CBCL). Using referral for either inpatient or outpatient services as the criterion for psychopathology, the CAS achieved a sensitivity of 78% and a specificity of 84%, based on discriminant analysis (Hodges et al., 1982). Combining CAS scores and CBCL scores in one discriminant analysis boosted sensitivity to 93% and specificity to 100% (no false positives). This result suggests that combining parent and child data (or alternatively, interview and rating scale data) may yield better discriminative power. Scores on the CAS overanxious scale have correlated significantly (r = .54, p < .001) with scores on the State-Trait Anxiety Scale for Children. CAS depression scores have also correlated significantly (r = .53, p < .001) with scores on the Child Depression Inventory.

The concordance between the CAS and the K-SADS has also been recently explored (Hodges, McKnew, Burbach, & Roebuck, 1987). Thirty clinically referred children aged 6 to 17 and their parents were interviewed separately using either the CAS or the K-SADS, then reinterviewed the next day with the other interview schedule. The order of interviewing was counterbalanced so about half the subjects were interviewed first with the CAS, whereas the other half were interviewed first with the K-SADS. Concordance between the two interview schedules was determined in four DSM-III diagnostic areas: ADD, conduct disorders, anxiety disorders, and affective disorders. Diagnoses were also made based on (a) the child only, (b) the parent only, (c) parent or child, and (d) parent and child consensus. Concordance between the CAS and K-SADS was moderately high for interviews with parents (average kappa = .62, range: .51 to .75), but lower for interviews with children (average kappa = .44, range: .36 to .52). Concordance was lower for anxiety disorders than other areas (kappa = .37 for the child interviews and .51 for the parent interviews). Taking all diagnoses from parent or child interviews reduced concordance slightly (average kappa = .54). Requiring parent-child consensus on diagnoses reduced concordance even more (average kappa = .46). Nevertheless, these results suggest moderately high concordance between the CAS and the K-SADS, particularly for parent interviews.

Overall, the CAS is a useful descriptive tool and diagnostic aid. It can be used with children as young as 7 years of age and it has a very simple format. The development of a parallel form for parents, a diagnostic index, and an addendum covering symptom onset and duration are useful additions even though they complicate the interview and extend the interviewing time required. The CAS depends on clinical inferences to a large extent, but is relatively easy for interviewers to learn.

Highly Structured Interviews

The following section reviews two highly structured interviews: the Diagnostic Interview for Children and Adolescents and the Diagnostic Interview Schedule for Children.

The Diagnostic Interview for Children and Adolescents.

The Diagnostic Interview for Children and Adolescents (DICA) was one of the first structured interviews for children and it has been widely used in clinical and epidemiological research. The original version, developed in 1969, was patterned after the Renard Diagnostic Interview and keyed to the ICD and Feighner diagnostic criteria (see Welner, Reich, Herjanic, Jung, & Amado, 1987, for a review). The DICA was revised in 1981 along the lines of the NIMH Diagnostic Interview Schedule (Robins, Helzer, Croughan, & Ratcliff, 1981) and was keyed to the then-new DSM-III criteria. Research using the earlier version (e.g., Herjanic & Campbell, 1977; Herjanic, Herjanic, Brown, & Wheatt, 1975) was pioneering in many ways, but is probably obsolete, at least with respect to the reliability and validity of the later DSM-III and DSM-III-R versions.

The revised DICA is highly structured and provides the interviewer with specific wording of questions and explicit categories for response coding. Most symptom items are coded 1 (No), 2 (Yes), or 3 (Uncertain). Responses coded "Uncertain" can be clarified by subsequent subquestions and recoded either "Yes" or "No." The role of clinical inference in conducting the interview and making symptoms ratings has been minimized, so the DICA can be administered by clinicians or lay interviewers. A moderate amount of instrument-specific training is required, however.

Parallel interview schedules have been developed for interviewing the child (DICA-C) and parent (DICA-P) about the child. The parent version covers demographic background information, pregnancy and childbirth, and medical and developmental history. A long section covers specific symptoms organized by diagnostic area (e.g., Attention Deficit Disorder, Conduct Disorder, Separation Anxiety Disorder). For each diagnosis, one or more questions have been written to cover each diagnostic criterion. The interview also includes questions about possible disorders in siblings and a brief family medical and psychiatric history. The child interview parallels the symptoms portion of the parent interview. Although the symptom sections of the interviews are quite long, a skip structure is employed to reduce interviewing time if few symptoms are present.

The DICA yields information on the presence/absence of more than 150 specific symptoms, as well as their severity, onset, duration, and associated impairments (see Herjanic & Reich, 1982). Diagnoses are made by directly comparing item responses to DSM criteria for symptoms, severity, onset, and duration. All DSM diagnoses applied to children and adolescents are covered. Unlike the K-SADS, in which parent and child responses are first reconciled, DICA diagnoses are formulated separately from the parent interview and the child interview.

To test interrater reliability, 10 interviewers independently coded two videotaped interviews with children. Agreement on symptom items averaged 85% (Herjanic & Reich, 1982). Test-retest reliability has been determined by having five psychiatrists code the same videotaped interview twice over a two- to three-month interval. Agreement over time averaged 89% (range: 80%–95%) for individual symptom items. More recently, 27 children admitted to an inpatient psychiatric unit were interviewed twice by two different interviewers, one to seven days apart (Welner, Reich, Herjanic, Jung, & Amado, 1987). Inter-interviewer agreement on the presence/absence of specific diagnoses was quite high (kappas ranged from .76 to 1.00).

Mother-father agreement was recently tested for a sample of 74 children (Sylvester, Hyde, & Reichler, 1987). Agreement regarding the presence of any diagnosis was moderately high (kappa = .54). Agreement was higher for oppositional/conduct disorder and attention deficits (range: .54–.61) than for anxiety disorders and depression (range: .33–.39). Parent-child agreement has also been determined using a sample of 84 children referred for outpatient services and their parents (Welner et al., 1987). For five diagnostic groupings (ADD, conduct disorders, affective disorders, enuresis, oppositional disorder), parent-child agreement on the presence/absence of the diagnosis averaged .62 (kappa statistic, range: .49–.80). This represents much higher parent-child agreement than has been found in previous studies (e.g., Reich, Herjanic, Welner, & Gandhy, 1982).

The validity of the original DICA was supported by its ability to discriminate significantly between matched samples of pediatric and psychiatric referrals (Herjanic & Campbell, 1977). The validity of the current version of the DICA-C was recently tested for 27 inpatients by comparing DICA diagnoses with independent discharge diagnoses formulated by clinicians (Welner et al., 1987). Agreement was moderate for three diagnostic groupings: attention deficit disorders (kappa = .50), conduct disorders (.43), and affective disorders (.52), but was low for anxiety/phobic disorders (.03) and adjustment disorders (−.18).

Two other recent studies have addressed the validity of the DICA. In one study, agreement between the DICA and best-estimate clinical diagnoses were determined for a sample of 30 children receiving inpatient services (Carlson, Kashani, Thomas, Vaidya, & Daniel, 1987). For six diagnostic areas (ADD, conduct disorder, oppositional disorder, affective disorder, overanxious disorder, and separation anxiety), agreement with the best-estimate diagnoses was low-moderate for the DICA-C (average kappa = .38, range: .15–.75) and the DICA-P (average kappa = .40, range: .05–.66). In the other study, the DICA was compared with scores on the Personality Inventory for Children (PIC), a measure of child personality completed by parents (Sylvester, Hyde, & Reichler, 1987). Scores greater than $T = 65$ on certain PIC scales (e.g., hyperactivity) were used to categorize children, then these categorizations were compared to their corresponding diagnosis (e.g., attention deficit disorder) derived from the DICA-C. This is a very stringent test of convergence because it involves comparing a parent-completed personality inventory with the child-completed diagnostic interview. There were significant relationships between the two instruments in many areas, although the degree of convergence was fairly low (average kappa = .28, range: .11 to .48).

In sum, the DICA has broad diagnostic coverage, and its moderate training requirements make it suitable for large-scale epidemiologic surveys involving many nonprofessional interviewers. Recent studies have generally supported the reliability and validity of the DICA. Furthermore, it is being widely used in diverse research studies in many areas, so there will undoubtedly be a growing body of findings regarding its performance in the near future.

The Diagnostic Interview Schedule for Children.

The NIMH sponsored the development of the Diagnostic Interview Schedule for Children (DISC) for use in epidemiologic studies of child and adolescent psychopathology (see Costello et al., 1982). The DISC is similar in design and purpose to the Diagnostic Interview Schedule (DIS), used in epidemiologic research on adult disorders (Robins et al., 1981), and its offspring, the DICA (see description above). The DISC is a highly structured diagnostic interview in which the order, wording, and coding of all items is specified. Like its predecessors, the DISC employs a skip structure to reduce interviewing time with children having few symptoms. Because it was designed for large-scale epidemiologic studies, the DISC can be administered by lay interviewers having two to three days of instrument-specific training. Parallel versions have been developed for separately interviewing children (DISC-C) and parents about their children (DISC-P). The child interview takes 40 to 60 minutes to complete with clinically referred children, whereas the parent version takes 60 to 70 minutes. A time frame of the last year is used for most items, and specific information about onset and duration is sought for many symptom items.

The DISC covers a broad range of symptoms as well as their severity and chronicity. Most items are coded 0-1-2, where 0 corresponds to *no or never*, 1 corresponds to *somewhat, sometimes, or a little*, and 2 corresponds to *yes, often, or a lot*. Descriptions and examples offered by the respondent are recorded verbatim for later editing. The DISC was originally keyed to the DSM-III and covers most psychiatric diagnoses applicable to children and adolescents. Some diagnoses (e.g., pica, autism) are derived from the parent interview alone. Diagnoses are generated by computer algorithms applied to edited DISC data. Diagnoses are derived separately from the DISC-C and DISC-P. Both interviews also yield quantitative symptoms scores in symptoms areas (e.g., overanxious, conduct disorder, attention deficits).

Interrater reliability has been tested by having three lay interviewers independently code videotaped interviews of 10 children (Costello, et al., 1984). Reliabilities averaged .98 for symptom scores (range: .94 to 1.00), indicating very little rater disagreement in how responses are coded. Test-retest reliability has been determined on 242 clinically referred children and their parents (Edelbrock et al., 1985). Parents and

children were interviewed twice at a median interval of nine days. For the parent interviews, test-retest reliability was .90 (intraclass correlation) for total symptom score and averaged .76 for symptom scales (range: .44 to .86). For the child interviews, reliability was strongly related to age. For total symptom scores, reliabilities were .39, .55 and .81 for children aged 6–9, 10–13 and 14–18, respectively. For symptom scores, reliabilities also increased with age and averaged .43, .60, and .71 for children aged 6–9, 10–13 and 14–18, respectively. For 21 DSM-III diagnoses having sufficient prevalence, test-retest reliability for the parent interview averaged *kappa* = .56 (range: .35 to .81). Reliabilities of diagnoses derived from the child interviews averaged .36 (range: .12 to .71).

Parent-child agreement on child symptom scores has also been examined for 299 parent-child dyads (Edelbrock, Costello, Dulcan, Conover, & Kalas, 1986). Only a moderate degree of agreement was found overall (average $r = .27$), but agreement was higher for behavior/conduct symptoms than affective/neurotic symptoms and was higher among older than younger children. Regardless of the child's age, parents reported significantly more behavior/conduct problems than their children reported about themselves. Children reported significantly more affective/neurotic problems and drug and alcohol abuse than their parents reported about their children. So, despite generally low *levels* of agreement, the *pattern* of disagreement seems consistent.

The validity of the DISC interviews has been supported by several lines of evidence. Costello, Edelbrock, and Costello (1985) compared matched samples of pediatric and psychiatric referrals and found that symptoms scores computed from both the DISC-P and DISC-C discriminated significantly between these criterion groups. Total symptom score derived from the DISC-P provided the best discrimination ($p < .001$). In a multiple discriminant analysis, symptoms scores derived from both parent and child interviews contributed significantly to the equation which correctly classified 77 of the 80 children. Based on the DISC-P, the psychiatric referrals obtained 51 diagnoses of severe disorders, compared to only two diagnoses in the pediatric group.

Symptoms scores derived from the DISC-C and DISC-P have also been shown to correlate significantly with other measures of child psychopathology, such as the parent and teacher versions of the Child Behavior Checklist. Total symptom score derived from the DISC-P, for example, has correlated $r = .70$ with total behavior problem score from the CBCL (Costello et al., 1985). The DISC-C has shown weaker, but significant relations to the CBCL ($r = .30$). Costello, Edelbrock, and Costello (1984, p. 591) have also found significant convergence between severe diagnoses from the DISC-P and CBCL scores above the normative range.

Edelbrock and Costello (1988) have also explored the relationship between DISC diagnoses and specific scales of the Child Behavior Profile. They found considerable convergence between the diagnoses of attention deficit disorders, conduct disorder, and depression/dysthymia and the scales labeled hyperactive, delinquent, and depressed, respectively. These relations were generally linear. An increasing score on the scale corresponded to an incrementally higher probability of obtaining the diagnoses. No diagnostic threshold was apparent. However, children scoring above the normative range ($T > 70$) on the scales were much more likely to receive the diagnosis than children scoring within the normative range. This suggests substantial convergence between two different ways of assessing child psychopathology.

In addition, the relations between the DISC and the K-SADS have recently been determined in a community sample of children (Cohen, O'Conner, Lewis, Velez, & Malachowski, 1987). One hundred children aged 9 to 12 who had been interviewed with the DISC were reinterviewed with the K-SADS three- to four-months later. Significant, although moderate, levels of agreement were obtained for many diagnoses.

In sum, the DISC is similar in structure and purpose to the DICA. It covers a broad range of symptoms and diagnoses and is suitable for use by lay interviewers. Several studies support the reliability and validity of the DISC, but because it is a relatively new interview schedule, more empirical tests need to be conducted.

Other Interviews.

Two recent efforts have expanded the range of interview schedules available for use. First, the Teacher Interview for Psychiatric Symptoms (TIPS) (Kerr & Schaeffer, 1987) is a semistructured interview designed to obtain diagnostic information from teachers. Modeled after the K-SADS and ISC, the TIPS comprises 46 questions about psychiatric symptoms that might be evident in school (e.g., general anxiety, attention deficits). The TIPS takes about 45 minutes to complete and can be administered over the telephone. The interview begins with questions about the teacher's own teaching experience and style, then moves on to specific child symptoms that parallel the ISC in format. The teacher is then asked 11 questions about the child's grooming, social popularity, school performance, and family problems. Overall, the TIPS

seems like a promising extension of the ISC and K-SADS.

Second, the Social Adjustment Inventory for Children and Adolescents (SAICA) is a new interview schedule for assessing children's adaptive functioning in several domains (John, Gammon, Prusoff, & Werner, 1987). The SAICA is a semistructured interview covering children's social and adaptive functioning in school, in their spare time, and with peers, siblings, and parents. It can be used to interview children and adolescents directly or to interview parents about their children. The SAICA is a very useful supplement to diagnostic assessment procedures.

SUMMARY

In the last five years, more work has been done on the development and testing of structured interviews for children and adolescents than all previous years. (A special section of the September 1987 issue of the *Journal of the American Academy of Child and Adolescent Psychiatry* provides a state-of-the-art appraisal and many new findings.) Nevertheless, structured interviewing with children is relatively new and most interview schedules are still evolving. Research on the reliability and validity of structured interviews is still needed. Many interview schedules are reliable enough for making global distinctions among groups. Whether they are reliable enough for idiographic description and diagnosis remains to be seen.

Validation efforts have increased dramatically in the past few years. The most common approaches to testing validity have been (a) comparing criterion groups, such as clinically referred and nonreferred samples; (b) determining convergent relations with other indices of child psychopathology, particularly child behavior rating scales; and (c) determining convergence between different interview schedules. Overall, most interview schedules have performed quite well, certainly well enough to warrant continued development and testing.

A range of applications has also been explored, including screening, description, and diagnosis. As screening tools, structured interviews are more costly and time consuming than checklists and rating scales. Their screening performance is also usually no better and often much worse than much cheaper paper-and-pencil assessment techniques. As descriptive tools, structured interviews are roughly comparable to checklists and rating scales in terms of reliability and information yield. However, they lack the psychometric development and normative standardization of many rating scales and are probably not the best choice if the goal is description only. The advantage of interviews lies primarily in their diagnostic applications. Unlike most checklists and rating scales, many interview schedules are keyed to specific diagnostic criteria and cover not only symptom presence and severity, but also the onset, duration, and associated impairments necessary for formal diagnoses.

Even so, no single interview schedule can be recommended for diagnostic assessments. Rather, different types of interviews seem suited to different purposes. Both the K-SADS and ISC were developed to select subjects for research on childhood depression and they serve that purpose very well. Both are focused on affective symptoms and provide precise and detailed information about symptom severity and chronicity. These interviews are semistructured and are intended for clinically sophisticated interviewers having extensive instrument-specific training. To the extent that they tap symptoms in other areas, the ISC and the K-SADS can also be recommended more generally for purposes of differential diagnosis among clinically referred samples.

The DISC and the DICA are opposite to the ISC and K-SADS. They are highly structured interviews in which the role of clinical judgment has been minimized. Both cover a broad range of symptoms and disorders and are suitable for large-scale studies employing lay interviewers. For these reasons, they seem more useful for describing symptom prevalence and distribution among nonreferred populations, rather than for purposes of differential diagnosis of identified cases.

Future Directions

Research on the reliability and validity of structured interviews for children will undoubtedly continue for many years. It seems unlikely that many new interview schedules will be developed, but rather that research will concentrate on the handful of interviews already available. The more highly developed and tested interview schedules, such as the K-SADS, CAS, DICA, and DISC, will become standard assessment and diagnostic tools in clinical and epidemiologic research. Although such studies will not be directed at testing the interviews themselves, their results will certainly contribute to the evaluation and ultimate refinement of the interview schedules.

Research using structured interviews will also have to face many unsolved problems and issues. A key question is whether children are reliable and valid reporters of their own social, emotional, and behavioral functioning. The ability to question children directly about themselves is a major strength of inter-

viewing and was one of the major stimuli to the development of structured interviews. However, many studies have obtained disappointingly low reliability from interviews with children. One study (Edelbrock et al., 1985) found that reliability of child reports was low for children below the age of 10, but increased to moderately high levels through middle childhood and adolescence. Parent-child agreement has also been low in most studies, although this depends on many factors, such as the area being assessed, the age of the children, and the clinical status of the respondents. Low parent-child agreement is not necessarily an indictment of the interview schedules because they may be accurately reflecting true differences in the way parents and children view child functioning. However, low agreement does raise the complex issue of how to deal with disparate data from different informants. Researchers have begun to try different strategies for integrating data from parent and child interviews, particularly when trying to formulate diagnoses (see Young, O'Brien, Gutterman, & Cohen, 1987).

A final issue involves taxonomic progress within child psychiatry. The diagnostic interviews are tied to the prevailing taxonomy of child disorders (i.e., the DSM). The validity of the interviews is simultaneously *built upon* and *limited by* the validity of the taxonomic system. Wholesale changes in the diagnostic interviews were mandated recently by the advent of the DSM-III-R (American Psychiatric Association, 1987) which embodies many substantive changes in the categories and criteria applied to children and youth. Some diagnostic interviews (e.g., DISC, DICA, K-SADS) have been rekeyed to the DSM-III-R, but research on their performance is not yet available.

REFERENCES

American Psychiatric Association. (1956). *Diagnostic and statistical manual of mental disorders* (1st ed.). Washington, DC: Author.

American Psychiatric Association. (1968). *Diagnostic and statistical manual of mental disorders* (2nd ed.). Washington, DC: Author.

American Psychiatric Association. (1980). *Diagnostic and statistical manual of mental disorders* (3rd ed.). Washington, DC: Author.

American Psychiatric Association. (1987). *Diagnostic and statistical manual of mental disorders* (3rd ed., rev.). Washington, DC: Author.

Carlson, G. A., Kashani, J., Thomas, M., Vaidya, A., & Daniel, A. E. (1987). Comparison of two structured interviews on a psychiatrically hospitalized population of children. *Journal of the American Academy of Child Psychiatry, 26*, 645–648.

Chambers, W., Puig-Antich, J., Hirsch, M., Paez, P., Ambrosini, P., Tabrizi, M. A., & Davies, M. (1985). The assessment of affective disorders in children and adolescents by semi-structured interview: Test-retest reliability of the K-SADS. *Archives of General Psychiatry, 42*, 696–702.

Cohen, P., O'Connor, P., Lewis, S., Velez, N., & Malachowski, B. (1987). Comparison of DISC and K-SADS interviews of an epidemiologic sample of children. *Journal of the American Academy of Child Psychiatry, 26*, 662–667.

Costello, E. J., Edelbrock, C., & Costello, A. J., (1985). The validity of the NIMH Diagnostic Interview Schedule for Children. *Journal of Abnormal Child Psychology, 13*, 579–595.

Costello, A. J., Edelbrock, C., Dulcan, M. K., Kalas, R., & Klaric, S. H. (1984). *Development and testing of the NIMH Diagnostic Interview Schedule for Children in a clinic population.* Final report (Contract # RFP–DB–81–0027). Rockville, MD: Center for Epidemiologic Studies, National Institute of Mental Health.

Costello, A. J., Edelbrock, C., Kalas, R., Kessler, M. D., & Klaric, S. H. (1982). *The NIMH Diagnostic Interview Schedule for Children (DISC).* Unpublished interview schedule. Pittsburgh: Department of Psychiatry, University of Pittsburgh.

Earls, F. (1980a). The prevalence of behavior problems in three-year-old children: A cross-national replication. *Archives of General Psychiatry, 37*, 1153–1157.

Earls, F. (1980b). The prevalence of behavior problems in three-year-old children: Comparison of mothers and fathers. *Journal of the American Academy of Child Psychiatry, 19*, 439–452.

Earls, F., Jacobs, G., Goldfein, D., Silbert, A., Beardslee, W., & Rivinus, T. (1982). Concurrent validation of a behavior problem scale for use with three-year-olds. *Journal of The American Academy of Child Psychiatry, 21*, 47–57.

Earls, F., & Richman, N. (1980a). Behavior problems of preschool children of West Indian born parents: A re-examination of family and social factors. *Journal of Child Psychiatry and Psychology, 21*, 108–117.

Earls, F., & Richman, N. (1980b). The prevalence of behavior problems in three-year-old children of West Indian born parents. *Journal of Child Psychology and Psychiatry, 21*, 99–107.

Edelbrock, C., & Costello, A. J. (1988). Convergence between statistically derived behavior problem syndromes and child psychiatric diagnoses. *Journal of Abnormal Child Psychology, 16*, 219–231.

Edelbrock, C., Costello, A. J., Dulcan, M. K., Conover, N. C., & Kalas, R. (1986). Parent-child agreement on child psychiatric symptoms assessed via structured interview. *Journal of Child Psychology and Psychiatry, 27*, 181–190.

Edelbrock, C., Costello, A. J., Dulcan, M. K., Kalas, R., & Conover, N. C. (1985). Age differences in the reliability of the psychiatric interview of the child. *Child Development, 56*, 265–275.

Endicott, J., & Spitzer, R. (1978). A diagnostic interview: The Schedule for Affective Disorders and Schizophrenia. *Archives of General Psychiatry, 35*, 837–844.

Freeman, M. (1971). A reliability study of psychiatric diagnosis in childhood and adolescence. *Journal of Child Psychology and Psychiatry, 12*, 43–54.

Group for the Advancement of Psychiatry. (1957). *The diagnostic process in child psychiatry.* New York: Author.

Group for the Advancement of Psychiatry. (1966). *Psychopathological disorders in childhood: Theoretical considerations and a proposed classification.* New York: Author.

Herjanic, B., & Campbell, W. (1977). Differentiating psychiatrically disturbed children on the basis of a structured interview. *Journal of Abnormal Child Psychology, 5*, 127–134.

Herjanic, B., Herjanic, M., Brown, F., & Wheatt, T. (1975). Are children reliable reporters? *Journal of Abnormal Child Psychology, 3*, 41–48.

Herjanic, B., & Reich, W. (1982). Development of a structured interview for children: Agreement between child and parent on individual symptoms. *Journal of Abnormal Child Psychology, 10*, 307–324.

Hodges, K., Kline, J., Stern, L., Cytryn, L., & McKnew, D. (1982). The development of a child assessment interview for research and clinical use. *Journal of Abnormal Child Psychology, 10*, 173–189.

Hodges, K., McKnew, D., Cytryn, L., Stern, L., & Kline, J. (1982). The Child Assessment Schedule (CAS) diagnostic interview: A report on reliability and validity. *Journal of the American Academy of Child Psychiatry, 21*, 468–473.

Hodges, K., McKnew, D., Burbach, D. J., & Roebuck, L. (1987). Diagnostic concordance between the Child Assessment Schedule (CAS) and the Schedule for Affective Disorders and Schizophrenia for School-Age Children (K-SADS) in an outpatient sample using lay interviewers. *Journal of the American Academy of Child Psychiatry*, *26*, 654–661.

John, K., Gammon, G. D., Prusoff, B., & Werner, V. (1987). The Social Adjustment Inventory for Children and Adolescents (SAICA): Testing of a new semistructured interview. *Journal of the American Academy of Child and Adolescent Psychiatry*, *26*, 916–921.

Kerr, M. M., & Schaeffer, A. L. (1987). *Teacher Interview for Psychiatric Symptoms (TIPS)*. Pittsburgh, PA: Author.

Kestenbaum, C. J., & Bird, H. (1978). A reliability study of the Mental Health Assessment Form for school age children. *Journal of the American Academy of Child Psychiatry*, *7*, 338–347.

Kovacs, M. (1982). *The Interview Schedule for Children (ISC)*. Unpublished interview schedule. Pittsburgh: Department of Psychiatry, University of Pittsburgh.

Kovacs, M. (1983). *The Interview Schedule for Children (ISC): Interrater and parent-child agreement*. Unpublished manuscript.

Kovacs, M., Feinberg, T. L., Crouse-Novak, M. A., Paulauskas, S. L., & Finkelstein, R. (1984). Depressive disorders in childhood: A longitudinal prospective study of characteristics and recovery. *Archives of General Psychiatry*, *41*, 229–237.

Langner, T., Gersten, J., McCarthy, E. D., Eisenberg, J. G., Greene, E. L., Herson, J. H., & Jameson, J. D. (1976). A screening inventory for assessing psychiatric impairment in children aged 6–18. *Journal of Consulting and Clinical Psychology*, *44*, 286–296.

Lapouse, R., & Monk, M. A. (1958). An epidemiologic study of behavior characteristics of children. *American Journal of Public Health*, *48*, 1134–1144.

Matarazzo, J. D. (1983). The reliability of psychiatric and psychologic diagnosis. *Clinical Psychology Review*, *3*, 103–145.

Orvaschel, H., Puig-Antich, J., Chambers, W., Tabrizi, M. A., & Johnson, R. (1982). Retrospective assessment of prepubertal major depression with the Kiddie-SADS-E. *Journal of the American Academy of Child Psychiatry*, *21*, 392–397.

Puig-Antich, J., Blau, S., Marx, N., Greenhill, L., & Chambers, W. (1978). Pre-pubertal major depressive disorder: A pilot study. *Journal of the American Academy of child Psychiatry*, *17*, 695–707.

Puig-Antich, J., & Chambers, W. (1978). *The Schedule for Affective Disorders and Schizophrenia for school-aged children*. Unpublished interview schedule. New York State Psychiatric Institute, New York, NY.

Puig-Antich, J., Chambers, W., Halpern, F., Hanlon, C., & Sachar, E. (1979). Cortisol hypersecretion in prepubertal depressive illness: A preliminary study. *Psychoneuroendocrinology*, *4*, 191–197.

Puig-Antich, J., Perel, J. M., Lupatkin, W., Chambers, W., Shea, C., Tabrizi, M. A., & Stiller, R. L., (1979). Plasma levels of imipramine (IMI) and desmethylimipramine (DSI) and clinical response in prepubertal major depressive disorder: A preliminary report. *Journal of the American Academy of Child Psychiatry*, *18*, 616–627.

Reich, W., Herjanic, B., Welner, Z., & Gandhy, P. R. (1982). Development of a structured psychiatric interview for children: Agreement on diagnosis comparing parent and child. *Journal of Abnormal Child Psychology*, *10*, 325–336.

Richman, N. (1977). Short-term outcome of behavior problems in preschool-aged children. In P. Graham (Ed.), *Epidemiological approaches in child psychiatry* (pp. 165–180). London: Academic Press.

Richman, N., & Graham, P. (1971). A behavioural screening questionnaire for use with three-year-old children. *Journal of Child Psychology and Psychiatry*, *12*, 5–33.

Richman, N., Stevenson, J., & Graham, P. (1975). Prevalence of behavioural problems in three-year-old children: An epidemiologic study in a London borough. *Journal of Child Psychology and Psychiatry*, *16*, 277–287.

Robins, L., Helzer, J. E., Croughan, J., & Ratcliff, K. S. (1981). National Institute of Mental Health Diagnostic Interview Schedule: Its history, characteristics, and validity. *Archives of General Psychiatry*, *38*, 381–389.

Rosen, B. M., Bahn, A. K., & Kramer, M. (1964). Demographic and diagnostic characteristics of psychiatric clinic patients in the USA. *American Journal of Orthopsychiatry*, *34*, 455–468.

Rutter, M., & Graham, P. (1968). The reliability and validity of the psychiatric assessment of the child: Interview with the child. *British Journal of Psychiatry*, *11*, 563–579.

Sandifer, M. G., Pettus, C. M., & Quade, D. (1964). A study of psychiatric diagnosis. *Journal of Nervous and Mental Disease*, *139*, 350–356.

Sylvester, C. E., Hyde, T. S., & Reichler, R. J. (1987). The Diagnostic Interview for Children and Personality Inventory for Children in studies of children at risk for anxiety disorders or depression.

Journal of the American Academy of Child and Adolescent Psychiatry, 26, 668–675.

Tarter, R., Templer, D., & Hardy, C. (1975). Reliability of the psychiatric diagnosis. *Diseases of the Nervous System, 36,* 30–31.

Welner, Z., Reich, W., Herjanic, B., Jung, K., & Amado, H. (1987). Reliability, validity, and parent-child agreement studies of the Diagnostic Interview for Children and Adolescents (DICA). *Journal of the American Academy of Child Psychiatry, 26,* 649–653.

Young, G., O'Brien, J., Gutterman, E., & Cohen, P. (1987). Research on the clinical interview. *Journal of the American Academy of Child and Adolescent Psychiatry, 26,* 613–620.

CHAPTER 15

STRUCTURED CLINICAL INTERVIEWS FOR ADULTS

Arthur N. Wiens

The term *interview* was derived from the French *entrevoir,* to have a glimpse of, and *s'entrevoir,* to see each other. The formal definition of the term is a meeting of persons face to face, especially one sought for the purpose of formal conference on some point. The term was first used in print in English in 1514 by the Duke of Suffolk, seeking a meeting with the King of England. It was later used in America, 1869, to describe "a meeting between a representative of the press and someone from whom he seeks to obtain statements for publication" (*Oxford English Dictionary,* 1971). Virtually all current definitions of the interview include reference to a face-to-face verbal exchange in which one person, the interviewer, attempts to elicit information or expressions of opinion or belief from another person, the interviewee.

INTERVIEW VERSUS CONVERSATION

Both an interview and conversation typically involve a face-to-face verbal exchange of information, ideas, attitudes, or feelings and contain messages exchanged through nonverbal as well as verbal modes of expression (Wiens, 1983). However, a crucial characteristic that distinguishes an interview from a conversation is that the interview is designed to achieve a consciously selected purpose. There may be no central theme in a conversation, but in an interview the content is directed toward a specific purpose and is likely to have unity, progression, and thematic continuity. If the purpose of the interview is to be achieved, one participant must assume and maintain responsibility for directing the interaction (asking questions)

toward the goal, and the other participant must facilitate achievement of the purpose by following the direction of the interaction (answering questions).

The roles of the two participants in a clinical interview are nonreciprocal because, in one form or another, the purpose of the interview is to give some benefit to the interviewee. Furthermore, whereas in conversation a person may behave in a spontaneous and unplanned manner, a clinical interviewer deliberately and consciously plans actions to further the purpose of the interview. A conversation may be started and terminated at will; however, an interview, once initiated, is generally continued until its purpose has been achieved or until the interviewer realizes that the purposes cannot be achieved. Stated in another way, the immediate purpose of most interviews is to encourage the interviewee to engage in some kind of self-exploration to satisfy a purpose explicitly or implicitly agreed upon by the interviewer and interviewee. In most interviews, the interviewer and interviewee agree on the objective to be reached, decide what topics need to be discussed, establish a relationship of trust that allows the interviewee to talk freely, and keep the discussion focused on relevant information. The interviewee usually does most of the talking, using about 80% of the talk time. If the percentage of talk time varies greatly from this, the interviewer probably is enjoying talking about himself or herself but is not learning much about the interviewee. A relatively unstructured interviewing style allows interviewees to discuss experiences largely on their own terms. In the case of personnel selection interviews this style could make it difficult to compare candidates; in the case of clinical interviews the unstructured approach could lead to problems in ascertaining whether diagnostic criteria have been met. An additional consideration in either a selection or clinical interview is the importance of details. A detailed inquiry or a persistent followup on an initially general question can bring to the foreground critical information about the interviewee.

THE CLINICAL INTERVIEW

Many clinicians have been heavily influenced by earlier psychoanalytic thought that placed considerable emphasis on the indirect techniques of interviewing and a free-flowing exchange between the clinician and patient. Generally, such unstructured interviews allow the clinician freedom to reword questions, to introduce new questions or to modify question order, and to follow patients' spontaneous sequence of ideas. It is often assumed that such spontaneous discussion allows patients to follow more nearly their natural train of thought and may permit them to bring out interview material that is more predictive of what they would say or do in real-life situations. The flexibility of the unstructured interview may allow clinicians to adapt their techniques to patients' particular situations. In some cases the interviewer may omit topics that do not seem applicable, and in other cases he or she may introduce related topics not originally planned. Many readers may have watched skilled clinician-interviewers elicit previously hidden facts, using attention to conflicts, dysphoric affects, defenses used by the patient, and symptom origins. The sophisticated data-reduction techniques and hypothesis testing carried out consciously or preconsciously in interviews by skilled clinicians have such practical value that development of these skills has become the primary pursuit of many clinicians (Young, O'Brien, Gutterman, & Cohen, 1987).

Experienced clinicians often assume that they can maintain best rapport with patients by formulating questions in words familiar to patients and habitually used by them, and by pursuing topics when patients indicate a readiness and willingness to discuss them. The unstructured clinical interview gives the clinician more discretion in formulating the wording and sequence of questions; accordingly, it requires a higher level of experience, skill, and training than that needed to follow a more standardized interview format. In particular, the clinician must have an overall conceptual grasp of theoretical context and considerable prior knowledge of the subject matter of the interview.

While some clinicians have espoused a spontaneous interview style, most experienced clinicians have adopted a semistandardized interviewing style or format. An observer listening to a clinician interviewing a series of patients soon discerns topic areas that the interviewer routinely introduces, and questions that he or she asks in almost the same way of every patient.

Furthermore, the topics to be covered in an initial clinical interview are relatively consistent from one clinician to the next. The general objective is to obtain a careful history that can be the foundation for the diagnosis and treatment of the patient's illness (Kaplan & Sadock, 1988). More specific objectives are to understand the individual patient's personality characteristics, including both strengths and weaknesses; to obtain insight into the nature of the interviewee's relationships with those closest to him or her, both past and present; and to obtain a reasonably comprehensive picture of the patient's development from the formative years to the present.

In preparing a written record of a clinical interview most clinicians begin by presenting *identifying information,* such as the patient's name, age, marital status, sex, occupation, race or ethnicity, place of residence and circumstances of living, history of prior clinical contacts, and referral and information sources. The *chief complaint,* or the problem for which the patient seeks professional help, is usually reviewed next, and is stated in the patient's own words or in the words of the person supplying this information. The intensity and duration of the presenting problem is noted, specifically the length of time each symptom has existed and whether there have been changes in quality and quantity from a previous state. It is also useful to include a description of the patient's appearance and behavior. In reviewing *present illness,* the clinician looks for the earliest and most disabling symptoms and for any precipitating factors leading to the chief complaint. Often the precipitating or stress factors associated with onset of symptoms may be subtle, requiring the clinician to draw on knowledge of behavior and psychopathology to help with inquiry regarding relevant life change events. The clinician should also report how the patient's symptoms have affected his or her life activities. It is important to review *past health history* for both physical and psychological problems—for example, to learn whether there are physical illnesses that might be affecting the patient's emotional state. Prior episodes of emotional and mental disturbances should be described. The clinician also needs to inquire about and report prescribed medication and alcohol and drug use. Possible organic mental syndromes must be noted. *Personal history* may include information about the patient's parents and other family members and any history of psychological or physical problems. The account of the patient's own childhood and developmental experiences may be quite detailed. Educational and occupational history is noted as well as social, marital, military, legal, and other experiences. The personal history should provide a comprehensive portrait of the patient independent of his or her illness (Siassi, 1984). The *mental status examination* is reviewed under the following headings: general appearance and behavior; mood, feelings, and affect; perception; speech and thought; sensorium and cognition; judgment; insight; and reliability. Finally, *recommendations* are presented about the kind of treatment the patient should receive for specific problems and target symptoms.

Topic areas to be covered are also relatively consistent among clinicians with different theoretical approaches. The interested reader may note commonalities between the description of the clinical interview and the assessment schema to which many behavioral interviewers refer. (Kanfer & Saslow, 1969). Kanfer and Saslow suggest examination of the following areas: analysis of the problem situation (including behavioral excesses, deficits, and assets); clarification of the problem situation that maintains the targeted behaviors; a motivational analysis; a developmental analysis (including biological, sociological, and behavioral spheres); a self-control analysis; an analysis of social relationships; and an analysis of the sociocultural-physical environment.

PURPOSE OF CLINICAL INTERVIEWS: DIAGNOSIS

The act of classification is basic to all science and to every other aspect of living. Accurate and reliable description that differentiates and predicts is the basis of hypothesis formation and testing in science (Wiens & Matarazzo, 1983). Diagnosis in clinical practice introduces order into the clinician's observations, with an attendant increase in meaningfulness and, ultimately, control (prevention and amelioration). Placing an object or organism or a set of behaviors into a certain class allows us to infer certain characteristics without needing to demonstrate each characteristic *de novo*. Classification can also help to put individual observations into a different perspective or context, and stimulate new questions for better treatment, prevention, control, and future research.

The purposes of the clinical interview and mental status examinations are to arrive at a diagnostic for-

mulation and a rational treatment plan. Several decades ago, the specific diagnosis assigned probably made little difference because the available treatments were highly limited and by necessity applied more or less to all patients (Siassi, 1984). However, as diagnostic criteria have become more detailed and some treatment procedures applied more selectively, specific treatment implications have become attached to such diagnoses as unipolar depression, acute schizophrenic episode, or elevator phobia. Careful diagnostic delineation is also critical for researchers who wish to study a homogeneous group of patients or who wish to define a group of patients who are comparable to those being studied by a researcher in another setting. Prevention or control must be based on understanding the development and maintenance of a given diagnostic condition. Reliable diagnosis enhances the search for commonalities across individual observations and allows for the development of abstractions not possible in the single case.

A caveat regarding psychiatric diagnosis must be kept in mind. Diagnoses are conventions to be adopted or discarded depending on whether they contribute usefully to functions of administration, treatment, research, or prevention. Like the term *disease,* a given diagnosis may not actually correspond to anything in nature at all and, just as diseases have come and gone, the diagnoses that we presently use may not survive; more useful ones may emerge. Diagnostic nomenclatures represent a way of thinking and communicating with each other. They should not be thought of as defining physical "reality," which will continue to be increasingly differentiated with advances in scientific understanding in the future.

While clinicians may have expressed some doubt about the usefulness of psychiatric diagnosis in the past (especially DSM-II) there has been a strong pragmatic reason for assigning a diagnosis to each patient. Miller, Bergstrom, Cross, and Grube (1981) randomly sampled psychologists listed in the *National Register of Health Service Providers in Psychology* (Council for the National Register, 1978) and reported that 90.6% used DSM-II to some extent in their practices. The overwhelming reason for using DSM-II was because it was required by third-party payers; 86.1% of those who used DSM-II endorsed this reason. Further, 42.9% reported that they used DSM-II because it was the only classification system available. While DSM-III was not yet available to the psychologists polled at the time the survey took place, nearly all practicing psychologists sampled agreed they soon would use DSM-III because they had no alternative. Probably most readers would agree that

DSM-III has had even heavier usage than the earlier DSM-II.

There is a further scientific and pragmatic reason to establish and refine diagnostic procedures and diagnostic specific treatments. One does not have to be too much of a seer to predict that the diagnosis-related groups (DRG) method of reimbursement is likely to be extended into the mental health arena. Managers for third-party payers are accumulating data on which treatment interventions work with which diagnostic group of patients, in which treatment setting, in how many treatment sessions, and so on. It seems likely that future treatment authorization will be tied to patient diagnosis and the documented effective treatment for that diagnostic condition. That is, different treatment protocols will be established for different patient diagnoses with corresponding pay schedules. Clinicians will need to know the needs of their patients and the preferred treatment indicated by science/research. The clinician will be asked the obvious questions: (a) What is your diagnosis? (b) What is your planned course of treatment? The opportunity exists now for the scientist/professional to help establish the diagnosis and treatment protocols.

HISTORICAL FOUNDATION

For many clinicians the most-used methods of diagnostic study in the past have been relatively open-ended history taking and the mental status examination, which does introduce some organization into the diagnostic interview and into classifying and reporting the information that is offered by the patient. Although certain information was to be obtained, the clinician was not expected to follow a rigid interview outline.

It seems clear that reliability in diagnosis would be enhanced by the use of more structured interviews than has often been the case in the past. Open-ended history taking is likely to omit important questions and leave significant aspects of patient functioning without review. Furthermore, the specific biases of individual clinicians are likely to lead them to over- or underemphasize certain aspects of history taking. A related concern is that an initial impression may lead one to miss diagnostic cues that are contrary to the expectations established on the basis of that first impression. All of us must be aware of how likely we are to see and observe what we are looking for in a clinical interview or any other situation. Subjective impressions have powerful effects. Try as one might to conduct an objective evaluation, an interview is essentially an interpersonal event. Therefore, subjec-

tive emotional reactions, whether conscious or unconscious, are inevitable. The clinician who takes a strong like or dislike to a patient must be particularly concerned about this reaction and must ask whether it is because the patient is very similar to the clinician or just different: not like me.

Ash (1949) showed 40 years ago that the open-ended diagnostic interview was not a reliable instrument across interviewers. Three psychiatrists participated in one interview and made separate diagnoses. There was only 45% agreement for major diagnostic categories and 20% for specific subcategories. However, as became abundantly clear in hindsight, a major aspect of the disagreement was that the interviewers often did not concur on the symptoms or behaviors diagnostic of a given psychiatric category. Thus, it was necessary to establish agreed-upon criteria before greater reliability in diagnosis could be achieved.

Diagnostic Criteria: DSM-III

There is little argument about the need for a common vocabulary of psychopathological behaviors and disorders (Siassi, 1984). The general consensus that clinicians need a rational, uniform, and systematic vocabulary has led psychiatrists for the past several decades to develop successive versions of the *Diagnostic and Statistical Manual,* culminating in the DSM-III (American Psychiatric Association, 1980), which provides multi-axial diagnostic formulations and is based on a psychobiosocial theory/model of behavior and psychopathology.

The diagnostic criteria in DSM-III are not general descriptions but specific, denotable features designed to assist clinicians in making a diagnosis. DSM-III attempts comprehensively to describe the specifiable features of each of the mental disorders and only rarely attempts to account for how the disturbance came about, unless the mechanism is included in the definition of the disorder. The text in the DSM-III manual begins with a clinical description for each psychiatric or psychological disorder, including its essential features, age at onset, course, typical level of impairment, complications, predisposing factors, prevalence, sex ratio, and family pattern. The discussion of each disorder ends with a box summary of the operationally denotable diagnostic criteria for that disorder. This classification system is still evolving; the reader may recall that DSM-III-R (American Psychiatric Association, 1987) has already been published.

A major test of the worth of the DSM-III—whether it provides a rational, uniform, and systematic vocabulary for clinicians—is whether clinicians using it arrive at the same diagnosis for a given patient. Extensive field trials were completed with the DSM-III before it was published, and the clinicians participating in these field trials generally agreed that the DSM-III was an improvement over DSM-II, that the multi-axial system was a useful addition, and that the diagnostic criteria were a major contribution; the participating clinicians agreed with the generally atheoretical approach taken in the description of the diagnostic categories. From a statistical perspective, the overall kappa coefficient of agreement for Axis I diagnoses of 281 adult patients was .78 for joint interviews and .66 for diagnoses made after separate interviews. Spitzer, Forman, and Nee (1979) indicate that, inasmuch as the kappa reliability coefficients are corrected for chance agreements, a high kappa (generally .70 and above) indicates good agreement on whether the patient has a disorder within that diagnostic class. Thus, with publication and use of the DSM-III, diagnosis is based on specific criteria for each disorder, so that when a given diagnosis is used we can know quite exactly what is meant because we know the precise criteria that have guided the diagnostician. Because each diagnostic entity is based on specific information, the interviewer has to proceed in a way that will allow those details to be obtained. Generally, this means that interviewing has to be more focused. Furthermore, the interviewer will usually have to obtain longitudinal as well as cross-sectional data: duration of symptoms is a diagnostic criterion for a number of mental disorders in DSM-III. Of course, this longitudinal focus also allows the interviewer to search for associations between life events (stressors) and symptoms.

Diagnostic Interview Schedules

In thinking about clinical criteria for diagnosis and sources of unreliability in diagnostic formulations, Spitzer, Endicott, and Robins (1975) noted five sources of unreliability and then determined that two of these contributed most heavily to diagnostic unreliability. The first source of unreliability they noted was *subject variance*, which occurs when patients actually have different conditions at different times. They gave the example of the patient who may show alcohol intoxication on admission to a hospital but develop delirium tremens several days later. A second source of unreliability is *occasion variance*, which occurs when patients are in different stages of the same condition at different times. An example of this would be a patient with a bipolar disorder who is depressed during one period of illness and manic during another. A third source of unreliability is *information variance*, which occurs when clinicians have different sources of information about their patients. Examples here include information from clinicians who talk with patients' families and those who do not, or from interviewers who question patients concerning areas of functioning and symptoms about which other interviewers do not ask. A fourth area of unreliability is *observation variance*, which occurs when clinicians notice different things although presumably observing the same patient behavior. Clinicians may disagree on whether a patient was tearful, hard to follow, or hallucinating. A fifth source of unreliability is *criterion variance*, which occurs when clinicians use varying diagnostic criteria (e.g., whether a formal thought disorder is necessary for the diagnosis of schizophrenia or precludes a diagnosis of affective disorder). Spitzer et al. (1975) concluded that the largest source of diagnostic variability by far was criterion variance. Their efforts in the development of DSM-III diagnostic criteria obviously reflected their confidence in this conclusion.

Their research efforts to reduce information variance (the second most important source of unreliability) led to the development of structured clinical interviews that reduce that portion of the unreliability variance based on different interviewing styles and coverage. The Research Diagnostic Criteria, or RDC (Spitzer, Endicott, & Robins, 1975) provide sets of specific inclusion and exclusion criteria for a large number of functional disorders, with particular emphasis on various ways of subtyping affective disorders. In following RDC, the clinician is required to use these criteria regardless of his or her own personal concept of the disorder. With this approach, the clinician's task is (a) to determine the presence or absence of specific clinical phenomena, and (b) to apply the comprehensive rules provided for making the diagnosis. A single patient can be categorized in different ways, such as by the presence or absence of endogenous psychopathology, situational stresses, psychotic features, and the like. The kappa values for the RDC were usually above .70, frequently above .80, and represent impressive levels of agreement. The RDC is an excellent tool available also to the researcher who wishes to study homogeneous patient groups. It is one of about 10 structured-interview guides distributed through Biometric Research of Columbia University.

Siassi (1984) concludes that the structured psychiatric interview has already become the foundation of much modern clinical research and that the clinical psychiatric interview and mental status examinations, as used in the past, will likely be replaced in the future by structured interview schedules for routine psychiatric examinations. This shift is supported by trends toward the use of operational criteria for diagnosis, well-defined taxonomies, almost exclusive use of structured examinations in research settings, and the growing influence of clinician-researchers. Further, the demand for accountability has also forced a problem-oriented type of recordkeeping system in most institutions, with emphasis on branch-logic systems of psychiatric decision making, and progress notes that reflect resolution of symptom-syndromes and changes in problem status rather than changes in psychodynamics. Finally, the impact of computers appears decisive in that they allow for more efficient retrieval of information than is possible with records of non-computerized narrative psychiatric interviews. Computers can also be used to apply an algorithm to yield highly reliable diagnoses from raw data (Siassi, 1984, p. 272).

The nature of a structured clinical interview is discussed by Edelbrock and Costello (1984), who note that it is essentially a list of target behaviors, symptoms, and events to be covered, and some guidelines or rules for conducting the interview and recording the data. Interview schedules vary in that some offer only general and flexible guidelines and others have strict and detailed rules (i.e., some are *semistructured* and others are *highly structured*). With the latter, wording and sequence of questions, recording responses, and rating responses are all specified and defined. The interviewer may be regarded as an interchangeable piece of the assessment machinery. Clinical judgment in eliciting and recording information is minimized and, given the same patient, different interviewers should obtain the same information. Clinical judgment may play more of a role in the semistructured interview with more latitude about what is asked, how it is asked, and how it is recorded. Edelbrock and Costello (1984) suggest that both types of interviews have some advantages. Highly structured interviews reduce the role of clinical inference and interpretation in the assessment and diagnostic process, and they typically yield more objective and quantifiable raw data. Alternatively, semistructured interviews are less stilted and permit a more spontaneous interview that can be tailored to the patient.

Edelbrock and Costello (1984) also conclude that structured interviews are here to stay, that they will become the standard assessment and diagnostic tools in clinical research and epidemiology and, that they will become more closely integrated into the training of mental health professionals and the delivery of

service. The authors also predicted that the interview would continue to evolve along the lines of increasing specialization of purpose, coverage, age, range, degree of structure, and interviewer qualifications. As diagnostic taxonomies evolve and become more differentiated, structured interviews will necessarily change in terms of their content. We can also expect results obtained via structured interviews to precipitate change in the diagnostic systems. Edelbrock and Costello noted another significant development: namely, the synergistic combination of structured interview data with data derived from other assessment methods such as checklists, rating scales, and self-report inventories. They expect multimethod assessment to yield a more comprehensive, reliable, and valid picture of the patient. Finally, they see a significant trend toward computer-assisted diagnosis, especially the use of the computer to sift through numerous bits of data relevant to diagnostic decision making.

Computer Development

Computers have long played a significant role in assessment. Much modern test construction has been dependent on the availability of computing resources. As test administration itself became more feasible with the advent of microcomputers, one of the questions raised concerned the comparability of data obtained with traditional paper-and-pencil administration and computerized administration. Lukin, Dowd, Plake, and Kraft (1985) obtained no significant differences between scores on measures of anxiety, depression, and psychological reactance across administration format. Most important, while producing results comparable to the pencil-and-paper assessment, the computerized administration was preferred over the pencil-and-paper administration by 85% of the subjects. This study, and others not reviewed here, supports the contention that computerized testing techniques provide results comparable to those of traditional assessments using individual tests.

It has been said that if the aircraft industry had evolved as spectacularly as the computer industry over the past 25 years, a Boeing 767 would cost $500 today, and it would circle the globe in 20 minutes on five gallons of fuel. Such performance would represent a rough analog of the reduction in cost, increase in speed of operation, and decrease in energy consumption of computers. The cost of computer logic devices is falling at the rate of 25% per year and the cost of computer memory at the rate of 40% per year. Computational speed has increased by a factor of 200 in 25 years. During the same period, the cost, energy consumption, and size of computers of comparable power have decreased by a factor of 10,000. The result is the personal computer, which for less than $500 can put at the disposal of an individual about the same basic computing power as a mainframe computer did in the early 1960s and as a minicomputer did in the early 1970s.

While psychological software has not kept pace with hardware development, the availability of new programs of interest to psychologists and other clinicians has been dramatic. Samuel E. Krug (1987) has compiled a product listing that includes more than 300 programs designed to assess or modify human behavior. Of these listings, 8% are categorized as structured interviews and are most likely to be described as intake interviews. The products in this category almost always are designed to be self-administered.

One of the earlier proponents of automated computer interviewing, John H. Greist (1984), observed that clinician training, recent experience, immediate distractions, and foibles of memory are among the factors that may compromise our competence as diagnosticians. Further, he stated that in virtually every instance in which computer interviews and clinicians have been compared, the computer outperforms the clinician in terms of completeness and accuracy. Erdman, Klein, and Greist (1985) suggest that one appeal of computer interviewing is the ability of the computer to imitate, even if only to a limited degree, the intelligence of a human interviewer. Like a human interviewer, the computer can be programmed to ask followup questions for problems that the respondent reports, and to skip followup questions in those areas of no problem. This branching capability leads to an interaction between computer and human (i.e., what happens in the interview depends on what the subject says). Thus, a computer interview can be tailored to the person using the program (e.g., not to ask a male subject about his own pregnancy). Of more interest is the capacity to ask followup questions in the subject's own words and to compare responses from different points in the interview. While it has been asserted that computers cannot detect flat affect, Erdman, Klein, and Greist (1985) note that it is possible to record simultaneously response latency and heart rate and use these variables to branch into questions/comments regarding emotional arousal. It does seem clear, however, that to date it has not been possible for the computer to report the many nonverbal cues that a human interviewer could observe and respond to. It must be acknowledged, however, that a human interviewer also remains oblivious to a great deal of information available in a two-person interaction.

DESCRIPTION OF ASSESSMENT METHODS

There are some general guidelines that should be considered in evaluating structured interviews. As noted by Spiker and Ehler (1984), these include the following: (a) sources of information should be specified in an effort to reduce information variance; (b) terms should be defined so that interviewers are consistent in their usage of them; (c) guidelines for determining the presence or absence of specified signs and symptoms should be given; (d) questions should be specified to ensure that necessary information is obtained to determine whether criteria for a given diagnosis have been met; and (e) information gathered should be in such a format that a given set of data will consistently lead to a given diagnosis.

Young et al. (1987) point out that efforts to reduce rater variability have formally consolidated into joint training, testing, and calibration of interviewers using standard procedures. The elements of the training programs will vary, particularly according to whether the interviewer is expected to formulate diagnoses. All training procedures attempt to ensure that interviewers have the skills to elicit and record the required information accurately and efficiently. This training involves monitoring interviews. If, in addition, the clinician/interviewer is to produce a diagnosis, it is necessary for him or her to know the diagnostic criteria thoroughly, have experience with differential diagnosis and have a well-developed understanding of the clinical manifestations that determine severity and clinical significance (Young et al., 1987, p. 617). A training program could include progressive steps, such as studying sample cases—videotaped and live interviews by trainees—and providing continual monitoring to maintain reliability. In the case of computer-administered interview schedules, a different criterion applies: namely, that the computer program has been sufficiently de-bugged so that it runs without error. This assumes, of course, that well-conceptualized questions went into the program in the first place.

Behavior checklists and patient questionnaires provide useful information for answering diagnostic questions, are often easy for different clinicians or even technicians to use, and often present data in such a way that it can be computer coded easily. Used by themselves, behavior checklists typically allow for only fairly general observations of an interviewee, so that additional procedures or clinician input is needed to arrive at a specific diagnosis.

The assessment methods described below were selected as illustrative of a number of structured interview applications. They are by no means an exhaustive listing or review. Included are general diagnostic interviews, psychosocial history interviews, specific-purpose interview schedules, and several behavior checklists and patient questionnaires.

Diagnostic Interview Schedule (DIS)

The Diagnostic Interview Schedule (DIS) (Robins, Helzer, Croughan, & Ratcliff, 1981) is a fully structured interview schedule designed to enable clinicians to make consistent and accurate DSM-III psychiatric diagnoses. It was designed to be administered by persons not professionally trained in clinical psychiatry, and all of the questions and the probes to be used are fully explained. It reminds interviewers not to omit critical questions, and presents well-tested phrasing for symptoms that are difficult to explain or potentially embarrassing to patients. Questions about symptoms cover both their presence or absence and severity (e.g., taking medication for the symptom, seeing a professional about the symptom, and having the symptom significantly interfere with one's life). In addition, the interview ascertains whether the symptom was explained entirely by physical illness or injury, or as a complication of the use of medication, illicit drugs, or alcohol. The age at which a given diagnostic symptom first appeared is also determined along with the most recent experience of the symptom. These questions are designed to help determine whether a disorder is current (i.e., the last two weeks, the last month, the last six months, or the last year). Demographic information including age, sex, occupation, race or ethnicity, education, marital status, and history of treatment is also determined. Current functioning is evaluated by ability within the last 12 months to work or attend school, maintain an active social life, act as head or co-head of a household, and get along without professional care for physical or emotional problems.

Aside from a few open-ended questions at the start of the interview to allow the interviewee the opportunity to voice the chief complaint and to give the interviewer some background for understanding answers to closed-ended questions, the interview is completely precoded. Symptoms assessed by the computer are precoded at five levels: (a) negative, the problem has never occurred; (b) present, but so minimal as to be of no diagnostic significance; (c) present and meets criteria for severity, but not relevant to the psychiatric diagnosis in question because every occurrence resulted from the direct or side effects of prescribed, over-the-counter, or illicit drugs or alco-

hol; (d) present and meets criteria for severity but not relevant to the psychiatric diagnosis in question because every occurrence resulted from medical illness or injury; (e) present, meets criteria for severity, and is relevant to the psychiatric diagnosis under consideration.

The DIS has been translated into different languages and its use is now underway, or planned, in about 20 different countries. Cross-national comparisons in psychiatric epidemiology are possible due to the growing number of population surveys in various countries that have used the DIS. Similarly, cross-cultural surveys of anxiety disorders and prevalence, symptomatic expression, and risk factors in alcoholism have been planned. Computerization of the DIS makes direct patient administration possible either in its entirety (18 sections) or one section at a time. The computer printout lists all DSM-III diagnoses for which the patient meets criteria. It also presents additional information about each diagnosis, including the recency of symptoms, duration, and age of onset, etc. In addition, the printout lists for the clinician what other diagnoses must be ruled out before this diagnosis can be assigned according to the DSM-III hierarchy.

Other well-known structured diagnostic interviews include the Present State Examination (Wing, Birley, & Cooper, 1967), the Renard Diagnostic Interview (Helzer, Robins, Croughan, & Welner, 1981), and The Schedule for Affective Disorders and Schizophrenia (Endicott & Spitzer, 1978).

Psychosocial History Interviews

While psychological testing and laboratory studies may be elective, considerable background information is almost always gathered from patients. The psychosocial history is seen as indispensable in the proper evaluation of a patient and as having a central role in clinical practice (Giannetti, 1987). The psychosocial history is seen as providing a biographical-historical perspective on the personality, the stresses and realities within which a person lives, and the nature of the relationships with those closest to the individual (i.e., the patient's individuality). It is an effort to get to know the particular individual who is presenting with a given problem. Psychological tests provide standardized estimates on a set of variables (personality, intellectual, symptomatic) against normative standards. The psychosocial history, on the other hand, provides information on the long series of external stimuli, events, and individuals with which the person has interacted, including the consequences of those interactions (Giannetti, 1987, p. 125).

The Giannetti On-Line Psychosocial History (GOLPH) (Giannetti, 1985) was written after the author reviewed clinical history outlines obtained from different service settings. A content analysis of the items from these outlines suggested that they could be sorted into 10 categories that were reasonably mutually exclusive and exhaustive (Giannetti, 1987):

1. Identifying demographic data/current living arrangements.
2. Family of origin
3. Client development
4. Educational history
5. Marital history/current family functioning
6. Occupational history/current financial circumstances
7. Military history
8. Legal/criminal history
9. Physical illnesses/current somatic symptoms
10. Psychological symptoms/treatments.

After these general categories were identified, items that could be reasonably obtained by self-report were written for each category. For example, items in 14 content areas were written for the general category of client development. The response alternatives to each item were researched so that they would be exhaustive, and the patient would have a minimum of "other" responses. Giannetti (1987) noted that it had been possible to limit "other" responses to approximately 2.5% of 2,400 response alternatives.

The GOLPH was designed to be administered after the clinician had met with the patient initially to discuss the reasons for seeking treatment. Knowing that a reasonably comprehensive historical review will be obtained using the structured psychosocial interview, the clinician is free to focus on the chief complaint and on establishing a therapeutic relationship. During the initial contact the clinician can also determine whether the patient will be unable to provide a valid self-report because of attention or memory deficits, psychosis, extreme anxiety, psychomotor retardation, or some other reason. The GOLPH is intended for individuals at least 16 years old, having a sixth-grade reading level, and seeking mental health services. It is estimated that most patients can complete the GOLPH in about the time it takes to complete an MMPI; administration can be interrupted and resumed. The program prints out a 3–12 page report; the first section is a narrative history under the general category headings noted above. It selects the appro-

priate personal pronouns and develops a sequence of response statements that turn into a narrative that is quite easy to read. The second section of the report is the followup summary in which the data are arranged in a format that allows for easy followup of positive symptoms and for consideration of the differential diagnostic implications of these data. The general history items in the first section of the printout report make the GOLPH pertinent to any situation requiring a history. The second section of the report is particularly relevant for a general psychiatric population, but it could be modified to specific clinical situations (e.g., behavioral medicine or neuropsychology) or to nonclinical evaluative contexts, such as in organizational or industrial settings (Giannetti, 1987, p. 142). The Giannetti On-Line Psychosocial History (GOLPH) is classified as a clinical assessment/ structured interview and is distributed by National Computer Systems, P.O. Box 1416, Minneapolis, MN 55440.

The IPS Social History can be administered on-line or in a paper-pencil format. It presents a series of questions which the respondent can answer by pressing numbers on the keyboard or by selecting response numbers in a question booklet. It is designed primarily for adults and takes 15 to 20 minutes to complete. From this administration, a narrative report can be produced immediately; the clinician can then refer to this report during a subsequent clinical interview. The program prepares a narrative printout under the following headings: current status, family history, educational history, military service, criminal history, alcohol and drug use history, personal relation/self-description, and psychological/medical history. The first heading, current status, contains items referring to age, sex, race or ethnicity, religion, marital status, children, place of residence, duration of current residence, members in household, economic status of neighborhood, employment, nature of occupation, income level, satisfaction with job, and perceived employer satisfaction. As is evident, many questions can be easily and systematically asked of a respondent, and the program can produce information-packed narrative summary paragraphs.

An example of a current status printout is reproduced below; it reflects the responses made by an individual who was being seen for psychological assessment as part of a job application process.

David F. is a 22-year-old white male who lists his religious affiliation as Protestant. He is presently single and has no children. David resides in an apartment and has lived at this location for less than one year with two other people. The economic status of the neighborhood is described as middle income. David is currently employed 32 hours per week and classifies his occupation as clerical. He earns $100.00 to $199.00 per week and is somewhat dissatisfied with his current occupation. In addition, David feels that his employer is very satisfied with the quality of his work.

The IPS Social History is distributed by Integrated Professional Systems, Inc., 5211 Mahoning Avenue, Suite 135, Youngstown, OH 44515.

The Psychological/Psychiatric Status Interview (PPSI) is designed for online computer administration of an initial psychological/psychiatric interview. The program interviews the patient with respect to presenting problems, current living situation, mental status, biological/medical status, interpersonal relations, and socialization. This program is designed specifically for computer administration of the interview and cannot be completed in a paper-and-pencil format. The PPSI provides the clinician with an organized data base on the client, which can be reviewed prior to a personal interview. The three- to five-page report may be printed or written to a text file. This structured interview essentially assumes that the respondent has come to a clinical service setting for help with a psychological/psychiatric problem. As noted above, a section of the narrative printout is devoted to a discussion of "presenting problem." With this particular interview, the respondent is also allowed to type into the program a narrative description of the problem that is at issue. The PPSI is also a combination of psychosocial history and diagnostic interview. It has had good patient acceptance; it has been especially helpful in gathering information from and in assessment of hearing-impaired individuals.

A unique feature of this structured interview is the manner in which it asks questions to complete a mental status examination. A sample mental status section is reproduced below; from this, the reader will be able to infer the questions that are the basis of the descriptive narrative.

John stated that he is oriented to person, place, and time. John indicated subjective experiences suggestive of attention/concentration difficulties. He indicated his attention often wanders. Statements indicative of subjective awareness of memory difficulties were not endorsed.

When visually presented three unrelated words (snake–city–priest) for 2 seconds each, John required only one presentation of the words before he could correctly identify all three words. When asked to identify the same words later (after approximately 15–20 minutes with no re-presentation of the words)

John was able to correctly select the word-triad from a set of six word-triads.

John rated his intellectual ability as above average. This rating is not consistent with his stated educational level (did not complete high school) and his reasons for this rating should be explored further. He indicated that he believes his current intellectual functioning is consistent with his level of functioning in the past. When asked what the saying, "People who live in glass houses shouldn't throw stones" means, John endorsed the response "People with faults shouldn't criticize others." His response to how a dog and a cat are alike was: "They are both animals." The endorsed answer for how reward and punishment are alike was "Both are responses to behavior." The ability to do simple addition appears to be intact. His endorsed responses to the addition problems were: $7 + 4 = $ "11;" $29 + 14 = $ "43." Simple subtraction skills appear to be intact. Answers given to subtraction problems were: $9 - 3 = $ "6;" $45 - 27 = $ "18." John was able to perform simple multiplication ($6 \times 7 = $ "42"). He correctly solved a simple division problem ($28/7 = $ "4").

Possible hallucinatory experiences may be present. He admitted seeing people or things that other people can't. He recently has had strange feelings inside or on his body. Further exploration of these experiences to ascertain if they represent hallucinations is indicated.

The possibility of delusional thinking is suggested. He indicated that he has been selected by God to fulfill a special purpose. These beliefs need to be further discussed with John to find out if there is a delusional component to his thought processes.

He did not endorse any items indicative of unusual thought content. John denied the presence of any extreme and unrealistic fears.

John described his current emotional state as feeling "nothing." The intensity of this feeling was described as mild and he experiences this feeling several hours each day. The feeling is most intense during the early evening hours. He did not identify any specific events which intensify the feeling. He has had this feeling for three to six months. Additional reported emotions include depression. John denied that he has had periods in which he felt very anxious and fearful for no apparent reason. Reported symptoms associated with a possible recent or current depressive emotional state include an increase in appetite. He denied any past or current suicidal ideation or behavior. He reported that he often has racing thoughts that are difficult to slow down.

Problematic behavior patterns may be present. He indicated that he has on at least one occasion spent so much money at one time that it created serious financial problems. He admitted that gambling has created problems in his life.

The Psychological/Psychiatric Status Interview is distributed by Psychologistics, Inc., P.O. Box 3896, Indialantic, FL 32903. This company also distributes several other structured interviews and report formats that are of interest to clinicians. One of these is the

Intake Evaluation Report-Clinician Version 2.0. It provides the clinician with a comprehensive checklist as a guide to use when evaluating the patient with respect to presenting problem, current situation, physical presentation, mental status, biological/medical status, interpersonal relations and socialization, diagnostic impressions, and recommendations. The checklist data are then typed into the computer program which organizes the obtained information in a manner useful for case conceptualization and treatment planning. The report may be printed out or written to a text file where, with the use of a word processor, it may be reformatted or revised to meet specific needs of the clinician.

Another program of interest is Session Summary designed to aid the clinician in completion of case notes and documentation of treatment. It may be completed by the clinician directly on the computer or by paper-and-pencil checklist. The checklist is included on the program disk and may be printed out by the user. The program generates a one-page narrative summary of the session.

The Termination/Discharge Summary was designed to assist the clinician in developing a concise, yet comprehensive, summary of the patient's evaluation/treatment. The program summarizes information in the areas of presenting problems, initial mental and physical status, evaluation results, the goals of treatment, outcomes of treatment, and termination or discharge recommendations. Changes in problem focus and/or intervention strategies are also documented. The summary may be completed directly on the computer or by paper-and-pencil checklist. The program generates a two-page narrative report providing documentation of the patient's treatment.

Krug (1987) listed 27 structured interviews in his psychware sourcebook. Other psychosocial history interviews in addition to the ones noted above are included in his listing. He also includes a number of specific-purpose interviews.

Specific Purpose Interview Schedules

Thus far, the discussion in this chapter has focused on patients most likely to be seen in mental health practices. The assessment of such patients has general significance for all patients, of course, as one can obtain information about overall level of emotional health and the possible presence of such universal and potentially debilitating symptoms as anxiety and depression. Fortunately, assessment procedures have been developed with other patient populations in mind as well.

The Comprehensive Drinker Profile (CDP) was first developed in 1971 as a structured intake interview procedure for assessing alcoholism in male inpatients. In its present form, the CDP is appropriate for use with both male and female clients entering any of a wide variety of treatment modalities in either inpatient or outpatient settings (Miller & Marlatt, 1984). The CDP provides an intensive and comprehensive history and status of the individual client with regard to his or her use and abuse of alcohol. It is intended to be administered as a structured clinical interview and normally requires one to two hours for completion. If necessary, however, the interview can be completed over more than one session. The authors note that for some clinical and research purposes it may be desirable to corroborate client self-report by interviewing collateral sources such as family and friends.

The CDP interview proceeds in a logistically structured order, following a particular sequence of question/information within three major sections (Miller & Marlatt, 1984, p. 3):

A. Demographic information
    Age and residence
    Family status
    Employment and income information
    Educational history
B. Drinking history
    Development of the drinking problem
    Present drinking pattern
    Pattern history
    Alcohol-related life problems
    Drinking settings
    Associated behaviors
    Beverage preferences
    Relevant medical history
C. Motivational information
    Reasons for drinking
    Effects of drinking
    Other life problems
    Motivation for treatment
    Drinking type ratings

The best time to conduct the CDP will vary with client populations. For inpatients requiring detoxification, it is best to wait a few days to a week until the major agitation and disorientation of withdrawal have subsided. It is also usually a good idea to clarify the individual's particular goal in seeking treatment (e.g., mitigation of a legal problem, disability) so that interview responses are not unduly oriented to achieving a particular goal. Finally, it may be necessary for the clinician to obtain blood-alcohol concentration (BAC) readings as it is quite difficult to judge intoxication from overt behavior alone. As a general guideline, a CDP interview should not proceed if the client's BAC exceeds 50 mg% (.050 g/100 ml) (Miller & Marlatt, 1984, p. 8).

Several sections of the CDP can be scored to derive quantitative indices. A quantitative index of strength of family history of alcoholism is derived by summing weighted scores of male and female blood relatives reported as problem drinkers or alcoholic. Numerical weights inversely reflect first-, second-, and third-degree relatives, so that relatives closer in the blood line contribute a higher weighted score than do more distant relatives. Alcohol consumption information is converted into standard units so that the actual amount of ethyl alcohol consumed can be measured across diverse beverages. It also provides a standard unit by which pretreatment and followup levels of consumption can be compared. A pattern of alcohol consumption across days and weeks can be calculated. A quantitative measure of physical dependence on alcohol is also derived. A wealth of information relevant to treatment selection and planning is provided by the CDP. This is consistent with the general treatment concept that alternative interventions should be available to best match patient characteristics with treatment modalities.

The Type A Structured Interview was developed by Friedman and Rosenman (1974) to elicit characteristics of the Type A syndrome. It consists of 22 questions and takes about 10 minutes to administer. Supervised training in administration is suggested because the interviewer must assess not only the specific content of answers, but also the general stylistics and mannerisms of the individual as he or she answers the questions. How something is said may be more important than what was actually said in assessing Type A characteristics. Typical characteristics of the Type A individual include the following:

1. A general expression of vigor and energy, alertness, and confidence.
2. A firm handshake and brisk walking pace.
3. Loud and/or vigorous voice.
4. Terse speech, abbreviated responses.
5. Clipped speech (a failure to pronounce the ending sounds of words).
6. Rapid speech and acceleration of speech at the end of a longer sentence.

7. Explosive speech (a general pattern of punctuating speech with certain words spoken emphatically) that may contain swear words.
8. Frequent interrupting with rapid responses given before another speaker has completed his or her question or statement.
9. Speech hurrying in the form of saying "yes, yes," "mm, mm," or "right, right" or nodding the head in assent while another person speaks.
10. Vehement reactions to questions relating to importance of time-progress (i.e., driving slowly, waiting in lines).
11. Use of clenched fist or pointing finger to emphasize verbalizations.
12. Frequent sighing, especially related to questions about work. It is important to differentiate this from the sighs of a depressed person.
13. Hostility directed at the interviewer or at the topics of the interview.
14. Frequent, abrupt, and emphatic one-word responses to questions (i.e., Yes! Never! Definitely! Absolutely!).

The Psychosocial Pain Inventory (PSPI) was developed to provide a standardized and reliable method of evaluating a number of psychosocial factors considered to be important in maintaining and exacerbating chronic pain problems (Heaton, Lehman, & Getto, 1980). The PSPI includes evaluation of the following factors: several forms of secondary gain, the effects of pain behavior on interpersonal relationships, the existence of stressful life events that may contribute to subjective distress or promote avoidance learning, and components of past learning history that familiarize the patient with the chronic invalid role and with its personal and social consequences. PSPI ratings also acknowledge that patients differ in the degree to which they are likely to be influenced by potential sources of secondary gain.

One section of the PSPI considers home or family responsibilities the patient discharged prior to the pain problem as compared to now. Comparison is made from "before" to "now" for those activities that were primarily the patient's responsibility; responses are graded from "less now" (i.e., the activity has decreased by no more than 25%) to "never now." Areas of activity the patient is asked about include housecleaning, clothes washing, clothes ironing, shopping, cooking, repair work (home), repair work (car), yard work, errands, caring for children, disciplining children, driving other family member, family finances, family correspondence, and others (specify). Early findings suggested that the PSPI has some value in predicting response to medical treatment for pain.

Behavior Checklists and Patient Questionnaires

As in each of the areas of discussion above, identification of structured information-gathering devices is illustrative and not exhaustive. This is especially true in the area of behavior checklists and patient questionnaires; literally, hundreds of them have been developed. Some devices that have been used to show changes in patients over time, especially as such changes might be related to treatment interventions, include observer rating scales and self-descriptive inventories. Examples of observer rating scales for adult patients are the Brief Psychiatric Rating Scale (Overall & Gorham, 1962), the Hamilton Depression Scale (Hamilton, 1967), the Wittenborn Psychiatric Rating Scale (Wittenborn, 1955), and the Nurses' Observation Scale for Inpatient Evaluation (Honigfeld & Klett, 1965).

Examples of self-descriptive inventories include the Beck Depression Inventory (Beck, Ward, Mendelson, Mock, & Erbaugh, 1961), the Hopkins Symptom Checklist (Derogatis, Lipman, Rickels, Uhlenhuth, & Covi, 1973) and the State-Trait Anxiety Inventory (Spielberger, Gorsuch, & Lushene, 1970). As the reader may reflect, questionnaires have been developed for many target-specific adult behavior problems, including social skills deficits, obsessive-compulsive behaviors, fears and phobias, anger, marital distress and dysfunction, ingestive disorders, sexual dysfunctions, and so on.

THEORETICAL AND METHODOLOGICAL CONSIDERATIONS

Much clinical research is difficult to do if reliable diagnoses cannot be achieved and clinicians disagree on patient classification. When researchers looked for sources of undependable information, or unreliability in diagnosis, it became apparent that *criterion variance* (application of different rules for assigning a diagnosis) and *information variance* (different interview data) were prime sources of unreliability. Continuing efforts to develop and improve specific, operationalized criteria for diagnoses have been broadly accepted and applied by clinicians. Paradoxically, procedures to clarify sources of erratic data in the

interview by standardizing the form of interviews have not been widely applied (Young et al., 1987).

Issues in Diagnosis

Diagnostic nomenclatures (e.g., DSM-III or DSM-III-R) represent a way of thinking and communicating. The DSM-III has provided a uniform and systematic vocabulary, and clinicians using its diagnostic criteria have achieved good agreement in diagnosis. Diagnostic agreement is achieved by using operationally defined criteria for the presence of a disorder and essentially substituting operational definitions for the varying and subjective judgments of clinicians. Parenthetically, it must be recognized that subjective judgments are never totally obviated, because even in deciding whether operational criteria have been met (e.g., was the patient inattentive?), subjective judgment is exercised. However, the more general issue here is the limitations inherent in operational definitions, namely, that reliance on a single operational definition confines our understanding of a concept (or diagnosis) to those aspects monitored by the particular set of rules and restricts opportunities to improve the rule system itself. By analogy, many psychologists are aware of the statement that "intelligence is what the intelligence test measures." They acknowledge the importance in developing concepts of cognitive functioning, of using procedures for study in addition to those included in intelligence tests. Research methologists warn against the use of single operational definitions in measurement systems. Each operational definition is inherently imperfect. Otherwise, the construct measured is self-evident and does not require the development of any measures. The use of multiple measures avoids reliance upon an assumed final, perfect operational definition and provides a framework for illuminating comparisons among measures. Using both structured interviews and rating scales provides a cross check so that errors and biases in each can be identified. In a similar fashion, the use of multiple probes (derived from operational definitions) within a structured interview improves reliability and validity (Young et al., 1987).

Gold (1986) acknowledges that the DSM-III has enormous influence and that its diagnostic codes are used by all mental health providers whose services are reimbursable by insurance companies. However, he is concerned that it is a reductionistic, symptom-based system that discourages practitioners from looking beyond the obvious. He notes, for example, that without objective verification one cannot be sure of the correct diagnosis if the symptoms of two disorders are similar. The example Gold uses is that of a grandiose delusion which could be seen in a manic or schizophrenic episode and that the correct differentiation is essential to institute the right treatment. He further observes that patient report regarding symptoms like "appetite" or "pain" depends on whether a patient is grateful for no appetite or has experienced pain so long it no longer seems unusual. Patients of differing ages and backgrounds display differing symptoms, for in sickness and in health, behavior is shaped by generation and culture, even by sex (Gold, 1986, p. 52).

Gold's major point is that the DSM-III encourages its users to believe that behavioral symptoms necessarily mean something psychiatric and leads clinicians not to consider organic conditions that can mimic psychiatric illnesses. Further, he asserts that the DSM-III categories do not parallel the biological subtypes that are being revealed in laboratory research (as in biological differences among depressed people). In the case of depression, it is necessary to differentiate primary and secondary affective disorders and to recognize that systemic medical diseases, CNS disorders, endocrine disorders, drug-induced disorders, and infections are major bases for secondary affective disorder. Gold suggests that at least 75 illnesses or conditions can cause symptoms of apparent mental disorder and psychiatric symptoms are often the first and only signs of a developing illness. He notes that in the diagnosis of cancer, that many types of tumors throughout the body can produce mental symptoms, which may be the only symptoms to appear for weeks, months, or years. In fact, he asserts that anyone who has an abrupt personality change, depression without a history of mood disorders, or weight loss of greater than 20 pounds—or who is unresponsive to standard psychiatric treatment—should be evaluated for cancer or other mimickers (Gold, 1986, p. 83). The most common mimickers of psychiatry, according to Gold (1986), are drug (illicit, prescribed, and over-the-counter) and alcohol reactions; endocrine disorders; and diseases of the central nervous system, infectious diseases, cancers, metabolic conditions, and nutritional and toxic disorders. Drugs, for example, must be considered in all psychiatric diagnoses, no matter how classically "psychiatric" the person may appear, because everybody takes them in one form or another. Because the brain is quicker to react than the rest of the body, mental and behavioral symptoms may outweigh or-

ganic signs as an indicator of reaction to environmental toxins. The generalization to be drawn for the construct of diagnosis, in the case of depression as an example, is that no one can conclude that a patient is in the midst of a major depressive episode without first ruling out possible organic causes.

Related to this generalization is the obvious truism that symptoms, particularly emotional symptoms, are not specific. First of all, the patient report of something like depressive symptoms is colored by the emotion itself; second, the depressive emotion may relate to infectious mononucleosis, a bad marriage, an enzyme deficiency, or other etiologies. Clearly, objective measures are needed to verify, or clarify, particular diagnoses. Laboratory tests have come to play a more important role in psychiatry in screening for medical illness, improving diagnostic reliability, monitoring treatment (especially through measurement of the blood levels of psychoactive drugs), and continuing research into mental illness. Kaplan and Sadock (1988) note a number of neuroendocrine tests (used particularly in depression), tests for sexually transmitted diseases, tests to assess plasma levels of psychotropic drugs, electroencephalography, evoked potentials, radioisotope brain scanning, and tests of regional blood flow.

In a paper on brain imaging in psychiatry, Andreasen (1988, p. 1387) concludes that brain imaging offers psychiatry a broad range of investigative techniques that fulfill the popular fantasy of being able to "read the mind," albeit in the form of "seeing the brain" both structurally and functionally. At present, brain imaging provides a modest amount of information that is useful in differential diagnosis, as in distinctions between depression and dementia. It has provided more information about possible pathophysiological mechanisms of major mental illnesses, including structural abnormalities in some forms of schizophrenia. Metabolic abnormalities, such as hypofrontality in schizophrenia or hyperfrontality in obsessional disorder, have also been observed. The long-term promise of brain imaging is substantial. It will permit the mapping of cerebral function in normal individuals so that we can achieve a better understanding of normal brain structure, physiology, chemistry, and functional organization. On the basis of this knowledge, the abnormalities underlying the major mental illnesses can also be mapped.

Andreasen's report gives further support to Wittenborn's (1984) hope that we are now at the threshold of important new knowledge of the relationships between neurochemical changes and behavior changes.

The properties of behavior that are included in these new relationships may be different from those that form the content of current assessments.

Issues in Structured Interviewing

Young et al. (1987, p. 614) review common sources of interview misinformation and in so doing delineate a number of variables that must be considered in the development of structured interviewing procedures. Regarding the structure of the interview, they note the following sources of misinformation:

Structure of the interview
  Lack of specificity in the question
  Complex and multidimensional concepts in question
  Sequence of questions
  Number of questions
  Question structure
  Unwarranted assumptions in the questions
  More than one question embedded in a single question
  Sensitive or threatening element in the questions
  Wording of the question (inexact terms, ambiguous or vague terms, complex terms and sentences, biased words)
Respondent sources of interview misinformation
  Need to give socially desirable answers
  Lack of understanding of the questions
  Memory lapses
  Experience of questioning as stressful
  No true opinion
  Differing emotional intensity among respondents
  Variable perceptions of the situation and purpose
  Timing of interview
Interviewer sources of misinformation
  Interviewer characteristics
  Preferences and biases
  Variable emotional intensity
  Variable verbal facility
  Variable understanding of the questions
  Recording errors

Test-retest reliability of structured interviews has been satisfactory and usually superior to traditional interview methods. However, the test-retest method, using different interviewers, faces fairly consistent methodological problems. These problems include clinical change in the patient (e.g., new symptoms or symptom remission); recall involving efforts to give the same response or omitting symptoms mentioned earlier; therapeutic effects of the first interview; greater symptom severity at the first interview; and regression to the mean. Then there is always the question of whether the diagnostic criterion that is being used is a valid yardstick.

Young et al. (1987) suggest that in the absence of biological markers, to designate discontinuities among diagnoses we resort to symptom grouping and enumeration as the basis for clinical diagnosis. Symptom designation involves more or less arbitrarily establishing cutting points for inclusion or exclusion from a diagnostic category. Where the cutting point is placed has an important effect on the percentage of correctly identified cases and noncases. In a study sample with many severe cases, the accuracy of identification will be high—certainly higher than in a general population sample including the full range of less severe and borderline cases.

Clinicians have been concerned that structured interviews are undergoing constant revision and that the lack of a final measure indicates an essential flaw in the instrument. A more positive view of this continuing modification is that the continuing efforts to improve the instrument attest to its importance and that it is reflecting the essential nature of the research process (i.e., gradual unfolding of knowledge and facts). It must again be recognized that diagnostic systems using specific operational criteria evolve over the years, so that an ideal, static nomenclature always remains elusive. Other clinicians may feel that current structured interviews are cumbersome, or that turning pages of an interview guide may interfere with the interviewer-patient relationship, or that the interviews take too long.

Perhaps the question of whether structured interviews in routine clinical use are beneficial for patients still has to be answered. Research has indicated that they increase by a factor of two to one the number of clinical observations (e.g., number of problem areas) and the amount of relevant patient information that is recorded. Clinicians using structured interviews tend not to be limited to the presenting symptoms in their diagnostic formulations; their results have higher reliability. Interviewers using structured interviews consider themselves equally as empathic as when using free-flowing interviews. With practice, they can use structured interviews with increasing efficiency, so that this method requires about the same amount of time as traditional interviews (Young et al., 1987).

There is evidence (Giannetti, 1987) that automated self-reports have advantages for both clinical practice and research. Patients accept and enjoy responding to online computerized questionnaires and frequently prefer them over clinical interviews or paper-and-pencil questionnaires. Even chronic and disturbed inpatients can answer computer-presented questions without assistance. There are indications that respondents are more likely to report socially undesirable behavior to a computer (e.g., reporting greater alcohol consumption to computers than to interviewers). Self-report and interviewer-collected history data show high agreement. Finally, it may be cost saving to complete interviews by computer rather than by traditional means.

Adams and Heaton (1987) call attention to a further administrative/research role of computers in clinical practice: creating and maintaining an informational data base. This data base might include information concerning patient demographics, referral sources, historical data, criterion test results (e.g., brain tests), psychological test findings, and clinical outcome. Such information is valuable in documenting the sources of patients, their demographic and base-rate profiles, the relationship of neuropsychological tests to other results, and the impact of testing, or other services, on patient outcome. Such data are of importance in quality assurance and in evaluation research. External reviewers and third-party agencies increasingly request data showing the accuracy of diagnosis and relationship to hospital/clinic utilization, more appropriate care, and improved outcome. As Adams and Heaton (1987) note, no amount of professional insistence on freedom to practice will substitute for such data, given the current climate in health services delivery. Once this view is accepted, it follows that the optimal way to gain control of the quality and accuracy of such data is to implement one's own system to generate the data.

SUMMARY

The clinical interview has been used for many years as a primary source of information about patients. Information obtained in the clinical interview has been used to determine diagnosis and treatment interventions. This has been true despite the observations made in systematic studies of the clinical interview that showed it often produced unreliable, or even misleading, data. A particular source of concern over the years has been the disagreement in diagnosis by different clinicians interviewing the same patient.

More recently, there has been a concerted effort to address two sources of undependable information about diagnoses: development of operationally defined diagnostic decision rules (DSM-III and DSM-III-R) to reduce criterion variance, and development of structured interviews to reduce information variance (i.e., to aid in obtaining the necessary facts from the patient to be able to assign a diagnosis). Structured diagnostic interviews have been used extensively in clinical and epidemiological research. The comprehensiveness of the information that can be collected with structured interviews is leading to their use in routine clinical practice. The availability of personal computers is contributing to their increased use in patient self-administration of various structured interviews, including psychosocial history interviews and diagnostic interviews. It is possible to predict with confidence that diagnostic criteria will continue to evolve and change until laboratory correlates of diagnoses are identified. It is also possible to predict that the use of structured interviews (computer administered), in clinical practice as well as research, will expand dramatically because of the wealth of information they provide the clinician.

REFERENCES

Adams, K. M., & Heaton, R. K. (1987). Computerized neuropsychological assessment: Issues and applications. In J. N. Butcher (Ed.), *Computerized psychological assessment* (pp. 355–365). New York: Basic Books.

American Psychiatric Association. (1980). *Diagnostic and statistical manual of mental disorders: DSM-III*. Washington, DC: Author.

American Psychiatric Association. (1987). *Diagnostic and statistical manual of mental disorders* (3rd ed., rev.). Washington, DC: Author.

Andreasen, N. C. (1988). Brain imaging: Applications in psychiatry. *Science, 239*, 1381–1388.

Ash, P. (1949). The reliability of psychiatric diagnosis. *Journal of Abnormal and Social Psychology, 44*, 272–277.

Beck, A. T., Ward, C. H., Mendelson, M., Mock, J., & Erbaugh, J. (1961). An inventory for measuring depression. *Archives of General Psychiatry, 4*, 561–571.

Council for the National Register of Health Service Providers in Psychology. (1978). *National register of health service providers in psychology*. Baltimore: Port City Press.

Derogatis, L. R., Lipman, R. S., Rickels, K., Uhlenhuth, E. H., & Covi, L. (1973). The Hopkins Symptom Checklist (HSCL): A measure of primary symptom dimensions. In P. Pichot (Ed.),

Psychological measurement in pharmacopsychiatry (Vol. 7). Basel: S. Karger.

Edelbrock, C., & Costello, A. J. (1984). Structured psychiatric interviews for children and adolescents. In G. Goldstein & M. Herson (Eds.), *Handbook of psychological assessment* (pp. 276–290). New York: Pergamon Press.

Endicott, J., & Spitzer, R. L. (1978). A diagnostic interview. *Archives of General Psychiatry, 35,* 837–844.

Erdman, H. P., Klein, M. H., & Greist, J. H. (1985). Direct patient computer interviewing. *Journal of Consulting and Clinical Psychology, 53,* 760–773.

Friedman, M., & Rosenman, R. H. (1974). *Type A behavior and your heart.* New York: Knopf.

Giannetti, R. A. (1985). *Giannetti on-line psychosocial history: GOLPH (Version 2.0).* Unpublished manuscript.

Giannetti, R. A. (1987). The GOLPH psychosocial history: Response-contingent data acquisition and reporting. In J. N. Butcher (Ed.), *Computerized psychological assessment* (pp. 124–144). New York: Basic Books.

Gold, M. S. (1986). *The good news about depression.* New York: Bantam Books.

Greist, J. H. (1984). Conservative radicalism: An approach to computers in mental health. In M. D. Schwartz (Ed.), *Using computers in clinical practice: Psychotherapy and mental health applications* (pp. 191–194). New York: Haworth Press.

Hamilton, M. (1967). Development of a rating scale for primary depressive illness. *British Journal of Social and Clinical Psychology, 6,* 278–296.

Heaton, R. K., Lehman, R. A. W., & Getto, C. J. (1980). *Psychosocial pain inventory.* Odessa, FL: Psychological Assessment Resources.

Helzer, J. E., Robins, L. N., Croughan, J. L., & Welner, A. (1981). Renard diagnostic interview. *Archives of General Psychiatry, 38,* 393–398.

Honigfeld, G., & Klett, C. (1965). The Nurses' Observation Scale for Inpatient Evaluation (NOSIE): A new scale for measuring improvement in chronic schizophrenia. *Journal of Clinical Psychology, 21,* 65–71.

Kanfer, F. H., & Saslow, G. (1969). Behavioral diagnosis. In C. M. Franks (Ed.), *Behavior therapy: Appraisal and status* (pp. 417–444). New York: McGraw-Hill.

Kaplan, H. I., & Sadock, B. J. (1988). *Synopsis of Psychiatry.* (Fifth Ed.). Baltimore: Williams & Wilkins.

Krug, S. E. (1987). *Psychware sourcebook, 1987–1988* (2nd ed.). Champaign, IL: MetriTech, Inc.

Lukin, M. E., Dowd, E. T., Plake, B. S., & Kraft, R. G. (1985). Comparing computerized versus traditional psychological assessment. *Computers in Human Behavior, 1,* 49–58.

Miller, L. S., Bergstrom, D. A., Cross, H. J., & Grube, J. W. (1981). Opinions and use of the DSM system by practicing psychologists. *Professional Psychology, 12,* 285–390.

Miller, W. R., & Marlatt, G. A. (1984). *Manual: Comprehensive Drinker Profile.* Odessa, FL: Psychological Assessment Resources.

Overall, J. E., & Gorham, D. R. (1962). The Brief Psychiatric Rating Scale. *Psychological Reports, 10,* 799–812.

Oxford English dictionary: The compact edition. (1971). Oxford: Oxford University Press.

Robins, L. N., Helzer, J. E., Croughan, J., & Ratcliff, K. (1981). National Institute of Mental Health Diagnostic Interview Schedule. *Archives of General Psychiatry, 38,* 381–389.

Siassi, I. (1984). Psychiatric interview and mental status examination. In G. Goldstein & M. Hersen (Eds.), *Handbook of psychological assessment* (pp. 259–275). New York: Pergamon Press.

Spielberger, C., Gorsuch, R., & Lushene, R. (1970). *The State-Trait Anxiety Inventory (STAI) test manual.* Palo Alto, CA: Consulting Psychologists Press.

Spiker, D. G., & Ehler, J. G. (1984). Structured psychiatric interviews for adults. In G. Goldstein & M. Hersen (Eds.), *Handbook of psychological assessment* (pp. 291–304). New York: Pergamon Press.

Spitzer, R. G., Endicott, J., & Robins, E. (1975). Clinical criteria for diagnosis and DSM-III. *American Journal of Psychiatry, 132,* 1187–1192.

Spitzer, R. L., Endicott, J., & Robins, E. (1978). Research diagnostic criteria rationale and reliability. *Archives of General Psychiatry, 35,* 773–782.

Spitzer, R. L., Forman, J. B. W., & Nee, J. (1979). DSM-III field trials: I. Initial interrater diagnostic reliability. *American Journal of Psychiatry, 136,* 815–817.

Wiens, A. N. (1983). The assessment interview. In I. B. Weiner (Ed.), *Clinical methods in psychology* (2nd ed.) (pp. 3–57). New York: Wiley.

Wiens, A. N. & Matarazzo, J. D. (1983). Diagnostic interviewing. In M. Hersen, A. E. Kazdin, & A. S. Bellack, A. S. (Eds.), *The clinical psychology handbook* (pp. 309–328). New York: Pergamon Press.

Wing, J. K., Birley, J. L. T., & Cooper, J. E. (1967). Reliability of a procedure for measuring and classifying "present psychiatric state." *British Journal of Psychiatry, 113,* 449–515.

Wittenborn, J. R. (1955). *Manual: Wittenborn Psychiatric Rating Scales.* New York: Psychological Corporation.

Wittenborn, J. R. (1984). Psychological assessment in treatment. In G. Goldstein & M. Hersen (Eds.), *Handbook of psychological assessment* (pp. 405–420). New York: Pergamon Press.

Young, G., O'Brien, J. D., Gutterman, E. M., & Cohen, P. (1987). Structured diagnostic interviews for children and adolescents. *Journal of the American Academy of Child and Adolescent Psychiatry; 26,* 611–620.

PART VII

PERSONALITY ASSESSMENT

CHAPTER 16

OBJECTIVE PERSONALITY ASSESSMENT

Laura S. Keller
James N. Butcher
Wendy S. Slutske

In his analysis of the impact of technological change on individuals and society, Mesthene (1970) described two extreme views of technology: as an "unalloyed blessing for man and society" or alternatively as "an almost unmitigated curse" (pp. 16–17). Those who favor the latter view stress the impersonal and potentially dehumanizing aspects of technology. Proponents of technological change emphasize its promise for "freeing man to pursue creative productivity" (Williams, 1977, p. 108). As an important component of psychology's technology, objective personality assessment has been both criticized and praised on the basis of extreme value positions such as these. Realistically, however, technological developments should be evaluated only in relation to their relevance and utility for the achievement of valued goals. Objective methods of personality assessment and their logical outgrowth, automated assessment methods, are particularly well suited to the achievement of practical goals in both research and applied psychological settings.

Objective assessment devices are characterized by the structured and standardized nature of their test stimuli, response options available to the subject, and scoring and interpretive strategies. Objective tests can be reliably and accurately administered, scored, and in some cases actually interpreted by nonprofessional workers or even by a machine. The latter is possible because of the huge amount of research data available on many popular objective personality instruments. These data have been incorporated into standardized systems of interpretive rules relating test scores to meaningful extra-test criteria. The reliability and standardization of data collected through objective personality inventories are ideal for research applications. In addition, the efficiency of such assessment methods is increasingly important in applied settings; limited funding and the current emphasis on accountability are making the cost/benefit ratios of various psychological technologies a standard concern.

HISTORICAL FOUNDATIONS

Throughout the history of mankind, various informal or formal methods have been used to classify, select, or predict the behavior of other human beings. As Ben-Porath and Butcher (in press) describe in their historical review, descriptions of personality assessment techniques can be found in the Bible, in ancient Chinese selection procedures, and in early Roman and Greek writings. They note three major divisions of personality assessment techniques, categorized by the type and source of data: (a) behavioral observations, (b) somatic examinations, and (c) verbal examinations.

Behavioral and Somatic Examinations

Behavioral observations lie at the base of most of our informal, personal strategies for assessing the character of those around us. They have also been used extensively in formal strategies for describing personality or predicting future behavior. Galton (1884) wrote of assessing individual character through observation of behavior, and Hartshorne and May (1928) described a series of behavioral tests designed to measure the personality trait of "honesty." The low correlations between the various single-situation honesty measures resulting from the latter test serves to point out a basic principle in objective personality testing: single items, whether they be behavioral observations or verbal responses, tend to be very unreliable and poor predictors of other individual descriptors or future behavior. Thus, *aggregation of information,* such as by grouping several observations across several situations, grouping information obtained by several different assessment methods, or simply by adding individual items together to form scales, is basic to the development of reliable, useful, descriptive and predictive personality measures.

Behavioral observations, such as performance-based tests for job selection or teachers' ratings of child classroom behavior, are widely used today. However, the trend has been toward directly measuring and changing behaviors in question rather than inferring underlying personality dispositions or predicting nonsampled behaviors from such measures. Although the boundaries are fuzzy, the contemporary uses of behavioral observation techniques are probably covered more appropriately in other chapters of this handbook, so will not be explored here.

Similarly, the use of somatic examinations to assess personality has lost popularity in the past few decades. The heyday of somatic assessment in the 1800s revolved around the techniques of phrenology, a systematized method of describing individual character and mental faculties through examining the size, shape, and form of the skull (Davies, 1955). Both this invalidated technique and the "somatotype" personality descriptors proposed by Sheldon (1940) have fallen into disfavor, leaving the somatic approach to personality assessment largely unused today. As Ben-Porath and Butcher (in press) point out, this area may see some new growth in the future with the expansion of new psychophysiological measures.

Verbal Personality Tests

The third category of personality tests, verbal examinations, has dominated the field of personality assessment this century. Verbal tests are traditionally divided into *projective techniques,* distinguished primarily by the unstructured nature of their response options, and *objective techniques,* which provide the responder with a limited set of structured response options. Although we will not discuss projective techniques in this chapter, it should be noted that the distinction is not as clear as it initially sounds: even in "objective" tests, "there is a 'projective' element involved in interpreting and responding to these verbal stimuli which must be recognized, in spite of the fact that the test situation is very rigidly structured as regards the ultimate response possibilities permitted" (Meehl, 1945, p. 299).

Although contemporary objective techniques had their roots in rating scales completed by individuals other than the subject being described, questionnaires completed by the test subject soon overshadowed rating scales in popularity. These *self-report inventories* were aggregates of "conventional culturally crystallized questions to which the subject must respond in one of a few fixed ways" (Meehl, 1945, p. 296). The first self-report inventories were developed in applied settings to aid psychologists in practical decision-making tasks. The Woodworth Personal Data Sheet (PDS) was constructed during World War I for mass psychiatric screening of military draftees (Woodworth, 1920). Designed to function as a standardized clinical interview, the PDS was a paper-and-pencil test consisting of questions about neurotic symptoms. The subject's score on this test was the total number of symptoms he or she endorsed.

After the war, many other inventories were developed for a variety of predictive purposes and by a variety of methods. Many, like the PDS, were developed through *rational* methods: items were selected, written, and/or grouped according to the test developer's theory of which items and scales should work for his or her purpose. However, researchers began to find that a priori predictions of how particular items would relate to criteria of interest were often disconfirmed in practice: "Surprising as it may be, there is simply too little empirical support for the notion that a sophisticated theoretical background boosts scale validity" (Burisch, 1984, p. 215).

A different method of test construction, the *empirical criterion keying* approach, dealt with this problem by asserting that a person's response "constitutes an intrinsically interesting and significant bit of verbal behavior, the non-test correlates of which must be discovered by empirical means" (Meehl, 1945, p. 297). Rather than grouping items into scales according to preconceived theoretical notions of relevant content, the empirical test constructor uses the *method of contrasted groups* to select items according to their significance in distinguishing between groups of people differing on the criterion of interest. For example, in constructing a "depression" scale for the MMPI, the responses of a group of diagnosed depressives were contrasted with those of a group of "normals." Items for which the frequency of endorsement differed significantly between the two groups were included in the scale. The Minnesota Multiphasic Personality Inventory (MMPI) (Dahlstrom, Welsh, & Dahlstrom, 1972, 1975; Hathaway & McKinley, 1940) and its "normal" personality counterpart, the California Psychological Inventory (CPI) (Baucom, 1985; Eysenck, 1985; Gough, 1975; Megargee, 1972), were both constructed largely through methods of empirical criterion keying. Empirical or "external" methods of test development and validation are particularly popular for practical uses involving selection or classification of individuals into predefined groups (Burisch, 1984).

A third method of personality test construction has gained in popularity as the computer technology necessary for its execution has become available. In the *factor analytic, internal consistency,* or *inductive* approach to test construction, homogeneous scales are developed by factor analyzing the inter-item correlations among a large pool of personality items. This approach tends to be used more often by personality researchers hoping to uncover the "basic dimensions" of personality than by practitioners, at least initially. The Guilford-Zimmerman Temperament Survey (Guilford & Zimmerman, 1956) and the Comrey Personality Scales (Comrey, 1970) were developed through internal consistency methods. However, the factor analytic method is best exemplified in the work of Cattell, the developer of the Sixteen Personality Factor Questionnaire or 16PF (Cattell, Eber, & Tatsuoka, 1970).

Cattell attempted to provide a comprehensive description of personality by factor analyzing ratings of individuals on a set of trait items derived from the set of all personality trait names in the English dictionary and the psychiatric literature. Cattell described the resultant factors as "primary source traits" of personality, which Anastasi (1988, p. 542) noted is "a designation that seems to imply more universality and stability of results than appear justified by the antecedent research." However, the 16PF has proved to be a popular instrument for "normal population" personality assessment, and over the years a large body of research data has accrued on its use (Butcher, 1985; Zuckerman, 1985). More recently, the 16PF has been expanded to include dimensions of pathological personality functioning as well. This new instrument, the Clinical Analysis Questionnaire (CAQ), is designed to provide a comprehensive assessment of every meaningful dimension of both normal and pathological functioning (Krug, 1980). Several other adaptations of the 16PF have been developed for particular

assessment purposes such as marriage counseling and job evaluation. However, the empirical validation research on these factorially developed instruments remains sketchy (Anastasi, 1988; Bolton, 1985; Butcher, 1985; Guthrie, 1985; McNair, 1978).

In the past two decades, test construction efforts have tended to combine several strategies in a multistep developmental process. Jackson (1971) presented a model test-construction strategy involving rational-theoretical selection of items based on the needs theory of Henry Murray (1938), followed by scale refinement through factorial internal consistency checks, and finally empirical validation against external criteria. Jackson's Differential Personality Inventory (DPI) (Jackson, 1972) and Personality Research Form (PRF) (Jackson, 1984) were constructed through this combination of rational, internal consistency, and empirical validation methodology. The inventories consist of relatively independent scales with high content homogeneity, and have also been designed to minimize the distorting effects of certain subject response styles. On reviewing the research literature of the past 10 years, however, we would tend to agree with Anastasi (1988) that "on the whole, the PRF is an excellent research instrument, but more information is needed to determine its effectiveness in practical situations" (p. 548).

Another of the "contenders to replace the MMPI monopoly" (Kleinmuntz, 1982, p. 242) is Millon's Clinical Multiaxial Inventory (MCMI). Like the PRF, the MCMI was developed using a mixture of scale construction methods. Item and scale content are linked to Millon's own clinical personality theory, but selection of the final item pool and scale composition were refined through a combination of internal consistency methods and external criterion checking. Millon set out to "draw upon the best features of the MMPI, minimize its limitations, and move forward to develop instruments that reflect advances of the past quarter of a century in psychopathology, diagnostic assessment, and test construction" (Millon, 1982, p. 1). Accordingly, the MCMI is distinguished by its brevity compared to comparable instruments, its link to a systematic clinical theory, the coordination of its interpretations with the current official psychiatric diagnostic system, its attempt to separate enduring personality characteristics from acute clinical symptom pictures, and its purported ability to discriminate among psychiatric groups. Because it was constructed with the latter goal in mind, the instrument is not recommended for use in "normal" populations or "for purposes other than diagnostic screening or clinical assessment" (p. 3). Although many authors (Butcher & Keller, 1984; Greer, 1984; Hess, 1985; Widiger,

1985; Widiger & Sanderson, 1987; Widiger, Williams, Spitzer, & Frances, 1985) have noted the lack of empirical validity information on the MCMI, in the past few years the data base on this instrument has been growing. While some researchers have found the MCMI to be useful and accurate for their purposes, broad concerns about its tendency to overpathologize compared to clinicians' judgments and its lack of correspondence to DSM-III diagnoses (American Psychiatric Association, 1980) have been raised. A revised form of the MCMI has been developed by Millon to incorporate new advances in his personality theory, to correspond to the revised diagnostic categories in the DSM-III-R, and to incorporate MCMI validation research (Millon, 1985a, 1986). The MCMI-II (Millon, 1987) includes two new personality disorder scales, new validity corrections, and a new item weighting system.

Despite the differences noted in test development strategies, in practice today most tests are either developed via a "mixed" strategy or, as is the case with the MMPI, their use has evolved to include a variety of approaches beyond their original developers' aims and methods. In general, research has failed to show that any particular one of these test construction methods results in significantly more valid or effective measurement devices than any other (Burisch, 1984; Goldberg, 1972; Hase & Goldberg, 1967).

CONTEMPORARY STATUS OF OBJECTIVE PERSONALITY TESTS

The proliferation of objective personality tests in the last half century attests to their practical advantages. For example, the ninth edition of the *Mental Measurements Yearbook* (Mitchell, 1985) categorizes 350 tests as personality instruments, 24.8% of all tests reviewed. Seventy-two percent of these were new since the last publication of the yearbook! Given these overwhelming numbers, we will not attempt in the space of this chapter to provide an overview of available tests. There are many other sources for such reviews including, of course, the *Ninth Mental Measurements Yearbook*. Anastasi (1988) also provides brief descriptions of many personality tests and measurement issues in her textbook on psychologica testing. As we described above, a wide variety of methods and measures has been subsumed under the broad and often vague category of "personality tests." Many of these methods, such as projective techniques, interest inventories, behavioral observations, diagnostic interviews, and peer assessments, are cov-

ered elsewhere in this volume. At present, self-report inventories represent by far the largest category of objective personality tests. Although it is not possible for us to provide a detailed evaluation of recent research and clinical applications of objective personality tests, we will try to provide a brief overview of general areas of current use. Our survey is designed to update the review of objective personality research provided by Butcher and Owen in 1978. Our survey of literature included all articles using one or more of the MMPI, MCMI, DPI, PRF, 16PF, or CAQ found in a computer search (MEDLINE and PSYCH ABSTRACTS) of the published literature from 1978 to early 1988. We recognize that some publications may have been missed inadvertently, and that the delay between publication and listing in these data bases has forced us to exclude much of the literature published in the past year. We chose these particular instruments because they are the most widely used objective measures, they are designed to cover a wide variety of personality dimensions, they represent different major methods of test development, and they include the measures used by Butcher and Owen (1978) in their review.

Survey of Recent Literature

Even a cursory look at the current literature indicates that either omnibus personality inventories or one or more of their scales are used as criterion measures for clinical and normal sample research on a routine basis. The MMPI scales, in particular, are often used as the standard against which other devices are compared, and current psychotherapeutic treatment outcome studies almost invariably use some aspect of the MMPI as part of their assessment strategy. Changes in MMPI or MCMI indices from pretreatment to posttreatment are often used as measures of treatment efficacy, and many studies utilize pretreatment MMPI or other test administrations to investigate the relationship between personality factors or level/type of pathology and subsequent treatment outcome.

In their comprehensive review of objective personality inventory research, Butcher and Owen (1978) noted several major areas of current interest: detection of alcohol and drug problems, personality assessment of medical patients, cross-cultural and subcultural applications, and development of various short forms and alternative forms of the MMPI. These content domains have continued to attract research interest. In particular, alcohol and drug abuse have been heavily researched. Much of the work continues to center on validation of the MMPI MacAndrew Addiction scale across diverse populations, although many other scales and strategies for differentiating alcoholics and/or drug addicts from various other groups are reported and sometimes compared to the MAC scale. The search continues for useful MMPI typologies to identify subgroups of chemical abusers sharing common treatment-relevant characteristics, and complex multivariate methods such as cluster analysis are increasingly popular tools for researchers searching for patient *types* rather than *the* addictive personality.

The current research on alcoholism is illustrative of a trend that can be seen across all areas of personality assessment research, namely the growing concern with demographic/cultural differences that might modify the validity of objective descriptors and predictors. Many of the research reports we saw were investigations of the generalizability of various scales or typologies to different socioeconomic classes, ethnic groups, and other nationalities, as well as of their generalizability across age and sex. International applications of the MMPI, for example, have dramatically increased in the past 10 years. There have been over 115 foreign language translations of the MMPI. The test is presently being used for clinical and research purposes in many countries, including such unlikely nations as the Soviet Union (Valsiner, 1982) and China (Song, 1981) that in the past had not been open to using personality scales for individual personality assessment. Objective personality tests are well suited for research investigating the factorial stability or universality of various *structure of personality* models across cultures, as well as describing salient cultural differences in personality test patterns.

Objective personality tests have been heavily used and researched in the medical field, particularly in investigating the psychogenic component of problem areas such as chronic pain, ulcers, asthma, irritable bowel syndrome, premenstrual syndrome, coronary heart disease, and recently even cancer. The MMPI and other tests have also been used to predict treatment outcome for other problems commonly encountered in behavioral medicine, such as obesity, anorexia, bulimia, smoking, and sexual dysfunction. As in other areas of research, many studies focus on describing mean group profiles in an attempt to describe *the* personality pattern characteristic of such individuals, whether it be cocaine abusers, infertile women, Hare Krishna devotees, head trauma patients, deep sea divers, shoplifters, or medical students (among many others). In the medical and psychiatric fields, such studies often suffer from the lack of empirical support for their assumption that these personality patterns are

risk factors for the particular problem syndrome rather than the result of it; more prospective studies are needed to address this issue. While group profiles are useful in contrasting different diagnostic groups to search for salient differences, group profiles tend to hide the large individual variation in personality types within particular diagnostic labels, ethnic groups, occupations, or other defined groups of individuals.

Fortunately, as in the alcohol and drug abuse literature, there is a growing trend to take individual differences into account by searching for distinctive personality subgroups within an overall diagnostic label. The latter approach, used in applications such as predicting surgery outcome for back pain patients, tries to identify subgroups of patients suffering from a particular physical disorder who share a common etiology or a common problem constellation. The hope is that particular patient subgroups might benefit differentially from treatment packages different from those most useful for other patients with another pattern of contributing factors. Although studies are still being conducted to discriminate *functional* medical problems from *organic* ones, the majority consensus these days is that personality instruments are not very useful in making such a black-and-white distinction. They may be more useful in describing a constellation of personality factors, coping styles, psychiatric problems, and physical complaints with implications for treatment planning.

Research on MMPI use in forensic settings has burgeoned in the last few years. Typological systems and special scales have been developed to predict recidivism, assess potential aggressiveness, and judge the legal competence of felons. Prediction of institutional adjustment using the MMPI-based Megargee classification of personality types (Megargee & Bohn, 1977) has received some further validational work, and other scales and configural rules have been researched as descriptors of major subtypes within the "criminal personality." In a somewhat related area of relevance to public safety, there is a growing body of research on the utility of personality tests in screening for highly stressful, highly responsible occupations such as police officer or airline pilot.

Efficiency and brevity of assessment are always of concern to practitioners and researchers. The literature reflects constant development of new instruments, or new scales from old instruments, designed to improve assessment of a particular area of interest. As Evans (1983) noted in his review of trends in the research published by the *Journal of Personality Assessment* over a 15-year span, the majority of these procedures disappear from sight after an initial published description. A particularly popular area for many years has been the effort to shorten the MMPI into a more efficient form. Several short forms continue to be used as criterion measures of psychological functioning, despite the general lack of external validity data justifying their use as equivalent forms of the MMPI (see cautions against short form use by Hoffman & Butcher, 1975; Streiner & Miller, 1986). Most of the studies we examined still evaluated the validity of short forms through correlations with long form scores, rather than looking at whether similar clinical decisions would be made based on the short versus long forms. Increasingly, clinical procedures are being streamlined by using computerized forms of many objective personality tests. The literature exploring the validity of such automated systems is certainly on the rise, but still all too scanty. The most extensive research program to evaluate computer-based interpretive reports has been conducted by Eyde, Kowal, and Fishburne (1987). Their article should serve as a model for future validity research.

Despite the age-old call for shorter, faster methods of assessment, the past few years have shown an interesting increase in studies advocating the combination of two or more personality instruments (such as the MMPI and MCMI) to provide a more thorough and detailed assessment than might be available from either test alone. If this trend truly reflects the needs of clinicians and their willingness to invest more time and energy to obtain greater accuracy of assessment, criticisms of the length of tests such as the MMPI may not be representative of most practitioners' views.

The research and clinical areas mentioned above provide a sample of the broad and varied current uses of objective personality instruments. Many other more specific studies were reported, and other topic areas, such as adolescent adjustment, family problems, relationship of personality test indices to other psychometric test data, prediction of response to psychopharmacologic treatment, custody evaluation, etc., are too numerous to explore in this brief survey.

Status of the MMPI

In the 10 years since Butcher and Owen (1978) published their survey of objective personality assessment, the MMPI has continued to be the most widely used and researched personality assessment instrument. Butcher and Owen found that 84% of the articles published between 1972 and 1977 employing a major clinical objective personality test utilized a 40-year-old inventory: the MMPI. Butcher and Keller (1984) found the same pattern was maintained between 1978 and 1982: 87% of the articles they surveyed utilized the MMPI. In both reviews, the 16PF came in a not-very-close second, and the newer DPI and MCMI had extremely little published research to validate their practical utility, beyond the original empirical studies the authors had utilized in constructing the tests.

In reviewing the literature since Butcher and Owen's survey, we found that the MMPI continues its strong domination of the published literature. This pattern varies a bit by population studied and focus of research; tests such as the 16PF and PRF are used most widely in normal populations and in more basic research on personality structure or descriptions of the intercorrelations of various personality measures. They may be viewed as more elegant instruments, both psychometrically and theoretically, than the MMPI, and their use in academic research probably reflects this. However, in clinical settings the extensive empirical validation literature on the MMPI is continuing to make it the most popular instrument. For practical decision-making applications, such validity data are essential, and are still largely missing on other objective personality instruments. Fortunately, in the past few years there has been a growing body of clinical research literature exploring the validity and utility of the MCMI, with some researchers finding it to be a very useful alternative or supplement to the MMPI in their settings. It is to be hoped that this trend will continue, with other instruments as well as the MCMI, so that psychologists will be able to make informed choices of appropriate assessment devices to be used for their particular purposes.

THE MMPI: AN EXAMPLE OF TEST EVOLUTION

The discussion above shows clearly that despite new developments in test construction that may hold promise for the future, the contemporary status of objective personality assessment is still largely synonymous with the contemporary status of the MMPI. There are several hundred new publications a year on the MMPI and the number of clinical applications involving the test appears to be growing substantially. Accordingly, we will discuss this cornerstone of contemporary objective personality measurement in more detail.

The MMPI, in one instrument, provides an example of the process of objective test development and the evolution of scale development and interpretive techniques over time. The story is largely one of adapting a preexisting instrument to the ever-changing needs of clinicians and researchers during the past four decades, a process which is continuing with the current development of the revised MMPI (MMPI-2). It is to the original authors' credit that this 45-year-old instrument has continued to prove useful for so many applications so far removed from its original purpose. Although the MMPI is classified as an empirically keyed test, the next sections make it clear that MMPI use has spanned all methods of objective test development and thus provides a good example of the practical integration of many approaches to objective personality assessment.

Original Item and Scale Development

In 1940 Hathaway and McKinley published the first of a number of articles detailing the development of a new paper-and-pencil personality test, the Minnesota Multiphasic Personality Inventory (MMPI), devised as an objective means of obtaining clinical-diagnostic information about clients in psychiatric and general medical settings (see Dahlstrom & Dahlstrom, 1980, for a collection of historically important articles on the MMPI). For the most part, scale development for the MMPI was empirical. The items selected for the scales were obtained, not according to some theoretical plan of the test developers, but through empirical item-analysis procedures designed to maximize discrimination between various predefined psychiatric groups versus "normal" individuals. The collection of scales was chosen to assess clinically relevant syndromes such as depression, hypochondriasis, sociopathy, schizophrenia, and hypomania, and to aid the clinician in arriving at a clinical diagnosis based on the diagnostic categories being used in the 1940s.

Unlike most personality inventories in existence at the time, the final selection of items for the MMPI scales followed a stringent empirical approach. However, the overall design of the MMPI cannot be called purely empirical, as selection of the original item pool was guided by preexisting ideas of appropriate content areas and themes relevant to psychiatric classification. The test authors initially collected over 1,000 items from a variety of sources such as clinical cases, textbooks, and previously published tests. These items were reduced to a pool of 504 items by eliminating those that the authors felt were redundant or were not considered promising for other reasons (again not a particularly empirical method). This reduced item pool was then administered to a group of individuals referred to as the "Minnesota normals": mostly visitors to the University of Minnesota Hospital not presently under a doctor's care, augmented by a group

of students attending conferences at the university, some medical patients, and a group of Work Progress Administration workers. The clinical scales were developed by determining which items differentiated the "normal" group from various clinical reference groups. These reference groups were composed of University of Minnesota Hospital psychiatric patients who had been diagnosed as having the symptoms or the problems defined by the diagnostic categories in use at the time, for example hysteria or psychasthenia. Care was taken in the accumulation of clinical cases to assure that the clinical problems within each group were homogeneous and clearly defined by the diagnostic criteria used in the study. Eight clinical scales were constructed by this method of contrasted groups: *Hs* (Hypochondriasis), *D* (Depression), *Hy* (Hysteria), *Pd* (Psychopathic Deviate), *Pa* (Paranoia), *Pt* (Psychasthenia), *Sc* (Schizophrenia), and *Ma* (Hypomania).

Hathaway and McKinley also departed from standard practice at the time by building several validity checks into their instrument from the beginning. Self-report instruments are notoriously vulnerable to invalidating effects of the subject's test-taking style or attitude, and almost every contemporary test includes one or more validity checks. In the MMPI, the "cannot say" scale is simply the total number of items which were not answered or were answered in both directions; too high a score lowers the scores on all scales and calls the validity of the test into question. The *L* scale (for "lie") was a rationally constructed scale, composed of items designed to tap an individual's unwillingness to admit to even commonly held, minor faults. The *F* scale measures deviance of responses compared to the normative sample; it is composed of items which less than 10% of the "Minnesota normals" answered in the keyed direction. Finally, the *K* scale was designed to identify subtle clinical defensiveness. It is the only validity scale in the MMPI to have been constructed empirically by the method of contrasted groups. A group of people with known psychopathology but normal MMPI profiles was compared with a group of nonpatients with normal profiles. The resulting *K* scale was later used to develop correction factors for defensiveness for several of the clinical scales (McKinley, Hathaway, & Meehl, 1948).

Two extra clinical scales, *Mf* (Masculinity/Femininity) and *Si* (Social Introversion), were added to the MMPI later. The *Si* scale was developed by Drake (1946) by contrasting socially participative female college students with other college women who were not involved in many extracurricular activities. *Mf* was originally designed to distinguish between homosexual and heterosexual men, but few items were found to work for this purpose. Hathaway and McKinely broadened this scale by adding items which distinguished between heterosexual men and women, and also added new items from a sex differences scale designed by Terman and Miles (1936). The addition of this scale brought the total number of items in the full MMPI to 550. (The total number of items in the Group Form booklet of the MMPI is 566, due to the inclusion of 16 repeated items. Although many clinicians and patients assume that these items represent an extra validity check, they were actually included only because their placement on the form made scoring simpler.)

Administration and Scoring of the MMPI

In most situations the MMPI is administered with a reusable booklet form (either the Group Form or Form R) and an answer sheet which can be either hand scored or machine scored. Other administration formats are available for special circumstances and include the original box form (each item is printed on a card and the subject is required to sort the cards into groups according to whether the items are true or false), audio forms for those with reading difficulties, foreign translations, and computer-administered versions. In the latter category, Richards, Fine, Wilson, and Rogers (1983) have even described "a voice recognition system developed to allow patients with no hand function to take the MMPI independently" (p. 167).

Raw scores for each MMPI scale are found by counting the number of item responses made in the keyed direction for that scale. Often several of the raw scores are "corrected" for defensiveness with a proportion of the K-scale value which has become a standard part of MMPI scoring procedure. Raw scores are then transformed into T-score units when they are plotted on the profile sheet (See Figure 16.1 for a sample MMPI-2 profile. The raw scores are noted across the bottom). Traditional MMPI T-scores are non-normalized standard scores with a mean of 50 and standard deviation of 10, based on the score distributions of the "Minnesota normal" sample. T-scores can also be computed using other normative groups as the reference population. The MMPI-2 incorporates a new nationally representative normative sample, and T-scores are computed using a new "uniform" transformation procedure which makes score levels more easily comparable across scales (Butcher, Dahlstrom,

Graham, Tellegen, & Kaemmer, 1989). T-score conversion tables also have been published based on norms for specific age groups, ethnic or racial groups, or for countries other than the United States (cf. Butcher & Pancheri, 1976; Colligan, Osborne, Swenson, & Offord, 1984; Dahlstrom, Lachar, & Dahlstrom, 1986; Dahlstrom, Welsh, & Dahlstrom, 1972). Scale elevations above two standard deviations from the mean (a score elevated above a T-score of 70) are generally considered clinically significant on the original MMPI. On the revised MMPI-2, the new normative group and T-scores lower this "clinically significant" cutoff to 65 (Butcher, Dahlstrom, Graham, Tellegen, & Kaemmer, 1989). (It should be noted that the normative tables provided by Colligan et al. use normalized T-scores rather than the traditional non-normalized standard scores, and thus are not easily interpretable using the extensive body of research based on the latter (Hsu, 1984; Miller & Streiner, 1986). Colligan and colleagues have been publishing research which will aid in direct interpretation of their normalized T-scores; in the meantime, their provision of a method to convert normalized T-scores back to linear scores may help in applying standard interpretive rules to their data [Osborne & Colligan, 1986].)

As with many other tests, computer scoring of MMPI records is becoming increasingly popular. There are several approaches to computer scoring of the subject's responses. Printed answer sheets can be key punched onto data cards or optically scanned and stored on a magnetic data tape, then entered into a scoring program. Alternatively, subject responses can be scored as the subject is taking the test interactively. Computer scoring, interpretation, and administration of objective personality tests such as the MMPI will be discussed in more detail later in this chapter and in Hanaker and Fowler's chapter in this handbook.

Subsequent Developments

Initially it was thought that simple scale elevations would directly reflect psychopathology measured by the individual MMPI scales. For example, depressed patients would be expected to show elevations on the Depression scale but not on the Schizophrenia scale. However, it was soon apparent that the MMPI did not perform very well as a means of classifying patients into strict diagnostic groups. Patients with elevations on one scale tended also to have elevations on other scales, some psychiatric patients did not have significant elevations on the appropriate scales, and some "normal" individuals did have elevations on one or more scales. As Graham (1987) notes, over-time

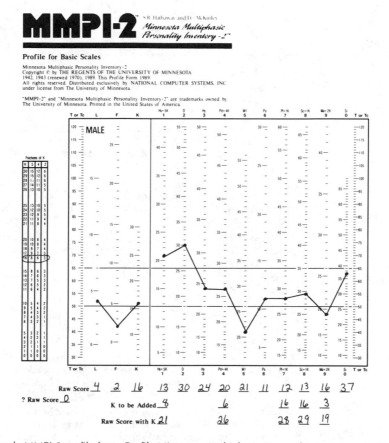

Figure 16.1. Sample MMPI-2 profile form. Profile Minnesota Multiphasic Personality Inventory-2. Copyright © by the Regents of the University of Minnesota 1942, 1943 (renewed 1970), 1989. This profile from 1989. Reproduced by permission of the publisher, the University of Minnesota Press.

interpretation of the MMPI has moved away from treating each scale as a measure of a known psychopathological category, instead of adopting a purely empirical approach:

> the MMPI is currently used in a way quite different from the way in which it was originally intended to be used. It is assumed that the clinical scales are measuring something, because reliable differences in scores are found among individuals from different reference groups. The new approach treats each MMPI scale as an unknown and, through experience and empirical research, the correlates of each scale are identified. When a person obtains a score on a particular scale, the clinician attributes to that person the characteristics and behaviors that through previous research and experience have been identified for other individuals with similar scores on that scale. . . . It is this new behavioral description approach to the utilization of the MMPI in everyday practice that

has led to the instrument's great popularity among practicing clinicians. (pp. 7–8)

As a result of this changing emphasis in MMPI interpretation, the 10 clinical scales are now usually referred to by numbers rather than by their original names (see Table 16.1).

Configural Interpretation.

The empirical correlate approach to interpretation of individual scales has also been expanded to interpretation of the overall pattern of scale scores obtained by an individual. Partly because of the intercorrelation among scales, but also presumably because of the overlap among characteristics of clinical syndromes, it was often found that several MMPI scales would be elevated together. Interpretation of a particular scale might vary depending on the relative elevations of

Table 16.1. Summary of Correlates of the MMPI Validity, Clinical, and Selected Special Scales

MMPI SCALE	SCALE CORRELATES
Validity Scales	
? (Cannot Say)	The number of items not answered or answered in both directions. A defensive or invalid profile with possible attenuation of scale scores is suggested if the ? raw score is 30 or more.
L (Lie)	Measures a rather unsophisticated or self-consciously "virtuous" test-taking attitude. Elevated scores suggest that the individual is presenting himself or herself in an overly positive light, attempting to create an unrealistically favorable view of his or her adjustment.
F (Infrequency)	Items on this scale are answered very infrequently by most people. A high score suggests not only an exaggerated pattern of symptom checking that is inconsistent with accurate self-appraisal, but also confusion, disorganization, or actual faking of mental illness.
K (Defensiveness)	High scores reflect an uncooperative attitude and an unwillingness or reluctance to disclose personal information or problems. Low scores suggest openness and frankness. *K* is positively correlated with intelligence and educational level, which should be taken into account in interpretation.
Clinical Scales	
1 (*Hs*, Hypochondriasis)	High scorers present numerous vague physical problems that tend to be chronic. They are generally unhappy, self-centered, whiney, complaining, hostile, and attention-seeking in their behavior.
2 (*D*, Depression)	Reflects depressed mood, low self-esteem, and feelings of inadequacy. High scorers are described as moody, despondent, pessimistic, distressed, high-strung, lethargic, over-controlled, and guilt-prone. Elevations may reflect great discomfort and need for change or symptomatic relief.
3 (*Hy*, Hysteria)	High scorers tend to rely on neurotic defenses such as denial and repression to deal with stress. They tend to be dependent, naive, outgoing, infantile, and narcissistic. Their interpersonal relations are often disrupted, and they show little insight into problems. High scorers show little interest in psychological processes and interpret psychological problems as physical ones. High levels of stress are often accompanied by the development of physical symptoms.
4 (*Pd*, Psychopathic Deviate)	Measures antisocial behavior, such as rebelliousness, disrupted family relations, impulsiveness, difficulties with school or work, legal involvement, and alcohol or drug abuse. Personality disorders are likely among high scorers: they are outgoing, sociable, and likeable as well as deceptive, manipulative, hedonistic, exhibitionistic, inclined toward poor judgment, unreliable, immature, hostile and aggressive. High scores usually reflect long-standing character problems that are highly resistant to change.
5 (*Mf*, Masculinity-Femininity)	High-scoring men are described as sensitive, aesthetic, passive, or feminine. They may show conflicts over sexual identity and low heterosexual drive. Low scoring men are viewed as masculine, aggressive, crude, adventurous, reckless, practical, and having narrow interests. Because the direction of scoring is reversed, high-scoring women are seen as masculine, rough, aggressive, self-confident, unemotional, and insensitive. Low-scoring women are viewed as passive, yielding, complaining, fault-finding, idealistic, and sensitive.
6 (*Pa*, Paranoia)	Elevations on this scale are often associated with being suspicious, aloof, shrewd, guarded, worrying, and overly sensitive. High scorers may project or externalize blame and harbor grudges against others. They are generally hostile and argumentative.
7 (*Pt*, Psychasthenia)	High scorers are tense, anxious, ruminative, obsessional, phobic, and rigid. They frequently are self-condemning and guilt prone, feel inferior and inadequate, overintellectualize and rationalize problems, and resist psychological interpretations.

Table 16.1. Summary of Correlates of the MMPI Validity, Clinical, and Selected Special Scales (*Continued*)

MMPI SCALE	SCALE CORRELATES
8 (*Sc*, Schizophrenia)	High scorers have an unconventional, schizoid life-style. They are withdrawn, shy, moody, and feel inadequate, tense, and confused. They may have unusual or strange thoughts, poor judgment, and erratic moods. Very high scorers may evince poor reality contact, bizarre sensory experiences, delusions, and hallucinations. They are generally uninformed and have poor problem-solving skills.
9 (*Ma*, Hypomania)	High scorers are viewed as sociable, outgoing, impulsive, overly energetic, and optimistic. They have liberal moral views, are flighty, may drink excessively, are grandiose, irritable, impatient, and rarely "follow through" with their plans. They are manipulative and exaggerate their self-worth. Very high scorers may show affective disorder, bizarre behavior, erratic mood, impulsive behavior, and delusions.
0 (*Si*, Social Introversion)	High scorers are viewed as introverted, shy, withdrawn, socially reserved, submissive, overcontrolled, lethargic, conventional, tense, inflexible, and guilt-prone. Low scorers are extroverted, outgoing, gregarious, expressive, aggressive, talkative, impulsive, uninhibited, spontaneous, manipulative, opportunistic, and insincere in social relations.
Special Scales	
A (Anxiety)	This scale defines the first and the largest factor dimension in the MMPI. It measures general maladjustment or emotional upset. High scores reflect anxiety, tension, lack of efficiency, and open expression of numerous psychological complaints.
R (Repression)	This factor scale relates to reliance on denial and repression. High scores reflect uninsightful, overcontrolled, and inhibited behavior. These individuals tend to avoid problems and appear overly conventional.
Es (Ego Strength)	This scale was originally developed to predict successful response to psychotherapy. Subsequent research has shown it to be an indicator of a person's overall level of functioning. High scores reflect effective functioning and the ability to withstand stress. Such individuals tend to have psychological resources that will help them to cope with problems.
MAC (MacAndrew Addiction)	This scale was developed to distinguish alcoholic from non-alcoholic psychiatric patients. High scores are also associated with other addictive problems such as drug abuse and pathological gambling; *MAC* serves as a measure of addiction-proneness.

Adapted from University of Minnesota Press (1984), *User's Guide for the Minnesota Report: Personnel Selection System*. Minneapolis, MN: Author.

other scales in the profile. Clinicians found that individuals with common MMPI profile patterns were often similar in terms of manifest problems, symptoms, and personality characteristics. The pattern or *configural approach* to MMPI interpretation came to be the preferred interpretive strategy (Halbower, 1955; Meehl, 1954). Several subsequent research programs have delineated actuarially based empirical descriptions of various MMPI patterns referred to as *code types*. For example, the individual whose profile is shown in Figure 16.1 has highest scale elevations on scales 2 (originally Depression) and 1 (originally Hypochondriasis), and therefore would be classified as

a 2–1. Correlates of this pattern could be looked up in one of many so-called cookbooks listing research results (Dahlstrom, Welsh, & Dahlstrom, 1972; Gilberstadt & Duker, 1965; Graham, 1987; Greene, 1980; Lachar, 1974; Lewandowski & Graham, 1972; Marks, Seeman, & Haller, 1974; Nelson & Marks, 1985). This work serves as the empirical basis of objective MMPI profile interpretation.

Another strategy for MMPI interpretation which combines information from several scales is the use of *objective rules* or *objective indices* to arrive at clinical decisions. This interpretive approach can use either actuarially derived discrimination rules such as the

Goldberg Index (Goldberg, 1965) or clinically compiled classification rules such as the Henrichs Rules (Henrichs, 1964, 1966) or the Meehl-Dahlstrom Rules (Meehl & Dahlstrom, 1960), designed to distinguish between neurotics and psychotics. In this approach the test interpreter, after scoring the record and drawing the profile, computes the index or classifies the profile according to the decision rules. For example, the Goldberg Index is computed by adding scales *L, Pa,* and *Sc* together and then subtracting scales *Hy* and *Pt* to get an index of the likelihood the patient is psychotic. As another example, if classification rules for combining scale scores confirm that a correctional inmate meets Megargee's "I" classification in his system for grouping criminal offenders (Megargee & Bohn, 1977), then the correlates and predictions relevant to that felony group would be applied to the case. An advantage of the objective classification approach is that it can readily be applied by a clerical worker or by a computer. Often, in fact, the rules become so complicated that automation is a distinct advantage in utilizing the research on such configural combinations.

Content-based Interpretation.

Although early MMPI research developments and clinical applications emphasized empirical correlates and objective interpretation of profiles, there were also advocates of *content-based interpretation* (Grayson, 1951; Harris & Lingoes, 1968; Koss & Butcher, 1973; Wiggins, 1969). Content interpretation takes us back to the rational method of test construction and interpretation; it assumes that the subject, in answering test items, is reacting and responding openly and directly to the item meaning and content. Consequently, the content of MMPI items might represent an important source of information that is not available through empirical test interpretation procedures. Several approaches to interpretation of MMPI content have been developed.

1. The *factor-analytic* approach. Several researchers have attempted to develop keys for factor dimensions within either the entire MMPI or within specific scales. Welsh (1956) and Block (1965) developed factor scales by intercorrelating the standard MMPI scales; their two primary factors are now scored by many clinicians and researchers as "*A*" (anxiety) and "*R*" (repression). Content-consistent subscales for *Mf* and *Si* were developed by Serkownek (see Schuerger, Foerstner, Serkownek, & Ritz, 1987) based on factor analyses of the items in these two scales. Others (cf. Comrey, 1957; Costa, Zonderman, McCrae, & Williams, 1985; Johnson, Butcher, Null, & Johnson,

1984; Stein, 1968) attempted to factor analyze the MMPI using item intercorrelations to arrive at homogeneous factor scales. While the factor analytic approach is not specifically oriented toward obtaining "pure" content dimensions, the research has produced a number of scales with homogeneous content.

2. The *rational* approach to content analysis. Several efforts to develop content scales by rational analysis have been attempted. One set of content scales, the Harris-Lingoes subscales for the MMPI (Harris & Lingoes, 1968), has become widely used in clinical and computerized MMPI interpretation. The Harris-Lingoes subscales are subsets of MMPI items on several MMPI scales: *D, Hy, Pd, Pa, Sc,* and *Ma.* The subscales were developed by reading through the items and placing "similar" items into content groups. A more systematic approach to developing content scales (Wiggins, 1969) included all of the MMPI items in the pool of potential contents and developed 13 homogeneous content scales for the MMPI. These scales are *HEA* (Health), *DEP* (Depression), *ORG* (Organic Symptoms), *FAM* (Family Problems), *AUT* (Authority Conflict), *FEM* (Feminine Interests), *REL* (Religious Fundamentalism), *HOS* (Manifest Hostility), *MOR* (Poor Morale), *PHO* (Phobias), *PSY* (Psychoticism), *HYP* (Hypomania), and *SOC* (Social Maladjustment). High scores on the content scales reflect high degrees of endorsement of the themes represented in the content scales. However, there have been relatively few studies establishing empirical correlates for the content scales. Thus, their interpretation must be based primarily upon rational or intuitive analysis of the scales by examining the "meanings" of the content dimensions reflected in the elevated scale.

3. The *critical item* approach to content interpretation. This approach assumes that individuals disclose personal problems through their response to individual items and suggests that certain item groups are more significant than others for reflecting important problem areas. Grayson (1951) first recommended the use of specific MMPI items as important signs of psychopathology. The items he suggested as "critical" for the assessment of psychopathology have been referred to as the "MMPI Critical Items," and have received widespread use despite the lack of empirical verification of their validity as problem indices. More recently Koss and Butcher (1973; Koss, Butcher & Hoffman, 1976), and Lachar and Wrobel (1979) have published empirically based critical items. The use of such critical items for fleshing out MMPI interpretations has gained wide acceptance. Although there are some problems with this interpretive approach (Koss, 1980), particularly the low reliability of single items,

this content-based procedure may add considerably to the empirical method of test interpretation.

Interpretation of special scales.

Current research and practice with the MMPI rely primarily on use of the validity scales, the clinical scales, the content scales and a number of special or experimental scales. Several hundred additional scales have been developed for the MMPI, primarily for specific purposes, such as measuring personality or behavioral characteristics like dominance or prejudice, or for predicting various symptom patterns such as drug abuse or chronic pain syndrome. Most of these additional scales have not attained wide use or acceptability. However, a few of the special scales have been widely researched and used clinically. Some of these experimental scales are the Ego Strength Scale (*Es*), a measure of tolerance for stress or ego strength (Barron, 1953); the Welsh Anxiety Scale (*A*), a factor scale designed as a measure of general maladjustment or anxiety (Welsh, 1956); the Welsh Repression Scale (*R*), another factor scale designed as a measure of overcontrol; and the MacAndrew Alcoholism Scale (*Mac*), a measure of an individual's proneness to addiction (MacAndrew, 1965). Table 16.1 provides a brief description of the basic validity and clinical scales for the MMPI, along with these four special scales. More detailed description of the many MMPI scales and scale combinations can be found in a number of useful texts (cf. Dahlstrom, Welsh, & Dahlstrom, 1972, 1975; Duckworth & Anderson, 1986; Graham, 1987; Greene, 1980).

It should be apparent that interpretation of the MMPI is a complicated process that requires professional training and access to a large amount of actuarial data. Later in this chapter we will illustrate the integration and application of all these interpretive methods to the case in Figure 16.1, through a report generated by the second author's computerized interpretive system.

Revision and Restandardization of the MMPI

In their overview of recent developments in the use of the MMPI, Butcher and Owen (1978) noted a number of problems and criticisms of the MMPI. Some of these problems involved the MMPI itself and centered around the apparent need for a revision and restandardization of the inventory; other problems involved the relative inactivity on the part of the test distributor in keeping up with the existing MMPI technology and in failing to provide necessary interpretive materials that had been developed for the MMPI. The problems cited included the need to update and broaden the MMPI item pool; the need for a new standardization of normal responses on a broader, more representative contemporary normative sample; and the need for more flexibility and willingness on the part of the test distributor to provide relevant test materials.

Since that review by Butcher and Owen a number of changes have taken place in the publication and distribution of the MMPI that may serve to rectify some of these problems. The major administrative change was that the University of Minnesota Press, the MMPI copyright holder, resumed responsibility for research and development of the instrument. The University Press contracted with National Computer Systems of Minneapolis to be the licensed distributor of the MMPI and to develop new profile sheets, scoring sheets, and other MMPI related materials to enhance clinical use of the test. The profile form illustrated in Figure 16.1 is an example of these updated materials.

In 1982 the University of Minnesota Press initiated a major research effort to revise, update, and restandardize the MMPI (Butcher, Graham, Dahlstrom, Tellegen, & Kaemmer, 1989). Some of the goals set for the redevelopment of the MMPI were the following:

1. To maintain the integrity of the existing validity, clinical and widely used special scales of the test.

2. To revise and reword the language of some of the existing items that were out of date, awkward, sexist, etc. Over the years language use has changed, and the content of some of the MMPI items has become antiquated.

3. To broaden the item pool to include other contents not now represented—for example, treatment compliance, amenability to change, relationship problems, work attitudes, etc.

4. To develop new, up-to-date norms for the MMPI. The original "Minnesota normals" represented a small, regional, somewhat parochial sample of adults living 40 years ago. Regional normative samples collected in North Carolina by Diehl (1977) and in southern Minnesota by Colligan et al. (1984) have indicated that the old norms are probably not representative of response patterns of contemporary "normal" people, but no nationwide standardization had ever been undertaken.

5. To include separate forms of the MMPI for adults and adolescents. New items were included for the adolescent form of the MMPI that are specific to problems of adolescents.

The MMPI project committee (James Butcher of the University of Minnesota, Grant Dahlstrom of the University of North Carolina, Jack Graham of Kent State University, and Auke Tellegen of the University of Minnesota) chose to conduct a program of research that was both conservative and expansive in scope: goals were to maintain the integrity of the original instrument while expanding its range of coverage, utility, and acceptability to clients.

To insure continuity with the original MMPI and its extensive research base, the committee decided to include the entire existing MMPI item pool (550 items) in the experimental booklet so that the original items and scales could be studied in modern samples of normals. It was possible for users involved in the restandardization research to continue to score and interpret the original MMPI scales while collecting responses on the new instrument. The 16 repeated items in the original MMPI were deleted and replaced with new items described below. This change would not affect scoring of the basic MMPI scales, as the repetitions were not scored in the original MMPI. About 14% of the original items were changed because of dated language or content, sexist or otherwise objectionable wording, or awkward grammar. In a few instances where items were so out of date as to be meaningless, new items were substituted. However, for comparison purposes, the original item was retained (along with the rewritten version) in the experimental booklets. Analyses presented by Ben-Porath and Butcher (1988) revealed that out of 82 rewritten items, only nine showed significant differences in endorsement percentage when compared to their original version, and none of these differences held across both sexes. Rewriting the items did not change any item-scale correlations significantly, and so had no real effect on the psychometric characteristics of the MMPI.

In addition to retaining the original items, some in updated form, the experimental MMPI booklet was expanded by the addition of 154 new items designed to address problem areas not well represented in the original version of the test. These additional items were selected rationally, through a broad sampling of views of MMPI experts as to which content domains needed further coverage. The separate adolescent form of the experimental MMPI booklet also contained the original 550 MMPI items, 50 new items dealing with treatment amenability, and 104 new items designed to provide better coverage of concerns and problems specific to adolescents.

The official MMPI-2 restandardization project involved an extensive collection of new MMPI, bio-graphical, demographic, and life event data on a *national* normative sample of adults (N = 2,600) and adolescents (still being tested). The new subject population for the MMPI-2 was obtained through a sampling of normal volunteers from several regions of the United States: Minnesota, Ohio, North Carolina, Pennsylvania, Washington, Virginia, and California. Efforts were made to obtain a sample representative of the U.S. population by matching sample characteristics to major demographic characteristics reported in the 1980 census. For a large subsample of the adult population, both members of married couples were tested and were asked to fill out behavioral and personality ratings of each other as well as assessing their marital relationship. The extra forms used in the national standardization provided descriptive data and MMPI response correlates that were not available for the original Minnesota normative sample.

The new norms for the MMPI obtained from this national sample will be eased into use in a conservative fashion. Clinicians and researchers will be provided with materials to allow direct comparison between old and new norms to insure continuity of interpretive strategies and research data. The MMPI-2 manual presents tables facilitating such comparisons (Butcher et al., 1989). Although the MMPI-2 booklet contains some of the new, experimental items which clinical studies have shown to be promising, the items contained in the original MMPI validity and clinical scales will be placed at the beginning of the booklet for those individuals who wish to use only the original scales.

Over time, however, it is likely that users will find many of the new inclusions in the MMPI-2 to be as useful or even more useful than the original MMPI scales. For example, content interpretation of the MMPI has been expanded and improved by the development of several new MMPI-2 content scales which include the dimensions represented by new items in the MMPI-2 item pool (See Table 16-2: Butcher, Graham, Williams, & Ben-Porath, 1989). These scales were developed by a multistage, multimethod approach starting with rational item groupings and then proceeding through statistical item-selection techniques to improve individual scale homogeneity and reduce scale intercorrelations. A number of studies aimed at testing and validating these scales against contemporary clinical populations have been conducted (Graham & Butcher, 1988; Keller & Butcher, in press). Some of the new items have already been shown to improve the discrimination of existing scales as well as to provide new content for assessing other problem areas. We will likely find, as new clinical

Table 16.2. MMPI-2 Content Scales

SCALE	DESCRIPTION OF CONTENT AND CORRELATES
ANX (*Anxiety*)	General symptoms of anxiety and tension; sleep and concentration problems; somatic correlates of anxiety; excessive worrying; difficulty making decisions; willingness to admit to these problems.
FRS (*Fears*)	Many specific fears and phobias including animals, high places, insects, blood, fire, storms, water, the dark, being indoors, dirt, etc.
OBS (*Obsessiveness*)	Excessive rumination, difficulty making decisions, compulsive behaviors, rigidity, feelings of being overwhelmed.
DEP (*Depression*)	Depressive thoughts, anhedonia, feelings of hopelessness and uncertainty, possible suicidal thoughts.
HEA (*Health Concerns*)	Many physical symptoms across several body systems: gastrointestinal, neurological, sensory, cardiovascular, dermatological, and respiratory. Reports of pain and of general worries about health.
BIZ (*Bizarre Mentation*)	Psychotic thought processes, auditory, visual, or olfactory hallucinations, paranoid ideation, delusions.
ANG (*Anger*)	Anger control problems, irritability, impatience, loss of control, past or potential abusiveness.
CYN (*Cynicism*)	Misanthropic beliefs, negative expectations about the motives of others, generalized distrust.
ASP (*Antisocial Practices*)	Cynical attitudes; problem behaviors; trouble with the law, stealing, belief in getting around rules and laws for personal gain.
TPA (*Type A*)	Hard-driving, work-oriented behavior; impatience; irritability; annoyance; feelings of time pressure; interpersonally overbearing.
LSE (*Low Self Esteem*)	Low self-worth; overwhelming feelings of being unlikable, unimportant, unattractive, useless, etc.
SOD (*Social Discomfort*)	Uneasiness around others; shyness; preference for being alone.
FAM (*Family Problems*)	Family discord, possible abuse in childhood, lack of love and affection in the family or marriage, feelings of hate for family members.
WRK (*Work Interference*)	Behaviors or attitudes likely to interfere with work performance, such as low self esteem, obsessiveness, tension, poor decision making, lack of family support, negative attitudes towards career or coworkers.
TRT (*Negative Treatment Indicators*)	Negative attitudes toward doctors and mental health treatment. Preference for giving up rather than attempting change. Discomfort discussing any personal concerns.

(Adapted from Butcher, Graham, Williams, and Ben-Porath, 1989)

populations are studied, that new items and scale-development strategies will add to and sometimes even replace traditional approaches to MMPI use.

Comments

MMPI scale development and interpretive strategies have increasingly incorporated methods, such as content analysis and factor analysis, that range far from the test's original empirical-criterion-keyed roots. However, the rationale for inclusion of these new methods and for revision of such tried-and-true personality tests remains the same: to provide a more efficient, accurate, reliable, and valid tool to aid psychologists in research and practical decision making. Many of the new developments with the MMPI, as well as with other objective personality tests, would not have been possible without the aid of another tool: the computer. The next sections will focus on the increasingly integral role of automation in the contemporary and future status of objective personality assessment technology.

AUTOMATED OBJECTIVE
PERSONALITY ASSESSMENT

In 1981, Greist and Klein reported that although 70% of state departments of mental health and 50% of community mental health centers used computers, very few of these employed them for clinical uses. Instead, computer technology had been introduced to meet management needs for information on resources, materials, facilities, staff, finances, patient population characteristics, and services provided. Such administrative and fiscal operations traditionally have been viewed as more amenable to automation than the less understood, less structured, and less specific techniques of clinical practice. Nevertheless, the literature of the past few years clearly demonstrates the growing use of computers as tools to aid in clinical as well as administrative decision making.

Johnson, Giannetti, and Williams (1976) described the history of computer use in mental-health care delivery as a progression from (a) automated patient data systems to (b) development of automated clinical techniques to (c) the development of interventionally relevant, decision-oriented strategies. Early computer applications (such as patient data management, test scoring, and interpretive programs designed to mimic traditional clinical practice) capitalized primarily on the speed, objectivity, and enormous memory capacity of the computer. More recent innovative applications have begun to utilize the flexibility and unique adaptive capabilities of computers, modifying old assessment strategies and developing new ones.

Automated Test Scoring
and Interpretation

Automated scoring of objective test answer sheets was one of the first clinical applications of computer technology, followed by computerized interpretation of standard psychological tests. Objective personality inventories are particularly amenable to automation because of their limited, structured response options and because of the standardized interpretive rules for these tests. The computer can store and access a much larger fund of interpretive literature and base-rate data than any individual clinician can master, contributing to the accuracy, objectivity, reliability, and validity of computerized reports. While any single clinician may do well to learn the norms and base rates of the client population he or she sees most often, a computer program can refer to a variety of population norms and, if programmed to do so, will always "remember" to tailor interpretive statements according to modify-ing demographic data such as education, marital status, and ethnicity.

Rome, Swenson, and colleagues (1962) at the Mayo Clinic developed the first computerized scoring and interpretive system for the MMPI. Since that time, their system has been expanded and many other, more complicated computerized interpretive systems have been developed, not only for the MMPI but also for instruments such as the 16PF (Karson & O'Dell, 1975, 1987), the MCMI (Millon, 1982, 1987), and even "a system of automated interpretation of coded visual-motor responses elicited by horizontally symmetrical, ambiguous, and indeterminate visual stimuli, i.e., by the ten Rorschach inkblots" (Piotrowski, 1980, p. 85; see also Exner, 1987). Hanaker and Fowler's chapter in this handbook provides a more thorough discussion of computerized interpretive systems. Reviews or discussions of some specific automated interpretive systems can be found in Adair (1978), Butcher (1978), Eyde (1985), Fowler (1985), Green (1982), Karson and O'Dell (1975, 1987), Nichols (1985), and Sundberg (1985a, 1985b). Butcher (1987) provides a comprehensive list of psychological software and services which were commercially available at the time of his review.

It should be noted that although the computer provides enormous advantages in the application of empirical scoring and interpretive rules to personality test data, currently available automated interpretations are not truly actuarial in nature. Actuarial prediction is "arrived at by some straight-forward application of an equation or table to the data . . . the defining property is that no judging or inferring or weighing is done by a skilled clinician" (Meehl, 1954, pp. 15–16). As discussed earlier, even the interpretation of the well-researched MMPI is subject to the experience and judgment of the individual clinician using it at the time; he or she must fill in the interpretive gaps left by the available "cookbooks" and modify standard interpretations as appropriate for moderating demographic variables, local base rates, or the particular purpose of the evaluation. Thus, currently available computerized interpretive systems are actually "a mixture of rules based on actuarially validated relationships and other rules culled from established clinical lore or from the expert author's personal experience with the test" (Vale & Keller, 1987, p. 72).

Unfortunately, the naive consumer may assume that a computerized interpretation is accurate simply because it is generated by a machine rather than a human. It is important to keep in mind that "the accuracy (validity) of these kinds of interpretations is dependent on the knowledge and skill of the clinician who generated the interpretive statements. The validity of these interpretations should not be assumed and needs to be demonstrated every bit as much as the validity of a test needs to be demonstrated" (Graham, 1987, p. 231). Ben-Porath and Butcher (1986) have suggested several questions that the potential user of a computerized test interpretation should consider:

(a) To what extent has the validity of this report been studied?
(b) To what extent does this report rely on empirical findings in generating its interpretation?
(c) To what extent does this report incorporate all of the currently validated descriptive information?
(d) Does the report take demographic variables into account?
(e) Are different versions available for various referral questions?
(f) Is the report internally consistent?
(g) Does the report include practical suggestions?
(h) Is the report periodically revised to reflect newly acquired information? (pp. 173–174)

The updated guidelines for computer-based tests and interpretations published by the American Psychological Association make it clear that it is the responsibility of the professional using a computerized test to evaluate its validity for the particular application in question (American Psychological Association, 1986). Validation of computerized interpretations is a complex endeavor which is generating considerable controversy and, fortunately, some new research studies at this time. For further discussion/debate of the issues, strategies, and difficulties in validation of automated interpretations, see Eyde, Kowal, and Fishburne (1987), Fowler and Butcher (1986), Matarazzo (1986a, 1986b), and Moreland (1985). It should also be noted that although there are numerous computer scoring programs available through commercial outlets for many contemporary objective personality tests, there is no assurance that these programs will generate scores or profiles that match those in the test handbooks. The user should never assume programs are error free; even the basic scores should be verified before use.

Figures 16.2 and 16.3 present a case description and sample computer-generated report for the man whose MMPI-2 profile appeared in Figure 16.1. This particular automated system, the Minnesota Report Adult Clinical System (Butcher, 1989a), illustrates a mixed actuarial and clinician-modeled interpretive program. The report is modeled on the interpretive style of James Butcher, incorporating all the strategies described earlier in this chapter: code type and indi-

vidual scale interpretation, content analysis using the new MMPI-2 scales as well as traditional subscale analysis, and utilization of well-researched special scales. The program is arranged hierarchically, first checking for a match to a codetype with well-researched actuarial correlates, then proceeding to individual scale interpretation if no such match is found. The computer program tailors interpretive statements according to the subject's population (mental health outpatient or inpatient, medical, chronic pain adult correctional, or college counseling), and according to demographic data such as education, sex, and marital status, which research has shown to be modifiers of interpretive rules. (The interpretive report illustrated in Figure 16.3 was generated for a chronic pain patient setting.) Statements are modified or added based on content scale scores as well. Profiles are plotted for the standard validity and clinical scales and for the MMPI-2 content scales. Indices and decision rules appropriate to the client's setting are reported, along with a list of the Koss-Butcher and Lachar-Wrobel critical items the client endorsed. Comparison between MMPI-2 and MMPI norms is facilitated by presentation of Welsh codes for both scoring systems on the clinical profile form page.

A general computerized report such as that shown above may not always be appropriate for the particular application needed by the test user. A human clinician can, of course, modify his or her narrative style (or the extent of information provided) based on the intended audience and the questions to be addressed by the report. With increasing frequency, authors of computerized interpretations are also designing computer programs to address the decision-relevant information needed for a particular application or setting, as well as tailoring reports to fit the norms of particular client populations. The Minnesota Report Personnel Selection System, for example, is a modification of Butcher's interpretive system specifically designed to aid in screening applicants for "highly responsible positions involving public trust and safety and for occupations involving high degrees of stress" (Butcher, 1989b, p. 2).

Users can select either a narrative interpretation geared to address possible work problems, or a shorter screening report rating the applicant on five dimensions: openness to evaluation, social facility, addiction potential, stress tolerance, and overall adjustment. The latter, shown in Figure 16.4 for the same individual described in Figures 16.2 and 16.3, illustrates a modification of a test interpretation to address only those areas of most direct concern for the testing application: in this case, the suitability of this individual for the "highly responsible position" of airline pilot. Another difference between this report and the Adult Clinical System interpretation is the inclusion of "content themes" based on configural rules combining scales with similar content. The report shown in Figure 16.4 would usually include scores and profiles for the validity, clinical, content and many special scales, just as in the Adult Clinical System. These were excluded here because of their redundancy with Figure 16.3.

These reports, based on a single expert's interpretive framework, represent only a few of the possible methods for constructing a computerized test interpretation. For example, Vale, Keller, and Bentz described developing a computer narrative report by starting with a list of important questions to be addressed by the interpretation, then writing a statement library based on the combined expertise of a committee of interpretive experts (Vale, Keller, & Bentz, 1986; Vale & Keller, 1987). They, along with Fowler (1987), give some further guidelines on strategies and issues in writing a computerized test interpretation system.

Online Assessment Using Standard Clinical Techniques

Although most automated testing systems have merely scored and interpreted test forms that were hand administered, the computer is increasingly being utilized as test administrator as well. Lushene, O'Neil, and Dunn (1974) first reported an online MMPI administration, scoring, and interpretive system, and several large clinical settings now routinely use computer-administered assessment devices. Teleprocessing of test responses is possible through commercial scoring services: users can enter subjects' test responses into a remote terminal and have the data transmitted to the central scoring service via regular phone lines, receiving almost instant turnaround on the test results. Alternatively, the test can be administered directly to the subject via the terminal and her or his responses can be sent to the scoring service without the need for an intermediary data-entry step.

Erdman and colleagues reviewed 21 studies of computerized patient interviews and concluded that they are "reliable, accurate, and highly acceptable to

Case Description

Mr. S. is a 48-year-old married Caucasian man who had been employed for 30 years as a mail carrier before suffering the gradual onset of low back pain over a three- to four-year period. He worked intermittently during these years but had been away from work on disability for two years by the time of this testing, which was part of his assessment for admission to an inpatient chronic pain rehabilitation program. Mr. S.'s pain and disability were considered to be in excess of organic findings. He was admitted to a three-week rehab program consisting of physical therapy, education, vocational counseling, family counseling, therapeutic recreation, stress management training, etc. During the program, staff collected history indicating the client had previous hospitalizations for "anxiety attacks" every year or so. He would check himself into hospitals for "rest" and minor tranquilizers. The internist who evaluated him during his chronic pain program speculated about "an element of malingering" in his clinical picture. The client was also evaluated by a psychiatrist, who suggested major depression camouflaged by somatization. He noted that some of the client's disability could be traced to secondary gain and attention-seeking. He was dependent on Ativan, but was weaned off of this and started on an anti-depressant medication instead. The client was cooperative during inpatient treatment but when he went back to work afterwards, his behavior was so withdrawn and unusual that he was rehospitalized on a psychiatric unit. Staff there evaluated him and concluded that his fear of the social and work responsibilities of his job were leading to use of "bizarre psychiatric symptoms as a way of controlling the situation." The MMPI clinical and content scales helped rule out actual psychotic processes in favor of more avoidant, anxious behaviors motivated by secondary gain and social discomfort. The client basically was hoping for retirement or continued disability rather than a return to work. When this was addressed directly and the client was given a great deal of support, stress management and assertiveness training, he was able to return to work and maintain employment during the several months of followup information available, despite continued vague somatic complaints.

Figure 16.2.

TM
MMPI-2

TM
MINNESOTA MULTIPHASIC PERSONALITY INVENTORY-2

By Starke R. Hathaway and J. Charnley McKinley

TM
THE MINNESOTA REPORT:
ADULT CLINICAL SYSTEM
INTERPRETIVE REPORT

By James N. Butcher

         Client ID: 0025297
       Report Date: 23-AUG-89
              Age: 48
              Sex: Male
          Setting: Chronic Pain
        Education: 12
   Marital Status: Married

Figure 16.3. Computer-generated narrative interpretation and score profile for the individual described in Figure 16.2. Reproduced by permission of the publisher, The University of Minnesota Press.

```
        TM                                                    page 1
MMPI-2                  TM
THE MINNESOTA REPORT:              ID: 0025297     REPORT DATE: 23-AUG-89
ADULT CLINICAL SYSTEM
INTERPRETIVE REPORT
```

PROFILE VALIDITY

This client's approach to the MMPI-2 was open and cooperative. The
resulting MMPI-2 profile is valid and probably a good indication of his
present level of personality functioning. This may be viewed as a positive
indication of his involvement with the evaluation.

SYMPTOMATIC PATTERNS

The client is exhibiting much somatic distress and may be experiencing a
problem with his psychological adjustment. His physical complaints are
probably extreme, possibly reflecting a general lack of effectiveness in
life. He is probably feeling quite tense and nervous, and may be feeling
that he cannot get by without help for his physical problems. He is likely
to be reporting a great deal of pain, and feels that others do not
understand how sick he is feeling. He may be quite irritable and may become
hostile if his symptoms are not given "proper" attention.

Many individuals with this profile have a history of psychophysiological
disorders. They tend to overreact to minor problems with physical symptoms.
Ulcers and gastrointestinal distress are common. The possibility of actual
organic problems, therefore, should be carefully evaluated. Individuals
with this profile report a great deal of tension and a depressed mood. They
tend to be pessimistic and gloomy in their outlook toward life.

The client seems to have a rather limited range of interests and tends to
prefer stereotyped masculine activities over literary and artistic pursuits
or introspective experiences. He tends to be somewhat competitive and needs
to see himself as masculine. He probably prefers to view women in
subservient roles. Interpersonally, he is likely to be intolerant and
insensitive, and others may find him rather crude, coarse, or narrow-minded.

In addition, the following description is suggested by the content of this
client's responses. He has difficulty managing routine affairs, and the
item content he endorsed suggests a poor memory, concentration problems, and
an inability to make decisions. He appears to be immobilized and withdrawn
and has no energy for life. He views his physical health as failing and
reports numerous somatic concerns. He feels that life is no longer
worthwhile and that he is losing control of his thought processes.

INTERPERSONAL RELATIONS

He appears to be somewhat passive-dependent in relationships. He may
manipulate others through his physical symptoms, and become hostile if
sufficient attention is not paid to his complaints. Marital unhappiness is
likely to be a factor in his present clinical picture. Many married persons
with this profile have difficulties with their marriage. They typically
show a diminished interest in sex. Moreover, his moodiness and whining are
likely to place additional strains on the marriage.

Figure 16.3. continued

He is somewhat shy, with some social concerns and inhibitions. He is a bit
hypersensitive about what others think of him and is occasionally concerned
over his relationships with others. He appears to be somewhat inhibited in
personal relationships and social situations, and may have some difficulty
expressing his feelings toward others.

BEHAVIORAL STABILITY

There are likely to be long-standing personality problems predisposing him
to develop physical symptoms under stress. His present disorder could
reflect, in part, an exaggerated response to environmental stress. Social
introversion-extraversion tends to be a very stable personality
characteristic over time. His interpersonal shyness is likely to continue
to be part of his personality pattern if retested at a later date.

DIAGNOSTIC CONSIDERATIONS

Individuals with this profile type are often seen as neurotic, and may
receive a diagnosis of Somatoform Disorder. Actual organic problems such as
ulcers and hypertension might be part of the clinical picture. Some
individuals with this profile have problems with abuse of pain medication or
other prescription drugs.

TREATMENT CONSIDERATIONS

He is likely to view his problems as physical and may not readily recognize
the psychological factors involved. He tends to somatize his difficulties
and to seek medical solutions rather than to deal with them psychologically.
He seems to tolerate a high level of psychological conflict and may not be
motivated to deal with his problems directly. He is not a strong candidate
for insight-oriented psychotherapy. Psychological treatment may progress
more rapidly if his symptoms are dealt with through behavior modification
techniques. However, with his generally pessimistic attitude and low energy
resources, he seems to have little hope of getting better. In any
intervention or psychological evaluation program involving occupational
adjustment, his negative work attitudes could become an important problem to
overcome. He holds a number of attitudes and feelings that could interfere
with work adjustment.

NOTE: This MMPI-2 interpretation can serve as a useful source of hypotheses
about clients. This report is based on objectively derived scale indexes
and scale interpretations that have been developed in diverse groups of
patients. The personality descriptions, inferences and recommendations
contained herein need to be verified by other sources of clinical
information since individual clients may not fully match the prototype. The
information in this report should most appropriately be used by a trained,
qualified test interpreter. The information contained in this report should
be considered confidential.

Figure 16.3. continued

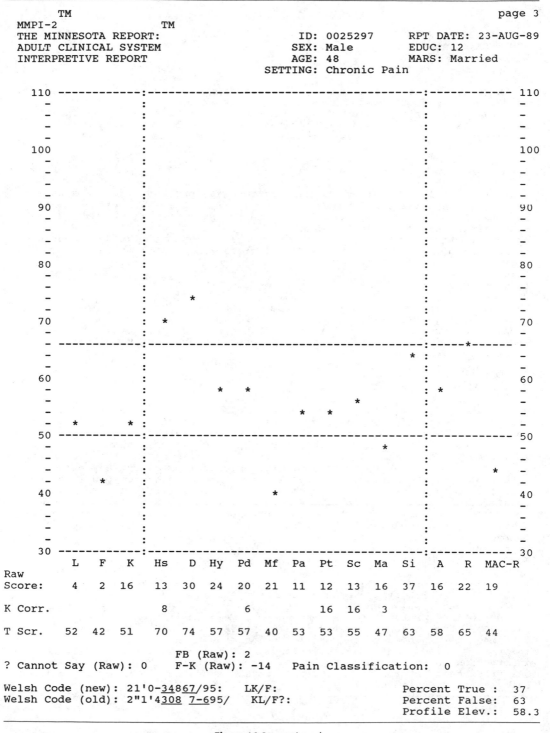

           TM   page 3
MMPI-2   TM
THE MINNESOTA REPORT: ID: 0025297   RPT DATE: 23-AUG-89
ADULT CLINICAL SYSTEM   SEX: Male   EDUC: 12
INTERPRETIVE REPORT   AGE: 48   MARS: Married
                                          SETTING: Chronic Pain

	L	F	K	Hs	D	Hy	Pd	Mf	Pa	Pt	Sc	Ma	Si	A	R	MAC-R
Raw Score:	4	2	16	13	30	24	20	21	11	12	13	16	37	16	22	19
K Corr.				8			6			16	16	3				
T Scr.	52	42	51	70	74	57	57	40	53	53	55	47	63	58	65	44

```
                             FB (Raw): 2
? Cannot Say (Raw): 0     F-K (Raw): -14    Pain Classification:  0

Welsh Code (new): 21'0-34867/95:     LK/F:              Percent True :  37
Welsh Code (old): 2"1'4308 7-695/    KL/F?:             Percent False:  63
                                                        Profile Elev.:  58.3
```

Figure 16.3. continued

```
        TM                                                          page 4
MMPI-2                      TM
THE MINNESOTA REPORT:                     ID: 0025297    RPT DATE: 23-AUG-89
ADULT CLINICAL SYSTEM                     SEX: Male      EDUC: 12
INTERPRETIVE REPORT                       AGE: 48        MARS: Married
                                     SETTING: Chronic Pain


                             Content Scales Profile
                 Butcher, Graham, Williams, and Ben-Porath (1989)
    110 -------------------------------------------------------------- 110
      -                                                                -
      -                                                                -
      -                                                                -
      -                                                                -
    100                                                                100
      -                                                                -
      -                                                                -
      -                                                                -
      -                                                                -
     90                                                                90
      -                                                                -
      -                                                                -
      -                                                                -
      -                                                                -
     80                                                                80
      -                                                                -
      -                                                                -
      -                                                                -
      -     *                *                                *        -
     70                                                                70
      -                                                                -
      - -------------------------------------------------------------  -
      -                                                                -
      -                                                                -
     60                                                    *           60
      -                                                       *        -
      -                             *        *                         -
      -                                *                               -
     50 ----------*------------------------------------------------- 50
      -                  *        *                            *       -
      -        *                  *                *                   -
      -                                                                -
      -                                                                -
     40                                                                40
      -                                                                -
      -                                                                -
      -                                                                -
      -                                                                -
     30 -------------------------------------------------------------- 30
         ANX FRS OBS DEP HEA BIZ ANG CYN ASP TPA LSE SOD FAM WRK TRT

Raw
Score:   15   2   5   3  15   1   5  13   9  10   2  13   7  19   3

T Score: 72  45  50  48  72  46  48  54  51  53  45  60  55  72  47
```

Figure 16.3. continued

```
        TM                                                            page 5
MMPI-2                    TM
THE MINNESOTA REPORT:                ID: 0025297      REPORT DATE: 23-AUG-89
ADULT CLINICAL SYSTEM
INTERPRETIVE REPORT
```

SUPPLEMENTARY SCORE REPORT

	Raw Score	T Score
Ego Strength (Es)	36	47
Dominance (Do)	18	55
Social Responsibility (Re)	16	39
Overcontrolled Hostility (O-H)	10	41
PTSD - Keane (PK)	7	48
PTSD - Schlenger (PS)	20	62
True Response Inconsistency (TRIN)	10	57T
Variable Response Inconsistency (VRIN)	9	65

Depression Subscales (Harris-Lingoes):

Subjective Depression (D1)	14	69
Psychomotor Retardation (D2)	11	81
Physical Malfunctioning (D3)	6	75
Mental Dullness (D4)	6	67
Brooding (D5)	2	51

Hysteria Subscales (Harris-Lingoes):

Denial of Social Anxiety (Hy1)	3	45
Need for Affection (Hy2)	4	40
Lassitude-Malaise (Hy3)	6	66
Somatic Complaints (Hy4)	6	67
Inhibition of Aggression (Hy5)	4	55

Psychopathic Deviate Subscales (Harris-Lingoes):

Familial Discord (Pd1)	1	45
Authority Problems (Pd2)	6	68
Social Imperturbability (Pd3)	4	52
Social Alienation (Pd4)	4	51
Self-Alienation (Pd5)	4	53

Paranoia Subscales (Harris-Lingoes):

Persecutory Ideas (Pa1)	3	58
Poignancy (Pa2)	3	55
Naivete (Pa3)	4	46

Figure 16.3. continued

	Raw Score	T Score
Schizophrenia Subscales (Harris-Lingoes):		
Social Alienation (Sc1)	3	51
Emotional Alienation (Sc2)	0	40
Lack of Ego Mastery, Cognitive (Sc3)	3	60
Lack of Ego Mastery, Conative (Sc4)	5	65
Lack of Ego Mastery, Def. Inhib. (Sc5)	1	47
Bizarre Sensory Experiences (Sc6)	3	55
Hypomania Subscales (Harris-Lingoes):		
Amorality (Ma1)	0	35
Psychomotor Acceleration (Ma2)	6	53
Imperturbability (Ma3)	2	41
Ego Inflation (Ma4)	3	50
Social Introversion Subscales (Ben-Porath, Hostetler, Butcher, & Graham):		
Shyness / Self-Consciousness (Si1)	9	62
Social Avoidance (Si2)	4	54
Alienation--Self and Others (Si3)	5	50

Uniform T scores are used for Hs, D, Hy, Pd, Pa, Pt, Sc, Ma, and the Content
Scales; all other MMPI-2 scales use linear T scores.

Figure 16.3. continued

CRITICAL ITEMS

The following critical items have been found to have possible significance in
analyzing a client's problem situation. Although these items may serve as a
source of hypotheses for further investigation, caution should be taken in
interpreting individual items because they may have been inadvertently
checked.

Acute Anxiety State (Koss-Butcher Critical Items)

    10. I am about as able to work as I ever was. (F)
    15. I work under a great deal of tension. (T)
   208. I hardly ever notice my heart pounding and I am seldom short of
        breath. (F)
   223. I believe I am no more nervous than most others. (F)
   301. I feel anxiety about something or someone almost all the time. (T)

Depressed Suicidal Ideation (Koss-Butcher Critical Items)

    38. I have had periods of days, weeks, or months when I couldn't take care
        of things because I couldn't "get going." (T)
   233. I have difficulty in starting to do things. (T)

Situational Stress Due to Alcoholism (Koss-Butcher Critical Items)

   264. I have used alcohol excessively. (T)
   489. I have a drug or alcohol problem. (T)

Mental Confusion (Koss-Butcher Critical Items)

    31. I find it hard to keep my mind on a task or job. (T)
   299. I cannot keep my mind on one thing. (T)
   325. I have more trouble concentrating than others seem to have. (T)

Persecutory Ideas (Koss-Butcher Critical Items)

    17. I am sure I get a raw deal from life. (T)
   124. I often wonder what hidden reason another person may have for doing
        something nice for me. (T)

Antisocial Attitude (Lachar-Wrobel Critical Items)

    35. Sometimes when I was young I stole things. (T)
   105. In school I was sometimes sent to the principal for bad behavior. (T)
   254. Most people make friends because friends are likely to be useful to
        them. (T)
   266. I have never been in trouble with the law. (F)

Figure 16.3. continued

Somatic Symptoms   (Lachar-Wrobel Critical Items)

33. I seldom worry about my health. (F)
53. Parts of my body often have feelings like burning, tingling, crawling,
    or like "going to sleep." (T)
57. I hardly ever feel pain in the back of my neck. (F)
142. I have never had a fit or convulsion. (F)
159. I have never had a fainting spell. (F)
176. I have very few headaches. (F)
224. I have few or no pains. (F)
247. I have numbness in one or more places on my skin. (T)
295. I have never been paralyzed or had any unusual weakness of any of my
     muscles. (F)
464. I feel tired a good deal of the time. (T)

Sexual Concern and Deviation (Lachar-Wrobel Critical Items)

121. I have never indulged in any unusual sex practices. (F)

Anxiety and Tension (Lachar-Wrobel Critical Items)

15. I work under a great deal of tension. (T)
17. I am sure I get a raw deal from life. (T)
223. I believe I am no more nervous than most others. (F)
261. I have very few fears compared to my friends. (F)
299. I cannot keep my mind on one thing. (T)
301. I feel anxiety about something or someone almost all the time. (T)
405. I am usually calm and not easily upset. (F)

Deviant Thinking and Experience (Lachar-Wrobel Critical Items)

122. At times my thoughts have raced ahead faster than I could speak
     them. (T)
427. I have never seen a vision. (F)

Depression and Worry (Lachar-Wrobel Critical Items)

10. I am about as able to work as I ever was. (F)
339. I have sometimes felt that difficulties were piling up so high that I
     could not overcome them. (T)
415. I worry quite a bit over possible misfortunes. (T)

Figure 16.3. continued

TM
MMPI-2

TM
MINNESOTA MULTIPHASIC PERSONALITY INVENTORY-2

By Starke R. Hathaway and J. Charnley McKinley

TM
THE MINNESOTA REPORT:
PERSONNEL SELECTION SYSTEM
SCREENING REPORT

By James N. Butcher


```
         Client ID:   0025297
        Report Date:  22-SEP-89
               Age:   48
               Sex:   Male
         Occupation:  Other
          Education:  12
```

Figure 16.4. Personnel screening computer-generated report for the individual described in Figures 16.2 and 16.3. Reproduced by permission of the publisher, The University of Minnesota Press.

```
       TM                                                        page 1
MMPI-2                TM
THE MINNESOTA REPORT:              ID: 0025297      REPORT DATE: 22-SEP-89
PERSONNEL SELECTION SYSTEM
SCREENING REPORT
```

OPENNESS TO EVALUATION

```
OVERLY      QUITE                   OVERLY
FRANK       OPEN       ADEQUATE     CAUTIOUS    GUARDED    INDETERMINATE

--X-------------------------------------------------------------------
```

SOCIAL FACILITY

```
                                  PROBLEMS
EXCELLENT    GOOD     ADEQUATE     POSSIBLE      POOR      INDETERMINATE

-----------------------------------------------------X-----------------------
```

ADDICTION POTENTIAL
(STANDARD LEVEL)

```
        NO APPARENT   PROBLEMS
LOW       PROBLEM     POSSIBLE      MODERATE     HIGH      INDETERMINATE

--------------X-------------------------------------------------------------
```

Figure 16.4. continued

```
        TM                                                        page 2
MMPI-2                  TM
THE MINNESOTA REPORT:                    ID: 0025297      REPORT DATE: 22-SEP-89
PERSONNEL SELECTION SYSTEM
SCREENING REPORT
```

                              _____

                                  STRESS TOLERANCE
                              _____

```
                                   PROBLEMS
HIGH         GOOD       ADEQUATE    POSSIBLE          LOW       INDETERMINATE

-------------------------------------------------------X-----------------------
```

                              _____

                                  OVERALL ADJUSTMENT
                              _____

```
                                   PROBLEMS
EXCELLENT    GOOD       ADEQUATE    POSSIBLE          POOR      INDETERMINATE

-------------------------------------------------------X----------------------
```

His MMPI-2 responses indicate that his psychological adjustment is likely to
be poor.

This applicant should be evaluated further to determine if he has adjustment
problems.

NOTE: This MMPI-2 report can serve as a useful guide for employment
decisions in which personality adjustment is considered important for
success on the job. The decision rules on which these classifications are
based were developed through a review of the empirical literature on the
MMPI-2 with "normal-range" individuals (including job applicants) and the
author's practical experience using the test in employment selection. The
report can assist psychologists and physicians involved in personnel
selection by providing an "outside opinion" about the applicant's
adjustment. The MMPI-2 should NOT be used as the SOLE means of determining
the applicant's suitability for employment. The information in this report
should be used by qualified test interpretation specialists ONLY.

Figure 16.4. continued

```
      TM                                                       page 3
MMPI-2                  TM
THE MINNESOTA REPORT:               ID: 0025297    REPORT DATE: 22-SEP-89
PERSONNEL SELECTION SYSTEM
SCREENING REPORT
```

CONTENT THEMES

The following content themes may serve as a source of hypotheses for further investigation. These content themes summarize similar item responses that appear with greater frequency with this applicant than with most people.

May be overly sensitive in interpersonal relationships.

May have low self-esteem that interferes with his taking on new tasks.

May show some discomfort in social situations.

May show irresponsible attitudes.

May sometimes disregard rules when it suits him.

May be prone to feeling anxious.

May show low energy or lack of enthusiasm.

May have problems with somatic distress.

May be overly sensitive to criticism.

May have a narrow pattern of interests.

May have negative attitudes or behaviors that would interfere with work adjustment.

Figure 16.4. continued

most patients" (Erdman, Greist, Klein, Jefferson, & Getto, 1981, p. 394). In general, concerns about the impersonality of such interactions have not proved justified. Reports show that patients usually enjoy the process and have even revealed more sensitive data to a computer than to a human interviewer (Erdman, Klein, & Greist, 1985; Greist & Klein, 1980, 1981; Johnson & Williams, 1980; Lucas, Mullins, Luna, & McInroy, 1977). However, the latter point illustrates that computer-administered versions of tests cannot necessarily be assumed to be parallel forms of paper-and-pencil versions. Moreland (1987) notes that "rather subtle differences between on-line and conventional test administrations can produce large differences in test scores produced by the two modes" (p. 33). For example, providing a clear "Cannot Say" option along with the "True" and "False" response options on the MMPI or CPI changes scores by producing more omitted items than on booklet forms where the "Cannot Say" option is not as obvious

(Biskin & Kolotkin, 1977; Lushene, O'Neil, & Dunn, 1974; Scissons, 1976).

Based on his review, Moreland concludes that if care is taken to make the computerized administrative format as similar as possible to the paper-and-pencil form, "non-equivalence is typically small enough to be of no practical consequence, if present at all" (p. 34). However, further research is needed to delineate the important parameters determining test equivalence, and to address individual differences in responses to computerized test administration.

Applications such as these and the many others described in the contemporary literature illustrate automated technology's potential for streamlining traditional objective personality assessment procedures. Computers can increase the accuracy and reliability of standardized administration, data collection, data storage, and application of objective decision rules. However, online technology also offers the possibility of more innovative uses than simply duplicating existing manual procedures. Some new uses include pro-gramming computers to mimic the human judgmental process, such as in the narrative interpretive schemes described above. The next sections will describe applications using the computer's capacity for dy-namic, adaptive systems of analysis to improve hu-man decision making.

Dynamic, Adaptive Assessment Strategies

Although Holtzman (1960) claimed that the clini-cian's uniquely human adaptive, creative, and intui-tive judgment could never be reproduced by a ma-chine, Kleinmuntz and McLean (1968) listed flexibility as one of the three main advantages of a computer—along with speed and objectivity. Accord-ing to them, "The ability of the computer to alter its activity as the result of the environment in which it is working is its greatest strength" (p. 75). In the case of an online test administration or interview, the com-puter can be programmed to choose one of several alternative content areas as a function of an individu-al's prior responses, much as a human interviewer would. Such a capability can be very useful in psychi-atric screening, both in tailoring specific assessment devices to maximize information about particular patients and in adapting a standardized interview sequence to the characteristics and needs of the indi-vidual subject. In addition, the flexibility and perfect memory of the computer make it possible for it to evaluate its own performance by specified criteria and to modify subsequent decisions and actions accord-ingly.

Branched Interviews
Most of the clinical work utilizing flexible assess-ment strategies has involved adaptive interviews. The growing utilization of large automated patient data systems requires collection of great quantities of information on each individual, but administration of the same lengthy interview to every subject can often be a wasteful and inefficient procedure. Certain re-sponses make other questions inappropriate or, on the other hand, may indicate the need for branching to more detailed questioning in specific topic areas. For example, asking an unemployed patient a series of questions relating to job performance would be an inefficient use of patient and interviewer time, and knowing that a patient is married may indicate the need to ask further questions about marital adjust-ment.

Several automated interview systems have been designed to deal with these problems. Stillman, Roth, Colby, and Rosenbaum (1969) described one of the first online psychiatric inventories, the Computer-Assisted Special Enquirer (CASE) developed at Stan-ford. The clinician entered interview questions and branching options into a terminal, using both multiple choice and narrative format items. This interview network was then presented to patients via an online terminal. Any particular patient received only about 50% of the total item pool due to the branching options. A computer-generated report indicated to the clinician which items were presented and what the responses to these were.

Erdman, Klein, and Greist (1985; Greist & Klein, 1980) at the University of Wisconsin have described adaptive administration of their computerized Social Adjustment Interview, which collects patient history information and evaluates current role functioning. Detailed questions later in the interview are condi-tional upon earlier answers to a standard set of demo-graphic items and the patient's choice of "two areas that are most involved in your problems right now" (1980, p. 165). Although the interview as a whole consists of more than 650 questions, the average single patient is likely to be presented with about 150 of these items. Erdman et al. reported excellent agreement between clinical evaluations and results of the computerized interview. Similarly, the computer-based Psychiatric Assessment Unit developed at the Veterans Administration Hospital in Salt Lake City (Johnson & Williams, 1980) has been reported to result in faster, cheaper, more accurate and consistent reports than the hospital's traditional assessment methods (Klingler, Miller, Johnson, & Williams, 1976, 1977).

Adaptive Test Administration
Adaptive administration of objective personality tests is not as well researched as flexible interview strategies. Although theoretically the branching abil-ity of the computer could make it possible to produce personality tests "tailored to each individual's needs and abilities" (Patience, 1977), thus far the applica-tion of adaptive testing strategies to achievement and ability testing (English, Reckase, & Patience, 1977; Vale & Weiss, 1975; Weiss, 1973) still greatly sur-passes their use in personality assessment. Many foresee personality assessment relying more and more in the future on individualized, tailored tests (e.g., Bartram & Bayliss, 1984; Ben-Porath & Butcher, 1986; Butcher, 1986; Butcher, Keller, & Bacon, 1985).

Research investigating the use of adaptive testing strategies in personality assessment falls roughly into four categories, based on the method used: (a) the prediction of full scores on the conventional paper-and-pencil form of the test, (b) the adaptive typological approach, (c) the countdown strategy, and (d) methods based on item response theory (IRT, also known as latent trait theory). In all four of these approaches, the majority of research has focused on examining the merits of altering extant personality assessment instruments (such as the MMPI) by applying adaptive testing methods.

Kleinmuntz and McLean (1968), pioneers in the use of adaptive testing in personality assessment, presented a model for a branched, interactive, computerized MMPI short form. Their program presented the subject with a subset of five items from each of the 15 scales to be estimated, on the basis of which a T-score was computed for each scale. Additional items were administered only for those scales that could not be clearly classified as "normal" or "abnormal" based on these T-scores, and the test ended when all scales could be so classified. Kleinmuntz and McLean's system cut the MMPI administration time drastically, but the correlations of their scale scores with the long form scores were not impressive.

More recently, Sanders (1985) explored the feasibility of developing individualized short forms of the MMPI. He used a two-stage approach, as did Kleinmuntz and McLean. Initially five items for each of 12 MMPI scales (the *Mf* scale was not scored) were administered via computer. Additional items were administered for each scale and entered into a stepwise multiple regression equation. When the predicted full-scale score was not altered significantly by the administration of additional items, item sampling for that scale was terminated and the computer went on to the next scale. The items that were administered for each scale were those that had the highest item-scale correlations. Sanders was successful in obtaining high correlations between predicted MMPI scale scores and full-scale scores, but the correlations between predicted and actual code types were not reported.

Clavelle and Butcher (1977) utilized an adaptive typological approach to predict MMPI code type membership, rather than estimating long form scale scores as Kleinmuntz and McLean (1968) and Sanders (1985) had done. Hoffman and Butcher (1975) have pointed out that even though good prediction of long form scale elevations can be achieved by several popular MMPI short forms, the congruence between code type classification based on the two forms is generally too low to be useful for practical clinical decision making. They suggested that instead of attempting to predict long form scale elevations, "a more fruitful clinical approach might be to use multivariate techniques, such as the discriminant function, to select a small subset of items for direct prediction of selected criteria or for specific decision problems" (p. 38).

Clavelle and Butcher implemented this suggestion by examining item responses for a large group of outpatients whose MMPI profiles fell into one of nine selected code type groups. Sixty-nine items which showed significant differences in endorsement frequency between these groups were used as predictor variables in a stepwise multiple discriminant function analysis with code type as the criterion. Accuracy of classification was assessed after administration of each block of 10 items. Results showed that classification accuracy tended to reach an asymptotic level after administration of a relatively small number of items, and in addition, certain blocks of code types tended to form higher order groups that were retained or excluded together. Clavelle and Butcher concluded that

> rather than continue with the administration of items of increasingly dubious discriminant value, it seems that a more efficient strategy would be to branch out to another set of items capable of providing the most additional information pertinent to a differentiation among the remaining code types. (p. 857)

Another approach which can also be considered typological, the countdown method, was described by Butcher, Keller, and Bacon (1985). When this strategy is applied to MMPI administration, it can be used to classify individuals more quickly as "normal" or "abnormal," i.e. whether their T-score on a particular scale is either less than 70 or is 70 or greater. Item administration for each scale is terminated when the number of unendorsed items equals the total number of items on the scale minus the cutoff (the number of endorsed items which correspond to a T-score of 70) plus one, or when the items answered in the keyed direction add up to the cutoff. For example, if a scale is 30 items long, and 20 endorsed items are required to obtain a T-score of 70 (the cutoff), as soon as an individual fails to endorse 11 items, administration of that scale can be terminated because there is no possibility of the subject exceeding a T-score of 70. That person has been classified as "normal" with complete accuracy as judged by full form scores.

Recently, Slutske, Ben-Porath, and Butcher (1988) described an implementation of the countdown method. They simulated an adaptive administration of the MMPI using data already collected from subjects who had completed the full paper-and-pencil version. In addition, they looked at the efficiency of ordering the items so that the least frequently endorsed items were presented first. They found that, particularly with a personnel selection sample, using the countdown method and administering items in ascending order of endorsement frequency resulted in a substantial savings in the number of items required. With a psychiatric sample, the most efficient way to administer items was to present the items most frequently endorsed by a normative sample first. Clearly, different approaches are required when dealing with individuals in which normal-range profiles are expected (personnel selection) versus when elevated profiles are more common (psychiatric sample). Slutske et al. suggest that the countdown strategy may be very useful for screening purposes where length of test is an issue.

A more psychometrically sophisticated adaptive testing technique, already extensively used in the areas of achievement and ability testing, is based on item-response theory (IRT). Briefly, according to Weiss (1985), IRT-based adaptive testing

> selects items that provide maximum levels of item information at an individual's currently estimated trait level. In addition, IRT-based methods of scoring tests permit estimation of individuals' trait levels based on their responses to one or more items. As a consequence, an item can be administered and an estimate can be made of the individual's level on the trait. After the administration of an item and estimation of trait, the new trait level is used to select the next item to be administered to that examinee. (p. 783)

The benefits of IRT-based adaptive testing are that it can decrease testing time by as much as 50% while maintaining or even improving on the precision of measurement obtained via conventional tests. For a concise review of this field, see Weiss (1985) or Weiss and Vale (1987).

The application of IRT-based adaptive testing to personality assessment is still a new and largely unexplored area. One of the first attempts to apply the IRT model to personality variables was a doctoral dissertation by Sapinkopf (1978). He compared the adaptive administration of several scales of the CPI to both the conventional paper-and-pencil format and to a nonadaptive computer-administered version. Sapinkopf found the adaptive strategy to be much more efficient than the other two methods in both the number of items and the testing time required, al-

though the reliabilities of two of the three adaptively administered CPI scales were lower than the reliabilities of the conventionally administered scales.

Carter (1982), again in a doctoral dissertation, investigated using a different IRT model to adaptively administer the MMPI. She obtained rather low correlations between the profiles obtained with the tailored and full-scale versions. In fact, her adaptively developed short form did not perform as well as two commonly used conventional short forms. Various reasons for the low correlations were suggested, including the possibility that using the more complicated IRT model employed by Sapinkopf (1977) might have resulted in more accurate estimates of full-scale scores with the same reduced number of items.

Carter and Wilkinson (1984) went on to identify those items on the MMPI which are "bad" according to latent trait models. Items which fit the model poorly have low or even negative discriminations: individuals low on the dimension being measured tend to endorse the item, while those high on the dimension do not, a result opposite to what is desired or expected. It was found that each of the basic MMPI scales had at least a few such items. It is interesting that the poorly fitting items according to their IRT analysis were the so-called subtle items originally identified by Weiner (1956), which some believe were included on the MMPI scales through chance correlations. Carter and Wilkinson concluded that the MMPI might be suitable for IRT-based adaptive administration if a two-parameter model (which takes item discriminations into account) is used.

Contrary to Carter and Wilkinson's conclusions, some experts believe that the application of IRT-based adaptive testing models to instruments such as the MMPI and CPI is inappropriate because these tests are empirically keyed and thus their scales are not unidimensional (cf. Ben-Porath and Butcher, 1986). The use of such tests results in the violation of some of the major assumptions of IRT, especially trait unidimensionality. Factorially derived personality assessment scales are much more appropriate for IRT methods, as these types of instruments are more likely to contain homogeneous, unidimensional scales.

It has recently been demonstrated (Reise & Waller, in press; Waller & Reise, in press) that adaptive testing using IRT works well for personality scales which meet the assumptions of the IRT model. The researchers used a computerized adaptive version of Tellegen's Multidimensional Personality Questionnaire (MPQ) (Tellegen, 1982), a factor analytically developed personality assessment instrument made up of 11 scales tapping various aspects of normal personality functioning. They were able to administer an individually tailored set of items chosen on the basis of the respondent's unique sequence of item endorsements and the difficulties and discriminations of the endorsed items. Reise and Waller found that it was possible to attain accurate trait estimates while maintaining an average item savings in excess of 40%.

There are several considerations in evaluating adaptively administered versions of objective personality tests. Just as with any computer-administered test, the equivalence of the adaptive version to the traditional paper-and-pencil version must be established empirically. The different response characteristics required may alter the nature of the instrument, and may make the norms developed on the traditional form inapplicable to the computer-administered version.

There are also considerations unique to adaptive versions of preexisting personality inventories. The adaptive administration of traditional instruments involves the rearrangement of the items within the inventory. Researchers in the area of achievement testing (Kingston & Dorans, 1984) have found context, or item-location effects, to be important on such tests as the Graduate Record Examination (GRE). Thus far, there are no studies investigating the importance of context for personality items.

Both of these considerations ultimately concern the validity of the modified versions of traditional personality assessment instruments. Additionally, many of the studies reviewed here were simulation studies: response data obtained from the conventional administration of personality assessment instruments were used to investigate the potential merits of adaptive versions of these tests. Until the adaptive versions are interactively administered to real subjects sitting at computer terminals, these studies must be considered preliminary. In addition, although attempts at modifying existing personality assessment instruments through adaptive testing strategies have been encouraging, it is likely that more benefit will be achieved from the development of new tests specifically designed for adaptive administration.

Development of New Assessment Strategies.

Johnson, Giannetti, and Williams (1979) noted that automation of standard clinical techniques does not take full advantage of the computer's capabilities and data bank. Accordingly, they attempted to construct a new inventory specifically designed for the computer. They took all the items in the data base of the Salt Lake City Veterans' Administration Hospital's computer-

ized Psychological Assessment Unit (approximately 2500 questions based on a large battery of standardized tests) and had expert clinicians categorize them rationally into content areas. They also took suggestions for items to be added for underrepresented content areas, and deleted redundant or overrepresented questions. The full question list was then administered to normal and psychiatric samples, and factor analysis was used to extract the empirical factors within each content domain. Only the items with the highest loadings on these factors were retained in the item pool. (This approach is similar to the multistage, multimethod strategy used in developing new content scales for the revised MMPI.) Johnson's group also added demographic and historical items at the beginning of the test as a basis for branching through the rest of the item pool, and empirically derived a dissimulation index to check on response validity. The preliminary version of the Psychological Systems Questionnaire (PSQ) consisted of 24 multiple choice demographic and branching items, 18 true-false dissimulation index items, and 729 true-false items which were scored on several factor analytically derived scales.

Several aspects of the PSQ's functioning illustrate the tremendous future potential of interactive computerized personality assessment. First, the demographic items at the beginning save time by allowing elimination of later items that are irrelevant or inappropriate. Second, the computer's ongoing computational ability allows it continually to calculate the individual's current standing on each scale throughout the entire test administration and to respond appropriately. For example:

> When a respondent is found to have scored high on a particular scale, he/she is asked for comments . . . the computer might say, "Mr. Jones, your test responses seem to indicate that you are very depressed. Would you care to make any comments about this?" These comments are then taken free-form from the typewriter keyboard. (Johnson, Giannetti, & Williams, 1979, p. 259)

This continuous scale-scoring ability may prove to be particularly useful in evaluating the validity of a patient's responses to an interactive self-report questionnaire. Evaluation of validity has always been a difficult problem in scoring self-report personality tests. The PSQ program was designed to print out cautionary reminders to the subject if the dissimulation index was getting high, and to terminate the test prematurely if the response pattern seemed completely invalid. Stout (1981) reports an even more sophisticated use of computer capabilities in ongoing evaluation of response validity. He suggests incorporation of ancillary data such as response latencies and key pressure into the computer's decision scheme. If certain latency patterns are found to be reliable indicators of invalidity or other unusual testing events, the computer could respond to these patterns appropriately. Stout lists examples, such as sudden high-speed responding as an indicator of randomness, or progressively longer response latencies as an indicator of fatigue. The computer could respond to such patterns either passively, by marking potentially invalid responses, or actively, by recommending a rest break, encouraging better cooperation and then readministering items, inserting extra items to check on the validity of earlier ones, switching to an alternate form more appropriate for the subject's capabilities, or signaling to a human examiner that something is amiss in the testing situation. Even computerized voice analysis might eventually be employed as a measure of test-taking attitude (Ben-Porath & Butcher, 1986).

Finally, one of the most important advantages of computerized testing systems is the computer's ability to utilize empirical data to modify its decision rules. If the computer is provided with information on the accuracy and utility of its decisions, it could be programmed to evaluate continually the relative contribution of particular items, actuarial formulas, etc., and drop or add variables and decision rules as appropriate. Computer systems will be ideal testing grounds for new measures and assessment strategies (Ben-Porath & Butcher, 1986; Butcher, Keller, & Bacon, 1985; Giannetti, Klingler, Johnson, & Williams, 1976).

CONCLUSION

D. J. Smail (1971) criticized what he saw as psychology's infatuation with technology, commenting that

> by becoming dazzled by statistical sophistication and technological efficiency, he [the psychologist] may forget to question the basis of his science and the ultimate purpose of his actions. In consequence he stands in danger of building around him an artificial world which, although possibly beautifully efficient within its own boundaries and elegant in its design, may bear no relation to anything that matters. (p. 173)

This review has attempted to show that, despite Smail's claims, personality assessment technology can and does have relevance to many things that matter. We pointed out at the beginning of this chapter that the value of technology lies in its utility as a tool to achieve valued goals. The extensive research and clinical literature on many objective personality tests attests to the practical value of these tools for contemporary psychological applications. Future developments, including new test construction methods and the increasing use of computer technology, will have to face the same empirical tests as have made or broken past assessment strategies. However, we believe that objective tests and their logical extension—automated methods—will play a major, successful role in the future of personality assessment technology.

REFERENCES

Adair, L. F. (1978). Review of MMPI computer services. In O. Buros (Ed.), *Eighth mental measurements yearbook*. Highland Park, NJ: Gryphon.

American Psychiatric Association. (1980). *Diagnostic and statistical manual of mental disorders* (3rd ed.). Washington, DC: Author.

American Psychological Association. (1986). *Guidelines for computer-based tests and interpretations*. Washington, DC: Author.

Anastasi, A. (1988). *Psychological testing* (6th ed.). New York: Macmillan.

Barron, F. (1953). An ego-strength scale which predicts response to psychotherapy. *Journal of Consulting Psychology, 17,* 327–333.

Bartram, D., & Bayliss, R. (1984). Automated testing: Past, present, and future. *Journal of Occupational Psychology, 57,* 221–237.

Baucom, D. H. (1985). Review of California Psychological Inventory. In J. V. Mitchell (Ed.), *The ninth mental measurements yearbook* (pp. 250–252). Lincoln: University of Nebraska Press.

Ben-Porath, Y. S., & Butcher, J. N. (1986). Computers in personality assessment: A brief past, an ebullient present, and an expanding future. *Computers in Human Behavior, 2,* 167–182.

Ben-Porath, Y. S., & Butcher, J. N. (1988, March). *Exploratory analyses of rewritten MMPI items.* Paper presented at the 23rd Annual Symposium on Recent Developments in the Use of the MMPI, St. Petersburg, Florida.

Ben-Porath, Y. S., & Butcher, J. N. (In press). The historical development of personality assessment. In C. E. Walker (Ed.), *Clinical psychology: Historical and research roots.* New York: Plenum Press.

Biskin, B. H., and Kolotkin, R. C. (1977). Effects of computerized administration on scores on the Minnesota Multiphasic Personality Inventory. *Applied Psychological Measurement, 1,* 543–549.

Block, J. (1965). *The challenge of response sets: Unconfounding meaning, acquiescence, and social desirability in the MMPI.* New York: Appleton-Century-Crofts.

Bolton, B. (1985). Review of the Adult personality Inventory. In J. V. Mitchell (Ed.), *The ninth mental measurements yearbook* (pp. 55–56). Lincoln: University of Nebraska Press.

Burisch, M. (1984). Approaches to personality inventory construction: A comparison of merits. *American Psychologist, 39,* 214–227.

Butcher, J. N. (1978). Present status of computerized MMPI reporting services. In O. Buros (Ed.), *Eighth mental measurements yearbook* (pp. 942–945). Highland Park, NJ: Gryphon.

Butcher, J. N. (1985). Review of Sixteen personality Factor Questionnaire. In J. V. Mitchell (Ed.), *The ninth mental measurements yearbook* (pp. 1391–1392). Lincoln: University of Nebraska Press.

Butcher, J. N. (1986, August). *Future directions in computerized psychological assessment procedures: The psychological clinic in the year 2001.* Paper presented at the 94th Annual Meeting of the American Psychological Association, Washington, DC

Butcher, J. N. (1987). *Computerized psychological assessment: A practitioner's guide.* New York: Basic Books.

Butcher, J. N. (1989a). *User's Guide for the MMPI-2 Minnesota Report: Adult Clinical System.* Minneapolis, MN: University of Minnesota, distributed by National Computer Systems.

Butcher, J. N. (1989b). *User's Guide for the MMPI-2 Minnesota Report: Personnel Selection System.* Minneapolis, MN: University of Minnesota, distributed by National Computer Systems.

Butcher, J. N., Graham, J. R., Dahlstrom, W. G., Tellegen, A. M., & Kaemmer, B. (1989). *MMPI-2 Manual for Administration and Scoring.* Minneapolis: University of Minnesota Press.

Butcher, J. N., Graham, J. R., Williams, C. L., & Ben-Porath, Y. S. (1989) *Development and Use of the MMPI-2 Content Scales.* Minneapolis, MN: University of Minnesota Press.

Butcher, J. N., & Keller, L. S. (1984). Objective personality assessment. In G. Goldstein & M. Hersen (Eds.), *Handbook of psychological assessment* (pp. 307–331). New York: Pergamon Press.

Butcher, J. N., Keller, L. S., & Bacon, S. F. (1985).

Current developments and future directions in computerized personality assessment. *Journal of Consulting and Clinical Psychology, 53,* 803–815.

Butcher, J. N., & Owen, P. L. (1978). Objective personality inventories: Recent research and some contemporary issues. In B. Wolman (Ed.), *Handbook of clinical diagnosis of mental disorders* (pp. 475–545). New York: Plenum Press.

Butcher, J. N., & Pancheri, P. (1976). *A handbook of cross-national MMPI research.* Minneapolis: University of Minnesota Press.

Carter, J. E. (1982). *A computerized adaptive version of the MMPI based on the Rasch model.* Unpublished doctoral dissertation, University of Chicago, Chicago Circle.

Carter, J. E., & Wilkinson, L. (1984). A latent trait analysis of the MMPI. *Multivariate Behavioral Research, 19,* 385–407.

Cattell, R. B., Eber, H. W., & Tatsuoka, M. M. (1970). *Handbook for the Sixteen Personality Factor Questionnaire (16PF).* Champaign, IL: Institute for Personality and Ability Testing.

Clavelle, P. R., & Butcher, J. N. (1977). An adaptive typological approach to psychiatric screening. *Journal of Consulting and Clinical Psychology, 45,* 851–859.

Colligan, R. C., Osborne, D., Swenson, W. M., & Offord, K. P. (1984). *The MMPI: A contemporary normative study.* New York: Praeger.

Comrey, A. L. (1957). Factors in the items of the MMPI. *American Psychologist, 12,* 437.

Comrey, A. L. (1970). *EDITS manual for the Comrey Personality Scales.* San Diego, CA: Educational and Industrial Testing Service.

Costa, P. T., Zonderman, A. B., McCrae, R. R., & Williams, R. B. (1985). Content and comprehensiveness in the MMPI: An item factor analysis in a normal adult sample. *Journal of Personality and Social Psychology, 48,* 925–933.

Dahlstrom, W. G., & Dahlstrom, L. (Eds.). (1980). *Basic readings on the MMPI: A new selection on personality measurement.* Minneapolis: University of Minnesota Press.

Dahlstrom, W. G., Lachar, D., & Dahlstrom, L. E. (1986). *MMPI patterns of American minorities.* Minneapolis: University of Minnesota Press.

Dahlstrom, W. G., Welsh, G. S., & Dahlstrom, L. E. (1972). *An MMPI handbook Vol. 1: Clinical interpretation* (rev. ed.). Minneapolis: University of Minnesota Press.

Dahlstrom, W. G., Welsh, G. S., & Dahlstrom, L. E. (1975). *An MMPI handbook Vol. 2: Research applications* (rev. ed.). Minneapolis: University of Minnesota Press.

Davies, J. D. (1955). *Phrenology fad and science: A 19th century American crusade*. New Haven, CT: Yale University Press.

Diehl, L. A. (1977). The relationship between demographic factors, MMPI scores and the social readjustment rating scale. *Dissertation Abstracts International, 38* (5–B), 2360.

Drake, L. E. (1946). A social I.E. scale for the MMPI. *Journal of Applied Psychology, 30,* 51–54.

Duckworth, J. C., & Anderson, W. P. (1986). *MMPI interpretation manual for counselors and clinicians* (3rd ed.). Muncie, IN: Accelerated Development.

English, R. A., Reckase, M. D., & Patience, W. M. (1977). Application of tailored testing to achievement measurement. *Behavior Research Methods and Instrumentation, 9,* 158–161.

Erdman, H. P., Greist, J. H., Klein, M. H., Jefferson, J. W., & Getto, C. (1981). The computer psychiatrist: How far have we come? Where are we heading? How far dare we go? *Behavior Research Methods and Instrumentation, 13,* 393–398.

Erdman, H. P., Klein, M. H., & Greist, J. H. (1985). Direct patient computer interviewing. *Journal of Consulting and Clinical Psychology, 53,* 760–773.

Evans, R. G. (1983). Who published what about whom? *Journal of Personality Assessment, 47,* 339–344.

Exner, J. E. (1987). Computer assistance in Rorschach interpretation. In J. N. Butcher (Ed.), *Computerized psychological assessment: A practitioner's guide* (pp. 218–235). New York: Basic Books.

Eyde, L. D. (1985). Review of the Minnesota Report: Personnel Selection System for the MMPI. In J. V. Mitchell (Ed.)., *The ninth mental measurements yearbook* (pp. 1005–1008). Lincoln: University of Nebraska Press.

Eyde, L. D., Kowal, D. M., & Fishburne, F. J. (1987, September). *Clinical implications of validity research on computer-based test interpretations of the MMPI*. Paper presented at the Symposium on Practical Test User Problems Facing Psychologists in Private Practice, New York, New York.

Eysenck, H. J. (1985). Review of California Psychological Inventory. In J. V. Mitchell (Ed.), *The ninth mental measurements yearbook* (pp. 252–253). Lincoln: University of Nebraska Press.

Fowler, R. D. (1985). Landmarks in computer-assisted psychological testing. *Journal of Consulting and Clinical Psychology, 53,* 748–759.

Fowler, R. D. (1987). Developing a computer-based test interpretation system. In J. N. Butcher (Ed.), *Computerized psychological assessment: A practitioner's guide* (pp. 50–63). New York: Basic Books.

Fowler, R. D., & Butcher, J. N. (1986). Critique of Matarazzo's views on computerized testing: All sigma and no meaning. *American Psychologist, 41,* 94–95.

Galton, F. (1884). Measurement of character. *Fortnightly Review, 42,* 179–185.

Giannetti, R. A., Klingler, D. E., Johnson, J. H., & Williams, T. A. (1976). The potential for dynamic assessment systems using on-line computer technology. *Behavior Research Methods and Instrumentation, 8,* 101–103.

Gilberstadt, H., & Duker, J. (1965). *A handbook for clinical and actuarial MMPI interpretation*. Philadelphia: Saunders.

Goldberg, L. R. (1965). Diagnosticians vs. diagnostic signs: The diagnosis of psychosis vs. neurosis from the MMPI. *Psychological Monographs, 79,* (Entire No. 602)

Goldberg, L. R. (1972). Parameters of personality inventory construction and utilization: A comparison of prediction strategies and tactics. *Multivariate Behavioral Research Monographs,* No. 72–2.

Gough, H. G. (1975). *California Psychological Inventory* (revised manual). Palo Alto, CA: Consulting Psychologists Press.

Graham, J. R. (1987). *The MMPI: A practical guide* (2nd ed.). New York: Oxford University Press.

Graham, J. R., & Butcher, J. N. (1988, March). *Differentiating schizophrenic and major affective disordered inpatients with the revised form of the MMPI*. Paper presented at the 23rd Annual Symposium on Recent Developments in the Use of the MMPI, St. Petersburg, Florida.

Graham, J. R., Schroeder, H. E., & Lilly, R. S. (1971). Factor analysis of items on the Social Introversion and Masculinity-Femininity scales of the MMPI. *Journal of Clinical Psychology, 27,* 367–370.

Grayson, H. M. (1951, June). *Psychological admissions testing program and manual*. Los Angeles: Veterans Administration Center, Neuropsychiatric Hospital.

Green, C. J. (1982). The diagnostic accuracy and utility of MMPI and MCMI computer interpretive reports. *Journal of Personality Assessment, 46,* 359–365.

Greene, R. L. (1980). *The MMPI: An interpretive manual.* New York: Grune & Stratton.

Greer, S. E. (1984). A review of the Millon Clinical Multiaxial Inventory. *Journal of Counseling and Development, 63,* 262–263.

Greist, J. H., & Klein, M. H. (1980). Computer programs for patients, clinicians, and researchers in psychiatry. In J. B. Sidowski, J. H. Johnson, & T. A. Williams (Eds.), *Technology in mental health care delivery systems* (pp. 161–181). Norwood, NJ: Ablex.

Greist, J. H., & Klein, M. H. (1981). Computers in psychiatry. In S. Arieti (Ed.), *American handbook of psychiatry* (2nd ed.) (Vol. 7, pp. 750–77). New York: Basic Books.

Guilford, J. P., & Zimmerman, W. S. (1956). Fourteen dimensions of temperament. *Psychological Monographs, 70* (Entire no. 417).

Guthrie, G. (1985). Review of Clinical Analysis Questionnaire. In J. V. Mitchell, Ed., *The ninth mental measurements yearbook* (pp. 340–341). Lincoln: University of Nebraska Press.

Halbower, C. C. (1955). *A comparison of actuarial versus clinical prediction to classes discriminated by MMPI.* Unpublished doctoral dissertation, University of Minnesota.

Harris, R. E., & Lingoes, J. C. (1968). *Subscales for the Minnesota Multiphasic Personality Inventory.* Unpublished manuscript. San Francisco: Langley Porter Clinic.

Hartshorne, H., & May, M. A. (1928). *Studies in the nature of character: Vol. 1. Studies in deceit.* New York: Macmillan.

Hase, H. D., & Goldberg, L. R. (1967). Comparative validity of different strategies of constructing personality inventory scales. *Psychological Bulletin, 67,* 231–248.

Hathaway, S. R., & McKinley, J. C. (1940). A multiphasic personality schedule (Minnesota): I. Construction of the schedule. *Journal of Psychology, 10,* 249–254.

Henrichs, T. (1964). Objective configural rules for discriminating MMPI profiles in a psychiatric population. *Journal of Clinical Psychology, 20,* 157–159.

Henrichs, T. (1966). A note on the extension of MMPI configural rules. *Journal of Clinical Psychology, 22,* 51–52.

Hess, A. K. (1985). Review of Millon Clinical Multiaxial Inventory. In J. V. Mitchell (Ed.), *The ninth mental measurements yearbook* (pp. 984–986). Lincoln: University of Nebraska Press.

Hoffman, N. G., & Butcher, J. N. (1975). Clinical limitations of three Minnesota Multiphasic Personality Inventory short forms. *Journal of Consulting and Clinical Psychology, 43,* 32–39.

Holtzman, W. H. (1960). Can the computer supplant the clinician? *Journal of Clinical Psychology, 16,* 119–122.

Hsu, L. M. (1984). MMPI T-scores: Linear versus normalized. *Journal of Consulting and Clinical Psychology, 52,* 821–823.

Jackson, D. N. (1971). The dynamics of structured personality tests: 1971. *Psychological Review, 78,* 229–248.

Jackson, D. N. (1972). *Differential Personality Inventory.* London, Ontario: Author.

Jackson, D. N. (1984). *Personality Research Form manual.* Port Huron, MI: Research Psychologists Press.

Johnson, J. H., Butcher, J. N., Null, C., & Johnson, K. N. (1984). Replicated item level factor analysis of the full MMPI. *Journal of Personality and Social Psychology, 47,* 105–114.

Johnson, J. H., Giannetti, R. A., & Williams, T. A. (1976). Computers in mental health care delivery: A review of the evolution toward interventionally relevant on-line processing. *Behavior Research Methods and Instrumentation, 8,* 83–91.

Johnson, J. H., Giannetti, R. A., & Williams, T. A. (1979). Psychological Systems Questionnaire: An objective personality test designed for on-line computer presentation, scoring, and interpretation. *Behavior Research Methods and Instrumentation, 11,* 257–260.

Johnson, J. H., & Williams, T. A. (1980). Using on-line computer technology to improve service response and decision-making effectiveness in a mental health admitting system. In J. B. Sidowski, J. H. Johnson, & T. A. Williams (Eds.), *Technology in mental health care delivery systems* (pp. 237–249). Norwood, NJ: Ablex.

Karson, S., & O'Dell, J. W. (1975). A new automated interpretation system for the 16PF. *Journal of Personality Assessment, 39,* 256–260.

Karson, S., & O'Dell, J. W. (1987). Computer-based interpretation of the 16PF: The Karson Clinical Report in contemporary practice. In J. N. Butcher (Ed.), *Computerized psychological assessment: A practitioner's guide* (pp. 198–217). New York: Basic Books.

Keller, L. S., & Butcher, J. N. (In press). *Assessment*

of chronic pain patients with the MMPI-2. Minneapolis, MN: University of Minnesota Press.

Kingston, N. M., & Dorans, N. J. (1984). Item location effects and their implications for IRT equating and adaptive testing. *Applied Psychological Measurement, 8,* 147–154.

Kleinmuntz, B. (1982). *Personality and psychological assessment.* New York: St. Martin's Press.

Kleinmuntz, B., & McLean, R. S. (1968). Computers in behavioral science: Diagnostic interviewing by digital computer. *Behavioral Science, 13,* 75–80.

Klingler, D. E., Miller, D. A., Johnson, J. H., & Williams, T. A. (1976). Strategies in the evaluation of an on-line computer-assisted unit for intake assessment of mental health patients. *Behavior Research Methods and Instrumentation, 8,* 95–100.

Klingler, D. E., Miller, D. A., Johnson, J. H., & Williams, T. A. (1977). Process evaluation of an on-line computer-assisted unit for intake assessment of mental health patients. *Behavior Research Methods and Instrumentation, 9,* 110–116.

Koss, M. P. (1980). Assessing psychological emergencies with the MMPI. In J. N. Butcher, G. Dahlstrom, M. Gunther, & W. Schofield (Eds.), *Clinical Notes on the MMPI.* Roche Psychiatric Service Institute Monograph Series. Nutley, NJ: Hoffman–LaRoche.

Koss, M. P., & Butcher, J. N. (1973). A comparison of psychiatric patients' self-report with other sources of clinical information. *Journal of Research in Personality, 7,* 225–236.

Koss, M. P., Butcher, J. N., & Hoffman, N. G. (1976). The MMPI critical items: How well do they work? *Journal of Consulting and Clinical Psychology, 44,* 921–928.

Krug, S. E. (1980). *Clinical Analysis Questionnaire Manual.* Champaign, IL: Institute for Personality and Ability Testing.

Lachar, D. (1974). *The MMPI: Clinical assessment and automated interpretation.* Los Angeles: Western Psychological Services.

Lachar, D., & Wrobel, T. A. (1979). Validation of clinicians' hunches: Construction of a new MMPI critical item set. *Journal of Consulting and Clinical Psychology, 47,* 277–284.

Lewandowski, D., & Graham, J. R. (1972). Empirical correlates of frequently occurring two-point MMPI code types: A replicated study. *Journal of Consulting and Clinical Psychology, 39,* 467–472.

Lucas, R. W., Mullins, P. J., Luna, C. B., &

McInroy, D. C. (1977). Psychiatrists and a computer as interrogators of patients with alcohol-related illnesses: A comparison. *British Journal of Psychiatry, 131,* 160–167.

Lushene, R. E., O'Neil, H. F., & Dunn, T. (1974). Equivalent validity of a completely computerized MMPI. *Journal of Personality Assessment, 38,* 353–361.

MacAndrew, C. (1965). The differentiation of male alcoholic outpatients from nonalcoholic psychiatric patients by means of the MMPI. *Quarterly Journal of Studies on Alcohol, 26,* 238–246.

Marks, P. A., Seeman, W., & Haller, D. (1974). *The actuarial use of the MMPI with adolescents and adults.* Baltimore: Williams and Wilkins.

Matarazzo, J. D. (1986a). Computerized psychological test interpretations: Unvalidated plus all mean and no sigma. *American Psychologist, 41,* 14–24.

Matarazzo, J. D. (1986b). Response to Fowler and Butcher on Matarazzo. *American Psychologist, 41,* 96.

McKinley, J. C., Hathaway, S. R., & Meehl, P. E. (1948). The MMPI: VI. The K scale. *Journal of Consulting Psychology, 12,* 20–31.

McNair, D. M. (1978). Review of the Clinical Analysis Questionnaire (CAQ). In O. K. Buros (Ed.), *Eighth mental measurements yearbook.* Highland park, NJ: Gryphon.

Meehl, P. E. (1945). The dynamics of "structured" personality tests. *Journal of Clinical Psychology, 1,* 296–303.

Meehl, P. E. (1954). *Clinical versus statistical prediction: A theoretical analysis and review of the evidence.* Minneapolis: University of Minnesota Press.

Meehl, P. E., & Dahlstrom, W. G. (1960). Objective configural rules for discriminating psychotic from neurotic MMPI profiles. *Journal of Consulting and Clinical Psychology, 24,* 375–387.

Megargee, E. I. (1972). *The California Psychological Inventory handbook.* San Francisco: Jossey-Bass.

Megargee, E. I., & Bohn, M. J. (1977). A new classification for criminal offenders, IV: Empirically determined characteristics of the ten types. *Criminal Justice and Behavior, 4,* 149–210.

Mesthene, E. G. (1970). *Technological change: Its impact on man and society.* New York: New American Library.

Miller, H. R., & Streiner, D. L. (1986). Differences in MMPI profiles with the norms of Colligan et al. *Journal of Consulting and Clinical Psychology, 54,* 843–845.

Millon, T. (1982). *Millon Clinical Multiaxial Inventory* (3rd ed.). Minneapolis, MN: National Computer Systems.

Millon, T. (1985a). The MCMI provides a good assessment of DSM-III disorders: The MCMI-II will prove even better. *Journal of Personality Assessment, 49,* 379–391.

Millon, T. (1985b). Response to Greer's review of the MCMI. *Journal of Counseling and Development, 63,* 631–632.

Millon, T. (1986). The MCMI and DSM-III: Further commentaries. *Journal of Personality Assessment, 50,* 205–207.

Millon, T. (1987). *Manual for the MCMI-II* (2nd ed.). Minneapolis, MN: National Computer Systems.

Mitchell, J. V. (Ed.) (1985). *The ninth mental measurements yearbook.* Lincoln: University of Nebraska Press.

Moreland, K. L. (1985). Validation of computer-based test interpretations: Problems and prospects. *Journal of Consulting and Clinical Psychology, 53,* 816–825.

Moreland, K. L. (1987). Computerized psychological assessment: What's available. In J. N. Butcher (Ed.), *Computerized psychological assessment: A practitioner's guide* (pp. 26–29).

Murray, H. A. (1938). *Explorations in personality.* Cambridge, MA: Harvard University Press.

Nelson, L. D., & Marks, P. A. (1985). Empirical correlates of infrequently occurring MMPI code types. *Journal of Clinical Psychology, 41,* 477–482.

Nichols, D. S. (1985). Review of the Minnesota report: Personnel Selection System for the MMPI. In J. V. Mitchell (Ed.), *The ninth mental measurements yearbook* (pp. 1008–1009). Lincoln: University of Nebraska Press.

Osborne, D. & Colligan, R. C. (1986). Linear equations for the development of non-normalized T-score tables based on the contemporary normative study of the MMPI. *Journal of Clinical Psychology, 42,* 482–484.

Patience, W. M. (1977). Description of components in tailored testing. *Behavior Research Methods and Instrumentation, 9,* 153–157.

Piotrowski, Z. A. (1980). CPR: The psychological X-ray in mental disorders. In J. B. Sidowski, J. H. Johnson, & T. A. Williams (Eds.), *Technology in mental health care delivery systems* (pp. 85–108). Norwood, NJ: Ablex.

Reise, S. P., & Waller, N. G. (in press). *Fitting the two-parameter model to personality data. Applied Psychological Measurement.*

Richards, J. S., Fine, P. R., Wilson, T. L., & Rogers, J. T. (1983). A voice-operated method for administering the MMPI. *Journal of Personality Assessment, 47,* 167–170.

Rome, H. P., Swenson, W. M., Mataya, P., McCarthy, C. E., Pearson, J. S., Keating, F. R., & Hathaway, S. R. (1962). Symposium on automation technics in personality assessment. *Proceedings of the Staff Meetings of the Mayo Clinic, 37,* 61–82.

Sanders, R. L. (1985). Computer-administered individualized psychological testing: A feasibility study. *International Journal of Man-Machine Studies, 23,* 197–213.

Sapinkopf, R. C. (1978). A computer adaptive testing approach to the measurement of personality variables. *Dissertation Abstracts International, 38* (10–B), 4993.

Schuerger, J. M., Foerstner, S. B., Serkownek, K., & Ritz, G. (1987). History and validities of the Serkownek subscales for MMPI scales 5 and 0. *Psychological Reports, 61,* 227–235.

Scissons, E. H. (1976). Computer administration of the California Psychological Inventory. *Measurement and Evaluation in Guidance, 9,* 22–25.

Sheldon, W. H. (1940). *The varieties of human physique: An introduction to constitutional psychology.* New York: Harper & Row.

Slutske, W. S., Ben-Porath, Y. S., & Butcher, J. N. (1988, March). *A real-data simulation study of adaptive MMPI administration.* Paper presented at the 23rd Annual Symposium on Recent Developments in the Use of the MMPI, St. Petersburg, Florida.

Smail, D. J. (1971). Statistical prediction and "cookbooks:" A technological confidence trick. *British Journal of Medical Psychology, 44,* 173–178.

Song, W. Z. (1981). *Application of the Minnesota Multiphasic Personality Inventory in some areas of the People's Republic of China.* Paper given at the Seventh International Conference on Personality Assessment, Honolulu, Hawaii.

Stein, K. B. (1968). The TSC scales: The outcome of a cluster analysis of the 550 MMPI items. In P. McReynolds (Ed.), *Advances in psychological assessment* (Vol. 1). Palo Alto, California: Science and Behavior Books.

Stillman, R., Roth, W. T., Colby, K. M., & Rosenbaum, C. P. (1969). An on-line computer system for initial psychiatric inventory. *American Journal of Psychiatry, 125,* 8–11.

Stout, R. L. (1981). New approaches to the design of computerized interviewing and testing systems. *Behavior Research Methods and Instrumentation, 13,* 436–442.

Streiner, D. L., & Miller, H. R. (1986). Can a good short form of the MMPI ever be developed? *Journal of Clinical Psychology, 42,* 109–113.

Sundberg, N. D. (1985a). Review of Behaviordyne Psychodiagnostic Laboratory Service for the Minnesota Multiphasic Personality Inventory (a computer-based test interpretation). In J. V. Mitchell (Ed.), *The ninth mental measurements yearbook* (pp. 1003–1005). Lincoln: University of Nebraska Press.

Sundberg, N. D. (1985b). Review of the Western Psychological Services computer based test report on the Minnesota Multiphasic Personality Inventory. In J. V. Mitchell (Ed.), *The ninth mental measurements yearbook* (pp. 1010–1011). Lincoln: University of Nebraska Press.

Tellegen, A. (1982). *Brief manual for the Differential Personality Questionnaire.* Minneapolis: Author.

Terman, L. M., & Miles, C. C. (1936). *Sex and personality: Studies in masculinity and femininity.* New York: McGraw-Hill.

Vale, C. D., & Keller, L. S. (1987). Developing expert computer systems to interpret psychological tests. In J. N. Butcher (Ed.), *Computerized psychological assessment: A practitioner's guide* (pp. 64–83).

Vale, C. D., Keller, L. S., & Bentz, V. J. (1986). Development and validation of a computerized interpretation system for personnel tests. *Personnel Psychology, 39,* 525–542.

Vale, C. D., & Weiss, D. J. (1975, October). *A study of computer-administered stradaptive ability testing.* (Research Report 75–5). Minneapolis: University of Minnesota, Psychometric Methods Program.

Valsiner, J. (1982). *Use of the MMPI in the Soviet Union.* Unpublished mimeographed materials.

Waller, N. B., & Reise, S. P. (in press). The development and implementation of computerized adaptive testing within the realm of normal range personality assessment. *Journal of Personality and Social Psychology.*

Weiner, H. (1956). Subtle and obvious keys for the MMPI. In G. S. Welsh & W. G. Dahlstrom (Eds.), *Basic readings on the MMPI in psychology and medicine* (pp. 195–204). Minneapolis: University of Minnesota Press.

Weiss, D. J. (1973, September). *The stratified adaptive computerized ability test* (Research Report 73–3). Minneapolis: University of Minnesota, Psychometric Methods Program.

Weiss, D. J. (1985). Adaptive testing by computer. *Journal of Consulting and Clinical Psychology, 53,* 774–789.

Weiss, D. J., & Vale, C. D. (1987). Computerized adaptive testing for measuring abilities and other psychological variables. In J. N. Butcher (Ed.), *Computerized psychological assessment: A practitioner's guide* (pp. 325–343). New York: Basic Books.

Welsh, G. S. (1956). Factor dimensions A and R. In G. S. Welsh & W. G. Dahlstrom (Eds.), *Basic readings on the MMPI in psychology and medicine.* Minneapolis: University of Minnesota Press.

Widiger, T. A. (1985). Review of Millon Clinical Multiaxial Inventory. In J. V. Mitchell (Ed.), *The ninth mental measurements yearbook* (pp. 986–988). Lincoln: The University of Nebraska Press.

Widiger, T. A., & Sanderson, C. (1987). The convergent and discriminant validity of the MCMI as a measure of the DSM-III personality disorders. *Journal of Personality Assessment, 51,* 228–242.

Widiger, T. A., Williams, J. B. W., Spitzer, R. L., & Frances, A. (1985). The MCMI as a measure of DSM-III. *Journal of Personality Assessment, 49,* 366–378.

Wiggins, J. S. (1969). Content dimensions in the MMPI. In J. N. Butcher (Ed.), *MMPI: Research developments and clinical applications.* New York: McGraw-Hill.

Williams, T. A. (1977). Computer technology in mental health care: "Toys" or tools? *Behavior Research Methods and Instrumentation, 9,* 108–109.

Woodworth, R. S. (1920). *Personal Data Sheet.* Chicago: Stoelting.

Zuckerman, M. (1985). Review of Sixteen Personality Factor Questionnaire. In J. V. Mitchell (Ed.), *The ninth mental measurements yearbook* (pp. 1392–1394). Lincoln: University of Nebraska Press.

CHAPTER 17

RORSCHACH ASSESSMENT

Philip Erdberg

The assessment technique that Hermann Rorschach introduced in 1921 has had its share of critics, but even they must concede the resilience of an instrument that, against considerable odds, has now survived well into its second half century. After Rorschach's death the year following its publication, the fledgling test was maintained by a few of his associates and then brought to America. There, it found itself with five groups of increasingly diverging adoptive parents whose differences ultimately became so extensive as to threaten its identity. Methodological criticism came from outside the Rorschach community as well, and there were even suggestions that the test be discarded entirely. But by the mid-1970s, a new consolidation had integrated the best of what had been learned during the half century of divergence, and the Rorschach now appears to have entered what may well be its healthiest years to date. The history of the test's development, a review of its elements, and some descriptions of new directions are the subjects of this chapter.

HISTORY AND DEVELOPMENT

The idea that associations to ambiguous visual stimuli could be of importance in understanding a person is an ancient one. Early writings suggest that the classical Greeks were interested in the interaction of ambiguity and the person's characterization of reality (Piotrowski, 1957). By the fifteenth century, both Da Vinci and Botticelli were postulating a relationship between creativity and the processing of ambiguous materials (Zubin, Eron, & Schumer, 1965). The use of inkblots as stimuli for imagination achieved substantial popularity in Europe during the nineteenth century. A parlor game called Blotto asked people to create responses to inkblots, and a book by

Justinius Kerner (1857) contained a collection of poetic associations to inkblot-like designs.

As the nineteenth century ended, several workers in the professional community were beginning to utilize inkblots in the study of a variety of psychological operations. Krugman (1940) reports that Binet and Henri were using inkblots to study visual imagination as early as 1895. Tulchin (1940) notes that Dearborn's work at Harvard (which resulted in 1897 and 1898 publications) employed inkblots as part of an experimental approach to the study of consciousness. Another American investigator, Whipple (1910), also utilized a series of inkblots as a way of studying what he called "active imagination." Rybakow (1910), working in Moscow, developed a series of eight blots to tap imaginative function, and Hens (1917), working at Bleuler's clinic in Zurich, used inkblots with a series of children, normal adults, and psychiatric patients.

The young Swiss psychiatrist, Hermann Rorschach, thus was not the first to involve inkblots in the study of psychological processes when he began his project in 1911. But his work was qualitatively different from anything that had preceded it in establishing a framework from which personality descriptions of substantial scope could be generated. Rorschach's preliminary but remarkably farsighted *Psychodiagnostik* was published in 1921. Tragically, he died within a year, at the age of 38, of complications of appendicitis.

It was three of Rorschach's friends, Walter Morgenthaler, Emil Oberholzer, and George Roemer, who insured that the insights and challenges of *Psychodiagnostik* were not lost. Morgenthaler had championed the book's publication against some resistance from the Bircher publishing house. Oberholzer followed up by insuring that an important posthumous paper (Rorschach & Oberholzer, 1923) was published, and all three continued to teach the test and encourage adherents. One of Oberholzer's students, David Levy, took the test to Chicago, where he established the first American Rorschach seminar in 1925.

Although each could have, neither Oberholzer nor Levy moved into a clear position as Rorschach's successor, and once in America, the test was adopted by five psychologists of very different backgrounds— Samuel Beck, Bruno Klopfer, Zygmunt Piotrowski, Marguerite Hertz, and David Rapaport. Of the five, only Beck, through the opportunity of a year's fellowship with Oberholzer in Zurich, was able to spend a significant amount of time with someone who had worked directly with Rorschach. With little in the way of common heritage or experience, the five Americans soon began diverging in directions consistent with their theoretical orientations. They ultimately produced five independent Rorschach systems, each attracting adherents and each generating a body of published literature and clinical lore. The history of the Rorschach from the late 1920s to the early 1970s is, to a large extent, the history of the development and elaboration of these five systems.

Beck completed the first American Rorschach dissertation in 1932. He followed it with a number of journal articles and published his *Introduction to the Rorschach Method* in 1937. He completed the elaboration of his system with additional books in 1944, 1945, and 1952, with revised editions published through 1967.

Klopfer had his first direct contact with the Rorschach in 1933. After a series of articles, which included a description of a scoring system (Klopfer & Sender, 1936), he published *The Rorschach Technique* with Douglas Kelley in 1942. Elaborations of his system occurred in books in 1954, 1956, and 1970.

Piotrowski was a member of a seminar offered by Klopfer in 1934, but within two years he was moving toward the creation of an independent system. His work culminated with the publication of *Perceptanalysis* in 1957.

Hertz, after a relatively brief interaction with Levy and Beck, utilized the Rorschach in her dissertation in 1932 and continued research with the test for the decade after at the Brush Foundation in Cleveland. Sadly, the nearly 3,000 cases she had amassed and the almost completed manuscript describing her system were inadvertently destroyed when the Foundation closed, and she never produced another book. However, her steady stream of journal articles and her

ongoing seminars led to the clear existence of a Hertz system by 1945.

Rapaport became interested in the Rorschach in the late 1930s and published a paper that described it in detail as part of a review of projective techniques in 1942. The first volume of *Diagnostic Psychological Testing* was published with Merton Gill and Roy Schafer in 1945, with the second volume following a year later. Schafer extended the system with additional books in 1948, 1954, and 1967, and Robert Holt edited a revised edition of the original two volumes in 1968.

With publication of Piotrowski's book in 1957, all five of the systems were essentially complete. Each was taught independently and, during this period of divergence, each accumulated its own body of research and clinical literature. When Exner did a comprehensive review of the five systems in 1969, he concluded that there were really five overlapping but clearly discrete tests. Each of the systematizers had taken Rorschach's ten inkblots and used some of the ideas in *Psychodiagnostik* to fashion an instrument consistent with his or her training and theoretical stance. Each asked the subject to respond to the cards and each attempted some sort of inquiry as a way of clarifying how the person had generated the response. Each had developed a format for coding or "scoring" various aspects of the percept. And each system then generated an interpretation on the basis of the data that had been gathered. But, at every level from administration to interpretation, there were major differences among the five systems.

These differences make sense in the context of the different theoretical positions and the resulting differences in methodology that the five systematizers brought to the various aspects of the Rorschach. At the coding level, Beck's rigorous positivism and behavioral training emerged in his insistence on normative and validational backing for the various scoring elements. Klopfer's phenomenological background allowed examiners greater leeway in using their own experience for reference in coding the same material. Rapaport, Hertz, and Piotrowski used methodological approaches between those of Beck and Klopfer. At the interpretive level, Rapaport's extensive utilization of psychoanalytic concepts separates his work from the somewhat less stringently theory-based interpretive strategies of the other four systems.

Trying to sort through all the ways the five systems differ one from another is an immense task. But a distinction suggested by Weiner (1977) addresses the crucial question that must be asked in order to characterize an approach: How does the system conceptualize the nature of Rorschach data? Weiner suggests that the Rorschach can be conceptualized either as a perceptual-cognitive task or as a stimulus to fantasy. The perceptual-cognitive stance assumes that the basic Rorschach task is to structure and organize an ambiguous stimulus field and that the way a person accomplishes this task is directly *representative* of real-world behavior that can be expected in other situations requiring the same kinds of operations. As an example, people who deal with the inkblots by breaking them into details that they then combine into meaningful relationships could be expected to deal with their day-to-day tasks in a similarly energetic, integrative manner. The focus in the perceptual-cognitive conceptualization of the Rorschach is not on the words but rather the structure of the person's responses, such as choice of location or integration of various blot areas. This reliably quantifiable description of Rorschach response structure is then utilized to generate descriptions of how the person is likely to behave elsewhere. These descriptions are based on the large body of validity studies that link Rorschach structural variables with nontest behavior.

The stimulus to fantasy approach, on the other hand, views the Rorschach as a vehicle that allows the person to project material about need states onto the ambiguity of the blots. The person's productions are seen as *symbolic* of internal dynamics. As an example, the percept of "two bitterly disappointed people" might be utilized to infer a state of interpersonal conflict on the part of the person producing the response. The focus in the stimulus-to-fantasy approach is on the actual words, and this content is utilized to derive hypotheses about internal states. Here the interpreter utilizes his or her theoretical framework and clinical experience to link symbols and dynamics.

There is some question about where Rorschach himself should be placed in terms of the perceptual-cognitive versus stimulus-to-fantasy distinction, but it is likely that he would have taken a middleground position that included both approaches. He had specifically criticized Hens' 1917 inkblot work for its focus solely on content and imagination. In doing this, he differentiated himself from Hens and, by implication, from most of the earlier inkblot work, the focus of which had been on verbalization and creative processes. Rorschach stated that his primary interest was what he called "the pattern of perceptive process," as opposed to the content of inkblot responses. *Psychodiagnostik* itself is almost totally in the perceptual-cognitive camp, with particular attention to issues of form, movement, and color. The 1923 posthumous

paper added the structural element of shading. And yet, Rorschach was well trained in the work of Freud and Jung. He almost certainly would have been comfortable with Freud's 1896 description of projection as a mechanism by which individuals endow external material with aspects of their own dynamics—and with Frank's classic 1939 paper which suggested that stimuli such as inkblots could serve as "projective methods" for eliciting this process. Indeed, Roemer (1967) states that Rorschach saw value in content analysis, citing a 1921 letter suggesting that he envisioned the technique as including both structural and symbolic material.

A review of their actual work in dealing with Rorschach material suggests that all five of the American systematizers also saw the data as having both perceptual-cognitive and symbolic components—but with real differences as to relative emphasis. Beck stayed closest to the structural aspects. Rapaport was most willing to place major emphasis on the verbalizations, and the other three were at varying points in between. As each system solidified and developed specialized terminology and literature, clinicians schooled in one approach could not easily communicate with those trained in another system because, increasingly, they lacked a shared language and body of knowledge.

The purpose of Exner's development of the Comprehensive System (1974, 1978, 1982, 1986a) was to provide the fragmented Rorschach community once more with a common methodology, language, and literature base. The accumulated literature of all five systems was reviewed, and some new research was undertaken. Using reliability and validity as criteria for inclusion, the project yielded a constellation of empirically defensible elements that forms the structural aspect of the system. Content analysis is a secondary but significant part of the Comprehensive System, and the approach to the handling of data as symbolic material can be characterized as dynamic but not specifically linked to any single theory of personality operation. What follows is a description of the elements of the Comprehensive System.

THE RORSCHACH ELEMENTS

A very frequent role for the Rorschach clinician is as consultant to the intervention process, offering data of value to the referring professional, whatever the setting. Typically the referral is made in the hope that personality assessment can supplement the observations made in clinical interaction and provide additional understanding of the person and guidance for intervention decisions. Because this is the way the Rorschach is often employed, it seems useful to present this review of its elements and their supporting literature in the format of a series of practical questions to which the test can validly be addressed.

How Does the Person Prefer to Cope with Need States

Faced with stressful situations, some individuals tend to utilize their internal resources to cope, while others are more apt to seek interaction with some aspect of their world. The Erlebnistypus (EB) first proposed by Rorschach (1921) provides an extraordinarily valuable indicator of which of these response tendencies is more likely for a particular person. A substantial number of studies (Exner, 1986a; Molish, 1967; and Singer & Brown, 1977, provide reviews) have lent support to Rorschach's hypothesis that individuals who use a preponderance of human movement (M) in formulating their Rorschach percepts (introversives) tend to utilize inner resources to deal with needs, while those who involve relatively more chromatic color (FC, CF, and C) in their responses (extratensives) are more likely to seek interaction with the environment during need states. Rorschach also identified a third response style, the ambient, to describe the person who does not have a clearly skewed introversive or extratensive profile.

A study described by Exner (1978) illustrates some behavioral correlates of the three styles and provides some reference points for contrasting them. A logical analysis task in which each move could potentially provide increasingly specific feedback about the combination of moves necesssary to reach a solution was given to academically matched college students whom the Rorschach had identified as either introversives, ambients, or extratensives. The students were scored on total moves to solution, total errors, total repeated moves, time between moves, and time to solution. The introversive group was characterized by fewer moves, longer times between moves, and fewer repeated moves and errors. The extratensive group had more moves and shorter times between moves than the introversives. The ambients had the greatest number of moves, the greatest number of repeated moves and errors, and, most important, took the longest amount of time to get to solutions.

We can speculate from these data that the introversive group used a more "thoughtful" approach, processing feedback internally, while the extratensive group utilized more interaction with the environment and less internal processing time. If we use time to solution as a measure of the efficiency of the problem-solving styles, the introversives and extratensives emerge as equally efficient although stylistically very different. It is only the ambients who are less efficient.

A substantial amount of data (Exner, 1986a, 1986b) on both normal and pathological adults is consistent with the problem-solving study described above in suggesting that ambients may be least able to cope with a variety of stressful situations. Within a normal sample, ambients made up only 23.8% of the group, with the remaining three quarters made up about equally of introversives and extratensives. In contrast, ambients accounted for 52.4% of an inpatient depressive sample, 56% of an outpatient character problem group, 41.9% of an inpatient schizophrenic sample, and 33.3% of a borderline personality disorder group.

The EB is very much an enduring trait that is predictive on an ongoing basis of the style individuals use in dealing with stressful situations. In one study, Exner (1986a) retested 39 clearly identified introversives and extratensives at one year. On retest, 38 of the 39 were still identifiable as displaying the Rorschach style that had characterized them a year earlier.

The issue of problem-solving style as described by the EB has far-ranging implications for the clinician. As an example, we might speculate that spouses whose styles are different would have difficulty when they needed to confront a problem as a couple, because one member's style of using interaction to "talk the problem through" might interfere with the other member's need for solitude to "mull things over."

Is the Person's Style Likely to Work? What Kinds of Problems Will it Meet?

Although the introversive and extratensive approaches are stylistically very different, they both represent task-oriented approaches for dealing with need states. They are both volitional strategies that the person calls up to handle problems. Consequently, Beck (1960) suggested that the summation of the human movement and color determinants (EA) could be utilized as a measure of the person's available psychological resources, those coping strategies the individual could decide to apply to some sort of stressful situation. A clue as to whether these organized strategies can be expected to work is provided by considering another summation, the *es*, and its relation to *EA*.

The *es*, a variable suggested by Exner (1986a) comprises the unorganized psychological material that impinges on the person in unexpected and often disorganizing ways. Using *EA* as a measure of accessible coping strategies and *es* as a measure of nondeliberate, intrusive psychological material, Exner developed the *D* score, a scaled difference score that is generated by comparing *EA* to *es*. When the *D* score is 0 or in the positive range, it suggests that

> *under most circumstances*, sufficient resources are available to be able to initiate and direct behavior in a deliberate and meaningful way, and that stimulus demands being experienced generally do not exceed the capacities of the subject for being able to control behavior. (p. 315)

If *D* is in the minus range, Exner suggests the likelihood of a situation in which "the frequency and/or intensity of stimulus demands exceeds the range of responses that can be formulated or implemented effectively" (p. 316).

If the *es* represents the totality of unorganized psychological material tapped by the Rorschach, a review of its components can be of value in describing more specifically the quality of the variables that have the potential for interfering with the person's deliberate coping style, be it introversive, extratensive, or ambient. Two Rorschach elements appear to be associated with disruptive ideation and four elements appear to be associated with intrusive affect. We will discuss each of these components of the *es* in detail.

Less validational data have been developed for the animal movement (*FM*) determinant than for most other Rorschach variables. The available studies are consistent in suggesting that *FM* is associated with the experience of unorganized ideation about need states intruding into consciousness with an intensity that demands action. What happens then may well depend on the extensiveness of the person's coping strategies for dealing with the need state to which he or she has been alerted. When the unorganized ideation reflected by *FM* is greater than the organized ideational style associated with *M*, the probability of more impulsive behavior may go up. Two studies (Exner & Murillo, 1975; Exner, Murillo, & Cannavo, 1973) found that when *FM* is greater than *M*, the likelihood of posthospitalization relapse is greater for a variety of psychiatric patients. We can speculate that one of the reasons for the relapsers' inability to operate outside the hospital involved their ongoing experience of

being alerted to need states for which they did not have sufficient coping and delaying strategies and to which they responded impulsively and inappropriately.

Another sort of disruptive ideational experience is that which appears to be associated with the use of inanimate movement (*m*) in formulating Rorschach percepts. While the *FM* experience seems to involve ideation about internal need states, *m* suggests ideation provoked by the experience of stressful situations over which the person feels little control. Subject groups as varied as Navy personnel under severe storm conditions, depressed psychiatric inpatients the day before a first ECT treatment, parachute trainees the evening before their first jump, and hospital patients the day before elective surgery all showed more *m* in the Rorschachs they produced at these times than in baseline records (Shalit, 1965; Exner, 1986a). A series of temporal consistency studies (Exner, 1986a) suggests that the test-retest correlations of *m* are notably lower than those of most other Rorschach variables, supporting the conceptualization of *m* as a situational or "state" variable.

The next group of Rorschach components associated with the individual's unorganized operations appears to involve the experience of painful emotion as opposed to disruptive ideation. Each component is reflective of a somewhat different type of distressing emotional experience, and it will be helpful to review each separately.

The use of the Rorschach's light-dark or shading features to formulate a percept involving texture (*FT*, *TF*, or *T*) appears to reflect the experience of a need for interpersonal contact that has more of an "emotional" than an "intellectual" quality. As an example, recently separated or divorced individuals who had not yet established new emotional relationships produced 2.7 times as much texture in their records as a group of demographically matched controls who rated their marriages at least average for stability and happiness (Exner, 1986a). Texture is the most frequent of the shading determinants, with most nonpatients producing one texture determinant. It would appear that the distribution of texture for several patient groups has a more bimodal quality, with members of these groups producing either no texture or more than one texture determinant. We can speculate that these extremes are associated with disruptions in effective interpersonal function, with the high-texture individuals manifesting greater than average interpersonal neediness and the no-texture individuals experiencing an unwillingness to seek relationships that have a meaningful affective component.

Another Rorschach variable that can contribute to

the amount of painful emotion impinging on the person involves the use of the shading features to formulate a percept of depth or dimensionality (*FV*, *VF*, or *V*). The use of this vista determinant appears associated with the sort of introspection that produces an unrealistically negative self-evaluation. Exner's data (1986a) suggest that vista is relatively rare (27%) in adult normals, while it occurs in 80% of an inpatient depressive sample. Exner and Wylie (1977), Exner (1986a), and Arffa (1982) have found that this generally rare variable is frequently present in the records of suicidal adults, adolescents, and children.

A third source of disruptive emotion is the experience that can be linked to the general use of the light-dark features of the blots (*FY*, *YF*, and *Y*). These diffuse shading determinants appear to suggest that the person is experiencing feelings of helplessness or resignation in the face of a stressful situation which demands action. Exner (1978) followed psychotherapy patients in a longitudinal study and found that those who were able to terminate by 18 months were characterized by significant decreases in the amount of diffuse shading in their records. Patients who were still in therapy at 18 months had about the same amount of diffuse shading as when they had begun treatment. We can hypothesize that diffuse shading is associated with some experience of helplessness in the face of stressful demands.

The final Rorschach variable that contributes to disruptive emotion involves the utilization of the white-gray-black features of the blots (*FC'*, *C'F*, and *C'*). This achromatic color determinant appears related to the experience of containing affect instead of allowing its discharge into the world. Exner (1986a) notes that several groups who could be expected to inhibit affective discharge—psychosomatics, obsessives, schizoids, and depressives who did not make suicide attempts—showed significantly more achromatic color in their Rorschachs than individuals whose behavior suggested less containment of affect (character disorders and depressives who made suicide attempts). It would appear that individuals who use achromatic color in producing their Rorschach percepts tend to internalize affect, and the pressure and disequilibrium that this painful limiting of emotional expression can produce is substantial.

These, then, are the sources of intrusive ideation and emotion that appear to have Rorschach correlates. When these disruptive elements predominate in a person's psychological operations, they can interfere significantly with the ability to utilize task-oriented coping strategies effectively.

What Is the Quality of the Person's Reality Testing?

The individual's ability to converge on percepts that are frequently seen or can be easily shared with others is a Rorschach indicator thought to be representative of accurate function in other day-to-day activities. Although there have been different methodologies used in the establishment of this indicator (Kinder, Brubaker, Ingram, & Reading, 1982; Exner, 1986a), it is fair to say that Rorschach and all the systematizers since have viewed "form quality" as an important variable. The consistent sense throughout all the systems is that form quality describes the individual's ability to operate conventionally and realistically in the world, a sort of conflict-free ego function. This skill manifests itself very early in normal development. It is fascinating to note that the perceptual accuracy of nonpatient 5-year-olds is virtually identical to that found for 16-year-olds and for adults (Exner & Weiner, 1982). Exner (1986a) provides an extensive review, suggesting that significant deficits in Rorschach form quality are likely to be associated with "major impairment" (p. 369).

Rorschach's original recommendation was that percepts be differentiated on the basis of "good" versus "poor" form. Elaborations of this basic dichotomy have allowed for greater specificity in describing the individual's reality testing. Using a modification of an approach suggested by Mayman (1970), Exner (1986a) divides good form responses into those involving superior articulation and those whose articulation is only ordinary. He divides nonconvergent form responses into those that are not commonly seen but that do not significantly misrepresent reality and those that distort it in arbitrary and very inaccurate ways. This sort of distinction can be of substantial value in the assessment of schizophrenia, where the specification of how badly reality is distorted may be diagnostic. Harder and Ritzler (1979), for example, found that a good form versus poor form dichotomy was unable to differentiate between psychotics and nonpsychotics in their inpatient sample, while approaches that made finer gradations within the good and poor form categories could differentiate the two groups quite accurately.

Exner's recent (1986a) development of the X−% was designed to provide a single measure that indicates how frequently the individual has significantly distorted the blot contours in the production of percepts. The mean X − % for Exner's nonpatient sample is 6%, while the mean for a sample of inpatient schizophrenics is 31%. An X−% greater than 20% suggests that the individual's disregard of the stimulus properties of the blots is so extensive that concern about his or her ability to operate accurately in other parts of daily life would be appropriate.

Another elaboration that may have substantial value in describing the person's reality testing is the distinction between perceptual accuracy in relatively affect-free situations (F+%) and accuracy in situations involving more affective complexity (X+%). Typically, these two indicators are highly correlated, but when they differ markedly, the divergence may have clinical significance. We can speculate, for example, that individuals whose affect-free reality testing is significantly better than their perceptual accuracy in emotionally toned situations might do well in structured hospital settings, but would tend to have difficulty if they were discharged into more ambiguous and complex environments.

How Mature and Complex Are the Person's Psychological Operations?

There are many of ways to approach the inkblots, some of them involving substantially more complexity than others. These distinctions appear to be of value in describing the sophistication of the person's psychological operations in day-to-day settings. Meili-Dworetzki (1956) found that as children increase in age, their location, selection, and integration of blot details become more complex. In a more recent study, Smith (1981) classified second- and sixth-grade students in terms of the Piagetian stages of cognitive development and found that children at the higher stages more frequently chose the whole blot as the location for their percepts and integrated various details into meaningful relationships ("two people looking at a butterfly"). Exner and Weiner (1982) found that these organized responses increased from 17% in the 5-year-old normative sample to 28% for their 16-year-olds, while vague percepts ("some kind of cloud") decreased from 32% to 7%. In the Comprehensive System, the scoring of developmental quality encompasses a range from very diffuse percepts to complex integration of form-dominated objects and may thus provide data about the sophistication with which the person approaches the world.

The use of blends, percepts in which more than one determinant is used in producing the response, appears to be associated with the complexity of the person's psychological operations as well. Exner

(1986a) suggests that although there may be a very modest relation to intelligence, what blends probably reflect specifically is psychological complexity and awareness of the intricacies of oneself and one's environment. He goes on to suggest that either a very large or very small number of blends may be problematical. The large numbers may be associated with an immobilizingly overcomplex style and the low-blend individual may be characterized by limited ability or willingness to entertain complex alternatives when responding to demands.

How Frequently Does the Person Attempt to Organize the Environment?

As noted above, an individual can either take a sort of "conservation of energy" approach to the Rorschach or attempt to organize the blot more energetically. The more conservative approach limits percepts to a single detail, while the more energetic style involves utilizing either the whole blot or integrating two or more details into a meaningful relationship. With only one possible exception (the whole percept on card V), responses involving wholes or the integration of details appear to represent a more organizationally challenging process. The frequency with which the person attempts this sort of energy-consuming integration (Zf) may provide a useful prediction of style in approaching the elements of the day-to-day world. Although Zf does have a modest correlation with intelligence (Exner, 1974), it would appear that other stylistic variables must play at least as great a part in determining how likely it is that the individual will attempt the synthesizing sorts of operations that this index reflects. For example, Exner (1986a) speculates that high Zf may be associated with a person's need for intellectual attainment or with a very precise way of dealing with detail. Low Zf, on the other hand, may reflect unwillingness to engage the complexity of the stimulus field.

How Efficient Are the Person's Attempts?

Whatever the frequency of the person's organizational attempts, it is equally important to know whether each attempt is likely to be efficient or not. An index developed by Exner (1974) can be of substantial value in describing the quality of the person's integrative efforts. This index, the Zd, provides a measure of whether, for any given number of organizational attempts, the overall complexity of an individual's integrative operation is greater, less, or about the same as that of a primarily nonpatient group studied by Wilson and Blake (1950). Individuals with a high positive Zd tend to bring in more complexity per organizational attempt than the Wilson and Blake sample, and they can be described as overincorporators. A high negative Zd implies that the individual has involved less complexity in organizational attempts than the normative sample did, an underincorporative style. A series of studies summarized by Exner (1986a) suggests that the Rorschach finding of under-incorporative or overincorporative style is associated with some quite consistent behavioral tendencies, whether the subjects were youngsters playing "Simon Says," high school students doing a perceptual-spatial task, college students guessing from incomplete verbal data, or adults doing a serial learning problem. The underincorporators were characterized by fast speed but many errors, responding before they had fully scanned and processed the data and guessing early as opposed to waiting for the appearance of additional data. The overincorporators tended to be much more cautious in their response style, waiting much longer before acting and needing more data, sometimes to the point of redundancy, to prompt their decisions. Both these extreme styles can be maladaptive. The under-incorporator runs the risk of inappropriate action by not processing all the relevant data. The overincorporators' need for "complete" data can be immobilizing, particularly in situations that involve time pressure or deadlines.

What Is the Extent and Quality of the Person's Self-Focus?

Several Rorschach variables provide information about self-image. We will review each of these in detail.

There is some suggestion that the use of the symmetrical properties of the blots to generate percepts involving pairs (2) or reflections (Fr or rF) is associated with self-focus. Exner (1973, 1986a) found that pair and reflection responses were positively associated with self-focused answers on a sentence completion task and with mirror-looking behavior in a group of engineering job applicants waiting for an interview. These findings led to the establishment of the Egocentricity Index, a weighted percentage of the number of reflections and pairs in a person's record. If someone's Egocentricity Index is significantly higher than the norm for his or her age group, it suggests the

likelihood of greater self-involvement. If it is notably lower than the age group mean, there is a likelihood of the sort of negative self-concept that is seen in depressed or suicidal individuals.

It would appear that one of the components of the Egocentricity Index, reflection responses, represents a somewhat more primitive and intense form of self-focus. Although frequencies for all groups are low, Exner and Weiner (1982) found that the percentage of reflection responses in the records of their nonpatient 5-year-olds was more than twice that of the 11-year-olds. Exner (1986a) reports that 32% of an outpatient character disorder sample have at least one reflection response, as opposed to an 8% figure for the adult nonpatients. He reports that individuals with reflection responses in their records were ranked negatively by their outpatient group therapy peers on items such as "would seek advice from" or "would tell problems to." We can speculate that reflections represent a particularly intense sort of self-focus that can lead to being viewed by others as unavailable or uninterested.

The presence of two Rorschach determinants, vista and form dimensionality (FD), suggest that the person is devoting some time to self-inspection. The form dimensionality determinant suggests a somewhat more objective version of this self-focus. As noted above, vista is associated with an intensely devaluing self-appraisal in which the person is unable to place positive and negative aspects in perspective.

Morbid content on the Rorschach also has implications for quite negative self-concept. Exner (1986a) reports the presence of at least one morbid content percept in 97% of an inpatient depressive sample as opposed to 47% of his nonpatient group. He reports that therapy patients who have three or more morbid content percepts were rated by their therapists as having more negative attitudes toward themselves and their presenting problems and less optimism about the future than patients without this Rorschach finding. Exner suggests that elevations in morbid content may indicate "that the self-image is conceptualized by the subject to include more negative and possibly damaged features than is commonplace and, second, that the orientation toward the self, and probably toward the environment, is marked by considerable pessimism" (p. 397).

How Actively or Passively Does the Person Interact with the World?

A differentiation of whether the person's movement responses are active ("someone building a house") or passive ("a bird gliding through the sky") appears to have substantial promise as a way of predicting a variety of important non-Rorschach behaviors. Exner (1974) found that acute schizophrenics, patients hospitalized for character disorders, and patients with a variety of diagnoses but a common history of assaultiveness were characterized by significantly more active movement responses. Inpatient schizophrenics and depressives had significantly more passive movement percepts. Even more important, though, was his finding that approximately 70% of psychiatric patients had a skewed active-passive mix, while about the same percentage of nonpatients had a more balanced mix of the two kinds of movement responses.

If the person's Rorschach active-passive balance is skewed one way or the other, a series of studies summarized by Exner (1986a) suggests the likelihood of cognitive inflexibility in a wide variety of situations. When the progress of adolescents treated for behavioral problems was evaluated by significant others, most of those rated as improved had shifted from a skewed to a more balanced active-passive ratio. Almost all of those rated as unimproved had not made this shift. Women whose active-passive mix was skewed were also characterized by a relatively rigid style when the actions of the central figure of their daydreams were evaluated. Women with more balanced active-passive ratios shifted much more frequently between active and passive modes for their daydreams' central figure. Psychoanalytically oriented therapists rated patients with skewed active-passive ratios lower for insight, progress, and overall session effectiveness and higher for redundancy than they did a group of patients with a more even distribution of active and passive percepts. High school students with balanced active-passive ratios were able to come up with significantly more unusual or "creative" uses for familiar objects both singly and in combination than an academically matched group of students with very skewed active-passive ratios. The common theme throughout these studies is that the Rorschach finding of a skewed distribution of active and passive percepts appears to be associated with the sort of cognitive rigidity that may limit the variety of the person's coping behaviors.

Two studies summarized by Exner (1986a) are of interest in suggesting correlates of the particular Rorschach finding of a skew in the direction of more passive percepts. When a measure of behavioral passivity was administered to the significant others of 279 outpatients, those with a passive skew in their Rorschachs were rated much higher for a variety of passive behaviors. Even more specifically, it would appear that when passive percepts for human movement (Mp) exceed active percepts (Ma), the person's ideation may be characterized by a sort of "magical thinking" which awaits the intervention of others at stressful times. Two groups of nonpatient adults, identified by the presence or absence of Mp greater than Ma, were asked to write endings for TAT stories in which the protagonist was portrayed as being in some sort of problematical situation. The Mp individuals brought new characters into their stories with significantly greater frequency. These "interveners," not the original protagonists, were significantly more often instrumental in initiating some sort of resolution. Exner describes this style as the "Snow White" feature: "being more likely to take flight into passive forms of fantasy as a defensive maneuver, and also being less likely to initiate decisions or behavior if the alternative that others will do so is available" (p. 374).

How Does the Person Respond to "Emotional" Experience?

Klopfer and Kelley (1942) and Beck et al. (1961) suggested that the proportion of responses given to the three fully chromatic blots may provide data about responsiveness to emotionally charged experiences in daily life. Nonpatients typically give about 40% of their responses for the 10 inkblots to these three cards. The Affective Ratio provides an index of how the person has responded to the three fully chromatic blots. It is formulated so that high scores mean the person has been proportionately over-responsive, and low scores mean that he or she has "backed away" from them. A series of studies summarized by Exner (1986a) suggests that as the Affective Ratio goes up, so does receptiveness to emotionally complex situations and willingness to involve this material in making decisions.

It is noteworthy that patients are often at the extremes of the Affective Ratio, with bimodal distributions suggesting that they either under-respond or over-respond to the fully chromatic blots (Exner, 1986a). When tested again after treatment, those patients who were rated by significant others as improved had moved into the normal range with much greater frequency than those rated as unimproved. It would appear that either under-responsiveness or over-responsiveness to the emotional parts of experience has the potential for generating maladaptive function.

If we view the Affective Ratio as providing a probability statement about how likely it is that emotional stimuli will be processed and responded to, an important next question concerns how well moderated the response will be when it does occur. The person's integration of form and color on the Rorschach appears to be associated with this sort of moderation. Form-dominated color (*FC*) percepts are associated with well-modulated affective responding, while color-dominated form or pure color percepts (*CF* or *C*) are more likely to be associated with more intense emotional displays. Gill (1966) found that ability to delay responses in a problem-solving task was associated with significantly more *FC* percepts. Individuals who could not delay their responses were characterized by significantly more *CF* and *C*. Adult nonpatients typically have about twice as much *FC* as *CF* and *C* in their records. Exner (1986a) reports that patient groups are more likely to be skewed outside of this normative 2:1 balance. Inpatient schizophrenics and depressives and outpatient character disorders were characterized by *CF* plus *C* greater than *FC*. Outpatients being treated for psychosomatic problems, on the other hand, frequently had *FC* four times greater than *CF* plus *C*, suggesting that they expend substantial amounts of energy insuring that any sort of emotional display will be very well modulated.

The configuration of the two kinds of data—one reflecting responsiveness to affective stimuli and the other predicting how well moderated the responses will be—can be of value in describing the person's overall approach to emotional experience. For example, we could speculate that a person who is over-responsive to emotionally charged situations (high Affective Ratio) and who does not mediate this material well (*CF* plus *C* greater than *FC*) would be likely to manifest relatively frequent episodes of poorly modulated emotional discharge.

What Is the Quality of Interpersonal Function?

Several Rorschach variables, including some newly developed ones, are of value in describing how an individual is likely to operate in the interpersonal world. Most people, patients and nonpatients alike, tend to give between four and six human-content percepts in the course of the 10 inkblots. Absence of human content is normatively unexpected and apt to be associated with significant interpersonal difficulties. Most human content involves whole humans, and percepts with human parts or mythical humans are substantially less frequent. They may suggest a less accurate understanding of the interpersonal world.

Another Rorschach variable that has interpersonal implications is the aggressive movement (*AG*) re-

sponse. Summarizing a series of studies with this variable, Exner (1986a) concludes that elevations in aggressive movement responses (often defined as *AG* greater than three) "signify an increased likelihood for aggressive behaviors, either verbal or nonverbal, and that they also indicate attitudes toward others that are more negative and/or hostile than is customary" (p. 405).

A composite variable developed by Exner (1986a), the Isolation Index, appears useful in its ability to identify individuals whose social network is tenuous and who are isolated and withdrawn. The presence of an elevated Isolation Index in the context of a record that has other suggestions of interpersonal discomfort—low Affective Ratio, absence of texture percepts, low number of whole humans—may describe an individual whose interpersonal competence and interest are significantly limited.

The hypervigilance index (Exner, 1987) was developed by analyzing Rorschach data to see whether it could discriminate that subset of therapy patients who were identified as avoiding close interpersonal relationships and who acted out their distrust of others by committing a good deal of energy to interpersonal vigilance. Individuals who are positive on this index devote a substantial amount of time to an apprehensive scanning of the interpersonal field, and their sense of pessimism and distrust concerning the motives of others is noteworthy.

A variable that Exner (1988) has recently termed cooperative projection (*COP*) can be scored for human or animal movement percepts in which there is a clearly cooperative relationship. *COP* percepts appear at least once in about 75% of nonpatient Rorschachs but in only 51% of outpatient records. Although research is still preliminary, *COP* appears to be a very stable variable that is associated with positive rankings by peers and possibly with favorable treatment outcome.

Is It Likely that the Person Is Schizophrenic?

After summarizing a substantial amount of conceptual and diagnostic literature on schizophrenia, Exner (1986a) concludes that it is the only syndrome that includes difficulties with both inaccurate perception and disordered thinking. The Rorschach has components that tap both of these areas, and a series of studies suggests that when indicators of both perceptual inaccuracy and cognitive slippage occur in the same individual, there is significant likelihood of a schizophrenic diagnosis. These studies led to the creation of the Schizophrenia Index, a constellation of five variables associated with both perceptual distortion and disordered thinking. In a series of six random draws, the Schizophrenia Index was able to identify on average about 80% of DSM-III diagnosed schizophrenics while never including more than 12% of the subjects from several other patient and nonpatient groups.

The Schizophrenia Index is a promising variable, but it must be used with a good deal of caution. The findings reported above suggest that it does have problems both in terms of false negatives and false positives. It missed on average some 20% of diagnosed schizophrenics, and it has some potential for calling false positives, particularly among schizoaffective disorders and amphetamine-related psychoses. Work is currently in progress (Exner, 1987, 1988) to improve the discriminative power of the Schizophrenia Index.

Is It Likely that the Person Is Suicidal?

More than a decade of research has now been completed using the Comprehensive System for the identification of suicidal individuals. The most recent data presented by Exner (1986a) describes findings on 101 individuals who had taken Rorschachs within the 60 days before their suicides. These records were contrasted with those of inpatient depressives, schizophrenics, and nonpatients, and a constellation of 12 variables was generated through a stepwise discriminant functions technique. These variables make up the Suicide Constellation. If a cutoff criterion of eight positive variables was employed, the Suicide Constellation identified 83% of the suicide group. If the suicidal individuals were classified in terms of the lethality of their attempt, the Suicide Constellation identified 92% of the highest lethality group. It falsely identified as suicidal 12% of the inpatient depressive group and 6% of the schizophrenics. Using the eight-variable cutoff, no individual in the nonpatient group was falsely called suicidal.

This constellation represents a notable improvement over previous psychometric suicide predictors, but two very significant cautions are in order. First, it is important to emphasize that the Exner data involve a 17% false negative and a 12% false positive rate. Second, demographic and situational variables play a major part in suicide, and Exner (1986a) cautions that test data alone may not account for a great deal of the variance in predicting this low base-rate phenomenon. Nonetheless, the Suicide Constellation data represent the most promising test approach so far, and a positive finding on the Suicide Constellation certainly implies that a thorough clinical assessment of the individual's potential for self-destructive behavior is indicated.

FUTURE DIRECTIONS

It is apparent from this summary of the scope of questions to which the Rorschach is appropriately addressed that the instrument can be of real value in helping the practicing clinician with the sorts of issues he or she faces on a daily basis. A study by Ritzler and Alter (1986) indicated that the test is now taught in 93% of American Psychological Association-approved graduate clinical psychology programs in the United States and Canada, and an increasing number of clinicians are seeking continuing education training (Exner, 1988). To a very great extent, it has been the availability of a current research base that has sparked the Rorschach's renaissance, and a substantial amount of work is currently in progress. Five major research areas are of particular importance.

Utilizing discriminant function techniques to specify stable ways to differentiate the Rorschachs of externally identified individuals—be they hypervigilant, perfectionistic, or violent—is a powerful methodology. This configural technique takes advantage of computer technology and allows very extensive utilization of the Rorschach's data yield.

The collection of normative data on a variety of clinically relevant groups is an equally important area on the research frontier. The availability of an increasing number of skilled Rorschach clinicians will undoubtedly lead to the accumulation of a substantial amount of important reference data over the next few years.

Advances in computer and psychophysiological technology now make possible increasingly sophisticated basic science research that will shed greater light on the way that Rorschach responses are generated. A series of studies (Exner, 1980) suggests that the blots are scanned very quickly and that the person processes substantially more data than he or she reports. What happens in the interim between the person's scanning of the blot and the articulation of a response appears to involve a very complex process that is the focus of substantial current research.

A fourth significant research area acknowledges that the Rorschach is typically utilized as part of a test battery. The study of its interaction with other personality instruments, and with cognitive and neuropsychological techniques, will be of substantial importance to practicing clinicians.

Finally, the Rorschach's potential as a rich source of content data continues to be an important area of study. A variety of workers are creating approaches that link Rorschach content material with constructs generated from formal theories of personality such as psychoanalysis.

SUMMARY

Perhaps the survival of Rorschach's deceptively simple technique can be traced to its unexpectedly comprehensive ability to tap the complexity of human psychological operation. It has been this very richness of data that has sometimes made for controversy as various workers have tried to decide how best to conceptualize and process the test's varied yield. Those years of divergence seem to be over. The integrative stance that currently characterizes Rorschach research and practice has turned the controversies into alternative and complementary approaches to a field whose breadth we are still charting after well over half a century.

REFERENCES

Arffa, S. M. (1982). Predicting adolescent suicidal behavior and the order of Rorschach measurement. *Journal of Personality Assessment*, *46*, 563–568.

Beck, S. J. (1937). Introduction to the Rorschach method: A manual of personality study. *American Orthopsychiatric Association Monograph*, No. 1.

Beck, S. J. (1944). *Rorschach's test. I. Basic processes*. New York: Grune & Stratton.

Beck, S. J. (1945). *Rorschach's test. II. A variety of personality pictures*. New York: Grune & Stratton.

Beck, S. J. (1952). *Rorschach's test. III. Advances in interpretation*. New York: Grune & Stratton.

Beck, S. J. (1960). *The Rorschach experiment: Ventures in blind diagnosis*. New York: Grune & Stratton.

Beck, S. J., Beck, A. G., Levitt, E., & Molish, H. B. (1961). *Rorschach's test. I. Basic processes* (3rd ed.). New York: Grune & Stratton.

Beck, S. J., & Molish, H. B. (Eds.). (1967). *Rorschach's test. II. A variety of personality pictures*. New York: Grune & Stratton.

Exner, J. E. (1973). The Self Focus Sentence Completion: A study of egocentricity. *Journal of Personality Assessment*, *37*, 437–455.

Exner, J. E. (1974). *The Rorschach: A comprehensive system* (Vol. I). New York: Wiley.

Exner, J. E. (1978). *The Rorschach: A comprehensive system. Vol. 2. Current research and advanced interpretation*. New York: Wiley.

Exner, J. E. (1986a). *The Rorschach: A comprehensive system. Vol. 1* (2nd ed.). *Basic foundations*. New York: Wiley.

Exner, J. E. (1986b). Some Rorschach data comparing schizophrenics with borderline and schizotypal personality disorders. *Journal of Personality Assessment*, *50*, 455–471.

Exner, J. E. (1987). *Alumni newsletter*. Asheville, NC: Rorschach Workshops.

Exner, J. E. (1988). *Alumni newsletter*. Asheville, NC: Rorschach Workshops.

Exner, J. E., & Murillo, L. G. (1975). Early prediction of post-hospitalization relapse. *Journal of Psychiatric Research*, *12*, 231–237.

Exner, J. E., Murillo, L. G., & Cannavo, F. (1973). Disagreement between patient and relative behavioral reports as related to relapse in nonschizophrenic patients. Washington, DC: Eastern Psychological Association.

Exner, J. E., & Weiner, I. B. (1982). *The Rorschach: A comprehensive system. Vol. 3. Assessment of children and adolescents*. New York: Wiley.

Exner, J. E., & Wylie, J. R. (1977). Some Rorschach data concerning suicide. *Journal of Personality Assessment*, *41*, 339–348.

Frank, L. K. (1939). Projective methods for the study of personality. *Journal of Psychology*, *8*, 343–389.

Gill, H. S. (1966). Delay of response and reaction to color on the Rorschach. *Journal of Projective Techniques and Personality Assessment*, *30*, 545–552.

Harder, D. W., & Ritzler, B. A. (1979). A comparison of Rorschach developmental level and form-level systems as indicators of psychosis. *Journal of Personality Assessment*, *43*, 347–354.

Hens, S. (1917). *Szynon phantasieprüfung mit formlosen klecksen be, schulkindern, normalen erwachsenen und geisteskranken*. [Szynon's imagination testing with formless inkblots on schoolchildren, normal adults and schizophrenics.] Unpublished dissertation, Zurich.

Kerner, J. (1857). Klexographien. [Inkblot graphics.] In R. Pissen (Ed.), *Kerners werke*. Berlin: Boag and Co.

Kinder, B., Brubaker, R., Ingram, R., & Reading, E. (1982). Rorschach form quality: A comparison of the Exner and Beck systems. *Journal of Personality Assessment*, *46*, 131–138.

Klopfer, B., Ainsworth, M. D., Klopfer, W. G., &

Holt, R. R. (1954). *Developments in the Rorschach technique. Vol. 1. Technique and theory*. Yonkers: World Book.

Klopfer, B., Ainsworth, M. D., Klopfer, W. G., & Holt, R. R. (Eds.). (1956). *Developments in the Rorschach technique. Vol. 2. Fields of application*. Yonkers: World Book.

Klopfer, B., & Kelley, D. (1942). *The Rorschach technique*. Yonkers: World Book.

Klopfer, B., Meyer, M. M., & Brawer, F. (Eds.). (1970). *Developments in the Rorschach technique. Vol. 3. Aspects of personality structure*. New York: Harcourt Brace Jovanovich.

Klopfer, B., & Sender, S. (1936). A system of refined scoring symbols. *Rorschach Research Exchange*, 1, 19–22.

Krugman, M. (1940). Out of the inkwell. *Rorschach Research Exchange*, 4, 91–101.

Mayman, M. (1970). Reality contact, defense effectiveness, and psychopathology in Rorschach form-level scores. In B. Klopfer (Ed.), *Developments in the Rorschach technique* (Vol. 3). New York: Harcourt Brace Jovanovich.

Meili-Dworetzki, G. (1956). The development of perception in the Rorschach. In B. Klopfer (Ed.), *Developments in the Rorschach technique* (Vol. 2). Yonkers: World Book.

Molish, H. B. (1967). Critique and problems of the Rorschach. A survey. In S. J. Beck & H. B. Molish (Eds.), *Rorschach's Test* (Vol. 2). New York: Grune & Stratton.

Piotrowski, Z. (1957). *Perceptanalysis*. New York: Macmillan.

Rapaport, D., Gill, M., & Schafer, R. (1945, 1946). *Diagnostic psychological testing*. Chicago: Yearbook Publishers.

Rapaport, D., Gill, M., & Schafer, R. (1968). *Diagnostic psychological testing* (rev. ed.). R. R. Holt (Ed.). New York: International Universities Press.

Roemer, G. (1967). The Rorschach and Roemer symbol test series. *Journal of Nervous and Mental Disorders*, 144, 185–197.

Rorschach, H. (1921). *Psychodiagnostik*. Bern: Bircher. (English translation, Bern: Hans Huber, 1942).

Rorschach, H., & Oberholzer, E. (1923). The application of the form interpretation test. *Zeitschrift fur die Gesamte Neurologie und Psychiatrie*, 82. Also in H. Rorschach (1942). *Psychodiagnostik*. Bern: Hans Huber.

Rybakow, T. (1910). *Atlas for experimental research on personality*. Moscow: University of Moscow.

Schafer, R. (1948). *The clinical application of psychological tests*. New York: International Universities Press.

Schafer, R. (1954). *Psychoanalytic interpretation in Rorschach testing*. New York: Grune & Stratton.

Schafer, R. (1967). *Projective testing and psychoanalysis*. New York: International Universities Press.

Shalit, B. (1965). Effects of environmental stimulation on the M, FM, and m responses in the Rorschach. *Journal of Projective Techniques*, 29, 228–231.

Singer, J. L., & Brown, S. L. (1977). The experience type: Some behavioral correlates and theoretical implications. In M. A. Rickers-Ovsiankina (Ed.), *Rorschach psychology*. Huntington, NY: Krieger Publishing Co.

Smith, N. M. (1981). The relationship between the Rorschach whole response and level of cognitive functioning. *Journal of Personality Assessment*, 45, 13–19.

Tulchin, S. H. (1940). The pre-Rorschach use of inkblot tests. *Rorschach Research Exchange*, 4, 1–7.

Weiner, I. B. (1977). Approaches to Rorschach validation. In M. A. Rickers-Ovsiankina (Ed.), *Rorschach psychology*. Huntington, NY: Krieger.

Whipple, G. M. (1910). *Manual of mental and physical tests*. Baltimore: Warwick and York.

Wilson, G., & Blake, R. (1950). A methodological problem in Beck's organizational concept. *Journal of Consulting Psychology*, 14, 20–24.

Zubin, J., Eron, L. D., & Schumer, F. (1965). *An experimental approach to projective techniques*. New York: Wiley.

PART VIII

BEHAVIORAL ASSESSMENT

CHAPTER 18

BEHAVIORAL ASSESSMENT OF CHILDREN

Thomas H. Ollendick
Ross Greene

The evaluation of effective treatment strategies depends on the development of sound assessment devices. Yet, while treatment strategies derived from behavioral principles have a long and rich tradition in clinical psychology (e.g., Holmes, 1936; Jones, 1924; Watson & Rayner, 1920), assessment procedures based on these same principles have been slower to evolve, particularly in the area of child behavioral assessment. Many behavioral assessment procedures for children have been adopted, sometimes indiscriminately, from those used with adults. This practice is of dubious merit and has frequently led to questionable findings. The need to focus greater attention on the development and evaluation of behavioral assessment procedures for children has been highlighted in several recent publications (e.g., Mash & Terdal, 1981, 1987; Ollendick & Hersen, 1984; Prinz, 1986).

As first described by Mash and Terdal (1981) and expanded on by Ollendick and Hersen (1984), child behavioral assessment can best be viewed as *an exploratory, hypothesis-testing process in which a range of specific procedures is used in order to understand a given child, group, or social ecology, and to formulate and evaluate specific intervention strategies*. As such, child behavioral assessment entails more than the identification of highly discrete target behaviors and their controlling variables. While the importance of direct observation of target behaviors should not be underestimated, more recent advances have incorporated a large range of assessment procedures, including behavioral interviews, self-reports, ratings by significant others, self-monitoring,

and behavioral observations. An approach combining these procedures can best be described as a multimethod one in which a composite "picture" of the child is obtained that is both informative and useful in the understanding and modification of specific behavior problems (Ollendick & Cerny, 1981).

Two other primary features characterize child behavioral assessment procedures: *first,* they must be sensitive to rapid developmental changes, and *second,* they must be validated empirically. Probably the most distinguishing characteristic of children is change. Whether such change is based on supposed stages of growth or assumed principles of learning, it has direct implications for the selection of specific assessment procedures and for their use in the evaluation of response to treatment. Behavioral interviews, self-reports, other-reports, self-monitoring, and behavioral observation are all affected by rapidly changing developmental processes. Further, some of these procedures may be more useful at one age period than another. For example, interviews may be more difficult to conduct and self-reports less reliable with younger children whereas self-monitoring and behavioral observations may be more reactive at older ages (Ollendick & Hersen, 1984). Age-related constraints are numerous and must be taken into consideration when selecting specific methods of assessment.

Just as child behavioral assessment procedures must be developmentally sensitive, they must also be validated empirically. All too frequently, professionals working with children have used assessment methods of convenience without sufficient regard for their psychometric characteristics, including their reliability, validity, and clinical utility. Although child behavior assessors have fared somewhat better in this regard, they too have tended to design and use highly idiosyncratic tools for assessment. As we have noted elsewhere (Ollendick & Hersen, 1984), comparison across studies is extremely difficult, if not impossible, and the advancement of an assessment technology, let alone an understanding of child behavior disorders, is not realized with such an idosyncratic approach.

While a multimethod approach that is based on developmentally sensitive and empirically validated procedures is espoused, it should be clear that a "test battery" approach is not being recommended. The specific devices to be used depend on a host of factors, including the age of the child, the nature of the referral question, and the personnel, time, and resources available (Ollendick & Cerny, 1981). Nonetheless, given the inherent limitations of the different procedures, as well as the desirability of obtaining as complete a picture of the child as possible, we recommend multimethod assessment whenever such is feasible. Any single procedure, including direct behavioral observation, is not sufficient to provide this composite view of the child. The multimethod approach is not only helpful in assessing specific target behaviors and in determining response to behavior change, but also in understanding child behavior disorders and advancing our database in this area of study.

Based on these considerations, we offer the following summary statements regarding child behavioral assessment:

1. Children are a special population. The automatic extension of adult behavioral assessment methods to children is not warranted and is often inappropriate. Age-related variables affect the choice of methods as well as the procedures employed.

2. Given rapid developmental change in children, normative comparisons are required to ensure that appropriate target behaviors are selected and that change in behavior is related to treatment, not to normal developmental change. Such comparisons require identification of suitable reference groups and information about the "natural course" of child behavior problems.

3. Thorough child behavioral assessment involves multiple targets of change, including overt behavior, affective states, and cognitive processes. Further, such assessment entails determining the context (e.g., familial, social, cultural) in which the child's behavior occurs and the *function* that the targeted behaviors serve.

4. Given the wide range of targets for change, multimethod assessment is desirable. Multimethod assessment should not be viewed simply as a test battery approach; rather, methods should be selected on the basis of their appropriateness to the referral question. Regardless of the measures used, they should be developmentally sensitive and empirically validated.

HISTORY AND DEVELOPMENT

As indicated earlier, adequate assessment of children's behavior problems requires a multimethod assessment approach in which data are gathered from self- and other-report sources as well as from direct behavioral observation. In this manner, important information from the cognitive and affective modalities can be combined with behavioral data to provide a more complete picture of the child. In addition, a multimethod approach provides the clinician with necessary information regarding the perceptions and reactions of significant others in the child's environment (e.g., parents, teachers). It should be noted, however, that this comprehensive assessment approach is of a relatively recent origin in the area of child behavioral assessment.

In its earliest stages, behavioral assessment of children relied exclusively on the identification and specification of discrete and observable target behaviors (cf. Ullmann & Krasner, 1965). As such, assessment was limited to gathering information from the motoric response modality. This early assessment approach followed logically from the theoretical assumptions of the operant school of thought which was in vogue at the time. Early on, behaviorally oriented psychologists posited that the only appropriate behavioral domain for empirical study was that which was directly observable (Skinner, 1953). Contending that the objective demonstration of behavior change following intervention was of utmost importance, behaviorists relied upon data that could be measured objectively. Hence, frequency, rate, and duration measures of the behaviors of interest were obtained. Although the existence of cognitions and affective states was not denied, they were not deemed appropriate subject matter for experimental analysis.

As treatment approaches with children were broadened to include cognitive and self-control techniques (e.g., Bandura, 1977; Kanfer & Phillips, 1970; Kendall & Hollon, 1980; Meichenbaum, 1977), it became apparent that assessment strategies would likewise have to expand into the cognitive and affective domains. Furthermore, even though operant techniques were shown to be highly efficacious in effecting behavior change under controlled conditions, the clinical significance and social validity of these changes were less evident. This state of affairs prompted behaviorists to expand their coverage and to pursue information from a variety of sources (e.g., significant other-report measures), even though these sources provided only indirect measures of behavior (Cone, 1978). The issue of the clinical significance of behavior change is especially crucial in child behavioral assessment because children are invariably referred for treatment by others (e.g., parents, teachers). Once the treatment goals have been identified adequately, the ultimate index of treatment efficacy lies in the referral source's perceptions of change. Hence, other-report measures become as important as direct observational ones.

More recently, the scope of behavioral assessment has been broadened further to incorporate the impact of large-scale social systems (e.g., schools, sociocultural influences) on the child's behavior (Patterson, 1976; Wahler, 1976). Although inclusion of these additional factors serves to complicate the assessment process, they are an indispensable part of child behavioral assessment. The ideologies and expectations of these seemingly distal social systems often have immediate and profound effects on individual behavior (see Winett, Riley, King, & Altman, 1989, for discussion of these issues).

In sum, child behavioral assessment has progressed from sole reliance on measurement of target behaviors to a broader approach that takes into account cognitive and affective processes of the child that mediate behavior change and the social contexts in which the target behaviors occur. The assessment techniques that accompany this approach include indirect behavioral measures, such as the behavioral interview, and self- and other-report instruments. These measures are utilized in addition to direct behavioral observation which remains the cornerstone of behavioral assessment (Mash & Terdal, 1981; Ollendick & Hersen, 1984).

THEORETICAL UNDERPINNINGS

Although behaviorism has had a historical development of its own, it is fair to state that the increased popularity of behavioral psychology has been partially spawned by dissatisfaction with the psychodynamic approach. A reflection of this dissatisfaction is that virtually all discussions of behavioral assessment are carried out through comparison and contrast with traditional assessment approaches (e.g., Bornstein,

Bornstein, & Dawson, 1984; Cone & Hawkins, 1977; Goldfried & Kent, 1972; Hayes, Nelson, & Jarrett, 1986; Mash & Terdal, 1981; Mischel, 1968; Ollendick & Hersen, 1984). Though such comparisons often result in oversimplification of both approaches, they are nevertheless useful and serve to elucidate the theoretical underpinnings of the behavioral approach. In this section, we will contrast the theoretical assumptions that guide behavioral and traditional assessment and discuss the practical implications of these assumptions for assessment.

The most fundamental difference between traditional and behavioral assessment approaches lies in the conception of personality and behavior. In the traditional assessment approach, personality is viewed as a reflection of underlying and enduring traits and behavior is assumed to be caused by these internal personality characteristics ("personologism"). In contrast, behavioral approaches have generally avoided references to underlying personality constructs, focusing instead on what the child does under specific conditions. From the behavioral perspective, the term *personality* refers to patterns rather than causes of behavior (Staats, 1975, 1986). Furthermore, behavior is viewed as a result of current environmental factors ("situationalism") or of current environmental factors interacting with organismic variables ("interactionism"). Thus, the current environment is stressed more in behavioral assessment than in traditional assessment. The focus of assessment is on what the child *does* in that situation rather than on what he or she *has* (Mischel, 1968). As a result, a lower level of inference is required in behavioral assessment than in traditional assessment.

It is important not to oversimplify the behavioral view of the causes of behavior, however. It has often been erroneously asserted that the behavioral approach focuses on external determinants of behavior at the exclusion of organismic states or internal cognitions and affects. To be sure, behavioral views of childhood disorders have emphasized the significant role of *current* environmental factors in the manifestation of behavior. However, intraorganismic variables that influence behavior are not ignored. This is evidenced by the array of self-report instruments tapping cognitive and affective modalities currently used in behavioral assessment. A thorough behavioral assessment should attempt to identify controlling variables, whether environmental or organismic in nature. As Mash and Terdal (1981) point out, "the relative importance of organismic and environmental variables and their interaction . . . should follow from a careful analysis of the problem" (p. 23).

The traditional conception of personality as made up of stable and enduring traits implies that behavior will be relatively consistent across situations and over time. The behavioral view, in contrast, has been one of situational specificity; that is, because behavior is in large part a function of situational determinants, a child's behavior will change as these situational factors are altered. Similarly, consistency of behavior across the temporal dimension is not necessarily expected. Hence, an aggressive act, such as a child hitting another child, would be seen from the traditional viewpoint as a reflection of underlying hostility, which, in turn, might be related to early life experiences or intrapsychic conflicts. Little or no attention is given to specific situational factors or the environmental context in which the aggressive act occurred. From the behavioral perspective, an attempt is made to identify those variables that elicit and maintain the aggressive act in that particular situation. That the child may aggress in a variety of situations is explained in terms of his or her learning history in which reinforcing consequences have been obtained for past aggressive acts, and not in terms of an underlying personality trait of hostility. From this analysis, it is clear that actual behavior is of primary importance to behaviorists, because it represents a sample of the child's behavioral repertoire in a given situation. From the traditional viewpoint, the behavior assumes importance only insofar as it is a *sign* of some underlying cause.

These differing assumptions have implications for the assessment process. In behavioral assessment, the emphasis on situational specificity necessitates an assessment approach that samples behavior across a number of settings. Hence, assessment of the child's behavior at home, in school, and/or on the playground is important in addition to information obtained in the clinic setting. Furthermore, the information obtained from these various settings likely will not, and in fact need not, be consistent. The child may behave aggressively in school and on the playground but not at home. This lack of consistent findings would be more problematic for the traditional approach. Similarly, the notion of temporal instability requires that the child's behavior be assessed at several points in time, whereas this would not be required from the traditional assessment standpoint.

At one point, it was relatively easy to differentiate behavioral from traditional assessment on the basis of the methods employed. Direct behavioral observation was the defining characteristic and often the sole assessment technique of the behavioral approach, whereas interviewing and projective techniques char-acterized traditional assessment. However, as behavioral assessment has matured and expanded to include a wider repertoire of assessment methods, differentiating behavioral and traditional assessments simply on the basis of assessment methods used has become more difficult. It is not uncommon for behaviorists to utilize information from interviews, self-report instruments, or even (though less commonly) projective techniques in assessment. Thus, there is much overlap in actual assessment practices. The difference between traditional and behavioral assessment lies, then, not in the methods employed, but rather in the manner in which data from assessment sources are utilized. Traditional approaches interpret assessment data as signs of underlying personality functioning. These data are used to diagnose and classify the child and to make prognostic statements. From the behavioral perspective, assessment data are utilized to identify target behaviors and their controlling conditions (again, be they overt or covert). Information obtained from assessment serves as a sample of the child's behavior under specific circumstances. This information guides the selection of appropriate treatment procedures. Because behavioral assessment is ongoing, such information serves as an index by which to evaluate continually the effects of treatment and to make appropriate revisions in treatment. Further, because assessment data are viewed as samples of behavior, the level of inference is low, whereas a high level of inference is required when one attempts to make statements about personality functioning from responses to interview questions or test items.

In addition to these differences, Cone (1986) has recently expanded on the nomothetic and idiographic distinction between traditional and behavioral assessment. Stated briefly, the nomothetic approach is concerned with the discovery of general laws as they are applied to large numbers of children. Usually, these laws provide heuristic guidelines as to how certain variables are related to one another. Such an approach can be said to be variable centered because it deals with particular characteristics (traits) such as intelligence, achievement, assertion, and so on. In contrast, the idiographic approach is concerned more with the uniqueness of a given child and is said to be child centered rather than variable centered. Unlike the nomothetic approach, the idiographic perspective emphasizes the discovery of relationships among variables uniquely patterned in each child. Of course, the idiographic approach is most akin to a behavioral perspective whereas the nomothetic approach is closely related to the traditional approach. As Mischel (1968) observed, "Behavioral assessment involves an exploration of the unique or idiosyncratic aspects of the single case, perhaps to a greater extent than any other approach" (p. 190). Cone (1986) illustrates how the idiographic/nomothetic distinction relates to the general activities of behavioral assessors by exploring five basic questions: What is the purpose of assessment? What is its specific subject matter? What general scientific approach guides this effort? How are differences accounted for? To what extent are currently operative environmental variables considered? Although further discussion of these important issues is beyond the scope of the present chapter, Cone's schema helps us recognize the pluralistic nature of behavioral assessment and calls our attention to meaningful differences in the diverse practices contained therein. As Cone (1986) concludes, "There is not one behavioral assessment, there are many" (p. 126). We agree.

In sum, traditional and behavioral assessment approaches operate under different assumptions regarding the child's behavior. These assumptions, in turn, have implications for the assessment process. Of paramount importance for child behavior assessors is the necessity of tailoring the assessment approach to the specific difficulties of the child in order to identify the problem accurately, specify treatment, and evaluate treatment success. Such tailoring requires ongoing assessment from a number of sources under appropriately diverse stimulus situations.

DESCRIPTION OF ASSESSMENT PROCEDURES

Multimethod behavioral assessment of children entails the use of a wide range of specific procedures. As behavioral approaches with children evolved from sole reliance on operant procedures to those involving cognitive and self-control procedures, the methods of assessment changed accordingly. The identification of discrete target behaviors has been expanded to include the assessment of cognitions and affects, as well as large-scale social systems that affect the child (e.g., families, schools, communities).

Information regarding these additional areas can be obtained most efficiently through behavioral interviews, self-reports, and other-reports. Cone (1978) has described these assessment methods as indirect ones; that is, while they may be used to measure behaviors of clinical relevance, they are obtained at a time and place different from that when the actual behaviors occurred. In both behavioral interviews and self-report questionnaires, a verbal representation of the behaviors of interest is obtained. Other-reports or

ratings by others are also included in the indirect category because they involve retrospective descriptions of behavior. Generally, a significant person in the child's environment (e.g., parent, teacher) is asked to rate the child based on previous observations (recollections).

As noted by Cone (1978), ratings such as these should not be confused with direct observation methods, which assess the behaviors of interest at the time and place of their occurrence. Of course, information regarding cognition and affects, as well as the situations or settings in which they occur, can also be obtained through direct behavioral observations, either by self-monitoring or through trained observers. In the sections that follow, both indirect and direct methods are reviewed briefly.

Behavioral Interviews

The first method of indirect assessment to be considered is the behavioral interview. Of the many procedures employed by behavioral clinicians, the interview is the most widely used (Swann & MacDonald, 1978) and is generally considered an indispensable part of assessment (Gross, 1984; Linehan, 1977). Behavioral interviews are structured to obtain detailed information about the target behaviors and their controlling variables, to begin the formulation of specific treatment plans, and to develop a relationship with the child and his or her family (Ollendick & Cerny, 1981). While the primary purpose of the behavioral interview is to obtain information, we have found that traditional "helping" skills including reflections, clarifications, and summary statements help put the child and his or her family at ease and greatly facilitate the collection of this information.

The popularity of the behavioral inteview may derive in part from a number of practical considerations, as well as to advantages it offers over other procedures (Gross, 1984). While direct observations of target behaviors are the hallmark of behavioral assessment, such observations are not always practical or feasible. At times, especially in outpatient therapy, the clinician must rely on the child's self-report as well as that of his or her parents to initiate assessment and treatment. Further, the interview allows the clinician to obtain a broad band of information regarding overall functioning as well as detailed information about specific areas. The flexibility inherent in the interview also allows the clinician to build a relationship with the child and his or her family and to obtain information that might otherwise not be revealed. As noted by Linehan (1977), some family members may be more likely to divulge information verbally in the context of a professional relationship than to write it down on a form to be entered into a permanent file.

In addition, the interview allows the clinician the opportunity to observe the family as a whole and obtain information about the context in which the problem behaviors of the identified client (i.e., the child) occurs. Several interrelated issues may arise when child behavioral assessment is expanded to include the family unit (Evans & Nelson, 1977; Ollendick & Cerny, 1981). First, children rarely refer themselves for treatment; invariably, they are referred by adults whose perceptions of problems may not coincide with those of the referred children. A second issue, related to the first, is the determination of when child behaviors are problematic and when they are not. Normative developmental comparisons are useful in this regard. It is not uncommon for parents to refer 5-year-olds who reverse letters, 3-year-olds who wet the bed, and 13-year-olds who are concerned about their physical appearance. Frequently, these referrals are based on parental uneasiness or unrealistic expectations rather than genuine problems (see Campbell, 1989, for further discussion of these issues). Finally, problematic family interactions (especially parent-child interactions) are frequently observed in families in which a particular child has been identified for treatment (cf. Patterson, 1976, 1982). These interactions may not be a part of the parents' original perception of the problematic behavior. However, assessment of such interactions allows the clinician the opportunity to observe the verbal and nonverbal behaviors of the family unit in response to a variety of topics and of family members in response to each other. Structured interviews assessing parent-child interactions have been developed by numerous researchers (e.g., Barkley, 1987).

Evaluation of parental perceptions and parent-child interactions may enable the clinician to conceptualize the problematic behavior and formulate possible treatment alternatives from a more comprehensive, integrated perspective. However, the above discussion is not meant to imply that the behavioral interview should be limited to the family; in many instances, the issues and practices described above should be extended to adults outside the family unit, such as teachers, principals, and physicians, and to environments beyond the home, including schools and day-care centers. For example, if a problem behavior is reported to occur primarily at school, assessing the perceptions and behavioral goals of a teacher and/or principal will be a necessity, and evaluating teacher-child interactions may prove similarly productive. Thus, the clinician should approach the behavioral interview with caution and avoid blind acceptance of the premise that a "problem" exists in the child. Information obtained in a comprehensive assessment may reveal that the behavior of the identified client is only a component of a more complex clinical picture involving parents, siblings, other adults, and/or systems.

In sum, an attempt is made during the behavioral interview to obtain as complete a picture as possible of the child, his or her family, and other important individuals and environments. While the interview is focused around specific target behaviors, adult-child interactions and adult perceptions of the problem may also be assessed. These perceptions should be considered tentative, however, and used primarily to formulate hypotheses about target behaviors and their controlling variables and to select additional assessment methods to explore target behaviors in greater depth (e.g., rating scales, self-reports, self-monitoring, and behavioral observations). The behavioral inteview is only the first step in the assessment process.

Ratings and Checklists

Following the initial behavioral interview(s) and the clarification of presenting complaints, significant others in the child's environment may be requested to complete rating forms or checklists. In general, these forms are useful in providing an overall description of the child's behavior, in specifying dimensions or response clusters that characterize the child's behavior, and in serving as outcome measures for the effectiveness of treatment. Many of these forms contain items related to such diverse areas of functioning as school achievement, peer relationships, activity level, and self-control. As such, they provide a potentially comprehensive and cost-effective picture of the child and his or her overall level of functioning. Further, the forms are useful in eliciting information that may have been missed in the behavioral interview (Novick, Rosenfeld, Bloch, & Dawson, 1966). Finally, the forms might prove useful in the search for the best match between various treatments (e.g., systematic desensitization, cognitive restructuring, and self-control) and types of children as described on these forms (Ciminero & Drabman, 1977).

The popularity of rating forms and checklists is supported by the number of forms currently available (McMahon, 1984). Two of the more frequently used forms are described here. One of the most widely researched scales is the Behavior Problem Checklist (Quay & Peterson, 1967, 1975) and its recent revision (Quay & Peterson, 1983). Based on Peterson's (1961) early efforts to sample diverse child behavior problems directly, the revised scale consists of 89 items, each rated on a three-point severity scale. While some of the items are quite general and require considerable inference (e.g., lacks self-confidence, jealous), others are more specific (e.g., cries, sucks thumb). Six primary dimensions or response clusters of child behavior have been identified on this scale: conduct problems, socialized aggression, attention problems, anxiety-withdrawal, psychotic behavior, and motor excess. It is interesting that the two primary problem clusters found on this checklist are similar to those in numerous factor analytic studies of other rating forms and checklists. These two factors or response clusters represent consistent dimensions of child behavior problems, reflecting externalizing (e.g., acting out) and internalizing (e.g., anxiety, withdrawal) dimensions of behavior (Achenbach, 1966).

While the Behavior Problem Checklist has a rather lengthy history and is one of the most researched scales, it does not include the rating of positive behaviors and, hence, does not provide a basis on which to evaluate more appropriate behaviors. A scale that does assess appropriate behaviors, as well as inappropriate ones, is the Child Behavior Checklist (Achenbach, 1978; Achenbach & Edelbrock, 1979, 1989). The scale, designed for both parents and teachers, contains both social competency and behavior problem items. Further, separate editions of the scale are available for boys and girls in each of three age ranges (4–5, 6–11, and 12–16 years), with considerable normative data available. Social competency items examine the child's participation in various activities (e.g., sports, hobbies, chores), social organizations (e.g., clubs, groups), and school (e.g., grades, placement, promotions). Responses to each item are scored on a three-point scale that reflects both the quantity and quality of competency-related behaviors. The behavior problem scale of the checklist consists of 118 items, each also rated on a three-point scale. As with Quay and Peterson's Behavior Problem Checklist, some of the items are general and require some inference (e.g., feels worthless, acts too young, and fears own impulses), while others are more specific and easily scored (e.g., wets bed, sets fires, and destroys own things). Factor analyses have revealed a variety of response clusters that differ with the age and sex of the child; nonetheless, broad-band grouping of the factors reflects the aforementioned internalizing and externalizing behavioral dimensions. This checklist also holds considerable promise in child behavioral assessment.

In addition to these more general rating forms, highly specific rating forms are also available for use in child behavioral assessment. Two such forms have been chosen for the purpose of illustration, one used in the assessment of an internalizing dimension (fears/anxiety), and the other employed in the assessment of an externalizing dimension (defiance/noncompliance).

The Louisville Fear Survey Schedule for Children (Miller, Barrett, Hampe, & Noble, 1972) contains 81 items that cover an extensive array of fears and anxieties found in children and adolescents. Each item is rated on a three-point scale by the child's parents. Responses to specific fear items can be used to subtype fearful children. For example, Miller et al. (1972) were able to differentiate among various subtypes of school-phobic children on the basis of this instrument.

The Home Situations Questionnaire (HSQ) (Barkley, 1981) contains 16 items representing situations in which noncompliant behavior may occur. For each situation, parents indicate whether noncompliant behavior is a problem and then rate each of the 16 problematic situations on a nine-point scale (mild to severe); thus, the scale assesses both the number of problem settings and the severity of noncompliant behavior. Situations include "in public places," "when asked to do homework," and "at bedtime." The scale is intended to serve more as a measurement of change in problem areas as a function of treatment than as a comparison with normal children. The HSQ has been shown to be sensitive to stimulant-drug effects (Barkley, Karlsson, Strzelecki, & Murphy, 1984), to discriminate behavior-problem from normal children (Barkley, 1981), and to be sensitive to the effects of parent-training programs (Pollard, Ward, & Barkley, 1983). The HSQ was selected for inclusion in this chapter because it may be used in conjunction with a comparion scale, the School Situations Questionnaire (SSQ) (Barkley, 1981), which is completed by teachers. This scale includes 12 school situations most likely to be problematic for clinic-referred children, including "during lectures to the class," "at lunch," and "on the bus." Teachers rate the occurrence and severity of noncompliant behavior on a scale identical to that of the HSQ. In earlier sections, we emphasized the importance of assessing child behavior in multiple environments; the HSQ and SSQ are representative of recent efforts to develop measures for this purpose.

In sum, a variety of other-report instruments are

available. As noted earlier, these forms must be considered indirect methods of assessment because they rely on retrospective descriptions of the child's behavior. For all of these scales, an informant is asked to rate the child based on past observations of that child's behavior. Global scales such as the Revised Behavior Problem Checklist and the Child Behavior Checklist comprehensively sample the range of potential behavior problems, while the more specific scales such as the Louisville Fear Survey Schedule for Children and the Home Situations Questionnaire provide highly detailed information about particular behaviors of direct interest. Both provide useful, but different, information in the formulation and evaluation of treatment programs.

Self-Report Instruments

Coincident with the collection of other-reports regarding the child's behavior, self-reports of attitudes, feelings, and behaviors may also be obtained from the child. Early behaviorists eschewed such data, maintaining that the only acceptable piece of data was observable behavior. To a large extent, this negative bias against self-report was an outgrowth of early findings indicating that reports of subjective states did not always coincide with observable behaviors (Finch & Rogers, 1984). While congruence in responding is, in fact, not always observed, contemporary researchers have cogently argued that the child's perceptions of his or her behavior and its consequences may be as important for behavior change as the behavior itself (Finch, Nelson, & Moss, 1983; Ollendick & Hersen, 1984). Furthermore, as we noted earlier, although different assessment procedures may yield slightly different information, data from these sources should be compared and contrasted in order to produce the best picture of the child and to derive meaningful treatment procedures and goals. Although self-report instruments have specific limitations, they can provide valuable information about the child and can be used as one index of change following treatment.

A wide variety of self-report instruments have been developed for use with children. Among these are specific measures of anger (Nelson & Finch, 1978), anxiety (Spielberger, 1973), assertion (Deluty, 1979; Ollendick, 1983a), depression (Kovacs, 1985), and fear (Scherer & Nakamura, 1968). Each of these instruments has been carefully developed and empirically validated. Three of the more frequently used instruments will be described briefly.

Spielberger's State-Trait Anxiety Inventory for Children (1973) consists of 20 items that measure *state* anxiety and 20 items that measure *trait* anxiety. The state form is used to assess the more transient aspects of anxiety, while the trait form is used to measure the more generalized aspects of anxiety. Combined, the two scales provide both process and outcome measures of change in self-reported anxiety. That is, the state form can be used to determine session-by-session changes in anxiety, while the trait form can be used as a pretreatment, posttreatment, and followup measure of reduction in generalized anxiety. A clear advantage of this instrument is that the state scale is designed so that responses to relatively specific anxiety-producing situations can be determined. For example, the child can be instructed to indicate how he or she feels "at this moment" about standing up in front of class, leaving home for summer camp, or being ridiculed by peers. Further, cognitive, motoric, and physiologic indicants of anxiety can be endorsed by the child (e.g., feeling upset, scared, mixed up, jittery, or nervous). Responses to the items are scored on a three-point scale (e.g., "I feel very scared . . . scared . . . not scared"). Finally, the extent of generalization of the anxiety response can be measured by the trait form. The Spielberger scales are most useful for middle-aged children (9–12), but have been used with both younger children and adolescents as well.

A second instrument that has been used frequently in child behavioral assessment is the Fear Survey Schedule for Children (Scherer & Nakamura, 1968) and its recent revision (Ollendick, 1983b; Ollendick, Matson, & Helsel, 1985). In the revised scale, designed to be used with younger and middle-age children, the child is instructed to rate his or her fear level to each of 80 items on a three-point scale. Children are asked to indicate whether a specific fear item (e.g., having to go to school, being punished by father, dark places, riding in a car) frightens them "not at all," "some," or "a lot." Factor analysis of the scale has revealed five primary factors: fear of failure or criticism, fear of the unknown, fear of injury and small animals, fear of danger and death, and medical fears. Further, it has been shown that girls report greater fear than boys, that specific fears change developmentally, and that the most prevalent fears of boys and girls have remained unchanged over the past 30 years. Such information is highly useful when determining whether a child of a specific age and gender is excessively fearful. Further, the instrument can be used to differentiate subtypes of specifically phobic youngsters whose fear of school is related to separation anxiety (e.g., death, having parents argue, being alone) from those whose fear is due to specific aspects of the school situation (e.g., taking a test, making a mistake, being sent to the principal). When information from this instrument is combined with that from parents on the Louisville Fear Survey Schedule for Children (Miller et al., 1972), a relatively complete picture of the child's characteristic fear pattern can be obtained.

The final self-report instrument ⁄to be reviewed is Kovac's (1985) Children's Depression Inventory (CDI). Within the last 10 years no other area in clinical child psychology has received more attention than depression in children. A multitude of issues regarding its existence, nature, assessment, and treatment have been examined (Cantwell, 1983; Rutter, 1986). One of the major obstacles to systematic investigations in this area has been the absence of an acceptable self-report instrument. The CDI, though still in a research form, appears to meet this need. The instrument is a 27-item severity measure of depression based on the well-known Beck Depression Inventory. Each of the 27 items consists of three response choices designed to range from mild depression to fairly severe and clinically significant depression. Kovacs reports that the instrument is suitable for middle-aged children and adolescents (8–17 years of age). We have found the instrument to be useful with younger children as well, especially when the items are read aloud and the response choices are depicted on a bar graph. Recently, Smucker, Craighead, Craighead, and Green (1968) have provided additional psychometric data on the CDI. Overall, they conclude that it is a reliable, valid, and clinically useful instrument for children and adolescents.

In sum, a variety of self-report instruments are available. As with other-report forms, self-reports should be used with appropriate caution and due regard for their specific limitations. Because they generally involve the child's retrospective rating of attitudes, feelings, and behaviors, they too, must be considered indirect methods of assessment (Cone, 1978). Nevertheless, they can provide valuable information regarding the child's own perception of his or her behavior.

Self-Monitoring

Self-monitoring differs from self-report in that it constitutes an observation of the *clinically relevant target behavior* at the time of its occurrence (Cone, 1978). As such, it is a direct method of assessment. Self-monitoring requires the child to observe his or her own behavior and then to record its occurrence systematically. Typically, the child is asked to keep a diary, place marks on a card, or push the plunger on a counter as the behavior occurs or immediately thereafter. Although self-monitoring procedures have been used with both children and adults, at least three considerations must be attended to when such procedures are used with younger children (Shapiro, 1984): The behaviors should be clearly defined, prompts to use the procedures should be readily available, and rewards for their use should be provided. Younger children may have difficulty remembering exactly what behaviors to monitor and how those behaviors are defined. For these reasons, it is generally considered desirable to provide the child a brief description of the target behavior, or better yet, a picture of it, and to have the child record only one or two behaviors at a time. In an exceptionally sensitive application of these guidelines, Kunzelman (1970) recommended the use of COUNTOONS, simple stick figure drawings that depict the specific behaviors to be self-monitored. Children are instructed to place a tally mark next to the picture when the behavior occurs. For example, a girl monitoring hitting her younger brother may be given an index card with a drawing of a girl hitting a younger boy and instructed to mark each time she does what the girl in the picture is doing. Of course, in a well-designed program, the girl might also be provided a picture of a girl and a younger boy sharing toys and asked as well to mark each time she emits the appropriate behavior. Such pictorial cues serve as visual prompts for self-monitoring. Finally, children should be reinforced following the successful use of self-monitoring.

In general, methods of self-monitoring are highly variable and depend on the specific behavior being monitored and its place of occurrence. For example, Shapiro, McGonigle, and Ollendick (1980) had mentally retarded and emotionally disturbed children self-monitor on-task behavior in a school setting by placing gummed stars on assignment sheets, while Ollendick (1981) had child ticquers simply place tally marks contingent on occurrences of tics on a colored index card carried in the child's pocket. In our clinical work, we have also used wrist counters with children whose targeted behaviors occur while they are "on the move." Such a device is not only easy to use, but serves as a visual prompt to self-record. The key to successful self-monitoring in children is the use of recording procedures that are uncomplicated.

In sum, self-monitoring procedures represent a direct means to obtain information about the target behaviors as well as their antecedents and consequences. While specific monitoring methods may vary, any procedure that allows the child to record presence of the targeted behaviors can be used. When appropriate procedures are used, self-monitoring represents a direct and elegant method of assessment.

Behavioral Observation

Direct observation of the child's behavior in the natural environment is the hallmark of child behavioral assessment. As described by Johnson and Bolstad (1973), the development of naturalistic observation procedures represents the major contribution of the behavioral approach to assessment and treatment of children. Naturalistic observations provide a direct sample of the child's behavior at the time and place of its occurrence. As such, it is the least inferential of the assessment methods described. However, behavioral observations in the naturalistic environment should not necessarily be viewed as better than these other methods of assessment. Rather, they should be viewed as complementary to the other methods, with each providing slightly different and potentially valuable information.

In behavioral observation systems, a single behavior or set of behaviors that have been identified as problematic (generally through the aforementioned procedures) are operationally defined, observed, and recorded in a systematic fashion. In addition, events that precede and follow the behaviors of interest are recorded and subsequently used in the development of specific treatment programs. Although Jones, Reid, and Patterson (1975) have recommended the use of "trained impartial observer-coders" for collection of these data, this is rarely possible in child behavioral assessment. Frequently, time constraints, lack of trained personnel, and insufficient resources mitigate against the use of highly trained and impartial observers. In some cases behavioral clinicians have used significant others in the child's environment (e.g., parents, teachers, siblings) or the children themselves as observers of their own behavior. Although not impartial, these observers can be trained adequately to record clearly defined observable behaviors in the natural environment. In other cases, behavioral clinicians have resorted to laboratory or analogue settings that are similar to, but not the same as, the natural environment. In these simulated settings, the child may be asked to behave as if he or she is angry with his or her parents, to role play assertive responding, or to approach a highly feared object. Behaviors can be directly observed or taped and reviewed retrospectively. The distinguishing characteristic of behavioral observations, whether made in the naturalistic environment or in simulated settings, is that a direct sample of behavior is obtained.

A wide variety of target behaviors have been examined using behavioral observation procedures. These behaviors have varied from relatively discrete behaviors like enuresis and tics that require simple recording procedures to complex social interactions that require extensive behavioral coding systems (e.g., O'Leary, Romanczyk, Kass, Dietz, & Santogrossi, 1971; Patterson, Ray, Shaw, & Cobb, 1969; Wahler, House, & Stambaugh, 1976).

The utility of behavioral observations in naturalistic and simulated settings was well illustrated in Ayllon, Smith, and Rogers' (1970) behavioral assessment of a school-phobic girl. In this case study, impartial observers in the child's home monitored the stream of events occurring on school days in order to delineate better the actual school-phobic behaviors and to determine the antecedent and consequent events associated with them. In this single-parent family, it was noted that the mother routinely left for work about one hour after the targeted girl (Valerie) and her siblings were to leave for school. Although the siblings left for school without incident, Valerie was observed to cling to her mother and refuse to leave the house and go to school. As described by Ayllon et al. (1970), "Valerie typically followed her mother around the house, from room to room, spending approximately 80 percent of her time within ten feet of her mother. During these times there was little or no conversation" (p. 128). Given her refusal to go to school, the mother took Valerie to a neighbor's apartment for the day. However, when the mother attempted to leave for work, Valerie followed her at a 10-foot distance. Frequently the mother had to return to the neighbor's apartment with Valerie in hand. This daily pattern was observed to end with the mother "literally running to get out of sight of Valerie" so that she would not follow her to work. During the remainder of the day, it was observed that Valerie could do whatever she pleased: "Her day was one which would be considered ideal by many grade school children—she could be outdoors and play as she chose all day long. No demands of any type were placed on her" (p. 129). Based on these observations, it appeared that Valerie's separation anxiety and refusal to attend school were related to her mother's attention and to the reinforcing environment of the neighbor's apartment where she could play all day.

However, because Valerie was also reported to be afraid of school itself, Ayllon et al. (1970) designed a simulated school setting in the home to determine the extent of anxiety or fear toward specific school-related tasks. (Obviously, observation in the school itself would have been desirable but was impossible because she refused to attend school.) Unexpectedly, little or no fear was evinced in the simulated setting; in fact, Valerie performed well and appeared to enjoy the school-related setting and tasks. In this case, these detailed behavioral observations were useful in ruling on differential hypotheses related to school refusal. They led directly to a specific and efficacious treatment program based on shaping and differential reinforcement principles. The utility of behavioral observations for accurate assessment and treatment programming has been noted in numerous other case studies as well (e.g., Ollendick & Gruen, 1972; Smith & Sharpe, 1970).

A major disadvantage of behavioral observations in the natural environment is that the target behavior may not occur during the designated observation periods. In such instances, simulated settings that occasion the target behaviors can be used. Simulated observations are especially helpful when the target behavior is of low frequency, when the target behavior is not observed in the naturalistic setting due to reactivity effects of being observed, or when the target behavior is difficult to observe in the natural environment due to practical constraints. Ayllon et al.'s (1970) use of a simulated school setting illustrated this approach under the latter conditions. A study by Matson and Ollendick (1976) illustrates this approach for low frequency behaviors. In this study, parents reported that their children bit either the parent or siblings when they "were unable to get their way or were frustrated." Direct behavioral observations in the home confirmed parental report, but it was necessary to observe the children for several hours prior to witnessing one incident of the behavior. Further, parents reported that their children were being "nice" while the observers were present and that the frequency of the biting behavior was much less than its usual rate. Accordingly, parents were trained in observation procedures and instructed to engage their children in play for four structured play sessions per day. During these sessions, the parents were instructed to occasion biting behavior by deliberately removing a preferred toy. As expected, the removal of favored toys in the structured situations resulted in increases in target behaviors, which were then possible to eliminate through behavioral procedures. The structured, simulated play settings maximized the probability that biting would occur and that it could be observed and treated under controlled conditions.

In sum, direct behavioral observation—either in the natural or controlled simulated environment—provides valuable information for child behavioral assessment. When combined with information gathered through behavioral interviews, self- and other-reports, and self-monitoring, a comprehensive picture of the child and his or her behaviors, as well as their controlling variables, is obtained. As with other assessment procedures, however, direct behavioral observation alone is not sufficient to meet the various behavioral assessment functions required for a thorough analysis of a child's problem behavior.

RESEARCH FINDINGS

As noted earlier, the use of assessment instruments and procedures that have been empirically validated is one of the primary characteristics of child behavioral assessment. However, the role of conventional psychometric standards in evaluating child behavioral assessment procedures is a controversial one (e.g., Barrios & Hartman, 1986; Cone, 1981, 1986; Cone & Hawkins, 1977; Mash & Terdal, 1981). Given the theoretical underpinnings of child behavioral assessment and the basic assumptions regarding situational specificity and temporal instability of behavior, traditional psychometric standards would appear to be of little or no value. After all, how can behaviors thought to be under the control of highly specific antecedent and consequent events be expected to be similar in different settings and at different times? Yet, if there is no consistency in behavior across settings and time, the prediction of behavior is impossible and the generalizability of findings obtained from any one method of assessment is meaningless. Such an extreme idiographic stance precludes meaningful assessment, except of a highly discrete behavior in a particular setting and at a specific point in time (Ollendick & Hersen, 1984).

Research findings suggest that we need not totally dismiss the notions of cross-situational and cross-temporal consistency of behavior (e.g., Bem & Allen, 1974). Although a high degree of behavioral consistency cannot be expected, we can expect a moderate degree of behavioral consistency across situations that involve similar stimulus and response characteristics and are temporally related. When the various procedures of the multimethod approach are used under these constraints, we can expect a modest relationship among the measures and a fair degree of predictability and generalizability. Under such circumstances, application of conventional psychometric standards to evaluation of child behavioral assessment procedures is less problematic and increasingly useful (Cone,

1977; Ollendick & Hersen, 1984). The value of psychometric principles has already been demonstrated for certain classes of behavior when measured through diverse methods like behavioral observation (e.g., Olweus, 1979), self-report (e.g., Ollendick, 1981), and other-report ratings (e.g., Cowen, Pederson, Barbigian, Izzo, & Trost, 1973). Further, when multiple methods of behavioral assessment have been used in the same studies, a modest degree of both concurrent and predictive validity has been reported (e.g., Gresham, 1982).

It is beyond the scope of the present chapter to review specific research findings related to the reliability, validity, and utility of the various procedures espoused in the multimethod approach. Nonetheless, brief mention will be made of specific directions of research and ways of enhancing the psychometric qualities of each procedure.

Behavioral Interviews

As noted by Evans and Nelson (1977), data based on retrospective reports obtained during the interview may possess both low reliability (agreement among individuals interviewed may differ and responses may vary over time) and low validity (reported information may not correspond to the "facts"). Such inaccurate or distorted recollections may result not only in delayed clarification of the presenting complaints, but in faulty hypotheses about causal agents and maintaining factors. For example, Chess, Thomas, and Birch (1966) reported that parents inaccurately reported that certain behavior problems developed at times predicted by popular psychological theories. For instance, problems with siblings were recalled to have begun with the birth of a younger sibling, and problems with dependency were reported to have begun when the mother became employed. In actuality, these behaviors were present prior to these events. In a similar vein, Schopler (1974) noted that many parents inaccurately blame themselves for their child's problematic behaviors and that many therapists inadvertently "buy into" this notion that parents are to blame. Such scapegoating accomplishes little in the understanding, assessment, and treatment of the child's problematic behavior (Ollendick & Cerny, 1981).

While the reliability and validity of general information about parenting attitudes and practices are suspect, recent findings suggest that parents and children can be reliable and valid reporters of current, specific information about problematic behaviors (e.g., Graham & Rutter, 1968; Gross, 1984; Herjanic, Herjanic, Brown, & Wheatt, 1973). The reliability

and validity of the information are directly dependent on the recency of the behaviors being discussed and the specificity of the information obtained. Thus, careful specification of precise behaviors and the conditions under which they are occurring is more reliable and valid than vague descriptions of current behaviors or general recollections of early childhood events (Ciminero & Drabman, 1977). When the interview is conducted along such guidelines, it is useful in specifying behaviors of clinical interest and in determining appropriate therapeutic interventions. As we have noted, however, it is only the first step in the hypothesis-generating process that is characteristic of child behavioral assessment.

Ratings and Checklists

As with behavioral interviews, issues related to reliability and validity are also relevant to ratings and checklists. Cronbach (1960) has noted that the psychometric quality of rating scales is directly related to the number and specificity of the items rated. Further, O'Leary and Johnson (1979) have identified four factors associated with item-response characteristics and raters that enhance the reliability and validity of such scales: (a) the necessity of using clearly defined reference points on the scale (i.e., estimates of frequency, duration, or intensity), (b) the inclusion of more than two reference points on the scale (i.e., reference points that quantify the behavior being rated), (c) a rater who has had extensive opportunities for observing the child being rated, and (d) more than one rater who has equal familiarity with the child.

The rating forms and checklists described earlier (Behavior Problem Checklist, Child Behavior Checklist, the Louisville Fear Survey Schedule for Children, and the Home Situations Questionnaire) incorporate these item and response characteristics and are generally accepted as reliable and valid instruments. For example, the interrater reliability of the Behavior Problem Checklist is quite high when raters are equally familiar with the children being rated and when ratings are provided by raters within the same setting (Quay, 1977; Quay & Peterson, 1983). Further, the stability of these ratings has been reported over two-week and one-year intervals. These findings have been reported for teachers in the school setting and parents in the home setting. However, when ratings of teachers are compared to those of parents, interrater reliabilities are considerably lower. While teachers seem to agree with other teachers and one parent tends to agree with the other parent, there is less agreement between parents and teachers. Such differences may be due to differential perceptions of behavior by parents and teachers or to the situational specificity of behavior, as discussed earlier. In the least, these findings support the desirability of obtaining information about the child in as many settings as possible.

The validity of the Behavior Problem Checklist has been demonstrated in numerous ways. It has been shown to distinguish clinic-referred children from nonreferred children, to be related to psychiatric diagnosis, other measures of behavioral deviances, prognosis, and the differential effectiveness of specific treatment strategies, and to reflect specific changes following therapeutic intervention (see Ollendick & Cerny, 1981, for a discussion of these findings).

Findings similar to those resulting from use of the Behavior Problem Checklist have been reported for the Child Behavior Checklist, the Louisville Fear Survey Schedule, and the Home Situations Questionnaire. These rating forms and checklists, as well as others, have been shown to possess sound psychometric qualities and to be clinically useful. They not only provide meaningful data about the child's adaptive and problem behaviors but are also useful in orienting parents, teachers, and significant others to specific problem or asset areas and in alerting them to observe and record specific behaviors accurately.

Self-Report Instruments

Of the various methods used in child behavioral assessment, the self-report method has received the least attention and empirical support. Traditionally, behavioral assessors have eschewed the use of self-report instruments, largely on the basis of their suspected low reliability and validity. As we have noted, however, such data can be meaningfully used to understand and describe the child, plan treatment, and evaluate treatment outcome.

As with interview and checklist or rating data, self-report of specific behaviors or events is more reliable and valid than more general, global reports of life experiences. Such self-reports of specific states can be used to specify discrete components of more general constructs (e.g., determining the exact fears of a fearful child and the exact situations that produce withdrawn behavior in an unassertive child). Illustratively, Scherer and Nakamura's (1968) Fear Survey Schedule for Children and its recent variation (Ollendick, 1983b) can be used to pinpoint very specific fears and classes of fear. Further, this instrument has been shown to be reliable over time, to possess

internal consistency and a meaningful factor structure, to distinguish between phobic and nonphobic children, and to discriminate among subtypes of phobic youngsters within a particular phobic group (Ollendick & Mayer, 1984).

Clearly, more research is needed in this area before the routine use of self-report instruments can be endorsed. Nonetheless, those instruments that measure specific aspects of behavior rather than global traits hold considerable promise for child behavioral assessment.

Self-Monitoring

In self-monitoring, the child observes his or her own behavior and then systematically records its occurrence. As with other measures, concerns related to the reliability and validity of this procedure remain. What is the extent of inter-observer agreement between a child who is instructed to monitor his or her own behavior and an objective observer? How accurate is the child in recording actual occurrences of behavior? How reactive is the process of self-monitoring?

The literature in this area is voluminous (see Shapiro, 1984, for an excellent review). Even though all necessary studies have not been conducted, the findings are in general agreement. *First,* children can be trained to be reliable and accurate recorders of their own behavior. The specific behaviors should be clearly defined, prompts to self-record should be available, and reinforcement for self-monitoring should be provided. Under such conditions, children's recordings closely approximate those obtained from observing adults. For example, in a study examining the effects of self-monitoring and self-administered overcorrection in the treatment of nervous tics in children, Ollendick (1981) showed that children who were provided clear prompts to self-record highly discrete behaviors were able to do so reliably. Estimates of occurrence very closely paralleled those reported by parents and teachers, even though children were unaware that these adults were recording their nervous tics. In another study, Ackerman and Shapiro (1985) demonstrated the accuracy of self-monitoring by comparing self-recorded data with a permanent product measure (the number of units produced in a work setting).

Second, self-monitoring may result in behavior change due to the self-observation process and result in altered estimates of the target behaviors. This effect is known as reactivity. Numerous factors have been shown to influence the occurrence of reactivity: specific instructions, motivation, goal-setting, nature of the self-recording device, and the valence of the target behavior (e.g., Nelson, 1977, 1981). Among the more important findings are that desirable behaviors (e.g., study habits, social skills) increase while undesirable behaviors (e.g., nervous tics, hitting) decrease following self-monitoring, and that the more obtrusive self-recording device is accompanied by greater behavior change. For example, Nelson, Lipinski, and Boykin (1978) found that hand-held counters produced greater reactivity than belt-worn counters. Holding a counter in one's hand was viewed as more obtrusive, contributing to pronounced reactivity. Reactivity is a concern in the assessment process, because it affects the actual occurrences of behavior. However, if one is aware of the variables that contribute to the reactive effects, self-monitoring can be used as a simple and efficient mechanism for data collection (Shapiro, 1984).

In short, self-monitoring has been found to be useful in the assessment of a wide range of child behavior problems across a wide variety of settings. When issues related to the reliability, accuracy, and reactivity of measurement are addressed, self-monitoring represents a clinically useful strategy that is highly efficient.

Behavioral Observation

As with other assessment strategies, behavioral observation procedures must possess adequate psychometric qualities and be empirically validated before their routine use can be endorsed. Although early behaviorists accepted the accuracy of behavioral observations based on their deceptively simplistic face validity, more recent investigators have enumerated a variety of problems associated with their reliability, validity, and clinical utility (e.g., Johnson & Bolstad, 1973; Kazdin, 1977). These problems include the complexity of the observation code, the exact recording procedures to be used (e.g., frequency counts, time sampling, etc.), observer bias, observer drift, and the reactive nature of the observation process itself (see Barton & Ascione, 1984, for further discussion of these issues). Our experience suggests that the greatest threat to the utility of observational data comes from the reactive nature of the observational process itself, especially when the observer is present in the natural setting. It is well known that the presence of an observer affects behavior, usually in socially desirable directions. Two strategies have been found to be useful in reducing such reactive effects: (a) recruiting and training observer-coders

already present in the natural setting (e.g., a teacher or parent), or (b) if this is not possible, planning extended observations so that children can habituate to the observers and so that the effects of reactivity are allowed to dissipate. However, it should be noted that several sessions of observations are required, since reactive effects have been observed for as long as six sessions (Johnson & Lobitz, 1974). Reactive effects, combined with the aforementioned practical issues of personnel, time, and resources, have led us to place greater emphasis upon recruiting observer-coders already present in the children's natural environment or training the children themselves as recorders of their own behavior.

In brief, behavioral observations are the most direct and least inferential method of assessment. Even though a variety of problems related to their reliability and validity are evident, behavioral observations are highly useful strategies and represent the hallmark of child behavioral assessment.

FUTURE DIRECTIONS

A number of directions for future research and development in child behavioral assessment may be evident to the reader. What follows is our attempt to highlight those areas that appear most promising and in need of greater articulation.

First, it seems to us that greater attention must be given to developmental factors as they affect the selection and evaluation of child behavioral assessment procedures. Although we have argued that these procedures should be developmentally sensitive, child behavioral assessors have frequently not attended to, or have ignored, this admonition. As we noted earlier, the most distinguishing characteristic of children is developmental change. Such change encompasses basic biological growth and maturity as well as affective, behavioral, and cognitive fluctuations that characterize children at different age levels. While the importance of accounting for developmental level when assessing behavior may be obvious, ways of integrating developmental concepts and principles into child behavioral assessment are less clear. Edelbrock (1984) has noted three areas for the synthesis of developmental and behavioral principles: (a) use of developmental fluctuations in behavior to establish normative baselines of behavior, (b) determination of age and gender differences in the expression and covariation of behavioral patterns, and (c) study of stability and change in behavior over time as related to such variables as age of onset and situational influences. Clearly, these areas of synthesis and integration are in their infancy and in need of considerably greater articulation (e.g., Harris & Ferrari, 1983; Ollendick & Hersen, 1983; Rutter & Garmezy, 1983; Sroufe & Rutter, 1984).

Second, and somewhat related to the first, greater attention must be focused on the incremental validity of the multimethod approach when used for children of varying ages. Throughout this chapter, we have espoused a multimethod approach consisting of interviews, self- and other-reports, self-monitoring, and behavioral observations. Quite obviously, some of these procedures may be more appropriate at certain age levels than at others. Further, the psychometric properties of these procedures may vary with age. If certain procedures are found to be less reliable or valid at different age levels, their indiscriminate use with children should not be endorsed. Inasmuch as these strategies are found to be inadequate, the combination of them in a multimethod approach would serve only to compound their inherent limitations (Mash & Terdal, 1981). The sine qua non of child behavioral assessment is that the procedures be empirically validated. Finally, the different procedures may vary in terms of their treatment utility. As noted recently by Hayes, Nelson, & Jarrett (1987), treatment utility refers to the degree to which assessment strategies are shown to contribute to beneficial treatment outcomes. More specifically, treatment utility addresses issues related to the selection of specific target behaviors and to the choice of specific assessment strategies. For example, we might wish to examine the treatment utility of using self-report questionnaires to guide treatment planning, above and beyond that provided by direct behavioral observation of children who are phobic of social encounters. All children could complete a fear schedule and be observed in a social situation, but the self-report data for only half of the children could be made available for treatment planning. If the children for whom self-reports were made available improved more than those whose treatment plans were based solely on behavioral observations, then the treatment utility of using self-report data would be established (for this problem with this age child). In a similar fashion, the treatment utility of interviews, role plays, and other devices could be evaluated (Hayes et al., 1987). Although the concept of treatment utility is relatively new, it shows considerable promise as a strategy to evaluate the incremental validity of our multimethod assessment approach. We should not necessarily assume that *more* assessment is *better* assessment.

Third, more effort must be directed toward the development of developmentally sensitive and empir-

ically validated procedures for the assessment of cognitive processes in children. In recent years, child behavioral assessors have become increasingly interested in the relation of children's cognitive processes to observed behaviors and affective experiences. The need for assessment in this area is further evidenced by the rapid increase of cognitive-behavioral treatment procedures with children (e.g., Kendall, Pellegrini, & Urbain, 1981; Meador & Ollendick, 1984). As noted by Kendall et al. (1981), there is a particularly pressing need to develop procedures that can examine the very cognitions and processes that are targeted for change in these intervention efforts. For example, the reliable and valid assessment of self-statements made by children in specific situations would facilitate the empirical evaluation of cognitive-behavioral procedures such as self-instructional training and cognitive restructuring (cf. Zatz & Chassin, 1983; Stefanek, Ollendick, Baldock, Francis, & Yaeger, 1987).

Fourth, we must concentrate additional effort on the role of the child in child behavioral assessment. All too frequently, "tests are administered *to* children, ratings are obtained *on* children, and behaviors are observed *in* children" (Ollendick & Hersen, 1984). This process views the child as a passive responder, someone who is largely incapable of actively shaping and determining the behaviors of clinical relevance. Although examination of these organismic variables is only beginning, it would appear that concerted and systematic effort must be directed to their description and articulation. The process described above also implies that child behavior (problematic or otherwise) occurs in a vacuum, and that the perceptions and behaviors of referral sources (parents, teachers) and characteristics of the environments in which behavior occurs are somehow less critical to assess. Recent efforts to develop reliable methods for assessing parent-child interactions are indicative of an increased awareness of the need to broaden the scope of assessment to include the specific individuals with whom, and environments in which, child behavior problems commonly occur. However, much additional work remains to be done in this area.

Fifth, and finally, we must continue to focus our attention on ethical issues in child behavioral assessment. A number of ethical issues regarding children's rights, proper and legal consent, professional judgment, and social values are raised in the routine practice of child behavioral assessment (Rekers, 1984). Are children capable of granting full and proper consent to a behavioral assessment procedure? At what age are children competent to give such consent? Is informed consent necessary? Or, might not informed consent be impossible, impractical, or countertherapeutic in some situations? What ethical guidelines surround the assessment procedures to be used? Current professional guidelines suggest that our procedures should be reliable, valid, and clinically useful. Do the procedures suggested in this chapter meet these professional guidelines? What are the rights of parents? Of society? It should be evident from these questions that a variety of ethical issues exist. Striking a balance among the rights of parents, society, and children is no easy matter but is one that takes on added importance in our increasingly litigious society.

In short, the future directions of child behavioral assessment are numerous and varied. Even though a technology for child behavioral assessment has evolved and is in force, we need to begin to explore the issues raised before we can conclude that the procedures are maximally productive and in the best interests of children.

SUMMARY

Child behavioral assessment strategies have been slow to evolve. Only recently has the chasm between child behavior therapy and assessment been narrowed. Increased awareness of the importance of developing assessment procedures that provide an adequate representation of child behavior disorders has spurred research into assessment procedures and spawned a plethora of child behavioral assessment techniques. The growing sophistication of child behavior assessment is witnessed by the appearance of self- and other-report strategies that take into account developmental, social, and cultural influences as well as cognitive and affective mediators of overt behavior. At the same time, attention to psychometric properties of assessment procedures has continued.

Certain theoretical assumptions guide child behavioral assessment. Foremost among these is the premise that behavior is a function of situational determinants and not a sign of underlying personality traits. To assess adequately the situational determinants and to obtain as complete a picture of the child as possible, a multimethod assessment approach is recommended utilizing both direct and indirect measures of behavior. Direct measures include self-monitoring as well as behavioral observation by trained observers in naturalistic or analogue settings. Indirect measures include behavioral interviewing and self- and other-report measures. These sources of information are considered indirect ones because they involve retrospective reports of previous behavior.

Even though direct behavioral observation remains the hallmark of child behavioral assessment, information from these other sources is considered not only valuable, but integral in the understanding and subsequent treatment of child behavior disorders. Hence, whereas the identification and specification of discrete target behaviors was once considered sufficient, thorough behavioral assessment involves serious consideration and systematic assessment of cognitive and affective aspects of the child's behavior and of developmental, social, and cultural factors that influence the child as well as direct observation of the problematic behavior.

Several areas of future research remain. These include clearer specification of developmental variables, a closer examination of the utility of the multimethod approach at different age levels, development of specific measures to examine cognitive processes in children, articulation of the role of the child in child behavioral assessment, and the continued development of ethical guidelines. While the basis for a technology of child behavioral assessment exists, considerable fine tuning remains to be done.

REFERENCES

Achenbach, T. M. (1966). The classification of children's psychiatric symptoms: A factor analytic study. *Psychological Monographs, 80,* 1–37.

Achenbach, T. M. (1978). The Child Behavior Profile—I. Boys aged 6–11. *Journal of Consulting and Clinical Psychology, 46,* 478–488.

Achenbach, T. M., & Edelbrock, C. S. (1979). The Child Behavior Profile—II. Boys aged 12–16 and girls aged 6–11 and 12–16. *Journal of Consulting and Clinical Psychology, 47,* 223–233.

Achenbach, T. M., & Edelbrock, C. S. (1989). Diagnostic, taxonomic, and assessment issues. In T. H. Ollendick & M. Hersen (Eds.), *Handbook of child psychopathology* (2nd ed.). New York: Plenum Press.

Ackerman, A. M., & Shapiro, E. S. (1985). Self-monitoring and work productivity with mentally retarded adults. *Journal of Applied Behavior Analysis, 17,* 403–407.

Ayllon, T., Smith, D., & Rogers, M. (1970). Behavioral management of school phobia. *Journal of Behavior Therapy and Experimental Psychiatry, 1,* 125–138.

Bandura, A. (1977). Self-efficacy: Toward a unifying theory of behavioral change. *Psychological Review, 84,* 191–215.

Barkley, R. A. (1981). *Hyperactive children: A hand-*

book for diagnosis and treatment. New York: Guilford Press.

Barkley, R. A. (1987). Defiant children: A clinician's manual for parent training. New York: Guilford Press.

Barkley, R. A., Karlsson, J., Strzelecki, E., & Murphy, J. (1984). Effects of age and Ritalin dosage on the mother-child interactions of hyperactive children. Journal of Consulting and Clinical Psychology, 52, 750–758.

Barrios, B., & Hartmann, D. P. (1986). The contributions of traditional assessment: Concepts, issues, and methodologies. In R. O. Nelson & S. C. Hayes (Eds.), Conceptual foundations of behavioral assessment. New York: Guilford Press.

Barton, E. J., & Ascione, F. R. (1984). Direct observations. In T. H. Ollendick & M. Hersen (Eds.), Child behavioral assessment: Principles and procedures. New York: Pergamon Press.

Bem, D. J., & Allen, A. (1974). On predicting some of the people some of the time: The search for cross-situational consistencies in behavior. Psychological Review, 81, 506–520.

Bornstein, P. H., Bornstein, M. T., & Dawson, B. (1984). Integrated assessment and treatment. In T. H. Ollendick & M. Hersen (Eds.), Child behavioral assessment: Principles and procedures. New York: Pergamon Press.

Campbell, S. B. (1989). Developmental perspectives in child psychopathology. In T. H. Ollendick & M. Hersen (Eds.), Handbook of child psychopathology (2nd ed.). New York: Plenum Press.

Cantwell, D. P. (1983). Childhood depression: A review of current research. In B. B. Lahey & A. E. Kazdin (Eds.), Advances in clinical child psychology (Vol. 5). New York: Plenum Press.

Chess, S., Thomas, A., & Birch, H. G. (1966). Distortions in developmental reporting made by parents of behaviorally disturbed children. Journal of the American Academy of Child Psychiatry, 5, 226–231.

Ciminero, A. R., & Drabman, R. S. (1977). Current developments in the behavioral assessment of children. In B. B. Lahey & A. E. Kazdin (Eds.), Advances in clinical child psychology (Vol. 1). New York: Plenum Press.

Cone, J. D. (1977). The relevance of reliability and validity for behavioral assessment. Behavior Therapy, 8, 411–426.

Cone, J. D. (1978). The behavioral assessment grid (BAG): A conceptual framework and taxonomy. Behavior Therapy, 9, 882–888.

Cone, J. D. (1981). Psychometric considerations. In M. Hersen & A. S. Bellack (Eds.), Behavioral assessment: A practical handbook (2nd ed.). Elmsford, NY: Pergamon Press.

Cone, J. D. (1986). Idiographic, nomothetic, and related perspectives in behavioral assessment. In R. O. Nelson & S. C. Hayes (Eds.), Conceptual foundations of behavioral assessment. New York: Guilford Press.

Cone, J. D., & Hawkins, R. P. (Eds.) (1977). Behavioral assessment: New directions in clinical psychology. New York: Brunner/Mazel.

Cowen, E. L., Pederson, A., Barbigian, H., Izzo, L. D., & Trost, M. A. (1973). Long-term follow-up of early detected vulnerable children. Journal of Consulting and Clinical Psychology, 41, 438–445.

Cronbach, L. J. (1960). Essentials of psychological testing. New York: Harper & Row.

Deluty, R. H. (1979). Children's Action Tendency Scale: A self-report measure of aggressiveness, assertiveness, and submissiveness in children. Journal of Consulting and Clinical Psychology, 41, 1061–1071.

Edelbrock, C. S. (1984). Developmental considerations. In T. H. Ollendick & M. Hersen (Eds.), Child behavioral assessment: Principles and procedures. Elmsford, NY: Pergamon Press.

Evans, I. M., & Nelson, R. O. (1977). Assessment of child behavior problems. In A. R. Ciminero, K. S. Calhoun, & H. E. Adams (Eds.), Handbook of behavioral assessment. New York: Wiley-Interscience.

Finch, A. J., Nelson, W. M., III, & Moss, J. H. (1983). A cognitive-behavioral approach to anger management with emotionally disturbed children. In A. J. Finch, W. M. Nelson, & E. S. Ott (Eds.), Cognitive behavioral approaches to treatment with children. Jamaica, NY: Spectrum Publications.

Finch, A. J., & Rogers, T. R. (1984). Self-report instruments. In T. H. Ollendick & M. Hersen (Eds.), Child behavioral assessment: Principles and procedures. Elmsford, NY: Pergmon Press.

Goldfried, M. R., & Kent, R. N. (1972). Traditional versus behavioral personality assessment: A comparison of methodological and theoretical assumptions. Psychological Bulletin, 77, 409–420.

Graham, P., & Rutter, M. (1968). The reliability and validity of the psychiatric assessment of the child—II. Interview with the parents. British Journal of Psychiatry, 114, 581–592.

Gresham, F. M. (1982). Social interactions as predictors of children's likeability and friendship patterns: A multiple regression analysis. *Journal of Behavioral Assessment, 4,* 39–54.

Gross, A. M. (1984). Behavioral interviewing. In T. H. Ollendick & M. Hersen (Eds.), *Child behavioral assessment: Principles and procedures.* Elmsford, NY: Pergamon Press.

Harris, S. L., & Ferrari, M. (1983). Developmental factors in child behavior therapy. *Behavior Therapy, 14,* 54–72.

Hayes, S. C., Nelson, R. O., & Jarrett, R. B. (1986). Evaluating the quality of behavioral assessment. In R. O. Nelson & S. C. Hayes (Eds.), *Conceptual foundations of behavioral assessment.* New York: Guilford Press.

Hayes, S. C., Nelson, R. O., & Jarrett, R. B. (1987). The treatment utility of assessment: A functional approach to evaluating assessment quality. *American Psychologist, 42,* 963–974.

Herjanic, B., Herjanic, M., Brown, F., & Wheatt, T. (1973). Are children reliable reporters? *Journal of Abnormal Child Psychology, 3,* 41–48.

Holmes, F. B. (1936). An experimental investigation of a method of overcoming children's fears. *Child Development, 1,* 6–30.

Johnson, S. M., & Bolstad, O. D. (1973). Methodological issues in naturalistic observations: Some problems and solutions for field research. In L. A. Hammerlynck, L. C. Handy, & E. J. Mash (Eds.), *Behavior change: Methodology, concepts, and practice.* Champaign, IL: Research Press.

Johnson, S. M., & Lobitz, G. K. (1974). Parental manipulation of child behavior in home observations. *Journal of Applied Behavior Analysis, 1,* 23–31.

Jones, M. C. (1924). The elimination of children's fears. *Journal of Experimental Psychology, 7,* 382–390.

Jones, R. R., Reid, J. B., & Patterson, G. R. (1975). Naturalistic observation in clinical assessment. In P. McReynolds (Ed.), *Advances in psychological assessment* (Vol. 3). San Francisco: Jossey-Bass.

Kanfer, F. H., & Phillips, J. S. (1970). *Learning foundations of behavior therapy.* New York: Wiley.

Kazdin, A. E. (1977). Artifact, bias, and complexity of assessment: The ABCs of reliability. *Journal of Applied Behavior Analysis, 4,* 7–14.

Kendall, P. C., & Hollon, S. D. (Eds.) (1980). *Cognitive-behavioral intervention: Assessment methods.* New York: Academic Press.

Kendall, P. C., Pellegrini, D. S., & Urbain, E. S. (1981). Approaches to assessment for cognitive-behavioral interventions with children. In P. C. Kendall & S. D. Hollon (Eds.), *Assessment strategies for cognitive-behavioral interventions.* New York: Academic Press.

Kovacs, M. (1985). *Children's Depression Inventory (CDI). Psychopharmacology Bulletin, 21,* 995–998.

Kunzelman, H. D. (Ed.). (1970). *Precision teaching.* Seattle: Special Child Publications.

Linehan, M. (1977). Issues in behavioral interviewing. In J. D. Cone & R. P. Hawkins (Eds.), *Behavioral assessment: New directions in clinical psychology.* New York: Brunner/Mazel.

Mash, E. J., & Terdal, L. G. (1981). Behavioral assessment of childhood disturbance. In E. J. Mash & L. G. Terdal (Eds.), *Behavioral assessment of childhood disorders.* New York: Guilford Press.

Mash, E. J., & Terdal, L. G. (Eds.) (1987). *Behavioral assessment of childhood disorders* (2nd ed.). New York: Guilford Press.

Matson, J. L., & Ollendick, T. H. (1976). Elimination of low frequency biting. *Behavior Therapy, 7,* 410–412.

McMahon, R. J. (1984). Behavioral checklists and rating forms. In T. H. Ollendick & M. Hersen (Eds.), *Child behavioral assessment: Principles and procedures.* Elmsford, NY: Pergamon Press.

Meador, A. E., & Ollendick, T. H. (1984). Cognitive behavior therapy with children: An evaluation of its efficacy and clinical utility. *Child and Family Behavior Therapy, 6,* 25–44.

Meichenbaum, D. H. (1977). *Cognitive-behavior modification.* New York: Plenum Press.

Miller, L. C., Barrett, C. L., Hampe, E., & Noble, H. (1972). Comparison of reciprocal inhibition, psychotherapy, and waiting list control for phobic children. *Journal of Abnormal Psychology, 79,* 269–279.

Mischel, W. (1968). *Personality and assessment.* New York: Wiley.

Nelson, R. O. (1977). Methodological issues in assessment via self-monitoring. In J. D. Cone & R. P. Hawkins (Eds.), *Behavioral assessment: New directions in clinical psychology.* New York: Brunner/Mazel.

Nelson, R. O. (1981). Theoretical explanations for self-monitoring. *Behavior Modification, 5,* 3–14.

Nelson, R. O., Lipinski, D. P., & Boykin, R. A. (1978). The effects of self-recorder training and the obtrusiveness of the self-recording device on the accuracy and reactivity of self-monitoring. *Behavior Therapy, 9,* 200–208.

Nelson, W. M., III, & Finch, A. J., Jr. (1978). *The Children's Inventory of Anger.* Unpublished manuscript, Xavier University.

Novick, J., Rosenfeld, E., Bloch, D. A., & Dawson, D. (1966). Ascertaining deviant behavior in children. *Journal of Consulting and Clinical Psychology, 30,* 230–238.

O'Leary, K. D., & Johnson, S. B. (1979). Psychological assessment. In H. C. Quay & J. S. Werry (Eds.), *Psychopathological disorders of children.* New York: Wiley.

O'Leary, K. D., Romanczyk, R. G., Kass, R. E., Dietz, A., & Santogrossi, D. (1971). *Procedures for classroom observations of teachers and parents.* Unpublished manuscript, State University of New York at Stony Brook.

Ollendick, T. H. (1981). Self-monitoring and self-administered overcorrection: The modification of nervous tics in children. *Behavior Modification, 5,* 75–84.

Ollendick, T. H. (1983a). Development and validation of the Children's Assertiveness Inventory. *Child and Family Behavior Therapy, 5,* 1–15.

Ollendick, T. H. (1983b). Reliability and validity of the Revised-Fear Survey Schedule for Children (FSSC-R). *Behaviour Research and Therapy, 21,* 685–692.

Ollendick, T. H., & Cerny, J. A. (1981). *Clinical behavior therapy with children.* New York: Plenum Press.

Ollendick, T. H., & Gruen, G. E. (1972). Treatment of a bodily injury phobia with implosive therapy. *Journal of Consulting and Clinical Psychology, 38,* 389–393.

Ollendick, T. H., & Hersen, M. (Eds.) (1983). *Handbook of child psychopathology.* New York: Plenum Press.

Ollendick, T. H., & Hersen, M. (Eds.) (1984). *Child behavioral assessment: Principles and procedures.* New York: Pergamon Press.

Ollendick, T. H., Matson, J. L., & Helsel, W. J. (1985). Fears in children and adolescents: Normative data. *Behaviour Research and Therapy, 23,* 465–467.

Ollendick, T. H., & Mayer, J. (1984). School phobia. In S. M. Turner (Ed.), *Behavioral treatment of anxiety disorders.* New York: Plenum Press.

Olweus, D. (1979). Stability of aggressive reaction patterns in males: A review. *Psychological Bulletin, 86,* 852–875.

Patterson, G. R. (1976). The aggressive child: Victim and architect of a coercive system. In E. J. Mash, L. A. Hammerlynck, & L. C. Hardy (Eds.), *Behavior modification and families.* New York: Brunner/Mazel.

Patterson, G. R. (1982). *Coercive family process.* Eugene, OR: Castalia.

Patterson, G. R., Ray, R. S., Shaw, D. A., & Cobb, J. A. (1969). *Manual for coding family interaction* (6th ed.). Unpublished manuscript, University of Oregon.

Peterson, D. R. (1961). Behavior problems of middle childhood. *Journal of Clinical and Consulting Psychology, 25,* 205–209.

Pollard, S., Ward, E., & Barkley, R. A. (1983). The effects of parent training and Ritalin on the parent-child interactions of hyperactive boys. *Child and Family Behavior Therapy, 5,* 51–69.

Prinz, R. (Ed.) (1986). *Advances in behavioral assessment of children and families.* Greenwich, CT: JAI Press.

Quay, H. C. (1977). Measuring dimensions of deviant behavior: The Behavior Problem Checklist. *Journal of Abnormal Child Psychology, 5,* 277–287.

Quay, H. C., & Peterson, D. R. (1967). *Manual for the Behavior Problem Checklist.* Champaign, IL: University of Illinois.

Quay, H. C., & Peterson, D. R. (1975). *Manual for the Behavior Problem Checklist.* Unpublished manuscript.

Quay, H. C., & Peterson, D. R. (1983). *Interim manual for the Revised Behavior Problem Checklist.* Unpublished manuscript, University of Miami.

Rekers, G. A. (1984). Ethical issues in child behavioral assessment. In T. H. Ollendick & M. Hersen (Eds.), *Child behavioral assessment: Principles and procedures.* Elmsford, NY: Pergamon Press.

Rutter, M. (1986). The developmental psychopathology of depression: Issues and perspectives. In M. Rutter, C. E. Izard, & P. B. Read (Eds.), *Depression in young people: Clinical and developmental perspectives.* New York: Guilford Press.

Rutter, M., & Garmezy, N. (1983). Developmental psychopathology. In E. M. Hetherington (Ed.), *Socialization, personality, and social development: Vol 4. Mussen's Handbook of child psychology.* New York: Wiley.

Scherer, M. W., & Nakamura, C. Y. (1968). A fear survey schedule for children (FSS-FC): A factor analytic comparison with manifest anxiety (CMAS). *Behaviour Research and Therapy, 6,* 173–182.

Schopler, E. (1974). Changes of direction with psychiatric children. In A. Davids (Ed.), *Child personality and psychopathology: Current topics* (Vol. 1). New York: Wiley.

Shapiro, E. S. (1984). Self-monitoring. In T. H. Ollendick & M. Hersen (Eds.), *Child behavioral assessment: Principles and procedures*. Elmsford, NY: Pergamon Press.

Shapiro, E. S., McGonigle, J. J., & Ollendick, T. H. (1980). An analysis of self-assessment and self-reinforcement in a self-managed token economy with mentally retarded children. *Journal of Applied Research in Mental Retardation, 1,* 227–240.

Skinner, B. F. (1953). *Science and human behavior.* New York: Macmillan.

Smith, R. E., & Sharpe, T. M. (1970). Treatment of a school phobia with implosive therapy. *Journal of Consulting and Clinical Psychology, 35,* 239–243.

Smucker, M. R., Craighead, W. E., Craighead, L. W., & Green, B. J. (1986). Normative and reliability data for the Children's Depression Inventory. *Journal of Abnormal Child Psychology, 14,* 25–39.

Spielberger, C. D. (1973). *Preliminary Manual for the State-Trait Anxiety Inventory for Children ("How I Feel Questionnaire").* Palo Alto, CA: Consulting Psychologist Press.

Sroufe, L. A., & Rutter, M. (1984). The domain of developmental psychopathology. *Child Development, 55,* 17–29.

Staats, A. W. (1975). *Social behaviorism.* Homewood, IL: Dorsey Press.

Staats, A. W. (1986). Behaviorism with a personality. In R. O. Nelson & S. C. Hayes (Eds.), *Conceptual foundations of behavioral assessment.* New York: Guilford Press.

Stefanek, M. E., Ollendick, T. H., Baldock, W. P., Francis, G., & Yaeger, N. J. (1987). Self-statements in aggressive, withdrawn, and popular children. *Cognitive Therapy and Research, 11,* 229–239.

Swann, G. E., & MacDonald, M. L. (1978). Behavior therapy in practice: A rational survey of behavior therapists. *Behavior Therapy, 9,* 799–807.

Ullmann, L. P., & Krasner, L. (Eds.) (1965). *Case studies in behavior modification.* New York: Holt, Rinehart, & Winston.

Wahler, R. G. (1976). Deviant child behavior in the family: Developmental speculations and behavior change strategies. In H. Leitenberg (Ed.), *Handbook of behavior modification and behavior therapy.* Englewood Cliffs, NJ: Prentice-Hall.

Wahler, R. G., House, A. E., & Stambaugh, E. E. (1976). *Ecological assessment of child problem behavior: A clinical package for home, school, and institutional settings.* Elmsford, NY: Pergamon Press.

Watson, J. B., & Rayner, R. (1920). Conditioned emotional reactions. *Journal of Experimental Psychology, 3,* 1–14.

Winett, R. A., Riley, A. W., King, A. C., & Altman, D. G. (1989). Preventive strategies with children and families. In T. H. Ollendick & M. Hersen (Eds.), *Handbook of child psychopathology* (2nd ed.). New York: Plenum Press.

Zatz, S., & Chassin, L. (1983). Cognitions of test-anxious children. *Journal of Consulting and Clinical Psychology, 51,* 526–534.

CHAPTER 19

BEHAVIORAL ASSESSMENT OF ADULTS

Stephen N. Haynes

INTRODUCTION

Assessment is an indispensable component in the behavioral analysis and treatment of adult behavior disorders. It provides the basis for diagnosis and classification, the identification of causal factors, the selection of intervention target behaviors, the selection of intervention goals, the design of intervention programs, and the evaluation of intervention effects. Most important, assessment is necessary for the continuing development of more powerful intervention procedures and the refinement of the conceptual models upon which those interventions are based (Goldfried, 1982; Haynes, 1978).

Behavioral assessment encompasses methods and concepts derived from and closely tied to behavioral construct systems (Nelson & Hayes, 1987). It includes diverse methods, such as naturalistic and analog observation, self-monitoring, psychophysiological measurement, interviews and questionnaires, product of behavior measures, manipulation, and critical event sampling. It is most frequently identified with an emphasis on observable and minimally inferential constructs, environmental determinism, and the quantification of psychological constructs (Haynes, 1984a).

Impact

Behavioral assessment is an active area of research and application. The most obvious indices of its status are the proliferation of books, published articles, symposia, and presentations at scientific conventions that have behavioral assessment as their focus. Al-

though no behavioral assessment books were published prior to the mid-1970s, several (Barlow, 1981; Bellack & Hersen, 1988; Ciminero, Calhoun, & Adams, 1977, 1986; Cone & Hawkins, 1977; Haynes, 1978; Haynes & Wilson, 1979; Hersen & Bellack, 1981; Keefe, Kopel & Gordon, 1978; Mash & Terdal, 1981; Nay, 1979; Nelson & Hayes, 1986) have been published in the last 15 years. Two journals (*Behavioral Assessment, Journal of Psychopathology and Behavioral Assessment*) were begun in 1979 and publish original research and methodological and review articles on behavioral assessment. Furthermore, an increasing number of graduate-level courses in psychology, education, and rehabilitation focus on behavioral assessment (see "Focus on Graduate Training" series in *Behavior Therapist,* 1987–1988).

The impact of behavioral assessment is also spreading across behavioral science disciplines, such as clinical psychology (Hersen, Kazdin, & Bellack, 1983), behavioral medicine and health psychology (Karoly, 1985; Keefe, & Blumenthal, 1982; Tryon, 1985), social work and psychiatry (see *Journal of Behavior Therapy and Experimental Psychiatry*), cognitive psychology (Merluzzi, Glass, & Genest, 1981), community psychology (Nietzel, Winett, MacDonald, & Davidson, 1977), developmental disorders (Sackett, 1978), pediatric medicine (Baer, 1986), and program evaluation (Alevizos, De Risi, Liberman, Eckman, & Callahan, 1978).

Derivation and Development

The historical derivations of behavioral assessment reflect the diversity of its methods. Naturalistic and analog behavioral observations were used in early Pavlovian, Watsonian, and other experimental psychological studies, and they can be traced to Hellenic and Egyptian eras (Alexander & Selesnick, 1966; Kazdin, 1978). These technologies for scientific inquiry have been adopted and refined by behavior analysts. Methodological refinements to behavioral observation, as well as other assessment procedures, have also come from adjunctive disciplines, such as ethology, social psychology, developmental psychology, and experimental psychology (e.g., Achenbach, 1974; Hutt & Hutt, 1970).

Other methods of behavioral assessment, such as questionnaires and interviews, have been adapted from traditional applied psychological disciplines such as educational, developmental, and clinical psychology. Their content and focus have been modified and refined by behavior analysts in order to increase their methodological and conceptual congruence with behavioral construct systems.

The development and application of behavioral assessment procedures have been strongly influenced by the methods and foci of behavioral interventions (Haynes, 1984a, 1984b; Kazdin, 1979; Miller, 1981; Russo, Bird, & Masek, 1980). Although interventions with adult disorders based on behavioral paradigms occurred in the 1950s and earlier (see Kazdin, 1978), extensive applications of behavioral paradigms did not take place until the 1960s (Bachrach, 1962; Bandura, 1969; Ullmann & Krasner, 1965; Wolpe, 1958). These interventions emphasized the manipulation of the client's interaction with his or her environment and necessitated the use of assessment procedures that differed procedurally and conceptually from those followed in traditional clinical interventions. In particular, traditional assessment methods, such as projective or global questionnaire measures, were not sufficiently specific, molecular, situationally sensitive, or congruent with this new emphasis on environmental and reciprocal determinism.

Behavioral assessment methods and focuses have also been influenced by advances in behavioral construct systems, particularly by an increasingly complex and comprehensive functional analysis of behavior disorders (Haynes & O'Brien, 1988). For example, the methods and focuses of behavioral assessment procedures have been affected by the hypothesized roles of stimulus-control factors in sleep disorders (Youkilis & Bootzin, 1981), cognitive factors in phobic disorders (Taylor & Agras, 1981), behavior chains in child behavior problems (Voeltz & Evans, 1982), temporally noncontiguous events in marital distress (Margolin, 1981), multiple and inter-

active causal factors (Haynes, 1987), and situational specificity in many behavior disorders (Kazdin, 1982a; McFall, 1982).

Another impetus for the development of behavioral assessment has been a dissatisfaction with traditional clinical assessment instruments and their underlying conceptual systems (McFall, 1986). The perceived stagnation of traditional clinical psychology—its failure to evolve more powerful conceptual models and intervention strategies—has been attributed, in part, to its emphasis on unobservable and highly inferential intrapsychic processes and causal factors. This emphasis was manifested in an almost exclusive reliance on verbal psychotherapy, the psychodynamic orientation of the prevalent diagnostic systems (DSM-I; DSM-II), and in the type of assessment instruments employed (Wolman, 1978). Highly inferential assessment instruments of questionable psychometric qualities were frequently used to identify hypothesized intrapsychic causal mechanisms and to provide trait-based personality descriptions.

Chapter Focus

The focus of this chapter is limited to one of many domains of applications of behavioral assessment— the assessment of adult behavior disorders. However, its widespread applicability renders such a limited focus artificial. Many advances in behavioral assessment technology and concepts occur first in limited areas of application before becoming more generalized. For example, a systems perspective was initially adopted in behavioral conceptualizations of family interaction (Vincent, 1980; Wahler, 1980), but has obvious relevance for the assessment of many adult behavior disorders (e.g., Haynes & Chavez, 1983; Miller, 1981). Therefore, advances in concepts and methods in other behavioral assessment domains will be considered when they are relevant to the assessment of adult behavior disorders.

The following section introduces the conceptual and methodological assumptions that underlie behavioral assessment. The functions of behavioral assessment are then considered, and the various behavioral assessment methods are described. Subsequent sections consider evaluative dimensions and current directions in behavioral assessment.

THEORETICAL AND METHODOLOGICAL BASES OF BEHAVIORAL ASSESSMENT

The goals, methods, and focuses of every assessment system are influenced by three sets of assumptions: (a) those concerning the *characteristics* of behavior disorders, (b) those concerning the *causes* of behavior disorders, and (c) those concerning *epistemology*—that is, the investigative strategies presumed to be most effective for studying the characteristics, causes, and treatment of behavior disorders. More extensive presentations of these issues can be found in publications by Bandura (1969), Eysenck (1986), Haynes (1978), Kanfer and Philips (1970), Mischel (1968), Nelson and Hayes (1986), and Wiggins (1973).

Assumptions Concerning the Characteristics of Behavior Disorders

There are several assumptions concerning the characteristics of behavior disorders that affect behavioral assessment strategies: (a) Behavior disorders can be expressed in cognitive, verbal, overt behavioral, and physiological response modes. (b) These response modes may demonstrate fractionation or low levels of covariation. (c) The degree of response-mode covariation varies across individuals, modes, and disorders. (d) There are individual differences in the topography of a behavior disorder. (e) Topographically dissimilar behaviors may demonstrate common variance (i.e., function as a *response class*). (f) Many behaviors are interdependent, and modification of one behavior is likely to affect others (Bandura, 1969, 1981; Haynes, 1978; Haynes & Wilson, 1979; Kanfer & Philips, 1970; Nelson & Hayes, 1986).

The multimodal nature of many adult behavior disorders suggests the need for assessment strategies with multiple focuses. Anxiety disorders, for example, may involve overt avoidance or escape behaviors, verbalizations of subjective fear and discomfort, and indices of physiological arousal and/or cognitive intrusions (Asterita, 1985; Taylor & Agras, 1981). Therefore, a comprehensive assessment necessitates the targeting of multiple components. The importance of multimodal assessment is further enhanced because the various components of behavior disorders frequently demonstrate low levels of covariation (Borkovec, Weerts, & Bernstein, 1977; Gannon & Haynes, 1986; Haynes & Wilson, 1979; Kaloupek & Levis, 1980). Inferences about one mode cannot be confidently drawn from measures of another. Furthermore, intervention programs may have differential effects across modes (e.g., Michelson & Mavissakalian, 1985).

There also are differences across individuals in the degree of covariation among response modes and in their clinical significance. Given that the apparent level of covariation among response modes is affected by the manner in which they are measured, some individuals will demonstrate a much higher degree of covariation among modes than will others (e.g., some persons with phobic behaviors, but not others, will demonstrate high correlations among physiological, verbal, and overt behavioral modes). Also, the dominant response of a behavior disorder for one individual (e.g., negative cognitive ruminations in depression) may play a relatively minor role for other individuals with the same disorder.

It is important to note that most behavior "disorders" are simply labels for a group of behaviors; the degree to which the behaviors that are included within these labels actually covary is usually undetermined. Furthermore, because they are controlled by different variables, covariance among these behaviors should not be expected. Only when labels are erroneously imbued with causal properties is covariance expected on an a priori basis (e.g., suggesting that low self-efficacy and sleep difficulties covary because they are both a result of "depression").

The preceding discussion emphasized the multiple components of behavior disorders. Additionally, covariation among structurally dissimilar behaviors (e.g., stealing, alcohol intake, and verbal aggression) also is frequently observed. Intervention effects are more likely to generalize to behaviors that covary or function as a response class. However, response covariation cannot be assumed, and the degree of covariation is likely to vary as a function of situational factors and to vary across individuals and intervention strategies (Patterson & Bechtel, 1977). In some cases, covariation among structurally dissimilar behaviors can facilitate assessment because some members of the response class may be more amenable than others to assessment. For example, high-frequency behaviors may sometimes be more easily assessed than their low-frequency covariates (Wahler, 1975).

Behaviors may also be part of *functional response classes*. That is, behaviors may be dissimilar in topography or statistically uncorrelated but be a function of similar maintaining factors. For example, for some people, alcohol and barbiturate ingestion, exercise and overeating, and behavioral relaxation may be part of the same functional *psychological arousal reduction* response class because they all serve to modify an internal state. The identification of functional response classes is important because behavioral interventions often attempt to substitute less problematic for more problematic behaviors in the same response class (e.g., teaching relaxation skills as a method of reducing anxiety associated overeating).

A significant advance in the conceptual foundations of behavioral construct systems has been the recognition of the interdependence of behaviors and behavior-environment interactions within their larger social systems. Behavior problems cannot be viewed independently from their environmental context. For example, the financial status, level and type of social support from family members, and extramarital relationships can affect an individual's level of marital distress (Stuart, 1980) and these mediating factors are affected by the behavior of the individual.

Perhaps more important, it is increasingly recognized that intervention programs can be affected by a client's social system and can have unintended effects (i.e., side effects). For example, reductions in the level of heterosexual anxiety of a college student may affect his or her study behavior and interaction with same-sex friends. In some cases, unintended effects contribute more to the evaluation of intervention outcome than do intended effects.

The adoption of a systems perspective (Vincent, 1980), in conjunction with the presumed lack of covariance among response modes within and between individuals, along with an assumption of between-person differences in the response mode of most clinical significance, necessitates a significant deviation from the limited focus often associated with behavioral assessment. Assessment targets and methods will necessarily vary across individuals and disorders. Consequently, assessment procedures must include multiple focuses and methods (Lazarus, 1976), including measurement of factors within a client's social system.

Assumptions About the Causes of Behavior Disorders

The most important determinants of the methods and focus of an assessment system are assumptions about the causes of behavior disorders. Although behavior analysts emphasize *functional* rather than *causal* relationships (see discussion in Haynes & O'Brien, 1988), most behavioral interventions attempt systematically to modify hypothesized controlling variables (e.g., early parent-child interactions cannot be modified but currently held irrational beliefs that are derived from those interactions can be; Ellis & Bernard, 1985). Therefore, identification of potential controlling (causal) variables is a primary goal of behavioral assessment.

There are several underlying assumptions about the nature of causal relationships that influence the focus of behavioral assessment. They include an emphasis on (a) contemporaneous reciprocal determinism; (b) the operation of mediational variables; (c) the importance of situational determinants of behavior; (d) multiple, idiosyncratic, and interactive causality; (e) temporal instability of causal factors; and (f) all causal relationships have limited domains, outside of which they are nonoperational.

The most important causal assumption is that of reciprocal determinism (Bandura, 1981). The probability, type, form, magnitude, and duration of behavior disorders are significantly affected by environmental events, such as social contingencies, cues, environmental stressors, and classical conditioning experiences (Eysenck & Martin, 1987) which, in turn, are influenced by the behavior of the individual (McFall & McDonel, 1986). For example, depression has been hypothesized to be caused by social reinforcement decrements that can be precipitated by the behavior of the depressed individual toward others (Lewinsohn, 1975). Similarly, insomnia may sometimes result from the presleep behaviors of the insomniac (Youkilis & Bootzin, 1981).

An emphasis on contemporaneous, rather than historical, causal factors is both theoretically and heuristically based. Behavior analysts presume, often without empirical justification, that a greater proportion of variance in the parameters (e.g., probability, magnitude, duration) of behavior disorders can be attributed to current rather than historical behavioral-environmental variables. Additionally, it is usually easier to manipulate contemporaneous than noncontemporaneous variables. For example, while the causal importance of early parental models for the development of paranoid behaviors in an adult may be recognized (Haynes, 1986), it may be easier for a therapist to intervene with more contemporaneous causal variables such as a restricted social network or social skills deficits.

The emphasis on environmental events as the primary causes of behavior disorders does not preclude a causal role for genetic, psychological, or cognitive variables. Indeed, evidence is quite strong for a significant causal role for organic and cognitive factors in behavior disorders, such as depression (Anisman & LaPierre, 1982), schizophrenia (Shapiro, 1981) and anxiety disorders (Merluzzi, Glass, & Genest, 1981). Behavior disorders must be considered final manifestations of multiple and interacting causal pathways. At the same time, an emphasis on the assessment of the functional relationships between a behavior disorder and environmental variables will, in many cases, result in the identification of important and clinically useful sources of behavioral variance.

The presumed causal role of behavior-environment interactions (McFall & McDonel, 1986) partially accounts for the emphasis on particular *assessment methods*. For example, naturalistic observation and self-monitoring are particularly well suited to measuring these interactions. Additionally, causal behavior-environment interactions are also the *focus* of assessment procedures such as interviews and questionnaires.

Congruent with a stress on environmental interactionism is an emphasis on the behavioral skills of clients. It is assumed that a client's behavioral repertoire (e.g., excesses, deficits, topography, content, timing) affects the probability, type, or degree of behavior disorders. For example, a behavior skills analysis might focus on deficits in social initiation skills for withdrawn or depressed individuals, verbal communication or negotiation skills for marital distress, time-management skills for habit problems (e.g., academic achievement, procrastination), sexual interaction skills for male or female sexual dysfunctions or disorders, or stress-reducing skills for sleep disorders and headaches (Adams & Sutker, 1984). Consequently, the assessment and enhancement of behavioral skills frequently becomes a major goal of intervention.

Mediational variables can play an important role in the genesis of behavior disorders (Bandura, 1981; Miller, 1981). For example, the parameters of depressive, ingestive, anxiety, or psychosomatic disorders, in the presence of biological or environmental precipitating stimuli, is not only mediated by an individual's behavioral skills, but also by social support systems and cognitive coping strategies (Billings & Moos, 1981). Consequently, the assessment of mediational variables is an important but frequently underemphasized component in the assessment of behavior disorders. It can facilitate the identification of intervention targets and also provide basic data for the development of prevention programs.

Behavioral construct systems also assume that a significant proportion of the variance in behavior can be accounted for by variance in situational stimuli (Schlundt & McFall, 1987). This is in contrast to the trait conceptualizations underlying most traditional clinical assessment procedures, which presume a higher degree of cross-situational consistency of behavior (McFall, 1982; Messick, 1981; Mischel, 1980).

Situational and trait models are not necessarily dichotomous, and neither can claim satisfactory predictive validity. Some degree of behavioral consistency across situations is not incompatible with situationally controlled variance, and a person × situation interactive model is probably a more accurate representation of behavioral variance than a model based on either component alone. Although situational factors exert considerable control over behavior, cross-situational consistencies in behavior probabilities and topography can, and frequently do, occur.

Further complicating the issue of behavioral consistency is the observation that the degree of situational control varies across behaviors, individuals, and situations (Haynes, 1979; Nelson, 1980). As noted by Nelson (1980), behaviors such as arithmetic abilities or automobile driving, which are associated with similar contingencies (or eliciting stimuli) across situations, are likely to demonstrate greater cross-situational stability than are behaviors such as social initiations or alcohol intake, which are associated with significant cross-situational variance in contingencies. Similarly, individuals with a history of stable contingencies for a particular behavior across situations (such as a person who has been consistently punished for aggressive behaviors in a variety of situations) are more likely to demonstrate cross-situational behavioral stability than are those with a less consistent contingency history. The person × situation interactive model of behavioral variance suggests that cross-situational behavior stability, while possible, cannot be assumed. Therefore, assessment procedures must sample a variety of potential antecedent and eliciting situations, although methods for their classification have not been developed (Schlundt & McFall, 1987).

A causal assumption that affects not only the focus of behavioral assessment but also enhances the role of assessment in the behavioral intervention process is that of multiple, idiosyncratic, and interactive determinism: there are multiple determinants of behavior disorders that will combine to form a complex matrix of potentiating, inhibiting, and mediating influences. As such, this pattern of determinants will vary across disorders and individuals. Univariate causal models cannot satisfactorily account for the onset, topography, duration, temporal and situational variance, or intensity of behavior disorders. There are multiple possible causes for a behavior disorder, and an instance of a disorder in an individual is usually the product of several interacting causal factors. Attempts to understand a behavior disorder through reference only to a limited domain of causal factors, such as response contingencies, cognitive processes, or biochemical dysfunctions, will usually result in an incomplete functional analysis or causal model (Haynes & O'Brien, in press).

Determinants are presumed to vary across disorders and across individuals manifesting the same disorder. This assumption contrasts with most nonbehavioral models (e.g., psychodynamic, gestalt, biochemical) that assume less variant models of causality. For example, the etiological role of potential causal factors (e.g., social contingencies, aversive environmental stimuli, decrements in environmental reinforcement, biochemical factors, and cognitive self-statements) will vary across "depressed" individuals (Billings & Moos, 1982).

In summary, the causal models underlying behavioral construct systems emphasize reciprocal determinism: multiple, idiosyncratic, temporally unstable, and interactive causal factors; situational factors; and mediating variables. These models have several implications for the methods and focus of behavioral assessment: (a) the importance of preinterventional behavioral assessment, (b) a multivariate and multimodal focus, (c) the use of multiple assessment methods, (d) a focus on contemporaneous causal variables, (e) situationally specific assessment, (f) a focus on the behavioral repertoires of clients, (g) the use of methods suitable for assessment in the natural environment, and (h) the assessment of variables that mediate the impact of environmental stressors. These causal models also have implications for the relationship between diagnosis and behavioral assessment, an issue that is discussed in the section "DSM-III-R and Behavioral Assessment."

Epistemological Assumptions

Therapy construct systems differ not only in their assumptions about the characteristics and causes of behavior, but also in their epistemology—assumptions about which *methods of inquiry* are more heuristic and the extent to which empiricism should be emphasized. The epistemology of behavioral construct systems emphasizes empirical hypothesis testing (Hay, 1982). During preintervention assessment, hypotheses are developed about target behaviors, intervention goals, determinants of behavior disorders, and preferred intervention strategies. These hypotheses are then tested during the assessment-intervention process.

The preferred method for hypothesis evaluation is through the application of empirical or scientific methods (Hersen & Barlow, 1976; Johnston & Pennypacker, 1980; Kazdin, 1982b, Kratochwill, 1978; Sidman, 1960). This application involves an emphasis on careful specification and measurement of dependent and independent variables, the use of assessment

instruments of known psychometric properties, careful control of measurement conditions, and serial measurement concomitant with systematic manipulation of independent variables.

The emphasis on empirical evaluation of hypotheses and intervention outcome strongly affects the role, methods, and focus of behavioral assessment. It mandates specification and quantification of variables, the continuing psychometric evaluation of assessment instruments, the use of minimally inferential variables, and assessment and intervention within controlled conditions. Quantification is stressed because it reduces susceptibility to interpretative biases inherent in the use of qualitative inferences and enhances confidence in the evaluation of causal hypotheses and intervention outcome. Therefore, behavioral interviewers often request information about the rates, durations, and magnitudes of target behaviors and particularly about their conditional probabilities (the probability that a specified behavior will occur given the occurrence of other events: [Haynes & Jensen, 1979]).

The most sensitive indicator of the viability of psychological construct systems is their degree of evolution over time. Construct systems based on an heuristic epistemology will evolve on dimensions of predictive validity and clinical utility; others will not. Behavioral construct systems have emphasized an epistemology that maximizes the use of heuristic constructs and empirical hypothesis testing. Behavioral construct systems are more likely to focus on observable, consensually verifiable and less inferential behaviors, behavioral goals, and causal relationships. Consequently, hypotheses, causal models, and intervention strategies can be systematically evaluated, supported, refined, and refuted. The causal role of more inferential variables, such as conflicts, complexes, needs, and impulses, is minimized. Assessment methods, such as naturalistic observation, behavioral self-monitoring, and psychophysiological assessment, attain increased status because they focus more on the measurable behaviors of clients than on their inferred psychological states.

Despite this strong emphasis on observables, inferential concepts are not alien to behavioral construct systems and are frequently the focus of behavioral assessment efforts. For example, behavior analysts make inferences about cognitive events, such as worry, attributions, and self-instructions, by measuring verbal and overt motor behavior (see Kendall & Hollon, 1981; Merluzzi et al., 1981), neurological functioning through neuropsychological assessments (Boll, 1981), or "anxiety" through behavioral avoidance tests or questionnaires (Bernstein, Borkovec, & Coles, 1986). Additionally, "feelings" of self-esteem, self-efficacy, inferiority, and rejection are often important *dependent* variables in behavioral intervention programs.

The emphasis on empiricism in behavioral assessment has been closely associated not only with particular assessment focuses and instruments, but also with careful control of the temporal and situational conditions under which assessment occurs. Single-subject experimental designs, such as reversal, replication, multiple baseline, simultaneous treatment, alternating treatment, and changing criterion, are particularly suited for clinical situations involving intensive study of individuals over extended periods of time (Hersen & Barlow, 1976; Kazdin, 1982b; Kratochwill, 1978). The purpose of these designs is to increase confidence in the causal inferences or internal validity of interventions—i.e., confidence that measured behavioral changes are a result of the variables being manipulated.

Behavior analysts are also adopting the statistical procedures applicable to the analysis of those interrupted time-series designs (Glass, Wilson, & Gottman, 1975; Gorsuch, 1983; Hartmann et al., 1980; Marascuilo, & Busk, 1988), although the inclusion of statistical procedures has been the subject of debate (Baer, 1977). The renewed emphasis in applied psychology on the intensive longitudinal study of single clients under systematically controlled conditions has been a major contribution of behavioral assessment.

The empirical emphasis of behavioral assessment has also had an indirect but important effect on the delivery of psychological services. It has accentuated the importance of professional accountability (Lloyd, 1983; O'Leary, 1979) and has provided a technology for the evaluation of service delivery and intervention outcome. The application of psychometrically evaluated assessment instruments within controlled settings and appropriate research designs can provide a strong test of the validity of clinical hypotheses and the efficacy of intervention (Bellack & Hersen, 1984).

An overzealous adoption of methodological empiricism, however, can have negative ramifications for a construct system. As noted by Glass and Kliegl (1983), many treatment outcome measures involve trivial quantifications and/or are devoid of psychometric validity and social or practical importance. Such exaggerated attempts at quantification demean methodological behaviorism and contribute to the perception that it often focuses on trivial events.

An excessive reliance on quantification can also reduce the creativity of psychological inquiry and the evolution of a psychological construct system. Our knowledge of functional relationships among behaviors and environmental events is elementary; such an early stage of scientific development requires an openness to new concepts and relationships. Although empiricism is the preferred method of evaluating hypotheses, and while the close examination of data can serve as a stimulus for new hypotheses, many ideas are generated from qualitative observations of phenomena. By supplementing quantitative with qualitative analyses, behavior analysts can insure that creativity and hypothesis generation are not hindered by an excessive reliance on empiricism.

Despite the dangers, the importance of the empirical bases of behavioral assessment cannot be understated. Psychological construct systems must be based on *methods of inquiry* rather than on conceptual assumptions. Psychological construct systems, such as gestalt, transactional analysis, person centered, and most psychoanalytic schools, have remained essentially unchanged for decades because they are defined by conceptual rather than methodological assumptions. In contrast, the rapid evolution of behavioral construct systems and the expanding array of available behavioral intervention strategies can be attributed to an emphasis on a set of *methods* for studying behavior rather than an emphasis on a prescribed set of *concepts* about the causes of behavior and the best methods of modifying it.

FUNCTIONS OF BEHAVIORAL ASSESSMENT

Assessment systems differ not only in their conceptual bases and methods, but also in their functions or the purposes for which they are applied (Ciminero, 1986). These functions affect the focus as well as the methods of assessment and can vary across settings, clients, behavior problems, and the intent of assessment (e.g., clinical outcome evaluation versus intervention design) (Hawkins, 1979). The functions of behavioral assessment include (a) identification of target behaviors, (b) identification of alternative behaviors, (c) identification of causal variables, (d) development of a functional analysis, (e) design of intervention strategies, (f) evaluation and modification of intervention strategies, and (g) facilitation of client-therapist interactions.

Identification of Target Behaviors

Clients or referral sources frequently present multiple behavior problems, exhibit multiple behavioral deficits, or are unable to pinpoint specific behavior problems or goals. Consequently, a major goal of the assessment process is to select behavior(s) (desirable and undesirable) upon which to focus intervention efforts (Barrios, 1988; Hawkins, 1986; Kanfer, 1985; Wilson & Evans, 1983; see special mini-series on target-behavior selection in *Behavioral Assessment,* 1985, *7,* 1–78). The bases for target-behavior selection include the frequency, intensity, duration, and magnitude of the behavior, the centrality of particular behaviors to the client's problems in living (i.e., "keystone behaviors") (Voeltz & Evans, 1982), the degree to which the behavior maximizes or minimizes the client's reinforcers, the values and goals of the client and the behavior analyst, the degree of danger to the client or others presented by the behavior, the functional relationships among behaviors, the probability of successful intervention, and a task analysis of treatment goals (Hawkins, 1986; Kanfer, 1985).

The principle that underlies most of the parameters of target-behavior selection outlined above is that of *shared variance.* Behaviors must be viewed within a systems perspective, and the degree to which a behavior exhibits covariation with other behaviors is an important determinant of whether it should be selected as a target behavior (Haynes, 1986b). For example, a behavior may be targeted because it is an easily modifiable member of a response class (e.g., "noncompliance" as a member in a class of adolescent antisocial behaviors) or because it functions as a causal variable for other behavior problems (e.g., intervention with marital communication deficits that may concomitantly help remediate inappropriate causal attributions). Thus, those behaviors whose modification is likely to have the greatest positive impact on other behaviors are often the most appropriate targets for intervention. The task of identifying these functional relationships among behaviors occurs through the functional analysis. It should also be stressed that the targets of intervention efforts with a particular client are almost always multiple and frequently change as a function of new information gathered in the natural course of the intervention (Evans, 1985; Kanfer, 1985).

Identification of Functional Classes

As noted earlier, many behaviors have similar functions (i.e., are triggered by the same discriminative stimuli or have similar reinforcing properties) and can, therefore, be considered as part of the same functional class (as with the example provided earlier of alcohol, marijuana, and barbiturate ingestion, overeating, and behavioral relaxation). Identification of functional classes of behaviors is useful because often some desirable elements in the class (e.g., behavioral relaxation) can be strengthened at the cost of undesirable elements in the same class (e.g., overeating).

Identification of Alternative Behaviors

In many cases, target-behavior selection is not confined to identification of undesirable target behaviors or classes of behaviors (such as multiple substance abuse or exhibitionism). It may also involve selection of behaviors that are positive alternatives to undesirable target behaviors or the selection of behaviors which reduce the probability or functional utility of problem behaviors (Goldfried, 1982; Hawkins, 1986). Kanfer (1985) refers to this class of target behaviors as those which are "instrumental" for altering the current problem situation toward a more effective future state" (p. 12). These are behaviors that may be members of the same response classes as the undesirable targeted behaviors. For example, positive self-efficacy statements may be a class of behaviors that are desirable alternatives to deprecatory self-statements in depression; enhanced assertive skills may be associated with a reduction in behaviors, such as aggressive outbursts or social avoidance, and self-induced relaxation skills may reduce sleep-onset latency, headache frequency, and magnitude of fear reactions.

Identification of positive behavioral goals is an important but often underemphasized function of behavioral assessment. It encourages the use of positive rather than negative contingencies, facilitates social acceptability of behavioral interventions, reduces the necessity of assessing low frequency or otherwise difficult-to-assess behaviors (e.g., stealing), and increases the probability of successful reduction of the targeted problem behaviors (Haynes, 1978).

Identification of Causal Variables

Because causal variables are frequently the target of intervention efforts, their identification is the most important function of behavioral assessment. For example, it is presumed that various psychophysiologic, anxiety, and stress-related disorders are a function of elevated levels of psychological or cognitive arousal. Therefore, these disorders are often treated with interventions, such as relaxation training, that are designed to change the magnitude or conditional probability of arousal.

Models of causality in behavioral construct systems are becoming increasingly complex along a number of dimensions (Haynes, 1988; Haynes & O'Brien, in press). In addition to an emphasis on the causal importance of contiguous antecedent and consequent environmental events (Kazdin, 1978), causal models now allow for multiple causal variables for a particular behavior disorder, variance in the weight of those variables across persons and time, temporally noncontiguous causal factors and additive, interactive, and nonlinear effects of causal factors. A wide array of environmental, cognitive, genetic, social system, and psychological variables are also recognized. Most important, causal relationships are often bidirectional (i.e., manifest *reciprocal determinism*) (Bandura, 1981). For example, "suspicious" behavior can be aversive to others, leading to their withdrawal which, in turn, can trigger additional paranoid behaviors (Haynes, 1986).

As noted in Haynes (1986b), there are several methods of deriving causal inferences, but all involve the identification of *conditional probabilities* for behavior problems, either through statistical association or manipulation. If there is a causal relationship between two events, the occurrence (or other parameter) of one must be related to the occurrence of the other. Thus, much effort in preintervention assessment is directed at identifying those conditional relationships (e.g., "In what situations do you tend to get headaches").

Development of a Functional Analysis

A functional analysis is the conceptually-based integration of results from preintervention assessment. It is "the identification of important, controllable, causal functional relationships applicable to identified target behavior(s)" (Haynes & O'Brien, in press). The functional analysis is a model of problem behaviors and represents a synthesis of a myriad of interacting behavioral, cognitive, and psychological causal factors, associated behavioral assets and deficits, situational sources of variance, the social system within which the client is embedded, and other mediating variables. In addition to identifying the pattern of relationships between and among these multiple causal factors, the functional analysis also specifies the strength of the relationship and the temporal sequence of various causal factors. Consequently, the functional analysis is the primary determinant of problem behavior selection and intervention design.

Despite its complexity and its central role in behavioral assessment, the functional analysis is the most subjective, inconsistently conceptualized, and least investigated aspect of behavioral assessment (Curran & Wessberg, 1981; Lewinsohn & Lee, 1981). How-

ever, it is becoming a more frequent topic of empirical investigation (Felton & Nelson, 1984) and conceptual discourse (Haynes & O'Brien, in press).

The Design of Intervention Strategies

The degree to which therapy construct systems stress the integration of assessment and intervention is a function of presumed differences in the characteristics and determinants of behavior problems within and between classes of behavior disorders. In behavioral construct systems, identification or classification of behavior problems or syndromes, such as "migraine headache," "depression," or "paranoia" is insufficient for treatment planning. Diagnostic categories provide only an imprecise picture of client functioning and indicate only an array of potential causal factors (Haynes, 1979, 1984a). Because of idiosyncratic behavioral determinants, identified in preintervention assessment, intervention programs can significantly vary across persons within diagnostic categories. Consequently, preintervention behavioral assessment is an integral component in the design of intervention strategies (Emmelkamp, 1986).

Although intervention decisions are primarily determined by causal models of targeted behavior disorders, they are also influenced by other factors. These include (a) the goals and resources of the client and behavior analyst, (b) competing behavior problems, (c) the relative effectiveness of interventions, (d) the potential side effects of an intervention, (e) social supports and other social and personal mediating variables, (f) the availability of alternate interventions, (g) ethical and social validity considerations, and (h) task analysis and cost-efficiency analysis (Haynes, 1986b).

In addition to designing intervention strategies, preintervention assessment is necessary to decide whether to intervene, and to select the components of intervention strategies. Examples of intervention components include specific items in desensitization hierarchies, instructional or situational variables in behavior rehearsal, or specific reinforcers in contingency management programs.

Evaluation and Modification of Intervention

Consistent with an emphasis on empirical hypothesis-testing epistemology and accountability, a major function of behavioral assessment is the evaluation of intervention outcome. This evaluation most frequently occurs through serial measurement, within carefully controlled conditions, of target behaviors before, during, and following interventions. However, the measurement of intervention outcome must not be confined to dependent variables (i.e., target variables). It is equally important that interventions be evaluated on the basis of their side effects (i.e., effects of intervention other than those involving the primary target behaviors) and generalization across situations, behaviors, and persons.

Serial assessment throughout intervention is also necessary to adjust intervention programs. Such program modifications may involve changes in target behaviors, intervention strategies, or components of intervention programs. Sometimes, intervention programs must also be interrupted to address mediating variables, such as client resistance or noncompliance.

The hypothesis-testing emphasis of behavioral construct systems stresses the evaluation not only of treatment outcome but also of the causal models (or functional analysis) upon which interventions are based as well as the internal validity of interventions. To address these issues, two questions must be answered: (a) Are effects of intervention the result of changes in the hypothesized causal variables? (b) Are the effects of intervention the result of the intended manipulations? These functions of assessment mandate that independent, as well as dependent, variables be measured (Peterson, Homer, & Wonderlich, 1982). For example, to attribute the causes of a successful program involving social skills and cognitive treatment in a case of excessive social avoidance, and to do so with validity, measures must be taken of manipulated independent variables such as positive outcome self-statements and level of social skills, in addition to dependent variables such as frequency of and comfort during social interactions.

As noted earlier, the evaluation of an intervention program is also affected by its *side effects*. Familiar examples include the effect of smoking cessation programs on weight gain, the effects of rapid smoking programs on cardiac arrhythmias associated with rapid smoking treatment, the effects of communication training on sexual satisfaction, and the side effects of medication. Consequently, assessment targets should include potential intervention side effects, both positive and negative.

Facilitating Client-Therapist Interaction

An often overlooked function of assessment is the establishment of a positive and facilitative relationship between the client and the behavior analyst. Clients' perceptions of the behavior analyst, of the assessment-intervention process, and of its underlying assumptions can affect their cooperation in the assessment and intervention process and the probability of successful intervention. The major vehicle for establishing a positive client-assessor relationship is the preintervention assessment interview (Haynes & Chavez, 1983). Although the variables affecting such a relationship have not been systematically studied, there has been emphasis on the importance of certain elements: keeping clients informed about the methods, intent, and rationale of the assessment process; the education of clients; and positive feedback to clients (Haynes, 1978).

Summary

Behavioral assessment has multiple functions that vary with the intent of assessment, and the relationship between these functions and the methods of assessment is complex. Furthermore, various assessment instruments have differential utility for these functions. For example, behavioral observation can be a powerful method of evaluating intervention outcome but is of limited use in facilitating positive client-assessor interactions. In contrast, the behavioral interview is an excellent vehicle for evaluating clients' perceptions of the intervention process, but may be less applicable for deriving quantitative indices of intervention outcome.

There are functions of behavioral assessment other than the ones described. These include providing data for differential diagnosis, gathering historical data on clients and their behavior problems, and gathering demographic or epidemiological data. These are secondary functions of the behavioral assessment of adult disorders because they contribute only indirectly to the development of a functional analysis and the design and evaluation of intervention strategies.

DSM-III-R AND BEHAVIORAL ASSESSMENT

DSM-III-R (American Psychiatric Association, 1987) is a frequently used multi-axial system for the classification of behavior disorders. In contrast to functional analysis, it is based on the structure or topography of behaviors (Adams & Haber, 1984; Eysenck, 1986; Morey, Skinner, & Blashfield, 1986) rather than their functional relationships. Consequently, it has been the subject of extensive criticism and debate (Hersen & Bellack, 1988; Behavioral assessment and DSM-III-R).

The relationship between DSM-III-R and behavioral assessment is influenced by several factors.

First, because the validity of any diagnostic system cannot exceed the validity of data upon which diagnostic decisions are made, behavioral assessment can make an important contribution to DSM-III-R diagnoses by providing valid data. Behavioral assessment methods are especially suited for deriving data for Axis IV—the psychological factors contributing to behavior disorders.

Second, the utility of behavioral assessment, other than for acquiring the data necessary for classification of behavior disorders, is influenced by the degree of which causal variables and, therefore, effective interventions, can be identified through structural classification (Haynes, 1979). This diagnostic category— causal variable relationship—is likely to vary across disorders and across persons within disorders. For some classes of behavior disorders, diagnosis may be sufficient to indicate causal variables or treatments. In most cases, however, causal factors and treatment recommendations cannot be inferred from DSM-III-R diagnoses (Haynes & O'Brien, 1988; Kanfer, 1985; Taylor, 1983). Therefore, additional assessment is usually necessary to acquire more molecular data so that functional analyses and intervention programs can be designed.

In summary, DSM-III-R provides a standardized nomenclature for communication between behavioral scientists and clinicians. Behavioral assessment can contribute to DSM-III-R diagnoses, even though the diagnostic categories are structurally based. However, in most cases structural classification of behavior is insufficient for the design of intervention programs. More important, the underlying assumptions of DSM-III-R diagnoses (i.e., structural typologies) are incompatible with many of the tenets of behavioral construct systems, and psychiatric labels can have a negative social and personal impact.

METHODS OF BEHAVIORAL ASSESSMENT

An appreciation of behavioral assessment methods and underlying concepts should be enhanced by delineation of the boundaries between behavioral and nonbehavioral assessment. However, these boundaries are increasingly indistinct and permeable (Barrett, Johnston, & Pennypacker, 1986; Bellack & Hersen, 1988). During the preparation of my book on behavioral assessment (Haynes, 1978) between 1973 and 1977, I did not find it difficult to distinguish behavioral from nonbehavioral assessment procedures. At that time there was considerable consensus among behavior analysts that behavioral assessment

methods included naturalistic observation, analog observation, self-monitoring, participant observation, psychophysiological methods, behavioral interviewing, and some behavioral questionnaires. These methods differed from traditional assessment methods in their structure, focus, specificity, level of inference, and/or underlying assumptions.

Behavioral assessment is becoming more inclusive and the factors that distinguish behavioral and nonbehavioral assessment less distinct (Barrett, Johnston, & Pennypacker, 1986). Perusal of recently published behaviorally oriented books and journal articles indicates that many of the assessment procedures used or advocated have not been traditionally associated with a behavioral construct system and are sometimes inconsistent with its underlying concepts. For example, assessment procedures recently used by behavior analysts include neuropsychological assessment, diaries, sociometric status, a projective method involving interpretation of patients' stories, traditional trait-based personality tests such as the IE scale, MMPI, the Beck Depression Inventory and other mood scales, and tests of academic achievement (see Barlow, 1981; Ciminero et al., 1986; Bellack & Hersen, 1988a; *Behavioral Assessment*).

The increasingly diffuse boundaries between behavioral and nonbehavioral assessment have several roots. First, behavior analysts are more frequently focusing on variables (e.g., cognitions, physiology, affect) that were excluded from earlier operantly influenced behavioral paradigms. This expanding focus has necessitated the use of a larger array of assessment instruments, many with greater inferential qualities. Second, there has been a moderation in the tendency of behavior analysts to reject automatically any assessment procedure identified with traditional clinical psychology. This has been replaced with a more reasoned appraisal of the applicability and psychometric qualities of traditional assessment instruments. Third, an early exclusionary emphasis on situational control of behavior has been replaced by a person × situation interactionist model; variance in behavior is partially associated with the person as well as situational variables, and cross-situational stability is sometimes observed. This conceptual modification has led to introduction into behavior assessment of some trait-based assessment instruments that are relatively insensitive to situational sources of variance.

A more disturbing determinant of the growing inclusiveness of behavioral assessment methods is an apparent reduction in the conceptual and methodological rigor of behavior analysts. Many seem unaware of the conceptual assumptions underlying the assessment procedures they use. For example, some behavior analysts fail to acknowledge assumptions inherent in administering an assessment instrument that provides a single "score" of some multifactor construct (e.g., "depression") that may demonstrate considerable situationally controlled variance. Also, many normatively derived assessment instruments (particularly questionnaires but also including behavioral coding systems) are applied without consideration of the degree to which they are useful for assessing the individual case at hand (Barrett et al., 1986; Cone, 1988). Similarly, there are frequently unacknowledged interpretative problems in administering an assessment instrument that provides a highly inferential or indirect measure of a construct (e.g., measures of irrational beliefs or cognitive distortion) or in administering an assessment instrument with unknown psychometric properties for the target population to which it is applied. Many behavior analysts also do not acknowledge the conceptual difficulties in interpreting data from an assessment instrument that was developed under a conceptual framework different from, and often incompatible with, a behavioral construct system (e.g., providing behavioral interpretations of scores from a locus-of-control scale) (Jensen & Haynes, 1986). Conceptual unsophistication is a particular concern because of its eventual impact on the evolution, viability, and empirical rigor of the behavioral construct system.

In view of these definitional difficulties, the focus of this chapter has been limited to those methods that have been traditionally associated with behavioral assessment or those methods that, although infrequently used, are congruent with behavioral construct systems. More extensive descriptions of behavioral or assessment instruments can be found in books by Bellack and Hersen (1988a) and Ciminero et al. (1986).

Behavioral assessment methods have been divided into three classes: (a) those primarily associated with behavioral construct systems, (b) those frequently used by behavior analysts but adopted from traditional nonbehavioral assessment systems, and (c) those less frequently used by behavior analysts but consistent with behavioral construct systems.

Assessment Methods Primarily Associated with Behavioral Construct Systems

Naturalistic Observation

The assessment method most congruent with behavioral construct systems is naturalistic observation using nonparticipant observers (i.e., those who are not normally part of the natural environment) (Hartmann & Wood, 1982; McIntyre et al., 1983). Typically, two or more trained observers enter the client's natural environment (e.g., hospital ward, home, classroom, bar, restaurant) several times on a predetermined schedule and systematically record occurrence or non-occurrence of preselected and predefined behaviors. Each observation session is often divided into smaller time-sampling periods (e.g., 10-, 15-, or 30-second periods). The observers may record occurrence or nonoccurrence of specified client behaviors (e.g., pain-referenced verbalizations or physical activity in a case of chronic pain) that occur during all or part of the sampling interval. They may also record behavior durations or behavior chains (e.g., sequential interaction between a depressed client and family members). The observers may note behaviors that are occurring at predetermined points in time (e.g., the behavior being emitted by a psychiatric inpatient at the end of serial 15-second intervals). Observers also may rate behaviors on established scales (Foster & Cone, 1986).

Behaviors sampled are those that (a) have potential etiological significance for identified behavioral problems (e.g., verbal contingencies emitted during distressed marital interaction), (b) provide a sensitive measure of problem behaviors and intervention outcome (e.g., frequency of social interaction by a depressed psychiatric inpatient), (c) indicate side effects and generalization of intervention, and/or (d) are goals or positive alternatives to undesirable behaviors. In all cases, these behaviors are carefully selected and defined prior to observation (Hartmann & Wood, 1982; Foster, Bell-Dolan, & Burge, 1988). Although observers usually focus on only one individual at a time, the interaction between two or more individuals is frequently monitored, and observation targets may be sequentially or randomly sampled from a group of potential subjects (e.g., rotation of targeted subjects among several individuals in a group or on a ward).

The training of observers and their method of observation have an important effect on the validity of derived data (Foster & Cone, 1980; Hartmann & Wood, 1982). Observers must be systematically trained to a satisfactory level of accuracy prior to observing target subjects. To reduce the probability of bias, drift, and other observer errors, inter-observer agreement should be evaluated frequently on a random schedule, retraining should be initiated when necessary, composition of observer teams should be changed, and observer awareness of the client's status (e.g., pre- or posttreatment) should be minimized (Haynes, 1978).

In open environments, such as a home, some constraints are often placed on the behavior of targeted individuals (McIntyre et al., 1983). For example, a dissatisfied marital couple being observed at home might be requested to remain within two rooms and to refrain from long telephone conversations, television viewing, and visits from friends during the observation sessions. While such constraints compromise the assessment environment and, therefore, the generalizability of the obtained data, they increase the efficiency of the observation process.

Naturalistic observation has been used in the assessment of a wide range of behavior problems, populations, and environments. Targeted behaviors and behavior problems have included interactions of distressed marital couples (Follingstad & Haynes, 1981), eating patterns of obese individuals (Brownell, 1981), pica (Mace & Knight, 1986), pain talk in cases of chronic pain (Fordyce & Laws, 1976), alcohol ingestion (Correa & Sutker, 1986), parent-infant interactions (Callahan, Brasted, & Hamilton, 1987) and stuttering (James, 1981). Other targeted behaviors have included leisure behavior of handicapped adults (Schleien, Wehman, & Kiernan, 1981), behaviors of institutional staff (Bassett & Blanchard, 1977) and foster grandparents (Fabray & Reid, 1978), restaurant skills of disabled individuals (Van den Pol et al., 1981), social and family interactions of depressed individuals (Hops et al., 1987; Lewinson & Lee, 1981). Naturalistic observation has also been used to assess approaches to feared or phobic objects (Waranch, Iwata, Wohl, & Nidiffer, 1981), self-help and work behaviors of institutionalized retarded and psychiatric inpatients (Cuvo, Leaf, & Borakove, 1978; Kazdin, 1984), behaviors of parents of problem children (Budd, Riner, & Brockman, 1983), and aggressive behaviors of schizophrenics (Matson & Stephens, 1977).

Environments in which naturalistic observation has occurred include homes (Jacobson, Elwood, & Dallas, 1981), schools, (Fagot, 1978), institutions for developmentally disabled psychiatric or geriatric parents (Schell et al., 1986), restaurants and cafeterias (Brownell, 1981), prisons (Bassett & Blanchard, 1977), hospital labor rooms (Anderson & Standley, 1977), neonatal intensive care units (Callahan, et al., 1987), and bathrooms (Cuvo et al., 1978). It is least applicable for the assessment of low frequency behaviors (e.g., stealing) and highly sensitive behaviors (e.g., sexual behaviors).

Several types of data can be derived from observation measures. The most frequent type is the rate or frequency of targeted behaviors (actually, the percentage of sampling intervals in which a behavior occurs). More important, observation can provide measures of the *conditional probabilities* of behaviors (the relative probability that a behavior will occur given the occurrence of other behaviors or events or given a particular situation or environment) or can be used to identify behavioral chains. For example, observation of marital interaction in the home can provide data on positive or negative reciprocity (the probability that one spouse will emit a positive or negative behavior following a positive or negative behavior emitted by the other) and the sequence of interactions preceding and during an argument (Jacobson & Margolin, 1979; Stuart, 1980).

Behavioral observation can also provide qualitative information (Weinrott, Reid, Bauske, & Brumett, 1981). Informal observation of clients can be a rich source of hypotheses concerning problem behaviors, response classes, behavior chains, associated behavior deficits and excesses, and other characteristics and determinants of behavior problems. Inclusion of a qualitative component in observation assessment can significantly facilitate functional analyses.

Naturalistic observation is probably the most powerful method of intervention outcome evaluation for many behavior problems. Its congruence with behavioral construct systems derives from its focus on behavior in the natural environment, its utility in detecting and measuring behavior-environment interactions, the quantitative properties of the obtained data, and the minimal level of inference associated with its use. However, like all assessment instruments, it varies in its applicability across behavior disorders and assessment functions and has several sources of error.

There are several sources of error variance in data obtained from naturalistic observation (Barrett, Johnston, & Pennypacker, 1986; Dorsey, Nelson, & Hayes, 1986; Fiske, 1978; Foster & Cone, 1986; Haynes, 1978; Sackett, 1978b; Suen & Ary, 1986; Wasik & Loven, 1980). These include (a) variance in the situational context in which observation occurs; (b) observer inaccuracy, bias, and drift; (c) errors in the behaviors selected for observation; (d) errors in the temporal parameters of observation (e.g., duration of sampling periods); (e) code complexity; and (f) insufficient definitional precision of codes. All sources of error are threats to the validity of inferences drawn from obtained data because these errors severely restrict the generalizability of the inference.

A major source of error in all assessment procedures, but particularly in naturalistic observation, is *reactivity* (Baum, Forehand, & Zegoib, 1979; Foster, Bell-Dolan, & Burge, 1988; Haynes & Horn, 1982).

An assessment process is reactive when it transiently or permanently modifies the targets of assessment. For example, the behavior of staff, spouses, and parents may be different when observers are present and when they are not. Therefore, reactivity is a threat to the external validity or situational and temporal generalizability of the acquired data. In the cases of socially sensitive behaviors (e.g., sexual or antisocial behaviors), naturalistic observation may be sufficiently reactive to preclude its use. Conceptual frameworks within which reactive effects of observation can be viewed and possible methods of minimizing them have been discussed in greater detail by Baum et al. (1979) and Haynes and Horn (1982).

Analog Observation

Analog observation involves the systematic observation of target subjects in analog situations—controlled environments that vary from the natural environment of the client (Haynes, 1978). For example, to evaluate possible communication difficulties, a distressed marital couple might be requested to discuss a problem in their relationship while being observed from behind a one-way mirror in an outpatient clinic (Jacobson et al., 1981). Similarly, an individual with heterosexual anxieties might be observed in a clinic waiting room while attempting to initiate and maintain a conversation with a confederate-stranger (e.g., Bellack, Hersen, & Lamparksi, 1979).

One form of analog assessment frequently used in the evaluation of social skills is *role playing*, in which a client is placed in an analog situation and responds to social stimuli typical of those encountered in the natural environment. Trained confederates are frequently used to provide carefully controlled stimuli to the client. For example, Greenwald (1977) presented heterosocially anxious females with audiotaped scenarios depicting social interaction with a male friend at a fast-food restaurant and other situations. The subjects role played each of these situations by responding to stimuli provided by the audiotape and a male confederate.

Another frequently used variation of analog assessment is the *behavior avoidance test* (BAT), in which subjects are asked to approach a feared object (Bernstein, 1973; Haynes & Wilson, 1979). For example, Mattick and Peters (1988) requested subjects with severe social phobias to engage in items from a hierarchy of feared behaviors (e.g., entering a crowded cafeteria with another person) while monitoring their subjective levels of discomfort.

Occasionally, assessment involves *behavior analogs*. The observed behavior is assumed to covary with the behavior of primary interest. For example, Lindsley (1960) monitored lever presses of psychiatric inpatients on a human operant response panel. Carter and Thomas (1973) had spouses in distressed marriages indicate the impact and intent of their verbal communication by pressing designated buttons. In these examples, the monitored responses (lever and button presses) were presumed to function as more easily observed and quantified analog measures, or covariates, of behaviors of primary interest (psychotic behavior and marital communication patterns).

Analog observation has been used in the assessment of a variety of behaviors and behavior problems, such as nonspecific social anxiety and social skills deficits (Bernstein, Borkovec, & Coles, 1986; Dow, Biglan, & Glaser, 1985; Merluzzi & Biever, 1987), dental anxiety (Wroblewski, Jacob, & Rehm, 1977), stuttering (James, 1981), heterosexual anxiety (Greenwald, 1977), alcohol ingestion, (Donovan & Marlatt, 1988), assertive responses of the elderly (Edinberg, Karoly, & Gleser, 1977), cigarette refusal skills (Hops et al., 1986), social competence in the mentally retarded (Castles & Glass, 1986), parent-child interaction (Hughes & Haynes, 1978), marital interaction (Haynes, Jensen, Wise, & Sherman, 1981; Markman, Floyd, Stanley, & Storaasli, 1988), speech anxiety (Fremouw & Zitter, 1978), small animal phobias (Barrera & Rosen, 1977), test anxiety (Goldfried, Linehan, & Smith, 1978), pain behaviors (Turner & Clancy, 1988), and eating disorders (Brownell, 1981).

A variety of measures have been taken in analog assessments. Most analog assessments involve direct observation of behavior using codes, sampling parameters, and procedures similar to those described for naturalistic observation. However, physiological, verbal self-report, questionnaire, qualitative observer impressions, and self-monitoring measures also are frequently taken.

The main advantage of analog assessment is that it provides a cost-efficient method of behavioral observation. The assessment environment and stimuli are arranged to increase the probability of occurrence of targeted behaviors and hypothesized etiological variables. This type of assessment increases the cost-effectiveness of the assessment method relative to that of naturalistic observation. Attempts to gather similar data in the natural environment can be extremely time consuming and costly, and many behaviors (e.g., social initiations by socially anxious clients) occur at a rate sufficiently low to preclude naturalistic observation. Because the physical environment and social stimuli associated with assessment are more carefully controlled than in naturalistic observation, behavioral variance attributable to situational stimuli is reduced, although external validity may be concomitantly reduced.

Several sources of error have been identified in analog assessment (Bellack, 1979; Bellack et al., 1979; Forehand & Atkeson, 1977; Hughes & Haynes, 1978; Kazdin, Esveldt-Dawson, & Matson, 1983). These include (a) instructional variables, (b) variance in situational stimuli, (c) reactivity, (d) demand factors, and (e) errors associated with the observers, sampling parameters, or other aspects of the data acquisition process.

The primary drawback to analog observation is that it is only an *indirect* measure of the individual's behavior in the setting of greatest importance—the natural environment. Although some studies have demonstrated significant correlations between behaviors emitted in analog and naturalistic settings, other studies have found low levels or correlation (see review by Haynes & Wilson, 1979). Generalization of behavior between naturalistic and analog settings cannot be assumed. Further, the degree or probability of generalization is likely to vary across subjects, target behaviors, settings, and observation methods.

Self-Monitoring

Self-monitoring involves the systematic self-observation and recording of parameters (e.g., occurrence, intensity) of specified behaviors and events (Bornstein, Hamilton, & Bornstein, 1986). Typically, the events and parameters to be recorded are first specified by the client and behavior analyst, and a recording form is developed. For low-rate behaviors (e.g., seizures, migraine headaches), clients may record every occurrence of the behavior. For high-rate or continuous behaviors (e.g., tics, blood pressure), monitoring most frequently occurs within specified time periods. When appropriate, there is also monitoring of topographic data (e.g., headache location and symptoms) or antecedent or consequent events (e.g., situations in which binge eating occurs and social reactions to attempts at social initiation).

Self-monitoring has been used in the assessment of numerous behaviors and behavior problems such as the eating patterns of obese (Brownell, 1981) or bulimic (Schlundt, Johnson, & Jarrell, 1986) individuals, cognitions (Merluzzi et al., 1981), smoking (Glasglow, Klesges, Godding, & Gegelman, 1983), bruxism (Rosen, 1981), blood pressure (Beiman, Graham, & Ciminero, 1978), caffeine intake (Bernard, Dennehy, & Keefauver, 1981), fuel conservation (Foxx & Hake, 1977), startle responses (Fair-bank, DeGood, & Jenkins, 1981), deviant sexual behavior (Foote & Laws, 1981), Raynaud's symptoms (Keefe, Surwit, & Pilon, 1981), hair pulling (Ottens, 1981), nausea associated with chemotherapy (Burish, Carey, Krozely, & Greco, 1987), arthritic pain (Varni, 1981), alcohol intake (Alden, 1988), drug intake (Donovan & Marlatt, 1988), seizures (Lubar & Shouse, 1977), and sleeping patterns of insomniacs (Bootzin & Engle-Friedman, 1981).

Several types of data can be acquired through self-monitoring. Clients can monitor overt motor behavior, verbal behavior, occurrence of environmental events associated with their behavior, physiological responses, cognitions, and affective responses. Durations and intensities, as well as frequencies, can also be monitored.

Self-monitoring has many advantages. It is applicable to a wide range of behavior problems, it is inexpensive, it is not time consuming, it can be used to gather data in the natural environment, and it can be used to derive quantitative indices of multiple-response modalities. It is one of the most cost efficient and clinically useful behavioral assessment procedures.

However, like other assessment strategies self-monitoring is subject to several general and idiosyncratic sources of error (Bornstein et al., 1986; Haynes, 1978; Nelson, 1977a, 1977b). Perhaps the most significant of those is observer bias, in which the recordings can be influenced by the expectancies and biases of the client, the social sensitivity associated with the targeted behavior, the contingencies associated with the targeted behavior, and the contingencies associated with the recordings. In some cases these biases may be so great as to compromise the validity of the data. For example, significant biases have been noted in the self-reported drinking behavior of alcoholics and eating behavior of obese individuals (Brownell, 1981).

Other sources of error variance include degree of prior training of the client in self-monitoring procedures, degree of specification of target behaviors, methods of time sampling and recording, contingencies associated with self-monitoring or submission of the acquired data to the behavior analyst, reaction from the client's social environment to the self-recording procedures, and characteristics (e.g., rate, duration) of the targeted behaviors and valence of the target behavior. As with other observation methods of assessment, reactivity is a particularly potent source of variance (Bornstein et al., 1986). The reactive impact of self-monitoring is frequently so great that self-monitoring is sometimes used as a method of intervention with clients. (e.g., Broden, Hall, & Mitts, 1971).

Participant Observation

Participant observation is a form of naturalistic or analog observation in which observers are normally part of the natural environment of the observed target (Haynes & Wilson, 1979; Margolin, Michelli, & Jacobson, 1988). Although the sampling and recording methods are usually similar to those described in "naturalistic observation" (involving structured behavior recording within discrete time samples), participant observers are usually less well trained than external observers and focus on a more restricted range of target events. For example, a staff member on a psychiatric ward might monitor the frequency and targets of social initiations by a patient during mealtime and recreation periods.

Although most frequently used in the assessment of children and institutionalized individuals, participant observation has also been used in the assessment of marital interactions (Margolin, Hattem, John, & Yost, 1985; Price & Haynes, 1980), food intake (Epstein & Martin, 1977), heterosexual social behaviors (Arkowitz, Lichtenstein, McGovern, & Hines, 1975), family interactions (Weinrott et al., 1981), caffeine intake (Bernard et al., 1981), alcohol intake (Donovan & Marlatt, 1988), deviant sexual behavior (Waranch et al., 1981), aggressive behavior (Matson & Stephens, 1977), and sexual dysfunction (Zeiss, 1978).

Reactive effects of participant observation are likely but have been infrequently studied (e.g., Price & Haynes, 1980). If the variables influencing reactivity outlined by Baum et al. (1979) and Haynes and Horn (1982) apply to participant observation, its reactive effects should be less than nonparticipant observation, as participant observation involves less change in the natural environment. However, the method of monitoring and the relationship between the observer and the target individual may affect the degree of reactivity. There are many situations (e.g., an individual monitoring the sexual or ingestive behavior of a spouse) in which participant observation might be expected to result in significant alterations of the monitored behavior or to affect the social interaction between the observer and target. Like self-monitoring, the reactive effects of participant observation may be used for therapeutic behavior change. For example, participant observation of the exchange of positive behaviors between spouses may result in an increase in the perceived rate of those behaviors.

The advantages of participant observation are similar to those of self-monitoring. It is inexpensive, applicable to a wide range of problem behaviors, populations, and environmental events, and can be used to gather data from the natural environment. However, like self-monitoring, the acquired data can also reflect observer biases (Christensen, Sullaway, & King, 1983; Margolin, 1983). Other sources of error include the degree of training of observers, the degree of specification of observation targets, and the methods of sampling and recording. Concern with possible biases and errors in participant observation and insufficient investigation of its psychometric properties have confined it to use as an adjunctive rather than a primary assessment instrument.

Psychophysiological Measures

A recent review (Haynes, Falkin, & Sexton-Radek, 1989) reported a dramatic increase in the use of psychophysiological assessment in behavior therapy since the 1960s. This trend can be attributed to four factors: (a) an increasing focus on physiological components of behavior problems and their interactions with behavioral and cognitive components, (b) an increasing involvement by behavior analysts in the analysis and treatment of medical-physiological disorders, (c) an increasing use of intervention procedures designed to modify physiological processes, and (d) advances in measurement technology. The focus of behavior analysts on physiological as well as cognitive and motoric components of behavior problems has encouraged adoption of psychophysiological (or electrophysiological) measurement methods. For example, obsessive-compulsive behavior problems (Mavissakalian & Barlow, 1981) have multiple components, frequently including autonomically and centrally mediated physiological responses, such as peripheral vasomotor constriction, heart rate acceleration, increases in skeletal muscle tension, and/or increases in skin conductance. As noted earlier in this chapter, physiological, cognitive, and motoric components of a syndrome frequently do not significantly covary, and assessment of all components is necessary for valid description, functional analysis, and intervention evaluation.

Impetus for the use of psychophysiological measurement techniques has also come from the increasing involvement of behavior analysts in the evaluation and treatment of psychosomatic and medical-psychological disorders (Davidson & Davison, 1980; Haynes & Gannon, 1981; Melamed & Siegel, 1980; Sturgis & Gramling, 1988). There is an increasing recognition of the etiological and mediational role of environmental and psychological factors in many organic disorders (see DSM-III-R) and of the significant psychological consequences frequently associated with organic disorders (Boll, 1981). The concepts and technology of behavioral construct systems are uniquely suited to the investigation and modification of these factors.

Psychophysiological measures used most frequently in behavioral assessment include brain wave patterns, eye movements, peripheral temperature, blood volume pulse, muscle tension, respiration, penile erections, skin conductance, and blood pressure. However, behavior analysts have more recently monitored biochemical variables, such as nicotine, cotinine, carbon monoxide, serum, and thiocyanate for smoking (Brown, Lichtenstein, McIntyre, & Harrington-Kostur, 1984; Foy, Rychtarik, & Prue, 1988) and blood alcohol, blood acetalaldehyde, and gamma-glutamyl transpeptidase for alcohol intake (Correa & Stuker, 1986). Most of these methods have been borrowed from the discipline of psychophysiology (Martin & Venables, 1980). With some notable exceptions (e.g., labial temperature measures: [Henson, Rubin, & Henson, 1979]), behavior analysts have made only minimal methodological contributions.

Medical-psychological disorders that have been assessed by behavior analysts with psychophysiological measurement methods include muscle-contraction headache (Blanchard et al., 1983; Haynes, 1981), migraine headache (Sturgis, Adams, & Brantley, 1981), essential hypertension (McCann, 1987), asthma (Alexander, 1981), dermatitis (Haynes, Wilson, & Britton, 1979), insomnia (Bootzin & Engle-Friedman, 1981), diabetes (Wing et al., 1985), sexual dysfunctions (McConagy, 1988), gastrointestinal dysfunctions (Walker & Sandman, 1981), diabetes (Green, 1978), pain (Chapman & Wykoff, 1981), hemophilia (Varni, 1981), and Raynaud's symptoms (Keefe et al., 1981). Psychophysiological methods have also been used in the assessment of behavior problems, such as alcoholism (Correa & Stuker, 1986), speech anxiety (Gatchel et al., 1978), anger (Hazaleus & Deffenbacher, 1986), smoking (Foy, Rychtarik, & Prue, 1988), pedophilia (Foote & Laws, 1981), bruxism (Rosen, 1981), marital interaction (Gottman & Levenson, 1986), hyperactivity (Wells, Conners, Imber, & Delamater, 1981), rape (Quinsey, Chaplin, & Varney, 1981), phobias and fears (Nietzel, Bernstein, & Russell, 1988), obsessive-compulsive disorders (Mavissakalian & Barlow, 1981), social-anxiety (McFall, 1982), post-traumatic stress disorder (Keane et al., 1985), and depression (Carson, 1986).

Many behavioral interventions, such as biofeedback, desensitization, relaxation training, operant conditioning of psychological responses, flooding (implosive) treatment, and specific imagery, are intended to modify some aspect of physiological functioning. Psychophysiological assessment methods are necessary to evaluate the process and outcomes of these interventions.

Each psychophysiological measurement method has common and unique sources of error associated with its technology (e.g., sensitivity, movement artifact, filtering, sensor placement, surface resistance). In addition, the generalizability of the obtained data is limited by the idiosyncracity of laboratory situations, sensor placement, time-sampling parameters, stimulus parameters, and reactivity. For example, the setting and temporal generalizability of laboratory occlusive measures of blood pressure of a hypertensive client will be influenced by the characteristics of the laboratory environment, the position of the client while blood pressure is taken, the placement and size of the occlusion cuff, exercise and dietary factors occurring immediately prior to measurement, types of stressors or other stimuli presented, instructions, methods of recording, and time-sampling parameters used.

Instruments Adapted from Traditional Clinical Assessment

Two behavioral assessment procedures (interviews and questionnaires) have been adopted from traditional applied psychological disciplines. In both cases, there are significant differences in format and content between behavioral and traditional applications that reflect differences in the underlying conceptual systems.

Because of the self-report nature of interviews and questionnaires and their association with traditional clinical psychology, they have been viewed skeptically by many behavior analysts. It was presumed that the probability of error, particularly biases associated with self-report measures, their nomothetic bases, and the degree of inference inherent in their interpretation, was sufficient to render them of little value as a primary data source. This blanket skepticism is being replaced by a recognition that error variance in questionnaires and interviews differs from, but probably does not exceed, that of other behavioral assessment methods. Furthermore, interviews and questionnaires can be useful adjuncts in a multimethod behavioral assessment program.

Behavioral Assessment Interviews

The interview is probably the most frequently used assessment instrument (Haynes, 1978; Haynes & Chavez, 1983; Haynes & Jensen, 1979; Linehan, 1977; Wiens, 1981). Almost every behavioral intervention involves preintervention verbal interaction with clients or significant individuals (e.g., teachers, staff, parents) from the client's environment.

The importance of the interview is a result of its multiple functions. Other assessment instruments have as their primary goal the derivation of data on the client's behavior or interactions with his or her environment. The assessment interview also serves these functions. Additionally, it is used to screen clients for therapy, evaluate and enhance clients' motivations for further assessment and intervention, select additional assessment strategies, inform clients about the assessment-intervention process, establish a positive relationship between the behavior analyst and client, and gather historical information (Haynes & Chavez, 1983; Morganstern, 1988). Thus, the assessment interview has a profound impact on assessment and intervention.

There are significant differences in the content and format of behavioral and nonbehavioral assessment interviews. Compared with nonbehavioral interviews, behavioral interviews tend to be more (a) systematic and structured, (b) focused on overt behavior and behavior-environment interactions, (c) attentive to situational sources of behavioral variance, (d) focused on current rather than historical behaviors and determinants, and (e) quantitative in orientation.

It is in the interview that a systems perspective of behavioral assessment is most apparent. Assessment focuses are becoming less confined to the analysis of discrete target behaviors and contingent and antecedent factors. Instead, the client is more frequently evaluated in the context of his or her larger social system. Also evaluated in the interview are other interactions in a client's social system, collateral changes potentially associated with intervention (such as changes in family interactions or occupational patterns), source of social support, mediational events, and behaviors that may covary with the targeted behaviors (response classes).

Despite its importance, the interview has been the assessment instrument least subjected to empirical evaluation. Although the interview has been subjected to investigation for other purposes, its psychometric properties as a behavioral assessment instrument have been infrequently studied. However, the behavioral assessment interview is becoming a more frequent topic of psychometric evaluation (e.g., Haynes,

Jensen, Wise, & Sherman, 1981; Watson, Tilleskjor, Hoodecheck-Schow, Purcel, & Jacobs, 1985).

Questionnaires

The questionnaire is probably the second most frequently used instrument in behavioral assessment (Emmelkamp, 1981; Wade, Baker, & Hartmann, 1979). Like the interview, it has been applied to the assessment of almost all adult behavior disorders (see review by Jensen & Haynes, 1986).

Many questionnaires used by behavior analysts (e.g., depression scales, marital satisfaction scales) are unaltered adoptions of those employed in traditional psychological assessment. Although some provide useful data to the behavior analyst, many have been adopted without sufficient attention to their underlying assumptions, psychometric properties, or applicability to targeted populations. Most traditional questionnaires are designed to measure some "personality trait" (e.g., "intelligence," "neuroticism," "depression") and do not satisfactorily attend to the situational variance of behavior or the heterogeneity within classes. In addition, many are based on psychodynamic etiological assumptions and do not provide measures of the multimodal components and determinants of specific targeted responses. Traditional questionnaires often provide a single index of a multifaceted syndrome. As a result, they are sometimes appropriate for initial screening or as a general index of program outcome but seldom have utility for most of the other functions of behavioral assessment.

Other questionnaires have been developed by behavior analysts. These target specific behavior problems, such as social skills deficits (Curran & Wessberg, 1981), obsessive-compulsive behaviors (Hodgson & Rachman, 1977), fears and phobias (Geer, 1965), anger (Novaco, 1975), marital distress and dysfunctions (LoPiccolo & Steger, 1974), and menstrual dysfunctions (Cox, 1977). Most have face validity, focus on more specific behaviors and events, and attend to situational determinants of behavior. However, their development and application have frequently violated standard psychometric principles. Many were rationally rather than empirically derived, were not subjected to internal homogeneity or factor analyses, and did not undergo multimethod validity evaluation prior to application. Such psychometric deficiencies hinder interpretation of their resultant scores.

When properly developed, evaluated, and applied, questionnaires can be an efficient and useful source of data. They are inexpensive to administer and score and have face validity for clients; their analysis and interpretation can be simplified through computer administration and scoring. However, because of the significant possibility of reporting biases, and the inferential difficulties in interpreting derived scores, questionnaire-derived, as well as interview-derived, data should be corroborated by data from other assessment procedures.

Adjunctive Methods

There are several other assessment methods that are less frequently used in behavior assessment but are consistent with its underlying concepts. These include product-of-behavior measures, manipulation, critical-event sampling, and computer-assisted assessment.

Product-of-Behavior Measures

Product-of-behavior measures are temporary or permanent records generated by target behaviors (Haynes & Wilson, 1979). For example, weight is a frequently used product-of-behavior measure for eating behavior and is frequently used in the evaluation of behavioral interventions with obesity (Brownell, 1981). Other product-of-behavior measures include tokens acquired and spent (as a measure of social and work behaviors of psychiatric inpatients) (Kazdin, 1984), grades or workbook performance (as measures of study behaviors), and blood urine composition (as measures for smoking or drug intake) (Glasglow et al., 1983; Stitzer et al., 1982).

Most product-of-behavior measures have the advantages of being relatively unobtrusive, permanent (or long lasting), and easily accessible. In many cases, these measures are minimally reactive and provide a quantitative index of behaviors emitted in the natural environment.

There are difficulties in interpreting product-of-behavior measures, however. Because the product-of-behavior index may reflect behaviors other than those targeted, the relationship between the product-of-behavior measure and the targeted behavior is frequently unclear. For example, weight changes may reflect targeted changes in eating patterns, but may also reflect changes in caloric expenditure, the intake of fluids or diuretics, hormonal changes, or the intake of stimulant medication or appetite suppressants. Because of these inferential problems, the external validity of the measures cannot be assumed. Also, because of the latency between some target behaviors and their products, some product-of-behavior measures may be insufficiently sensitive to behavior change.

Manipulation

One of the most potentially useful but least frequently used methods of assessment is manipulation of hypothesized controlling events. Changes in dependent variables that occur concomitantly with manipulation of hypothesized causal factors are powerful bases for deriving causal inferences. This has been a primary method of causal analysis of many empirically based psychological disciplines, such as experimental psychology (Kling & Riggs, 1971), experimental psychopathology (Maher, 1966), and the experimental analysis of behavior (Honig, 1966).

Although manipulation is consistent with an hypothesis-testing epistemology, it has been infrequently used as a preintervention assessment strategy. Several examples of manipulation were reviewed by Mavissakalian and Barlow (1981) in their discussion of behavioral assessment strategies for obsessive-compulsive disorders. For example, in studies by Rachman, compulsive hand washers first touched contaminated objects. They were then allowed (a) to wash their hands immediately afterwards, (b) were forced to delay hand-washing, or (c) had their hand washing interrupted. Multimethod assessment was used to evaluate the effects of these manipulations. Manipulation has also been used to assess the effect of social stimuli on the drinking behavior of alcoholics by systematically manipulating these stimuli in simulated bars (Donovan & Marlatt, 1988; Miller, 1981).

Manipulation of hypothesized antecedent stimuli can also be useful in the functional analysis of medical-psychological disorders. For example, the exposure of headache clients to various stressors in a laboratory with simultaneous monitoring of electomyographic responses from multiple cephalic sites may help identify specific antecedents and localized muscle tension responses associated with head pain. Controlled presentation of laboratory stimuli may also help identify precipitants of blood pressure increases of hypertensives, anxiety arousing stimuli for fearful subjects, or the efficacy of potential reinforcers.

The greatest advantage of assessment via manipulation is that it can provide powerful confirmatory or disconfirmatory data on hypothesized controlling stimuli, both antecedent and consequent. Alternative methods of evaluating these relationships are limited to self-report unless they occur at a rate sufficient for observation. The primary disadvantages of manipulation reside in threats to internal and external validity. Care must be taken to design manipulation strategies (e.g., controlling sequence, duration, intensity, expectancy factors) so that valid causal inferences may be drawn. More important, the external validity, or setting generality, of the observed relationships cannot be assumed when manipulations occur in analog settings.

Computer-Assisted Assessment

Computer-assisted assessment is similar in content and procedure to both interviews and questionnaires. Typically, a client sits in front of a video monitor upon which questions or other visual stimuli are presented. His or her responses are made via an adjacent keyboard. The interactive computer system operates as a decision tree, and stimuli presented are a function of previous client responses. For example, if a client indicates problems with sleep-onset insomnia, a series of questions might be presented concerning the client's sleeping environment, presleep cognitions, or diet.

Preliminary research (Angle, 1981; Angle, Ellinwood, Hay, Johnson, & Hay, 1977; Angle, Hay, Hay, & Ellinwood, 1977; Kleinmuntz, 1972) suggests that computer-assisted assessment can facilitate the collection and analysis of massive amounts of data and is well received by clients. In addition, errors associated with bias, fatigue, or procedural variance in assessment interviews are reduced.

The main drawbacks to computer-assisted assessment appear to be technological and financial. The initial investment for a computer and its programming can be considerable, although it may be cost efficient over an extended period of time. In addition, because computer programs tend to be somewhat specialized, it is difficult to develop an interactive program with sufficient sensitivity and flexibility to address satisfactorily the myriad of problems and controlling variables presented in most clinical situations.

Critical-Event Sampling

Another potentially useful but infrequently used method of behavioral assessment involves automated recording in the natural environment during problematic periods for clients (Haynes, 1978; Margolin, 1981). For example, tape recorders can be self-actuated by a distressed marital couple during verbal altercations at home or by a heterosocially anxious individual while on a date.

A related procedure involves retrospective analysis of critical events. Foster, DeLawyer, and Guevremont (1986), for example, conducted structured interviews with fifth- to eighth-grade students to identify incidents that affected their liking of peers.

Critical-event sampling in the natural environment can be cost and time efficient, because much sampling is limited to periods when there is a high probability of problematic interactions in the natural environment. Similar information would be costly to acquire through psychological observation. Quantitative indices may be derived from these recordings, and they can also provide a rich source of qualitatively derived hypotheses.

Because there has been limited psychometric evaluation of this assessment procedure, sources and degree of error can only be estimated. As with many other assessment instruments, critical-event sampling may have significant reactive effects. For example, critical-event sampling of verbal altercations of distressed marital couples was attempted in one study (Follingstad & Haynes, 1981), but the procedure had obvious reactive effects on marital interaction. Furthermore, the audiotapes returned to the investigators were not random samples of marital altercations— couples sometimes erased recordings they did not like or failed to record at designated times.

EVALUATION

The applicability of classical psychometric principles to behavioral assessment is a subject of debate (Cone, 1988; Nelson, 1983). However, assessment systems and instruments can be evaluated on a number of important dimensions, including applicability and utility, reliability, validity, and sources of error variance. The evaluation of any assessment instrument is complicated because its psychometric properties cannot be assumed to be stable and are not necessarily generalizable across populations, settings, or assessment functions. The psychometric evaluation of behavioral assessment is rendered even more difficult because it is composed of a set of divergent procedures, each of which is associated with idiosyncratic attributes and psychometric characteristics. Because of this complexity, the following section only highlights major evaluative dimensions in behavioral assessment. More comprehensive examinations of particular assessment methods can be found in books by Ciminero et al. (1986), Haynes (1978), and Nelson and Hayes (1987).

Applicability and Utility

The applicability and utility of an assessment instrument refers to the degree to which it is useful for deriving clinically useful information on particular populations, behaviors or behavior disorders, can be applied in particular situations, and/or is useful for particular assessment purposes. In considering the applicability and utility of behavioral assessment instruments, several evaluative dimensions, such as clinical utility, cost effectiveness, utility for developing a functional analysis, and utility for DSM-III-R diagnoses are particularly important considerations.

There can be little doubt that many behavioral assessment instruments have empirical utility—they provide powerful methods of multimethod and multimodal evaluation of intervention effects and hypothesized functional relationships. In contrast, the clinical utility of many behavioral assessment instruments has been questioned where service delivery rather than research is the prime focus (Barlow, 1980; Emmelkamp, 1981; Hayes, Nelson, & Jarret, 1987; Haynes, 1984b; Margolin, 1981; Strosahl & Linehan, 1986). Surveys of behavior therapists in clinical practice have suggested that their use of behavioral assessment instruments is frequently limited to interviews and trait-based questionnaires (Swan & MacDonald, 1979).

The limited clinical application of behavioral assessment methods can be attributed to several factors (Haynes, 1984a): (a) Many behavioral assessment instruments (particularly psychopsychological and observational methods) are time consuming to apply and have a relatively unfavorable cost-effectiveness ratio (Alevizos et al., 1978; McIntyre et al., 1983; Wicramesekera, 1981). (b) Many behavior analysts are inadequately trained in the application of behavioral assessment instruments (O'Leary, 1979). (c) The type of information provided by the assessment instruments (e.g., observed behavior rates) is not always useful in formulating functional analyses and designing intervention programs (Foster & Cone, 1980; Hayes et al., 1987). (d) Adequate assessment instruments have not been developed for many problem behaviors encountered by clinicians (such as paranoia, hypochondriasis, psychosomatic disorders). (e) The financial contingency systems operating in private practice and social service agencies often reward client contacts for therapy more than for assessment (Haynes, Lemsky, & Sexton-Radek, 1987a,b).

Several additional issues in the clinical utility of behavioral assessment are worthy of consideration. First, like all assessment instruments, behavioral assessment instruments are differentially useful across disorders. Perhaps the most important determinant of an instrument's utility in deriving a functional analysis for a particular disorder is the degree to which the disorder has a functional relationship with environmental variables. For some behavior disorders (such as marital distress, phobias, and aggression), evidence supports a strong functional relationship between the disorder and behavioral, cognitive, and environmental variables. For other disorders (such as depression or migraine headaches), controlling variables appear to be shared among environmental and organic factors. Finally, for many other behavior disorders (such as schizophrenia, paranoia, or asthma), a functional relationship with behavioral-environmental factors is possible but undemonstrated. Therefore, the utility of behavioral assessment (or any psychological assessment) in deriving pretreatment functional analyses is affected by the proportion of variance in the targeted disorder accounted for by variance in behavioral, cognitive, environmental factors or their interactions. However, even when environmental determinants play a minor role, behavioral assessment is a very powerful system for intervention evaluation.

Second, specific behavioral assessment instruments are differentially useful in formulating functional analyses and in their applicability for the other purposes of assessment (Haynes, 1984a, 1984b; Nelson & Hayes, 1986). Some instruments, such as the interview, are more useful for developing than for testing hypotheses. Others, such as naturalistic or analog observation, may be more suitable for hypothesis testing than for hypothesis development (see discussions by Gottman, 1985; Jacobson, 1985; Weiss & Frohman, 1985), although suggestions for improving the clinical utility of these instruments have been offered (e.g., Foster, Bell-Dolan, & Burge, 1988).

Considering the alternatives (e.g., nonbehavioral interviews and objective and projective tests), behavioral assessment is, despite its deficiencies, the most powerful and clinically useful assessment system. It provides the clinician with a set of procedures amenable to the multimethod and multimodal assessment of most adult disorders, in most settings and for most purposes. No other assessment system approaches such diversity of utility. Because of its empirical analysis, it is particularly suited to the clinician who adopts a functional, hypothesis testing, and accountability orientation.

Reliability

Reliability is a complex concept referring to the stability or consistency of measures derived from repeated administrations of a measurement instrument across similar situations (external reliability) or from the degree or pattern of covariance of elements within an instrument (internal reliability) (McFall & McDonel, 1986). Reliability is a particularly important attribute of an instrument because it sets the upper limit to its validity.

The application of traditional reliability concepts to behavioral assessment poses difficulties because of differences between traditional and behavioral conceptual systems in assumptions about the situational and temporal stability of behavior (Haynes, 1978; Strosahl & Linehan, 1986). Coefficients of reliability for measures of a presumably stable phenomenon (one demonstrating cross-situational stability such as IQ or locus of control) provide indices of the validity or degree-of-error variance of those measures. Coefficients of reliability for measures of events with expected situational or temporal instability (e.g., eating patterns, marital interaction, autonomic arousal) may be indicative either of error variance associated with the measurement instruments or of true variance in the phenomenon measured.

For example, staff observations of a psychiatric inpatient may demonstrate considerable day-to-day variability in the frequency with which he or she initiates social interaction with other patients. This measured variability may accurately reflect the patient's behavior or may reflect varying levels of diligence by the observers, the use of different observers on different days, variance in the times or settings in which the patient's social behavior is sampled, functional dissimilarity of the situations, or insufficient specification of the observation codes.

The probability that measured variance is a function of true behavior variability (i.e., is accurate) rather than error variance in the measurement instrument can be enhanced by careful control of sources of error. Thus, care in construction and application of assessment instruments, such as the use of highly trained observers, careful training of patients in self-monitoring procedures, careful specification of target events, specifically worded questionnaire and interview items, coding of situational factors, and consistency in the timing and setting of assessment can reduce the impact of methodological errors. Also, use of criterion measures (such as a second observer) can help evaluate sources of error variance attributable to the measurement instruments.

Low indices of reliability, even if attributable to true instability of the target behavior rather than measurement error, have important implications for the interpretation of the measure. There is an inverse relationship between the degree of stability of a target behavior and the number of times that behavior must be measured in order to derive an accurate estimate of its parameters (Foster, Bell-Dolan, & Burge, 1988; Haynes, 1978). This means, for example, that we must spend many more days observing on-unit social interactions of an inpatient who demonstrates day-to-day variability in his or her social interactions than of an inpatient who demonstrates day-to-day consistency in this behavior. Therefore, we expect differences across persons in the temporal stability of target behaviors, and the frequency of measurement must be a function of the stability of measures obtained and cannot be determined on an a priori basis.

Criterion-Referenced Validity

Because assessment instruments differ in the degree to which they accurately measure the phenomena they are intended to measure, their validity is frequently evaluated by comparing resulting indices with those derived from other independently evaluated assessment instruments. This process is referred to as criterion-referenced validity evaluation and can be either concurrent or predictive. Concurrent validity is the degree of correlation between two instruments administered at the same time. For example, the *concurrent validity* of an interview with a woman reporting orgasmic dysfunction might be indicated by the degree of correlation between the interview, questionnaires, or sexual partner reports of sexual behavior. *Discriminant validity* is a form of concurrent validity measuring the degree to which an assessment instrument can differentiate groups classified on the basis of naturally occurring phenomena. For example, the discriminant validity of an analog measure of marital communication might be the degree to which it could successfully discriminate couples seeking marital therapy from those not seeking marital therapy. *Predictive validity* is the degree to which an assessment instrument can predict measures taken at a later time. For example, the predictive validity of psychophysiological measures of stress responses of headache patients could be indicated by the degree to which these measures are associated with the outcome of relaxation/biofeedback training (Blanchard et al., 1983).

The types of validity noted above are derived from traditional psychometric principles and require the administration of standardized instruments to a large number of subjects. However, behavioral assessment instruments are often developed specifically to measure important behaviors of a single client (e.g., parent observation of study behavior by a child) and are, therefore, not amenable to the same nomothetically based psychometric considerations (Cone, 1988). Nevertheless, issues of validity (sometimes referred to as *accuracy*) are still of concern because the behavior analyst is interested in the degree to which the obtained measures reflect the target behavior rather than other sources of variance (e.g., the degree to which the measures of study behavior reflect actual study behavior rather than level of attention by the parent).

One measure of the validity or accuracy of observation methods is inter-observer agreement (although often considered a measure of reliability). In this method, two observers simultaneously record target behaviors, and the degree of agreement between the two is calculated (formulae for calculating inter-observer agreement coefficients are summarized in Foster & Cone, 1986).

There is considerable variability in the extent to which behavioral assessment instruments have been subjected to criterion-referenced validity evaluations. Some, such as interviews (Haynes & Chavez, 1983; Morrell, King, & Martin, 1986) and naturalistic observation (Hartmann & Wood, 1982), have undergone very little criterion validity or accuracy evaluation (other than inter-observer agreement). Others, such as behavioral questionnaires and analog observation, have been the subject of more extensive evaluation (see reviews in Bellack & Hersen, 1988a; Ciminero et al., 1986; Nelson & Hayes, 1986) but often within a nomothetic framework.

The results of these evaluations have been mixed, reflecting both the methodological difficulties inherent in applying this psychometric concept to behavioral assessment instruments and the early developmental stage of many behavioral assessment methods. For example, several validity evaluations of analog assessment procedures (Bellack, 1979; Curran et al., 1980; De Armas & Brigham, 1986, Jacobson et al., 1981) have noted problems in the external validity or setting generalizability of the obtained measures. In particular, analog measures of social behavior frequently do not correlate highly with other measures of the same phenomenon or with the same measure administered in a different setting.

Behavior analysts have frequently ascribed an inherent validity to behavioral observation. Observation measures were presumed to be valid because they are minimally inferential and were assumed simply to reflect the behavior of the targeted individual at the time of observation. Differences between behavioral observation and another measure of the same phenomenon (e.g., discrepancies between questionnaire-measured phobic behavior and an individual's motor behavior in the presence of a phobic stimulus) were presumed to be indicative of invalidity of the nonob-servation measure, or of the fact that they were measures of uncorrelated response modalities. However, behavioral observation measures are no longer presumed to be inherently valid. Measures derived from behavioral observation can reflect methodological variance as well as true behavior variance, and low coefficients of agreement with other measures can as readily be indicative of time sampling, definitional, situational, and inferential errors in the observation measure. Consequently, validity assessment is as important for observational as for nonobservational measures.

In summary, a large number of studies have reported data indicating that behavioral assessment instruments can provide data with a satisfactory degree of criterion-referenced validity (Ciminero et al., 1986). However, inferences of validity of any assessment instrument should be drawn cautiously. Validity and reliability are not stable properties of an assessment instrument; neither can they automatically be generalized across populations, settings, methods of administration, or functions of assessment. Furthermore, low indices of criterion validity have been reported in some studies, and many behavioral assessment instruments have undergone insufficient validity evaluation (Conger & Keane, 1981).

Content Validity

Content validity refers to the degree to which the content of an assessment instrument (items on a questionnaire, situations sampled, codes in an observation system) adequately samples the targeted construct (Goldfried, 1982; Haynes, 1978; Linehan, 1980). For example, a behavioral interview with adequate content validity for preintervention assessment of depressed clients should focus on typical sources of reinforcement, recent changes in reinforcement rate or stimulus control parameters, social consequences for depressive behavior, associated cognitive or attributive behaviors, environmental stimuli preceding depressive episodes, coping behaviors, and social supports (Lewinsohn & Lee, 1981). In addition, content validity is also affected by methods of sampling, data reduction, and data analysis used by the assessor (Linehan, 1980).

The structure and content of a content-valid instrument varies with the purposes of assessment. For example, an observational system to assess the effects of a token system on the self-care behaviors of hospitalized patients should adequately sample those self-care behaviors, potential side effects, and mediating variables such as token stealing or staff-patient interactions. However, different behaviors might be sampled in an observation system directed at the same patients but intended to evaluate the general and specific effects of pharmacological intervention.

Although content validity is a qualitative dimension of an assessment instrument, it can be enhanced through careful instrument construction and evaluation. Most behavioral assessment instruments are constructed rationally or analytically—the developer selects elements of the instrument (e.g., questions, observation codes) on the basis of his or her theoretical preconceptions (Conger, Wallander, Mariotto, & Ward, 1980). As a result, the instruments sometimes more closely reflect the developer's preconceptions than empirically determined characteristics and determinants of the targeted behavior problem.

Rational derivations can be supplemented with alternative methods of constructing assessment instruments. These methods involve examination of previously used items, or comparing groups varying on the dimension of interest (e.g., comparing social initiation responses of socially skilled and socially unskilled individuals) and interviews with persons from the target population or professionals who work with them. The social and external validity of identified items can also be examined, and tests for redundancy and internal homogeneity can be conducted (Conger et al., 1980; Spence, 1981).

Content validity of a behavioral assessment instrument decreases over time because the instrument is based on an evolving conceptualization of the targeted disorder. As our understanding of the characteristics and determinants of behavior problems increases, the content validity of assessment instruments based on earlier conceptualizations diminishes.

Generalizability

Generalizability is an alternative conceptual and statistical process for identifying sources of variance in an obtained score (Coates & Thoresen, 1978; Cronbach, Gleser, Nanda, & Rajaratnam, 1972; Foster & Cone, 1980; Hartmann & Wood, 1982). Through analysis of variance procedures, proportions of variance can be assigned to sources (facets), such as observers, situations, or time. Although still infrequently used in behavioral assessment, analysis of variance is an heuristic psychometric model for conceptualizing and analyzing the reliability and validity of an assessment instrument and identifying sources of variance.

TRENDS

Behavioral assessment is an evolutionary conceptual and methodological system characterized by an ongoing process of refinement. Contrasted to its use in the 1980s, behavioral assessment in the 1990s will have a significantly greater empirical basis, clinical applicability, breadth of focus, and conceptual sophistication. These changes stimulate, as well as reflect, developments in behavioral construct systems. There are several major areas of change in behavioral assessment: (a) an expanding focus of assessment, (b) the increased application of psychometric and research design principles, (c) a reanalysis of the conceptual foundations of behavioral assessment, (d) an examination of the clinical decision-making processes, and (e) technological advances in measurement.

An Expanding Focus

The array of variables, functional relationships, and target behaviors included in behavioral construct systems is expanding. There is an increased focus on behavioral chains, temporally extended and noncontiguous determinants, predictor and mediating variables, community and environmental settings, cognitive and physiological variables, treatment generalization, side effects, and social systems. As noted throughout this chapter, behavioral assessment is also being used with an expanding range of adult behavioral disorders (e.g., Parks & Hollon, 1988).

There has been a strong emphasis in behavioral assessment on a SORC (stimulus, organism, response, contingency) model (e.g., Goldfried, 1982), which emphasizes four potential determinants of behavior problems and classes of intervention targets and strategies. The SORC model has served to contrast behavioral with traditional conceptual systems and to emphasize the multifaceted qualities and determinants of behavior problems.

Recent conceptual advances suggest that the SORC model, although originally heuristic, may unnecessarily limit the range of identifiable behavioral relationships and controlling variables. A number of studies have pointed to the etiological importance of *extended interactions* or *behavioral chains* (Cromwell & Peterson, 1981; Gottman, 1979; Margolin, 1981, 1983; McFall, 1982; Miller, 1981; Vincent, 1980; Voeltz & Evans, 1982) and the clinical utility of examining *response classes* (Mash, 1979; Miller, 1981). For example, marital satisfaction and distress may be predicted more accurately from an analysis of extended periods of interactions (Margolin, 1981) than from assessment of only recent interactions. Similarly, paranoid ideation may be functionally related to multiple interactions across a range of interpersonal interactions (Haynes 1986a) rather than to transient or situationally specific interpersonal experiences.

In a similar vein, an analysis of the *social system* within which a client is imbedded may often help identify important causal factors or mediators of intervention outcome (Winett, 1985). As in the case of marital distress (Margolin, Michelli, & Jacobson, 1988), sources of variance for a behavior problem may reside in interactions (e.g., spouse-child, spouse–in-law) external to the client or dyad of interest.

Behavioral etiological conceptualizations and assessments have stressed controlling variables in close temporal proximity to the target behavior (Russo, et al., 1980). For example, most systems for naturalistic observation attend to those antecedent stimuli that immediately (e.g., within 60 seconds) precede target responses. In fact, the structure of most behavioral observation systems and associated methods of data analysis makes it difficult to identify controlling events that occur more than a few minutes prior to a target behavior. More recently, the etiological role of controlling events that are less temporally contiguous to target behaviors is being recognized (Haynes, 1986, 1988). Many adult behavior disorders, such as obsessive-compulsive behaviors, sleep disorders, elevated blood pressure, or sexual dysfunctions, may be functionally associated with events that occurred hours, days, or months previously.

An emphasis on *cost-effectiveness* evaluations of interventions (Yates, 1985), and a recognition of the idiosyncratic nature of behavior disorders and individuals' responses to intervention have resulted in a greater interest in identifying and measuring variables that predict or *mediate intervention outcome* (Blanchard, 1981; Cooke & Meyers, 1980). A wide range of predictors or mediators have been suggested, including social supports, cognitive factors, previous intervention experiences, self-reinforcement and self-control skills, and etiology-intervention congruence (Haynes, 1984a). The focus on predictors and mediators of intervention outcome has several potential benefits. First, it may facilitate the efficient dissemination of psychological services. Second, clients can be matched more effectively to intervention programs. Third, the potential effectiveness of interventions can be increased through identification and modification of mediational factors.

One important mediational variable that has come under closer scrutiny is *treatment compliance* (some-

times called procedural reliability) (Billingsley, White, & Munson, 1980; Blanchard, 1981; Brownell, 1981; Johnson, Wildman, & O'Brien, 1980; Peterson, Homer, & Wonderlich, 1982; Shapiro & Shapiro, 1983) or the degree to which clients emit the prescribed behaviors designed to effect modification of the target problem(s). Examples of behavioral intervention prescriptions include practicing relaxation at home for treatment of anxiety disorders and altering the stimulus-control aspects of the home environment in treatments of insomnia or obesity. Assessment of compliance with intervention prescriptions is particularly important because treatment compliance is a major determinant of intervention outcome; it contributes to the understanding of the etiology of targeted disorders.

Behavior analysts also have expanded the focus of *outcome evaluations*. In early intervention studies, evaluation of outcome was usually limited to effects on the main target variables (Ullmann & Krasner, 1965). However, a more thorough evaluation of intervention outcome would assess the degree of generalization of the treatment effects across behaviors, persons, or settings (Blanchard, 1981; Russo, Cataldo, & Cushing, 1981), other side effects of the intervention (Epstein & Martin, 1977), the perceived validity or significance by the client of the associated behavior changes (Kazdin, 1977; Lebow, 1982; Wolf, 1978), and the cost-efficiency of intervention (Haynes, 1986b).

An increased attention to *cognitive factors* and other more inferential constructs in behavioral assessment (Doyne et al., 1983; Van Egeren, Haynes, Franzen, & Hamilton, 1983; Gottman & Levenson, 1986; Lewinsohn & Lee, 1981; Merluzzi et al., 1981; Miller, 1981) has resulted from an increased emphasis on intervention outcome predictor variables, cognitive intervention strategies (e.g., "rational" interventions, covert modeling, and covert reinforcement), and the etiological role of cognitions. Cognitions are assumed to function as antecedent stimuli for behavior (e.g., self-deprecatory thought preceding social withdrawal), as consequences for behavior (e.g., self-delivered punishment following failure experiences), as the primary defining characteristics of behavior problems (e.g., obsessive ruminations), as mediators of the impact of environmental stimuli (e.g., outcome expectancies as a mediator of surgery stress), and/or as significant mediators of treatment outcome (e.g., perceived credibility of an intervention).

The recent emphasis in psychological construct systems on cognitive factors, such as imagery, expectations, self-statements, and beliefs, has been the subject of criticism (e.g., Sampson, 1981). Their role and significance for behavior problems remains highly inferential, and methods for their assessment are in early stages of development (e.g., Kendall & Hollon, 1981). Moreover, cognitive variables are frequently assumed to be the terminal points rather than simply elements in causal chains. Behavior analysts are sometimes insufficiently cognizant of the fact that cognitions also function as dependent variables and neglect to search for their social learning or situational determinants.

The focus of behavioral assessment also reflects the expanding applications of behavioral interventions. For example, interventions in the community (Alevizos et al., 1978; Carr, Schnelle, & Kirchner, 1980; Foxx & Hake, 1977; Hawkins, 1979; Jones, 1979; Lloyd, 1983; Nietzel et al., 1977; O'Donnell, 1977; Palmer, Lloyd, & Lloyd, 1977) have focused on such problems as energy conservation, police activities, pollution, facility utilization, and program evaluation.

Behavioral assessment strategies are being applied also to an expanding number of clinical behavior problems. These include pain (Chapman & Wykoff, 1981), dermatological disorders (Haynes et al., 1979), obsessive-compulsive disorders (Emmelkamp & Kwee, 1977), post-traumatic stress disorders (Fairbank et al., 1981), hemophilia (Varni, 1981), hemodialysis (Maher, 1981), and problems of the elderly (Edinburg et al., 1977). These areexciting advances in the conceptual bases and clinical applicability of behavioral assessment. Although they significantly complicate the assessment process and the functional analysis of behavior problems, there can be little doubt that the resulting benefits of more powerful conceptual models and intervention power outweigh the cost of increased assessment efforts.

An unavoidable concomitant of an expansion in target variables, functional relationships, and methods is an increasingly diffuse boundary between behavioral and nonbehavioral assessment. As noted by Bellack and Hersen (1988a), many traditional, nonbehavioral assessment instruments are very reliable and valid, and many behavioral assessment methods are highly inferential and focus on unobservable variables. Yet, despite this overlap, differences in emphasis remain. Behavioral assessment methods, *relative* to nonbehavioral assessment methods and constructs, retain their emphasis on an idiographic approach, minimization of inferences, and a careful control of sources of error.

Epistemological Advances

The most important elements of a psychological construct system are not the assumptions about behavior and its determinants, but the *methods of inquiry* that enabled the derivation of those concepts. Although there is an obvious interdependence between concepts and methodology, advances in methods of inquiry determine the long-term utility and viability of a psychological construct system. It is an emphasis on an empirical methodology that most forcefully discriminates behavioral from most nonbehavioral construct systems.

The empirical orientation of behavioral construct systems has promoted a close examination of the temporal and situational structure within which measurement and intervention occur. Confidence in the inference derived from assessment is influenced not only by the validity of the instruments used, but also by the degree to which threats to internal and external validity are minimized by the structure of their administration.

The empirical bases of behavioral assessment are evolving in several areas: (a) an emphasis on the psychometric properties of behavioral assessment instruments, (b) an emphasis on standardization and norm development, (c) a refinement of procedures for the statistical analysis of time-series designs, and (d) the development of research designs useful in clinical situations.

As noted earlier in this chapter, an initial emphasis on the face validity of assessment instruments and a rejection of traditional psychometric principles was partly responsible for the proliferation of behavioral assessment instruments that were constructed on a nonempirical basis. This emphasis has been replaced with a more judicious application of psychometric principles to the development and evaluation of assessment instruments. Behavior analysts are increasingly concerned with principles, such as internal and external reliability (Haynes et al., 1979; Jacobson et al., 1981), factor structure (Galassi & Galassi, 1980), criterion and content validity (Bellack et al., 1979; Foster & Cone, 1980), applicability and utility (Barlow, 1980; Nelson & Hayes, 1987), and sources of error (Baum, Forehand, & Zegoib, 1979). Although there are difficulties in applying traditional psychometric concepts to behavioral assessment methods, their thoughtful application can increase confidence in the validity and applicability of derived measures.

The need for standardization of measurement instruments and development of norms has been noted by a number of authors (Goldfried, 1982; Hartmann, Roper, & Bradford, 1979; Haynes & Chavez, 1983; Korchin & Schulberg, 1981; Mash, 1979; McFall, 1977; O'Leary, 1979). There are significant differences across researchers in the assessment instruments used, and normative data for most assessment instruments are unavailable. The result is that data derived from most behavioral assessment instruments must be interpreted subjectively rather than empirically. This condition is probably unavoidable in early phases of any technological enterprise. But a movement toward standardization and development of norms is now beginning.

There also is increasing attention to the development and application of statistical procedures, particularly for deriving inferences about intervention effects and behavior causality (Edgington, 1982; Gardner, Hartmann, & Mitchell, 1982; Gorsuch, 1983; Hartmann et al., 1980; Horne, Yang, & Ware, 1982; Huitema, 1985; Kratochwill & Piersel, 1983; Notarius, Krokoff, & Markham, 1981; Wampold & Worsham, 1986). Statistical issues are a particular concern in behavioral assessment because multiple measures are often taken frequently across time. Although there is appropriate concern that increased reliance on statistical inference might be accompanied by less careful control of sources of experimental variance (Michael, 1974; Sidman, 1960), the judicious use of statistical procedures within carefully controlled experimental designs can frequently facilitate a more sensitive evaluation of treatment effects and causal relationships.

In summary, an epistemology that stresses the use of an empirically based scientific method for evaluating intervention effects and the functional analysis of behavior and behavior problems is one of the most exciting attributes of behavioral assessment and behavioral construct systems. Although an emphasis on method rather than theory has been criticized, it is this epistemological orientation that is responsible for the continued viability and evolution of behavioral methods and concepts.

A Conceptual Reanalysis

The growing inclusiveness of behavioral assessment and its decreased methodological distinctiveness has spawned a healthy reexamination of its assumptions and conceptual foundations (e.g., McFall, 1986; Nelson & Hayes, 1986). For example, Cone (1986) and Strosahl and Linehan (1986) examined the as-

sumptions, assets, and liabilities associated with idiographic and nomothetic assessment methods: the sources of behavioral variance associated with each, their area of overlap and distinctiveness, and the inductive or deductive reasoning processes associated with each. Evans (1985) examined the assumptions and methodological implications of the triple-response mode (verbal, overt behavioral, psychological). He also discussed the role, measurement, and validation of behavioral constructs. Gannon and Haynes (1987) discussed discordance between cognitive and psychological response modes as an explanatory concept for the development of psychophysiologic disorders. Barrett, Johnston, and Pennypacker (1986) addressed the units of measurement used in behavioral assessment and advocated closer adherence to less inferential, precisely measurable, behavioral variables characteristic of experimental behavioral analysis. McFall and McDonel (1986) reviewed situational and person sources of behavioral variability. They examined methodologies for ascribing sources of behavior variance, inferential errors in past research, the role of moderator variables, and an interactional perspective (person × situation). McFall and McDonel suggest a multifaceted approach to understanding behavioral variance, characterized by more careful delineation of the purposes, strengths, benefits, and domain of particular conceptual models. Haynes and O'Brien (in press) offered a new definition for the functional analysis in behavioral assessment and suggested methods of derivation and integration.

The high proportion of published articles in behavioral assessment that have a conceptual focus is indicative of its evolutionary nature and the interdependence between assessment and theory. The underlying bases, presumptions, and postulates are still malleable, and conceptual boundaries have yet to be defined. Theory certainly affects assessment and theory development and testing is also affected by the power of available assessment methods (see Mini-Series: The linkage between theory and assessment method, *Behavioral Assessment*, pp. 3–104). While this malleability presents definitional problems in the discipline, it also offers exciting opportunities for development.

Clinical Decision Making

The major functions of behavioral assessment require not only the careful administration of valid assessment instruments, but also the integration by the behavior analysts of the acquired information for the purpose of clinical decision making. From data acquired in the assessment phase, behavior analysts must select target behaviors, construct causal models, and design intervention programs. However, despite its importance, this decision-making process has undergone little empirical scrutiny. There are no empirically-derived guidelines for selecting target behaviors, developing functional analyses, or designing intervention programs (Haynes, 1986b).

More recently, investigators have been addressing the clinical decision-making process. For example, Wilson and Evans (1983) and Hay, Hay, Angle, and Nelson (1979) investigated the reliability of target behavior selection. Felton and Nelson (1984) investigated the inter-assessor agreement in the selection of causal variables and in the design of intervention strategies. As these studies suggest, clinical decision making in behavioral assessment will be a topic of increased empirical evaluation.

Technological Advances in Measurement

To facilitate data recording in the natural environment and to reduce sources of measurement error that occur when people record behavioral events, advances have been made in the development of automated data collection instruments. Recording devices have been miniaturized, telemetric and automatic recording procedures have been developed for monitoring physiological responses in the natural environment, and computer analysis techniques have been developed to analyze acquired data. Some examples include (a) the monitoring of electroencephalographic patterns of insomniacs at home through portable recording devices or through the use of the home telephone as a data modem (Burnett et al., 1985); (b) the automatic monitoring of blood pressure and heart rate throughout the day through the use of portable recording devices (Agras, Southam, & Taylor, 1983; Holden & Barlow, 1986; Keefe & Blumenthal, 1982); (c) the monitoring of peak-expiratory-flow-rate outside the clinic through the use of a relatively inexpensive portable apparatus (Alexander, 1981); (d) the monitoring of carbon monoxide levels of individuals on smoking programs throughout the day by having subjects exhale in polyvinyl bags (Martin & Fredericksen, 1980), and (e) computerized observation recording and data reduction systems. An expanded discussion of technological advances in behavioral assessment is provided by Rugh, Gable, and Lemke (1986).

SUMMARY

Behavioral assessment is an increasingly viable conceptual and methodological system. It is the topic of many books, research and review articles, journals, symposia, and graduate-level courses, and it is having an impact on many fields of applied psychology. The derivations of behavioral assessment reflect the diversity of its methods and have been influenced by traditional technologies of scientific inquiry, traditional methods of clinical assessment, the methods and focus of behavioral intervention, and a dissatisfaction with traditional clinical construct systems.

There are many assumptions that affect the methods, focus, and goals of behavioral assessment. These include presumptions of (a) low levels of covariation among multimodal components of behavior disorders, (b) interdependence of many behaviors, (c) individual differences in behavioral covariations, (d) environmental interactionism, (e) the importance of mediational and situational factors as sources of behavior control, (f) multiple and idiosyncratic determinants of behavior disorders, and (g) the heuristic value of methodological empiricism.

Assessment methods and focuses are also affected by their functions. These include (a) identification of target behaviors, (b) identification of alternative behaviors, (c) identification of causal variables, (d) development of a functional analysis, (e) design of intervention strategies, (f) evaluation of target behaviors, and (g) identification of causal relationships. These functions vary across clients, disorders, and the purpose of the assessment. Furthermore, the various assessment methods are differentially applicable to these functions.

Because behavioral assessment emphasizes the validity of acquired data, it can contribute to DSM-III-R diagnoses. However, diagnostic systems, such as the DSM-III-R, based on the structure of behavior, will usually not provide sufficient information for the design of intervention programs. Consequently, additional assessment will be necessary to identify important functional relationships.

The boundaries between behavioral and nonbehavioral assessment methods are becoming increasingly indistinct and permeable. This appears to be a result of the growing focus on unobservable variables, a more reasoned appraisal of traditional clinical assessment instruments, and a reduction of the conceptual and methodological rigor of behavior analysts. Assessment methods most often associated with or consistent with a behavioral paradigm include naturalistic observation, analog observation, self-monitoring, participant observation, psychophysiological measures, behavioral interviews, behavioral questionnaires, product-of-behavior measures, manipulation, critical-event sampling, and computer-assisted assessment. Each assessment method is associated with idiosyncratic areas of applicability, utility, and sources of error. The reactive effects sometimes associated with assessment are a particularly salient source of error for many instruments.

An early emphasis on the inherent and face validity of behavioral instruments is being replaced by judicious psychometric evaluations. Particular attention is being focused on their applicability, utility, reliability, criterion-related validity, content validity, and generalizability. Although the application of some psychometric principles is problematic, the clinical utility, content validity, and external validity of certain instruments is of particular concern.

Perhaps the greatest asset of behavioral measurement systems is that they are conceptually and methodologically evolutionary. This is reflected in an expanding focus of behavioral assessment to include a wider array of controlling and covarying events, especially extended interactions, behavioral chains, response classes, noncontemporaneous controlling events, and mediational variables. Intervention outcome variables have also been expanded to include generalization, side effects, predictors, and cost-efficiency evaluations. Behavioral assessment methods are also being applied to an increasing number of target disorders. The empirical bases of behavioral assessment are also expanding through increased application of psychometric principles, a recognition of the need for standardization and norm development, the study of clinical decision making, and the application of statistical and design principles.

REFERENCES

Achenbach, T. M. (1974). *Developmental psychopathology*. New York: Ronald.

Adams, H. E., & Haber, J. D. (1984). The classification of abnormal behavior. In H. E. Adams & P. B. Sutker (Eds.), *Comprehensive handbook of psychopathology*. New York: Plenum Press.

Adams, H. E., & Sutker, P. B. (Eds.) (1984). *Comprehensive handbook of psychopathology*. New York: Plenum Press.

Agras, W. S., Southam, M. A., & Taylor, C. B. (1983). Long-term persistence of relaxtion-induced blood pressure lowering during the working day. *Journal of Consulting and Clinical Psychology, 51*, 792–794.

Alden, L. E. (1988). Behavioral self-management controlled drinking strategies in a context of secondary prevention. *Journal of Consulting and Clinical Psychology, 56*, 280–286.

Alevizos, P., De Risi, W., Liberman, R., Eckman, T., & Callahan, E. (1978). The behavior observation instrument: A method of direct observation for program evaluation. *Journal of Applied Behavior Analysis, 11*, 243–257.

Alexander, A. N. (1981). Asthma. In S. N. Haynes & L. R. Gannon (Eds.), *Psychosomatic disorders: A psychophysiological approach to etiology and treatment*. New York: Praeger.

Alexander, F. G., & Selesnick, S. T. (1966). *The history of psychiatry: An evaluation of psychiatric thought and practice from prehistoric times to the present*. New York: Harper & Row.

American Psychiatric Association. (1987). *Diagnostic and statistical manual of mental disorders* (3rd ed., rev.). Washington, DC: Author

Anderson, B. J., & Standley, K. (1977). Manual for naturalistic observation of the childbirth environment. *Catalog of Selected Documents in Psychology, 7*, 6.

Angle, H. V. (1981). The interviewing computer: A technology for gathering comprehensive treatment information: *Behavior Research Methods and Instrumentation, 13*, 607–612.

Angle, H. V., Ellinwood, E. H., Hay, W. M., Johnson, T., & Hay, L. R. (1977). Computer-aided interviewing in comprehensive behavioral assessment. *Behavior Therapy, 8*, 747–754.

Angle, H. V., Hay, L. R., Hay, W. M., & Wellinwood, E. H. (1977). Computer assisted behavioral assessment. In J. D. Cone & R. P. Hawkins (Eds.), *Behavioral assessment: New directions in clinical psychology*. New York: Brunner/Mazel.

Anisman, H., & LaPierre, Y. (1982). Neurochemical aspects of stress and depression: Formulations and caveats. In R. W. J. Neufeld (Ed.), *Psychological stress and psychopathology*. New York: McGraw-Hill.

Arkowitz, H., Lichtenstein, E., McGovern, K., & Hines, P. (1975). The assessment of social competency in males. *Behavior Therapy, 6*, 3–14.

Asterita, M. F. (1985). *The physiology of stress*. New York: Human Sciences Press.

Bachrach, A. J. (Ed.). (1962). *Experimental foundations of clinical psychology*. New York: Basic Books.

Baer, D. M. (1977). Perhaps it is better not to know. *Journal of Applied Behavior Analysis, 10*, 167–172.

Baer, D. M. (1986). Advances and gaps in a behavioral methodology of pediatric medicine. In N. A. Krasnegor, J. D. Arasteh, & M. F. Cataldo (Eds.), *Child health behavior: A behavioral pediatrics perspective* (pp. 54–69). New York: Wiley.

Bandura, A. (1969). *Principles of behavior modification*. New York: Holt, Rinehart, and Winston.

Bandura, A. (1981). In search of pure unidirectional determinants. *Behavior Therapy, 12,* 315–328.

Barlow, D. H. (1980). Behavior therapy: The next decade. *Behavior Therapy, 11,* 315–328.

Barlow, D. H. (1981). *Behavioral assessment of adult disorders*. New York: Guilford Press.

Barrera, M., Jr., & Rosen, G. M. (1977). Detrimental effects of a self-reward contracting program on subjects' involvement in self-administered desensitization. *Journal of Consulting and Clinical Psychology, 45,* 1180–1181.

Barrett, B. H., Johnston, J. M., & Pennypacker, H. S. (1986). Behavior: Its units, dimensions, and measurement. In R. O. Nelson & S. C. Hayes (Eds.), *Conceptual foundations of behavioral assessment* (pp. 156–200). New York: Guilford Press.

Barrios, B. A. (1988). On the changing nature of behavioral assessment. In A. S. Bellack & M. Hersen (Eds.), *Behavioral assessment. A practical handbook* (3rd ed.). (pp. 3–41). Elmsford, NY: Pergamon Press.

Bassett, J. E., & Blanchard, E. B. (1977). The effect of the absence of close supervision on the use of response cost in a prison token economy. *Journal of Applied Behavior Analysis, 10,* 375–379.

Baum, C. G., Forehand, R., & Zegoib, L. E. (1979). A review of observer reactivity in adult-child interactions. *Journal of Behavioral Assessment, 1,* 167–177.

Behavioral assessment and DSM-III-R. (1988). *Behavioral Assessment, 10,* 43–121.

Beiman, J., Graham, L. E., & Ciminero, A. R. (1978). Self-control progressive relaxation training as an alternative nonpharmacological treatment for essential hypertension: Therapeutic effects in the natural environment. *Behavior Research and Therapy, 16,* 371–375.

Bellack, A. S. (1979). A critical appraisal of strategies for assessing social skill. *Behavioral Assessment, 1,* 157–176.

Bellack, A. S., & Hersen, M. (Eds.). (1984). *Research methods in clinical psychology*. Elmsford, NY: Pergamon Press.

Bellack, A. S., & Hersen, M. (Eds.). (1988a). *Behavioral assessment. A practical handbook*. (3rd ed.). Elmsford, NY: Pergamon Press.

Bellack, A. S., & Hersen, M. (1988b). Future directions of behavioral assessment. In Bellack, A. S. & Hersen, M. (Eds.). *Behavioral assessment. A practical handbook* (3rd ed.). (pp. 610–615). Elmsford, NY: Pergamon Press.

Bellack, A. S., Hersen, M., & Lamparski, D. (1979). Role-play tests for assessing social skill: Are they valid? Are they useful? *Journal of Consulting and Clinical Psychology, 47,* 335–342.

Bernard, M. E., Dennehy, S., & Keefauver, L. W. (1981). Behavioral treatment of excessive coffee and tea drinking: A case study and partial replication. *Behavior Therapy, 12,* 543–548.

Bernstein, D. A. (1973). Situational factors in behavioral fear assessment: A progress report. *Behavior Therapy, 4,* 41–48.

Bernstein, D. A., Borkovec, T. D. & Coles, M. G. H. (1986). Assessment of anxiety. In A. R. Ciminero, C. S. Calhoun, & H. E. Adams (Eds.), *Handbook of behavioral assessment* (2nd ed.) (pp 353–403). New York: Wiley.

Biever, J., & Merluzzi, T. V. (1987). Role-playing procedures for the behavioral assessment of social skill: A validity study. *Behavioral Assessment, 9,* 361–377.

Billings, A. G., & Moos, R. H. (1981). The role of coping responses and social resources in attenuating the impact of stressful life events. *Journal of Behavioral Medicine, 4,* 139–157.

Billings, A. G., & Moos, R. H. (1982). Psychosocial theory and research on depression: An integrative framework and review. *Clinical Psychology Review, 2,* 213–237.

Billingsley, F., White, O. R., & Munson, R. (1980). Procedural reliability: A rationale and an example. *Behavioral assessment, 2,* 229–241.

Blanchard, E. B. (1981). Behavioral assessment of psychophysiologic disorders. In D. H. Barlow (Ed.), *Behavioral assessment of adult disorders*. New York: Guilford Press.

Blanchard, E., Andrasik, F., Arena, J. R., Neff, D. R., Saunders, N. L., Jurish, S. E., Teders, S. J., & Rodichok, L. D. (1983). Psychophysiological responses as predictors of response to behavioral treatment of chronic headache. *Behavior Therapy, 14,* 357–575.

Boll, T. J. (1981). Assessment of neuropsychological disorders. In D. H. Barlow (Ed.), *Behavioral assessment of adult disorders*. New York: Guilford Press.

Bootzin, R. R., & Engle-Friedman, M. (1981). The assessment of insomnia. *Behavioral assessment, 3,* 107–126.

Borkovec, T. D., Weerts, T. C., & Bernstein, D. A. (1977). Assessment of anxiety. In A. R. Ciminero, K. S. Calhoun, & H. E. Adams (Eds.), *Handbook of behavioral assessment*. New York: Wiley.

Bornstein, P. H., Hamilton, S. B., & Bornstein, M. T. (1986). Self-monitoring procedures. In A. R. Ciminero, C. S. Calhoun, & H. E. Adams (Eds.), *Handbook of behavioral assessment* (pp 176–222). New York: Wiley.

Broden, M., Hall, R. F., & Mitts, B. (1971). The effect of self-recording on the classroom behavior of two eighth-grade students. *Journal of Applied Behavior Analysis, 4,* 191–199.

Brown, R. A., Lichtenstein, E., McIntyre, K. O., & Harrington-Kostur, J. (1984). Effects of nicotine fading and relapse prevention on smoking cessation. *Journal of Consulting and Clinical Psychology, 52,* 307–308.

Brownell, K. D. (1981). Assessment of eating disorders. In D. H. Barlow (Ed.), *Behavioral assessment of adult disorders*. New York: Guilford Press.

Budd, K. S., Riner, L. S., & Brockman, M. P. (1983). A structured observation system for clinical evaluation of parent training. *Behavioral Assessment, 5,* 373–393.

Burish, T. G., Carey, M. P., Krozely, M. G., & Greco, F. A. (1987). Conditioned side effects induced by cancer chemotherapy: Prevention through behavioral treatment. *Journal of Consulting and Clinical Psychology, 55,* 42–48.

Burnett, K. F., Taylor, C. B., Thoresen, C. E., Rosekind, M. R., Miles, L. E., & DeBusk, R. F. (1985). Toward computerized scoring of sleep using ambulatory recordings of heart rate and physical activity. *Behavioral Assessment, 7,* 261–271.

Callahan, E. J., Brasted, W. S., & Hamilton, S. A. (1987). Assessment of parent-child interaction in the neonatal intensive care unit. *Behavioral Assessment, 9,* 333–347.

Carr, A. F., Schnell, J. F., & Kirchner, R. E., Jr. (1980). Police crackdowns and slowdowns: A naturalistic evaluation of changes in police traffic enforcement. *Behavioral Assessment, 2,* 33–41.

Carson, T. P. (1986). Assessment of depression. In A. R. Ciminero, K. S. Calhoun, & H. E. Adams (Eds.), *Handbook of behavioral assessment* (pp. 404–445). New York: Wiley.

Carter, R. D., & Thomas, E. J. (1973). Modification of problematic marital communication using corrective feedback and instruction. *Behavior Therapy, 4,* 100–109.

Castles, E. E., & Glass, C. R. (1986). Empirical generation of measures of social competence for mentally retarded adults. *Behavioral Assessment, 8,* 319–330.

Chapman, C. R., & Wyckoff, M. (1981). The problem of pain: A psychobiological perspective. In S. N. Haynes & L. R. Gannon (Eds.), *Psychosomatic disorders: A psychophysiological approach to etiology and treatment*. New York: Praeger.

Christensen, A., Sullaway, M., & King, C. E. (1983). Systematic error in behavioral reports of dyadic interaction: Egocentric bias and content effects. *Behavioral Assessment, 5,* 129–140.

Ciminero, A. R. (1986). Behavioral assessment: An overview. In A. R. Ciminero, K. S. Calhoun, & H. E. Adams (Eds.), *Handbook of behavior assessment* (2nd ed.) (pp. 446–495). New York: Wiley.

Ciminero, A. R., Calhoun, K. S., & Adams, H. E. (Eds.). (1977). *Handbook of behavioral assessment*. New York: Wiley.

Ciminero, A. R., Calhoun, K. S., & Adams, H. E. (Eds.). (1986). *Handbook of behavioral assessment*. New York: Wiley.

Coates, T. J., & Thoresen, C. E. (1978). Using generalizability theory in behavioral observation. *Behavior Therapy, 9,* 157–162.

Cone, J. D. (1986). Idiographic, nomothetic and related perspectives in behavioral assessment. In R. O. Nelson & S. C. Hayes (Eds.), *Conceptual foundations of behavioral assessment,* (pp. 111–128). New York: Guilford.

Cone, J. D. (1988). Psychometric considerations and the multiple models of behavioral assessment. In A. S. Bellack & M. Hersen (Eds.), *Behavioral assessment: A practical handbook* (3rd ed.). (pp. 42–66). Elmsford, NY: Pergamon Press.

Cone, J. D., & Hawkins, R. P. (Eds.). (1977). *Behavioral assessment: New directions in clinical psychology*. New York: Brunner/Mazel.

Conger, A. J., Wallander, J. L., Mariotto, M. J., & Ward, D. (1980). Peer judgments of heterosexual-social anxiety and skill: What do they pay attention to anyhow? *Behavioral Assessment, 2,* 243–259.

Conger, J. C., & Keane, S. P. (1981). Social skills intervention in the treatment of isolated or withdrawn children. *Psychological Bulletin, 90,* 478–495.

Cooke, C. J., & Meyers, A. (1980). The role of predictor variables in the behavioral treatment of obesity. *Behavioral assessment, 2,* 59–69.

Correa, E. I., & Sutker, P. B. (1986). Assessment of alcohol and drug behaviors. In A. R. Ciminero,

K. S. Calhoun, & H. E. Adams (Eds.), *Handbook of behavioral assessment* (2nd ed.) (pp 446–495). New York: Wiley.

Cox, D. J. (1977). Menstrual symptom questionnaire: Further psychometric evaluation. *Behaviour Research and Therapy, 15,* 506–508.

Cromwell, R. E., & Peterson, G. W. (1981). Multisystem-multimethod assessment: A framework. In E. E. Filsinger & R. A. Lewis (Eds.), *Assessing marriage: New behavioral approaches.* Beverly Hills, CA: Sage Publications.

Cronbach, L. J., Gleser, C. C., Nanda, H., & Rajaratman, N. (1972). *The dependability of behavioral measurements: Theory of generalizability for scores and profiles.* New York: Wiley.

Curran, J. P., Monti, P. M., Corriveau, D. P., Hay, L. R., Hagerman, S., Zwick, W. R., & Farrell, A. D. (1980). The generalizability of a procedure for assessing social skills and social anxiety in a psychiatric population. *Behavioral Assessment, 2,* 389–401.

Curran, J. P., & Wessberg, H. W. (1981). Assessment of social inadequacy. In D. H. Barlow (Ed.), *Behavioral assessment of adult disorders.* New York: Guilford Press.

Cuvo, A. J., Leaf, R. B., & Borakove, L. A. (1978). Teaching janitorial skills to the mentally retarded: Acquisition, generalization, and maintenance. *Journal of Applied Behavior Analysis, 11,* 345–355.

Davidson, P. O., & Davison, S. M. (1980). *Behavioral medicine: Changing health lifestyles.* New York: Brunner/Mazel.

De Armas, A., & Brigham, T. A. (1986). Moderated role-play validity: Do some subjects role play more naturally than others? *Behavioral Assessment, 8,* 341–347.

Donovan, D. M., & Marlatt, G. A. (1988). *Assessment of addictive disorders.* New York: Guilford Press.

Dorsey, B. L., Nelson, R. O., & Hayes, S. C. (1986). The effects of code complexity and of behavioral frequency on observer accuracy and interobserver agreement. *Behavioral Assessment, 8,* 349–363.

Dow, M. G., Biglan, A., & Glaser, S. R. (1985). Multimethod assessment of socially anxious and socially nonanxious women. *Behavioral Assessment, 7,* 273–282.

Doyne, E. J., Chambless, D. L., & Buetler, L. E. (1983). Aerobic exercise as a treatment for depression in women. *Behavior Therapy, 14,* 434–440.

Edgington, E. S. (1982). Nonparametric tests for single-subject multiple schedule experiments. *Behavioral Assessment, 4,* 83–91.

Edginton, E. S. (1984). Statistics and single case analysis. In M. Hersen, R. M. Eisler, & P. M. Miller (Eds.), *Progress in behavior modification:* (Vol. 16, pp. 83–119). New York: Academic Press.

Edinberg, M. A., Karoly, P., & Gleser, G. C. (1977). Assessing assertion in the elderly: An application of the behavior analytic model of competence. *Journal of Clinical Psychology, 33,* 869–874.

Ellis, A., & Bernard, M. E. (1985). *Clinical applications of rational-emotive therapy.* New York: Plenum Press.

Emmelkamp, P. M. G. (1981). The current and future status of clinical research. *Behavioral Assessment, 3,* 249–253.

Emmelkamp, P. M. G., & Kwee, K. C. (1977). Obsessional ruminations: A comparison between thought stopping and prolonged exposure in imagination. *Behavior Research and Therapy, 15,* 441–444.

Emmelkamp, P. M. (1986). Behavior therapy with adults. In S. L. Garfield & A. E. Bergin (Eds.), *Handbook of psychotherapy and behavior change* (3rd ed.). New York: Wiley.

Epstein, L. H., & Martin, J. E. (1977). Compliance and side effects of weight regulation groups. *Behavior Modification, 1,* 551–558.

Evans, I. M. (1985). Building systems models as a strategy for target behavior selection in clinical assessment. *Behavioral Assessment, 7,* 21–32.

Eysenck, H. J. (1986). A critique of contemporary classification and diagnosis. In T. Millon & G. L. Klerman (Eds.), *Contemporary directions in psychopathology: Toward the DSM-IV* (pp 73–98). New York: Guilford Press.

Eysenck, H. J., & Martin, I. (1987). *Theoretical foundations of behavior therapy.* New York: Plenum Press.

Fabray, P. L., & Reid, D. H. (1978). Teaching foster grandparents to train severely handicapped persons. *Journal of Applied Behavior Analysis, 11,* 111–123.

Fagot, B. I. (1978). Reinforcing contingencies for sex-role behaviors: Effect of experience with children. *Child Development, 49,* 30–36.

Fairbank, J. A., DeGood, D. E., & Jenkins, C. W. (1981). Behavioral treatment of a persistent post-traumatic startle response. *Journal of Behavior Therapy and Experimental Psychiatry, 12,* 321–324.

Felton, J. L., & Nelson, R. O. (1984). Inter-assessor

agreement on hypothesized controlling variables and treatment proposals. *Behavioral Assessment, 6,* 199–208.

Fiske, D. W. (1978). *Strategies for personality research: The observation versus interpretation of behavior.* San Francisco: Jossey-Bass.

Follingstad, D. R., & Haynes, S. N. (1981). Naturalistic observation in assessment of behavioral marital therapy. *Psychological Reports, 49,* 471–479.

Foote, W. E., & Laws, D. R. (1981). A daily alternation program for organismic reconditioning with a pedophile. *Journal of Behavior Therapy and Experimental Psychiatry, 12,* 267–273.

Fordyce, W. E., & Laws, D. R. (1976). *Behavioral methods for chronic pain and illness.* Saint Louis: C. V. Mosby.

Forehand, R., & Atkeson, B. M. (1977). Generality of treatment effects with parents as therapists: A review of assessment and implementation procedures. *Behavior Therapy, 8,* 575–593.

Foster, S. L., Bell-Dolan, D. J., & Burge, D. A. (1988). Behavioral observation. In A. S. Bellack & M. Hersen (Eds.), *Behavioral assessment. A practical handbook* (3rd ed.) (pp. 119–160). Elmsford, NY: Pergamon Press.

Foster, S. L., & Cone, J. D. (1980). Current issues in direct observation. *Behavioral Assessment, 2,* 313–338.

Foster, S. L., & Cone, J. D. (1986). Design and use of direct observation systems. In A. R. Ciminero, C. S. Calhoun, & H. E. Adams (Eds.), *Handbook of behavioral assessment* (2nd ed.) (pp 253–324). New York: Wiley.

Foster, S. L., DeLawyer, D. D., & Guevremont, D. C. (1986). A critical incidents analysis of liked and disliked peer behaviors and their situational parameters in childhood and adolescence. *Behavioral Assessment, 8,* 115–133.

Foxx, R. M., & Hake, D. R. (1977). Gasoline conservation: A procedure for measuring and reducing the driving of college students. *Journal of Applied Behavior Analysis, 10,* 61–74.

Foy, D. W., Rychtarik, R. G., & Prue, D. M. (1988). Assessment of appetitive disorders. In A. S. Bellack, & M. Hersen (Eds.). *Behavioral assessment: A practical handbook* (3rd ed.) (pp. 542–577). Elmsford, NY: Pergamon Press.

Fremouw, W. J., & Zitter, R. E. (1978). A comparison of skills training and cognitive restructuring—relaxation for the treatment of speech anxiety. *Behavior Therapy, 9,* 248–259.

Galassi, M. D., & Galassi, J. P. (1980). Similarities and differences between two assertion measures: Factor analysis of college self-expression scale and the Rathus assertiveness inventory. *Behavioral Assessment, 2,* 43–57.

Gannon, L. R., & Haynes, S. N. (1987). Cognitive-physiological discordance as an etiological factor in psychophysiologic disorders. *Advances in Behavior Research and Therapy, 8,* 223–236.

Gardner, W., Hartmann, D. P., & Mitchell, C. (1982). The effects of serial dependence on the use of X2 for analyzing sequential data in dyadic interactions. *Behavioral Assessment, 4,* 75–82.

Gatchel, R. J., Korman, M. N., Weis, C. B., Smith, D., & Clark, L. (1978). A multiple-response evaluation of EMG biofeedback performance during training and stress-induction conditions. *Psychophysiology, 15,* 253–258.

Geer, J. H. (1965). The development of a scale to measure fear. *Behaviour Research and Therapy, 3,* 45–53.

Glasglow, R. E., Klesges, R. C., Godding, P. R., & Gegelman, R. (1983). Controlled smoking, with or without carbon monoxide feedback, as an alternative for chronic smokers. *Behavior Therapy, 14,* 386–397.

Glass, G. V., & Kliegl, R. M. (1983). An apology for research integration in the study of psychotherapy. *Journal of Consulting, and Clinical Psychology, 51,* 28–41.

Glass, G. V., Wilson, V., & Gottman, J. M. (1975). Design and analysis of time-series experiments. Boulder, CO: Colorado Associated University Press.

Goldfried, M. R. (1982). Behavioral assessment, an overview. In A. S. Bellack, M. Hersen, & A. E. Kazdin (Eds.). *International handbook of behavior modification and therapy* (pp. 81–107). New York: Plenum Press.

Goldfried, M. R., Linehan, M. M., & Smith, J. L. (1978). Reduction of test anxiety through cognitive restructuring. *Journal of Consulting and Clinical Psychology, 46,* 32–39.

Gorsuch, R. L. (1983). Three methods for analyzing limited time series (N of 1) data. *Behavioral Assessment, 5,* 141–145.

Gottman, J. M. (1979). *Marital interaction: Experimental investigation.* New York: Academic Press.

Gottman, J. M. (1985). Observational measures of behavior therapy outcome: A reply to Jacobson. *Behavioral Assessment, 7,* 317–322.

Gottman, J. M., & Levenson, R. W. (1986). Assessing the role of emotion in marriage. *Behavioral Assessment, 8,* 31–48.

Green, L. (1978). Temporal and stimulus factors in

self monitoring by obese persons. *Behavior Therapy, 9,* 328–341.

Greenwald, D. P. (1977). The behavioral assessment of differences in social skill and social anxiety for female college students. *Behavior Therapy, 8,* 925–237.

Hartmann, D. P., Gottman, J. M., Jones, R. R., Gardner, W., Kazdin, A. E., & Vaught, R. S. (1980). Interrupted time series analysis and its application to behavioral data. *Journal of Applied Behavior Analysis, 13,* 543–559.

Hartmann, D. P., Roper, B. L., & Bradford, D. C. (1979). Some relationships between behavioral and traditional assessment. *Journal of Behavior Assessment, 1,* 3–21.

Hartmann, D. P., & Wood, D. D. (1982). Observation methods. In A. S. Bellack, M. Hersen, & A. E. Kazdin (Eds.), *International handbook of behavior modification and therapy.* New York: Plenum Press.

Hawkins, R. P. (1979). The functions of assessment: Implications for selection and development of devices for assessing repertoires in clinical educational and other settings. *Journal of Behavioral Assessment, 12,* 501–516.

Hawkins, R. P. (1986). Selection of target behaviors. In R. O. Nelson & S. C. Hayes (Eds.), *Conceptual foundations of behavioral assessment* (pp. 331–383). New York: Guilford Press.

Hay, L. R. (1982). Teaching behavioral assessment to clinical psychology students. *Behavioral Assessment, 4,* 35–40.

Hay, W. M., Hay, L. R., Angle, H. V., & Nelson, R. O. (1979). The reliability of problem identification in the behavioral interview. *Behavioral Assessment, 1,* 107–118.

Hayes, S. L., Nelson, R. O., & Jarret, R. B. (1987). The treatment utility of assessment: A functional approach to evaluate assessment quality. *American Psychologist, 42,* 963–974.

Haynes, S. N. (1978). *Principles of behavioral assessment.* New York: Gardner Press.

Haynes, S. N. (1979). Behavioral variance, individual differences and trait theory in a behavioral construct system: A reappraisal. *Behavioral Assessment, 1,* 41–49.

Haynes, S. N. (1981). Muscle contraction headache. In S. N. Haynes & L. R. Gannon (Eds.), *Psychosomatic disorders: A psychophysiological approach to etiology and treatment.* New York: Praeger.

Haynes, S. N. (1984a). Behavioral assessment. In M. Hersen, A. E. Kazdin, & A. S. Bellack (Eds.), *The Clinical psychology handbook.* Elmsford, NY: Pergamon Press.

Haynes, S. N. (1984b). Behavioral assessment of adults. In G. Goldstein & M. Hersen (Eds.), *Handbook of psychological assessment.* Elmsford, NY: Pergamon Press.

Haynes, S. N. (1986a). A behavioral model of paranoid behaviors. *Behavior Therapy, 17,* 266–287.

Haynes, S. N. (1986b). The design of intervention programs. In R. O. Nelson & S. Hayes (Eds.), *Conceptual foundations of behavioral assessment* (pp. 386–429). New York: Guilford Press.

Haynes, S. N. (1988). Causal models and the assessment-treatment relationship in behavior therapy. *Journal of Psychopathology and Behavioral Assessment. 10,* 171–183.

Haynes, S. N. & Chavez, R. (1983). The interview in the assessment of marital distress. In E. E. Filsinger (Ed.), *A sourcebook of marriage and family assessment.* Beverly Hills, CA: Sage Publications.

Haynes, S. N., Falkin, S., & Sexton-Radek, K. (1989). Psychophysiological measurement in behavior therapy. In G. Turpin (Ed.), *Handbook of clinical psychophysiology.* London: Wiley.

Haynes, S. N., Follingstad, D. R., & Sullivan, J. C. (1979). Assessment of marital satisfaction and interaction. *Journal of Consulting and Clinical Psychology, 47,* 789–791.

Haynes, S. N., & Gannon, L. R. (1981). *Psychosomatic disorders: A psychophysiological approach to etiology and treatment.* New York: Praeger.

Haynes, S. N., & Horn, W. F. (1982). Reactive effects of behavioral observation. *Behavioral Assessment, 4,* 369–385.

Haynes, S. N., & Jensen, B. J. (1979). The interview as a behavioral assessment instrument. *Behavioral Assessment, 1,* 97–106.

Haynes, S. N., Jensen, B. J., Wise, E., & Sherman, D. (1981). The marital intake interview: A multimethod criterion validity assessment. *Journal of Consulting and Clinical Psychology, 43,* 379–387.

Haynes, S. N., & O'Brien, W. (1988). The Gordian Knot of DSM-III-R use: Integrating principles of behavior classification and complex causal models. *Behavioral Assessment 10,* 95–105.

Haynes, S. N., & O'Brien, W. O. (in press). The functional analysis in behavioral assessment. *Clinical Psychology Review.*

Haynes, S. N., & Wilson, C. C. (1979). *Behavioral assessment.* San Francisco: Jossey-Bass.

Haynes, S. N., Wilson, C. C., & Britton, B. T. (1979). Behavioral intervention with atopic dermatitis. *Biofeedback and Self Regulation, 4,* 195–209.

Hazaleus, S. L., & Deffenbacher, J. L. (1986). Relaxation and cognitive treatments of anger. *Journal of Consulting and Clinical Psychology, 54,* 222–226.

Henson, D. E., Rubin, H. B., & Henson, C. (1979). Consistency of the labial temperature change of human female eroticism. *Behaviour Research and Therapy, 17,* 226–240.

Hersen, M., & Barlow, D. H. (1976). *Single case experimental designs: Strategies for studying behavior change.* Elmsford, NY: Pergamon Press.

Hersen M., & Bellack, A. S. (Eds.). (1981). *Behavioral assessment: A practical handbook* (2nd ed.). Elmsford, NY: Pergamon Press.

Hersen, M., & Bellack, A. S. (1988). DSM-III and behavioral assessment. In A. S. Bellack, & M. Hersen (Eds.). *Behavioral assessment: A practical handbook* (3rd ed.) (pp. 67–84). Elmsford, NY: Pergamon Press.

Hersen, M., Kazdin, A. E., & Bellack, A. S. (Eds.). (1983). *The clinical psychology handbook.* Elmsford, NY: Pergamon Press.

Hodgson, R., & Rachman, S. (1977). Obsessional-compulsive complaints. *Behaviour Research and Therapy, 15,* 389–395.

Holden, A. E., & Barlow, D. H. (1986). Heart rate and heart rate variability recorded in vivo in agoraphobics and nonphobics. *Behavior Therapy, 17,* 26–42.

Honig, W. K. (1966). *Operant behavior: Areas of research and application.* New York: Appleton-Century-Crofts.

Hops, H., Biglan, A., Sherman, L., Arthur, J., Friedman, L., & Osteen, V. (1987). Home observations of family interactions of depressed women. *Journal of Consulting and Clinical Psychology, 55,* 341–346.

Hops, H., Weissman, W., Biglan, A., Thompson, R., Faller, C., & Severson, H. H. (1986). A taped situation test of cigarette refusal skill among adolescents. *Behavioral Assessment, 8,* 145–154.

Horne, G. P., Yang, M. C. K., & Ware, W. B. (1982). Time series analysis for single-subject designs. *Psychological Bulletin, 91,* 178–189.

Hughes, H. M., & Haynes, S. N. (1978). Structured laboratory observation in the behavioral assessment of parent-child interactions: A methodological critique. *Behavior Therapy, 9,* 428–447.

Huitema, B. E. (1985). Autocorrelation in applied behavior analysis: A myth. *Behavioral Assessment, 7,* 107–118.

Hutt, S. J., & Hutt, C. (1970). *Direct observation and measurement of behavior.* Springfield, IL: Charles C. Thomas.

Jacobson, N. S. (1985). The uses versus abuses of observational measures. *Behavioral Assessment, 7,* 323–330.

Jacobson, N. S., Elwood, R. W., & Dallas, M. (1981). Assessment of marital dysfunction. In D. H. Barlow (Ed.), *Behavioral assessment of adult disorders.* New York: Guilford Press.

Jacobson, N. S., & Margolin, G. (1979). *Marital therapy: Strategies based on social learning and behavior exchange principles.* New York: Guilford Press.

James, J. E. (1981). Behavioral self-control of stuttering using time-out from speaking. *Journal of Applied Behavior Analysis, 14,* 25–37.

Jensen, B. J., & Haynes, S. N. (1986). Self-report questionnaires. In A. R. Ciminero, C. S. Calhoun, & H. E. Adams (Eds.), *Handbook of behavioral assessment* (2nd ed.) (pp. 150–175). New York: Wiley.

Johnson, W. G., Wildman, H. E., & O'Brien, T. (1980). The assessment of program adherence: The achilles' heel of behavioral weight reduction? *Behavioral Assessment, 2,* 291–301.

Johnston, J. M., & Pennypacker, H. S. (1980). *Strategies and tactics of human behavioral research.* Hillsdale, NJ: Lawrence Erlbaum.

Jones, R. R. (1979). Program evaluation design issues. *Behavioral Assessment, 1,* 51–56.

Kallman, W. M., & Feuerstein, M. J. (1986). Psychophysiological procedures. In A. R. Ciminero, C. S. Calhoun, & H. E. Adams (Eds.), *Handbook of behavioral assessment* (2nd ed.) (pp. 325–350). New York: Wiley.

Kaloupek, D. B., & Levis, D. J. (1980). The relationship between stimulus specificity and self-report indices in assessing fear of heterosexual social interaction: A test of the unitary response hypothesis. *Behavioral Assessment, 2,* 267–281.

Kanfer, F. H. (1985). Target selection for clinical change programs. *Behavioral Assessment, 7,* 7–20.

Kanfer, F., & Phillips, J. S. (1970). *Learning foundations of behavior therapy.* New York: Wiley.

Karoly, P. (1985). The logic and character of assessment in health psychology: Perspectives and possibilities. In P. Karoly (Ed.), *Measurement strategies in health psychology* (pp. 3–45). New York: Wiley.

Katz, E. R., Varni, J. W., & Jay, S. M. (1984). Behavioral assessment and management of pediatric pain. In M. Hersen, R. M. Eisler, & P. M. Miller (Eds.), *Progress in behavior modification* (Vol. 18, pp. 164–194). New York: Academic Press.

Kazdin, A. E. (1977). Assessing the clinical and applied importance of behavior change through social validation. *Behavior Modification, 1,* 427–452.

Kazdin, A. E. (19/8). *History of behavior modification.* Baltimore: University Park Press.

Kazdin, A. E. (1979). Situational specificity: The two edged word of behavioral assessment. *Behavioral Assessment, 1,* 57–75.

Kazdin, A. E. (1982a). Symptom substitution, generalization, and response covariation: Implications for psychotherapy outcome. *Psychological Bulletin, 91,* 349–365.

Kazdin, A. E. (1982b). *Single-case research designs: Methods for clinical and applied settings.* New York: Oxford University Press.

Kazdin, A. E. (1984). *Behavior modification in applied settings.* Homewood, IL: Dorsey Press.

Kazdin, A. E., Esveldt-Dawson, K., & Matson, J. L. (1983). The effects of instructional set on social skills performance among psychiatric inpatient children. *Behavior Therapy, 14,* 413–423.

Keane, T. M., Fairbanks, J. A., Caddell, J. M., Zimering, R. T., & Bender, M. E. (1985). A behavioral approach to assessing and treating posttraumatic stress disorder in Vietnam veterans. In C. R. Figley (Ed.), *Trauma and its wake* (pp. 257–294). New York: Brunner/Mazel.

Keefe, F. J., & Blumenthal, J. A. (1982). *Assessment strategies in behavioral medicine.* New York: Grune & Stratton.

Keefe, F. J., Kopel, S. A., & Gordon, S. B. (1978). *A practical guide to behavioral assessment.* New York: Springer.

Keefe, F. J., Surwit, R. S., & Pilon, R. N. (1981). Collagen vascular disease: Can behavior therapy help? *Journal of Behavior Therapy and Experimental Psychiatry, 12,* 171–175.

Kendall, P. C., & Hollon, S. D. (1981). *Assessment strategies for cognitive-behavioral interventions.* New York: Academic Press.

Kleinmuntz, B. (1972). *Computer in personality assessment.* Morristown, NJ: General Learning Press.

Kling, J. W., & Riggs, L. A. (1971). *Experimental Psychology.* New York: Holt, Rinehart, & Winston.

Korchin, S. J., & Schulberg, D. (1981). The future of clinical assessment. *American Psychologist, 36,* 1147–1158.

Kratochwill, T. R. (Ed.). (1978). *Single subject research: Strategies for evaluating change.* New York: Academic Press.

Kratochwill, T. R., & Piersel, W. C. (1983). Time-series research: Contributions to empirical clinical practice. *Behavioral Assessment, 5,* 165–176.

Lazarus, A. A. (1976). *Multimodal behavior therapy.* New York: Springer.

Lebow, J. (1982). Consumer satisfaction with mental health treatment. *Psychological Bulletin, 91,* 244–259.

Lewinsohn, P. M. (1975). The behavioral study and treatment of depression. In M. Hersen, R. M. Eisler, & P. M. Miller (Eds.), *Progress in behavior modification* (Vol. 1). New York: Academic Press.

Lewinsohn, P. M., & Lee, W. M. (1981). Assessment of affective disorders. In D. H. Barlow (Ed.), *Behavioral assessment of adult disorders,* New York: Guilford Press.

Lindsley, O. R. (1960). Characteristics of the behavior of chronic psychotics as revealed by free-operant conditioning methods. *Disease of the Nervous System, 21,* 66–78.

Linehan, M. M. (1977). Issues in behavioral interviewing. In J. D. Cone & R. P. Hawkins (Eds.), *Behavioral assessment: New directions in clinical psychology.* New York: Brunner/Mazel.

Linehan, M. M. (1980). Content validity: Its relevance to behavioral assessment. *Behavioral Assessment, 2,* 147–159.

Lloyd, M. E. (1983). Selecting systems to measure client outcome in human service agencies. *Behavioral Assessment, 5,* 55–70.

LoPiccolo, J., & Steger, J. C. (1974). The sexual interaction inventory: A new instrument for assessment of sexual dysfunction. *Archives of Sexual Behavior, 3,* 585–595.

Lubar, J. R., & Shouse, M. N. (1977). Use of biofeedback in the treatment of seizure disorders and hyperactivity. In B. Lahey & A. E. Kazdin (Eds.), *Advances in clinical child psychology.* New York: Plenum Press.

Mace, F. C., & Knight, D. (1986). Functional analysis and treatment of severe pica. *Journal of Applied Behavior Analysis, 19,* 411–416.

Maher, B. (1966). *Introduction to research in psychopathology.* New York: McGraw-Hill.

Maher, B. (1981). Psychological intervention in hemodialysis. Invited address at Southern Illinois University, Carbondale, Illinois.

Marascuilo, L. A., & Busk, P. L. (1988). Combining statistics for multile-baseline AB replicated ABAB designs across subjects. *Behavioral Assessment, 10,* 1–28.

Margolin, G. (1981). Practical applications of behavioral marital assessment. In E. E. Filsinger & R. A. Lewis (Eds.), *Assessing marriage: New behavioral approaches.* Beverly Hills, CA: Sage Publications.

Margolin, G. (1983). An international model for the behavioral assessment of marital relationships. *Behavioral Assessment, 5,* 103–127.

Margolin, G., Hattem, D., John, R. S., & Yost, K. (1985). Perceptual agreement between spouses and outside observers when coding themselves and a stranger dyad. *Behavioral Assessment, 7,* 235–247.

Margolin, G., Michelli, J., & Jacobson, N. (1988). Assessment of marital dysfunction. In A. S. Bellack & M. Hersen (Eds.), *Behavioral assessment, A practical handbook* (3rd ed.) (pp. 441–489). Elmsford, NY: Pergamon Press.

Markman, H. J., Floyd, F. J., Stanley, S. M., & Storaasli, R. D. (1988). Prevention of marital distress: A longitudinal investigation. *Journal of Consulting and Clinical Psychology, 56,* 210–217.

Martin, I., & Venables, P. H. (Eds.). (1980). *Techniques in psychophysiology.* New York: Wiley.

Martin, J. E., & Fredericksen, L. W. (1980). Self-tracking of carbon monoxide levels by smokers. *Behavior Therapy, 11,* 577–587.

Mash, E. J., (1979). What is behavioral assessment? *Behavioral assessment of childhood disorders.* New York: Guilford Press.

Mash, E. J., & Terdal, L. G. (1981). *Behavioral assessment of childhood disorders.* New York: Guilford Press.

Matarazzo, J. D., & Wiens, A. N. (1972). *The interview: Research on its anatomy and structure.* Chicago, IL: Aldine-Atherton.

Matson, J. L., & Stephens, R. M. (1977). Overcorrection of aggressive behavior in a chronic psychiatric patient. *Behavior Modification, 1,* 559–564.

Mattick, R. P., & Peters, L. (1988). Treatment of severe social phobia: Effects of guided exposure with and without cognitive restructuring. *Journal of Consulting and Clinical Psychology, 56,* 251–260.

Mavissakalian, M. G., & Barlow, D. H. (1981). Assessment of obsessive-compulsive disorders. In D. H. Barlow (Ed.), *Behavioral assessment of adult disorders.* New York: Guilford Press.

Merluzzi, T. V., Glass, C. R., & Genest, M. (1981). *Cognitive Assessment.* New York: Guilford Press.

McCann, B. S. (1987). The behavioral management of hypertension. In M. Hersen, R. M. Eisler, & P. M. Miller (Eds.), *Progress in behavior modification* (Vol. 21, pp. 191–229). Newbury Park: Sage.

McConagy, N. (1988). Sexual dysfunction and deviation. In A. S. Bellack & M. Hersen, (Eds.). *Behavioral assessment: A practical handbook* (3rd ed.) (pp. 490–540). Elmsford, NY: Pergamon Press.

McFall, R. M. (1977). Behavioral training: A skill acquisition approach to clinical problems. In J. T. Spence, R. Carson, & J. Thibaut (Eds.), *Behavioral approaches to therapy* (pp 330–367). Morristown, NJ: General Learning Press.

McFall, R. M. (1982). A review and reformulation of the concept of social skills. *Behavioral Assessment, 4,* 1–33.

McFall, R. M. (1986). Theory and method in assessment: The vital link. *Behavioral Assessment, 8,* 3–10.

McFall, R. M. & McDonel, E. (1986). The continuing search for units of analysis in psychology: Beyond persons, situations and their interactions. In R. O. Nelson & S. C. Hayes (Eds.), *Conceptual foundations of behavioral assessment* (pp. 201–241). New York: Guilford Press.

McIntyre, T. J., Bornstein, P. H., Isaacs, C. D., Woody, D. J., Bornstein, M. T., Clucas, T. J., & Long, G. (1983). Naturalistic observation of conduct-disordered children: An archival analysis. *Behavior Therapy, 14,* 375–385.

Melamed, B. G., & Siegel, L. J. (1980). *Behavioral medicine: Practical applications in health care.* New York: Springer.

Merluzzi, T. V., & Biever, J. (1987). Role-playing procedures for the behavioral assessment of social skill: A validity study. *Behavioral Assessment, 9,* 361–377.

Merluzzi, T. V., Glass, C. R., & Genest, M. (1981). *Cognitive assessment.* New York: Guilford Press.

Messick, S. (1981). Constructs and their vicissitudes in educational and psychological measurement. *Psychological Bulletin, 89,* 575–588.

Michael, J. (1974). Statistical inference for individual organism research: Some reactions to a suggestion by Gentile, Roden, and Klein. *Journal of Applied Behavior Analysis, 7,* 627–628.

Michelson, L., & Mavissakalian, M. (1985). Psychophysiological outcome of behavioral and pharmacological treatments of agoraphobia. *Journal of*

Consulting and Clinical Psychology, 53, 229–236.

Miller, P. M. (1981). Assessment of alcohol abuse. In D. H. Barlow (Ed.), *Behavioral assessment of adult disorders.* New York: Guilford Press.

Mini-Series: The linkage between theory and assessment method. (1986). *Behavioral Assessment, 8,* 3–104.

Mischel, W. (1968). *Personality and assessment.* New York: Wiley.

Mischel, W. (1980). *Introduction to personality.* New York: Holt, Rinehart, & Winston.

Morey, L. C., Skinner, H. A., & Blashfield, R. K. (1986). Trends in the classification of abnormal behavior. In A. R. Ciminero, C. S. Calhoun, & H. E. Adams (Eds.), *Handbook of behavioral assessment* (2nd ed.). (pp. 47–78). New York: Wiley.

Morganstern, K. P. (1988). Behavioral interviewing. In A. S. Bellack & M. Hersen (Eds.). *Behavioral assessment: A practical handbook* (3rd ed.). (pp. 86–118). Elmsford, NY: Pergamon Press.

Morrell, E. M., King, A. C., & Martin, J. E. (1986). The validity of cardiac inpatient self-report of smoking. *Behavioral Assessment, 8,* 365–371.

Nay, W. F. (1979). *Multimethod clinical assessment.* New York: Gardner Press.

Nelson, R. O. (1977a). Methodological issues in assessment via self-monitoring. In J. D. Cone & R. P. Hawkins (Eds.), *Behavioral assessment: New directions in clinical psychology.* New York: Brunner/Mazel.

Nelson, R. O. (1977b). Assessment and therapeutic functions in self-monitoring. In M. Hersen, R. M. Eisler, & P. M. Miller (Eds.), *Progress in behavior modification* (Vol. 5). New York: Academic Press.

Nelson, R. O. (1980). The use of intelligence tests within behavioral assessment. *Behavioral Assessment, 2,* 417–423.

Nelson, R. O. (1983). Behavioral assessment: Past, present, and future. *Behavioral Assessment, 5,* 195–206.

Nelson, R. O., & Hayes, S. C. (1986). *Conceptual foundations of behavioral assessment.* New York: Guilford Press.

Nietzel, M. T., Bernstein, D. A., & Russell, R. L. (1988). Assessment of anxiety and fear. In A. S. Bellack & M. Hersen (Eds.), *Behavioral assessment: A practical handbook* (3rd ed.) (pp. 280–312). Elmsford, NY: Pergamon Press.

Nietzel, M. T., Winett, R. A., MacDonald, M. L., & Davidson, W. S. (1977). *Behavioral approaches to community psychology.* Elmsford, NY: Pergamon Press.

Notarius, C. I., Krokoff, L. J., & Markham, H. J. (1981). Analysis of observational data. In E. E. Filsinger & R. A. Lewis (Eds.), *Assessing marriage: New behavioral approaches.* Beverly Hills: Sage Publications.

Novaco, R. W. (1975). *Anger control: The development and evaluation of an experimental treatment.* Lexington, MA: Lexington Books.

O'Donnell, C. R. (1977). Behavior modification in community settings. In M. Hersen, R. M. Eisler, & P. M. Miller (Eds.), *Progress in behavioral modification: Volume 4* (pp 69–118). New York: Academic Press.

O'Leary, K. D. (1979). Behavioral assessment. *Behavioral Assessment, 1,* 31–36.

Ollendick, T. H., & Hersen, M. (1984). *Child behavioral assessment: Principles and procedures.* Elmsford, NY: Pergamon Press.

Ottens, A. J. (1981). Multifaceted treatment of compulsive hair pulling. *Journal of Behavior Therapy and Experimental Psychiatry, 12,* 77–80.

Palmer, M. H., Lloyd, M. E., & Lloyd, K. E. (1977). An experimental analysis of electricity conservation procedures. *Journal of Applied Behavior Analysis, 10,* 665–671.

Parks, C. W., Jr., & Hollon, S. D. (1988). Cognitive assessment. (1988). In A. S. Bellack & M. Hersen (Eds.), *Behavioral assessment: A practical handbook* (3rd ed.) (pp. 161–211). Elmsford, NY: Pergamon Press.

Patterson, G. R., & Bechtel, C. G. (1977). Formulating the situational environment in relation to states and traits. In R. B. Cattell & P. M. Greger (Eds.), *Handbook of modern personality therapy.* Washington, DC: Halstead.

Peterson, L., Homer, A. L., & Wonderlich, S. A. (1982). The integrity of independent variables in behavior analysis. *Journal of Applied Behavior Analysis, 15,* 477–492.

Price, M. G., & Haynes, S. N. (1980). The effects of participant monitoring and feedback on marital interaction and satisfaction. *Behavior Therapy, 11,* 134–139.

Quinsey, V. L., Chaplin, T. C., & Varney, G. (1981). A comparison of rapists' and non-sex offenders' sexual preference for mutually consenting sex, rape, and physical abuse of women. *Behavioral Assessment, 3,* 127–135.

Rosen, J. C. (1981). Self-monitoring in the treatment of diurnal bruxism. *Journal of Behavior Therapy and Experimental Psychiatry, 12,* 347–350.

Rugh, J. D., Gable, R. S., & Lemke, R. R. (1986). Instrumentation for behavioral assessment. In A. R. Ciminero, C. S. Calhoun, & H. E. Adams (Eds.), *Handbook of behavioral assessment* (2nd ed.) (pp. 79–108). New York: Wiley.

Russo, D. C., Bird, B. L., & Masek, B. J. (1980). Assessment issues in behavioral medicine. *Behavioral Assessment, 2*, 1–18.

Russo, D. C., Cataldo, M. F., & Cushing, P. J. (1981). Compliance training and behavioral covariation in the treatment of multiple behavior problems. *Journal of Applied Behavior Analysis, 14*, 209–222.

Sackett, G. P. (Ed.). (1978a). *Observing behavior, Vol. 1: Theory and applications in mental retardation.* Baltimore: University Park Press.

Sackett, G. P. (Ed.). (1978b). *Observing behavior, Vol. 2: Data collection and analysis methods.* Baltimore: University Park Press.

Sampson, E. E. (1981). Cognitive psychology as ideology. *American Psychologist, 36*, 730–743.

Schleien, S. J., Wehman, P., & Kiernan, J. (1981). Teaching leisure skills to severely handicapped adults: An age-appropriate darts game. *Journal of Applied Behavior Analysis, 14*, 513–519.

Schell, R. M., Pelham, W. E., Bender, M. E., Andree, J. A., Law, T., & Robbins, F. R. (1986). The concurrent assessment of behavioral and psychostimulant interventions: A controlled case study. *Behavioral Assessment, 8*, 373–384.

Schlundt, D. G., Johnson, W. G., & Jarrell, M. P. (1986). A sequential analysis of environmental, behavioral, and affective variables predictive of vomiting in bulimina nervosa. *Behavioral Assessment, 8*, 253–269.

Schlundt, D. G., & McFall, R. M. (1987). Classifying social situations: A comparison of five methods. *Behavioral Assessment, 9*, 21–42.

Shapiro, D. A., & Shapiro, D. (1983). Comparative therapy outcome research: Methodological implications of meta-analysis. *Journal of Consulting, and Clinical Psychology, 51*, 42–53.

Shapiro, S. A. (1981). *Contemporary theories of schizophrenia.* New York: McGraw-Hill.

Sidman, M. (1960). *Tactics of scientific research.* New York: Basic Books.

Spence, S. H. (1981). Validation of social skills of adolescent males in an interview conversation with a previously unknown adult. *Journal of Applied Behavior Analysis, 15*, 493–503.

Stitzer, M. L., Bigtelow, G. E., Liebson, I. A., & Hawthorne, J. W. (1982). Contingent reinforcement for benzodiazepine-free urine: Evaluation of a drug abuse treatment intervention. *Journal of Applied Behavior Analysis, 15*, 493–503.

Strosahl, K. D., & Linehan, M. M. (1986). Basic issues in behavioral assessment. In A. Ciminero, K. S. Calhoun, & H. E. Adams (Eds.), *Handbook of behavioral assessment* (pp. 12–46). New York: Wiley.

Stuart, R. B. (1980). *Helping couples change.* New York: Guilford Press.

Sturgis, E. T., Adams, H. E., & Brantley, P. J. (1981). The parameters, etiology, and treatment of migraine headaches. In S. N. Haynes & L. Gannon (Eds.), *Psychosomatic disorders: A psychophysiological approach to etiology and treatment.* New York: Praeger.

Sturgis, E. T., & Arena, J. G. (1984). Psychophysiological assessment. In M. Hersen, R. M. Eisler, & P. M. Miller (Eds.), *Progress in behavioral modification* (Vol. 17, pp. 3–30). New York: Academic Press.

Sturgis, E. T., & Gramling, S. (1988). Psychophysiological assessment. In A. S. Bellack, & M. Hersen (Eds.), *Behavioral assessment: A practical handbook* (3rd ed.) (pp. 213–251). Elmsford, NY: Pergamon Press.

Suen, H. K., & Ary, D. (1986). Poisson cumulative probabilities of systematic errors in single-subject and multiple-subject time sampling. *Behavioral Assessment, 8*, 155–169.

Swan, G. E., & MacDonald, M. L. (1979). Behavior therapy in practice: A national survey of behavior therapists. *Behavior Therapy, 9*, 799–807.

Taylor, C. B. (1983). DSM-III and behavioral assessment. *Behavioral Assessment, 5*, 5–14.

Taylor, C. B., & Agras, W. S. (1981). Assessment of phobia. In D. H. Barlow (Ed.), *Behavior assessment of adult disorders.* New York: Guilford Press.

Thompson, J. K., & Figueroa, J. L. Critical issues in the assessment of headache. In M. Hersen, R. M. Eisler, & P. M. Miller (Eds.), *Progress in behavior modification* (Vol. 15, pp. 81–113). New York: Academic Press.

Turkat, I. (1986). In A. Ciminero, K. S. Calhoun, & H. E. Adams (Eds.), *Handbook of behavioral assessment* (pp. 109–149). New York: Wiley.

Turner, J. A., & Clancy, S. (1988). Comparison of operant behavioral and cognitive-behavioral group treatment for chronic low back pain. *Journal of Consulting and Clinical Psychology, 56*, 261–266.

Tryon, W. W. (1985). *Behavioral assessment in behavioral medicine*. New York: Springer.

Ullmann, L. P., & Krasner, L. (1965). *Case studies in behavior modification*. New York: Holt, Rinehart, & Winston.

Van den Pol, R. A., Iwata, B. A., Ivancic, M. T., Page, T. J., Neef, N. A., & Whitley, F. P. (1981). Teaching the handicapped to eat in public places: Acquisition, generalization, and maintenance of restaurant skills. *Journal of Applied Behavior Analysis, 14*, 61–69.

Van Egeren, L., Haynes, S. N., Franzen, M., & Hamilton, J. (1983). Cognitive factors in sleep-onset insomnia. *Behavioral Medicine, 6*, 217–232.

Varni, J. P. (1981). Self-regulation techniques in the management of chronic arthritic pain in hemophilia. *Behavior Therapy, 12*, 185–294.

Vincent, J. P. (1980). *Advances in family intervention, assessment, and theory*. Greenwich, CT: JAI Press.

Voeltz, L. M., & Evans, I. M. (1982). The assessment of behavioral interrelationships in child behavior therapy. *Behavioral Assessment, 4*, 131–165.

Wade, T. C., Baker, T. B., & Hartmann, D. P. (1979). Behavior therapists' self-reported views and practices. *Behavior Therapist, 2*, 3–6.

Wahler, R. G. (1975). Some structural aspects of deviant child behavior. *Journal of Applied Behavior Analysis, 8*, 27–42.

Wahler, R. G. (1980). The insular mother: Her problems in parent-child treatment. *Journal of Applied Behavior Anaysis, 13*, 207–219.

Walker, B. B., & Sandman, C. A. (1981). Disregulation of the gastrointestinal system. In S. N. Haynes & L. R. Gannon (Eds.), *Psychosomatic disorders: A psychophysiological approach to etiology and treatment*. New York: Praeger.

Wampold, B. E., & Worsham, N. L. (1986). Randomization tests for multiple-baseline designs. *Behavioral Assessment, 8*, 135–143.

Waranch, H. R., Iwata, B. A., Wohl, M. K., & Nidiffer, F. D. (1981). Treatment of regarded adult's mannequin phobia through *in vivo* desensitization and shaping approach responses. *Journal of Behavior Therapy and Experimental Psychiatry, 12*, 359–362.

Wasik, B. H., & Loven, M. D. (1980). Classroom observation data: Sources of inaccuracy and proposed solutions. *Behavioral Assessment, 2*, 211–277.

Watson, C. G., Tilleskjor, C., Hoodecheck-Schow, E. A., Purcel, J., & Jacobs, L. (1985). Do alcoholics give valid self-reports? *Journal of Studies on Alcohol, 45*, 344–348.

Weinrott, M. R., Reid, J. B., Bauske, B. W., & Brumett, B. (1981). Supplementing naturalistic observations with observer impressions. *Behavioral Assessment, 3*, 151–159.

Weiss, R. L., & Frohman, P. E. (1985). Behavioral observation as outcome measures: Not through a glass darkly. *Behavioral Assessment, 7*, 309–316.

Wells, K. C., Connors, C. K., Imber, L., & Delamater, A. (1981). Use of single-subject methodology in clinical decision-making with a hyperactive child on the psychiatric inpatient unit. *Behavioral Assessment, 3*, 359–369.

Wicramesekera, I. E. (1981). Clinical research in a behavioral medicine private practice. *Behavioral Assessment, 3*, 265–271.

Wiens, A. N. (1981). The assessment interview. In I. B. Wiener (Ed.), *Clinical methods in psychology*. New York: Wiley.

Wiggins, J. S. (1973). *Personality and prediction: Principles of personality assessment*. Reading, MA: Addison-Wesley.

Wilson, F. E., & Evans, I. M. (1983). The reliability of target behavior selection in behavioral assessment. *Behavioral Assessment, 5*, 15–32.

Winett, R. A. (1985). Ecobehavioral assessment in health lifestyles: Concepts and methods. In P. Karoly (Ed.), *Measurement strategies in health psychology* (pp. 147–181). New York: Wiley.

Wing, R. R., Epstein, L. H., Nowalk, M. P., Koeske, R., & Hagg, S. (1985). Behavior change, weight loss, and physiological improvements in type II diabetic patients. *Journal of Consulting and Clinical Psychology, 53*, 111–122.

Wolfe, M. M. (1978). Social validity: The case of subjective measurement or how applied behavior analysis is finding its heart. *Journal of Applied Behavior Analysis, 11*, 203–214.

Wolman, B. B. (1978). *Clinical diagnosis of mental disorders*. New York: Plenum Press.

Wolpe, J. (1958). *Psychotherapy by reciprocal inhibition*. Stanford, CA: Stanford University Press.

Wroblewski, P. F., Jacob, T., & Rehm, L. P. (1977). The contribution of relaxation to symbolic modeling in the modification of dental fears. *Behaviour Research and Therapy, 15*, 113–117.

Yates, B. T. (1985). Cost-effectiveness analysis and cost-benefit analysis: An introduction. *Behavioral Assessment, 7*, 207–234.

Youkilis, H. D., & Bootzin, R. R. (1981). A psycho-physiological perspective of the etiology and treatment of insomnia. In S. N. Haynes & L. R. Gannon (Eds.), *Psychosomatic disorders: A psy-*

chophysiological approach to etiology and treatment. New York: Praeger.

Zeiss, R. A. (1978). Self-directed treatment for premature ejaculation. *Journal of Consulting and Clinical Psychology, 46,* 1234–1241.

PART IX

ASSESSMENT AND INTERVENTION

CHAPTER 20

PSYCHOLOGICAL ASSESSMENT IN TREATMENT

J. R. Wittenborn

INTRODUCTION

At one time most therapy for problem behavior was organized and directed on the supposition that the problem behavior per se served some basic, underlying disposition, possibly motivational, possibly neurochemical. There were three assumptions: (a) Problem behavior could serve to express or implement the underlying predisposition. (b) The elimination of one implementing behavior would not necessarily prevent the emergence of another expression that could also be a problem. (c) The proper object of treatment must be the modification of the underlying predisposition. Recently, it has become acceptable to regard some explicit delimited behavior as the object of treatment. With this shift from an emphasis on hypothesized disposition to concern for the actual problem behavior, it has become possible to compare the efficacy of various treatments with respect to the attainment of the specified behavioral objective.

Usually therapies or treatments imply a course of action that has a corrective, restorative, or remedial role with respect to some overt behavioral objective. Basic initial instruction in motor skills, communication via spoken or written language, and factual knowledge are generally considered educational objectives and not included among the aims of treatment. Any listing of behavioral objectives that might be called goals of treatment is arbitrary and certainly incomplete. Nevertheless, there are some major classes of objectives: (a) the modification of affect that is inappropriate for the circumstances, (b) the elimination of unnecessary and maladaptive behavior and the acquisition of adaptive modes of response, (c) the

modification of affect or specifiable behaviors that are regarded as symptomatic of a diagnosable psychopathology whether or not the symptom behavior is maladaptive, and (d) the acquisition of skills that have been lost or had not been acquired under the conditions in which such learning usually occurs. A definition of treatment may include the constructive modification of behavior that is a source of distress to the individual or to others, that is alien to or a pronounced exaggeration of some aspect of his or her normal personality, or that is contrary to the requirements of law or the conventions of society. The present review is limited to controlled investigations of adults who have been treated by psychotherapy or psychotropic drugs.

The Sample

The selection of devices appropriate for the assessment of treatment-related change, as well as the interpretation of the findings, must be approached with an awareness of the characteristics of the sample. Such characteristics of patients as their age, sex, social relationships, economic commitments, opportunities, marital status, friendships, and familial associations can play a role that has supportive, limiting, or provocative functions. In addition to specifying pertinent features of any clinical sample, it is conventional to provide a diagnosis for each patient. Diagnoses, although controversial, serve to remind the clinician of features of the illness that may have been overlooked, provide a guide to prognostic speculation, and afford some economy of description. As a part of diagnosis, the clinician should consider limitations in the patient's premorbid competence.

In designing the investigation, selecting practicable assessment devices, and maintaining the therapeutic regimen, the relevant limiting factors may include memory faults, failures in orientation, delusional disorders, sensory-motor impairments, or social-emotional predispositions. The conditions under which the patient lives and the presence of responsible others can also impose realistic limitations on both the treatment and the assessment of its effects.

All clinical samples are heterogeneous, and the degree of this heterogeneity, as well as its sources, can be important. Unrecognized or uncorrected heterogeneity in the sample reduces the sensitivity of all research. If sources of heterogeneity pertinent to the efficacy of treatment are known before the trial, some effort is usually made to eliminate them. If pretreatment heterogeneities cannot be eliminated from the sample, some investigators seek to randomize them so that the biasing influence will be equally distributed among the treatments under comparison. Other investigators, however, will choose to stratify identifiable sources of heterogeneity and to assign them equally to treatments under comparison. With such provisions, the contribution of the stratified factors to changes in the patient may be calculated, their tendency to interact with any treatment identified, and their confounding with intertreatment comparisons minimized by statistical procedures.

Pertinent characteristics of the sample include the kinds of behaviors that are the immediate causes for the patient's being in treatment. These behaviors serve as obvious and objective criteria of efficacy. Behaviors that are not a target of therapy but may qualify therapeutic effect should be assessed also so that their biasing effect may be weighed and eliminated by appropriate data analysis.

Selection of Assessment Devices

Standard test performances, ratings of observed behavior, ratings of observers' opinions, and inventories for self-description can reflect some of the behavioral changes expected from theoretical considerations or from prior experience with the proposed treatment. Ad hoc inventories or checklists that represent pertinent aspects of behavior not represented by standard assessment devices may be desirable for evaluating treatment-related behavior changes. Self-descriptive inventories and observer rating scales often have the same descriptive titles and highly similar, if not identical, content for their behavioral referents. Despite this similarity in content, such inventories and scales do not distinguish among individuals in the same way and should not be regarded as equivalent or interchangeable.

Most investigators tend to rely heavily on a common group of assessment devices. The use of a common pool of assessment devices may confer the advantage of a degree of comparability among studies. This possible advantage is only incidental, however, and investigators must remain critically evaluative of the appropriateness of any assessment considered for their particular purposes. Uncertainty concerning the practicability of an assessment procedure for the sample of patients or the conditions of the study should be resolved before any selection becomes final.

It is important to select assessment procedures that not only reflect the behavioral content of the patient's symptoms, but also discriminate within a sufficiently broad range of severity to show either an increase or a decrease. If the range of severity sampled by the test cannot show an appreciable increase or decrease for the level of severity that the sample presents, the scope of the test is insufficient for the task.

All tests and assessment procedures considered for inclusion in the investigation should be pretested on a small sample of the population proposed for the investigation. Such pretesting provides guidance for anticipating the qualifications of personnel necessary for the assessment, for estimating the amount of training and supervision they must have, and for providing the general conditions under which reliable assessments can be made. If pretesting reveals that the proposed assessment procedures will be impracticable under the conditions of the inquiry, the investigator will be spared embarrassment and the loss of time and effort that could have been involved if this very practical aspect of the investigation had been disregarded.

Investigators should consider the characteristics of their samples, the physical and social context in which the treatment is conducted, and the behavior to be modified when they select devices to assess therapeutic efficacy. Usually it is possible to choose assessment devices that have been used by prior investigators in similar situations to reflect changes consequent to the treatment; these findings can provide some basis for anticipating the possible results when the same assessment devices are applied in the proposed investigation.

The number of assessment devices can be critical. If too few are applied, they may not reflect pertinent changes during the course of treatment, and a potentially effective treatment may go unrecognized. If too many assessment devices are applied, the burden on patients and staff may be excessive, and some of the scores will not reflect the treatment-related changes.

Data Analysis and Interpretation

When numerous assessments have been made and only a modest portion of them shows a significant drug effect, the investigator may have difficulty deciding whether the observed discriminations are true and verifiable evidence of therapeutic effect or merely the kind of chance contrasts that occur in most series of trials. In such cases, a multivariate discriminant analysis is often used to show whether the set of tests generates a significant discrimination. If the entire set of tests is a significant discriminator, then some of the individual tests that meet a criterion for statistical significance are probably truly significant discriminators and not fortuitous unconfirmable events. The number of assessment devices or separate scores should not exhaust the number of degrees of freedom available for testing the significance of a multivariate discriminator. In general, the larger the number of separate scores to be analyzed, the larger should be the number of patients available for the analysis.

As an alternative, some investigators have found it practical to reduce the number of potential criteria by a preliminary factor analysis. This step in data reduction can lead to the use of factor scores as criteria of efficacy. It can also identify the criteria that are good measures of the factors. In exploratory studies, it can be useful also to use two independent measures of each aspect of expected change. Mutually confirmatory findings can be reassuring to the investigator, while inconsistent findings alert the investigator to the hazard of overconfident generalization.

There are numerous advantages to providing both a representative set of promising criteria and a sufficiently large sample, particularly when the investigation is exploratory in nature and there are no applicable precedents to guide the way. For example, samples of ample size offer the advantage of permitting the group to be split into two comparable subsamples for analytical purposes. If the two subsamples generate corresponding, mutually confirming indications of change in some particular respect, the investigator may assume that the finding is not a sampling artifact.

One persisting problem in comparing the efficacy of treatments is the interpretation of negative results. What does it mean when the inquiry reveals no difference between two treatments? It could mean that the treatments were equally effective, that neither treatment was effective, that the criteria of treatment effect were inappropriate, or that the assessments were conducted in an improper manner and were unable to show consistent differences between any treatment groups. Other interpretations of negative results could be applicable. Perhaps the two treatment groups were exposed to confounding influences that would obscure any differences. Perhaps the assessments were delayed until a spontaneous remission had erased all contrasts. The difficulties in interpreting inconclusive results and the logical impossibility of proving the null hypothesis strongly suggest that investigators avoid experimental designs where a substance under assessment is compared with a standard treatment of known efficacy and no placebo comparison is included. An investigational treatment may have therapeutic merit even though it is inferior to the standard treatment, and under these conditions an answer to the efficacy question requires a placebo comparison. If an investigational treatment happens to be superior to a standard treatment control, the implications are unambiguously supportive, regardless of the availability of a placebo control.

PSYCHOTHERAPY

Definitions of psychotherapy appear to have varied over time. The term *psychotherapy* once referred to the nonphysical interventions of a psychiatrist or, in some quarters, a psychoanalyst. Later, psychotherapy included the interventions of psychologists, particularly if they were working in a medical setting or under the direction of a psychiatrist. Concurrently, counseling was becoming increasingly psychotherapeutic in nature. Eventually, psychotherapy was practiced by psychologists working independently, usually under the licensure of a state agency. The implicit, if not explicit, goal of psychotherapy was often described as strengthening or fulfilling the potential of the patient's personality. This growth or restructuring of the personality was expected to bring some amelioration, if not remission, of psychopathological symptoms and the emergence of behavior forms that were satisfactory from the standpoint of the patient or others. During this period there seemed to be as much concern for philosophical orientation as for method per se.

Method, to whatever extent it was explicated, expressed a definitive point of view, e.g., the nondirective method developed by Rogers and his associates (Rogers, 1942), the classical psychoanalytic methods or their modifications (Freud, 1935), or the eclectic Meyerian psychobiological orientation (Meyer, 1951). In most traditional psychotherapeutic interventions, the procedure involved a series of interviews between the therapist and patient. The focus was on affect and motive, and the objective for patients was the acquisition of a new understanding of their behavior ("insight") and the development of a more effective life style than they had before therapy. The efficacy of these various interventions was assumed, and, with one or two exceptions, controlled evaluations of such procedures were nonexistent.

Among the various alternative psychotherapeutic procedures that emerged were methods that focused on the modification of problem behaviors. The method described as *behavior modification* usually distinguished among discrete problem behaviors (Franks & Barbrack, 1983). When the goal of therapy was approached as modification of one or more discrete target behaviors, reports of controlled systematic assessment of psychotherapeutic efficacy began to appear in the literature. One important procedure for such focused intervention became known as desensitization. In this procedure, a nonresponse or an aversive response in a context that formerly provoked symptomatic problem responses was effected by means of a program, often ad hoc, contrived by the therapist, wherein responses avoidant or incompatible with the problem behavior were elicited and reinforced. Some greatly circumscribed aversive learning is reminiscent of some of the early methods of Watson (1925). Desensitization and other methods that focus on the avoidance of undesired responses and place relatively little emphasis on insight and motivational modifications could be truly called a program of behavior modification. Other programs, often referred to as cognitive, were concerned with modifying the manner in which patients viewed themselves and their problem behavior, but did not necessarily involve the patient in the circuity of dynamic formulations and motivational modifications.

There were three desiderata for inclusion of reports in the present review of assessment in psychotherapy: (a) the therapeutic method was explicitly described, (b) the criteria were changes objectively and reliably defined before treatment, and (c) the significance of change was stated in terms of formal comparisons between the treatment sample and a control sample drawn without bias from the common patient population. The control sample was untreated or treated by an alternative method. This review of controlled studies of psychotherapetic efficacy could not presume to be comprehensive, but it is usefully representative of the kinds of studies that meet the present

criteria. The 25 studies selected for review were roughly classified in terms of both the method (desensitization, cognition, or neither) and objectives (reduction of anxiety manifestations; reduction of phobic, obsessive, compulsive symptoms; reduction of depression; or objective unspecified).

In most of the studies, some assessment procedures failed to show a significant contrast between the respective treatments under comparison. This failure could result from many factors other than the possibility that the method of treatment was not effective for the behavior assessed, particularly in the sample under investigation. For this reason, assessment procedures that offered no discriminations will be disregarded. For the present purposes, the de facto objective of therapy was the behavior shown to be responsive to the procedure. It is of interest, therefore, to review the assessments that offered some discrimination, but it must be recognized that it may not be possible to replicate all of the findings.

With few exceptions the psychotherapeutic studies selected for review are well designed, well conducted, and intelligently reported, and they contrast favorably with the comparable literature published prior to 1960. The quality of the recent research appears to be a consequence of four developments: (a) the general acceptance of group psychotherapy, which makes it relatively easy to form a sample of patients exposed to a common psychotherapeutic situation; (b) the development and acceptance of relatively limited explicit therapeutic procedures; (c) the acceptance of limited therapeutic goals comprising behavioral changes specifiable prior to therapy; and (d) the general acceptance of multivariate concepts and methods of analysis among clinical investigators.

The various methods of desensitization are conspicuous among the widely accepted explicit psychotherapeutic interventions. Among the 10 studies in which the therapeutic objective was behaviorally explicit, desensitization was a principal method in nine. In each of these inquiries, the efficacy of desensitization was compared with one to four other methods, usually including a nontherapy control. For eight of these nine studies, the objective was the amelioration of handicapping anxiety, for example, in written examinations, in public speaking, or in the elimination of a phobic or compulsive reaction. These manifestations yielded to the method of desensitization; the assessment procedures that displayed one or more significant contrasts are listed in Table 20.1 according to the frequency of their use. Because most of these assessments were used and found to discriminate in only one of the studies included in the present review, they may

Table 20.1. Assessments That Distinguished Desensitization Effects on Anxious, Phobic, or Compulsive Manifestations

ASSESSMENT	FREQUENCY OF USE	SOURCE OF PROCEDURE
Grade Point Average	4	From school records
Anxiety Differential	3	Husek & Alexander, 1963
Adjective Checklist for Anxiety	2	Zuckerman, 1960
*Personal Report of Confidence of Speaker	1	Paul, 1966
Worry-Emotionality Scale (Worry)	1	Liebert & Morris, 1967
Cognitive Interference Questionnaire	1	Sarason, unpublished, 1976
Exam Behavior Scale from Effective Study Test	1	Brown, 1975
10-item Anagram Test	1	ad hoc, Kirkland & Hollandsworth, Jr., 1980
Suinn Test Anxiety Behavior Scale	1	Suinn, 1969
Test Anxiety Scale	1	Sarason, 1972
Timed Behavioral Checklist for Performance Anxiety	1	Paul, 1966
Word Count	1	From Recorded Speech Sample
Duration of Silences	1	From Recorded Speech Sample
Number of "ah" Statements	1	From Recorded Speech Sample
Social Anxiety Scale	1	Watson & Friend, 1969
*Beck Depression Inventory	1	Beck & Beamesderfer, 1974
*State-Trait Anxiety Inventory Trait Anxiety Scale	1	Spielberger, Gorsuch, & Lushene, 1970
Complaints	1	ad hoc, McLean & Hakstian, 1979
Goals	1	ad hoc, McLean & Hakstian, 1979
Social	1	ad hoc, McLean & Hakstian, 1979
Average Satisfaction	1	ad hoc, McLean & Hakstian, 1979
Mood	1	ad hoc, McLean & Hakstian, 1979
Dropout Rate	1	
Stress Tolerance Test in Standard Situation	1	Lazarus, 1961
Washing Time in Standard Situation	1	Foa, Steketee, & Milby, 1980
Digit Symbol	1	Brown, 1969
Digit Symbol	1	Meichenbaum, 1972
Achievement Anxiety Test-Debilitating Anxiety	1	Alpert & Haber, 1960
Frustration Thermometer Scores	1	McReynolds & Tori, 1972
Fear Rating	1	Tori & Worell, 1973
Approach Test	1	ad hoc, Tori & Worell, 1973

*Assessments that distinguished both desensitization and cognitive methods.

not all prove to discriminate in other similar inquiries. Nevertheless, it is apparent that many assessment procedures can be sensitive to the differential effects of various psychotherapeutic approaches. These assessment procedures would seem to be promising candidates for further use when the desensitization approach is applied to the amelioration of the particular neurotic manifestations modified in the studies under review.

A second major approach that lends itself to controlled inquiry is concerned with patients' recognition and reconceptualization of their problem behaviors. These approaches are somewhat diversified in their specifics and range from the approach advocated by Beck (1967) to the rational-emotive approach endorsed by Ellis (1962). Eight studies involved a cognitive type approach. These studies are of particular interest because they suggest that the cognitive approaches have been preferred for the psychotherapy of depressed affect. In contrast, among the studies presently reviewed the desensitization approach was applied one time only to the treatment of depression, but desensitization was frequently used for the amelioration of symptoms often accompanying depression: that is, anxious, phobic, or compulsive behaviors. Because desensitization has been applied to the elimination or modification of neurotic behavior and the cognitive approach has been applied most often to the amelioration of depression, it is not surprising to learn that the effects of these contrasting methods have been shown by different assessment procedures. With few exceptions, the devices that have proven sensitive when the cognitive approach has been compared with other approaches (Table 20.2) are different from those found to be differentiating in the desensitization studies (Table 20.1).

An explicitly defined behavioral objective or a definite, well-specified procedure is not necessary to compare the efficacy of various psychotherapies. There were four acceptable studies that had no definite behavioral objective and methods that were either described vaguely or conformed with neither of the two major classes of approach. The discriminating assessments for these studies are listed in Table 20.3.

PHARMACOTHERAPY

The effects of pharmacotherapy are usually examined in terms of symptom reduction, behavioral changes shown by psychological tests, a diversity of physiological indices, and miscellaneous untoward responses often anticipated from the pharmacology of the drug under consideration. With the increasing pharmacologic and neurochemical sophistication, there is a growing tendency to regard medication from the standpoint of its pharmacodynamics, pharmaco-

kinetics, and its mode of action, including the neurophysiology of the neurotransmitters involved. Unfortunately, the metabolic and anatomical bases for behavioral disorders are not sufficiently known to permit the selection of treatment on the basis of its neurophysiological effects. The probable behavioral effects of a drug may involve a diverse spectrum, only a part of which corresponds with any current, generally accepted constellation of psychopathology.

When psychopathology is ameliorated by pharmacotherapeutic intervention, the conclusion often drawn is that the psychopathology was a manifestation of some metabolic disorder that was corrected by the pharmacotherapeutic intervention. In most cases, this seems to be a gratuitous inference. A pharmacologic intervention that happens to modify certain behavioral capacities in a therapeutically desirable manner may be no more than a fortunate coincidence and may tell us nothing about the etiology of the disorder or of its implementing physiology. Nevertheless, some knowledge of the mode of action of pharmacotherapeutic substances can be of value in anticipating the

Table 20.2. Assessments That Distinguished the Effects of Cognitive Approaches

ASSESSMENT	FREQUENCY OF USE	SOURCE OF PROCEDURE
*Beck Depression Inventory	4	Beck & Beamesderfer, 1974
Hamilton Rating Scale for Depression	3	Hamilton, 1967
Anxiety Scale	2	Similar to Walk's fear thermometer, 1956
MMPI-D	2	Hathway & Meehl, 1951
*Personal Report of Confidence	2	Paul, 1966
MMPI-Sc	1	Hathaway & Meehl, 1951
Hopelessness Scale	1	Heimberg, 1961
Miskimins Seld-Goal-Other II	1	Miskimins, 1972; Miskimins & Braucht, 1971
Discussion for Therapy Group 10-minutes	1	ad hoc, Fuchs & Rehm, 1977
Pleasant Events Schedule	1	MacPhillamy & Lewinsohn, 1972
Self-Evaluation Questionnaire	1	ad hoc, Fuchs & Rehm, 1977
Self-Reinforcement	1	ad hoc, Fuchs & Rehm, 1977
Self-Control Attitudes and Beliefs Test	1	ad hoc, Fuchs & Rehm, 1977
*State-Trait Anxiety Inventory Trait Anxiety Scale	1	Spielberger, Gorsuch, & Lushene, 1970
Eysenck Personality Inventory Neuroticism Scale	1	Eysenck & Eysenck, 1968
Item 4 from Fear Survey Scale	1	Reynolds, 1967
Irrational Beliefs Test	1	Jones, 1969
Idea Inventory	1	Kassinove, Crisci, & Tiegerman, 1977
Multiple Affect Adjective Check List: Anxiety Scale, Depression Scale	1	Zuckerman, Lubin, & Robins, 1965
Approach Behavior Test	1	ad hoc, Biran & Wilson, 1981
Efficacy Expectations	1	Bandura, Adams, & Beyer, 1977
Performance Fear	1	ad hoc, Biran & Wilson, 1981
Heart Rate	1	
Skin Potential	1	

* Assessments that distinguished both desensitization and cognitive methods.

Table 20.3. Assessments that Distinguished the Effects of Methods Other Than Desensitization or Cognitive

ASSESSMENT	FREQUENCY OF USE	SOURCE OF PROCEDURE
Acceptance of Other Scale	1	Guerney, 1977
Self-Feeling Awareness Scale	1	Guerney, 1977
Mother-Daughter Situation Questionnaire Expressive Skill	1	Ely, Guerney, & Stover, 1973
Adolescent-Parent Communication Checklist	1	Beaubien, 1970
Personal Orientation Inventory	1	Shostrom, 1964
Secord-Jourard Body-Cathexis Scale	1	Jourard & Remy, 1957
Dosamentes-Alperson Expressive Movement Scale	1	Dosamantes-Alperson, 1975
Post Session Questionnaire	1	Soeken, Manderscheid, Flatter, & Silbergeld, 1981
Semistructured Interview of Basic Demography	1	ad hoc, Meyer, Derogatis, Miller, Reading, Cohen, Park, & Whitmarch, 1981
Hopkins Symptom Checklist	1	Derogatis, Lipman, Rickels, Uhlenhuth, & Covi, 1973

possible spectrum of behavioral effects and selecting criteria for the assessment of these effects. Some of the medications seem to have a relatively direct effect on behavior via their influence on mediating brain structures. For example, some drugs appear to affect the metabolism of certain brain cells; others affect the mobilization or removal of some neurotransmitters (Bloom, 1986). The study of neurotransmitters and neuroreceptors is currently of great interest in pharmacotherapy, possibly because it helps account for the behavioral distinctions among the effects of some drugs. These neurophysiological investigations may eventually be useful in selecting devices for the assessment of efficacy.

Studies of the efficacy of psychotropic drugs have far exceeded studies of the efficacies of psychotherapies in number and—until recently, perhaps—in the quality of design, execution, and data analysis as well. In a large measure, current psychotherapy and pharmacotherapy share the objective of modifying behavior, particularly those behavioral qualities that are referred to as symptomatic (presumably of some unverified intrinsic disorder), but these behavioral qualities are, in truth, the immediate and tangible reason for the patient's seeking treatment. Therefore, the modification of these manifest behaviors may be a proper, if not sufficient, object of both psychotropic drug and behavior modification therapies.

The demand for treatments that are in some way more efficacious and involve fewer or different side effects than substances currently available provides the major imperative for evaluative drug studies.

Federal law requires that tests for efficacy and safety be conducted for all prospective pharmacotherapies, whether new or modification of existing therapies.

The requirements for proper clinical investigation of psychotropic substances have been set forth by an international committee (Wittenborn, 1977), and, with minor modifications, have been accepted by investigators in most nations that support an appreciable pharmaceutical industry. This and other publications (Wittenborn, 1971) illuminate the general criteria for the development of evidence to support a claim of efficacy for new psychotropic medications.

In general, studies of psychotropic substances are focused on some recognized, diagnostically sanctionable mental disease entity, and psychotropic medication is assessed in terms of the alleviation of symptoms and judgments of overall improvement. An overall judgment of improvement implies that an underlying diagnosable psychopathological disease has, at least in part, remitted.

Because of the great number and diversity of reports of drug trials, a comprehensive list of the assessments that have been used to show treatment-related changes would exceed the limits of the present review. The Early Clinical Drug Evaluation Units Program (ECDEU) of the U.S. Mental Health Administration has provided a manual (Guy, 1976) describing assessment devices recommended for use in the assessment of psychotropic substances. These devices are concerned with the symptoms of functional, as contrasted with organic, disorders and are presented under several headings. The devices listed in Table 20.4 are from the ECDEU Manual (Guy, 1976) and were selected because of their common use in studies of adult patients.

Almost all studies of the effect of psychotropic substances include some provision for assessing undesired effects. The procedures commonly used for this purpose vary with the type of drug under investigation. In addition to measures of vital signs, kidney function, and blood chemistry, investigators commonly include various other metabolic and behavioral assessments. For example, there may be methods for assessing adverse neurological effects, such as represented by the Abnormal Involuntary Movement Scale from the ECDEU Manual (Guy, 1976) and a diversity of devices for assessing other undesired central nervous system effects that can impair everyday behavior, particularly its psychomotor aspects. Although undesired behavioral effects may be surveyed by a simple checklist, additional procedures are usually required.

In a review of controlled studies of behavioral toxicity, Wittenborn (1980) reported the incidence with which various assessments showed detracting behavioral changes in consequence of different classes of psychotropic medication. For example, Wittenborn, Flaherty, McGough, Bossange, and Nash (1976) reported a study in which normal subjects were used to show that a standard daily dose of imipramine had a significantly detracting effect on

such practical performances as the Digit Symbol Substitution Test (DSST) and latency and accuracy of response in a vigilance test. Psychomotor responses to psychotropic medication are not invariably detracting, however. They can vary with the aspect of behavior examined as well as with the drug under scrutiny. As early as 1961, Wittenborn, Plante, Burgess, and Livermore reported that in depressed patients iproniazid had an enhancing effect on such behaviors as performance on the WAIS Similarities, numerical ability as represented by the Differential Aptitude Test (DAT), and latency of response in a reaction time situation. Obviously, standard tests of mental ability and psychomotor performance have a place in the assessment of psychotropic substances. Whether such tests show ameliorating or detracting effects of medication will depend upon the drug and the patient's condition (the therapeutic effect may be confounded with the detracting effects of the drug) as well as numerous other factors. The literature is voluminous and difficult to organize (Wittenborn, 1978, 1979).

Current investigations of the efficacy of psychotropic substances can draw on a large and diversified literature of prior studies. Some caveats are implicit in this literature. For example, the meaning of a rating scale score can depend on the professional role and orientation of the user (Wittenborn, Plante, & Burgess, 1961), and there are cultural differences in symptom constellations (Wittenborn, 1966a). There

Table 20.4. Selected Assessments from the ECDEU Manual

OBSERVER RATING SCALES FOR ADULT PATIENTS	SOURCE OF ASSESSMENT DEVICE
Brief Psychiatric Rating Scale (BPRS)	Overall & Gorham, 1962
Hamilton Depression Scale (HAMD)	Hamilton, 1967
Hamilton Anxiety Scale (HAMA)	Hamilton, 1959
Wittenborn Psychiatric Rating Scale (WITT)	Wittenborn, 1955
Nurses' Observation Scale for Inpatient Evaluation	Honigfeld & Klett, 1965
Self-Descriptive Inventories	
Self-Report Symptom Inventory (SCL-90)	Derogatis, 1977
Self-Rating Anxiety Scale (SAS)	Zung, 1971
Beck Depression Inventory (BECK)	Beck & Beamesderfer, 1974
Clyde Mood Scale (CLYDE)	Clyde, 1963
Hopkins Symptom Checklist (HSCL)	Derogatis, Lipman, Rickels, Uhlenhuth, & Covi, 1973
Profile of Mood States (POMS)	McNair, Lorr, & Droppleman, 1971
Scales for Geriatric Patients	
Crichton Geriatric Rating Scale (CRICHT)	Robinson, 1964
Sandoz Clinical Assessment-Geriatric (SCAG)	Shader, Harmatz & Salzman, 1974
Standard Tests	
Wechsler Adult Intelligence Scale (WAIS)	Wechsler, 1955
Wechsler Memory Scale (WMEM)	Wechsler & Stone, 1945
Memory for Designs Test	Graham & Kendall, 1960

is a large literature on factors that qualify the efficacy of medication: for example, the importance of the presence or absence of a dependent self-critical personality in depressed women treated with imipramine (Wittenborn, 1966b), or the importance of class status in response to antidepressant medication (Downing & Rickels, 1972).

There has been an increasing number of well-controlled studies of the effects of psychotropic substances on memory, perception, mental alacrity, and psychomotor responses of normal subjects. Although most diagnosable behavioral disorders may involve impairment in one or more of these areas of behavior, such impairments have been either disregarded or accorded no more than secondary significance in traditional claims of therapeutic efficacy. The seeming paradox between this detracting effect on many forms of behavior and the ameliorating effect on the target symptoms has not been explicated by suitable research. Suggestive leads have been reported. For example, Desai, Taylor-Davies, and Barnett (1983) found that diazepam was associated with an enhancement of short-term memory among normal subjects with high anxiety, but the memory of subjects with low anxiety was impaired by diazepam. Such findings serve incidentally to remind us that the direction and magnitude of drug-related change in memory can vary with the intrasample distribution of a third variable.

At present, the effect of psychotropic substances on the various kinds of behavior measured by familiar tests is best examined by the use of normal volunteers. In this way it is possible to avoid confounding the therapeutic effects expected of patients with the concurrent detracting effects commonly reported. Recent reviews of drug effects on memory (Wittenborn, 1988) and psychomotor behavior of normal volunteers (Wittenborn, 1987) make it possible to compare the responses to various tests when the subjects have received a given psychotropic substance. It is possible also to compare responses elicited by various drugs in

Table 20.5. A Summary of Psychomotor Responses to Eleven Drugs

PSYCHOMOTOR TEST	BARBITURATES	ALCOHOL	LORAZEPAM	AMITRIPTYLINE	DIAZEPAM	SCOPOLAMINE	PROPRANALOL	NITRAZEPAM	TEMAZEPAM	CAFFEINE	AMPHETAMINES
Saccadic eye movements		−	−		−−			−−	−−		+
Tracking	−	−−−−	−	−−	−−−−−−	−		n	n	n	+
DSST	−	−			−−−−−−−−−	n	n				
Digit copying	−		−n		−−−		−n				
Reaction time—simple		−	−		−−−nn			−−			+
Body sway	−	−−−	−−−	−−	−−n			−	n	n	
Tapping		−	−−		−−−−−−n					n	n
Maddox Wing		−−	−n		n			−	n		
CFF		−	−−	−	−−−		−	nn	nn	n	n
Reaction time—complex	−	−−nn	−−	−n		−nnn		n	n	n	
Nystagmus		−−	−	n						n	
Hand steadiness		−−	n		n					−n	
Attention		−			nn	−					+
Nonsignificant	0	2	3	2	8	4	2	4	6	7	2
Enhancements	0	0	0	0	0	0	0	0	0	0	4
Impairments	5	20	16	6	30	3	5	4	2	1	0
Total	5	22	19	8	38	7	7	8	8	8	6
Portion of comparisons impaired	1.00	0.91	0.84	0.75	0.79	0.43	0.71	0.50	0.25	0.13	0

n: Nonsignificant comparisons.

+: Enhancements of tested behavior.

−: Impairments of tested behavior.

Table 20.6. Drug Response Summary for Memory Tests

TEST	DIAZEPAM	LORAZEPAM	TRIAZOLAM	OXAZEPAM	FLURAZEPAM	ALCOHOL	CAFFEINE	SCOPOLAMINE	NICOTINE	PROPRANOLOL	TRIPROLIDINE
Verbal recall	----- -----	----	-	-n		+--	n	-	++	n	
Verbal recall delayed	--------			--			n		+		
Paired associates	--		-			-		-			
Verbal recog. delayed	--n		-	--			n				
Arithmetic	---n	-	-	--		-n	n			+	
Number recall	----			-n		n	n	-			
Digit span	n	-n	-		-		n				
Numbers in sequence							+	--	+nn		
DSST	----- ----n	----	----	-	-n	----	+	n		n	----
Symbol copying	---	-n	--	--			+			-n	--
Visual recall	-n	-	-		-						
Nonsignificant	5	2	0	2	1	2	6	1	2	3	0
Enhancements	0	0	0	0	0	1	3	0	4	1	0
Impairments	39	12	11	9	5	7	0	5	0	1	5
Total	44	14	11	11	6	10	9	6	6	5	5
Portion of comparisons impaired	.89	.86	.00	.92	.83	.70	.00	.83	.00	.20	1.00

n: Nonsignificant comparisons.

+: Enhancements of tested behavior.

−: Impairments of tested behavior.

terms of a given test. These two reviews were based on well-controlled studies. On the assumption that lack of significant findings tends to be a result of a diversity of irrelevant factors, only those studies that include at least one significant drug-placebo comparison were considered. The material offered in Table 20.5 for psychomotor tests and in 20.6 for memory tests was further restricted by requiring that each test entered in the table must have been used in at least five separate comparisons and that each drug included in the tables must have been tested by five separate comparisons. A given study may have compared several drugs on the basis of a given test. It is possible also that a given study may have evaluated a given drug on the basis of several tests.

Table 20.5 shows that 13 different tests of psychomotor performance were used to examine the effects of 11 different drugs. Table 20.6 indicates that 11 different tests of memory were used to examine the effects of 11 different drugs. From the data in these tables, it is apparent that all drugs are not equal in their effect on behavior. For example, data in Table 20.5 show that barbiturates, alcohol, and lorazepam had a detracting effect in 100%, 91%, and 84%, respectively, of the psychomotor tests applied. In contrast, caffeine and amphetamine impaired response on only 13% and 0% of the psychomotor tests applied. In Table 20.6, the data indicate that lorazepam and alcohol had an impairing effect in 86% and 70%, respectively, of the memory tests applied; in contrast, caffeine and nicotine had no detracting effect on memory test scores.

Seven drugs were used in testing both memory and psychomotor behavior. Scopolamine had a detracting effect in 83% of the memory trials, but in only 43% of the psychomotor trials. Propranalol had a detracting effect in only 20% of the memory trials, but had a detracting effect in 71% of the psychomotor trials. Thus, we see that there was a great contrast between scopolamine and propranalol in their effects on memory. In the diazepam trials, 89% of the memory assessments and 79% of the psychomotor assessments showed impairment (Table 20.7). In contrast, the alcohol trials showed impairment in 70% of the memory assessments and in 91% of the psychomotor assessments.

Most of the comparisons reviewed in Tables 20.5 and 20.6 indicate a drug-related impairment of behavior. For four of the drugs, however, the comparisons showed unmistakeable enhancement. Amphetamines have been used and misused to preserve effective psychomotor behavior during excessively long hours of continuous effort, and many users rely on caffeine to retain mental alertness and to combat minor fatigue. Nicotine under proper conditions can enhance memory (Peeke & Peeke, 1984; Warburton, Wesnes, Shergold, & James, 1986). Apparently the enhancing effect of nicotine can be usefully described as a state-dependent learning phenomenon. If material is learned in the presence of nicotine effects, i.e., smoking, memory for this material will be best if recall is required in the presence of nicotine. Material learned in the absence of nicotine, but recalled in its presence is not enhanced and may be impaired. Alcohol, which ordinarily detracts from both psychomotor response and memory, can, under certain conditions, protect the materials presented during the acquisition phase from confounding with experiences immediately subsequent to the material presented for learning. Thus, if its use is properly timed, the detracting effect of alcohol can be used to provide a retrograde facilitating effect on the retention of the material presented during the acquisition phase (Parker, Birnbaum, Weingartner, Hartley, Stillman, & Wyatt, 1980). In addition, retrograde facilitation of the recall of material presented for learning has been effected by interpolating diazepam immediately after the acquisition phase, but well before the recovery phase of the learning paradigm. Thus, the assessment of treatment-mediated behavior change is meaningful only in the total context of the procedure (Hinrichs, Ghoneim, & Mewaldt, 1984).

Clinical psychopharmacology has provided an active area for the formal evaluation of treatment effects, and both government and industry have provided support for the required studies. The blessing that this situation confers upon the development of formal assessment procedures for the evaluation of psychotropic substances is limited by two conservative influences. One is the discouraging suspicion of the FDA when confronted with a new concept of assessment or unfamiliar approaches to data analysis; the other is the growing attitude of the pharmaceutical industry that clinical tests of efficacy and safety are a product to be delivered as scheduled and available at a price that is competitive. In addition, the product must meet prior specifications with respect to characteristics of the sample, including presenting symptoms, the size of the sample, the identity of the assessment devices employed, and the method by which the data are analyzed. In this kind of a marketplace the extensive use of familiar assessments or their modifications can be expected, but there is little encouragement for innovation. This total situation can be discouraging to

Table 20.7. A Comparison of Detracting Effects of Various Psychotropic Substances on Memory and Psychomotor Behavior

| DRUG | MEMORY (M) | | | | | PSYCHOMOTOR (P) | | | | | PORTION − (M) PORTION − (P) |
	−	n	+	SUM	PORTION −	−	n	+	SUM	PORTION −	
scopolamine	5	1	0	7	.83	4	3	0	7	.43	1.93
diazepam	39	5	0	44	.89	30	8	0	38	.79	1.13
flurazepam	5	1	0	6	.83	4	1	0	5	.80	1.04
lorazepam	12	2	0	16	.86	18	3	0	21	.86	1.00
alcohol	7	2	1	10	.70	20	2	0	22	.91	.77
propranolol	1	3	1	5	.20	5	2	0	7	.71	.28
caffeine	0	6	3	9	.00	1	7	0	8	.13	.00

n: Number of trials with no drug-related impairment of behavior.
+: Number of trials with drug-related enhancement of behavior.
−: Number of trials with drug-related impairment of behavior.

the investigator impatient to participate in the advancement of methodology or an increasingly comprehensive understanding of behavioral effects.

TREATMENT-RELATED CHANGES IN GERIATRIC SAMPLES

Within the last two decades there have been conspicuous changes in the way in which people over 60 years of age view themselves and are viewed by others. The average life expectancy for most persons has increased, and accordingly, there is an increased interest in the treatment of behavioral problems among the elderly.

The usual diversity of mental problems may be found among the old, but age brings an important shift in the relative prevalence of problems. For the most part, behavioral difficulties of the elderly seem to be related to impairment of mental faculties. Conspicuous also are dysphoric changes in affect that may be realistic responses to the accelerating loss in their capacities and the diminished significance of the role they can play. Because diminution of mental faculties, particularly memory, is probably the single most common basis for a concern on the part of patients and their associates, many treatments have been sought and evaluated from the standpoint of their potential for retarding, ameliorating, and possibly reversing what had appeared to be an irreversible deteriorating process.

Pharmacotherapy

It is amply evident that most therapists regard drugs as the treatment of choice for the problems of the elderly and do not consider this group to be desirable candidates for psychotherapy (Kucharski, White, & Schratz, 1979). In addition to the antipsychotic, antidepressant, and anti-anxiolytic medications that are prescribed for the general population, there are several substances that offer some promise for ameliorating those deteriorating mental changes that, for most persons, accompany advancing years.

The literature presents considerable diversity in the kinds of behavioral losses experienced by old people, the medications that have been subject to clinical trial, and the findings of pertinent reports. Reports of a comprehensive review of this literature (Wittenborn, 1981a, 1981b) lend themselves to our present interest. This review was limited to studies of the efficacy of pharmacotherapy for samples of patients over 65 years of age. All of the samples comprised persons described as experiencing some degree of impairment, which ranged from minimal to major. Samples of primarily psychotic patients or patients suffering from functional disorders uncomplicated by evidence of mental impairment were excluded, as were samples of patients whose impairment was a consequence of stroke, trauma, or toxic influences. Only controlled investigations that provided explicit tests of statistical significance of intertreatment group contrasts were included.

Table 20.8 identifies the 28 tests that discriminated in at least one study and indicates the frequency with which they were used and were discriminated. The literature identified 42 additional tests that failed to discriminate. Formal mental tests were not major contributors to the evidence of therapeutic efficacy. This modest evidence of the pertinence of mental tests for displaying drug-related behavioral changes in the elderly may be partly due to the kinds of studies in which the tests were applied and also to the kinds of patients treated and the conditions under which the treatment occurred. Regardless of the explanation for these particular results, the value of mental tests for assessing pharmacotherapy for the elderly remains to be shown and may require approaches relating population characteristics to test requirements in a way that was not always provided by studies included in the present series.

The review distinguished the rating scales and inventories on the basis of whether the device was sufficiently standard to have a name or whether it was an ad hoc procedure designed to serve the needs of the investigation. There were 24 named scales. Ten were used more than once, and 14 were used one time only. The 10 named scales used more than once provided some significant discriminations in one half of the studies in which they were applied (Table 20.9). The named scales that were used in a single study were significant discriminators in only 3 (21%) of the 14 studies in which they were used. The 16 unnamed or ad hoc scales were significant discriminators in 71% of the applications. These findings suggest that investigators may sometimes resort to the use of a known procedure even though it may not be wholly appropriate for their purposes. The findings indicate that an ad hoc assessment designed to reflect the anticipated changes can be discriminating, despite its lack of a background of successful use that often supports the familiar named procedures.

Findings for the named scales are summarized in Table 20.10. It is strikingly apparent that only observer rating scales were effective in showing significant differences between treatment groups, and that

Table 20.8. Testing Procedures That Distinguished* Between the Responses of Drug and Placebo Groups (Geriatrics)

SCORE	USED	DISCRIMINATED	SCORE	USED	DISCRIMINATED
Orientation	13	5	Wechsler Adult	1	1
Digit Span	12	2	Intelligence Scale—		
Digit Symbol Substitution	7	2	Comprehension		
Test			Wechsler Memory—	1	1
Abstractions	6	2	Visual		
Writing Performance	5	1	Paired Associate—	1	1
General Information	5	1	Pictorial		
Successive Subtractions	5	1	Digit Copying	1	1
Wechsler Memory	5	1	Bourdon-Wiersma	1	1
Learning Associates			Cancellation		
Gottschaldt Hidden	2	1	Spoke Test	1	1
Figures			Figure Perception	1	1
Bender-Gestalt	4	1			
Raven	4	1	Yerkes-Spatial	1	1
Vocabulary	4	1	Visualizing		
			Delayed Recall	1	1
Finger Tapping	3	2	Object Memory	1	1
Critical Flicker Fusion	3	2	Apraxia	1	1
Similarities	3	1			
Short-Term Memory	3	1			
Krakau Visual Acuity	2	2			
Test					

*42 scored behaviors were tested without any significant discriminations.

none of the well-known self-report inventories provided any discrimination. There are various possible explanations for the failure of self-report inventories in the studies of the elderly. Perhaps elderly subjects were too distractible in the testing situation or their comprehension was limited. It is also possible that old people are particularly unrealistic in identifying the specific nature of their failures and in recognizing specific improvements.

An increasing portion of the population is now surviving more than 70 years. Among these, senior persons many will suffer the devastation of Alzheimer's disease or other memory impairments. Currently the memory aspects of age-related changes have become a major interest among psychopharmacologists and behavioral methodologists. In response to

this situation, the pharmaceutical industry offers substances in the hope that they may have an ameliorating, if not restorative, effect on memory losses. Unfortunately, most investigations fail to show significant therapeutic efficacy.

While the drug industry has been modifying the substances submitted for clinical testing, the methodologists have sought to improve the sensitivity of instruments for the assessment of behavioral changes, particularly in memory functions. Perhaps the most comprehensive program of test development has been undertaken by Thomas Crook and his associates who have formed Memory Assessment Clinics, Incorporated, in Bethesda, Maryland. They have organized an inclusive battery of memory tests and are in the process of securing a large body of normative data

Table 20.9. Incidence of Discriminating Use

RATING SCALES	NUMBER OF SCALES	NUMBER OF COMPARISONS*	COMPARISONS WITH SIGNIFICANT DISCRIMINATION	PORTION WITH SIGNIFICANT DISCRIMINATION
Named scales—Multiple use	10	36	18	.50
Named scales—Single use	14	14	3	.21
Unnamed scales	16	17	12	.71

*More than one scale might be applied in a single study.

Table 20.10. Named Rating Scales Used in More Than One Placebo-Controlled Study of Psychotropic Drug Effects in Old People

RATING SCALE	NUMBER OF STUDIES INVOLVED	STUDIES WITH AT LEAST ONE MODIFIED BEHAVIOR*	PORTION WITH AT LEAST ONE MODIFIED BEHAVIOR*
Nurses' Observation Scale for Inpatient Evaluation (NOSIE)	7	3	.43
Profile of Mood Scales (POMS)**	5	0	.00
Sandoz Clinical Assessment-Geriatrics (SCAG)	4	4	1.00
Brief Psychiatric Rating Scale (BPRS)	3	2	.67
Crichton Royal Behavior Scale	2	2	1.00
Stockton Geriatric Rating Scale	2	0	.00
Barabee-Hyde Hospital Adjustment Rating Scale	2	0	.00
Beck Depression Rating Scale**	2	0	.00
Taylor Manifest Anxiety Scale (TMAS)**	2	0	.00
SCAGlike Scales	7	7	1.00

*At least one scorable component with a significant drug-placebo contrast in change.
**Self-descriptive.

suitable for showing differences between age groups. (Descriptions of the memory assessment battery of Dr. Crook's group and copies of their latest reports may be obtained by writing to the authors.) These tests appear to be modifications of earlier testing procedures; whether these modifications will be appreciably more sensitive than their antecedents remains to be seen. It is possible that the standard use of a comprehensive battery of assessments for a large sample could reveal patterns of memory performance. Such patterns of performance could be examined for changes in the course of deteriorating disease or in response to effective therapies.

Psychotherapy

Elderly patients may be regarded by many psychiatrists as undesirable candidates for psychotherapy (Ford & Sbordone, 1980; Kucharski et al., 1979), but there is an appreciable literature describing psychotherapeutic-like interventions in the care of elderly who suffer from behavioral disturbances or disabilities. Much of this literature describes how such intervention might be or has been conducted. Unfortunately, most of these accounts have an anecdotal quality, present few if any systematic comparisons, and do not qualify as reports of controlled investigations.

In addition to this literature, which usually refers to small samples or illustrative case descriptions, there are a few reports of systematic studies based on adequate samples, conventional designs, and analyses of the significance of intergroup differences in mean change. The literature of relatively strong studies is quite small, however, and the present review is based on the strongest available reports. Two studies were concerned with reality orientation therapy, but the methods used differed somewhat. A third study was concerned with the efficacy of individualized treatment for patients approached from the standpoint of their excess disabilities. The fourth study described the use of brief psychotherapy providing sessions limited to 15 minutes, and the fifth study examined the efficacy of a daily program of physical stimulation wherein patients were maintained in an enriched program of activity. In these five investigations, improvement in the patients' performance in practical respects, such as self-care, communication, and social interaction as well as the diminution of affective disturbance and various indications of dementia, were central among the therapeutic objectives. The discriminating assessments indicating therapeutic efficacy are listed in Table 20.11.

The five studies on which Table 20.11 is based represent, but may not include all, the appropriate studies that might be found in the literature. Nevertheless, they suggest that benefits can result from psychotherapy with geriatric patients and that these differentiating benefits may be detected by the use of formal assessment procedures.

Table 20.11. Assessments Sensitive to Psychotherapies in Geriatric Samples

ASSESSMENT	FREQUENCY OF USE	SOURCE OF PROCEDURE
Mental Status Exam	1	Bower, 1967
Therapist's Rating	1	Godbole & Verinis, 1974
Zung Depression Scale	1	Zung, 1965
Scale of Excess Disability	1	Brody, Kleban, Lawton, & Silverman, 1971
Test of Reality Orientation with Geriatric Patients (TROG)	1	Johnson, McLaren, & McPherson, 1981
Florida State Hospital Behavior Rating Sheet	1	Harris, 1976

COMMENTS FOR THE FUTURE

Minor modifications of traditional assessment, whether tests, inventories, or rating scales, are much in evidence. It is not yet clear, however, that significant advances have been made in the definition and assessment of target behaviors, Clinical observations and published case descriptions have generated ways of thinking that have become traditional, and these familiar ways of thinking have determined our expectations and directed our observations with self-confirming consequences. This situation is inimical to advancements. If we are to continue our advancements in the amelioration of behavioral problems, we must break out of the views that have become stereotyped and challenge the adequacy, if not the pertinence, of our therapeutic goals and our criteria for therapeutic gain.

At the very least, further advances in the identification and the research evidence of psychotherapeutic efficacy will require evaluative review of the content of the assessment devices in current use. Perhaps we have been blinded by our own limited conceptions of the nature of the behavior that one should attempt to change. Perhaps our criteria do not sufficiently reflect the patient's expectations concerning him- or herself and others at the time treatment is sought. Is it possible that the criteria in common use neglect the importance of the desires and expectations of others who are a part of the patient's interpersonal environment? It is the patient's discomfort or the discomfort of others who share his life that brings the patient into treatment, but the criteria in common use may not reflect these qualities of distress sufficiently to show changes generated by effective therapy. Moreover, our criteria may not reflect some of the areas in which the therapy has not provided desired amelioration of the distress.

If we find that the patient's distress involves features that are either disregarded or insufficiently represented by assessment procedures in current use, we should not hesitate to attempt to devise practicable assessment procedures that are sensitive to all aspects of the patient's distress. It is possible that the psychotherapist also has disregarded pertinent aspects of the patient's situation. Those who develop assessment procedures should not hesitate to represent new and different criteria of potential significance even though the psychotherapists do not currently consider those aspects to be prime objectives.

Our understanding of the neurochemical mechanisms involved in behavior, particularly disordered behavior, appears to be on the threshold of new concepts which almost certainly will stimulate significant revisions in our approaches to the assessment of behavior disorders and their modification. As the neurophysiologists offer us hope that we can expect new drugs designed to intervene in neurological processes involved in the generation of explicit behavior, we must anticipate changes in the methods by which the efficacy of such intervention is assessed. The behavior that reflects modified neurophysiologic functions may not correspond in any direct and obvious manner with the behavioral manifestations that therapists seek to modify. It would seem to be a most remarkable coincidence if the behaviors in which we wish to intervene were found to correspond closely with any natural neurophysiologic pattern. It is possible that we will find it useful to perceive socially relevant behavior in terms of components which we do not now recognize as pertinent, but which may have the advantage of a close correspondence with neurophysiologic functions. If components of the therapist's target behavior are identified as expressions of known neurophysiologic functions directly responsive to drugs, it may be most expeditious for us to measure these components as a primary step and as a secondary step to weight them according to their involvement with the target behavior.

Advancement in treatment must be defined in terms of criteria. Irrelevant criteria, or obtuse or misused assessments can deny advancement.

NOTES

The preparation of this manuscript was supported in part by a grant from the Cape Branch Foundation, Dayton, New Jersey.

REFERENCES

Alpert, R., & Haber, R. N. (1960). Anxiety in academic achievement situations. *Journal of Abnormal and Social Psychology*, *61*, 207–215.

Axelrod, J. (1986, December). Transduction of neurotransmitter and hormone signals: Anterior pituitary and thyroid cells. In S. H. Snyder (Chair), *Plenary Nobel Laureate lecture*. Fifteenth convention of the Collegium Internationale Neuro-Psychopharmacologicum, San Juan, Puerto Rico.

Bandura, A., Adams, N. E., & Beyer, J. (1977). Cognitive processes mediating behavioral change. *Journal of Personality and Social Psychology*, *35*, 125–129.

Beck, A. T. (1967). *Depression: Clinical, experimental and theoretical aspects*. New York: Harper & Row.

Beck, A. T., & Beamesderfer, A. (1974). Assessment of depression: The depression inventory. In P. Pinchot (Ed.), *Psychological measurement in pharmacopsychiatry* (Vol. 7). Basel: S. Karger.

Baubien, C. O. (1970). *Adolescent-parent communication styles*. Unpublished doctoral dissertation, Pennsylvania State University.

Biran, M., & Wilson, G. T. (1981). Treatment of phobic disorders using cognitive and exposure methods: A self-efficacy analysis. *Journal of Consulting and Clinical Psychology*, *49*, 886–889.

Bloom, F. E. (1986, December). Molecular mechanisms of psychopathology. In W. E. Bunney, (Chair), *Plenary Nobel Laureate Lecture*. Fifteenth convention of the Collegium Internationale Neuro-Psychopharmacologicum, San Juan, Puerto Rico.

Bower, H. M. (1967). Sensory stimulation and the treatment of senile dementia. *Medical Journal of Australia*, *1*, 1113–1119.

Brody, E. M., Kleban, M. H., Lawton, M. P., & Silverman, H. A. (1971). Excess disabilities of mentally impaired aged: Impact of individualized treatment. *Gerontologist*, *11*, 124–133.

Brown, M. (1969). *A set of eight parallel forms of the digit symbol test*. Unpublished set of tests, University of Waterloo, Waterloo, Ontario, Canada.

Brown, W. F. (1975). *Effective study test: Manual of directions*. San Marcos, TX: Effective Study Materials.

Clyde, D. J. (1963). *Manual for the Clyde Mood Scale*. Miami: Clyde Computing Service.

Derogatis, L. R. (1977). *SCL-90, administration, scoring, and procedures manual for the revised version*. Baltimore, MD: Johns Hopkins University School of Medicine.

Derogatis, L. R., Lipman, R. S., Rickels, K., Uhlenhuth, E. H., & Covi, L. (1973). The Hopkins Symptom Checklist (HSCL): A Measure of primary symptom dimensions. In P. Pichot (Ed.), *Psychological measurement in pharmacopsychiatry* (Vol. 7). Basel: S. Karger.

Desai, N., Taylor-Davies, A., Barnett, D. B. (1983). The effects of diazepam and oxprenolol on short term memory in individuals of high and low state anxiety. *British Journal of Clinical Pharmacology*, *15*, 197–202.

Dosamantes-Alperson, E. (1975). *The Dosamantes-Alperson Expressive Movement Scale*. Unpublished test, California State University, Los Angeles, CA.

Downing, R. W., & Rickels, K. (1972). Predictors of amitriptyline response in outpatient depressives. *Journal of Nervous and Mental Disease*, *154*, 248–263.

Ellis, A. (1962). *Reason and emotion in psychotherapy*. New York: Lyle Stuart.

Ely, A., Guerney, B. G., Jr., & Stover, L. (1973). Efficacy of the training phase of conjugal therapy. *Psychotherapy: Theory, research and practice*, *10*, 201–207.

Eysenck, H. J., & Eysenck, S. B. G. (1968). *Manual: Eysenck Personality Inventory*. San Diego: Educational and Industrial Testing Service.

Foa, E. B., Steketee, G., & Milby, J. B. (1980). Differential effects of exposure and response prevention in obsessive-compulsive washers. *Journal of Consulting and Clinical Psychology*, *48*, 71–79.

Ford, C. V., & Sbordone, R. J. (1980). Attitudes of psychiatrists toward elderly patients. *American Journal of Psychiatry*, *137*, 571–575.

Franks, C. M., & Barbrack, C. R. (1983). Behavior therapy with adults: An integrative approach. In M. Hersen, A. E. Kazdin, & A. S. Bellack (Eds.), *The clinical psychology handbook*. Elmsford, NY: Pergamon Press.

Freud, S. (1935). *A general introduction to psychoanalysis.* New York: Liveright Publishing Corp.

Fuchs, C. Z., & Rehm, L. P. (1977). A self-control behavior therapy program for depression. *Journal of Consulting and Clinical Psychology, 45,* 206–215.

Godbole, A., & Verinis, J. S. (1974). Brief psychotherapy in the treatment of emotional disorders in physically ill geriatric patients. *Gerontologist, 15,* 143–148.

Graham, F. K., & Kendall, B. S. (1960). Memory for Designs Test: General revised manual. *Perceptual and Motor Skills,* Monograph Supplement, *11,* 147–188.

Guerney, B. G., Jr. (1977). *Relationship enhancement: Skill-training programs for therapy, problem prevention, and enrichment.* San Francisco: Jossey-Bass.

Guy, W. (Ed.). (1976). *ECDEU Assessment manual for psychopharmacology* (rev. ed.). (DHEW Publication No. ADM 76-338). Washington, DC: U.S. Government Printing Office.

Hamilton, M. (1959). The Assessment of anxiety states by rating. *British Journal of Medical Psychology, 32,* 50–55.

Hamilton, M. (1967). Development of a rating scale for primary depressive illness. *British Journal of Social and Clinical Psychology, 6,* 278–296.

Harris, C. (1976). The Florida State Hospital Patient Behavior Rating Sheet. In J. Cone & R. Hawkins (Eds.), *Behavior assessment: New directions in clinical psychology.* New York: Brunner Mazel.

Hathaway, S. R., & Meehl, P. E. (1951). *An atlas for the clinical use of the MMPI.* Minneapolis: University of Minnesota Press.

Heimberg, L. (1961). *Development and construct validation for an inventory for the measurement of future time perspective.* Unpublished master's thesis, Vanderbilt University.

Hinrichs, J. V., Ghoneim, M. M., & Mewaldt, S. P. (1984). Diazepam and memory: Retrograde facilitation produced by interference reduction. *Psychopharmacology, 84,* 158–162.

Honigfeld, G., & Klett, C. (1965). The Nurses' Observation Scale for Inpatient Evaluation (NOSIE): A new scale for measuring improvement in chronic schizophrenia. *Journal of Clinical Psychology, 21,* 65–71.

Husek, T., & Alexander, S. (1963). The effectiveness of anxiety differential in examination stress situations. *Educational Psychological Measurements, 23,* 309–318.

Johnson, C. H., McLaren, S. M., & McPherson, F. M. (1981). The comparative effectiveness of three versions of "classroom" reality orientation. *Age and Ageing, 10,* 33–35.

Jones, R. G. (1969). *A factored measure of Ellis' irrational belief system, with personality and maladjustment correlates.* Doctoral Dissertation, Texas Technological College. (University Microfilms, No. 69-6443).

Jourard, S. M., & Remy, R. M. (1957). Individual variance scores: An index of the degree of differentiation of the self and the body image. *Journal of Clinical Psychology, 13,* 62–63.

Kassinove, H., Crisci, R., & Tiegerman, S. (1977). Developmental trends in rational thinking. *Journal of Community Psychology, 5,* 266–274.

Kirkland, K., & Hollandsworth, J. G., Jr. (1980). Effective test taking: Skills-acquisition versus anxiety reduction techniques. *Journal of Consulting and Clinical Psychology, 48,* 431–439.

Kucharski, L. T., White, R. M., Jr., & Schratz, M. S. (1979). Age bias, referral for psychological assistance and the private physician. *Journal of Gerontology, 34,* 423–428.

Lazarus, A. A. (1961). Group therapy of phobic disorders by systematic desensitization. *Journal of Abnormal and Social Psychology, 63,* 504–510.

Liebert, R. M., & Morris, L. W. (1967). Cognitive and emotional components of test anxiety: A distinction and some initial data. *Psychological Reports, 20,* 975–978.

MacPhillamy, D. J., & Lewinsohn, P. M. (1972, September). *The measurement of reinforcing events.* Paper presented at the meeting of the American Psychological Association, Honolulu.

McLean, P. D., & Hakstian, A. R. (1979). Clinical depression: Comparative efficacy of outpatient treatments. *Journal of Consulting and Clinical Psychology, 47,* 818–836.

McNair, D. M., Lorr, M., & Droppleman, L. F. (1971). *Manual for the Profile of Mood States.* San Diego: Educational and Industrial Testing Services.

McReynolds, W. T., & Tori, C. (1972). A further assessment of attention-placebo effects and demand characteristics in studies of systematic desensitization. *Journal of Consulting and Clinical Psychology, 38,* 261–264.

Meichenbaum, D. H. (1972). Cognitive modification of test-anxious college students. *Journal of Consulting and Clinical Psychology, 39,* 370–380.

Meyer, A. (1951). The collected papers of Adolf

Meyer. In E. E. Winters (Ed.), *Mental Hygiene* (Vol. 4). Baltimore: Johns Hopkins University Press.

Meyer, E., III, Derogatis, L. R., Miller, M. J., Reading, A. J., Cohen, I. H., Park, L. C., & Whitmarsh, G. A. (1981). Addition of time-limited psychotherapy to medical treatment in a general medical clinic. *Journal of Nervous and Mental Disease, 169,* 780–790.

Miskimins, R. W. (1972). *Manual: MSGO II.* Fort Collins, CO: Rocky Mountain Behavioral Science Institute.

Miskimins, R. W., & Braucht, G. N. (1971). *Description of the Self.* Fort Collins, CO: Rocky Mountain Behavioral Science Institute.

Overall, J. E., & Gorham, D. R. (1962). The Brief Psychiatric Rating Scale. *Psychological Reports, 10,* 799–812.

Parker, E. S., Birnbaum, I. M., Weingartner, H., Hartley, J. T., Stillman, R. C., & Wyatt, R. J. (1980). Retrograde enhancement of human memory with alcohol. *Psychopharmacology, 69,* 219–222.

Paul, G. L. (1966). *Insight vs. desensitization in psychotherapy: An experiment in anxiety reduction.* Stanford: Stanford University Press.

Peeke, S. C., & Peeke, H. V. S. (1984). Attention, memory and cigarette smoking. *Psychopharmacology, 84,* 205–216.

Reynolds, D. J. (1967). *The Temple Fear Survey Inventory.* Unpublished manuscript, Temple University.

Robinson, R. A. (1964). The diagnosis and prognosis of dementia. In W. F. Anderson (Ed.), *Current achievements in geriatrics.* London: Cassell.

Rogers, C. R. (1942). *Counseling and psychotherapy.* Boston: Houghton-Mifflin.

Sarason, I. G. (1972). Experimental approaches to test anxiety: Attention and the use of information. In C. D. Speilberger (Ed.), *Anxiety: Current trends in theory and research* (Vol. 2). New York: Academic Press.

Sarason, I. G. (1976). *Cognitive Interference Questionnaire.* Unpublished instrument. Seattle, WA: University of Washington.

Shader, R. I., Harmatz, J. S., & Salzman, C. (1974). A new scale for clinical assessment in geriatric populations: Sandoz Clinical Assessment Geriatric (SCAG). *Journal of American Geriatric Society, 22,* 107–113.

Shostrom, E. L. (1964). A test for the measurement of self-actualization. *Educational and Psychological Measurement, 24,* 207–218.

Snyder, S. H. (1986, December). Multiple receptors for multiple messengers. In O. J. Rafaelsen (Chair), *Plenary Nobel Laureate Lecture.* Fifteenth convention of the Collegium Internationale Neuro-Psychopharmacologicum, San Juan, Puerto Rico.

Soeken, D. R., Manderschied, R. W., Flatter, C. H., & Silbergeld, S. (1981). A controlled study of quantitative feedback in married-couples brief group psychotherapy. *Psychotherapy: Theory, Research and Practice, 18,* 204–218.

Spielberger, C., Gorsuch, R., & Lushene, R. (1970). *The State-Trait Anxiety Inventory (STAI) test manual.* Palo Alto, CA: Consulting Psychologists Press.

Suinn, R. M. (1969). The STABS, a measure of test anxiety for behavior therapy: Normative data. *Behavior Research and Therapy, 7,* 335–339.

Tori, C., & Worell, L. (1973). Reduction of human avoidant behavior: A comparison of counterconditioning, expectancy, and cognitive information approaches. *Journal of Consulting and Clinical Psychology, 41,* 269–278.

Walk, R. D. (1956). Self-ratings of fear in a fear-invoking situation. *Journal of Abnormal and Social Psychology, 52,* 171–178.

Warburton, D. M., Wesnes, K., Shergold, K., & James, M. (1986). Facilitation of learning and state dependency with nicotine. *Psychopharmacology, 89,* 55–59.

Watson, J. B. (1925). *Behaviorism.* New York: W. W. Norton.

Watson, D., & Friend, R. (1969). Measurement of social-evaluative anxiety. *Journal of Consulting and Clinical Psychology, 33,* 448–457.

Wechsler, D. (1955). *Manual for the Wechsler Adult Intelligence Scale.* New York: Psychological Corporation.

Wechsler, D., & Stone, C. P. (1945). Manual for Wechsler Memory Scale. *Journal of Psychology, 19,* 87–95.

Wittenborn, J. R. (1955). *Manual: Wittenborn Psychiatric Rating Scale.* New York: Psychological Corporation.

Wittenborn, J. R. (1966a). Psychiatric syndromes as a cultural phenomenon. *Proceedings of the 5th International Congress of the Collegium Internationale Neuro-Psychopharmacologicum,* Washington 1966, Excerpta Medica International Congress Series 129.

Wittenborn, J. R. (1966b). The assessment of clinical change. In J. O. Cole & J. R. Wittenborn (Eds.),

Pharmacotherapy of depression. Springfield, IL: Charles C. Thomas.

Wittenborn, J. R. (1971). The design of clinical trials. In J. Levine, B. C. Schiele, & L. Bouthilet (Eds.), *Principles and problems in establishing the efficacy of psychotropic agents*. Washington, DC: U.S. Government Printing Office. Public Health Service Publication No. 2138.

Wittenborn, J. R. (Ed.), (1977). Guidelines for clinical trials of psychotropic drugs. *Pharmakopsychiatrie Neuro-Psychopharmakologie, 4,* 205–264.

Wittenborn, J. R. (1978). Behavioral toxicity in normal humans as a model for assessing behavioral toxicity in patients. In M. A. Lipton, A. DiMascio, & K. F. Killam (Eds.), *Psychopharmacology: A generation of progress*. New York: Raven Press.

Wittenborn, J. R. (1979). Effects of benzodiazepines on psychomotor performance. *British Journal of Clinical Pharmacology, 7,* 61S–67S.

Wittenborn, J. R. (1980). Behavioral toxicity of psychotropic drugs. *Journal of Nervous and Mental Disease, 168,* 171–176.

Wittenborn, J. R. (1981a). The assessment of behavioral changes in geriatric patients. *Psychopharmacology Bulletin, 17,* 96–103.

Wittenborn, J. R. (1981b). Pharmacotherapy for age-related behavioral deficiencies. *Journal of Nervous and Mental Disease, 169,* 139–156.

Wittenborn, J. R. (1987). Psychomotor tests in psychopharmacology. In I. Hindmarch & P. D. Stonier (Eds.), *Human psychopharmacology measures and methods* (Vol. 1). Chichester: Wiley.

Wittenborn, J. R. (1988). Assessment of the effects of drugs on memory. In I. Hindmarch & H. Ott (Eds.), *Benzodiazepine Receptor Ligands, Memory and Information Processing*. Berlin: Springer-Verlag.

Wittenborn, J. R., Flaherty, C. F., Jr., McGough, W. E., Bossange, K. A., & Nash, R. J. (1976). A comparison of the effect of imipramine, nomifensine, and placebo on the psychomotor performance of normal males. *Psychopharmacology, 51,* 85–90.

Wittenborn, J. R., Plante, M., & Burgess, F. (1961). A comparison of physicians' and nurses' symptom ratings. *Journal of Nervous and Mental Disease, 133,* 514–518.

Wittenborn, J. R., Plante, M., Burgess, F., & Livermore, N. (1961). The efficacy of electroconvulsive therapy, iproniazid and placebo in the treatment of young depressed women. *Journal of Nervous and Mental Disease, 133,* 316–332.

Zuckerman, M. (1960). The development of an affect adjective checklist for the measurement of anxiety. *Journal of Consulting Psychology, 24,* 457–462.

Zuckerman, M., Lubin, B., & Robins, S. (1965). Validation of the Multiple Affect Adjective Check List in clinical situations. *Journal of Consulting Psychology, 29,* 594.

Zung, W. W. K. (1965). A Self-rating depression scale. *Archives of General Psychiatry, 12,* 63–70.

Zung, W. W. K. (1971). A rating instrument for anxiety disorders. *Psychosomatics, 12,* 371–379.

CHAPTER 21

TESTING AND INDUSTRIAL APPLICATION

Robert Gatewood
Robert Perloff

The assessment of individuals has been the main focus of the related fields of industrial psychology and personnel/human resource management since their beginning approximately 80 years ago. One primary use of such assessment has been for selection with the purpose of measuring individual differences among job applicants and identifying those with greater amounts of the knowledge and abilities necessary for job performance. A second major purpose of individual assessment has been the identification of training needs of employees. In this, tests are used as diagnostic instruments in order to identify weaknesses of employees in the performance of job tasks. Training programs are then used to correct the deficiencies.

Primarily since the 1950s, assessment has broadened from the concentration on knowledge and abilities to other characteristics of individuals and other organizational purposes. After the development of personality inventories in clinical psychology, these instruments began to be used in selection and career development. Attitude measurement of employees has also become widespread with the resulting data used diagnostically. These measurements indicate the positive and negative perceptions of employees about specific organizational features such as supervisory behavior, compensation, and physical facilities. Results indicate areas in possible need of modification. Testing of vision, hearing, and strength related to the performance of specific job activities has been widely carried out. Recently, honesty testing by use of either polygraphs or paper-and-pencil tests has also become popular, mainly because of the magnitude of embezzlement and theft within organizations. Similarly, there is currently much discussion about testing both job applicants and employees for alcohol and drug use.

The purpose of this chapter is to present an overview of many of the currently used assessment devices within organizations. In doing this, we will describe the nature of the major types of devices that are used, indicate the purposes of the assessment, and summarize research regarding the use of such devices in organizations. When appropriate, statements will also be made concerning the legal implications of these assessment devices. With the passage of the various equal employment opportunity laws, much attention has been given to the impact of assessment devices on minority groups. Such attention has, obviously, had major implications for using these devices in making employment decisions.

ASSESSMENT OF KNOWLEDGE, SKILLS, AND ABILITIES

As indicated previously, the assessment of knowledge, skills, and abilities has been useful in selection, training needs assessment, and career development.

The most-often used types of devices have been achievement and aptitude tests, the interview, personality inventories, and performance tests. We will briefly discuss each of these.

Achievement and Aptitude Tests

Achievement and aptitude tests are paper and pencil, usually group-administered, tests of knowledge and ability. The distinction between achievement and aptitude is made primarily on the basis of the use of the test results (Anastasi, 1982). Achievement test results are used to assess present levels of knowledge or ability. Aptitude test results are used to predict future performance of individuals. Essentially, the two types are very similar in content.

Cognitive Tests

Cognitive tests are devices discussed in other chapters as intelligence tests. The history of the use of such tests in selection has been extensive. However, the frequency of use has diminished since the early 1970s when several Supreme Court decisions found that the defendant companies, which used the tests as a standard part of their selection programs, were guilty of race discrimination under the Civil Rights Act of 1964. Subsequent research, however, using criterion-related validity data accumulated over multiple studies, has generally supported the use of cognitive tests in selection for a variety of jobs. Such support is based on both demonstrated validity and the relatively low adverse impact of the tests.

The validity of cognitive tests has been demonstrated in validity generalization studies. The principle of validity generalization holds that the commonly observed variation among validity coefficients, of the same predictor-criterion combination across different organizations, is not due to organizational differences but rather to methodological deficiencies within the validity studies, such as small sample size, unreliability of the measures used, restriction in range, etc. Correcting such deficiencies has produced evidence of the stability of validity coefficients across organizations. Thus, the conclusion of such research is that variation in validity coefficients is artificial and that the validity of a predictor can be generalized across organizations for similar jobs (Schmidt & Hunter, 1984). In such cases, an additional validity study is unnecessary.

Cognitive ability tests have been included frequently in validity generalization studies, partially because of the extensive number of studies that have been reported for these tests. Results, in general, have supported their use in selection. For example, Schmidt, Hunter, and Pearlman (1981), based on an analysis of data from approximately 370,000 clerical workers, showed that the validities of seven cognitive abilities were essentially constant across five different task-defined clerical job families. In a related study, Hunter (1980) used meta-analyses on the results of over 500 criterion-related validity studies of jobs that constituted a representative sample of jobs in the *Dictionary of Occupational Titles* (U.S. Department of Labor, 1977). His conclusion was that cognitive ability tests were valid for all jobs and job families.

Some recent studies (e.g. Algera, Jansen, Roe, & Vijn, 1984; Kemery, Mossholder, & Roth, 1987), however, have criticized the statistical limitations of the meta-analytic procedures that were used in the Schmidt and Hunter studies. The general nature of these criticisms is that the previous statements of the omnibus validity of cognitive tests could be overly optimistic and that scientific prudence is recommended in the interpretation of validity generalization studies.

A second critical topic concerning the use of such tests in selection assessment is the adverse impact they may have on various demographic groups. The evidence in this regard is in general agreement that cognitive tests are not inherently discriminatory. *Differential validity* is the term used to describe the hypothesis that employment tests are less valid for minority than nonminority group members. This concept was thought to be feasible in the years after the early Supreme Court decisions. However, various studies have consistently disclaimed the possibility of the concept. For example, Boehm (1977) examined 31 studies in which 583 validity coefficients were reported. These studies were also scored on methodological characteristics. For the most part, differential validity was observed only in those studies with several methodological limitations. For the methodologically sound studies, no differences in validity coefficients between African-Americans and white groups were observed.

Hunter, Schmidt, and Hunter (1979) examined 781 pairs of validity coefficients in another study of differential validity. The pairs were made up of the correlations between the same predictor variable and criterion variable for both a white and an African-American group of workers. These correlations ranged from approximately −.37 to +.55. Graphs of the pattern of these coefficients were drawn for each

Table 21.1. Comparison of Eight Selection Methods with Standardized Tests

SELECTION METHODS

	Biographical Data	Interview	Peer Evaluation	Self-Assessment	Reference Checks	Academic Performance	Expert Judgment	Projective Techniques
Validity	Equal	Less	Equal	Less	Less	Less	Less	Less
Adverse Impact	Equal or Less	Equal	Presumed to Be More	Less	Equal	Equal	Unknown	Less
Feasibility	Equal	Equal	Less	Less	Less	Less	Less	Less

Note. From "Validity and Fairness of Some Alternative Employee Selection Procedures" by R. Reilly and G. Chao, 1982, *Personnel Psychology, 35,* 1–62. Reprinted by permission.

group. The two curves looked almost identical, meaning that the test acted in the same manner, for both African-Americans and whites.

Reilly and Chao (1982) examined the related issue of adverse impact of tests in comparison to eight other types of selection measures (see Table 21.1). Three characteristics of selection tests were studied: validity, adverse impact, and feasibility (e.g., ease of gathering and scoring data, cost of doing so, and reliability). None of the eight alternative types of selection measures was judged to be superior to tests in terms of validity. Also only two (or possibly three) of the eight demonstrated less adverse impact, and none were judged as more feasible to use. Therefore, it was not apparent that any of the other selection methods was superior; in fact, most were clearly inferior to tests when all three characteristics were taken into account.

It must be noted that other tests in addition to cognitive ability tests were included in many of these studies of differential validity and adverse impact. However, it is generally thought that these conclusions hold true for cognitive tests specifically.

Mechanical Tests

Mechanical tests generally measure either (a) knowledge about or skill in using tools, machines, and electrical equipment; or (b) verbal and mathematical ability to follow directions or make calculations. Within this general format, a wide variety of tests is available. These tests can have a broad array of topics or may be narrowly focused on one specific topic.

One of the most often used broad-topic tests is the Bennet Mechanical Comprehension Test. This paper-and-pencil test has six different forms plus a Spanish language edition. The items of this test contain objects which are almost universally familiar in American culture: airplanes, carts, steps, pulleys, seesaws, gears, etc. The questions measure the respondent's ability to perceive and understand the relationship of physical forces and mechanical elements in practical situations. While requiring some familiarity with these common tools and objects, the questions purportedly assume no more technical knowledge than can be acquired through everyday experience in an industrial society such as ours. Items are pictures with a brief accompanying question. For example, a sample item is a picture of two men carrying a weighted object hanging down from a plank and it asks, "Which man carries more weight?" Because the object is closer to one man than to the other, the correct answer is the man closer to the object. There are 60 such items on each of the alternate forms. Another frequently used general test is the MacQuarrie Test for Mechanical Ability. This is also a paper-and-pencil test that requires about 30 minutes to administer. It contains seven subtests: tracing, tapping, dotting, copying, location, blocks, and pursuit. The nature of some of these subtests is as follows. The tracing test requires the test taker to draw a line through small openings in a series of vertical lines. The dotting test requires placing one dot in each of a series of small squares spaced irregularly.

Examples of specific tests are the Purdue Trade Tests. These are also paper-and-pencil tests. Tests such as the Test for Electricians, the Trade Information Test in Welding, and the Trade Information Test in Engine Lathe Operation are multiple choice questionnaires of technical knowledge in these areas. Example questions are the following: "Cutting oil should be used when cutting screw threads in (a) brass, (b) cast iron, (c) steel, (d) copper." "Conductors of electricity are most often made of (a) iron, (b) brass, (c) lead, (d) copper."

Other tests are performance types. The Hand-Tool Dexterity Test is designed to measure manipulative skill important in factory jobs and industrial apprentice training. The test uses a wooden frame approximately $9'' \times 9'' \times 18''$ in size. On the left-hand upright are mounted four bolts of each of three sizes. Using wrenches and screwdrivers, the test taker takes apart the 12 fastenings according to a prescribed sequence and reassembles the nuts, washers, and bolts on the right-hand upright.

Mechanical ability tests have proven to be valid in selection for specific jobs and useful for diagnosing deficiencies in knowledge of mechanical principles and techniques. For example, Ghiselli (1973) reviewed the use of various tests in selection studies from 1920 through 1971. In doing this, he grouped jobs into eight general occupations and tests into five general types (Table 21.2). Two of these types of tests were those measuring spatial and mechanical abilities and those measuring motor abilities. The former demonstrated relatively high validity coefficients for managerial, service, vehicle, trades and crafts, and industrial occupations. The latter were useful for selection in service, vehicle, trades and crafts, and industrial occupations.

Clerical Tests

Traditionally, clerical jobs have been thought of as those similar to bookkeeping, typing, filing, and recordkeeping positions. The analyses that have been done of these types of jobs have indicated that they consist of extensive checking or copying of words and numbers and the orderly movement and placement of objects such as files and reports. Therefore, clerical ability tests have predominantly measured perceptual speed and accuracy in the processing of verbal and numerical data.

Perhaps the most widely used clerical ability test is the Minnesota Clerical Test. The test is a brief, easily administered and easily scored instrument. It has two separately timed and scored subtests: number checking and name checking. In each subtest there are 200 items. Each item consists of a pair of numbers or names. The respondent is to compare the pair and place a check on a line between the two entries of the pair if these two entries are identical. If the two entries are different, no mark is placed on the line. The entries in the numbers subtest range from 3 through 12 digits; the entries in the names subtest range from 7 through 16 letters. The score is the number right minus the number wrong.

Although the two subtests are related, they do measure separate abilities (Selover, 1949). The names subtest has been found to be correlated with speed of reading, spelling, and group measures of intelligence. The numbers subtest has been related to the verification of arithmetic computations. Scores on the subtests are only slightly related to either educational level or experience in clerical positions.

Ghiselli's (1973) study (Table 21.2) found that this type of test is related to training and work performance for clerical, managerial, protective, trades and crafts, and industrial occupations.

Interview

The interview has been one of the most often used selection devices, as it can be applied to all job groups. However, periodic reviews of the use of this method in terms of the prediction of future job performance of applicants have generally found widespread deficiencies. These have been in both reliability among interviewers in their assessment of applicants and also the validity of predictions (Schmitt, 1976). These disparities, in turn, have led to an extensive study of factors of the interview that have impeded the evaluation of interviewers. We will summarize these areas of study in this section. A more complete discussion of the interview is presented by Eder and Ferris (1989).

One source of difficulty with the interview has been its use in assessing a wide variety of characteristics of applicants (Gatewood & Feild, 1990). Depending on the specific job of interest, some of the characteristics that have been assessed are job knowledge, personality traits, future work motivation, adjustment to incumbent workers, verbal ability, and career development potential. While such a diversity of characteristics is theoretically possible to measure, reviews have agreed that there is evidence to support the assessment of only a few of these. Ulrich and Trumbo (1965) concluded that "the interviewer is all too frequently asked to do the impossible because of limitations on the time, information, or both.

Table 21.2. Validity Coefficients for Occupations

	TRAINING	PERFORMANCE
All Managers		
Intellectual abilities	.30	.27
Spatial and mechanical abilities	.28	.22
Perceptual accuracy	.23	.25
Motor abilities	.02	.14
Clerical Occupations		
Intellectual abilities	.47	.28
Spatial and mechanical abilities	.34	.17
Perceptual accuracy	.40	.29
Motor abilities	.14	.16
Sales Occupations**		
Intellectual abilities		.19
Spatial and mechanical abilities		.18
Perceptual accuracy		.04
Motor abilities		.12
Protective Occupations		
Intellectual abilities	.42	.22
Spatial and mechanical abilities	.35	.18
Perceptual accuracy	.30	.21
Motor abilities		.14
Service Occupations		
Intellectual abilities	.42	.27
Spatial and mechanical abilities	.31	.13
Perceptual accuracy	.25	.10
Motor abilities	.21	.15
Vehicle Occupations		
Intellectual abilities	.18	.16
Spatial and mechanical abilities	.31	.20
Perceptual accuracy	.09	.17
Motor abilities	.31	.25
Trades and Crafts		
Intellectual abilities	.41	.25
Spatial and mechanical abilities	.41	.23
Perceptual accuracy	.35	.24
Motor abilities	.20	.19
Industrial Occupations		
Intellectual abilities	.38	.20
Spatial and mechanical abilities	.40	.20
Perceptual accuracy	.20	.20
Motor abilities	.28	.22

From "The Validity of Aptitude Tests in Personnel Selection" by E. E. Ghiselli, 1973, *Personnel Psychology, 26,* pp. 461–477.
**No data on training available.

. . . When the task was limited . . . acceptable validity was achieved" (p. 114). Three main types of characteristics have been identified as appropriately measured in the interview: job knowledge, personal relations (sociability, verbal fluency, etc.), and work habits (dependability, stability of performance of job tasks, ability to coordinate simultaneous projects, etc.) (Schmitt, 1976).

A number of factors only peripherally related to job performance have been shown to influence the assessment evaluations of interviewers. Physical attractiveness of the applicant and personal liking of the applicant by the interviewer are two such factors (Keenan, 1977). A variety of nonverbal behaviors of the applicant, such as eye contact, head movement, smiling, hand movement, and general body posture have also been identified. The disproportionate influence of any negative information obtained about the interviewee has also been determined (Rowe, 1963). Related to this is the finding that frequently the interviewer makes an overall assessment of the acceptability of the applicant within the first few minutes of the interview (Ulrich & Trumbo, 1965). In addition, contrast effects associated with previous applicants (Valenzi & Andrews, 1973) are among many information processing factors that have been studied (Dreher & Sackett, 1983).

Several court cases, ruling on claims of discrimination due to the interview, have yielded opinions about specific features of the content and process of the interview. Pointed out as sources of discrimination have been the following: having all male and/or all white interviewers, not using a structured or written interview format, not having stated criteria for employment decisions, and not using uniformity in applying selection criteria (Arvey, 1979). Also, research has determined that females are given lower evaluations than comparable male applicants when the jobs of interest are those frequently thought of as "male" jobs (Haetner, 1977).

In terms of improving the psychometric properties of the interview, Langdale and Weitz (1973) concluded that the reliability of assessments increased as the interviewers were given more information about the job to be filled. Osburn, Timmrick, and Bigby (1981) noted higher interviewer accuracy when interviewees were rated on scales keyed to specific behavioral job dimensions. Other research by Arvey, Miller, Gould, and Burch (1987), Latham and Saari (1984), and Weekly and Gier (1987) has documented that when job information is used to develop interview questions as well as to evaluate interviewee answers, interview validity can also be enhanced. The use of a panel rather than a single interviewer has also been linked to increased validity (Arvey & Campion, 1982).

These and related findings have served as the basis for recommendations intended to improve the reliability and validity of the interview. Gatewood and Feild (1990) summarized the main suggestions:

1. restrict the number of applicant characteristics assessed.

2. adopt a semistructured format by predetermining major questions.
3. use job-related questions based on job analysis.
4. use multiple questions for each characteristic assessed.
5. develop a formal scoring system with specified decision rules.
6. use trained, interview panels.

Personality Inventories

The use of personality information in selection is one of the most complex and apparently contradictory topics in the assessment of applicants. On the one hand, there is a body of research that argues that personality characteristics are related to job success. On the other hand, the demonstrated empirical evidence supporting the validity of personality measures in selection is, at best, inconsistent.

Concerning the relationship of personality to job performance, Grimsley and Jarrett (1975) concluded that differences in drive, energy, social adjustment, self-confidence, social aggressiveness, and emotional stability are evident between more and less successful managers. Similarly, a longitudinal study of managers at AT&T found personality differences between those managers who had been promoted to middle-management positions and those who remained at lower managerial positions during an eight-year period (Bray, Campbell, & Grant, 1979).

In opposition to these findings, various reviews have produced the conclusion that as a predictive device, personality tests have had low demonstrated validity. Guion and Gottier (1965) stated that in their review the number of significant findings was barely above the chance level of occurrence. Kinslinger (1966) found that the frequency of methodological shortcomings in studies using projective techniques prevented any positive judgment of their validity. Recently, Schmitt, Gooding, Noe, and Kirsch (1984) reported an average validity coefficient of .15 for self-report personality inventories as determined by meta-analysis. Ghiselli (1973) reported slightly higher coefficients (.16 to .31) across his various occupations (Table 21.2).

For the most part, personality assessment for selection has borrowed heavily from the instruments commonly used for clinical assessment. For example, the MMPI has been used even though the intent of this instrument was not to assist in industrial selection decisions. Other self-report, multiple-choice inventories have also been heavily used, e.g., the California

Psychological Inventory, the Edwards Personal Preference Scale, and the Guilford-Zimmerman Temperament Scale. Projective devices, such as the Rorschach Inkblot Test and the Thematic Apperception Test have also been utilized. Other tests, McClelland's variation of the TAT (McClelland, 1961) and the Miner Sentence Completion Scale (Miner, 1977), have been developed specifically for industrial use.

One explanation for the low validity of personality tests has focused on the inappropriateness of using clinical measures in industrial applications. For example, self-report inventories have been criticized for the ease with which they can be "faked" by respondents. Job applicants, unlike clinical subjects, have a self-serving purpose in presenting responses that convey a socially desirable image. It is generally believed that an applicant should be social, self-confident, aggressive, able to work on multiple projects simultaneously, etc. Studies have demonstrated respondents' ability to change responses on this type of inventory upon demand (Lanyon & Goodstein, 1982). Projective techniques have been criticized for the unreliability of scoring and the cost involved in their use. Partially in response to these criticisms, the Miner Sentence Completion Scale uses a simple, direct scoring system and also limits the amount of responses possible.

Some recent work has been more positive in conclusions about the use of personality data. Cornelius (1983) reviewed studies using projective devices. He concluded that these tests, especially McClelland's TAT and Miner's test, have demonstrated empirical validity. Similarly, Hogan, Carpenter, Briggs, and Hansson (1985) have stated that self-report inventories using broadly defined personality constructs and many items for each measurement scale also have demonstrated validity. In addition, assessment centers, a form of work-sample test that is discussed subsequently in this chapter, have included personality traits among the various dimensions that are measured. Our tentative conclusion, based on all the evidence to date, is that personality measures which are carefully designed for use in organizational situations can provide valid assessments.

Performance Tests

Performance tests are assessment devices that present testing situations that closely resemble actual parts of a job and require the individual to complete some activity under structured testing conditions. The term *motor* is used if the test requires the physical manipulation of equipment or materials, for example operating a machine, installing a piece of equipment, or making a product. The term *verbal* is applied if the testing situation is primarily language or people oriented, for example, simulating an interrogation, editing a manuscript for grammatical errors, or explaining a decision in how to train subordinates. The term *work sample* is frequently used for performance tests that assess nonmanagers. *Assessment centers* are performance tests most often given to managers and professional staff. Both types are used not only for selection but also for diagnosis of training needs.

Work Sample

Most commonly, a work sample has been used for clerical staff, technicians, and skilled craftsmen. Specific tests require typing, welding, wiring connections, cutting and nailing boards, and mixing chemicals. In some cases, the testing procedures are quite elaborate in design. Robinson (1981) describes the building of an $8' \times 12'$ shed that included 25 common and expensive construction errors. For testing, individuals were required to walk through the shed and note all construction errors. The essential requirement in the design of work samples is that they mirror critical job tasks and include systematic scoring procedures. Gatewood and Feild (in press) provide a description of necessary steps in doing this. These include performing a thorough job analysis, obtaining ratings of critical or frequent tasks, designing testing situations that reflect the job in terms of equipment and demands, using either a process or a product scoring system, and training judges in the use of the scoring procedure.

Evaluations of the use of these tests in selection programs have been overwhelmingly positive and have identified several benefits in their use. Gordon and Kleiman (1976) compared work sample and ability tests in relation to success in a police training course using three different samples. In each sample, the work sample test was superior. Schmidt, Greenthol, Hunter, Berner, and Seaton (1977) compared scores of minority and nonminority applicants on both written and work samples for positions as metal trade apprentices. A difference in scores between the two groups was identified for only one of three performance tests but for all five of the written tests. Cascio and Phillips (1979) found that work samples can serve as realistic job previews. That is, the work sample can provide a representative preview of the actual job, including positive and negative aspects. A portion of those applicants finding the job unsuitable removed themselves from the selection program. The net effect was to reduce the turnover rate among new hires, resulting in considerable saving for the organization.

Assessment Centers

An assessment center (AC) consists of a standardized evaluation of behavior based upon multiple assessments. Multiple, trained observers and techniques are used to accomplish this. The development of an AC starts with a job analysis that identifies clusters of job activities that make up the important parts of the job. Each cluster should be specific and observable, and consist of job tasks that can be logically related. These job clusters are referred to as *dimensions,* and it is these that are measured by the assessment center devices. Table 21.3 provides a brief list of dimensions commonly used in ACs.

The concept of an AC calls for each of these dimensions to be measured by several different assessment devices. The assessors then meet for an evaluation session which is intended to develop overall dimension ratings and a global assessment rating across all dimensions. Many assessment devices previously discussed in this text are utilized: mental ability tests, indepth interviews, personality inventories, and achievement tests. The distinguishing feature of ACs is the use of work simulations. Two of the

most commonly used simulations are the In-Basket and the Leaderless Group Discussion LGD.

The In-Basket is a paper-and-pencil test that is intended to replicate administrative tasks. The name of the device is taken from the "in- and out-baskets" that are on some managers' desks and are used to hold organizational memos coming to and going from the manager. An in-basket assessment can consist of up to 30 such memos, each of which requires a direct response from the assessee. In responding, the assessee writes on memo pads/stationery specific actions to be taken, even naming individuals to be involved in these actions. Typically, three hours are allotted for completion. An in-depth interview is administered to the assessee on completion of the in-basket segment and both the oral and written information is used in forming assessments of dimensions of interest. The most commonly used dimensions are planning and organizing, ability to delegate, decisiveness, independence, and initiative.

The LGD is designed to represent those managerial dimensions that require the interaction of small groups of individuals to solve a problem. In the LGD, participants are tested in groups of six. These six are seated around a conference table usually placed in the middle of the room. AC assessors are seated along the

Table 21.3. Behavioral Dimensions Frequently Measured in Assessment Centers

Oral Communication	Effective expression in individual or group situations (includes gestures and nonverbal communications)
Planning and Organizing	Establishing a course of action for self and/or others to accomplish a specific goal; planning proper assignments of personnel and appropriate allocation of resources
Delegation	Utilizing subordinates effectively; allocating decision making and other responsibilities to the appropriate subordinates
Control	Establishing procedures to monitor and/or regulate processes, tasks, or activities of subordinates and job activities and responsibilities; taking action to monitor the results of delegated assignments or projects
Decisiveness	Readiness to make decisions, render judgments, take action, or commit oneself
Initiative	Active attempts to influence events to achieve goals; self-starting rather than passive acceptance. Taking action to achieve goals beyond those called for; originating action.
Tolerance for Stress	Stability of performance under pressure and/or opposition
Adaptability	Maintaining effectiveness in varying environments, with various tasks, responsibilities, or people
Tenacity	Staying with a position or plan of action until the desired objective is achieved or is no longer reasonably attainable

From *Assessment Centers and Managerial Performance* by G. Thorton, III, and W. Byham, 1982, New York, Academic Press.

walls of the room to observe and record the behavior of the participants. The problem presented to the group commonly is an allocation-of-resource dilemma in which there are more demands for the resource than supply. Each participant is asked to play a specific role and is provided brief background information that specifies position in the organization and needs concerning the use of the resource. The group is usually given 1½ hours to arrive at a decision about the allocation. Common dimensions assessed are oral communication, tolerance for stress, persuasiveness, and adaptability.

Validity of assessment ratings have been demonstrated with such criteria as career advancement and work performance (Thornton & Byham, 1982). Another positive feature of ACs is their generally favorable support by courts and the EEOC in alleged discrimination cases. For example, in the much-publicized sex discrimination case against AT&T's promotion policies, ACs were identified as a method to use in modifying these policies (Assessment & Development, 1973). Criticism of the use of ACs has centered on two aspects: (a) their cost relative to that of more conventional assessment devices (Hinrichs, 1978), and (b) the low reliability of ratings of the same dimension across various AC exercises (Sackett & Dreher, 1982).

ASSESSMENT OF ATTITUDES

As mentioned previously, the measurement of attitudes of employees has become of great interest to organizations. Such data are used to diagnose strengths and weaknesses in organizational programs and physical facilities as well as to monitor changes in the work force over time. Scarpello and Vandenberg (in press) have summarized the construction and use of attitude assessment instruments. Although there is obviously a large number of specific topics that have been assessed, we will discuss three of the most frequently measured: job satisfaction, organizational commitment, and job content.

Job Satisfaction

Locke (1976) has defined job satisfaction "as a pleasurable or positive emotional state resulting from the appraisal of one's job or job experiences" (p. 1300). While this definition is generally accepted by both researchers and practitioners, there is no certainty that the measurement of satisfaction reflects this definition, according to Organ and Near (1985).

They point out that job satisfaction is typically measured with instruments modeled after attitude scales. Because psychologists have viewed attitudes as an assemblage of cognition, affective, and action tendencies, factors other than emotional states have entered into the measurement of satisfaction. After reviewing these instruments, Organ and Near concluded that "the items on most job attitude scales tend to focus on the job itself or the facets of the job (e.g., supervision, the task, pay), not on the feelings of the respondent" (p. 244). The wording and format of the items usually require a cognitive evaluation of the work situation. For example the respondent may be asked to judge various aspects of the job relative to how much of this aspect there should be in an ideal job or how much of this aspect he or she expected from the job.

The instruments used to measure job satisfaction are generally classified into two groups: measures of overall satisfaction and measures of satisfaction of specific job facets. Both types typically employ Likert-type items as measuring devices. Cook, Hepworth, Wall, and Warr (1981) have reviewed and illustrated the major instruments. Our comments are partially based on their presentation.

Somewhat surprisingly, measures of overall satisfaction differ widely among the instruments reviewed in terms of number of items and content of questions. Items range from 4 to 38. Content varies from questions about a worker's emotional reactions to the job as a whole, to cognitive reactions of organizational or supervisory functioning, to evaluations of specific intrinsic and extrinsic features of blue-collar jobs. In this type of instrument, responses to all items are summed to produce a total score: the measurement of overall satisfaction. Reported reliabilities, generally internal consistency, are usually at least .80. Most of the instruments that were reviewed also described criterion and construct validity data.

A variety of organizational topics (see Table 21.4) are measured in the 29 instruments of facet satisfac-

Table 21.4. Scales of Job Satisfaction Facet Measures

supervision	social needs
company as a whole	autonomy
nature of work	personal growth
extent of work	esteem needs
co-workers	subordinates
working conditions	intrinsic rewards
pay	extrinsic rewards
promotions	friends' attitudes
security	family attitudes

From *The Experience of Work* by S. D. Cook, S. J. Hepworth, T. D. Wall, and P. B. Warr, 1981, New York, Academic Press.

tion, with various combinations of topics constituting each instrument. Most often measured were satisfaction with pay, promotions, and supervision. More recent instruments have focused on job content/tasks also. As with the overall satisfaction measures, most of the reported reliability estimates for these facet measures are of internal consistency. These estimates are usually .80+ and frequently .90+. This is to be expected due to the homogeneity of content of specific facet scales. Validity data are reported in terms of correlations with other satisfaction measures and correlations among the various scales of an instrument.

Much research has been addressed to the correlates of job satisfaction, especially in terms of work outputs and actions. Among these the relationship of satisfaction to productivity has been the most controversial. It had generally been assumed by managers in organizations and several writers during the 1950s and 1960s that satisfaction is positively correlated with productivity, but reviews of empirical studies by Herzberg, Mausner, Peterson, and Capwell (1957), and Vroom (1964) failed to identify any such relationship. However, recent work by Organ (1977) and Petty, McGee, and Cavender (1984) have disagreed with these conclusions. The latter work applied meta-analysis to studies reported in major journals between 1964 and 1983. A corrected correlation of .31 was found between satisfaction and performance, with 77% of the variance among studies accounted for, using the meta-analytic corrections. The authors concluded that the two variables are, in fact, correlated and the determined correlation is probably an underestimate due to restriction in range caused by various organizational factors. They stated that this new evidence is partially attributable to the more complete data on reliability and variance reported in recent studies.

For other variables, a consistent, inverse relationship has been found between satisfaction and absenteeism and turnover (Herzberg et al., 1957; Vroom, 1964), complaints and grievances (Locke, 1976), output variability, (Locke, 1976), and fatigue, headaches, and ill health (Burke, 1970).

Organizational Commitment

Steers (1977) defined commitment to an organization as the relative strength of an individual's identification with and involvement in that organization. Three factors of such identification have been specified. One is an individual's strong belief in and acceptance of the organization's goals. A second is the individual's willingness to exert considerable effort

on behalf of the organization. The third is the individual's desire to maintain membership.

The concept is frequently measured by multiple-item scales using five- or seven-point ratings, as in the commonly used assessment instrument described below (Porter, Steers, Mowday, & Boulian, 1974):

> This 15-item questionnaire was designed to measure . . . commitment. . . . Included in this instrument are items pertaining to the subject's perceptions concerning his loyalty toward the organization, his willingness to exert a great deal of effort to achieve organizational goals, and his acceptance of the organization's values. All items represent statements to which the subject responds on 7-point Likert scales, ranging from "strongly disagree" to "strongly agree." (p. 605)

Randall (1987) has reviewed commitment studies and has described positive and negative correlates of low, moderate, and high commitment for both the employee and the organization. The following summarizes this work. For individual employees, low commitment can promote originality and innovation but negatively affect career advancement in the organization. Moderate commitment enhances employees' feelings of belonging, security, and efficacy but may also retard advancement. High levels often can help advance an individual's career and/or compensation because organizations reward such loyalty. However, individual growth may be hindered and mobility limited. High levels can also lead to stress in family relationships.

For the organization, a low level of employee commitment may lead to functional turnover of non-productive employees but it has also been linked to general patterns of higher tardiness, absenteeism, turnover, and lower quality work. Moderate levels have been linked to a lessening of these problems and to an increase in job satisfaction. However, lesser amounts of spontaneous cooperation and willingness to change also frequently occur. Finally, high commitment is shown in a general willingness to accept demands for greater effort and performance. Negative consequences are reduced flexibility, lack of critical review, and unethical behavior.

Job Content

Theories of motivation and satisfaction have specified that the nature of work activities, as viewed by the worker, are critical to specific work outcomes. Because of this, many organizational change programs assess workers' perceptions of job activities as a basis for making adjustments in work demands. Such changes are intended to prompt more positive job satisfaction, commitment, and performance. There are numerous assessment devices and accompanying change programs. One of the most researched of these is the Job Characteristics Model (Hackman & Oldham, 1980).

There are five key job characteristics which are measured through self-report questionnaires that use multiple-item scales and Likert-type response formats. These are *skill variety, task significance, task identity, autonomy,* and *feedback.* Low scale scores on these characteristics are indicative of jobs that can be successfully modified through redesign of work activities. The model holds that these job characteristics affect three critical psychological states of the worker: experienced meaningfulness of work, experienced responsibility for outcomes of work, and knowledge of the actual results of the work. These three critical states, in turn, influence a number of personal and work outcomes: high internal work motivation, high quality work performance, high satisfaction with the work, and low absenteeism and turnover.

However, this path from perceptions of job characteristics to outcome variables is moderated by *growth-need strength.* This characteristic reflects the employee's desire for personal challenges, accomplishment, and learning on the job. Individuals with high needs are more likely to respond positively to jobs that provide increases in the basic five job characteristics. If an employee's need is low, an enriched job may increase personal tension, stress, and job dissatisfaction. Therefore, self-report questionnaires are also administered to employees to measure growth-need strength using multiple-item, Likert-type scales. There have been numerous published studies describing the success of this model (Hackman & Oldham, 1980).

ASSESSMENT OF PHYSIOLOGICAL RESPONSES

There are three reasons for the assessment of specific physical characteristics of individuals in work situations: to enhance selection decisions, to assist in the diagnosis of poor performance of existing employees, or to provide information for medical insurance. In this section, we will briefly discuss the procedures for four types of physiological assessment: vision, hearing, honesty, and drug-use testing.

Vision Testing

Visual sensitivity includes several separate functions. For industrial work the most important are color discrimination, near acuity at reading (13 to 16 inches), far acuity (usually measured at 20 feet), depth perception, and muscular balance of the eyes (phoria). The most common measure of vision is the Snellen Chart which contains rows of letters of gradually decreasing size. It is intended to measure only far acuity. Accuracy in reading the letters of this chart has been found to be affected by many factors in a normal employment testing situation: amount of illumination, distance from chest, position of examinee's head, etc. For this reason more accurate and complete visual measures are taken by using specially designed instruments such as the Ortho-Rater, the AO Sight Screener, and the Keystone Telebinocular. These instruments provide measures of all the visual characteristics mentioned above.

Hearing Testing

The most important aspect of hearing for industrial work is auditory acuity—the faintest sound that the individual can just barely hear. The most reliable measurement of this involves electronic audiometers. With these, one ear at a time is tested; the subject receiving the sound through a headphone pressed against the ear. The examiner increases the decibel level of the transmitted sound until the subject indicates that sound has been heard. This sound threshold is then remeasured by starting with a clearly audible sound and decreasing the decibel level until the subject reports no hearing. At each sound wave frequency, the subject's hearing loss in decibels can be determined from the audiometer dial. This dial has been calibrated at "normal hearing" for the population. Normal hearing levels have been determined through testing a large, representative sample of people.

Honesty Testing

A major concern of many businesses is the cost of employee theft, estimated in the millions of dollars. Consequently, a whole industry has grown to assist in measuring the honesty of applicants and employees. There are two major types of assessment devices that are used: the polygraph that measures physiological responses accompanying verbal answers, and paper-and-pencil, self-report inventories. Research on these devices has, in general, not been supportive of their use. In fact, approximately 30 states have forbidden or limited the use of the polygraph in employment decisions and the U.S. Congress has passed the Employee Polygraph Protection Act of 1988 which greatly restricted the use of the polygraph in employment situations. Therefore, our purpose in this section is merely to describe these assessment devices, not to advocate their use.

The most common polygraph examination uses readings of three types of physiological data. One set of readings, the electrodermal channel, displays changes in palmar skin resistance or galvanic skin response. The second set, the *cardio* channel, records heart rate and some changes in pulse volume. The third channel is connected pneumatically or electrically to an expandable belt around the respondent's chest and records respiration.

There are usually three types of questions used in the examination. One type is the irrelevant, nonemotional question, such as "Are you six feet tall?" A second type is the emotional control question. Such questions are designed to elicit an emotional reaction, preferably of guilt. Questions such as "Did you ever lie to escape punishment?" are frequently asked. The third type is specifically about the behavior of interest, usually the stealing or damage of company goods. To detect lying, the polygrapher looks for evidence of autonomic disturbance associated with the answers to the last type of question. Most polygraph examiners make an overall judgment of lying based on both the polygraph information and other data, such as the demeanor of the respondent, the examiner's knowledge of evidence, etc.

The major difficulty with the use of the polygraph is the identification of a large number of false positives due to other factors besides guilt that can trigger emotional reactions in respondents. Also, there are considerable legal and psychological issues accompanying the inappropriate assessment of an individual as being guilty of lying.

Paper-and-pencil tests question the respondent's attitudes toward theft and other defalcations. Statements similar to the following, which require "yes" or "no" answers, are used.

Should a person be fired if caught stealing more than $10?
Most of your friends have stolen something in their lives.
The courts are too easy on law breakers.

Other types of questions ask respondents about the frequency of theft in society (What percentage of people take more than $5 per week from their employer?), personal ruminations about theft (Have you ever thought about taking some money from any place where you worked?), perceived ease of theft (How easy is it to steal and not be caught?), and assessment of one's own honesty (In comparison to others, how honest are you?).

Sackett and Harris (1984) reviewed 10 of the most popularly used tests. Although the measures demonstrated high reliabilities (.90+), a major limitation was the methodological deficiency of validity studies. In general, test scores were related to admission of guilt or having been caught in a dishonest act. Such a criterion is not a measure of honesty but rather a limited measure of dishonesty.

Drug Testing

According to some estimates, drug abuse costs organizations as much as $25 billion annually through absenteeism, mistakes, damage, injury, and sick leave. Not included in this figure are increased insurance costs. In response, the testing of applicants and employees has become more frequent in an attempt to identify individuals who use drugs. Such testing is more common in public institutions than in private, particularly since President Reagan's Executive Order of September 15, 1986, which authorized drug testing of federal employees. However, this practice is growing in the private sector in which it has been recently estimated that approximately one third of the Fortune 500 firms require some testing. Such testing is controversial with a few court cases having been heard and, undoubtedly, more to follow.

There are several drug testing procedures, of which the two most often used are the following. The Immunoassay Test attempts to determine whether drugs are in a person's system on the basis of the reaction of the urine specimen to certain antibodies created by the immune system of laboratory animals. This test can detect both the presence and absence of drugs as well as the amount of drugs in a person's system. However, it cannot determine when the drug was taken, how much was taken (although rough estimates can be made), the specific substance used among a drug group, and, most important, how much job performance impairment was caused.

A much more precise test is the Gas Chromatography/Mass Spectrometry Test. This test can separate complex mixtures of drugs and other substances into their pure parts. When a mixture, such as an extract of drugs from urine, is injected into the testing instrument, each drug will move through the instrument in gas form at a different speed. When a particular drug reaches the end of the instrument and enters the mass spectrometer, it is separated from other drugs and is in a pure form. Such testing is more accurate than an immunoassay test, can search for many different drugs, and can identify a specific one from a group. However, it is much more expensive than the immunoassay and is still limited in that it cannot determine the time of drug use or the level of job performance impairment. In most situations, the immunoassay test is the general assessment device, with the gas chromatography test being used for further evaluation of those individuals testing positive on the first.

At the heart of the legal question is the issue of invasion of privacy. By their very nature, drug assessment procedures are intrusive upon the individual. Coupled with this concern is the inability of the tests to measure intoxication of work impairment. Therefore, the argument against drug testing is that in the absence of evidence of the individual's inability to perform work safely and efficiently, employers are invading the off-work time of employees and are attempting to regulate their private lives.

Hartstein (1987) has provided the following general directives to employers in using drug testing:

1. Seek employee/union input in an attempt to secure employee support for the program.
2. Limit testing to reasonable circumstances such as pre-employment or when there is a reasonable suspicion of drug use, preferably based on poor job performance.
3. Select testing methods carefully to provide multiple, different testing analyses.
4. Select a testing laboratory carefully.
5. Use a consent form whenever possible.
6. Specify procedures by which an employee may appeal or challenge a positive test of drug use.

ASSESSMENT OF CORPORATE CULTURE

A relatively recent phenomenon has been the assessment of the organization as a whole rather than the individuals within the organization. Pettigrew (1979) describes culture and its importance:

> In order for people to function within any given setting, they must have a continuing sense of what that reality is all about in order to be acted upon. Culture is the system of such publicly and collectively accepted meanings operating for a given group at a given time. This system . . . interprets a people's own situation to themselves. (p. 574)

Deal and Kennedy (1982) write:

> Whether weak or strong, culture has a powerful influence throughout an organization; it affects practically everything—from who gets promoted and what decisions are made, to how employees dress and what sports they play. Because of this impact, we think that culture also has a major effect on the success of the business. (p. 4)

Assessment of an organization's culture is made by gathering data about five factors. The business environment is the competitive marketplace defined by the organization's products, competitors, customers, technologies, government influences, etc. This is the single most important factor. Values are the basic beliefs of an organization, the definition of success. Heroes are those people who personify the culture's values and as such provide role models for others. Rites and rituals are the systematic and programmed routines of day-to-day life in the company that show employees what is meant by success and what is expected of them. Trice and Beyer (1984) discuss rites of passage, degradation, enhancement, renewal, conflict reduction, and integration as the main organizational rituals. Finally, the communication network is the main carrier of information, values, and rituals. This network is populated by individuals who assume the roles of storytellers, spies, priests, cabals, and whispers.

Data for assessment are gathered by studying several organizational characteristics. One is the physical setting which is the manifest statement to the world of its values and beliefs. Also of importance is what the company says about itself in annual reports, brochures, recruiting pamphlets, etc. A third source of information is how the company greets strangers. A fourth is observing how employees spend their time. Last, it is necessary to interview employees as to the history of the company, reasons for its success, and the kinds of people who work there. In doing this, it is necessary to gather data about career paths, lengths of time in specific jobs, the content of messages, and the anecdotes and stories that are regularly discussed.

Deal and Kennedy (1982) describe four of the main cultures. The *tough guy, macho* culture is a world of individuals who take high risks and get quick feedback on whether actions were right or wrong. The *work hard/play hard* culture is one characterized by a high level of activity with relatively low risk. The *bet-your-company* culture is one with a high-risk, slow-feedback environment characterized by big stakes decisions. The *process* culture is a world of little or no feedback and measurement of results but rather an emphasis on the appropriateness of actions.

REFERENCES

Algera, J. A., Jansen, P. G. W., Roe, R. A., & Vijn, P. (1984). Validity generalization: Some critical remarks on the Schmidt and Hunter procedure. *Journal of Occupational Psychology, 57*, 197–210.

Anastasi, A. (1982). *Psychological testing* (5th ed.) (p. 394) New York: Macmillan.

Arvey, R., (1979). Unfair discrimination in the employment interview: Legal and psychological aspects. *Psychological Bulletin, 86*, 736–765.

Arvey R., & Campion, J. (1982). The employment interview: A summary and review of recent research. *Personnel Psychology, 35*, 281–322.

Arvey, R. D., Miller, H. E., Gould, R., & Burch, P. (1987). Interview validity for selecting sales clerks. *Personnel Psychology, 40*, 1–12.

Assessment & Development. (1973). Landmark AT&T-EEOC consent agreement increases assessment center usage, 1–2.

Boehm, V. (1977). Differential validity: A methodological artifact? *Journal of Applied Psychology, 62*, 146–154.

Bray, D. W., Campbell, R. J., & Grant, D. L. (1979). *Formative years in business*. Huntington, NY: Robert E. Krieger Publishing.

Burke, R. J. (1970). Occupational and life strains, satisfaction, and mental health. *Journal of Business Administration, 1*, 35–41.

Cascio, W., & Phillips, N. (1979). Performance testing: A rose among thorns? *Personnel Psychology, 32*, 751–766.

Cook, J. D., Hepworth, S. J., Wall, T. D., & Warr, P. B. (1981). *The experience of work*. New York: Academic Press.

Cornelius, E. T. (1983). The use of projective techniques in personnel selection. *Research in personnel and human resources management*. Greenwich, CT: JAI Press.

Deal, T. E., & Kennedy, A. A. (1982). *Corporate cultures*. Reading, MA: Addison-Wesley.

Dreher, G., & Sackett, P. (1983). Commentary. In G. Dreher, & P. Sackett, (Eds.), *Perspectives on employee staffing and selection*. Homewood, IL: Richard D. Irwin.

Eder, R. W., & Ferris, G. R., (Eds.). (1989). *The employment interview: Theory, research, and practice*. Beverly Hills, CA: Sage Publications.

Gatewood, R. D., & Feild, H. S. (in press). *Human Resource Selection* (2nd Ed.) Hinsdale, IL: Dryden Press.

Ghiselli, E. E. (1973). The validity of aptitude tests in personnel section. *Personnel Psychology, 26*, 461–477.

Gordon, M. F., & Kleiman, L. S. (1976). The prediction of trainability using a work sample test and an aptitude test: A direct comparison. *Personnel Psychology, 29*, 243–253.

Guion, R. M., & Gottier, R. F. (1965). Validity of personality measures in personnel selection. *Personnel psychology, 18*, 135–164.

Grimsley, G., & Jarrett, H. (1975). The relation of past managerial achievements to test measures obtained in the employment situation: Methodology and results—II. *Personnel Psychology, 28*, 215–231.

Hackman, J. R., & Oldham, G. (1980). *Work redesign*. Reading, MA: Addison-Wesley.

Haetner, J. (1977). Race, age, sex, and competence as factors in employer selection of the disadvantaged. *Journal of Applied Psychology, 62*, 199–202.

Hartstein, B. A. (1987). Drug testing in the work place: A primer for employers. *Employee Relations Law Journal, 12*, 577–607.

Herzberg, F., Mausner, B., Petersen, R. O., & Capwell, D. F. (1957). *Job attitudes: Review of research and opinion*. Pittsburgh: Psychological Service of Pittsburgh.

Hinrichs, J. R. (1978). An eight-year follow-up of a management assessment center. *Journal of Applied Psychology, 63*, 596–601.

Hogan, R., Carpenter, B., Briggs, S., & Hanson, R. (1985). Personality assessment and personnel selection. In H. J. Bernardin, & D. A. Bownes (Eds.), *Personality assessment in organizations*. New York, NY: Praeger.

Hunter, J. E. (1980). *Validity generalization for 12,000 jobs: An application of synthetic validity and validity generalization to the General Aptitude Test Battery (GATB)*. Washington, DC: U.S. Employment Service, U.S. Department of Labor.

Hunter, J. E., Schmidt, F. L., & Hunter, R. (1979). Differential validity of employment test by race: A comprehensive review and analysis. *Psychological Bulletin, 85*, 721–735.

Keenan, A. (1977). Some relationships between interviewers' personal feeling about candidates and their general evaluation of them. *Journal of Occupational Psychology, 50*, 275–283.

Kemery, E. R., Mossholder, K. W., & Roth, L. (1987). The power of the Schmidt and Hunter additive model of validity generalization. *Journal of Applied Psychology, 72*, 30–37.

Kinslinger, H. J. (1966). Application of projective

techniques in personnel psychology since 1949. *Psychological Bulletin, 66*, 134–149.

Langdale, J. A., & Weitz, J. (1973). Estimating the influence of job information on interviewer agreement. *Journal of Applied Psychology, 57*, 23–27.

Latham, G. P., & Saari, L. M. (1984). Do people do what they say? Further studies on the situational interview. *Journal of Applied Psychology, 69*, 569–573.

Lanyon, R. I., & Goodstein, L. D. (1982). *Personality assessment* (2nd ed.). New York: NY: Wiley.

Locke, E. A. (1976). The nature and causes of job satisfaction. In M. D. Dunnette (Ed.), *Handbook of industrial and organizational psychology*. Chicago: Rand McNally College Publishing Co.

McClelland, D. C. (1961). *The achieving society*. Princeton, NJ: D. Van Nostrand.

Miner, J. B. (1977). *Motivation to manage: A ten-year update on the "studies in management education" research*. Atlanta, GA: Organizational Measurement Systems Press.

Organ, D. W. (1977). A reappraisal and reinterpretation of the satisfaction causes performance hypothesis. *Academy of Management Review, 2*, 46–53.

Organ, D. W., & Near, J. P. (1985). Cognition vs. affect in measures of job satisfaction. *International Journal of Psychology, 20*, 241–253.

Osburn, H. G., Timmrick, C., & Bigby, D. (1981). Effect of dimensional relevance and accuracy of simulated hiring decisions by employment interviewers. *Journal of Applied Psychology, 66*, 159–165.

Pettigrew, A. M. (1979). On studying organizational cultures. *Administrative Science Quarterly, 24*, 570–581.

Petty, M. M., McGee, G. W., & Cavender, J. W. (1984). A meta-analysis of the relationships between individual job satisfaction and individual performance. *Academy of Management Review, 9*, 712–721.

Porter, L., Steers, R. T., Mowday, R. T., & Boulian, P. V. (1974). Organizational commitment, job satisfaction and turnover among psychiatric technicians. *Journal of Applied Psychology, 59*, 603–609.

Randall, D. M. (1987). Commitment and the organization: The organization man revisited. *Academy of Management Review, 12*, 460–471.

Reilly, R., & Chao, G. (1982). Validity and fairness of some alternative employee selection procedures. *Personnel Psychology, 35*, 1–62.

Robinson, D. (1981). Content-oriented personnel selection in a small business setting. *Personnel Psychology, 34*, 77–87.

Rowe, P. (1963). Individual differences in selection decisions. *Journal of Applied Psychology, 47*, 305–307.

Sackett, P. R., & Dreher, G. F. (1982). Constructs and assessment center dimensions: Some troubling empirical findings. *Journal of Applied Psychology, 67*, 401–410.

Sackett, P., & Harris, M. (1984). Honesty testing for personnel selection: A review and critique. *Personnel Psychology, 37*, 221–246.

Scarpello, V. G., & Vandenberg, R. (in press). Some issues to consider when surveying employees' opinions. In J. Jones, B. Steffy, & D. Bray (Eds.), *Applying psychology in business: The manager's handbook*. Lexington, MA: Lexington Books.

Schmidt, F. L., Greenthol, A., Hunter, J., Berner, J., & Seaton, F. (1977). Job sample vs. paper-and-pencil trade and technical tests: Adverse impact and examiner attitudes. *Personnel psychology, 30*, 187–197.

Schmidt, F. L., Hunter, J. E., & Pearlman, K. (1981). Task differences as moderators of aptitude test validity in selection: A red herring. *Journal of Applied Psychology, 66*, 166–185.

Schmidt, F. L., & Hunter, J. E. (1984). A within-setting empirical test of the situational specificity hypothesis in personnel selection. *Personnel Psychology, 37*, 317–326.

Schmitt, N. (1976). Social and situational determinants of interview decisions: Implications for the employment interview. *Personnel Psychology, 29*, 79–101.

Schmitt, N., Gooding, R., Noe, R., & Kirsch, M. (1984). Metanalysis of validity studies published between 1964 and 1982 and the investigation of study characteristics. *Personnel Psychology, 37*, 407–422.

Selover, R. B. (1949). Review of the Minnesota Clerical Test. In O. K. Buros (Ed.), *The third mental measurements yearbook* (pp. 635–636). New Brunswick, NJ: Rutgers University Press.

Steers, R. M. (1977). *Organizational effectiveness: A behavioral view*. Santa Monica, CA: Goodyear.

Thornton, G. C., III, & Byham, W. C. (1982). *Assessment centers and managerial performance*. New York: Academic Press.

Trice, H. M., & Beyer, J. M. (1984). Studying organizational cultures through rites and ceremonies. *Academy of Management Review, 9*, 653–669.

Ulrich, L., & Trumbo, D. (1965). The selection interview since 1949. *Psychological Bulletin, 63*, 100–116.

U.S. Department of Labor. (1977). *Dictionary of*

occupational titles (4th ed.). Washington, DC: U.S. Government Printing Office.

Valenzi, E., & Andrews, I. R. (1973). Individual differences in the decision process of employment interviewers. *Journal of Applied Psycholoogy, 58,* 49–53.

Vroom, V. H. (1964). *Work and motivation.* New York: Wiley.

Weekly, J. A., & Gier, J. A. (1987). Reliability and validity of the situational interview for a sales position. *Journal of Applied Psychology, 72,* 484–487.

PART X
SPECIAL TOPICS

CHAPTER 22

PSYCHOLOGICAL ASSESSMENT OF MINORITY GROUP MEMBERS

Antonio E. Puente

Little doubt is evident in either the professional or the lay literature regarding the contribution of psychology to the understanding of abnormal behavior. The doubt that is expressed is sparse and often politically motivated. This acceptance has arisen largely because empirically-based psychological principles are the foundation for assessment strategies in general psychopathology.

To those involved with the understanding of psychopathology in general, and measurement strategies of abnormal behavior in particular, one source of continuing concern is individual differences. Indeed, individual differences and diversity are often viewed as impediments to the development of general principles of behavior.

Beyond the theoretical and practical concerns raised by individual differences are the issues of confounding or measurement errors. Of significance is the lack of understanding and sensitivity for larger group differences. Few would question the basic ability of specific psychological tests (e.g., Halstead-Reitan) to assist in the discrimination or classification of specific diagnostic groups (i.e., those with organic brain dysfunction). Practitioners who do question their validity may not be examining the correct criterion variables. Regardless, expert diagnosticians are in agreement about the potential for classification of behavior through testing. In contrast, few would agree that affiliation with specific demographic groups (nondiagnostic) would be of great value in diagnostic classification. Presumably, this assumption is based on the concept that psychopathology (or for that matter abilities or any other behavioral variable) is

relatively free from the contamination of these potential confounds (Westermeyer, 1987a). Thus, this perspective suggests that other (nondiagnostic) group membership, while possibly important in some capacity, would have little or no effect on nosological issues. Such a belief is deeply rooted in nonempirical foundations, and its beginnings lie in a number of historical trends, none well documented or acknowledged. Thus, speculation rather than definitive analysis is the source for the following observation.

Few attempts have been made to understand the behavior of individuals in minority groups, possibly because it did not matter. Brislin (1988) and others have cogently argued that psychologists for too long have categorically shown poor understanding of behavioral traits and patterns of individuals who do not belong to groups associated with mainstream America. This limited perspective of the nature of behavior was first addressed by the late Frank Beach (1950) in his now classic article, "The Snark was a Boojum." In more contemporary terms, Robert Guthrie's (1976) book, *Even the Rat was White,* cites clear evidence not only of restricted sampling but of limited understanding of many other species (in the case of Beach) or other racial and ethnic groups (in the case of Guthrie).

One direct outcome of this situation, shown in recent statistics, suggests that few individuals appear interested in studying how understanding racial and ethnic group membership may contribute to understanding behavior. The article by the American Psychological Association's (APA) Committee for Human Resources, "The Changing Face of American Psychology," (Howard, Pion, Gottfredson, Flattau,

Oskane, Pfafflin, Bray, & Burstein, 1986) underscores the paucity of minorities pursuing study and being associated with all areas of psychology. Of special concern is the limited number of minorities in graduate schools and in faculty positions. These trends persist a decade after the historical report in 1978 by the President's Commission on Mental Health. Among other observations, this group concluded not only that minority groups are not adequately served but that too few professionals are available to deal with the issues relevant to nonmajority concerns.

The lack of understanding combined with the lack of resources to solve the problem will clearly lead to further complications of an already complex issue. Nevertheless, the common denominator is limited understanding. This limited understanding of minority populations has resulted in overrepresentation of minority groups in several distinct psychopathology groups. Maheady, Towne, Algozzine, Mercer, and Ysseldyke (1983) and others have observed that members of minority or underrepresented groups tend to be overrepresented in special education programs, especially programs for the mildly handicapped. While it is unclear that "fairer" tests will produce less overrepresentation, it is certain that this trend persists.

The *overrepresentation* of minority groups in handicapped conditions has, in turn, resulted in negative stereotypes. Such stereotypes in the short term encourage the assignment of individuals to incorrect diagnostic groups (e.g., learning disabled). In the long term, this stereotypical and grossly incorrect data base may eventually serve as a foundation for potentially incorrect theories and research programs on racial and ethnic differences (e.g., Jensen, 1980). While all valid programs of enquiry should exist (Kuhn, 1970), constraints on the scientific process fueled by emotional and unempirical variables have little value for the discipline, for the science, for society, and most of all, for members of minority groups.

The purpose of this chapter will be to avoid such an orientation by focusing as much as possible on the data that are available. Initially, this contribution will focus on providing both historical and clinical background of testing of minority group members. Standard clinical and psychometric practices involving individuals of minority groups will be presented and critiqued. Suggestions for theoretical shifts as well as practical clinical and psychometric approaches will be outlined, with cognizance of the potential pitfalls that presently exist.

This chapter is intended for North American audiences. Numerous limitations in the available data set, whether clinical or otherwise, would make a more geographically ambitious approach unworkable. Nevertheless, the approach (though not necessarily the data) should be considered a model for workers in other cultures, groups, or locations (e.g., Native Indians in mainstream Brazilian culture) in order to address the issues of psychological assessment of minority group members.

An initial step in understanding members of minority groups is to define such groups. According to a system often cited by psychopathology textbooks, individuals are different from larger groups if they are not members of that group. Group composition can be determined by social, legal, biological, statistical, and behavioral variables. Possibly the easiest and most socially acceptable variable is biological, such as color of skin. However, other variables may also play a role. Statistical methods define group memberships by numerical scores obtained, while social and legal approaches may use societal tradition to define membership. Behavioral variables represent the most robust method as they should be free of bias due to the use of empirical behavioral methods to determine group composition. As a consequence, it would appear logical that minority group composition is determined as much as possible on behavioral and not other variables because we are essentially interested in behavior. Such an approach reduces confusion and highlights what is important—the behavior of the minority group member.

Standard practices have used overt and obvious variables to classify members into minority groups. For example, if an individual is not white (Caucasian) in North America he or she must belong to a minority group. One need look no further than the disciplines of animal behavior and neuropsychology to realize that gross morphological signs are often not well correlated with clear behavioral patterns. For this chapter, Brislin's (1988) classification system for human diversity is adopted. Contrary to popular belief, only three races exist. These include Caucasian (e.g., white), Black, and Indian. The Indian race can be subdivided into Native-American (e.g., Cherokee, Incas, etc.) and Asian (e.g., Japanese, Chinese, etc.). Ethnicity is another variable that can be used to differentiate mainstream from minority groups. Here, ethnicity is defined as a collective identity (e.g., Jew, Italian, etc.). Next, group composition can be determined by culture (e.g., southern, urban, etc.). This variable implies that groups can be defined according to social and personal identification. While less understood and accepted, other variables could also assist in determining group membership. These include but should not be limited to gender, sex, physical status (e.g., disability), social class, and religion.

In the area of psychological assessment, race has been the most widely studied of the previous variables. Sex, and to a lesser degree, ethnicity have been considered as potential variables. However, culture, gender, physical status, social class, and religion have rarely been considered important in understanding human behavior. Whether this neglect is due to collective wisdom or ignorance is not known (nor is it the focus of this chapter). However, as much as possible the named variables should be addressed in the psychological assessment of minority groups.

Regardless of the variable used, minority group membership will be defined as indicated previously by groups who are both politically powerless and sparsely represented in scientific inquiry. However, what may be a minority group in terms of ethnicity in 1990 may not be by the year 2,000. Census figures suggest, for example, that by the year 2025 there may be more Hispanics than traditional Caucasian (white, Anglo-Saxon) Americans.

A necessary outcome of appropriately defining group membership is the implication that a minority member will engage in behavior that is different from the mainstream norm but not necessarily abnormal. Thus, clearer understanding of human behavior is the goal. Such an understanding is not only academically useful but also contains treatment implications. The importance of minority group membership for psychological treatment has been outlined by Sue and Zane (1987), while Lawson (1987) has reported its implications for psychopharmacological intervention. Caution should be inserted here. Careful between-group comparison often implies limited concern for within-group analysis. Using the Hispanic population in the United States as an example, the behavioral patterns of Cubans, Mexicans, and Puerto Ricans may actually differ more from each other than the entire group of Hispanic differs from Caucasians. Thus, within-minority group analysis will eventually become as important as minority versus majority group comparisons.

HISTORICAL FOUNDATIONS

The origins of mental testing can be traced to Galton's *Inquiries into Human Faculty and Its Development* in 1883 (Boring, 1950). In order to assess potential human defects (and not sins as had commonly been the case prior to Galton), this British pioneer developed the "mental test." While the test intended to measure such variables as color discrimination and auditory reaction time, the purpose of establishing the Anthropometric Laboratory at the International Health Exhibition in London was to determine the range of human abilities. Together with the founding of the journal *Biometrika* and the Eugenics Laboratory, Galton attempted to develop the concept of racial improvement (Schultz, 1981).

The discrimination of acceptable and nonacceptable human characteristics has, unfortunately, found its way into present-day mental testing, possibly by way of James McKeen Cattell. After obtaining his Ph.D. from Wundt, Cattell came into contact with Galton (Boring, 1950), who in turn, had enormous influence both directly (e.g., with numerous students) and indirectly (e.g., as editor of *Science*) on the study of mental ability in the U.S. However, it was not until the appearance of Henry H. Goddard at Vineland Training School in New Jersey, and later Lewis Terman at Stanford University that systematic assessment of psychological abilities became part of mainstream psychology.

Using "the evidence of mental tests," Terman (1916) indicated that "the average intelligence of women and girls is as high as that of men and boys" (pg. 68). Nevertheless, he concluded later in his book, *The Measurement of Intelligence*, that the "dullness" seen in "Indians, Mexicans, and negroes raises the question of racial differences in mental tasks." Terman suggested "Children of the group should be segregated in special classes and given instruction which is concrete and practical. They cannot master abstraction, but they can often be made efficient workers, able to look out for themselves" (p. 92). He continued, "There is no possibility at present of convincing society that they should be allowed to reproduce, although from a eugenics point of view they constitute a grave problem because of their unusually prolific breeding" (p. 92).

Such an orientation is observed if not directly, at least as an undercurrent, in Goddard's work and later in Robert Yerkes' groundbreaking work with the Army Alpha and Beta tests during World War I. These tests were meant to classify A (intelligent) and D and E (feebleminded) individuals with a mean mental age of 13.08. (This score may have prompted Goddard to term any adult with less than 13 years of mental age as "moron.") However, both immigrants and non-whites tended to score lower, prompting Yerkes (1923) to write in *Atlantic Monthly* about non-inherited racial differences. This conclusion readily supported the racist conclusion of Madison Grant who considered Nordics superior to other races. Based on these observations, Yerkes and others encouraged strict immigration laws especially for "the negro." To curtail the reproduction of those already in the United States, several American followers of Galton (namely John H. Noyer and Victoria Woodhull) established a center for American eugenics in Cold Spring Harbor with financial support from the Carnegie Institution (Leahey, 1987). One of the greatest proponents of eugenics, Henry Goddard, published his famous book *The Kallikak Family, A Study in the Heredity of Feeblemindedness* (1912). This book, probably more than any published work of the time, was used for the control of reproduction by minorities.

Reflecting the influence of this and similar works, sterilization and vasectomy became common phenomena. According to Leahy, one of the greatest landmark decisions on the issue was that of a mental patient, Carrie Buck. After giving birth to a retarded child out of wedlock, the "feebleminded" Buck was involuntarily sterilized. She, in turn, sued the state of Virginia but lost in a split decision at the Supreme Court level.

It seems as though unempirical (and presently considered unethical) approaches to the measurement of abilities are never easily resolved scientifically. Earlier in this century, this issue was far from being resolved academically. Approximately 50 years later, Stephen Jay Gould (1981) continues to argue that such strong conclusions have indeed been based on weak data.

Unfortunately, this approach to the understanding of minority behavior, at best weak and spurious, was the foundation for the Jewish genocide by the Nazis. However, not until 1954 did the judicial branch in this country make strides to erase this previously accepted and now embarrassing "scientific" orientation. The *Brown* case in 1954 allowed for desegregating of races in the school system. However, cases specifically referring to minorities and testing did not surface until the 1970s (Reschly, 1984). Generally, the plaintiff in these cases represented the three major minority groups of the time—African-American, Hispanic, and Native-American—who had been poorly and unethically classified as retarded. For example, Spanish-speaking Hispanics were often placed in handicapped classes based solely on verbal IQ scores.

While most of the cases were won or favorably settled out of court, it was not until the legislative aspect of the litigation-legislation cycle occurred

(Bersoff, 1981) that reform began to be developed and later implemented. According to Reschly (1984), the federal Education for All Handicapped Children Act of 1975 "was the most important and most widely applicable legislative act." This act opened the road for later litigation meant to define more succinctly the spirit of this law.

Perhaps linked to these legal efforts, psychologists have become increasingly aware of the need to document human abilities more carefully. In his introduction to the special issue, "Cultural Factors in Understanding and Assessing Psychopathology" (*Journal of Consulting and Clinical Psychology*), James Butcher (1987) stated that "the application of psychological procedure and methods with patients for different cultural backgrounds raises numerous methodological issues." Issues such as psychological equivalence, test reliability and validity, and test utility were some of the factors that Butcher considered critical. This chapter attempts to build on this new-found scientific interest in an effort to determine the needs, limitations, and directions associated with the psychological assessment of minority populations in North America.

ASSESSMENT METHODS

This section of the chapter will focus on specific assessment methods, examining in turn standard measures, culturally sensitive methods, and behavioral assessment methods. As feasible, each section will cover a variety of tests or assessment strategies including application (and/or translation), norms, limitations and cautions, and suggestions for use.

Standard Measures

Interview.

The interview, whether structured or unstructured, remains not only the initial step of any psychological assessment but also the most commonly used method for obtaining information. The interview is a frequently used method for obtaining data in cross-cultural contexts. As Zubin (1965) and others have pointed out, however, the unstructured interview poses problems since it may yield unreliable data resulting from a host of uncontrolled factors.

Structured interviews may help in avoiding these pitfalls. Numerous interview methods, including several presented in this chapter, seem generally well suited for use with minority populations, especially since they are often based on objective diagnostic criteria (e.g., Research Diagnostic Criteria). Several of these methods are found in Table 22.1.

Although many of these structured interviews have been well studied and validated, validity studies often use the judgment of the clinician as the criterion variable. Further, it is well accepted that cultural and ethnic variables—such as behavior patterns, nonverbal cues, translation equivalence, gender differences, and general cultural beliefs—are often misunderstood by even the most sensitive clinician (Westermeyer, 1987a).

One way to avoid this complication is to use interview methods that either have been formally validated or are in current use with these populations. For example, the Present State Examination was an interview used for the international pilot study of psychopathology (World Health Organization, 1973). Another method is that of using a translator or someone knowledgeable about minority groups. However, even this approach has limitations. It is not unusual for the translator to be a lay person with limited understanding of psychological principles as well as an individual with personal interest in the patient. Further, translators may be fluent in one but not necessarily both languages, or worse yet, not understand the culture in question. Distortion or misconception further impairs data gathering, especially with severely disorganized patients.

In order to bridge the gap between patient and psychologist, rapport should be established. Westermeyer (1987b) suggested that interviews may take up to twice the usual time of a standard interview. Also, the clinician should make sure that ambiguous (whether real or imagined) questions or answers is classified. Confrontation, the hallmark of some structured interview methods, should be avoided if possible since it may adversely affect client-clinician rapport.

By far the most important aspect of any diagnostic interview is to place the client in his or her *own* and not the psychologist's context. Otherwise, a patient's behavior could be incorrectly interpreted as maladaptive (Adebimpe, 1981). To avoid erroneous conclusions, the psychologist must put special emphasis on understanding the patient's culture, race, ethnicity, or social context that grants him or her membership in a minority group. Not only must that context be understood but it should be understood as it relates to the patient's relationship to majority culture (e.g., Mexican migrant worker employed as a field hand in Colorado). Finally, and possibly most important, the clinician must understand his or her own limitations in other sociocultural situations. To enhance his or her understanding of others, the psychologist must become aware of, and possibly experience, other cultures and ethnic behavior patterns and cognitions.

Intellectual.

Tests which attempt to measure the construct of intelligence are not only the most commonly used psychological tests (see chapters 4, 5, and 6) but also the most vehemently criticized. The literature is replete with controversies about the efficacy of the construct of intelligence and its measurability, and strong and often emotional arguments have been levied against tests of intelligence by members of minority groups. Before these arguments are considered, the most commonly used tests of intelligence will be reviewed relative to their applicability to minority populations.

The application of intelligence tests to children of minority populations has yielded the most empirical data as well as the most controversy. Of the tests applicable to children, the Wechsler Intellectual Scale for Children-Revised (WISC-R) is one of the most popular psychometric tests of intelligence. Nevertheless, conflicting and nonconclusive evidence has resulted from use of intelligence tests with minorities. For example, in one thorough review of the literature, the race of the examiner did not seem to affect the

Table 22.1. Several Structured Interview Applicable to Minority Populations

Interview	References
Brief Psychiatric Rating Scale	Overall & Gorham (1962)
Inpatient Multidimensional Rating	Lorr & Lett (1969)
Mental Status Schedule	Spitzer, Endicott, & Flenn (1967)
Present State Examination	Wing (1970)
Structural Clinical Interview (DSM III)	Spitzer & William (1983)
International Classification of Disease	World Health Organization (in press)
Interview (for ICD-10)	
Mini-Method Station Examination	Folstein, Folstein & McHugh (1975)

validity of intelligence scores in African-American children (Graziano, Varca, & Levy, 1982). Using the criteria outlined by Jensen (1980) for determining bias in testing, Sandoval (1979) concluded that the "WISC-R appears to be non-biased for minority group children." Other factors are presented by Sandoval to explain observed minority versus majority group scores. These findings are supported by Ross-Reynolds and Reschly (1983) in a study involving Anglo, African-American, Hispanic, and Native-American Papago. While no bias in the WISC-R was found against African-American and Hispanics, ceiling effects influenced the response pattern of the Papagos.

Language, however, may be confounded in bilingual children and thus needs to be clarified prior to the administration of the WISC-R. Sandoval (1979) examined the evidence of cultural bias for Anglo, Hispanic, and African-American children. Further, the Spanish version of the WISC-R, does not have acceptable norms for each cultural or ethnic group and should be used with extreme caution. Concern is also cited by Dana (1984) who indicated that the WISC-R is biased for traditional Native-American children. He indicated that a pattern of spatial > sequential > conceptual > acquired knowledge exists across both ages and tribes.

Lampley and Rust (1986) examined the validity of the Kaufman Assessment Battery for Children and found that African-Americans scored significantly lower on this test. These findings are supported by others (e.g., Sandoval & Mielle, 1979). Nevertheless, these conclusions are in direct contrast to those of Hickman and Reynolds (1986–87) who reported that "blacks did not perform significantly better in the test form developed solely on their own item statistic."

It seems that regardless of the data, contrasting interpretations abound. An interesting and eloquent attack on these issues was leveled by George Jackson, chair, Association of Black Psychologists, in 1975. A more balanced perspective on this issue is presented by Cole (1981) as well as Reynolds and Brown (1984). Additional commentaries and rebuttals are found in the 1985 article by Jensen in *Behavioral and Brain Sciences*.

Little information is found for adult intelligence testing with the *Weschler Adult Intelligence Scale-Revised* (WAIS-R). For example, in the first edition of this *Handbook*, Lindenmann and Matarazzo (1984) indicated that the Army Alpha was developed for literates and the Army Beta for the non-English speaking. The implicit assumption is that non-English-speaking individuals were illiterate. Of course,

if the dominant language becomes that of the client, then it is the psychologist who is illiterate.

Using both the WAIS and the WAIS-R, Whitworth and Gibbons (1986) reported that differences were found using both tests and that the most significant differences appeared to be the conversion of race to scale scores. Reynolds, Chastain, Kaufman, and McLean (1987) reanalyzed the data for the 1981 standardized sample of the WAIS-R and reported a 14½ point difference between whites and African-Americans on the Full Scale IQ. In attempting to resolve these discrepancies, Grubb (1987) examined the IQ differences in profoundly and severely mentally retarded individuals using Weschler's test. He reported no differences between whites and African-Americans in this sample of subjects and concluded that lower IQ scores of African-Americans were not biologically determined and, instead, were attributable to other factors.

Unfortunately, few data other than the results of the Weschler tests exist on measures of intellectual abilities. While one might expect that such tests as the Raven Progressive Matrices and the Beta would be less ethnically biased, the data provide little support for this (or contradictory) views. For example, using "minority group offenders," Hiltonsmith and colleagues (1984) reported that these subjects actually scored lower on the Beta than on the WAIS-R.

Achievement, Aptitude, and Interest

Achievement tests are widely used in educational as well as clinical settings. However, as with many other psychometric instruments, relatively few data on minorities are available. In chapter 7 of the *Handbook*, there is a comprehensive review of achievement tests. Of the tests discussed in that chapter, the California Achievement Test (in education) and the Wide Range Achievement Test (in education and clinical application) are two of the most frequently used tests which have been applied to nonmajority samples of the United States population. Initial findings regarding test bias in these measures reflect the conclusions outlined by Fox and Zirkin (1984) in the first edition of this *Handbook*. Specifically, they suggest that while attention should be paid to the possibility of such bias, and while it may be intuitive that such bias would exist (at least on specific items), these tests should not be considered biased. This conclusion is in direct contrast to others, however. For example, Weiss (1987), considered the Scholastic Aptitude Test especially biased in the verbal section. While Golden Rule procedures have been applied to reduce such biases, the reliability and validity of these tests may be in jeopardy (Linn & Drasgow, 1987a). Thus, conflicts exist in terms of having a useful but unbiased test of achievement.

For tests of interest, even fewer data exist. While separate scales for sex are the rule and not the exception for measures of occupation it is generally assumed that other variables are of little importance. The same applies for interest surveys. For example, the Kuder Occupational Interest Survey (Form DD) (Kuder, 1966) as well as the Holland Interest Inventories (1978) consider academic major, occupational status, and even personality type, but not cultural, race, or ethnic factors. The Strong-Campbell is available in Spanish but the norms presumably are from non-Spanish-speaking samples. In a recent study, Drasgow and Hulin (1987) attempted to answer the question of whether scores on the Job Description Index (a vocational measure) varied across different Hispanic populations. Specifically, they compared bilingual Mexicans in Mexico City to other Hispanics residing elsewhere. While few differences were noted between the New York and Miami samples, large differences were noted between the U.S. and Mexican samples. Drasgow and Hulin concluded that both linguistic *and* cultural measurement equivalence must be addressed in measures of vocational interest.

While it is assumed that ethnicity, race, and related variables have been explored by the Educational Testing Service and related psychological test corporations, again few scientific data exist in the public domain regarding tests of aptitude. Terman (1916) helped develop the now widely used Stanford Achievement Test for pre-college screening with no reference to minority groups. At the college level, the College Advanced Placement Examination is also widely used and accepted. However, data on minority populations is still lacking for both of these instruments.

Personality.

Tests of personality could be generally categorized as one of two types—projective or objective. Projective or cognitive-perceptual tests (e.g., Rorschach) are quite commonly used with minority members because of their inherent ease of administration and superficial adaptability and interpretation. According to preliminary analyses by Exner and Sciara (personal communication, July 7, 1989), the Rorschach, an internationally accepted measure of cognitive-perceptual status, does not appear to be biased against Asian-Americans, African-Americans, or Mexican-Americans.

In contrast, limitations of test adaptability are more readily accounted for with objective measures. Clearly, the best example is the Minnesota Multiphasic Personality Inventory (MMPI). The homogeneity of the original MMPI sample limits its ready application to minority groups. According to Dahlstrom, Welsh, and Dahlstrom (1972), the normals used in the original MMPI sample were Caucasian, married, rural, blue-collar workers, with an eighth-grade education. However, Dahlstrom, Diehl, and Lachar (1986), and Lachar and Dahlstrom (1986) have suggested that even when important demographic variables are taken into account (e.g., race and socioeconomic status), approximately 12% to 13% of the total variance of the basic scales is accounted for. Still, the popularity of the test has resulted in translation into approximately 100 languages (Butcher, 1984; Williams, 1987), and a wealth of cross-cultural, ethnic, and racial studies based on research using this instrument have been published.

In an excellent review of ethnicity and the MMPI, Greene (1987) did an exhaustive examination of studies. Over 100 studies were analyzed according to type of scale and item level across groups including African-American–white, Hispanic–white, and Asian-American–Native-American. Greene concluded that too many variables and too few adequately completed studies prevent conclusions of bias. The variables in question include subject parameters, ethnic group membership profile validity, moderator variable, and scores analyzed. Additional methodological considerations include appropriate statistical analyses, adequate sample size, and validity of statistical (versus clinical) significance. Based on his review, Greene provided the following four conclusions:

1. At this stage of our understanding, it is too premature to develop norms for specific ethnic and racial groups.
2. Subjects have to be identified with an ethnic group using subjective self (not clinician or experimenter) identification.
3. Empirical and not clinical differences should be emphasized.
4. Finally, more research needs to be focused on the special scales of the MMPI.

As exhaustive as the review is and as heuristic as Greene's conclusions may be, others advocate different orientations. For example, Gynther (1981), Gynther and Green (1980), and others argue that specific norms—and, in some cases, items—be developed, using an empirical methodology rather than a review of the literature.

Better understanding of ethnic, cultural, and race differences and their application to interpretation of *t* scores, specific scale scores, or patterns preclude widespread use of the MMPI with minorities. For example, it seems foolish to group all Hispanics together as Greene and others have done. As Sue and Zane (1987) have indicated, being culturally sensitive is being aware of within-group heterogeneity. Further, little understanding appears evident in the MMPI research with regard to differences among culture, ethnicity, and race. Until such issues, as well as those outlined by Greene (1987), are resolved, not only will the MMPI data as it now stands be premature; it will be incorrect. According to a recent announcement from the Restandardization Committee of the University of Minnesota Press (1989) concerning the MMPI-2, published in 1989, the revised version will have "national norms that are much more representative of the present population of the U.S." (p. 4). Whether this implies that a representative number of minorities included in the normative sample remains to be seen.

Neuropsychological.

It is often assumed that brain functions are not affected by non-neurological variables. To determine the current status of that assumption, the table of contents was reviewed in three major textbooks used to teach introduction to neuropsychology textbooks—Lezak (1987), Golden (1981), and Wedding, Horton, and Webster (1986). The review suggests that issues of culture, ethnicity, and race have not been addressed to date. Even more revealing are the reference sections of the books, which indicate that very few articles on these issues exist. A review of the existing journal literature also exposes the paucity of references surrounding neuropsychological assessment and the effects of culture, ethnicity, and race. In *Reliability and Validity in Neuropsychological Assessment,* Franzen (1989) presents an excellent overview of issues concerning most measures of neuropsychological ability. While different forms of validity are considered, no mention is made of the application of the tests to minority group members.

Most of the sparse data that do exist on this topic are found in the non-neuropsychological literature. For example, Lopez and Romero (1988) assessed intellectual functions in Spanish-speaking adults using both the WAIS and the Puerto Rican version of the WAIS. While the authors report that differences did exist, test equivalence is generally elusive and its application for

these tests to a neuropsychological sample would be at best haphazard. On a more theoretical note, Drasgow (1972) addressed test-item bias and differential validity by using a "profoundly" biased test. However, in this case (as with all others), no direct or indirect mention is made of neuropsychological tests.

Anecdotal and clinical evidence indicate that these variables may have little, if any, effect on specific sensory and possibly motor measures. Some support for this contention exists. For example, Roberts and Hamsher (1984) administered both the Facial Recognition and Visual Naming Tests of the Multilingual Aphasia Examination to African-Americans in a consultation setting. They reported negligible racial bias. In contrast, Adams, Boake, and Crain (1982) found that bias did exist with regard to several variables, including ethnicity, in neuropsychological performance. In both brain-damaged and non-samples, African-Americans and Mexican-Americans exhibited more errors than did white subjects. One may extrapolate from early (though questionable) motor learning studies on race that motor measures may be affected by race. However, as implied, the data are questionable because of numerous methodological and theoretical issues. Other individual variables are definitely affected. Language, for example, is a difficult variable to measure across groups because it contains syntactical, grammatical, and cultural content that often precludes a direct translation/interpretation of a specific concept. For example, the location in a sentence of nouns and verbs differs across certain languages. Another example involves the Spanish alphabet which contains two additional letters, ñ and ll. Cognitive styles may similarly be affected because of variables which directly affect cognitive manipulations, such as specific style of analysis of information. Additionally, indirect variables may play a role. Asians or Hispanics not acculturated to North American norms may find it difficult to permit a professional to examine "their minds." In certain subcultures, this probing is allowed only by medicine men, witch doctors, or "curanderos." Thus, it may be impossible to obtain valid data because of the client's fear of testing.

While few individual neuropsychological tests have been adapted or translated, the two most widely used batteries, the Halstead-Reitan and Luria-Nebraska Neuropsychological Batteries, have been used with diverse populations. Both of these batteries have been translated into Spanish (HRNB by Melendez; Luria-Nebraska by Puente and colleagues) and are presently being used in other cultures. The Luria-Nebraska has been successfully adapted for Chinese-speaking subjects. Of the two, the Halstead-Reitan may prove, at least initially, to be more adaptable since the focus is less on language function than in the Luria-Nebraska. In both cases, however, the lack of data from diverse populations is presently hindering their application.

The data that do exist, though extremely sketchy, may indicate the direction for future research. For example, complications are introduced in a report on sex, age, developmental variables, and cognitive functioning by Denno, Meijs, Nachsshon, and Aurand (1982). Differences were noted on a variety of cognitive tests (e.g., Stanford-Binet) but only for 4- and 8-year-olds. Specifically, "white males scored the highest on all tests, followed by white females, black females and black males." Thus, variables such as sex and age may interact with race (and other variables). If these studies are found to be valid examples of neuropsychological measures, then a clear and easy identification of variables contributing to diversity of neuropsychological performance may not be feasible.

Culturally Sensitive Measures

One method of avoiding test bias with regard to culturally different populations is to use instruments that are sensitive to and factor out cultural variables. Of the attempts to diminish test bias, the most significant effort has been by Cattell. His Culture-Fair Intelligence Test measures intellectual abilities that allegedly factor out culture.

Cattell's basic aim was to factor out both cultural and educational variables from intellectual factors. Items were developed on common rather than culturally specific knowledge. Based on initial speculation, Cattell suggested that fluid intelligence was a function of biological factors including genetic and constitutional ones. In contrast, crystallized intelligence was a result of the development of fluid intelligence through environmental and cultural opportunities. While the Culture-Fair Test has been regularly used in the United States, its popularity has extended to non–North American populations. To date the instrument has been used with Nigerian (Nenty, 1986), Bulgarian (Paspalanova & Shtetinski, 1985), Italian (Stepanile, 1982), Spanish (Ortega-Esteban, Ledesma-Sanz, Lopez-Sanchez, & Prieto-Adanez, 1983), Israeli (Zeidner, 1987), and Indian (Ravishankar, 1982) groups. Unfortunately, the test has been shown to exhibit bias in some (e.g., Nigerian) though not all populations. In addition, these studies were completed with individuals residing in their own culture. It would be interesting to explore the efficacy of this test with minority cultures residing in the United States.

While this thrust is promising in theory, additional research both in the United States and abroad will have to occur prior to its wider clinical acceptance.

Of all standardized tests, the WAIS has received most attention with regard to cultural standardization. Two excellent examples are the Canadian and Puerto Rican versions of the test. Violato (1984) administered the standard or a revised version of the WAIS to 101 Canadians. The revised version contained eight items that were changed to increase face validity for Canadians. While bias effects were limited, the author did suggest that changes for Canadian administration of the WAIS were necessary. The WAIS has also been translated and standardized with Puerto Rican populations (1980). It was assumed that all translations would be appropriate; this assumption, however, is incorrect. Puerto Rican, Chicano, Mexican, Latin American, South American, and Castilian Spanish not only have their own dialects and idiosyncracies but in many cases, their own language. Thus, the Puerto Rican translation of the WAIS has limited usefulness with non–Puerto Rican subjects. Further, though yet to be researched, the issue of norms needs to be addressed. For example, Puerto Rican norms may differ from Argentinean norms. Also, there is the question of when an individual, from one culture but residing in another, becomes acculturated enough to be administered the "new" culture's tests. These and related questions remain to be answered.

Other tests of intellectual ability which are purported to be culture-reduced or fair include Raven's Progressive Matrices—both Coloured and Standard versions—as well as the Peabody Picture Vocabulary Test, the Quick Test, and the Army Beta. However, little evidence exists on the ability of these tests to be culture free. With the Picture Vocabulary Test serving as an example, several of the pictures on this test are useful for North American but not British populations. Another interesting example is that of the Luria-Nebraska Neuropsychological Battery. Certain sections and stimuli are deemed culture free or culture reduced; but several of the visual stimuli come from Denmark and not Nebraska, making clear identification of specific items (e.g., nutcracker) an often difficult if not impossible task.

Behavioral Assessment

In another section of this *Handbook*, chapters on behavioral assessment are found. One major focus of this type of assessment is the assumption that behavioral, versus psychometric, approaches to assessment reduce the risk of focusing on psychic and nonobservable attributions. Psychometric focus may increase the potential for incorrect understanding of the behavior in question and, of course, is more likely to introduce bias in the assessment process. The reader is directed not only to these chapters but to an excellent book by Hayes and Nelson (1986) for clarification of procedures and purposes of behavioral assessment.

Behavioral assessment focuses on empirically based methods of understanding behavior and, thus, the application to minority populations seems obvious. If psychometric tests are riddled with questions of culture, race, and ethnicity, then an assessment procedure which focuses on the behavior, and places the individuals in question in their environmental context, would seem an excellent alternative. Hence, it is surprising to note that this application has not been considered and researched adequately.

What scientific literature does exist is limited and, at best, preliminary. For example, Slate (1983) attempted to compare three nonbiased "behavioral" measures in retarded and nonretarded children across race and social class. Unfortunately, the results are so convoluted that they preclude an adequate understanding of any of these measures. Further, the possibility exists that behavioral measures may themselves be biased. Letherman, Williamson, Moody, and Wozniaz (1986) examined the effects of race of rater on the rating of the social skills of African-American and white children. The results support earlier findings that the race of the child affects the ratings received. In addition, the researchers reported that racial bias effects were noted with both African-American and white raters.

While intuitive support exists for the use of behavioral assessment with non-mainstream populations, complications are evident in the literature. First, little data and even less clinical application of this approach are available. In addition, initial studies suggest that bias may still be present both in terms of the rated and the rater.

THEORETICAL ISSUES

Bias

Kenneth Eells pioneered the concept of bias in mental measurement, specifically the mental test. While his work focused only on whites, it did address the importance of difference—in this case, social class—in assessment of mental function (Eells, 1951). Although the reasons for doing so are not entirely clear, some workers in the psychometric field generalized his findings to other populations, namely African-Americans. This generalization, an incorrect one, launched a wave of poorly developed and executed studies on bias in testing.

One of the most controversial figures in mental bias research is Arthur Jensen, of the University of California at Berkeley; his most controversial book is *Bias in Mental Testing* (1980). According to Jensen, mental testing has been criticized because of one or more of the following reasons;

1. Cultural bias
2. Specific test items
3. Inability to define or measure intelligence
4. Tests that measure too narrow a range of abilities
5. Failure to measure innate capacity
6. IQ tests that measure only learned skills
7. IQs that are inconsistent
8. Test scores that are contaminated by extraneous factors
9. Misuses, abuses, and undesirable consequences of testing

According to Jensen (1980), these criticisms are largely unfounded and probably due to other factors. As he wrote, "Anxiety about one's own status, or the importance of the traits measured by tests, or sympathy for the less fortunate, may prompt the acceptance of criticisms of tests without evidence" (p. 23).

Unfortunately, such critiques tend to focus on IQ tests and are emotionally interpreted. They complicate the question and prevent adequate understanding of the valid issues.

In a more objective manner, Reynolds and Brown (1984) presented a set of reasons which are applicable to bias for a wider range of tests. These include;

1. Inappropriate content.
2. Inappropriate standardization samples.
3. Examiner and language bias.
4. Inequitable social consequences.
5. Measurement of different constructs.
6. Differential predictive validity.

Regardless of the source of bias, the definition of bias must also be considered. Unfortunately, numerous definitions are available in the literature—some more heuristic than others. The following are two samples of the many available.

Eells (1951): [Bias results from] differences in the extent to which the child being tested has had the opportunity to know and become familiar with the specific subject matter or specific process required by the test item. (pg. 54)

Jensen (1980): Psychometric bias is a set of statistical attributes conjointly of a given test and two or more specified subpopulations (p. 375)

Flaugher (1978) has suggested that test bias can mean more than simple knowledge or psychometric deficiencies. Indeed, bias could be represented in a wide variety of concerns including, but not limited to, both psychometric issues (mean differences, differential validity, item content, internal validity) and test usage (overinterpretation, sexism, selection model, and atmosphere). He concluded that in 1978 the research was promising, but the results were still disappointing.

Among the more current research findings, an excellent example is Drasgow's (1972) article, "Biased Test Items and Differential Validity." In this review, the author addresses differences between majority and minority groups in validity coefficients. The results of his study provide support for earlier findings suggesting that validity coefficients may not prove useful in examining test bias. He concludes: "Test scores *can* be used to predict criterion performance for minority group members. Nevertheless, *it may be inappropriate to compare test scores for minority group members with test scores for majority group members*" [italics added] (p. 529). In a similar vein, Cole (1981) concluded in her article, "Bias in Testing," that "there is not large-scale, consistent bias against minority groups." Nevertheless, both "subtle aspects of the testing situation" and presumably more refined understanding still evade workers in the field. In contrast, Humphries (1986) has argued that even if items differ between groups, these items should not be labeled as biased if adequate measurement properties are taken into account.

Despite these opinions, many questions still need to be formulated and answered. Until then, as Reynolds and Brown have concluded, the verdict on test bias is still not in.

Acculturation

If a minority group does poorly on a test, relative to a majority group, two interpretations may be used to account for the discrepancy. A rather emotional one is provided by Jensen (1980)—that the difference is accounted for by biological factors such as genetics. A less popular interpretation used by researchers studying integration of an immigrant group into a majority or mainstream culture is that of acculturation.

Assimilation into a larger, more mainstream culture allows an individual to understand and adjust to the cultural, social, and psychological requirements of that culture. Conversely, those who do not adapt are considered to exhibit greater degrees of psychopathology. An illustration of the lack of adaptation was reported by Hoffman, Dana, and Bolton (1985) who found that Sioux Native-Americans with strong ties to tribal values and language were more likely to exhibit psychopathology as measured by the MMPI. These findings have also been replicated with other minority groups, including Hispanics (e.g., Montgomery & Oroz, 1984). Focusing on cognitive style and intelligence, Gonzales and Roll (1985) reported differences between Mexican-Americans and whites on several test measures. However, no group difference were observed between Anglo-Americans and a subgroup of the original sample of Mexican-Americans who had been shown to be acculturated to Anglo-American culture.

One method to determine whether acculturation has been achieved and thus controlled is to administer an acculturation scale. Marin, Sabogal, Marin, and Otero-Sabogal (1987) have developed a 12-item scale which measures acculturation in Hispanic populations. The validation criteria included generation, length of residence in the United States, age at arrival, ethnic self-identification, and an acculturation index. These findings have been extended to children (e.g., Franco, 1983) as well as to other cultural groups such as Asian-Americans, (Suinn, Rickard-Figueroa, Lew, & Vigil, 1987). Preliminary findings suggest that age (younger), sex (male), and length of exposure to the predominant culture (Burnam, Telles, Karno, & Hough, 1987) as well as cultural awareness and ethnic loyalty (Padilla, 1985) are critical factors in the acculturation process. Fradd and Hallman (1983) concluded that until an individual has been taught strategies to build bridges from a previous to a current domain of knowledge, the validity of test measures is questionable.

Social Policy

Whether tests are biased or culturally free, whether an individual belongs to a minority or a majority group, whether different groups are biologically equal or unequal, group differences exist. To deny the obvious would be foolish. Certain minority groups perform differently, at times worse, than majority groups on specific items, tasks, or tests. Such apparent differences drive social policy. Academic psychology would undoubtedly prefer to research these problems and discrepancies more thoroughly before allowing findings to affect the judicial and legislative process, because the data for any of these questions are at best inconclusive and at worst confusing.

However, policy must be and will be made in the absence of adequate data and in the presence of emotion (see Bersoff, 1981). This reality could explain why Cole (1981) concluded that test bias research is likely to have only a small impact on complex social policy issues. Regardless, there are issues that relate to the available data. In the first edition of this *Handbook,* Reschly (1984) addresses the concept of fairness. According to him, two approaches have been adopted. Equal treatment implies no bias or documentation in selection procedures and that all candidates, regardless of demographic affiliation, are treated equally. An alternative to this approach is equal outcomes, which implies that selection should match population demographics. Regardless of the approach and the data, the North American society has adopted in principle the concept of fairness. The question remaining is which method described by Reschly will be chosen and what, if any, implications will the current paucity of data and lack of scientific agreement have on social policy formation and implementation.

To assist policy makers, researchers need to place greater importance on studying issues of race, culture, ethnicity, and related variables. The findings must then be applied to broaden our limited understanding of differences in psychological test performance of minority group members. Of course, there is the issue of who is to pursue these questions, both in academic and research settings. In the seminal article, "The Changing Face of American Psychology" (Howard et al., 1986), the future for minority group representation is presented as quite dismal. While women have made significant strides, African-Americans, Hispanics, Asian-Americans, and Native-Americans, continue to lose ground in terms of representation in graduate school ranks. Similar trends exist in academic ranks, and presumably in clinical settings as well. Programs within the American Psychological Association, including the Minority Fellowship Program and the Minority Neuroscience Fellowship Program, may aid talented minorities to pursue graduate training. Unfortunately, undergraduate majors in psychology mirror the same trend. Indeed, by the time minorities have chosen a college, they most likely have committed to a course of study. Simply put, despite the urgency of the questions raised, the future for a better understanding of psychological assessment of minority group members looks bleaker than its past.

SUMMARY

Understanding human behavior requires an understanding of human diversity. Unfortunately, historical foundations have dictated an incorrect understanding of how culture, race, ethnicity, and related demographic variables affect human behavior. This situation is evident in the traditional and current use of psychological tests to measure such variables as intelligence, achievement, abilities, aptitude, personality, and neuropsychological function.

Two factors appear to have guided this incorrect measurement of human diversity. First, pioneers such as Terman not only suggested that minorities were inferior but that their "proliferation should be controlled." Legislation and adjudication addressing minority bias continues to this day even at the level of the Supreme Court. Second, few researchers, academicians, or clinicians have devoted time and effort to answering pertinent questions on human diversity, and even fewer have studied psychological assessment of diversity. Recently published statistics indicate that fewer minorities than in earlier years are pursuing graduate training in psychology or the study of human diversity. The lack of interested personnel is mirrored in faculty and clinical positions throughout North America.

The obvious outcome is a field lacking in adequate data. The data that are available are clouded not only by a host of methodological problems but by researchers' gross misunderstanding of minority group members (including but not limited to within-group heterogeneity), especially in the context of majority group behavior patterns. Regardless of the absence of data, social policy continues forward. Thus, much effort needs to be directed to the areas of research, teaching, and services to minority group members. Until additional adequate information is available, caution should be used in the application of present knowledge of the psychological assessment of minority group members.

REFERENCES

Adams, R. L., Boake, C., & Crain, C. (1982). Bias in a neuropsychological test classification related to education, age, and ethnicity. *Journal of Consulting and Clinical Psychology, 50,* 143–145.

Adebimpe, V. R. (1981). Overview: White norms and psychiatric diagnoses of black patients. *American Journal of Psychiatry, 138,* 279–285.

Beach, F. (1950). The snark was a bojum. *American Psychologist, 5,* 115–124.

Bersoff, D. N. (1981). Testing and the law. *American Psychologist, 36,* 1047–1056.

Boring, E. G. (1950). *A history of experimental psychology* (2nd ed.). Englewood Cliffs, NJ: Prentice-Hall.

Brislin, R. W. (1988). Increasing awareness of class, ethnicity, culture, and race by expanding students' own experience. In E. S. Cohan (Ed.), *The G. Stanley Hall Lecture Series* (Vol. 8, pp. 137–180). Washington, DC: American Psychological Association.

Burnam, M. A., Telles, C. A., Karno, M., & Hough, R. L. (1987). Measurement of acculturation in a community population of Mexican Americans. *Hispanic Journal of Behavior Science, 9,* 105.

Butcher, J. N. (1984). Current developments in MMPI use: An international perspective. In J. N. Butcher & C. D. Spielberger (Eds.), *Advances in personality assessment.* Hillsdale, NJ: Erlbaum.

Butcher, J. N. (1987). Introduction to the special series: Cultural factors in understanding and assessing psychopathology. *Journal of Consulting and Clinical Psychology, 55,* 459–460.

Butchner, J. N., Braswell, L., & Raney, D. (1982). A cross-cultural comparison of American Indian, black & white inpatients on the MMPI and persisting symptoms. *Journal of Consulting and Clinical Psychology, 51,* 587–594.

Cattell, R. R., (1963). Theory of fluid and crystallized intelligence: A critical experiment. *Journal of Educational Psychology, 54,* 1–22.

Cole, N. S. (1981). Bias in testing. *American Psychologist, 36,* 1067–1077.

Dahlstrom, W. G., Diehl, L. A., & Lachar, D. (1986). MMPI correlates of the demographic characteristics of black and white normal adults. In W. G. Dahlstrom, D. Lachar, & L. E. Kahlstrom (Eds.), *MMPI patterns of American minorities* (pp. 104–138). Minneapolis: University of Minnesota Press.

Dahlstrom, W. G., Lachar, D., & Dahlstrom, L. E. (Eds.). (1986). *MMPI patterns of American minorities.* Minneapolis: University of Minnesota Press.

Dahlstrom, W. G., Welsh, G. S., & Dahlstrom, L. E. (1972). *An MMPI handbook. Volume I: Clinical interpretation.* Minneapolis: University of Minnesota Press.

Dana, R. H. (1984). Intelligence testing of American Indian children: Sidesteps in quests of ethical practice. *White Cloud Journal, 3,* 35–43.

Denno, D., Meijs, B., Nachshon, I., & Aurand, S. (1982). Early cognitive functioning: Sex and race differences. *International Journal of Neuroscience, 16,* 159–172.

Drasgow, F. (1972). Biased test items and differential validity. *Psychological Bulletin, 92,* 526–531.

Drasgow, F., & Hulin, C. L. (1987). Cross-cultural measurement. *Revista Interamericana de Psicologia, 21,* 1–24.

Eells, K. (1951). *Intelligence and cultural differences.* Chicago: University of Chicago Press.

Faust, D., & Ziskin, J. (1988). The expert witness in psychology and psychiatry. *Science, 241,* 31–35.

Flaugher, R. L. (1978). The many definitions of test bias. *American Psychologist, 33,* 671–679.

Fox, C. H., & Zirkin, B. (1984). Achievement tests. In G. Goldstein & M. Hersen (Eds.), *Handbook of psychological assessment.* New York: Pergamon Press.

Fradd, S., & Hallman, C. L. (1983). Implications of psychological and educational research for assessment and instruction of culturally and linguistically different students. *Learning Disability Quarterly, 6,* 468–478.

Franco, J. N. (1983). An acculturation scale for Mexican-American children. *Journal of General Psychology, 108,* 175–181.

Franzen, M. D. (1989). *Reliability and validity in neuropsychological assessment.* New York: Plenum Press.

Goddard, H. H. (1912). *The Kallikak family: A study in the heredity of feeble-mindedness.* New York: Macmillan.

Golden, C. J. (1981). *Diagnosis and rehabilitation in clinical neuropsychology* (2nd ed.). Springfield, IL: Charles C. Thomas.

Gonzales, R. R., & Roll, S. (1985). Relationship between acculturation, cognitive style, and intelligence: A cross-sectional study. *Journal of Cross-Cultural Psychology, 16,* 190–205.

Gould, S. J. (1981). *The mismeasurement of man.* New York: W. W. Norton & Company.

Grazianu, W., Varca, P., Levy, J. (1982). Race of examiner effects and the validity of intelligence tests. *Review of Educational Research, 52,* 469–497.

Greene, R. L. (1987). Ethnicity and MMPI performance: A review. *Journal of Consulting and Clinical Psychology, 55,* 497–512.

Grubb, N. J. (1987). Intelligence at the low end of the curve: Where are the racial differences? *Journal of Black Psychology, 14,* 25–34.

Guthrie, R. (1976). *Even the rat was white.* New York: Harper & Row.

Gynther, M. D. (1981). In the MMPI an appropriate

device for blacks. *Journal of Black Psychology, 7,* 67–75.

Gynther, M. D., & Green, S. B. (1980). Accuracy may make a difference but does a difference make for accuracy? A response to Pritchard and Rosenblatt. *Journal of Consulting and Clinical Psychology, 48,* 268–272.

Hayes, S. C., & Nelson, R. O. (Eds.). (1986). *The conceptual foundations of behavioral assessment.* New York: Guilford Press.

Hickman, J. A., & Reynolds, C. R. (1986–1989). Are race differences in mental test scores an artifact of psychometric methods? A test of Harrington's experimental model. *Journal of Special Education, 20,* 409–430.

Hiltonsmith, R. W. (1984). Predicting WAIS-R scores from the Revised Beta for low functioning minority group offenders. *Journal of Clinical Psychology, 40,* 1063–1066.

Hoffmann, T., Dana, R., & Bolton, B. (1985). Measured acculturation and MMPI-168 performance of Native American adults. *Journal of Cross Cultured Psychology, 16,* 243–256.

Holland, J. L. (1979). *The self-directed search professional manual.* Palo Alto, CA: Consulting Psychologists Press.

Howard, A., Pion, G. M., Gottfredson, G. D., Flattau, P. E., Oskame, S., Pfafflin, S. M., Bray, D. W., & Burstein, A. G. (1986). The changing face of American psychology: A report from the Committee on Employment and Human Resources. *American Psychologist, 41,* 1311–1327.

Humphries, L. G. (1986). An analysis and evaluation of test and item bias in the prediction context. *Journal of Applied Psychology, 71,* 327–333.

Jackson, G. D. (1975). On the report of the Ad Hoc Committee on educational tests with disadvantaged students: Another psychological view from the Association of Black Psychologists. *American Psychologist, 30,* 88–93.

Jensen, A. (1980). *Bias in mental testing.* New York: Free Press.

Jensen, A. R. (1986). Construct-validity and test bias. *Phi Delta Kappan, 58,* 340–346.

Kuder, G. F. (1966). *General manual: Occupational interest survey form DD.* Chicago: Science Research Association.

Kuhn, T. S. (1970). *The structure of scientific revolutions* (2nd ed.). Chicago: University of Chicago Press.

Lachar, D., Dahlstrom, W. G., & Moreland, K. L. (1986). Relationship of ethnic background and other demographic characteristics to MMPI patterns in psychiatric samples. In W. G. Kahlstrom, D. Lackar, & L. E. Dahlstrom (Eds.), *MMPI patterns of American minorities* (pp. 139–178). Minneapolis: University of Minnesota Press.

Lampley, D. A., & Rust, J. V. (1986). Validation of the Kaufman Assessment Battery for Children with a sample of preschool children. *Psychology in the Schools, 23,* 131–137.

Lawson, W. B. (1987). Racial and ethnic factors in psychiatric research. *Hospital and Community Psychiatry, 37,* 50–54.

Leahey, T. H. (1987). A history of psychology (2nd ed.). Englewood Cliffs, NJ: Prentice-Hall.

Lethermun, V. R., Williamson, D. A., Moody, S. C., & Wozniak, P. (1986). Racial bias in behavioral assessment of children's social skills. *Journal of Psychopathology and Behavioral Assessment, 8,* 329–332.

Lezek, M. D. (1987). *Neuropsychological assessment* (2nd ed.). New York: Oxford University Press.

Lindenmann, J. E., & Matarazzo, J. D. (1984). Intellectual assessment of adults. In G. Goldstein & M. Hersen (Eds.), *Handbook of psychological assessment* (pp. 77–79). New York: Pergamon Press.

Linn, R. L., & Drasgow, F. (1987). Implications of the Golden Rule settlement for test construction. *Educational Measurement Issues and Practice, 6,* 13–17.

Lopez, S., & Romero, A. (1988). Assessing the intellectual functioning of Spanish-speaking adults: Comparison of the EIWA and the WAIS. *Professional Psychology: Research and Practice, 19,* 263–270.

Maheady, L., Towne, R., Algozzine, B., Mercer, J., & Ysseldyke, J. (1983). Minority overrepresentation: A case for alternative practices prior to referral. *Learning Disability Quarterly, 6,* 448–456.

Marin, G., Sabogal, F., Marin, B., & Otero-Sabogal, R. (1984). Development of a short acculturation scale for Hispanics. *Hispanic Journal of Behavioral Sciences, 9,* 183–205.

Montgomery, G. T., & Orozlo, S. (1984). Validation of a measure of acculturation for Mexican Americans. *Hispanic Journal of Behavioral Sciences, 6,* 53–63.

Nenty, H. J. (1986). Cross-culture bias analysis of Cattell Culture-Fair Intelligence Test. *Perspectives in Psychological Researches, 9,* 1–16.

Olmedo, E. L. (1981). Testing linguistic minorities. *American Psychologist, 36,* 1078–1085.

Ortega-Esteban, J., Ledesma-Sanz, A., Lopez-Sanchez, F., & Prieto-Adanez, G. (1983). Profit of the academically successful student in the Spanish universities. *Sciencia Pegagogica Experimentalis, 20,* 62–82.

Padilla, A. M. (1985). Acculturation and stress among immigrants and later generation individuals. *Spanish-Speaking Mental Health Research Center: Occasional Paper, 20,* 11–60.

Paspalanova, E., & Shtetinski, D. (1985). Standardization of the CF 2A Intelligence Test of Cattell for Bulgarian population. *Psikhologiia Bulgaria,* 1985, 12–22 (translation).

Prasse, D. (1979). Federal legislation and school psychology: Impact and implication. *Professional Psychology, 9,* 592–601.

President's Commission on Mental Health. (1978). *A report to the President from the President's Commission on Mental Health.* Washington, DC: U.S. Government Printing Office.

Ravishankar, V. (1982). A correlational study of Cattell's personality factor B. and I. Q. as measured by his culture free test. *Indian Psychological Review, 22,* 9–11.1

Reschly, D. J. (1984). Aptitude tests. In G. Goldstein & M. Hersen (Eds.). *Handbook of psychological assessment.* New York: Pergamon Press.

Reschly, D. J. (1988). Larry P. Larry P. Why the California shy fell an IQ testing. *Journal of School Psychology, 26,* 199–205.

Restandardization Committee of the University of Minnesota Press. (1989). MMPI-2 Minnesota Multiphasic Personality Inventory. *Critical Items, 4* (2), 1–4.

Reynolds, C. R., & Brown, R. T. (1984). Bias in mental testing. In C. R. Reynolds & R. T. Brown (Eds.), *Perspectives on bias in mental testing.* New York: Plenum Press.

Reynolds, C. R., Chastain, R. L. Kaufman, A. S., & McLean, J. E. (1987). Demographic characteristic of IQ among adults: Analysis of the WAIS-R standardization sample as a function of the stratification variables. *Journal of School Psychology, 25,* 323–342.

Roberts, R. J., & Hamsher, K. D. (1984). Effects of minority status on facial recognition and naming performance. *Journal of Clinical Psychology, 40,* 539–545.

Ross-Reynolds, J., & Reschly, D. J. (1983). An investigation of the item bias on the WISC-R with four sociocultural groups. *Journal of Consulting and Clinical Psychology, 51,* 144–146.

Sandoval, J. (1979). The WISC-R and internal evidence of test bias with minority group. *Journal of Consulting and Clinical Psychology, 47,* 919–927.

Sandoval, J., & Mielle, M. P. W. (1980). Accuracy of judgments of WISC-R item difficulty for minority groups. *Journal of Consulting and Clinical Psychology, 48,* 249–253.

Scarr, S. (1988). Race and gender as psychological variables: Social and ethical issues. *American Psychologist, 43,* 56–60.

Schratz, M. M. (1978). A developmental investigation of sex differences in spatial (visual-analytic) and mathematical skills in three ethnic groups. *Developmental Psychology, 14,* 365–380.

Schultz, D. (1981). *A history of modern psychology* (3rd ed.). New York: Academic Press.

Slate, N. (1983). Nonbiased assessment of adaptive behavior: Comparison of three instruments. *Exceptional Children, 50,* 67–70.

Spitzer, R. L., Endicott, J., & Fleiss, W. (1967). Instruments and recording forms for evaluating psychiatric status and history: Rationale, method of development and description. *Comprehensive Psychiatry, 8,* 321–343.

Spitzer, R. L., & Williams, J. B. W. (1980). Classification of mental disorders and DSM-III. In H. I. Kaplan, A. M. Freedman, & B. J. Sadock (Eds.), *Comprehensive textbook of psychiatry-III.* Baltimore: William and Wilkins.

Stepanile, C. (1982). Contributo per una taratura intaliana del test culture fair di Cattell. *Bollettino di Applicata, (161–164),* 81–86. (Translation)

Sue, S., & Zane, N. (1987). The role of culture and cultural techniques in psychotherapy. *American Psychologist, 42,* 37–45.

Suinn, R. M., Richard-Figueroa, K., Len, S., & Vigil, P. (1987). The Suinn-Law Asian Self-Indentity Acculturation Scale: An initial report. *Educational and Psychological Measurement, 6,* 103–112.

Terman, L. W. (1916). *The measurement of intelligence.* Boston: Houghton-Mifflin Company.

Triandis, H. C. (1982). Acculturation and biculturation indices among relatively accultured Hispanic youths. *Revista Interamericana de Psicologia, 16,* 140–149.

Violato, C. (1984). The effects of Canadianization of American-biased items on the WAIS and WAIS-R information subtests. *Canadian Journal of Behavioral Science, 16,* 36–41.

Wedding, D., Horton, A. M., & Webster, J. (1986). *The neuropsychology handbook.* New York: Springer.

Weiss, J. (1987). The Golden Rule bias reduction principle: A practical reform. *Educational Measurement Issues and Practice, 6,* 23–25.

Weschler, D. A. (1960). *Escala de Inteligencia de Weschler-Adultos.* New York: Psychological Corporation.

Westermeyer, J. (1987a). Cultural factors in clinical assessment. *Journal of Consulting and Clinical Psychology, 55,* 471–478.

Westermeyer, J. (1987b). Clinical considerations in cross-cultural diagnosis. *Hospital and Community Psychiatry, 38.* 160–165.

Whitworth, R. H., & Gibbons, R. T. (1986). Cross-racial comparison of the WAIS and WAIS-R. *Educational and Psychological Measurement, 46,* 1041–1049.

Williams, C. L. (1987). Issues surrounding psycho-logical testing of minority patients. *Hospital and Community Psychiatry, 38,* 184–189.

Williams, T. S. (1983). Some issues in the standardized testing of minority students. *Journal of Education, 165,* 192–208.

World Health Organization. (1973). *International pilot project on schizophrenia.* Geneva, Switzerland: Author.

Yerkes, R. N. (1923, March). Testing the human mind. *Atlantic Monthly,* pp. 358–370.

Zeidner, M. (1987). Test of the cultural bias hypothesis: Some Israeli findings. *Journal of Applied Psychology, 72,* 38–48.

Zubin, J. (1965). Cross-national study of diagnosis of the mental disorder: Methodology and planning. *American Journal of Psychiatry, 125,* 12–20.

CHAPTER 23

COMPUTER-ASSISTED PSYCHOLOGICAL ASSESSMENT

L. Michael Honaker
Raymond D. Fowler

The growing impact of computers on every aspect of life in our society also affects all the professions. In psychology, the availability of computers has had a profound effect on every aspect of psychological assessment from test construction and standardization to scoring and interpretation. This chapter traces the history and development of computer use in the asssessment process and summarizes the primary assessment applications that are available today. The major research, as well as ethical and legal issues associated with the use of computers in psychological assessment are also discussed.

The recent dramatic increase in the availability and accessibility of computer-assisted assessment services has led many to view the application of the computer to psychological testing as a new development. But the first computer-based test interpretation systems were developed around 1960 and services to clinicians based on these systems were available soon afterward. As Krug (1987a) observes, "There's no denying that after little more than a quarter of a century, computer testing has become an overnight sensation" (p. 15).

The growth in computer-based assessment has been the product of rapid improvement of computer systems (followed by lower costs and greater availability) and increased psychometric sophistication. The early systems used large, expensive mainframe computers and were developed to assist in limited components of the assessment process. These early systems (e.g., Swenson & Pearson, 1964) served primarily to provide rapid scoring of test results and brief, screening-oriented descriptions of the scores. In the late 1950s the speed of the computer in accomplishing these tasks became necessary due to a demand for psychological testing that was expanding faster than the availability of psychologists (Fowler, 1985). As computers became more sophisticated and accessible and the emphasis on actuarial-based interpretation of test scores increased, computers were employed as adjuncts for the *entire* assessment process. In addition to scoring and other simple clerical tasks, subsequent systems (e.g., Johnson & Williams, 1980) were developed to administer and provide sophisticated interpretations for most of the major psychological assessment procedures. Today, with the advent of cheap and powerful microcomputers and the growing computer and psychometric sophistication of psychologists, computers are used to administer, score, and interpret complete, individually tailored batteries of psychological evaluation procedures. Initially, practitioners had rather limited access to computers and programs; now they can select from a variety of inexpensive computer systems and hundreds of assessment-related software products.

The history of compter-assisted assessment can be viewed as occurring in three phases. Each phase represents an increase in accessibility of computer services to the clinician and parallels improvements in computer technology. A description of the highlights associated with each of these phases shows how rapidly computer-assisted assessment has progressed in the last couple of decades.

PHASE I
MAINFRAME COMPUTERS AND
MAIL-IN SCORING AND
INTERPRETATION SERVICES
(1960 TO EARLY 1970s)

Computers were largely a World War II development and did not begin to appear on college campuses until the mid-1950s. The early computers were quite expensive and large, often housed in several rooms or even an entire floor of a campus building. Psychologists, especially those interested in statistics and psychometrics, were among the first faculty members to use them.

Around 1960, mental health administrators in collaboration with major computer manufacturers, began exploring applications of computer technology to mental health delivery (Johnson, Giannetti, & Williams, 1976). This collaboration resulted in two major applications. One class of application involved administrative systems designed to reduce paper work and monitor the vast amount of data generated in a hospital setting (Graetz, 1966). Concurrent with the development of these administrative systems, behavioral scientists began to explore methods of using the computer to assist in the psychological assessment process.

The first major computer-assisted psychological assessment program became operational in the early 1960s at the Mayo Clinic in Rochester, Minnesota (Swenson & Pearson, 1964, Swenson, Rome, Pearson, & Brannick, 1965). The Mayo system was developed to deal with a practical problem: a large intake of patients and a small psychology staff. The Mayo system provided the referring physician with scores on the Minnesota Personality Inventory (MMPI) and a brief interpretation of each scale elevation. Although simple, it provided a practical means to screen large numbers of medical patients who otherwise might have had no psychological or psychiatric assessment. The work at the Mayo Clinic accelerated the development of new computer-based test interpretation (CBTI) systems by demonstrating that they worked in an applied setting.

Soon after the Mayo system became operational, other CBTI systems for the MMPI were developed. They were different in style and approach, but the general goals of all were similar. Whereas the Mayo system was designed to generate a brief scale-by-scale printout for screening purposes, the new systems were intended to produce detailed narrative clinical reports based on a configural interpretation of the MMPI.

The first CBTI system to receive widespread professional use, developed by Fowler (1964, 1965, 1969) at the University of Alabama, became operational in 1963. Fowler's intent was to design a system that simulated the decision-making processes of a skilled MMPI interpreter and produced a report similar in style and content to one written by a clinician. In 1965, the Roche Psychiatric Service Institute (RPSI), established by Roche Laboratories to make the Fowler system nationally available, initiated the first MMPI mail-in CBTI service for psychologists and psychiatrists. During the 17 years RPSI operated, over 1.5 million MMPI reports were generated and approximately one fourth of the eligible psychiatrists and clinical psychologists in the United States used the service to some extent.

Two other significant CBTI systems for the MMPI were also developed during this period. Interpretive systems developed by Caldwell (1971) and by Finney and his colleagues at the University of Kentucky (Finney, 1965, 1966) were psychodynamically oriented and based on high point configurations and various combinations of clinical and special scales. An important feature of their programs was the inclusion of a detailed discussion of treatment implications.

By the early 1970s, there were at least seven commercial MMPI interpretation services (Fowler, 1972). Additionally, other psychologists had developed computer programs which scored and/or interpreted several other tests, including the Rorschach (Piotrowski, 1964), the Holtzman Ink Blot Test (Gorham, 1967), the Sixteen Personality Factor Questionnaire (Eber, 1964; Karson & O'Dell, 1975), the Thematic Apperception Test (Smith, 1968), the California Psychological Inventory (Finney, 1966), and others.

During this initial phase, the utility of the computer as an aid to scoring and/or interpretation of psychological tests was clearly established. However, access to computer technology for the average psychologist was limited to mail-in services and the computer had relatively little impact on mental health delivery systems in general. As noted by Lanyon (1971), the period was "essentially pre-technological."

PHASE II
MINICOMPUTERS AND
INTERVENTIONALLY RELEVANT
AUTOMATION TECHNIQUES
(EARLY 1970s TO EARLY 1980s)

In the 1970s, use of minicomputer systems in mental health facilities gradually became widespread. These systems had much greater computing power than the original mainframe computers, were much smaller in size, and could be obtained at a fraction of the cost of the larger systems (e.g., $26,000 vs. $500,000, Johnson & Williams, 1978). By 1974, at least 57% of the mental health centers had access to a computer (Johnson, Giannetti, & Nelson, 1976).

In the early 1970s many clinicians remained skeptical of the computer's usefulness in mental health delivery. A possible reason for this skepticism was that the initial developers "had not consulted with clinicians regarding what was really needed to assist them in performing a better job" (Johnson, Giannetti, & Williams, 1976, p. 86). Partially in response to the practitioners' discontent, developers of psychological computer systems began to focus on applications which aided the clinician in real-life clinical decision making, a goal which was called the "development of interventionally relevant automation techniques" (Johnson, Giannetti, & Williams, 1976). An outgrowth of this goal was the development of sophisticated computer systems designed to assist clinicians in their total performance of mental health care delivery. An integral part of these systems was onsite use of the computer for direct computer administration, scoring, and interpretation of psychological evaluation procedures.

The first large-scale demonstration of online testing and interpretation took place at the Veterans Administration Hospital in Salt Lake City, Utah, in the early 1970s (Johnson & Williams, 1980). By 1973, Johnson (a clinical psychologist), Williams (a psychiatrist), and their colleagues had developed computer programs to administer, score, and interpret several psychometric and social history intruments. These programs became part of a comprehensive computer-based Psychiatric Assessment Unit (PAU) which was designed "as a means for optimizing assignment of patients into the treatment system in order to improve both individual care and facilities utilization" (Johnson & Williams, 1975, p. 389). The system employed a mainframe computer with 13 terminals and was used as part of an intake process at the Utah hospital to assess an average of 17 patients per day.

For each patient, the PAU computer software could administer a battery of tests selected by a testing coordinator. Most battteries included the MMPI, a test of intelligence and memory, a social history and problem checklist, the Beck Depression Inventory, and a structured mental status examination conducted by an interviewer and recorded on the terminal (Johnson & Williams, 1975). *Onsite* computer administration, scoring, and interpretation of a complete test battery was a marked advance over previous systems.

Also, empirical evaluation of the system (e.g., Klinger, Miller, Johnson, & Williams, 1976, 1977) suggested that PAU assessments were more internally consistent, twice as fast, and half as costly as traditional evaluations. The PAU was definitely successful in demonstrating the utility and intervention relevance of computer-assisted assessment.

Perhaps the most important contribution to evolve from the PAU was the development of a commercial computer system based on the pioneering PAU concepts. In 1977, members of the original PAU group founded Psych Systems, the first company to market hardware and software systems to administer, score, and interpret a battery of psychological instruments. Initially minicomputer-based systems capable of supporting two to sixteen terminals were offered. The software, known as Fasttest, was part of a turnkey system and eventually contained 30 assessment instruments, including measures of intelligence, vocational interest, personality, social history, medical history, and alcohol abuse.

By the early 1980s, there were 320 Psych Systems owners with more than 700 test terminals in operation (Fowler, 1985). The success of Psych Systems in marketing relatively expensive ($60,000–$100,000) systems primarily to independent practitioners demonstrated that there was a demand in the mental health profession for interactive, onsite testing. The apparent increased acceptance of in-office computers as an adjunct to the assessment process, the demonstrated commerical marketability of assessment programs, and the introduction of microcomputer technology set the stage for the next phase of development of computer-assisted assessment.

PHASE III
MICROCOMPUTERS AND THE COMMERCIALIZATION OF SOFTWARE DEVELOPMENT (LATE 1970s to PRESENT)

In the late 1970s and early 1980s, low-cost yet powerful personal microcomputers became available. Clinicians could now purchase a complete computer system, including software, for as little as $2,500. This new, easily accessible technology spawned an explosion of assessment software development, initially by individuals or small entrepreneurial companies and later by major test publishers.

CompuPsych was one of the first of the new companies to recognize and successfully address the need for an inexpensive microcomputer system dedicated to psychological assessment. Incorporated in June of 1980, their main product was the Psychometer, a small, portable microcomputer designed specifically for the administration, scoring, and interpretation of psychological evaluation procedures. The first Psychometer was shipped in May, 1981, and included programs for the MMPI and the Jenkins Activity Survey (Carol Watson, personal communication, December 13, 1988).

Although the Psychometer achieved some success, many practitioners were reluctant to purchase the system because it was limited to assessment functions. Many clinicinas were (and are) attracted to the microcomputer technology because of its office management (e.g., billing) and word-processing capabilities as well as for automated assessment. Accordingly, other companies, including Psych Systems, began to develop and market software for the major commercial microcomputers already in the marketplace, such as Apple and Tandy Radio Shack (TRS), and later IBM.

Psychological Assessment Resources (PAR) (founded by Bob Smith in 1978) was one of the first to market assessment software for the standard microcomputers. In 1980, PAR begin marketing TRS and Apple scoring software for the MMPI (Smith, personal communication, December 20, 1988). Also in 1980, Precision People (founded by Diane and John Trifelleti), (Trifelleti, personal communication, December 15, 1988) began marketing a microcomputer program for scoring and interpreting the Wechsler Intelligence Scale for Children-Revised (WISC-R). PAR's MMPI programs and the WISC-R by Precision People represent two of the first successful clinical assessment programs marketed at the national level for major microcomputer systems. Today, PAR has become a major developer and distributor of psychological assessment products and is an active participant in the advancement of computerized assessment. Also, Precision People continues to be a major developer of clinical assessment software and serves as a distributor for their own and others' psychological assessment programs.

Duthie (personal communication, December 15, 1988) formed Psychological Software Specialists (PSS) in 1982. In the same year PSS was one of the first (in addition to PAR) to publish a catalogue which listed a selection of assessment software for major commercial microcomputers. The catalogue included programs developed by PSS, individual software developers, and other newly formed software companies specializing in psychological applications. PSS was eventually purchased by Applied Innovations and Duthie currently markets software through a new company, Pacific Psychological.

In 1982, two other companies were formed which also contributed to the early development of microcomputer assessment software. In August 1982, Honaker, Harrell, and Rainwater founded Psychologistics, a company for the development and marketing of assessment software for mental health practitioners. Their initial products were Apple programs for scoring and interpreting the WISC-R and an online psychosocial history. In the same year, Sergio Docette started Applied Innovations (AI) to develop interactive screening instruments for a wide range of populations (Pratt, personal communication, December 12, 1988). AI purchased Duthie's programs in 1982 and also began development of their own systems. Currently, both Psychologistics and AI continue to develop and market psychological assessment software for Apple and IBM microcomputers.

By 1984, there were several small companies whose primary goal was the development and marketing of assessment software. The continued success for some of these companies demonstrated that the computer had become an accepted component of the assessment process. By this time, approximately 39% of individual clinicians (psychologists and psychiatrists) owned or had access to a computer and 43% of these practitioners either currently used or had an interest in computer assessment procedures (Levitan, Shook, & Willis, 1984). A guide developed by the Association for the Measurement and Evaluation in Guidance (1984) contained 112 software lisitings for 72 instruments. In Krug's (1984) *Psychware*, he described 190 computer based products that had implications for assessing and modifying behavior.

In 1983 and 1984, the success of this new technology attracted the attention of major test publishers. One of the first major efforts came from National Computer Systems (NCS). NCS purchased CompuPsych in 1983 and concurrently began work on a computer-based assessment system for IBM microcomputers. Their efforts resulted in the introduction of the Microtest system in January, 1985, which included software for the administration and interpretation of the MMPI, Career Assessment Inventory, and the Millon Clinical Multiaxial Inventory (Maruish, personal communication, December 13, 1988). Shortly afterward, NCS purchased Psych Systems. NCS later expanded their Microtest to include several other assessment programs and today they continue to be a major developer and distributor of assessment software for IBM microcomputers. They also continue to support owners of the Psych Systems (Fasttest) and CompuPsych (psychometer) systems.

From the mid-1980s to the present, numerous individuals, small companies and major test publishers entered the assessment software market. Krug (1987a) listed 72 separate suppliers of over 300 computer-based products with assessment applications. Although most of these products are for the administration/interpretation of traditional paperpencil tests, developers are now beginning to develop and market assessment procedures specifically designed for computer administration (e.g., Honaker, Harrell, & Ciminero, 1987; Johnson, Giannetti, Williams, 1979; Krug, 1985; Weiss, 1985). Over the last three decades, the computer clearly has become an accepted and integral component of the assessment process.

CURRENT STATUS OF COMPUTER-ASSISTED ASSESSMENT

Currently, the microcomputer can be used to administer, score, and/or interpret most of the psychological assessment procedures that are used by clinicians. There are computer programs that administer the major personality tests, some intelligence tests, and stuctured interviews directly on the computer. Once the assessment procedure is administered, either on the computer or in the traditional manner, the computer can quickly and accurately score the results as well as perform complex psychometric analyses. Many programs also provide a detailed interpretation including diagnostic hypotheses and treatment recommendations. In essence, software programs can quickly, reliably, and accurately do many of the clerical tasks of assessment that can be very time consuming and error ridden when done in the traditional manner.

An overview of the purposes and functions of microcomputers today is included in Table 23.1 which contains a taxonomy of computer-based psychological service products. (For an excellent detailed discription of many of the functions listed in Table 23.1, see Moreland, 1987). The types of assessment programs most available to and most frequently used by clinicians fall into one of three areas: personality evaluation, cognitive assessment, and interviewing. In the following sections, some of the major applications in these areas will be discussed. The examples of available software are not meant to be exhaustive and a more extensive listing is included in Krug (1987a).

(Addresses for the software companies mentioned in the following review are listed in Appendix A.)

PERSONALITY ASSESSMENT

Programs designed to assist personality evaluation represent by far the largest number of assessment software applications available today. These programs account for close to 45% of the products listed in Krug (1987a). Most provide scoring and/or interpretive reports and some also permit interactive test administration.

Online Administration

Interactive administration of personality assessment procedures has been of keen interest to many researchers throughout the history of computer use in psychology. Because of their relatively simple verbal stimulus characteristics and limited response options, the initial focus was on objective personality tests, including the MMPI (e.g., Dunn, Lushene, & O'Neil, 1972), the California Psychological Inventory (CPI) (Scissons, 1976), the Eysenck Personality Inventory (Katz & Dalby, 1981a), and the 16PF (Karson & O'Dell, 1975), to name a few. Recently, attempts have also been made to administer some projective techniques, such as the Rorschach (Miller, 1986) and Draw-A-Man (Levy & Barowsky, 1986), by computer. Automated administration of projective procedures requires significant changes in the response options available to the examinee and current approaches are not likely to be equivalent to the traditional procedure (see later discussion). Consequently, interactive objective tests have received a major portion of researchers' interest and are the applications most available to the practitioner.

Today, programs are available which administer many of the major objective personality tests, including the MMPI (National Computer Systems), California Psychological Inventory (Consulting Psychologists Press), Personality Inventory for Children (PIC) (Western Psychological Services), 16PF (Integrated Professional Systems), Adult Personality Inventory (Krug, 1985) and Millon Clinical Multiaxial Inventory (NCS). The majority of the interactive administration systems are developed and marketed by the publishers of the tests because test items are copyrighted and can be stored on magnetic media only by permission.

Computer administration of objective tests parallels

Table 23.1. Taxonomy of Computer-Based Psychological Software

1. Purpose
   a. *Assessment.* Programs designed to diagnose or evaluate by means of tests, histories, self-descriptions, or standardized observations.
   b. *Behavior Change.* Programs designed to help individuals eliminate unwanted behaviors or initiate new ones. Examples include counseling, weight control, negotiation, and stress management. None of these systems is included in this chapter.
2. Type of Assessment Instrument
   a. *Standardized tests.* Includes published and unpublished psychometric instruments. Examples include personality (MMPI), cognitive (WAIS-R), and vocational interest (Strong-Campbell).
   b. *Interviews, rating scales and checklists.* Standard information recorded by the client or for the client by an observer. Examples include medical and social histories, symptom checklists, behavioral observations, and clinician checklists.
   c. *Screening and integrative systems.* These are more complex programs that take the information from several sources and combine them. Examples include an initial screener to sample possible problem areas and an integrated report writer to combine results of several instruments into a single report.
   d. *Computer-dependent systems.* These programs are assessment procedures developed specifically for the computer and cannot be implemented effectively without the computer. An example is the computer adaptive testing procedures used for assessment of abilities.
3. Function and Output
   a. *Scoring.* The instrument is scored and appropriate norms are applied.
   b. *Score calculations.* Statistical manipulations of the scores are performed to aid psychometric analysis of the results.
   c. *Profile generation.* Scores are presented in some graphic format.
   d. *Descriptive report.* Statements about the meaning of scales or scale elevations are provided.
   e. *Interpretive report.* A report, usually in narrative form, is provided to describe the particular individual in terms of test performance.
   f. *Integrated report.* A report that contains information from various sources, including different tests, histories, demographic data, and behavioral observations is provided.
   g. *Used modified report.* The program produces a report that is developed specifically by the user or a report that has been modified in part by the user.
4. Administration Mode
   a. *Clinical.* The instrument is administered in the traditional manner by a clinician (for example, the Rorschach or WAIS-R) or self-administered on an answer sheet.
   b. *Interactive.* The items are presented on a computer screen, and the client responds on the keyboard.
5. Processing Mode
   a. *Remote.* The computer is located away from the site of administration, and data are mailed or transmitted by telephone; the test is not interactive.
   b. *Dial-in (teleprocessing).* The test is administered in the usual way and transmitted by data terminal to a mainframe computer for processing.
   c. *Optical scanning.* The test is administered on special answer sheets which are read into the computer by an optical scanner.
   c. *Punch-in.* The test is administered in the usual clinical or paper-pencil manner, and the responses are entered in an onsite computer for processing.
   d. *Online.* The test is administered, scored, and the report generated by the computer.

This table is based on an Appendix presented in Fowler (1985, p. 759).

the administration of the traditional procedures with some slight modifications. Usually items are presented one at a time on the computer monitor with the response options listed beneath the item. The response options are those presented in the test booklet (e.g., true or false), although sometimes an additional option to skip the item is also listed. (It is important to note that this additional option is a modification of the regular test procedure which may affect the equivalency of the computer version, e.g., White, Clements, & Fowler, 1985.) Examinees respond by pressing one

of the keys on the keypad which corresponds to the option they wish to endorse.

For most programs, the presentation order of items is identical to that for the traditional test. However, some psychologists (e.g., Butcher, Keller, & Bacon, 1985) have suggested that adaptive testing procedures that are possible on the computer can modify and improve the administration process. Computer-adaptive testing (CAT) maximizes administration time by administering only those items necessary to obtain an accurate estimate of the measured attribute (Weiss,

1985; Weiss & Vale, 1987). Preliminary investigations (Ben-Porath, Waller, Slutske, & Butcher 1988) have found that computer adaptive administration of the MMPI-2 is a feasible alternative to traditional, full-length administration for some of the content scales. The CAT procedures appear promising but further verification of their applicability and validity is needed before adaptive approaches are widely adopted with current personality tests.

The computer's capacity for increased control of the assessment process is the primary reason for use of the computer for interactive personality evaluation (Krug, 1987b). The computer insures that standard administration procedures are followed and that response integrity is maintained. Instructions and items are presented in the same manner for all examinees and the computer will accept only scorable responses to the items. The computer increases the potential for reliability in administration procedures, thus more closely approximating the carefully controlled conditions under which the test was developed and decreases scoring errors (Krug, 1987b).

Researchers have also identified additional advantages to interactive personality assessment procedures. Honaker, Harrell, and Buffaloe (1988) found that computer administration requires significantly less time to complete than paper-pencil administration. Also, most examinees generally view the computer-based personality tests more positively than the traditional version and when given a choice, express preference for the computer (e.g., Harrell & Lombardo, 1984; Honaker, Harrell, & Buffaloe, et al., 1988).

Another benefit for online administration is the potential for accurate recording of ancillary measures on the computer which may add additional important information about the subject's test-taking behavior. Stout (1981) suggested that reaction times and keypress force may reflect emotional reactions to the test items and also may be useful validity indicators. The implications of the ancillary data have yet to be explored systematically but computer administration does provide a reliable means for recording the data and makes examination of possible correlates possible.

A potential disadvantage of computer administration is that test modifications necessary for computerization may result in changes in how the examinee responds to the test items. As will be discussed in detail later in this chapter, these changes may create a situation in which the normative and validity data for the traditional test cannot be generalized to the computer version. Another disadvantage is that online administration of personality assessment procedures ties up the computer and may not be a cost-effective use of computer time (Moreland, 1987, p. 31).

Scoring and Interpretation

As seen in the history of computer use in psychology, programs for scoring and/or interpretation of personality tests, particularly the MMPI, have long been an integral component of computerized assessment. The majority of personality programs available today provide interpretive output although many focus also on scoring.

Scoring software, with the exception of that which provides online administration, necessitates that the test be administered first in the traditional manner. For objective tests, the actual responses are typed or optically scanned into the computer. The program then tallies the raw scores for scales and converts the scale scores to standard scores based on test norms. For most projective tests (e.g., Rorschach [Exner, 1987]), scores based on the subject's responses represent the raw data input, and appropriate score ratios, percentiles etc., are computed in addition to standard scores. Some projective programs (e.g., Bender Report [Psychometric Software]) provide scoring prompts which guide the clinician through the scoring process. The prompts describe the criteria for scorable responses, which are endorsed as present or absent by the clinician. The program then computes raw scores and appropriate standard scores.

Some important variations in scoring procedures of the software should be noted. First, some programs use a table look-up procedure which roughly parallels the noncomputer procedure used to convert raw scores to standard scores. Other systems employ formulas which convert raw scores to standard scores based on the mean and standard deviation for the scale. If the test scores are not normally distributed (i.e., the MMPI) and the formula does not correct for deviations from normality, the latter procedure can produce standard score values which are different from those obtained with traditional procedures. For example, one program examined by Honaker produced differences compared to the traditional tabled values as large as 10 T-scores for some of the scales.

A second significant variation is that some scoring programs employ norms different from those traditionally used for the test. This occurs most often when the program developer does not have permission from the publisher to use the test norms or there are additional norms available for the test which may be more accessible or more appropriate for the software application. For example, some MMPI scoring programs use the newly developed Mayo clinic norms (Colligan, Osborne, Swenson, & Offord, 1983) rather than the traditional University of Minnesota norms. Programs which use the Mayo norms will produce somewhat different T-score values for several of the scales because these norms are based on normalized, rather than linear, T-scores and are developed from a more recent sample.

Aside from these variations in scoring procedures, accuracy and speed are often cited as primary advantages of scoring software (e.g., Greene, 1980; Klett, Schaefer, & Plemel cited in Moreland, 1987). Also, programs provide additional scores that are not often obtained with traditional scoring because of time considerations. Most MMPI programs provide scoring for many of the special scales that can be very time consuming to obtain when scored in the traditional manner. Although the reliability and validity for some of these auxiliary scales have not been well established, these additional scores may help the clinician better understand the overall test results (Graham, 1987).

Computer programs for interpretation of personality tests represent the most widely available assessment software. Several different programs are available for all major tests. The majority have been designed for objective tests as opposed to projective techniques. For example, Krug (1987a) identified at least 19 different reports for the MMPI and eight for the 16PF, but only two each for the Rorschach and projective drawings.

Computer reports provide a range of different levels of interpretive aid ranging from a simple printout of the test scores to a complete interpretive narrative report, including diagnostic hypotheses and treatment recommendations, based on complex evaluation of score combinations. The reports include interpretive statements that are modeled after an expert clinician (e.g., Karson & O'Dell, 1987) or based on empirically demonstrated correlates of score elevations (e.g., Lachar, 1987). However, most represent a combination of both (e.g., Butcher, 1987; Exner, 1987) and rely heavily on "clinical lore" which Wiggins (1973) has defined as the total body of information available to a clinician "from a variety of sources including published research, theoretical writings, and the cumulative experience of one clinician or many" (p. 200).

Fowler (1987; cf. Butcher et al., 1985; Moreland, 1987; Roid & Gorsuch, 1984; Vale & Keller, 1987) describes five types of computer-based reports. The scoring/profile report simply presents scores, often in graphic format to simplify comprehension of the results. The descriptive report provides information about what scales measure and how scale elevations are interpreted. Complex analysis and interactions of test score patterns are addressed in the interpretive report. These reports are often presented in a narrative format similar to that written by a clinician. Interpretive statements are designed to describe the particular individual's profile rather than just state correlates associated with generic scale elevations. The summary report brings together information from different assessment procedures and presents in a single report a brief synopsis of the results from each source. The most sophisticated computer report is the integrated report, which attempts to duplicate the process of a clinician's interpretation of a battery of tests. Information from each of the tests is compared and interpretive statements are modified based on these comparisons. Currently, computer reports are limited primarily to scoring, descriptive, or interpretive types. To date, no successful integrated report has been developed.

Most reports use an "omnibus" interpretive strategy designed to address a broad range of test score information that is applicable to a variety of clinical settings (Vale & Keller, 1987). Some reports are more focused and are designed to be used with specific populations or to address specific questions. For example, the Minnesota Personnel Screening Report (NCS) focuses on MMPI interpretations relevant to personnel decisions and is tailored to the specific occupation being screened (Butcher, 1987). Similarly, the MMPI Medical Report (Integrated Professional Systems) includes interpretation of special medically relevant scales and is designed specifically for a hospital or medical outpatient setting.

Computer reports usually are based on a fixed set of decision rules that cannot be modified by the user. This inflexibility does not allow the clinician to make adjustments based on differing base rates that may be encountered in a particular setting where the program is used. One program available in the cognitive assessment area (Wechsler Memory Scale Report [Psychometric Software]) does provide the clinician with the option to modify the decision rules that determine when statements are printed and to change the actual content of the statements. This flexibility has not yet been built into programs for personality assessment reports.

The opportunity to define assessment objectives of the report is another option that is possible with the computer but currently has limited availability. For example, Krug's (1985) TEST PLUS program for the Adult Personality Inventory allows the user to define an ideal profile for a particular setting and the program compares the individual's profile with this model. The clinician can define a standard of performance which guides the program's decision-making process. Similar procedures which allow the clinician to affect the computer output interactively have not been implemented for other personality test reports.

Computer-based reports can offer several advantages over traditional techniques (Butcher, 1987; Vale & Keller, 1987). First, the computer offers standardization, reliability, and accuracy of results. Interpretations from the same scores will always be identical and the report's accuracy will not change from report to report. The objectivity, quickness, and the availability of an "outside opinion" represent additional advantages. The reports are not subject to interpretive bias and can provide the user with up-to-date interpretations which parallel those given by an expert clinician. Another benefit is the quick turnaround of reports which can be more time and cost effective than traditional procedures. Finally, examination of the validity of computer, as opposed to clinician, reports should be easier because explicit rules are used reliably to generate interpretations (Vale & Keller, 1987).

The last advantage has also proved to be a potential problem for computer-derived reports. The validity and accuracy of interpretive programs have come under much more scrutiny than the interpretations provided by clinicians, due partly to the reliability and potential "visibility" of computer based interpretations. As will be discussed later in this chapter, empirical examination of most interpretive systems is limited at best and their validity has not been clearly established. Another possible disadvantage of computer reports is the potential misuse by individuals not properly trained to evaluate the report. Problems with clients and nonprofessionals reading the reports are obvious, but also of concern are psychologists using computerized reports for tests that they do not know adequately.

COGNITIVE ASSESSMENT

Computer programs which assist in various aspects of cognitive assessment represent the second largest group of software systems currently available. Krug (1987a) lists 97 separate software products in the cognitive/ability assessment area. Intellectual assessment software has been the main clinical application, although some pioneering efforts have begun in neuropsychological assessment.

INTELLECTUAL ASSESSMENT

Software systems for the scoring and interpretation of standard intelligence tests were among the first commercially available programs for today's standard microcomputers and have been the primary focus of software development. Some successful attempts have also been made to produce programs for online administration of traditional intellectual assessment procedures.

Online Administration

The importance of standard administration procedures in intelligence testing (e.g., Sattler, 1988, pp. 109–110) and the computer's capacity to control stimulus presentation and record information reliably would seem to make computers ideal for cognitive assessment. However, traditional, omnibus intelligence tests utilize complex stimulus material, particularly for the evaluation of performance abilities. Also, the responses tapped by standard intelligence tests, particularly those associated with the examination of nonverbal, visual-motor abilities, are difficult to duplicate on the computer. The complexity and response requirements have thus far hindered the development of systems for *complete* online microcomputer administration of the traditional, omnibus intelligence evaluation procedures (e.g., Wechsler scales, Stanford-Binet). Consequently, computer administration programs available today for traditional intelligence tests are limited primarily to those which assess verbal skills (e.g., Shipley Institute of Living Scale [Western Psychological Services]).

Pioneering attempts to automate the WAIS were first reported by Elwood (1969, 1972). His work served as an impetus for further research, including examination of computer-assisted administration of the Peabody Picture Vocabulary Test (e.g., Elwood & Clark, 1978; Knights, Richardson, & McNarry, 1973; Overton & Scott, 1972), the Slosson Intelligence Test (Hedl, O'Neil, & Hansen, 1973), and the Raven's Progressive Matrices (e.g., Gilberstadt, Lushene, & Buegel, 1976). Many of these initial systems required equipment in addition to the computer and thus did not find their way into common use.

One of the few successful software systems for online administration of an intelligence test is a program marketed by Research Psychologists Press (RPP) for the Multidimensional Aptitude Battery (MAB) (Jackson, 1984). The MAB is a relatively new instrument designed to assess intellectual abilities in a multiple-choice format. Scales used in the MAB parallel closely those found on the WAIS-R, and MAB scores correlate highly with their respective WAIS-R counterparts. These high correlations, as well as the calibration procedures used to equate MAB and WAIS-R scores, suggest that the MAB can be considered a parallel form of the WAIS-R. The MAB is administered to an individual or group in a paper-and-pencil format. The Verbal subtests can also be administered online by a RPP computer program, which yields results parallel to those obtained in the traditional format (Harrell, Honaker, Hetu, & Oberwager, 1987). Although the Performance subtests are not presented on the screen, the program provides the option for examinees to type in responses while viewing the test booklet.

It is interesting to note that one of the primary considerations for Jackson (1984, p. 6) in the development of the MAB, was to create an instrument "permitting . . . automated administration." That an eminent test developer would have this goal in mind reflects the strong impact computers are beginning to have not only on the assessment process but also on test development.

The limited success of attempts to computerize traditional tests totally suggests that online evaluation of intelligence may depend on the development of tests designed specifically for the computer. New tests could be developed which optimize not only the stimulus control capabilities of the computer but also take advantage of the computer's capacity to do complex computations. For example, Weiss (1985) recently introduced the Minnesota Computerized Adaptive Testing System (MCATS) which allows the user to develop a CAT procedure for "virtually any test designed to measure one (or more) unidimensional variables" (p. 788). The MCATS introduces the technology for the development of a completely computer-based measure of intellectual abilities, although this capacity has yet to be realized on a large scale.

Scoring and Interpretation

The majority of computer applications for intellectual assessment provide scoring or score computations and interpretive reports for tests that are first administered in the traditional manner. Scoring functions include actual computation of raw scores, conversion of raw scores to standard scores, and/or psychometric calculations for description and evaluation of the standard scores. Raw score computation is limited to those few procedures which are administered online (see above). Conversion of raw scores to standard

scores is somewhat more prevalent, but this function is available only on programs developed or authorized by the test publishers because test norms are copyrighted. The most prevalent scoring function is the psychometric evaluation of standard scores.

The prevalence of programs that provide psychometric analysis of test scores is the result of increased emphasis on statistically based approaches for interpreting intelligence tests. These approaches are based on classic test theory (e.g., Ghiselli, 1964) and have been described in detail by Sattler (1988) and others (e.g., Gregory, 1987; Kaufman, 1979). The central premise of these approaches is that scores obtained from an intelligence test reflect both the subject's actual ability and error of measurement. The error necessitates that specific scores be interpreted as a range of scores that represent an estimate of the examinee's true ability. Also, differences between scores that may reflect cognitive strengths or weaknesses can be intepreted only if one can assume that the difference is reliable and not due to error. Accordingly, only statistically significant differences are viewed as important. The practical consequence of these approaches is that competent interpretation of intelligence tests has become dependent on considerable statistical manipulation of obtained scores, over and beyond "simple" scoring and conversion to standard scores. These analyses are very time consuming and potentially error ridden when done by hand but can be accomplished on the computer quickly and accurately.

The psychometric data provided by current programs include both descriptive and evaluative information that has been emphasized by the statistically based interpretive models. Descriptive statistics include percentile ranks, grade and age equivalents for scores, and confidence intervals for obtained and predicted scores (i.e., the range of scores expected in a retest situation). Several programs provide additional evaluation of the scores, which can be quite complex when not done by computer. Included are analyses of possible statistically significant differences between scores and individual scores compared to the mean of several other scores. An evaluation of the abnormality of these differences (i.e., the frequency with which these differences are expected to occur in a normal population) is also performed. Examination of patterns of performance across different scores, computation of factor scores and possible significant differences, comparison of current performance to that on other tests, and computation of demographically based estimates of intellectual functioning are features included in some of the programs.

The statistical analyses serve as the basis for the interpretive reports produced by intellectual assessment software. Most reports are descriptive in nature and delineate in narrative form the information implied by the statistical manipulations. These reports usually focus on the level of intellectual functioning relative to others and suggested areas of cognitive strengths and weaknesses. In addition to descriptive information, some programs include clinical (e.g., Precision People), educational (e.g., Report Writer [Psychological Assessment Resources]), vocational (e.g., Honaker & Harrell, 1984; WAIS-Riter [Southern Micro Systems]), and/or neuropsychological (e.g., Wechsler Interpretation System [Applied Innovations]) implications of the scores. A few of the programs include the option of typing in behavioral observations of the examinee. These observations are printed out in narrative form as part of the report.

By far the largest number of programs in the area are written for the Weschler scales—at least 15 (Krug, 1987a). However, programs are also available for all the major intelligence assessment procedures (e.g., Kaufman Assessment Battery for Children, Stanford-Binet, Slosson Intelligence Test; see Krug, 1987a). Most programs are written for one specific test. However, an interesting feature of some software is the capability to interpret scores from several different assessment instruments. For example, the Report Writer program marketed by PAR provides interpretive reports for a variety of cognitive instruments, including the WAIS-R/WISC-R, Stanford-Binet, WRAT-R, Trail Making Test, Symbol Digit Modalities Test, and the Woodcock-Johnson Achievement Test.

Use of computer programs to aid in administration and scoring of intelligence assessment procedures appears to offer some advantages over traditional procedures. The reliability and accuracy of calculations would seem to be a definite asset of the computer. Westby (1984) reported that in a study evaluating 252 Wechsler protocols, scoring programs produced no errors in age computation, conversion of raw scores to scale scores, summation of scale scores, and conversion of scaled score totals to IQs. However, when these same protocols were scored by doctoral graduate students, one third of the protocols included one or more computation errors. The mechanical scoring errors resulted in as much as a 16-point difference between the obtained and actual Full Scale IQ. Similar score variations resulting from clerical scoring errors on the Wechsler scales have been reported by others (e.g., Ryan, 1983; Miller, Chansky, & Gredler, 1970). Westby's results suggest that use of the computer for scoring and calculations could help eliminate these errors. Considering the important impact that IQ results can have on placement and treatment decisions, the increased accuracy offered by the computer represents a significant advantage over traditional procedures.

There is also suggestive evidence that online administration of intelligence tests is perceived positively by examinees. For example, Harrel et al. (1987) reported that college students rated computer administration of the MAB more favorably than traditional administration. Additional research is needed to ascertain whether this positive reaction is found in other populations and across individuals.

NEUROPSYCHOLOGICAL ASSESSMENT

Application of computer technology to neuropsychological evaluation procedures is somewhat limited compared to that seen in other areas of assessment, although the number of commercial software products more than doubled in the last couple of years (Krug, 1987a).

Neuropsychological assessment usually entails administration of a battery of tests designed to ascertain patterns of functional strengths and weaknesses (Lezak, 1983). However, as is true with intelligence testing, the stimulus and response complexity necessitated by components of many of the tests makes it difficult to duplicate these procedures with today's computer technology. Consequently, only a few of the procedures have been transferred successfully to online administration.

Swiercinsky (1983) produced the first complete computerized neuropsychological assessment battery. His system, SAINT, included 10 subtests which were computerized variations of traditional paper-pencil procedures. The system served to demonstrate the feasibility of online administration of some neuropsychological tests. However, its limited availability, lack of demonstrated validity, and rather rudimentary use of the computer's technology has made it unacceptable by today's standards (Golden, 1987). Other developers have focused on the administration of individual tests rather than complete batteries. Programs have been created for traditional neuropsychological tests such as the Halstead Category Test (e.g., PAR; Wang Neurological Laboratory [WNL]), the Finger Tapping Test (e.g., WNL), and the Wisconsin Card Sorting Test (e.g., PAR). Because there has been no adequate demonstration that computer versions of these procedures yield results equivalent to the traditional formats (e.g., Honaker, Harrell, Roman, & Cooley, 1988), these programs should perhaps be viewed as research versions. Other online software is available for tests which have been designed specifically for the computer (e.g., Life Science Associates) but normative data and validity data for these systems are either limited or absent.

Scoring and interpretive programs are available for individual neuropsychological tests such as the Wechsler Memory Scale (e.g., Psychometric Software) and the Bender-Gestalt (e.g., Precision People) and also for test batteries such as the Halstead-Reitan (e.g., Integrated Professional Systems) and the Luria-Nebraska (e.g., Western Psychological Services). However, the utility and validity of many of the battery programs have been severely questioned by some in the neuropsychological community. Adams and Heaton (1985) indicated that "none of the programs to date has produced results that are either satisfactory or equal in accuracy to those achieved by human clinicians" (p. 790). Similarly, Golden (1987) characterized the use of computers in neuropsychology as "at present more of a promise than a reality" (p. 344).

The lack of acceptance of scoring and interpretive computer applications which have been developed for neuropsychological test batteries rests partly on the goals of the existing programs and the consequent criteria by which the programs are judged. A primary focus of the programs evaluated by Adams and Heaton (1985) and Golden (1987) is the prediction and location of cerebral damage. The game of "lesion, lesion, where is the lesion" has been discarded by neuropsychologists (Lezak, 1983) and currently the focus is more on detailed functional analysis of deficits and strengths. Thus, even if the existing programs were successful in meeting the goal of locating cerebral damage, they would not address the type of information which would be most helpful to the neuropsychologist. Golden (1987) suggests that computer programs which help identify patterns of performance across tests may be most useful.

A second contributing factor to the strong criticisms of neuropsychological software is the apparent misperception that the computer programs developed in this area are designed to replace the clinician. As Golden (1987) observes, "Why psychologists are so eager for such programs is not clear. If the tests could be interpreted by computers, it is obvious there would be a much smaller need for psychologists" (p. 347). There is, of course, no evidence that the advent of computer-based testing has reduced the need for psychologists. On the contrary, the current boom in psychological assessment, which is now a significant factor in the practice of psychology, is a direct outcome of the availability of computer software that facilitates the assessment process.

The criticisms of neuropsychological programs have spurred the development of new systems designed to avoid the problems of previous programs. Golden (1987) noted this aim in describing his development of an online assessment battery called the Nebraska Neuropsychological Examination (NENE). The goals of the yet to be completed system are to implement a more detailed evaluation of abilities than that previously available and to optimize use of the functions (e.g., memory, graphics, timing) available in today's microcomputers. Also, Russell recently (January, 1988) introduced the Halstead-Reitan-Russell Battery software (HRRB [Scientific Psychology, Inc.]). The HRRB is a coordinated set of tests designed to measure the cortical functions relevant to neuropsychological applications. Consistent with Golden's (1987) emphasis on the examination of performance patterns, the HRRB scoring program transforms test scores into coordinated scale scores that can be used to identify deficit areas readily. The reports produced by the program are designed specifically to *aid* the clinician in interpretation (it is interesting to note that in promotional materials, Russell emphasizes that the HRRB is not an interpretive system).

The NENE and HRRB represent the continued interest that neuropsychologists have in utilizing the benefits offered by the computer. As indicated by Adams and Heaton (1987), the computer potentially offers several promising applications to neuropsychology which are just beginning to be realized. Golden (1987) observes: "Work currently in progress is encouraging, and I expect that the next decade will see a quantum leap in the sophistication and usefulness of computerized material available in neuropsychology" (p. 354).

COMPUTERIZED INTERVIEWS

One of the earliest uses of computer technology (e.g., Slack, Hicks, Reed, & Van Cura, 1966) was to gather information in a structured-interview format. Researchers have examined the feasibility and utility of computer interviews for a variety of areas, including psychiatric histories (e.g., Maultsby & Slack, 1971; Carr, Ghosh, & Ancill, 1983), psychosocial histories (e.g., Giannetti, 1987), mental status (e.g.,

Slack, 1971), alcohol and drug use (e.g., Erdman, Klein, & Greist, 1983; Skinner & Allen, 1983), suicide risk (e.g., Greist, Gustafson et al., 1973), and sexual dysfunction (Greist & Kline, 1980). Currently available is microcomputer software that can administer and provide printout summaries for a variety of interviews, including psychosocial histories (e.g., Giannetti On-Line Psychosocial History, GOLPH [NCS]; Psychosocial History Report [Psychometric Software]), developmental histories (e.g., Developmental History Report [Psychometric Software]), mental status (e.g., Psychological-Psychiatric Status Interview [Psychologistics]), chemical dependency (e.g., Honaker et al., 1987) and diagnostic interviews for children/adolescents (e.g., Stein, 1987) and adults (e.g., Fowler, Finkelstein, Penk, Bell, & Itzig, 1987).

Computerized interviews elicit information from the patient by presenting questions directly on the computer screen in a multiple-choice or true-false format. Usually, patients respond by pressing one of the number keys that corresponds to the option they wish to endorse. In some programs, fill-in-the blank questions are used in addition to the objective-question format. For these questions, the patients must type in their responses using the computer keyboard like a typewriter.

The basic presentation of a computerized interview is similar to a structured, paper-pencil or clinician interview. Questions usually are administered in a standard sequence and format, but interivew programs also have "branching" capabilities which allow the program to skip inappropriate questions or to present more detailed questions concerning a certain area. For example, questions about an individual's marital relationship would not be administered if the person endorsed "single" in response to a question on marital status. Similarly, if frequent alcohol use was indicated, detailed questions concerning drinking patterns could be presented.

The question composition of automated interviews is usually static and the clinician wishing to use a computerized interview is limited to the content areas and questions programmed by the developers. To address these limitations, some developers have recently introduced programs which allow users to develop their own computerized interviews (e.g., Q-Fast [StatSoft]) or allow the clinician to modify and/or add questions to an exisitng interview (e.g., Psychosocial History Report [Psychometric Software]).

The output from interview programs is usually descriptive rather than interpretive, and presents the information given by the interviewee in a variety of formats. Some programs produce a "bullet" report. These reports (e.g., Basic Interview Series [Psych Solutions Associates]; Child Diagnostic Screening Battery [Reason House]) simply list the options endorsed by the client, usually grouped under rationally derived content headings. Other programs (e.g., GOLPH [NCS]; Psychological-Psychiatric Status Interview [Psychologistics]) produce a more sophisticated narrative summary of the information which parallels the written summary done by a clinician. Diagnostic hypotheses (e.g., GOLPH [NCS]) and/or treatment recommendations (e.g., Alcohol Assessment and Treatment Profile [Psychologistics]) are sometimes included as part of the report. Some programs compute summary scores based on rational or empirical grouping of the item content (e.g., Fowler, et al., 1987; Honaker et al., 1987).

Research on the utility of computerized interviews suggests that they offer several advantages over those conducted in the traditional manner. As emphasized by Erdman, Klein, and Greist (1985), computerized interviews are 100% reliable and will always address the same content areas. Consequently, the automated interview often produces more complete data than the clinician (e.g., Angle, Ellinwood, & Carroll, 1978; Angle, Johnsen, Grebenkemper, & Ellinwood, 1979; Carr et al., 1983; Climent, Plutchik, & Estrada, 1975; Greist, VanCura, & Kneppreth, 1973; Simmons & Miller, 1971). Although the computer's comprehensiveness is due partly to its inability to forget to ask questions, patients also appear to be more willing to divulge information, particularly of a personal, sensitive nature, to the unemotional, nonjudgmental computer. Greist and Klein (1980) found that subjects were more likely to indicate the presence of sexual problems when interviewed by computer than when interviewed by a psychiatrist. Similar findings regarding other personally sensitive issues (e.g., drinking, criminal record, etc.) have been found by other investigators (e.g., Carr et al. 1983; Lucas, Mullins, Luna, & McInroy, 1977). Another apparent advantage of the computer is that many (but not all) patients view the computer favorably and even express a preference for the computer over traditional interview methods (e.g., Carr et. al., 1983; Helzer, Robins, Croughan, & Ratcliff, 1981; Lucas, 1977; Skinner & Allen, 1983; see review in Stein, 1987).

Despite some clear benefit to the use of computer-based interviewing, the approach is not without disadvantage. Some patients (as well as some clinicians) feel that computers "dehumanize" the assessment process. This potential negative reaction emphasizes the importance of not assuming that computer interviews can be used for all patients. A second disadvantage is that current programs are limited to obtaining structured, verbal material and are relatively inflexible in the wording of questions (Erdman et., 1985). Consequently, much of the nonverbal data that clinicians often use during the interview to guide question asking and interpretation of responses is not available for the computer. Also, the standardized wording of the questions may be beyond the reading level of the patient or worded in a manner that is not understood. Although it is possible to program variations in the reading level, wording, and language of questions (e.g., Bloom, White, Beckley, & Slack, 1978), these options are not available in programs generally available to the clinician. Presently, it is clear that computer interviews can not replace the clinical interviewer but instead are useful adjuncts to the data-gathering process.

A final disadvantage is that use of the computer for online administration of any assessment procedure ties up the computer for as much as an hour or more. Consequently, the system is unavailable for word processing, billing, and other office maintenance procedures.

Clinician Checklists

Related to the use of computers for interviewing are *clinician checklist* programs. These programs provide a structured set of questions that are answered directly by the clinician. They are designed to help organize data collection and produce narrative summaries of procedures conducted regularly by the clinician. An example is the Intake Evaluation Report (IER) (Honaker & Harrell, 1988), composed of a series of multiple-choice, fill-in-the-blank questions that pertain to information often obtained during an initial interview or extended mental status exam. Topic areas include presenting problem, current situation, physical presentation, mental status, biological/medical status, interpersonal relations and socialization, diagnostic impressions, and recommendations. The program also allows the clinician to add comments concerning areas not covered by the IER questions. Once the clinician has completed the intake interview, the IER can be completed directly on the computer by the clinician in less than five minutes, or a paper-pencil version can be filled in and typed into the computer later. The program produces a two- to three-page report which summarizes the clinician's reponses to the questions in a narrative format. At the end of the report, areas not covered during the initial

intake are listed so that they can be addressed in future sessions.

The clinician report programs provide many of the advantages offered by computerized interviews and circumvent some of the disadvantages. Like online interviews, the checklists provide a reliable, standardized method for data collection. However, because the information is obtained directly by the clinician, issues concerning the loss of nonverbal data and the client's understanding of the questions are attenuated. Also, the relatively quick data entry leaves the computer free for other tasks.

RESEARCH ISSUES

The expanded use of computers to replace or aid the traditional psychological assessment procedure has resulted in many research questions. Two major issues concern the equivalency of computerized testing and traditional formats, and the validity of the information produced by computers.

Equivalency

When a traditional assessment procedure is converted to computer administration, the stimulus presentation and the response requirements must be modified to conform to the computer. A test item appearing normally in the context of several items in a test booklet is instead presented by itself on a computer monitor. Written or verbalized reactions to an assessment stimulus are replaced by key presses on a computer keyboard. For some assessment procedures (e.g., interviews, projective tests), a clinician is replaced by a computer. It is possible that these modifications may produce changes in how the examinee responds to the evaluation. The computerized format may no longer reflect the same psychological constructs as those tapped by the original procedure and the procedures cannot be considered equivalent. To this extent the validity and normative data for the traditional procedure cannot be generalized to the computer format.

Equivalence between tests can be evaluated along both psychometric and experiential dimensions (Honaker, 1988). Psychometric equivalence requires that both procedures yield essentially identical information about the examinee. For traditional psychological tests, this requirement necessitates that both administration formats produce scores that have equal means, standard deviations, and rankings, and that correlate equally well with external criteria. Experiential equivalency refers to similarities in the perceptual, emotional, and attitudinal reactions that examinees have in response to the two formats. When two administration procedures are experienced differently, it is possible that other components of the evaluation process, in addition to or instead of the psychometric equivalence of the test itself, may be affected differentially. For example, if one format creates more anxiety and discomfort, examinees exposed to this format may be less willing to continue in the evaluation process or may develop less positive perceptions of the psychological intervention than examinees exposed to a different format.

Psychometric Equivalence

In general, research has not established that computerized tests are psychometrically equivalent to their traditional counterparts. Additionally, for some procedures (e.g., interviews) there is strong evidence for nonequivalence. There are many unanswered questions, the most important being how individual differences in examinees and variations in the human-computer interface affect the equivalence of computerized tests (Honaker, 1988). Also, most studies have not addressed all the criteria for equivalence and have usually ignored possible differences in variances and criterion validity between computerized and traditional procedures. Finally, much of the research is based on nonclinical populations and may not be generalizable to clinical situations. A brief review of the specific research findings for each of the main clinical assessment procedures should provide the reader with some idea of the incompleteness of our current knowledge and directions for further research.

Personality Assessment. The majority of studies examining the equivalence of computerized assessment has addressed online administration of personality evaluation procedures. Researchers have focused primarily on objective procedures, such as the 16PF (e.g., Harrell & Lombardo, 1984), Firo-BC (Katz & Dalby, 1981b) and CPI (e.g., Scissons, 1976), although some examinations of projective techniques, including the Rorschach (e.g., Miller, 1986) and Draw-A-Man (Levy & Barowsky, 1986), have been reported. The largest number of studies have been conducted with the MMPI and thus the current status of equivalency research for personality assessment software is best reflected by these studies.

MMPI equivalency research has produced inconsistent and imcomplete findings (Honaker, 1988). Some researchers (e.g., Biskin & Kolotkin, 1977; Lambert, Andrews, Rylee, & Skinner, 1987; Lushene, O'Neil, & Dunn, 1974; White et al., 1985) have found that computerized MMPI administration produces significant mean score differences on one or more scales. Other researchers (e.g., Honaker, Harrell, & Buffaloe, 1988; Rozensky, Honor, Rasinski, Tovian, & Herz, 1986; Russell, Peace, & Mellsop, 1986) have found no score differences acrosss modes. The computer does appear to yield equal ranking of scores (e.g., White et al., 1985) and appears to yield score reliability that is equal to or slightly better than the traditional format (e.g., Honaker, Harrell, & Buffaloe, 1988). However, there has been little examination of possible variations in score distributions that may result from the two formats and evaluation of criterion validity of the computer procedures is totally absent. In general, research has not established that the two administration modes yield equivalent results, and Honaker (1988) concludes that "until further systematic studies are completed, a clinician must be cautious in assuming that the scores obtained from computer administration of the MMPI have the same meaning for a particular patient as scores obtained in the traditional format" (p. 576).

The status of the MMPI equivalency research is somewhat discouraging because the number of studies on the MMPI far exceeds that done for any other assessment instrument. It is clear that additional research is needed.

Intellectual Assessment. Examination of the equivalency of computer-administered intelligence evaluation procedures is limited. Initial exploration of the WAIS (e.g., Elwood, 1969, 1972) and the Peabody Picture Vocabulary Test (Knights et al., 1973; Overton & Scott, 1972) suggested that automated (by means other than or in addition to the computer) procedures for intelligence tests were reliable and correlated well with their traditional counterparts. However, in at least one study (e.g., Knights et al., 1973), mean score differences were found between the administration formats. Only a few studies have examined completely computerized systems. In an early unpublished dissertation by Hedl (cited in Hedl et al., 1973), computer administration of the Slosson Intelligence Test correlated highly with examiner administration and exhibited parallel concurrent validity with the WAIS. Similarly, Harrell et al. (1987) found that a computerized version of the MAB Verbal subtests produced mean scores, standard deviations, and rankings that were parallel to those obtained in the traditional manner. Both studies employed college students, a characteristic which may attenuate the generalizability of their results.

Because of the paucity of research, one cannot assume that computer administration is equivalent to the regular administration of traditional intelligence tests. Also, there is evidence that intelligence is one of the individual characteristics that affects the equivalency of computerized procedures. Johnson and Baker (1973) found that subjects of lower intellectual ability did not perform as well on a computer-administered concept formation task as they did when the task was human administered. Subjects with above average ability performed equally well under both administration conditions. These findings suggest that computer-administered cognitive tests may be differentially equivalent, depending on the intellectual level of the examinee. Other possibly important variables, which may affect the equivalency of computerized cognitive and ability tasks, have also been identified, including the presence of timed components of the test (Greaud & Green, 1986) and the type of response measured by the test (Honaker, Harrell, Roman, & Cooley, 1988).

Interviews. Several studies have shown that computerized interviews yield more information than those conducted in the traditional manner (but it should be noted that this is not true for all computer interviews [Skinner & Allen, 1983]). Also, patients appear more willing to divulge personally sensitive information in computer interviews. Although this willingness is generally viewed as an advantage of using the computer (e.g., Erdman et al., 1985), these findings indicate that a computer interview is not equivalent to the traditional interview. Accordingly, the information obtained may not be interpretable in the same manner as the material derived in a regular interview. It appears that the additional data obtained by the computer are valid (e.g., Carr et al., 1983), but it is not clear how the added information affects the clinical process.

The more detailed findings provided by the computer may serve to evaluate more effectively, and thus facilitate treatment (Angle, 1981). The added symptoms that are endorsed on the computer may also distract the clinician. Usually, symptoms that occur infrequently are perceived as more "abnormal" and thus clinically important. However, information obtained from computer interviews may lead us to find that behaviors previously seen as unusual actually occur with some frequency in the clinical population. Our norms for certain symptoms, particularly those of a personally sensitive nature, may have to be revised. In general, now that it is established that some people are more willing to endorse symptoms on some computer interviews, research needs to evaluate the clinical importance and implications of this additional information.

Experimental Equivalence

In addition to the absence of clearly established psychometric equivalence, there is increasing evidence that the computer and traditional formats are experienced differently by examinees. But it is not clear what effect these differences have on the assessment process.

Studies have found that computer administration is perceived more positively than the traditional procedures for most major assessment applications. Many (but not all) individuals rate the computer as more comfortable, interesting, quicker, relaxing, and easier (e.g., Bresolin, 1984; Honaker, Harrell, & Buffaloe, 1988; Rozensky et al. 1986). Also, several studies (e.g., Carr et al. 1983; Helzer et al., 1981; Honaker, Harrell, & Buffaloe, 1988; Lucas, 1977; Russell et al., 1986; White et al., 1985) have found that when given a choice, most (but again, not all) examinees express a preference for computer administration.

Thus, the computer does not appear to be experientially equivalent to regular assessment procedures, but two questions remain relatively unaddressed. First, what variables affect perceptions and attitudes toward the computer? Previous computer experience and perceived ease of taking the test on the computer have been identified as important (e.g., Burke, Normand, & Raju, 1987; Hoffer & Green, 1985), but to date, no study has systematically evaluated the impact of these or any other variables. Second, what effects, if any, does nonequivalence have on the assessment process? One preliminary study (Barron, Daniels, & O'Toole, 1987) suggests that computer, compared to clinician, administration of an intake battery did not result in different expectations regarding treatment. However, participants in the study were college students who were receiving class credit for their participation; this constraint seriously limits the generalizability of these results to other populations. Also, there has been no direct examination of whether experiential differences affect the psychometric equivalence of the computerized test or how computer administration of one test may affect the examinee's reactions to other procedures that are not computerized (see Honaker, 1988).

Validity

The accuracy and validity of information produced by computer assessment systems has received considerably more public attention than the question of equivalency. In fact, much of the controversy concerning computerized testing has focused on this issue (e.g., Fowler & Butcher, 1986; Matarazzo, 1986).

A primary concern of critics regarding computer-based test interpretation (CBTI) is that for many programs there are few, if any, published reports of empirically demonstrated validity (Lanyon, 1984; Matarazzo, 1983). This criticism is accurate for most software systems on the market today but is less true for some CBTI programs. For example, recent reviews of CBTIs for the MMPI (e.g., Moreland, 1985, 1987) have identified several studies evaluating the validity of different CBTI systems. These studies have shown that computer MMPI reports are rated as accurate by clinicians familiar with the patient (e.g., Green, 1982; Lachar, 1974), are rated as more accurate than "phony" reports (e.g., Moreland & Onstad, 1985), and show acceptable external criterion validity (e.g., Hedlund, Morgan, & Master, 1972). Validity research is also available for CBTI systems for the PIC (Lachar, 1987), Rorschach (Exner, 1987), and 16PF (Karson & O'Dell, 1987). Contrary to the critics' claims, there are published findings that support the validity of some CBTI reports.

However, there are methodological flaws in most of the validation research, and only portions of the CBTIs, not the entire systems, have been examined (Moreland, 1985). An important methodological concern is the criteria by which the accuracy of CBTI reports are judged. Criteria employed have included accuracy ratings given by professionals familiar with the patient (e.g., Green, 1982), reports written by clinicians (e.g., Johnson, Giannetti, & Williams, 1978), interpretations given by an expert (e.g., Karson & O'Dell, 1987), and ratings provided on symptom checklists (e.g., Hedlund et al., 1972). A major difficulty with these criteria is their potential lack of reliability (Lanyon, 1987) and the consequent difficulty of generalizing the findings to actual clinical decisions.

In general, proponents and critics agree that there is a need for considerably more evaluation of the validity of CBTI reports, but there are differences in the suggested directions for this additional research. Two primary areas of disagreement concern which criteria should be employed to evaluate the accuracy of CBTI reports and what components of the report need the most attention. Moreland (1985) implies that CBTI systems should be evaluated in light of their accuracy in predicting external behavioral criteria: validity is a function of how well each statemet provided in the report corresponds to patient behaviors observed by the clinician. A similar, yet slightly different, focus is suggested by Lanyon (1987) who emphasizes "narrow band," empirically verifiable predictions, such as clinical diagnoses, as appropriate criteria. Both Lanyon and Moreland indicate that the focus should be placed on individual statements in the report and that all statements should be examined. In sharp contrast, Vale and Keller (1987) indicate that prediction accuracy of external behavioral correlates is "perhaps somewhat more ambitious than is necessary or desirable" (p. 79). Instead, CBTIs should be considered expert systems and should be evaluated according to how well they agree with the expert they are supposed to emulate. The complete report should be evaluated relative to how well the narrative addresses relevant assessment questions in a manner similar to that of an expert clinician. Similar emphasis on report utility and the importance of the total narrative has also been proposed by Krug (1987b).

Variations in the suggested criteria for evaluation of CBTI systems could reflect different perceptions regarding the function of the computer in the assessment process. If the computer is perceived as a *substitute* for the clinician, then demonstration that the computer report provides the same information and makes the same decisions as the clinician is appropriate. This approach emphasizes the speed and reliability that is afforded by the computer. The CBTI is simply an automated clone that is quicker and more consistent than the clinician. Another perspective is that the computer provides a *method for improving*, instead of just duplicating, the decision-making capabilities of the clinician. From this viewpoint, emphasis is placed on the computer's capacity to store information, perform complex multivariate analysis of data, and produce reliable acturial predictions. A CBTI is not only quicker and more reliable, but potentially more accurate than the expert clinician. Examination of the criterion validity of the CBTI *and clinician* reports becomes important because demonstration of improvement for the CBTI must have a standard for comparison (i.e., the clinician report).

Both *criterion validity* and *expert similarity* validation strategies are needed to establish the accuracy of CBTI systems. The two strategies can be used concurrently or sequentially to determine the validity of existing systems or to aid in the development of new systems. For most current systems, it would be helpful to show that the reports are at least as accurate as expert clinicians. To accomplish this, Vale and Keller (1987) suggest several strategies, including having experts reconstruct the profile based on the CBTI and directly comparing clinician and CBTI interpretations of the same profile. If the goal of the system is to develop a quick and reliable substitute for the expert, validation work is complete once the CBTI and expert show 100% agreement. This approach assumes that the expert clinician's interpretations are accurate, which may be an unjustified assumption. Use of this strategy alone cannot produce an accurate interpretive system unless it has first been established that the expert's judgements are valid. This issue is attenuated somewhat when the expert's interpretations are based on established actuarial relationships, such as seen in Lachar's (1987) PIC system and Exner's (1987) CBTI for the Rorschach. However, actuarial data are not available for all profile types and cross-validation of the actuarial relationships is usually absent. Also, most actuarially based systems include a significant proportion of "clinical judgment" statements which reflect the expert opinions of the author of the system (e.g., Butcher, 1987; Exner, 1987).

The expert-simulation approach to validation essentially maintains the status quo and produces improvements in assessment accuracy only to the degree that the emulated expert (or experts) improves. To optimize the potential of the CBTI systems, further evaluation of the criterion validity of computer statements is needed in addition to verification that the CBTI and experts agree. CBTI systems may make it easier to investigate test-criteria relationships because the computer reliably uses explicit rules to generate interpretations. Examination of the accuracy of statements made on the basis of these relationships can serve to improve the accuracy of the CBTI *and* can increase our knowledge base for the test.

Complete validation of a CBTI system necessitates examination of variations in accuracy for different populations and base rates (Lanyon, 1987). Establishing the validity for a wide variety of populations with different base rates for the characteristics addressed by the test may prove to be an insurmountable task if CBTI systems continue to be developed in their current fashion. Today, most programs are *closed systems* that do not allow the user to modify or replace either the decision rules or the corresponding interpretive statements. In fact, for most systems the user does not know what rules are used as the basis for interpretation because of proprietary concerns of the developers. Creation of open system programs which allow clinicians to modify the rules or statements based on local norms and base rates may help to improve the accuracy of the CBTI for specific locations. Open programs may also decrease the need for the developer to validate the CBTI for all populations and base rates.

The development of interactive, artificial-intelligence-based, expert systems for test interpretation is another alternative that should be explored. Although CBTIs have been called expert systems (e.g., Vale & Keller, 1987), current systems lack several characteristics often found in the expert systems that have been applied successfully to other fields (e.g., medicine). As described by Chabris (1987), "A true expert system must be capable of performing three basic services: not only problem solving but also interactive explanation and knowledge acquisition (learning)" (p. 108). Currently, CBTIs can serve as an aid to problem solving, but they do not provide explanations of how conclusions were derived or change as a result of new data provided by the user. The knowledge acquisition function of a true expert-system CBTI could serve to enhance the accuracy of information output by the system and would provide a built-in mechanism for correcting for population and base rate differences.

It should be noted that the validity of a CBTI report is dependent on the validity of the test for which the report is written (Fowler, 1985). If the test has well-established empirical relationships between test variables and behavior, report statements based on these empirical findings are more likely to prove valid; therefore, for some CBTIs research will need to focus first on the validity of the test itself. This is particularly true for instruments developed specifically for the computer, as some of these tests are quite new and have little, if any, validity data.

The utility of CBTI systems is another validity issue that must be addressed in future research (Krug, 1987b; Lanyon, 1987). We need to ascertain the impact of CBTIs on the decision-making process of the clinician. Do the CBTI narratives add any useful information beyond the profile scores? If so, what? Do they have discriminative validity? What type of narrative report is most useful? Do some CBTI reports include statements which are harmful to the examinee—that is, are they safe (Vale & Keller, 1987)? To date, these questions have not been addressed.

Given the general lack of established validity for CBTI reports, a related concern is whether clinicians attribute more validity to a computerized report than is warranted. In a preliminary examination of this question, Honaker, Hector, and Harrell (1986) asked clinical psychology graduate students and practicing clinicians to rate the accuracy of MMPI reports that were randomly labeled as either clinician or computer generated. There was no difference in the accuracy ratings for the two types of reports, although reports of either type which deliberately contained an inaccurate statement were rated as less accurate. Also, in response to questions regarding the utility of the reports, clinicians were considerably more critical of reports labeled as computer produced. These findings fail to support the critics' claims that computer reports are viewed as more credible than is warranted. However, further exploration with nonprofessionals and professionals not trained in MMPI interpretation is needed as well as examination of reports for other tests.

In general, the present status of validation research emphasizes that CBTIs should be regarded as adjuncts to the assessment process and not as replacements for the clinician. Although studies for some CBTI systems have been favorable (Moreland, 1987), most systems have not been evaluated properly, if at all. Also, the studies that have been completed have methodological problems that may attenuate the generalizability of their findings. As stated in the American Psychological Association (APA) (1986) guidelines for computer-based testing, computer reports are considered professional to professional *consultations* and "should be used only in conjunction with professional judgment" (p. 12).

ETHICAL, LEGAL AND PROFESSIONAL ISSUES

New technological developments within a profession usually result in ethical, legal, and professional issues that must be resolved. Although many clinicians feared that computer-based testing would lead to serious problems in all three areas, the problems have been relatively few.

Ethical Issues

Ethical issues concerning computer-based testing and interpretation were first raised in the mid-1960s when mail-in MMPI and 16PF services began to be offered. Since the Ethical Principles of the American Psychological Association prohibited mail-order psychological services to clients, a committee was asked to determine whether mail-in test interpretation services should also be prohibited. The committee concluded that such services were different from the proscribed mail-order services because the reports were provided directly to professionals and not to clients seeking psychological services. The committee recognized, however, that the new technology raised issues not covered in the Ethical Standards, and recommended a set of guidelines for CBTI services. These guidelines, which were designed specifically to deal with mail-in services, were subsequently adopted as APA's official position (APA, 1966).

With the advent of microcomputers and the greatly increased availability and variety of testing software and services, the 1966 guidelines were no longer sufficient, and revised guidelines that were broader in scope were adopted (APA, 1986). These guidelines draw extensively from the Standards for Educational and Psychological Testing (APA, AERA, & NCME, 1985), an interorganizational statement on the use of tests, and relate those standards to two important APA documents: the Ethical Principles of Psychologists (APA, 1981) and the Standards for Providers of Psychological Services (APA, 1977). The guidelines address the responsibilities of test authors, software authors, and test publishers as well as the professional who uses the software and services. Because the revised Guidelines are relatively new, the degree to which they will resolve potential problems remains to be seen. The original Guidelines seem to have functioned well. During the quarter century that computer-based test reports have been available, few ethical complaints have been made and no psychologist has been found guilty of malpractice or of ethical violations associated with CBTI use.

Legal Issues

Although virtually all widely used psychological tests are protected by copyright, violations such as making photocopies of test items for teaching purposes or creating short forms for screening purposes have been commonplace over the years, and until recently publishers were fairly relaxed about enforcement. When psychologists first began to develop assessment software it was not clear how the copyright laws applied to such activities, and many scoring and interpretation systems were developed without permission (but without objection) from publishers. As publishers began to develop CBTI systems for their own tests, they began to defend their rights more vigorously and some litigation has resulted. It seems clear that there is no legal and ethical way in which test materials that are under copyright protection may be copied or otherwise made part of a computer system without permission from the copyright holders, and violators are likely to face legal action.

Professional Issues

The question of who is qualified to use psychological tests was further complicated by the availability of computer-based reports. Psychiatrists played an active part in the early development of psychological tests, including the Rorschach, TAT, and MMPI, and test publishers have traditionally made clinical psychological tests available to physicians for purchase, but most do not avail themselves of that opportunity. The first mail-in services, following the policies of the test publishers, made computer-based test reports equally available to licensed psychologists and physicians and they were used extensively by both groups without significant objections.

When online systems became available, enabling clinicians both to administer and to interpret tests on their own and others' patients, some psychologists raised objections that psychiatrists who purchased and used these systems were practicing psychology and were therefore in violation of ther licensing laws. However, most state licensing laws specifically exempt physicians from resrictions on the use of psychological tests (so long as they do not use the title psychologist when administering such tests). Some state psychological associations have developed or considered restrictive guidelines (e.g., Ohio Psychological Association, 1983), but these standards are not binding on other professions. In the state of Kansas, the Office of the Attorney General issued an opinion which states that professionals who are not psychologists may use psychological tests and interpretations, provided that such work is consistent with their training and with any applicable professional code of ethics (Opinion, 80-130).

At the present time, online testing systems are accessible to psychiatrists but apparently have been purchased by relatively few. Most psychiatrists obtain their psychological testing through referral to psychologists or by using mail-in services.

Some of the professional issues raised have broad public policy implications. Matarazzo (1986), in a strongly worded critique of computer-based testing, expressed concern that the availability of computer testing software would prove economically seductive to mental health professionals, leading them to offer testing to too many patients and clients, thus contributing to an escalation of health care costs which would be passed on to all Americans. In reply, Fowler and Butcher (1986) observed that computers reduced cost of testing to more manageable levels, and that "testing, when done appropriately and economically, can lower health care costs by improving diagnosis and treatment."

The ubiquitous question—"Can the computer supplant the clinician?"—has been visited and revisited for a quarter of a century. Fowler and Butcher (1986) note that computer-based reports cannot supplant the clinician and were not intended to do so, just as "an

on-board computer may add a dimension of accuracy and speed to the decisions of a pilot, but is not a substitute for the pilot." Rather than leading to technological unemployment of psychologists, computer-based testing has been accompanied by greatly expanded interest and involvement in testing on the part of psychologists. In the late 1950s, interest in testing had so diminished that few psychologists were willing to do psychological evaluations and testing courses were dropped in many graduate programs. Twenty-five years later, Moreland and Dahlstrom (1983) found that 91% of the psychologists they surveyed do assessment as part of their practice and more than half use computer scoring (10%) and interpretation (45%) services. It is likely that that number is even greater today.

There is a growing consensus that computer-assisted testing and interpretation can be a time- and cost-effective aid in psychological assessment, but few believe today that the computer will supplant the clinician. As Fowler and Butcher (1986) noted, "There must be a clinician between the computer and client." Computers can produce psychological reports, but a psychological assessment requires the integration of test material with a whole range of other data including history, interviews, and behavioral observations. Even the very best psychological reports, whether they are written by a clinician or generated by a computer, are of little value without a competent clinician who can put the results into the context of the patient's life. A report from well-designed interpretation system that is based on a valid test can provide a useful source of hypotheses for the clinician, but it is the task of the clinician to examine those hypotheses in light of the clinical history and behavioral observations. Computer technology can assist clinicians by providing useful, cost-effective ways to give the public better and more efficient services.

REFERENCES

Adams, K. M., & Heaton, R. K. (1985). Automated interpretation of neuropsychological test data. *Journal of Consulting and Clinical Psychology, 53*, 790–802.

Adams, K. M., & Heaton, R. K. (1987). Computerized neuropsychological assessment: Issues and applications. In J. N. Butcher (Ed.), *Computerized psychological assessment* (pp. 355–365). New York: Basic Books.

American Psychological Association. (1966). Interim standards for automated test scoring and interpretation services. *American Psychologist, 22*, 1141.

American Psychological Association (1977). *Standards for providers of psychological services.* Washington, DC: Author.

American Psychological Association (1981). *Ethical principles of pschologists.* Washington, DC: Author.

American Psychological Association (1986). *Guidelines for computer-based tests and interpretations.* Washington, DC: Author.

Angle, H. V. (1981). The interviewing computer: A technology for gathering comprehensive treatment information. *Behavior Research Methods & Instrumentation, 13*, 607–612.

Angle, H. V., Ellinwood, E. H., & Carroll, J. (1978). Computer interview problem assessment of psychiatric patients. In F. H. Orthner (Ed.), *Proceedings: Second Annual Symposium on Computer Application in Medical Care.* New York: Institute of Electrical and Electronic Engineers.

Angle, H. V., Johnsen, T., Grebenkemper, N. S., & Ellinwood, E. H. (1979). Computer interview support for clinicians. *Professional Psychology, 10*, 49–57.

Association for Measurement and Evaluation in Guidance. (1984). *Guide to microcomputer software in testing and assessment.* Washington, DC: Author.

Barron, M. R., Daniels, J. L., & O'Toole, W. M. (1987). The effect of computer-conducted initial intake interviews on client expectancy. *Computers in Human Behavior, 3*, 21–28.

Ben-Porath, Y. S., Waller, N. G., Slutske, W. S., & Butcher, J. N. (1988, August). *A comparison of two methods of adaptive administration of the MMPI-2 content scales.* Paper presented at the meeting of the American Psychological Association, Atlanta, GA.

Biskin, B. H., & Kolotkin, R. L. (1977). Effects of computerized administration on scores of the Minnesota Multiphasic Personality Inventory. *Applied Psychological Measurement, 1*, 543–549.

Bloom, S. M., White, R. J., Beckley, R. F., & Slack, W. V. (1978). CONVERSE: A means to write, edit, administer, and summarize computer-based dialogue. *Computers and Biomedical Research, 11*, 167–175.

Bresolin, M. J., Jr. (1984). *A comparative study of computer administration of the Minnesota Multiphasic Personality Inventory in an inpatient psychiatric setting.* Unpublished doctoral dissertation, Loyola University, Chicago, IL.

Burke, M. J., Normand, J., & Raju, N. S. (1987). Examinee attitudes toward computer-administered testing. *Computers in Human Behavior, 3*, 95–107.

Butcher, J. N. (1987). Computerized clinical and personality assessment using the MMPI. In J. N. Butcher (Ed.), *Computerized psychological assessment* (pp. 161–197). New York: Basic Books.

Butcher, J. N., Keller, L. S., & Bacon, S. F. (1985). Current developments and future directions in computerized personality assessment. *Journal of Consulting and Clinical Psychology, 53*, 803–815.

Caldwell, A. B. (1971, April). *Recent advances in automated interpretation of the MMPI.* Paper presented at the Sixth Annual MMPI Symposium, Minneapolis, MN.

Carr, A. C., Ghosh, A., & Ancill, R. J. (1983). Can a computer take a psychiatric history? *Psychological Medicine, 13*, 151–158.

Chabris, C. F. (1987). *Artificial intelligence and Turbo Pascal.* Homewood, IL: Dow Jones-Irwin.

Climent, C. E., Plutchik, R., & Estrada, H. (1975). A comparison of traditional and symptom checklist-based histories. *American Journal of Psychiatry, 132*, 450–453.

Colligan, R. C., Osborne, D., Swenson, W. M., & Offord, K. P. (1983). *The MMPI: A contemporary normative study.* New York: Praeger.

Dunn, T. G., Lushene, R. E., & O'Neil, H. F., Jr. (1972). Complete automation of the MMPI and a study of its response latencies. *Journal of Consulting and Clinical Psychology, 39*, 381–387.

Eber, H. W. (1964, September). Automated personality description with 16PF data. In Dregor, R. M. (Chair), *Computer reporting of personality test data.* Symposium presented at the meeting of the American Psychological Association, Los Angeles, CA.

Elwood, D. J. (1969). Automation of psychological testing. *American Psychologist, 24*, 287–289.

Elwood, D. J. (1972). Validity of an automated measure of intelligence in borderline retarded subjects. *American Journal of Mental Deficiency, 7*, 90–94.

Elwood, D. J., & Clark, C. L. (1978). Computer administration of Peabody Picture Vocabulary Test to young children. *Behavior Research Methods & Instrumentation, 10*, 43–46.

Erdman, H., Klein, M. H., & Greist, J. H. (1983). The reliability of a computer interview for drug use/abuse information. *Behavior Research Methods & Instrumentation, 15*, 66–68.

Erdman, H., Klein, M. H., & Greist, J. H. (1985). Direct patient computer interviewing. *Journal of Consulting and Clinical Psychology, 53*, 760–773.

Exner, J. E., Jr. (1987). Computer assistance in Rorschach interpretation. In J. N. Butcher (Ed.), *Computerized psychological assessment* (pp. 218–235). New York: Basic Books.

Finney, J. C. (1965, September). *Purposes and usefulness of the Kentucky program for the automatic interpretation of the MMPI*. Paper presented at the meeting of the American Psychological Association, Chicago.

Finney, J. C. (1966). Programmed interpretation of the MMPI and CPI. *Archives of General Psychiatry, 15*, 75–81.

Fowler, D. R., Finkelstein, A. Penk, W., Bell, W., & Itzig, B. (1987). An automated problem-rating interview: The DPRI. In J. N. Butcher (Ed.), *Computerized psychological assessment* (pp. 87–107). New York: Basic Books.

Fowler, R. D. (1964, September). *Computer processing and reporting of personality test data*. Paper presented at the meeting of the American Psychological Association, Los Angeles.

Fowler, R. D. (1965, September). *Purposes and usefulness of the Alabama program for the automatic interpretation of the MMPI*. Paper presented at the meeting of the American Psychological Association, Chicago.

Fowler, R. D. (1969). Automated interpretation of personality test data. In J. N. Butcher (Ed.), *MMPI: Research developments and clinical applications* (pp. 105–125). New York: McGraw-Hill.

Fowler, R. D. (1972). Automated psychological test interpretation: The status in 1972. *Psychiatric Annals, 2*, 10–28.

Fowler, R. D. (1985). Landmarks in computer-assisted psychological assessment. *Journal of Consulting and Clinical Psychology, 53*, 748–759.

Fowler, R. D. (1987). Developing a computer-based test interpretation system. In J. N. Butcher (Ed.), *Computerized psychological assessment* (pp. 50–63). New York: Basic Books.

Fowler, R. D., & Butcher, J. N. (1986). Critique of Matarazzo's views on computerized testing: All sigma and no meaning. *American Psychologist, 41*, 94–96.

Ghiselli, E. E. (1964). *Theory of psychological measurement*. New York: McGraw-Hill.

Giannett, R. A. (1987). The GOLPH psychosocial history: Response-contingent data acquisition and reporting. In J. N. Butcher (Ed.), *Computerized psychological assessment* (pp. 124–144). New York: Basic Books.

Gilberstadt, H., Lushene, R., & Buegel, B. (1976). Automated assessment of intelligence: The TAPA test battery and computerized report writing. *Perceptual and Motor Skills, 43*, 627–635.

Golden, C. J. (1987). Computers in neuropsychology. In J. N. Butcher (Ed.), *Computerized psychological assessment* (pp. 344–354). New York: Basic Books.

Gorham, D. R. (1967). Validity and reliability studies of a computer-based scoring system for inkblot responses. *Journal of Consulting Psychology, 31*, 65–70.

Graetz, R. E. (1966). The computer: A new tool for psychiatry. *Hospital and Community Psychiatry, 17*, 26–28.

Graham, J. R. (1987). *The MMPI: A practical guide*. New York: Oxford University Press.

Greaud, V. A., & Green, B. F. (1986). Equivalence of conventional and computer presentation of speed tests. *Applied Psychological Measurement, 10*, 23–34.

Green, C. J. (1982). The diagnostic accuracy and utility of MMPI and MCMI computer interpretive reports. *Journal of Personality Assessment, 46*, 359–365.

Greene, R. L., (1980). *The MMPI: An interpretive manual*. New York: Grune & Stratton.

Gregory, R. J. (1987). *Adult intellectual assessment*. Boston: Allyn and Bacon.

Greist, J. H., Gustafson, D. H., Stauss, F. F., Rowse, G. L., Laughren, T. P., & Chiles, J. A. (1973). A computer interview for suicide risk prediction. *American Journal of Psychiatry, 130*, 1327–1332.

Greist, J. H., & Klein, M. H. (1980). Computer programs for patients, clinicians, and researchers in psychiatry. In J. B. Sidowski, J. H. Johnson, & T. A. Williams (Eds.), *Technology in mental health care delivery systems* (pp. 161–182). Norwood, NJ: Ablex.

Greist, J. H., Van Cura, L. J., & Kneppreth, N. P. (1973). A computer interview for emergency room patients. *Computers and Biomedical Research, 6*, 257.

Harrell, T. H., & Lombardo, T. A. (1984). Validation of an automated 16PF administration procedure. *Journal of Personality Assessment, 48*, 638–642.

Harrell, T. H., Honaker, L. M., Hetu, M., & Oberwager, J. (1987). Computerized versus traditional administration of the Multidimensional Aptitude

Battery-Verbal Scale: An examination of reliability and validity. *Computers in Human Behavior, 3*, 129–137.

Hedl, J. J., O'Neil, H. F., & Hansen, D. N. (1973). Affective reactions toward computer-based intelligence testing. *Journal of Consulting and Clinical Psychology, 40*, 217–222.

Hedlund, J. L., Morgan, D. W., & Master, F. D. (1972). The Mayo Clinic Automated MMPI Program: Crossvalidation with psychiatric patients in an army hospital. *Journal of Clinical Psychology, 28*, 505–510.

Helzer, J. E., Robins, L. N., Croughan, J. L., & Ratcliff, K. S. (1981). National Institute of Mental Health Diagnostic Interview Schedule: Its history, characteristics and validities. *Archives of General Psychiatry, 38*, 381–389.

Hoffer, P. J., & Green, B. F. (1985). The challenge of competence and creativity in computerized psychological testing. *Journal of Consulting and Clinical Psychology, 53*, 826–838.

Honaker, L. M. (1988). The equivalency of computerized and conventional MMPI administration: A critical review. *Clinical Psychology Review, 8*, 561–577.

Honaker, L. M., & Harrell, T. H. (1984). *WAIS-Report* [Computer program]. Indialantic, FL: Psychologistics.

Honaker, L. M., & Harrell, T. H. (1988). *Microcomputer system for the Intake Evaluation Report* [Computer program]. Indialantic, FL: Psychologistics.

Honaker, L. M., Harrell, T. H., & Buffaloe, J. D. (1988). Equivalency of Microtest computer MMPI administration for standard and special scales. *Computers in Human Behavior, 4*, 323–337.

Honaker, L. M., Harrell, T. H., & Ciminero, A. (1987). *Chemical Dependency Assessment Profile* [Computer program]. Indialantic, FL: Psychologistics.

Honaker, L. M., Harrell, T. H., Roman, P., & Cooley, D. S. (1988, March). *Equivalency of computer versus traditional administration of the Finger Tapping Test: A re-evaluation.* Paper presented at the meeting of Southeastern Psychological Association, New Orleans, LA.

Honaker, L. M., Hector, V. S., & Harrell, T. H. (1986). Perceived validity of computer- versus clinician-generated MMPI reports. *Computers in Human Behavior, 2*, 77–83.

Jackson, D. N. (1984). *Manual for the Multidimensional Aptitude Battery.* Port Huron, MI: Research Psychologists Press.

Johnson, E. S., & Baker, R. F. (1973). The computer as experimenter: New results. *Behavioral Science, 18*, 377–385.

Johnson, J. H., Giannetti, R. A., & Nelson, M. S. (1976). The results of a survey on the use of technology in mental health centers. *Hospital and Community Psychiatry, 27*, 387–388.

Johnson, J. H., Giannetti, R. A., & Williams, T. A. (1976). Computers in mental health care delivery: A review of the evolution toward interventionally relevant on-line processing. *Behavior Research Methods & Instrumentation, 8*, 83–91.

Johnson, J. H., Giannetti, R. A., & Williams, T. A. (1978). A self-contained microcomputer system for psychological testing. *Behavior Research Methods & Instrumentation, 10*, 579–581.

Johnson, J. H., Giannetti, R. A., & Williams, T. A. (1979). Psychological systems questionnaire: An objective personality test designed for on-line computer presentation, scoring, and interpretation. *Behavior Research Methods & Instrumentation, 11*, 257–260.

Johnson, J. H., & Williams, T. A. (1975). The use of on-line computer technology in a mental health admitting system. *American Psychologist, 30*, 388–390.

Johnson, J. H., & Williams, T. A. (1978). Using a microcomputer for on-line psychiatric assessment. *Behavior Research Methods & Instrumentation, 10*, 576–578.

Johnson, J. H., & Williams, T. A. (1980). Using on-line computer technology in a mental health admitting system. In J. B. Sidowski, J. H. Johnson, & T. A. Williams (Eds.), *Technology in mental health care delivery systems* (pp. 237–249). Norwood, NJ: Ablex.

Karson, S., & O'Dell, J. W. (1975). A new automated interpretation system for the 16PF. *Journal of Personality Assessment, 39*, 256–260.

Karson, S., & O'Dell, J. W. (1987). Computer based interpretation of the 16PF: The Karson Clinical Report in contemporary practice. In J. N. Butcher (Ed.), *Computerized psychological assessment* (pp. 198–217). New York: Basic Books.

Katz, L., & Dalby, J. T. (1981a). Computer and manual administration of the Eysenck Personality Inventory. *Journal of Clinical Psychology, 37*, 586–588.

Katz, L., & Dalby, J. T. (1981b). Computer-assisted and traditional psychological assessment of elementary-school-aged children. *Contemporary Educational Psychology, 6*, 314–322.

Kaufman, A. S. (1979). *Intelligent testing with the WISC-R*. New York: Wiley-Interscience.

Klett, B., Schaefer, A., & Plemel, D. (1985, May). Just how accurate are computer-scored tests? *The VA Chief Psychologist, 8*, 7.

Klingler, D. E., Miller, D. A., Johnson, J. H., & Williams, T. A. (1976). Strategies in the evaluation of an on-line computer-assisted unit for intake assessment of mental health patients. *Behavior Research Methods & Instrumentation, 9*, 95–100.

Klinger, D. E., Miller, D. A., Johnson, J. H., & Williams, T. A. (1977). Process evaluation of an on-line computer-assisted unit for intake assessment of mental health patients. *Behavior Research Methods & Instrumentation, 9*, 110–116.

Knights, R. M., Richardson, D. H., & McNarry, L. R. (1973). Automated vs. clinical administration of the Peabody Picture Vocabulary Test and the Coloured Progressive Matrices. *American Journal of Mental Deficiency, 78*, 223–225.

Krug, S. E. (1984). *Psychware: A reference guide to computer-based products in psychology, education, and business*. Kansas City, MO: Test Corporation of America.

Krug, S. E. (1985). *TEST PLUS: A microcomputer based system for the Adult Personality Inventory*. [Computer program]. Champaign, IL: MetriTech.

Krug, S. E. (1987a). *Psychware Sourcebook 1987–1988*. Kansas City, MO: Test Corporation of America.

Krug, S. E. (1987b). Microtrends: An orientation to computerized assessment. In J. N. Butcher (Ed.), *Computerized psychological assessment* (pp. 15–25). New York: Basic Books.

Lachar, D. (1974). Accuracy and generalization of an automated MMPI interpretation system. *Journal of Consulting and Clinical Psychology, 42*, 267–273.

Lachar, D. (1987). Automated assessment of child and adolescent personality: The Personality Inventory for Children (PIC). In J. N. Butcher (Ed.), *Computerized psychological assessment* (pp. 261–291). New York: Basic Books.

Lambert, M. E., Andrews, R. H., Rylee, K., & Skinner, J. R. (1987). Equivalence of computerized and traditional MMPI administration with substance abusers. *Computers in Human Behavior, 3*, 139–143.

Lanyon, R. I. (1971). Mental health technology. *American Psychologist, 26*, 1071–1076.

Lanyon, R. I. (1984). Personality assessment. *Annual Review of Psychology, 35*, 667–701.

Lanyon, R. I. (1987). The validity of computer-based personality assessment products: Recommendations for the future. *Computers in Human Behavior, 3*, 225–238.

Levitan, K. B., Shook, D. G., & Willis, E. A. (1984). *Survey of practitioners' information technology needs and uses in psychology and psychiatry*. Silver Spring, MD: KBL Group.

Levy, A. J., & Barowsky, E. I. (1986). Comparison of computer-administered Harris-Goodenough Draw-A-Man Test with standard paper-and-pencil administration. *Perceptual and Motor Skills, 63*, 395–398.

Lezak, M. D. (1983). *Neuropsychological assessment*. New York: Oxford.

Lucas, R. W. (1977). A study of patients' attitudes to computer interrogation. *International Journal of Man-Machine Studies, 9*, 69–86.

Lucas, R. W., Mullins, P. J., Luna, C. B., & McInroy, D. C. (1977). Psychiatrists and a computer as interrogators of patients with alcohol-related illnesses: A comparison. *British Journal of Psychiatry, 131*, 160–167.

Lushene, R. E., O'Neil, H. F., & Dunn, T. (1974). Equivalent validity of a completely computerized MMPI. *Journal of Personality Assessment, 38*, 353–361.

Matarazzo, J. D. (1983, July 22). Computerized psychological testing. *Science, 221*, 323.

Matarazzo, J. D. (1986). Computerized clinical psychological test interpretation: Unvalidated plus all mean and no sigma. *American Psychologist, 41*, 14–24.

Maultsby, M. C., & Slack, W. V. (1971). A computer-based psychiatry history system. *Archives of General Psychiatry, 25*, 570–572.

Miller, F. E. (1986). The development and evaluation of an online computer-assisted Rorschach Inkblot Test. *Journal of Personality Assessment, 50*, 222–228.

Miller, C. K., Chansky, N. M., & Gredler, B. R. (1970). Rater agreement on WISC protocols. *Psychology in the Schools, 7*, 190–193.

Moreland, K. L. (1985). Validation of computer-based test interpretations: Probems and prospects. *Journal of Consulting and Clinical Psychology, 53*, 816–825.

Moreland, K. L. (1987). Computerized psychological assessment: What's available. In J. N. Butcher

(Ed.), *Computerized psychological assessment* (pp. 26–49). New York: Basic Books.

Moreland, K. L., & Dahlstrom, W. G. (1983). Professional training with and use of the MMPI. *Professional Psychology: Research and Practice, 14*, 218–223.

Moreland, K. L., & Onstad, J. A. (1985, March). *Validity of the Minnesota Clinical Report I: Mental health outpatients.* Paper presented at the 20th Annual MMPI Symposium, Honolulu.

Ohio Psychological Association (1983). *Ethical principles related to computerized testing.* Columbus, OH: Author.

Overton, G. W., & Scott, K. G. (1972). Automated and manual intelligence testing: Data on parallel forms of the Peabody Picture Vocabulary Test. *American Journal of Mental Deficiency, 76*, 639–643.

Piotrowski, Z. A. (1964). A digital computer administration of inkblot test data. *Psychiatric Quarterly, 38*, 1–26.

Roid, G. H., & Gorsuch, R. L. (1984). Development and clinical use of test-interpretive programs on microcomputers. In M. D. Schwartz (Ed.), *Using computers in clinical practice* (pp. 141–149). New York: Haworth.

Rozensky, R. H., Honor, L. F., Rasinski, K., Tovian, S. M., & Herz, G. I. (1986). Paper-and pencil versus computer-administered MMPIs: A comparison of patients' attitudes. *Computers in Human Behavior, 2*, 111–116.

Russell, G. K. G., Peace, K. A., & Mellsop, G. W. (1986). The reliability of a microcomputer administration of the MMPI. *Journal of Clinical Psychology, 42*, 120–122.

Ryan, J. J. (1983). Scoring reliability on the WAIS-R. *Journal of Consulting and Clinical Psychology, 51*, 149–150.

Sattler, J. M. (1988). *Assessment of children.* San Diego, CA: Author.

Scissons, E. H. (1976). Computer administration of the California Psychological Inventory. *Measurement and Evaluation in Guidance, 9*, 22–25.

Simmons, E. M., & Miller, O. W. (1971). Automated patient history-taking. *Hospitals, 45*, 56–59.

Skinner, H. A., & Allen, B. A. (1983). Does the computer make a difference? Computerized versus face-to-face versus self-report of alcohol, drug, and tobacco use. *Journal of Consulting and Clinical Psychology, 51*, 267–275.

Slack, W. V. (1971, January 8). Computer based interviewing system dealing with nonverbal behavior as well as keyboard responses. *Science*, 84–87.

Slack, W. V., Hicks, G. P., Reed, C. Z., & Van Cura, L. J. (1966). A computer-based medical history system. *New England Journal of Medicine, 274*, 194–198.

Smith, M. S. (1968). The computer and the TAT. *Journal of School Psychology, 6*, 206–214.

Stein, S. J. (1987). Computer-assisted diagnosis for children and adolescents. In J. N. Butcher (Ed.), *Computerized psychological assessment* (pp. 145–158). New York: Basic Books.

Stout, R. L. (1981). New approaches to the design of computerized interviewing and testing systems. *Behavior Research Methods & Instrumentation, 13*, 436–442.

Swenson, W. M., & Pearson, J. S. (1964). Automation techniques in personality assessment—A frontier in behavioral science and medicine. *Methods of Information in Medicine, 3*, 34–36.

Swenson, W. M., Rome, H. P., Pearson, J. S., & Brannick, T. L. (1965). A totally automated psychologist: Experience in a medical center. *Journal of the American Medical Association, 191*, 925–927.

Swiercinsky, D. P. (1983). *Users' manual: SAINT-II system for administration and interpretation of neuropsychological tests.* Liberty, MO: Compu-Psych.

Vale, C. D., & Keller, L. S. (1987). Developing expert computer systems to interpret psychological tests. In J. N. Buthcer (Ed.), *Computerized psychological assessment* (pp. 325–343). New York: Basic Books.

Weiss, D. J. (1985). Adaptive testing by computer. *Journal of Consulting and Clinical Psychology, 53*, 774–789.

Weiss, D. J., & Vale, C. D. (1987). Computerized adaptive testing for measuring abilities and other psychological variables. In J. N. Butcher (Ed.), *Computerized psychological assessment* (pp. 325–343). New York: Basic Books.

Westby, L. (1984). *An examination of mechanical errors in WISC-R and WAIS-R scoring.* Unpublished manuscript.

White, D. M., Clements, C. B., & Fowler, R. D. (1985). A comparison of computer administration with standard administration of the MMPI. *Computers in Human Behavior, 1*, 153–162.

Wiggins, J. S. (1973). *Personality and prediction: Principles of personality assessment.* Reading, MA: Addison-Wesley.

APPENDIX A

Software Vendors

This appendix includes a listing of the software companies mentioned in this chapter. The list is not exhaustive, and inclusion does not imply endorsement by the authors. See Krug (1987) for a more comprehensive description of the available software and suppliers.

Applied Innovations (AI), South Kingston Office Park, Wakefield, RI 02879

Consulting Psychologists Press, P. O. Box 60070, Palo Alto, CA 94306

Integrated Professional Systems, 5211 Mahoning Avenue, Suite 135, Youngstown, OH 44515

Life Science Associates, 1 Fenimore Road, Bayport, NY 11705

National Computer Systems (NCS), Professional Assessment Services, P.O. Box 1416, Minneapolis, MN 55440

Pacific Psychological, 710 George Washington Way, Suite G-3, Richland, WA 99352

Precision People, 3452 North Ride Circle S., Jacksonville, FL 32217

Psych Solutions Associates, P. O. Box 10262, Baltimore, MD 21234

Psychological Assessment Resources (PAR), P.O. Box 998, Odessa, FL 33556

Psychologistics, P.O. Box 3896, Indialantic, FL 32903

Psychometric Software, 2050 South Patrick Drive, Indian Harbour Beach, FL 32937

Reason House, 204 East Joppa Road, Suite 10, Towson, MD 21204

Research Psychologists Press (RPP), P.O. Box 984, Port Huron, MI 48061

Scientific Psychology, 2477 SW 19th Terrace, Miami, FL 33145

Southern Micro Systems, P. O. Box 2097, Burlington, NC 27216

StatSoft, 2325 East 13th Street, Tulsa, OK 74104

Wang Neuropsychological Laboratory, 1720 La Luna Court, San Luis Obispo, CA 93401

Western Psychological Services, 12031 Wilshire Boulevard, Los Angeles, CA 90025

Author Index

SUBJECT INDEX

ABOUT THE EDITORS AND CONTRIBUTORS

THE EDITORS

Gerald Goldstein (Ph.D., University of Kansas, 1962) is Director of the Neuropsychology Research Program at the Highland Drive VA Medical Center in Pittsburgh, and Professor of Psychiatry and Psychology at the University of Pittsburgh. He has authored and coauthored numerous articles, chapters and books in the area of clinical neuropsychology, which is his major research interest. He is Editor of *Neuropsychology Review*, and serves on the editorial board of the *Journal of Clinical and Experimental Neuropsychology*, the *Journal of Psychopathology and Behavioral Assessment*, the *Archives of Clinical Neuropsychology* and *The Clinical Neuropsychologist*. He is a member of the American Board of Clinical Neuropsychology and Past President of the Division of Clinical Neuropsychology of the American Psychological Association.

Michel Hersen (Ph.D.) is Professor of Psychiatry and Psychology at the University of Pittsburgh School of Medicine. He is Past President of the Association for Advancement of Behavior Therapy. He has coauthored and coedited 64 books, including *Single Case Experimental Designs*, published by Pergamon Press. He has also published more than 174 scientific journal articles and is coeditor of several psychological journals, including *Behavior Modification, Clinical Psychology Review, Journal of Anxiety Disorders, Journal of Family Violence*, and *Journal of the Multihandicapped Person*. Dr. Hersen is the recipient of several research grants from the National Institute of Mental Health, the Department of Education, the National Institute of Disabilities and Rehabilitation Research, and the March of Dimes Birth Defects Foundation.

THE CONTRIBUTORS

James N. Butcher (Ph.D., University of North Carolina at Chapel Hill, 1964) is currently Professor of Psychology in the Department of Psychology at the University of Minnesota. He has maintained an active research program in the areas of: personality assessment, abnormal psychology, cross-cultural personality factors, and computer based personality assessment. Professor Butcher is a member of the University of Minnesota Press' MMPI Consultative Committee. Since 1982 the committee has been actively engaged in a large scale project to revise and restandardize the MMPI. He is also an Associate Editor for the Journal of Consulting and Clinical Psychology: Psychological Assessment and advisory editor for Contemporary Psychology, and serves as consulting editor for numerous other journals in psychology and psychiatry.

Anthony J. Costello (Medical Training at the University of Cambridge and University College Hospital, London 1959). His post-graduate training was at The Royal Free Hospital, The Institute of Psychiatry and the Maudsley Hospital, and The Hospital for Sick Children, all in London, England. He is now Professor of Psychiatry and Director of Child and Adolescent Psychiatric Services at the University of Massachusetts Medical Center, Worcester. His main interests are in assessment and recording of child behavior and he has explored a wide range of techniques ranging from electronic recording of mother-infant interaction to structured interviewing.

Craig Edelbrock (Ph.D., Oregon State University, 1976) is Associate Professor and Director of Research in the Department of Psychiatry and Behavioral Sciences at the University of Massachusetts Medical

School in Worcester. His major interests are developmental psychopathology and the assessment of children's behavioral disorders. He currently serves on the editorial boards of *Psychological Assessment,* the *Journal of Abnormal Child Psychology,* the *Journal of Clinical Child Psychology,* and the *Journal of Child Psychology and Psychiatry.*

Philip Erdberg (Ph.D., University of Alabama, 1969), is a diplomate in clinical psychology of the American Board of Professional Psychology. He has been a consulting psychologist for a variety of schools, agencies, and treatment facilities in northern California since 1971. Dr. Erdberg is the author of two current chapters on the Rorschach and has been an instructor with Rorschach Workshops since 1977. He has taught in academic, clinical, and post-doctoral settings. His current research interest is the combined utilization of the Rorschach and the MMPI. Dr. Erdberg is president-elect of the Society for Personality Assessment.

Jack M. Fletcher (Ph.D., University of Florida, 1978) is Associate Professor of Pediatrics in the Department of Pediatrics, University of Texas Medical School at Houston. He is also an adjunct Associate Professor of Psychology at the University of Houston. Dr. Fletcher has published widely on the neuropsychology of learning disabilities and brain injuries in children.

Raymond D. Fowler (Ph.D., Pennsylvania State University, 1957) is Chief Executive Officer of the American Psychological Association. He previously chaired the psychology departments at the University of Alabama (1965–1983) and the University of Tennessee (1987–1989). His computer-based interpretation system for the MMPI developed in the early 1960s was the first to be widely used in this country and in Europe. Dr. Fowler has written numerous articles on personality assessment, alcoholism and criminal behavior. He is currently Editor of the *American Psychologist.*

Michael D. Franzen (Ph.D.) is Director of Neuropsychology at West Virginia University Health Sciences Center where he is an Associate Professor of Behavioral Medicine and Psychiatry. He is also an Associate Professor of Psychology at West Virginia University. His research interests include the application of psychometric evaluation methods to clinical neuropsychology, and the application of behavioral

methodology and assessment strategies to neuropsychological assessment. His other research interests include medical neuropsychology and the effect of psychiatric conditions on cognitive functions.

Robert Gatewood (Ph.D., Purdue University) is currently an Associate Professor of Management at the University of Georgia. His major areas of professional interest are in human resource selection and human resource planning. He has presented papers at the national meetings of the Academy of Management and the American Psychological Association, and has published several journal articles.

Charles Golden (Ph.D.) is currently a Professor and Director of Clinical Neuropsychology in the Department of Psychology, Sociology, and Anthropology at Drexel University in Philadelphia. Dr. Golden's primary area of research and practice is clinical neuropsychology and the development of new test instruments in that field. He is best known for his work on the Luria-Nebraska Neuropsychology battery. He is the author of 20 books and 30 chapters in such areas as neuropsychology, forensics, statistics, research methodology, and clinical psychology.

Ross W. Greene (Ph.D., Virginia Polytechnic Institute and State University, 1989) is presently a Visiting Assistant Professor of Psychology at Virginia Tech. His research interests include school transitions, use of sociometric status and other social learning variables in the prediction of long-term adjustment of children, and asssessment and treatment of externalizing disorders in children and adolescents.

Kerry deS. Hamsher (Ph.D., University of Iowa, 1977) is Associate Professor of Neurology at the University of Wisconsin Medical School, Milwaukee Clinical Campus, and Director of Neuropsychology at Sinai Samaritan Medical Center, Milwaukee, Wisconsin. His major areas of interest include the development of neuropsychological assessment instruments, diagnostic nosology, cognitive deficits in aphasia, sequencing aspects of memory, and clinical research in neuropsychology. He has authored and co-authored many research articles and other works, and he is on the board of consulting editors for several journals.

Jo-Ida C. Hansen (Ph.D., University of Minnesota, 1974) is Professor of Psychology, Director of the Center for Interest Measurement Research, and Director of the Counseling Psychology Program at the University of Minnesota. She has authored many articles in Journals and has presented papers on vocational interest measurement at national and international meetings. She is co-author of the Strong-Campbell Interest Inventory; author of the *Interpretive Guide to the SCII*, and was project director for the 1981 and 1985 revisions of the SCII.

Stephen N. Haynes (Ph.D., University of Colorado, 1971) is Professor and Director of the Clinical Studies Program at the University of Hawaii. Dr. Haynes has published numerous books and articles in the areas of behavioral assessment, psychophysiological disorders and psychopathology.

L. Michael Honaker (Ph.D., University of Alabama, 1982) is Associate Professor of Psychology and Associate Director of Clinical Training at the Florida Institute of Techology School of Psychology. He has conducted numerous workshops on computer use in clinical psychology at the national and regional level, has developed several widely used computerized assessment instruments and has published both empirically based and review articles on computerized assessment, which is his major research interest.

Lynda J. Katz (Ph.D. University of Pittsburgh, 1977) is Associate Professor of Psychiatry and Education at the University of Pittsburgh, School of Medicine, Western Psychiatric Institute and Clinic and Director, Neuropsychological Assessment and Rehabilitation Services Department. Dr. Katz is Project Director of RSA funded training grants in the area of Psychiatric Rehabilitation and a NIDDR funded Post Doctoral training grant in Rehabilitation Research. Major areas of interest are Neuropsychological Assessment, Psychiatric Rehabilitaiton and Learning Disabilities. She is a Consulting Editor for Rehabilitation Counseling Bulletin. Among Dr. Katz's most recent publications are those in the areas of Learning Disabilities, Psychiatric Rehabilitation, and Vocational Assessment.

Alan S. Kaufman (Ph.D., Columbia University, 1970) is Research Professor at The University of Alabama. A Fellow of four divisions of APA, Dr. Kaufman has authored or coauthored over 200 articles, chapters, reviews, tests, and books on psychological assessment. Dr. Kaufman presently serves on the editorial boards of nine professional journals in the areas of clinical psychology, school psychology, spe-

cial education, and clinical neuropsychology. He was a co-winner of a 1988–89 Award for Excellence by the Mensa Education & Research Foundation.

Laura S. Keller (Ph.D., University of Minnesota, 1988) is a staff psychologist in the Adult Outpatient Program at Human Services, Inc., in Washington County, Minnesota. During her graduate training in clinical psychology, she worked as a research assistant on the University of Minnesota's national MMPI Restandardization Project and was also employed as a research associate at Assessment Systems Corporation in St. Paul, Minnesota, developing automated psychological test interpretive reports. She has co-authored several journal articles and chapters on objective personality assessment and automated psychological assessment, and is the author of a new MMPI-2 monograph to be published by the University of Minnesota Press, *Assessment of Chronic Pain Patients with the MMPI-2,* along with Dr. James Butcher.

James E. Lindemann (Ph.D., The Pennsylvania State University, 1954) is Professor of Medical Psychology at the Crippled Children's Division of the Oregon Health Sciences University. His major interests are in physical disability, cognitive and social development, and rehabilitation planning. He is the author of *Psychological and Behavioral Aspects of Physical Disability* and (with Sally J. Lindemann) of *Growing Up Proud: A Parent's Guide to the Psychological Care of Children with Disabilities.*

Joseph D. Matarazzo (Ph.D., Northwestern University, 1952) is Professor and Chair, Department of Medical Psychology, School of Medicine, Oregon Health Sciences University, Portland, Oregon. He currently is the President of the American Psychological Association and the author of the *Fifth Edition of Wechsler's Measurement and Appraisal of Adult Intelligence,* has published many articles on psychology as a science and a profession, and serves on the editorial board of a number of scientific and scholarly journals.

Robert W. Motta (Ph.D., Hofstra University, New York 1975) is an Associate Professor of Psychology. He is the Director of the Doctoral Program in School–Community Psychology at Hofstra and is the Supervisor of the Educational Counseling Program in Hofstra's Clinical and School Doctoral Program. Dr. Motta is currently (1989–1990) the president of the

New York State Psychological Association (NYSPA)–School Psychology Division and is the former secretary–treasurer of the NYSPA School Division. He has authored a number of articles and book chapters on childhood behavioral and learning problems including a recent chapter on assessment of children with developmental disabilities. He is currently pursuing research on the effects of parental Posttraumatic Stress Disorder on their children's behavior and emotional adjustment.

Thomas H. Ollendick (Ph.D., Purdue University, 1971) is currently Professor of Psychology and Director of Clinical Training at Virginia Polytechnic Institute and State University. He has held former positions at the Devereux Foundation, Indiana State University, and Western Psychiatric Institute and Clinic. He has co-authored and authored several books, research articles and chapters and is currently on the editorial board of several journals and on the Executive Committee of AABT and is President-Elect of APA's Section I on Clinical Child Psychology.

Mitchel D. Perlman, Ph.D., received his doctoral degree (Clinical Psychology) in 1986 from California School of Professional Psychology–San Diego. His teaching and professional interest lay in psychodiagnostic assessment encompassing cognitive, emotional, and forensic domains. Integrating his research experience with his therapeutic expertise, Dr. Perlman sits on the advisory board of Alvarado Parkway Institute Psychiatric Hospital for Children & Adolescents.

Robert Perloff (Ph.D., Ohio State University, 1951) has been active on a number of fronts in the field of testing and measurement and has published a number of articles in testing and the fields of program evaluation. He is former President of the Eastern Psychological Association, the Evaluation Research Society, and the American Psychological Association, and is now president of the American Psychological Foundation. His current position is Distinguished Service Professor of Business Administration and of Psychology at the Katz Graduate School of Business of the University of Pittsburgh.

Antonio E. Puente (Ph.D., University of Georgia, 1978) is Associate Professor of Psychology of the University of North Carolina at Wilmington and in private practice in Wilmington, North Carolina. He has authored or co-authored several books and scien-

tific publications in the area of clinical neuropsychology, which is his major research and clinical interest. Dr. Puente is on editorial and review boards of several journals, on the board of several professional organizations as well as being active on APA committees for minority issues.

Mark D. Reckase (Ph.D., Syracuse University, 1972) is Assistant Vice President of the Assessment Programs Area of The American College Testing Program (ACT). Before coming to ACT, he was Associate Professor of Educational Psychology at the University of Missouri–Columbia. He has authored and coauthored many articles and book chapters on psychometric theory and statistical analysis, and for the past fifteen years has performed funded research on statistical models of test performance for the Office of Naval Research.

Daniel J. Reschly (Ph.D., University of Oregon, 1971) is Professor of Psychology and Professional Studies in Education and Director of the School Psychology Graduate Program at Iowa State University. Reschly has authored numerous articles dealing with psychological testing, the mildly handicapped, minority students, and legal guidelines. He has edited the *School Psychology Review* and served as President of the National Association of School Psychologists in 1984–85.

Recent work has focused on assessment and interventions in social competence, particularly adaptive behavior assessment with the mildly handicapped.

Robert F. Sawicki (Ph.D., Kent State University, 1983) is Clinical Director of the Head Injury Program at the Institute for Rehabilitation and Research and Clinical Assistant Professor in the Department of Rehabilitation at Baylor College of Medicine. His research interests are in scale construction in neuropsychological assessment and the neuropsychology of neurological disorders.

Shawn Shea (M.D., University of North Carolina at Chapel Hill, 1980) is the Director of the Continuous Treatment Team at Monadnock Family Services in Keene, New Hampshire. He is the past Medical Director of the Diagnostic and Evaluation Center and the Associate Director of Residency Training at Western Psychiatric Institute and Clinic. He is the author of the book *Psychiatric Interviewing: The Art of Understanding*. He is also the author of various articles concerning interviewing training and regularly presents several workshops on advanced interviewing at the American Psychiatric Association Annual Meeting.

Gregory T. Slomka (Ph.D. University of Pittsburgh, 1986) is Clinical Coordinator of Assessment Services within Neuropsychological Assessment and Rehabilitation Service at Western Psychiatric Institute and Clinic, Pittsburgh, Pennsylvania. His major interests lie in developmental neuropsychology and the application of neuropsychology testing in multiply disabled populations. He has authored a number of chapters on the neuropsychological assessment of children and the developmentally disabled.

Wendy S. Slutske (B.S., University of Wisconsin, 1986) is currently a graduate student in the Clinical Psychology Program at the University of Minnesota and a Research Assistant on the MMPI Restandardization Project.

H. Gerry Taylor (Ph.D., University of Iowa, 1975) is an Associate Professor of Pediatrics at Case Western Reserve University School of Medicine and Director of Pediatric Psychology at Rainbow Babies and Childrens Hospital, Cleveland, Ohio. Dr. Taylor is actively involved in the assessment of children with learning and neurological disorders. The major objective of his research is to clarify cognitive deficits as an aid to improved understanding of etiology, associated academic and behavior problems, and treatment.

Julia R. Vane (Ph.D., New York University, 1951) was a Professor of Psychology at Hofstra University until her death in December, 1988. She was Chair of the Department of Psychology and Director of the Doctoral Program in Clinical and School Psychology at Hofstra. She was a Diplomate in Clinical and in School Psychology. She has published the well-known Vane Kindergarten Test and the Vane Language Test and has authored a number of articles in the area of behavioral and clinical assessment. She is past president of the Nassau County Psychological Association, past president of the Division of School Psychology of the APA, a member of the New York State Board for Psychology, and a member of the Commissioner's Task Force on Professional Education in New York State. She has been a consulting editor for the *Journal of Educational Research,* the *Journal of School Psychology* and the *Journal of Clinical Psychology.*

Arthur N. Wiens (Ph.D., University of Portland, 1956) is Professor of Medical Psychology and Chairman of the Clinical Training Committee in the Department of Medical Psychology, Oregon Health Sciences University. He has a long-time interest in research on the interview and in teaching interviewing skills. He co-authored *The Interview: Research on its Anatomy and Structure* and *Non-Verbal Communication: The State of the Art.*

J. Richard Wittenborn (Ph.D., University of Illinois, 1942), University Professor of Psychology and Education at Rutgers University, has published numerous reports describing the conceptualization and quantification of various aspects of human behavior, including the development of rating scales and the design of clinical investigation. He has been active in the development of psychopharmacology at both the national and international levels and is currently engaged in the study of changes in human behavior.

Pergamon General Psychology Series

Editors: **Arnold P. Goldstein,** Syracuse University
Leonard Krasner, Stanford University &
SUNY at Stony Brook

*Out of print in original format. Available in custom reprint edition.